Lecture Notes in Artificial Intelligence 9119

Subseries of Lecture Notes in Computer Science

T0181118

More information about this series at http://www.springer.com/series/1244

Leszek Rutkowski · Marcin Korytkowski
Rafał Scherer · Ryszard Tadeusiewicz
Lotfi A. Zadeh · Jacek M. Zurada (Eds.)

Artificial Intelligence and Soft Computing

14th International Conference, ICAISC 2015
Zakopane, Poland, June 14–18, 2015
Proceedings, Part I

 Springer

Editors

Leszek Rutkowski
Częstochowa University of Technology
Częstochowa
Poland

Marcin Korytkowski
Częstochowa University of Technology
Częstochowa
Poland

Rafal Scherer
Częstochowa University of Technology
Częstochowa
Poland

Ryszard Tadeusiewicz
AGH University of Science and Technology
Krakow
Poland

Lotfi A. Zadeh
University of California
Berkeley, California
USA

Jacek M. Zurada
University of Louisville
Louisville, Kentucky
USA

ISSN 0302-9743   ISSN 1611-3349   (electronic)
Lecture Notes in Artificial Intelligence
ISBN 978-3-319-19323-6   ISBN 978-3-319-19324-3   (eBook)
DOI 10.1007/978-3-319-19324-3
Library of Congress Control Number: 2015939285

LNCS Sublibrary: SL7 – Artificial Intelligence

Springer Cham Heidelberg New York Dordrecht London
© Springer International Publishing Switzerland 2015

Printed on acid-free paper

Springer International Publishing AG Switzerland is part of Springer Science+Business Media
(www.springer.com)

Preface

This volume constitutes the proceedings of the 14th International Conference on Artificial Intelligence and Soft Computing, ICAISC 2015, held in Zakopane, Poland, during June 14–18, 2015. The conference was organized by the Polish Neural Network Society in cooperation with the University of Social Sciences in Łódź, the Institute of Computational Intelligence at the Częstochowa University of Technology, and the IEEE Computational Intelligence Society, Poland Chapter. Previous conferences took place in Kule (1994), Szczyrk (1996), Kule (1997), and Zakopane (1999, 2000, 2002, 2004, 2006, 2008, 2010, 2012, 2013, and 2014) and attracted a large number of papers and internationally recognized speakers: Lotfi A. Zadeh, Hojjat Adeli, Rafal Angryk, Igor Aizenberg, Shun-ichi Amari, Daniel Amit, Piero P. Bonissone, Jim Bezdek, Zdzisław Bubnicki, Andrzej Cichocki, Włodzisław Duch, Pablo A. Estévez, Jerzy Grzymala-Busse, Martin Hagan, Yoichi Hayashi, Akira Hirose, Kaoru Hirota, Hisao Ishibuchi, Er Meng Joo, Janusz Kacprzyk, Jim Keller, Laszlo T. Koczy, Adam Krzyzak, Soo-Young Lee, Derong Liu, Robert Marks, Evangelia Micheli-Tzanakou, Kaisa Miettinen, Henning Müller, Ngoc Thanh Nguyen, Erkki Oja, Witold Pedrycz, Marios M. Polycarpou, José C. Príncipe, Jagath C. Rajapakse, Šarunas Raudys, Enrique Ruspini, Jörg Siekmann, Roman Słowiński, Igor Spiridonov, Boris Stilman, Ponnuthurai Nagaratnam Suganthan, Ryszard Tadeusiewicz, Ah-Hwee Tan, Shiro Usui, Fei-Yue Wang, Jun Wang, Bogdan M. Wilamowski, Ronald Y. Yager, Syozo Yasui, Gary Yen, and Jacek Zurada. The aim of this conference is to build a bridge between traditional artificial intelligence techniques and so-called soft computing techniques. It was pointed out by Lotfi A. Zadeh that "soft computing (SC) is a coalition of methodologies which are oriented toward the conception and design of information/intelligent systems. The principal members of the coalition are: fuzzy logic (FL), neurocomputing (NC), evolutionary computing (EC), probabilistic computing (PC), chaotic computing (CC), and machine learning (ML). The constituent methodologies of SC are, for the most part, complementary and synergistic rather than competitive." These proceedings present both traditional artificial intelligence methods and soft computing techniques. Our goal is to bring together scientists representing both areas of research. This volume is divided into six parts:

- Neural Networks and Their Applications,
- Fuzzy Systems and Their Applications,
- Evolutionary Algorithms and Their Applications,
- Classification and Estimation,
- Computer Vision, Image, and Speech Analysis,
- Workshop: Large-Scale Visual Recognition and Machine Learning.

The conference has attracted a total of 322 submissions from 39 countries and after the review process, 142 papers have been accepted for publication. The ICAISC 2015 hosted the Workshop: Large-Scale Visual Recognition and Machine Learning organized by

- Marcin Korytkowski, Częstochowa University of Technology, Poland,
- Rafał Scherer, Częstochowa University of Technology, Poland,
- Sviatoslav Voloshynovskiy, University of Geneva, Switzerland.

The Workshop was supported by the project "New Perspectives on Intelligent Multimedia Management With Applications in Medicine and Privacy Protecting Systems" cofinanced by a grant from Switzerland through the Swiss Contribution to the Enlarged European Union, and supported by the project "Innovative methods of retrieval and indexing multimedia data using computational intelligence techniques" funded by the National Science Centre. I would like to thank our participants, invited speakers, and reviewers of the papers for their scientific and personal contribution to the conference. The following reviewers were very helpful in reviewing the papers:

R. Adamczak	A. Dzieliński	J. Kacprzyk
H. Altrabalsi	P. Dziwiński	W. Kamiński
S. Amari	S. Ehteram	T. Kaplon
T. Babczyński	A. Fanea	A. Kasperski
M. Baczyński	B. Filipic	V. Kecman
A. Bari	I. Fister	E. Kerre
M. Białko	C. Frowd	P. Klęsk
L. Bobrowski	M. Gabryel	J. Kluska
L. Borzemski	A. Gawęda	L. Koczy
J. Botzheim	M. Giergiel	Z. Kokosinski
T. Burczyński	P. Głomb	A. Kołakowska
R. Burduk	Z. Gomółka	J. Konopacki
K. Cetnarowicz	M. Gorawski	J. Korbicz
L. Chmielewski	M. Gorzałczany	P. Korohoda
W. Cholewa	G. Gosztolya	J. Koronacki
M. Choraś	D. Grabowski	M. Korytkowski
K. Choros	E. Grabska	J. Kościelny
P. Cichosz	K. Grąbczewski	L. Kotulski
R. Cierniak	C. Grosan	Z. Kowalczuk
P. Ciskowski	M. Grzenda	M. Kraft
S. Concetto	J. Grzymala-Busse	M. Kretowski
B. Cyganek	J. Hähner	D. Krol
J. Cytowski	H. Haberdar	B. Kryzhanovsky
R. Czabański	R. Hampel	A. Krzyzak
I. Czarnowski	Z. Hendzel	A. Kubiak
J. de la Rosa	F. Hermann	E. Kucharska
K. Dembczynski	Z. Hippe	J. Kulikowski
J. Dembski	A. Horzyk	O. Kurasova
N. Derbel	M. Hrebień	V. Kurkova
G. Dobrowolski	E. Hrynkiewicz	M. Kurzyński
W. Duch	I. Imani	J. Kusiak
L. Dutkiewicz	D. Jakóbczak	N. Labroche
L. Dymowa	A. Janczak	J. Liao

A. Ligęza	K. Patan	B. Strug
F. Liu	A. Pieczyński	P. Strumiłło
H. Liu	A. Piegat	M. Studniarski
M. Ławryńczuk	Z. Pietrzykowski	R. Sulej
J. Łęski	P. Prokopowicz	J. Swacha
B. Macukow	A. Przybył	P. Szczepaniak
K. Madani	A. Radzikowska	E. Szmidt
L. Magdalena	E. Rafajłowicz	M. Szpyrka
W. Malina	E. Rakus-Andersson	J. Świątek
R. Mallipeddi	M. Rane	R. Tadeusiewicz
J. Mańdziuk	A. Rataj	H. Takagi
U. Markowska-Kaczmar	L. Rolka	Y. Tiumentsev
M. Marques	F. Rudziński	A. Tomczyk
A. Materka	A. Rusiecki	V. Torra
R. Matuk Herrera	L. Rutkowski	F. Trovo
J. Mazurkiewicz	S. Sakurai	M. Urbański
V. Medvedev	N. Sano	C. Uzor
J. Mendel	J. Sas	T. Villmann
J. Michalkiewicz	A. Sashima	E. Volna
Z. Mikrut	R. Scherer	R. Vorobel
S. Misina	P. Sevastjanov	M. Wagenknecht
W. Mitkowski	A. Sędziwy	T. Walkowiak
W. Mokrzycki	J. Silc	L. Wang
O. Mosalov	W. Skarbek	J. Wąs
T. Munakata	A. Skowron	B. Wilamowski
H. Nakamoto	E. Skubalska-Rafajłowicz	M. Witczak
G. Nalepa	K. Slot	M. Wozniak
M. Nashed	D. Słota	M. Wygralak
A. Nawrat	A. Słowik	R. Wyrzykowski
F. Neri	R. Słowiński	G. Yakhyaeva
M. Nieniewski	C. Smutnicki	J. Yeomans
R. Nowicki	A. Sokołowski	J. Zabrodzki
A. Obuchowicz	T. Sołtysiński	S. Zadrożny
G. Onwubolu	B. Starosta	D. Zakrzewska
S. Osowski	J. Stefanowski	A. Zamuda
A. Owczarek	E. Straszecka	R. Zdunek
G. Paragliola	V. Štruc	

Finally, I thank my coworkers Łukasz Bartczuk, Piotr Dziwiński, Marcin Gabryel, Marcin Korytkowski, and the conference secretary Rafał Scherer, for their enormous efforts to make the conference a very successful event. Moreover, I would like to appreciate the work of Marcin Korytkowski who designed the Internet submission system.

June 2015

Leszek Rutkowski
President of the Polish Neural Network Society

A. Ligęza
F. Liu
H. Liu
M. Ławryńczuk
J. Łęski
B. Macukow
K. Madani
L. Magdalena
W. Malina
R. Mallipeddi
J. Mańdziuk
U. Markowska-Kaczmar
M. Marques
A. Materka
R. Matuk Herrera
J. Mazurkiewicz
V. Medvedev
J. Mendel
J. Michalkiewicz
Z. Mikrut
S. Misina
W. Mitkowski
W. Mokrzycki
O. Mosalov
T. Munakata
H. Nakamoto
G. Nalepa
M. Nashed
A. Nawrat
F. Neri
M. Nieniewski
R. Nowicki
A. Obuchowicz
G. Onwubolu
S. Osowski
A. Owczarek
G. Paragliola

K. Patan
A. Pieczyński
A. Piegat
Z. Pietrzykowski
P. Prokopowicz
A. Przybył
A. Radzikowska
E. Rafajłowicz
E. Rakus-Andersson
M. Rane
A. Rataj
L. Rolka
F. Rudziński
A. Rusiecki
L. Rutkowski
S. Sakurai
N. Sano
J. Sas
A. Sashima
R. Scherer
P. Sevastjanov
A. Sędziwy
J. Silc
W. Skarbek
A. Skowron
E. Skubalska-Rafajłowicz
K. Slot
D. Słota
A. Słowik
R. Słowiński
C. Smutnicki
A. Sokołowski
T. Sołtysiński
B. Starosta
J. Stefanowski
E. Straszecka
V. Štruc

B. Strug
P. Strumiłło
M. Studniarski
R. Sulej
J. Swacha
P. Szczepaniak
E. Szmidt
M. Szpyrka
J. Świątek
R. Tadeusiewicz
H. Takagi
Y. Tiumentsev
A. Tomczyk
V. Torra
F. Trovo
M. Urbański
C. Uzor
T. Villmann
E. Volna
R. Vorobel
M. Wagenknecht
T. Walkowiak
L. Wang
J. Wąs
B. Wilamowski
M. Witczak
M. Wozniak
M. Wygralak
R. Wyrzykowski
G. Yakhyaeva
J. Yeomans
J. Zabrodzki
S. Zadrożny
D. Zakrzewska
A. Zamuda
R. Zdunek

Finally, I thank my coworkers Łukasz Bartczuk, Piotr Dziwiński, Marcin Gabryel, Marcin Korytkowski, and the conference secretary Rafał Scherer, for their enormous efforts to make the conference a very successful event. Moreover, I would like to appreciate the work of Marcin Korytkowski who designed the Internet submission system.

June 2015

Leszek Rutkowski
President of the Polish Neural Network Society

Organization

ICAISC 2015 was organized by the Polish Neural Network Society in cooperation with the University of Social Sciences in Łódź, the Institute of Computational Intelligence at Częstochowa University of Technology, and the IEEE Computational Intelligence Society, Poland Chapter and with technical sponsorship of the IEEE Computational Intelligence Society.

ICAISC Chairpersons

Honorary chairmen

Lotfi A. Zadeh	University of California, Berkeley, USA
Hojjat Adeli	The Ohio State University, USA
Jacek Żurada	University of Louisville, USA

General chairman

Leszek Rutkowski	Częstochowa University of Technology, Poland

Co-chairmen

Włodzisław Duch	Nicolaus Copernicus University, Poland
Janusz Kacprzyk	Polish Academy of Sciences, Poland
Józef Korbicz	University of Zielona Góra, Poland
Ryszard Tadeusiewicz	AGH University of Science and Technology, Poland

ICAISC Program Committee

Rafał Adamczak, Poland
Cesare Alippi, Italy
Shun-ichi Amari, Japan
Rafal A. Angryk, USA
Jarosław Arabas, Poland
Robert Babuska, Netherlands
Ildar Z. Batyrshin, Russia
James C. Bezdek, Australia
Marco Block-Berlitz, Germany
Leon Bobrowski, Poland
Piero P. Bonissone, USA

Bernadette Bouchon-Meunier, France
Tadeusz Burczynski, Poland
Andrzej Cader, Poland
Juan Luis Castro, Spain
Yen-Wei Chen, Japan
Wojciech Cholewa, Poland
Fahmida N. Chowdhury, USA
Andrzej Cichocki, Japan
Paweł Cichosz, Poland
Krzysztof Cios, USA
Ian Cloete, Germany

Erkki Oja, Finland
Stanisław Osowski, Poland
Nikhil R. Pal, India
Maciej Patan, Poland
Witold Pedrycz, Canada
Leonid Perlovsky, USA
Andrzej Pieczyński, Poland
Andrzej Piegat, Poland
Vincenzo Piuri, Italy
Lech Polkowski, Poland
Marios M. Polycarpou, Cyprus
Danil Prokhorov, USA
Anna Radzikowska, Poland
Ewaryst Rafajłowicz, Poland
Sarunas Raudys, Lithuania
Olga Rebrova, Russia
Vladimir Red'ko, Russia
Raúl Rojas, Germany
Imre J. Rudas, Hungary
Enrique H. Ruspini, USA
Khalid Saeed, Poland
Dominik Sankowski, Poland
Norihide Sano, Japan
Robert Schaefer, Poland
Rudy Setiono, Singapore
Pawel Sevastianow, Poland
Jennie Si, USA
Peter Sincak, Slovakia
Andrzej Skowron, Poland
Ewa Skubalska-Rafajłowicz, Poland
Roman Słowiński, Poland
Tomasz G. Smolinski, USA
Czesław Smutnicki, Poland
Pilar Sobrevilla, Spain
Janusz Starzyk, USA
Jerzy Stefanowski, Poland

Vitomir Štruc, Slovenia
Pawel Strumillo, Poland
Ron Sun, USA
Johan Suykens, Belgium
Piotr Szczepaniak, Poland
Eulalia J. Szmidt, Poland
Przemysław Śliwiński, Poland
Adam Słowik, Poland
Jerzy Świątek, Poland
Hideyuki Takagi, Japan
Yury Tiumentsev, Russia
Vicenç Torra, Spain
Burhan Turksen, Canada
Shiro Usui, Japan
Michael Wagenknecht, Germany
Tomasz Walkowiak, Poland
Deliang Wang, USA
Jun Wang, Hong Kong
Lipo Wang, Singapore
Zenon Waszczyszyn, Poland
Paul Werbos, USA
Slawo Wesolkowski, Canada
Sławomir Wiak, Poland
Bernard Widrow, USA
Kay C. Wiese, Canada
Bogdan M. Wilamowski, USA
Donald C. Wunsch, USA
Maciej Wygralak, Poland
Roman Wyrzykowski, Poland
Ronald R. Yager, USA
Xin-She Yang, United Kingdom
Gary Yen, USA
John Yen, USA
Sławomir Zadrożny, Poland
Ali M.S. Zalzala, United Arab Emirates

ICAISC Organizing Committee

Rafał Scherer   Secretary
Łukasz Bartczuk   Organizing Committee Member
Piotr Dziwiński   Organizing Committee Member
Marcin Gabryel   Finance Chair
Marcin Korytkowski   Databases and Internet Submissions

Contents – Part I

Neural Networks and Their Applications

Parallel Approach to the Levenberg-Marquardt Learning Algorithm
for Feedforward Neural Networks 3
  Jarosław Bilski, Jacek Smoląg, and Jacek M. Żurada

Microarray *Leukemia* Gene Data Clustering by Means of Generalized
Self-Organizing Neural Networks with Evolving Tree-Like Structures ... 15
  Marian B. Gorzałczany, Jakub Piekoszewski, and Filip Rudziński

Innovative Types and Abilities of Neural Networks Based on Associative
Mechanisms and a New Associative Model of Neurons 26
  Adrian Horzyk

Complexity of Shallow Networks Representing Finite Mappings 39
  Věra Kůrková

Probabilistic Neural Network Training Procedure with the Use of
SARSA Algorithm 49
  Maciej Kusy and Roman Zajdel

Extensions of Hopfield Neural Networks for Solving
of Stereo-Matching Problem 59
  Łukasz Laskowski, Jerzy Jelonkiewicz, and Yoichi Hayashi

Molecular Approach to Hopfield Neural Network 72
  *Łukasz Laskowski, Magdalena Laskowska, Jerzy Jelonkiewicz,
  and Arnaud Boullanger*

Toward Work Groups Classification Based on Probabilistic Neural
Network Approach 79
  *Christian Napoli, Giuseppe Pappalardo, Emiliano Tramontana,
  Robert K. Nowicki, Janusz T. Starczewski, and Marcin Woźniak*

Adaptation of RBM Learning for Intel MIC Architecture............. 90
  *Tomasz Olas, Wojciech K. Mleczko, Robert K. Nowicki,
  Roman Wyrzykowski, and Adam Krzyzak*

Using an Artificial Neural Network to Predict Loop
Transformation Time 102
  Marek Palkowski and Wlodzimierz Bielecki

Using Parity-N Problems as a Way to Compare Abilities of Shallow,
Very Shallow and Very Deep Architectures 112
   *Paweł Różycki, Janusz Kolbusz, Tomasz Bartczak,
   and Bogdan M. Wilamowski*

Product Multi-kernels for Sensor Data Analysis 123
   Petra Vidnerová and Roman Neruda

Fuzzy Systems and Their Applications

A Fuzzy Approach to Competitive Clusters Using Moore Families 137
   *Victor Gerardo Alfaro-Garcia, Anna Maria Gil-Lafuente,
   and Anna Klimova*

A Fingerprint Retrieval Technique Using Fuzzy Logic-Based Rules 149
   Rosario Arjona and Iluminada Baturone

Initial Comparison of Formal Approaches to Fuzzy and Rough Sets..... 160
   Adam Grabowski and Takashi Mitsuishi

Comparative Approach to the Multi-Valued Logic Construction
for Preferences... 172
   *Krystian Jobczyk, Antoni Ligęza, Maroua Bouzid,
   and Jerzy Karczmarczuk*

Learning Rules for Type-2 Fuzzy Logic System in the Control of
DeNOx Filter 184
   Marcin Kacprowicz, Adam Niewiadomski, and Krzysztof Renkas

Selected Applications of P1-TS Fuzzy Rule-Based Systems 195
   Jacek Kluska

Fuzzy Agglomerative Clustering 207
   Michal Konkol

An Exponential-Type Entropy Measure on Intuitionistic Fuzzy Sets 218
   Yessica Nataliani, Chao-Ming Hwang, and Miin-Shen Yang

Comparative Analysis of MCDM Methods for Assessing the Severity of
Chronic Liver Disease 228
   Andrzej Piegat and Wojciech Sałabun

Solving Zadeh's Challenge Problems with the Application of
RDM-Arithmetic 239
   Marcin Pluciński

The Directed Compatibility Between Ordered Fuzzy Numbers - A Base
Tool for a Direction Sensitive Fuzzy Information Processing 249
   Piotr Prokopowicz and Witold Pedrycz

Learning Rules for Hierarchical Fuzzy Logic Systems with Selective
Fuzzy Controller Activation 260
    Krzysztof Renkas, Adam Niewiadomski, and Marcin Kacprowicz

A New Approach to the Rule-Base Evidential Reasoning
with Application 271
    Pavel Sevastjanov, Ludmila Dymova, and Krzysztof Kaczmarek

Bias-Correction Fuzzy C-Regressions Algorithm 283
    Miin-Shen Yang, Yu-Zen Chen, and Yessica Nataliani

Interval Type-2 Locally Linear Neuro Fuzzy Model Based on Locally
Linear Model Tree 294
    Zahra Zamanzadeh Darban and Mohammad Hadi Valipour

Evolutionary Algorithms and Their Applications

Hybrids of Two-Subpopulation PSO Algorithm with Local Search
Methods for Continuous Optimization 307
    Aneta Bera and Dariusz Sychel

Parallel Coevolutionary Algorithm for Three-Dimensional Bin Packing
Problem 319
    Wojciech Bożejko, Łukasz Kacprzak, and Mieczysław Wodecki

Adaptive Differential Evolution: SHADE with Competing Crossover
Strategies 329
    Petr Bujok and Josef Tvrdík

A Parallel Approach for Evolutionary Induced Decision Trees.
MPI+OpenMP Implementation 340
    Marcin Czajkowski, Krzysztof Jurczuk, and Marek Kretowski

Automatic Grammar Induction for Grammar Based
Genetic Programming 350
    Dariusz Palka and Marek Zachara

On the Ability of the One-Point Crossover Operator to Search the
Space in Genetic Algorithms 361
    Zbigniew Pliszka and Olgierd Unold

Multiple Choice Strategy for PSO Algorithm Enhanced with
Dimensional Mutation 370
    Michal Pluhacek, Roman Senkerik, Ivan Zelinka,
    and Donald Davendra

A Hybrid Differential Evolution-Gradient Optimization Method 379
    Wojciech Rafajłowicz

On the Tuning of Complex Dynamics Embedded into Differential
Evolution   389
    Roman Senkerik, Michal Pluhacek, Ivan Zelinka, Donald Davendra,
    Zuzana Kominkova Oplatkova, and Roman Jasek

Classification and Estimation

Mathematical Characterization of Sophisticated Variants
for Relevance Learning in Learning Matrix Quantization
Based on Schatten-p-norms.   403
    Andrea Bohnsack, Kristin Domaschke, Marika Kaden,
    Mandy Lange, and Thomas Villmann

Adaptive Active Learning with Ensemble of Learners and Multiclass
Problems   415
    Wojciech Marian Czarnecki

Orthogonal Series Estimation of Regression Functions in Nonstationary
Conditions   427
    Tomasz Galkowski and Miroslaw Pawlak

A Comparison of Shallow Decision Trees Under Real-Boost Procedure
with Application to Landmine Detection Using Ground Penetrating
Radar   436
    Przemysław Klęsk, Mariusz Kapruziak, and Bogdan Olech

A New Interpretability Criteria for Neuro-Fuzzy Systems for Nonlinear
Classification   448
    Krystian Łapa, Krzysztof Cpałka, and Alexander I. Galushkin

Multi-class Nearest Neighbour Classifier for Incomplete
Data Handling.   469
    Bartosz A. Nowak, Robert K. Nowicki, Marcin Woźniak,
    and Christian Napoli

Cross-Entropy Clustering Approach to One-Class Classification   481
    Przemysaw Spurek, Mateusz Wójcik, and Jacek Tabor

Comparison of the Efficiency of Time and Frequency Descriptors Based
on Different Classification Conceptions   491
    Krzysztof Tyburek, Piotr Prokopowicz, Piotr Kotlarz,
    and Repka Michał

CNC Milling Tool Head Imbalance Prediction Using Computational
Intelligence Methods   503
    Tomasz Żabiński, Tomasz Mączka, Jacek Kluska, Maciej Kusy,
    Piotr Gierlak, Robert Hanus, Sławomir Prucnal, and Jarosław Sęp

Computer Vision, Image and Speech Analysis

A Feature-Based Machine Learning Agent for Automatic Rice and
Weed Discrimination   517
  Beibei Cheng and Eric T. Matson

Relation of Average Error in Prolate Spheroidal Wave Functions
Algorithm for Bandlimited Functions Approximation to Radius of
Information   528
  Michał Cholewa

Algebraic Logical Meta-Model of Decision Processes -
New Metaheuristics   541
  Ewa Dudek-Dyduch

Specific Object Detection Scheme Based on Descriptors Fusion Using
Belief Functions   555
  Mariem Farhat, Slim Mhiri, and Moncef Tagina

Video Key Frame Detection Based on SURF Algorithm   566
  Rafał Grycuk, Michał Knop, and Sayantan Mandal

Automatic Diagnosis of Melanoid Skin Lesions Using Machine Learning
Methods   577
  Katarzyna Grzesiak-Kopeć, Leszek Nowak, and Maciej Ogorzałek

An Edge Detection using 2D Gaussian Function in
Computed Tomography   586
  Michal Knas, Robert Cierniak, and Olga Rebrova

Facial Displays Description Schemas for Smiling vs. Neutral Emotion
Recognition   594
  Karolina Nurzyńska and Bogdan Smołka

Image Segmentation in Liquid Argon Time Projection
Chamber Detector   606
  Piotr Płoński, Dorota Stefan, Robert Sulej, and Krzysztof Zaremba

Massively Parallel Change Detection with Application to Visual
Quality Control   616
  Ewaryst Rafajłowicz and Karol Niżyński

A Fuzzy Logic Approach for Gender Recognition from Face Images
with Embedded Bandlets   626
  Zain Shabbir, Absar Ullah Khan, Aun Irtaza,
  and Muhammad Tariq Mahmood

Interpretation of Image Segmentation in Terms
of Justifiable Granularity   638
  Piotr S. Szczepaniak

Information Granules in Application to Image Recognition   649
  Krzysztof Wiaderek, Danuta Rutkowska,
  and Elisabeth Rakus-Andersson

Can We Process 2D Images Using Artificial Bee Colony?   660
  Marcin Woźniak, Dawid Połap, Marcin Gabryel, Robert K. Nowicki,
  Christian Napoli, and Emiliano Tramontana

Workshop: Large-Scale Visual Recognition and Machine Learning

Improving Effectiveness of SVM Classifier for Large Scale Data   675
  Jerzy Balicki, Julian Szymański, Marcin Kępa, Karol Draszawka,
  and Waldemar Korłub

Reducing Time Complexity of SVM Model
by LVQ Data Compression   687
  Marcin Blachnik

Secure Representation of Images Using Multi-layer Compression   696
  Sohrab Ferdowsi, Sviatoslav Voloshynovskiy, Dimche Kostadinov,
  Marcin Korytkowski, and Rafał Scherer

Image Indexing and Retrieval Using GSOM Algorithm   706
  Marcin Gabryel, Rafał Grycuk, Marcin Korytkowski,
  and Taras Holotyak

Multi-layer Architecture For Storing Visual Data Based on WCF and
Microsoft SQL Server Database   715
  Rafał Grycuk, Marcin Gabryel, Rafał Scherer,
  and Sviatoslav Voloshynovskiy

Object Localization Using Active Partitions
and Structural Description   727
  Mateusz Jadczyk and Arkadiusz Tomczyk

Supervised Transform Learning for Face Recognition   737
  Dimche Kostadinov, Sviatoslav Voloshynovskiy, Sohrab Ferdowsi,
  Maurits Diephuis, and Rafał Scherer

Fast Dictionary Matching for Content-Based Image Retrieval   747
  Patryk Najgebauer, Janusz Rygał, Tomasz Nowak,
  Jakub Romanowski, Leszek Rutkowski, Sviatoslav Voloshynovskiy,
  and Rafał Scherer

Recognition and Modeling of Atypical Children Behavior   757
  Aleksandra Postawka and Przemysław Śliwiński

Intelligent Fusion of Infrared and Visible Spectrum for Video
Surveillance Application 768
    Rania Rebai Boukhriss, Emna Fendri, and Mohamed Hammami

Visual Saccades for Object Recognition 778
    Janusz A. Starzyk

Improving Image Processing Performance Using Database User-Defined
Functions 789
    Michal Vagač and Miroslav Meličerčík

Author Index 801

Contents – Part II

Data Mining

Improvement of the Multiple-View Learning Based on the
Self-Organizing Maps 3
   Tomasz Galkowski, Artur Starczewski, and Xiuju Fu

Natural Language Processing Methods Used for Automatic Prediction
Mechanism of Related Phenomenon 13
   Krystian Horecki and Jacek Mazurkiewicz

Visual Exploration of Data with Multithread MIC Computer Architectures   25
   Piotr Pawliczek, Witold Dzwinel, and David A. Yuen

Random Forests with Weighted Voting for Anomalous Query Access
Detection in Relational Databases................................... 36
   Charissa Ann Ronao and Sung-Bae Cho

Performance Evaluation of the Silhouette Index..................... 49
   Artur Starczewski and Adam Krzyżak

Convex Nonnegative Matrix Factorization with Rank-1 Update for
Clustering 59
   Rafał Zdunek

Bioinformatics, Biometrics and Medical Applications

On the Convergence of Quantum and Distributed Computational
Models of Consciousness 71
   Susmit Bagchi

Nature-Inspired Algorithms for Selecting EEG Sources for Motor
Imagery Based BCI 79
   Sebastián Basterrech, Pavel Bobrov, Alexander Frolov,
   and Dušan Húsek

PROCESS: Projection-Based Classification of Electroencephalograph
Signals 91
   Krisztian Buza, Júlia Koller, and Kristóf Marussy

Feature Extraction of Palm Vein Patterns Based on Two-Dimensional
Density Function 101
   Mariusz Kubanek, Dorota Smorawa, and Taras Holotyak

Segmentation Based Feature Selection on Classifying Proteomic
Spectral Data 112
  Hsun-Chih Kuo and Sheng-Tzung Yeh

SOM vs FCM vs PCA in 3D Face Recognition 120
  Sebastian Pabiasz, Janusz T. Starczewski, and Antonino Marvuglia

The Fuzzified Quasi-Perceptron in Decision Making Concerning
Treatments in Necrotizing Fasciitis 130
  Elisabeth Rakus-Andersson, Janusz Frey, and Danuta Rutkowska

Mobile Fuzzy System for Detecting Loss of Consciousness and Epileptic
Seizure 142
  Paweł Staszewski, Piotr Woldan, and Sohrab Ferdowsi

Customization of Joint Articulations Using Soft Computing Methods ... 151
  Arkadiusz Szarek, Marcin Korytkowski, Leszek Rutkowski,
  Magdalena Scherer, Janusz Szyprowski, and Dimce Kostadinov

A New Method for the Dynamic Signature Verification Based on the
Stable Partitions of the Signature 161
  Marcin Zalasiński, Krzysztof Cpałka, and Meng Joo Er

New Fast Algorithm for the Dynamic Signature Verification Using
Global Features Values 175
  Marcin Zalasiński, Krzysztof Cpałka, and Yoichi Hayashi

Concurrent Parallel Processing

Parallelization of a Block Cipher Based on Chaotic Neural Networks ... 191
  Dariusz Burak

Acceleration of Neighborhood Evaluation for a Multi-objective Vehicle
Routing 202
  Szymon Jagiełło, Jarosław Rudy, and Dominik Żelazny

A Concurrent Inconsistency Reduction Algorithm for the Pairwise
Comparisons Method 214
  Konrad Kułakowski, Radosław Juszczyk, and Sebastian Ernst

OpenCL Implementation of PSO Algorithm for the Quadratic
Assignment Problem 223
  Piotr Szwed, Wojciech Chmiel, and Piotr Kadłuczka

Agent Systems, Robotics and Control

Towards a Better Understanding and Behavior Recognition of
Inhabitants in Smart Cities. A Public Transport Case 237
  Radosław Klimek and Leszek Kotulski

Aspects of Structure and Parameters Selection of Control Systems
Using Selected Multi-Population Algorithms   247
    Krystian Łapa, Jacek Szczypta, and Rajasekar Venkatesan

Optimization of Controller Structure Using Evolutionary Algorithm   261
    Andrzej Przybył, Jacek Szczypta, and Lipo Wang

Multi-Criteria Fuel Distribution: A Case Study   272
    Jarosław Rudy and Dominik Żelazny

A Robust Heuristic for the Multidimensional A-star/Wavefront Hybrid
Planning Algorithm   282
    Igor Wojnicki, Sebastian Ernst, and Wojciech Turek

Human-Agent Interaction Design for Decreasing Indebtedness   292
    Saori Yamamoto and Yugo Takeuchi

Artificial Intelligence in Modeling and Simulation

Fuzzy Xor Classes from Quantum Computing   305
    Anderson Ávila, Murilo Schmalfuss, Renata Reiser,
    and Vladik Kreinovich

New Method for Non-linear Correction Modelling of Dynamic Objects
with Genetic Programming   318
    Łukasz Bartczuk, Andrzej Przybył, and Petia Koprinkova-Hristova

Clustering Algorithm Based on Molecular Dynamics with Nose-Hoover
Thermostat. Application to Japanese Candlesticks   330
    Leszek J. Chmielewski, Maciej Janowicz, and Arkadiusz Orłowski

Improving the Analysis of Context-Aware Information via Marker-Based
Stigmergy and Differential Evolution   341
    Mario G.C.A. Cimino, Alessandro Lazzeri, and Gigliola Vaglini

Modeling Manufacturing Processes with Disturbances - A New Method
Based on Algebraic-Logical Meta-Models   353
    Ewa Dudek-Dyduch

A New Approach to Nonlinear Modeling Based on Significant Operating
Points Detection   364
    Piotr Dziwiński and Eduard D. Avedyan

An Application of Differential Evolution to Positioning Queueing
Systems   379
    Marcin Gabryel, Marcin Woźniak, and Robertas Damaševičius

Experimental Evaluation of Selected Approaches to Covariance Matrix
Regularization   391
    Przemysław Głomb and Michał Cholewa

A New Approach to Security Games 402
 Jan Karwowski and Jacek Mańdziuk

Proposal of a Context-Aware Smart Home Ecosystem 412
 Radosław Klimek and Grzegorz Rogus

Computational Models of Immediate and Expected Emotions for
Emotional BDI Agents 424
 Hanen Lejmi-Riahi, Fahem Kebair, and Lamjed Ben Said

A Graph Grammar Tool for Generating Computational Grid
Structures 436
 Wojciech Palacz, Iwona Ryszka, and Ewa Grabska

Assessment of Fertilizer Nitrogen Requirement of Sugar Beetroot Using
Info-Gap Theory 448
 Andrzej Piegat and Karina Tomaszewska

Geometric Approach in Local Modeling: Learning of Mini-models
Based on n-Dimensional Simplex 460
 Marcin Pietrzykowski and Andrzej Piegat

Immune Optimal Design of 2-D and 3-D Structures 471
 Arkadiusz Poteralski, Mirosław Szczepanik, and Tadeusz Burczyński

Swarm and Immune Computing of Dynamically Loaded Reinforced
Structures 483
 Arkadiusz Poteralski, Mirosław Szczepanik, Radosław Górski,
 and Tadeusz Burczyński

The Setup Method of the Order with the Help of the Rough Sets
Convention 495
 Aleksandra Ptak, Henryk Piech, and Nina Zhou

ALMM Solver: The Idea and the Architecture 504
 Krzysztof Rączka, Ewa Dudek-Dyduch, Edyta Kucharska,
 and Lidia Dutkiewicz

Graph-Based Optimization of Energy Efficiency of Street Lighting 515
 Adam Sędziwy and Leszek Kotulski

Extended AMUSE Algorithm and Novel Randomness Approach for
BSS Model Aggregation with Methodology Remarks 527
 Ryszard Szupiluk, Tomasz Ząbkowski, and Krzysztof Gajowniczek

Various Problems of Artificial Intelligence

Constraint Optimization Production Planning Problem. A Note on
Theory, Selected Approaches and Computational Experiments   541
    Weronika T. Adrian, Nicola Leone, Antoni Ligęza, Marco Manna,
    and Mateusz Ślażyński

Investigating the Mapping between Default Logic and Inconsistency-
Tolerant Semantics   554
    Abdallah Arioua, Nouredine Tamani, Madalina Croitoru,
    Jérôme Fortin, and Patrice Buche

Automated Discovery of Mobile Users Locations with Improved
K-means Clustering   565
    Szymon Bobek, Grzegorz J. Nalepa, and Olgierd Grodzki

Capturing Dynamics of Mobile Context-Aware Systems with Rules and
Statistical Analysis of Historical Data   578
    Szymon Bobek, Mateusz Ślażyński, and Grzegorz J. Nalepa

Reasoning over Vague Concepts   591
    Mustapha Bourahla

Parallel Simulated Annealing Algorithm for Cyclic Flexible Job Shop
Scheduling Problem   603
    Wojciech Bożejko, Jarosław Pempera, and Mieczysław Wodecki

Transactional Forward Chaining: A Functional Approach   613
    Konrad Grzanek

Metasets and Opinion Mining in New Decision Support System   625
    Magdalena Kacprzak, Bartłomiej Starosta,
    and Katarzyna Węgrzyn-Wolska

Practical Approach to Interoperability in Production Rule Bases with
SUBITO   637
    Krzysztof Kaczor

Measuring Complexity of Business Process Models Integrated
with Rules   649
    Krzysztof Kluza

On Perturbation Measure for Binary Vectors   660
    Maciej Krawczak and Grażyna Szkatuła

A Quick Method for Dynamic Difficulty Adjustment of a Computer
Player in Computer Games   669
    Ewa Lach

UCT-Based Approach to Capacitated Vehicle Routing Problem   679
  Jacek Mańdziuk and Cezary Nejman

An Improved Magnetotactic Bacteria Moment Migration Optimization
Algorithm.   691
  Hongwei Mo, Jingwen Ma, and Yanyan Zhao

SBVRwiki a Web-Based Tool for Authoring of Business Rules   703
  Grzegorz J. Nalepa, Krzysztof Kluza, and Krzysztof Kaczor

Classification in Sparse, High Dimensional Environments Applied to
Distributed Systems Failure Prediction   714
  José M. Navarro, Hugo A. Parada G., and Juan C. Dueñas

Balanced Support Vector Regression.   727
  Marcin Orchel

Adaptation Mechanism of Feedback in Quaternion Kalman Filtering
for Orientation Estimation   739
  *Przemysław Pruszowski, Agnieszka Szczęsna, Andrzej Polański,
  Janusz Słupik, and Konrad Wojciechowski*

Using Graph Grammar Systems with Memory in Computer
Aided Design   749
  Iwona Ryszka and Barbara Strug

Software Framework for Modular Machine Learning Systems   760
  Marcin Korytkowski, Magdalena Scherer, and Sohrab Ferdowsi

Using Co-occurring Graph Patterns in Computer Aided Design
Evaluation   768
  Barbara Strug

Parallel Cost Function Determination on GPU for the Vehicle Routing
Problem   778
  *Mieczysław Wodecki, Wojciech Bożejko, Szymon Jagiełło,
  and Jarosław Pempera*

A DSS Based on Hybrid Meta-Heuristic ILS-VND for Solving the
1-PDTSP   789
  Hiba Yahyaoui and Saoussen Krichen

On Enhancing the Label Propagation Algorithm for Sentiment Analysis
Using Active Learning with an Artificial Oracle   799
  *Anis Yazidi, Hugo Lewi Hammer, Aleksander Bai,
  and Paal Engelstad*

Author Index   811

Neural Networks and Their Applications

Parallel Approach to the Levenberg-Marquardt Learning Algorithm for Feedforward Neural Networks

Jarosław Bilski[1(✉)], Jacek Smoląg[1], and Jacek M. Żurada[2,3]

[1] Institute of Computational Intelligence, Częstochowa University of Technology, Częstochowa, Poland
{Jaroslaw.Bilski,Jacek.Smolag}@iisi.pcz.pl
[2] Information Technology Institute, University of Sociel Sciences, Łódź, Poland
[3] Department Electrical and Computer Engineering, University of Louisville, Louisville, KY 40292, US
jacek.zurada@louisville.edu

Abstract. A parallel architecture of the Levenberg-Marquardt algorithm for training a feedforward neural network is presented. The proposed solution is based on completely new parallel structures to effectively reduce high computational load of this algorithm. Detailed parallel neural network structures are explicitly discussed.

1 Introduction

Feedforward neural networks have been investigated by many scientists e.g. [1], [10], [19], [23], [26], [37], [39]. Gradient methods have been often used to train feedforward networks, see e.g. [14], [24], [38]. In the traditional approach neural networks learning algorithms, like other learning algorihms [25], [28], [29], [31], [34], are implemented on a serial computer. Due to the computational complexity of the learning algorithm, the serial implementation is very time consuming and slow. The Levenberg Marquart algorithm [15], [22] is one of the most effective learning methods, but requires particularly complex calculations. Unfortunately, for very large networks the computational load of the Levenberg-Marquardt algorithm makes it impractical. A suitable solution to this problem is the use of high performance dedicated parallel structures, see eg. [2] - [9], [32], [33]. This paper presents a new concept of parallel realisation of the Levenberg-Marquardt learning algorithm. A single iteration of the parallel architecture requires much fewer computation cycles than a serial implementation. The efficiency of this new architecture is very satisfying and is explained in the last part of the paper.

A sample structure of the feedforward network is shown in Fig. 1. The network has L layers, N_l neurons in each $l - th$ layer and N_L outputs. The input vector contains N_0 input signals. The equation (1) describes the recall phase of the network

$$s_i^{(l)}(t) = \sum_{j=0}^{N_{l-1}} w_{ij}^{(l)}(t)\, x_i^{(l)}(t),$$

$$y_i^{(l)}(t) = f(s_i^{(l)}(t)). \tag{1}$$

L. Rutkowski et al. (Eds.): ICAISC 2015, Part I, LNAI 9119, pp. 3–14, 2015.
DOI: 10.1007/978-3-319-19324-3_1

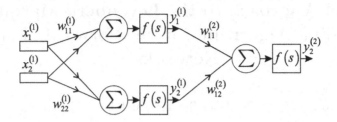

Fig. 1. Feedforward neural network sample structure

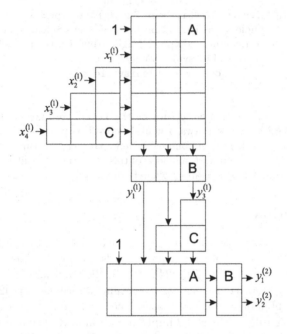

Fig. 2. Pipelined version of recall phase of the feedforward network

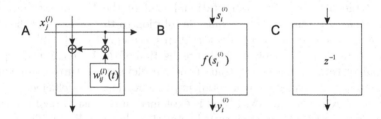

Fig. 3. The structures of recall phase processing elements

The parallel realisation of the recall phase algorithm uses the architecture which requires many simple processing elements. The pipelined version of the parallel realisation of the feedforward network in recall phase (1) is depicted in Fig. 2 and its processing elements (PE) in Fig. 3. Two main kinds of functional processing elements are used in the proposed solution. The aim of the processing elements A is to create matrices which contain values of weights in all layers. The input signals are entered parallelly into the rows of the elements, multiplied by weights and finally the received results are summed in the columns. The activation function for each neuron in the $l - th$ layer is calculated after determination of product $\mathbf{w}_i^{(l)}\mathbf{x}^{(l)}$ in the processing element of type B. Additional processing element C is used to delay transferred data. Thus the structure operates in a pipeline flow and next results can be obtained after only one step. The outputs of neurons in the previous layer act the same time as inputs to the next layer. The output $\mathbf{y}^{(L)}$ for the last layer is the output of the whole network.

The Levenberg-Marquard method [15], [22] is used to train the feedforward network. The following goal criterion is minimized

$$
E\left(\mathbf{w}\left(n\right)\right) = \frac{1}{2}\sum_{t=1}^{Q}\sum_{r=1}^{N_L} \varepsilon_r^{(L)2}\left(t\right) = \frac{1}{2}\sum_{t=1}^{Q}\sum_{r=1}^{N_L} \left(y_r^{(L)}\left(t\right) - d_r^{(L)}\left(t\right)\right)^2 \tag{2}
$$

where $\varepsilon_i^{(L)}$ is defined as

$$
\varepsilon_r^{(L)}(t) = \varepsilon_r^{(Lr)}(t) = y_r^{(L)}(t) - d_r^{(L)}(t) \tag{3}
$$

and $d_r^{(L)}(t)$ is the $r - th$ desired output in the $t - th$ probe.

The Levenberg-Marquardt algorithm is a modification of the Newton method and is based on the first three elements of the Taylor series expansion of the goal function. In the classical case a change of weights is given by

$$
\Delta\left(\mathbf{w}(n)\right) = -\left[\nabla^2\mathbf{E}\left(\mathbf{w}(n)\right)\right]^{-1}\nabla\mathbf{E}\left(\mathbf{w}(n)\right) \tag{4}
$$

this requires knowledge of the gradient vector

$$
\nabla\mathbf{E}\left(\mathbf{w}(n)\right) = \mathbf{J}^T\left(\mathbf{w}(n)\right)\varepsilon\left(\mathbf{w}(n)\right) \tag{5}
$$

and the Hessian matrix

$$
\nabla^2\mathbf{E}\left(\mathbf{w}(n)\right) = \mathbf{J}^T\left(\mathbf{w}(n)\right)\mathbf{J}\left(\mathbf{w}(n)\right) + \mathbf{S}\left(\mathbf{w}(n)\right) \tag{6}
$$

where $\mathbf{J}\left(\mathbf{w(n)}\right)$ in (5) and (6) is the Jacobian matrix

$$
\mathbf{J}(\mathbf{w}\left(n\right)) = \begin{bmatrix} \frac{\partial\varepsilon_1^{(L)}(1)}{\partial w_{10}^{(1)}} & \frac{\partial\varepsilon_1^{(L)}(1)}{\partial w_{11}^{(1)}} & \cdots & \frac{\partial\varepsilon_1^{(L)}(1)}{\partial w_{ij}^{(k)}} & \cdots & \frac{\partial\varepsilon_1^{(L)}(1)}{\partial w_{N_L N_{L-1}}^{(L)}} \\ \vdots & \vdots & \vdots & \vdots & \vdots & \vdots \\ \frac{\partial\varepsilon_{N_L}^{(L)}(1)}{\partial w_{10}^{(1)}} & \frac{\partial\varepsilon_{N_L}^{(L)}(1)}{\partial w_{11}^{(1)}} & \cdots & \frac{\partial\varepsilon_{N_L}^{(L)}(1)}{\partial w_{ij}^{(k)}} & \cdots & \frac{\partial\varepsilon_{N_L}^{(L)}(1)}{\partial w_{N_L N_{L-1}}^{(L)}} \\ \vdots & \vdots & \vdots & \vdots & \vdots & \vdots \\ \frac{\partial\varepsilon_{N_L}^{(L)}(Q)}{\partial w_{10}^{(1)}} & \frac{\partial\varepsilon_{N_L}^{(L)}(Q)}{\partial w_{10}^{(1)}} & \cdots & \frac{\partial\varepsilon_{N_L}^{(L)}(Q)}{\partial w_{ij}^{(k)}} & \cdots & \frac{\partial\varepsilon_{N_L}^{(L)}(Q)}{\partial w_{N_L N_{L-1}}^{(L)}} \end{bmatrix}. \tag{7}
$$

The errors $\varepsilon_i^{(lr)}$ in the hidden layers are calculated as follows

$$\varepsilon_i^{(lr)}(t) \triangleq \sum_{m=1}^{N_{l+1}} \delta_i^{(l+1,r)}(t) w_{mi}^{(l+1)}, \tag{8}$$

$$\delta_i^{(lr)}(t) = \varepsilon_i^{(lr)}(t) f'\left(s_i^{(lr)}(t)\right). \tag{9}$$

On this basis, the components of the Jacobian matrix for each weight can be determined

$$\frac{\partial \varepsilon_r^{(L)}(t)}{w_{ij}^{(l)}} = \delta_i^{(lr)}(t) x_j^{(l)}(t). \tag{10}$$

It should be noted that derivatives (10) are computed in a similar way it is done in the classical backpropagation method, except that each time there is only one error given to the output. In this algorithm, the weights of the entire network are treated as a single vector and their derivatives form the Jacobian matrix $\mathbf{J}$.

The $\mathbf{S}(\mathbf{w}(n))$ component (6) is given by the formula

$$\mathbf{S}(\mathbf{w}(n)) = \sum_{t=1}^{Q} \sum_{r=1}^{N_L} \varepsilon_r^{(L)}(t) \nabla^2 \varepsilon_r^{(L)}(t). \tag{11}$$

In the Gauss-Newton method it is assumed that $\mathbf{S}(\mathbf{w}(n)) \approx 0$ and that equation (4) takes the form

$$\Delta(\mathbf{w}(n)) = -\left[\mathbf{J}^T(\mathbf{w}(n)) \mathbf{J}(\mathbf{w}(n))\right]^{-1} \mathbf{J}^T(\mathbf{w}(n)) \varepsilon(\mathbf{w}(n)). \tag{12}$$

In the Levenberg-Marquardt method is is assumed that $\mathbf{S}(\mathbf{w}(n)) = \mu\mathbf{I}$ and that equation (4) takes the form

$$\Delta(\mathbf{w}(n)) = -\left[\mathbf{J}^T(\mathbf{w}(n)) \mathbf{J}(\mathbf{w}(n)) + \mu\mathbf{I}\right]^{-1} \mathbf{J}^T(\mathbf{w}(n)) \varepsilon(\mathbf{w}(n)). \tag{13}$$

By defining

$$\begin{aligned}\mathbf{A}(n) &= -\left[\mathbf{J}^T(\mathbf{w}(n)) \mathbf{J}(\mathbf{w}(n)) + \mu\mathbf{I}\right] \\ \mathbf{h}(n) &= \mathbf{J}^T(\mathbf{w}(n)) \varepsilon(\mathbf{w}(n))\end{aligned} \tag{14}$$

the equation (13) is as follows

$$\Delta(\mathbf{w}(n)) = \mathbf{A}(n)^{-1}\mathbf{h}(n). \tag{15}$$

The equation (15) can be solved using the QR factorization

$$\mathbf{Q}^T(n) \mathbf{A}(n) \Delta(\mathbf{w}(n)) = \mathbf{Q}^T(n) \mathbf{h}(n), \tag{16}$$

$$\mathbf{R}(n) \Delta(\mathbf{w}(n)) = \mathbf{Q}^T(n) \mathbf{h}(n). \tag{17}$$

This paper used the Householder reflection method for the QR factorization. Operation of the Levenberg-Marquardt algorithm is described below. In practice, the algorithm is implemented in 5 steps:

1. The calculation of the network outputs for all input data, errors and the goal criterion.
2. The calculation the Jacobian matrix, by applying the backpropagation method for each error individually.
3. The calculation of $\Delta\left(\mathbf{w}(n)\right)$ by using the QR factorization.
4. The recalculation of the goal criterion (2) for $\mathbf{w}(n) + \Delta\left(\mathbf{w}(n)\right)$. If the goal criterion is less than the one calculated in step 1, then μ should be reduced β times, the new weight vector remains and the algorithm returns to Step 1. Otherwise, the μ value should be increased β times and the algorithm goes back to step 3.
5. The algorithm terminates when the gradient falls below a preset value or the goal function falls below a preset value.

2   Parallel Realisation

First, the errors in all neurons using backpropagation are calculated assuming that each time only one error is given to the output and than the Jacobian matrix is determined. This is accomplished by the structure shown in Fig. 4. Its processing elements are shown in Fig. 5. The A processing elements are used to calculate the error $\varepsilon_r^{(L)}$ (3) in the output layer. The B elements transfer the errors to the linear part of neurons (9), and the D processing elements compute errors

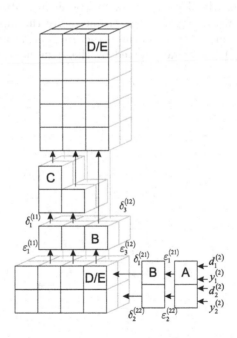

Fig. 4. The structure showing how to propagate error back and compute the Jacobian matrix elements

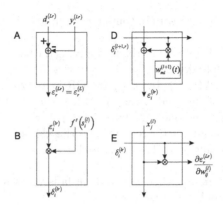

Fig. 5. The processing elements for propagating error back and computing the Jacobian matrix elements

$\varepsilon_i^{(lr)}$ in the hidden layers (8). The E processing elements determine the elements of the Jacobian matrix (10). It should be noted that at the same time all rows of the Jacobian matrix for all output errors of a single sample are determined. This is achieved by the use of L parallel layers. The structure shown in Fig. 4 starts operation immediately after the calculation of the outputs perfomed by the structure in Fig 2 for the data of the first sample. The $\mathbf{A}(n)$ matrix (14) is calculated based on the Jacobian matrix. These calculations are performed by the structure shown in Fig. 6. In the same figure the internal structure of the individual processing elements in this structure is also shown. At the same time, the vector $\mathbf{h}(n)$ (14) is determined by the structure shown in Figure 7.

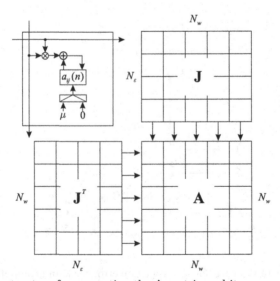

Fig. 6. The structure for computing the $\mathbf{A}$ matrix and its processing element

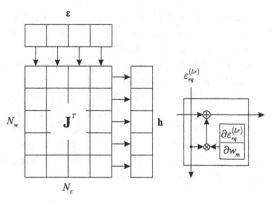

Fig. 7. The structure for computing the **h** vector and its processing element

After calculating the $\mathbf{A}(n)$ matrix and the $\mathbf{h}(n)$ vector, the equation (15) is solved. The equation (15) can be solved using the QR factorization . This will be achieved by the use of the Hauseholder reflections. The parallel structure calculating matrices $\mathbf{R}$ and $\mathbf{Q}^T\mathbf{h}$ is shown in Fig. 8. Elements A2 transform

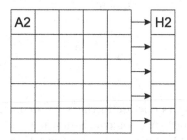

Fig. 8. The general structure for parallelization of the QR decomposition

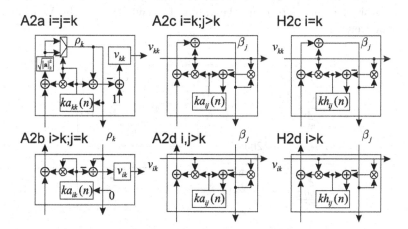

Fig. 9. The processing elements of the QR decomposition

the elements of the **A** matrix and elements H2 transform the elements of the **h** vector. This step performs a sequence of the Householder reflection so as to reset the elements below the main diagonal of the **A** matrix. First, the elements in the first column are reset, then the second and so on, until the last but one. The **A** matrix and the **h** vector are transformed. The vectors used to perform reflections are based on the columns of the **A** matrix, except that it includes the elements from the main diagonal to the end of the column. It should be noted that the QR decomposition process requires the $N_w - 1$ matrix reflections. The A2 and H2 processing elements will operate differently depending on the phase (k) of the process (Fig. 9). The A2a and A2b elements determine the module of the **a** subvector and, on this basis, calculate the value

$$\rho_k = \begin{cases} \|\mathbf{a}_k\|_2 & for\ a_{kk} \leq 0 \\ -\|\mathbf{a}_k\|_2 & for\ a_{kk} > 0, \end{cases} \tag{18}$$

and the reflection vector

$$\mathbf{v}_k = \begin{bmatrix} \mathbf{0} \\ \bar{\mathbf{v}}_k \end{bmatrix}. \tag{19}$$

The **v** vector is transmitted to the elements A2c and A2d which in the next columns calculate the values of the reflected vectors $\bar{\mathbf{a}}$

$$\bar{\mathbf{a}} = \mathbf{a} - \mathbf{v}\beta \tag{20}$$

where

$$\beta = \frac{\mathbf{v}^T \mathbf{a}}{\gamma} \tag{21}$$

$$\gamma = v_1. \tag{22}$$

The H2c and H2d elements operate in the same manner on the **h** vector. The construction of all the processing elements is shown in Fig. 9. After determination of the **R** matrix and the $\mathbf{Q}^T\mathbf{h}$ vector the equation (17) is solved. This is realized by the structure shown in Fig. 10. Its elements are also shown in this figure. The A3a and A3b elements determine the value of $\Delta(\mathbf{w}(n))$, and the W elements update the weights.

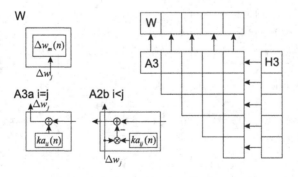

Fig. 10. The structure for computing the weight vector **w** and its processing element

3   Conclusion

In this paper the parallel realisation of the Leveberg-Marquardt learning algorithm for a feedforward neural network is proposed. It is assumed that all multiplications and additions are performed within the same time unit. To make the presentation of the results simple, graphs only for the neural network shown in Fig. 1 with variable neuron number in the hidden layer are presented. We can compare computational performance of the parallel implementation of the Levenberg-Marquardt learning algorithm with a sequential solution for a two-layer network with two inputs, one output, up to $N = 100$ neurons in the hidden layer and up to $Q = 100$ samples of the learning data of a neural network. Computational complexity of the serial Levenberg-Marquardt learning algorithm is of order $\mathcal{O}(N^3)$ and equals $TS = 21\frac{1}{3}N^3 + 72N^2 + 48\frac{2}{3}N + 32N^2Q + 38NQ + 10Q$. In the presented parallel architecture each epoch requires only $TP = 16N^2 + 53N + 2Q + 15$ time units (see Fig. 11). Performance factor ($PF = TS/TP$) of parallel realisation of the Levenberg-Marquardt learning algorithm achieves nearly 330 for $N = 100$ neurons in the hidden layer, $Q = 100$ samples of the learning data and it grows fast when these numbers grow, see Fig. 11. It has been observed that the performance of the proposed solution is promising. An analogous parallel approach can be used for other advanced learning algorithms of feedforward neural networks, see eg. [1], [7]. In the future research we plan to design parallel realisation of learning of other structures including probabilistic neural networks [27] and various fuzzy [11], [17], [20], [35], [36], [40], and neuro-fuzzy structures [12], [13], [16], [18], [21], [30].

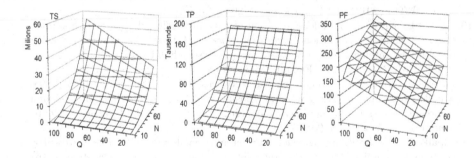

Fig. 11. Number of times cycles in a) classical (serial), b) parallel implementation and c) performance factor

References

1. Bilski, J.: The UD RLS algorithm for training the feedforward neural networks. International Journal of Applied Mathematics and Computer Science 15(1), 101–109 (2005)

2. Bilski, J., Litwiński, S., Smoląg, J.: Parallel realisation of QR algorithm for neural networks learning. In: Rutkowski, L., Siekmann, J.H., Tadeusiewicz, R., Zadeh, L.A. (eds.) ICAISC 2004. LNCS (LNAI), vol. 3070, pp. 158–165. Springer, Heidelberg (2004)

3. Bilski, J., Smoląg, J.: Parallel realisation of the recurrent RTRN neural network learning. In: Rutkowski, L., Tadeusiewicz, R., Zadeh, L.A., Zurada, J.M. (eds.) ICAISC 2008. LNCS (LNAI), vol. 5097, pp. 11–16. Springer, Heidelberg (2008)

4. Bilski, J., Smoląg, J.: Parallel realisation of the recurrent Elman neural network learning. In: Rutkowski, L., Scherer, R., Tadeusiewicz, R., Zadeh, L.A., Zurada, J.M. (eds.) ICAISC 2010, Part II. LNCS (LNAI), vol. 6114, pp. 19–25. Springer, Heidelberg (2010)

5. Bilski, J., Smoląg, J.: Parallel realisation of the recurrent multi layer perceptron learning. In: Rutkowski, L., Korytkowski, M., Scherer, R., Tadeusiewicz, R., Zadeh, L.A., Zurada, J.M. (eds.) ICAISC 2012, Part I. LNCS (LNAI), vol. 7267, pp. 12–20. Springer, Heidelberg (2012)

6. Bilski, J., Smoląg, J.: Parallel approach to learning of the recurrent Jordan neural network. In: Rutkowski, L., Korytkowski, M., Scherer, R., Tadeusiewicz, R., Zadeh, L.A., Zurada, J.M. (eds.) ICAISC 2013, Part I. LNCS (LNAI), vol. 7894, pp. 32–40. Springer, Heidelberg (2013)

7. Bilski, J.: Parallel Structures for Feedforward and Dynamical Neural Networks (in Polish). AOW EXIT (2013)

8. Bilski, J., Smoląg, J., Galushkin, A.I.: The parallel approach to the conjugate gradient learning algorithm for the feedforward neural networks. In: Rutkowski, L., Korytkowski, M., Scherer, R., Tadeusiewicz, R., Zadeh, L.A., Zurada, J.M. (eds.) ICAISC 2014, Part I. LNCS (LNAI), vol. 8467, pp. 12–21. Springer, Heidelberg (2014)

9. Bilski, J., Smoląg, J.: Parallel Architectures for Learning the RTRN and Elman Dynamic Neural Networks. IEEE Transactions on Parallel and Distributed Systems PP(99) (2014), doi:10.1109/TPDS.2014.2357019

10. Chu, J.L., Krzyżak, A.: The recognition of partially occluded objects with support vector machines, convolutional neural networks and deep belief networks. Journal of Artificial Intelligence and Soft Computing Research 4(1), 5–19 (2014)

11. Cpałka, K., Rutkowski, L.: Flexible Takagi-Sugeno Fuzzy Systems. In: Proceedings of the Int. Joint Conference on Neural Networks, Montreal, pp. 1764–1769 (2005)

12. Cpałka, K., Łapa, K., Przybył, A., Zalasiński, M.: A new method for designing neuro-fuzzy systems for nonlinear modelling with interpretability aspects. Neurocomputing 135, 203–217 (2014)

13. Cpalka, K., Rebrova, O., Nowicki, R., et al.: On design of flexible neuro-fuzzy systems for nonlinear modelling. International Journal of General Systems 42(6), Special Issue: SI, 706–720 (2013)

14. Fahlman, S.: Faster learning variations on backpropagation: An empirical study. In: Proceedings of Connectionist Models Summer School, Los Atos (1988)

15. Hagan, M.T., Menhaj, M.B.: Training feedforward networks with the Marquardt algorithm. IEEE Transactions on Neural Networks 5(6), 989–993 (1994)

16. Korytkowski, M., Nowicki, R., Rutkowski, L., Scherer, R.: AdaBoost Ensemble of DCOG Rough–Neuro–Fuzzy Systems. In: Jędrzejowicz, P., Nguyen, N.T., Hoang, K. (eds.) ICCCI 2011, Part I. LNCS, vol. 6922, pp. 62–71. Springer, Heidelberg (2011)

17. Korytkowski, M., Rutkowski, L., Scherer, R.: From ensemble of fuzzy classifiers to single fuzzy rule base classifier. In: Rutkowski, L., Tadeusiewicz, R., Zadeh, L.A., Zurada, J.M. (eds.) ICAISC 2008. LNCS (LNAI), vol. 5097, pp. 265–272. Springer, Heidelberg (2008)
18. Korytkowski, M., Scherer, R.: Negative Correlation Learning of Neuro-fuzzy System Ensembles. In: Rutkowski, L., Scherer, R., Tadeusiewicz, R., Zadeh, L.A., Zurada, J.M. (eds.) ICAISC 2010, Part I. LNCS (LNAI), vol. 6113, pp. 114–119. Springer, Heidelberg (2010)
19. Laskowski, L., Jelonkiewicz, J.: Self-Correcting Neural Network for stereo-matching problem solving. Fundamenta Informaticae 138, 1–26 (2015)
20. Łapa, K., Przybył, A., Cpałka, K.: A new approach to designing interpretable models of dynamic systems. In: Rutkowski, L., Korytkowski, M., Scherer, R., Tadeusiewicz, R., Zadeh, L.A., Zurada, J.M. (eds.) ICAISC 2013, Part II. LNCS (LNAI), vol. 7895, pp. 523–534. Springer, Heidelberg (2013)
21. Łapa, K., Zalasiński, M., Cpałka, K.: A new method for designing and complexity reduction of neuro-fuzzy systems for nonlinear modelling. In: Rutkowski, L., Korytkowski, M., Scherer, R., Tadeusiewicz, R., Zadeh, L.A., Zurada, J.M. (eds.) ICAISC 2013, Part I. LNCS (LNAI), vol. 7894, pp. 329–344. Springer, Heidelberg (2013)
22. Marqardt, D.: An algorithm for last-sqares estimation of nonlinear paeameters. J. Soc. Ind. Appl. Math., 431–441 (1963)
23. Patan, K., Patan, M.: Optimal training strategies for locally recurrent neural networks. Journal of Artificial Intelligence and Soft Computing Research 1(2), 103–114 (2011)
24. Riedmiller, M., Braun, H.: A direct method for faster backpropagation learning: The RPROP Algorithm. In: IEEE International Conference on Neural Networks, San Francisco (1993)
25. Romaszewski, M., Gawron, P., Opozda, S.: Dimensionality reduction of dynamic msh animations using HO-SVD. Journal of Artificial Intelligence and Soft Computing Research 3(3), 277–289 (2013)
26. Rumelhart, D.E., Hinton, G.E., Williams, R.J.: Learning internal representations by error propagation. In: Rumelhart, D.E., McCelland, J. (red.) Parallel Distributed Processing, ch. 8, vol. 1. The MIT Press, Cambridge (1986)
27. Rutkowski, L.: Multiple Fourier series procedures for extraction of nonlinear regressions from noisy data. IEEE Transactions on Signal Processing 41(10), 3062–3065 (1993)
28. Rutkowski, L.: Identification of MISO nonlinear regressions in the presence of a wide class of disturbances. IEEE Transactions on Information Theory 37(1), 214–216 (1991)
29. Rutkowski, L., Jaworski, M., Pietruczuk, L., Duda, P.: Decision trees for mining data streams based on the gaussian approximation. IEEE Transactions on Knowledge and Data Engineering 26(1), 108–119 (2014)
30. Rutkowski, L., Przybył, A., Cpałka, K., Er, M.J.: Online speed profile generation for industrial machine tool based on neuro-fuzzy approach. In: Rutkowski, L., Scherer, R., Tadeusiewicz, R., Zadeh, L.A., Zurada, J.M. (eds.) ICAISC 2010, Part II. LNCS (LNAI), vol. 6114, pp. 645–650. Springer, Heidelberg (2010)
31. Rutkowski, L., Rafajlowicz, E.: On optimal global rate of convergence of some nonparametric identification procedures. IEEE Transactions on Automatic Control 34(10), 1089–1091 (1989)
32. Smoląg, J., Bilski, J.: A systolic array for fast learning of neural networks. In: Proc. of V Conf. Neural Networks and Soft Computing, Zakopane, pp. 754–758 (2000)

33. Smoląg, J., Rutkowski, L., Bilski, J.: Systolic array for neural networks. In: Proc. of IV Conf. Neural Networks and Their Applications, Zakopane, pp. 487–497 (1999)
34. Starczewski, A.: A clustering method based on the modified RS validity index. In: Rutkowski, L., Korytkowski, M., Scherer, R., Tadeusiewicz, R., Zadeh, L.A., Zurada, J.M. (eds.) ICAISC 2013, Part II. LNCS (LNAI), vol. 7895, pp. 242–250. Springer, Heidelberg (2013)
35. Starczewski, J., Rutkowski, L.: Connectionist structures of type 2 Fuzzy Inference Systems. In: 4th International Conference on Parallel Processing and Applied Mathematics, Nalenczow, Poland (2001)
36. Starczewski, J., Rutkowski, L.: Interval type 2 neuro-fuzzy systems based on interval consequents. In: Neural Networks and Soft Computing. Advances In Soft Computing, pp. 570–577 (2003)
37. Tadeusiewicz, R.: Neural Networks (in Polish). AOW RM (1993)
38. Werbos, J.: Backpropagation through time: What it does and how to do it. Proceedings of the IEEE 78(10) (1990)
39. Wilamowski, B.M., Yo, H.: Neural network learning without backpropagation. IEEE Transactions on Neural Networks 21(11), 1793–1803 (2010)
40. Zalasiński, M., Cpałka, K.: New approach for the on-line signature verification based on method of horizontal partitioning. In: Rutkowski, L., Korytkowski, M., Scherer, R., Tadeusiewicz, R., Zadeh, L.A., Zurada, J.M. (eds.) ICAISC 2013, Part II. LNCS (LNAI), vol. 7895, pp. 342–350. Springer, Heidelberg (2013)

Microarray *Leukemia* Gene Data Clustering by Means of Generalized Self-organizing Neural Networks with Evolving Tree-Like Structures

Marian B. Gorzałczany[(✉)], Jakub Piekoszewski, and Filip Rudziński

Department of Electrical and Computer Engineering
Kielce University of Technology
Al. 1000-lecia P.P. 7, 25-314 Kielce, Poland
{m.b.gorzalczany,j.piekoszewski,f.rudzinski}@tu.kielce.pl

Abstract. The paper presents the application of our clustering technique based on generalized self-organizing neural networks with evolving tree-like structures to complex cluster-analysis problems including, in particular, the sample-based and gene-based clusterings of microarray *Leukemia* gene data set. Our approach works in a fully unsupervised way, i.e., without the necessity to predefine the number of clusters and using unlabelled data. It is particularly important in the gene-based clustering of microarray data for which the number of gene clusters is unknown in advance. In the sample-based clustering of the *Leukemia* data set, our approach gives better results than those reported in the literature and obtained using a method that requires the cluster number to be defined in advance. In the gene-based clustering of the considered data, our approach generates clusters that are easily divisible into subclusters related to particular sample classes. It corresponds, in a way, to subspace clustering that is highly desirable in microarray data analysis.

Keywords: Microarray cancer gene data · Gene expression data clustering · Generalized self-organizing neural networks with evolving tree-like structures · Cluster analysis · Unsupervised learning

1 Introduction

Microarray technologies have been playing an increasingly important role in genomic research (see, e.g., [11]). They make possible to measure the level of expression or activity of tens of thousands of genes simultaneously in different experimental samples (in general, under different experimental conditions). The resulting data are usually represented in the form of the so-called gene expression data matrix. Its rows represent genes and its column - various specific samples. Thus, each cell of the matrix represents a numeric level of the expression of a given gene in a given sample. One of the essential steps in interpreting the meaning of such immense amount of biological information is to discover clusters of genes that manifest similar expression patterns (coexpressed and possibly

L. Rutkowski et al. (Eds.): ICAISC 2015, Part I, LNAI 9119, pp. 15–25, 2015.
DOI: 10.1007/978-3-319-19324-3_2

coregulated genes). In general, however, it is meaningful to cluster both genes and samples into homogeneous groups [8].

This paper presents both gene-based and sample-based clusterings of *Leukemia* human cancer microarray data set by means of our original approach that employs generalized self-organizing neural networks (SONNs) with evolving tree-like structure and with dynamically defined neighborhood (SONNs with DDN for short) presented in [5]. It is worth stressing that our approach works in a fully unsupervised way, i.e., using unlabelled data and without a predefined number of clusters which is particularly important in the gene-based clustering of microarray data where the number of gene clusters is unknown in advance. First, the clustering process using SONNs with DDN is outlined (its more detailed presentation can be found in [5]). Then, the operation of the proposed networks on two- and three-dimensional benchmark data sets [12] that contain data groups of various shapes and densities is shown. Finally, their application to the clustering of the afore-mentioned human cancer microarray data set, i.e., *Lukemia* [4] is presented and compared with an alternative solution.

2 Generalized SONNs with DDN for Data Clustering - An Outline [5]

In the course of learning that controls the evolution of tree-like structures of generalized SONNs with DDN, they are able to: a) automatically adjust the number of neurons in the network by removing low-active neurons from the network and adding new neurons in the areas of existing high-active neurons in order to take over some of their activities, b) disconnect the tree-like structures into subnetworks, and c) reconnect some of the subnetworks preserving the no-loop spanning-tree properties. These mechanisms enable them to detect data clusters of various shapes and densities including both volumetric as well as thin, shell, piece-wise linear, polygonal, etc. kinds of clusters. Each detected cluster is represented by a single disconnected subnetwork. Therefore, the number of automatically generated subnetworks is equal to the number of clusters. Moreover, our approach also generates a multi-point prototype for each cluster; that prototype is represented by the collection of neurons belonging to a given subnetwork. Such prototypes can be directly used in clustering/classification tasks by employing the well-known nearest multi-prototype approach [2], [1]. The application of our approach to the clustering of several synthetic and real (coming from the UCI repository [10]) benchmark data sets has been presented in [5]. Our approach is a generalization of our earlier solutions to automatic determination of the number of clusters and their prototypes in data sets [6], [7].

The point of departure for the idea of the generalized SONNs (see [5] for details) is the conventional SONN with one-dimentional neighborhood (i.e., the neuron chain) with n inputs $x_1, x_2, \ldots, x_n$ and m neurons with outputs $y_1, y_2, \ldots, y_m$, respectively. $y_j = \sum_{i=1}^{n} w_{ji} x_i$, $j = 1, 2, \ldots, m$ and w_{ji} are weights connecting the i-th input of the network with the output of the j-th neuron. Using vector notation ($\boldsymbol{x} = (x_1, x_2, \ldots, x_n)^T$, $\boldsymbol{w}_j = (w_{j1}, w_{j2}, \ldots, w_{jn})^T$),

$y_j = \boldsymbol{w}_j^T \boldsymbol{x}$. The learning data set contains L input vectors $\boldsymbol{x}_l$ ($l = 1, 2, \ldots, L$). In the first stage of any Winner-Takes-Most (WTM) learning algorithm that can be applied to the considered network, the neuron j_x winning in the competition of neurons when learning vector $\boldsymbol{x}_l$ is presented to the network must be determined in the following way (assuming the normalization of learning vectors):

$$d(\boldsymbol{x}_l, \boldsymbol{w}_{j_x}) = \min_{j=1,2,\ldots,m} d(\boldsymbol{x}_l, \boldsymbol{w}_j), \tag{1}$$

where $d(\boldsymbol{x}_l, \boldsymbol{w}_j)$ is a distance measure between $\boldsymbol{x}_l$ and $\boldsymbol{w}_j$; throughout this paper, the Euclidean distance measure $d_E(\boldsymbol{x}_l, \boldsymbol{w}_j) = \sqrt{\sum_{i=1}^{n} (x_{li} - w_{ji})^2}$ will be applied. The WTM learning rule is following:

$$\boldsymbol{w}_j(k+1) = \boldsymbol{w}_j(k) + \eta_j(k) N(j, j_x, k)[\boldsymbol{x}(k) - \boldsymbol{w}_j(k)], \tag{2}$$

where k is the iteration number, $\eta_j(k)$ is the learning coefficient, and $N(j, j_x, k)$ is the neighborhood function:

$$N(j, j_x, k) = e^{-\frac{d_{tpl}^2(j, j_x)}{2\lambda^2(k)}} \tag{3}$$

with $\lambda(k)$ being the radius of the neighborhood and $d_{tpl}(j, j_x)$ representing the topological distance between the neurons no. j_x and no. j. The neighborhood of a given neuron in the tree-like topology of our generalized SONNs is defined along the arcs (being the pieces of the conventional SONN with one-dimensional neighborhood) emanating from that neuron as shown in Fig. 1 (see [5] for details). Therefore, $d_{tpl}(j, j_x) = 1$ for all j-th neurons being direct neighbors of the j_x-th one as illustrated in Fig. 1. In turn, $d_{tpl}(j, j_x) = 2$ for all j-th neurons being second along all paths starting at the j_x-th one (see Fig. 1), etc.

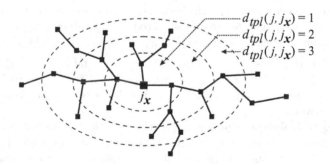

Fig. 1. Examples of neighborhood of the j_x-th neuron [5]

In order to implement three mechanisms, listed as a), b), and c) in the first paragraph of this section, five operations are activated (under some conditions) after each learning epoch.

Operation 1 (first component of mechanism a)) - the removal of single, low active neurons: The neuron no. j_r is removed from the network (preserving the network continuity - see [5] for details) if its activity - measured by the number of its wins win_{j_r} - is below an assumed level win_{min}, i.e., $win_{j_r} < win_{min}$. win_{min} is experimentally selected parameter (usually, $win_{min} \in \{2, 3, 4\}$).

Operation 2 (mechanism b)) - the disconnection of the network (subnetwork) into two subnetworks: The disconnection of two neighboring neurons j_1 and j_2 takes place if the following condition is fulfilled: $d_E(\boldsymbol{w}_{j_1}, \boldsymbol{w}_{j_2}) > d_{coef} d_{E,avr}$ where $d_{E,avr} = \frac{1}{P} \sum_{p=1}^{P} d_{E,p}$ is the average distance between two neighboring neurons for all pairs p, $p = 1, 2, \ldots, P$, of such neurons, and d_{coef} is experimentally selected parameter (a distance coefficient) governing the disconnection operation (usually, $d_{coef} \in [3, 4]$).

Operation 3 (second component of mechanism a)) - the removal of small-size subnetworks: A subnetwork of m_s neurons is removed from the system if $m_s < m_{s,min}$, where $m_{s,min}$ is experimentally selected parameter (usually, $m_{s,min} \in \{3, 4\}$).

Operation 4 (third component of mechanism a)) - the insertion of additional neurons into the neighborhood of high-active neurons in order to take over some of their activities. *Case 4a*: A new neuron, labelled as (new), is inserted between two neighboring and high-active neurons j_1 and j_2 (i.e., their numbers of wins win_{j_1} and win_{j_2} are above an assumed level win_{max}: $win_{j_1}, win_{j_2} > win_{max}$). win_{max} is experimentally selected parameter (usually $win_{max} \in \{2, 3, 4\}$ and $win_{max} \geq win_{min}$, where win_{min} is defined in Operation 1). The weight vector $\boldsymbol{w}_{(new)}$ of the new neuron is calculated as follows: $\boldsymbol{w}_{(new)} = \frac{\boldsymbol{w}_{j_1} + \boldsymbol{w}_{j_2}}{2}$. *Case 4b*: A new neuron (new) is inserted in the neighborhood of high-active neuron j_1 surrounded by less-active neighbors (i.e., $win_{j_1} > win_{max}$ and $win_j < win_{max}$ for j such that $d_{tpl}(j, j_1) = 1$). The weight vector $\boldsymbol{w}_{(new)} = [w_{(new)1}, w_{(new)2}, \ldots, w_{(new)n}]^T$ is calculated as follows: $w_{(new)i} = w_{j_1 i}(1 + \xi_i)$, $i = 1, 2, \ldots, n$, where ξ_i is a random number from the interval $[-0.01, 0.01]$ (see [5] for details).

Operation 5 (mechanism c)) - the reconnection of two selected subnetworks: Two subnetworks S_1 and S_2 are reconnected by introducing topological connection between neurons j_1 and j_2 ($j_1 \in S_1$, $j_2 \in S_2$) after fulfilling condition $d_E(\boldsymbol{w}_{j_1}, \boldsymbol{w}_{j_2}) < d_{coef} \frac{d_{E,avr_{S_1}} + d_{E,avr_{S_2}}}{2}$. $d_E(\boldsymbol{w}_{j_1}, \boldsymbol{w}_{j_2})$ and d_{coef} are the same as in Operation 2. $d_{E,avr_{S_1}}$ and $d_{E,avr_{S_2}}$ are calculated for subnetworks S_1 and S_2, respectively, in the same way as $d_{E,avr}$ is calculated in Operation 2 for the considered network.

According to Kohonen's comments [9], the selection of learning parameters is mainly based on experimental results taking into account that the learning coefficient $\eta(k)$ and the neighborhood radius $\lambda(k)$ should be some monotonically decreasing functions of time ($\lambda(k)$ can also be constant in time). Based on that, in the experiments presented below, the learning parameters are defined as follows: $\eta_j(k) = \eta(k)$ of (2) is linearly decreasing over the learning horizon (which includes 10.000 epochs) from $7 \cdot 10^{-4}$ to 10^{-6}, $\lambda(k) = \lambda$ of (3) is equal to 2, the initial number of neurons in the network is equal to 2, $win_{min} = 2$, $win_{max} = 4$, $m_{s,min} = 2$, and $d_{coef} = 4$.

3   Clustering of Two- and Three-Dimensional Benchmark Data Sets

The so-called Fundamental Clustering Problem Suite (FCPS) [12] is a collection of benchmark data sets that, for different reasons, pose difficult problems to clustering algorithms. We selected two benchmark sets from FCPS, one two-dimensional (*Lsun* data set) and one three-dimensional (*Atom* data set) to illustrate the performance of our approach. According to [12], main clustering problems in *Lsun* are different variances in clusters and in *Atom* - linearly non-separable data of different densities and variances.

Figs. 2 and 3 present the performance of our clustering technique applied to particular data sets. The figures are arranged in the same way, i.e., parts a) of them represent the data, parts b), c), d), e), and f) show the evolution of the tree-like structures of the generalized SONNs at different stages of the learning process, and parts g) and h) - the plots of the number of neurons (g) and the number of subnetworks (clusters) (h) vs. epoch number. It can be seen that our approach, in an automatic way, increases the number of neurons in particular networks (starting from the initial numbers of two neurons) and detects the correct numbers of data clusters in both sets by disconnecting the tree-like structures of the generalized SONNs into appropriate number of subnetworks.

4   Clustering of *Leukemia* Cancer Microarray Data Set

The performance of our approach will now be validated in the clustering of a data set coming from microarray experiments. The benchmark human cancer microarray data set, i.e., *Leukemia* [4] is considered. It is typical for microarray gene expression data sets that they contain thousands of original genes (in our case, 7.129) and a small number of samples (in our case, 72 including two classes called ALL with 47 samples and AML with 25 samples). Additionally, many of the original genes are noisy and redundant. In order to filter out such genes, various preprocessing methods are applied (see, e.g., [3] for details) yielding reduced subset of genes (3.571 for *Leukemia* data set) that are used in experiments. As already mentioned in the introduction (see also [8]), in gene expression data analysis it is meaningful to consider both the sample-based and gene-based clusterings. In the first case, the samples are the objects and the genes are the features, whereas in the second case it is quite opposite. Due to a very small number of data samples, the parameter win_{max} that (together with win_{min}) controls the overall number of neurons in the network is reduced to win_{min}, i.e., $win_{max} = win_{min} = 2$. For the same reason, the distance coefficient is slightly reduced ($d_{coef} = 3$). The remaining parameters are unchanged.

Figs. 4, 5, 6, and 7 present the performance of our clustering algorithm applied to the considered data set. Figs. 4 and 5 show the plots of the number of neurons and the number of subnetworks (clusters) vs. epoch number for the sample-based and gene-based clusterings, respectively. As far as the sample-based clustering is concerned, the number of clusters in data set and the cluster assignments

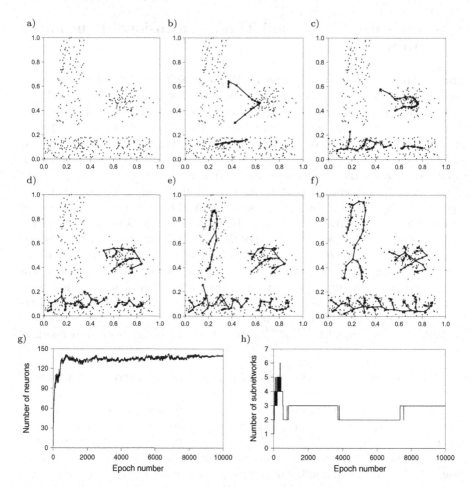

Fig. 2. *Lsun* data set (a) and the evolution of the generalized SONN in it in learning epochs: b) no. 5, c) no. 50, d) no. 100, e) no. 500, and f) no. 10 000 (end of learning), as well as plots of the number of neurons (g) and the number of subnetworks (clusters) (h) vs. epoch number

of particular data samples are known. Therefore, a direct verification of the obtained results is possible. However, it should be stressed that our approach does not use the knowledge on the cluster assignments and the cluster number during its operation. That knowledge is used after the completion of the learning to evaluate the obtained results. Fig. 4b shows that our approach detects the correct (equal to 2) number of sample clusters in the considered data set. The percentage of correct decisions, equal to 98.6%, regarding the cluster assignments of particular data samples is higher than in the case of an alternative approach presented in [3] (93.14%) which additionally requires the cluster number to be defined in advance.

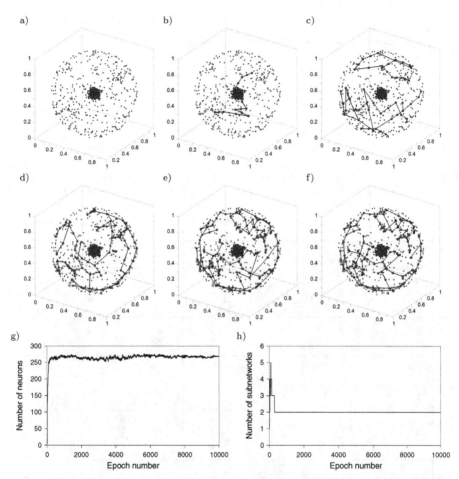

Fig. 3. *Atom* data set (a) and the evolution of the generalized SONN in it in learning epochs: b) no. 5, c) no. 50, d) no. 100, e) no. 500, and f) no. 10 000 (end of learning), as well as plots of the number of neurons (g) and the number of subnetworks (clusters) (h) vs. epoch number

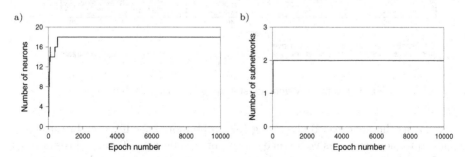

Fig. 4. Plots of the number of neurons (a) and the number of subnetworks (clusters) (b) vs. epoch number for the sample-based clustering of the *Leukemia* data set

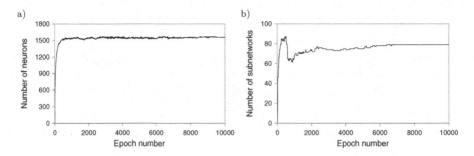

Fig. 5. Plots of the number of neurons (a) and the number of subnetworks (clusters) (b) vs. epoch number for the gene-based clustering of the *Leukemia* data set

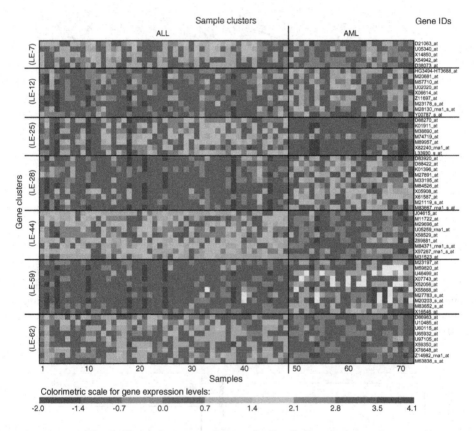

Fig. 6. Exemplary gene clusters in the *Leukemia* data set

As far as the gene-based clustering (or, to be more specific, the clustering of gene expression levels) is concerned, our approach detects 79 gene clusters (see Fig. 5b). Fig. 6 presents the pseudocolor image of some of them. Each of those clusters can be easily divided into two subclusters related to ALL and AML samples. Therefore, the results generated by our approach correspond, in a way,

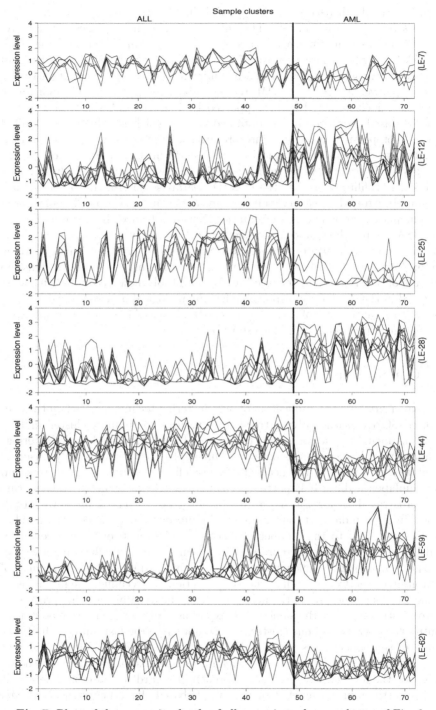

Fig. 7. Plots of the expression levels of all genes in each gene cluster of Fig. 6

to the so-called subspace clustering which is highly desirable in microarray data analysis (see discussion in [8]). The subspace clustering captures clusters created by a subset of genes across a subset of data samples (in our case, ALL and AML samples separately). Fig. 7 shows the plots of the expression levels of all genes in the gene clusters of Fig. 6 confirming the compactness of particular clusters (as well as ALL and AML related subclusters). The pseudocolor image of particular clusters of Fig. 6 (supported by Fig. 7) can be used in a deeper genetics-based discussion of the obtained results which is - due to the limited space - not possible here. The interpretation of the obtained gene clusters is possible on the basis of statistical analysis performed with the use of specialized and dedicated software. In our experiments, we use two publicly available functional profiling tools, i.e., the DAVID (Database for Annotation, Visualization and Integrated Discovery) software, available on the server of Laboratory of Immunopathogenesis and Bioinformatics, National Cancer Institute at Frederick, USA (http://david.abcc.ncifcrf.gov) and the 'g:Profiler' software, available on the server of Institute of Computer Science, University of Tartu, Estonia (http://biit.cs.ut.ee/gprofiler). We can only mention here that, for instance, in the case of 'LE-7' gene cluster (see Fig. 6), both tools indicate that all the genes collected in the cluster are responsible for one biological process named 'cell cycle'. In turn, in the case of 'LE-28' gene cluster, 7 out of 10 genes are responsible for biological process named 'defense response', etc.

5   Conclusions

The paper presents the application of our clustering technique based on the generalized SONNs with evolving tree-like structures to complex cluster-analysis problems including, in particular, the sample-based and gene-based clusterings of microarray *Leukemia* gene data set. Our approach works in a fully unsupervised way, i.e., without the necessity to predefine the number of clusters and using unlabelled data. It is particularly important in the gene-based clustering of microarray data for which the number of gene clusters is unknown in advance. In a given data set, our approach, in automatic way, detects the number of clusters (equal to the number of disconnected subnetworks) and generates multi-prototypes for them (represented by neurons in particular subnetworks). It is performed by the implementation of automatic adjustment of the number of neurons in the network as well as the disconnection and reconnection mechanisms of the tree-like structures of the network during the dynamic learning process. It is worth stressing that the same set of experimentally selected parameters that control the operation of our clustering technique (see the last paragraph of Section 2 of the paper) gives very good clustering results for completely different types of data sets such as FCPS benchmarks and microarray data. It shows, in a way, the low sensitivity of our approach in regard to those parameters. It is also worth emphasizing that in the sample-based clustering of the *Leukemia* data set our approach gives much higher percentage of correct decisions than the alternative technique of [3] which additionally requires the cluster number to be defined in advance. Moreover, our approach exhibits also interesting features as far as the gene-based clustering of the *Leukemia* data set is concerned. Namely, it generates clusters that are easily divisible into subclusters related to particular sample classes; it, in a way, corresponds to subspace clustering which is highly desirable in microarray data analysis [8].

References

1. Bezdek, J.C., Keller, J., Krisnapuram, R., Pal, N.R.: Fuzzy Models and Algorithms for Pattern Recognition and Image Processing. Springer Science & Business Media, New York (2005)
2. Bezdek, J.C., Reichherzer, T.R., Lim, G.S., Attikiouzel, Y.: Multiple-prototype classifier design. IEEE Trans. Systems, Man and Cybernetics, Part C 28(1), 67–79 (1998)
3. Cho, H., Dhillon, I.S.: Coclustering of human cancer microarrays using minimum sum-squared residue coclustering. IEEE/ACM Trans. Computational Biology and Bioinformatics 5(3), 385–400 (2008)
4. Golub, T.R., et al.: Molecular classification of cancer: class discovery and class prediction by gene expression monitoring. Science 286, 531–537 (1999)
5. Gorzałczany, M.B., Piekoszewski, J., Rudziński, F.: Generalized tree-like self-organizing neural networks with dynamically defined neighborhood for cluster analysis. In: Rutkowski, L., Korytkowski, M., Scherer, R., Tadeusiewicz, R., Zadeh, L.A., Zurada, J.M. (eds.) ICAISC 2014, Part II. LNCS (LNAI), vol. 8468, pp. 713–725. Springer, Heidelberg (2014)
6. Gorzałczany, M.B., Rudziński, F.: Cluster analysis via dynamic self-organizing neural networks. In: Rutkowski, L., Tadeusiewicz, R., Zadeh, L.A., Żurada, J.M. (eds.) ICAISC 2006. LNCS (LNAI), vol. 4029, pp. 593–602. Springer, Heidelberg (2006)
7. Gorzałczany, M.B., Rudziński, F.: WWW-newsgroup-document clustering by means of dynamic self-organizing neural networks. In: Rutkowski, L., Tadeusiewicz, R., Zadeh, L.A., Zurada, J.M. (eds.) ICAISC 2008. LNCS (LNAI), vol. 5097, pp. 40–51. Springer, Heidelberg (2008)
8. Jiang, D., Tang, C., Zhang, A.: Cluster analysis for gene expression data: a survey. IEEE Trans. Knowledge and Data Engineering 16(11), 1370–1386 (2004)
9. Kohonen, T.: Self-Organizing Maps, 3rd edn. Springer, Berlin (2001)
10. Machine Learning Database Repository, University of California at Irvine, ftp.ics.uci.edu
11. Schena, M.: Microarray Analysis. John Wiley & Sons (2003)
12. Ultsch, A.: Clustering with SOM: U*C. In: Proc. Workshop on Self-Organizing Maps, Paris, France, pp. 75–82 (2005)

Innovative Types and Abilities of Neural Networks Based on Associative Mechanisms and a New Associative Model of Neurons

Adrian Horzyk[✉]

Department of Automatics and Biomedical Engineering, AGH University of Science and Technology, Mickiewicza Av. 30, 30-059 Cracow, Poland
horzyk@agh.edu.pl

Abstract. This paper presents a new concept of representation of data and their relations in neural networks which allows to automatically associate, reproduce them, and generalize about them. It demonstrates an innovative way of developing emergent neural representation of knowledge using a new kind of neural networks whose structure is automatically constructed and parameters are automatically computed on the basis of plastic mechanisms implemented in a new associative model of neurons - called as-neurons. Inspired by the plastic mechanisms commonly occurring in a human brain, this model allows to quickly create associations and establish weighted connections between neural representations of data, their classes, and sequences. As-neurons are able to automatically interconnect representing similar or sequential data. This contribution describes generalized formulas for quick analytical computation of the structure and parameters of ANAKG neural graphs for representing and recalling of training sequences of objects.

Keywords: Associative mechanisms · As-neurons · ANAKG neural graphs · Knowledge engineering · Knowledge representation · Artificial neural associative systems · Associative neural networks · Emergent cognitive systems

1 Introduction

Brains are well-developed biological machines that efficiently represent and process big-data. The principle of operation of the human mind is not based on numerical computational processes, but on active associative context-sensitive consolidation of many pieces of information which forms knowledge and allows generalization and creativity [14] [31]. Generalization is indispensable for modelling and operation of knowledge and intelligence [8]. In the current stage of development of neural networks, we have many structures, models of neurons, and training methods that enable approximation, association, prediction, regression, recognition, and classification [3] [21] [29]. The majority of artificial neuron models represents weighted sums which are used to compute output values using various activation functions [21] [29]. Artificial neural networks (ANNs) are trained using external algorithms [17] [21] [29] which usually do not exist in real

© Springer International Publishing Switzerland 2015
L. Rutkowski et al. (Eds.): ICAISC 2015, Part I, LNAI 9119, pp. 26–38, 2015.
DOI: 10.1007/978-3-319-19324-3_3

brains [16] [19]. Biological neurons use internal, plastic, and local adaptation mechanisms which enable them to represent frequently repeated combinations of similar input stimuli and connect these representations to reproduce their sequence. Current investigations in neurobiology [15] [16] [19] [20] provide insight into universal plastic mechanisms which enable neurons to automatically change their connections and parameters to consolidate and represent frequent and similar combinations of object features and their sequences.

The essence of intelligence is the ability to memorize, reproduce, and generalize about frequent and similar patterns which define objects, actions, and their sequences, which allows to predict and control future events. As brains have insufficient resources to memorize every pattern [7] [16] [19] [25] [26], they prefer to represent and memorize only classes of patterns representing subgroups of similar objects. Classes are represented in neurons as combinations of their most frequent and representative features. Such connected neurons can represent statements, rules, and algorithms based on the most frequent and similar sequences of training objects. This unified, simplified, and consolidated representation of objects and their sequences is fundamental for knowledge representation, generalization, creativeness, and managing big-data on the fly [14] [22] [23] [24]. This kind of representation allows to quickly recognize similar objects and their sequences as well as recall other corresponding pieces of information. Thus, neural representations of classes of objects can be activated by various pieces of the objects defining these classes. The previously activated neurons can temporarily influence potential future activity of other connected neurons (Fig. 2-3) and thus control them and represent a context for their subsequent possible activations. This control can not only strengthen the influence of other inputs - in effect enabling or accelerating their activity - but also inhibit their influence and decelerate or even stop their activity due to inhibitory connections. This feature defines the possibility to control neuronal activity within the context of previous objects, events, and thoughts in brains [12] [16] [19].

Human languages help to share important information, define rules, methods, and algorithms, as well as allow to describe things and actions precisely to avoid misunderstandings. They make way for human cooperation which relies strongly on communication, knowledge, and intelligence. They allow people to solve problems on the basis of previously solved tasks which were somehow similar to the currently solved problems. Solutions are usually described by algorithms in the form of a sequence of steps [9] [11] [12]. Such steps are performed under the conditions of given contexts defined by various circumstances. Our brains can consolidate sequential relations, dependencies, rules, conditions, and develop complex algorithms using consolidated neural representations of objects defined by their subsets of features. This paper informs about neural associative processes and describes a generalized universal model for associative context-sensitive consolidation of training sequences of objects which can represent things and procedures in general.

A neuron represents an object or its part when it activates as a result of a time-spread combination of input stimuli triggered by the object. Thus, each

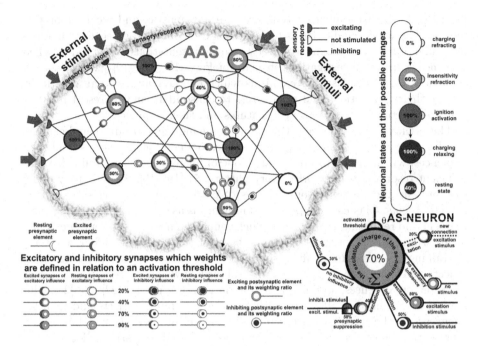

Fig. 1. As-neurons capable of representation of most frequent and repeatable combinations of input stimuli and their sequences

neuron represents an infinite set of time-spread combinations of input stimuli that can activate it. This set can contain similar as well as differing combinations, which allows neurons to automatically generalize about objects and create representations of their classes. As a result, similar objects produce similar neural reactions, and similarly affect other connected neurons. Connections between neurons also enable to represent various time-spread sequences of objects (e.g. sentences, rules, or algorithms). The preceding objects in each sequence - that are represented in a neural network and have triggered activity of other neurons - create an activity context for subsequent objects represented by other neurons only if these neurons are connected together and can influence their states as a result of their activity. Connections between as-neurons described in this paper are automatically created if their activity occurs in short intervals [12], e.g. for as-neurons representing objects of each training sequence. This feature of as-neurons enables their network automatic, consolidated, and context-sensitive representation of time-spread sequences of classes of objects that as-neurons already represent. Synaptic weights are presented as a percentage of threshold values (Fig. 1) because it is important to notice how much each weight influences the activation of a postsynaptic as-neuron. Connections and synaptic weights between as-neurons enable to differentiate various influences of the context formed by the activity of other presynaptic neurons. This allows to produce different context-sensitive reactions of a neural network constructed from as-neurons. Furthermore, associative consolidation of representations of various sequences in a single neural graph sometimes triggers generalized reactions that have not been trained (Fig. 3). This kind of generalization can be sometimes intuitively interpreted as creativity [11] [12].

This paper describes a generalized associative model of neurons (as-neurons) (Fig. 1) for an upgraded fast automatic construction of ANAKG neural graphs - introduced in [11] and [12] - capable of representing and consolidating training sequences of objects. An introduced associative method for automatic development of ANAKG neural graphs constructed from as-neurons is very fast because it demands only a single browse through a training sequence set (S). All parameters and connections are automatically computed locally by as-neurons and synapses. This is possible if the training sequence set is fully defined and available before starting the adaptation process [11] [13]. In nature, due to emotions, needs, and other circumstances, the thinking processes favour and many times rehearse specific training patterns, which are trained at various moments and contexts. In machine learning, we lack such redundant information, treat data in the same way, and build a computational model quickly for a precise number of training patterns [5] [6] [21] [29]. These circumstances can force adaptation methods to work differently. In order to use the time-dependent mechanisms of biological neurons for efficient machine learning, we have to intelligently speed up or slow down the simulation time of as-neurons to automatically produce appropriate connections between them. We also need to substitute the initial structure and connections of biological neurons - inherited and naturally developed - with fast plastic mechanisms which let as-neurons quickly develop an artificial structure representing classes of training objects, their relations and sequences.

2   Active Associative Mechanisms in Neural Networks

Association is usually defined as a connection or relation between two or more objects [2] [3] [18] [30] [32]. Brains contain reactive neurons [16], which allow us to consider a special kind of associations - active associations - which automatically trigger relationships between neural representations of object classes via automatic reactivity of neurons and their ability to stimulate neurons representing other object classes in diverse ways. Stimulated neurons can be activated, which automatically triggers recalling of sequences of associated neural representations of other object classes through weighted neural connections. Such active associations are modelled in a new kind of systems - called artificial neural associative systems (aas-systems) - defined in [11] and [12]. Among other elements, the aas-systems are built from reactive as-neurons that enable to automatically create active associations between neural representations of object classes reproducing their context-sensitive relationships with other classes. In aas-systems, the capabilities observed in brains can be adapted to tasks of machine learning and cooperation with contemporary computers by introducing new kinds of sensory receptors not occurring in nature [12].

Associative systems exhibit a few important features that determine and define active associations in neural graphs: similarity, sequence, frequency, uniqueness, parallelism, and time-dependency of associative processes. These processes are controlled by local dependencies transmitted through connections and by the flow of time. They can also activate plastic mechanisms reconstructing associations. Similar neurons, which are often connected together and can stimulate each other, usually represent similar objects defined by similar feature values. Representation of object sequences is very important because it allows to associate even totally different objects which are somehow related. In an aas-system representing sequences of objects, the as-neurons representing them form new connections or strengthen the existing ones to reproduce these sequences. It is sometimes impossible to unambiguously represent all correlated sequences of objects in aas-systems. Varying frequencies of presenting individual sequences during training of the aas-systems play an important role in the adaptation process: frequently occurring training sequences of objects will be more strongly represented and more easily recalled than those that occur more rarely. Moreover, this enables to forget less frequent and correlated sequences. This mechanism automatically manages knowledge of aas-systems. On the other hand, unique objects and unique combinations of common objects create unique contexts for easy recalling of sequences. To demonstrate how it works in your brain, you can try to put together two or three common objects in a unique (untypical) configuration and place them on your desk when you leave thinking about something you would like to remember when you come back. When you come back you will immediately remember what you wanted when you see this unique (untypical) object configuration you left on your desk. ANAKG neural graphs - parts of aas-systems - adequately connect neural representations of objects and strengthen the connections reproducing their frequencies, sequences, and uniqueness. Additional connections are used to reproduce the contexts of recently presented objects that activated the as-neurons which represent them. This allows for automatic sequential context-sensitive recalling of associated objects (Fig. 2-3) [11].

$$\delta_{S,\widehat{S}} = \sum_{\{S\rightsquigarrow\widehat{S} \,:\, (\cdots\rightsquigarrow S\rightsquigarrow\cdots\rightsquigarrow\widehat{S}\rightsquigarrow\cdots)\in\mathbb{S}\}} \left(\frac{1}{1+\frac{\Delta t - t_a^{\widehat{S}}}{\omega}}\right)^{\gamma} \tag{1}$$

$$w_{S,\widehat{S}} = \frac{\eta_S \cdot \delta_{S,\widehat{S}} \cdot \theta_{\widehat{S}}}{\eta_S + (\eta_S - 1) \cdot \delta_{S,\widehat{S}}} \tag{2}$$

$$f_{\widehat{S}}(t) = \pm\theta_{\widehat{S}} \cdot \left(\frac{t}{\omega} - 1\right)^{\gamma} \tag{3}$$

$$\widehat{X}_{\widehat{S}}^{t_2} = R_{\widehat{S}}^{\Delta t}\left(X_{\widehat{S}}^{t_1}\right) = \mathrm{sgn}\left(X_{\widehat{S}}^{t_1}\right) \cdot f_{\widehat{S}}\left(f_{\widehat{S}}^{-1}\left(\left|X_{\widehat{S}}^{t_1}\right|\right) + \Delta t\right) =$$
$$= \mathrm{sgn}\left(X_{\widehat{S}}^{t_1}\right) \cdot \theta_{\widehat{S}} \cdot \left(\sqrt[\gamma]{\frac{\left|X_{\widehat{S}}^{t_1}\right|}{\theta_{\widehat{S}}}} - \frac{\Delta t}{\omega}\right)^{\gamma} \tag{4}$$

$$X_{\widehat{S}}^{t_2} = g\left(X_{\widehat{S}}^{t_1}\right) = \begin{cases} \sum\limits_{S \rightsquigarrow \widehat{S}} w_{S,\widehat{S}} \cdot x_S^{t_2} + R_{\widehat{S}}^{t_2-t_1}\left(X_{\widehat{S}}^{t_1}\right) & \text{if } \left|X_{\widehat{S}}^{t_1}\right| < \theta_{\widehat{S}} \\ \sum\limits_{S \rightsquigarrow \widehat{S}} w_{S,\widehat{S}} \cdot x_S^{t_2} + R_{\widehat{S}}^{t_2-(t_1+t_r)}\left(-\theta_{\widehat{S}}\right) & \text{if } X_{\widehat{S}}^{t_1} \geq \theta_{\widehat{S}} \wedge t_2 > t_1 + t_r \\ -\theta_{\widehat{S}} & \text{if } X_{\widehat{S}}^{t_1} \geq \theta_{\widehat{S}} \wedge t_2 \leq t_1 + t_r \end{cases} \tag{5}$$

$$x_S^{t_2} = h\left(X_S^{t_2-t_a^S-t_s}\right) = \begin{cases} 1 \text{ if } X_S^{t_2-t_a^S-t_s} \geq \theta_{\widehat{S}} \\ 0 \text{ if } X_S^{t_2-t_a^S-t_s} < \theta_{\widehat{S}} \end{cases} \tag{6}$$

$$t_a^S = T(X_S, \theta_S) = \left\lceil \frac{t_a^{MAX}}{1 + \frac{X_S - \theta_S}{\theta_S}} \right\rceil \tag{7}$$

where

$S \rightsquigarrow \widehat{S}$ - a synaptic weighted connection between as-neurons S and $\widehat{S}$,

$\delta_{S,\widehat{S}}$ - efficiency of synaptic connection at activating postsynaptic as-neuron $\widehat{S}$ through presynaptic as-neuron S accordingly to the time interval of their activations,

θ_S - an activation threshold of as-neuron S,

η_S - a number of activations of presynaptic as-neuron S,

ω - maximum time necessary to gradually relax each as-neuron from its most excited state to its resting state,

t_s - time necessary to propagate a stimulus along a connection and through a synapse from a presynaptic as-neuron S to a postsynaptic as-neuron $\widehat{S}$,

t_r - absolute refraction time in which as-neurons are unsusceptible for any stimulations,

t_a^S - computed relative activation time of as-neuron S according to its above-threshold excitation level determined by its activation threshold θ_S $(0 < t_a \leq t_a^{MAX})$,

t_a^{MAX} - maximum activation time of as-neurons when $X_S = \theta_S$,

t_1 - the moment of the last update of a neuronal state,

t_2 - the current moment of a neuronal state update,

$f_{\widehat{S}}(t)$ - concave continuously decreasing functions used to define relaxation function R of as-neurons,

$R_{\widehat{S}}^{\Delta t}$ - a relaxation function that gradually turns the as-neuron $\widehat{S}$ to its resting state, where Δt is the relaxation period from its last update during which no external stimuli occurred,

$x_S^{t_2}$ - an input stimulus distributed from as-neuron S to synapses, where t_2 is a moment of its influence on postsynaptic as-neurons via these synapses,

$h(X_S^t)$ - a function that determines the presynaptic influence of as-neuron S accordingly to the activation threshold of this as-neuron.

The context of past events should not last infinitely, their influence on recalling of following objects has to be gradually reduced and stopped (4). Consequently, the neurons need a built-in mechanism which will gradually reduce their excitation (3). In biological neurons, such a mechanism is called relaxation [16] [19], during which neurons return back to their resting states after the stimulations have failed in activating them or after the activations precede the refraction period. An associative model of neurons (as-neurons) (Fig. 1) augments the models of artificial neurons [21] [29] and spiking neurons [15] by additional features and functions that enable as-neurons to automatically connect and represent classes of objects and their sequences allowing for context-sensitive recalling, generalization, and creativeness [14]. The as-neurons weigh and add input stimuli (2), use activation thresholds $\theta_{\hat{S}}$, relax, refract (5), start plastic processes to change weights (2), and automatically connect to other as-neurons, whose activities often occur in similar periods [11] [12]. The synchronisation of firing of as-neurons usually suggests that object classes represented by these as-neurons are semantically related (e.g. they are similar, define the same class, or follow one another), so they should be connected or their connections should be strengthened. In this way, related object classes represented by as-neurons can be conditionally recalled according to the strength of synaptic connections between them.

As-neurons work in parallel in time, but their activations are often not synchronized, so they need a special simulation environment. Due to the limitations of today's computers, some simplified models have also been proposed [11] [12] to enable and accelerate an adaptation process of aas-systems. These models assume updating in discrete moments of simulation time and accomplish the main associative goals which allow to automatically influence representation and relationships of other data. Thus, aas-systems are automatically internally programmed by training data relationships - not by external training algorithms. They use plastic mechanisms that can automatically react to input data and represent these relationships in synaptic weights, connections, and thresholds. External stimulations of any time-spread combination of as-neurons (directly or via sensory receptors) recall an active associative reaction of the aas-system according to the relationships in the represented training data. This results in stimulation of other connected as-neurons as well. Upon activation, they produce an answer built from the represented classes of objects in a sequence arising from the moments of their activations (Fig. 3). Frequently activated as-neurons can newly interconnect or strengthen their existing connections in order to remember the result of associative recalling and make it available for the future. In this way, aas-systems - a kind of emergent cognitive systems - can develop new internal associations according to external and internal stimuli. This process resembles the ability to recall self-developed conclusions during thinking in people.

Brains have the built-in ability to develop initial neural structures. Aas-systems lack genetically inherited structures, so we have to use some extra rules to quickly develop these structures for various training data. This often proves advantageous, because the structures can be created according to a given task without the limitations introduced by e.g. inherited types of receptors or an imposed initial structure. The aas-system structures can be automatically optimized and specialized in associating given training data. New as-neurons are created as a consequence of external input stimuli which have not produced activation of any existing as-neuron. The axon of as-neuron S connects to as-neuron $\widehat{S}$ if as-neuron $\widehat{S}$ is activated in short period ($\leq \omega$) after as-neuron S has been activated and this connection is reinforced when this sequence of activations is repeated in the future. In the ANAKG neural graphs only $\delta_{S,\widehat{S}}$ (1) and η_S have to be computed during a single browse through a training sequence set. Weights (2) can be computed at the end of this fast adaptation process. The construction process of ANAKGs has been precisely described in [11], [12], and [14].

3 Generalization of Training Sequences

This section describes an experiment in which a training sequence set called 'Monkey': "*I have a monkey. My monkey is very small. It is very lovely. It likes to sit on my head. It can jump very quickly. It is also very clever. It learns quickly. My monkey is lovely.*" was used to develop an ANAKG graph shown in Fig. 2. New as-neurons represented each new word. Words from each sentence were presented with an interval of 20 units of simulation time. Connections were established between all as-neurons in each sequence of words (sentence) so that each as-neuron representing a word in a sequence was connected to all as-neurons representing all following words in this sequence. If the same word occurred in many sequences, the same neuron represented it. This process naturally combined and interlaced all training sequences taking into account contexts of previous words in each sentence. This also aggregated representations of all the same words in all training sequences. The amount of activations of all presynaptic as-neuron η_S was computed according to the number of repetitions of words of all training sequences (Tab. 1). They served to compute the efficiencies of all synaptic connections $\delta_{S,\widehat{S}}$ (1) at activating postsynaptic as-neurons $\widehat{S}$ by stimulations of presynaptic as-neurons S according to the time interval of their activations (Tab. 1). Weights were computed according to formula (2) introduced in the previous section (Tab. 2). Other constants were set according to the average times described by Kalat in [16], assuming that each unit of simulation time conforms to approximately 1 ms of biological neuron operation in the following way: maximal relaxation time $\omega = 100$, maximal charge time of excited as-neurons that achieved their activation thresholds $t_a^{MAX} = 15$, connection and synaptic transmission time $t_s = 5$, absolute refraction time $t_r = 3$, and activation thresholds of all as-neurons $\theta = 1$. Gamma constant $\gamma = 4$ allowed to achieve appropriate concave shape of function (3) used for relaxation (4).

The constructed ANAKG neural graph allowed for external stimulation of any as-neuron, as-neuron combination, or sequence to elicit an ANAKG reaction. Depending on the breadth of a context of initializing external stimulations of as-neurons, we could obtain various behaviours and answers. The ANAKG neural graph answers were constructed from sequences of objects represented by activated as-neurons. In the constructed ANAKG graph (Fig. 2), as-neuron MONKEY was stimulated and activated two times in $t = 0$ and $t = 20$. The first activation of as-neuron MONKEY has stimulated connected as-neurons

Table 1. $\delta_{S,\widehat{S}}$ (1) and η_S values computed for training sequence set 'Monkey'

PRESYNAPTIC AS-NEURON	η	Σδ	A	ALSO	CAN	CLEVER	DOG	HAVE	HEAD	I	IS	IT	JUMP	LEARNS	LIKES	LOVELY	MONKEY	MY	ON	QUICKLY	SIT	SMALL	TO	VERY
A	2						0,534											1,000					1,000		
ALSO	2		1,000			0,534	0,310																0,534		1,000
CAN	1										1,000									0,310				0,534
CLEVER	1																							
DOG	1																							
HAVE	2		1,534	1,000			0,192										0,534						0,310		
HEAD	1																							
I	2		0,844	0,534			0,126	2,000									0,310						0,192		
IS	4			1,000		0,310											1,534						0,534		2,534
IT	5			0,534	1,000	0,192	0,085				2,000		0,534	1,000	1,000	0,310		0,126	0,192	0,726	0,310		0,534	1,154
JUMP	1																			0,534				1,000
LEARNS	1																		1,000					
LIKES	1					0,126												0,192	0,310		0,534	1,000		
LOVELY	2																							
MONKEY	3										2,000						0,534					0,310		0,534
MY	3										1,000	1,067					0,310	2,000				0,192		0,310
ON	1							0,534											1,000					
QUICKLY	2																							
SIT	1							0,310											0,534	1,000				
SMALL	2					1,000																		
TO	1							0,192										0,310	0,534	1,000				
VERY	4					1,000											1,000			1,000		1,000		

Table 2. $w_{S,\widehat{S}}$ (2) values computed for training sequence set 'Monkey'

PRESYNAPTIC AS-NEURON	θ	w	A	ALSO	CAN	CLEVER	DOG	HAVE	HEAD	I	IS	IT	JUMP	LEARNS	LIKES	LOVELY	MONKEY	MY	ON	QUICKLY	SIT	SMALL	TO	VERY
A	1						0,421											0,667					0,667		
ALSO	1		0,667			0,421	0,269																0,421		0,667
CAN	1										1,000									0,310				0,534
CLEVER	1																							
DOG	1																							
HAVE	1		0,868	0,667			0,175										0,421						0,269		
HEAD	1																							
I	1		0,593	0,421			0,118	1,000									0,269						0,175		
IS	1			0,571		0,252											0,713						0,381		0,874
IT	1			0,374	0,556	0,167	0,080				0,769		0,374	0,556	0,556	0,248		0,114	0,167	0,459	0,248		0,374	0,600
JUMP	1																			0,534				1,000
LEARNS	1																		1,000					
LIKES	1					0,126												0,192	0,310		0,534	1,000		
LOVELY	1																							
MONKEY	1										0,857						0,394					0,257		0,394
MY	1										0,600	0,624					0,394	0,257		0,857			0,170	0,257
ON	1							0,534											1,000					
QUICKLY	1																							
SIT	1							0,310											0,534	1,000				
SMALL	1					0,667																		
TO	1							0,192										0,310	0,534	1,000				
VERY	1					0,571											0,571			0,571		0,571		

IS, VERY, SMALL, and LOVELY but did not result in further activations of other as-neurons. The second activation of as-neuron MONKEY triggered a sequence of activations of the as-neurons representing words: MONKEY IS VERY LOVELY (Fig. 2-3). Notice, that this sequence of words had not been used during construction and adaptation of this ANAKG graph, so it came into being as a result of generalization of all training sequences. The ANAKG neural graphs are universal and can consolidate and generalize sequences representing anything.

This example shows a new kind of generalization and highlights the importance of neuron relaxation common in biological neural networks. Without the relaxation of as-neurons, this result and a similar kind of network answers would be impossible. Moreover, these as-neurons produced this sequence of activations automatically as an answer to external stimulations of single as-neuron MONKEY. Stimulating an initial sub-sequence of any training sequence in almost all cases causes recalling of the remainder of this training sequence. Given a context, the differing length of the initial sub-sequence depends on the training frequency and uniqueness of the recalled sequence. Rare and more correlated sequences demand

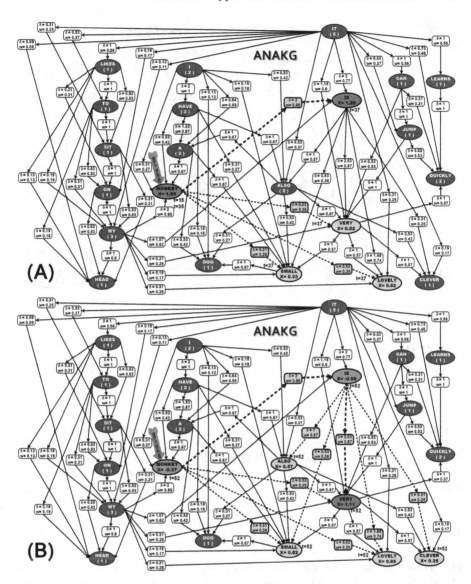

Fig. 2. A developed ANAKG graph for the presented training sequence set: (A) two sequential external stimulations of as-neuron MONKEY in simulation time: t=0 and t=20 result in activation of as-neuron IS, (B) as-neuron IS together with the previous contextual excitation coming from as-neuron MONKEY activates as-neuron VERY

a wider context for initial recalling than sequences that have a more unique initial sequence or have been trained more frequently than the others. The context for recalling of subsequent as-neurons in a sequence is formed based on below-threshold excitations that enable as-neurons activations in the immediate future (Fig. 2-3).

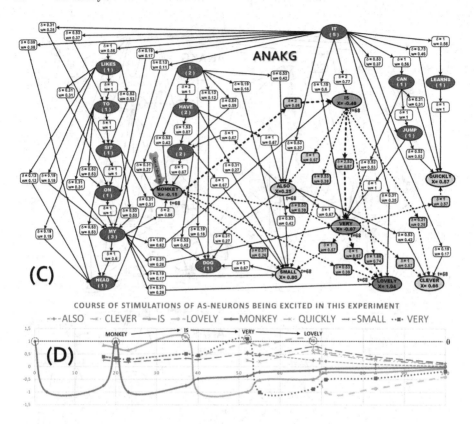

Fig. 3. The automatically stimulated and activated as-neurons: (C) as-neuron VERY together with the previous contextual excitations coming from as-neurons MONKEY and IS activates as-neuron LOVELY (Fig. 2), (D) time chart of the as-neuron excitations, activities, and refractions, presenting an ANAKG answer to the external stimulations of as-neuron MONKEY represented by sequentially activated as-neurons

4   Summary and Conclusions

This paper extends the abilities of commonly used neural networks in the field of artificial intelligence. It introduces a new kind of neurons and adaptation strategies. The presented adaptation strategy uses novelty parameters regarding the numbers of activations of as-neurons and time-dependent delta parameters that measure the efficiency of synaptic connection between presynaptic and postsynaptic as-neurons accordingly to the time interval of their activations. This paper also presents generalized formulas to quickly construct and adapt ANAKG neural networks to represent training sequence sets. A single browse through a training sequence set allows to construct a structure and compute all parameters of this network. This work shows that this kind of neural networks can not only remember a great part of training sequences but also generalize about them. The ANAKG neural networks as well as aas-systems are not intended to precisely remember training data but rather to represent the knowledge about trained objects, generalize about them, and even get creative answers. Knowledge is always the generalization of trained objects, facts, and rules. Our brains also do not precisely remember all the trained objects, facts, and rules, but represent classes of objects and only the most important or frequent facts and rules. This limitation is necessary if we want to process big-data and form knowledge on their basis. The precision of representation of classes of objects and represented facts and rules depends on the number and kind of perception elements (receptors) as well as the number of neurons that can be used to represent them. However, knowledge more capable of generalizing comes into being when objects are well aggregated and their sequences are appropriately consolidated. Such knowledge makes an indispensable background for intelligent processing and intelligence.

The experiments confirmed the adaptive and generalizing abilities of the presented ANAKG neural graphs. The obtained results demonstrate the associative capabilities that can be modelled and used in the field of artificial intelligence. These investigations have shown new possible directions of investigation that can spark the creation of new neural associative models of knowledge representation and extend the capabilities of artificial intelligence, knowledge mining, and emergent cognitive systems. This research was supported by AGH 11.11.120.612.

References

[1] Anderson, J.R., Lebiere, C.: The Newell test for a theory of cognition. Behavioral and Brain Science 26, 587–637 (2003)
[2] Arik, S.: Global asymptotic stability analysis of bidirectional associative memory neural networks with time delays. IEEE Transactions on Neural Networks, 580–586 (2005), doi:10.1109/TNN.2005.844910
[3] Borowik, B.: Associative Memories. MIKOM, Warsaw (2002)
[4] Cassimatis, N.L.: Adaptive Algorithmic Hybrids for Human-Level Artificial Intelligence (2007)
[5] Dudek-Dyduch, E., Tadeusiewicz, R., Horzyk, A.: Neural Network Adaptation Process Effectiveness Dependent of Constant Training Data Availability. Neurocomputing 72, 3138–3149 (2009)
[6] Dudek-Dyduch, E., Kucharska, E., Dutkiewicz, L., Rączka, K.: ALMM solver - a tool for optimization problems. In: Rutkowski, L., Korytkowski, M., Scherer, R., Tadeusiewicz, R., Zadeh, L.A., Zurada, J.M. (eds.) ICAISC 2014, Part II. LNCS (LNAI), vol. 8468, pp. 328–338. Springer, Heidelberg (2014)
[7] Duch, W.: Towards comprehensive foundations of computational intelligence. In: Duch, W., Mandziuk, J. (eds.) Challenges for Computational Intelligence. SCI, vol. 63, pp. 261–316. Springer, Heidelberg (2007)
[8] Duch, W.: Brain-inspired conscious computing architecture. Journal of Mind and Behaviour 26, 1–22 (2005)
[9] Hawkins, J., Blakeslee, S.: The Essence of Intelligence. One Press, Helion (2006)
[10] Hecht-Nielsen, R.: Confabulation Theory: The Mechanism of Thought. Springer (2007)
[11] Horzyk, A.: How Does Generalization and Creativity Come into Being in Neural Associative Systems and How Does It Form Human-Like Knowledge? Neurocomputing, 238–257 (2014), doi:10.1016/j.neucom.2014.04.046

[12] Horzyk, A.: Artificial Associative Systems and Associative Artificial Intelligence, pp. 1–276. EXIT, Warsaw (2013)

[13] Horzyk, A.: Information Freedom and Associative Artificial Intelligence. In: Rutkowski, L., Korytkowski, M., Scherer, R., Tadeusiewicz, R., Zadeh, L.A., Zurada, J.M. (eds.) ICAISC 2012, Part I. LNCS, vol. 7267, pp. 81–89. Springer, Heidelberg (2012)

[14] Horzyk, A: Human-Like Knowledge Engineering, Generalization and Creativity in Artificial Neural Associative Systems. AISC 11156. Springer (2015)

[15] Izhikevich, E.: Neural excitability, spiking, and bursting. Int. J. Bifurcat. Chaos 10, 1171–1266 (2000)

[16] Kalat, J.W.: Biological grounds of psychology. PWN, Warsaw (2006)

[17] Kucharska, E., Dudek-Dyduch, E.: Extended learning method for designation of co-operation. In: Nguyen, N.T. (ed.) TCCI XIV 2014. LNCS, vol. 8615, pp. 136–157. Springer, Heidelberg (2014)

[18] Larose, D.T.: Discovering knowledge from data. Introduction to Data Mining. PWN, Warsaw (2006)

[19] Longstaff, A.: Neurobiology. PWN, Warsaw (2006)

[20] Nowak, J.Z., Zawilska, J.B.: Receptors and Mechanisms of Signal Transfer. PWN, Warsaw (2004)

[21] Rutkowski, L.: Techniques and Methods of Artificial Intelligence. PWN, Warsaw (2012)

[22] Rutkowski, L., Jaworski, M., Pietruczuk, L., Duda, P.: A new method for data stream mining based on the misclassification error. IEEE Trans. on Neural Networks and Learning Systems (2014)

[23] Rutkowski, L., Jaworski, M., Pietruczuk, L., Duda, P.: The CART decision trees for mining data streams. Information Sciences 266, 1–15 (2014)

[24] Rutkowski, L., Jaworski, M., Duda, P., Pietruczuk, L.: Decision trees for mining data streams based on the Gaussian approximation. IEEE Trans. on Knowledge and Data Engineering 26(1), 108–119 (2014)

[25] Tadeusiewicz, R., Rowinski, T.: Computer science and psychology in information society, AGH (2011)

[26] Tadeusiewicz, R.: New Trends in Neurocybernetics. Computer Methods in Materials Science 10(1), 1–7 (2010)

[27] Tadeusiewicz, R., Figura, I.: Phenomenon of Tolerance to Damage in Artificial Neural Networks. Computer Methods in Material Science 11(4), 501–513 (2011)

[28] Tadeusiewicz, R.: Neural Networks as Computational Tool with Interesting Psychological Applications. In: Computer Science and Psychology in Information Society, pp. 49–101. AGH Printing House (2011)

[29] Tadeusiewicz, R., Korbicz, J., Rutkowski, L., Duch, W. (eds.): Neural Networks in Biomedical Engineering. Monograph: Biomedical Engineering – Basics and Applications, vol. 9. Exit, Warsaw (2013)

[30] Tetko, I.V.: Associative Neural Network. Neural Proc. Lett. 16(2), 187–199 (2002)

[31] Wang, P.: Rigid flexibility. The Logic of Intelligence. Springer (2006)

[32] Sha, Z., Li, X.: Mining local association patterns from spatial dataset. In: 7th Int. Conf. on Fuzzy Systems and Knowledge Discovery (2010)

Complexity of Shallow Networks Representing Finite Mappings

Věra Kůrková[✉]

Institute of Computer Science, Czech Academy of Sciences
Pod Vodárenskou věží 2, 18207 Prague, Czech Republic
vera@cs.cas.cz

Abstract. Complexity of shallow (one-hidden-layer) networks representing finite multivariate mappings is investigated. Lower bounds are derived on growth of numbers of network units and sizes of output weights in terms of variational norms of mappings to be represented. Probability distributions of mappings whose computations require large networks are described. It is shown that due to geometrical properties of high-dimensional Euclidean spaces, representation of almost any randomly chosen function on a sufficiently large domain by a shallow network with perceptrons requires untractably large network. Concrete examples of such functions are constructed using Hadamard matrices.

Keywords: Shallow feedforward networks · Signum perceptrons · Finite mappings · Model complexity · Hadamard matrices

1 Introduction

Although originally biologically inspired neural networks were introduced as multilayer computational models, later one-hidden-layer architectures became dominant in applications (see, e.g., [1] and the references therein). Recently, new learning algorithms were developed for networks with more than one hidden layers called deep networks [2, 3]. To distinguish them from deep networks, one-hidden-layer networks became called shallow networks.

In practical implementations, feedforward networks compute functions on finite domains in $\mathbb{R}^d$ representing discretized data sets or images. It was proven that shallow networks with many types of computational units have "universal representation property", i.e., they can exactly represented any finite mapping. Ito [4] proved this property for networks with perceptrons with any sigmoidal activation function and Michelli [5] verified this property for networks with Gaussian radial units.

However, proofs of the universal representation capability of shallow networks require potentially unlimited numbers of hidden units. These numbers representing model complexities are critical factors for practical implementations. Upper bounds on model complexities of shallow networks in dependence on their input dimensions, types of units, functions to be approximated, and accuracies of

© Springer International Publishing Switzerland 2015
L. Rutkowski et al. (Eds.): ICAISC 2015, Part I, LNAI 9119, pp. 39–48, 2015.
DOI: 10.1007/978-3-319-19324-3_4

approximation have been studied using tools from nonlinear approximation theory (see, e.g., [6–10] and references therein). These bounds were used to obtain descriptions of classes of functions which can be efficiently computed by shallow networks. On the other hand, limitations of computational capabilities of shallow networks are much less understood. Only few lower bounds on rates of approximation by these networks are known. Moreover, the bounds are mostly non-constructive and hold for types of computational units that are not commonly used [11, 12].

In this paper, we investigate complexities of shallow networks representing finite mappings. Mappings on finite subsets of d-dimensional spaces $\mathbb{R}^d$ (corresponding to pixels of patterns to be recognized or scattered data to be classified) represent common tasks performed by feedforward networks. We use the concept of variational norm tailored to a dictionary from theory of approximation as a tool to obtain lower bounds on numbers of units or sizes of output weights in shallow networks representing finite mapping. We prove that when the size of a dictionary of computational units is "relatively small" then almost any mapping on a sufficiently large domain cannot be tractably represented by a shallow network with units from the dictionary. We apply general results to the dictionary of signum perceptron. We illustrate existential results on distributions of functions whose representations require networks with large model complexities with a concrete construction of such functions based on Hadamard matrices. Our results present a seeming paradox: although almost randomly chosen function on a large domain cannot be tractably represented by shallow perceptron networks, finding concretee constructions of such functions is difficult. This paradox reminds situation in coding theory where "almost any code we cannot think about is good". Also in neurocomputing, it seems that practical tasks lead to computations of functions which are far from being random, they have some structures which can be efficiently computed by shallow networks with properly chosen types of units.

The paper is organized as follows. Section 2 contains basic concepts on shallow networks and dictionaries of computational units. Section 3 reviews universal representation property of shallow networks and introduces variational norms as a tool for investigation of network complexity. In Section 4, estimates of probabilistic distributions of sizes of variational norms are proven. In section 5, concrete examples of functions which cannot be tractably represented by perceptron networks are constructed using Hadamard matrices. Section 6 is a brief discussion.

2 Preliminaries

Shallow networks (one-hidden-layer networks with single linear outputs), compute input-output functions from sets of the form

$$\operatorname{span}_n G := \left\{ \sum_{i=1}^n w_i g_i \,|\, w_i \in \mathbb{R},\, g_i \in G \right\},$$

where G, called a *dictionary*, is a set of functions computable by a given type of units, the coefficients w_i are output weights, and n is the number of hidden units. This number can be interpreted as a measure of *model complexity*. By

$$\text{span}\, G := \bigcup_{n \in \mathbb{N}} \text{span}_n\, G$$

is denoted the set of functions computable by one-hidden-layer networks with units from the dictionary G with any number of hidden units. Typical dictionaries used in neurocompting are parameterized families of functions, i.e., they have the form $G_\phi(X, U)$, where $\phi : X \times U \to \mathbb{R}$ is a function of two variables, where $X \subset \mathbb{R}^d$ represents the set od inputs and $U \subset \mathbb{R}^r$ the set of parameters which are optimized during learning.

In this paper, we focus on capabilities of shallow networks to represent functions on finite domains in $\mathbb{R}^d$. For $X \subset \mathbb{R}^d$, we denote by

$$\mathcal{F}(X) := \{f \,|\, f : X \to \mathbb{R}\}$$

the linear space of real-valued functions on X. When $X \subset \mathbb{R}^d$ is finite, $\mathcal{F}(X)$ is isomorphic to the finite dimensional Euclidean space $\mathbb{R}^{\text{card}\, X}$ and we call its elements *finite mappings*. So, on $\mathcal{F}(X)$ we have the Euclidean inner product defined as

$$\langle f, g \rangle := \sum_{u \in X} f(u)g(u)$$

and the Euclidean norm

$$\|f\| := \sqrt{\langle f, f \rangle}.$$

To distinguish the inner product $\langle ., . \rangle$ on $\mathcal{F}(X)$ from the inner product on $X \subset \mathbb{R}^d$, we denote the latter as $u \cdot v := \sum_{i=1}^d u_i v_i$. By $\mathcal{B}(X)$ we denote the subset of $\mathcal{F}(X)$ formed by $\{-1, 1\}$-valued functions, i.e.,

$$\mathcal{B}(X) = \{f : X \to \{-1, 1\}\}.$$

The most common type of computational units are *perceptrons*, which compute functions of the form $\sigma(v \cdot . + b) : X \to \mathbb{R}$, where $\sigma : \mathbb{R} \to \mathbb{R}$ is an *activation function*. It is called *sigmoid* when it is monotonic increasing and $\lim_{t \to -\infty} \sigma(t) = 0$ and $\lim_{t \to \infty} \sigma(t) = 1$. Important types of activation functions are the *Heaviside function* defined as

$$\vartheta(t) := 0 \text{ for } t < 0 \quad \text{and} \quad \vartheta(t) := 1 \text{ for } t \geq 0$$

and the *signum function* $\text{sgn} : \mathbb{R} \to \{-1, 1\}$, defined as

$$\text{sgn}(t) := -1 \text{ for } t < 0 \quad \text{and } \text{sgn}(t) := 1 \quad \text{for } t \geq 0.$$

We denote by $H_d(X)$ the dictionary of functions on $X \subset \mathbb{R}^d$ computable by *Heaviside perceptrons*, i.e.,

$$H_d(X) := \{\vartheta(v \cdot . + b) : X \to \{0, 1\} \,|\, v \in \mathbb{R}^d, b \in \mathbb{R}\},$$

and by $P_d(X)$ the dictionary of functions on X computable by *signum percep-trons*, i.e.,

$$P_d(X) := \{\operatorname{sgn}(v \cdot . + b) : X \to \{-1,1\} \mid v \in \mathbb{R}^d, b \in \mathbb{R}\}.$$

Note that $H_d(\mathbb{R}^d)$ is the *set of characteristic functions of half-spaces* of $\mathbb{R}^d$. From technical reasons, in our arguments we use the signum activation function as all units from $P_d(X)$ have the same norm equal to $(\operatorname{card} X)^{1/2}$. From the point of view of model complexity, there is only a minor difference between networks with units from the dictionary of signum perceptrons $P_d(X)$ and the dictionary of Heaviside perceptrons $H_d(X)$, as $\operatorname{sgn}(t) = 2\vartheta(t) - 1$ and $\vartheta(t) = \frac{\operatorname{sgn}(t)+1}{2}$. So any network having n signum perceptrons can be replaced with a network having $n + 1$ Heaviside perceptrons.

Another widespread type of computational units are kernel units. For $X \subseteq \mathbb{R}^d$, $U \subseteq \mathbb{R}^r$, and a kernel $K_d : X \times U \to \mathbb{R}$, we denote by $F_{K_d}(X,U)$ the dictionary of *kernel units with parameters in* U, i.e.,

$$F_{K_d}(X,U) := \{K_d(.,u) : X \to \mathbb{R} \mid u \in U\}.$$

When $X = U$, we write shortly $F_{K_d}(X)$. In *Support Vector Machines (SVMs)*, $U = \{u_i, i = 1,\ldots,l\}$ is the set of input points from the training sets $\{(u_i, v_i), i = 1,\ldots,l\}$ of input-output pairs. The dictionary of Gaussian kernel units with width $1/a$ and centers in U is denoted

$$S_d^a(X,U) := \{e^{-a\|.-u\|^2} : X \to \mathbb{R} \mid u \in U\}.$$

3   Universal Representation Property

Many shallow networks have universal approximation property holding for all continuous functions on compact subsets of $\mathbb{R}^d$ (see, e.g., [13]). For finite domains, even stronger universal representation property holds for shallow networks of many commonly used types. The following proposition by Ito [4, p.71] gives a condition on a general dictionary formed by a parameterized family of functions $G_\phi(X)$ on a finite domain $X \subset \mathbb{R}^d$ guaranteeing that a shallow network with units from the dictionary $G_\phi(X)$ can exactly represent any function on X.

Proposition 1. *Let $\phi : \mathbb{R}^d \times \mathbb{R}^r \to \mathbb{R}$ and $X = \{x_1,\ldots,x_n\} \subset \mathbb{R}^d$. If there exists $Y = \{y_1,\ldots,y_n\} \subset \mathbb{R}^r$ such that $\det M(\phi)_{i,j} \neq 0$, where $M(\phi)_{i,j} = \phi(x_i,y_j)$, then for all $f : X \to \mathbb{R}$ there exist coefficients $w_1,\ldots,w_n$ such that for all $x \in X$, $f(x) = \sum_{j=1}^m w_j\phi(x,y_j)$.*

So when a dictionary $G_\phi(X)$ satisfies the assumption of Proposition 1, then any mapping on X can be exactly represented by a shallow network with $n = \operatorname{card} X$ units from $G_\phi(X,Y)$. Ito [4] applied Proposition 1 to Heaviside percep-trons for which he constructed for any finite domain $X = \{x_1,\ldots,x_n\}$ a set of parameters $Y = \{y_1 = (v_1,b_1),\ldots,y_n = (v_n,b_1)\}$ such that $\det M(\phi)_{i,j} \neq 0$, where $\phi(x_i, y_j) = \vartheta(v_j \cdot x_i + b_j)$. Using an approximation of the Heaviside function by a sufficiently steep sigmoidal, he showed that the condition holds for perceptrons with any sigmoidal activation function. So the universal representation property holds for shallow sigmoidal perceptron networks.

For dictionaries formed by kernel units, where the kernel is symmetric strictly positive definite, the condition of Proposition 1 obviously holds with $x_i = y_i$. So in particular, it holds for the Gaussian kernel $S_d^a(X, X)$.

Although shallow networks with the most common computational units are universal representers, for practical applications such exact representations might be untractably large. The proof of Proposition 1 assumes that the number of units is as large as the number of points in the finite domain. Nevertheless, often the requirement of an exact representation can be relaxed to a reasonably good approximation. In such cases, estimates of speed of decrease of approximation errors with increasing numbers of network units are needed. Such estimates have been studied in terms of a variational norm of a function to be approximated, which is tailored to a given dictionary G (see, e.g., [9] and the references therein).

For a bounded subset G of a normed linear space $(\mathcal{X}, \|.\|_{\mathcal{X}})$, *G-variation (variation with respect to the set G)*, denoted by $\|.\|_G$, is defined as

$$\|f\|_G := \inf \left\{ c \in \mathbb{R}_+ \mid f/c \in \mathrm{cl}_{\mathcal{X}} \, \mathrm{conv} \, (G \cup -G) \right\} ,$$

where $-G := \{-g \mid g \in G\}$, $\mathrm{cl}_{\mathcal{X}}$ denotes the closure with respect to the topology induced by the norm $\| \cdot \|_{\mathcal{X}}$, and conv denotes the convex hull.

Besides of being a crucial factor in estimates of rates of approximation, variational norm tailored to a dictionary also can be used to obtain lower bounds on model complexity. For a finite dictionary G, G-variation of a function $f \in \mathrm{span}\, G$ is equal to the minimal sum of absolute values of coefficients in all possible representations of f as linear combinations of elements of G. More precisely, by [6, Proposition 2.3] for G with $\mathrm{card}\, G = m$ and $f \in \mathrm{span}\, G$ we have

$$\|f\|_G = \min \left\{ \sum_{i=1}^{m} |w_i| \,\middle|\, f = \sum_{i=1}^{m} w_i \, g_i, \, w_i \in \mathbb{R}, \, g_i \in G \right\} . \tag{1}$$

So if a function has a large variation with respect to a finite set G, then each its representation by a network with units from G has either large number of units or some units have large output weights. Note that also in theory of circuit complexity, classes of functions defined by constraints on both numbers of gates and sizes of weights have been investigated. In particular, the class $\widehat{LT_2}$ of depth-2 polynomial size threshold gate circuits with weights being polynomially bounded integers plays an important role [14].

To describe classes of functions with large variations, we use the following lower bound on variational norm from [6, 10]. By $G^{\perp}$ is denoted the *orthogonal complement of G*.

Theorem 1. *Let $(\mathcal{X}, \|.\|_{\mathcal{X}})$ be a Hilbert space and G its bounded subset. Then for every $f \in \mathcal{X} \setminus G^{\perp}$, $\|f\|_G \geq \dfrac{\|f\|^2}{\sup_{g \in G} |g \cdot f|}$.*

Theorem 1 implies that functions which are not correlated with any element of the dictionary G (or in other words, which are almost orthogonal to all its elements) have large variations.

4   Probability Distributions of Variations

In this section, we describe distributions of values of G-variations of real-valued functions and $\{-1,1\}$-valued functions on finite domains. We show that the distributions depend on the size of the domain X and the dictionary $G(X)$. Using estimates of sizes of dictionaries formed by perceptrons, we show that almost any function on a sufficiently large domain cannot be tractably represented by shallow perceptron networks.

The following theorem shows that when a dictionary $G(X)$ is not "too large", then for "sufficiently large" domains X, almost any randomly chosen function has large $G(X)$-variation. We denote by $B_r(X) = \{f \in \mathcal{F}(X) \mid \|f\| = r\}$ the sphere of radius r in $\mathcal{F}(X)$.

Theorem 2. *Let d be a positive integer, $X \subset \mathbb{R}^d$ with $\operatorname{card} X = m$, $G(X)$ a subset of $\mathcal{F}(X)$ with $\operatorname{card} G(X) = k$ such that for all $g \in G(X)$, $\|f\| = r$, and $b > 0$. Then*
(i) for μ a uniform probability measure on $B_r(X)$,

$$\mu(\{f \in \mathcal{F}(X) \mid \|f\|_{G(X)} \geq b\}) \geq 1 - 2k\,e^{-\frac{m}{2b^2}};$$

(ii) for $G(X) \subset \mathcal{B}(X)$ and any $f \in \mathcal{B}(X)$

$$\Pr(\|f\|_{G(X)} \geq b) \geq 1 - 2k\,e^{-\frac{m}{2b^2}}.$$

Both parts of Theorem 2 follow from the geometric lower bound on variational norm given in Theorem 1 and from geometrical properties of high-dimensional Euclidean spaces. For large domains X, the space $\mathcal{F}(X)$ is isometric with the Euclidean space $\mathbb{R}^{\operatorname{card} X}$. With $\operatorname{card} X = m$ increasing, the probabilistic measures of sets of vectors correlated with elements of $G(X)$ are decreasing exponentially fast. Estimates of sizes of these measures follow from the concentration of measure phenomenon and from Chernoff bound on sums of independently identically distributed (i.i.d.) random variables from probability theory (for details of proofs see [15] and [16]). Thus the measure of the set of functions with variations larger than b is at least $1 - 2\operatorname{card} G(X)\,e^{-\frac{m}{2b^2}}$. For example, setting $b = m^{1/4}$, we get $1 - 2\operatorname{card} G(X)\,e^{-\frac{m^{1/2}}{2}}$. For a "relatively small" dictionary and large domain X, this bound is close to 1.

Such "relatively small" dictionaries are dictionaries of kernel units centered at data points, which are used in SVM. These dictionaries have the same number of elements as the number of points in the set X, i.e., $k = \operatorname{card} G(X) = \operatorname{card} X = m$. So for a dictionary $F(X) = F_{K_d}(X, X)$ with $\|g\| = r$ for all $g \in F_{K_d}(X, X)$, Theorem 2 implies that

$$\mu(\{f \in \mathcal{F}(X) \mid \|f\|_{F(X)} \geq b\}) \geq 1 - 2m\,e^{-\frac{m}{2b^2}}.$$

Setting $b = m^{1/4}$, we get $\mu(\{f \in \mathcal{F}(X) \mid \|f\|_{F(X)} \geq m^{1/4}\}) \geq 1 - 2m\, e^{-\frac{m^{1/2}}{2}}$. For example, when the domain X is the d-dimensional Boolean cube $X = \{0,1\}^d$, i.e., $m = 2^d$, this lower bound implies that almost any function of the Euclidean norm equal to r has $F_{K_d}(X)$-variation at least $2^{d/4}$.

Also the dictionaries of signum perceptrons $P_d(X)$ are small enough to obtain from Theorem 2 estimates showing untractability of representations of finite mappings on sufficiently large domains. Upper bounds on card $P_d(X)$ depending on the dimension d and the size m of the domain X follow from estimates of numbers of dichotomies (i.e., partitions into two subsets) of finite subsets of $\mathbb{R}^d$. Various such estimates were derived by several authors (see the references in the discussion after [17, Theorem 1]) starting from results by Schläfli [18]. We use the following estimate, based on a result from [17].

Theorem 3. *For every d and every $X \subset \mathbb{R}^d$ such that* card $X = m$,

$$\text{card}\, P_d(X) \leq 2 \sum_{i=0}^{d} \binom{m-1}{i} \leq 2\frac{m^d}{d!}.$$

Combining Theorems 2 and 3, we derive the next corollary.

Corollary 1. *Let d be a positive integer, $X \subset \mathbb{R}^d$ with* card $X = m$, $f \in \mathcal{B}(X)$, *and $b > 0$. Then*

$$\Pr\left(\|f\|_{P_d(X)} \geq b\right) \geq 1 - 4\frac{m^d}{d!}e^{\frac{-m}{2b^2}}.$$

For example, for $m = 2^d$ and $b = 2^{d/4}$, we obtain a lower bound $1 - 4\frac{2^{d^2}}{d!}e^{-2^{d/2-1}}$.

5   Construction of Functions with Large Variations

The results derived in the previous section are existential. They imply that implementation of almost any randomly chosen binary classification task by a perceptron network requires untractably large number of units or sizes of output weights. In this section, we construct an example of a class of such functions.

To construct functions, which cannot be represented by shallow perceptron networks of low model complexities, we use Hadamard matrices. Recall that a *Hadamard matrix* of order m is an $m \times m$ square matrix M with entries in $\{-1,1\}$ such that any two distinct columns (or equivalently rows) of M are orthogonal. Note that this property is invariant under permutating rows or columns and under sign flipping all entries in a column or a row. Two distinct rows of a Hadamard matrix differ in exactly $m/2$ positions. Hadamard matrices were first studied by Sylvester [19] who observed that if M is a Hadamard matrix of order m, then $\begin{vmatrix} M & M \\ M & -M \end{vmatrix}$ is a Hadamard matrix of order $2m$. He proved that for every positive integer k, there exists a Hadamard matrix of order 2^k that can be constructed recursively starting from the matrix $H_2 = \begin{vmatrix} 1 & 1 \\ 1 & -1 \end{vmatrix}$ and repeating

the operation $H_{2^{k+1}} := \begin{vmatrix} H_{2^k} & H_{2^k} \\ H_{2^k} & -H_{2^k} \end{vmatrix}$. Matrices constructed by this recursion are called *Hadamard-Sylvester* matrices. Thus for every k, there exists a Hadamard matrix of order 2^k. The Hadamard conjecture proposes that a Hadamard matrix of order $4k$ exists for every positive integer k.

The next theorem gives a lower bound on variation with respect to signum perceptrons of a $\{-1, 1\}$-valued function constructed using a Hadamard matrix.

Theorem 4. *Let M be an $m \times m$ Hadamard matrix, $\{x_i \mid i = 1, \ldots, m\} \subset \mathbb{R}^d$, $\{y_j \mid j = 1, \ldots, m\} \subset \mathbb{R}^d$, $X = \{x_i \mid i = 1, \ldots, m\} \times \{y_j \mid j = 1, \ldots, m\}$, and $f_M : X \to \{-1, 1\}$ be defined as $f_M(x_i, y_j) =: M_{i,j}$. Then $\|f_M\|_{P_d(X)} \geq \frac{\sqrt{m}}{log_2 m}$.*

To prove the theorem we use the following lemma by Lindsay (see, e.g., [20, p.88]). It provides a useful tool for estimating the differences between the numbers of +1s and −1s in submatrices of Hadamard matrices.

Lemma 1 (Lindsey). *Let m be a positive integer and M an $m \times m$ Hadamard matrix. Let A and B be subsets of the set of indices of rows, columns, resp., of M. Then $\left| \sum_{a \in A} \sum_{b \in B} M_{a,b} \right| \leq \sqrt{n \operatorname{card} A \operatorname{card} B}$.*

Proof of Theorem 4. To derive a lower bound on $S_d(X)$-variation of f_M, we use Theorem 1 which implies that $\|f_M\|_{P_d(X)} \geq \frac{\|f_M\|^2}{\sup_{g \in P_d(X)} \langle f_M, g \rangle} = \frac{m^2}{\sup_{g \in P_d(X)} \langle f_M, g \rangle}$. To estimate $\sup_{g \in G} \langle f_M, g \rangle$, we define for each $g \in P_d(X)$ an $m \times m$ matrix $M(g)$ such that $M(g)_{i,j} = g(x_i, y_j)$. It is easy to check that $\langle f_M, g \rangle = \sum_{i,j} M_{i,j} M(g)_{i,j}$.

Farther, we reorder both matrices M and $M(g)$ by permuting their rows and columns using suitable permutations in such a way that in the matrix $\bar{M}$ obtained by reordering of M, each row and each column starts with a (possibly empty) initial segment of −1s followed by a (possibly empty) segment of 1s. This property allows us to estimate $|\langle f_M, g \rangle| = |\sum_{i,j=1}^{m} \bar{M}_{i,j} \bar{M}(g)_{i,j}|$. For each row $i = 1, \ldots, m$ let k_i denotes the last column, where $M_{i,k_i} = -1$, i.e., $M_{i,j} = -1$ for all $j \leq k_i$ and $M_{i,j} = 1$ for all $j > k_i$. Using Lindsay lemma and a partition of the matrix $M(g)$ into four submatrices where all entries are either −1 or 1, we obtain an upper bound $m\sqrt{m}$ on the difference of +1s and −1s. Iterating the procedure at most $\log_2 m$-times, we obtain an upper bound $m\sqrt{m} \log_2 m$. Thus $\|f_M\|_{P_d(X)} \geq \frac{m^2}{m\sqrt{m} \log_2 m} = \frac{\sqrt{m}}{\log_2 m}$. □

Applying Theorem 4 to the domain in the form of a discrete cube $\{0, 1\}^d$, where d is even, we obtain the following corollary.

Corollary 2. *Let d be an even integer and M be an $2^{d/2} \times 2^{d/2}$ Hadamard matrix, and $f_M : X \to \{-1, 1\}$ be defined as $f_M(x_l, y_r) =: M_{i,j}$, where $x_l, x_r \in \{0, 1\}^{d/2}$ such that $x_{l,i} = x_i$ and $x_{r,i} = x_{d/2+i}$. Then $\|f_M\|_{P_d(X)} \geq \frac{2^{d/2}}{d}$.*

So by Corollary 2 any representation of the function f_M by a shallow signum perceptron network requires the number of units or sizes of some output weights depending on d exponentially.

6 Discussion

We investigated limitations of capabilities of shallow networks to represent finite mappings. Taking advantage of the concept of variational norm tailored to a dictionary from theory of approximation, we described classes of functions whose representations require networks with large model complexities. We described probability distributions of values of variational norms. We proved that when the size of a dictionary is considerably smaller than $\exp^{\frac{\operatorname{card} X}{2b^2}}$, where X is the domain, then almost any function on X has $G(X)$-variation larger than b. Combining our results with estimates of sizes of dictionaries of perceptrons, we proved that almost any function on $\{0, 1\}^d$ cannot be tractably represented by perceptron networks. We illustrated our existential results by a concrete example of a class of such functions constructed using Hadamard matrices. Our results show a seeming paradox related to perceptron networks - although for large input dimension d, almost any randomly chosen function on the Boolean cube $\{0, 1\}^d$ requires a network with the number of perceptrons or sizes of their output weights depending on d exponentially, it is quite difficult to find concrete examples of such functions. We constructed such function using properties of Hadamard matrices which represent a rather extreme type of matrices as concerns distribution of their entries $+1$s and -1s and properties of codes which they generate.

Acknowledgments. This work was partially supported by the Czech Grant Agency grant 15-18108S and institutional support of the Institute of Computer Science RVO 67985807.

References

1. Fine, T.L.: Feedforward Neural Network Methodology. Springer, Heidelberg (1999)
2. Hinton, G.E., Osindero, S., Teh, Y.W.: A fast learning algorithm for deep belief nets. Neural Computation 18, 1527–1554 (2006)
3. Bengio, Y.: Learning deep architectures for AI. Foundations and Trends in Machine Learning 2, 1–127 (2009)
4. Ito, Y.: Finite mapping by neural networks and truth functions. Mathematical Scientist 17, 69–77 (1992)
5. Micchelli, C.A.: Interpolation of scattered data: Distance matrices and conditionally positive definite functions. Constructive Approximation 2, 11–22 (1986)
6. Kůrková, V., Savický, P., Hlaváčková, K.: Representations and rates of approximation of real-valued Boolean functions by neural networks. Neural Networks 11, 651–659 (1998)

7. Kainen, P.C., Kůrková, V., Vogt, A.: A Sobolev-type upper bound for rates of approximation by linear combinations of heaviside plane waves. Journal of Approximation Theory 147, 1–10 (2007)

8. Kainen, P.C., Kůrková, V., Sanguineti, M.: Complexity of Gaussian radial-basis networks approximating smooth functions. J. of Complexity 25, 63–74 (2009)

9. Kainen, P.C., Kůrková, V., Sanguineti, M.: Dependence of computational models on input dimension: Tractability of approximation and optimization tasks. IEEE Trans. on Information Theory 58, 1203–1214 (2012)

10. Kůrková, V.: Complexity estimates based on integral transforms induced by computational units. Neural Networks 33, 160–167 (2012)

11. Maiorov, V.: On best approximation by ridge functions. J. of Approximation Theory 99, 68–94 (1999)

12. Maiorov, V., Pinkus, A.: Lower bounds for approximation by MLP neural networks. Neurocomputing 25, 81–91 (1999)

13. Pinkus, A.: Approximation theory of the MLP model in neural networks. Acta Numerica 8, 143–195 (1999)

14. Roychowdhury, V., Siu, K.Y., Orlitsky, A.: Neural models and spectral methods. In: Roychowdhury, V., Siu, K., Orlitsky, A. (eds.) Theoretical Advances in Neural Computation and Learning, pp. 3–36. Springer, New York (1994)

15. Kůrková, V.: Representations of highly-varying functions by one-hidden-layer networks. In: Rutkowski, L., Korytkowski, M., Scherer, R., Tadeusiewicz, R., Zadeh, L.A., Zurada, J.M. (eds.) ICAISC 2014, Part I. LNCS (LNAI), vol. 8467, pp. 67–76. Springer, Heidelberg (2014)

16. Kůrková, V., Sanguineti, M.: Complexity of shallow networks representing functions with large variations. In: Wermter, S., Weber, C., Duch, W., Honkela, T., Koprinkova-Hristova, P., Magg, S., Palm, G., Villa, A.E.P. (eds.) ICANN 2014. LNCS, vol. 8681, pp. 331–338. Springer, Heidelberg (2014)

17. Cover, T.: Geometrical and statistical properties of systems of linear inequailities with applictions in pattern recognition. IEEE Trans. on Electronic Computers 14, 326–334 (1965)

18. Schläfli, L.: Theorie der vielfachen Kontinuität. Zürcher & Furrer, Zürich (1901)

19. Sylvester, J.: Thoughts on inverse orthogonal matrices, simultaneous sign successions, and tessellated pavements in two or more colours, with applications to Newton's rule, ornamental tile-work, and the theory of numbers. Philosophical Magazine 34, 461–475 (1867)

20. Erdös, P., Spencer, J.H.: Probabilistic Methods in Combinatorics. Academic Press (1974)

Probabilistic Neural Network Training Procedure with the Use of SARSA Algorithm

Maciej Kusy$^{(\boxtimes)}$ and Roman Zajdel

Faculty of Electrical and Computer Engineering, Rzeszow University of Technology,
al. Powstancow Warszawy 12, 35-959 Rzeszow, Poland
{mkusy,rzajdel}@prz.edu.pl

Abstract. In this paper, we present new probabilistic neural network (PNN) training procedure for classification problems. Proposed proce- dure utilizes the State-Action-Reward-State-Action algorithm (SARSA in short), which is the implementation of the reinforcement learning method. This algorithm is applied to the adaptive selection and com- putation of the smoothing parameter of the PNN model. PNNs with different forms of the smoothing parameter are regarded. The prediction ability for all the models is assessed by computing the test error with the use of a 10-fold cross validation (CV) procedure. The obtained results are compared with state-of-the-art methods for PNN training.

Keywords: Probabilistic neural network · Reinforcement learning · SARSA · Smoothing parameter · Prediction ability

1 Introduction

Probabilistic neural network is a radial basis function based data classifier pro- posed by Specht [1]. It is applied in medical diagnosis and prediction [2–4], image classification and recognition [5–7], earthquake magnitude prediction [8] or classification in a time-varying environment [9].

The training process of PNN relies on the adaptive selection and computation of the smoothing parameter (sigma, or σ in short). The value of sigma must be estimated on the basis of the PNN's classification performance. There are four possible categories of the PNN classifiers. They differ in the approaches for the choice of the smoothing parameter: a single parameter for the whole PNN, a vector of σs where each element relates to the class of the data, a vector of σs which are associated with all input variables, and the matrix of the smoothing parameters, where each entry refers to a particular data attribute and a class. Different procedures have been proposed up to this date to find an optimal smoothing parameter of the PNN model, e.g.: (1) the conjugate gradient procedure for iterative optimization of the set of sigmas related to each data attribute [10]; (2) the conjugate gradient and the approximate Newton algorithms for optimal smoothing parameters associated with each data attribute and class [5]; (3) the golden section search method and the swarm intelligence algorithm for a self-adaptive PNN with the single sigma and the matrix of the

© Springer International Publishing Switzerland 2015
L. Rutkowski et al. (Eds.): ICAISC 2015, Part I, LNAI 9119, pp. 49–58, 2015.
DOI: 10.1007/978-3-319-19324-3_5

smoothing parameters [11]; (4) the particle swarm optimization algorithm that avoids gradient computation for PNN with σ-parameter calculated with respect to all features and class indices [12].

This study is an extension of our work presented in [13] and [14]. In those papers we developed PNN training procedures which use three reinforcement learning (RL) algorithms: $Q(0)$-, $Q(\lambda)$-, and stateless Q-learning. In this article, we propose new RL-based training procedure for the PNN model. This procedure utilizes the SARSA algorithm [17, 18] for the choice and computation of the smoothing parameter. This solution is applied to all four categories of the PNN classifiers. The results are verified in the classification problems of UCI machine learning repository data sets [15].

This paper is organized as follows. Section 2 presents the probabilistic neural network highlighting the differences in all four types of the PNNs. In Section 3, the basis of the SARSA algorithm is discussed. Section 4 describes the proposed procedure. In Section 5, we present empirical results along with the illustration of the training process for the PNN model. The article is concluded in Section 6.

2   Probabilistic Neural Network

Probabilistic neural network is a feedforward model. In the first layer, PNN is composed of n nodes which represent the attributes of an input vector $\mathbf{x} \in \mathbb{R}^n$. The second layer, called the pattern layer, consists of the neurons whose number is equal to the cardinality of the data set. These neurons are activated by means of radial basis functions computed between training records and a test vector. Pattern neurons feed the signal to the next, summation layer. There are G neurons in the summation layer, where G represents the number of classes. Each gth neuron ($g = 1, \ldots, G$) acquires the inputs measured over all the examples of the gth class. Therefore, l_g hidden neurons constitute the input for the gth summation neuron. Finally, the output layer determines the category for the vector $\mathbf{x}$ in accordance with the Bayes's theorem on the basis of the outputs of all the summation layer neurons

$$G^* (\mathbf{x}) = \arg\max_g \{y_g (\mathbf{x})\}, \tag{1}$$

where $G^* (\mathbf{x})$ denotes the predicted class for the pattern $\mathbf{x}$ and $y_g (\mathbf{x})$ is the summation layer signal. $y_g (\mathbf{x})$ is a probability density function (PDF) for gth class, which defines a concentration of the data of class g around the vector $\mathbf{x}$. In real classification problems, a data set distribution is usually unknown. Therefore, some approximation of the PDF must be determined. The Gaussian function is a common choice for $y_g (\mathbf{x})$. In such a case, $y_g (\mathbf{x})$ can be treated as aggregate of l_g number of PDFs, which are used for the activation of pattern layer neurons. Depending on the form of the Gaussian PDF, which requires an appropriate choice of the smoothing parameter, four PNN classifiers can be distinguished. They are shortly characterized below.

In the simplest case, when the smoothing parameter takes the form of a scalar, the summation layer signal depends on the same value of σ for all pattern neurons in the hidden layer

$$y_g\left(\mathbf{x}\right) = \frac{1}{l_g \left(2\pi\right)^{n/2} \sigma^n} \sum_{i=1}^{l_g} \exp\left(-\frac{1}{2\sigma^2}\left(\mathbf{x}_i^{(g)} - \mathbf{x}\right)^T \left(\mathbf{x}_i^{(g)} - \mathbf{x}\right)\right), \qquad (2)$$

where $\mathbf{x}_i^{(g)}$ is the ith training vector $(i = 1, \ldots, l_g)$ from the class g and $\mathbf{x}$ is an unknown test sample.

In the second case, the smoothing parameter takes the values from the set $\{\sigma^{(1)}, \ldots, \sigma^{(G)}\}$, where each gth element relates to each gth class index. Then the summation layer signal is defined as follows

$$y_g\left(\mathbf{x}\right) = \frac{1}{l_g \left(2\pi\right)^{n/2} \left(\sigma^{(g)}\right)^n} \sum_{i=1}^{l_g} \exp\left(-\frac{1}{2\left(\sigma^{(g)}\right)^2}\left(\mathbf{x}_i^{(g)} - \mathbf{x}\right)^T \left(\mathbf{x}_i^{(g)} - \mathbf{x}\right)\right), \qquad (3)$$

where $\sigma^{(g)}$ denotes the smoothing parameter associated with gth class.

Third possibility of the smoothing parameter representation considers the number of input variables. Thus, $y_g\left(\mathbf{x}\right)$ is determined on the basis of $\sigma_1, \ldots, \sigma_n$. The following summation layer signal is obtained

$$y_g\left(\mathbf{x}\right) = \frac{1}{l_g \left(2\pi\right)^{n/2} \sqrt{\det \Sigma_V}} \sum_{i=1}^{l_g} \exp\left(-\frac{1}{2}\left(\mathbf{x}_i^{(g)} - \mathbf{x}\right)^T \left(\Sigma_V\right)^{-1} \left(\mathbf{x}_i^{(g)} - \mathbf{x}\right)\right),$$
$$(4)$$

where $\Sigma_V = \text{diag}\left(\sigma_1^2, \ldots, \sigma_n^2\right)$ is the covariance matrix and σ_j refers to jth variable for $j = 1, \ldots, n$.

Finally, the smoothing parameter can be determined for each jth data attribute and each gth class separately. In such a case, we have $G \cdot n$ parameters: $\sigma_1^{(1)}, \ldots, \sigma_n^{(G)}$. Therefore, the summation layer signal is computed as follows

$$y_g\left(\mathbf{x}\right) = \frac{1}{l_g \left(2\pi\right)^{n/2} \sqrt{\det \Sigma_{CV}}} \sum_{i=1}^{l_g} \exp\left(-\frac{1}{2}\left(\mathbf{x}_i^{(g)} - \mathbf{x}\right)^T \left(\Sigma_{CV}\right)^{-1} \left(\mathbf{x}_i^{(g)} - \mathbf{x}\right)\right),$$
$$(5)$$

where $\Sigma_{CV} = \text{diag}\left((\sigma_1^{(g)})^2, \ldots, (\sigma_n^{(g)})^2\right)$ is the covariance matrix and $\sigma_j^{(g)}$ stands for the smoothing parameter related to jth variable and the gth class.

We can observe that considering the summation neuron signals (2)–(5), the following PNN classifiers are created:

- the network with scalar σ (in short: PNNS);
- the network with G-dimensional sigma vector: $\boldsymbol{\sigma}_C = \left[\sigma^{(1)}, \ldots, \sigma^{(G)}\right]$ (in short: PNNC);
- the network with n-dimensional sigma vector: $\boldsymbol{\sigma}_V = \left[\sigma_1, \ldots, \sigma_n\right]$ (in short: PNNV);
- the network with $(G \times n)$-dimensional sigma matrix $\boldsymbol{\sigma}_{CV}$ consisting of $\sigma_j^{(g)}$ elements for $j = 1, \ldots, n$ and $g = 1, \ldots, G$ (in short: PNNCV).

The PNN model with the smoothing parameter computed for each data coordinate and class creates the most general form of this network. However, this type of the network is computationally the most demanding since $G \times n$ matrix of the smoothing parameters must be stored.

3   SARSA Algorithm

SARSA is one the reinforcement learning algorithms, which allows the agent to learn a policy of interaction with an unknown environment through a trial and error method. The agent explores this environment and selects an action to perform. Depending on the effect of this action, the agent obtains a reward. Its goal is to maximize the discounted sum of future reinforcements r_t received in long run in any time step t, which is usually formalized as $\sum_{t=0}^{\infty} \gamma^t r_t$, where $\gamma \in [0,1]$ is the agent's discount rate [16].

SARSA computes the Q–table of all $Q(s,a)$ values by successive approximations. $Q(s,a)$ represents the expected pay-off that an agent can obtain in state s after it performs action a. In time step t, the Q–table is updated for a state-action pair (s_t, a_t) according to the following formula [17]

$$Q_{t+1}(s_t, a_t) = Q_t(s_t, a_t) + \alpha \, \Delta_t, \tag{6}$$

where $\alpha \in (0,1]$ is the learning rate and

$$\Delta_t = r_t + \gamma Q_t(s_{t+1}, a_{t+1}) - Q_t(s_t, a_t) \tag{7}$$

is the temporal differences error. This error requires the value of a single element of Q_t in the state s_{t+1} after the action a_{t+1} is performed. Therefore, the update of the action value function for s_t and a_t must be held until in the state s_{t+1}, the action a_{t+1} is executed.

The formula in (6) will be used as the basis of the algorithm for the PNN's smoothing parameter optimization presented in the next section.

4   Proposed Procedure

For the adaptation of the smoothing parameter, the SARSA algorithm is proposed for PNN, PNNC, PNNV, and PNNCV models.

The main idea of the algorithm for the choice of the optimal value of the smoothing parameter is to train the network on the training set and then test it on the independent test set. The training error E and the test error $\check{E}$ are computed on the training and test subsets, respectively. The following error measure is assumed

$$E = \frac{1}{l} \sum_{i=1}^{l} m_i, \tag{8}$$

where m_i is the misclassification error defined as follows

$$m_i = \begin{cases} 1 & \text{if } G^*(\mathbf{x}_i) \neq \hat{G}_i \\ 0 & \text{if } G^*(\mathbf{x}_i) = \hat{G}_i \end{cases}, \tag{9}$$

where $G^*(\mathbf{x}_i)$ is defined in (1), $\mathbf{x}_i$ is the ith input element and $\hat{G}_i$ is its corresponding output. The error measure (8) computed for the training set is assumed to be the state in SARSA algorithm.

In Algorithm 1, we present the procedure of applying the SARSA method for the adaptive choice of $\boldsymbol{\sigma}_{CV}$ for the PNNCV classifier. The procedure starts with an arbitrary initialization of all the elements of $\boldsymbol{\sigma}_{CV}$ with the same values

$$\sigma_0 = \underset{\sigma \in [\sigma_{0\_l}, \sigma_{0\_u}]}{\arg \min} \{E(\sigma)\}, \tag{10}$$

where σ_{0_l} and σ_{0_u} are the lower and upper bounds of the initial value of the smoothing parameter, respectively. Such an initialization of the smoothing parameter allows us find an approximate value of sigma which minimizes the training error defined in (8). For PNNS, the smoothing parameter is initialized with a scalar σ_0, while for PNNC and PNNV, it is initialized with the vectors $\boldsymbol{\sigma}_C$ and $\boldsymbol{\sigma}_V$ of the same σ_0 values, respectively. The test error computed according to (8) for initial smoothing parameter values is assigned to the minimum test error $E_{\min}$. The action value function Q is initialized with zeros [16]. After the initialization process, the main loop begins (steps **6** and **7**). This loop runs over: the maximum number of training steps $t_{\max}$, each jth variable, and gth class index. In the first iteration (steps **9** and **10**), the $s_{j,1}^{(g)}$ state is observed by computing the training error value according to (8). For this state, the action $a_{j,1}^{(g)}$ is chosen using ϵ-greedy method with $Q_{j,0}^{(g)}$ as the argument. Then, in step **12**, the smoothing parameter is updated in the following way

$$\sigma_{j,t}^{(g)} = \sigma_{j,t-1}^{(g)} + a_{j,t}^{(g)}. \tag{11}$$

Afterwards, for a new value of the smoothing parameter, the training and test errors are computed (step **13**). Next, in step **14**, the training error $E_{j,t}^{(g)}$ becomes the state of the system in $t+1$ time step. For this state, the corresponding $a_{j,t+1}^{(g)}$ is selected (step **15**). If an actual test error is smaller than the minimum one, both $\sigma_{j,\min}^{(g)}$ and $E_{\min}$ are updated (steps **16**–**19**). The reinforcement signal is calculated in step **20** using

$$r_t = E_{j,t-1}^{(g)} - E_{j,t}^{(g)}, \tag{12}$$

where $E_{j,t-1}^{(g)}$ and $E_{j,t}^{(g)}$ are the previous and actual training error values, respectively. The reinforcement signal r_t follows the changes of the training error: it is positive and negative when the error decreases and increases, respectively. In steps **21** and **22**, the actualization of the action value function is performed.

This algorithm is also used for PNNS, PNNC, and PNNV but for these models, the main loop (steps **6** and **7**) runs over $t_{\max}$, $t_{\max} \cdot G$, and $t_{\max} \cdot n$ iterations, respectively.

---

1 Initialize for $g := 1, \ldots, G$, $j := 1, \ldots, n$, $s \in S$, $a \in A$:

2     $\sigma_{j,0}^{(g)} = \sigma_0$ according to (10)

3     $E_{\min} := \breve{E}_{j,0}^{(g)}$ according to (8)

4     $Q_{j,0}^{(g)}(s,a) := 0$

5 Assume the maximum number of training steps $t_{\max}$

6 **for** $t := 1$ **to** $t_{\max}$ **do**

7   **foreach** g **and** j **do**

8   **if** $t = 1$ **then**

9           $s_{j,1}^{(g)} := E_{j,0}^{(g)}$ according to (8)

10   Choose action $a_{j,1}^{(g)}$ at state $s_{j,1}^{(g)}$ using a policy based on $Q_{j,0}^{(g)}$

11   **end**

12   Apply action $a_{j,t}^{(g)}$: $\sigma_{j,t}^{(g)} := \sigma_{j,t-1}^{(g)} + a_{j,t}^{(g)}$

13   Calculate $E_{j,t}^{(g)}$ and $\breve{E}_{j,t}^{(g)}$ according to (8)

14        $s_{j,t+1}^{(g)} := E_{j,t}^{(g)}$

15   Choose action $a_{j,t+1}^{(g)}$ at state $s_{j,t+1}^{(g)}$ using a policy based on $Q_{j,t-1}^{(g)}$

16   **if** $\breve{E}_{j,t}^{(g)} < E_{\min}$ **then**

17           $\sigma_{j,\min}^{(g)} := \sigma_{j,t}^{(g)}$

18           $E_{\min} := \breve{E}_{j,t}^{(g)}$

19   **end**

20        $r_t := E_{j,t-1}^{(g)} - E_{j,t}^{(g)}$

21        $\triangle_t := r_t + \gamma Q_{j,t-1}^{(g)} \left(s_{j,t+1}^{(g)}, a_{j,t+1}^{(g)} \right) - Q_{j,t-1}^{(g)}(s_{j,t}^{(g)}, a_{j,t}^{(g)})$

22   Update: $Q_{j,t}^{(g)}(s_{j,t}^{(g)}, a_{j,t}^{(g)}) := Q_{j,t-1}^{(g)}(s_{j,t}^{(g)}, a_{j,t}^{(g)}) + \alpha\triangle_t$

23   **end**

24 **end**

Algorithm 1. SARSA algorithm for σ_{CV} parameter adaptation

5 Empirical Results and Discussion

In the simulations, six UCI machine learning repository [15] medical data sets are used: dermatology (D), diagnostic breast cancer (DBC), Haberman survival (HS), cardiotocography (CTG), Pima Indians diabetes (PID), and Wisconsin breast cancer (WBC).

We use the following settings for Algorithm 1: the symmetric set of actions $A = \{-1, -0.1, -0.01, 0.01, 0.1, 1\}$, lower and upper bounds for σ_0: $\sigma_{0\_l} = 1$ and $\sigma_{0\_u} = 10$, maximum number of training steps $t_{\max} = 100$, greedy parameter $\epsilon = 0.05$, discount rate $\gamma = 0.995$, learning rate $\alpha = 0.02$. The values of the above parameters are obtained experimentally. A 10-fold cross validation procedure is utilized to assess the prediction ability of the PNN models.

Table 1 presents CV error $\breve{E}$ expressed in terms of the percentage of misclassified examples for PNNS, PNNC, PNNV, and PNNVC in the classification problems of considered data sets. We also provide the classification results for these models available in literature.

It can be observed that except for the PID and HS data classification problems conducted respectively by means of PNNS and PNNV, the CV error values obtained for PNN models trained using the SARSA algorithm reach lower values than the ones presented in the reference studies. For the D and WBC data set classification tasks, the error is reduced 3.4 and 4.7 times for PNNS and PNNV, respectively. For the proposed approach, the PNNV model has the highest prediction ability in five out of six classification problems. In turn, the PNNS model is the "worst" predictor among the tested ones.

In Fig. 1 and Fig. 2, we show the plots of the training error (E), the test error $(\breve{E})$, the reinforcement signal (r), and the smoothing parameter (σ) as the function of time steps. The plots are depicted for exemplary single run selected out of 10 cross validation folds for the HS and WBC data classification problems performed with the use of PNNS. In these figures, the training error changes along with the modifications of the reinforcement signal. The increase of E makes r reach a negative value. In the opposite case, when the training error decreases, the reinforcement signal takes a positive value. The magnitude of r signal is proportional to the change of the error, in accordance with (12). In both plots, we can also notice that after $t_{\max}$ iterations, the lowest training error is obtained. Thus, the proposed approach minimizes the training error, which is assumed. However, in WBC classification task, the time step when the lowest E is achieved is not accompanied with the lowest value of the test error $\breve{E}$ (Fig. 2).

Table 1. CV test error results (in %) obtained for proposed PNN training algorithm. Rows labeled "r. w." contain reference work results in format: [ref]:value.

Model		Data sets					
		D	DBC	HS	CTG	PID	WBC
PNNS	SARSA	**8.12**	**6.15**	**23.19**	7.67	28.25	**2.06**
	r. w.	[19]:30.69	[19]:7.31	[20]:25.66	n/a	[21]:**21.95**	[22]:2.34
PNNC	SARSA	7.03	5.09	20.24	7.06	26.67	1.62
	r. w.	n/a	n/a	n/a	n/a	n/a	n/a
PNNV	SARSA	**1.67**	**2.11**	21.58	3.62	**21.22**	**1.03**
	r. w.	[14]:2.55	[14]:2.26	[14]:**21.04**	n/a	[11]:24.71	[11]:4.87
PNNCV	SARSA	**5.31**	**2.63**	**18.26**	6.35	**23.45**	**1.03**
	r. w.	[19]:6.49	[19]:4.62	[14]:18.53	n/a	[12]:26.30	[12]:1.05

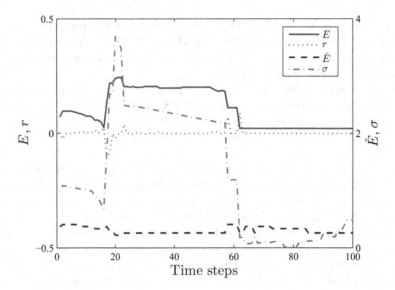

Fig. 1. Illustration of the training process for HS data set classification problem performed by PNNS

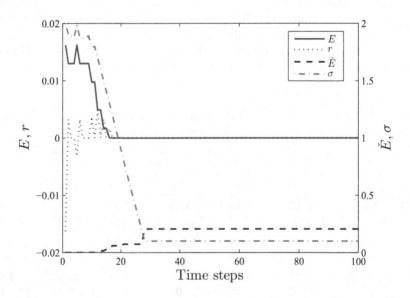

Fig. 2. Illustration of the training process for WBC data set classification problem performed by PNNS

6   Conclusions

In this article, we proposed the application of the SARSA algorithm to the selection and adaptation of the smoothing parameter for the probabilistic neural network. Four categories of the PNN models were regarded for which sigma was chosen as follows: a single parameter for the whole PNN, a single parameter for each class, a single parameter for each data attribute, and a single parameter for each attribute and class. The PNN classifiers were tested on the UCI machine learning repository data sets by assessing their prediction ability using a 10-fold CV procedure. The achieved results were referred to the outcomes available in literature. In thirteen out of fifteen compared pairs of results (SARSA vs "r. w."), the prediction ability of PNN trained by meas of the proposed algorithm was higher than the one obtained by the state-of-the-art methods. The presented contribution confirmed that the proposed reinforcement learning method can be implemented to the automatic adaptation of the PNN's model parameter.

In the future research, we will focus on different representation of the reinforcement signal used in the training process of PNN. Furthermore, the comparison of the proposed approach with the multilayer perceptron, radial basis function network, support vector machines and deep leaning architectures will be considered.

Acknowledgements. This work was supported by the Rzeszow University of Technology under Grant No. KPE/DS/2015 and Grant KIiA/DS/2015.

References

1. Specht, D.F.: Probabilistic neural networks. Neural Networks 3, 109–118 (1990)
2. Maglogiannis, I., Zafiropoulos, E., Anagnostopoulos, I.: An intelligent system for automated breast cancer diagnosis and prognosis using SVM based classifiers. Applied Intelligence 30, 24–36 (2009)
3. Mantzaris, D., Anastassopoulos, G., Adamopoulos, A.: Genetic algorithm pruning of probabilistic neural networks in medical disease estimation. Neural Networks 24, 831–835 (2011)
4. Orr, R.K.: Use of a Probabilistic Neural Network to Estimate the Risk of Mortality after Cardiac Surgery. Medical Decision Making 17, 178–185 (1997)
5. Chtioui, Y., Panigrahi, S., Marsh, R.: Conjugate gradient and approximate Newton methods for an optimal probabilistic neural network for food color classification. Optical Engineering 37, 3015–3023 (1998)
6. Kyriacou, E., Pattichis, M.S., Pattichis, C.S., et al.: Classification of atherosclerotic carotid plaques using morphological analysis on ultrasound images. Applied Intelligence 30, 3–23 (2009)
7. Ramakrishnan, S., Selvan, S.: Image texture classification using wavelet based curve fitting and probabilistic neural network. International Journal of Imaging Systems and Technology 17, 266–275 (2007)
8. Adeli, H., Panakkat, A.: A probabilistic neural network for earthquake magnitude prediction. Neural Networks 22, 1018–1024 (2009)

9. Rutkowski, L.: Adaptive Probabilistic Neural Networks for Pattern Classification in Time-Varying Environment. IEEE Transactions on Neural Networks 15, 811–827 (2004)

10. Specht, D.F., Romsdahl, H.: Experience with adaptive probabilistic neural networks and adaptive general regression neural networks. In: IEEE International Conference on Neural Networks, Orlando, pp. 1203–1208 (1994)

11. Georgiou, L.V., Pavlidis, N.G., Parsopoulos, K.E., Alevizos, P.D., Vrahatis, M.N.: New Self-adaptive Probabilistic Neural Networks in Bioinformatic and Medical Tasks. International Journal on Artificial Intelligence Tools 15, 371–396 (2006)

12. Georgiou, L.V., Alevizos, P.D., Vrahatis, M.N.: Novel Approaches to Probabilistic Neural Networks Through Bagging and Evolutionary Estimating of Prior Probabilities. Neural Processing Letters 27, 153–162 (2008)

13. Kusy, M., Zajdel, R.: Probabilistic neural network training procedure based on Q(0)-learning algorithm in medical data classification. Applied Intelligence 41, 837–854 (2014)

14. Kusy, M., Zajdel, R.: Application of Reinforcement Learning Algorithms for the Adaptive Computation of the Smoothing Parameter for Probabilistic Neural Network. IEEE Transactions on Neural Networks and Learning System (in print), doi:10.1109/TNNLS.2014.2376703

15. UCI Machine Learning Repository, archive.ics.uci.edu/ml/datasets.html

16. Sutton, R.S., Barto, A.G.: Reinforcement learning: An Introduction. MIT Press, Cambridge (1998)

17. Rummery, G., Niranjan, M.: On line q-learning using connectionist systems. Technical Report CUED/F-INFENG/TR 166, Cambridge University Engineering Department (1994)

18. Singh, S.P., Sutton, R.S.: Reinforcement Learning with Replacing Eligibility Traces. Machine Learning 22, 123–158 (1996)

19. Chang, R.K.Y., Loo, C.K., Rao, M.V.C.: A Global k-means Approach for Autonomous Cluster Initialization of Probabilistic Neural Network. Informatica 32, 219–225 (2008)

20. Chandra, B., Naresh Babu, K.V.: An Improved Architecture for Probabilistic Neural Networks. In: International Conference on Neural Networks, San Jose (2011)

21. Temurtas, H., Yumusak, N., Temurtas, F.: A comparative study on diabetes disease diagnosis using neural networks. Expert Systems with Applications 36, 8610–8615 (2009)

22. Azar, A.T., El-Said, S.A.: Probabilistic neural network for breast cancer classification. Neural Computing & Applications 23, 1737–1751 (2013)

Extensions of Hopfield Neural Networks for Solving of Stereo-Matching Problem

Łukasz Laskowski[1](✉), Jerzy Jelonkiewicz[1], and Yoichi Hayashi[2]

[1] Czestochowa University of Technology,
Department of Computer Engineering, Poland
lukasz.laskowski@kik.pcz.pl
[2] Meiji University, Department of Computer Science, Japan

Abstract. Paper considers three Hopfield based architectures in the stereo matching problem solving. Together with classical analogue Hopfield structure two novel architectures are examined: Hybrid-Maximum Neural Network and Self Correcting Neural Network.Energy functions that are crucial for the network performance and working algorithm are also presented.All considered structures are tested to compare their performance features. Two of them are particularly important: accuracy and computational time. For the experiment real and simulated stereo images are used. Obtained results lead to the conclusion about feasibility of considered architectures in the stereo matching problem solving for real time applications.

Keywords: Hopfield neural network · Artificial neuron · Spin-glass · Molecular magnet

1 Introduction

Stereovision is a natural way of determining the distance by humans. Although not new, this idea is still a subject of intensive research. Simplified model of human sight can be presented as two parallel cameras, and this model (named parallel stereovision system) will be considered for the stereo matching problem. Such systems have been widely applied in numerous fields such as cartography, psychology, neurophysiology, visually impaired support, a vehicle driving support, robots navigation, and a lot of others. This wide application field of the stereovision systems is due to its unquestionable advantages: do not emit any radiation, like microwave, not any physical contact with environment is necessary, like in the case of white cane, and is easy to apply. Figure 1 illustrates the geometry of a parallel stereovision system [15,13,36].

The system is composed of two cameras. In a parallel stereovision, the optical axes of cameras are located parallelly and perpendicularly to the baseline, connecting the centres of the cameras. Consequently, the image of the observed point W with coordinates (x, y, z) has different positions in planes of left and right cameras. It is easy to notice that the smaller difference in positions of images of point W, the further point W is located from the point of (0,0,0) (point of

© Springer International Publishing Switzerland 2015
L. Rutkowski et al. (Eds.): ICAISC 2015, Part I, LNAI 9119, pp. 59–71, 2015.
DOI: 10.1007/978-3-319-19324-3_6

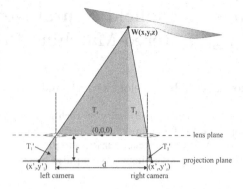

Fig. 1. The geometry of a parallel stereovision system

reference (0,0,0) is located between lens centres). The expressions on real coordinates can be written as equation 1.

$$
\begin{cases}
\frac{x'_l}{f} = \frac{x + \frac{d}{2}}{z} \\
\frac{x'_r}{f} = \frac{x - \frac{d}{2}}{z} \\
\frac{y'_l}{f} = \frac{y'_r}{z} = \frac{y}{z}
\end{cases}
\quad ; \tag{1}
$$

Hence, the distance to the observed point is inversely proportional to the difference in position of this point on image plane left and right (disparity). A closer look at the equation 1 shows that it seems to be possible to determine the distance to each point at an observed scene (depth analysis [15]). The problem seems to be trivial but it is not, in fact. The real scene contains large numbers of points. The main problem lies in finding the corresponding points in left and right pictures. Finding the points in the left and the right images which correspond to the same physical point in space is called the stereo correspondence problem. The complexity of the correspondence problem depends on the complexity of the scene and can involve complex computations. In theory, general solution may not exist, given the ambiguity which results from textureless regions, occlusion, specularities, etc. From a computational point of view, trying to match each of the pixels in one image to each of the pixels in the other image is extremely difficult due to massive number of comparisons. There are some simplifications that can help reduce the number of false matches, but many unsolved problems still exist in stereo matching [10]. It is worth noting, that stereo-correspondence still remains one of the most complicated vectorial optimization problem [6,8,7,35,29,41,30,20,21,37,38]. The main problems include the following: occlusion, discontinuity of depth, discontinuity of periphery, regularity, and repetitiveness. For this reason, the stereo-matching problem is one of the most complex task in the computer vision, and it is vital important in terms of its performance efficiency.

The paper compares performance efficiency of classical Continuous Hopfield Neural Network (CHNN) with two new networks: Hybrid-Maximum Neural

Network (HMNN) and Self Correcting Neural Network (SCNN) in stereo-matching problem solving. The first one is widely presented in the literature [6,16,17,18], while the other two are described in [25,22,24,23]. The architecture, energy functions (the energy of network forms changes in the course of the network's work), and working algorithm are presented in the paper. Considered networks are compared in terms of their accuracy and computational requirements.The tests results, based on testing real images, are included in the comparison. The accuracy of the solution and the efficiency are discussed. The depth maps, obtained by each investigated network, are also shown in the paper.

1.1   Background

In the literature, one can find a few types of algorithms for solving the stereo correspondence problems [3]. The main ones are as follows:

- **Feature based** algorithms [14] which find correspondences between some selected features of the images, such as edge pixels, line segments, or curves.
- **Phase based** algorithms - based on the Fourier phase information which can be considered as a sort of gradient-based optical flow method, with time derivative approximated by the difference between the left and right Fourier phase images, [12]. This idea became really applicable with the introduction of localized frequency filters called Gabor filters. This method computes the convolution between Gabor kernels and the left and right image parts. In order not to get trapped in some local minimum hierarchical methods were used here [40].
- **Energy based** algorithms - this kind of approach based on minimization of energy function representing a given problem (in this case stereo - matching problem of course), [33]. These kinds of methods seem to be the most universal, powerful and developed.
- **Area based** algorithms [28] are based on dividing images on sub-areas, which are fitted. These methods are well adapted for relatively textured areas. However, they generally assume that the observed scene is locally fronto-parallel, which causes problems for slanted surfaces and in particular near the occluding contours of the objects. Finally, the matching process does not take into account very important edge information which should be used to get reliable and accurate dense maps.

Nowadays algorithms in their basic forms, as described above, are rarely used mostly for very basic problems. Researchers try to merge different types of solutions in order to get as many advantages from all types of algorithms as possible and avoid their weaknesses. A very interesting development of area-based algorithm was purposed by Sun [42]. The author developed stereo matching algorithm which produces a dense disparity (depth) map by using cross correlation, rectangular sub-regioning (RSR) and 3D maximum-surface techniques in a coarse-to-fine (pyramid) scheme. Correlation is achieved by using the box filtering technique and by segmenting the stereo images into rectangular sub-images at different levels of the pyramid. The disparity map for the stereo images is found in the 3D correlation coefficient volume by obtaining the global 3D maximum - surface rather than simply choosing the position that gives the local maximum correlation coefficient value for each pixel. The 3D maximum-surface is obtained using a two-stage dynamic programming (TSDP) technique. This method seems to be very promising, but rectangular segmenting can generate false fitting.

The use of energy method to weekly calibrated stereo pictures was presented by Alvarez et al. [3]. At first, the authors found a simplified expression of the disparity that allows it estimation from a stereo pair of images by means of an energy minimisation approach. The estimation process assumes that the epipolar geometry is known and it is included in the energy model. The energy function is minimised by means of a gradient descent method. The results of the experiments are very promising, but gradient minimisation can work slowly with a risk of being trapped in local minimum of energy.

The various intelligent systems [4,5,9,19,2,34,11,31,39] can be applied to energy minimization, especially Hopfield-like neural nets [16,17,18]. The ability of the Hopfield network to solve the optimisation problems relies on its steepest descent dynamics and guaranteed convergence to local minima of the energy landscape. The advantage of Hopfield-like neural networks over the gradient minimisation methods lies in their fast operation. This is due to massively parallel computations - so important for real- time systems. This kind of system was used in stereo-matching problem solving [26]. In [32], the authors described a driving support system based on stereoscopy and Hopfield-like analog neural nets. Unfortunately, they did not include any clear depth map that could result from the application of their system, so it is difficult to estimate the efficiency of their system. Also, the form of energy function is unclear. It is worth noting that the authors reduced the computation time by the elimination of a certain number of neurons. We have tested the continuous Hopfield-based neural network with our own defined energy function. Presented further results of simulation were fairly good. The only noticed drawback of this implementation was quite a long computation time.

Discrete asynchronous Hopfield neural net, used for solving stereo-matching problem, was described in [43] by Sun and al. The authors presented very good results of stereo matching by using a Hopfield-like net. Our attempt to repeat results presented in [43] failed.

Despite some drawbacks of Hopfield's network's work performance, quoted here, it seems that such structures are the best way of solving the stereo-matching problem. The ability of Hopfield's-like structures to operate in parallel enables fast and accurate performance. It is very important for real-time systems.

Looking at the state-of-the-art-of stereovision matching with the use of Hopfield-like networks, one can have an impression that this domain has been well explored. However, none of the networks, described in the above- mentioned articles, work in an efficient enough way. Unfortunately, our attempt to apply them in the stereo-matching process each time resulted in the number of errors of the network's work performance exceeding 20 % (the way of error calculation and experimental conditions were described in section 3), which practically eliminates those methods of solving the stereo-matching problem. The subject presented here is so wide and complicated that it is still possible to improve the efficiency of such systems, to work out better architecture of nets and decrease the number of errors of the stereo-matching process.

2   Novel Architectures

Here we present two novel architectures of Hopfield-based neural networks: Hybrid-Maximum Neural Network and Self-Correcting Neural Network. Both architectures are extensions of a classical analogue Hopfiled neural networks.

2.1   Hybrid-Maximum Neural Network (HMNN)

The main idea that stays behind proposed network is to combine slow but accurate analog Hopfield neural network with much faster Maximum Neural Network [44]. The additional advantage of a maximum network is that stereo matching is reciprocally unique thanks to network's architecture. Unfortunately, the accuracy of solution found by the Maximum Neural Network is much worse than in the case of analog Hopfield- like network.

However, it is possible to combine the precision of work performance of the analog Hopfield network with the speed of maximum neural network's operation. The hybrid neural network contains both the analog Hopfield network and the maximum neural network. The architecture of the novel network shows Fig.2.

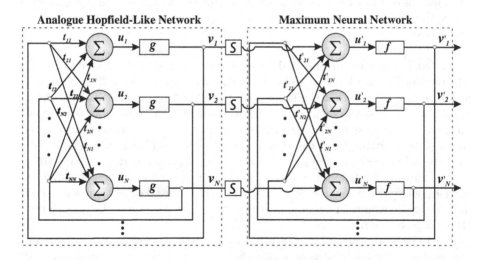

Fig. 2. An architecture of Hybrid-Maximum Neural Network

In the first stage of the HMNN's work performance, the analog Hopfield neural network is looking for the attraction area of the global minimum. Having found it, the network is switched to its maximum mode thanks to the block of switching function S (see Fig. 2).The switching follows a given number of iteration (determined empirically). The switching function can be defined as follows:

$$f(v_{ij}, it) = \begin{cases} v_{ij} & \text{for } it = it_{max} \\ 0 & \text{for } it \neq it_{max} \end{cases} , \qquad (2)$$

where it is an iteration number, it_{max} is assumed maximum number of iteration in continuous mode. In maximum mode, the network is quickly evaluating towards the global minimum and the term of uniqueness is kept automatically thanks to the maximum activation function (all terms are described in the further section).

2.2   Self-Correcting Neural Network (SCNN)

Proposed here neural structure was inspired by Dual Mode Neural Network introduced by S. Lee and J. Park in [27]. The structure presented here is a further modification of this kind of network. Dual mode neural networks in original expression was not fitted to solve stereo matching problem, mainly because of using discrete Hopfield network in the basic layer. That is the reason why the authors decided to use only the main architecture of dual mode networks, modifying the layers operation. Architecture of the SCNN was depicted in fig. 3.

As can be seen, this kind of structure consists of two kinds of neurons: neurons in the basic layer and neurons in the supervising layer. The function of these two kinds of neurons is completely different. The additional neuron neu_{00} is still active (potential equal 1) and its role is to supply external currents to neurons in the basic layer.

The basic layer is implemented by continuous Hopfield-like neural network. The proposed network consists of $n \times n$ neurons for one epipolar lines in an image. It is easy to note that the target system will consist of n networks working in parallel - each network will implement stereo-matching problem for one epipolar line. n is dimension of images ($width = height = n$). Each neuron neu_{ik} is responsible for fitting i-point in right image to k-point in left image. The higher the external potential of neu_{ik}, the better fitting of points is. In the final configuration only for corresponding points i in right image to k in left image potential of neu_{ik} will equal 1, for the rest point external potential of neurons will equal 0. It is very convenient to represent neurons as a matrix, named Fitting Matrix (FM), depicted in fig. 4.

As can be easily concluded, one in FM means fitting of points, values between zero and one (for continuous activation function, used here) can be interpreted as probability of stereo-matching of points.

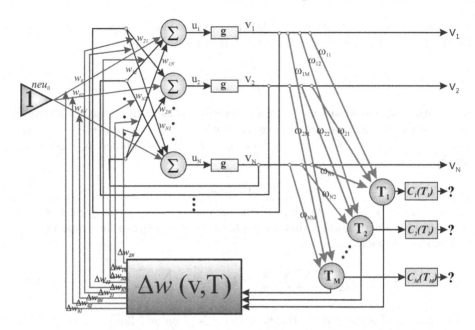

Fig. 3. The architecture of Self Correcting Neural Network (SCNN)

v_{ik}

i

Left image

$k \longrightarrow$ 1   2   3   4   5 ... n

Right image

	1	2	3	4	5	n
1	0	1	0	0	0	0
2	0	0	0	1	0	0
3	0	0	1	0	0	0
4	0	0	0	0	1	0
5	0	0	0	0	0	0
n	0	0	0	0	0	1

Fig. 4. The fitting matrix for Hopfield-like neural network for solving stereo matching problem

The Hopfield computational energy H associated with the network state v is given by (3)

$$H(t) = -\frac{1}{2}\sum_i\sum_k\sum_j\sum_l w_{ij}v_{ik}v_{jl} - \sum_i\sum_k I_{ik}v_{ik} + \frac{1}{\tau}\sum_i\sum_k L(v_{ik}), \quad (3)$$

where w is the weight matrix, I_i is the firing threshold of neuron i, v_i being the external state of neuron i. In equation 3 L is expressed by (4)

$$L(x) = \int_{\frac{1}{2}}^{x} g^{-1}(\eta)d\eta. \tag{4}$$

In equation (4) τ is a positive constant (interpreted as neuron relaxation time) and g is a continuous activation function with $v_i(w) = g(u_i(w))$, u_i is internal potential of neuron i. In the present work g is the sigmoidal function, expressed by (5)

$$g(x) = \frac{1}{1 + e^{-\alpha x}}, \tag{5}$$

where value of α adjusts the slope of the sigmoidal curve. In the present work $\alpha = 50$. It is worth noting, that for high value of α, (3) can be simplified to following expression:

$$H(t) = -\frac{1}{2} \sum_i \sum_k \sum_j \sum_l w_{ik,jl} v_{ik} v_{jl} - \sum_i \sum_k I_{ik} v_{ik}. \tag{6}$$

The equation of motion of the Hopfield model is given as follows:

$$\frac{du_{ik}}{dw} = \sum_j \sum_l w_{ik,jl} v_{jl} + I_{ik} - \frac{u_{ik}}{\tau}. \tag{7}$$

Because of using not-parallel systems for implementation of considered structure, the equation of dynamic for Hopfield network must be discretized by means of a numerical method. In this case Euler discretization was used [1]:

$$u_{ik}(t+1) = u_{ik}(t) + \Delta t \left(\sum_j \sum_l w_{ik,jl} v_{jl}(t) + I_{ik} - \frac{u_{ik}(t)}{\tau} \right) \tag{8}$$

In (8) Δt is a time step. In the presented design the value 10^{-3} has been chosen, which has been determined to be small enough for the Euler rule to provide satisfying accuracy.

The role of basic layer is to minimize their energy function, defined by weight connections between neurons. With the use of (6) initial weights between distinguished neurons in basic layer can be calculated. In original expression of dual mode networks initial weights were put randomly. Heuristic filling of weight matrix significantly accelerates the algorithm working and makes it more efficient. It is certain that the network considered here will find solution not worse than the classic continuous Hopfield network. Basic layer minimizes the energy function iteratively. The state of neurons is continuously updated and fed back to the network, and the network will eventually reach a stable state and an approximate optimum solution will be achieved.

In the case of classical Hopfield-like networks it is often impossible to make all assumption of solution in energy function (for example correspondence of edge in depth map to edge in image). Considered SCNN gives us the possibility to check the solution and the weight correction.

The supervising layer can be built with different neurons - their type depends on problem specification. Thanks to using supervising neurons the reached solution, obtained by basic layer, is verified. Each neuron controls one of the conditions of syntactic correctness. If the condition for a given neuron is not met, the range of weight modification is calculated, and connection weights are modified (which means also modification of energy function). After the modification, basic layer is starting minimization procedure once again. This procedure is repeated until the solution is satisfying, in the sense of problem expression. This means that the objective function is minimized while maintaining all conditions of the solution syntactic correctness.

3   Experimental Results

The stereovision system was tested using Dtest environment written by the authors, implemented in C++ in the Linux environment.

The resolution of the input stereo-images is 100×100. The images are calibrated in order to find corresponding lines, before starting the stereo matching procedure. This process allows for scanning of the pictures line-by-line, which decreases the complexity of the method. To verify the efficiency of the proposed method, an experiment was performed using both simulated and real images. Simulated images enabled the error calculation. Applied average relative error seems to be the most appropriate. In the simulated images expected value for each scene point $\bar{d}_{ik}$ is known. The error is calculated automatically in the Dtest program after loading the model depth map (for the whole picture) or after loading the model neuron activity map (for selected image line). The error of the stereo matching process can be calculated only for simulated pictures (possibility of neurons activity map determination). The experimental results for simulations of considered networks presents fig. 5.

It shows networks accuracy expressed by the error value as well as their required computational time, indicated by number of epochs needed to reach stable state. As can be clearly seen, the best network in terms of obtained accuracy (error is only 4,37%) seems to be the SCNN. However this impressive result was reach at the cost of long computational time - up to 180 epochs were required. Lower computational time was needed for the CHNN but accuracy in this case is a few times worse. A much faster but having accuracy as poor as the previous one is the HMNN. When consider both performance parameters, unquestioned leader is the SCNN although its required computational time can a drawback in real-time systems.

Origin picture	The name of network	Obtained depth map	Error	Epochs number
	*Analogue Hopfield-like neural network*		19.89%	83
	Hybrid Maximum Neural Network		20.04%	60
	Self-Correcting Neural Network	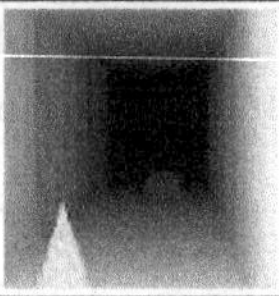	4.37	179

Fig. 5. The evaluation of results of working neural networks investigated in the present publication

4   Conclusion

This study compares three architectures: classical Hopfield neural network (CHNN) and novel Hybrid-Maximum Neural Network (HMNN) and Self Correcting Neural Network (SCNN) in stereo-matching problem solving. The stereo correspondence problem has been formulated as an optimisation task where an energy function of the network (dual function) is minimised. The energy function represents the mapping of all constraints of the solution. The advantage of using a Hopfield-like neural networks is that a global match is automatically achieved. It is because all the neurons are interconnected in a feedback loop so the output of one affects the input of all the others. The convergence to the stable state is guaranteed for the continuous Hopfield-like network with the continuous activation function. The parallel execution capability of this structure is also its unquestioned advantage in terms of possible parallel computing.

The most common problem with optimisation of the Hopfield-like networks is possible trapping in local minima of energy. Fortunately, it can be solved by using a supervising layer. Thanks to interconnection weights modification, done by the supervising neurons, local minima can be left. The promising properties of considered artificial neural network was tested both on simulated and real stereo images.

The experimental results also indicate significant advantage of the supervising neurons for interconnection weights modification. A comparative analysis performed for all three considered networks proves that the SCNN is the most accurate but requires longer computational time. Presented analysis lead to the conclusion that the weights correction based on the obtained solution is essential to reach a correct solution of stereo correspondence problem. This approach can be crucial for applications requiring really high accuracy.

References

1. Abe, S.: Global convergence and suppression of spurious states of the hopfield neural networks. IEEE Transactions on Circuits and Systems I: Fundamental Theory and Applications 40(4), 246–257 (1993)
2. Al-askar, H., Lamb, D., Hussain, A.J., Al-Jumeily, D., Randles, M., Fergus, P.: Predicting financial time series data using artificial immune system-inspired neural networks. Journal of Artifcial Intelligence and Soft Computing Research 5(1), 45–68 (2015)
3. Alvarez, L., Weickert, J., Sanchez, J., Deriche, R.: Dense disparity map estimation respecting image discontinuities: a PDE and scale-space based approach. Technical Report RR-INRIA/RR-3874-FR+ENG-3874, INRIA, Rocquencourt (2000)
4. Anand, K., Raman, S., Subramanian, K.: Implementing a neuro fuzzy expert system for optimising the performance of chemical recovery boiler. Journal of Artifcial Intelligence and Soft Computing Research 4(2/3), 249–263 (2014)
5. Bali, S., Jha, D., Kumar, D., Pham, H.: Fuzzy multi-objective build-or-buy approach for component selection of fault tolerant software system under consensus recovery block scheme with mandatory redundancy in critical modules. Journal of Artifcial Intelligence and Soft Computing Research 4(2/3), 98–119 (2014)
6. Cierniak, R.: New neural network algorithm for image reconstruction from fanbeam projections. Neurocomputing 72(13-15), 3238–3244 (2009), Hybrid Learning Machines (HAIS 2007)/Recent Developments in Natural Computation (ICNC 2007)
7. Cpalka, K.: A new method for design and reduction of neuro fuzzy classification systems. IEEE Transactions on Neural Networks 20(4), 701–714 (2009)
8. Cpalka, K., Rutkowski, L.: Flexible takagi sugeno neuro fuzzy structures for nonlinear approximation. WSEAS Transactions on Systems 5, 1450–1458 (2005)
9. Das, P., Pettersson, F., Dutta, S.: Pruned-bimodular neural networks for modelling of strength-ductility balance of hsla steel plates. Journal of Artifcial Intelligence and Soft Computing Research 4(4), 354–372 (2014)
10. Dunk, A., Haffegee, A., Alexandrov, V.N.: Selection methods for interactive creation and management of objects in 3d immersive environments. In: Sloot, P., van Albada, D., Dongarra, J. (eds.) ICCS. Procedia Computer Science, vol. 1, pp. 2609–2617. Elsevier (2010)
11. El-Laithy, K., Bogdan, M.: Synchrony state generation: an approach using stochastic synapses. Journal of Artificial Intelligence and Soft Computing Research 1, 17–25 (2011)
12. Fleet, D., Jepson, A.: Computation of component image velocity from local phase information. International Journal of Computer Vision 5(1), 77–104 (1990)
13. Gabryel, M., Korytkowski, M., Scherer, R., Rutkowski, L.: Object detection by simple fuzzy classifiers generated by boosting. In: Rutkowski, L., Korytkowski, M., Scherer, R., Tadeusiewicz, R., Zadeh, L.A., Zurada, J.M. (eds.) ICAISC 2013, Part I. LNCS, vol. 7894, pp. 540–547. Springer, Heidelberg (2013)
14. Grimson, E.: Computational experiments with a feature based stereo algorithm (1984)

15. Hartley, R., Zisserman, A.: Multiple View Geometry in Computer Vision, 2nd edn. Cambridge University Press (2004) ISBN: 0521540518
16. Hopfield, J., Feinstein, D., Palmer, R.: Unlearning has a stabilizing effect in collective memories. Nature 304, 158–159 (1983)
17. Hopfield, J., Tank, D.: Neural computation of decisions in optimization problems. Biological Cybernetics 52(3), 141–152 (1985)
18. Hopfield, J., Tank, D.: Computing with neural circuits: A model. Science 233, 624–633 (1986)
19. Katiyar, R., Pathak, V.K., Arya, K.: Human gait recognition system based on shadow free silhouettes using truncated singular value decomposition transformation model. Journal of Artifcial Intelligence and Soft Computing Research 4(4), 283–301 (2014)
20. Korytkowski, M., Nowicki, R., Rutkowski, L., Scherer, R.: AdaBoost ensemble of DCOG rough–neuro–fuzzy systems. In: Jędrzejowicz, P., Nguyen, N.T., Hoang, K. (eds.) ICCCI 2011, Part I. LNCS, vol. 6922, pp. 62–71. Springer, Heidelberg (2011)
21. Korytkowski, M., Rutkowski, L., Scherer, R.: From ensemble of fuzzy classifiers to single fuzzy rule base classifier. In: Rutkowski, L., Tadeusiewicz, R., Zadeh, L.A., Zurada, J.M. (eds.) ICAISC 2008. LNCS (LNAI), vol. 5097, pp. 265–272. Springer, Heidelberg (2008)
22. Laskowski, Ł.: Hybrid-maximum neural network for depth analysis from stereo-image. In: Rutkowski, L., Scherer, R., Tadeusiewicz, R., Zadeh, L.A., Zurada, J.M. (eds.) ICAISC 2010, Part II. LNCS, vol. 6114, pp. 47–55. Springer, Heidelberg (2010)
23. Laskowski, L.: Objects auto-selection from stereo-images realised by self-correcting neural network. In: Rutkowski, L., Korytkowski, M., Scherer, R., Tadeusiewicz, R., Zadeh, L.A., Zurada, J.M. (eds.) ICAISC 2012, Part I. LNCS, vol. 7267, pp. 119–125. Springer, Heidelberg (2012)
24. Laskowski, L.: A novel hybrid-maximum neural network in stereo-matching process. Neural Computing and Applications 23(7-8), 2435–2450 (2013)
25. Laskowski, L., Jelonkiewicz, J.: Self-correcting neural network for stereo-matching problem solving. Fundamenta Informaticae 138, 1–26 (2015)
26. Lee, J.J., Shim, J.C., Ha, Y.H.: Stereo correspondence using the hopfield neural network of a new energy function. Pattern Recognition 27(11), 1513–1522 (1994)
27. Lee, S., Park, J.: Dual-mode dynamics neural network for combinatorial optimization. Neurocomputing 8(3), 283–304 (1995), Optimization and Combinatorics, Part I-III
28. Nishihara, H.K.: Readings in computer vision: Issues, problems, principles, and paradigms, pp. 63–72. Morgan Kaufmann Publishers Inc., San Francisco (1987)
29. Nowicki, R., Pokropińska, A.: Information criterions applied to neuro-fuzzy architectures design. In: Rutkowski, L., Siekmann, J.H., Tadeusiewicz, R., Zadeh, L.A. (eds.) ICAISC 2004. LNCS (LNAI), vol. 3070, pp. 332–337. Springer, Heidelberg (2004)
30. Nowicki, R., Rutkowska, D.: Neuro–fuzzy systems based on Gödel and Sharp implication. In: Proceedings of Intern. Conference Application of Fuzzy Systems and Soft Computing — ICAFS 2000, Siegen, Germany, pp. 232–237 (June 2000)
31. Nowicki, R., Scherer, R., Rutkowski, L.: A method for learning of hierarchical fuzzy systems. In: Sincak, P., et al. (eds.) Intelligent Technologies – Theory and Applications, pp. 124–129. IOS Press, Amsterdam (2002)
32. Pajares, G., Cruz, J., Aranda, J.: Relaxation by hopfield network in stereo image matching. Pattern Recognition 31(5), 561–574 (1998)

33. Paragios, N., Deriche, R.: Geodesic active regions and level set methods for motion estimation and tracking. Computer Vision and Image Understanding 97(3), 259–282 (2005)
34. Redi, J., Gastaldo, P., Zunino, R.: A two-layer neural system for reduced-reference visual quality assessment. Journal of Artificial Intelligence and Soft Computing Research 1, 27–41 (2011)
35. Rutkowski, L., Przybył, A., Cpałka, K., Er, M.J.: Online speed profile generation for industrial machine tool based on neuro-fuzzy approach. In: Rutkowski, L., Scherer, R., Tadeusiewicz, R., Zadeh, L.A., Zurada, J.M. (eds.) ICAISC 2010, Part II. LNCS (LNAI), vol. 6114, pp. 645–650. Springer, Heidelberg (2010)
36. Rygał, J., Najgebauer, P., Nowak, T., Romanowski, J., Gabryel, M., Scherer, R.: Properties and structure of fast text search engine in context of semantic image analysis. In: Rutkowski, L., Korytkowski, M., Scherer, R., Tadeusiewicz, R., Zadeh, L.A., Zurada, J.M. (eds.) ICAISC 2012, Part I. LNCS, vol. 7267, pp. 592–599. Springer, Heidelberg (2012)
37. Scherer, R.: Neuro-fuzzy relational systems for nonlinear approximation and prediction. Nonlinear Analysis 71, e1420–e1425 (2009)
38. Scherer, R., Rutkowski, L.: A fuzzy relational system with linguistic antecedent certainty factors. In: Rutkowski, Kacprzyk (eds.) Proceedings of the Sixth International Conference on Neural Network and Soft Computing, Zakopane, Poland, June 11-15, 2002. Advances in Soft Computing, pp. 563–569. Springer, Physica-Verlag (2003)
39. Scherer, R., Rutkowski, L.: Neuro-fuzzy relational classifiers. In: Rutkowski, L., Siekmann, J.H., Tadeusiewicz, R., Zadeh, L.A. (eds.) ICAISC 2004. LNCS (LNAI), vol. 3070, pp. 376–380. Springer, Heidelberg (2004)
40. Singh, M., Hassan, M.: Hierarchical optimisation for non-linear dynamical systems with non-separable cost functions. Automatica 14(1), 99–101 (1978)
41. Starczewski, J., Scherer, R., Korytkowski, M., Nowicki, R.: Modular type-2 neuro-fuzzy systems. In: Wyrzykowski, R., Dongarra, J., Karczewski, K., Wasniewski, J. (eds.) PPAM 2007. LNCS, vol. 4967, pp. 570–578. Springer, Heidelberg (2008)
42. Sun, C.: Fast algorithms for stereo matching and motion estimation. In: Australia-Japan Advanced Workshop on Computer Vision, September 9-11 (2003)
43. Sun, C., Jones, R., Talbot, H., Wu, X., Cheong, K., Beare, R., Buckley, M., Berman, M.: Measuring the distance of vegetation from powerlines using stereo vision. IS-PRS Journal of Photogrammetry and Remote Sensing 60(4), 269–283 (2006)
44. Takefuji, Y., Lee, K.C., Aiso, H.: An artificial maximum neural network: a winner-take-all neuron model forcing the state of the system in a solution domain. Biological Cybernetics 67(3), 243–251 (1992)

Molecular Approach to Hopfield Neural Network

Łukasz Laskowski[1,2(✉)], Magdalena Laskowska[2], Jerzy Jelonkiewicz[1],
and Arnaud Boullanger[3]

[1] Czestochowa University of Technology, Department of Computer Engineering, Al.
A.K. 36, 42-200 Czestochowa, Poland
lukasz.laskowski@kik.pcz.pl
[2] Czestochowa University of Technology, Institute of Physics, Al. Armii Krajowej 19,
PL-42-200 Czestochowa, Poland
[3] Université Montpellier II, Chimie Moléculaire et Organisation du Solide, Institut
Charles Gerhardt, UMR 5253 CC 1701, 2 Place E. Bataillon, F-34095 Montpellier
Cedex 5, France

Abstract. The present article puts forward a completely new technology development , a spin glass-like molecular implementation of the Hopfield neural structure. This novel approach uses magnetic molecules homogenously distributed in mesoporous silica matrix, which forms a base for a converting unit, an equivalent of a neuron in the Hopfield network. Converting units interact with each other via a fully controlled magnetic fields, which corresponds to weighted interconnections in the Hopfield network. This novel technology enables building fast, high-density content addressable associative memories. In particular, it is envisaged that in the future this approach can be scaled up to mimic memory with human-like characteristics. This would be a breakthrough in artificial brain implementations and usher in a new type of highly intelligent beings. Another application relates to systems designed for multi-objective optimization (multiple criteria decision making).

Keywords: Hopfield neural network · Artificial neuron · Spin-glass · Molecular magnet

1 Introduction

The Hopfield's concept of neural computation led to a breakthrough in the Neural Networks domain, allowing for the construction of auto-associative memories [11] or systems for multi-criterion optimization [12]. His idea was based on the minimization properties of a spin glass, which manifests itself as a slow drift of the system towards its global energy function (Hamiltonian) minimum. The energy landscape of such systems is fully determined by couplings between contributed atomic spins. For this reason the evolution on the system depends on continuous adjustment of the atom spins orientation in response to magnetic fields either external once or those exerted by other atoms. The only possible stable state of the atomic spins corresponds to the local energy minimum. Interestingly, this property can be used to build neural computational systems. The Hopfield's idea

© Springer International Publishing Switzerland 2015
L. Rutkowski et al. (Eds.): ICAISC 2015, Part I, LNAI 9119, pp. 72–78, 2015.
DOI: 10.1007/978-3-319-19324-3_7

was simple: the problem's description can be given by the couplings (or so-called interconnection's strengths) in the sense that the energy minimum corresponds to the solution (where the interconnections create the energy landscape), that is the solution in the form of the minimum-energy configuration of a spin glass is found as a result of its relaxation. However, some practical implementations of this idea have not met expectations so far. In many fields (e.g. associative memories) Hopfield networks have been applied, providing better than any other solution. Nevertheless, due to constraints of these systems, they could only mimic the original Hopfield's concept. From this point of view, spin glasses seem to be a promising candidate for working implementation of the Hopfield network. Unfortunately, its implementation turned out to be challenging, since both the determination of couplings between neurons as well as checking the spin states of neurons are hardly possible.

In the present article we show a completely new technology development aiming at the hardware implementation of artificial neurons based on molecular techniques. The technology refers to a spin glass-like hardware implementation of the Hopfield neural structure. The point of the idea is an arrays of magnetic molecules magnetically coupled through electrodes and interconnection devices capable of transmitting magnetic fields. In particular, this novel approach uses homogenously distributed magnetic molecules inside SBA-15 mesoporous silica matrix. Such a material creates converting units that are equivalent to neurons in the Hopfield network with weighted interconnections between them. Individual converting units interact with one another by means of exchange interactions and controlling of electrons coherence. It is possible to control a magnetic field using spin-wave in dielectric [21] and to tune Fermi electron coherency level. Having built all the necessary elements of a neural network one can arrange them as part of Hopfield-like networks. These networks work in the same way as their physical precursor - spin glass - with all their advantages: fully parallel processing (extremely fast calculations, unavailable for any existing system) and efficiency. Importantly, no external power supply is necessary in the process of drifting to energy minimum - the system is self-polarized. Some power is needed only for setting the initial states (if necessary) or setting the interconnections. This novel technology enables fast, high density content addressable associative memory implementation. Ultimately, it is expected that the proposed approach can be scaled up to mimic memory with human-like characteristics.

The considered technology can significantly influence research and application areas, mainly artificial intelligence [3,4,9,13,2,22,10,20,26]. For instance a straightforward application seems to be a content addressable associative memory (CAAM). This kind of memory, implemented on the molecular scale, offers both high capacity and instant access, which in turn opens up new and unprecedented possibilities for artificial intelligence. It is easy to realize that molecular CAAM, with all kind of patterns and ease to learn new ones, can move forward the artificial intelligence research.

The technology, being a subject of the article, will also offer new opportunities for solving multi-criterion optimization problems [5,8,7,23,18,27,19,14,15,24,25].

Such problems, involving more than one objective function to be optimized simultaneously, what can be extremely difficult to solve. Problems of this type can be found in mathematics, engineering or economics. Vector optimization problems arise, for example, in decision making, statistics, functional analysis, approximation theory, multi-object programming or cooperative game theory. As it was proved, the Hopfield networks are very efficient in solving such problems, but also disappointingly slow. As a result, solutions can be found at the expense of computational time. When using a real parallel system, like the one described in the paper, a solution can be found instantly. Another possible application field for the molecular Hopfield network relates to a human-like expert system where fast and multi-criteria inference is needed.

2   The Structure of Molecular Neural Network

The proposed solution employs an enlarged Ising model of a spin glass. The model of the spin glass is implemented with the use of molecular neurons localized in the thin film of hexagonally arranged mesoporous silica SBA-15. As for the real Ising model, the system performance depends on interactions between converting units (or network nodes - basic units of a spin-glass neural networks). In the scheme under discussion, SBA-15 mesoporous silica thin film is activated by magnetic molecules (molecular magnets Mn_{12} [6]). Silica SBA-15 has a form of thin and long rods with walls made of amorphous silica (SiO_2). The rods arrangement is regular, in this case hexagonal. The structure of these species is shown in fig. 1.

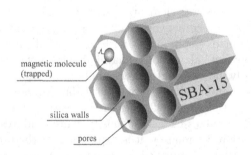

Fig. 1. The structure of SBA-15 type mesoporous silica

This material can be deposited on a substrate (e.g. silicon wafers) in the form of a thin film. An interesting feature of this layout is that it is possible to obtain 2D hexagonal structure (mesopores arranged vertically on the substrate surface), which is presented in fig. 2.

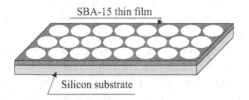

Fig. 2. 2D hexagonally arranged SBA-15 thin film on a silicon wafer substrate

Such an arrangement allows the construction of the basic elements - converting units, equivalents of neurons. Converting units must be bi-stable structures. Their main feature allow for generalisation.

Thanks to our novel method of thin films preparation, we obtained "one body" two state structure of converting units. We are also capable of obtaining restricted activation of silica structure - one pore contains only one molecular magnet. This structure can be acquired by using two layer silica thin films. First layer is not porous and contains precursor groups. Homogenous distribution of such units Is particularly important. Second silica layer is mesoporous. When diameter of a single pore is about 4.2 nm or 2.5 nm (depending on surfactant type), after activation by Mn_{12} molecular magnets it is high probable, that each pore contains single molecular magnet. The procedure of such films preparation has been depicted in 3.

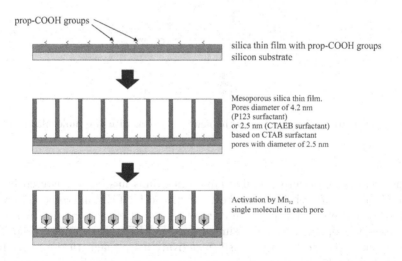

Fig. 3. Preparing of double layer silica thin films activated by molecular magnets

The interactions between molecules in two different pores are negligibly small due to shielding by silica walls. In this case a single pore containing magnetic molecule plays role of converting unit.

The interaction strengths between converting units are determined by the coherence of Fermi electrons. These, in turn, are spin-polarized due to exchange interaction with magnetic molecules inside converting units. Also magnetic moment of magnetic molecules can be switched by this interactions. Electrons polarization decays quickly with distance from converting unit. Nonetheless, the magnetic field of a converting unit can be preserved by transforming the spin polarization into a spin wave transported in dielectric. In order to control magnetic interactions between molecules our team proposed a coherence controller. This idea is based on a spin-FET (field-effect transistor) design [1] with a system of electrodes controlling the Fermi electrons coherence. This concept has not been published yet and is the subject of a patent proposal. For the purpose of device testing, we also plan to use electrodes of various thicknesses up to 1μm, placed between converting units, as a rigid weighted interconnections. The thickness of electrodes is then related to the strength of the interaction between converting units (or simply the interconnections), i.e., for thinner electrodes the interaction is stronger. Schematic representation of the network with two molecular neurons is depicted in fig. 4.

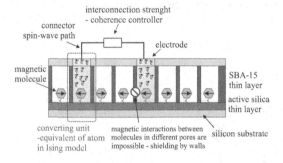

Fig. 4. Schematic representation of the neural network with two molecular neurons

The technology of active double layer silica films has been mastered by our team. Geometry of such films has been confirmed by TEM microscope imaging and X-Ray scattering. The physical-chemistry properties were checked by Raman spectroscopy supported by DFT simulations, SQUID magnetometry and EPR spectroscopy. Also technology of silica activation by magnetic ions has been tested before [16,17]. Having well-investigated basic material, it is almost certain, that molecular neural network will be created in the nearest time.

3 Conclusion

In the paper we have presented completely novel hardware implementation of an artificial neuron - single-molecule-magnet based neuron. Our idea seems to be feasible from the technological point of view. Authors mastered the technology of the thin SBA-15 film deposition on the silicon substrate. The geometrical and physical properties of these layers were confirmed by series of experiments. Considering the current status of research it is our belief a successful realization of a molecular neuron is just a matter of time.

Aknowledgement. Financial support for this investigation has been provided by the National Centre of Science (Grant-No: 2011/03/D/ST5/05996).

References

1. Agnihotri, P., Bandyopadhyay, S.: Analysis of the two-dimensional datta–das spin field effect transistor. Physica E: Low-dimensional Systems and Nanostructures 42(5), 1736–1740 (2010)
2. Al-askar, H., Lamb, D., Hussain, A.J., Al-Jumeily, D., Randles, M., Fergus, P.: Predicting financial time series data using artificial immune system-inspired neural networks. Journal of Artifcial Intelligence and Soft Computing Research 5(1), 45–68 (2015)
3. Anand, K., Raman, S., Subramanian, K.: Implementing a neuro fuzzy expert system for optimising the performance of chemical recovery boiler. Journal of Artifcial Intelligence and Soft Computing Research 4(2/3), 249–263 (2014)
4. Bali, S., Jha, D., Kumar, D., Pham, H.: Fuzzy multi-objective build-or-buy approach for component selection of fault tolerant software system under consensus recovery block scheme with mandatory redundancy in critical modules. Journal of Artifcial Intelligence and Soft Computing Research 4(2/3), 98–119 (2014)
5. Cierniak, R.: New neural network algorithm for image reconstruction from fan-beam projections. Neurocomputing 72(13-15), 3238–3244 (2009), Hybrid Learning Machines (HAIS 2007)/Recent Developments in Natural Computation (ICNC 2007)
6. Cornia, A., Mannini, M., Sainctavit, P., Sessoli, R.: Chemical strategies and characterization tools for the organization of single molecule magnets on surfaces. Chem. Soc. Rev. 40, 3076–3091 (2011)
7. Cpalka, K.: A new method for design and reduction of neuro fuzzy classification systems. IEEE Transactions on Neural Networks 20(4), 701–714 (2009)
8. Cpalka, K., Rutkowski, L.: Flexible takagi sugeno neuro fuzzy structures for nonlinear approximation. WSEAS Transactions on Systems 5, 1450–1458 (2005)
9. Das, P., Pettersson, F., Dutta, S.: Pruned-bimodular neural networks for modelling of strength-ductility balance of hsla steel plates. Journal of Artifcial Intelligence and Soft Computing Research 4(4), 354–372 (2014)
10. El-Laithy, K., Bogdan, M.: Synchrony state generation: an approach using stochastic synapses. Journal of Artificial Intelligence and Soft Computing Research 1, 17–25 (2011)
11. Hopfield, J., Feinstein, D., Palmer, R.: Unlearning has a stabilizing effect in collective memories. Nature 304, 158–159 (1983)
12. Hopfield, J., Tank, D.: Computing with neural circuits: A model. Science 233, 624–633 (1986)

13. Katiyar, R., Pathak, V.K., Arya, K.: Human gait recognition system based on shadow free silhouettes using truncated singular value decomposition transformation model. Journal of Artifcial Intelligence and Soft Computing Research 4(4), 283–301 (2014)
14. Korytkowski, M., Nowicki, R., Rutkowski, L., Scherer, R.: AdaBoost ensemble of DCOG rough–neuro–fuzzy systems. In: Jędrzejowicz, P., Nguyen, N.T., Hoang, K. (eds.) ICCCI 2011, Part I. LNCS, vol. 6922, pp. 62–71. Springer, Heidelberg (2011)
15. Korytkowski, M., Rutkowski, L., Scherer, R.: From ensemble of fuzzy classifiers to single fuzzy rule base classifier. In: Rutkowski, L., Tadeusiewicz, R., Zadeh, L.A., Zurada, J.M. (eds.) ICAISC 2008. LNCS (LNAI), vol. 5097, pp. 265–272. Springer, Heidelberg (2008)
16. Laskowski, L., Laskowska, M.: Functionalization of sba-15 mesoporous silica by cu-phosphonate units: Probing of synthesis route. Journal of Solid State Chemistry 220, 221–226 (2014)
17. Laskowski, L., Laskowska, M., Balanda, M., Fitta, M., Kwiatkowska, J., Dzilinski, K., Karczmarska, A.: Mesoporous silica sba-15 functionalized by nickel-phosphonic units: Raman and magnetic analysis. Microporous and Mesoporous Materials 200, 253–259 (2014)
18. Nowicki, R., Pokropińska, A.: Information criterions applied to neuro-fuzzy architectures design. In: Rutkowski, L., Siekmann, J.H., Tadeusiewicz, R., Zadeh, L.A. (eds.) ICAISC 2004. LNCS (LNAI), vol. 3070, pp. 332–337. Springer, Heidelberg (2004)
19. Nowicki, R., Rutkowska, D.: Neuro–fuzzy systems based on Gödel and Sharp implication. In: Proceedings of Intern. Conference Application of Fuzzy Systems and Soft Computing — ICAFS 2000, Siegen, Germany, pp. 232–237 (June 2000)
20. Nowicki, R., Scherer, R., Rutkowski, L.: A method for learning of hierarchical fuzzy systems. In: Sincak, P., et al. (eds.) Intelligent Technologies – Theory and Applications, pp. 124–129. IOS Press, Amsterdam (2002)
21. Oliver, T., Buettner, J., Bauer, M., Demokritov, S., Kivshar, Y., Grimalsky, V., Rapoport, Y., Slavin, A.: Linear and nonlinear diffraction of dipolar spin waves in yttrium iron garnet films observed by space- and time-resolved brillouin light scattering (1999)
22. Redi, J., Gastaldo, P., Zunino, R.: A two-layer neural system for reduced-reference visual quality assessment. Journal of Artificial Intelligence and Soft Computing Research 1, 27–41 (2011)
23. Rutkowski, L., Przybył, A., Cpałka, K., Er, M.J.: Online speed profile generation for industrial machine tool based on neuro-fuzzy approach. In: Rutkowski, L., Scherer, R., Tadeusiewicz, R., Zadeh, L.A., Zurada, J.M. (eds.) ICAISC 2010, Part II. LNCS (LNAI), vol. 6114, pp. 645–650. Springer, Heidelberg (2010)
24. Scherer, R.: Neuro-fuzzy relational systems for nonlinear approximation and prediction. Nonlinear Analysis 71, e1420–e1425 (2009)
25. Scherer, R., Rutkowski, L.: A fuzzy relational system with linguistic antecedent certainty factors. In: Rutkowski, Kacprzyk (eds.) Proceedings of the Sixth International Conference on Neural Network and Soft Computing, Zakopane, Poland, June 11-15, 2002. Advances in Soft Computing, pp. 563–569. Springer, Physica-Verlag (2003)
26. Scherer, R., Rutkowski, L.: Neuro-fuzzy relational classifiers. In: Rutkowski, L., Siekmann, J.H., Tadeusiewicz, R., Zadeh, L.A. (eds.) ICAISC 2004. LNCS (LNAI), vol. 3070, pp. 376–380. Springer, Heidelberg (2004)
27. Starczewski, J., Scherer, R., Korytkowski, M., Nowicki, R.: Modular type-2 neuro-fuzzy systems. In: Wyrzykowski, R., Dongarra, J., Karczewski, K., Wasniewski, J. (eds.) PPAM 2007. LNCS, vol. 4967, pp. 570–578. Springer, Heidelberg (2008)

Toward Work Groups Classification Based on Probabilistic Neural Network Approach

Christian Napoli[1]([✉]), Giuseppe Pappalardo[1], Emiliano Tramontana[1],
Robert K. Nowicki[2], Janusz T. Starczewski[2], and Marcin Woźniak[3]

[1] Department of Mathematics and Informatics, University of Catania,
Viale A. Doria 6, 95125 Catania, Italy
{napoli,pappalardo,tramontana}@dmi.unict.it
[2] Institute of Computational Intelligence, Czestochowa University of Technology,
Al. Armii Krajowej 36, 42-200 Czestochowa, Poland
Robert.Nowicki@iisi.pcz.pl, Janusz.Starczewski@iisi.pcz.pl
[3] Institute of Mathematics, Silesian University of Technology,
Kaszubska 23, 44-101 Gliwice, Poland
Marcin.Wozniak@polsl.pl

Abstract. This paper presents the application of some Computational Intelligence methods for obtaining a classifier analysing employees to form work groups. The proposed bio-inspired solution analyses employees using data gathered from their professional attitudes and skills, then suggests how to form groups of human resources within a company that can effectively work together. The same proposed tool provides employers with a fair and effective means for employee evaluation. In our approach, employee profiles are processed by a dedicated Radial Basis Probabilistic Neural Network based classifier, which finds non-explicit custom-created groups. The accuracy of the classifier is very high, revealing the potential efficacy of the proposed bio-inspired classification system.

1 Introduction

Nowadays, Computational Intelligence (CI) is one of the fast developing fields of science, and many of the newly proposed CI solutions and methods are bio-inspired. Nature itself is among the best teachers. Generally, nature-inspired mechanisms that solve parallel and complex tasks help increasing efficiency and precision of the implemented solutions. I.e., Evolutionary Computation (EC) methods consist in simulating the behavior of real organisms into the process of optimization and positioning. Previously, [21] and [22] have presented the application of genetic based methods to dynamic system positioning. NoSQL database systems and queue positioning models like in [5] are efficient applications of EC methods; [10], [25] , [24] and [18] proposed dedicated Evolutionary Strategy (ES) solutions, and [23] described a dedicated Cuckoo Search Algorithm (CSA). Moreover, CI can be applied to create learning sets for Artificial Intelligence (AI) control systems [11], [6] or image processing [26] and [28]. In [19], CI was used to assist in finding move method refactoring opportunities in large software systems. Other fields of application for CI techniques and neural networks have been

© Springer International Publishing Switzerland 2015
L. Rutkowski et al. (Eds.): ICAISC 2015, Part I, LNAI 9119, pp. 79–89, 2015.
DOI: 10.1007/978-3-319-19324-3_8

used in [16], [17], [7], [4], [20]. All these projects used some bio-inspired methods to efficiently perform sophisticated tasks, whereas other common methods have low efficiency or are inapplicable due to complex differential and integral models.

This paper discusses a dedicated bio-inspired classifier for the creation of work groups. Our model autonomously finds groups of workers, in public administrations or companies, consisting of collaborative networks of people who share a common vision and goal. Moreover, since often novel groups of employees coming from several branches have to be created in order to achieve some new goals, or for special tasks, we propose an automatic system that unveils professional affinities among employees, in order to create efficient teams. The found 'non-explicit' groups of employees, who possibly work on different areas or branches, could form a successful team because of the similarities underlying some of their attributes, such as interest, skill, competence, etc.

In this paper we aim to emulate a decision making process by means of mutual information theory indexes and Radial Basis Probabilistic Neural Networks (RBPNNs) in order to unveil the underlying affinities in human groups of employees. Our solution is based upon Radial Basis Neural Networks (RBNN), which are well known for their capability to classify, cluster and generalize datasets by creating a model of the input sets even for partial input data [9]. Moreover, RBNNs can be continuously trained to recognize novel features, hence can easily cope with a changing dataset, as previously shown in [3]. Let us now present the collaborative group theory, our relation model and the classifier.

2   Affinity-Oriented Collaborative Groups

It is possible to represent a collaborative network as a graph describing the collaborative relations among the agents represented as nodes in the network. In a work-related collaborative network, nodes are employees and arcs are professional relations among different employees in terms of collaborations, office dependencies or hierarchies involved to perform a task (e.g. employees of an area are connected with their area manager).

Collaborative networks, like social networks, follow a *scale-free* behavior (see [2]). A few nodes act as important hubs (i.e. employees who hold key positions or play important roles with major responsibilities). These hubs have a large number of relations with other employees (sometimes in different departments), hence the work of such hubs widely reflects that of collaborative networks. I.e. generally, the distribution of a complex job handled by the employees in different departments follows a scale-free pattern.

Moreover, the emerging *small-world* properties are important characteristics to consider in order to understand the social dynamics involved in the work flow and the related management [1]. Both the scale-free behavior and small-world properties make it difficult to analyze the network with conventional means, e.g. a stationary or analytical model describing job-related area. The analysis is complex because of an uncontrolled growing number of parameters.

In order to obtain a fair evaluation of human resources, one can choose affine employees as a sampling cluster, i.e. the aim is to measure the performance of an employee with respect to the mean behavior of other employees. However, a sampling cluster should not trivially map a department or an office, because results would be affected by the mutual interactions of people under evaluation. Therefore, an appropriate employee clustering for a collaborative network becomes paramount for gaining accurate human performance measures. Moreover, successful positioning of new human resources, as well as their relocation or assignment to a different position within a company are critical decisions. Therefore, homogeneous and harmonious work groups that share a common background as well as professional attitudes and complementary skills need to be properly created, possibly, with little effort.

3 Collaborative Network Dynamics

Section 2 has described the theoretical grounds for collaborative networks. Let us now present definitions and mathematical models of the collaborative network, which can be represented as a graph whereby the nodes are the employees and the arcs professional connections like dependencies, collaborations and interactions.

We state that *employee* is an element in an employee pool $\mathcal{U}$, which consists of all the employees in the analyzed company. In order to formalize the structure and functions in collaborative networks we need to define the following:

- *employee*: $u_i \in \mathcal{U} = \{$employees set$\}$,
- *feature*: $f \in \mathcal{F} = f(\mathcal{U}) = \{f : \mathcal{U} \to \{0, 1\}\}$,
- *relation*: $r \in \mathcal{R} = \{r : \mathcal{U} \times \mathcal{U} \to \{0, 1\}\}$,
- *category*: an equivalence class $\mathscr{C}$ of $\mathcal{U}$ with respect to several features or relations.

It is then possible to define $\mathcal{F}$ as a finite set of *features* related to an employee. If the feature list of an employee u shows a feature f then $f(u) = 1$, otherwise $f(u) = 0$. Examples of features can be the gender (1 if male or 0 if female), the academic degree (1 if achieved or 0 if not), each of several responsibilities (1 if accountable for, otherwise 0), a professional achievement (1 if completed or 0 if still in completion or non compatible with the professional figure), etc. Moreover, it is possible to define a mutual interaction r_f among two employees u_1 and u_2 so that $r_f(u_1, u_2) = 1$ when a professional relation exists (an edge in the collaborative network links u_1 and u_2). In the same way, relation r_g indicates whether two employees are members of the same group (i.e. they are part of an existing team, office, division, etc.). Then, it is possible to define *categories* as classes of equivalence $\mathscr{C}$ among employees according to groups, relations, employee features, or other kinds of provided data. Therefore, categories can be used to model partitions of employees according to their features, skills, groups, area of interests, etc.

The collaborative network graph is mathematically defined as $G = (\mathcal{U}, A)$, where the vertexes set is $V = \{v_i \sim u_i \in \mathcal{U}\}$, and the arcs set is

$$A = \{a(v_i, v_j) : r_c(u_i, u_j) + r_g(u_i, u_j) \geq 1\}, \tag{1}$$

whereby $(u_i, u_j) \in \mathcal{U} \times \mathcal{U} \setminus \{u_i\}$ identifies a pair of employees, and where r_c and r_g are two relations. Basing on the given definition of relations, $r_c(u_i, u_j) = 1$ if employees u_i and u_j have professional relations, otherwise $r_c(u_i, u_j) = 0$ if they do not share any professional collaboration. Similarly, $r_g(u_i, u_j) = 1$ if the two employees belong to one team or an explicitly defined area within the company, otherwise $r_g(u_i, u_j) = 0$. If there is a finite number of arcs $a \in A$ that connect two vertexes $v_0, v_n \in V$, then it exists at least one path $P_G(v_0, v_n) = \{a(v_i, v_j)\}_{v_0}^{v_n}$ where $a(v_i, v_j)$ are arcs from v_i to v_j, and the *length* $l_{0,n}$ is given as the cardinality $|P_G(v_0, v_n)|$, when $P_G(v_0, v_n) \neq \emptyset$, that is the number of arcs, from v_0 to v_n, used to form a path.

The *graph distance* $d_G : V \times V \to \mathbb{R}_0^+$, is

$$d_G(v_0, v_n) = \begin{cases} 0 & v_0 = v_n \\ \min\{l_{0,n}\} & P_G(v_0, v_n) \neq \emptyset \\ +\infty & P_G(v_0, v_n) = \emptyset \end{cases} . \tag{2}$$

The given definition of arcs and graph distance allows us to consider the existence of two different kinds of relations: when a pair of employees are linked by an arc $a \in A$, indeed the distance is 1, otherwise the distance is the minimum number of hops separating the pair. On the other hand, if the employees belong to the same group, $(r_g = 1)$ the distance is cut down to 1.

With this definition of distance it is possible to unveil the professional affinity of one employee with other employees. For our model, employees with similar interests and skills should have a very small distance, whereas employees having very high distances perform very different jobs and need not collaborate. The defined distance will be used as an adjunct parameter (other than employee features) for the developed classifier.

The feature set $\mathcal{F}$ has to be profiled for each employee. Moreover, $\mathcal{F}$ can be a basis for a Hilbert space where the employees can be classified according to their features. Thanks to the formalism that we have just introduced, we can attribute a natural number to each employee, so that it will be possible to compare employee pairs $u_0, u_n \in \mathcal{U} \subset \mathbb{N}$. For each employee u_i we define a feature vector ϕ_i consisting of boolean values, each identifying the presence or absence of a certain feature for the employee profile

$$\phi_i = [f_1(u_i), f_2(u_i), ..., f_N(u_i)] \; \forall \, f_\alpha \in \mathcal{F}, u_i \in \mathcal{U}. \tag{3}$$

Then, it is possible to define a *feature distance*

$$d_{\mathcal{F}}(u_0, u_n) = \frac{1}{\sum_\alpha \delta(f_\alpha(u_0), f_\alpha(u_n))}, \tag{4}$$

whereby δ represents the delta of Kronecker and conventionally $\langle \phi_0 | \phi_n \rangle = 0 \Rightarrow d_{\mathcal{F}}(u_0, u_n) = +\infty$. The aim of such a defined distance is to obtain significant and coherent information about the behavioral proximity or affinity among employees in a given collaborative network. Distances d_G, $d_{\mathcal{F}}$ are then used to pilot the RBPNN classifier in order to create collaborative work groups on demand. In this case, distances and similarity indexes among selected employees are used in to qualify affinity when forming a new team.

4   The Implemented RBPNN Classifier

For the purpose of work group member classification, we use a dedicated system based on Probabilistic Neural Networks (PNN). These networks have a topology similar to common Feed Forward Neural Networks (FFNN) with Back Propagation Training Algorithm (BPTA). The primary difference lies in the activation function that, instead of being i.e. a sigmoid function, is a statistical distribution or a significant mathematical function. The selection of a transfer function is indeed decisive for the speed of convergence in approximation and classification problems (please see [8]). The kinds of activation functions used for PNNs have to meet some important properties to preserve the generalization abilities. In addition, these functions have to preserve the decision boundaries of the PNNs. This kind of neural architecture if correctly trained can generate a model for the latent features [15] for which there is a non explicit link among employees [13].

For the proposed RBPNN model both the input and the first hidden layer exactly match the PNN architecture. Input neurones are used as distribution units that supply the same input values to all the neurones in the first hidden layer, and such neurones are called *pattern units*. Each pattern unit performs the dot product ($\cdot$) of the input pattern vector $\mathbf{u}$ by a weight vector $\mathbf{W}^{(0)}$, and then performs a nonlinear operation on the result. This nonlinear operation gives output $\mathbf{x}^{(1)}$ that is handed to the following summation layer. While the common sigmoid function is used for a standard FFNN with BPTA, for PNNs the activation function is exponential, therefore for the j-th neurone the output is computed as

$$\mathbf{x}_j^{(1)} = \exp\left(\frac{||\mathbf{W}^{(0)} \cdot \mathbf{u}||}{2\sigma^2}\right), \tag{5}$$

where $||.||$ represents the *norm* operation and σ the statistical distribution spread, see [10], [23] or [24] for CI-related exponential distributions. In our model, while preserving the PNN topology, to obtain RBPNN capabilities, the activation function has been substituted with a Radial Basis Function (RBF), which satisfies all the conditions stated before. Then, there exists the equivalence between the $\mathbf{W}^{(0)}$ vector of weights and the centroids vector of a RBNN, which in our classifier are computed as the statistical centroids of all the given input sets.

We name ρ the chosen RBF, then the new output of the first hidden layer for the j-th neurone is

$$\mathbf{x}_j^{(1)} \triangleq \rho\left(\frac{||\mathbf{u} - \mathbf{W}^{(0)}||}{\beta}\right), \tag{6}$$

where β is the distribution shape control parameter, quite similar to σ used in (5). The second hidden layer in our RBPNN is a PNN. It computes weighted sums of received values from the preceding neurones. This second hidden layer is called summation layer with the output of the k-th summation unit

$$\mathbf{x}_k^{(2)} = \sum_j \mathbf{W}_{jk} \mathbf{x}_j^{(1)}, \tag{7}$$

where $\mathbf{W}_{jk}$ represents the weight matrix. Such weight matrix consists of a weight value for each connection from the j-th pattern units to the k-th summation unit. These summation units work as the neurones of a linear perceptron network. The training for the output in the applied model is performed similarly to RBNNs. However, the layer size and number of summation units is smaller than in RBNNs, the training is therefore simplified and the speed greatly increased (see [12]).

Our dedicated RBPNN topology enables us to distribute to its various layers the different parts of the classified input. While the pattern layer is just a nonlinear processing layer, the summation layer selectively sums the output of the first hidden layer. The output layer fulfills the nonlinear mapping such as classification, approximation and prediction. In fact, the first hidden layer of our RBPNN is responsible for the fundamental task, which is the classification of the employees into workgroups, see [29].

In order to properly classify the input dataset, i.e. employees into their collaborative groups, the size of the input layer is so as to match the number N_F of features given to the RBPNN, whereas the size of the pattern units matches the number of employees N_S. The number of the summation units in the second hidden layer is equal to the number of output units, these should match the number of groups N_G we are interested in to have the employees classified. Figure ?? shows our RBPNN model and its main characteristics, which are important for the applied bio-inspired adaptive learning process.

To create the RBPNN classifier we used an actor-critic reinforcement learning architecture with BPTA. Decision correctness evaluation in the applied RBPNN is performed with respect to the human-made choices, where ξ is the error function. We consider that this evaluation is performed by a stationary agent (*critic*). It is possible both to use the *critic* in order to filter the effectiveness of RBPNN outputs and to train an *adaptive critic*, which in the long run simulates the decisions of the human *critic* and then diminishes the need for human driven control. The *adaptive critic* needs to learn and this learning process is done by BPTA, which uses ξ as error function. For this reason the *adaptive critic* can be trained by means of the traditional gradient descent algorithm so that the weight modification Δw_{ij} is

$$\Delta w_{ij} = -\mu \frac{\partial \xi}{\partial w_{ij}} = -\mu \frac{\partial \xi}{\partial \tilde{f}_i} \frac{\partial \tilde{f}_i}{\partial \tilde{u}_i} \frac{\partial \tilde{u}_i}{\partial w_{ij}}, \tag{8}$$

where $\tilde{f}_i$ is activation of i-th neuron, μ the learning rate, and $\tilde{u}_i$ is the i-th input to the neurone weighted as

$$\tilde{u}_i = \sum_j w_{ij} \tilde{f}_j(\xi_i). \tag{9}$$

The results of the adaptive critic determines whether or not to continue the training of the RBPNN with new data, as well as whether the last training results should be saved or discarded.

5   Experimental Setup

The proposed RBPNN classifier has been tested using data collected in anonymous form from public and private companies. Datasets describe up to 200 employees and 32 groups for each one of the analysed companies, for a total of 7 companies. The profiles were characterized using 250 different boolean features that compose coded profile values passed to the RBPNN classifier as input sets. The dataset contains all boolean values for the features of each examined employee, work groups memberships for the employee and his/her professional relations within the company. Figure 1 shows boolean diagrams representing each company, where employee profiles were coded to test our classifier. The intrinsic structure of the dataset prevents us from considering only a reduced portion of the feature list for an employee: a piece of information is usually largely spread over a certain number of variables (a boolean value expresses the gender, the academic degree, professional achievements, previous projects, etc.). Although data are anonymous, employees have been identified with a unique ID. These IDs are used to characterize the links among employees themselves and reported by the classifier as IDs pairs. On the other hand, the memberships of employees to work groups are indirectly identified from the list of employees in each group. In RBPNN input data (coded employee profiles) preprocessing, for each employee the relative feature list has been associated to a list of memberships, this contributes to realize a statistically driven classifier that identifies the main concerns regarding the group chosen by the employees. Starting from the profile features, the described RBPNN was then used to determine potentially most efficient collaborative groups for future projects.

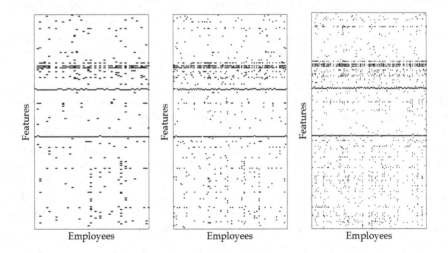

Fig. 1. The feature list representation for each employee in a company, where each diagram represents a different company. In the charts, each row represents a different profile feature, while columns are the different employees.

Fig. 2. Group membership reconstruction, for each of the analyzed companies, performed by our RBPNN: green dots show the correct associations, while black dots give the associations that the RBPNN was unable to reproduce

Initially, we have asked our RBPNN model to correctly reconstruct the groups from the input sets. For this, both the employee profile features and the membership to work groups were provided to the network during the training step. Therefore, the RBPNN has learnt how to reproduce the correct paths of the collaborative network model (see Section 3) to associate the lists of profile features with existent work groups. Figure 2 shows the results of the associations. Our RBPNN model was able to correctly attribute employees to the proper groups with an error less than 1%. As a remarkable side effect of such an architecture, while a few work groups were not assigned, no false positive occurred. Then, after the RBPNN has been trained with the first dataset, we have asked it to assign employees into new work groups. In this case, RBPNN results were successively compared to assignments made by a human employer, unaware of the RBPNN results. Finally, Table 1 summarises the main statistical values, which show that the proposed RBPNN classifier can efficiently build collaborative work groups for various companies. The table orderly reports three case studies, respectively with 50, 100 and 197 analysed employees, and the related number of total employee-group combinations, number of correctly given results on those combinations and the overall ratio of correctness. Moreover, along with such information also the number of correct assignments is reported, as well as the number of missed or unmatched assignments. The classification results are very promising and show the power of our presented solution.

Table 1. The bio-inspired RBPNN classifier examinations results for each analysed company

	analysed employees profiles		
Case study	**50**	**100**	**197**
Total combinations	1600	3200	6304
Correct results	1593	3182	6261
Wrong results	7	13	43
Correct assignments	11	17	34
Unmatched assignments	6	13	27
Missed assignments	1	5	16
Assignments correctness	61.11%	48.57%	44.16%
Overall correctness	**99.56%**	**99.44%**	**99.32%**

6   Conclusions

In this work the employees, intended as the nodes of a collaborative network in various companies, have been grouped by a bio-inspired RBPNN classifier. The classifier is statistically driven by means of categories with a probabilistic meaning. Our RBPNN contributes to identify the most appropriate conceivable model to have affinity-oriented work groups. Our model can represent the underlying affinities among employees. The RBPNN classifier can be continuously trained to reflect the changes that affect the company while time goes on, using new employee profiles. New features and data can be continuously fed into the RBPNN, hence possible work group suggestions can be either confirmed, changed or withdrawn by the RBPNN according to recent activities. Thus, the presented solution can perform a refined analysis and advices can be given at any time. The proposed classifier could be integrated with the company servers handling employees data, by providing the employers with a useful tool for preemptive work group testing and hypothetical simulations of new human resource assets. Very large input data sets could be handled by further improving the classifier using e.g. some fast aggregation methods (see [27], [14]).

Acknowledgements. This work has been partially supported by project PRISMA PON04a2 A/F funded by the Italian Ministry of University and Research within PON 2007-2013 framework.

References

1. Ahn, Y., Han, S., Kwak, H., Moon, S., Jeong, H.: Analysis of topological characteristics of huge online social networking services. In: Proceedings of World Wide Web, pp. 835–844. ACM (2007)
2. Barabási, A.L.: Scale-free networks: a decade and beyond. Science 325(5939), 412–413 (2009)
3. Bonanno, F., Capizzi, G., Napoli, C.: Some remarks on the application of rnn and prnn for the charge-discharge simulation of advanced lithium-ions battery energy storage. In: 2012 International Symposium on Power Electronics, Electrical Drives, Automation and Motion (SPEEDAM), pp. 941–945. IEEE (2012)
4. Bonanno, F., Capizzi, G., Lo Sciuto, G., Napoli, C., Pappalardo, G., Tramontana, E.: A cascade neural network architecture investigating surface plasmon polaritons propagation for thin metals in openMP. In: Rutkowski, L., Korytkowski, M., Scherer, R., Tadeusiewicz, R., Zadeh, L.A., Zurada, J.M. (eds.) ICAISC 2014, Part I. LNCS (LNAI), vol. 8467, pp. 22–33. Springer, Heidelberg (2014)
5. Borowik, G., Woźniak, M., Fornaia, A., Giunta, R., Napoli, C., Pappalardo, G., Tramontana, E.: A software architecture assisting workflow executions on cloud resources. International Journal of Electronics and Telecommunications 61(1), 17–23 (2015)
6. Capizzi, G., Bonanno, F., Napoli, C.: Recurrent neural network-based control strategy for battery energy storage in generation systems with intermittent renewable energy sources. In: 2011 International Conference on Clean Electrical Power (ICCEP), pp. 336–340 (2011)
7. Capizzi, G., Napoli, C., Paternò, L.: An innovative hybrid neuro-wavelet method for reconstruction of missing data in astronomical photometric surveys. In: Rutkowski, L., Korytkowski, M., Scherer, R., Tadeusiewicz, R., Zadeh, L.A., Zurada, J.M. (eds.) ICAISC 2012, Part I. LNCS, vol. 7267, pp. 21–29. Springer, Heidelberg (2012)
8. Duch, W.: Towards comprehensive foundations of computational intelligence. In: Duch, W., Maíndziuk, J. (eds.) Challenges for Computational Intelligence. SCI, vol. 63, pp. 261–316. Springer, Heidelberg (2007)
9. Duch, W., Jankowski, N.: Survey of neural transfer functions. Neural Computing Surveys 2(1), 163–212 (1999)
10. Gabryel, M., Nowicki, R.K., Woźniak, M., Kempa, W.M.: Genetic cost optimization of the $GI/M/1/N$ finite-buffer queue with a single vacation policy. In: Rutkowski, L., Korytkowski, M., Scherer, R., Tadeusiewicz, R., Zadeh, L.A., Zurada, J.M. (eds.) ICAISC 2013, Part II. LNCS (LNAI), vol. 7895, pp. 12–23. Springer, Heidelberg (2013)
11. Gabryel, M., Woźniak, M., Nowicki, R.K.: Creating learning sets for control systems using an evolutionary method. In: Rutkowski, L., Korytkowski, M., Scherer, R., Tadeusiewicz, R., Zadeh, L.A., Zurada, J.M. (eds.) SIDE 2012 and EC 2012. LNCS, vol. 7269, pp. 206–213. Springer, Heidelberg (2012)
12. Huang, D., Ma, S.: A new radial basis probabilistic neural network model. In: Proceedings of Conference on Signal Processing, vol. 2. IEEE (1996)
13. Liben-Nowell, D., Kleinberg, J.: The link-prediction problem for social networks. Journal of the American Society for Information Science and Technology 58(7), 1019–1031 (2007)
14. Marszałek, Z., Połap, D., Woźniak, M.: On preprocessing large data sets by the use of triple merge sort algorithm. In: Proceedings of International Conference on Advances in Information Processing and Communication Technologies - IPCT 2014, Santa Barbara, California, USA, pp. 65–72. The IRED, Seek Digital Library (2014)

15. Miller, K., Griffiths, T., Jordan, M.: Nonparametric latent feature models for link prediction. In: Advances in Neural Information Processing Systems, vol. 22, pp. 1276–1284 (2009)
16. Napoli, C., Bonanno, F., Capizzi, G.: Exploiting solar wind time series correlation with magnetospheric response by using an hybrid neuro-wavelet approach. Proceedings of the International Astronomical Union 6(S274), 156–158 (2010)
17. Napoli, C., Bonanno, F., Capizzi, G.: An hybrid neuro-wavelet approach for long-term prediction of solar wind. Proceedings of the International Astronomical Union 6(S274), 247–249 (2010)
18. Napoli, C., Pappalardo, G., Tramontana, E.: A hybrid neuro–wavelet predictor for QoS control and stability. In: Baldoni, M., Baroglio, C., Boella, G., Micalizio, R. (eds.) AI*IA 2013. LNCS, vol. 8249, pp. 527–538. Springer, Heidelberg (2013)
19. Napoli, C., Pappalardo, G., Tramontana, E.: Using modularity metrics to assist move method refactoring of large systems. In: 2013 7th International Conference on Complex, Intelligent, and Software Intensive Systems (CISIS), pp. 529–534. IEEE (2013)
20. Napoli, C., Pappalardo, G., Tramontana, E., Marszałek, Z., Połap, D., Woźniak, M.: Simplified firefly algorithm for 2d image key-points search. In: 2014 IEEE Symposium on Computational Intelligence for Human-like Intelligence, pp. 118–125. IEEE (2014)
21. Nowak, A., Woźniak, M.: Analysis of the active module mechatronical systems. In: Proceedings of Mechanika 2008 - ICM 2008, Kaunas, Liethuania, pp. 371–376. Kaunas University of Technology Press (2008)
22. Nowak, A., Woźniak, M.: Multiresolution derives analysis of module mechatronical systems. Mechanika 6(74), 45–51 (2008)
23. Woźniak, M.: On applying cuckoo search algorithm to positioning $GI/M/1/N$ finite-buffer queue with a single vacation policy. In: Proceedings of the 12th Mexican International Conference on Artificial Intelligence - MICAI 2013, pp. 59–64. IEEE (2013)
24. Woźniak, M., Kempa, W.M., Gabryel, M., Nowicki, R.K.: A finite-buffer queue with single vacation policy - analytical study with evolutionary positioning. International Journal of Applied Mathematics and Computer Science 24(4), 887–900 (2014)
25. Woźniak, M., Kempa, W.M., Gabryel, M., Nowicki, R.K., Shao, Z.: On applying evolutionary computation methods to optimization of vacation cycle costs in finite-buffer queue. In: Rutkowski, L., Korytkowski, M., Scherer, R., Tadeusiewicz, R., Zadeh, L.A., Zurada, J.M. (eds.) ICAISC 2014, Part I. LNCS (LNAI), vol. 8467, pp. 480–491. Springer, Heidelberg (2014)
26. Woźniak, M., Marszałek, Z.: An idea to apply firefly algorithm in 2D image key-points search. In: Dregvaite, G., Damasevicius, R. (eds.) ICIST 2014. CCIS, vol. 465, pp. 312–323. Springer, Heidelberg (2014)
27. Woźniak, M., Marszałek, Z., Gabryel, M., Nowicki, R.K.: Modified merge sort algorithm for large scale data sets. In: Rutkowski, L., Korytkowski, M., Scherer, R., Tadeusiewicz, R., Zadeh, L.A., Zurada, J.M. (eds.) ICAISC 2013, Part II. LNCS (LNAI), vol. 7895, pp. 612–622. Springer, Heidelberg (2013)
28. Woźniak, M., Połap, D.: Basic concept of cuckoo search algorithm for 2D images processing with some research results: An idea to apply cuckoo search algorithm in 2D images key-points search. In: Proceedings of the 11th International Conference on Signal Processing and Multimedia Applications - SIGMAP 2014, Setubal, Portugal, pp. 164–173. SciTePress - INSTICC (2014)
29. Zhao, W., Huang, D., Guo, L.: Optimizing radial basis probabilistic neural networks using recursive orthogonal least squares algorithms combined with micro-genetic algorithms. In: Proceedings of Neural Networks, vol. 3. IEEE (2003)

Adaptation of RBM Learning
for Intel MIC Architecture

Tomasz Olas[1]([⊠]), Wojciech K. Mleczko[2], Robert K. Nowicki[2], Roman Wyrzykowski[1],
and Adam Krzyzak[3]

[1] Institute of Computer and Information Sciences, Czestochowa University of Technology,
ul. Dabrowskiego 73, 42-200 Czestochowa, Poland
{olas,roman}@icis.pcz.pl
http://www.icis.pcz.pl
[2] Institute of Computational Intelligence, Czestochowa University of Technology,
Al. Armii Krajowej 36, 42-200 Czestochowa, Poland
{wojciech.mleczko,robert.nowicki}@iisi.pcz.pl
http://www.iisi.pcz.pl
[3] Department of Computer Science and Software Engineering,
Concordia University, Montreal, Canada
krzyzak@cs.concordia.ca
http://www.concordia.ca/cs

Abstract. In the paper, the parallel realization of the Boltzmann Restricted Machine (RBM) is proposed. The implementation intends to use multicore architectures of modern CPUs and Intel Xeon Phi coprocessor. The learning procedure is based on the matrix description of RBM, where the learning samples are grouped into packages, and represented as matrices. The influence of the package size on convergence of learning, as well as on performance of computation, are studied for various number of threads, using conventional CPU and Intel Phi architectures. Our research confirms a potential usefulness of MIC parallel architecture for implementation of RBM and similar algorithms.

Keywords: Restricted Boltzman Machine · Parallel programming · Multicore architectures · Intel Xeon Phi architecture

1 Introduction

The Intel Xeon Phi coprocessor is the first generation product (codenamed Knights Corner) of the Intel MIC (Many Integrated Core) architecture. It combines many Intel CPU cores onto a single chip [10]. Intel Xeon Phi architecture is targeted for highly parallel, High Performance Computing (HPC) workloads, and offers a high peak performance (more than 1 Tflops at double-precision) with a high memory bandwidth (more than 300 GB/s). A key attribute of this architecture is that unlike GPU accelerators [50] Intel Xeon Phi coprocessors can execute applications compiled from the same C/C++ or Fortran code as conventional Intel Xeon CPU solutions.

In this work, the Intel MIC architecture is applied to implement the learning phase of Restricted Boltzmann Machine. This process could be described in various versions.

© Springer International Publishing Switzerland 2015
L. Rutkowski et al. (Eds.): ICAISC 2015, Part I, LNAI 9119, pp. 90–101, 2015.
DOI: 10.1007/978-3-319-19324-3_9

However, it can be assumed that use of multicore architectures like Intel MIC will be the most effective when the version applying matrix operations is chosen. Such a description of RBM and learning process has been selected and implemented.

Neural networks possess a natural parallelism that can be implemented on various physical architectures [3,4,5,6,7,8,37,49]. In fact, the perceptron proposed by Frank Rosenblatt [39] was implemented as a parallel electro-mechanical device. The authors of this paper applied many signal processors connected by dedicated serial bus to realize a fast neural network [1]. Nowadays, artificial neural networks are implemented in structures built from single molecules [31], e.g. distributed in mesoporous silica matrix [29,30]. The Restricted Boltzmann Machine [21,45] is the one of sophisticated types of neural networks, which can process the probability distribution, and is applied to filtering, image recognition, and modelling [14]. The RBMs are also components of deep belief networks [9,23].

2 Intel MIC Architecture

The Intel Xeon Phi coprocessor comprises of up to 61 processor cores connected by a high performance 512-bit bidirectional ring interconnect. Each core is capable of 4-way hyper-threading, which gives up to 244 logical cores [46]. An important component of the Intel Xeon Phi coprocessorâĂŹs core is its SSE (Streaming SIMD Extensions) vector processing unit (VPU). The VPU features 512-bit wide registers with support for the Initial Many-Core Instructions (IMCI) instruction set. Thus, the VPU can execute 16 single-precision or 8 double-precision instructions per cycle. Each instruction can be a floating point multiply-add, which gives 32 single-precision or 16 double-precision floating point operations per cycle.

The Intel Xeon Phi coprocessor implements a leading-edge, very high bandwidth memory subsystem. The memory controllers and the PCIe client logic provide a direct interface to GDDR5 memory on the coprocessor and the PCIe bus, respectively. The coprocessor has over 6 GB of on-board memory (maximum 16GB). Each core contains a 32KB, 8-way set associative L1 cache, and 512KB, 8-way L2 cache. The high-speed bidirectional ring connects together all the cores, caches, memory controllers and PCIe client logic of Intel Xeon Phi coprocessors. As a result, caches are fully coherent and implement the x86 memory model. The L1 and L2 caches provide an aggregate bandwidth that is approximately 15 and 7 times, respectively, faster compared to the aggregate on-board memory bandwidth. Hence, the effective utilization of the caches is key to achieving high performance on Intel Xeon Phi coprocessors.

The main advantage of Xeon Phi accelerator is that it is built to deliver a general-purpose programming environment similar to that provided for Intel CPUs. The coprocessor is supported by a rich development environment that includes compilers from C/C++, Fortran and OpenCL languages, numerous libraries such as threading libraries (OpenMP, Cilk Plus, etc.) and high performance math libraries (e.q., MKL library), performance characterizing and tuning tools (e.g., Intel VTune Amplifier), and debuggers.

In principle, programming applications for Intel Xeon Phi coprocessors is not significantly different from programing for conventional Intel x86 processors. However, after empirical performance and programmability studies performed by many researchers [15,42,47,48] it is clear that to achieve high performance, Intel Xeon Phi still needs help from programmers, and that merely relying on compilers with traditional programming models is still far from reality. In fact, high degree of parallelism of Xeon Phi accelerators is best suited to applications that are structured to use the parallelism. Almost all codes would gain from some tuning beyond the initial base performance to achieve higher performance. This can range from minor modifications to major restructuring to expose and exploit parallelism through multiple tasks, use of vectors, and reduce communication overheads. The hidden benefit [38] is that this "transforming-and-tuning" approach doubles advantages of programming investments for Intel Xeon Phi coprocessors that generally apply directly to any general-purpose processor as well, offering more forward scaling to future computing architectures.

3   Introduction to Restricted Boltzmann Machine Learning

3.1   Definition of RBM

The Restricted Boltzmann Machine is the two layer recurrent neural network. The input values are presented on the layer called "visible" as vector $\mathbf{v}_0(t) = [v_{10}(t), \ldots, v_{i0}(t), \ldots, v_{M0}(t)]$. M is the number of inputs, t indicates the specific sample. The data are transmitted to the layer called "hidden", as depicted in Figure 1. Given an observed state [22], the energy of the joint configuration of the visible and hidden units (v, h) is given by:

$$E\left(\mathbf{v}, \mathbf{h}\right) = \sum_{i \in visible} b_{vi}v_i - \sum_{j \in hidden} b_{hj}h_j - \sum_{i,j} v_i h_j w_{ij}, \tag{1}$$

where v_i, h_j are the binary states of visible unit i and hidden unit j, b_{vi}, b_{hj} are their biases and w_{ij} is the weight between them. The network assigns a probability to every possible pair of a visible and a hidden vector via this energy function: where v_i, h_j are the binary states of visible unit i and hidden unit j, b_{vi}, b_{hj} are their biases and w_{ij} is

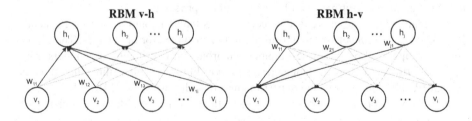

Fig. 1. Schematic representation of a Restricted Boltzmann Machine (RBM) - bidirectionally

the weight between them. The network assigns a probability to every possible pair of a visible and a hidden vector via this energy function:

$$p\left(\mathbf{v}, \mathbf{h}\right) = \frac{1}{Z} e^{-E(\mathbf{v},\mathbf{h})}, \tag{2}$$

where the *partition function* Z, is given by summing over all possible pairs of visible and hidden vectors:

$$Z = \sum_{\mathbf{v},\mathbf{h}} e^{-E(\mathbf{v},\mathbf{h})}, \tag{3}$$

The probability that the network assigns to a visible vector, $\mathbf{v}$, is given by summing over all possible hidden vectors:

$$p\left(\mathbf{v}\right) = \frac{1}{Z} \sum_{\mathbf{h}} e^{-E(\mathbf{v},\mathbf{h})}, \tag{4}$$

Given a random input configuration $\mathbf{v}$, the state of the hidden unit j is set to 1 with probability:

$$P\left(h_j = 1 | \mathbf{v}\right) = \sigma \left(b_{hj} + \sum_i v_i w_{ij} \right), \tag{5}$$

where $\sigma(x)$ is the logistic sigmoid function $\frac{1}{1+\exp(-x)}$. Similarly, given a random hidden vector the state of the visible unit i can be set to 1 with probability:

$$P\left(v_i = 1 | \mathbf{h}\right) = \sigma \left(b_{vi} + \sum_i h_j w_{ij} \right). \tag{6}$$

The probability that the network assigns to a training image can be raised by adjusting the weights and biases to lower the energy of that image and to raise the energy of other images, especially those that have low energies and therefore make a big contribution to the partition function. The derivative of the log probability of a training vector with respect to a weight is surprisingly simple.

$$\frac{\partial \log p(\mathbf{v})}{\partial w_{ij}} = \langle v_i h_j \rangle_0 - \langle v_i h_j \rangle_\infty, \tag{7}$$

where $\langle \cdot \rangle_0$ denotes the expectations for the data distribution (p_0) and $\langle \cdot \rangle_\infty$ denotes the expectations for the model distribution (p_∞) [32]. It can be done by starting at any random state of the visible units and performing alternating Gibbs sampling for a very long time. One iteration of alternating Gibbs sampling consists of updating all of the hidden units in parallel using equation 5 followed by updating all of the visible units in parallel using equation 6 [21].

To solve this problem, Hinton proposed a much faster learning procedure âĂŞ the Contrastive Divergence algorithm [21],[22]. Using this procedure can be applied in order to correct the weights and bias of the network:

$$\Delta w_{ij} = \eta \left(\langle v_i h_j \rangle_0 - \langle v_i h_j \rangle_\infty \right), \tag{8}$$

$$\Delta b_{\mathrm{v}i} = \eta (v_{i0} - v_{i\infty}), \tag{9}$$

$$\Delta b_{\mathrm{h}j} = \eta (h_{j0} - h_{j\infty}), \tag{10}$$

4   Adaptation of RBM Learning to Multicore Architecture Using Learning with Accumulation

To adapt RBM to multicore architecture we will apply the procedures described in section 3.1 to a package of learning samples. As a consequence, the weight adjustment will be calculated and applied once for all the samples in the package. The size of a package is denoted by u, and it should be correlated with the number of threads in the available multicore architecture. The resulting number of packages is specified as $\tau_{\max}$. If the number of samples is less than $u\tau_{\max}$ the last package is smaller, but for the sake of clarity the case will be omitted. This idea could be implemented in various ways. In our research, the method has been applied where values of all the samples assigned to the τ–th package are represented by a single matrix $\mathbf{V}_0(\tau)$, i.e. [26,40]

$$\mathbf{V}_0(\tau) = \begin{bmatrix} v_{01} \left(\tau u - u + 1 \right) & \cdots & v_{0M} \left(\tau u - u + 1 \right) \\ \vdots & \ddots & \vdots \\ v_{01} \left(\tau u \right) & \cdots & v_{0M} \left(\tau u \right) \end{bmatrix}. \tag{11}$$

Then, matrix $\mathbf{H}_0(\tau)$ consists the values on hidden layer for all samples in package number τ, i.e.

$$\mathbf{H}_0(\tau) = \begin{bmatrix} h_{01} \left(\tau u - u + 1 \right) & \cdots & h_{0N} \left(\tau u - u + 1 \right) \\ \vdots & \ddots & \vdots \\ h_{01} \left(\tau u \right) & \cdots & h_{0N} \left(\tau u \right) \end{bmatrix} \tag{12}$$

and it is calculated using matrix operation which can be easily parallelized using common libraries such as OpenMP. This process is illustrated on Fig. 2. The subsequent steps of RBM are processed in the same way. Note that for package number τ occurs $t = \tau u - u + 1, \ldots, \tau u$.

The weights between visible and hidden layers are updated once after processing the whole package of samples, so the size of the package has direct influence on the frequency of an update. The matrix of updates derived for package τ can be written down as

$$\Delta \mathbf{W}(\tau) = \eta \left(\mathbf{V}_0^T(\tau) \mathbf{H}_0(\tau) - \mathbf{V}_\infty^T(\tau) \mathbf{H}_\infty(\tau) \right), \tag{13}$$

or as

$$\Delta \mathbf{W}(\tau) = \eta \left(\mathbf{V}_0^T(\tau) \mathbf{H}_0(\tau) - \mathbf{V}_\infty^T(\tau) \mathbf{H}_\infty(\tau) \right) + \alpha \Delta \mathbf{W}(\tau - 1) \tag{14}$$

and it is applied as follows

$$\mathbf{W}(\tau + 1) = \mathbf{W}(\tau) + \Delta \mathbf{W}(\tau). \tag{15}$$

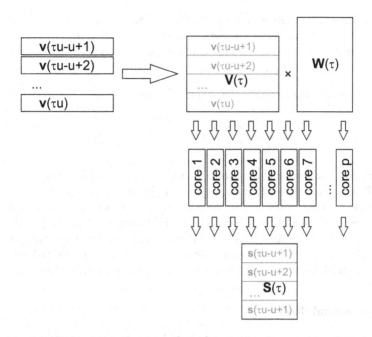

Fig. 2. Parallel processing of matrix operation in RBM implementation

Obviously $\Delta w_{ij}(0) = 0$. The biases are updated in the same way, i.e.

$$\Delta \mathbf{B}_v(\tau) = \eta \left(\mathbf{V}_0(\tau) - \mathbf{V}_\infty(\tau) \right) \tag{16}$$

and

$$\Delta \mathbf{B}_h(\tau) = \eta \left(\mathbf{H}_0(\tau) - \mathbf{H}_\infty(\tau) \right), \tag{17}$$

or

$$\Delta \mathbf{B}_v(\tau) = \eta \left(\mathbf{V}_0(\tau) - \mathbf{V}_\infty(\tau) \right) + \alpha \Delta \mathbf{B}_v(\tau - 1) \tag{18}$$

and

$$\Delta \mathbf{B}_h(\tau) = \eta \left(\mathbf{H}_0(\tau) - \mathbf{H}_\infty(\tau) \right) + \alpha \Delta \mathbf{b}_h(\tau - 1). \tag{19}$$

The research using both parallel and sequence implementations indicates that the frequency of weights update is significant for the obtained results (see Fig. 3).

5 Parallel Implementation and Experimental Results

5.1 Details of Parallel Implementation

The proposed algorithms are implemented in C++ language using the OpenMP standard for parallelizing computation. The important step is transformation of computation in such a way that efficient implementations of matrix and vector operations available in the BLAS library can be utilized. For example, the operation of summing elements of a matrix is replaced with a matrix-vector multiplication, where the vector contains all ones. It is illustrated by the following code:

```
cblas_dgemv(CblasRowMajor, CblasTrans, numcases, numhid,
            -1.0, nh, numhid, one, 1, 0.0, db, 1);
cblas_dgemv(CblasRowMajor, CblasTrans, numcases, numhid,
            1.0, ph, numhid, one, 1, 1.0, db, 1);
```

which is responsible for computing the expression given below:

$$db_j = \sum_i^{numcases} ph_{ij} - \sum_i^{numcases} nh_{ij}. \tag{20}$$

All the codes are compiled using Intel C++ Compiler available in Intel Parallel Studio XE 2015 environment. Additionally, the Intel Math Kernel Library (MKL) are used for the efficient implementation of BLAS routines, as well as for generating pseudorandom numbers in particular, the SIMD-oriented Fast Mersenne Twister pseudorandom number generator $VSL\_BRNG\_SFMT19937$ is utilized. All experiments are performed in double precision, with an extensive usage of vectorization (512-bit AVX-512 vector extension for Intel Xeon Phi, and 256-bit AVX2 standard for Intel CPUs).

5.2 Experimental Results

In this section, we investigate experimentally both convergence and performance of the proposed method of parallizing the RBM learning on multicore architecture. For test purposes, we use the MNIST database of handwritten digits, available at [25].

Fig. 3 shows the learning error for 100 epochs depending on the package size u. For the tested problem, it can be concluded that initially the learning error is quickly decreasing with increasing in the package size. The minimal error corresponds to the package size of about 60 samples. Further increase in the package size results in a slow increase of the learning error.

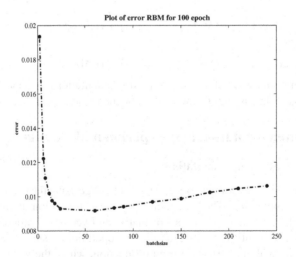

Fig. 3. Influence of the package size on error learning for 100 epochs

All the experiments were performed on Intel Xeon Phi and Intel CPU platforms managed by the MICLAB project [24]. One node of the testing platform consists of two 12-core processors Intel Xeon E5-2695 v2 2.40GHz (30 MB L3 cache), equipped with 128GB ECC RAM memory (1866MHz) providing 2×59.7 GB/s memory bandwith. Each node is also equipped with two coprocessors Intel Xeon Phi 7120P with 61 cores. The coprocessors have 16 GB on-board memory with 352 GB/s memory bandwith. The peak performance of this platform is given by 1208.3 Gflop/s for a single coprocessor and 480.8 Gflop/s for two CPUs in one node.

Table 1 contains execution times for proposed version of the algorithm investigated in this work, both for a node with two CPUs and a single coprocessor, with different numbers of threads. In our experiments, the number of threads is up to 48 for two CPUs (using hyperthreading), and up to 240 for Intel Xeon Phi. In our experiments, the package size is selected as 120 or 240. Analyzing these results we conclude that for the investigated sizes of the problem the execution time on two CPUs is shorter than on a single coprocessor.

Table 1. Execution time for RBM parallizing on Intel CPUs and Intel Xeon Phi coprocessor

package size	$u = 1$	$u = 120$		$u = 240$	
version	sequential	sequential	parallel (shortest time)	sequential	parallel (shortest time)
2 x Intel Xeon	591.2	85.02	9.04 (24 threads)	82.48	7.78 (48 threads)
Intel Xeon Phi	5670.2	507.85	37.55 (60 threads)	433.42	26.78 (120 threads)

Fig. 4 presents speedup of the package version of the algorithm for different sizes of package, depending on the number of threads, separately for CPU and coprocessor. In the second case, for each size of package the number of threads belongs to the following set: 60, 120, 180, 240. These values correspond to executing 1, 2, 3 and 4 threads per core, respectively. The conclusion is that speedup increases with the package size, both for CPUs and coprocessor.

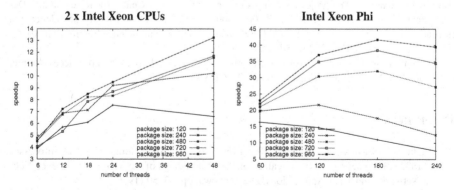

Fig. 4. Speedup for RBM learing depending on package size and number of threads, for CPUs and coprocessor

The performance results achieved in these experiments are in favour of CPUs against coprocessor. At the same time, our preliminary experiments show that to utilize fully the computing power of coprocessor it is necessary to increase considerably the size of investigated problems. For example, instead of data used in current experiments, we should consider learning problems with 8000 neurons, 4000 neurons in hidden layer, package size is 240. For this problem the execution time on one Intel Xeon Phi is twice shorter than on two CPUs (301 seconds for 240 threads running on Intel Xeon Phi versus 665 seconds for 24 threads running on two CPUs).

6   Conclusions and Future Work

In the paper, we propose the method for paralizing the Boltzmann Restricted Machine learning. This method allows to use multicore architectures of modern general-purpose processors and Intel Xeon Phi coprocessors, the first generation product of Intel MIC architecure. The learning procedure is based on the matrix description of RBM, where the learning samples are grouped into packages, and represented as matrices. In the performed experiments, for conventional CPU and Intel Phi architecures, we investigate the convergence of learning and performance of computation depending on the package size and number of threads. The results achieved for the rather small tested problem could be considered as satisfying in case of conventional CPU architectures. At the same time, the preliminary results show that to utilize the high computational power offered by about 60 cores of Intel Xeon Phi architecture it is required to solve larger problems corresponding, e.g., to 8000 neurons. Other directions of future works include investigation of further optimization strategies for parallizing RBM learning, as well as possibility to use the hybrid environment provided by CPUs and coprocessors. The promising approach to the learning problem which should be considered is using various types of computational intelligence systems [2,11,12,13,16,17,18,19,20,27,41,43,44] including neural networks, in particular convolutional neural networks [28]. Such systems and their parallel implementation on Intel MIC architecture can be useful in many applications, such as face recognition [33,34,35,36].

Acknowledgements. The project was supported by the National Centre for Research and Development under project No. POIG.02.03.00.24-093/13, by the Polish Ministry of Science and Education under Grant No. BS-1-112-304/99/S, and by the National Science Centre (Poland) under decision number DEC-2012/05/B/ST6/03620.

The authors are grateful to Czestochowa University of Technology for granting access to Intel CPU and Xeon Phi platforms managed by the MICLAB project.

References

1. Bilski, J., Nowicki, R., Scherer, R., Litwiński, S.: Application of signal processor TMS320c30 to neural networks realisation. In: Proceedings of the Second Conference Neural Networks and Their Applications, Czêstochowa, pp. 53–59 (1996)
2. Bilski, J., Smolag, J.: Parallel architectures for learning the RTRN and Elman dynamic neural networks. IEEE Transactions on Parallel and Distributed Systems PP(99) (2014)

3. Bilski, J., Litwiński, S., Smoląg, J.: Parallel realisation of QR algorithm for neural networks learning. In: Rutkowski, L., Siekmann, J.H., Tadeusiewicz, R., Zadeh, L.A. (eds.) ICAISC 2004. LNCS (LNAI), vol. 3070, pp. 158–165. Springer, Heidelberg (2004)

4. Bilski, J., Smoląg, J., Galushkin, A.I.: The parallel approach to the conjugate gradient learning algorithm for the feedforward neural networks. In: Rutkowski, L., Korytkowski, M., Scherer, R., Tadeusiewicz, R., Zadeh, L.A., Zurada, J.M. (eds.) ICAISC 2014, Part I. LNCS (LNAI), vol. 8467, pp. 12–21. Springer, Heidelberg (2014)

5. Bilski, J., Smoląg, J.: Parallel realisation of the recurrent RTRN neural network learning. In: Rutkowski, L., Tadeusiewicz, R., Zadeh, L.A., Zurada, J.M. (eds.) ICAISC 2008. LNCS (LNAI), vol. 5097, pp. 11–16. Springer, Heidelberg (2008)

6. Bilski, J., Smoląg, J.: Parallel realisation of the recurrent elman neural network learning. In: Rutkowski, L., Scherer, R., Tadeusiewicz, R., Zadeh, L.A., Zurada, J.M. (eds.) ICAISC 2010, Part II. LNCS (LNAI), vol. 6114, pp. 19–25. Springer, Heidelberg (2010)

7. Bilski, J., Smoląg, J.: Parallel realisation of the recurrent multi layer perceptron learning. In: Rutkowski, L., Korytkowski, M., Scherer, R., Tadeusiewicz, R., Zadeh, L.A., Zurada, J.M. (eds.) ICAISC 2012, Part I. LNCS, vol. 7267, pp. 12–20. Springer, Heidelberg (2012)

8. Bilski, J., Smoląg, J.: Parallel approach to learning of the recurrent Jordan neural network. In: Rutkowski, L., Korytkowski, M., Scherer, R., Tadeusiewicz, R., Zadeh, L.A., Zurada, J.M. (eds.) ICAISC 2013, Part I. LNCS, vol. 7894, pp. 32–40. Springer, Heidelberg (2013)

9. Chu, J.L., Krzyzak, A.: The recognition of partially occluded objects with support vector machines and convolutional neural networks and deep belief networks. Journal of Artificial Intelligence and Soft Computing Research 4(1), 5–19 (2014)

10. Intel Corporation: Intel Xeon Phi Coprocessor System Software Developer's Guide. Technical report, The Intel Corporation (June 2013)

11. Cpałka, K., Rutkowski, L.: Flexible Takagi-Sugeno fuzzy systems. In: Proc. IEEE International Joint Conference on Neural Networks (IJCNN), vol. 3, pp. 1764–1769 (2005)

12. Cpałka, K., Łapa, K., Przybył, A., Zalasiński, M.: A new method for designing neuro-fuzzy systems for nonlinear modelling with interpretability aspects. Neurocomputing 135, 203–217 (2014)

13. Cpałka, K., Rebrova, O., Nowicki, R., Rutkowski, L.: On design of flexible neuro-fuzzy systems for nonlinear modelling. International Journal of General Systems 42(6), 706–720 (2013)

14. Dourlens, S., Ramdane-Cherif, A.: Modeling & understanding environment using semantic agents. Journal of Artificial Intelligence and Soft Computing Research 1(4), 301–314 (2011)

15. Fang, J., Varbanescu, A.L., Sips, H.: Benchmarking Intel Xeon Phi to Guide Kernel Design. Delft University of Technology Parallel and Distributed Systems Report Series, No. PDS-2013-005, pp. 1–22 (2013)

16. Gabryel, M., Korytkowski, M., Scherer, R., Rutkowski, L.: Object detection by simple fuzzy classifiers generated by boosting. In: Rutkowski, L., Korytkowski, M., Scherer, R., Tadeusiewicz, R., Zadeh, L.A., Zurada, J.M. (eds.) ICAISC 2013, Part I. LNCS, vol. 7894, pp. 540–547. Springer, Heidelberg (2013)

17. Galkowski, T., Rutkowski, L.: Nonparametric fitting of multivariate functions. IEEE Transactions on Automatic Control 31(8), 785–787 (1986)

18. Gałkowski, T.: Kernel estimation of regression functions in the boundary regions. In: Rutkowski, L., Korytkowski, M., Scherer, R., Tadeusiewicz, R., Zadeh, L.A., Zurada, J.M. (eds.) ICAISC 2013, Part II. LNCS, vol. 7895, pp. 158–166. Springer, Heidelberg (2013)

19. Galkowski, T., Pawlak, M.: Nonparametric function fitting in the presence of nonstationary noise. In: Rutkowski, L., Korytkowski, M., Scherer, R., Tadeusiewicz, R., Zadeh, L.A., Zurada, J.M. (eds.) ICAISC 2014, Part I. LNCS (LNAI), vol. 8467, pp. 531–538. Springer, Heidelberg (2014)

20. Gaweda, A.E., Scherer, R.: Fuzzy number-based hierarchical fuzzy system. In: Rutkowski, L., Siekmann, J.H., Tadeusiewicz, R., Zadeh, L.A. (eds.) ICAISC 2004. LNCS (LNAI), vol. 3070, pp. 302–307. Springer, Heidelberg (2004)
21. Hinton, G.: Training products of experts by minimizing contrastive divergence. Neural Computation 14(8), 1771–1800 (2002)
22. Hinton, G.: A practical guide to training restricted Boltzmann machines. Momentum 9(1), 926 (2010)
23. Hinton, G., Osindero, S., Teh, Y.W.: A fast learning algorithm for deep belief nets. Neural Computation 18(7), 1527–1554 (2006)
24. http://miclab.pl: MICLAB Pilot laboratory of massively parallel systems. Web Page (2015)
25. http://yann.lecun.com/exdb/mnist/: The mnist database of handwritten digits
26. Karpathy, A., Toderici, G., Shetty, S., Leung, T., Sukthankar, R., Fei-Fei, L.: Large-scale video classification with convolutional neural networks. In: 2014 IEEE Conference on Computer Vision and Pattern Recognition (CVPR), pp. 1725–1732 (June 2014)
27. Korytkowski, M., Rutkowski, L., Scherer, R.: From ensemble of fuzzy classifiers to single fuzzy rule base classifier. In: Rutkowski, L., Tadeusiewicz, R., Zadeh, L.A., Zurada, J.M. (eds.) ICAISC 2008. LNCS (LNAI), vol. 5097, pp. 265–272. Springer, Heidelberg (2008)
28. Krizhevsky, A.: One weird trick for parallelizing convolutional neural networks. arXiv preprint arXiv:1404.5997 (2014)
29. Laskowski, L., Laskowska, M.: Functionalization of SBA-15 mesoporous silica by cu-phosphonate units: Probing of synthesis route. Journal of Solid State Chemistry 220, 221–226 (2014)
30. Laskowski, L., Laskowska, M., Balanda, M., Fitta, M., Kwiatkowska, J., Dzilinski, K., Karczmarska, A.: Mesoporous silica SBA-15 functionalized by nickel-phosphonic units: Raman and magnetic analysis. Microporous and Mesoporous Materials 200, 253–259 (2014)
31. Laskowski, Ł., Laskowska, M., Jelonkiewicz, J., Boullanger, A.: Spin-glass implementation of a Hopfield neural structure. In: Rutkowski, L., Korytkowski, M., Scherer, R., Tadeusiewicz, R., Zadeh, L.A., Zurada, J.M. (eds.) ICAISC 2014, Part I. LNCS (LNAI), vol. 8467, pp. 89–96. Springer, Heidelberg (2014)
32. Le Roux, N., Bengio, Y.: Representational power of restricted boltzmann machines and deep belief networks. Neural Computation 20(6), 1631–1649 (2008)
33. Pabiasz, S., Starczewski, J.: Face reconstruction for 3D systems. In: Rutkowska, D., Cader, A., Przybyszewski, K. (eds.) Selected Topics in Computer Science Applications, pp. 54–63. Academic Publishing House EXIT (2011)
34. Pabiasz, S., Starczewski, J.T.: Meshes vs. depth maps in face recognition systems. In: Rutkowski, L., Korytkowski, M., Scherer, R., Tadeusiewicz, R., Zadeh, L.A., Zurada, J.M. (eds.) ICAISC 2012, Part I. LNCS, vol. 7267, pp. 567–573. Springer, Heidelberg (2012)
35. Pabiasz, S., Starczewski, J.T., Marvuglia, A.: A new three-dimensional facial landmarks in recognition. In: Rutkowski, L., Korytkowski, M., Scherer, R., Tadeusiewicz, R., Zadeh, L.A., Zurada, J.M. (eds.) ICAISC 2014, Part II. LNCS (LNAI), vol. 8468, pp. 179–186. Springer, Heidelberg (2014)
36. Pabiasz, S., Starczewski, J.T.: A new approach to determine three-dimensional facial landmarks. In: Rutkowski, L., Korytkowski, M., Scherer, R., Tadeusiewicz, R., Zadeh, L.A., Zurada, J.M. (eds.) ICAISC 2013, Part II. LNCS, vol. 7895, pp. 286–296. Springer, Heidelberg (2013)
37. Patan, K., Patan, M.: Optimal training strategies for locally recurrent neural networks. Journal of Artificial Intelligence and Soft Computing Research 1(2), 103–114 (2011)
38. Reinders, J.: An Overview of Programming for Intel Xeon Processors and Intel Xeon Phi Coprocessors. Technical report, The Intel Corporation (2012)
39. Rosenblatt, F.: The perceptron: A probabilistic model for information storage and organization in the brain. Psychological Review 65(65), 386–408 (1958)

40. Russakovsky, O., Deng, J., Su, H., Krause, J., Satheesh, S., Ma, S., Huang, Z., Karpathy, A., Khosla, A., Bernstein, M., et al.: Imagenet large scale visual recognition challenge. arXiv preprint arXiv:1409.0575 (2014)
41. Rutkowski, L., Przybył, A., Cpałka, K., Er, M.J.: Online speed profile generation for industrial machine tool based on neuro-fuzzy approach. In: Rutkowski, L., Scherer, R., Tadeusiewicz, R., Zadeh, L.A., Zurada, J.M. (eds.) ICAISC 2010, Part II. LNCS (LNAI), vol. 6114, pp. 645–650. Springer, Heidelberg (2010)
42. Saule, E., Kaya, K., Çatalyürek, Ü.V.: Performance Evaluation of Sparse Matrix Multiplication Kernels on Intel Xeon Phi. In: Wyrzykowski, R., Dongarra, J., Karczewski, K., Waśniewski, J. (eds.) PPAM 2013, Part I. LNCS, vol. 8384, pp. 559–570. Springer, Heidelberg (2014)
43. Scherer, R., Rutkowski, L.: A fuzzy relational system with linguistic antecedent certainty factors. In: Rutkowski, L., Kacprzyk, J. (eds.) Proceedings of the Sixth International Conference on Neural Network and Soft Computing. Advances in Soft Computing, pp. 563–569. Springer, Heidelberg (2003)
44. Scherer, R.: Neuro-fuzzy relational systems for nonlinear approximation and prediction. Nonlinear Analysis 71, e1420–e1425 (2009)
45. Smolensky, P.: Information processing in dynamical systems: Foundations of harmony theory. In: Rumelhart, D.E., McLelland, J.L. (eds.) Parallel Distributed Processing: Explorations in the Microstructure of Cognition. Foundations, vol. 1, pp. 194–281. MIT (1986)
46. Staff, C.I., Reinders, J.: Parallel Programming and Optimization with Intel® Xeon Phi^{TM} Coprocessors: Handbook on the Development and Optimization of Parallel Applications for Intel® Xeon Coprocessors and Intel® Xeon Phi^{TM} Coprocessors. Colfax International (2013)
47. Szustak, L., Rojek, K., Gepner, P.: Using Intel Xeon Phi coprocessor to accelerate computations in MPDATA algorithm. In: Wyrzykowski, R., Dongarra, J., Karczewski, K., Waśniewski, J. (eds.) PPAM 2013, Part I. LNCS, vol. 8384, pp. 582–592. Springer, Heidelberg (2014)
48. Szustak, L., Rojek, K., Olas, T., Kuczynski, L., Halbiniak, K., Gepner, P.: Adaptation of MPDATA heterogeneous stencil computation to Intel Xeon Phi coprocessor. Scientific Programming (in press, 2015)
49. Tambouratzis, T., Chernikova, D., Pázsit, I.: Pulse shape discrimination of neutrons and gamma rays using Kohonen artificial neural networks. Journal of Artificial Intelligence and Soft Computing Research 3(2), 77–88 (2013)
50. Wyrzykowski, R., Szustak, L., Rojek, K.: Parallelization of 2d MPDATA EULAG algorithm on hybrid architectures with GPU accelerators. Parallel Computing 40(8), 425–447 (2014)

Using an Artificial Neural Network to Predict Loop Transformation Time

Marek Palkowski[✉] and Wlodzimierz Bielecki[✉]

West Pomeranian University of Technology in Szczecin
Faculty of Computer Science and Information Systems
Zolnierska 49, 71210 Szczecin, Poland
{mpalkowski,wbielecki}@wi.zut.edu.pl
http://www.wi.zut.edu.pl

Abstract. Automatic software parallelization is a key issue for high performance computing. There are many algorithms to transform program loop nests to multithreaded code. However, the time of a transformation process is usually unknown, especially for transitive closure based algorithms. The computational complexity of transitive closure calculation algorithms is relatively high and may prevent applying corresponding transformations. The paper presents the prediction of loop transformation time by means of an artificial neural network for the source-to-source TRACO compiler. The analysis of a loop nest structure and dependences is used to estimate the time of TRACO transformations. The training of a Feed-Forward Neural Network is used to make a decision about transformation time. Experiments with various NAS Parallel Benchmarks show promise for the use of neural networks in automatic code parallelization and optimization.

Keywords: Artificial neural networks · Automatic loop nest parallelization · Parallel computing · Iteration space slicing · Transitive closure

1 Introduction

Automatic loop nest parallelization is recognized as a crucial transformation for achieving high performance for nested loop computations. One of popular techniques is Iteration Space Slicing introduced by Pugh and Rosser being implemented in the TRACO compiler. The slice of computations is represented as following chains of dependences (i.e. transitive dependences) to reach all statement instances which can affect the result.

Extracting parallelism by means of TRACO relies on the transitive closure of an affine dependence relation describing all the dependences in a loop nest. Algorithms aimed at calculating transitive closure are presented in papers [1–4] and they are out of the scope of this paper. The time and memory complexities of calculating transitive closure depend considerably on the number and kind of dependence relations representing all the dependences in a loop nest.

© Springer International Publishing Switzerland 2015
L. Rutkowski et al. (Eds.): ICAISC 2015, Part I, LNAI 9119, pp. 102–111, 2015.
DOI: 10.1007/978-3-319-19324-3_10

In many cases, when the number of dependence relations is more than several hundreds, known algorithms [1–4] fail to produce transitive closure due to limited resources of computers or because the time required for calculating transitive closure is not acceptable in practice (from several hours to several days).

In this paper, we explore the use of machine learning to automatically build a sufficiently accurate model based on a small number of empirical transitive closure calculations, which can be useful in predicting the time of loop nest optimization. For training a neural network, we take into account the structure of a loop nest, the number of dependence relations, and the character of dependences. The output of the model is a predicted class of possible transformation time. Experiments with NAS benchmarks were carried out to analyse the accuracy of the neural network decisions.

2   Loop Transformations Based on Transitive Closure

A dependence analysis is required for correct loop parallelization. Two statement instances I and J are *dependent* if both access the same memory location and if at least one access is a write. The TRACO algorithms require an exact representation of loop-carried dependences and consequently an exact dependence analysis which detects a dependence if and only if it actually exists. To describe and implement the algorithm, we chose the dependence analysis proposed by Pugh and Wonnacott [17], where dependences are represented with dependence relations.

A dependence relation is a tuple relation of the form [*input list*]→[*output list*]: *formula*, where *input list* and *output list* are the lists of variables and/or expressions used to describe input and output tuples and *formula* describes the constraints imposed upon *input list* and *output list* and it is a Presburger formula built of constraints represented with algebraic expressions and using logical and existential operators [17].

Standard operations on relations and sets are used, such as intersection (∩), union (∪), difference (-), domain (dom R), range (ran R), relation application ($S' = R(S)$: $e' \in S'$ iff exists e s.t. $e \to e' \in R, e \in S$). In detail, the description of these operations is presented in [18, 17].

We would like only to note that positive transitive closure for a given relation R, R^+, is defined as follows [18]

$$R^+ = \{e \to e' : e \to e' \in R \lor \exists e'' s.t. \ e \to e'' \in R \land e'' \to e' \in R^+\}. \quad (1)$$

It describes which vertices e' in a dependence graph (represented by relation R) are connected with vertex e.

Transitive closure, R^*, is defined as follows [18]: $R^* = R^+ \cup I$, where I the identity relation. It describes the same connections in a dependence graph (represented by R) that R^+ does plus connections of each vertex with itself.

TRACO uses the transitive closure of a loop nest dependence graph to implement algorithms presented in paper [5] allowing us to generate parallel code representing synchronization-free slices.

Definition 1. Given a dependence graph defined by a set of dependence relations, a slice S is a weakly connected component of this graph, i.e., a maximal subgraph such that for each pair of vertices in the subgraph there exists a forward or backward path.

The algorithm presented in paper [10] allows us to generate fine-grained parallel code representing a legal (free) loop statement instances schedule. The free schedule function is defined as follows.

Definition 2 [11]. The *free schedule* is the function that assigns discrete time of execution to each loop nest statement instance as soon as its operands are available, that is, it is mapping $\sigma\colon LD \to \mathbb{Z}$ such that

$$\sigma(p) = \begin{cases} 0 \ \textit{if there is no } p_1 \in LD \ \textit{s.t. } p_1 \to p \\ 1 + max(\sigma(p_1), \sigma(p_2), ..., \sigma(p_n)); p, p_1, p_2, ..., p_n \in LD; \\ p_1 \to p, p_2 \to p, ..., p_n \to p, \end{cases} \quad (2)$$

where $p, p_1, p_2, ..., p_n$ are loop nest statement instances, LD is the loop nest domain, $p_1 \to p, p_2 \to p, ..., p_n \to p$ mean that the pairs p_1 and p, p_2 and p, ..., p_n and p are dependent, p represents the destination and $p_1, p_2, ..., p_n$ represent the sources of dependences, n is the number of operands of statement instance p (the number of dependences whose destination is statement instance p).

In all parallelization algorithms, TRACO uses transitive closure whose calculation takes most time during a loop nest transformation process. Hence, it is very important to predict transitive closure calculation time before the application of a transformation to justify its usage. If this time is not acceptable in practice, we renounce the use of a corresponding transformation.

3   Neural Network Structure

For the studied approach we propose a neural network consisting of seven input neurons, hidden neurons and one output neuron. The structure of the network is presented in Figure 1.

To predict the time of transitive closure computation, the number of dependence relations and the kind of each dependence are analysed by means of the three input neurons. We distinguish between data flow and non-uniform dependences. Data flow (true) dependence (RAW: Read After Write) is described as follows: a statement *S2* is flow dependent on *S1* if and only if *S1* modifies a resource that *S2* reads and *S1* precedes *S2* in execution. This kind of dependences is more difficult to remove than anti and output ones. Non-uniform dependences are described with relations for which one or more differences between the corresponding output and input relation tuples are not constants.

The rest of input neurons describe the structure of a loop nest: the numbers of statements, loops, and parameters. The last input neuron takes into account whether loops are perfectly or imperfectly nested.

An output neuron value is within one of six classes representing transitive closure computation time. The classes are explained in Table 1.

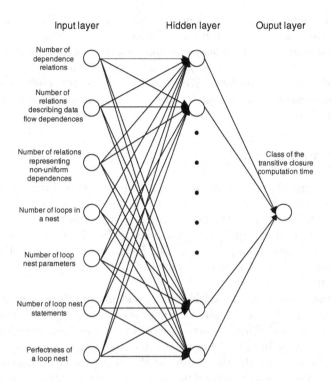

Fig. 1. Feed-Forward Neural Network structure

Table 1. Input and output layer details

Neuron	Type	Data Type	Details
Number of dependence relations		Integer	minimum = 1
Percentage of relations representing flow dependences		Float	minimum = 0, maximum = 1
Percentage of relations representing no-uniform dependences	Input	Float	minimum = 0, maximum = 1
Number of statements		Integer	minimum = 1
Number of parameters		Integer	minimum = 0
Number of loops in a nest		Integer	minimum = 1
Perfectness of a loop nest		Boolean	True - perfectly nested loops, False - imperfectly nested loops.
Class of transitive closure computation time	Output	Integer	0 s.t. 0 ≤ t <0.1 seconds, 1 s.t. 0.1≤ t <0.5 seconds, 2 s.t. 0.5 ≤ t <1 seconds, 3 s.t. 1 ≤ t <5 seconds, 4 s.t. 5 ≤ t <100 seconds, 5 s.t. t ≥ 100 seconds.

A decision engine has been implemented by means of PyBrain - a modular Machine Learning Library for Python. *"PyBrain, as its written-out name already suggests, contains algorithms for neural networks, for reinforcement learning (and the combination of the two), for unsupervised learning, and evolution. Since most of the current problems deal with continuous state and action spaces, function approximators (like neural networks) must be used to cope with the large dimensionality"* [6].

4   Experimental Study

To evaluate the quality of the neural network, we have experimented with NAS Parallel Benchmarks 3.3 (NPB) [14] being developed at the NASA Ames Research Centre to study performance of parallel supercomputers. Benchmarks are derived from computational fluid dynamics applications, they consist of five kernels and three pseudo-applications [14]. From 431 loop nests of the NAS benchmark suite, TRACO is able to analyse 257 loop nests, and dependences are available in 134 loop nests.

In this paper, we examine transitive closure calculation time taken by the approach to transitive closure computation presented in paper [15]. This approach is based on a modified Floyd-Warshall algorithm where basis dependence distance vectors are used for the calculation of relations describing self-dependences.

For studied loop nests, the time taken for the calculation of transitive closure is from several milliseconds to several hours, details are presented in Figure 2. For most loop nests, the time of transitive closure calculations takes one or less than one second, but there are benchmarks for which the time of transitive closure calculation is not acceptable in practice.

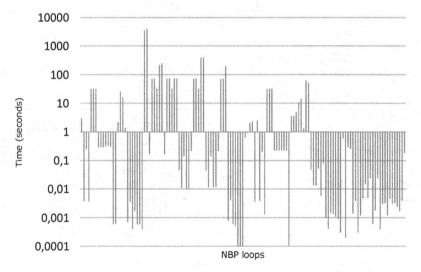

Fig. 2. Transitive closure computation time distribution for NPB loop nests

The number of dependence relations is a basic factor impacting the time of transitive closure calculation, but this time is not defined by a linear function. For example, the dependences of the benchmarks *SP_rhs.f2p_3* and *SP_rhs.f2p_4* are described with 699 and 507 relations, respectively, and the time of transitive closure calculation for these benchmarks takes 4.8 and 10.8 seconds, respectively.

The Tanh Layer has been chosen for hidden and output layers. The corresponding activation function is defined as follows:

$$y(u) = \frac{e^u - e^{-u}}{e^u + e^{-u}} \tag{3}$$

The Softmax and Sigmoid Layers are also acceptable for the considered network. The Linear Layer has been considered as the worst one because transitive closure calculation time depends on the input data in a nonlinear way. For the hidden layer, we have chosen 49 neurons. The configuration of a network, using the Pybrain library, is presented in Listing 1.

```python
from pybrain.datasets            import ClassificationDataSet
from pybrain.utilities           import percentError
from pybrain.tools.shortcuts     import buildNetwork
from pybrain.supervised.trainers import BackpropTrainer
from pybrain.structure.modules   import TanhLayer

alldata = ClassificationDataSet(7, 1, nb_classes=6)

# alldata.addSample(inp, outp)

tstdata, trndata = alldata.splitWithProportion( 0.25 )

trndata._convertToOneOfMany( )
tstdata._convertToOneOfMany( )

fnn = buildNetwork(7, 49, 1, outclass=TanhLayer)

trainer = BackpropTrainer( fnn, dataset=trndata, momentum=0.1,
    verbose=False, weightdecay=0.01)

for i in range(100):
    trainer.trainEpochs(1)

trnresult = percentError( trainer.testOnClassData(), trndata['
    class'] )
tstresult = percentError( trainer.testOnClassData(dataset=
    tstdata ), tstdata['class'] )
```

Listing 1. A Pybrain script of the configuration of the network

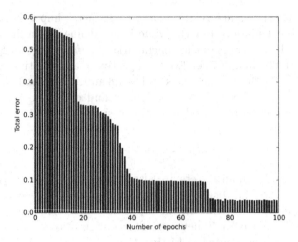

Fig. 3. Total error and the number of epochs

We have trained the network with three sizes of the test data and 100 epochs. The number of epochs is dictated by the total error defined by the sum of errors over all training sets. The total error describes a decent guess as to whether a network can be better if it were given longer to train. If the total error changed a lot from one iteration to the next, that would be a sign that it had not settled down to a final state. We have observed a stability of that factor between 60 and 80 epochs. Figure 3 illustrates this fact.

When all data is splitted with 0.5 proportion (equal sizes of the test and train data sets), the best results are predictably reached. Specially, we observe good recognition between two classes for the shortest transformation times, see Figure 4a. Train and test errors amount 25.9% and 19.8%, respectively (28 misses for all data set). A lower accuracy takes place for the following proportion: 30% test data and 70% train data, see Figure 4b. Train and test errors constitute 22.4% and 28.8%, respectively (34 misses). The prediction is still interesting for the smallest test data (20%), see Figure 4c. Train and test errors amount 34.6% and 23.1%. Although the sensitivity of the network is lower (43 misses), we can observe that many predictions are fall in neighbour classes.

It is notable that the predictions of the longest transformation time (class 5) are missed. This can be explained due to a small data set falling in this class. Only few loop nests for the considered benchmark suite fall in this class. For these benchmarks, the network outputs class 4, the nearest class for those cases. A transformation of more complex loop nest classes may not be justified in practice, hence the compiler does not generate any optimized code.

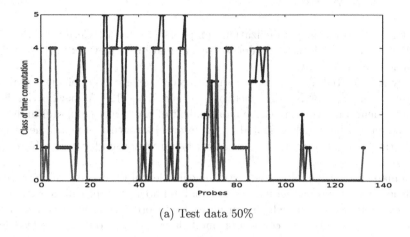

(a) Test data 50%

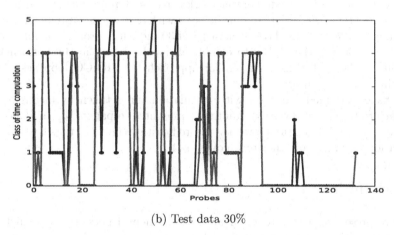

(b) Test data 30%

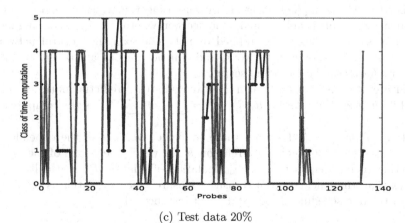

(c) Test data 20%

Fig. 4. Transformation time prediction for NAS Parallel Benchmarks. Real and predicted loop nest classes are marked with the blue and red lines, respectively.

5 Related Work

Well-known automatic parallelization compilers (Pluto [7], Cetus [8], Par4All [9]) do not offer any decision model. A transformation framework for these tools is enabled automatically.

Strey A. and Riehm J. presented an automatic generation of efficient parallel programs from EpsiloNN neural network specifications [12]. A specification language for neural networks must be independent of the target computer architecture and should be closely oriented to the internal structure of neural networks. Hence, this approach unfortunately cannot be directly used for source-to-source compilers.

Rahman et al. [13] explore the use of machine learning to automatically build a sufficiently accurate model based on a small number of empirical executions of parametrically tiled code, which can be useful in predicting effective tile sizes. With this purpose, a fully connected, multi-layer perceptron (MLP), feed forward neural network is used. That network consists of an input layer with three input parameters (tile sizes), an output layer with one output - predicted execution time, and one hidden layer consisting of 30 hidden neurons. The advantage of that approach is the ability to exhibit all local minima in the performance distribution. We will consider a similar approach for TRACO loop nest tiling algorithms in the future.

We have examined a dataset with calculation times taken by means of the approach to transitive closure computation presented in paper [15]. In analogues way, we may build neural networks to predict the time of transitive closure calculation by means of other techniques [1–4].

6 Conclusion

We have presented a way to build an artificial neural network to predict the time of transitive closure calculation. Using such a prediction, an optimizing compiler (based on implementing algorithms using the transitive closure of a dependence relation) is able to make the decision whether a corresponding loop nest transformation has to be applied or not. The examined neural network is based on a Feed-Forward network, and can be used as a strategy to fully substitute for a standard random search.

In future, we indent to study neural networks for the prediction of the calculation of the power k of relation R, R^k ($R^k = \underbrace{R \circ R \circ ...R}_{k}$, "$\circ$" is the composition operation). Relation R^k describes those connected vertices in the dependence graph, represented by dependence relation R, for which the length of each path connecting them is equal to k. The calculation of relation R^k is usually more complex than the calculation of transitive closure. Such a relation is required to build the free schedule of loop statement instances [10].

References

1. Kelly, W., Pugh, W.: Transitive closure of infinite graphs and its applications. Int. J. Parallel Programming 24, 579–598 (1996)
2. Verdoolaege, S.: Integer Set Library - Manual (2011), http://www.kotnet.org/~skimo//isl/manual.pdf
3. Wlodzimierz, B., Tomasz, K., Marek, P., Beletska, A.: An Iterative Algorithm of Computing the Transitive Closure of a Union of Parameterized Affine Integer Tuple Relations. In: Wu, W., Daescu, O. (eds.) COCOA 2010, Part I. LNCS, vol. 6508, pp. 104–113. Springer, Heidelberg (2010)
4. Verdoolaege, S., et al.: Transitive Closures of Affine Integer Tuple Relations and their Overapproximations, Rapport de recherch RR-7560, INRIA (2011), http://hal.inria.fr/inria-00578052
5. Beletska, A., Bielecki, W., Cohen, A., Palkowski, M., Siedlecki, K.: Coarse-grained loop parallelization: Iteration space slicing vs affine transformations. Parallel Computing 37, 479–497 (2011)
6. Schaul, T., et al.: PyBrain. Journal of Machine Learning Research 11, 743–746 (2010)
7. Bondhugula, U., Hartono, A., Ramanujan, J., Sadayappan, P.: A practical automatic polyhedral parallelizer and locality optimizer. In: ACM SIGPLAN Programming Languages Design and Implementation, PLDI 2008 (2008)
8. Chirag, D., Hansang, B., Seung-Jai, M., Seyong, L., Eigenmann, R., Midkiff, S.: Cetus: A Source-to-Source Compiler Infrastructure for Multicores. IEEE Computer, 36–42 (2009)
9. Amini, M., et al.: Par4All: From Convex Array Regions to Heterogeneous Computing. In: 2nd International Workshop on Polyhedral Compilation Techniques (IMPACT 2012), Paris, France, 01/201 (2012)
10. Bielecki, W., Palkowski, M., Klimek, T.: Free scheduling for statement instances of parameterized arbitrarily nested af ne loops. Parallel Computing 38(9), 518–532 (2012)
11. Darte, A., Robert, Y., Vivien, F.: Scheduling and Automatic Parallelization. Birkgauser (2000)
12. Strey, A., Riehm, J.: Automatic Generation of Efficient Parallel Programs from EpsiloNN Neural Network Specifications (1997)
13. Rahman, M., Pouchet, L., Sadayappan, P.: Neural Network Assisted Tile Size Selection. In: 5th International Workshop on Automatic Performance Tuning (iWAPT 2010), Berkeley, CA, USA (2010)
14. NAS Parallel Benchmarks (2013), http://www.nas.nasa.gov
15. Bielecki, W., Kraska, K., Klimek, T.: Using basis dependence distance vectors in the modified Floyd Warshall algorithm, Journal of Combinatorial Optimization (April 2014)
16. Pugh, W., Rosser, E.: Iteration space slicing and its application to communication optimization. In: International Conference on Supercomputing, pp. 221–228 (1997)
17. Pugh, W., Wonnacott, D.: An exact method for analysis of value-based array data dependences. In: Banerjee, U., Gelernter, D., Nicolau, A., Padua, D.A. (eds.) LCPC 1993. LNCS, vol. 768, pp. 546–566. Springer, Heidelberg (1994)
18. Kelly, W., Maslov, V., Pugh, W., Rosser, E., Shpeisman, T., Wonnacott, D.: The omega library interface guide. Technical report, College Park, MD, USA (1995)

Using Parity-N Problems as a Way to Compare Abilities of Shallow, Very Shallow and Very Deep Architectures

Paweł Różycki[1][(✉)], Janusz Kolbusz[1], Tomasz Bartczak,
and Bogdan M. Wilamowski[2]

[1] University of Information Technology and Management in Rzeszow,
Sucharskiego 2, 35-225 Rzeszow, Poland
{prozycki,jkolbusz}@wsiz.rzeszow.pl
[2] Auburn University, Auburn, AL 36849-5201 USA
tbartczak10@gmail.com, wilambm@auburn.edu
http://wsiz.rzeszow.pl

Abstract. This paper presents a new concept of a dual neural network which is hybrid of linear and nonlinear network. This approach allows for solving the problem of Parity-3 with only one sigmoid neuron or Parity-7 with 2 sigmoid neurons that is shown in the analytical and experimental manner. The paper describes the architecture of ANN, presents an analytical way of choosing the weights and the number of neurons, and provides the results of network training for different ANN architectures solving the Parity-N problem.

Keywords: Parity-N problem · ANN architecture · Summator in output layer

1 Introduction

Artificial Neural Networks (ANNs) are currently used in many different applications. We likely see them every day, but dont realize that they are there. When you watch the weather forecast on the news or view it on the Internet or you mobile phone, few of us realize that ANNs were likely used to generate the forecast [1–3]. In industry, ANNs are used to control induction [4–6], permanent magnet [7, 8], and stepper motors [9]. Additionally, they are used in robotics [10], motion control [11], battery control [12], job scheduling [13], and networking [14]. Some more advanced ANNs are used in highly complex, dynamic systems such as oil wells [15, 16]. Although their uses vary, you can see that ANNs are found almost everywhere. An enormous amount of research has been devoted to ANN research over the past several decades. Much research has focused on training algorithms such as Error Back Propagation (EBP) [17, 18], the Levenberg Marquardt (LM) algorithm [19, 20], and the Neuron by Neuron (NBN) algorithm [21–23]. Other

This work was supported by the National Science Centre, Cracow, Poland under Grant No. 2013/11/B/ST6/01337.

© Springer International Publishing Switzerland 2015
L. Rutkowski et al. (Eds.): ICAISC 2015, Part I, LNAI 9119, pp. 112–122, 2015.
DOI: 10.1007/978-3-319-19324-3_11

research has seized opportunities to optimize training algorithms and network architecture. This research has produced improvements in algorithms such as momentum [24] and flat-spot elimination [25] for EBP. We have also seen the architecture progression from the Multi-Layer Perceptron (MLP) to the Bridged Multi-Layer Perceptron (BMLP) to Fully Connected Cascade (FCC) architecture [26] and finally to Dual Neural Networks (DNN) [27]. All of this research has produced many advances in the methods used to train ANNs as well as improvements in architecture design which have significantly improved efficiency [27–29]. However, considering ANN architectures the key question is how many neurons should be used or how much compact ANN can be. Another important problem is how to train such minimal networks: if appropriate methods exists and how many patterns is needed. A good measure of ANN power is possibility of resolve Parity-N problem, the special case of classification, using a particular number of neurons. The implementations of ANN in selected architectures able to solve some Parity-N problems are presented in three next chapters. Chapter 2 shows examples of minimal MLP networks that are able to resolve selected Parity-N problem. Chapters 3 and 4 presents implementations of such problems using BMLP and FCC, respectively. For all of these architectures methodology for design of solution for particular Parity-N problem are also presented with the special reference to use the summator in output layer in the place of sigmoidal neuron. Note that also in the case of approximation/regression last neuron should be linear. Chapter 5 shows the method for reduction of number of weights in the ANN designed in previous chapters by inserting summator of input. Chapter 6 shows results of experiments for training designed ANN.

2   Design of Shallow MLP Architecture with One Hidden Layer

The MLP is the oldest and the best known and studied architecture. It is a feedforward ANN which contains neurons with the same, usually sigmoidal, activation function. In such ANN all inputs are connected to all neurons in the first hidden layer and all neurons outputs in the hidden layers are connected to neurons in the next layer. The most common architecture uses only one hidden layer. Such network with n_h neurons in hidden layer is able to resolve Parity-N problem described by equation:

$$N = n_h \tag{1}$$

Figure 1 shows samples of architectures that are able to resolve Parity-N problem. As one may see from equation 1, the Parity-2 problem can be resolved by two hidden neurons. Figure 1.a shows the most common implementation with hard threshold neurons. As shown in Table 1.a. in this case the output is equal to expected values so the hard threshold output neuron can be replaced by simpler summator. Such implementation is shown in Figure 1.b. Moreover, all input weights are equal 1 so an input of each hidden neuron is the same. Therefore,

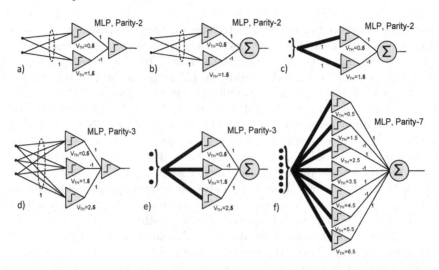

Fig. 1. Minimal MLP architecture to resolve Parity-2 problem: (a) with sigmoidal output, (b) with summator output, (c) with bus on input; to resolve Paruty-3 problem: (d) with sigmoidal output, (e) with summator output bus on input and (f) to resolve Parity-7 problem.

input is redrawn as a bus in Figure 1.c. Figures 1.d,e show similar implementation for solution of Parity-3 problem. Output calculations for this problem is shown in Table 1.b.

As it can be seen in Table 1 solutions for successive Parity-N problems can be found by adding neurons with threshold values equal 0.5, 1.5, 2.5, 3.5,... that can be generalized as $n - 0.5$ and corresponding output weights 1, -1, 1, -1,... that can be generalized as $(n \bmod 2)2 - 1$, where n is the number of the given neuron. Figure 1.f. shows implementation of Parity-7 problem for such calculated neurons and weights.

Table 1. States for MLP architecture solving (a) Parity-2 problem with two hidden neurons and (b) Parity-3 problem with three hidden neurons

a)

Number of ones on inputs	Neuron 1 output TH=0.5 (o1)	w1	Neuron 2 output TH=1.5 (o2)	w2	Output o1w1 +o2w2
0	0		0		0
1	1	1	0	-1	1
2	1		1		0

b)

Number of ones on inputs	Neuron 1 output TH=0.5 (o1)	w1	Neuron 2 output TH=1.5 (o2)	w2	Neuron 3 output TH=2.5 (o3)	w3	Output o1w1 +o2w2+o3w3
0	0		0		0		0
1	1		0		0		1
2	1	1	1	-1	0	1	0
3	1		1		1		1

3   Design of Very Shallow BMLP Architecture with One Hidden Layer

The BMLP architecture is modified MLP with additional direct connections between inputs and all neurons in entire network. These additional cross-layer connections improve significantly the power of network. The BMLP network with n_h neurons in one hidden layer allow to resolve the Parity-N problem for N given by equation:

$$N = 2n_h + 1 \qquad (2)$$

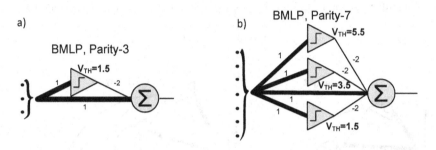

Fig. 2. Minimal BMLP implementation solving Parity-3 problem (a) and Parity-7 problem (b)

In Figure 2 is shown implementation of solutions for Parity-3 problem and Parity-7 and Table 2 corresponding output calculations. The same as for MLP in the case of BMLP output are equal to expected values therefore hard threshold neuron is not needed. As it can be seen, in general the given Parity-N problem can be resolved using $floor(N/2)$ neurons with threshold values 1.5, 3.5, 5.5 ... and output weight equal to -2.

Table 2. States for BMLP architecture solving (a) Parity-3 problem with one hidden neuron and (b) Parity-7 problem with three hidden neurons

a)

Number of ones on input in	Neuron 1 output TH=1.5 (o1)	w1	Output in+o1w1
0	0		0
1	0		1
2	1	-2	0
3	1		1

b)

Number of ones on input in	Neuron 1 output TH=5.5 (o1)	w1	Neuron 2 output TH=3.5 (o2)	w2	Neuron 3 output TH=1.5 (o3)	w3	Output in+o1w1+o2w2 +o3w3
0	0		0		0		0
1	0		0		0		1
2	0		0		1		0
3	0		0		1		1
4	0	-2	1	-2	1	-2	0
5	0		1		1		1
6	1		1		1		0
7	1		1		1		1

4   Design of Very Deep FCC Architecture

The FCC is special case of the BMLP network with only a single neuron in each hidden layer. Again all inputs are fully connected with all neurons. As can be found in [26] the FCC is actually the best architecture and most compact. It allows to solve given Parity-N problem using the fewest number of neurons. Research has shown that the largest Parity-N problem that a FCC network can solve using n neurons is defined by:

$$N = 2^n - 1 \qquad (3)$$

It means that Parity-15 problem can be solved using four neurons. In fact, as shown in Table 3 and in Figure 3 the output neuron can be replaced by summator therefore nh neurons in hidden layers are able to solve Parity-N problem given by:

$$N = 2^{(n_h+1)} - 1 \qquad (4)$$

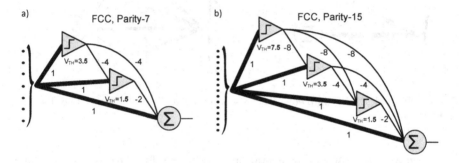

Fig. 3. Minimal FCC implementation solving Parity-7 problem (a) and Parity-15 problem (b)

Implementation of FCC architecture solving Parity-7 problem and Parity-15 problem are shown in Figure 3. Note that FCC is special case of BMLP so implementation of FCC solution for Parity-3 problem has been already shown in previous chapter (Figure 2.a). Design of FCC architecture able to solve Parity-N problem should be started from last hidden neuron. Note that the number of needed neurons can be calculated from equation 4. It means that one hidden neuron is able to solve up to Parity-3 problem, two hidden neurons up to Parity-7 problem, and four hidden neurons up to Parity-31 problem. The number of needed hidden neurons is therefore given by:

$$n_h = ceil(\log_2(N+1) - 1) \qquad (5)$$

In order to design FCC network able to resolve Parity-N problem the threshold of given neuron can be calculated as $2^n - 0.5$ and weight is equal -2^n where n is number of hidden neuron counting from output. Example of such design for Parity-15 is shown in Table 3 where design for Parity-3 and Parity-7 are marked in dark.

Table 3. States for FCC architecture solving Parity-15 problem

Number of ones on Inputs (In)	Neuron 3			Neuron 2			Neuron 1			Output in+o3w3+o2w2+o1w1
	Input In	output TH=7.5 (o3)	(w3)	Input in+o3w3	Output TH=3.5 (o2)	(w2)	Input in+o3w3+o2w2	Output TH=1.5 (o1)	(w1)	
0	0	0	-8	0	0	-4	0	0	-2	0
1	1	0	-8	1	0	-4	1	0	-2	1
2	2	0	-8	2	0	-4	2	1	-2	0
3	3	0	-8	3	0	-4	3	1	-2	1
4	4	0	-8	4	1	-4	0	0	-2	0
5	5	0	-8	5	1	-4	1	0	-2	1
6	6	0	-8	6	1	-4	2	1	-2	0
7	7	0	-8	7	1	-4	3	1	-2	1
8	8	1	-8	0	0	-4	0	0	-2	0
9	9	1	-8	1	0	-4	1	0	-2	1
10	10	1	-8	2	0	-4	2	1	-2	0
11	11	1	-8	3	0	-4	3	1	-2	1
12	12	1	-8	4	1	-4	0	0	-2	0
13	13	1	-8	5	1	-4	1	0	-2	1
14	14	1	-8	6	1	-4	2	1	-2	0
15	15	1	-8	7	1	-4	3	1	-2	1

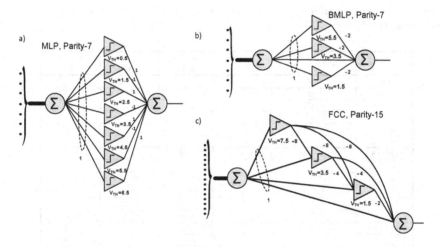

Fig. 4. Architectures with reduced number of weights: (a) implementation of MLP for Parity-7 problem, (b) implementation of BMLP for Parity-7 problem, (c) implementation of FCC for Parity-15 problem

Table 4. Number of hidden neurons and number of weights needed for solving Parity-N problems

Architecture	Number of hidden neurons	Number of weights (standard approach)	Reduced number of weights
MLP (1-hidden layer)	$n_h = N$	$n_w = Nn_h + 2n_h + 1$	$n_w = N + 3n_h + 1$
BMLP (1-hidden layer)	$n_h = \text{floor}(N/2)$	$n_w = N(n_h + 1) + 2n_h + 1$	$n_w = N + 3n_h + 2$
FCC	$n_h = \text{ceil}(\log_2(N+1)-1)$	$n_w = N(n_h + 1) + ((n_h + 2)(n_h + 1))/2$	$n_w = N + 2n_h + ((n_h + 2)(n_h + 1))/2$

5   Architectures with Reduced Number of Weights

In the case of Parity-N problems the networks can be further reduced. As shown in previous chapters each hidden neuron takes all inputs with the same weight equal to one. It means that the neuron takes as an input the sum of input values, therefore N connections from inputs to given neuron can be replaced by one connection with the value of sum of these inputs. Implementations of this approach for selected Parity-N problems with MLP, BMLP and FCC using input summator are shown in Figure 4. In this way the number of weights in network can be significantly reduced especially for large networks. It means simpler and cheaper implementation. The number of weights comparison between implementation using standard approach and reduced implementation is shown in Table 4. Note that the standard FCC implementation for Parity-15 problem require 70 weights while reduced implementation requires only 31 weights. The same problem implemented in MLP require 256 weights using standard approach and only 61 weights in reduced network.

Table 5. Comparison training of MLP, BMLP and FCC architectures (success maximum error=0.001)

Parity-N	Architecture	# neurons	Success Rate	Ave. Iteration	Ave. Time [ms]
Parity-3	MLP	4	1	11.54	3.10
Parity-3	MLP	3*	1	7.41	5.14
Parity-3	MLP	3**	0.87	16.15	9.32
Parity-3	BMLP/FCC	2	1	11.77	3.44
Parity-3	BMLP/FCC	1*	1	4.39	1.87
Parity-3	BMLP/FCC	1**	1	3.87	2.51
Parity-5	MLP	6	0.69	13.57	6.87
Parity-5	MLP	5*	1	12.46	11.70
Parity-5	MLP	5**	0.67	32.76	24.02
Parity-5	BMLP	3	0.64	14.39	8.04
Parity-5	BMLP	2*	0.65	14.98	8.60
Parity-5	BMLP	2**	0.76	40.70	27.49
Parity-5	FCC	3	0.28	22.93	12.73
Parity-5	FCC	2*	0.66	12.95	6.66
Parity-5	FCC	2**	0.74	19.76	12.42
Parity-7	MLP	8	0.98	56.14	144.71
Parity-7	MLP	7*	1	25.46	61.00
Parity-7	MLP	7**	0.91	144.97	92.65
Parity-7	BMLP	4	0	-	-
Parity-7	BMLP	3*	0.69	79.72	91.33
Parity-7	BMLP	3**	0.77	62.46	39.49
Parity-7	FCC	3	0	-	-
Parity-7	FCC	2*	0.33	165.39	141.91
Parity-7	FCC	2**	0.36	23.75	17.83
Parity-7	FCC	4	0.21	68.57	63.00
Parity-7	FCC	3*	0.87	49.26	56.23
Parity-7	FCC	3**	0.90	31.54	21.13

* plus summator on output

** plus summator on output and on input (reduced number of weights)

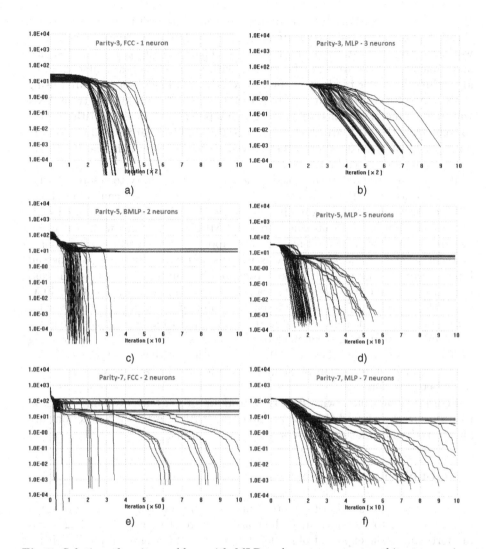

Fig. 5. Solution of parity problem with MLP and super compact architectures using the newest NBN software [16] (a) Parity-3 problem (8 patterns) solved with 1 sigmoidal neurons - FCC architecture, (b) Parity-3 problem (8 patterns) solved with 3 sigmoidal neurons - MLP architecture, (c) Parity-5 problem (32 patterns) solved with 2 sigmoidal neurons - BMLP architecture, (d) Parity-5 problem (32 patterns) solved with 6 sigmoidal neurons - MLP architecture, (e) Parity-7 problem (128 patterns) solved with 2 sigmoidal neurons - FCC architecture, (f) Parity-7 problem (128 patterns) solved with 8 sigmoidal neurons - MLP architecture.

6   Training Architectures

Previous chapters show how to design networks in several architectures for Parity-N problems. As shown, analytically calculated weights for these network allow to resolve given problems. The separate issue is if such designed and dimensioned network can be trained with success using available training algorithms. In order to check it several experiments have been prepared using NBN 2.08 software [16]. This is a tool written in C++ dedicated to train ANN with many different architectures using many popular training algorithms. Due to comparing the MLP architecture with BMLP and FCC architectures that are not layer-by-layer architectures, the NBN algorithm has been chosen. Results of experiments are shown in Table 5.

Results confirm analytical considerations about possibility to resolve Parity-N problem using particular ANN architectures. However, as it can be observed, the deep architectures are more difficult to train. For Parity-7 the minimal FCC architecture with 3 neurons but also the BMLP architecture with 4 neurons are unable to train if all used neurons are bipolar. This is because of vanishing gradient problem [30]. Note that this issue is less visible if summator instead bipolar neuron is used in output layer (denoted by * in the Table 5). In this case these deep architectures are able to train with success rates equals 0.33 for FCC and 0.69 for BMLP. The positive impact of summator can be also observer for MLP architecture. It allows to reduce number of iteration needed to solve given problem. The reduction of number of weights has also the impact on training results (denoted by **). For the MLP architecture it gives a bit worse results due to significant reduction of weights while for BMLP and FCC it allows to reach better result.

Figure 5 shows plots with details of training process achieved in NBN 2.08 tool. It can be observed that the architectures with cross-layer connections are able to train much faster with less number of neurons.

7   Conclusions

Based on the studies of Parity-N problems one can conclude that power of ANN is proportional to its width in shallow architectures (see Eq. (1) and (2)) and proportional to the exponent of its depth in deep architectures (Eq. (4)). Therefore, one may recommend usage of deep architectures, but these architectures are very difficult to train. The proposed very shallow architectures are much easier to train. They have also reduced number of neurons.

References

1. Mandal, S., Choudhury, J., Bhadra, S., De, D.: Growth Estimation with Artificial Neural Network Considering Weather Parameters Using Factor and Principal Component Analysis. In: Proceedings of the 10th International Conference on Information Technology, Rourkela (2007)

2. Quan, Y.: Research on weather forecast based on neural networks. In: Proceedings of the 3rd World Congress on Intelligent Control and Automation, Beijing (2000)
3. Ghate, V.N., Dudu, S.V.: Cascade neural-network-based fault classifier for three-phase induction motor. IEEE Transactions on Industrial Electronics 58(5), 1555–1563 (2011)
4. Orlowska-Kowalska, T., Dybkowski, M., Szabat, K.: Adaptive sliding-mode neuro-fuzzy control of the two-mass induction motor drive without mechanical sensors. IEEE Transactions on Industrial Electronics 57(2), 553–564 (2010)
5. Pucci, M., Cirrincione, M.: Neural MPPT control of wind generators with induction machines without speed sensors. IEEE Transactions on Industrial Electronics 58(1), 37–47 (2011)
6. El-Sousy, F.F.M.: Hybrid H based wavelet-neural-network tracking control for permanent-magnet synchronous motor servo drives. IEEE Transactions on Industrial Electronics 57(9), 3157–3166 (2010)
7. Xia, C., Guo, C., Shi, T.: A neural-network-identifier and fuzzy-controller-based algorithm for dynamic decoupling control of permanent-magnet spherical motor. IEEE Transactions on Inductrial Electronics 57(8), 2868–2878 (2010)
8. Le, Q.N., Jeon, J.W.: Neural-network-based low-speed-damping controller for stepper motor with an FPGA. IEEE Transactions on Industrial Electronics 57(9), 3167–3180 (2010)
9. Juang, C.-F., Chang, Y.-C., Hsiao, C.-M.: Evolving gaits of a hexapod robot by recurrent neural networks with symbiotic species-based particle swarm optimization. IEEE Transactions on Industrial Electronics 58(7), 3110–3119 (2011)
10. Tsa, C.-C.I., Huang, H.-C., Lin, S.-C.: Adaptive neural network control of a self-balancing two-wheeled scooter. IEEE Transactions on Industrial Electronics 57(4), 1420–1428 (2010)
11. Charkhgard, M., Farrokhi, M.: State-of-charge estimation for lithium-ion batteries using neural networks and EKF. IEEE Transactions on Industrial Electronics 57(12), 4178–4187 (2010)
12. Yahyaou, A., Fnaiech, N., Fnaiech, F.: A Suitable Initialization Procedure for Speeding a Neural Network Job-Shop Scheduling. IEEE Transactions on Industrial Electronics 58(3), 1052–1060 (2011)
13. Machado, V., Neto, A., de Melo, J.D.: A neural network multiagent architecture applied to industrial networks for dynamic allocation of control strategies using standard function blocks. IEEE Transactions on Industrial Electronics 57(5), 1823–1834 (2010)
14. Lu, C.-H.: Wavelet fuzzy neural networks for identification and predictive control of dynamic systems. IEEE Transactions on Industrial Electronics 58(7), 3046–3058 (2011)
15. Wilamowski, B.M., Kaynak, O.: Oil well diagnosis by sensing terminal characteristics of the induction motor. IEEE Transactions on Industrial Electronics 47(5), 1100–1107 (2000)
16. Wilamowski, B.M., Yu, H.: NNT - Neural Networks Trainer (2015), http://www.eng.auburn.edu/~wilambm/nnt/index.htm (accessed February 1, 2015)
17. Rumelhart, D.E., Hinton, G.E., Williams, R.J.: Learning representations by back-propagating errors. Nature 323, 533–536 (1986)
18. Werbos, P.J.: Back-propagation: Past and future. In: Proceedings of International Conference on Neural Networks, San Diego (1988)
19. Levenberg, K.: A method for the solution of certain problems in least squares. Quarterly of Applied Mathematics 2, 164–168 (1944)

20. Hagan, M.T., Menha, M.B.J.: Training feedforward networks with the Marquardt algorithm. IEEE Transactions on Neural Networks 5(6), 989–993 (1994)
21. Wilamowski, B.M., Cotton, N.J., Kaynak, O., Dundar, G.: Computing gradient vector and jacobian matrix in arbitrarily connected neural networks. IEEE Transactions on Industrial Electronics 55(10), 3784–3790 (2008)
22. Wilamowski, B.M., Yu, H.: Improved Computation for Levenberg Marquardt Training. IEEE Transactions on Neural Networks 21(6), 930–937 (2010)
23. Wilamowski, B.M., Yu, H.: Neural Network Learning Without Backpropagation. IEEE Transactions on Neural Networks 21(11), 1793–1803 (2010)
24. Phansalkar, V.V., Sastry, P.S.: Analysis of the back-propagation algorithm with momentum. IEEE Transactions on Neural Networks 5(3), 505–506 (1994)
25. Wilamowski, B.M., Torvik, L.: Modification of gradient computation in the back-propagation algorithm. In: ANNIE 1993 - Artificial Neural Networks in Engineering, St. Louis (1993)
26. Hunter, D.S., Yu, H., Pukish, M.S., Kolbusz, J., Wilamowski, B.M.: Selection of Proper Neural Network Sizes and Architectures – A Comparative Study. IEEE Transactions on Industrial Informatics 8(2), 228–240 (2012)
27. Hunter, D.S., Wilamowski, B.M.: Parallel Multi-Layer Neural Network Architecture with Improved Efficiency. In: Proceedings of the 4th International Conference on Human System Interaction, Yokohama (2011)
28. Trenn, S.: Mulit-layer Perceptrons: Approximation Order and Necessary Number of Hidden Units. IEEE Transactions on Neural Networks 19(5), 836–844 (2008)
29. Wilamowski, B.M.: Neural Network Architectures and Learning Algorithms. IEEE Industrial Electronics Magazine, 56–63 (December 2009)
30. Hochreiter, S.: The Vanishing Gradient Problem During Learning Recurrent Neural Nets and Problem Solutions. Int. J. Unc. Fuzz. Knowl. Based Syst. 06, 107 (1998)

Product Multi-kernels for Sensor Data Analysis

Petra Vidnerová[✉] and Roman Neruda

Institute of Computer Science
Academy of Sciences of the Czech Republic,
Pod vodárenskou věží 2, Praha 8,
Czech Republic
{petra,roman}@cs.cas.cz

Abstract. Regularization networks represent a kernel-based model of neural networks with solid theoretical background and a variety of learning possibilities. In this paper, we focus on its extension with multi-kernel units. In particular, we describe the architecture of a product unit network, and we propose an evolutionary learning algorithm for setting its parameters. The algorithm is capable to select different kernels from a dictionary and to set their parameters, including optimal split of inputs into individual products. The approach is tested on real-world data from sensor networks area.

Keywords: Regularization networks · Multi-kernel models · Product units · Sensor data

1 Introduction

The problem of *learning from examples* (also called *supervised learning*) is a subject of great interest at present. The need for a good supervised learning technique stems from a wide range of application areas, covering various approximation, classification, and prediction tasks.

In this paper we study one such learning technique – the so-called *regularization network* (RN). RNs are feed-forward neural networks with one hidden layer. They benefit from a good theoretical background, their architecture has been proved to be the solution of the problem of learning from examples when formulated as a regularized minimization problem (see [1–4]).

The paper [5] showed that the performance of the RN learning depends significantly on the choice of kernel function. Moreover, the choice of kernel function always depends on a particular task at hand. Different kernel functions are suitable for different data types, but one often has to deal with heterogeneous data, in the sense that attributes differ in type or quality, or that the character of data differs in different parts of the input space. Therefore, we propose network architectures using composite types of kernels that might better reflect the heterogeneous character of data. These kernel types include either a sum of selected kernel functions or a tensor product of functions operating on a split subsets of input variables. This split, as well as the types and parameters of kernel functions, are adaptively set by an original neuro-evolutionary learning algorithm, in our case.

© Springer International Publishing Switzerland 2015
L. Rutkowski et al. (Eds.): ICAISC 2015, Part I, LNAI 9119, pp. 123–133, 2015.
DOI: 10.1007/978-3-319-19324-3_12

Our approach can be ranked among the so called *multi-kernel* models. Recently, this area has been a subject of extensive research [6–9], and it includes a wide range of algorithms, mostly designed only for the support vector machines (SVM) learning. In our research we apply the multi-kernel approach to regularization neural networks with different kernel units. Kůrková et al have studied theoretical properties of kernel units with variable and fixed widths [10–13].

The approach is tested on a real-world data from the area of sensor networks for air pollution monitoring. We use data from De Vito et al [14], [15] that describe a supervised learning approximation problem. The data contain tens of thousands measurements of gas multi-sensor devices recording concentrations of several gas pollutants. The measurements are labeled by conventional air pollution monitoring stations. The data are described in detail in Section 5.

The paper is organized as follows. In the next section, the regularization network is introduced. In Section 3 the product kernel functions are introduced. Section 4 describes the genetic parameter search. Section 5 contains results of our experiments. Conclusion can be found in Section 6.

2   Regularization Networks and Kernels

In order to develop regularization networks we formulate the problem of supervised learning as a function approximation problem. We are given a set of examples $\{(\boldsymbol{x}_i, y_i) \in R^d \times R\}_{i=1}^N$ obtained by random sampling of some real function f, and we would like to find this function. Since this problem is ill-posed, we have to add some *a priori* knowledge about the function f. We usually assume that the function is *smooth*, in the sense that two similar inputs correspond to two similar outputs, and that the function does not oscillate too much. This is the main idea of the regularization theory, where the solution is found by minimizing the functional (1) containing both the data and smoothness information.

$$H[f] = \frac{1}{N} \sum_{i=1}^N (f(\boldsymbol{x}_i) - y_i)^2 + \gamma \Phi[f], \tag{1}$$

where Φ is called a *stabilizer* and $\gamma > 0$ is *the regularization parameter* controlling the trade-off between the closeness to data and the smoothness of the solution. The regularization approach has sound theoretical background, it was shown that for a wide class of stabilizers the solution has a form of feed-forward neural network with one hidden layer, called *regularization network*, and that different types of stabilizers lead to different types of regularization networks [16, 4].

Poggio and Smale in [4] proposed a learning algorithm derived from the regularization scheme (1). They choose the hypothesis space as a Reproducing Kernel Hilbert Space (RKHS) $\mathcal{H}_K$ defined by an explicitly chosen, symmetric, positive-definite kernel function $K_{\boldsymbol{x}}(\boldsymbol{x}') = K(\boldsymbol{x}, \boldsymbol{x}')$. The stabilizer is defined by means of norm in $\mathcal{H}_K$, so the problem is formulated as follows:

$$\min_{f \in \mathcal{H}_K} H[f], \quad \text{where } H[f] = \frac{1}{N} \sum_{i=1}^N (y_i - f(\boldsymbol{x}_i))^2 + \gamma \|f\|_K^2. \tag{2}$$

The solution of minimization (2) is unique and has the form

$$f(\boldsymbol{x}) = \sum_{i=1}^{N} w_i K_{\boldsymbol{x}_i}(\boldsymbol{x}), \qquad (N\gamma I + K)\boldsymbol{w} = \boldsymbol{y}, \tag{3}$$

where I is the identity matrix, K is the matrix $K_{i,j} = K(\boldsymbol{x}_i, \boldsymbol{x}_j)$, and $\boldsymbol{y} = (y_1, \ldots, y_N)$.

The solution (3) can be represented by a neural network with one hidden layer, where the hidden units realize kernel functions, and an output linear layer. The choice of a kernel function and types of typical kernels are discussed in the next section.

Once the *meta-parameters* γ and the type of kernel function are fixed, the algorithm is simple and efficient (it reduces to the problem of solving linear system of equations). We perform the search for optimal meta-parameters by genetic algorithm that will be described in Section 4.

3   Multi-Kernels

The kernel function used in a particular application of regularization network is typically supposed to be given in advance, for instance chosen by a user. It reflects our prior knowledge or assumption about the problem and its solution. Therefore its choice is crucial for the quality of the solution and should be always done according to the given task.

What is common to all kernel methods is the way the data are seen by the learning algorithm. Data are not represented individually, but through a set of pair-wise comparisons, realized by the kernel function [6]. The data set $T = \{(\boldsymbol{x}_i, y_i) \in \mathbb{R}^d \times \mathbb{R}\}_{i=1}^{N}$ is presented by $N \times N$ matrix of pair-wise comparisons $K_{ij} = K(\boldsymbol{x}_i, \boldsymbol{x}_j)$ (i.e. matrix K in eq. (3)).

In this context, kernels are often understood as measures of similarity, i.e. the higher $K(\boldsymbol{x}, \boldsymbol{y})$ is, the more similar data points $\boldsymbol{x}$ and $\boldsymbol{y}$ are. The prior knowledge of the problem may suggest suitable similarity measure.

In theory, mostly symmetric and positive-definite functions are considered as kernels. In practice, wider range of functions can be considered, for example in [17], it was demonstrated that kernels which are only conditionally positive definite can possibly outperform classical kernels.

Common examples of kernel functions are:

 - linear $K(\boldsymbol{x}, \boldsymbol{y}) = \boldsymbol{x}^T \boldsymbol{y}$
 - polynomial $(\boldsymbol{x}, \boldsymbol{y}) = (\gamma \boldsymbol{x}^T \boldsymbol{y} + r)^d, \gamma > 0$
 - Gaussian radial basis function $(\boldsymbol{x}, \boldsymbol{y}) = exp(-\gamma||\boldsymbol{x} - \boldsymbol{y}||^2), \gamma > 0$
 - sigmoid $(\boldsymbol{x}, \boldsymbol{y}) = \tanh(\gamma \boldsymbol{x}^T \boldsymbol{y} + r)$

Here, γ, d and r are parameters of the kernel.

All kernels mentioned above work with numerical data. It was pointed out in [18] that kernels make it possible to work with nonvectorial data. This is due to the fact that kernels automatically provide a vectorial representation of the data in the feature space. Some examples on nonvectorial kernels may be found in [19].

In recent years, several methods have been proposed to combine multiple kernels instead of using a single one [7]. These multi-kernel algorithms are mainly designed for SVM learning.

One motivation for multi-kernel approach stems from the multi-modal nature of data. Each set of these features may require a different notion of similarity (i.e., a different kernel). Instead of building a specialized kernel for such applications, is it possible to define just one kernel for each of these modes and linearly combine them.

In our previous work [20–22], we have also proposed composite types of kernel functions to be used in RN learning. Following the reasoning of Aronszajn's breakthrough paper [23], where products, sums and linear combinations of reproducing kernels are considered, it can be easily shown that these types of kernels can be used as activation functions in the regularization networks (cf. [20]). Moreover, kernel functions that are created as a combination of simpler kernel functions might better reflect the character of data.

Let $K_1, \ldots, K_k$ be kernel functions defined on $\Omega_1, \ldots, \Omega_k$ ($\Omega_i \subset \mathbb{R}^{d_i}$), respectively. Let $\Omega = \Omega_1 \times \Omega_2 \times \cdots \times \Omega_k$. The kernel function K defined on Ω that satisfies:

$$K(\boldsymbol{x}_1, \boldsymbol{x}_2, \ldots, \boldsymbol{x}_k, \boldsymbol{y}_1, \boldsymbol{y}_2, \ldots, \boldsymbol{y}_k) = K_1(\boldsymbol{x}_1, \boldsymbol{y}_1) K_2(\boldsymbol{x}_2, \boldsymbol{y}_2) \cdots K_k(\boldsymbol{x}_k, \boldsymbol{y}_k), \quad (4)$$

where $\boldsymbol{x}_i \in \Omega_i$, we call a *product kernel*.

By a *sum kernel* we mean a kernel function K that can be expressed as $K(\boldsymbol{x}, \boldsymbol{y}) = K_1(\boldsymbol{x}, \boldsymbol{y}) + K_2(\boldsymbol{x}, \boldsymbol{y})$, where K_1 and K_2 are kernel functions.

We can combine different kernel functions or two kernel functions of the same type but with different parameters, such as two Gaussians of different widths (note that in this case the Gaussians have the same center).

4   Evolution of Kernels

In our approach we use genetic algorithms (GA) [24] that represent a sound and robust technique to find approximate solutions to optimization and search problems. The use of GA gives us versatility, thus with suitable solution encoding, we can search for different type of kernel units, including product kernels within the framework of one algorithm. The genetic algorithms typically work with a population of *individuals* embodying abstract representations of feasible solutions. Each individual is assigned a *fitness* that expresses a measure of how good solution it represents. The better the solution, the higher the fitness value.

The population evolves towards better solutions. The evolution starts from a population of completely random individuals and iterates in generations. In each generation, the fitness of each individual is evaluated. Individuals are stochastically selected from the current population (based on their fitness), and modified by means of operators *mutation* and *crossover* to form a new population. The new population is then used in the next iteration of the algorithm.

4.1   Encoding

We work with individuals encoding the parameters of the RN learning algorithm. They are the type of kernel function, its additional parameters, and the regularization parameter. When the type of the kernel function is known in advance, the individual consists only of the kernel's parameter (i.e. the width in case of Gaussian kernel) and the regularization parameter.

In case of simple kernel function, the individual is encoded as $I = \{K, p, \gamma\}$, where K is the type of kernel function, and p is a kernel parameter, i.e.

$$I = \{\text{Gaussian}, \text{width} = 0.5, \gamma = 0.01\}.$$

For product kernel function, the individual is $I = \{K_0, p_0, K_1, p_1, i_1, \ldots, i_n, \gamma\}$, where K_0, K_1 are the types of kernel functions, p_0, p_1 are kernel parameters, and $i_1, \ldots, i_n \in \{0, 1\}$ is an index of kernel by which the i-th attribute is processed, i.e

$$I = \{\text{Gaussian}, 0.84, \text{Inverse\_Multiquadric}, 1.58, [0, 0, 1, 0, 1, 1, 1, 1], \gamma = 0.2\}.$$

4.2   Operators

New generations of individuals are created using the operators of *selection*, *crossover* and *mutation*. Mutation operator is implemented as a standard biased mutation introducing small random perturbation to numerical values of existing individuals (by adding a small random float drawn from normal distribution).

The crossover for individuals representing simple kernels of the same type operates as a version of arithmetic crossover, where kernel parameter and γ are subject to the operator. In our case, the new parameters are chosen randomly from the interval formed by the old values, i.e.

$$\gamma = (1 - r)\gamma_1 + r\gamma_2,$$

where $r \in \langle 0, 1 \rangle$ is a random number, γ_1 and γ_2 are parents' values, and γ is the offspring value.

In case of product kernels, the attribute vectors are combined by a one-point crossover and the subkernels are interchanged.

4.3   Fitness

The performance of the resulting network is measured by a *crossvalidation error*, that is generally used as an estimate of a real generalization ability. Then, it can be stated that we search for such meta parameters that optimize the crossvalidation error. As a selection method we use the standard *tournament selection*, where two individuals are randomly selected and the one with the lower crossvalidation error is selected for reproduction.

5 Experimental Results

5.1 Sensor Data

The dataset used for our experiments consists of real-world data from the application area of sensor networks for air pollution monitoring. The data contain tens of thousands measurements of gas multi-sensor MOX array devices recording concentrations of several gas pollutants collocated with a conventional air pollution monitoring station that provides labels for the data. The data are recorded in 1 hour intervals, and there is quite a large number of gaps due to sensor malfunctions. For our experiments we have chosen data from the interval of March 10, 2004 to April 4, 2005, taking into account each hour where records with missing values were omitted. There are altogether 5 sensors as inputs and we have chosen three target output values representing concentrations of CO, NO_2 and NOx.

Table 1. Overview of data sets sizes

Task	train set	test set	Task	train set	test set
sparse CO	1224	6120	CO i1-5	1469	5875
sparse NO2	1233	6160	NO2 i1-5	1479	5914
sparse NOx	1233	6163	NOx i1-5	1480	5916

Table 2. Task 1: Experiment on sparse measurements

Crossvalidation errors

	Gaussian kernel		Product kernels		Sum kernels	
Task	E_{avg}	stddev	E_{avg}	stddev	E_{avg}	stddev
CO	0.152	0.000	**0.148**	0.002	0.152	0.003
NO2	0.429	0.003	**0.407**	0.009	0.434	0.012
NOx	0.227	0.000	**0.207**	0.006	0.229	0.005

Training errors

	Gaussian kernel		Product kernels		Sum kernels	
Task	E_{avg}	stddev	E_{avg}	stddev	E_{avg}	stddev
CO	0.132	0.002	**0.123**	0.005	0.128	0.010
NO2	0.308	0.002	**0.277**	0.025	0.312	0.003
NOx	0.139	0.001	**0.135**	0.011	0.139	0.002

Testing errors

	Gaussian kernel		Product kernels		Sum kernels	
Task	E_{avg}	stddev	E_{avg}	stddev	E_{avg}	stddev
CO	0.136	0.001	**0.134**	0.002	0.138	0.006
NO2	**0.334**	0.002	0.343	0.011	0.338	0.004
NOx	**0.158**	0.001	**0.158**	0.008	0.160	0.005

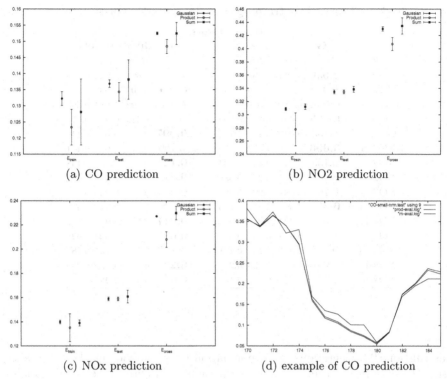

(a) CO prediction

(b) NO2 prediction

(c) NOx prediction

(d) example of CO prediction

Fig. 1. Task 1: Comparison of training, test and crossvalidation errors for various kernels. Prediction of CO values on test data.

In the first experiment, we use spare measurements for training, i.e. the training data consists of 4 samples per day. The rest is then used for testing. This task is easier, since we predict small intervals between measurements.

The second experiment divides the whole time period into five intervals. Then, only one interval is used for training, the rest is again utilized for testing. We considered three different choices of the training part selection. This task may be more difficult, since the prediction is performed also in different parts of the year than the learning, e.g. the model trained on data obtained during winter may perform worse during summer (as was suggested by experts in the application area).

Table 1 brings overview of data sets sizes. All tasks have 5 input values and 1 output (predicted value). All values are normalized between $\langle 0, 1 \rangle$.

5.2   Models and Setting

For both tasks, the genetic algorithm described in the previous section was applied. In the first experiment, regularization networks with Gaussian, product and sum kernels were evolved. In the second experiment, only Gaussian and product kernels were evolved. Among possible subkernels, there were Gaussian, Multiquadric, Inverse-Multiquadric, and Sigmoid functions. Genetic algorithm

Table 3. Task 2: Comparison of **training** errors for networks trained on single epochs

Training errors

Task	Gaussian kernel				Product kernels			
	E_{avg}	stddev	min	max	E_{avg}	stddev	min	max
CO-i1	**0.050**	0.000	0.050	0.050	0.051	0.002	**0.049**	0.055
CO-i2	0.049	0.000	0.049	0.049	**0.046**	0.002	**0.043**	0.050
CO-i3	**0.054**	0.000	**0.053**	0.054	0.056	0.003	0.054	0.065
CO-i4	**0.333**	0.001	0.332	0.334	0.347	0.016	**0.325**	0.378
CO-i5	0.133	0.000	0.132	0.133	**0.097**	0.018	**0.077**	0.142
NO2-i1	**0.096**	0.002	0.093	0.101	0.100	0.015	**0.091**	0.141
NO2-i2	0.133	0.001	0.131	0.134	**0.122**	0.014	**0.105**	0.148
NO2-i3	0.388	0.001	0.384	0.389	**0.314**	0.077	**0.214**	0.434
NO2-i4	0.297	0.002	0.295	0.299	**0.287**	0.012	**0.265**	0.307
NO2-i5	**0.375**	0.001	0.374	0.376	0.389	0.032	**0.330**	0.435
NOx-i1	0.018	0.000	0.018	0.018	**0.017**	0.001	**0.016**	0.020
NOx-i2	0.026	0.000	0.026	0.027	**0.025**	0.002	**0.021**	0.028
NOx-i3	0.156	0.001	0.154	0.158	**0.152**	0.019	**0.121**	0.184
NOx-i4	0.231	0.002	0.229	0.234	**0.230**	0.017	**0.203**	0.258
NOx-i5	0.106	0.023	0.087	0.132	**0.095**	0.011	**0.083**	0.122

was run for 300 generations, with population of 20 individuals. We were also using the elite mechanism heuristics with the size of elite set to 2 individuals. For fitness evaluation, the 10 folds crossvalidation is used.

Errors are computed as follows:

$$E = 100 \frac{1}{N} \sum_{i=1}^{N} \|\boldsymbol{y}_i - f(\boldsymbol{x}_i)\|^2,$$

each computation was repeated 10 times, average errors and their standard deviations were computed.

5.3   Results

Results of the first experiment can be found in Tab. 2 and Fig. 5.1. For second experiment see Tab. 3, Tab. 4, and Fig. 5.3.

In the first task, training was performed only on 4 values per day, the rest of data was left for testing. Tab. 2 lists crossvalidation, training and test errors for networks with evolved Gaussian kernels, product kernels and sum kernels. In terms of crossvalidation and training errors, product kernels provide best fitting. Their generalization ability in terms of test error is more or less the same as for other kernels.

For the second task, the data are divided to 5 epochs, one epoch is used for training, the rest for testing. This is a more difficult tasks, since the prediction is made in periods that were not seen during learning. Training and test errors

Table 4. Task 2: Comparison of **test** errors for networks trained on single epochs.

| | Testing errors | | | | | | | |
| Task | Gaussian kernel | | | | Product kernels | | | |
	E_{avg}	stddev	min	max	E_{avg}	stddev	min	max
CO-i1	**0.210**	0.005	0.205	0.217	0.214	0.020	**0.192**	0.248
CO-i2	1.134	0.007	1.116	1.142	**0.878**	0.088	**0.709**	0.988
CO-i3	0.233	0.009	0.221	0.254	**0.228**	0.019	**0.197**	0.267
CO-i4	**0.326**	0.002	**0.323**	0.329	0.749	0.512	0.433	1.921
CO-i5	**0.296**	0.005	0.287	0.301	0.321	0.050	**0.204**	0.374
NO2-i1	**2.151**	0.052	2.096	2.267	2.263	0.540	**1.189**	2.997
NO2-i2	5.260	0.045	5.161	5.319	**3.928**	1.447	**2.661**	6.874
NO2-i3	**0.718**	0.004	**0.709**	0.721	1.033	0.218	0.764	1.351
NO2-i4	0.735	0.011	0.726	0.757	**0.734**	0.069	**0.669**	0.908
NO2-i5	**0.678**	0.024	**0.655**	0.735	0.913	0.183	0.709	1.302
NOx-i1	2.515	0.015	2.495	2.538	**2.409**	0.159	**2.093**	2.658
NOx-i2	3.113	0.019	3.081	3.139	**2.495**	0.068	**2.416**	2.592
NOx-i3	1.105	0.008	1.088	1.114	**0.956**	0.267	**0.730**	1.689
NOx-i4	**0.952**	0.008	0.941	0.970	1.256	0.520	**0.774**	2.610
NOx-i5	**0.730**	0.102	0.642	0.850	0.748	0.091	**0.544**	0.856

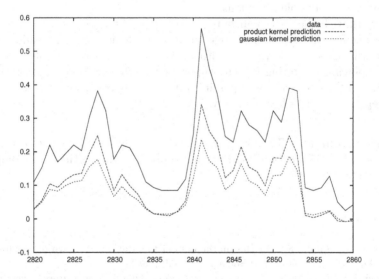

Fig. 2. Task 2: Example of prediction of CO concentration during 40 hours (in period not used for training).

are listed in Tab. 3 and Tab. 4, respectively. Gaussian and product kernels were evolved. Results are similar to the first experiment. In terms of training errors, product kernels were better in 10 cases from 15. In terms of testing errors, products were superior only in 7 cases. Note, that if we compare minimal instead of average values, the product kernels are winning in almost in all cases (except

1 in case of training errors, except 3 in case of test errors). That may indicate there is still space for improvement for the optimal product kernel search.

It is also interesting to note that the resulting product networks are mainly combinations of Gaussian and Inverse-Multiquadric functions.

6   Conclusion

In this work we have proposed a model of product kernel units that constitute a multi-kernel regularization network. A learning algorithm for setting parameters of such a network has been described. This algorithm combines an optimization of linear combination weights of kernel functions with evolutionary search for optimal input split into product kernels, and for the form of kernel functions from the dictionary. The performance of the model has been tested on a real-world approximation problem from sensor measurements of air chemical compounds. The results show that product kernels can provide better results when compared to single-kernel regularization network models.

For the future work we plan to elaborate the evolutionary algorithm in order to address the major drawback of slow performance for large data sets. A hybridization with gradient type local search embedded into evolutionary algorithm might be one of possible directions.

The work with the particular data showed several interesting properties that are relevant for the application area. In order to achieve better results on the data, it will be advisable to deal with missing data in a reasonable way, such as by employing clustering or semi-supervised methods. Also, some statistical properties of the data, such as a possible differences between summer and winter measurements requires further study.

Acknowledgements. This work was partially supported by the Czech Grant Agency grant 15-18108S and institutional support of the Institute of Computer Science RVO 67985807.

References

1. Cucker, F., Smale, S.: On the mathematical foundations of learning. Bulletin of the American Mathematical Society 39, 1–49 (2001)
2. Girosi, F.: An equivalence between sparse approximation and support vector machines. Technical report, Massachutesetts Institute of Technology, A.I. Memo No. 1606 (1997)
3. Girosi, F., Jones, M., Poggio, T.: Regularization theory and Neural Networks architectures. Neural Computation 2(7), 219–269 (1995)
4. Poggio, T., Smale, S.: The mathematics of learning: Dealing with data. Notices of the AMS 50, 536–544 (2003)
5. Kudová, P.: Learning with kernel based regularization networks. In: Information Technologies - Applications and Theory, Košice, Prírodovedecká fakulta Univerzity Pavla Jozefa Šafárika, 83–92 (2005)

6. Vert, J.P., Tsuda, K., Scholkopf, B.: A primer on kernel methods. Kernel Methods in Computati onal Biology, 35–70
7. Gönen, M., Alpaydin, E.: Multiple kernel learning algorithms. J. Mach. Learn. Res. 12, 2211–2268 (2011)
8. Cortes, C.: Invited talk: Can learning kernels help performance? In: Proceedings of the 26th Annual International Conference on Machine Learning, ICML 2009, pp. 1:1–1:1. ACM, New York (2009)
9. Kloft, M., Blanchard, G.: The local rademacher complexity of lp-norm multiple kernel learning. In: Shawe-Taylor, J., Zemel, R., Bartlett, P., Pereira, F., Weinberger, K. (eds.) Advances in Neural Information Processing Systems 24, pp. 2438–2446. Curran Associates, Inc. (2011)
10. Kainen, P.C., Kůrková, V., Sanguineti, M.: Complexity of gaussian radial-basis networks approximating smooth functions. Journal of Complexity 25, 63–74 (2009)
11. Kůrková, V., Kainen, P.C.: Kernel networks with fixed and variable widths. In: Dobnikar, A., Lotrič, U., Šter, B. (eds.) ICANNGA 2011, Part I. LNCS, vol. 6593, pp. 12–21. Springer, Heidelberg (2011)
12. Kůrková, V.: Some comparisons of networks with radial and kernel units. In: Villa, A.E.P., Duch, W., Érdi, P., Masulli, F., Palm, G. (eds.) ICANN 2012, Part II. LNCS, vol. 7553, pp. 17–24. Springer, Heidelberg (2012)
13. Kůrková, V., Kainen, P.C.: Comparing fixed and variable-width gaussian networks. Neural Networks 57, 23–28 (2014)
14. Vito, S.D., Massera, E., Piga, M., Martinotto, L., Francia, G.D.: On field calibration of an electronic nose for benzene estimation in an urban pollution monitoring scenario. Sensors and Actuators B: Chemical 129(2), 750–757 (2008)
15. De Vito, S., Fattoruso, G., Pardo, M., Tortorella, F., Di Francia, G.: Semi-supervised learning techniques in artificial olfaction: A novel approach to classification problems and drift counteraction. IEEE Sensors Journal 12(11), 3215–3224 (2012)
16. Poggio, T., Girosi, F.: A theory of networks for approximation and learning. Technical report, Cambridge, MA, USA, A. I. Memo No. 1140, C.B.I.P. Paper No. 31 (1989)
17. Boughorbel, S., Tarel, J.P., Boujemaa, N.: Conditionally positive definite kernels for svm based image recognition. In: ICME, pp. 113–116 (2005)
18. Schoelkopf, B., Smola, A.J.: Learning with Kernels. MIT Press, Cambridge (2002)
19. Shawe-Taylor, J., Cristianini, N.: Kernel Methods for Pattern Analysis. Cambridge University Press (2004)
20. Kudová, P., Šámalová, T.: Sum and product kernel regularization networks. In: Rutkowski, L., Tadeusiewicz, R., Zadeh, L.A., Żurada, J.M. (eds.) ICAISC 2006. LNCS (LNAI), vol. 4029, pp. 56–65. Springer, Heidelberg (2006)
21. Vidnerová, P., Neruda, R.: Evolutionary learning of regularization networks with product kernel units. In: SMC, pp. 638–643. IEEE (2011)
22. Vidnerová, P., Neruda, R.: Evolving sum and composite kernel functions for regularization networks. In: Dobnikar, A., Lotrič, U., Šter, B. (eds.) ICANNGA 2011, Part I. LNCS, vol. 6593, pp. 180–189. Springer, Heidelberg (2011)
23. Aronszajn, N.: Theory of reproducing kernels. Transactions of the AMS 68, 337–404 (1950)
24. Mitchell, M.: An Introduction to Genetic Algorithms. MIT Press, Cambridge (1996)

Fuzzy Systems and Their Applications

A Fuzzy Approach to Competitive Clusters Using Moore Families

Victor Gerardo Alfaro-Garcia[1(✉)], Anna Maria Gil-Lafuente[1], and Anna Klimova[1]

Faculty of Economics and Business
University of Barcelona, Barcelona, Spain
valfaro06@gmail.com, amgil@ub.edu, klimova4919@hotmail.com

Abstract. Our investigation applies a fuzzy grouping model in order to identify potential enterprise clusters based on their characteristic manufacturing activities in a specific city. The aim is to create clusters towards the construction of competitive advantages, cost reduction and economies of scale. We utilize tools of Fuzzy Sets Theory, evaluating productive capacities of local enterprises under Moore Families. Results conclude in 16 different clusters formed by 2, 3, 4 and 5 firms located in 6 different zones of a specific city. This work seeks to shed light in the conformation of groups under uncertain conditions, and the deep examination of the manufacturing activities in a specific territory for decision and policy making.

Keywords: Fuzzy clustering · Multiple criteria evaluation · Group decision-making · Moore families

1 Introduction

In the last decades the economic openness and globalization has simplified trade barriers making economies more dependent on each other and so affecting the competitiveness of organizations and regions. In this context, governments have been reflecting about competitiveness and sustainable growth, focusing their efforts on the promotion of economic policy as dominating key element to boost the regional development within a worldwide economic context. Competitiveness as center of development strategy has focused the development of cluster initiatives and programs [1] in order to develop competitive environments and create competitive advantages for the existing industrial and business tissues. In this sense, the cluster empowerment initiatives are directed to promote economic development, improve microeconomic business environment, increment productivity and stimulate entrepreneurship and the entry of new business [2,3]. Also, location plays a major role highlighting the conditions of the region as geographic area forming an integrated economic space, which offers distinctive qualities to boost growth.

The objective pursued in this work is especially relevant to emergent economies such as the Mexican market, which since the 1980's has been transiting from a

© Springer International Publishing Switzerland 2015
L. Rutkowski et al. (Eds.): ICAISC 2015, Part I, LNAI 9119, pp. 137–148, 2015.
DOI: 10.1007/978-3-319-19324-3_13

closed economy to an open market strategy. Such external and internal economic liberation has affected in a certain degree to all the enterprises within the territory. The increasing commercial openness and free market treaties signed by the nation have increased the competitive environment in a way that productivity and higher quality of manufactured goods needs to be continuously pursed in order to retain market share.

Our object of study resides in the Mexican city of Morelia, which manufacturing activities have always had a specific weight in the regional context but their qualitative evolution and the policy programs to enhance the productive sectors have not been able to substantially stimulate the potential economic growth of the city. An integral perspective of the industrial tissue is needed in order to surpass the current challenges that the city presents.

In this regard, one of the points on which the decision and policy making process are based on, resides on knowing the competitive advantages of zones and regions, their peculiarities and specificities in order to lead to fruitful cooperation, strategic alliances and added value activities of their enterprise network. In this order of ideas, the primary target of this work consists on finding the possible affinities of enterprises in each zone of a specific city by analysing their manufacturing activities. By doing so firms can identify potential clusters allowing positive synergies and policy makers can lead to infrastructure optimal utilization and suitable development plans.

2   Theoretical Framework

2.1   Competitive Advantages and Clusters

Porter [3] defines an industry cluster as "a set of industries related through buyer-supplier relationships or common technologies, common buyers, distribution channels or common workplace." The author describes two types of clusters: vertical and horizontal clusters. The firsts are made of industries linked through relationships between buyers and sellers, while horizontal groupings are the result of the existence of inter-connections between companies of the same level, in order to share resources.

In recent definitions geographic concentration has been included as an important characteristic of a cluster. Authors like Jacobs & De Man [4] propose three definitions related to the concept of a cluster. The regional cluster, composed of spatially concentrated industries, the sectoral cluster, composed of sectors or groups of sectors and the network clusters, integrated by chains of value.

Porter [5] redefines the concept of cluster incorporating geographic concentration as an important element, as "geographic concentrations of interconnected companies, specialized suppliers, service providers, related industries firms and associated institutions; competing in particular fields but also cooperating". Such definition will be adopted for the purposes of the present research.

The OECD [6] has defined the cluster as a grouping, or local productive system (LPS) in a same region that operate in similar business lines and whose relations foster the development of multiple interdependencies between them, strengthening their competitiveness in a wide variety of areas, such as: training, financial resources, technological development, product design, marketing, distribution and tourism.

It is widely convened that clusters contribute to economic growth as they facilitate an environment of innovation and entrepreneurship that enables profitable growth through increased efficiency, quality and differentiation in goods and services. Such characteristics have a direct impact on competitiveness.

2.2 Studied City

Morelia is a city located in the centre of the Mexican Republic; it is the capital of the state of Michoacán de Ocampo. It is immersed in the Mega – region called "Greater Mexico City", where approximately 45 million people live and generates \$290,000 million in LRP, more than half of the whole nation, Florida [7]. In economic aspects, the city has an overall gross domestic product of 7,774.5 dollars per capita, when the mean in the republic is 9,980 dollars. The city raised its gross domestic product from the 2003 to 2008 by 15 %. The main economic activities of the city are tourism, education and commerce. The city reaches 1,606,399 economically active citizens which 1,554,720 are employed.

Despite the laudable touristic, educational and cultural indicators, the development of the industrial tissue is incipient. In terms of industry, the city has over 16 mining economical units, where around 100 people work, 3143 manufactur-

Table 1. Total Manufacturing Enterprises with 50 Employees or More. *Source:* Inegi [8]

A_1	GS Alimentos de México	C_2 Arpillas de Exportación
A_2	Rafias Industriales	C_3 Sacos de Propileno Especializados
A_3	Sigma Alimentos de Occidente	C_4 Quimic
A_4	Estación la Antigua Valladolid	C_5 Fundidora Morelia
A_5	Infasa	D_1 Harinera Michoacana
A_6	Alstom Mexicana	D_2 Matec
A_7	Andritz Hidro	D_3 El Pino
A_8	De Acero	D_4 Polystrech Ortiz
A_9	Molinos Morelia	D_5 Trico Casa Grande
A_{10}	Tron Hermanos	E_1 Bebidas Purificadas de Michoacán
A_{11}	La Universal Impresora	E_2 Congeladora y Empacadora Nacional
A_{12}	Michoacana de Plásticos	E_3 Fabrica de Trenzados Marinos
A_{13}	Placoyt	F_1 Internacional de Sacos y Arpillas
A_{14}	Agro Metálica Michoacana	F_2 Grupo Papelero Scribe
A_{15}	Comprovet	G_1 Kimberly y Clark de México
A_{16}	Fabricación de Escobas.	G_2 La Voz de Michoacán
B_1	Afrima de Michoacán	G_3 Resinas Sintéticas
B_2	Favetex	G_4 Cartonera de Morelia
B_3	Industrias Jafher	G_5 Fabricas la Central
C_1	Aarhuskarlshamn México	G_6 ULTM de Morelia

ing enterprises where 14,606 people work. In 2008 only 16 licenses for industrial land use were petitioned. The city has an industrial park where 180 enterprises offer around 9,000 employments, most of the enterprises established have only distributing activity and the manufacturing enterprises are small or medium size companies.

In the present study we will take into count all the manufacturing enterprises from the studied city with 51 or more employees. A total of 41 firms were retrieved from the National Statistical Directory of Economic Units [8]. By generating clusters of medium and large enterprises we endorse economies of scale, identification of weak and strong industries and in time, incentive policies.

3   Methodology

We propose the use of Affinities theory and Moore families. Such combination allows us to know the role of the interacting variables at a certain significance level. According to Kaufmann and Gil-Aluja [11] the affinity concept is defined as "those homogeneous characteristics grouped at certain levels, in ordered structures, which link elements of two set of different nature and are related to the phenomena they represent". In this sense, the affinity concept is the core of the mathematical application, which is supported on two main aspects: homogeneity and relationship. The first one refers to each group linked into the selected level. According to the requirements of each characteristic –elements of one of the sets– a more or less high level will be assigned that defines the threshold at which homogeneity exist. The second one expresses the need to link the elements of each of the sets by certain rules of nature, human will and so on [11]. Based on this concept, the methodological procedure is assembled in two steps: the first starts from the original matrix to describe the fuzzy subset [9] and transform it to a Boolean matrix [10] with a threshold $\alpha = n$; in the second phase we proceed to propose an algebraic approach, in which the relation between affinities in Moore families is based [11]. We proceed to define each of the mathematical procedures.

3.1   The Fuzzy Subset of Thresholds

From main matrix of the fuzzy relationship [R], it is possible to demonstrate the range of possibilities to solve several problems of decision, provided that a threshold is established for each criterion, which expresses the degree, from which is considered to possess the required criteria [12]. Hence, fuzzy subset of thresholds is defined:

$$[U] = \begin{array}{cc} C_1 & \boxed{u_1} \\ C_2 & \boxed{u_2} \\ C_3 & \boxed{u_3} \\ \cdots & \boxed{\cdots} \\ C_n & \boxed{u_n} \end{array}$$

$$u_1 \in [0,1], i = 1, 2, \cdots, n$$

This fuzzy subset of thresholds enables a fuzzy relation [R] , to be converted into its Boolean matrix [B], if it is established that:

$$\text{If:} \quad r_{ij} \geq u_i \quad \text{then} \quad b_{ij} = 1; r_{ij} < u_i \quad \text{then} \quad b_{ij} = 0$$
$$j = 1, 2, \ldots, m$$
$$i = 1, 2, \ldots, n$$

Where b_{ij} represents the elements of the Boolean Matrix [B].

3.2 Moore Families

Starting from the concept of "power set" [12], given finite set E_1, its stronger set (power set), $\prod E_1$, is designed as the set formed by all possible combination of its elements taken 1 by 1, 2 by 2, ... m by m, if m is its cardinal. In this way, the set obtained is given by:

$$E_1 = \{a, b, c, \ldots, m\} \tag{1}$$

And set of all its parts or power set is given by:

$$\prod(E_1) = \{\emptyset, a, b, c, \ldots, m, ab, ac, bc, \ldots, mm, E_1\} \tag{2}$$

It is a family of $\prod(E_1)$, as $F(E_1)$, therefore: $F(E_1) \in \prod(E_1)$, if $F(E_1)$ verifies: (1) $E_1 \in F(E_1)$; (2) the intersection of the number of parts of $prod(E_1)$ belongs $F(E_1)$, belongs too $F(E_1)$, is defined by:

$$(A \in F(E_1), B \in F(E_1)) \Rightarrow (A \cap B \in F(E_1)), \tag{3}$$

Therefore $F(E_1)$ is a Moore family.

From a Moore family a Moore closing can be constructed. The Moore closing is a functional application, in which all the components from the subset $A \in E_1$ are made to correspond with a MA, such that:

$$MA = \bigcap_{F \in F_A(E_1)} F \tag{4}$$

Where $F_A(E_1)$ represents the subset of the elements of $F(E_1)$ that contains A and F all elements of $F_A(E_1)$. Note that mathematically to make a Moore closing must be satisfied by the properties of: Extensivity: $\forall A \in \prod(E_1) : A \in MA$; Idempotence: $\forall A \in \prod(E_1) : M(MA) = MA$; Isotony: $\forall A, B \in \prod(E_1) : A \subset B \Rightarrow (MA \subset MB)$, must be satisfied.

3.3 Studied Variables

In the present study we propose seventeen variables that will be used to create clusters of enterprises in different zones within the studied city. Each variable represents the main economic activities that can be developed by a constituted manufacturing firm in the city of Morelia [13]. These variables were chosen as they represent a unified classification system in the Mexican territory, thus results could be repeated and compared with other cities. Table 2. Contains the main manufacturing activities to be evaluated. Table 3. Presents the intensity in which a firm develops a certain manufacturing activity, such intensity is represented with a value between 0 and 1. Being 1 the total capacity of a firm to perform a certain manufacturing activity and 0 the lack of capacity to perform a certain manufacturing activity. The values were calculated based on information retrieved from the National Institute of Statistics [8]. Table 4. Presents the different zones in which firms are located within the city.

Table 2. Manufacturing activities. *Source:* [13]

V_1 Apparel manufacturing
V_2 Machinery and equipment manufacturing
V_3 Beverage and tobacco industries
V_4 Chemical industry
V_5 Food industry
V_6 Petroleum and coal products manufacturing
V_7 Plastic and rubber industry
V_8 Electric appliances, accessories and electric power generation equipment manufacturing
V_9 Basic metal industry
V_{10} Metal products manufacturing
V_{11} Other manufacturing industries
V_{12} Non-metallic mineral products manufacturing
V_{13} Paper industry
V_{14} Printing and related industries
V_{15} Furniture, mattresses and blinds manufacturing
V_{16} Textile inputs manufacturing, and textiles finishing
V_{17} Textile products manufacturing, except apparel

Table 3. Manufacturing Activities Evaluated by Firm. *Source:* Self-elaborated

	V_1	V_2	V_3	V_4	V_5	V_6	V_7	V_8	V_9	V_{10}	V_{11}	V_{12}	V_{13}	V_{14}	V_{15}	V_{16}	V_{17}
A_1			0.5	0.6	1												
A_2												0.4			0.2	0.8	1
A_3			0.4	0.6	1												
A_4						1	0.4										
A_5		0.3			1							0.2					
A_6	0.5							1	0.7			0.7					
A_7	0.3							1	0.5			0.5					
A_8									0.6	1		0.6					
A_9				0.3	1												
A_{10}				0.5	1							0.6					

Table 3. (*Continued*)

	V_1	V_2	V_3	V_4	V_5	V_6	V_7	V_8	V_9	V_{10}	V_{11}	V_{12}	V_{13}	V_{14}	V_{15}	V_{16}	V_{17}
A_{10}				0.5	1						0.6						
A_{11}												0.3					
A_{12}			0.6			1											
A_{13}			0.3			1											
A_{14}	0.6	1									0.2						
A_{15}	0							0.6	1		0.2						
A_{16}	0.5										1						
B_1				0.2	1												
B_2	1	0.7															
B_3														1	0.4	0.7	
C_1			0.4	0.6	1												
C_2														0.3	0.6	1	
C_3							0.5									0.6	1
C_4			0.6	1	0.7												
C_5									1	0.7							
D_1				0.4	1												
D_2														0.3	1	0.6	
D_3			1														
D_4				0.4		1											
D_5				1													
E_1		1	0.5	0.6													
E_2			0.6	0.4	1												
E_3											0.3			0.3	0.6	1	
E_4															0.2	0.7	1
E_5													1				
F_1													1				
F_2														1			
F_3				1			0.6										
F_4													1				
F_5				1													
F_6	0.3									0.5	1						
F_7	0.7	1									0.6						

Table 4. Manufacturing Firms by Zones of the Studied City *Source:* Self-elaborated

Zone	Manufacturing firms
A Industrial Park	A_1 A_2 A_3 A_4 A_5 A_6 A_7 A_8 A_9 A_{10} A_{11} A_{12} A_{13} A_{14} A_{15} A_{16}
B Technologic Institute	B_1 B_2 B_3
C Pedregal	C_1 C_2 C_3 C_4 C_5
D Industrial Colony	D_1 D_2 D_3 D_4 D_5
E State University	E_1 E_2 E_3 E_4 E_5
F South West	F_1 F_2 F_3 F_4 F_5 F_6 F_7

4   Results

Boolean matrices with fuzzy subsets of thresholds are generated according to the models stated in the methodology section. The threshold level is set at $\alpha \geq 0,4$, i.e. the enterprises that develop a specific manufacturing activity with a minimum intensity of 0,4 are included in the model. This threshold is taken firstly with an intention to build clusters capable of generating synergies at different levels, stressing the main intention of building economies of scale, therefore cost reduction.

Table 5. Boolean Matrices by Zones. *Source:* Self-elaborated

B Technologic Institute $\alpha = 0.4$

	V_1	V_2	V_5	V_{15}	V_{17}
B_1	0	0	1	0	0
B_2	1	1	0	0	0
B_3	0	0	0	1	1

C Pedregal $\alpha = 0.4$

	V_3	V_4	V_5	V_7	V_9	V_{10}	V_{16}	V_{17}
C_1	0	1	1	0	0	0	0	0
C_2	0	0	0	0	0	0	1	1
C_3	0	0	0	1	0	0	1	1
C_4	1	1	1	0	0	0	0	0
C_5	0	0	0	0	1	1	0	0

A Industrial Park $\alpha = 0.4$

	V_1	V_2	V_3	V_4	V_5	V_6	V_7	V_8	V_9	V_{10}	V_{11}	V_{14}	V_{16}	V_{17}
A_1	0	0	1	1	1	0	0	0	0	0	0	0	0	0
A_2	0	0	0	0	0	0	0	0	0	0	0	0	1	1
A_3	0	0	0	1	1	0	0	0	0	0	0	0	0	0
A_4	0	0	0	0	0	1	0	0	0	0	0	0	0	0
A_5	0	0	0	1	0	0	0	0	0	0	0	0	0	0
A_6	1	0	0	0	0	0	0	1	1	0	1	0	0	0
A_7	0	0	0	0	0	0	0	1	1	0	1	0	0	0
A_8	0	0	0	0	0	0	0	0	1	1	1	0	0	0
A_9	0	0	0	0	1	0	0	0	0	0	0	0	0	0
A_{10}	0	0	0	1	1	0	0	0	0	0	1	0	0	0
A_{11}	0	0	0	0	0	0	0	0	0	0	0	1	0	0
A_{12}	0	0	0	1	0	0	1	0	0	0	0	0	0	0
A_{13}	0	0	0	0	0	0	1	0	0	0	0	0	0	0
A_{14}	1	1	0	0	0	0	0	0	0	0	0	0	0	0
A_{15}	0	0	0	0	0	0	0	0	1	1	0	0	0	0
A_{16}	1	0	0	0	0	0	0	0	0	0	1	0	0	0

D Industrial Colony $\alpha = 0.4$

	V_4	V_5	V_7	V_{16}	V_{17}
D_1	0	1	0	0	0
D_2	0	0	0	1	1
D_3	1	0	0	0	0
D_4	0	0	1	0	0
D_5	0	1	0	0	0

E State University $\alpha = 0.4$

	V_3	V_4	V_5	V_{13}	V_{16}	V_{17}
E_1	1	1	1	0	0	0
E_2	1	0	1	0	0	0
E_3	0	0	0	0	1	1
E_4	0	0	0	0	1	1
E_5	0	0	0	1	0	0

F South West $\alpha = 0.4$

	V_1	V_2	V_4	V_7	V_{11}	V_{12}	V_{13}	V_{14}
F_1	0	0	0	0	0	0	1	0
F_2	0	0	0	0	0	0	0	1
F_3	0	0	1	1	0	0	0	0
F_4	0	0	0	0	0	0	1	0
F_5	0	0	1	0	0	0	0	0
F_6	0	0	0	0	1	1	0	0
F_7	1	1	0	0	1	0	0	0

Continuing with the procedure, Moore Families are obtained by setting a threshold of $\alpha \geq 0, 4$, following the criteria defined in previous sections:

Table 6. Moore families. *Source :* Self-elaborated

A Industrial Park	C Pedregal	F South West
$E_1, \varnothing$	$E_1, \varnothing$	$E_1, \varnothing$
$V_1\ V_8\ V_9\ V_{11}, A_6$	$V_7\ V_{16}\ V_{17}\ , C_3$	$V_1\ V_2\ V_{11}\ , F_7$
$V_4\ V_5\ V_{11}\ , A_{10}$	$V_9\ V_{10}\ , C_5$	$V_{11}\ V_{12}\ , F_6$
$V_9\ V_{10}\ V_{11}, A_8$	$V_{16}\ V_{17}, C_2$	$V_4\ V_7\ , F_3$
$V_8\ V_9\ V_{11}, A_7$	$V_4\ V_5\ , C_1$	V_{14}, F_2
$V_3\ V_4\ V_5\ , A_1$	$V_{14}, C_2\ C_3$	$V_{13}, F_1\ F_4$
$V_3\ V_{11}, A_{16}$	$V_{16}, C_2\ C_3$	$V_{11}, F_6\ F_7$
$V_9\ V_{10}, A_{15}$	$V_5, C_1\ C_4$	$V_4, F_3\ F_5$
$V_1\ V_2, A_{14}$	$V_4, C_1\ C_4$	$E_2, \varnothing$
$V_4\ V_7, A_{12}$	V_3, C_4	
$V_4\ V_5, A_3$	$E_2, \varnothing$	
$V_{16}\ V_{17}, A_2$		
V_{14}, A_{11}		
$V_{11}, A_6\ A_7\ A_8\ A_{10}\ A_{16}$		
$V_{10}, A_8\ A_{15}$		
$V_9, A_6\ A_7\ A_8\ A_{15}$		
$V_8, A_6\ A_7$		
$V_7, A_{12}\ A_{13}$		
V_6, A_4		
$V_5, A_1\ A_3\ A_9\ A_{10}$		
$V_4, A_1\ A_3\ A_5\ A_{10}\ A_{12}$		
$V_1, A_6\ A_{14}\ A_{16}$		
	$E_2, \varnothing$	

E State University	D Industrial Colony	B Technologic Institute
$E_1, \varnothing$	$E_1, \varnothing$	$E_1, \varnothing$
$V_{16}\ V_{17}, A_4$	$V_{16}\ V_{17}, D_2$	$V_{15}\ V_{17}, B_3$
$V_3, V_4\ V_5, E_1$	V_4, D_3	$V_1\ V_2, B_2$
V_3, V_5, E_2	$V_5, D_1\ D_5$	V_5, B_1
$V_{17}, E_3\ E_4$	V_7, D_4	$E_2, \varnothing$
$V_{16}, E_3\ E_4$	$E_2, \varnothing$	
V_{13}, E_5		
$V_3, E_1\ E_2$		
	$E_2, \varnothing$	

4.1 Analysis of Results

The totality of the manufacturing firms with 50 employees or more of the studied city were introduced to the mathematical model. Results for each zone show similar behaviour, grouping the majority of the enterprises in the second level, i.e. one firm that develops one or more manufacturing activity, however not linked with any other firm. The rest of the levels present a larger amount of firms related to each other. Only Zone A. presents the capacity of conforming clusters with 3 or more enterprises. See Table 7.

Table 7. Aggregated Results (*G: Groups, F: Firms, MA: Manufacturing Activities. Source:*) Self-elaborated

	A Industrial Park			C Pedregal			F South West	
	G F	MA	G F		MA	G F		MA
Level 1	E_1 E_1	E_1	E_1 E_1		E_1	E_1 E_1		E_1
Level 2	13 1	1,2,3,4	5 1		1,2,3	4 1		1,2,3
Level 3	3 2	1	4 2		1	3 2		1
Level 4	1 3	1	E_2 E_2		E_2	E_2 E_2		E_2
Level 5	2 4	1						
Level 6	2 5	1						
Level 7	1 3	1	E_2 E_2		E_2			

	E State University			D Industrial Colony			B Technologic Institute	
	G F	MA	G F		MA	G F		MA
Level 1	E_1 E_1	E_1	E_1 E_1		E_1	E_1 E_1		E_1
Level 2	4 1	1,2,3	3 1		2	3 1		1,2
Level 3	2 2	1	1 2		1	E_2 E_2		E_2
Level 4	E_2 E_2	E_2	E_2 E_2		E_2			

Zone A. being the zone with the largest attraction of manufacturing firms, has achieved 6 levels of groups. The main manufacturing activities displayed are V_1, V_4, V_5, V_9 and V_{11}, showing a preponderance of metal and chemical industry in the zone. The largest groups of enterprises that could create clusters because of their characteristic manufacturing activities are groups of 5 enterprises: A_1, A_3, A_5, A_{10}, A_{12} and A6, A_7, A_8, A_{10}, A_{16}.

Zone B. is the zone with the least amount of enterprises; no group was created be-cause of the dissimilar manufacturing characteristics that firms develop in that specific zone of the city.

Zone C. Presents 2 levels of groups. Main manufacturing activities are V_4, V_4 and V_{16}, V_{17}, i.e. Textile, chemical and food manufacturing activities, 4 different groups of 2 related firms were assembled: C_1, C_4 and C_2, C_3.

Zone D. Exhibits 2 levels of groups. The preponderant manufacturing activity is V5: food industry. Only one cluster was defined: D_1, D_5.

Zone E. Shows 2 levels of groups. Main manufacturing activities are Textile and Beverage and tobacco industries. Clusters were found to be possible: E_3, E_4 and E_1, E_2.

Zone F. Presents 2 levels of groups, the main manufacturing activities in the zone are Paper Industry and other manufacturing activities. From these preponderant activities 2 clusters were generated: F_1, F_4 and F_6, F_7.

Results have a variety of implications; at first instance the preponderant manufacturing activities of firms are concentrated in a few categories. This fact narrows the possibility of large clusters of enterprises. However this opens a new discussion and research agenda as to evaluate the causalities of the poor development of certain manufacturing activities, this could result in opportunities for the progress of the city. The industrial park, as the zone with the largest amount of groups has been effective at attracting enterprises that share common manufacturing activities; however other zones present potential clusters, further research needs to be conducted in order to evaluate the incentives needed to promote the growth of these industries and zones.

5 Conclusion

Results show clusters of enterprises conformed by affinity relationships. Localization within the studied city and related manufacturing activities were the variables chosen to generate groups with a homogeneity level of 60 %. A total of 16 different clusters were obtained in 6 different zones of the city. The preponderant manufacturing activities of the city are concentrated in a few categories such as food, chemical, textile and other manufacturing activities.

Our model is founded on the basic principles of Moore Families, the processes al-low us to group different variables with a certain level of significance. The present work tries to shed a light in the academic world by offering a group based model in which subjective and relative factors are intrinsic for the decision making process. Also this analysis tries to aid decision makers so they can create common policies due to the results of the grouping processes. Further research needs to be conducted, firstly to study the nature of the variables stated to know whether they need to be weighted, and if this weight plays a significant role on the results obtained; secondly further research needs to be conducted in order to analyse results under Galois Group theory in order to achieve a better visualization of the results implications. The model we present can be applied to different locations and it may allow optimizing the process of grouping firms under subjective and uncertain conditions.

References

1. Ketels, C.I.: Recent research on competitiveness and clusters: what are the implications for regional policy? Cambridge Journal of Regions, Economy and Society 6(2), 269–284 (2013)
2. Porter, M.: What is strategy? Harvard Business Review 74(6), 61–78 (1996)
3. Porter, M.E.: The Competitive Advantage of Nations. Harvard Business Review 68, 73–93 (1990)
4. Jacobs, D., De Man, A.: Clusters Industrial policy and firm strategy. Analys & Strategic Mangement (1996)
5. Porter, M.: Clusters and the New Economics of Competition. Harvard Business (2000)
6. OCDE.: Primer Foro sobre Clusters Locales. International Conference on Territorial Development. Organizacin para la Cooperación y el Desarrollo Económico (2001)
7. Florida, R.: Who's Your City? Basic Books, USA (2008)

8. INEGI.: Directorio Estadístico Nacional de Unidades Económicas, http://www.inegi.org.mx
9. Gil Lafuente, J.: Marketing para el nuevo milenio: nuevas técnicas para la gestión comercial en la incertidumbre, p. 476. Ediciones Pirámide, Barcelona (1997)
10. Gil Lafuente, A.M.: Nuevas estrategias para el análisis financiero en la empresa, p. 480. Ariel, Barcelona (2001)
11. Gil Aluja, J.: Elements for a theory of decision in uncertainty, p. 347. Kluwer Academic Publishers, Dordrecht (1999)
12. Gil Aluja, J.: Towards a new paradigm of investment selection in uncertainty. Fuzzy Sets and Systems 84(2), 187–197 (1996)
13. INEGI. North American Industry Classification System, Mexico. Methodological synthesis. SCIAN 2013 (2013), http://www3.inegi.org.mx (retrieved 2014)

A Fingerprint Retrieval Technique Using Fuzzy Logic-Based Rules

Rosario Arjona$^{(\boxtimes)}$ and Iluminada Baturone

Microelectronics Institute of Seville (IMSE-CNM),
University of Seville and Spanish National Research Council (CSIC), Seville, Spain
{arjona,lumi}@imse-cnm.csic.es

Abstract. This paper proposes a global fingerprint feature named QFingerMap that provides fuzzy information about a fingerprint image. A fuzzy rule that combines information from several QFingerMaps is employed to register an individual in a database. Error and penetration rates of a fuzzy retrieval system based on those rules are similar to other systems reported in the literature that are also based on global features. However, the proposed system can be implemented in hardware platforms of very much lower computational resources, offering even lower processing time.

Keywords: Fingerprint retrieval · Fuzzy rules · Low computational cost

1 Introduction

A fingerprint identification system requires to compare the query fingerprint against all the fingerprints registered in a database. This operation can be very time consuming if the comparison process is complex and the database is large (several millions of fingerprints can be registered in forensic and government applications) [1]. The objective of retrieval techniques is to apply a complex comparison process to a small number of registered individuals instead of considering the whole database.

Several retrieval techniques have been proposed in the literature. They can be grouped into techniques based on *Exclusive Classification* and based on *Continuous Classification*. In the *Exclusive Classification*, fingerprints are grouped into pre-defined disjoint classes (each fingerprint is associated to one class). The most common fingerprint classification, which was proposed in [2] and extended in [3], distinguishes five fingerprint classes (arch, whorl, tended arch, left loop, and right loop). The problem is that most of fingerprints are only distributed into three classes (right loop, left loop, and whorl) and the number of comparisons are not reduced enough for a large fingerprint database [1]. In addition, determining the correspondence between a fingerprint and a class is usually a fuzzy and ambiguous operation, even for a human. *Continuous Classification* is more suitable to cope with such fuzziness. It consists of two phases: (1) in the indexing phase, a numeric vector (an index) is stored in the database to register a fingerprint; (2) in the retrieving phase, a list of M candidates are selected

© Springer International Publishing Switzerland 2015
L. Rutkowski et al. (Eds.): ICAISC 2015, Part I, LNAI 9119, pp. 149–159, 2015.
DOI: 10.1007/978-3-319-19324-3_14

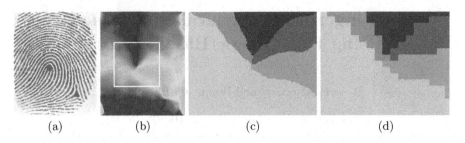

(a)   (b)   (c)   (d)

Fig. 1. Features extracted from a fingerprint image: (a) Singular points, (b) Directional image, (c) Segmented directional image of the window depicted in (b), and (d) QFingerMap.

among the N stored candidates based on a simple comparison process between the N stored indices and the index of the query fingerprint [4].

Fingerprints, which are represented by ridges (defined by black colors in Fig. 1(a)) and valleys (defined by bright colors in Fig. 1(a)), are captured with a high variability because individuals do not always place their fingers on the sensors in the same way. Hence, the extraction of distinctive as well as simple indices to be stored and compared is not an easy task. Local features such as the traditional minutiae (which mean small details) require a detailed analysis of the fingerprint image to detect endings (ridges which end) and bifurcations (ridges which are divided into two ridges). In contrast, global features require a coarser analysis. An example is the directional image (also known as orientation image, field or map, or directional field or map), which contains the ridge orientations at the pixels (orientations are represented by colors in Fig. 1(b)). Other global features are the singular points (depicted in Fig. 1(a)): cores which are the points where ridges converge (represented by a circle in Fig. 1(a)) or deltas which are the points where ridges diverge (represented by a triangle in Fig. 1(a)).

Minutiae give high accuracy for identification purposes [5] [6] [7], but the extraction process of minutiae is complex. Fuzzy rule-based systems have been proposed for minutiae extraction [8], selection of the optimal set of minutiae [7], and minutia-based fingerprint matching [9]. For a retrieval application, whose objective is to find a small number of candidates with very low effort, global features offer acceptable recognition results with low computational complexity [10] [11] [12] [13]. Fuzzy rule-based systems have also been employed for directional image description [14], and to classify fingerprints based on textures [15].

This paper proposes a new global feature named QFingerMap that provides fuzzy information of the fingerprint image. Instead of registering the finger of an individual by a crisp index, a finger is registered by a fuzzy rule whose antecedent part considers the QFingerMaps that can be extracted from it. Given a query finger, several rules will be activated at certain degree. A list of possible candidates can be obtained from the activation degree of the rules.

The paper is organized as follows. Section 2 describes the extraction of the feature QFingerMap and the fuzzy rule base that employs it. Section 3 summarizes the design decisions taken to extract QFingerMaps and evaluates the performance of the rule base with two fingerprint databases. Results are compared to other approaches proposed in literature. Finally, Section 4 gives conclusions.

2   Fuzzy Retrieval System

2.1   Fuzzy Fingerprint Feature

As commented in Introduction, the directional image contains information about the tangent directions, $D(i,j)$, to the ridges at the pixels of the fingerprint. Horizontal, G_x, and vertical, G_y, gradients can be computed by using different filters such as Sobel, Gaussian, or Prewitt. The values of G_x and G_y are usually obtained after the convolution of a window centered at each pixel with the horizontal and vertical filter matrix. The fingerprint image should be enhanced, and gradient values should be combined, averaged, and smoothed in order to remove incorrect directions because the computation of the directional image is sensitive to noise in fingerprint images. The method reported in [16], and implemented in [17], can be summarized as follows:

$$D(i,j) = \frac{\pi}{2} + \frac{\arctan\left(\frac{sin2theta(i,j)}{cos2theta(i,j)}\right)}{2} \qquad (1)$$

where:

$$sin2theta(i,j) = \frac{G_{xy}(i,j)}{\sqrt{G_{xy}(i,j)^2 + (G_{xx}(i,j) - G_{xy}(i,j))^2}} \qquad (2)$$

$$cos2theta(i,j) = \frac{G_{xx}(i,j) - G_{xy}(i,j)}{\sqrt{G_{xy}(i,j)^2 + (G_{xx}(i,j) - G_{xy}(i,j))^2}} \qquad (3)$$

$$G_{xx}(i,j) = G_x(i,j) \cdot G_x(i,j) \,; G_{xy}(i,j) = G_x(i,j) \cdot G_y(i,j) \,; \\ G_{yy}(i,j) = G_y(i,j) \cdot G_y(i,j) \qquad (4)$$

The direction values are obtained after applying three Gaussian filters to the computation of: (1) gradient values (G_x and G_y); (2) covariance data of the image gradients (G_{xx}, G_{xy} and G_{yy}); and (3) sine and cosine of the double angles (*sin2theta* and *cos2theta*).

Since most of discrimination information in the directional image is around the convex core, let us consider a window of BxC pixels centered at the convex core (as depicted in Fig. 1(b)). If such a window is employed to extract a global feature and each direction value is encoded with 8 bits, the number of bits to store per fingerprint is BxCx8. An study was carried out to simplify not only the number of bits to store (in order to reduce memory requirements of the retrieval system) but also the computational cost of extracting the fingerprint feature (in order to reduce processing time and/or hardware cost).

The first simplification considered to reduce memory is to cluster the continuous direction values in the range $[0°, 180°]$ into several representative directions. For example, if 8 representative directions are considered, the result is that the number of bits to store is reduced to $BxCx3$ (plus 8x8 to store the values of the representative directions). Clustering techniques have been employed to classify fingerprints [18]. However, those clustering techniques, which are based on a genetic algorithm, increase the processing time considerably. The clustering algorithm considered in our case is K-means, which finds K representative directions, $V = (v_1, v_2, ..., v_K)$, among the BxC directions, by minimizing the following target function.

$$J[V; X] = \sum_{i=1}^{K} \sum_{j=1}^{BxC} d(x_j, v_i) \tag{5}$$

where $d(x_j, v_i)$ is the distance between the directions and the representative directions (or prototypes).

The K-means algorithm with different values of K was applied to directional images of the fingerprints of two databases. One of them is the public and standard database FVC 2000 DB2a [19], with 800 fingerprints (from 100 fingers and 8 samples from each finger) captured by a capacitive sensor. The other database was created by the authors for on-line recognition. It consists of 560 fingerprints (from 112 fingers and 5 samples from each finger) captured by an optical sensor. An interesting result is that the prototypes found for each fingerprint are, in general, different from the representative directions of another fingerprint. However, the values are similar. For example, for $K=8$, the mean values of the representative directions found in the fingerprints of the FVC 2000 DB2a were $13.37°$, $35.15°$, $51.65°$, $68.57°$, $84.98°$, $101.48°$, $117.71°$, and $139.53°$, while they were $15.20°$, $39.33°$, $56.94°$, $76.19°$, $97.24°$, $117.89°$, $138.74°$, and $164.26°$ for the fingerprints of the on-line database. Since the mean values were very similar for many fingerprints, the second simplification considered was to employ a set of K fixed and equispaced prototypes. For example, for $K=8$, the following prototypes are considered: $11.25°$, $33.75°$, $56.25°$, $78.75°$, $101.25°$, $123.75°$,

Table 1. Processing to obtain symbols from gradient values

IF	THEN
$(\|G_x\| = 0\ OR\ \|G_y\| \geq 2.413 \cdot \|G_x\|)\ AND\ G_x \cdot G_y \geq 0$	Symbol is 0
$(\|G_x\| = 0\ OR\ \|G_y\| \geq 2.413 \cdot \|G_x\|)\ AND\ G_x \cdot G_y < 0$	Symbol is 1
$(\|G_x\| = 0\ OR\ \|G_y\| < 0.414 \cdot \|G_x\|)\ AND\ G_x \cdot G_y \geq 0$	Symbol is 2
$(\|G_x\| = 0\ OR\ \|G_y\| < 0.414 \cdot \|G_x\|)\ AND\ G_x \cdot G_y < 0$	Symbol is 3
$(\|G_y\| < \|G_x\|\ AND\ \|G_y\| \geq 0.414 \cdot \|G_x\|)\ AND\ G_x \cdot G_y \geq 0$	Symbol is 4
$(\|G_y\| < \|G_x\|\ AND\ \|G_y\| \geq 0.414 \cdot \|G_x\|)\ AND\ G_x \cdot G_y < 0$	Symbol is 5
$(\|G_y\| \geq \|G_x\|\ AND\ \|G_y\| < 2.413 \cdot \|G_x\|)\ AND\ G_x \cdot G_y \geq 0$	Symbol is 6
$(\|G_y\| \geq \|G_x\|\ AND\ \|G_y\| < 2.413 \cdot \|G_x\|)\ AND\ G_x \cdot G_y < 0$	Symbol is 7

146.25°, and 168.75°. Each prototype can be represented by a symbol from 0 to 7, encoded with 3 bits.

The main advantage of the second simplification is the high reduction of computational cost. Not only the prototypes should not be computed (using Equation (5)) but also no trigonometric, powering or square-rooting operations are needed. Once gradient values, G_x and G_y, are obtained, they are compared to determine directly which symbol is associated to each pixel. Hence, complex operations and subsequent clustering is reduced to simple comparisons between gradient values as shown in Table 1.

As in any technique that calculates directional images, smoothing process is also required to obtain homogeneous direction regions. Among the wide set of filters that can be used to perform smoothing [1], a non linear filter based on maximum operator has been selected. It considers the neighboring pixels inside a SxS window centered at the analyzed pixel and assigns it the symbol value with the highest number of occurrences inside the window. The result after smoothing with a 27x27 window is shown in Fig. 1(c) (each representative direction is defined by a color).

The third simplification considered to reduce memory is to apply downsampling in order to remove possible redundant information. A simple way is to take 1 between n consecutive pixels (downsampling by a factor of n), being the pixels swept in the BxC window of the segmented directional image from left to right and from up to bottom. Fig. 1(d) shows the result after applying a downsampling factor of 8.

The simplifications considered result in a fuzzy fingerprint feature that is advantageous in terms of memory required to be stored as well as processing time to be extracted. This feature is named QFingerMap because it is a map of directions whose extraction process is quick. Table 2 shows a comparison in terms of memory and processing time between the initial and final fingerprint features commented above. The results in the first row correspond to a global feature obtained from a 129x129 window centered at the convex core and formed by the direction values calculated as in Equations 1 to 4 and post-processed as done in [17]. The results in the second row correspond to a QFingerMap obtained from a 129x129 window, using 8 representative directions, and a downsampling factor of 8 (as shown in Fig. 1(d)). While the directional image was extracted using a platform with an Intel i7 processor running at 3.20 GHz, the QFingerMap was extracted using dedicated hardware in a Field Programmable Gate Array (FPGA) running at 25 MHz. The gain in memory and time does not mean a loss of distinctiveness, as will be described in Section 3.

2.2   Fuzzy Rule Base

A QFingerMap is invariant to translations because it is centered at the convex core but it changes if the finger is placed on the sensor with a different orientation. Fig. 2 illustrates examples of QFingerMaps extracted from fingerprints from the same and different fingers. Hence, several QFingerMaps should be extracted from the same finger to take into account the variability of the captures.

Table 2. Comparison between features based on directional image and QFingerMap

Fingerprint Feature	Platform	Memory (bits)	Time (ms)	Gain in Memory	Gain in Time
Directional Image	Intel i7 @ 3.20 GHz	129x129x8	240	x1	x1
QFingerMap	Virtex 6 FPGA @ 25 MHz	17x17x3	23	x154	x10

Table 3. Classification fuzzy rules for the retrieval system

IF	THEN
QFM' is QFM_{11} OR ... OR QFM' is QFM_{1R}	Individual 1
...	...
QFM' is QFM_{N1} OR ... OR QFM' is QFN_{NR}	Individual N

If R is the number of captures considered, QFM_{t1}, ..., QFM_{tR} are extracted to register the finger of the t-th individual. An intuitive way to evaluate if a query QFingerMap, QFM', corresponds to a registered individual is to apply the if-then rules in Table 3. The if-then rules can be seen as classification rules based on matching fuzzy patterns [20] where the fuzzy patterns are the QFingerMaps. The rules' antecedents used in the fuzzy system employed with the FVC 2000 DB2a combines three QFingerMaps for each individual. If one fingerprint image is captured from each individual in the enrollment process, the first QFingerMap in the rule's antecedent is extracted from that image, the second QFingerMap is extracted from that image rotated 11.25° clockwise, and the third QFingerMap is extracted from the image rotated 11.25° counterclockwise. The rules' antecedents used in the on-line database only employs one QFingerMap for each fingerprint image (because the sensor employed forced the user to introduce the finger always with the same orientation).

Since a QFingerMap is a fuzzy fingerprint feature, if the query QFingerMap has been extracted from the finger of the t-th individual, QFM' should be similar to at least one of the QFM_{t1}, ..., QFM_{tR}, but, surely, it will not be identical to any of them. The similarity between two QFingerMaps can be evaluated by

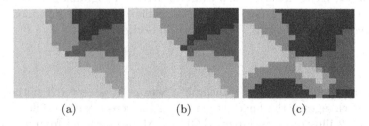

(a)   (b)   (c)

Fig. 2. (a) and (b) QFingerMaps of fingerprints from the same finger but different captures, and (c) from a different finger.

using many measures. In our case, since the retrieval process should be fast, the following simple measure has been selected.

$$similarity(QFM', QFM) = 1 - \frac{1}{W} \sum_{i=1}^{W} d_i(QFM', QFM) \qquad (6)$$

where $QFM' = (v'_1, ..., v'_W)$, $QFM = (v_1, ..., v_W)$, and

$$d_i(QFM', QFM) = \begin{cases} 1 \text{ if } v'_i \neq v_i \\ 0 \text{ otherwise} \end{cases} \qquad (7)$$

Similarity ranges from 0, which means that all the symbols (or representative directions, v_i and v'_i) assigned to the pixels in the same location are different, to 1, which means that all the symbols are the same. For example, Fig. 3 shows the similarities between a query QFingerMap and the QFingerMaps in two rules' antecedents.

The rules' antecedents combine the similarity degrees between QFingerMaps by a disjunctive conjunction, OR. As usual in fuzzy rule bases, the s-norm maximum has been selected as OR operator. Hence, the activation degree of each rule is computed as follows.

$$activation\_degree_{rule_t} =$$
$$max_{r=1,...,R}\left\{ similarity(QFM', QFM_{tr}) \right\} \qquad (8)$$

The conclusion provided by the rule base can be an individual or a set of candidates (M). In the first case, the consequence (the individual) of the most activated rule is selected. In the second case, a set of M individuals are given, each of them with the certainty of being the true candidate given by the activation degree of its corresponding rule, as illustrated in Fig. 3.

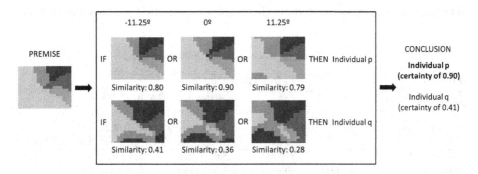

Fig. 3. Example of inference with two fuzzy rules.

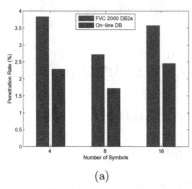 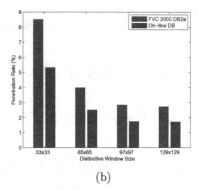

(a)   (b)

Fig. 4. (a) Influence of number of symbols and (b) distinctive window size of QFingerMaps in the Penetration Rate.

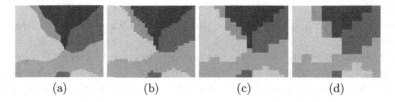

(a)   (b)   (c)   (d)

Fig. 5. (a)-(d) Influence of several downsampling factors in the extraction of a QFingerMap: (a) 1, (b) 4, (c) 8, and (d) 16.

3 Design and Evaluation of the Fuzzy Retrieval System

The design decisions taken to extract the QFingerMaps and define the rules were based on evaluating the main performance indicators of a retrieval system. Performance indicators depend on the indexing scenario. In a *Non Incremental Search* scenario (where the candidate list is truncated to M) there is a trade-off between *Error Rate* and *Penetration Rate*. *Error Rate* is the percentage of searched fingerprints (rules in this case) whose mate is not present in the candidate list and *Penetration Rate* is the portion of the rule base that the system

Table 4. Time to search among 2000 individuals

Feature	Time (ms)	Platform
QFingerMap	23	Virtex 6 FPGA @ 25 MHz
Orientations and Frequencies [12]	67	Intel Pentium 4 @ 2.26 GHz
Orientations and Frequencies [10]	1.6	Intel Core 2 Quad @ 2.26 GHz
Minutiae [6]	1400	Intel Xeon @ 1.7 GHz (PCI @ 33 MHz)
Minutiae Triplets [5]	1000	Sun Ultra 2 @ 143 MHz
Minutiae Cylinder Code [21]	90000	Intel Pentium 4 @ 2.8 GHz

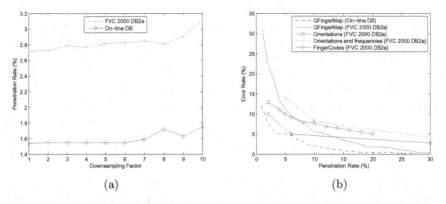

Fig. 6. (a) Penetration Rate depending on downsampling factor. (b) Tradeoff between Penetration Rate and Error Rate for different fingerprint features.

has to search on the average (M/N). The objective is a low *Error Rate* with a low *Penetration Rate* but the problem is that *Error Rate* increases as M is smaller. In an *Incremental Search* scenario, there are not retrieval errors because the candidate list is not truncated. The search finishes as soon as the true mate is retrieved. The worst case is when the corresponding mate is in the rule with the lowest activation degree. For an *Incremental Search* scenario, the only performance indicator is *Penetration Rate* [4].

The recognition and discrimination capability offered by QFingerMaps depend on the number of symbols considered. Fig. 4(a) shows the Penetration Rates obtained for different number of symbols (representative directions) and fingerprint databases. 4, 8 and 16 symbols were studied. 4 symbols offered limited information to distinguish individuals. 8 symbols offered finer information. 16 symbols did not imply to improve the discrimination capability because they increased intra-class variations, that is, representations of captures from the same finger were more different. Hence, 8 symbols were selected as the best option.

The resulting image after the symbol assignation should be smoothed to remove isolated and noisy direction values. Several smoothing window sizes were analyzed: 3x3 smoothing, 9x9 smoothing, and 27x27 smoothing. The last smoothing was selected because a 27x27 window provided good performance for the different types of sensors analyzed.

The influence of the size of the singular area (BxC) in the Penetration Rates was also analyzed. The best results were provided by a 129x129 window as illustrated in Fig. 4(b). Smaller window sizes did not contain information enough while sizes larger than 129x129 could not be analyzed in many fingerprint images. For example, enlarging the window size from 129x129 to 257x257 implies increasing the number of fingerprint images with uncompleted windows from 18.6% to 100% in the FVC 2000 DB2a database, and from 4.1% to 48.2% in the fingerprint database created for on-line recognition. For most fingerprint sensors, which capture a fingerprint size of approximately, 300x300 pixels, 129x129 is a suitable size.

Fig. 5 shows different QFingerMaps resulting from different downsampling factors applied to a 129x129 window. If the downsampling factor is high, discriminative information is removed. This is illustrated in terms of Penetration Rate in Fig. 6(a). A downsampling factor of 8 was selected, which means a QFingerMap with 17x17 symbols. If the symbols are encoded with 3 bits then the 17x17 symbol vector requires 867 bits (17x17x3 bits), as shown in Table 2.

According to a non incremental search scenario, the tradeoff between Error Rate and Penetration Rate was evaluated. Fig. 6(b) shows the results obtained with the two databases considered and compares the results with other approaches reported in the literature [11] [12] [13]. The designed fuzzy retrieval system offers competitive performance.

The first row in Table 4 shows the time to search among 2000 individuals using the proposed technique implemented in a FPGA working at 25 MHz. The other rows in Table 4 show the time reported in the literature using other techniques based on both global and local features, implemented in other hardware platforms.

4   Conclusions

Despite the simplicity of the fingerprint feature proposed, processing of fuzzy information by using fuzzy rules is able to find the individual in a database with competitive error and penetration rates. This has been analyzed with two fingerprint databases. The fuzzy retrieval system implemented in a Virtex 6 FPGA provides low processing time even working at low frequency.

Acknowledgments. This work has been partially supported by TEC2011-24319 and IPT-2012-0695-390000 projects from the Ministry of Economy and Competitiveness of the Spanish Government (with support from the PO FEDER-FSE). The work of R. Arjona has been supported by a Post-Doc Fellowship from the Regional Government of Andalusia.

References

1. Maltoni, D., Maio, D., Jain, A.K., Prabhakar, S.: Handbook of Fingerprint Recognition. Springer (2009)
2. Galton, F.: Finger Prints. Macmillan and Co. (1892)
3. Henry, E.: Classification and Uses of Finger Prints. George Routledge and Sons (1892)
4. Cappelli, R., Ferrara, M.: A Fingerprint Retrieval System based on Level-1 and Level-2 Features. Expert Systems with Applications: An International Journal 38(12), 10465–10478 (2012)
5. Bhanu, B., Tan, X.: Fingerprint Indexing based on Novel Features of Minutiae Triplets. IEEE Transactions on Pattern Analysis and Machine Intelligence 25(5), 616–622 (2003)
6. Chung, Y., Kim, K., Kim, M., Pan, S., Park, N.: A Hardware Implementation for Fingerprint Retrieval. In: Khosla, R., Howlett, R.J., Jain, L.C. (eds.) KES 2005. LNCS (LNAI), vol. 3683, pp. 374–380. Springer, Heidelberg (2005)

7. Iancu, I., Constantinescu, N.: Intuitionistic Fuzzy System for Fingerprints Authentication. Applied Soft Computing 13, 2136–2142 (2013)
8. Sagai, V.K., Koh Jit Beng, A.: Fingerprint Feature Extraction by Fuzzy Logic and Neural Networks. In: 6th International Conference on Neural Information Processing (ICONIP 1999), vol. 3, pp. 1138–1142. IEEE Press, New York (1999)
9. Chen, X., Tian, J., Yang, X.: A New Algorithm for Distorted Fingerprints Matching Based on Normalized Fuzzy Similarity Measure. IEEE Transactions on Image Processing 15(3), 767–776 (2006)
10. Cappelli, R.: Fast and Accurate Fingerprint Indexing based on Ridge Orientation and Frequency. IEEE Transactions on Systems, Man, and Cybernetics, Part B: Cybernetics 41(6), 1511–1521 (2011)
11. de Boer, J., Bazen, A.M., Gerez, S.H.: Indexing Fingerprint Databases based on Multiple Features. In: Proceedings of the 12th Annual Workshop on Circuits, Systems and Signal Processing Workshop (ProRISC 2001), pp. 300–306 (2001)
12. Jiang, X., Liu, M., Kot, A.C.: Fingerprint Retrieval for Identification. IEEE Transactions on Information Forensics and Security 1(4), 532–542 (2006)
13. Leung, K.C., Leung, C.H.: Improvement of Fingerprint Retrieval by Statistical Classifier. IEEE Transactions on Information Forensics and Security 6(1), 59–69 (2011)
14. Arjona, R., Gersnoviez, A., Baturone, I.: Fuzzy Models for Fingerprint Description. In: Petrosino, A. (ed.) WILF 2011. LNCS, vol. 6857, pp. 228–235. Springer, Heidelberg (2011)
15. Galar, M., Sanz, J., Pagola, M., Bustince, H., Herrera, F.: A Preliminary Study on Fingerprint Classification Using Fuzzy Rule-based Classification Systems. In: Proceedings of the IEEE International Conference on Fuzzy Systems (FUZZ-IEEE), pp. 554–560 (2014)
16. Bazen, A.M., Gerez, S.H.: Systematic Methods for the Computation of the Directional Fields and Singular Points of Fingerprints. IEEE Transactions on Pattern Analysis and Machine Intelligence 24(7), 905–919 (2002)
17. Software Implementation for Directional Image Extraction (2011), http://www.csse.uwa.edu.au/~pk/research/matlabfns/FingerPrints/ridgeorient.m
18. Cappelli, R., Lumini, A., Maio, D., Maltoni, D.: Fingerprint Classification by Directional Image Partitioning. IEEE Transactions on Pattern Analysis and Machine Intelligence 21(5), 402–421 (1999)
19. Fingerprint Verification Competition-onGoing (2013), https://biolab.csr.unibo.it/fvcongoing/UI/Form/Home.aspx
20. Pedrycz, W.: Fuzzy Sets in Pattern Recognition: Methodology and Methods. Pattern Recognition 23(1/2), 121–146 (1990)
21. Cappelli, R., Ferrara, M., Maltoni, D.: Minutia Cylinder-Code: A New Representation and Matching Technique for Fingerprint Recognition. IEEE Transactions on Pattern Analysis and Machine Intelligence 32, 2128–2141 (2010)

Initial Comparison of Formal Approaches to Fuzzy and Rough Sets

Adam Grabowski[✉] and Takashi Mitsuishi

[1] Institute of Informatics, University of Białystok
Ciołkowskiego 1M, 15-245 Białystok, Poland
adam@math.uwb.edu.pl
[2] University of Marketing and Distribution Sciences, Kobe
3-1 Gakuen Nishimachi, Nishi-ku, Kobe 655-2188, Japan
takashi_mitsuishi@red.umds.ac.jp

Abstract. Fuzzy sets and rough sets are well-known approaches to incomplete or imprecise data. In the paper we compare two formalizations of these sets within one of the largest repositories of computer-checked mathematical knowledge – the Mizar Mathematical Library. Although the motivation was quite similar in both developments, these approaches – proposed by us – vary significantly. Paradoxically, it appeared that fuzzy sets are much closer to the set theory implemented within the Mizar library, while in order to make more feasible view for rough sets we had to choose relational structures as a basic framework. The formal development, although counting approximately 15 thousand lines of source code, is by no means closed – it allows both for further generalizations, building on top of the existing knowledge, and even merging of these approaches. The paper is illustrated with selected examples of definitions, theorems, and proofs taken from rough and fuzzy set theory formulated in the Mizar language.

1 Introduction

Through the years, we can observe the evolution of mathematics from the classical paper-based model in the direction of use of computers. As fuzzy set theory proposed by Zadeh [24] offered new mathematical insight for the real data in the world of uncertain or incomplete information, dealing mainly with those contained in digital archives, it is not surprising that similar methods will be used in order to obtain the properties of objects within the theory itself.

The original approach to fuzzy numbers met some criticism and various ways of improvement were offered as yet. But usually computers serve as an assistant offering calculations – why not to benefit from their more artificial intelligence strength? We try to address some issues concerned with the digitization of this specific fragment of fuzzy set theory, representing a path to ordered fuzzy numbers, so it can be considered as a case study in a knowledge management, being a work on fuzzy sets in the same time.

The paper is organized as follows. In the next section we describe a kind of scenario for our formalization. The third section is devoted specifically to the

© Springer International Publishing Switzerland 2015
L. Rutkowski et al. (Eds.): ICAISC 2015, Part I, LNAI 9119, pp. 160–171, 2015.
DOI: 10.1007/978-3-319-19324-3_15

situation in the area of computer-checked formalization of mathematics and contains a brief primer to formal fuzzy sets; in the fourth we gave a brief description of the alternative approach – rough set theory. The other two sections explain specific issues we met during our work with a more detailed study of dissimilarities between approaches, while the final brings some concluding remarks and the plans for future work.

2   The Motivation: Bridging a Route to OFNs

Usually, the formalization challenge should have a sort of a lighthouse – clearly visible target; sometimes, especially for a larger group of collaborators it is a tough theorem or chosen textbook. We aimed at getting to the OFN because only from broader perspective one can see if the developed approach was really flexible and reusable. Obviously, we aim also at the formal comparison of the two models. Ordered Fuzzy Numbers (OFN) were introduced by Kosiński, Prokopowicz and Ślęzak in 2002 [15,16] as the extension of the parametric representation of convex fuzzy numbers. Unquestionable advantage of OFN is that, in contrast to classical fuzzy numbers proposed by Dubois and Prade [2], they do not suffer from unexpected and uncontrollable results of repeatedly applied operations.

In this approach, an ordered fuzzy number is defined as a pair of continuous functions, (f, g) which domains are the intervals $[0, 1]$ and values are in $\mathbb{R}$. The continuity of both functions implies their images are bounded intervals, call them UP and $DOWN$, respectively. We can mark boundaries as $UP = [l_A, 1_A^-]$ and $DOWN = [1_A^+, p_A]$. In general, the functions f, g need not to be invertible, only continuity is required. If we add the constant function on the interval $[1_A^-, 1_A^+]$ with its value equal to 1, we might define the membership function

$$\mu(x) = \mu_{up}(x), \text{ if } x \in [l_A, 1_A^-] = [f(0), f(1)], \tag{1}$$
$$\mu(x) = \mu_{down}(x), \text{ if } x \in [1_A^+, p_A] = [g(1), g(0)] \text{ and}$$
$$\mu(x) = 1 \text{ when } x \in [1_A^-, 1_A^+]$$

if

1. $f \leq g$ are both invertible, i.e. inverse functions $f^{-1} =: \mu_{up}$ and $g^{-1} =: \mu_{down}$ exist and
2. f is increasing, and g is decreasing.

The membership function obtained in this way $\mu(x), x \in \mathbb{R}$ represents a mathematical object which reminds a convex fuzzy number in the classical sense [12].

3   Fuzzy Sets Treated Formally

We were surprised that within the rough set theory the notion of a rough set is not formally chosen as unique. On the one hand, it is a class of abstraction with respect to the rough equality, on the other – the pair of approximation operators. As both theories have much in common, we expected the same from fuzzy sets. But – the membership function itself can be just treated as a fuzzy set. Obviously, there is something unclear with the domain vs. support of a function (as what we call 'fuzzy sets' in fact is a fuzzy subset), but it is not that dangerous. As the first author developed the formalization of rough sets, he could make the decision of how much of the existing apparatus should be used also in this case. Eventually all relational structure framework [8] was dropped as completely useless here. Surprisingly to us, [11] used term "formalization" to describe algebraic model of fuzzy relations – and this representation strongly depends on relational structures. It should be remembered that we do much more – the language we use should be understandable by computers, hence the choice of the approach is determined by other means. We could take the Cartesian product of the original set and the corresponding function, but it is enough to deal only with the latter one. All the operations on fuzzy sets actually are concerned with the membership functions, which initially seemed to be a little bit controversial, but we found it rather useful.

"Computer certification" is a relatively new term describing the process of the formalization via rewriting the text in a specific manner, usually in a rigorous language. Now this idea, although rather old (taking Peano, Whitehead and Russell as protagonists), gradually obtains a new life. As the tools evolved, the new paradigm was established: computers can potentially serve as a kind of oracle to check if the text is really correct. Hence such activity extends perspectives of knowledge reusing. The problem with computer-driven formalization is that it draws the attention of researchers somewhere at the intersection of mathematics and computer science, and if the complexity of the tools will be too high, only software engineers will be attracted and all the usefulness for an ordinary mathematician will be lost. But here, at this border, where there are the origins of MKM – Mathematical Knowledge Management, the place of fuzzy sets can be also. To give more or less formal definition, according to Wiedijk [23], *the formalization* can be seen presently as "the translation into a formal (i.e. rigorous) language so computers check this for correctness."

Among many available systems which serve as a proof-assistant we have chosen Mizar. The Mizar system [9] consists of three parts – the formal language, the software, and the database. The latter, called Mizar Mathematical Library (MML for short) established in 1989 is considered one of the largest repositories of computer checked mathematical knowledge. The basic item in the MML is called a Mizar article. It reflects roughly a structure of an ordinary paper, being considered at two main layers – the declarative one, where definitions and theorems are stated and the other one – proofs. Naturally, although the latter is the larger, the earlier needs some additional care.

As far as we know, this is the first attempt to formalize fuzzy sets in such extent using any popular computerized proof assistant. The formalization work started as described in [5] was completed by the first author and accepted to Mizar database under the name FUZNUM_1 at the end of 2014 [4]. Earlier development – by the second author – was accepted under MML identifier `FUZZY_1` in 2001 [17] and passed the massive redesign to follow new expressive power of the Mizar language.

Recall that a fuzzy set A over a universe X is a set defined as

$$A = \{(x, \mu_A) : x \in X\},$$

where $\mu_A \in [0, 1]$ is membership degree of x in A.

Because the notions in the MML make a natural hierarchy (as the base set theory is the Tarski-Grothendieck set theory, which is basically Zermelo-Frankel set theory with the Axiom of Choice where the axiom of infinity is replaced by Tarski's axiom of existence of arbitrarily large, strongly inaccessible cardinals) of the form: functions $\to$ relations = subsets of Cartesian product $\to$ sets, so it is a binary relation, i.e. subset of Cartesian product $X \times X$.

Zadeh's approach assumes furthermore that μ_A is a function, extending a characteristic function χ_A. So, for arbitrary point x of the set A, the pair (x, μ_A) can be replaced just by the value of the membership function $\mu_A(x)$, which is in fact, formally speaking, the pair under consideration. Then all operations can be viewed as operations on functions, which appeared to be pretty natural in the set-theoretic background taken in the MML as the base. All basic formalized definitions and theorems can be tracked under the address http://mizar.org.

```
definition let C be non empty set;
  mode FuzzySet of C is Membership_Func of C;
end;
```

Of course, `Membership_Func` is not uniquely determined for C – the keyword `mode` starts the shorthand for a type[1] in Mizar, that is, in fact C variable can be read from the corresponding function rather than vice versa.

We collected translations of selected formalized notions in Table 1.

Table 1. Formalized notions and their formal translations

The notion	Formal counterpart
the membership function	`Membership_Func of C`
fuzzy set	`FuzzySet of C`
$\chi_A(x)$	`chi(A,X).x`
α-set	`alpha-set C`
supp C	`support C`
$F \cap G$	`min (F,G)`
$F \cup G$	`max (F,G)`
cF	`1_minus F`

As we can read from Table 1, there are standard operations of fuzzy sets available, usually taken componentwise (note that `F.x` stands for the value of the function F on an argument x). The support of a membership function shouldn't be defined because it was used already by the theory of formal power series.

---

[1] Most theorem provers are untyped, the Mizar language has types.

Note that the Mizar repository extensively uses a difference between functions and partial functions; (`Function of X, Y` and `PartFunc of X, Y` in Mizar formalism); because in case of partial functions only the inclusion of the domain in the set X is required, hence the earlier type expands to the latter automatically. Of course all such automation techniques are turned on after proving corresponding properties formally.

4   Rough Sets as the Structural Counterpart

Another extension of classical set theory, dealing with the situation of incomplete or uncertain information, is the rough set theory. There no space here to discuss pros and cons of both approaches, although both can be feasible in the same situation (rough-fuzzy hybridization). As the origins seem to very similar, at least at the very first sight, we could expect also the same lines of formalizing code. Much to our surprise it wasn't so.

The literature of machine-aided formalization of mathematics makes a clear distinction between classical (sometimes called also *concrete*) mathematics and abstract one. The difference is in dealing with the notion of a structure (the latter one uses such notion while the earlier doesn't) – pretty technical notion which can be viewed as partial function.

Both fuzzy and rough set theory extends the ordinary set theory in the direction of partial membership; clearly in rough case it is more probability-oriented. Even in very informal form, one can see clear correspondence between membership function and basic notions of ZF – essentially membership function *per se* can be expressed in this language.

The Bayesian content in RST can be easily observed under formal code of

```
definition
   let A be finite Tolerance_Space;
   let X be Subset of A;
   func MemberFunc (X, A) -> Function of the carrier of A, REAL means
:: ROUGHS_1:def 9
   for x being Element of A holds
      it.x = card (X /\ Class (the InternalRel of A, x)) /
        (card Class (the InternalRel of A, x));
   correctness;
end;
```

which informally can be read as

$$\mu_X(x) = \frac{|X \cap [x]_R|}{|[x]_R|}$$

In other words, the primitive notion is the indiscernibility relation establishing a relational structure, and the membership function is build by counting cardinalities of corresponding classes of abstraction (remember Pawlak's original idea was to have equivalence relation for that). Of course, given a tolerance space, its μ_X is determined uniquely, hence contrary to the `mode` as in fuzzy case, here we have keyword `func` which is a (language) function – both its existence and uniqueness can be proven.

5 Extending the Ordinary Set Theory

In the usual informal mathematical jargon it is easy to say that e.g., two objects are identical up to the isomorphism, formal language has to deal somehow with it. The classical example is the parallel treatment of lattices – both in the sense of relational structures equipped by the partial ordering and corresponding algebraic structure – tools which offer automated discovery of facts are usually specialized (including those based on the equational calculus).

In the fuzzy set theory similar dualism can be noticed at the very beginning – some people treat fuzzy sets as the pair of the set and corresponding membership function. On the other hand, also axiomatical approaches to obtain fuzzy sets without ZF as an intermediate step are known; it is a kind of interesting research direction but we decide to put the stress on the reusability of knowledge.

Fuzzy sets are subsets of ordinary sets; as we can take membership function just as χ of ordinary sets, it clearly shows the feasibility of this approach. Of course, it is impossible then, at least without any additional preparing work, to find the common bottom ground for ordinary sets and fuzzy sets; however all sets can be made fuzzy in view of the simple lemma cited below:

```
theorem
  for C being non empty set holds
    chi(C,C) is FuzzySet of C;
```

After this, we can choose from all fuzzy sets in this very broad sense those ones which membership function has values only 0 or 1 – i.e. crisp sets (which can be also mapped back to classical bivalent sets by appropriate α-cuts).

Original approach was not very carefully chosen but we can revise articles (this is the policy like Wikipedia has however the process of submissions and revisions is supervised by the Library Committee of the Association of Mizar Users). Of course, from purely formal point of view, the Cartesian product of the set and a singleton cannot be equal to the original set regardless of the approach we will choose.

6 Attributes Defining Fuzzy Numbers

Remembering that a fuzzy number is a convex, normalized fuzzy set on the real line $\mathbb{R}$, with exactly one $x \in \mathbb{R}$ such that $\mu_A(x) = 1$ and μ_A is at least segmentally continuous, we defined it as the Mizar type:

```
definition
  mode FuzzyNumber is f-convex strictly-normalized continuous
    FuzzySet of REAL;
end;
```

As all types are constructed as radix types with added optional adjectives, the generalization, especially that automated-driven (by cutting the adjectives in the assumptions), is possible and quite frequently used. Some of the adjectives are a little bit stronger that others, with the quoted below as example:

```
definition let C be non empty set;
          let F be FuzzySet of C;
   attr F is strictly-normalized means :SNDef:
     ex x being Element of C st
       F.x = 1 &
       for y being Element of C st F.y = 1 holds y = x;
end;
```

Observe that this adjective means that a fuzzy set is also normalized in normal sense. Due to automatic clustering of attributes after *registering* this quite natural and easy property this won't need any additional reference.

```
registration let C be non empty set;
   cluster strictly-normalized -> normalized for FuzzySet of C;
   coherence;
end;
```

The proof of the above registration is trivial (note `coherence`; without any additional explanations the Mizar checker knows it is logically true taking into account only definitional expansions of the corresponding definitions and first order logic). As all Mizar types should have non-empty denotation (i.e. an example object should be constructed), it would force us to define both triangular and trapezoidal fuzzy sets. The natural definition is usually written in form similar to Eq. (1), i.e. conditional definition of parts of the function. We used intervals `[.a,b.]` and `AffineMaps` to save some work (e.g., affine maps are proven to be continuous, one-to-one, and monotone real maps under underlying assumptions). The operator `+*` glues two functions if their domains are disjoint; if not, then the ordering of gluing counts.

```
definition let a,b,c be Real;
   assume a < b & b < c;
   func TriangularFS (a,b,c) -> FuzzySet of REAL equals
:: FUZNUM_1:def 7
     AffineMap (0,0) | (REAL \ ].a,c.[)
       +* (AffineMap (1/(b-a),-a/(b-a)) | [.a,b.])
       +* (AffineMap (-1/(c-b),c/(c-b)) | [.b,c.]);
   correctness;
end;
```

The assumptions on the ordering of real variables a, b, c seem to be unnecessary here and potentially they can be removed (as if a is not less than c, then the first part is just the affine map equal to zero for any real argument, hence fuzzy set, but not of triangular shape); we kept this as needed to prove the continuity of this fuzzy set afterwards. However, we can define this in a more natural way, avoiding somewhat cryptic `AffineMap` – per cases, but of course the compatibility property should be proved (to show that both definienses describe the same notion); such construction is called *redefinition*.

```
definition
  let a,b,c be Real;
  assume a < b & b < c;
  redefine func TriangularFS (a,b,c) -> FuzzySet of REAL means
  for x being Real holds
    ((x <= a or c <= x) implies it.x = 0) &
    (a <= x & x <= b implies it.x = (x-a)/(b-a)) &
    (b <= x & x <= c implies it.x = (c-x)/(c-b));
  correctness;
  compatibility;
end;
```

Note that we can define this more generally, without assuming that the universe is just the set of all real numbers. Many properties of fuzzy numbers are just properties of fuzzy sets over the real universe and they are automatically recognized so. Within such framework, the target type of OFN was introduced as

```
definition
  mode OrderedFuzzyNumber -> element means :OFNDef:
    ex f, g being continuous PartFunc of REAL, REAL st
    dom f = [. 0,1 .] & dom g = [. 0,1 .] & it = [f,g];
  existence;
end;
```

and to encode Eq. (1) we applied similar techniques as in defining triangular fuzzy sets; essentially we used three intervals taking on the intermediate the constant map with the value 1.

- `[.inf UP OFN, sup UP OFN.]`,
- `[.inf DOWN OFN, sup DOWN OFN.]`,
- `AffineMap (0, 1) | [.sup UP OFN, inf DOWN OFN.]`.

Then the corresponding membership function should be again the result of the gluing operation applied to inverse functions limited to these intervals where instead of writing f^{-1} we used (`up-part OFN`)". Significant issue is that the converse of the function always exists as it is just a relation; in case of invertible function the converse is also a function.

As we noticed right under the definition of triangular fuzzy set, some restrictions (i.e. assumptions) are artificial. To show something more meaningful however, they are really needed within the proofs of the uniqueness of the peak and the continuity of the resulting fuzzy set as a whole.

```
theorem :: FUZNUM_1:29
  for a,b,c being Real st a < b & b < c holds
    TriangularFS (a,b,c) is strictly-normalized;
```

Paradoxically, most of the real technical obstacles we met during proving the continuity of the map glued from segmentally continuous parts, i.e. in the theorem

```
theorem :: FUZNUM_1:30
  for a,b,c being Real st a < b & b < c holds
    TriangularFS (a,b,c) is continuous;
```

where the main step was the following lemma:

```
theorem :: FUZNUM_1:23
  for f,g being PartFunc of REAL, REAL st
  f is continuous & g is continuous &
  ex x being object st dom f /\ dom g = {x} &
  for x being object st x in dom f /\ dom g holds f.x = g.x holds
    ex h being PartFunc of REAL, REAL st
    h = f +* g & for x being Real st
    x in dom f /\ dom g holds h is_continuous_in x;
```

which can be understood as the fact that gluing of two continuous real functions which coincide at a singleton returns again a continuous real function – pretty straightforward at first sight.

Of course, once the continuity of glued maps is established, defining another Mizar functor TrapezoidalFS to construct trapezoidal fuzzy set is a similar routine work.

7   Remarks on Approaches' Dissimilarities

From the viewpoint of automated proof-assistant, we were surprised that the basic difference between two approaches can be found even at the very first stage: the definitions of types *rough set* and *fuzzy set*. In fact, as we noticed before in Sec. 3, rough sets in Mizar can be treated either as a pair of the two approximation operators or the classes of abstraction with the respect to the given indiscernibility relation. The formal definition of a fuzzy set is even simpler that the classical one (see Sec. 3) – just certain membership function. Rough sets are more abstract while fuzzy sets are strongly tied with the set theory, specifically Zermelo-Fraenkel in the case of our framework (as many mathematicians claim).

Rough sets have more purely algebraic flavour, it is quite natural that they use in a significant way the automation provided by the Mizar system. In case of fuzzy sets, where concrete computations are more important [13], it is not so.

Some natural questions concerning these concrete pieces of Mizar code devoted to extensions of ordinary set theory may arise:

– Is there any other (closer to set-theoretical origins) formal definition of rough sets? On the one hand, fuzzy sets seem naturally extending classical set theory – contrary to approximation spaces. As far as we know, nobody formalized them in any other leading proof assistants (although set-theoretical axiomatic formalism is given by Bryniarski [1]);

- How to cope with the universe on which fuzzy sets are defined? According to Mizar Tarski-Grothendieck formalism, the function's value outside its domain is equal to the empty set (or zero, which is the same taking into account von Neumann definition of naturals), but we can aim at the clear distinction between a fuzzy set and the other one defined only on the support of the previous one;
- The transition from classical part to structural formalism is relatively easy (in other proof-assistants they may be called *setoids*), but the opposite direction is not that straightforward; recall that groups can be defined as ordered tuples, but in real mathematical practice this is not the case;
- It is interesting that – contrary to rough sets [7] – we don't see a clear way of generalization of the classical notion of a fuzzy set, while there are lots of such within rough set theory: from equivalence relations to tolerances, partitions vs. coverings, etc. Even mereology as a theory of a part of a whole as a primitive notion instead of an element is quite feasible in case of Pawlak's sets, so maybe because both approaches are formalized in a highly structured database, automated provers can discover new results and mark already existing similarities automatically [6];
- As the gluing of maps defined on unit interval into topological space (called *paths*) is the very basic notion in algebraic topology and homotopy theory, it would be interesting to explore the correspondence between these two important topics and OFNs.

In our opinion, we made some significant progress on the certification of fuzzy sets and numbers, but our primary aim was to get the formal net of notions correct and reusable and we hope to benefit from it in our future work. It is worth noticing here that although in the current paper we focus on declarative part – definitions and theorems, all proofs can be tracked either at the home page of the Mizar project (http://mizar.org) or offline after the installation of the Mizar system.

Although it is possible in Mizar to prove theorems without proving lemmas they depend on before, we aimed at the formalization of all the content just from its basics. The other issue is that the theorems which are "conditionally" proven will not be accepted as a part of the Mizar Mathematical Library, so they are formally useless in some sense. Such approach can be useful, however, from the viewpoint of more advanced topics (preliminaries can be just stated without proving).

8   Conclusion and Further Work

Computer certification of proofs seems to be an emerging trend and some corresponding issues can be raised. We are assured that there are some visible pros of our approach, as for example, automated removal of repetitions, and also the need of writing a sort of preliminary section vanishes in the Mizar code. Also as we explained before, the type system enables us to search for possible generalizations (including a kind of reverse mathematics at the very end); the use of automated knowledge discovery tools is much easier due to internal information exchange format, which at the same time offers direct translations for a number of formats (including close to the English-like human-oriented language), not limited to the Mizar source code.

There are of course drawbacks we should remember of: first of all, the syntax. The Mizar language, although pretty close to natural language, is still an artificial (a kind of programming) language. Of course, main problem with the formalization is making proper formal background – lemmas and theorems – which can be really time-consuming, hence the stress on reusability of available knowledge. We argue that the formalization itself can be very fruitful and creative as long as it extends the horizons of the research and make new results possible. Furthermore, the more the database larger is, the formalization can be more feasible. Good example here (other than the aforementioned) are BCK algebras which are already formalized – this can start the development of fuzzy logic within MML. Even if the formalized content concerning fuzzy sets is not that big as of now (there is about 15 thousand lines of Mizar code on fuzzy and rough sets comparing with 2.5 million of lines in the whole MML), the basics are already done, and it can serve both as a good starting point for further development, including rough-fuzzy hybridization [3], as well as from translated existing content we can try to obtain new results.

Regardless of the gains of the availability of the topic to majority of popular proof assistants one can ask a question of assurance of the correctness of the proofs; Urban's [22] tools translating Mizar language into the input of first-order theorem-provers (TPTP – Thousands of Problems for Theorem Provers), proof simplification via lemma extraction [21] or XML interface providing information exchange between various math-assistants are already in use, so not only proof-checkers other than the Mizar verifier can analyze it, but additionally it can allow for some time-consuming proofs to be done by computer. Of course, still all these achievements are subject to careful human supervising in order to provide the proper research background.

References

1. Bryniarski, E.: Formal conception of rough sets. Fundamenta Informaticae 27(2/3), 109–136 (1996)
2. Dubois, D., Prade, H.: Operations on fuzzy numbers. International Journal of System Sciences 9(6), 613–626 (1978)
3. Dubois, D., Prade, H.: Rough fuzzy sets and fuzzy rough sets. International Journal of General Systems 17(2–3), 191–209 (1990)
4. Grabowski, A.: The formal construction of fuzzy numbers. Formalized Mathematics 22(4), 313–319 (2014)
5. Grabowski, A.: On the computer certification of fuzzy numbers. In: Ganzha, M., Maciaszek, L., Paprzycki, M. (eds.) Proceedings of Federated Conference on Computer Science and Information Systems, FedCSIS 2013, pp. 51–54 (2013)
6. Grabowski, A.: Automated discovery of properties of rough sets. Fundamenta Informaticae 128(1-2), 65–79 (2013)

7. Grabowski, A.: On the computer-assisted reasoning about rough sets. In: Dunin-Kęplicz, B., Jankowski, A., Szczuka, M. (eds.) Monitoring, Security and Rescue Techniques in Multiagent Systems. Advances in Soft Computing, vol. 28, pp. 215–226 (2005)
8. Grabowski, A., Jastrzębska, M.: Rough set theory from a math-assistant perspective. In: Kryszkiewicz, M., Peters, J.F., Rybiński, H., Skowron, A. (eds.) RSEISP 2007. LNCS (LNAI), vol. 4585, pp. 152–161. Springer, Heidelberg (2007)
9. Grabowski, A., Korniłowicz, A., Naumowicz, A.: Mizar in a nutshell. Journal of Formalized Reasoning 3(2), 153–245 (2010)
10. Kacprzak, M., Kosiński, W.: On lattice structure and implications on ordered fuzzy numbers. In: Proc. of EUSFLAT 2011, pp. 267–274 (2011)
11. Kawahara, Y., Furusawa, H.: An algebraic formalization of fuzzy relations. Fuzzy Sets and Systems 101, 125–135 (1999)
12. Klir, G.J.: Fuzzy arithmetic with requisite constraints. Fuzzy Sets and Systems 91, 165–175 (1997)
13. Koleśnik, R., Prokopowicz, P., Kosiński, W.: Fuzzy calculator – useful tool for programming with fuzzy algebra. In: Rutkowski, L., Siekmann, J.H., Tadeusiewicz, R., Zadeh, L.A. (eds.) ICAISC 2004. LNCS (LNAI), vol. 3070, pp. 320–325. Springer, Heidelberg (2004)
14. Korniłowicz, A.: On rewriting rules in Mizar. Journal of Automated Reasoning 50(2), 203–210 (2013)
15. Kosiński, W., Prokopowicz, P., Ślęzak, D.: Fuzzy numbers with algebraic operations: algorithmic approach. In: Kłopotek, M., Wierzchoń, S.T., Michalewicz, M. (eds.) Intelligent Information Systems, IIS 2002, Poland, pp. 311–320 (2002)
16. Kosiński, W., Prokopowicz, P., Ślęzak, D.: Ordered fuzzy numbers. Bulletin of the Polish Academy of Sciences, Sér. Sci. Math. 51(3), 327–338 (2003)
17. Mitsuishi, T., Endou, N., Shidama, Y.: The concept of fuzzy set and membership function and basic properties of fuzzy set operation. Formalized Mathematics 9(2), 351–356 (2001)
18. Moore, R., Lodwick, W.: Interval analysis and fuzzy set theory. Fuzzy Sets and Systems 135(1), 5–9 (2003)
19. Naumowicz, A., Korniłowicz, A.: A brief overview of MIZAR. In: Berghofer, S., Nipkow, T., Urban, C., Wenzel, M. (eds.) TPHOLs 2009. LNCS, vol. 5674, pp. 67–72. Springer, Heidelberg (2009)
20. Pawlak, Z.: Rough Sets: Theoretical Aspects of Reasoning about Data. Kluwer, Dordrecht (1991)
21. Pąk, K.: Methods of lemma extraction in natural deduction proofs. Journal of Automated Reasoning 50(2), 217–228 (2013)
22. Urban, J., Sutcliffe, G.: Automated reasoning and presentation support for formalizing mathematics in Mizar. In: Autexier, S., Calmet, J., Delahaye, D., Ion, P.D.F., Rideau, L., Rioboo, R., Sexton, A.P. (eds.) AISC 2010. LNCS, vol. 6167, pp. 132–146. Springer, Heidelberg (2010)
23. Wiedijk, F.: Formal proof – getting started. Notices of the AMS 55(11), 1408–1414 (2008)
24. Zadeh, L.: Fuzzy sets. Information and Control 8(3), 338–353 (1965)

Comparative Approach to the Multi-Valued Logic Construction for Preferences

Krystian Jobczyk[1,2], Antoni Ligęza[2], Maroua Bouzid[1], and Jerzy Karczmarczuk[1]

[1] University of Caen,
Maréchal Juin 6, 14200 Caen, France
{krystian.jobczyk,maroua.bouzid-mouaddib,jerzy.karczmarczuk}@unicaen.fr
[2] AGH University of Science and Technology,al. Mickiewicza 30,30-059 Kraków,
Poland
ligeza@agh.edu.pl

Abstract. This paper is aimed at the giving of a comparative approach to the preferences modelling. This approach is conceived to grasp the fuzzy nature of preferences what determines the choice two fuzzy logic formalisms for their representation discussed by P. Hajek and L. Godo. These two (appropriately modified) formalism are used to propose two formalism for preferences: *Fuzzy Modal Preferential Logic* (FMPL) and *Comparative Possibilistic Multi-Modal Propositional Logic* (CPMPL). We also justify some metalogical properties of both systems such as their completeness and we discuss a satisfiability problem for them. In result, we propose a short juxtaposition of the properties of the considered systems.

Keywords: Fuzzy logic for preferences · Multi-valued logic for preferences · Preferences modelling

1 Introduction

Different aspects of *preferences modelling* are considered in temporal knowledge representation. On one one hand, preferences and their representation are discussed in the context of the temporal planning issue as its specific constraints type – see for example: [8], [10], sometimes in term of STPP and STPPU— like in [11]. On the other hand, other approaches—such as: [15], [13] expose an epistemic or a game-theoretic nature of preferences. It is usually discussed there in terms of different variants of epistemic logic or logic of action. All the approaches refer, however, to the *fuzzy nature* of preferences partially and indirectly. The recent attempt for modelling user's preferences on attributes from [3] seems to be too algebraic and relatively narrow approach.

The lack of the exact multi-valued or fuzzy logic system for preferences representation and–as result–lack of a knowledge about its properties forms a main motivation of this paper. Therefore, we propose a new formalism of multi-valued logic and fuzzy logic for preferences modeling in this paper. For this purpose, we

© Springer International Publishing Switzerland 2015
L. Rutkowski et al. (Eds.): ICAISC 2015, Part I, LNAI 9119, pp. 172–183, 2015.
DOI: 10.1007/978-3-319-19324-3_16

especially adopt a formalism of systems involved in a newly interpreted modal necessity proposed and developed by L.Godo and F. Esteva in [4], in [6] and [7]– retrospectively discussed also in [5]. This approach allows us to apply a multi-valued modal systems with a decreasing or increasing degree of necessity of the modal operators to the preferences. It has been shown in [4] that if a set S of such degrees taken from a fuzzy set [0,1] is finite, then systems of possibilistic logic with modal operators with necessity (possibility) degrees from S remain complete.

1.1   Goal and a Novelty of the Paper

The first aim of this paper is a putting forward proposal of a new *Fuzzy-Modal Preferential Logic* FMPL as suitable for preferences representation. In order to expose the advantages of this newly proposed system we intend to compare FMPL with some alternative fuzzy system being an appropriate modification of the Hajek's *comparative possibilistic multi-modal propositional logic* CPMPL — considered in [5]— but without reference to preferences. For this purpose we justify a handful of properties of both systems such as completeness, model checking problem and its complexity. We show these properties in terms of the newly proposed interval semantics. In other words, this paper proposes an answer of the following questions:

- How to construct a multi-valued logic for preferences?
- Which (useful) properties have this system?
- Why a multi-valued system seems to be more comfortable than an alternative fuzzy comparative one?

1.2   Terminological Background and Methodological Remarks

All of the considered frames in our interval-based semantics will be based on an order $\langle S, \leq \rangle$ which:

- is strongly discrete, i.e. there are only finitely many points between any two points,
- the order contains the least element,
- for any a, b, $c \in$ S, if $a \leq c$ and $b \leq c$, then either $a \leq b$ or $b \leq a$.

We will consider a finite set $\mathcal{A} = \{1, \ldots, m\}$ of agents such that each agent is endowed with a set of a local states L_i and $i \in \mathcal{A}$. If e is an environment of an agent the set of local states is denoted by L_e. Each agent is equipped with a set of local actions and protocolar functions that produce a transition relation t. In such a framework we adopt the following definitions.

Definition 1. *Let $\mathcal{L}$ be a given language. An interval-based interpreted system* IBIS *is a tuple* (S, s_0, t, Lab) *such that*

S *is a set of global states (which can be points or intervals) reachable from the initial state* s_0,

t is a standard transition relation between states, and
Lab is a labeling function, which for an interval $I = s_1, s_2, \ldots, s_k$ *is defined:*
$Lab(I) = Lab(s_1, s_2, \ldots, s_k) = (\hat{s}_1, \hat{s}_2, \ldots, \hat{s}_k)$, *where terms* $\hat{s}_i$ *represents the point* s_i *in* $\mathcal{L}$, *for* $i < k$. *In particular pairs* $(a, b) \in S^2$ *are associated to formulas pair* $(\hat{a}, \hat{b})$.

Definition 2. *An interval is a finite path in* IBIS, *or as a sequence* $I = s_1 s_s \ldots s_k$ *such that* $s_i t s_{i+1}$ *for* $1 \leq i \leq k - 1$ *and a transition* t.

Definition 3. *A generalized Kripke frame is a tuple* $M = (S, s_0, t, Lab)$, *where* s_0, t *and Lab are as above and* $S \subseteq L_e \times L_1 \times \ldots L_m$ *is a set of reachable (in any way) global states. It easy to see that an unravelling generalized Kripke frame is an IBIS.* [1]

Definition 4. *(Model checking). Given a logic* $\mathcal{L}$, *a generalized Kripke frame* M, *an interval* $I = s_0 \ldots s_k$ *and a formula* $\phi \in \mathcal{L}$, *the model checking problem for* $\mathcal{L}$ *amounts to checking whether or not it holds* $M, I \models \phi$.

In a model checking procedure for a newly constructed FMPL we make use of the reduction method to the Boolean quantified satisfiability problem recognized as a PSpace-problem from [9]. We use a standard logical notation.

1.3   Paper's Organization

The paper is organized as follows. In Section 2 we introduce a multi-valued logic for preferences (FMPL) representation by means of the necessity definition proposed by Godo and Hajek. We check completeness of this system and perform its model checking for the interval-based semantics. In Section 3 we consider comparative fuzzy preferential logic CPMPL as the alternative system for preferences and we will discuss its difficulties. We expose the conditional nature of the completeness proof, the difficulties with an interval-based semantics construction for CPMPL and undefinability of a CPMPL-satisfiability problem in this semantics type. In section 4 we give a short juxtaposition of properties of both systems. In the last section of the paper we formulate conclusions and we sketch a promising research direction in this area.

2   Fuzzy Modal Preferential Logic

It has just been mentioned that preferences are often expressed in terms of modal-epistemic logic and represented by relations being some types of orders– especially in many game-theoretic approaches where they are interpreted in infinite game trees. In this paragraph we intend to understand preferences in a 'broader' sense and represent them by partial orders rejecting a linearity condition for them. We adopt such a way of their understanding because such a

---

[1] For clarity, we omit the detailed definition of unravelling.

generality ensures more flexibility with respect to the incomparable worlds. This *manouvre* is also dictated by a purely meta-logical properties of the formalism that we use for preferences representation. Indeed, partial orders represent the modal system S4 which shows to have much more comfortable properties such as completeness (in a multi-modal version as $S4_m$, i.e. S4 with m-modalities) than S4.3 – suitable for linear orders.

We also intend to expose a fuzzy nature of preferences — often formulated with a different degree of a certainty in many practical situations as the one described below.

Example 1. We can prefer to go to the theater today afternoon with a preference $\frac{3}{10}$ and whenever, but not today-with a preference $\frac{7}{10}$ and only in our birthday we are strongly motivated with a preference = 1 (modal necessity) to go to the theater.

It is clear that a modal representation of preferences seems to be too sharp in this matter because—as based on two-valued reasoning. However, it seems to be reasonable to restrict a *spectrum* of possible fuzzy values associated with our preferences to their finite set $S \subseteq [0,1]$. This *manouvre* will turn out reasonable from the technical point of view, as well. In essence, it ensures completeness of the considered system.

2.1   Fuzzy Modal Preferential Logic FMPL — Syntax and Semantics

It has already been said that preferences will be represented by us in an interval-based semantics as transitive and reflexive orders. Moreover, we decided to interpret their in a fuzzy manner. It will be reflected in types of operators that we introduce. In essence, we want to consider operators of a type $[\text{Pref}]_i^\alpha \phi$ read: "an agent i (strongly) prefers ϕ with a degree $\alpha \in [0,1]$", and $\langle \text{Pref} \rangle_i^\alpha \phi$ "an agent i weakly prefers ϕ with a degree α"

A language $\mathcal{L}$ of FMPL is given by a grammar:

$$\phi \; := \; p \,|\, \neg\phi \,|\, \phi \wedge \psi \,|\, [\text{Pref}]_i^\alpha \phi \,|\, \langle \text{Pref} \rangle_i^\alpha \phi$$

Axioms: The axioms of FMPL are: the axioms of Boolean propositional calculus, and

$[\text{Pref}]_i^\alpha (\phi \to \chi) \to ([\text{Pref}]_i^\alpha \phi \to [\text{Pref}]_i^\alpha \chi)$ (axiom K)

$[\text{Pref}]_i^\alpha \phi \to [\text{Pref}]_i^\alpha [\text{Pref}]_i^\alpha \phi$ (axiom 4)

$[\text{Pref}]_i^\alpha \phi \to \phi$ (axiom T)

As inference rules we adopt *Modus Ponens* and the inference rule for $[\text{Pref}]_i^\alpha$ operator: from $\phi \to \psi$ infer $[\text{Pref}]_i^\alpha \phi \to [\text{Pref}]_i^\alpha \psi$ for some $\alpha \in G$, with G being a finite subset of $[0,1]$. The finiteness of G is important for the satisfiability of FMPL, and it enables the completeness for the point-wise semantics [4,5]. This will be discussed in the context of interval-based semantics.

As usual, we define FMPL as the smallest theory in a language $\mathcal{L}(\text{FMPL})$ which contains the above axioms and closed on the above inference rules.

FMPL in An Interval-Based Semantics and Satisfiability Problem.
We intend to interpret this FMPL in an interval-based semantics. It will be
based on an inductive definition of satisfaction for formulas of $\mathcal{L}$(FMPL) that
we will introduce below. For this purpose assume as given an IBIS with a labeling
function Lab defined earlier. Recall that if an interval $I = s_1 \ldots s_k$, than $Lab(I) =$
$Lab(s_1 \ldots s_k) = (\widehat{s_1} \ldots, \widehat{s_1})$, where $\widehat{s_i}$ represents a point s_i in a given language.
Assume also that $\sim_i$ is an accessibility relation between intervals (for some agent
i). For two given intervals, say $I = s_1 \ldots s_k$ and $I' = s_1' \ldots s_l'$ we only assume
wrt $\sim_i^\alpha$ the following: $I \sim_i^\alpha I'$ means that $k \leq l$ and j-local states of I and I'
are identical (for $j \leq k$).

Naturally, the necessity degrees α — associated to modal formulas of FMPL
— should be reflected in the accessibility relation $\sim_i$ interpreting these formulas.
We will write: $I \sim^\alpha I'$ iff the relation $\sim (I, I')$ is associated to a value at least
α (symb: $\alpha \leq \| \sim (I, I')\|$. In terms of a convention of Hajek we can say that
intervals I and I' are at least α-similar [5]. It is easy to observe that $\sim_i^\alpha$ is a
partial order, hence it can be an appropriate representation for preferences in
the light of earlier arrangements.

Definition 5. *(Satisfaction) Given a formula $\phi \in \mathcal{L}$(FMPL), an IBIS and an
interval I we define inductively the fact that ϕ is satisfied in IBIS and in an
interval I (symb.$I \models \phi$) as follows:*
   IBIS, $I \models p$ iff $p \in Lab(I)$ for all $p \in Var$.
   IBIS, $I \models \neg\phi$ iff if its not such a case that IBIS, $I \models \phi$.
   IBIS, $I \models \phi \wedge \psi$ iff there is such a case that IBIS, $I \models \phi$ and IBIS, $I \models \psi$.
   *IBIS, $I \models [\text{Pref}]_i^\alpha \phi$, where $i \in A$, iff for all $I \sim_i^\alpha I'$ it holds IBIS, $I' \models \phi$ for
a fixed α.*
   *IBIS, $I \models \langle \text{Pref} \rangle_i^\alpha \phi$, where $i \in A$, iff there is such I' that $I \sim_i^\alpha I'$ and it holds
IBIS, $I' \models \phi$ for a fixed α.*

The key clause of the above definition is this one referring to the modal oper-
ators $[\text{Pref}]_i^\alpha \phi$ and $\langle \text{Pref} \rangle_i^\alpha \phi$. These conditions assert that such modal formulas
are satisfied in an interval I and model IBIS iff the same formula ϕ holds in all
intervals accessible from this I in the sense of the accessible relation $\sim_i$ by an
agent i.

*Example 2. Consider a formula $[\text{Pref}]_i^\alpha \phi$ and intervals I^k of the form: $s_1 s_2 \ldots s_k$
(for $k = 1, 2, \ldots 5$) that are labeled by a formula ϕ, and an interval $s_1 \ldots s_6$, which
is not labeled by ϕ. Assume that $I \sim_i I^k$ and $I \sim_i s_1 \ldots s_6$ for some accessibility
relation $\sim_i$. It is easy to observe that a formula $[\text{Pref}]_i^\alpha \phi$ is not satisfied in I
because not for all intervals accessible from, say I^{access}, it holds $I^{\text{access}} \models \phi$. In
fact, $s_1 \ldots s_6 \not\models \phi$ (due to above satisfaction definition).*

We intend to justify the PSpace completeness of satisfiability problem for
FMPL. The proof uses a reduction of a satisfiability problem for FMPL to the
satisfiability problem for $S4_m$ that is known as PSpace-complete, [2]. In the
proof we adopt the proof ideas from [9]. This proof idea requires, however, some
additional justification. In fact, we said that accessibility relations in IBIS are

associated to one of a values from a finite $G \in [0.1]$ in our case. Hence we will consider a slightly modified key relationships between accessibility relations in Kripke frames of the form $K = \langle W, S_1 \ldots, S_k \rangle$ and in IBIS in the form: $I_1 S_i I_2$ in K $\iff$ $I_1 \sim_i^\alpha I_2$ in IBIS, for $\alpha \in G$ and $i \leq k$. It means that we will consider only intervals et least α-similar to the initial ones in satisfaction condition for formulas of FMPL.

Theorem 1. *(Satisfiability + Completeness) FMPL is complete wrt the interval IBIS-based semantics. The satisfiability problem for FMPL is PSpace-complete.*

Proof. (Outline) This proof uses a reduction of a satisfiability problem for FMPL to the satisfiability problem for $S4_m$ what can be deduced as PSpace-complete because of the satisfiability problem for S4 — known as PSpace-complete, [2]. In the proof we adopt the proof ideas from [9].

In order to reduce the case of $S4_m$ to the case of FMPL, it suffices to show that $IBIS, I \models_{FMPL} \phi \iff M \models_{S4_m} f(\phi)$ for some model M and a bijection f that transforms the formulas of $FMPL$ into formulas of $S4_m$ replacing each box-operator $[\ ]_j \phi$ of $S4_m$ by $[\text{Pref}]_i^\alpha \phi$, where $j \in \{1, \ldots, m\}$ and $\text{card}\{G\} = m$.

($\rightarrow$) Assume first that ϕ is satisfied in a model $IBIS = (S, s_0, \sim_i^\alpha, t, Lab)$ and in an interval I. We aim at giving of such a Kripke model $\mathcal{M}$ that $f(\phi)$ is satisfied in it. This situation is, however, easy because it is enough to assume that a domain $|M|$ of $\mathcal{M}$ consists of the intervals from IBIS such that it holds for all i: $I_1 S_i I_2 in \mathcal{M} \iff I_1 \sim_i^\alpha I_2 in \text{IBIS}$ for a fixed $\alpha \in G$. One can inductively check that $f(\phi)$ is satisfied in the Kripke model $\mathcal{M}$.

($\leftarrow$) Assume now that $(M, \omega) \models f(\phi)$ for $\mathcal{M} = (W, \omega_0, S_1, \ldots, S_m)$ and that M contains only the relations in ϕ. We can construct a model IBIS $= \langle W \bigcup \{s_0\}, s_0, t, Lab \rangle$ with a new point s_0 as an initial one. A transition relation t is not empty because it contains (s_0, t) for some t-due to its definition. We finally define $Lab(s_0, \omega) = \pi(\omega)$. It remains only to justify by induction that ϕ is satisfied in the interval $s_0 \omega$ in IBIS.

We analyze only the case of the modal box-operator. For this purpose we assume inductively that $IBIS, s_0 \omega \models \phi \iff M, \omega \models f(\phi)$. We want to prove that IBIS, $s_0 \omega \models [\text{Pref}]_i^\alpha \phi$, or that $\forall s' w' (s_0 \omega \sim^\alpha s' w' \wedge s' w' \models \phi)$ for some fixed α. Assume also that $M, \omega \models [\text{Pref}]_i^\alpha f(\phi)$, which is equivalent to $\forall \omega'(\omega S \omega' \wedge \omega' \models f(\phi))$. Meanwhile $\omega S \omega' \iff (s' = s_0$ and $s_0 \omega \sim^\alpha s' \omega')$ for all ω' and the relation S. Therefore we have $\forall \omega'(s' = s_0$ and $s_0 \omega \sim^\alpha s' \omega' \wedge \omega' \models f(\phi))$. The induction assumption allows us to deduce that $\forall s' \omega'(s' = s_0 \wedge s_0 \omega \sim^\alpha s' \omega' \wedge s' \omega' \models \phi)$ what proves this case.

The above procedure has been carried out for the fixed parameter $\alpha \in G \subseteq [0, 1]$. The same reasoning can be used for each parameter $\beta \in G$. The finiteness of G ensures that the complexity of the satisfiability problem for FMPL remains PSpace-complete. □

Note that an assuming of a linearity condition for preferences changes a complexity of the satisfiability problem. In fact, it holds the following theorem:

Theorem 2. *The satisfiability problem for for FMPL with a linearity condition for preferences is NP-complete.*

Proof. In essence, such a system can form a kind of a multi-modal S4.3$_m$ for some finite m. It has been shown in [2] that a satisfiability problem for S4.3 — even for the Horn clauses — is NP-complete.   □

One can raise a question whether a finiteness condition imposed on a set of necessity degree can ensure a completeness of FMPL wrt the interval based semantics with discrete finite intervals, like in a pointwise semantics in [4]. This is not obvious, since it requires at least a density condition for the space of intervals. How inappropriate is the condition of a finite discreteness imposed on intervals, can be seen from the fact that S4remains complete wrt the Cantor set. Recall that this set can be defined as a set of all real numbers represented as $\sum_{i=1}^{\infty} a_i/3^i$ for $a_i \in \{0, 2\}$.

Theorem 3. *Assume that FMPL is such that a set of necessity degrees G has one fixed value α. Then it is complete wrt the Cantor space.*

Proof. It immediately follows from the fact that S4 is complete wrt to the Cantor space [14] and from the fact that such a restricted FMPL can be translated to S4.   □

3   Comparative Multi-modal Preferential Logic and Its Difficulties

As it has been mentioned before, the preferences have a comparative nature. It means that having a preference, say $Pref_1$, with respect to a subject or activity A, we can have a possibility to compare $Pref_1$ with some other, say $Pref_2$, wrt to the same preference object or activity. In essence, we are usually willing to formulate our preferences *against* the other alternative ones.

Example 3. We put a preference P_1: 'going to the cinema today' with a value $\frac{3}{10}$ against a preference P_2 'goint to the cinema tomorrow" with a values $\frac{4}{25}$.

In the light of the above statements it seems to be reasonable to consider a new alternative approach to the preferences representation that will be more suitable for such a comparative nature of preferences. In fact: some A can be more preferable than B and B more than C *etc.* It remains to chose only the appropriate formal representation for such a property. The so-called *comparative possibilistic modal propositional logic* CPMPL with a one binary modality ∇–interpreted as $\|\phi \nabla \chi\| = 1$ iff possibility of ϕ is less than or equal to the possibility of χ–described in [5] can be suitable for such a task from the purely theoretical point of view.

In this section we introduce a slightly modified version of CPMPL as suitable for preferences representation. Secondly, we comparatively examine both FMPL and CPMPL in further subsections. This presentation will be, however, aimed at the exposing of the advantages of the earlier multi-valued preferential approach because–as we will argue later–this new comparative fuzzy approach is not so convenient as one can think. On the other hand, we observe an interesting fact that a rejecting of a linearity condition is not required to preserve a completeness in a case of CPMPL-formalism.

3.1 Comparative Possibilistic Multi-modal Preferential Logic-Syntax and Semantics

As this alternative fuzzy approach to the preferences representation we adopt a multi-modal system CPMPL proposed in [6]–in a slight modified version. CPMPL is built in a language given by a grammar:

$\phi ::= \phi \mid \neg\phi \mid \phi \wedge \chi \mid \phi \bigtriangleup \chi$.

Because a comparison between preferences is both a transitive relation (if A is weaker preferable than B and B weaker than C, than than A is weaker preferable than C) and a linear one (either A is more preferable than B, or B is more preferable than A), we adopt the following **axioms system**:

- axioms of propositional calculus,
- $(\phi\bigtriangleup\chi) \rightarrow ((\chi\bigtriangleup\psi) \rightarrow (\phi\bigtriangleup\psi))$,   (transitivity)
- $(\phi\bigtriangleup\chi) \vee (\chi\bigtriangleup\phi)$,   (linearity)
- $(\phi\bigtriangleup\chi) \rightarrow ((\phi \vee \chi)\bigtriangleup(\chi \vee \psi))$ (disjunction)
- $(\phi\bigtriangleup\chi) \rightarrow [\,](\phi\bigtriangleup\chi)$ (boxing 1).

As inference rules we adopt *Modus Ponens* and necessitation rule of the form: from $\phi \rightarrow \chi$ deduce $\phi\bigtriangleup\chi$.

CPMPL will be interpreted by us in a Kripke frames $\mathcal{K} = (W, \mu, e)$, where $W \neq \emptyset$ is a set of states, μ is a probability measure and $e : \mathcal{L}(CPMPL) \mapsto [0,1]$ is a standard fuzzy evaluation function. We adopt the following interpretation of formulas in a model $\mathcal{K}$: $\|\phi\bigtriangleup\chi\|_M = \mu(\phi) \leq \mu(\chi)$ (probability of χ is greater than probability of ϕ) for $w = \|\phi\|_K$ and $v = \|\chi\|_K$.

Example 4. Assume that ϕ_C = 'It is preferable to visit a cinema today' and χ_T = It is preferable to visit a theather today' and $\|\phi_C\| = \frac{45}{100}$ and $\|\phi_T\| = \frac{21}{100}$. Than $\|\phi_T\| = \mu(visiting\ a\ cinema) = \frac{21}{100} \leq \frac{45}{100} = \mu(visiting\ a\ theater)$ and $\|\phi_T\bigtriangleup\chi_C\|$ is satisfied in some model K.

3.2 Completeness of CPMPL

It has been shown in [6](see also: [5]) that CPMPL is complete wrt to the proposed semantics. This proof leads by an reinterpretation of this system in some fuzzy tense system, called MTL in [6]. The proof idea bases on a translation * of the language $\mathcal{L}$(CPMPL) into the language $\mathcal{L}$(MTL) such that: $p^* = p$, $(\phi\bigtriangleup\chi)^* = [\,](\phi^* \rightarrow F\chi^*)$, where F is a temporal operator 'always in the future' of LTL and $[\,]$ is a normal modal box-type operator. We omit the details of the proof that can be easily found in [6], pp. 16-17. Meanwhile we will propose a short outline of the new completeness proof of this system.

Idea of our proof will be based on the alternative translation of formulas of CPMPL into propositional variables of so-called Rational Pavelka Logic RPL. The idea of translation is easy: bimodal formula, say $\odot(k, j)$, is represented by double-indexed propositional variable $p_{k,j}$; unary modal operator, say $\odot j$,–by a singularly indexed propositional variable p_j.

Our proof-similar to the ideas of of completeness proof for Rational Pavelka logic from [5] will be essentially based on the definition of so-called *truth degree* and *provability degree* defined as: $\|\phi\|_T = inf\{\|\phi\|_M : M$ is a model of $T\}$ and $|\phi|_T = sup\{r : T \vdash (\widehat{r} \to \phi)\}$ *(resp.)* for an arbitrary formula $\phi \in \mathcal{L}(RPL)$. In such a terminological framework, the Pavelka style of completeness proofs consists of a proving of a unique equality:

$$\|\phi|_T = |\phi\|_T \,^2.$$

In order to prove the CPMPL-completeness we also adopt the following lemmas (without their proofs).

Lemma 1. *([5], p. 130) If $T \nvdash \widehat{r} \to \phi$ then the theory $T \cup \{\phi \to \widehat{r}\}$ is consistent.*

Lemma 2. *([5], p. 81) Let T be consistent and complete. Then the evaluation $e(p_i) = |p_i|$ is a model for T.*

Theorem 4. Completeness *CPMPL is complete wrt to the proposed semantics. More precisely, for each theory T in a language $\mathcal{L}(CPMPL)$ and a formula ϕ of this language it holds: $|\phi|_T = \|\phi\|_T$.*

Proof. (Short outline). For a use of the proof we should make a simple translation of the bi-modal CPMPL-formulas $\phi \bigtriangleup \chi$ into the propositional variables $p_{\phi,\chi}$ similarly as it has been made by a translation of the formulas of fuzzy probability system FP discussed in [5], p. 235.

In order to justify the theorem we have to justify that both $|\phi|_T \leq \|\phi\|_T$ and $\|\phi\|_T \leq |\phi|_T$. Meanwhile, the proof for $|\phi|_T \leq \|\phi\|_T$ (soundness) is routine. In order to prove the converse we must show that for each rational $r < \|\phi\|$, $T \vdash \widehat{r} \to \phi$, where $\widehat{r}$ is a representation of r in a language of CPMPL. By a transposition it is enough to show that if T does *not* prove $\widehat{r} \to \phi$, than $\|\phi\| \leq r$. Assume therefore that $T \nvdash \widehat{r} \to \phi$ what means that $T \cup \{\phi \to \widehat{r}\}$ is consistent and it must have a complete Lindenbaum extension, say T'. Then-by the above lemma– an evaluation $e(p_i) = |p_i|$ and $e(\phi \to \widehat{r}) = 1$, thus $e(\phi) \leq r$. In particular, it means that $e(p_{\phi, chi}) = |p_{\phi,\chi}|$ and $e((\phi \bigtriangleup \chi) \to \widehat{r}) = 1$, thus $e(\phi \bigtriangleup \chi) \leq r$ what finishes our proof. □

Remark 1. Note that the translation of the formulas can be also carried out in two steps. Firstly, we can represent a CPMPL-formulas $\phi \bigtriangleup \chi$ by an unary modal operator $P(\phi|\chi)$ for a conditional probability-read as: 'probability of χ under a condition ϕ' in the appropriate language. In the second step, we can represent $P(\phi|\chi)$ by a single propositional variable $p_{\phi,\chi}$.

3.3 Further Properties of CPMPL and Its Difficulties....

We have just shown how to arrive at the completeness theorem *via* method of formulas translation. It is not difficult to observe that the above proof is essentially based on the earlier lemmas and the same translation between formulas of CPMPL and formulas of Pavelka's system. This situation seems to correspond well with

---

² It exactly means that a formula ϕ is equally provable in a theory T as satisfiable in its models.

the situation exposed in [6] of the similarly conditioned proving of completeness of CPMPL *via* referring to a fuzzy tense logic. Hence, one can state that a completeness proof for CPMPL cannot be so direct like in a case of FMPL where we make use of the direct translation to better-known completeness of $S4.3_m$. Moreover, the CPMPL-completeness does not solve the model checking problem. This problem will be shortly discussed in this subsection together with further properties of CPMPL and its difficulties such as interval-based semantics construction.

Interval-Based Semantics Construction. The pointwise Kripke fuzzy semantics for CPMPL has already been introduced in outline. The interval-based semantics construction seems to be, however, more problematic one for the following reasons–if it is possible at all.

• Assuming that formulas ϕ and χ (from $\phi \triangle \chi$) will be interpreted in intervals, say I_1 and I_2 (*resp.*), it is not clear how to define relationships between I_1 and I_2. Fuzzy logic semantics-in a contrast with a modal logic one-is not necessary based on the accessibility relations between states or intervals.

• It is not clear whether the relations of intervals for CPMPL-formulas have/or should have more temporal or spatial nature.

• Even if the interval-based semantics construction is possible, it is not clear which of the spatial-temporal interval relations (for example of Allen's sort) can be suitable for an interpretation of $\phi \triangle \chi$. It appears that this formula requires more a quantitative interpretation approach than the qualitative one. Indeed, $\phi \triangle \chi$ can be much better semantically interpreted by a fact that a *measure* of an interval I_1 (associated with ϕ) is *smaller* than a *measure* of I_2 associated with χ than by the temporal-spatial relationships between I_1 and I_2 such as: *meet, overlap, begin etc.*

Satisfiability Problem. In order to consider a satisfiability problem for CPMPL return to the idea of the representation of a formula $\phi \triangle \chi$ by $[\,](\phi \to F\chi)$ for F being a temporal 'future' operator of linear temporal logic LTL. Such a representation justifies that a CPMPL-satisfiability problem is not only more complicated than a model checking for LTL, but also for our FMPL that does not contain such 'mixed' modalities. Meanwhile, it is known that the model checking for LTL is in PSpace and–even–PSpace-hard. This first fact was solved via reduction to the formulas satisfiability problem(see: [12], p. 15); the second one-by a reduction to the tiling problem (see: [12], p. 18-19). It allows us to formulate the following

Corollary 1. *The satisfiability problem for CPMPL is (at least) in PSpace and is even (at least) PSpace-hard.*

The direct justification of this fact should be, however, (at least) slightly more complicated that the satisfiability proof for FMPL and systems with separate, non-combined modalities.

All the above remarks on the CPMPL-satisfiability problem refer to the pointwise semantics. Meanwhile–in the light of the exposed difficulties with the interval-based semantics construction–the CPMPL-satisfiability problem for this semantics type cannot be even formulated.

4   FMPL *versus* Comparative Fuzzy Preferential Logic

We venture to formulate a handful of comparative remarks on both systems for
preferences representation. There are handful similarities between them, but also
a handful of differences. Both FMPL and CPMPL are complete and the completeness can be obtained by a referring to the other systems earlier recognized as
complete ones and *via* an appropriate formulas translation. CPMPL grasps the
comparative nature of preferences, but it has worst technical and meta-logical
properties. The detailed comparison is given in the table below.

Properties	Fuzzy-Modal Preferential Logic	Comparative Multi-M. Preferential Logic
• *completeness*	yes	yes
• *proof of completeness*	*via* formulas translation, use-ful in a model checking prob-lem solving	*via* formulas translation
• *nature of logic*	multi-valued	fuzzy
• *comparative nature of preferences*	non-reflected	reflected
• *semantics type*	pointwise, interval-based	only pointwise
• *nature of semantics*	Kripke modal	Kripke fuzzy
• *satisfiability problem*	PSPACE	(at least) PSPACE
• *satisfiability prob-lem for interval-based semantics*	in PSPACE, PSPACE-hard	non exists
• *ability for a combina-tion with other system (for actions, temporal re-lations etc.)*	high	restricted, non direct

5   Further Implementations and Concluding Remarks

In this paper we put forward a comparative analysis of two 'candidatures' for a
role of the appropriate multi-valued/fuzzy logic for preferences representation.
In order to single out the best logic, we considered a handful of their properties
such as completeness, satisfiability problems and a problem of the interval-based
semantics construction. We concluded that–although a comparative fuzzy preferential logic better grasp the comparative nature of preferences than the alternative system–it shows worst meta-logical properties. It turns out that *Fuzzy-Modal
Preferential Logic* shows a better ability for a combination with other systems
for actions, temporal relations *etc.*

This last property–a system's ability to be combined–is especially important
from the point of view of a long term goal of our research. In future we just intend
to develop hybrid models for temporal reasoning with preferences and other
constraints. FMPL seems to be also more able to be extended to a new system

with preferences for two agents groups that can express the mutually inconsistent preferences. It appears that the Allen's detecting inconsistency algorithm from [1] can be easily implemented for such a system. This issue requires, however, a more detailed analysis.

References

1. Allen, J.F.: Maintaining knowledge about temporal intervals. Communications of ACM 26(11), 832–843 (1983)
2. Chen, C.-C., Li, I.-P.: The computational complexity of the satisfiability of modal Horn clauses for modal propositional logics. Theoretical Computer Science 129, 95–121 (1994)
3. Glodeanu, C.V.: Exploring user's preferences in a fuzzy setting. Electronic Notes in Theoretical Computer Science 303, 37–57 (2014)
4. Godo, L., Esteva, H., Rodriquez, R.: A modal account of similarity-based reasoning. International Journal of Approximate Reasoning 4 (1997)
5. Hajek, P.: Metamathematics of Fuzzy Logic. Kluwer Academic Publishers, Dordrecht (1998)
6. Hajek, P., Hramancova, D.: A qualitative fuzzy possibilistic logic. International Journal of Approximate Reasoning 12, 1–19 (1995)
7. Hajek, P., Hramancova, D., Esteva, F., Godo, L.: On modal logics for qualitative possibility in a fuzzy setting. In: Proceeding of the Tenth Conference on Uncertainty in Artificial Intelligence, pp. 278–285 (1994)
8. Khatib, L., Morris, P., Morris, R., Rossi, F.: Temporal reasoning about preferences. In: Proceedings of IJCAI 2001, pp. 322–327 (2001)
9. Lomuscio, A., Michaliszyn, J.: An epistemic halpern-shoham logic. In: Proceedings of IJCAI 2013, pp. 1010–1016 (2013)
10. Morris, R., Morris, P., Khatib, L., Yorke-Smith, N.: Temporal planning with preferences and probabilities. In: Proceedings of ICAPS 2005 Workshop on Constraint Programming for Planning and Schedulling, Monterey, CA, pp. 1–7 (2005)
11. Rossi, F., Yorke-Smith, N., Venable, K.: Temporal reasoning with preferences and uncertainty. In: Proceedings of AAAI, vol. 8, pp. 1385–1386 (2003)
12. Schnobelen, P.: The complexity of temporal logic model checking. In: Proceedings of 4th Int. Workshop Advanced in Modal Logic, vol. 4, pp. 1–44 (2002)
13. van Benthem, J.: Dynamic logic for belief revision. Journal of Applied Non-Classical Logics 17(2), 119–155 (2007)
14. Benthem, J.v., Bezhanishvili, G.: Modal logic of space. In: Handbook of Spatial Logics, pp. 217–298. Springer (2007)
15. van Benthem, J., Gheerbrant, A.: Game: Solution, epistemic dynamics, and fixed-point logics. Fundamenta Informaticae 100, 19–41 (2010)

Learning Rules for Type-2 Fuzzy Logic System in the Control of DeNOx Filter

Marcin Kacprowicz[1,2(✉)], Adam Niewiadomski[1], and Krzysztof Renkas[1]

[1] Institute of Information Technology,
Lodz University of Technology, Łódź, Poland
[2] Institute of Social Sciences and Computer Science,
Higher Vocational State School in Wloclawek, Włocławek, Poland
marcin.kacprowicz@dokt.p.lodz.pl,
adam.niewiadomski@p.lodz.pl,
800561@edu.p.lodz.pl

Abstract. Imperfect methods of aquiring knowledge from experts in order to create fuzzy rules are generally known [16,4,25]. Since this is a very important part of fuzzy inference systems, this article focuses on presenting new learning methods for fuzzy rules. Referring to earlier work, the authors extended learning methods for fuzzy rules on applications of Type-2 fuzzy logic systems to control filters reducing air pollution. The filters use Selective Catalytic Reduction (SCR) method and, as for now, this process is controlled manually by a human expert.

Keywords: Fuzzy controler · Learning fuzzy rules · Higher order fuzzy logic system · Selective Catalytic Reduction (SCR) · Air pollution

1 Introduction: Emission of Industrial Gases and Fuzzy Control

1.1 Characteristics of the Problem

Nitrogen oxides are by-products of industrial production processes. In general, one might say they are a by-product of burning fuels. These gases are emitted into the atmosphere, despite their considerably harmful effect on humans and nature. Therefore, nitrogen oxide emission must be minimized. One of the means of neutralizing it is the use of ammonia (NH_3). The so-called Selective Catalytic Reduction (SCR) is one of the most popular methods of neutralizing nitrous oxide originating from burning fuels. The use of SCR is based on injecting heated ammonia into the combustion chamber, where consequently a chemical reaction takes place.

The amount added to the SCR filter of ammonia is adjusted by a valve, and adjustments (settings) of the valve are dependent on the amount of nitrogen oxides. As for now, the process, in particular, adjustments of ammonia valve (its opening angle), are still supervised by a human expert. As has been shown in [9] the process of Selective Catalytic Reduction (SCR) is a non-linear process that

© Springer International Publishing Switzerland 2015
L. Rutkowski et al. (Eds.): ICAISC 2015, Part I, LNAI 9119, pp. 184–194, 2015.
DOI: 10.1007/978-3-319-19324-3_17

is affected by many factors, which results in problems in the control system in a traditional way based on linear models. Therefore, because of non-linearity of the process, we propose to apply dedicated fuzzy logic systems (FLS) to control efficiently SCR processes, and to limit, at least partially, human participation in the process, see Fig. 1.

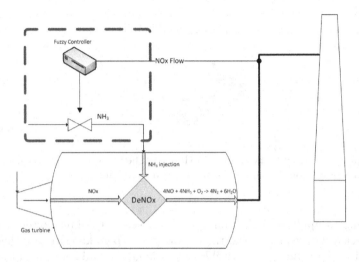

Fig. 1. A general schema of Selective Catalytic Reduction filter system. The red line bounds the part of the system, the fuzzy logic is proposed to be applied to.

1.2   Selective Catalytic Reduction (SCR) System

The DeNOx filtration system is based on a chemical reaction between nitrous oxides (NO_x) and ammonia (NH_3). As a result of a chemical reaction involving these substances clean nitrogen and water are obtained. Factory fumes containing nitrous oxides are pushed into a chamber where subsequently ammonia is injected, upon being heated in a tank prior to that. Ammonia gas in the process is a reducer separating molecules of NO_x to nitrogen N_2 and water H_2O. Because ammonia used in the process is both an extremely detrimental and relatively expensive compound, the appropriate dosage for both ecological and financial reasons is crucial for the architecture of the system.

Therefore, ammonia is supplied to the reactor through the ammonia valve. The valve control signals, in particular, angles of its opening, are computed by a traditional controller and supervised by a human operator, who makes his/her decisions on the base of "NO_x Flow" taken from exhaust gases, in particular, from sensors located in the final part of the exhaust (in the chimney), see Fig.1.

1.3   Related Work

Publication [3] describes some types of uncertainty that must be handled in power management systems. The authors show numerous problems encountered

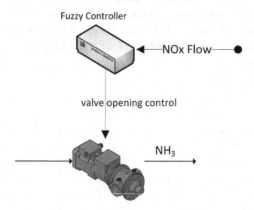

Fig. 2. A part of a general schema of SCR (Fig. 1). The fuzzy controller output adjusts the valve that is responsible for ammonia injected to exhaust gases.

when trying to apply optimization methods. Despite the great interest in the world of science-based solutions, the majority of expert knowledge rather than optimization algorithms is well visible. Traditional methods of control lead to a compromise to reach acceptable solutions. Fuzzy logic provides a framework for discussion of modeling such solutions. Examples of fuzzy logic systems applications are broadly known, e.g. [18]. Another work on FLSs in the industry and the environment is [2]. Because of non-linearity of those processes, fuzzy logic is proposed as one of the most hopeful methods, and the authors postulate to use it when indexing industries, in terms of the level of air and water pollution. Publications that deal with the general problem of fuzzy sets and fuzzy controllers are [14,23,19,21]. The authors [10] present rules and ideas for Interval Type-2 fuzzy logic systems. They introduce the concept of upper and lower membership functions. Higher order fuzzy logic systems are also described in [20,11,15]. The main problem and dedicated fuzzy logic systems for SCR described in this article on FLS was presented in [12,7] and we reproduce them in Sections 1.3 and 2 for the convenience of the reader.

2   Dedicated Type-2 Fuzzy Logic Systems for SCR

In this article, implementing the Type-2 fuzzy logic system (as stated by Mamdani in traditional mining i.e. Type-1 which was proposed and formalized by Mendel) is proposed as a means of controlling the dosage of ammonia (NH_3) in the reaction chamber. Decisions are made based on input data containing information on the concentration of NO and NO_2. Input data is fuzzified, with the use of IF-THEN rules combined with the fuzzy inference methods allowing for inference, and eventually the result of inference is obtained in the form of Type-2 fuzzy sets, which are defuzzified in order to come up with an exact figure determining the degree (percentage-wise) to which the ammonia dosage valve should open. The controller allows for the configuration of the inference method, as well as specifying the manner in which the rules are activated. Input data concerning the concentration of NO and NO_2 is obtained from sensors located at the SCR system outlet, see in Fig. 1.

The data they provide is recorded at 2 second intervals. Such a frequency results from legal regulations pertaining to the greenhouse gases emissions and the technical capabilities of controlling the ammonia dosage valve. According to current regulations limit, the total concentration of nitrogen oxides and dioxides is limited to 400 mg/m^3.

2.1 Input and Output Type-2 Fuzzy Sets

The values of NO_x concentration read from sensors are fuzzified to linguistic expressions: *Low, Medium, High, Higher than acceptable.*Type-2 fuzzy sets representing these labels are given in Figure 4. The output of the controller is the desired angle of the ammonia valve opening, and is described by linguistic labels: *Low, Medium, High, Very High.* Type-2 fuzzy sets representing these labels are depicted in Fig. 3.

The input data (samples) are fuzzified to Type-2 fuzzy sets presented in Fig. 4. The result of inference, the output Type-2 fuzzy sets representing angles of the ammonia valve opening, are illustrated in Fig. 3.

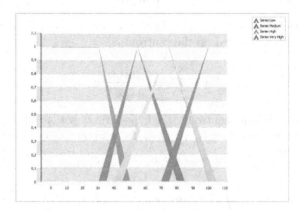

Fig. 3. Type-2 fuzzy sets for linguistic variables of output data which describe the valve opening angle to determine the amount of ammonia (the x value represents the angle of valve opening in percent)

2.2 IF-THEN Rules

On the basis of Type-2 fuzzy set of input and output expert determines sixteen fuzzy rules. They represent the linguistic values of the input data and Output.

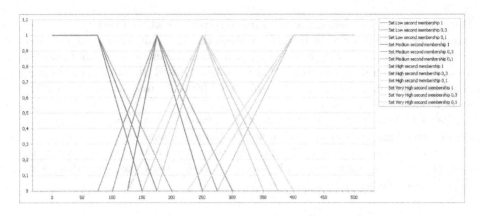

Fig. 4. Type-2 fuzzy sets for linguistic values of input data on NO and NO$_2$ (in mg/m^3)

We present some of them.

IF (NO IS Low) AND (NO$_2$ IS Low) THEN Valve opening angle IS Low

IF (NO IS Medium) AND (NO$_2$ IS Low) THEN Valve opening angle IS Low

IF (NO IS High) AND (NO$_2$ IS Low) THEN Valve opening angle IS Medium

IF (NO IS Higher Than Acceptable) AND (NO$_2$ IS Low) THEN Valve opening angle IS High

2.3   Type Reduction and Defuzzification

The type reduction operation on a Type-2 fuzzy set A in a discrete $X = \{x_1, \ldots, x_N\}$, $N \in \mathbb{N}$, is based on the centroid [8]:

$$C_A = \frac{\sum_{i=1}^{N} x_i \mu_A(x_i)}{\sum_{i=1}^{N} \mu_A(x_i)} \tag{1}$$

Using Extension Principle, centroid of a Type-2 fuzzy set $\widetilde{A} = \{\langle x, \mu_{\widetilde{A}}(x) \rangle \colon x \in X\}$ in X such that $\mu_{\widetilde{A}}(x_i) = \int_{u \in J_{x_i}} f_{x_i}(u)/u$, and $J_x \subseteq [0, 1]$ is the set of all primary memberships of x_i to $\widetilde{A}$, is given:

$$C_{\widetilde{A}} = \int_{\theta_1 \in J_{x_1}} \cdots \int_{\theta_N \in J_{x_N}} [f_{x_1}(\theta_1) \overset{T}{*} \ldots \overset{T}{*} f_{x_N}(\theta_N)] \bigg/ \frac{\sum_{i=1}^{N} x_i \theta_i}{\sum_{i=1}^{N} \theta_i} \tag{2}$$

where $\theta \in [\underline{J}_x, \bar{J}_x]$, and T is a T-norm. The defuzzification process in designed fuzzy controllers is based on the Height Method:

$$y^* = \frac{\sum_{i=1}^{m} y_i \mu_{Ci*}}{\sum_{i=1}^{m} \mu_{Ci*}} \tag{3}$$

where y^* is a real output value, μ_{Ci*} is the value of i-th fuzzy rule activation, and y_i is an element of Y with the highest membership [12].

3 Dedicated Modifications of Type-2 Fuzzy Logic Systems Architecture for SCR

Learning of fuzzy rules is performed using the training data. In this case, the use of filter DeNOx, we have two inputs and one output, but the proposed new methods of learning fuzzy rules can be extended to any number of inputs and outputs through each other's kernels can be a universal tool in improving the efficiency of fuzzy logic systems

3.1 Fuzzy Rules Learning

Fuzzy rules for Type-2 fuzzy controllers, in general, are determined by experts basing on their own experience. That does not guarantee optimal solution and was an impact to extends the research of the possibility of learning rules. Suppose we have two inputs, x_1, x_2, and one output y represented by Type-2 fuzzy sets $X, Y, \mu_{x_1}, \mu_{x_2} : X \longrightarrow [0, 1], \mu_y : Y \longrightarrow [0, 1]$. Based on Type-2 set of inputs it can be generate n rules IF-THEN where $n = \prod_{i=1}^{k} F_{x_i}$, k is number of inputs and F_x is a count of Type-2 fuzzy sets in k-th input. Each rule can have one successor from among j where $j = F_y$ is a number of output Type-2 fuzzy sets. Training data are represented by three element sets, i.e. x_1, x_2 and y, where x_1 and x_2 are inputs values, and y is the expected output value. Learning rules is based on the analysis of each of three element set. On the basis of influence of rules (possible to be created) that are activated, counter of the successor of this rule is increased. Three algorithms for selecting successors were presented in [7] for FLS and now extended to a Type-2 FLS presented: SR_I, SR_{II} and SR_{III}.

Algorithm 1. Learning Rule I (SR_I)

1: **for all** consequent **do**
2:     **if** activation Value of Primary Membership For Consequent == maxActivationValue **then**
3:         $consequentCounter \leftarrow consequentCounter + 1$

Algorithm 2. Learning Rule II (SR_{II})

1: **for all** consequent **do**
2:     **if** activation Value of Primary Membership For Consequent > 0 **then**
3:         $consequentCounter \leftarrow consequentCounter + 1$

Algorithm 3. Learning Rule III (SR_{III})

1: **for all** consequent **do**
2:     **if** activation Value of Primary Membership For Consequent > 0 **then**
3:         $consequentCounter \leftarrow consequentCounter + activationValueForConsequentofPrimaryMembership$

Other learning rules methods are shown in [22,6,1].

3.2 Type-2 Fuzzy Logic Systems with and without Learning Rules: Pros and Cons

Of course, learning rules has some cons, however taking into account gains from the use of learning rules it can be said that they significantly improves the results of fuzzy systems. All pros and cons are presented in Table 1

Table 1. Pros and cons of learning fuzzy rules

Pros	Cons
It does not require the expert	Learning data are necessary as an additional step in system so it is more costly
Improve of results is very likely	
Methods of learning work quickly	May not cover all possible cases
It can work in adaptive mode	Sensitive to changes in time the scope of data during operation
A significant increase in correlation to expected results given by expert, see Table 2	

4 Experiment

The experiment is conducted on six sets of samples. Three sets of ten thousand samples and three sets of one hundred thousand samples are applied. The results obtained are compared with the expert's propositions. For each sample two vectors are created: E - a vector containing the outcomes proposed by the expert, C - vector containing the outcomes calculated by the controller. Both vectors are of the same length and they are compared using three methods. The first method is minimum-maximum method, the second is Pearson Correlation Coefficient (PCC) and the other one is Mean Absolute Percentage Error (MAPE).

$$\text{min-max}(E, C) = \frac{\sum_{i=1}^{n} \min\{e_i, c_i\}}{\sum_{i=1}^{n} \max\{e_i, c_i\}} \tag{4}$$

where $E = \{e_1, e_2, ..., e_n\}$, $C = \{c_1, c_2, ..., c_n\}$, c_i is the actual value computed by the fuzzy controller and e_i is the forecast value given by human experts. Values of min-max(E, C) represent similarity of vectors E and C. The largest possible value of min-max(E, C) is 1 – it would mean that vectors are identical, so the values proposed by the controller are all equal to the values of ammonia valve opening angle proposed by human experts.

$$r_{(E,C)} = \frac{\sum_{i=1}^{n} (e_i - \bar{e})(c_i - \bar{c})}{\sqrt{\sum_{i=1}^{n} (e_i - \bar{e})^2} \sqrt{\sum_{i=1}^{n} (c_i - \bar{c})^2}} \tag{5}$$

where $r \in [-1; 1]$, $\bar{e} = \frac{1}{n} \sum_{i=1}^{n} e_i$ and $\bar{c} = \frac{1}{n} \sum_{i=1}^{n} c_i$. Value of PCC represent correlation between vectors E and C. Value -1 means complete negative correlation, 0 means no correlation and 1 mean complete positive correlation. The mean absolute percentage error (MAPE), also known as mean absolute percentage deviation (MAPD), is a measure of accuracy of a method for constructing fitted time series values in statistics, specifically in trend estimation.

$$M = \frac{1}{n} \sum_{i=1}^{n} \left| \frac{c_i - e_i}{c_i} \right| \tag{6}$$

4.1 Learning Fuzzy Rules from Data

The research is performed using Type-2 fuzzy controller with two inputs and one output. Of course, solution which is presented can be extend for any number of inputs and outputs. Listing (1.1) presents an algorithm for learning rules which is the best of three that have been created and tested. Differences between algorithms rely on the way of calculating the counters in each rule. In the best method (Algorithm I) presented on listing (1.1) only counter of set which has the biggest degree of membership is incremented. In the end, the algorithm chooses the consequent of a rule whose counter is the biggest. The other two methods are presented in listings (1.1) and (1.2). Included codes are in fact a method of representing algorithms.

Listing 1.1. Learning algorithm of fuzzy rules for a fuzzy controller. The learning algorithm is compatible with Algorithm I and II. The difference lies in the fact that in Algorithm I, the counter is incremented only for a set having the highest degree of activation, whereas in Algorithm II, each counter is incremented which has a degree of activation greater than 0.

```
foreach (learningData){
//Type−2 fuzzy set name, primary belong to Type−2 fuzzy set
Dictionary<string, double> uy =
    CountMembershipForAllFuzzySets(y);
//Type−2 fuzzy set name, primaty belong to Type−2 fuzzy set
Dictionary<string, double> ux1 =
    CountMembershipForAllFuzzySets(x1);
//Type−2 fuzzy set name, primary belong to Type−2 fuzzy set
Dictionary<string, double> ux2 =
    CountMembershipForAllFuzzySets(x2);
foreach (rules){
 foreach (ux1){
  if (ux1.Value.PrimaryMembership == 0){
  continue;
 }
 foreach (ux2){
  if (ux2.Value.PrimaryMembershi == 0){
  continue;
 }
 foreach (uy){
  if (uy.Value.PrimaryMembershi == 0){
  continue;
 }
 foreach (fuzzySets in rules){
  if (rules.x1.FuzzySetName == ux1.FuzzySetName &&
  rules.x2.FuzzySetName == ux2.FuzzySetName){
   if(uy.Value.PrimaryMembershi is MAX){
  rules.y[uy.FuzzySetName] += 1;
}}}}}}}
```

Listing 1.2. Learning algorithm consequent with Algorithm III where the counter is not incremented but the value of membership is increased instead.

```
...
rules.y[uy.FuzzySetName] += uy.Value.PrimaryMembershi;
...
```

The use of the methods in evaluation is commented in Table 2, in rows 2, 3 and 4, respectively.

4.2   Results

For each of the methods presented by listings (1.1) and (1.2), test on Type-2 fuzzified controller were conducted. The best results are shown here: Table 2. In this case the best results, meaning the highest resemblance and Pearson Correlation Coefficient and lowermost percent of error (MAPE) for vectors E and C are shown in bold. A difference of 0.005 should be interpreted as 40 tonnes (forty tonnes) nitrous oxide emitted into the atmosphere per year. The difference between the controller supplied with a learning of rules provided by an expert and by learning rules discussed in this article amount to $0.9420 - 0.9240 = 0.018$, which is comparable to 144 tonnes (one hundred forty four tonnes) of NO_2 emitted into the atmosphere per year.

Table 2. Values of min-max(E, C) similarity, the Pearson correlation coefficient (PCC) and the mean absolute percentage error (MAPE) of outputs computed by Type-2 fuzzy controllers to expert proposals

	min-max(E, C)	PCC	MAPE	Remarks
1.	0.9290	0.9240	16,379%	Type-2 Fuzzy Logic Systems, without rules learning
2.	**0.9360**	**0.9420**	**8,146%**	**Type-2 Fuzzy Logic Systems, with rules learning via Algorithm I**
3.	0.9330	0.9380	9,157%	Type-2 Fuzzy Logic Systems, with rules learning via Algorithm II
4.	0.9350	0.9400	8,561%	Type-2 Fuzzy Logic Systems, with rules learning via Algorithm III

5   Summary and Future Work

This article presents the new use of Type-2 fuzzy logic systems to control Selective Catalytic Reduction (SCR). Its task is to complement a human expert in making decisions. This paper is a continuation of research on fuzzified control in SCR. Extending work on it was based on adding learning methods to creating fuzzy rules in Type-2 fuzzy logic controllers. In prior research FLS learning methods were tested. The results obtained by the use of Type-2 fuzzy logic controller with a learning method in place are better than the results of Type-2 fuzzy logic controller whose rules of operation were created by an expert, see Table 2

All tests and results show that learning methods allow for better modelling of humans' perceptions of reality. In addition, they show the possibilities and directions of a search for new alternative ways to describe reality. Another conclusion that can be drawn from tests is that learning fuzzy rules allow to achieve better results than the fuzzy controller with rules from an expert.

Learning the rules can also be used in the hierarchical fuzzy controllers [5,24,17,13]. Due to the large quantity of rules in this type of systems can potentially greatly improve the performance of such solutions.

These conclusions lead to the final conclusion that further research on applications of FLSs to manage data on the environment pollution, and additionally, complying with official legal requirements, are reasonable and worth continuing.

References

1. Casillas, J., Cordon, O., Herrera, F.: Improving the wang and mendel's fuzzy rule learning method by inducing cooperation among rules (2000)
2. Christian, R.A., Lad, R.K., Deshpande, A.W., Desai, N.G.: Fuzzy MCDM approach for addressing composite index of water and air pollution potential of industries. International Journal of Digital Content Technology and its Applications 1, 4–71 (2008)
3. Cirstea, M.N.: Neural and fuzzy logic control of drives and power systems. Newnes (2002)
4. Cordon, O., Herrera, F., Villar, P.: Generating the knowledge base of a fuzzy rule-based system by the genetic learning of the data base. IEEE Transactions on Fuzzy Systems 9(4), 667–674 (2001)
5. Gegov, A.E., Frank, P.M.: Hierarchical fuzzy control of multivariable systems. Fuzzy Sets and Systems 72, 299–310 (1995)
6. Hammell, R., Sudkamp, T.: Learning fuzzy rules from data. In: The Application of INformation Technologies (Computer Science) to Mission Systems (1998)
7. Kacprowicz, M., Niewiadomski, A.: On dedicated fuzzy logic systems for emission control of industrial gases. In: Trends in Logic XIII (2014)
8. Karnik, N.N., Mendel, J.M.: Centroid of a type-2 fuzzy set. Information Sciences 132, 195–220 (2001)
9. Kuropka, J.: The test with ammonia nitrogen oxide reduction catalysts granular (in Polish, Badanie redukcji tlenkw azotu amoniakiem na katalizatorach ziarnistych). Ochrona rodowiska pp. 15–18 (1994)
10. Liang, Q., Mendel, J.M.: Interval type-2 fuzzy logic systems: Theory and design. IEEE Transactions on Fuzzy Systems 8, 535–550 (2000)
11. Mendel, J.M.: Uncertain Rule-Based Fuzzy Logic Systems: Introduction and New Directions. Prentice Hall (2001)
12. Niewiadomski, A., Kacprowicz, M.: Higher order fuzzy logic in controlling selective catalytic reduction systems. Bulletin of the Polish Academy of Sciences Technical Sciences 62(4), 743–750 (2014)
13. Renkas, K., Niewiadomski, A.: Hierarchical fuzzy logic systems: Current research and perspectives. In: Rutkowski, L., Korytkowski, M., Scherer, R., Tadeusiewicz, R., Zadeh, L.A., Zurada, J.M. (eds.) ICAISC 2014, Part I. LNCS, vol. 8467, pp. 295–306. Springer, Heidelberg (2014)

14. Rutkowska, D., Pilinski, M., Rutkowski, L.: Neural networks, genetic algorithms and fuzzy systems (in Polish, Sieci neuronowe, algorytmy genetyczne i systemy rozmyte). Scientific Publishing PWN, Warsaw-Lodz (1997)
15. Rutkowski, L.: Methods and techniques of artificial intelligence (in Polish, Metody i techniki sztucznej inteligencji). Scientific Publishing PWN, Warsaw (2009)
16. Serrurier, M., Sudkamp, T., Dubois, D., Prade, H.: Fuzzy inductive logic programming: Learning fuzzy rules with their implication. In: The 14th IEEE International Conference on Fuzzy Systems, FUZZ 2005, pp. 613–618 (2005)
17. Shahmaleki, P., Mahzoon, M.: Designing a hierarchical fuzzy controller for backing-up a four wheel autonomous robot. Proceedings of the American Control Conference (ACC 2008) (FrB17.5), June 11-13, pp. 4893–4897 (2008)
18. Smoczek, J.: Interval arithmetic-based fuzzy discrete-time crane control scheme design. Bulletin of the Polish Academy of Sciences Technical Sciences 61(4), 863–870 (2013)
19. Starczewski, J.T.: Extended triangular norms on gaussian fuzzy sets. In: Montseny, E., Sobrevilla, P. (eds.) EUSFLAT Conf., pp. 872–877. Universidad Polytecnica de Catalunya (2005)
20. Starczewski, J.T.: A triangular type-2 fuzzy logic system. In: IEEE International Conference on Fuzzy Systems, pp. 1460–1467 (2006)
21. Starczewski, J.T.: On defuzzification of interval type-2 fuzzy sets. In: Rutkowski, L., Tadeusiewicz, R., Zadeh, L.A., Zurada, J.M. (eds.) ICAISC 2008. LNCS (LNAI), vol. 5097, pp. 333–340. Springer, Heidelberg (2008)
22. Wang, L., Mendel, J.M.: Generating fuzzy rules by learning from examples. IEEE Transactions on Fuzzy Systems 22, 1414–1427 (1992)
23. Yager, R.R., Filev, D.P.: Fundamentals of modeling and fuzzy control (in Polish: Podstawy modelowania i sterowania rozmytego). Scientific and Technical Publishing, Warsaw (1995)
24. Zadeh, L.A.: Fuzzy logic = computing with words. IEEE Transactions on Fuzzy Systems 4(2) (May 1996)
25. Zhang, W.B., Liu, W.J.: IFCM:fuzzy clustering for rule extraction of interval type-2 fuzzy logic system. In: 46th IEEE Conference on Decision and Control, p. 5318 (2007)

Selected Applications of P1-TS Fuzzy Rule-Based Systems

Jacek Kluska[(✉)]

Faculty of Electrical and Computer Engineering, Rzeszów University of Technology,
Powstańców Warszawy 12, 35-959 Rzeszów, Poland
jacklu@prz.edu.pl

Abstract. In this paper, some results concerning analytical methods of fuzzy modeling, especially so called P1-TS fuzzy rule-based systems are described. The basic notions and facts concerning the theory of fuzzy systems are briefly recalled, including a method for overcoming or at least weakening the curse of dimensionality. A P1-TS system performing the function of the fuzzy JK flip-flop, as well as optimal controller for the 2nd order dynamical plant are described. Next, we show how to use the idea of P1-TS system for identification of some class of nonlinear dynamical systems. We briefly characterize FPGA hardware implementation of the P1-TS system. A result of a mobile robot navigation system design is described, as well. Finally, we show how to obtain a highly interpretable fuzzy classifier as a medical decision support system, by using both the theory of P1-TS system with a large number of inputs in conjunction with the idea of meta-rules, and gene expression programming method.

Keywords: Analytical theory of fuzzy systems · Fuzzy modeling · Fuzzy control · Fuzzy Petri nets · Fuzzy hardware · Diagnostics

1 Introduction

Fuzzy logic has been successfully applied in numerous fields such as control systems engineering, industrial automation, robotics, economics, environmental engineering, consumer electronics, image processing, medicine, and power engineering, e.g. in vehicles, antiskid braking systems, robot navigation systems, air conditioners, cameras, camcorders, elevators, household equipment, etc. Microprocessor chips specializing in fuzzy information processing have also been manufactured, for example NLX230, AL220 or 68HC12. According to the Web of Science database during the years 1969-2014 the keywords "fuzzy modeling" and "fuzzy control" occur in the literature for more than 12 500 times. However, there are very few works on analytical approach to the synthesis and analysis of fuzzy logic systems. The exception is the book of Ying [1], where the author has rightly pointed out that the fuzzy systems developed are mostly treated as (magic) black boxes with little analytical understanding and explanation. In this work we intend to show that analytical theory is still needed and development of such theory brings benefits and is useful in various fields.

© Springer International Publishing Switzerland 2015
L. Rutkowski et al. (Eds.): ICAISC 2015, Part I, LNAI 9119, pp. 195–206, 2015.
DOI: 10.1007/978-3-319-19324-3_18

2 Basic Properties of P1-TS Systems

Let us consider a simple fuzzy rule-based system with the inputs constituting a vector $\mathbf{z} = [z_1, \ldots, z_n]^T \in D^n = \times_{k=1}^n [-\alpha_k, \beta_k]$, $(\alpha_k + \beta_k > 0)$, and the output S. Suppose any input has assigned 2 linear, complementary membership functions of fuzzy sets

$$N(z_k) = (\alpha_k + \beta_k)^{-1}(\beta_k - z_k), \quad P(z_k) = 1 - N(z_k), \quad k = 1, 2, \ldots, n, \quad (1)$$

where $z_k \in [-\alpha_k, \beta_k]$. The rules have the following form

$$\text{If } z_1 \text{ is } A_{i_1} \,\&\, \ldots \,\&\, z_n \text{ is } A_{i_n}, \text{ then } S = q_{i_1, \ldots, i_n}, \quad q_{i_1, \ldots, i_n} \in \mathbb{R}, \quad (2)$$

where $A_{i_k} \in \{N_{i_k}, P_{i_k}\}$ and $i_1, \ldots, i_n \in \{0, 1\}$. Such a system we will call P1-TS system [3]. One can show that for any function $f_0 : D^n \to \mathbb{R}$ given by

$$f_0(\mathbf{z}) = \sum_{(p_1, \ldots, p_n) \in \{0,1\}^n} \theta_{p_1, \ldots, p_n} z_1^{p_1} \cdots z_n^{p_n}, \quad \theta_{p_1, \ldots, p_n} \in \mathbb{R}, \quad (3)$$

there exists such a P1-TS system, for which $S(\mathbf{z}) = f_0(\mathbf{z})$, for any $\mathbf{z} \in D^n$. What's more, one can find the consequents of rules $q_1, \ldots, q_{2^n}$ by solving 2^n algebraic equations. A unique solution always exists, if and only if, the hyperrectangle D^n has a non-zero volume [2].

The vector

$$\mathbf{g}(\mathbf{z}) = [1, \ldots, (z_1^{p_1} \cdots z_n^{p_n}), \ldots, (z_1 \cdots z_n)]^T \in \mathbb{R}^{2^n}, \quad p_k \in \{0, 1\}, \quad (4)$$

we call a *generator* of the P1-TS rule-based system and

$$\mathbf{\Omega} = [\mathbf{g}(\boldsymbol{\gamma}_1), \ldots, \mathbf{g}(\boldsymbol{\gamma}_{2^n})] \in \mathbb{R}^{2^n} \times \mathbb{R}^{2^n}, \quad (5)$$

is its *fundamental matrix*, where $\boldsymbol{\gamma}_j$ is a vertex of the hyperrectangle D^n. The matrix $\mathbf{\Omega}$ is called fundamental one, since it is always nonsingular for $\alpha_k + \beta_k > 0$, $(k = 1, \ldots, n)$. Nonfuzzy output of the P1-TS system can be expressed as follows

$$S(\mathbf{z}) = \mathbf{g}^T(\mathbf{z})(\mathbf{\Omega}^T)^{-1}\mathbf{q} = f_0(\mathbf{z}). \quad (6)$$

In practice, the rules may be *contradictory* and/or *incomplete* and the systems may have many outputs. In all such cases one can generalize the results on transformation of rules into equations similar to (3)–(6). Furthermore, for a large number of input variables, we can use *meta-rules*, which are equivalent to subsets of individual rules in the form of (2). More complicated results can be obtained for the systems with membership functions for input variables, that are polynomials of the 2nd or higher degree [2]. However, here we will limit ourselves to the systems with the simplest fuzzy sets as in (1).

It is well known that the fuzzy systems suffer from the curse of dimensionality [4]. So, what to do, if we want to use the vector $\mathbf{g}$ and the matrix $\mathbf{\Omega}$, where $\dim \mathbf{g} = 2^n$, and $\dim \mathbf{\Omega} = 4^n$ for the system with n input variables? With the help comes recursion. Namely, one can show that for $k + 1$ input variables, the generator can be obtained as follows

$$\mathbf{g}_{k+1} = \begin{bmatrix} 1 \\ z_{k+1} \end{bmatrix} \otimes \mathbf{g}_k \in \mathbb{R}^{2^{k+1}}, \quad \mathbf{g}_0 = 1, \quad k = 0, 1, 2, \ldots, \tag{7}$$

and the fundamental matrix

$$\boldsymbol{\Omega}_{k+1} = \begin{bmatrix} 1 & 1 \\ -\alpha_{k+1} & \beta_{k+1} \end{bmatrix} \otimes \boldsymbol{\Omega}_k \in \mathbb{R}^{2^{k+1} \times 2^{k+1}}, \quad \boldsymbol{\Omega}_0 = 1, \quad k = 0, 1, 2, \ldots, \tag{8}$$

where "$\otimes$" denotes the Kronecker product [2]. Furthermore, using recursion and Kronecker product one can compute the inverse of the fundamental matrix

$$\boldsymbol{\Omega}_{k+1}^{-1} = \frac{1}{\alpha_{k+1} + \beta_{k+1}} \begin{bmatrix} \beta_{k+1} & -1 \\ \alpha_{k+1} & 1 \end{bmatrix} \otimes \boldsymbol{\Omega}_k^{-1}, \quad k = 0, 1, 2, \ldots \tag{9}$$

In this way, it is possible to perform the synthesis or analysis of the rule-based systems with a number of inputs equal to 10 or more. Such a number of input variables causes rather serious problems in practical applications, if we use the traditional approach to the fuzzy rule-based systems [4], [5]. The use of symbolic computations is particularly productive for the above recursive matrix calculus.

3   P1-TS System as Fuzzy JK Flip-Flop

Owing to analytical theory we can easily obtain a model of the fuzzy JK flip-flop (or fuzzy RS flip-flop) as a discrete-time dynamic system. Fuzzy JK flip-flop with the inputs J and K, where J denotes the Set-input, and K is the Reset-input, and the output Q, can be described in several ways [10], [11]. For example we can use multiple-inputs-multiple-output P1-TS system description in the matrix form [2] as follows

$$\text{If } [J(t), K(t), Q(t)] = \begin{bmatrix} N_1 & N_2 & N_3 \\ P_1 & N_2 & N_3 \\ N_1 & P_2 & N_3 \\ P_1 & P_2 & N_3 \\ N_1 & N_2 & P_3 \\ P_1 & N_2 & P_3 \\ N_1 & P_2 & P_3 \\ P_1 & P_2 & P_3 \end{bmatrix}, \text{ then } Q(t+1) = \begin{bmatrix} 0 \\ 1 \\ 0 \\ 1 \\ 1 \\ 1 \\ 0 \\ 0 \end{bmatrix}, \tag{10}$$

where $J, K, Q \in [0, 1]$, and $t = 0, 1, 2, \ldots$ The fuzzy sets N_k and P_k are interpreted as *near zero*, and *near one*, respectively. For $J, K, Q \in \{0, 1\}$ the system of rules (10) describes the binary JK flip-flop (by $N_k \equiv 0$ and $P_k \equiv 1$). Many variants of fuzzy JK flip-flops have been developed [11]. Some of them were implemented as synchronous systems, while others (super–fast) – as asynchronous ones [12]. The fuzzy JK flip-flop can be used as the basic element for storing a "fuzzy token" in the fuzzy Petri net (FPN) [13]. Such a net can be both a formal model for process control and/or fault diagnosis of discrete event systems [14]. What is more, FPN can be designed and made as a very fast hardware device.

4   P1-TS System as Optimal Controller

In many publications the fuzzy logic controller was compared with the classical one by using simulations, taking into account numerical parameters of the plant. In contrast to those works we will use an analytical approach, i.e. we will use symbols instead of specific numbers. Suppose the second order plant

$$\ddot{y}(t) + 2\xi\omega_0\dot{y}(t) + \omega_0^2 y(t) = k_0 u(t), \qquad \xi > 0, \qquad y(0), \ \dot{y}(0), \qquad (11)$$

is controlled in the closed-loop by the P1-TS system, as shown in Fig. 1. In the control engineering practice, the typical design requirements refer to the quality of transient processes which should be obtained in the closed-loop feedback system by some fixed reference signal. One can check that there exists such a P1-TS system performing the controller function, for which the closed-loop system is asymptotically stable, and the plant output converges to the setpoint w_0 without oscillations, even if $\xi < 1$. This means that for the reference signal $w(t) = w_0$, $(t \geqslant 0)$, one obtains the desired transient response

$$y(t) = w_0 + (y_0 - w_0) e^{-\lambda t}, \qquad (12)$$

where $\lambda > 0$ and depending on this parameter we can ensure a sufficiently fast step response. Assuming the control error $\varepsilon(t) = w(t) - y(t)$, the inputs of the rule-based system as $z_1 = \dot{\varepsilon}(t)$, $z_2 = \varepsilon(t)$, $z_3 = \ddot{\varepsilon}(t)$ and the output signal of the P1-TS system $S = \dot{u}(t)$, we obtain the optimal rules, i.e. the rules for which the overall system is critically damped. This means that after applying such rules, the step response $y(t)$ of the closed-loop system is in the form of (12). After defining the fuzzy sets on the appropriate universes containing 0, we obtain the optimal fuzzy rules as shown in Table 1, where

$$k_p = 2\xi\omega_0\lambda k_0^{-1}, \quad T_i = k_0 \left(\omega_0^2\lambda\right)^{-1}, \quad T_d = \lambda k_0^{-1}. \qquad (13)$$

It is clear that both the control error and its derivatives are from intervals containing zero. Thus, $-\alpha_2 \leqslant z_2 = \varepsilon(t) \leqslant \beta_2$, $-\alpha_1 \leqslant z_1 = \dot{\varepsilon}(t) \leqslant \beta_1$, $-\alpha_3 \leqslant z_3 = \ddot{\varepsilon}(t) \leqslant \beta_3$, where $0 < \alpha_k \approx \beta_k$ for $k = 1, 2, 3$. This means that interpretation of the labels used in antecedents of the fuzzy rules is as follows: N_k is "negative", and P_k - "positive" for $k = 1, 2, 3$. The proof of the optimality of the rules can be performed either in time- or frequency domain. In time domain we should

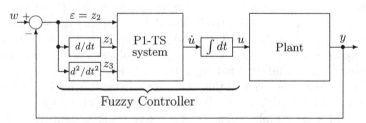

Fig. 1. The colsed-loop control system

Table 1. Look-up-table for the optimal P1-TS system performing the function of the controller.

$\dot{\varepsilon}(t),\varepsilon(t) \setminus$ $\ddot{\varepsilon}(t) \to$ $\downarrow$	N_3	P_3
N_1, N_2	$-T_d\alpha_3 - T_i^{-1}\alpha_2 - k_p\alpha_1$	$T_d\beta_3 - T_i^{-1}\alpha_2 - k_p\alpha_1$
N_1, P_2	$-T_d\alpha_3 + T_i^{-1}\beta_2 - k_p\alpha_1$	$T_d\beta_3 + T_i^{-1}\beta_2 - k_p\alpha_1$
P_1, P_2	$-T_d\alpha_3 + T_i^{-1}\beta_2 + k_p\beta_1$	$T_d\beta_3 + T_i^{-1}\beta_2 + k_p\beta_1$
P_1, N_2	$-T_d\alpha_3 - T_i^{-1}\alpha_2 + k_p\beta_1$	$T_d\beta_3 - T_i^{-1}\alpha_2 + k_p\beta_1$

consider the appropriate integro-differential equation. This proof follows from the results (3)–(6) in case of $n = 3$ inputs (z_1, z_2, z_3) by assumption that all coefficients $\theta_{(.)}$ at the nonlinear components of equation (3) are equal to zero, by taking into account the differential equation defining the plant (11), the required step response (12) as the optimality condition, the system structure shown in Fig. 1, and the rules in Table 1 together with the definition of coefficients (13).

It must be stressed that the assessment of the closed-loop system behavior does not depend on numerical values of the plant (ξ, ω_0, k_0) or accuracy of the simulations.

5   Identification of Some Class of Nonlinear Dynamic Systems

Identification and modeling of dynamic systems based on the measurement data is important for engineering practice. Suppose that the observed trajectory of the n-th order dynamic system is known in the discrete-time, i.e. the values of the coordinates $z_j(t_1),\ldots,z_j(t_{K+1})$ for $j = 1,\ldots,n$ are given. One can show that, as a result of a learning process that resembles a well-known Widrow-Hoff learning procedure for the feedforward neural networks, we get a P1-TS system, whose behavior can be described by the following system of nonlinear differential equations [2]

$$\frac{dz_j}{dt} = \mathbf{g}^T(z_1,\ldots,z_n)\left(\sum_{k=1}^{K}\mathbf{g}_{t_k}\mathbf{g}_{t_k}^T\right)^{-1}[\mathbf{g}_{t_1},\cdots,\mathbf{g}_{t_K}]\,\mathbf{d}_j\,, \qquad (14)$$

where

$$\mathbf{g}_{t_k} = \mathbf{g}(z_1(t_k),\cdots,z_n(t_k)),\quad k = 1,2,\ldots,K, \qquad (15)$$

is the generator of the P1-TS rule-based system and

$$\mathbf{d}_j = [\Delta z_1/\Delta t_1,\ldots,\Delta z_K/\Delta t_K]^T \in \mathbb{R}^K,\; j = 1,2,\ldots,n, \qquad (16)$$

where $\Delta z_k = z_j(t_{k+1}) - z_j(t_k)$, $\Delta t_k = t_{k+1} - t_k$ for $k = 1,2,\ldots,K$. The above system is an approximation of the following one

$$\frac{dz_k}{dt} = a_{k,0} + \sum_{i=1}^{n}a_{k,i}z_i + \sum_{\substack{i,j=1 \\ i<j}}^{n}a_{k,i,j}z_iz_j + \cdots + a_{k,1,2,\ldots,n}z_1z_2\cdots z_n, \qquad (17)$$

for $k = 1, \ldots, n$. The modeling error can be made arbitrarily small for a sufficiently dense sampling of the measured signals. The above class of nonlinear dynamic systems is seemingly simple; it also comprises some class of chaotic systems, e.g. Chen's attractor described by the following nonlinear differential equations

$$\begin{cases} \dot{x} = a\,(y - x)\,, \\ \dot{y} = (c - a)\,x - xz + cy, \\ \dot{z} = xy - bz, \end{cases} \tag{18}$$

where the constants are $a = 35$, $b = 3$, and $c = 28$. One can show that this system can be modeled by the zero-order 3-input-3-output P1-TS system [2].

6   Hardware Implementation of P1-TS System

Since P1-TS system has many applications, it is worthwhile to implement it as a hardware device. The basis for the hardware implementation is the following result [2]

$$S_n\,(q_1, \ldots, q_{2^n}) = N_n\,(z_n)\,S_{n-1}\,(q_1, \ldots, q_{2^{n-1}}) + P_n\,(z_n)\,S_{n-1}\,(q_{2^{n-1}+1}, \ldots, q_{2^n})\,, \tag{19}$$

for $n = 1, 2, \ldots$, where $S_0\,(x) = x$, $\forall\, x \in \mathbb{R}$. Here $S_n\,(q_1, \ldots, q_{2^n})$ denotes the output of the system with the inputs $(z_1, \ldots, z_n)$ by the consequents of the rules $[q_1, \cdots, q_{2^n}]^T$, whereas $N_n\,(z_n)$ and $P_n\,(z_n)$ are membership functions for $z_n \in [-\alpha_n, \beta_n]$, the output $S_{n-1}\,(q_1, \ldots, q_{2^{n-1}})$ of the system is computed for the inputs $z_1, \ldots, z_{n-1}$ and by the consequents of the rules $[q_1, \cdots, q_{2^{n-1}}]^T$, and $S_{n-1}\,(q_{2^{n-1}+1}, \ldots, q_{2^n})$ is the output of the system with inputs $z_1, \ldots, z_{n-1}$ and by the consequents of the rules $[q_{2^{n-1}+1}, \ldots, q_{2^n}]^T$.

The FPGA implementation of the P1-TS system, which operates according to the formula (19) was described in [6]. It is worth noting that the FPGA logic resources are independent of the number of inputs, and the number of inputs is limited only by available memory storing the consequents of the rules. Here we quote only the results concerning the processing speed of the P1-TS system, which has the form of a software module for a variety of microprocessor-based controllers, and FPGA hardware device. In case of 4 input variables, the processing time is $36\,700\,\mu s$ for GE Fanuc VersaMax controller, $2\,400\,\mu s$ for Siemens S7-1200 PLC, and $139\,\mu s$ for a very fast PLC of Beckhoff (CP6607). The completely on-chip-P1-TS-system process the same information during $10.35\,\mu s$. It should be noted that the literature does not provide similar results concerning Takagi-Sugeno systems for the number of inputs greater than 3, which is a consequence of the curse of dimensionality [5]. Table 2 shows the propagation times of the P1-TS system as a hardware device with 4, 8, 12 and 16 inputs. It is clear that any program implementation is many times slower than a hardware device. In the next section we will show that the hardware implementation can be used as a real-time control system.

Table 2. Propagation times of the P1-TS hardware prototype based on Xilinx Spartan-6 FPGA chip

Number of inputs	Clock cycles	Propagation time [μs]
4	932	10.35
8	15 932	177.02
12	251 822	2 798.02
16	4 030 142	44 779.35

7   Mobile Robot Navigation Problem Using P1-TS System

Let us consider the navigation problem for a two-wheeled mobile robot, having two independent drives: the left (l) and the right (r). Robot movement is forced by the direct control systems, which are responsible for the execution of the appropriate number of wheel revolutions, according to the preset number of pulses per time unit, u_l and u_r, respectively. The robot position and the target point are known. The robot should go to the destination point and simultaneously avoid obstacles, whose location is unknown a priori. The obstacles are detected by the infra-red (IR) proximity sensors, which are coupled to the m-bit independent registers: z_1 (for the obstacles to the left of the robot), z_2 (for the obstacles to the right of the robot), and z_3 (for obstacles in front of the robot), where z_1, z_2, $z_3 \in [0, a]$, where $a = 2^m - 1$. In the universe $[0, a]$ we define the membership functions of fuzzy sets: $N_1(z_1)$ - there is *no obstacle to the left* of the robot, $N_2(z_2)$ - there is *no obstacle to the right* of the robot, and $N_3(z_3)$ - there is *no obstacle in front* of the robot, and naturally, $P_i(z_i) = 1 - N_i(z_i)$ are their complements, ($i = 1, 2, 3$). Next, we define the inputs z_4 and z_5. The variable $z_4 \in [-\pi, \pi]$ is the angle between the line perpendicular to the robot axle and a distance line between the robot and the goal point, whereas $z_5 \in [0, D]$ is the distance between the robot and the goal point. Finally, we define the fuzzy sets for the inputs z_4 and z_5: A_1 - the angle z_4 is *negative*, A_2 - the angle z_4 is *near zero*, A_3 - the angle z_4 is *positive*, B_1 - the distance z_5 is *small*, B_2 - the distance z_5 is *big*. The membership functions of fuzzy sets A_i are triangular and make strong fuzzy partition on $[-\pi, \pi]$, whereas $B_1 = N_4(z_4)$, and $B_2 = 1 - N_4(z_4)$, so that the interpretation of all fuzzy sets is simple.

The navigator should combine obstacle avoidance and goal-seeking behaviors. We can design the behaviors independently and next combine them by a soft switching function according to the situation around the robot. The architecture of the navigation system is shown in Fig. 2. Every wheel is moved by a DC motor coupled with a gear. We assume that DC motors are controlled by PID controllers working at the lowest control level. The inputs of the controllers are signals $u_l \in [-C, C]$ and $u_r \in [-C, C]$, where C is the maximal value of pulses per second.

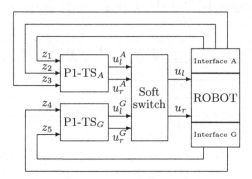

Fig. 2. Navigation system for the mobile robot

Table 3. Look-up-table for the P1-TS$_A$ fuzzy system for the robot working in the obstacle avoidance mode

Rule	z_1 (right)	z_2 (left)	z_3 (front)	Decision	$\left(u_l^A, u_r^A\right)$
R_1	N_1	N_2	N_3	go ahead	(C, C)
R_2	P_1	N_2	N_3	turn left	$(-C, C)$
R_3	N_1	P_2	N_3	turn right	$(C, -C)$
R_4	P_1	P_2	N_3	go ahead	(C, C)
R_5	N_1	N_2	P_3	turn left	$(-C, C)$
R_6	P_1	N_2	P_3	turn left	$(-C, C)$
R_7	N_1	P_2	P_3	turn right	$(C, -C)$
R_8	P_1	P_2	P_3	turn left	$(-C, C)$

Now we will investigate the obstacle avoidance mode. By formulating the fuzzy rules for this mode, which should be performed by the P1-TS$_A$ system, the following decisions can be taken: "*go ahead*" or "*turn left*" or "*turn right*". The fuzzy rules are given in Table 3. According to analytical theory of P1-TS systems we immediately obtain the following control actions

$$u_l^A = \frac{C}{a^3} \left(a^3 - 2a^2 z_1 - 2a^2 z_3 + 2a z_1 z_2 + 2a z_1 z_3 + 2a z_2 z_3 - 4 z_1 z_2 z_3\right), \quad (20)$$

$$u_r^A = \frac{C}{a^2} \left(a^2 - 2a z_2 + 2 z_1 z_2\right). \quad (21)$$

Now let us consider the goal seeking mode. The fuzzy rules for the P1-TS$_G$ system are given in Table 4, where the coefficient $\eta \in (0, 1)$, say $\eta = 0.05$. Finally, we obtain the following control actions

$$u_l^G = C \left(\eta + \frac{z_4 - \eta |z_4|}{\pi} + \frac{1 - \eta}{D} z_5 - \frac{1 - \eta}{\pi D} |z_4| z_5\right), \quad (22)$$

Table 4. Look-up-table for the P1-TS$_G$ fuzzy system for the robot working in the goal seeking mode

Rule	z_4 (angle)	z_5 (distance)	Decision	$\left(u_l^G, u_r^G\right)$
R_1	A_1	B_1	turn left	$(-C, C)$
R_2	A_2	B_1	go ahead slowly	$(\eta C, \eta C)$
R_3	A_3	B_1	turn right	$(C, -C)$
R_4	A_1	B_2	turn left	$(-C, C)$
R_5	A_2	B_2	go ahead	(C, C)
R_6	A_3	B_2	turn right	$(C, -C)$

$$u_r^G = C\left(\eta - \frac{z_4 + \eta\,|z_4|}{\pi} + \frac{1-\eta}{D}z_5 - \frac{1-\eta}{\pi D}\,|z_4|\,z_5\right), \qquad (23)$$

for the navigation system working in the goal seeking mode. Once the rule bases for the P1-TS systems are gathered, the two behaviors can be combined as follows

$$u_l = \rho u_l^A + (1-\rho)\,u_l^G, \qquad u_r = \rho u_r^A + (1-\rho)\,u_r^G, \qquad (24)$$

where the coefficient $\rho \in [0,1]$ is a constant or $\rho = \mathfrak{s}(x_1, \ldots, x_6)/a$ by some t-conorm $\mathfrak{s}$, e.g. maximum. Observe that explicitly obtained control actions can be easily implemented as a small, inexpensive and very fast hardware device, e.g. described in Section 6.

8   P1-TS Model as Medical Decision Support System

To show further advantages of the use of the analytical theory of fuzzy systems, we will consider an example which requires the use of a large number of variables. For $D^n = [0,1]^n$ the P1-TS system processes the information expressed by a continuous multi-valued logic. Its rules are therefore highly interpretable. When the number of inputs of the rule-based system is large, we are rather interested in the *meta-rules* than in the individual rules, since the number of individual rules is usually 2^n. The meta-rule is equivalent to k rules of the form (2), where $2 \leqslant k \leqslant 2^n$. Suppose the inputs of the P1-TS system are $x_1, \ldots, x_n \in [0,1]$ and the consequents of the rules are from the set $\{0,1\}$. Let us define new input variables $z_1, \ldots, z_{2n}$ as follows: $z_{2k-1} = x_k$, $z_{2k} = 1 - x_k$, for $k = 1, \ldots, n$. Then, the crisp output of this system can be expressed in the form of sum of products

$$S = \sum_{i=1}^{M}\prod_{i \in P_i} z_i, \quad M \leqslant 2^{2n}, \qquad (25)$$

where $P_i \in 2^{\{1, \ldots, 2n\}}$, and from (25) one can unambiguously read the meta-rules which are equivalent to the set of original rules in the form of (2).

Taking into account the equation (25) and using gene expression programming method [8] we can construct a classifier as P1-TS system with highly interpretable meta-rules. In [7] such a classifier was obtained, as a medical decision support system which is able to predict peri-operative complications in patients suffering from cancer [9]. The P1-TS system was built for the data set containing 107 patients, each described by 8 attributes: age (x_1), BMI (x_2), comorbidities (x_3), previous operations (x_4), hormonal status (x_5), histology of tumor (x_6), histologic grade (x_7), and FIGO stage (x_8). The output variable was bivalent one, i.e. $S \in \{present, absent\}$, where $S = present$ denotes occurrence of intra- or post-operative complications. The dataset was obtained from the Clinical Department of Obstetrics and Gynecology of Rzeszów State Hospital in Poland. Three types of predictors were proposed: (1) - the original attribute $x_i \in \{x_{i,min}, \ldots, x_{i,max}\} \subset \mathbb{R}$ and there is no recommendation to split this universe into subintervals, (2) - the original attribute $x_i \in \{x_{i,min}, \ldots, x_{i,max}\} \subset \mathbb{R}$ and there are recommendations to split this universe into some number of subsets, and (3) - the original attribute $x_i \in \{label_1, \ldots, label_r\}$, where $r \geqslant 2$. Next, the attributes x_i were linearly transformed into new variables z_k. Finally, 42 new input variables were obtained: $z_1, \ldots, z_{42}$. As one can see, a half of the variables of z-type are redundant, but these variables are proposed to be used to facilitate the process of seeking expressions in the form of sum of products (or product of sums) of the input variables. Even if we consider only 21 variables, it is evident that the use of 2^{21} individual rules becomes meaningless, so we must use the meta-rules. The number and complexity of the meta-rules can be adjusted by setting up the appropriate parameters for the gene expression programming algorithm. Several different models with the same minimal testing error were received. Let us quote, for example

$$S = z_{12}z_{29} + z_{20}z_{29} + z_{24}z_{42}. \tag{26}$$

Thus, according to the analytical theory the equation (26) we can immediately express in the form of 3 meta-rules [7]:

1. If BMI is near the lower bound of overweight and cancer is moderately differentiated, then complications are present;
2. If comorbidities are absent and cancer is moderately differentiated, then complications are present;
3. If hormonal status is post-menopausal and cervical cancer is not of IIB stage, then complications are present.

The decision trees and C5 algorithm as the competitive "white-box" classifiers, proved to be worse than the proposed P1-TS system. In the literature one can find a lot of fuzzy classifiers constructed using evolutionary algorithms. However, the fuzzy rule-based classifiers with several tens of variables are rather absent.

9   Conclusion

Generally, the article demonstrates some of the author's experiences concerning applications of the P1-TS rule-based systems. Some results on analytical methods in fuzzy modeling and control were described. Although the fuzzy sets used in this system are the simplest, we showed that there is considerable number of applications of such systems, especially in control and technical or medical diagnostics. Only the basic results concerning the theory of P1-TS systems are briefly recalled, including a method of weakening the curse of dimensionality in fuzzy systems. A model of the fuzzy JK flip-flop, as a generalization of the binary flip-flop was described, that can be used for the fuzzy Petri net synthesis. We showed that P1-TS system performing a function of the fuzzy controller in the feedback loop for the linear 2nd order plant, can be easily designed to behave optimally in the sense of requirements, that are generally acceptable in the automatic control engineers community. It should be noted that to show this fact, we do not need numerical simulations. Our result can be easily generalized for some class of the nonlinear dynamic plants. Furthermore, the identification method for a certain class of nonlinear dynamic systems was described and a result of a mobile robot navigation system design was given. Fully hardware implementation of the P1-TS system was characterized, where the number of inputs is much greater than in the fuzzy systems so far described in the literature. The presented system is very fast and cheap. Owing to analytical approach to the navigation system design, we obtained the control actions, which can be easily implemented as a hardware device. It was shown how to obtain a highly interpretable classifier in the form of P1-TS system with several dozen of inputs, by using both analytical methods of fuzzy modeling, and gene expression programming method. It seems that analytical theory is still needed and development of this theory brings benefits and is useful in various fields [15], [16], [17], [18], [19], [20], [21].

References

1. Ying, H.: Fuzzy control and modeling. Analytical foundations and applications. IEEE Press, New York (2000)
2. Kluska, J. (ed.): Analytical Methods in Fuzzy Modeling and Control. STUDFUZZ, vol. 241. Springer, Heidelberg (2009)
3. Kluska, J.: Transformation lemma on analytical modeling via Takagi–Sugeno fuzzy system and its applications. In: Rutkowski, L., Tadeusiewicz, R., Zadeh, L.A., Żurada, J.M. (eds.) ICAISC 2006. LNCS (LNAI), vol. 4029, pp. 230–239. Springer, Heidelberg (2006)
4. Pedrycz, W., Gomide, F.: Fuzzy Systems Engineering: Toward Human-Centric Computing. Wiley-IEEE Press (2008)
5. McKenna, M., Wilamowski, B.M.: Implementing a Fuzzy System on a Field Programmable Gate Array. In: Int. Joint Conf. Neural Networks, Washington DC, July 15-19, pp. 189–194 (2001)
6. Kluska, J., Hajduk, Z.: Hardware implementation of P1-TS fuzzy rule-based systems on FPGA. In: Rutkowski, L., Korytkowski, M., Scherer, R., Tadeusiewicz, R., Zadeh, L.A., Zurada, J.M. (eds.) ICAISC 2013, Part I. LNCS, vol. 7894, pp. 282–293. Springer, Heidelberg (2013)
7. Kluska, J., Kusy, M., Obrzut, B.: The Classifier for Prediction of Peri-operative Complications in Cervical Cancer Treatment. In: Rutkowski, L., Korytkowski, M., Scherer, R., Tadeusiewicz, R., Zadeh, L.A., Zurada, J.M. (eds.) ICAISC 2014, Part II. LNCS (LNAI), vol. 8468, pp. 143–154. Springer, Heidelberg (2014)

8. Ferreira, C.: Gene Expression Programming: A New Adaptive Algorithm for Solving Problems. Complex Systems 13(2), 87–129 (2001)
9. Kusy, M., Obrzut, B., Kluska, J.: Application of gene expression programming and neural networks to predict adverse events of radical hysterectomy in cervical cancer patients. Medical & Biological Engineering & Computing 51(12), 1357–1365 (2013)
10. Hirota, K., Ozawa, K.: The concept of fuzzy flip-flop. IEEE Trans. SMC 19, 980–987 (1989)
11. Gniewek, L., Kluska, J.: Family of fuzzy J-K flip-flops based on bounded product, bounded sum and complementation. IEEE Trans. SMC, Part B 28(6), 861–868 (1998)
12. Kluska, J., Hajduk, Z.: Digital implementation of fuzzy Petri net based on asynchronous fuzzy RS flip-flop. In: Rutkowski, L., Siekmann, J.H., Tadeusiewicz, R., Zadeh, L.A. (eds.) ICAISC 2004. LNCS (LNAI), vol. 3070, pp. 314–319. Springer, Heidelberg (2004)
13. Gniewek, L., Kluska, J.: Hardware implementation of fuzzy Petri net as a controller. IEEE Trans. SMC, Part B 34(3), 1315–1324 (2004)
14. Kluska, J., Hajduk, Z., Gniewek, L.: Synthesis of the Fuzzy Petri Nets as Hardware Devices for Control and Diagnostics, Pomiary, Automatyka, Kontrola R.52(6 bis), 5–7 (2006)
15. Lughoffer, E., Buchtala, O.: Reliable All-Pairs Evolving Fuzzy Classifiers. IEEE Trans. Fuzzy Syst. 21(4), 625–641 (2013)
16. Piegat, A., Olchowy, M.: Does an Optimal Form of an Expert Fuzzy Model Exist? In: Rutkowski, L., Scherer, R., Tadeusiewicz, R., Zadeh, L.A., Zurada, J.M. (eds.) ICAISC 2010, Part I. LNCS, vol. 6113, pp. 175–184. Springer, Heidelberg (2010)
17. Smoczek, J.: Evolutionary Optimization of Interval Mathematics–Based Design of a TSK Fuzzy Controller For Anti–Sway Crane Control. Int. J. Appl. Math. Comput. Sci. 23(4), 749–759 (2013)
18. Smoczek, J.: P1-TS fuzzy scheduling control system design using local pole placement and interval analysis. Bull. Pol. Ac. Sci.: Tech. 62(3), 455–464 (2014)
19. Ulu, C.: Exact analytical inverse mapping of decomposable TS fuzzy systems with singleton and linear consequents. Applied Soft Computing 23, 202–214 (2014)
20. Ulu, C., Güzelkaya, M., Eksin, I.: Exact Inversion of TSK Fuzzy Systems With Linear Consequents. In: XXIV Int. Conf. Information, Communication and Automation Technologies (ICAT), Sarajevo, pp. 1–4 (2013)
21. Soltani, M., Chaari, A., Hmida, F.B.: A Novel Fuzzy C–Regression Model Algorithm Using a New Error Measure and Particle Swarm Optimization. Int. J. Appl. Math. Comput. Sci. 22(3), 617–628 (2012)

Fuzzy Agglomerative Clustering

Michal Konkol[(✉)]

NTIS - New Technologies for the Information Society
and Department of Computer Science and Engineering,
University of West Bohemia,
Univerzitni 8, 306 14 Plzen, Czech Republic
nlp.kiv.zcu.cz,
konkol@kiv.zcu.cz

Abstract. In this paper, we describe *fuzzy agglomerative clustering*, a brand new fuzzy clustering algorithm. The basic idea of the proposed algorithm is based on the well-known hierarchical clustering methods. To achieve the soft or fuzzy output of the hierarchical clustering, we combine the single-linkage and complete-linkage strategy together with a *fuzzy distance*. As the algorithm was created recently, we cover only some basic experiments on synthetic data to show some properties of the algorithm. The reference implementation is freely available.

Keywords: Hierarchical Clustering · Fuzzy Clustering · Agglomerative Clustering

1 Introduction

Clustering algorithms became a very important tool for many fields including biology [1], marketing [2], or natural language processing [3]. They simply analyse the input data and create groups of similar objects. There are two basic types of clustering algorithms: hard and soft. The hard clustering algorithms are older and allow each object to be part of only one cluster. The soft clustering algorithms allow each object to be part of multiple clusters. The fuzzy clustering algorithms have the same output as a soft clustering, but also include a measure of a membership of objects in the clusters. Very often the terms soft and fuzzy are interchangeable. The fuzzy clustering seems to be more natural as the world is usually not black and white.

An example can be taken from the natural language processing field. Currently, word clusters became an important feature in multiple tasks. Soft clustering can be used to include a word in multiple clusters, because it can have multiple distinct meanings [4].

Our algorithm is motivated by the Web People Search task [5,6,7]. The input of this task is a set of web pages, that are returned for a person name query (e.g. John Doe) by the search engine. The goal is to group pages related to the same person. The hard hierarchical clustering is usually used, because it is possible to adaptively change the convergence criterion and the number of clusters is found automatically [8]. The problem is, that a web page can be related to multiple persons (e.g. a Facebook page with a list of people with the same name). Thus we need to incorporate a soft clustering to fully solve this task.

© Springer International Publishing Switzerland 2015
L. Rutkowski et al. (Eds.): ICAISC 2015, Part I, LNAI 9119, pp. 207–217, 2015.
DOI: 10.1007/978-3-319-19324-3_19

In this paper we propose *fuzzy agglomerative clustering*, which is a novel algorithm for the fuzzy clustering based on hierarchical clustering principles. The fuzzy output of the algorithm is achieved through a combination of single-linkage and complete-linkage strategies in one algorithm together with a *fuzzy distance*. The fuzzy distance is used for points that are already included in a cluster and thus cannot be added to another cluster in a standard (hard) hierarchical clustering.

The rest of the paper is organized as follows. We summarize the related work in section 2. The detailed description of our algorithm is given in section 3. The experiments are covered in section 4. The last section summarizes our contribution and shows some paths of our future research.

2   Related Work

There are multiple types of algorithms referred to as hierarchical fuzzy clustering. The first type [9] are standard hard hierarchical algorithms extended for use on fuzzy data.

The second type [10,11,12] is based on another fuzzy clustering algorithm, which generates a high number of fuzzy clusters. These clusters are then merged using standard hierarchical clustering. Very often the fuzzy clusters are generated using fuzzy C-means with a desired number of clusters much higher then the expected number of clusters in the data.

The last type are hierarchical clustering algorithms adapted to produce fuzzy clusters. Our algorithm belongs to this group. We are only aware of one (other) algorithm of this type [13]. This algorithm uses a very different approach and the results should be different from our algorithm.

3   Proposed Algorithm

First, we would like to introduce our mathematical notation and definition of the task. We follow with outline of some of the problems connected with fuzzy hierarchical clustering and present the basic idea behind our solution. Then we give an in-depth description of our algorithm.

The input of a clustering algorithm is a set of points $P = \{p_i \in \mathbb{R}^k | i \leq N\}$, where N is the number of data objects represented as k-dimensional vectors. The output is a set of clusters $C = \{C_i \subseteq P | i \leq M\}$, where M is the number of clusters in the output and each cluster C_i is a set of points. The clusters created by a standard hard clustering algorithm are partition of input points, i.e. $\bigcup C_i = P$, $C_i \cap C_j = \emptyset \; \forall i \neq j$. For fuzzy clustering $\bigcup C_i = P$, but the second property $C_i \cap C_j = \emptyset \; \forall i \neq j$ is not mandatory. The output of fuzzy clustering algorithm can be enhanced with membership values $\mu(p, C_i) \; \forall p \in C_i$, which determines how likely (or how much) the point belongs to a cluster. The indices used for points and clusters (e.g. i in C_i) are used only to distinguish different clusters and do not imply any order.

We use $d_{a,b}$ to denote distance or dissimilarity between a and b, where a (resp. b) can be both a point or a cluster. Further in the paper, we use only the term distance even though we do not need the triangle inequality property of distance metrics.

We use the symbol $=$ to denote both equality and assignment and the particular meaning should be clear from the context.

3.1   The Basic Idea

If we want to go from hard hierarchical clustering to fuzzy hierarchical clustering, many problems arise. We will focus on these problems and later we will describe our idea how to solve them.

Imagine we are clustering points in $\mathbb{R}^1$ using Euclidean distance and we are currently in situation (a) or (b) depicted on Fig. 1. In both situations, we have eight points $p_1, \ldots, p_8$ and two clusters $C_1 = \{p_1, p_2, p_3, p_4\}$, $C_2 = \{p_5, p_6, p_7, p_8\}$. The numbers on the top of the line sections are the distances between neighbouring points. This particular situation can arise using various strategies for the hard hierarchical clustering – *single-*, *complete-* or *average-linkage*. Now, if we want to have a fuzzy clustering we would (in some cases) like to have point p_5 simultaneously in clusters C_1 and C_2, i.e. we want to add point p_5 to cluster C_1.

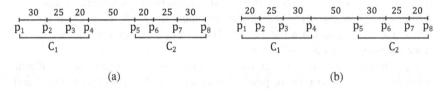

(a)   (b)

Fig. 1. Example

Now consider that we are using single-linkage. The distance d_{p_5, C_1} is equal to d_{C_1, C_2}. The problem is, that we need to decide, if we want to add point p_5 to cluster C_1 or if we want to merge clusters C_1 and C_2. The later is hard clustering. If we choose the former, in situation (a) we will gradually add points p_6, p_7, p_8 to C_1. In situation (b) we have two options. We can update the distances between clusters as usually, which leads to the same situation as in (a). Or we can ignore the change of distances between clusters when adding points that already belong to some cluster and we will merge clusters C_1 and C_2 right in the next step. In all cases, we get C_1 and C_2 merged. There is no possibility to control the *fuzziness*, i.e. how many points should be added.

With the complete-linkage strategy $d_{p_5, C_1} \neq d_{C_1, C_2}$, but if we choose to add point p_5 to C_1, we will gradually add points p_6, p_7, p_8 to C_1 again, in both situations.

Similar problems are common for all hierarchical clustering algorithms as far as we know.

We solve these problems by combining single-linkage and complete-linkage in one algorithm. We use complete-linkage for distances between clusters (e.g. d_{C_1, C_2}). We use the single-linkage for distances between points and clusters (e.g. d_{p_5, C_1} or d_{p_1, p_2}). This is still not enough to solve these problems, but opens some possibilities. We propose a measure of membership $\mu(p_i, C_j)$ which measures the relatedness between cluster C_j and point p_i. The details will be covered in the next section. The important property is, that the membership of points decreases as we gradually add points, e.g.

$\mu(p_5, C_1)$ could be 0.4, $\mu(p_6, C_1)$ could be 0.25, etc. We use this function to gradually increase distance between points, so d_{p_7,C_1} could become greater than d_{C_1,C_2} even though d_{C_1,C_2} is acquired with the complete-linkage strategy. To distinguish these altered distances, we call them *fuzzy distances* in this paper. Our approach allows parametrization which controls fuzziness.

We believe it is possible to switch from single-linkage to some other strategy, e.g. average-linkage. We use the single-linkage, because it is the most intuitive strategy.

3.2 The Algorithm

At the beginning, we start with $C = \emptyset$. We will also need a set of points U, that are already in a cluster, i.e. $U = \{p_j \in P | \exists i \leq |C| : p_j \in C_i \in C\}$. We use $\bar{U} = P \setminus U$ for unused points. The $|C|$ denotes the current number of clusters during the algorithm. It is 0 at the beginning and M at the end.

We remember all distances between points $d_{p_i,p_j}, p_i, p_j \in P$, between points and clusters $d_{p_i,C_j}, p_i \in P, C_j \in C$, and between clusters $d_{C_i,C_j}, C_i, C_j \in C$. It is necessary to define a set of usable distances D, because we want to skip specific distances, e.g. distance d_{p_i,C_j} if $p_i \in C_j$. We finish the initialization by computing distances between points $d_{p_i,p_j}, p_i, p_j \in P, i \neq j$ and adding them to D. We assume that for each distance $d_{a,b} \in D$ we also know the a and b. The set D can be seen as distance matrix, where we use only some cells.

The algorithm loops until it converges. The loop consists of three steps – find minimum value $d_{a,b}$ in D, merge corresponding elements a and b (points and/or clusters), recompute distances where necessary. The first step in the loop, finding the minimum value of D, is straightforward. The interesting part is the second and third step. We distinguish four cases based on the minimum value $d_{a,b} = \min D$.

- merging two points, i.e. $a, b \in P$
- merging unused point and cluster, i.e. $a \in \bar{U}, b \in C$ (or $a \in C, b \in \bar{U}$)
- merging used point and cluster, i.e. $a \in U, b \in C$ (or $a \in C, b \in U$)
- merging clusters, i.e. $a, b \in C$

We cover these cases in the following subsections.

3.3 Merging Two Points

The minimal distance in D is $d_{a,b} = \min D$, where $a, b \in P$. Firstly, update the set of usable distances D. We do not want to merge the same points again, so we set $D = D \setminus \{d_{a,b}, d_{b,a}\}$.

We (optionally) remove combinations of a and b with other points from D (this operation is very cheap with proper implementation). We do this because of implementation reasons as it is faster to find the minimum of D and merging a (resp. b) with some other point will usually not change the result. Mathematically, we set $D = D \setminus \{d_{x,p} \in D | (x = a \vee x = b) \wedge p \in P\}$. We mark the points a and b as used points, i.e. $U = U \cup \{a, b\}$, and create new cluster $C_{new} = \{a, b\}$.

Now we need to compute some new distances. We start with unused points $p \in \bar{U}$. For all these points we compute the distance using (1) and add this distance to D,

$D = D \cup \{d_{p,C_{new}}\}$. Then we follow with the distances between our new cluster C_{new} and all the other clusters $C_{other} \in C$ using (2) and we again add this distance to D, $D = D \cup \{d_{C_{other},C_{new}}\}$. We also define distances $d_{a,C_{new}} = d_{a,b}$ and $d_{b,C_{new}} = d_{a,b}$, but we do not add these distances to D, because C_{new} already contains a and b.

$$d_{p,C_{new}} = \min\{d_{p,a}, d_{p,b}\} \tag{1}$$

$$d_{C_{other},C_{new}} = \max\{d_{C_{other},a}, d_{C_{other},b}\} \tag{2}$$

Then we need to compute the fuzzy distances. First, we need to define function $d_{min}(u)$ by (3), where $u \in U \subset P \wedge u \neq a \wedge u \neq b$. The membership $\mu(u, C_{new})$ of used point u in cluster C_{new} is defined by (4). The distance $d_{u,C_{new}}$ is defined by (5). The $t(\mu)$ function is defined by (6), where m is the fuzziness parameter. As the algorithm picks shortest distances first $d_{min}(u) < \min\{d_{u,a}, d_{u,b}\}$ and $\mu(u, C_{new}) \in [0, 0.5]$ and $t(\mu) > 1$. As $m \to \infty$ all points are added to all clusters with uniform membership. As $m \to 1$ the algorithm becomes a hard clustering. We have chosen the $t(\mu)$ function arbitrary, because of its desirable properties, e.g. $t(\mu) > 1$ for $\mu \in [0, 1)$, $t(\mu) \to \infty$ if $\mu \to 0$, smooth function, etc. The function $t(\mu)$ is shown on Fig. 2 for some values of m.

$$d_{min}(u) = \min\{d_{u,C_i} | u \in C_i \in C\} \tag{3}$$

$$\mu(u, C_{new}) = 1 - \frac{\min\{d_{u,a}, d_{u,b}\}}{\min\{d_{u,a}, d_{u,b}\} + d_{min}(u)} \tag{4}$$

$$d_{u,C_{new}} = t(\mu(u, C_{new})) \min\{d_{u,a}, d_{u,b}\} \tag{5}$$

$$t(\mu) = 1 - \log_m(\mu) \tag{6}$$

We have computed new fuzzy distances for $d_{u,C_{new}}$. But we need to compute fuzzy distances $d_{a,C_{other}}$ (resp. $d_{b,C_{other}}$) for all $C_{other} \in C, other \neq new$ using (7) and (8). Note that $d_{min}(a) = d_{a,b}$. At the end we add the new cluster to C, i.e. $C = C \cup C_{new}$.

$$\mu(a, C_{other}) = 1 - \frac{d_{a,C_{other}}}{d_{a,C_{other}} + d_{a,b}} \tag{7}$$

$$d_{a,C_{other}} = t(\mu(a, C_{other})) d_{a,C_{other}} \tag{8}$$

3.4   Merging Unused Point and Cluster

In this situation $a \in \bar{U}$ and $b \in C$, we will mark $C_b = b$ to show that b is a cluster. We merge a and C_b, $C_b = C_b \cup \{a\}$. Then we follow the same steps as in the previous section, but with slightly different formulas. We remove a from D, $D = D \setminus \{d_{a,C_b}\}$ and also (optionally) $D = D \setminus \{d_{a,p} \in D | p \in P\}$. We add a to used points, $U = U \cup \{a\}$.

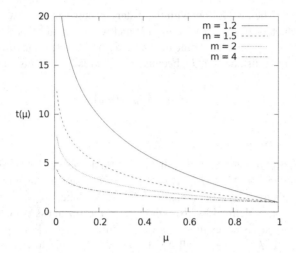

Fig. 2. The $t(\mu)$ function for some values of fuzziness parameter m

Then we update the distances d_{p,C_b} for all $p \in \bar{U}$ using (9) and d_{C_{other},C_b} for all $C_{other} \in C, other \neq b$.

$$d_{p,C_b} = \min\{d_{p,a}, d_{p,C_b}\} \qquad (9)$$

$$d_{C_{other},C_b} = \max\{d_{a,C_{other}}, d_{C_b,C_{other}}\} \qquad (10)$$

We follow with the fuzzy distances d_{u,C_b} for all $u \in U, u \neq a$. The corresponding formulas (11) and (12) are slightly changed compared to the previous section, but have the same logic. And finally, we need to update fuzzy distances $d_{a,C_{other}}$ using formulas (13) and (14).

$$\mu(u,a) = 1 - \frac{d_{u,a}}{d_{u,a} + d_{min}(u)} \qquad (11)$$

$$d_{u,C_b} = \min\{t(\mu(u,a))d_{u,a}, d_{u,C_b}\} \qquad (12)$$

$$\mu(a, C_{other}) = 1 - \frac{d_{a,C_{other}}}{d_{a,C_{other}} + d_{a,C_b}} \qquad (13)$$

$$d_{a,C_{other}} = t(\mu(a, C_{other}))d_{a,C_{other}} \qquad (14)$$

3.5   Merging Used Point and Cluster

In this situation $a \in U \subset P$ and $b \in C$, we will mark $C_b = b$ to show that b is a cluster. Firstly, we add a to C_b, $C_b = C_b \cup \{a\}$. Then we recompute distances again, but only d_{u,C_b} where $u \in U, u \neq a$ using (15) and (16). We use a different definition of membership in (16) if compared to (12). Instead of using the membership corresponding to a, we use membership corresponding to C_b. We do this, because there is always (at least) one point $p \in U$, that has a property $d(p, a) = d_{min}(p)$. For such a point, the membership would be always 0.5. As the algorithm would continue, we would have such point in each step (of this type) and that would be undesirable behavior.

$$\mu(u, C_b) = 1 - \frac{d_{u,C_b}}{d_{u,C_b} + d_{min}(u)} \tag{15}$$

$$d_{u,C_b} = \min\{t(\mu(u, C_b))d_{u,a}, d_{u,C_b}\} \tag{16}$$

3.6 Merging Two Clusters

This is the simplest situation. We have $a, b \in C$. To denote that a and b are clusters, we use $C_a = a$ and $C_b = b$. We simply recompute distances d_{p,C_a} using (17), where $p \in P$. We use (18) for distances d_{C_{other},C_a}, where $C_{other} \in C, other \neq a$. Then we merge the clusters, $C_a = C_a \cup C_b$, and remove C_b from C, $C = C \setminus \{C_b\}$.

$$d_{p,C_a} = \min\{d_{p,C_a}, d_{p,C_b}\} \tag{17}$$

$$d_{C_{other},C_a} = \max\{d_{C_{other},C_a}, d_{C_{other},C_b}\} \tag{18}$$

3.7 Convergence and Complexity

Consider the situation, when we ignore the already used points. Then the algorithm is the standard hard agglomerative clustering with complexity $N(N-1)$. In our algorithm, we need one extra iteration for each point, that is already in a cluster and is going to be added to another one. The number of extra iterations cannot be guessed ahead, but we can find an upper bound.

The upper bound for complexity is given by $\frac{N(N-1)}{2}(N-2)N+N^2$. The $\frac{N(N-1)}{2}$ is the maximum number of clusters, that can be possibly created, i.e. all possible pairs in a set of N elements. The maximum number of clusters is multiplied by $N - 2$, because we can add $N - 2$ points to each pair of points, i.e. to have all points in all clusters. And finally multiplied by N, which is the cost of merging. The additional N^2 is needed to merge the clusters, where each cluster consists of all points.

We propose a rule, that each point can merge with another point, only if both points are not used in another cluster. This rule reduces the $\frac{N(N-1)}{2}$ to $\frac{N}{2}$. This rule can affect the results in some cases, but only a very little for reasonably large data. The final complexity is then $O(N^3)$. In comparison to the hard agglomerative clustering, we increase the complexity from $O(N^2)$ in sake fuzzy output.

The convergence is usually faster and lies between $O(N^2)$ and $O(N^3)$. It depends on the clustered data and the fuzziness parameter μ, i.e. how many shared points are in the clusters.

3.8   Implementation

We have implemented the proposed algorithm in the Brainy machine learning library [14]. The reference implementation is based on a distance matrix, that stores all the necessary distances.

4   Experiments

First, we experimentally evaluate the complexity of the algorithm. Fig. 3 shows the relation between data size and computation time. We tested three values of μ: 1 (no fuzziness), 1.2 (reasonably fuzzy), 10 (extremely fuzzy). We can see, that in the case of extreme fuzziness $\mu = 10$ (i.e. 'all points in all clusters') the computation time grows rapidly with more data. It is very important, that for reasonable fuzziness $\mu = 1.2$ the computation time is significantly lower and much closer to the hard clustering $\mu = 1$.

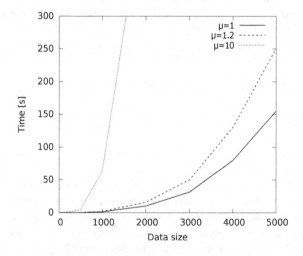

Fig. 3. The relation between data size and time

The second experiment that we provide shows only a sample output of our algorithm on the synthetic data. Fig. 4 shows two clusters randomly sampled from two Gaussian distributions. Points that belong to the first cluster are marked by a circle. Points that belong to the second cluster are marked by a cross. Crossed circles are points that belong to both clusters. You can see the output for various settings of fuzziness.

We are aware, that this experiment is not sufficient for any claims or proofs. We only hope it shows some potential of the proposed algorithm. We are going to do proper experiments to compare the proposed algorithm with other algorithms, but it is out of the scope of this preliminary study.

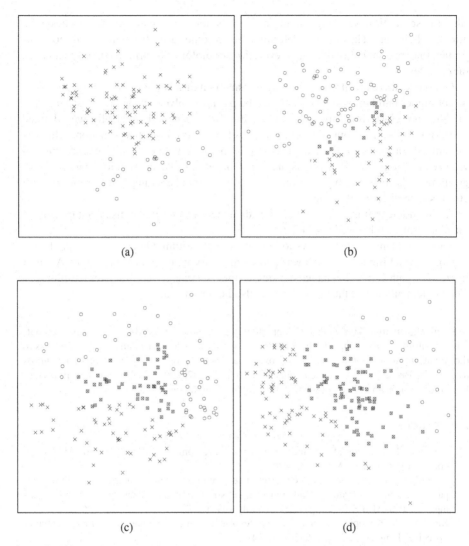

Fig. 4. Clustering points of two clusters randomly sampled from two Gaussian distributions using fuzziness (a) 1.01, (b) 1.1, (c) 1.2, (d) 1.3

5 Discussion and Future Work

In this paper, we proposed a fuzzy agglomerative clustering. Since we came up with this algorithm very recently, we carried out only a few synthetic tests of the algorithm. They show some basic behavior of the algorithm, but an in-depth experimental study is yet to be done.

The algorithm have some desirable properties, which come from its hierarchical nature. It is possible to use plenty of various distance and dissimilarity metrics. It is possible to use multiple stopping conditions, so it is not necessary to know (or guess) the number of clusters. The output is deterministic. In some cases, the hierarchy is more important than the final clusters, e.g. in evolutionary biology the structure helps to analyse the samples.

Of course, there are also disadvantages. The main disadvantage is too high complexity for higher number of objects. This can be partially solved by canopy clustering [15] or other pre-clustering approaches. Compared to other mathematically well-defined clustering algorithms, our algorithm does not have any objective function, which is minimized (or maximized). Thus it is impossible to say, that the clusters are optimal with regard to given criteria. It is also known, that all the hierarchical clustering algorithms fails for some types of input, i.e. single-linkage strategy has problems with clusters with different densities.

At the moment, it is hard to tell, if the advantages outweigh the disadvantages and if the algorithm will be used in practice.

There are many different ways to improve the algorithm. One of them is the definition of the $t(\mu)$ function, which was chosen arbitrary without any deep study. Another interesting path can be to change the single-linkage strategy (e.g. for average-linkage). The implementation of the algorithm can also be optimized.

Acknowledgements. This work was supported by grant no. SGS-2013-029 Advanced computing and information systems, by the European Regional Development Fund (ERDF). Access to the MetaCentrum computing facilities provided under the program "Projects of Large Infrastructure for Research, Development, and Innovations" LM2010005, funded by the Ministry of Education, Youth, and Sports of the Czech Republic, is highly appreciated.

References

1. Legendre, P., Legendre, L.: Numerical ecology. Developments in Environmental Modelling, vol. 24. Elsevier B.V., Amsterdam (2012)
2. Russell, S., Lodwick, W.: Fuzzy clustering in data mining for telco database marketing campaigns. In: 18th International Conference of the North American Fuzzy Information Processing Society, NAFIPS 1999, pp. 720–726 (July 1999)
3. Brychcín, T., Konopík, M.: Semantic spaces for improving language modeling. Computer Speech & Language 28(1), 192–209 (2014)
4. Lin, D., Wu, X.: Phrase clustering for discriminative learning. In: Proceedings of the Joint Conference of the 47th Annual Meeting of the ACL and the 4th International Joint Conference on Natural Language Processing of the AFNLP, ACL 2009, vol. 2, pp. 1030–1038. Association for Computational Linguistics, Stroudsburg (2009)
5. Artiles, J., Gonzalo, J., Sekine, S.: The semeval-2007 weps evaluation: Establishing a benchmark for the web people search task. In: Proceedings of the Fourth International Workshop on Semantic Evaluations (SemEval 2007), pp. 64–69. Association for Computational Linguistics, Prague (2007)
6. Artiles, J., Gonzalo, J., Sekine, S.: Weps 2 evaluation campaign: overview of the web people search clustering task. In: 18th WWW Conference on 2nd Web People Search Evaluation Workshop, WePS 2009 (2009)
7. Artiles, J., Borthwick, A., Gonzalo, J., Sekine, S., Amigó, E.: Weps-3 evaluation campaign: Overview of the web people search clustering and attribute extraction tasks. In: CLEF 2010 LABs and Workshops, Notebook Papers, September 22-23, Padua, Italy (2010)

8. Delgado, A.D., Martínez, R., Fresno, V., Montalvo, S.: A data driven approach for person name disambiguation in web search results. In: Proceedings of COLING 2014, the 25th International Conference on Computational Linguistics: Technical Papers, pp. 301–310. Dublin City University and Association for Computational Linguistics, Dublin (2014)
9. GhasemiGol, M., Sadoghi Yazdi, H., Monsefi, R.: A new hierarchical clustering algorithm on fuzzy data (fhca). International Journal of Computer and Electrical Engineering IJCEE 2(1), 134–140 (2010)
10. Rodrigues, M.E.S.M., Sacks, L.: A scalable hierarchical fuzzy clustering algorithm for text mining. In: Proceedings of the 5th International Conference on Recent Advances in Soft Computing (2004)
11. Treerattanapitak, K., Jaruskulchai, C.: Generalized agglomerative fuzzy clustering. In: Huang, T., Zeng, Z., Li, C., Leung, C.S. (eds.) ICONIP 2012, Part III. LNCS, vol. 7665, pp. 34–41. Springer, Heidelberg (2012)
12. Frigui, H., Krishnapuram, R.: Clustering by competitive agglomeration. Pattern Recogn. 30(7), 1109–1119 (1997)
13. Bank, M., Schwenker, F.: Fuzzification of agglomerative hierarchical crisp clustering algorithms. In: Gaul, W.A., Geyer-Schulz, A., Schmidt-Thieme, L., Kunze, J. (eds.) Challenges at the Interface of Data Analysis, Computer Science, and Optimization. Studies in Classification, Data Analysis, and Knowledge Organization, pp. 3–11. Springer, Heidelberg (2012)
14. Konkol, M.: Brainy: A machine learning library. In: Rutkowski, L., Korytkowski, M., Scherer, R., Tadeusiewicz, R., Zadeh, L.A., Zurada, J.M. (eds.) ICAISC 2014, Part II. LNCS(LNAI), vol. 8468, pp. 490–499. Springer, Heidelberg (2014)
15. McCallum, A., Nigam, K., Ungar, L.H.: Efficient clustering of high-dimensional data sets with application to reference matching. In: Proceedings of the Sixth ACM SIGKDD International Conference on Knowledge Discovery and Data Mining, KDD 2000, pp. 169–178. ACM, New York (2000)

An Exponential-Type Entropy Measure on Intuitionistic Fuzzy Sets

Yessica Nataliani[1], Chao-Ming Hwang[2], and Miin-Shen Yang[1(✉)]

[1] Department of Applied Mathematics, Chung Yuan Christian University,
Chung-Li 32023, Taiwan
[2] Department of Applied Mathematics, Chinese Culture University,
Yangminshan, Taipei, Taiwan
msyang@math.cycu.edu.tw

Abstract. Entropy of an intuitionistic fuzzy set (IFS) is used to indicate the degree of fuzziness for IFSs. In this paper we deal with entropies of IFSs. We first review some existing entropies of IFSs and then propose a new entropy measure based on exponential operations for an IFS. Finally, comparisons are made with some existing entropies to show the effectiveness of our proposed one.

Keywords: Fuzzy sets · Intuitionistic fuzzy sets · Fuzziness · Entropy

1 Introduction

A fuzzy set, proposed by Zadeh [21], is a generalization of an ordinary set in which it allows the membership value of an element in a fuzzy set to be between 0 and 1. In fuzzy systems, measuring the fuzziness of a fuzzy set is an important step, and the entropy of a fuzzy set is a measure of the fuzziness of a fuzzy set. De Luca and Termini [8] first introduced the axiom construction for entropy of fuzzy sets with reference to Shannon's probability entropy. Yager [19] defined the degree of fuzziness of a fuzzy set in terms of a lack of distinction between the fuzzy set and its complement. Ebanks [10] suggested five properties for entropy of fuzzy sets. Liu [15] gave some axiom definitions of entropy and also defined a δ-entropy.

An intuitionistic fuzzy sets (IFS), introduced by Atanassov [1], is a generalization of a fuzzy set. Since an IFS can present the degrees of both membership and non-membership with a degree of hesitancy, the knowledge and semantic representation becomes more meaningful and applicable [2,3]. These IFSs have been widely studied and applied in various areas [4,7,9,12-14,16]. Burillo and Bustince [5] first gave axioms of entropy for IFSs. Szmidt and Kacprzyk [15] proposed an entropy measure for IFSs in which it is defined as the ratio of intuitionistic fuzzy cardinalities. Hung [11] proposed some formulas of fuzzy entropies induced by distances between two IFSs.

In this paper, we propose a new entropy measure on IFSs based on exponential operations. The axioms for the entropy of IFSs are also considered and discussed. Some comparisons are performed to assess the performance of the proposed entropy with some existing entropy measures. The results indicate that the proposed method is

© Springer International Publishing Switzerland 2015
L. Rutkowski et al. (Eds.): ICAISC 2015, Part I, LNAI 9119, pp. 218–227, 2015.
DOI: 10.1007/978-3-319-19324-3_20

superior in performance to others. The remainder of the paper is organized as follows. In Section 2, we review several existing entropies for IFSs. We then propose a new entropy measure on IFSs. Examples are given and comparisons are made between these entropy measures for IFSs in Section 3. Finally, conclusions are stated in Section 4.

2   A New Entropy Measure on Intuitionistic Fuzzy Sets

The following notations are used in this section; $R^+ = [0, \infty)$; X is the universal set; $FS(X)$ is the class of all fuzzy sets of X; $\mu_A(x)$ is the membership function of A in $FS(X)$; $P(X)$ is the class of all crisp subsets of X; $[a]$ is the fuzzy set of X for which $\mu_{[a]}(x) = a$, $\forall x \in X$; F is a subclass of $FS(X)$ with (1) $P(X) \subseteq F$, (2) $[\frac{1}{2}] \in F$, and (3) $A, B \in F \Rightarrow A \cup B \in F, A^c \in F$, where A^c is the complement of A in F with $\mu_{A^c}(x) = 1 - \mu_A(x), \forall x \in X$. A fuzzy set A^* is said to be crisper than A if $\mu_{A^*}(x) \geq \mu_A(x)$ when $\mu_A(x) \geq 1/2$, and $\mu_{A^*}(x) \leq \mu_A(x)$, when $\mu_A(x) \leq 1/2$. In the following, we shall describe those aspects of IFSs, given by Atanassov [1], which are needed in our discussion.

Definition 2.1 (Atanassov [1]) An intuitionistic fuzzy set (IFS) A in X is defined as $A = \{(x, \mu_A(x), \nu_A(x)) \mid x \in X\}$ where $\mu_A : X \rightarrow [0,1]$ and $\nu_A : X \rightarrow [0,1]$ with the condition $0 \leq \mu_A + \nu_A(x) \leq 1, \forall x \in X$. The numbers $\mu_A(x)$ and $\nu_A(x)$ denote the degree of membership and non-membership of x to A, respectively.

Let X be a universal set and let $IFS(X)$ be the class of all IFSs in X. For any fuzzy set A' in X, it should be a special case of $IFS(X)$ in which it can be defined as $A' = \{(x, \mu_{A'}(x), \nu_{A'}(x)) \mid x \in X\}$ where $\mu_{A'}(x) \in [0,1]$ and $\nu_{A'}(x) = 1 - \mu_{A'}(x)$. For any A in $IFS(X)$, the number $\pi_A(x) = 1 - \mu_A(x) - \nu_A(x)$ is called the intuitionistic index of x in A. It is a hesitancy degree of x to A. Obviously, $0 \leq \pi(x) \leq 1$ is for each $x \in X$. Some basic operations on $IFS(X)$ are described in the following definition (see also De et al. [6]).

Definition 2.2 If A and B are in $IFS(X)$, then

(i) $A \subseteq B$ if and only if $\forall x \in X, \mu_A(x) \leq \mu_B(x)$ and $\nu_A(x) \geq \nu_B(x)$;

(ii) $A = B$ if and only if $\forall x \in X, \mu_A(x) = \mu_B(x)$ and $\nu_A(x) = \nu_B(x)$;

(iii) $A \cap B = \{(x, \min\{\mu_A(x), \mu_B(x)\}, \max\{\nu_A(x), \nu_B(x)\}) \mid x \in X\}$;

$A \cup B = \{< x, \max\{\mu_A(x), \mu_B(x)\}, \min\{\nu_A(x), \nu_B(x)\} > \mid x \in X\}$.

Based on similar axioms about entropy of fuzzy sets in De Luca and Termini [8], Szmidt and Kacprzyk [17] gave the axioms of entropy for IFSs as follows.

Definition 2.3 (Szmidt and Kacprzyk [17]) A real function $E : IFS(X) \to [0,1]$ is called the entropy on $IFS(X)$, if E satisfies the following properties:

(P1) $E(A) = 0$ if A is a crisp set;

(P2) $E(A) = 1$ if $\mu_A(x) = \nu_A(x)$ for all $x \in X$;

(P3) $E(A) \leq E(B)$ if $A \leq B$ (i.e. A is the sharpness of B);

i.e., $\mu_A(x) \leq \mu_B(x)$ and $\nu_A(x) \geq \nu_B(x)$ for $\mu_B(x) \leq \nu_B(x)$ or

$\mu_A(x) \geq \mu_B(x)$ and $\nu_A(x) \leq \nu_B(x)$ for $\mu_B(x) \geq \nu_B(x)$.

(P4) $E(A) = E(A^c)$ where $A^c = \{(x, \nu_A(x), \mu_A(x)) | x \in X)\}$.

Based on a similar definition of σ-entropy for a fuzzy set in $FS(X)$ from Liu [15], we can define σ-entropy for an IFS A in $IFS(X)$ as follows.

Definition 2.4 Let E be an entropy on $IFS(X)$. If, for any $A \in IFS(X)$, we have $E(A) = E(A \cap D) + E(A \cap D^c)$, for all $D \in P(X)$. Then, the entropy E is called a σ-entropy for an IFS $A \in IFS(X)$.

Assume that $X = \{x_1, ..., x_n\}$. Let F be an IFS in $IFS(X)$. We review the following entropies for any $A \in IFS(X)$ as follows.

(a) Burillo and Bustince [5] defined an entropy of an IFS F as follows:

$$E_{BB}(F) = \sum_{i=1}^{n} \pi_F(x_i) \tag{1}$$

(b) Szmidt and Kacprzyk [17] defined an entropy of an IFS F as follows:

$$E_{SK}(F) = \sum_{i=1}^{n} \frac{\min(\mu_F(x_i), \nu_F(x_i) + \pi_F(x_i))}{\max(\mu_F(x_i), \nu_F(x_i) + \pi_F(x_i))} \tag{2}$$

(c) Hung [11] defined an entropy of an IFS F as follows:

$$E_E(A) = 1 - \sqrt{\frac{1}{n} \sum_{i=1}^{n} (u_{A(x_i)} - \nu_{A(x_i)})^2} \tag{3}$$

(d) Hung [11] defined another entropy of an IFS F as follows:

$$E_H(A) = 1 - \frac{1}{n} \sum_{i=1}^{n} | u_{A(x_i)} - \nu_{A(x_i)} | \tag{4}$$

Based on the condition $0 \leq u_A(x_i) + \nu_A(x_i) \leq 1$, we can modify equation (4) as follows:

$$E_{H'}(A) = 1 - \frac{\sum_{i=1}^{n} |u_{A(x_i)} - v_{A(x_i)}|}{\sum_{i=1}^{n} t_i} \tag{5}$$

where $t_i = u_A(x_i) + v_A(x_i), i = 1, ..., n$, by refitting n to $\sum_{i=1}^{n} t_i$, Thus, we have

$$E_{H'}(A) = 1 - \frac{\sum_{i=1}^{n} |u_{A(x_i)} - v_{A(x_i)}|}{\sum_{i=1}^{n} t_i} = 1 - \frac{\sum_{i=1}^{n} |u_{A(x_i)} - v_{A(x_i)}| I_{[u_{A(x_i)} \geq v_{A(x_i)}]} + |u_{A(x_i)} - v_{A(x_i)}| I_{[u_{A(x_i)} < v_{A(x_i)}]}}{\sum_{i=1}^{n} t_i}$$

$$= 1 - \frac{\sum_{i=1}^{n} |2u_{A(x_i)} - t_i| I_{[u_{A(x_i)} \geq \frac{t_i}{2}]} + |2v_{A(x_i)} - t_i| I_{[u_{A(x_i)} < \frac{t_i}{2}]}}{\sum_{i=1}^{n} t_i} = \frac{\sum_{i=1}^{n} (t_i - (2u_{A(x_i)} - t_i)) I_{[u_{A(x_i)} \geq \frac{t_i}{2}]} + (t_i - (2v_{A(x_i)} - t_i)) I_{[u_{A(x_i)} < \frac{t_i}{2}]}}{\sum_{i=1}^{n} t_i}$$

$$= \frac{2\sum_{i=1}^{n} (t_i - u_{A(x_i)}) I_{[u_{A(x_i)} \geq \frac{t_i}{2}]} + (t_i - v_{A(x_i)}) I_{[u_{A(x_i)} < \frac{t_i}{2}]}}{\sum_{i=1}^{n} t_i} = \frac{\sum_{i=1}^{n} v_{A(x_i)} I_{[u_{A(x_i)} \geq \frac{t_i}{2}]} + u_{A(x_i)} I_{[u_{A(x_i)}(x_i) < \frac{t_i}{2}]}}{\frac{1}{2} \sum_{i=1}^{n} t_i}$$

According to the above derivation, we propose a new entropy $E_N(A)$ for an IFS A based on exponential operations as follows:

$$E_N(A) = \frac{\sum_{i=1}^{n} (1 - e^{-v_{A(x_i)}}) I_{[u_{A(x_i)} \geq \frac{t_i}{2}]} + (1 - e^{-u_{A(x_i)}}) I_{[u_{A(x_i)} < \frac{t_i}{2}]}}{\sum_{i=1}^{n} (1 - e^{-\frac{t_i}{2}})} \tag{6}$$

We first claim that the proposed $E_N(A)$ is entropy of IFSs.

Property 1 $E_N(A)$ is entropy of IFSs.

Proof: If A is a crisp set, then $u_A(x_i) = 0$ or 1.

If $u_A(x_i) = 1$, then $v_A(x_i) = 0$ and $1 - e^{-v_A(x_i)} = 0$.

If $u_A(x_i) = 0$, then $1 - e^{-u_A(x_i)} = 0$. Hence,

$$E_N(A) = \frac{\sum_{i=1}^{n} (1 - e^{-v_{A(x_i)}}) I_{[u_{A(x_i)} \geq \frac{t_i}{2}]} + (1 - e^{-u_{A(x_i)}}) I_{[u_{A(x_i)} < \frac{t_i}{2}]}}{\sum_{i=1}^{n} (1 - e^{-\frac{t_i}{2}})} = 0.$$

If $u_A(x_i) = v_A(x_i) = \frac{t_i}{2}$ for all i, then $E_N(A) = \frac{\sum_{i=1}^{n} (1 - e^{-v_{A(x_i)}}) I_{[u_{A(x_i)} \geq \frac{t_i}{2}]} + (1 - e^{-u_{A(x_i)}}) I_{[u_{A(x_i)} < \frac{t_i}{2}]}}{\sum_{i=1}^{n} (1 - e^{-\frac{t_i}{2}})} = 1.$

If $u_B(x_i) \leq v_B(x_i)$, then $u_A(x_i) \leq u_B(x_i) \leq t_i/2$. Hence, $1 - e^{-u_A(x_i)} \leq 1 - e^{-u_B(x_i)}$.

If $u_B(x_i) \geq v_B(x_i)$, then $u_A(x_i) \geq u_B(x_i) \geq t_i/2$ and $v_A(x_i) \leq v_B(x_i)$.

Hence, $1-e^{-v_A(x_i)} \leq 1-e^{-v_B(x_i)}$, and then we have that $E_N(A) \leq E_N(B)$.

Finally, we have

$$E_N(A) = \frac{\sum_{i=1}^{n}(1-e^{-v_A(x_i)})I_{[u_A(x_i)\geq\frac{t_i}{2}]} + (1-e^{-u_A(x_i)})I_{[u_A(x_i)<\frac{t_i}{2}]}}{\sum_{i=1}^{n}1-e^{-\frac{t_i}{2}}}$$

$$= \frac{\sum_{i=1}^{n}(1-e^{-v_A(x_i)})I_{[v_A(x_i)<\frac{t_i}{2}]} + (1-e^{-u_A(x_i)})I_{[v_A(x_i)\geq\frac{t_i}{2}]}}{\sum_{i=1}^{n}1-e^{-\frac{t_i}{2}}} = E_N(A^c).$$

Thus, the proof is completed.   □

We may say that the proposed entropy $E_N(A)$ replaces the membership functions $v_A(x_i)$ with $1-e^{-v_A(x_i)}$ and $u_A(x_i)$ with $1-e^{-u_A(x_i)}$. In fact, an exponential-type distance had been successfully used in clustering algorithms by Wu and Yang [18] and Yang and Wu [20] where they had claimed that it has robustness for clustering. We next claim that $E_N(A)$ is also a σ-entropy for an IFS A in $IFS(X)$.

Property 2 The proposed entropy $E_N(A)$ is σ-entropy on IFSs.

Proof: By Definition 2.4, we need to prove that $E_N(A) = E_N(A \cap D) + E_N(A \cap D^c)$ for all $D \in P(X)$. Assume that the universal set X is discrete with $X = \{x_1, x_2, ..., x_n\}$. We mention that D is a crisp set with the membership function $u_D(x_i) \in \{0,1\}$. Thus, we have

$$E_N(A \cap D) = \frac{\sum_{i=1}^{n}(1-e^{-v_{A\cap D}(x_i)})I_{[u_{A\cap D}(x_i)\geq\frac{t_i}{2}]} + (1-e^{-u_{A\cap D}(x_i)})I_{[u_{A\cap D}(x_i)<\frac{t_i}{2}]}}{\sum_{i=1}^{n}(1-e^{-\frac{t_i}{2}})} = \frac{\sum_{i=1}^{n}(1-e^{-\frac{t_i}{2}+u_{A\cap D}(x_i)})I_{[u_{A\cap D}(x_i)\geq\frac{t_i}{2}]} + (1-e^{-u_{A\cap D}(x_i)})I_{[u_{A\cap D}(x_i)<\frac{t_i}{2}]}}{\sum_{i=1}^{n}(1-e^{-\frac{t_i}{2}})}$$

$$= \frac{\sum_{i=1}^{n}(1-e^{-\frac{t_i}{2}+u_A(x_i)})I_{[u_A(x_i)\geq\frac{t_i}{2},u_D(x_i)\geq\frac{t_i}{2}]} + (1-e^{-u_A(x_i)})I_{[u_A(x_i)<\frac{t_i}{2},u_D(x_i)\geq\frac{t_i}{2}]}}{\sum_{i=1}^{n}(1-e^{-\frac{t_i}{2}})} = \frac{\sum_{i=1}^{n}(1-e^{-v_A(x_i)})I_{[u_A(x_i)\geq\frac{t_i}{2},u_D(x_i)\geq\frac{t_i}{2}]} + (1-e^{-u_A(x_i)})I_{[u_A(x_i)<\frac{t_i}{2},u_D(x_i)\geq\frac{t_i}{2}]}}{\sum_{i=1}^{n}(1-e^{-\frac{t_i}{2}})}$$

Similarly, $E_N(A \cap D^c) = \dfrac{\sum_{i=1}^{n}(1-e^{-v_A(x_i)})I_{[u_A(x_i)\geq\frac{t_i}{2},u_{D^c}(x_i)\geq\frac{t_i}{2}]} + (1-e^{-u_A(x_i)})I_{[u_A(x_i)<\frac{t_i}{2},u_{D^c}(x_i)\geq\frac{t_i}{2}]}}{\sum_{i=1}^{n}(1-e^{-\frac{t_i}{2}})}$

Hence,

$$E_N(A \cap D) + E_N(A \cap D^c) = \frac{\sum_{i=1}^{n}(1-e^{-v_A(x_i)})I_{[u_A(x_i)\geq\frac{t_i}{2},u_D(x_i)\geq\frac{t_i}{2}]} + (1-e^{-u_A(x_i)})I_{[u_A(x_i)<\frac{t_i}{2},u_D(x_i)\geq\frac{t_i}{2}]}}{\sum_{i=1}^{n}(1-e^{-\frac{t_i}{2}})}$$

$$+ \frac{\sum_{i=1}^{n}(1-e^{-v_A(x_i)})_{[u_A(x_i)\geq\frac{t_i}{2},u_{D^c}(x_i)\geq\frac{t_i}{2}]} + (1-e^{-u_A(x_i)})_{[u_A(x_i)<\frac{t_i}{2},u_{D^c}(x_i)\geq\frac{t_i}{2}]}}{\sum_{i=1}^{n}(1-e^{-\frac{t_i}{2}})}$$

$$= \frac{\sum_{i=1}^{n}(1-e^{-v_A(x_i)})_{[u_A(x_i)\geq\frac{t_i}{2}]} + (1-e^{-u_A(x_i)})_{[u_A(x_i)<\frac{t_i}{2}]}}{\sum_{i=1}^{n}(1-e^{-\frac{t_i}{2}})} = E_N(A)$$

Thus, the proof is completed.   □

3   Comparisons and Results

The linguistic hedges, like "very", "more or less", "slightly", are used to represent the modifiers of linguistic variables. Let

$$F = \{(x, u_A(x), 1-(1-v_A(x))) \mid x \in X\}$$

be an IFS in X. For any positive real number n, De et al. [6,7] defined the IFS F^n as follows:

$$F^n = \{(x, (u_A(x))^n, 1-(1-v_A(x))^n) \mid x \in X\}.$$

Using the above operation, they also defined the concentration and dilation of F as follows:

Concentration: CON(F)= F^2

Dilation: DIL(F)= $F^{1/2}$

The concentration and dilation are mathematic models frequently used for modifies. Thus, we can use these mathematic operators to define the linguistic hedges as follows:

Very F=CON(F)= F^2, more or less F=DIL(F)= $F^{1/2}$ and very very F= F^4.

We consider an IFS F in $X = \{6,7,8,9,10\}$ defined by Hung [11] with $F = \{(6,0.1,0.8),(7,0.3,0.5),(8,0.6,0.2),(9,0.9,0.0),(10,1.0,0.0)\}$. By taking into account the characterization of linguistic variables, we regarded F as "Large" on X. Using the above operations, we have that

$F^{1/2}$ can be treated as "More or less Large",

F^2 can be treated as "Very Large",

F^4 can be treated as "Very very Large",

We generate the following IFSs:

$F^{1/2} = \{(6,0.316,0.552),(7,0.548,0.293),(8,0.775,0.106),(9,0.949,0.0),(10,1.0,0.0)\}$

$F^2 = \{(6,0.01,0.96),(7,0.09,0.75),(8,0.36,0.36),(9,0.81,0.0),(10,1.0,0.0)\}$

$F^4 = \{(6,0.0,0.998),(7,0.008,0.938),(8,0.13,0.59),(9,0.656,0.0),(10,1.0,0.0)\}$

We now use these IFSs to compare E_H, E_E, E_{BB}, E_{SK} and E_N, respectively. The comparison results are shown in Table 1.

Table 1. Results of the measures of fuzziness with different entropies

IFSs	E_H	E_E	E_{BB}	E_{SK}	E_N
$F^{1/2}$	0.378	0.297	0.462	0.319	0.344
F	0.360	0.293	0.600	0.307	0.301
F^2	0.316	0.226	0.660	0.301	0.227
F^4	0.191	0.163	0.668	0.176	0.114

According to the results of Table 1, we can see that

$$E_H(F^{1/2}) \geq E_H(F) \geq E_H(F^2) \geq E_H(F^4)$$

$$E_E(F^{1/2}) \geq E_E(F) \geq E_E(F^2) \geq E_E(F^4)$$

$$E_{BB}(F^{1/2}) \leq E_{BB}(F) \leq E_{BB}(F^2) \leq E_{BB}(F^4)$$

$$E_{SK}(F^{1/2}) \geq E_{SK}(F) \geq E_{SK}(F^2) \geq E_{SK}(F^4)$$

$$E_N(F^{1/2}) \geq E_N(F) \geq E_N(F^2) \geq E_N(F^4)$$

From the viewpoint of concentration and dilation operators, a good entropy measure on these IFSs should have the following requirement:

$$E(F^{1/2}) \geq E(F) \geq E(F^2) \geq E(F^4) \tag{7}$$

Based on Table 1, the entropy measures E_H, E_E, E_{SK} and E_N satisfy (7), but E_{BB} fails.

We next make the comparison for E_H, E_E, E_{SK} and E_N. We consider an another IFS F_2 in $X = \{6,7,8,9,10\}$ defined by

$$F_2 = \{(6,0.3,0.5),(7,0.2,0.4),(8,0.1,0.3),(9,1.0,0.0),(10,1.0,0.0)\}.$$

We can generate the following AIFSs:

$$F_2^{1/2} = \{(6,0.548,0.293),(7,0.447,0.225),(8,0.316,0.163),(9,1.0,0.0),(10,1.0,0.0)\}$$

$$F_2^2 = \{(6,0.09,0.75),(7,0.04,0.64),(8,0.01,0.51),(9,1.0,0.0),(10,1.0,0.0)\}$$

$$F_2^4 = \{(6,0.008,0.938),(7,0.002,0.87),(8,0.0,0.76),(9,1.0,0.0),(10,1.0,0.0)\}$$

We use these IFSs to compare E_H, E_E, E_{SK} and E_N, respectively. The comparison results are shown in Table 2.

Table 2. Results of the measures of fuzziness with different entropies

IFSs	E_H	E_E	E_{SK}	E_N
$F_2^{1/2}$	0.474	0.17 7	0.419	0.374
F_2	0.480	0.200	0.158	0.344
F_2^2	0.248	0219	0.105	0.095
F_2^4	0.008	0.084	0.002	0.005

According to the results of Table 2, we have

$$E_H(F_2^{1/2}) \le E_H(F_2) \ge E_H(F_2^2) \ge E_H(F_2^4)$$
$$E_E(F_2^{1/2}) \le E_E(F_2) \ge E_E(F_2^2) \ge E_E(F_2^4)$$
$$E_{SK}(F_2^{1/2}) \ge E_{SK}(F_2) \ge E_{SK}(F_2^2) \ge E_{SK}(F_2^4)$$
$$E_N(F_2^{1/2}) \ge E_N(F_2) \ge E_N(F_2^2) \ge E_N(F_2^4)$$

Hence, the order of the entropy measures E_{SK} and E_N presents better than others. Finally, we compare only for E_{SK} and E_N. We consider an another IFS F_3 in $X = \{6,7,8,9,10\}$ defined by

$$F_3 = \{(6,0.1,0.2),(7,0.1,0.3),(8,0.1,0.4),(9,0.11,0.2),(10,0.11,0.3)\}$$

We can generate the following IFSs:

$$F_3^{1/2} = \{(6,0.316,0.106),(7,0.316,0.163),(8,0.316,0.225),(9,0.332,0.106),(10,0.332,0.163)\}$$
$$F_3^2 = \{(6,0.01,0.36),(7,0.01,0.51),(8,0.01,0.64),(9,0.012,0.36),(10,0.012,0.51)\}$$
$$F_3^4 = \{(6,0.0,0.59),(7,0.0,0.76),(8,0.0,0.87),(9,0.0,0.59),(10,0.0,0.76)\}$$

We use these IFSs to compare E_{SK} and E_N. The comparison results are shown in Table 3.

Table 3. Results of the measures of fuzziness with E_{SK} and E_N

IFSs	E_{SK}	E_N
$F_2^{1/2}$	0.802	0.665
F_2	0.804	0.567
F_2^2	0.530	0.050
F_2^4	0.286	0.000

According to the results of Table 3, we have

$$E_{SK}(F_3^{1/2}) \leq E_{SK}(F_3) \geq E_{SK}(F_3^2) \geq E_{SK}(F_3^4)$$
$$E_N(F_3^{1/2}) \geq E_N(F_3) \geq E_N(F_3^2) \geq E_N(F_3^4)$$

Obviously, the order of the entropy measure E_N presents better than E_{SK}. From the previous comparisons, the proposed entropy E_N is actually better for presenting the measure of fuzziness for IFSs.

To give more perspective viewpoints for E_{SK} and E_N, we may consider to analyze their equations as follows. For the previously considered IFS F_3 with

$$F_3 = \{(6,0.1,0.2),(7,0.1,0.3),(8,0.1,0.4),(9,0.11,0.2),(10,0.11,0.3)\},$$

We have that

$$v_A(x_i) > u_A(x_i), \ (u_A(x_i))^{\frac{1}{2}} > 1-(1-v_A(x_i))^{\frac{1}{2}}, \forall i \ \text{ and } \ \sum_{i=1}^{n} \frac{1-v_A(x_i)}{1-u_A(x_i)} > \sum_{i=1}^{n} \frac{1-(u_A(x_i))^{\frac{1}{2}}}{(1-v_A(x_i))^{\frac{1}{2}}}.$$

In this case, the equation of E_{SK} should have

$$E_{SK}(A) = \sum_{i=1}^{n} \frac{\min(u_A(x_i),v_A(x_i))+\pi_A(x_i)}{\max(u_A(x_i),v_A(x_i))+\pi_A(x_i)} = \sum_{i=1}^{n} \frac{1-\max(u_A(x_i),v_A(x_i))}{1-mix(u_A(x_i),v_A(x_i))}$$

$$= \sum_{i=1}^{n} \frac{1-v_A(x_i)}{1-u_A(x_i)} > \sum_{i=1}^{n} \frac{1-(u_A(x_i))^{\frac{1}{2}}}{1-(1-(1-v_A(x_i))^{\frac{1}{2}})} = E_{SK}(A^{\frac{1}{2}}).$$

That is, $E_{SK}(F_3^{1/2}) < E_{SK}(F_3)$. This means that E_{SK} is not good for presenting the measure of fuzziness for the IFS F_3 on the base of analyzing the equation of E_{SK}. On the other hand, we may analyze the equation of E_N as follows. In general, if $u_A(x_i) \leq t_i/2$, then $E_N(A)$ will be an increasing function of $u_A(x_i)$. In this case, if $u_A(x_i)$ is small, then $E_N(A)$ is small too. If $u_A(x_i) > t_i/2$, then $E_N(A)$ will be an increasing function of $v_A(x_i)$. In this case, if $v_A(x_i)$ is small, then $E_N(A)$ is small too. Hence, data from dilation to concentration will imply that $E_N(A)$ becomes small.

4   Conclusions

There had several entropy measures on IFSs proposed in literatures for measuring the fuzziness of IFSs. In this paper we proposed an exponential-type entropy measure on IFSs. The hedges, like "very", "highly", "more or less", with linguistic variables are used for the comparisons of our proposed entropy with several existing methods. The results show that our proposed one presents better measure for the fuzziness of IFSs.

References

1. Atanassov, K.: Intuitionistic fuzzy sets. Fuzzy Sets and Systems 20, 87–96 (1986)
2. Atanassov, K.: New operations defined over the intuitionistic fuzzy sets. Fuzzy Sets and Systems 61, 137–142 (1994)
3. Atanassov, K.: Intuitionistic Fuzzy Sets: Theory and Applications. Physica-Verlag, Heidelberg (1999)
4. Atanassov, K., Georgeiv, G.: Intuitionistic fuzzy prolog. Fuzzy Sets and Systems 53, 121–128 (1993)
5. Burillo, P., Bustince, H.: Entropy on intuitionistic fuzzy sets and interval valued fuzzy sets. Fuzzy Sets and Systems 78, 305–316 (1996)
6. De, S.K., Biswas, R., Roy, A.R.: Some operations on intuitionistic fuzzy sets. Fuzzy Sets and Systems 114, 477–484 (2000)
7. De, S.K., Biswas, R., Roy, A.R.: An application of intuitionistic fuzzy sets in medical diagnosis. Fuzzy Sets and Systems 117, 209–213 (2001)
8. De Luca, A., Termini, S.: A definition of a non-probabilitistic entropy in the setting of fuzzy sets theory. Information and Control 20, 301–312 (1972)
9. Deschrijver, G., Kerre, E.E.: On the position of intuitionistic fuzzy set theory in the framework of theories modelling imprecision. Information Sciences 177, 1860–1866 (2007)
10. Ebanks, B.R.: On measures of fuzziness and their representation. J. Math. Anal. Appl. 94, 24–37 (1983)
11. Hung, W.L.: A note on Entropy of intuitionistic fuzzy sets. Internat. J. Uncertainty, Fuzziness and Knowledge-Based System 11, 627–633 (2003)
12. Hung, W.L., Yang, M.S.: On the j-divergence of intuitionistic fuzzy sets with its application to pattern recognition. Information Sciences 178, 1641–1650 (2008)
13. Hwang, C.M., Yang, M.S.: New construction for similarity measures between intuitionistic fuzzy sets based onlower, upper and middle fuzzy sets. International Journal of Fuzzy Systems 15, 359–366 (2013)
14. Hwang, C.M., Yang, M.S., Hung, W.L., Lee, M.G.: A similarity measure of intuitionistic fuzzy sets based on Sugeno integral with its application to pattern recognition. Information Sciences 189, 93–109 (2012)
15. Liu, X.: Entropy, distance measure and similarity measure of fuzzy sets and their relations. Fuzzy Sets and Systems 52, 305–318 (1992)
16. Pankowska, A., Wygralak, M.: General IF-sets with triangular norms and their applications to group decision making. Information Sciences 176, 2713–2754 (2006)
17. Szmidt, E., Kacprzyk, J.: Entropy for intuitionistic fuzzy sets. Fuzzy Sets and Systems 118, 467–477 (2001)
18. Wu, K.L., Yang, M.S.: Alternative c-means clustering algorithms. Pattern Recognition 35, 2267–2278 (2002)
19. Yager, R.R.: On the measure of fuzziness and negation. Part 1: Membership in the unit interval. Internat. J. General System 5, 189–200 (1979)
20. Yang, M.S., Wu, K.L.: A similarity-based robust clustering method. IEEE Trans. on Pattern Analysis and Machine Intelligence 26, 434–448 (2004)
21. Zadeh, L.A.: Fuzzy sets. Information and Control 8, 338–356 (1965)

Comparative Analysis of MCDM Methods for Assessing the Severity of Chronic Liver Disease

Andrzej Piegat and Wojciech Sałabun[✉]

Department of Artificial Intelligence Methods and Applied Mathematics,
Faculty of Computer Science and Information Technology,
West Pomeranian University of Technology, Szczecin, Poland
{apiegat,wsalabun}@wi.zut.edu.pl

Abstract. The paper presents the Characteristic Objects method as a potential multi-criteria decision-making method for use in medical issues. The proposed approach is compared with TOPSIS and AHP. For this purpose, assessment of the severity of Chronic Liver Disease (CLD) is used. The simulation experiment is presented on the basis of the Model For End-Stage Liver Disease (MELD). The United Network for Organ Sharing (UNOS) and Eurotransplant use MELD for prioritizing allocation of liver transplants. MELD is calculated from creatinine, bilirubin and international normalized ratio of the prothrombin time (INR). The correctness of the selection is examined among randomly selected one million pairs of patients. The result is expressed as a percentage of agreement between the assessed method and MELD selection. The Characteristic Objects method is completely free of the rank reversal phenomenon, obtained by using the set of characteristic objects. In this approach, the assessment of each alternative is obtained on the basis of the distance from characteristic objects and their values. As a result, correctness of the selection obtained by using the Characteristic Objects method is higher than those obtained by TOPSIS or AHP techniques.

Keywords: Fuzzy Set Theory · MCDM · COMET · AHP · TOPSIS

1 Introduction

Many decision-making methods and tools have been developed to support a medical decision making. However, any improvement in medical decision making is very important, because it can contribute to generating substantial benefits for both patients and health care providers [20]. The Analytic Hierarchy Process (AHP) and Technique for Order of Preference by Similarity to Ideal Solution (TOPSIS) are examples of multi-criteria decision-making (MCDM) methods using in the medical field [2,4,6,8,18,20,21,24]. Unfortunately, the rank reversal phenomenon is still the main shortcoming of MCDM methods [7,41,44]. The commonly used rank reversal definition emphasizes that this issue occurs when the rankings for the alternatives are changed with either the addition or removal of an alternative. As a result, decision-makers cannot be sure, which solution is correct. Additionally, there is no research to estimate the correctness of mentioned methods.

© Springer International Publishing Switzerland 2015
L. Rutkowski et al. (Eds.): ICAISC 2015, Part I, LNAI 9119, pp. 228–238, 2015.
DOI: 10.1007/978-3-319-19324-3_21

In the paper, the Characteristic Objects method is presented as a potential multi-criteria decision-making method for use in medical issues. The proposed approach is compared with TOPSIS and AHP in respect to the correctness of assessments. For this purpose, the simulation experiment is presented on the basis of the Model For End-Stage Liver Disease (MELD), the reference model for assessing Chronic Liver Disease [13,14,45]. It was initially developed to predict death within three months of surgery in patients who had undergone a TIPS procedure [22]. Subsequently it is found to be useful in determining prognosis and prioritizing for receipt of a liver transplant [13,14]. Today, the United Network for Organ Sharing (UNOS) and Eurotransplant use MELD for prioritizing allocation of liver transplants [12]. The right select of patients is extremely important to successfully transplant a liver and save a life. Therefore, the MCDM methods will be verified by the proposed experiment.

The rest of the paper is organized as follows: Section 2 describes TOPSIS technique and Section 3 presents the AHP method. Afterward, Section 4 introduces the description of the Characteristic Objects Method. The simulation experiment and its results are presented in Section 5. Finally, Section 6 shows concluding remarks.

2   TOPSIS Procedure

TOPSIS technique is a commonly used MCDM method [16,17,18,29,42,43]. The classical TOPSIS method is based on the idea that the best alternative should have the shortest geometric distance from the positive ideal solution (PIS) and the longest distance from the negative ideal solution (NIS) [9,10,19]. PIS and NIS are easiest to identify when all of the criteria are monotonic (either increasing/profit attributes or decreasing/cost attributes). This is a common assumption when using TOPSIS.

A decision-making problem is based on m alternatives, A_1, A_2, A_3, ..., A_m, and n monotonic criteria, C_1, C_2, C_3, ..., C_n. Using these data, an original score of the decision matrix $D[x_{ij}]_{mxn}$ is created, where x_{ij} is the evaluation of alternative A_i for criterion C_j. Finally, $W = (w_1, w_2, w_3, ..., w_n)$ is the vector of criteria weights, where $\sum_{j=1}^{n} w_j = 1$. With the above assumptions, TOPSIS is performed using the following six steps [39]:

Step 1. Evaluation matrix – decision maker creates an evaluation matrix $D[x_{ij}]_{mxn}$ consisting of m alternatives and n criteria.

Step 2. Normalization – normalize the evaluation matrix $D[x_{ij}]_{mxn}$ using the normalization formula, defined for profit attributes by equation (1) and for cost attributes by equation (2) [23,39]:

$$r_{ij} = \frac{x_{ij} - min_i(x_{ij})}{max_i(x_{ij}) - min_i(x_{ij})} \tag{1}$$

$$r_{ij} = \frac{max_i(x_{ij}) - x_{ij}}{max_i(x_{ij}) - min_i(x_{ij})} \tag{2}$$

Step 3. Inclusion of weight – calculate the weighted normalized decision matrix defined by equation (3) for each element in the matrix:

$$v_{ij} = w_j \cdot r_{ij} \tag{3}$$

Step 4. Positive and Negative Ideal Solution (PIS and NIS) – determine the PIS using equation (4) and the NIS using equation (5):

$$V_j^+ = \{v_1^+, v_2^+, v_3^+, \ldots, v_n^+\} = \{(max_i(v_{ij})|j \in K_b)(min_i(v_{ij})|j \in K_c)\} \tag{4}$$

$$V_j^- = \{v_1^-, v_2^-, v_3^-, \ldots, v_n^-\} = \{(min_i(v_{ij})|j \in K_b)(max_i(v_{ij})|j \in K_c)\} \tag{5}$$

where K_b is a set of benefit criteria and K_c is a set of cost criteria.

Step 5. Euclidean distance – calculate the Euclidean distance as the following: the $i - th$ alternative and the NIS alternative (6) or the PIS (7) alternative:

$$D_i^- = \sqrt{\sum_{j=1}^{n}(v_{ij} - v_j^-)^2} \tag{6}$$

the $i - th$ alternative and the PIS alternative (7):

$$D_i^+ = \sqrt{\sum_{j=1}^{n}(v_{ij} - v_j^+)^2} \tag{7}$$

Step 6. Alternatives ranking – calculate the relative closeness to the ideal condition using equation(8):

$$C_i = \frac{D_i^-}{D_i^- + D_i^+} \tag{8}$$

3   The Analytic Hierarchy Process

The Analytic Hierarchy Process (AHP) is a popular method for organizing and analyzing decision problems. The applications of AHP are numbered in the thousands [1,5,15,33,34,35,36,38]. The AHP has been used to medical decision making, such as diagnosis, therapy, treatment, organ transplantation, and health care evolution. The procedure for using the AHP can be summarized as the following five steps [1,33,37,40]:

Step 1. Organizing problem hierarchically – in this step, the problem is structured as a tree. The overall goal of the decision-making problem is located at the highest level. Afterwards, on the next levels are located criteria and sub-criteria. The last level contains the alternatives.

Step 2. Development of judgment matrices by pairwise comparisons – the judgment matrices of criteria or alternatives can be defined from the pairwise comparisons of criteria at the same level or all possible alternatives in the respect of particular criterion. The pairwise comparisons are done in terms of which element dominates the other.

Step 3. Consistency checking – after making all the pair-wise comparisons, the consistency is determined by using the eigenvalue, λ_{max}, to calculate the consistency index (CI) as follows (9):

$$CI = \frac{\lambda_{max} - n}{n - 1} \qquad (9)$$

where n is a size of judgment matrix. Judgment consistency can be checked by taking the consistency ratio (CR). Saaty calculated the CR as the ratio of the CI to a random index (RI). The CR is acceptable, if it does not exceed 0.10. If it is greater, the judgment matrix is inconsistent. To obtain a consistent matrix, judgments should be reviewed and improved.

Step 4. Calculating local priorities from judgment matrices – several methods for deriving local priorities from judgment matrices have been developed, such as the eigenvector method (EVM), the logarithmic least squares method (LLSM) and the weighted least squares method (WLSM). In this paper, the local weights of criteria and the local scores of alternatives will be derived by using EVM.

Step 5: Alternatives ranking – the final step is to obtain global priorities by aggregating all local priorities with the application of a simple weighted sum. Then the final ranking of the alternatives is determined on the basis of these global priorities.

4   Characteristic Objects Method

The COMET method is a very simple approach, but to be able to understand better this technique, the basic knowledge on the Fuzzy Sets Theory is necessary [26,28]. The basic concept of COMET method was proposed by prof. Piegat [26,27]. The formal notation of COMET method is presented in the five following steps [27,30,31,32].

Step 1. Define the space of the problem – an expert determines dimensionality of the problem by selecting number r of criteria, $C_1, C_2, ..., C_r$. Subsequently, the set of fuzzy numbers for each criterion C_i is selected, i.e., $\tilde{C}_{i1}, \tilde{C}_{i2}, ..., \tilde{C}_{ic_i}$. In this way, the following result is obtained (10):

$$\begin{aligned}
C_1 &= \{\tilde{C}_{11}, \tilde{C}_{12}, ..., \tilde{C}_{1c_1}\} \\
C_2 &= \{\tilde{C}_{21}, \tilde{C}_{22}, ..., \tilde{C}_{2c_1}\} \\
&\cdots\cdots\cdots\cdots\cdots\cdots\cdots\cdots \\
C_r &= \{\tilde{C}_{r1}, \tilde{C}_{r2}, ..., \tilde{C}_{rc_r}\}
\end{aligned} \qquad (10)$$

where $c_1, c_2, ..., c_r$ are numbers of the fuzzy numbers for all criteria.

Step 2. Generate the characteristic objects – The characteristic objects (CO) are obtained by using the Cartesian Product of fuzzy numbers cores for each criteria as follows (11):

$$CO = C(C_1) \times C(C_2) \times ... \times C(C_r) \qquad (11)$$

As the result of this, the ordered set of all CO is obtained (12):

$$
\begin{aligned}
CO_1 &= C(\tilde{C}_{11}), C(\tilde{C}_{21}), ..., C(\tilde{C}_{r1}) \\
CO_2 &= C(\tilde{C}_{11}), C(\tilde{C}_{21}), ..., C(\tilde{C}_{r2}) \\
&\cdots\cdots\cdots\cdots\cdots\cdots\cdots\cdots\cdots\cdots\cdots \\
CO_t &= C(\tilde{C}_{1c_1}), C(\tilde{C}_{2c_2}), ..., C(\tilde{C}_{rc_r})
\end{aligned} \tag{12}
$$

where t is a number of CO (13):

$$
t = \prod_{i=1}^{r} c_i \tag{13}
$$

Step 3. Rank the characteristic objects – the expert determines the Matrix of Expert Judgment (MEJ). It is a result of pairwise comparison of the characteristic objects by the expert knowledge. The MEJ structure is as follows (14):

$$
MEJ = \begin{pmatrix} \alpha_{11} & \alpha_{12} & ... & \alpha_{1t} \\ \alpha_{21} & \alpha_{22} & ... & \alpha_{2t} \\ ... & ... & ... & ... \\ \alpha_{t1} & \alpha_{t2} & ... & \alpha_{tt} \end{pmatrix} \tag{14}
$$

where α_{ij} is a result of comparing CO_i and CO_j by the expert. The more preferred characteristic object gets one point and the second object get zero point. If the preferences are balanced, the both objects get half point. It depends solely on the knowledge of the expert and can be presented as (15):

$$
\alpha_{ij} = \begin{cases} 0.0, & f_{exp}(CO_i) < f_{exp}(CO_j) \\ 0.5, & f_{exp}(CO_i) = f_{exp}(CO_j) \\ 1.0, & f_{exp}(CO_i) > f_{exp}(CO_j) \end{cases} \tag{15}
$$

where f_{exp} is an expert mental judgment function.

Afterwards, the vertical vector of the Summed Judgments (SJ) is obtained as follows (16):

$$
SJ_i = \sum_{j=1}^{t} \alpha_{ij} \tag{16}
$$

The last step assigns to each characteristic object an approximate value of preference. In the result, the vertical vector P is obtained, where $i-th$ row contains the approximate value of preference for CO_i. This algorithm is presented as a fragment of Matlab code:

```
1: k = length(unique(SJ));
2: P = zeros(t,1);
3: for i = 1:k
4:     ind = find(SJ == max(SJ));
5:     P(ind) = (k - i) / (k - 1);
6:     SJ(ind) = 0;
7: end
```

In line 1, the number k is obtained as a number of unique value of the vector SJ. In line 2, the vertical vector P of zeros is created (with identical size as vector SJ). In line 4, the index with maximum value from vector SJ is obtained. This index is used to assign the value of preference to adequate position in vector P (based on the principle of indifference of Laplacea). In line 6, the maximum value of the vector SJ is reset.

Step 4. The rule base – each characteristic object and value of preference is converted to a fuzzy rule as follows, general form (17) and detailed form (18):

$$IF\ CO_i\ THEN\ P_i \tag{17}$$

$$IF\ C(\tilde{C}_{1i})\ AND\ C(\tilde{C}_{2i})\ AND\ ...\ THEN\ P_i \tag{18}$$

In this way, the complete fuzzy rule base is obtained.

Step 5. Inference and final ranking – The each one alternative is a set of crisp numbers corresponding to criteria $C_1, C_2, ..., C_r$. It can be presented as follows (19):

$$A_i = \{a_{1i}, a_{2i}, ..., a_{ri}\} \tag{19}$$

Each single alternative activates a specified number of fuzzy rules, and for each rule the fulfillment degree of the conjunctive complex premise is determined. Fulfillment degrees of all activated rules sum up to one. The preference of alternative is computed as sum of the product of all activated rules, as their fulfillment degrees, and their values of the preference. The final ranking of alternatives is obtained by sorting the preference of alternatives.

5 The Experiment and Results

The Model For End-Stage Liver Disease (MELD) is the reference model for assessing the severity of Chronic Liver Disease (CLD). This model was developed on the basis of three parameters: creatinine, bilirubin and international normalized ratio of the prothrombin time (INR)[14,45]. Further studies confirmed the practical accuracy of this system [3,11,13]. The formula of MELD is presented as (20):

$$MELD = 9.57ln(CRE) + 3.78ln(BIL) + 11.2ln(INR) + 6.43 \tag{20}$$

where, BIL is serum bilirubin (mg/dl), CRE is serum creatinine (mg/dl), and INR is international normalized ratio of the prothrombin time.

In the paper, the severity of CLD will be assessed in simulated groups of two randomly selected patients. Each patient is described as a set of three medical results (CRE, BIL, INR). The MELD score allows to assess, which patient in each group is more dying, in a reliable way. Subsequently, three MCDM methods are used to make the same assessment. If the result from MCDM method points the same patient as a MELD score, then it is counted as the correct answer. In this study, the correctness is defined as a percentage of the correct answer in the respect to all trials. The number of trials (the number of groups) is selected as one million. Thereby, the mean error of correctness will be not bigger than 0.05 percent. Serum bilirubin, serum creatinine and INR must be included in appropriate intervals, $CRE \in [88.4, 500]\mu mol/l$, $BIL \in [17.1, 1000]\mu mol/l$, and $INR \in [1, 10]$. For formula (20) these values must be converted from SI units to US units (for serum creatinine $1mg/dl = 88.4\mu mol/l$ and for serum bilirubin $1mg/dl = 17.1\mu mol/l$).

TOPSIS technique is simple to use, but weights of criteria must be identified. The easiest approach is to adapte weights from formula (20). The sum of all weights must be equal to one. In that way, we obtain the following weights: $w_{CRE} = 0.3898$, $w_{BIL} = 0.1540$, $w_{INR} = 0.4562$. Subsequently, formulas (1-8) are used to obtain the final results for one million pairs of patients.

AHP application requires a consistent judgment matrix. For this purpose, the judgment matrix will be filled by the ratio of a first value to second for three attributes. This approach guarantees the CR rate at 0.00. The weights of criteria from the linear model are also used to construct judgment matrix in the AHP method. In effect, the values of weights are returned exactly the same as in TOPSIS method. Afterwards, in the same manner the rest of judgment matrices are obtained. It allows for use the step 3 and step 4 of AHP method.

In the COMET method the most important is generating characteristic objects. For this purpose, fuzzy numbers (FNs) must be defined. Figures 1, 2 and 3 show FNs for CRE, BIL, and INR. Each criterion is evaluated with two linguistic values: *low* and *high*. The linguistic value *low* has a convex membership function, and *high* has a concave membership functions. Quadratic membership functions are determined as (21-26):

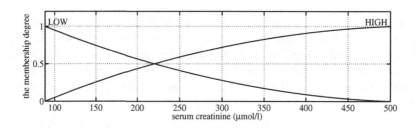

Fig. 1. The set of two fuzzy numbers for serum creatinine

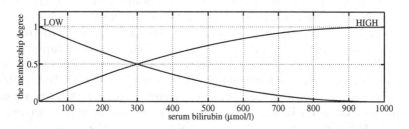

Fig. 2. The set of two fuzzy numbers for serum bilirubin

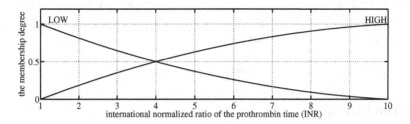

Fig. 3. The set of two fuzzy numbers for INR

$$\mu_L(CRE) = \frac{CRE^2}{204402} - \frac{103CRE}{19404} + \frac{1089}{761} \tag{21}$$

$$\mu_H(CRE) = 1 - \mu_L(CRE) \tag{22}$$

$$\mu_L(BIL) = \frac{BIL^2}{933319} - \frac{7BIL}{3322} + \frac{7510}{7251} \tag{23}$$

$$\mu_H(BIL) = 1 - \mu_L(BIL) \tag{24}$$

$$\mu_L(INR) = \frac{INR^2}{108} - \frac{23INR}{108} + \frac{65}{54} \tag{25}$$

$$\mu_H(INR) = 1 - \mu_L(INR) \tag{26}$$

The assessment of each patient is obtained on the basis of the distance from the nearest characteristic objects and their values of assessments. The eight characteristic objects are presented in Table 1. The comparison of correctness of analyzed MCDM methods is presented in Table 2. The worst correctness is obtained by using TOPSIS method. The result for TOPSIS is equal 80.53 ± 0.04 percent. Quite good results were obtained by using AHP method, 93.32 ± 0.03 percent, but the best result was obtained by using COMET method. The correctness of COMET method for assessing the severity of CLD is equal 96.63 ± 0.02 percent. These good results were obtained by using only eight characteristic objects. Identification of COMET method required only 28 simple questions with three possibilities of an answer (15). On the other hand, AHP method needs 3,000,001 questions by using Saaty's scale (minimum 17 possibilities). Further work is planned to test, more detailed, effectiveness of MCDM methods.

Table 1. The eight characteristic objects and their assessments of COMET method

O_i	Creatinine	Bilirubin	INR	SJ	Rank	Assessment
O_1	low	low	low 0.5	8		0/7
O_2	low	low	high 3.5	5		3/7
O_3	low	high	low 1.5	7		1/7
O_4	low	high	high 5.5	3		5/7
O_5	high	low	low 2.5	6		2/7
O_6	high	low	high 6.5	2		6/7
O_7	high	high	low 4.5	4		4/7
O_8	high	high	high 7.5	1		7/7

Table 2. The comparison of correctness of MCDM methods for experiment

MCDM method	Number of correct answers	Number of incorrect answers
TOPSIS	805,345	194,655
AHP	933,165	66,835
COMET	966,309	33,691

6   Conclusion

This study proposes a new multi-criteria decision-making method to solve medical problems, which is called the Characteristic Objects Method (COMET). Moreover, the COMET method is completely free from the rank reversal phenomenon, because all preferences are identified on characteristic objects and not on compared alternatives. Therefore, the assessing of alternatives are invariable in the respect to number of alternatives and their attributes.

Multi-Criteria Decision-Making (MCDM) methods are very rarely tested, because there is no certain reference to obtain a final ranking. This paper considers the problem of assessing the severity of Chronic Liver Disease (CLD). As a reference model is used MELD score. The MELD model is calculated from serum creatinine, serum bilirubin and INR. Based on MELD model it has been demonstrated that COMET method is better to use in medical problems than TOPSIS or AHP. The COMET method was compared with TOPSIS and AHP in respect to correctness of answer for simulated groups (one million pairs of patients).

References

1. Blair, A.R., Mandelker, G.N., Saaty, T.L., Whitaker, R.: Forecasting the resurgence of the u.s. economy in 2010: An expert judgment approach. Socio-Economic Planning Sciences 44(3), 114–121 (2010)
2. Boran, F.E., Gen, S., Kurt, M., Akay, D.: A multi-criteria intuitionistic fuzzy group decision making for supplier selection with TOPSIS method. Expert Systems with Applications 36(8), 11363–11368 (2009)
3. Cholongitas, E., Marelli, L., Shusang, V., Senzolo, M., Rolles, K., Patch, D., Burroughs, A.K.: A systematic review of the performance of the model for end-stage liver disease (MELD) in the setting of liver transplantation. Liver Transplantation 12(7), 1049–1061 (2006)
4. Dolan, J.G., Isselhardt, B.J., Cappuccio, J.D.: The Analytic Hierarchy Process in Medical Decision Making: A Tutorial. Medical Decision Making 9(1), 40–50 (1989)
5. Dong, Y., Zhang, G., Hong, W.C., Xu, Y.: Consensus models for AHP group decision making under row geometric mean prioritization method. Decision Support Systems 49(3), 281–289 (2010)
6. Figueira, J., Greco, S., Ehrgott, M.: Multiple Criteria Decision Analysis: State of the Art Surveys. Springer, New York (2004)
7. Garca-Cascalesa, M.S., Lamata, M.T.: On rank reversal and TOPSIS method. Mathematical and Computer Modelling 56(5-6), 10–19 (2012)
8. Hsu, P.F., Hsu, M.G.: Optimizing the information outsourcing practices of primary care medical organizations using entropy and TOPSIS. Quality and Quantity 42(2), 181–201 (2008)

9. Hwang, C.L., Lai, Y.J., Liu, T.Y.: A new approach for multiple-objective decision-making. Computers and Operations Research 20(8), 889–899 (1993)
10. Hwang, C.L., Yoon, K.P.: Multiple attribute decision making: Methods and applications. Springer, New York (1981)
11. Ioannou, G.N., Perkins, J.D., Carithers Jr., R.L.: Liver transplantation for hepatocellular carcinoma: Impact of the MELD allocation system and predictors of survival. Gastroenterology 134(5), 1342–1351 (2008)
12. Jung, G.E., Encke, J., Schmidt, J., Rahmel, A.: Model for end-stage liver disease. New basis of allocation for liver transplantations. Chirurg 79(2), 157–163 (2008)
13. Kamath, P.S., Kim, W.: The model for end-stage liver disease (MELD). Hepatology 45(3), 797–805 (2007)
14. Kamath, P.S., Wiesner, R.H., Malinchoc, M., Kremers, W., Therneau, T.M., Kosberg, C.L., D'Amico, G., Dickson, E.R., Kim, W.R.: A model to predict survival in patients with end-stage liver disease. Hepatology 33(2), 464–470 (2001)
15. Karami, E.: Appropriateness of farmers adoption of irrigation methods: The application of the AHP model. Agricultural Systems 87(1), 101–119 (2006)
16. Kim, Y., Chung, E.S., Jun, S.M., Kim, S.U.: Prioritizing the best sites for treated wastewater instream use in an urban watershed using fuzzy TOPSIS. Resources Conservation and Recycling 73, 23–32 (2013)
17. Kuo, R.J., Wu, Y.H., Hsu, T.S.: Integration of fuzzy set theory and TOPSIS into HFMEA to improve outpatient service for elderly patients in Taiwan. Journal of the Chinese Medical Association 75(7), 341–348 (2012)
18. La Scalia, G., et al.: Multi-criteria decision making support system for pancreatic islet transplantation. Expert Systems with Applications 38(4), 3091–3097 (2011)
19. Lai, Y.J., Liu, T.Y., Hwang, C.L.: TOPSIS for MODM. European Journal of Operational 76(3), 486–500 (1994)
20. Liberatore, M.J., Nydick, R.L.: The analytic hierarchy process in medical and health care decision making: A literature review. European Journal of Operational Research 189(1), 194–207 (2008)
21. Lin, C.T., Tsai, M.C.: Location choice for direct foreign investment in new hospitals in China by using ANP and TOPSIS. Quality and Quantity 44(2), 375–390 (2010)
22. Malinchoc, M., Kamath, P.S., Gordon, F.D., Peine, C.J., Rank, J., ter Borg, P.C.: A model to predict poor survival in patients undergoing transjugular intrahepatic portosystemic shunts. Hepatology 31(4), 864–871 (2000)
23. Milani, A.S., Shanian, A., Madoliat, R., Nemes, J.A.: The effect of normalization norms in multiple attribute decision making models: A case study in gear material selection. Structural and Multidisciplinary Optimization 29(4), 312–318 (2005)
24. Padilla-Garrido, N., et al.: Multicriteria Decision Making in Health Care Using the Analytic Hierarchy Process and Microsoft Excel. Medical Decision Making (first published on May 14, 2014)
25. Piegat, A.: Fuzzy Modeling and Control. Springer, New York (2001)
26. Piegat, A., Sałabun, W.: Nonlinearity of human multi-criteria in decision-making. Journal of Theoretical and Applied Computer Science 6(3), 36–49 (2012)
27. Piegat, A., Sałabun, W.: Identification of a Multicriteria Decision-Making Model Using the Characteristic Objects Method. Applied Computational Intelligence and Soft Computing (2014)
28. Sałabun, W.: The use of fuzzy logic to evaluate the nonlinearity of human multi-criteria used in decision making. Przeglad Elektrotechniczny (Electrical Review) 88(10b), 235–238 (2012)
29. Sałabun, W.: The mean error estimation of TOPSIS method using a fuzzy reference models. Journal of Theoretical and Applied Computer Science 7(3), 40–50 (2013)

30. Sałabun, W.: Application of the Fuzzy Multi-criteria Decision-Making Method to Identify Nonlinear Decision Models. International Journal of Computer Applications 89(15), 1–6 (2014)
31. Sałabun, W.: Reduction in the number of comparisons required to create matrix of expert judgment in the COMET method. Management and Production Engineering Review 5(3), 62–69 (2014)
32. Sałabun, W.: The Characteristic Objects Method: A New Distance-based Approach to Multicriteria Decision-making Problems. Journal of Multi-Criteria Decision Analysis 21(3-4) (first published on July 4, 2014)
33. Saaty, T.L.: Decision making the analytic hierarchy and network processes (AHP/ANP). Journal of Systems Science and Systems Engineering 13(1), 1–35 (2004)
34. Saaty, T.L.: Time dependent decision-making; dynamic priorities in the AHP/ANP: Generalizing from points to functions and from real to complex variables. Mathematical and Computer Modelling 46(78), 860–891 (2007)
35. Saaty, T.L.: Decision making the analytic hierarchy and network processes (AHP/ANP). International Journal Services Sciences 1(1), 83–98 (2008)
36. Saaty, T.L., Brandy, C.: The encyclicon, volume 2: a dictionary of complex decisions using the analytic network process. RWS Publications, Pittsburgh (2009)
37. Saaty, T.L., Shang, J.S.: An innovative orders-of-magnitude approach to AHP-based mutli-criteria decision making: Prioritizing divergent intangible humane acts. European Journal of Operational Research 214(3), 703–715 (2011)
38. Saaty, T.L., Tran, L.T.: On the invalidity of fuzzifying numerical judgments in the analytic hierarchy process. Mathematical and Computer Modelling 46(78), 962–975 (2007)
39. Shih, H.S., Shyur, H.J., Lee, E.S.: An extension of TOPSIS for group decision making. Mathematical and Computer Modelling 45(7-8), 801–813 (2007)
40. Sipahi, S., Timor, M.: The analytic hierarchy process and analytic network process: an overview of applications. Management Decision 48(5), 775–808 (2010)
41. Soltanifar, M., Shahghobadi, S.: Survey on rank preservation and rank reversal in data envelopment analysis. Knowledge-Based Systems 60, 10–19 (2014)
42. Sun, Y.F., Liang, Z.S., Shan, C.J., Viernstein, H., Unger, F.: Comprehensive evaluation of natural antioxidants and antioxidant potentials in Ziziphus jujuba Mill. var. spinosa (Bunge) Huex H. F. Chou fruits based on geographical origin by TOPSIS method. Food Chemistry 124(4), 1612–1619 (2011)
43. Taleizadeh, A.A., Akhavan Niaki, S.T., Aryanezhad, M.B.: A hybrid method of Pareto, TOPSIS and genetic algorithm to optimize multi-product multiconstraint inventory control systems with random fuzzy replenishments. Mathematical and Computer Modeling 49(5-6), 1044–1057 (2009)
44. Wang, Y.M., Luoc, Y.: On rank reversal in decision analysis. Mathematical and Computer Modelling 49(5-6), 1221–1229 (2009)
45. Wiesner, R.H., McDiarmid, S.V., Kamath, P.S., Edwards, E.B., Malinchoc, M., Kremers, W.K., Krom, R.A., Kim, W.R.: MELD and PELD: application of survival models to liver allocation. Liver Transplantation 7(7), 567–580

Solving Zadeh's Challenge Problems
with the Application of RDM-Arithmetic

Marcin Pluciński[✉]

Faculty of Computer Science and Information Technology,
West Pomeranian University of Technology,
Żołnierska 49, 71-062 Szczecin, Poland
mplucinski@wi.zut.edu.pl

Abstract. The paper presents a simple method of CwW that is based on RDM-models of intervals and on the multidimensional RDM-interval arithmetic. The method is explained on the example of popular Zadeh's challenge problem known as 'Balls in a box' problem. On the base of presented calculations, the general methodology of solving CwW problems with the application of simplified RDM-models of quantifiers is formulated.

Keywords: Computing with Words · Interval arithmetic · RDM-arithmetic · Zadeh's challenge problems

1 Introduction

Computing with Words (CwW) is very important for decision-making, where very often, apart from numerical data, linguistic information provided by a problem expert is at disposal. Using linguistic and numerical information together enables a more effective decision-making than using only numerical one. Additionally, the linguistic information provided by the problem expert can be much more important and informative for the problem solving than numerical data, because accuracy of numerical data can be sometimes very low, although this data can make impression of a great precision.

The idea of CwW, created by prof. Lotfi Zadeh, has been presented in numerous publications after 1990 [17–22, 24, 26]. From the very beginning CwW has been connected with fuzzy and interval arithmetic [3–5, 9].

CwW is rather a very difficult mathematical area and at present its development phase can be evaluated as a beginning state. This opinion is supported by the fact that practical possibilities of the present CwW are rather limited. Prof. Lotfi Zadeh has formulated many popular challenge problems. These problems can be found in his publications, eg. [25], and some of them are listed below.

- Tall Swedes
  Most Swedes are tall. How many are short? What is the average height of Swedes?

© Springer International Publishing Switzerland 2015
L. Rutkowski et al. (Eds.): ICAISC 2015, Part I, LNAI 9119, pp. 239–248, 2015.
DOI: 10.1007/978-3-319-19324-3_22

- Temperature
  Usually the temperature in my city is not very low and not very high. What is the average temperature?
- Flight delay
  Usually most United Airlines flights from San Francisco leave on time. What is the probability that my flight will be delayed?
- Balls in a box
  A box contains about 20 balls of various sizes. Most are large. What is the number of small balls? What is the probability that a ball drawn at random is neither small nor large?

The above problems may seem very easy for non-specialists. However, it is not true. Many persons cannot solve them and such ability may be very important for autonomous thinking. If simple CwW examples cannot be solved, then, how more complex tasks could be?

Solutions of Zadeh's CwW-problems are in the scientific literature rather rare. Examples can be [1, 13–15]. These papers show how complicated are problems of autonomous thinking. They require considerable theoretical knowledge and each solution takes many pages. Therefore, industrial engineers or common economists can have difficulties with its application.

The paper presents a less complicated method of CwW that is based on RDM-models of intervals and on the multidimensional RDM-interval arithmetic. The method will be explained on the base of the last listed above problem, known as 'Balls in a box' problem.

2   RDM-Model of an Interval

The description of intervals with an application of RDM-models can be an interesting alternative to the commonly used interval arithmetic described by Moore [6, 7]. The author of the RDM-model concept is prof. Andrzej Piegat [10–12]. This concept allows to overcome many faults of the interval arithmetic such as:

- the excess width effect,
- the dependency problem,
- difficulties in solving of even simplest interval equations, and others.

These faults are described in greater detail in [2, 16]. Among others, they result from such features of the interval arithmetic as: nonexistence of additive and multiplicative inverse of intervals and failure to meet the distributivity law.

The RDM-arithmetic has almost the same mathematical properties as conventional arithmetic [8]. As a result, complicated problems can be solved thanks to possibility of a formulas transformation. The RDM-arithmetic provides complete, multidimensional problem solutions from which various simplified representations as: a cardinality distribution, a span of a solution or an expected value of a solution can be derived.

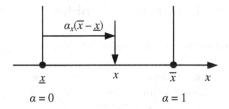

Fig. 1. The meaning of the RDM-variable α in the RDM-model of an interval

The RDM-arithmetic introduces an internal RDM-variable $\alpha \in [0,1]$, which has a meaning of a relative-distance-measure (RDM), Fig. 1. An interval X can be described as:

$$X = [\underline{x}, \overline{x}] = \underline{x} + \alpha_x(\underline{x} - \overline{x}), \quad \alpha_x \in [0,1]. \tag{1}$$

For example, the interval $A = [1,4]$ with use of the RDM-model has the form:

$$A = 1 + 3\alpha_A, \quad \alpha_A \in [0,1].$$

Thanks to RDM-variables, inside of intervals can also take part in calculations.

One of the greatest advantages of the RDM-arithmetic, is a possibility of taking into account dependencies between intervals. In real problems, they are very common. Such dependencies can be taken into account by means of RDM-variables.

For example in the classic interval arithmetic, as a result of subtracting two identical intervals we have:

$$Y = X - X = [\underline{x}, \overline{x}] - [\underline{x}, \overline{x}] = [\underline{x} - \overline{x}, \overline{x} - \underline{x}]. \tag{2}$$

If $A = [1,4]$:

$$A - A = [1,4] - [1,4] = [-3,3].$$

In the RDM-arithmetic, we can introduce two RDM-variables $\alpha_{x1}, \alpha_{x2} \in [0,1]$:

$$Y = X - X = (\underline{x} + \alpha_{x1}(\overline{x} - \underline{x})) - (\underline{x} + \alpha_{x2}(\overline{x} - \underline{x})) = (\alpha_{x1} - \alpha_{x2})(\overline{x} - \underline{x}). \tag{3}$$

The result is a function of two RDM-variables α_{x1} and α_{x2}: $Y = f(\alpha_{x1}, \alpha_{x2})$. We can calculate from it many parameters, eg. an interval lower and upper bound. The function value is the smallest for $\alpha_{x1} = 0$ and $\alpha_{x2} = 1$ – in that way we can get the lower bound of the resulting interval which is equal $\underline{x} - \overline{x}$. The function value is the greatest for $\alpha_{x1} = 1$ and $\alpha_{x2} = 0$ – in that way we can get the upper bound of the resulting interval which is equal $\overline{x} - \underline{x}$.

If, however, we know that in the formula we have the same interval X, we can assume that $\alpha_{x1} = \alpha_{x2} = \alpha_x$. Then:

$$Y = X - X = (\underline{x} + \alpha_x(\overline{x} - \underline{x})) - (\underline{x} + \alpha_x(\overline{x} - \underline{x})) = 0, \tag{4}$$

what is consistent with common sense, but unattainable for the classic interval arithmetic.

3 Solution of 'Balls in a box' Problem

First, let us recall the problem that we want to solve.

"A box contains about 20 balls of various sizes. Most are large. What is the number of small balls? What is the probability that a ball drawn at random is neither small nor large? [25]"

First of all, let's define the quantifier *most*. A proposal of such definition can be found in prof. Zadeh's papers [19, 23] and the membership function of the quantifier is presented in Fig. 2a. The quantifier *most* describes the ratio of large balls to all balls in the box. In the paper, there will be used a simplified, interval form of it, Fig. 2b.

A simplified form of the quantifier *most* can be described using the variable m which has the sense of part of the whole (PofW). RDM-model of the variable m has the form:

$$m = \frac{2}{3} + \frac{1}{3}\alpha_m, \quad \alpha_m \in [0, 1].$$ (5)

The quantifier $NOT(most)$ will also be used in the solution. It can be interpreted as the minority of the whole, whereas the quantifier *most* has a sense of the majority of the whole. It can be defined as:

$$NOT(m) = 1 - m = \frac{1}{3} - \frac{1}{3}\alpha_m, \quad \alpha_m \in [0, 1].$$ (6)

It should be noticed that the RDM-variable α_m enables modeling of the dependency between quantifiers *most* and $NOT(most)$, and for their RDM-models holds:

$$m + NOT(m) = 1.$$ (7)

The dependency is illustrated in Fig. 3.

The last question of the task suggests that there are large, small and other balls in the box. Let us define them as a medium-sized balls. Since we don't

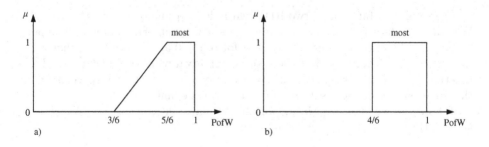

Fig. 2. The membership function of the linguistic quantifier *most* (a) and its simplified form (b)

Fig. 3. Illustration of the connection between RDM-models of quantifiers *most* and *NOT(most)*

have any information about amounts of small and medium balls, let's create an additional variable s in the form of RDM-model:

$$s = \alpha_s, \quad \alpha_s \in [0, 1], \tag{8}$$

which determines what part of not large balls represent small ones.

Respectively, the RDM-model:

$$NOT(s) = 1 - \alpha_s, \quad \alpha_s \in [0, 1], \tag{9}$$

determines what part of not large balls represent medium ones.

The probability of the medium ball drawing can be calculated as:

$$p = NOT(m) \cdot NOT(s) = \left(\frac{1}{3} - \frac{1}{3}\alpha_m\right) \cdot (1 - \alpha_s), \quad \alpha_m \in [0, 1], \alpha_s \in [0, 1]. \tag{10}$$

The plot of the function $p = f(\alpha_m, \alpha_s)$ is presented in Fig. 4.

The value of the function of the possibility distribution of the medium ball drawing probability will be proportional to the contour lines length. From formula (10) we can find:

$$\alpha_s = 1 - \frac{3p}{1 - \alpha_m} \quad \text{and} \quad \frac{d\alpha_s}{d\alpha_m} = \frac{-3}{(1 - \alpha_m)^2},$$

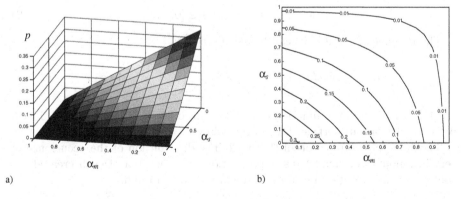

a)

b)

Fig. 4. The plot of the function $p = f(\alpha_m, \alpha_s)$ in the form of a surface (a) and in the form of contour lines (b)

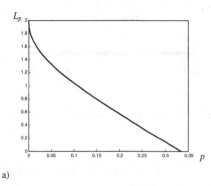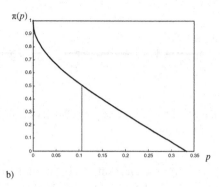

a)   b)

Fig. 5. The plot of contour lines length as a function of the probability p (a) and the possibility distribution of the medium ball drawing probability (b)

and then the length of contour lines can be calculated as:

$$L_p = \int_0^{1-3p} \sqrt{1 + \left(\frac{d\alpha_s}{d\alpha_m}\right)^2} \, d\alpha_m \, . \tag{11}$$

The plot of contour lines length as a function of the probability p is presented in Fig. 5a. For $p = 0$ the length is equal 2. In Fig. 5b, we can see the possibility distribution of the medium ball drawing probability. The expected value of the possibility equals approximately 0.1058.

As an answer to the second question, we can say that the probability of the medium ball drawing can be known approximately as $p \in [0, \frac{1}{3}]$ and it can be expressed linguisticaly as *about* 0.1.

Now, let's calculate the number of small balls. As before, we can assume that the total amount of balls 'about 20' is described by the variable b in the form of RDM-model:

$$b = 16 + 8 \cdot \alpha_b, \quad \alpha_b \in [0, 1] \, . \tag{12}$$

The number of small balls can be calculated as:

$$n = b \cdot NOT(m) \cdot s = (16 + 8\alpha_b) \cdot \left(\frac{1}{3} - \frac{1}{3}\alpha_m\right) \cdot \alpha_s \, . \tag{13}$$

The variable n is the function of 3 RDM-variables: $n = f(\alpha_m, \alpha_s, \alpha_b)$. Fig. 6 presents 3D contour surfaces for integer values of n.

The value of the function of the possibility distribution of the occurrence of certain amounts of small balls is proportional to the area of such created 3D contour surfaces, Fig. 6. From the formula (13) we can find:

$$\alpha_b = \frac{\frac{3}{8}n}{(1 - \alpha_m)\alpha_s} - 2 \, ,$$

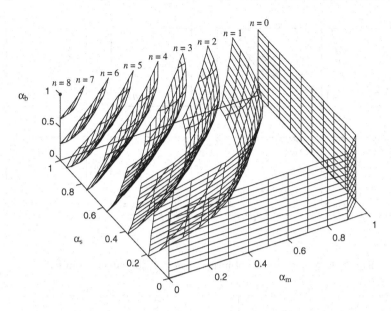

Fig. 6. 3D contour surfaces of the function $n = f(\alpha_m, \alpha_s, \alpha_b)$ for integer values of n

and then the area of each 3D contour surface can be calculated as:

$$A_n = \iint_D \sqrt{1 + \left(\frac{d\alpha_b}{d\alpha_m}\right)^2 + \left(\frac{d\alpha_b}{d\alpha_s}\right)^2} \, d\alpha_m d\alpha_s , \qquad (14)$$

where: D – area defined by the projection of a 3D contour surface onto the plane $\alpha_m \times \alpha_s$. Examples of such areas for integer values of n are presented in Fig. 7.

The area D is limited on the plane $\alpha_m \times \alpha_s$ by following lines:

– for $n < 5\frac{1}{3}$:

$$\alpha_m = 0, \quad \alpha_s = 1, \quad \alpha_s = \frac{3n}{16(1 - \alpha_m)}, \quad \alpha_s = \frac{n}{8(1 - \alpha_m)},$$

– for $n \geq 5\frac{1}{3}$:

$$\alpha_m = 0, \quad \alpha_s = 1, \quad \alpha_s = \frac{n}{8(1 - \alpha_m)}.$$

The plot of the area of 3D contour surfaces as a function of n is presented in Fig. 8a. In Fig. 8b, we can see the possibility distribution of the of the occurrence of certain amounts of small balls.

Finally, we can say that the numer of small balls belongs to the interval $[0, 8]$. The expected value of the possibility equals approximately 2.149, but because the number of balls must be an integer value we can say that the most possible number equals 2.

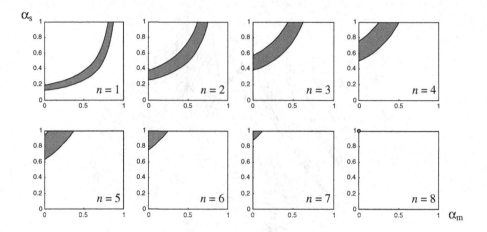

Fig. 7. Exemplary areas of integration (14) for integer values of n

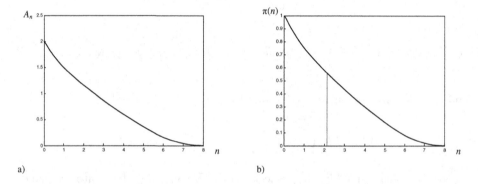

a)   b)

Fig. 8. The plot of the area of 3D contour surfaces as a function of n (a) and the possibility distribution of the occurrence of certain amounts of small balls (b)

The task can be also solved under the assumption that the RDM variable α_b can only take values:

$$\alpha_b \in \left\{0, \frac{1}{8}, \frac{2}{8}, \frac{3}{8}, \frac{4}{8}, \frac{5}{8}, \frac{6}{8}, \frac{7}{8}, 1\right\}$$

to assure that the number of balls will always be integer – see (12). The expected value for such created possibility distribution function is equal approximately 1.8, so assuming that the number of balls must be an integer value we can also say that the most possible number equals 2.

4   Conclusions

The paper has described a CwW approach based on simplified RDM-models of linguistic quantifiers. Presented calculations are not complicated and obtained results are consistent with common sense.

On the basis of the presented example, the following, general algorithm of solving CwW problems with the application of simplified RDM-model of quantifiers can be formulated.

1. Determine variables and RDM-models of linguistic quantifiers occurring in the problem.
2. Determine general formulas enabling the problem solving.
3. Find the solution as a function of RDM-variables.
4. Determine the possibility distribution of the solution and calculate the expected value.

Such methodology is simple and can also be applied to other CwW problems.

References

1. Aliev, R., Pedrycz, W., Fazlollahi, B., Huseynov, O.H., Alizadeh, A.V., Guirimov, B.G.: Fuzzy logic-based generalized decision theory with imperfect information. Information Sciences 189, 18–42 (2012)
2. Dymova, L.: Soft computing in economics and finance. Springer, Heidelberg (2011)
3. Hansen, E.R.: A generalized interval arithmetic. In: Nickel, K. (ed.) Interval Mathematics. LNCS, vol. 29, pp. 7–18. Springer, Heidelberg (1975)
4. Hanss, M.: Applied fuzzy arithmetic. Springer, Heidelberg (2005)
5. Kaufmann, A., Gupta, M.M.: Introduction to fuzzy arithmetic. Van Nostrand Reinhold, New York (1991)
6. Moore, R.E.: Interval analysis. Prentice Hall, Englewood Cliffs (1966)
7. Moore, R.E., Kearfott, R.B., Cloud, M.J.: Introduction to interval analysis. Society for Industrial and Applied Mathematics, Philadelphia (2009)
8. Landowski, M.: Differences between Moore's and RDM interval arithmetic. In: Angelov, P., et al. (eds.) Intelligent Systems'2014. AISC, vol. 322, pp. 331–340. Springer, Heidelberg (2015)
9. Piegat, A.: Fuzzy modeling and control. Physica Verlag, Heidelberg (2001)
10. Piegat, A., Landowski, M.: Is the conventional interval-arithmetic correct? Journal of Theoretical and Applied Computer Science 6(2), 27–44 (2012)
11. Piegat, A., Landowski, M.: Two interpretations of multidimensional RDM interval arithmetic: multiplication and division. International Journal of Fuzzy Systems 15(4), 486–496 (2013)
12. Piegat, A., Landowski, M.: Multidimensional approach to interval-uncertainty calculations. In: New Trends in Fuzzy Sets, Intuitionistic Fuzzy Sets, Generalized Nets and Related Topics, pp. 137–152. System Research Institute of Polish Academy of Sciences, Warsaw (2013)
13. Rajati, M.R., Mendel, J.M., Wu, D.: Solving Zadeh's Magnus challenge problem on linguistic probabilities via linguistic weighted averages. In: Proceedings of IEEE International Conference on Fuzzy Systems (FUZZ-IEEE), pp. 2177–2184 (2011)
14. Rajati, M.R., Wu, D., Mendel, J.M.: On solving Zadeh's tall Swedes problem. In: Proceedings of 2011 World Conference on Soft Computing (2011)
15. Rajati, M.R., Mendel, J.M.: Lower and upper probability calculations using compatibility measures for solving Zadeh's challenge problems. In: Proceedings of IEEE International Conference on Fuzzy Systems, pp. 1–8 (2012)

16. Sevastjanov, P., Dymova, L.: A new method for solving interval and fuzzy equations: linear case. Information Sciences 17, 925–937 (2009)
17. Zadeh, L.A.: Fuzzy logic = computing with words. IEEE Transactions on Fuzzy Systems 4(2), 103–111 (1996)
18. Zadeh, L.A.: Linguistic characterization of preference relations as a basis for choice in social systems. In: Fuzzy Sets, fuzzy Logic, and Fuzzy Systems, pp. 336–354. World Scientific Publishing Co., Inc. (1996)
19. Zadeh, L.A.: A new direction in AI – toward a computational theory of perceptions. AI Magazine 22(1), 73–84 (2001)
20. Zadeh, L.A.: From computing with numbers to computing with words – from manipulation of measurements to manipulation of perceptions. International Journal of Applied Mathematics and Computer Science 12(3), 307–324 (2002)
21. Zadeh, L.A.: A note on web intelligence, world knowledge and fuzzy logic. Data & Knowledge Engineering 50, 291–304 (2004)
22. Zadeh, L.A.: Generalized theory of uncertainty (GTU) – principal concepts and ideas. Computational Statistics & Data Analysis 51, 15–46 (2006)
23. Zadeh, L.A.: Computations with imprecise probabilities. In: Proceedings of 7-th International Conference on Applications of Fuzzy Systems and Soft Computing (ICAFS 2008), pp. 1–3 (2008)
24. Zadeh, L.A.: Computing with words and perceptions – a paradigm shift. In: Proceedings of the 2009 IEEE International Conference on Information Reuse and Integration, pp. viii–x (2009)
25. Zadeh, L.A.: Computing with Words: Principal concepts and ideas. Springer (2012)
26. Zadeh, L.A., Kacprzyk, J.: Computing with Words in Information/Intelligent Systems 1: Foundations. Studies in Fuzziness and Soft Computing, vol. 33. Physica-Verlag HD (1999)

The Directed Compatibility Between Ordered Fuzzy Numbers - A Base Tool for a Direction Sensitive Fuzzy Information Processing

Piotr Prokopowicz[1]($\boxtimes$) and Witold Pedrycz[2]

[1] Institute of Mechanics and Applied Computer Science
Kazimierz Wielki University, Bydgoszcz, Poland
piotrekp@ukw.edu.pl
[2] Department of Electrical and Computer Engineering
University of Alberta, Edmonton, Canada
pedrycz@ee.ualberta.ca

Abstract. The Ordered Fuzzy Numbers (OFN) were defined over 10 years ago as a tool for processing fuzzy numbers. This model has an additional feature used in processing, namely direction. It allows to define arithmetical operations in a new way. Proposed methods retain the basic computational properties of the operations known for the real numbers. Apart from a good calculations, OFNs also offer new possibilities for processing imprecise information. The new property - a direction - has a major impact on the calculations, but gives also a new potential for processing data in the fuzzy systems. We can include to the fuzzy value some more interpretation than membership value. If we want take into account this additional information in the processing of fuzzy system, we need the methods which are sensitive for the direction.

This publication presents the basic tool for processing a fuzzy statement 'A is B' where A and B are OFNs. It can be called a compatibility of A with B. New proposition is sensitive for the direction and bases on the conception of the *Direction Determinant* proposed in previous studies on the topic.

Keywords: Directed fuzzy compatibility · Fuzzy statement · Ordered Fuzzy Numbers · Kosinski's Fuzzy Numbers · Direction Determinant

1 Introduction

Fuzzy sets [1, 2] are useful tool for an imprecise information processing. They allow for use of a formal model to the situation described linguistically. In some cases that may be the only way due to the incomplete knowledge of the subject as well as inaccuracy of the available data. For inaccurate quantitative processing specific form of fuzzy sets - the fuzzy numbers are used (usually convex fuzzy numbers). Unfortunately, common calculation mechanisms cause that the already small number of basic arithmetic operations can easily lead to a drastic increase of imprecision of results. Therefore, its practical usefulness could be lost.

© Springer International Publishing Switzerland 2015
L. Rutkowski et al. (Eds.): ICAISC 2015, Part I, LNAI 9119, pp. 249–259, 2015.
DOI: 10.1007/978-3-319-19324-3_23

Model of the Ordered Fuzzy Numbers is helpful here, as it introduces convenient and flexible the computing mechanisms eliminating main calculations defects. This model takes into account the order of the characteristic parts of a fuzzy number (hence the name contains the word 'Ordered') giving the fuzzy number an additional feature - direction. Thanks to consideration of the order when performing operations we get the opportunity to reduce the imprecision of the following operations. This model has a number of properties that were presented in the publications [9, 15, 22].

The fuzzy statement 'A is B' where A and B are fuzzy sets is a base for the analysis where we want to apply the fuzzy sets and their imprecise mechanisms. Calculation result of this statement can be called a similarity or compatibility of A with B. The idea of compatibility and similarity between fuzzy sets was discussed in the many publications (for example [4, 7, 8]). However, in this paper we focus on the OFN model. In the most situations if we want use the OFNs instead of the fuzzy sets or numbers, we can ignore the direction and use the same methods. But, if we want take into account additional information contained in the new model, we need the methods which are sensitive for the direction. Presentation of such method is the goal of this paper. However first, the Ordered Fuzzy Numbers will be recalled, as they are unusual model of fuzzy information. Before introducing a formal definition (in the next section), it can be useful to clarify a background concept of OFNs.

It is not new observation [3] that the each convex membership function of fuzzy number could be split into two parts: a first is non-decreasing and a second non-increasing (see Fig.1). The OFNs evolved from such point of view. However, in the new model an order between non-decreasing and non-increasing part of fuzzy number is independent from the domain values. Such assumptions leads to new possibilities in the calculations and processing of imprecise data. Some of them presents this paper.

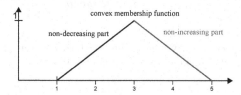

Fig. 1. A convex membership function and its parts

The name 'Ordered Fuzzy Numbers' can cause an ambiguous reception of the ideas behind. An 'Order' in the name may be interpreted as suggestion that the mathematical order was introduced to the general model of fuzzy numbers. It should be clarified, the intentions of the authors was to emphasize the individual order of parts of fuzzy number independent from the domain of its membership function.

To honor the late Professor Witold Kosiński, his work, the contribution and commitment to the development, analysis and popularization of the "Ordered Fuzzy Numbers" model in further part of this paper and in future works the name "Kosinski's Fuzzy Numbers" (KFN for short) will be used instead.

2 Kosinski's Fuzzy Numbers (KFN)

In the series of papers [9, 10, 14–18] were introduced and developed main concepts of the idea of Kosinski's Fuzzy Numbers. Following these papers fuzzy number will be identified with the pair of functions defined on the interval $[0, 1]$.

Definition 1. *The Kosinski's Fuzzy Number (KFN in short) A is an ordered pair of two continuous functions*

$$A = (f_A, g_A) \tag{1}$$

called the up-part and the down-part, respectively, both defined on the closed interval $[0, 1]$ with values in $\mathbf{R}$.

If the both functions f and g are monotonic (Fig.2a), they are also invertible and possess the corresponding inverse functions defined on a real axis with the values in $[0, 1]$. Now, if these two opposite functions are not connected, we linking them with constant function (with the value 1). In such way we receive an object which directly represents the classical fuzzy number. For the finalization of transformation, we need to mark an order of f and g with an arrow on the graph (see Fig.2b). Notice that pairs (f, g) and (g, f) are the two different Kosinski's Fuzzy Numbers, unless $f = g$. They differ by their orientation or direction.
The interpretations for this orientation and its relations with the real world problems are explained in the [16] and [18].

For the later use it will be more convenient to adopt the following indications of KFN boundaries:
$$UP = (s, 1^-)$$
$$CONST = [1^-, 1^+) \tag{2}$$
$$DOWN = [1^+, e)$$

For monotonous f and g we may point the membership function:
$\mu(x) = f^{-1}(x)$, if $x \in [f(0), f(1)] = [s, 1^-]$, and
$\mu(x) = g^{-1}(x)$, if $x \in [g(1), g(0)] = [1^+, e]$ and
$\mu(x) = 1$ when $x \in [1^-, 1^+]$.

It is worth to point out that a class of Kosinski's Fuzzy Numbers represents the whole class of convex fuzzy numbers with continuous membership functions (regarding "classical fuzzy numbers" [3, 5, 6, 12]).

Calculations on Kosinski's Fuzzy Numbers were analyzed and discussed among others in the papers [11, 15, 22].

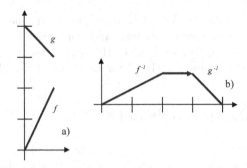

Fig. 2. a)Kosinski's Fuzzy Number, b)The Kosinski's Fuzzy Number as a convex fuzzy number with an arrow

2.1   Additional Aspects of the KFNs

Key element of the new model is an order of the parts of fuzzy number, which is independent from the real numbers universe. This feature will be called a 'Direction'. An example of real world interpretation for the new property was presented in [16, 18]. KFNs are considered in these papers as the results of observation in a time, which passes regardless of the values of the analyzed data. Thus, the time dependence can be a natural interpretation of the Direction.

Introducing Direction, however, has also other consequences. There is some inconsistency with the convex fuzzy numbers. This is understandable since the KFNs are a specific extension of classic model and thus unprecedented elements appear - the improper OFNs. This aspect was commented in [9, 10, 22]. However, thanks to the new property, also new potential for the practical use of OFN appears. We get a new quality associated with the Direction. The work [23, 24] present the practical use in modeling financial data, and [25] diversity of opinions in social networks. In [28] the application of KFNs for ant colony optimization algorithm is presented.

3   'Direction' in the Processing of Imprecise Data

The statement 'A is B' where A and B are fuzzy sets is a base for the analysis where we want to apply the fuzzy sets and their imprecise mechanisms. We can use the KFNs instead. We could also ignore the direction and use the same methods as for fuzzy sets. However, if we want take into account additional information - represented by the direction - we need the methods which are sensitive for the direction. In the next part of this publication the **directed fuzzy compatibility** counting method is presented. It uses basic ideas presented in [26] defined as a Direction Determinant. As it is important element of proposition, the main ideas of the Direction Determinant are presented in the next subsection.

We start with supporting structure, which will simplify further description.

3.1 PART Function

The PART function as the result presents the information about part of KFN, which contains the given argument.

Definition 2. *For the KFN A defined on X the PART function $X \rightarrow Y$ is determined as follows:*

$$PART_A(x) = y = \begin{cases} CONST_A : x \in CONST_A, \\ UP_A : x \in UP_A, \\ DOWN_A : x \in DOWN_A, \\ NONE_A : x \in NONE_A. \end{cases} \quad (3)$$

where:
$x \in X, Y = \{CONST_A, UP_A, DOWN_A, NONE_A\}$,
$CONST_A$ – a subset of X for which the membership function of A number is equal to 1;
UP_A – a subset of X for which the inverse of the up-part has values;
$DOWN_A$ – a subset of X for which the inverse of the down-part has values;
$NONE_A$ – a subset of X for which the membership function of A number is 0.

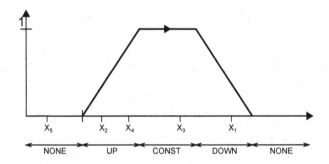

Fig. 3. Parts of the support of KFN

Figure 3 illustrate the effect of $PART$ function. For this example we have the following results: $PART(x_1) = DOWN$, $PART(x_2) = UP$, $PART(x_3) = CONST$, $PART(x_4) = UP$, $PART(x_5) = NONE$

Fuzzy numbers are fuzzy sets defined over the space (or subspace) of real numbers. Thus the sets UP, CONST and DOWN can be treated as numerical intervals.

3.2 The Direction Determinant

It is worth noting that the direction of the KFN is an additional property in comparison with the classical fuzzy numbers and it has a different meaning than the degree of membership. Thus, if we want processing an information contained in the KFN, we need additional parameter which will represent a new property. The proposition is **direction determinant** (see [26]). The purpose of this parameter is to represent a kind of direction 'intensity' of the argument. The direction determinant is connected with a particular KFN and is defined only for its support.

Definition 3. *Let A denote the OFN, and x is an element of the support.* **Proportional direction determinant** *of x in relation to A marked as dir_x^A is calculated as a the result of directional function $D : suppA \rightarrow (-1; 1)$ for the argument x in the following way:*

$$dir_x^A = D_A(x) = \begin{cases} 0 & : for \;\; PART(x) = CONST \\ \frac{(x-1^-)}{(1^- - s)} & : for \;\; PART(x) = \;\; UP \\ \frac{(x-1^+)}{(e-1^+)} & : for \;\; PART(x) = \;\; DOWN \end{cases} \qquad (4)$$

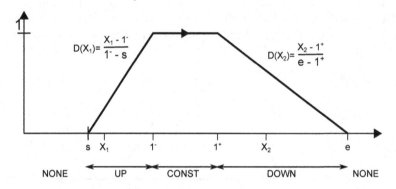

Fig. 4. Proportional direction determinant calculations

The above-mentioned determinant is called proportional, because it is calculated from the ratio of the position of support of the considered argument in relation to the whole fuzzy boundary of OFN, to which this argument belongs. It is well illustrated on Fig.4.

Such approach is connected with one of the useful interpretations of the direction of KFN [16]. A partial membership at the fuzzy boundaries can represent the imprecise concept of "now". If we treat this imprecision as symmetrical, then our fuzzy "now" in the context includes as much time forward as backwards. Hence, UP and $DOWN$ in the scale of time (independently of the arguments) are equal. Thus, there is a reason for calculating the determinant of the element situated on UP or $DOWN$ to the proportion of the respective intervals and not only to the value.

It is worth noting that, if the degree of membership is equal to zero, the direction determinant is undefined, because the argument is not a part of function domain D (the value is outside the KFN support). It should also be noted that for the arguments in the $CONST$ interval, we have the direction determinant that is equal to zero, what is justified, as these are the values about which we have no doubt - their membership is full (equal to 1). According to this intuition we should also expect (and this is taken into account) that, the closer the arguments are to the kernel of fuzzy number, their direction 'intensity' (that is the direction determinant) is smaller.

Presented parameter is a tool for defining methods which are **sensitive to the direction**. It means the processing imprecise data methods, which gives different results if the data described by KFNs differs only by the direction.

4 Compatibility Between Two Kosinski's Fuzzy Numbers

In this section the new idea for calculating compatibility between two KFNs will be presented. Since we search methods which are sensitive to the direction, a solution is to include into processing the Direction Determinant. Thus, as the result of fuzzy statement A *is* B a pair of values is proposed. First, is a truth value in classical fuzzy meaning - the value from interval $[0, 1]$, which indicates a degree of compatibility between two pieces of imprecise data represented by the KFNs. The second is, mentioned above, the Direction Determinant.

Definition 4. *For Kosinski's Fuzzy Numbers A and B the result of statement 'A is B' called* **directed fuzzy compatibility** *and labeled $COMP_{AB}$ is composed of two values: truth value T_{AB} and Direction Determinant D_{AB} calculated as follows:*

$$COMP_{AB} = (T_{AB}, D_{AB}) \tag{5}$$

$$T_{AB} = max(min(\mu_A(x), \mu_B(x))) : x \in \mathbf{X} \tag{6}$$

If T_{AB} is zero, then D_{AB} is unspecified, else

$$D_{AB} = D_B(x_0), \ x_0 = x : \mu_B(x) = T_{AB} \tag{7}$$

where: $X \subset \mathbf{R}$ – a domain of given KFNs, $\mu_A(x)$, $\mu_B(x)$ – membership functions of A and B, D_B – Direction Determinant of B for given x.

Figure 5 shows the result of compatibility of A with B, when A is a singleton. For this example truth value is $T_{AB} = 0,25$ and Direction Determinant is $D_{AB} = -0,75$. The D_{AB} can be interpreted as an indication of shifts of A to B. The negative values means the shift in the direction of *up-part* of B, the positive - shift in the direction of *down-part* of B. Such behavior can be also understand as a kind of directed relative dependence between values.

As Kosinski's Fuzzy Number are an extension of classical fuzzy numbers, the result of fuzzy statement 'A is B' should be extension of the classical solution. What is important, the boundary dependencies for truth values are preserved in the new proposition. Especially, when there is no shared part of the support

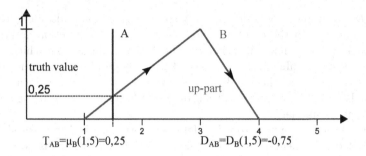

Fig. 5. The compatibility of singleton with a general KFN

between the numbers A and B, the truth value of result is zero. On the other hand, when A is the same number as B, the truth value is equal to one regardless of the directions of the numbers. In addition to these results, we also achieve intuitive behavior of results with partial compatibility.

It is understandable that the statement 'A is B' in a context of truth value is symmetrical. However, if we want use a direction sensitive methods we need a tool which gives us different results in such context as in the new proposition.

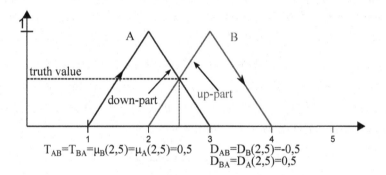

Fig. 6. The compatibility between two KFNs with the same direction

The examples on the Figs.6 and 7 presents the results of directed fuzzy compatibility with different directions of the KFNs. We can observe for both cases truth value results are the same. But the difference is specified just by the Direction Determinant.

However, for opposite orientation of KFNs (see Fig.7) the Direction Determinants are the same. As we remember, the determinant part of the result indicates shift of A to B. For 'A is B' A is shifted to B in the direction of *down-part* of B, and for the 'B is A' B is shifted to A in the direction of *down-part* of A. So, both shifts in the context of parts of KFNs have the same direction .

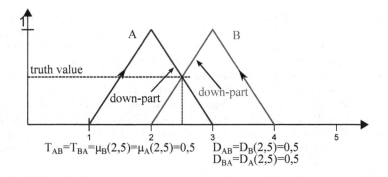

Fig. 7. The compatibility between the KFNs with the opposite directions

5   Summary

In this paper the method for calculating compatibility between two Kosinski's Fuzzy Numbers was proposed. It bases on the idea of the Direction Determinant, which is a kind of a direction measure of argument for the given KFN. As a result of compatibility the two values are generated. One represents the truth value in typical sense for fuzzy sets, the second is above mentioned determinant. However, it should be noted that the main result is the truth value, so according to the Definition 4 if the truth value of compatibility is equal to 1, it is mean we not analyzing the Direction Determinants. We calculate this determinant only when truth is more then 0 and less than 1. Such solution preserves the boundary dependencies, as if the truth value is 0, we have no compatibility (so the direction is not relevant), and with the truth value equal to 1, we have full compatibility regardless of the direction.

Presented Definition 4 can be used as a base tool for the *direction sensitive methods*. It gives good flexibility. If we need to take into account a direction in processing, we should use the Direction Determinant as a part of it. However, if we want use the KFNs in the processing only for their good calculations properties, then we can ignore the Direction Determinant and use only the truth values.

References

1. Zadeh, L.A.: Fuzzy sets. Information and Control 8, 338–353 (1965)
2. Zadeh, L.A.: The concept of a linguistic variable and its application to approximate reasoning. Part I, II, III. Information Sciences 8, 199–249 (1975)
3. Nguyen, H.T.: A note on the extension principle for fuzzy sets. J. Math. Anal. Appl. 64, 369–380 (1978)
4. Kacprzyk, J.: Compatibility relations for the representation of associations between variables in knowledge-based systems, and their use in approximate reasoning. Fuzzy Sets and Systems 42, 273–291 (1991)
5. Pedrycz, W., Gominde, F.: An Introduction to Fuzzy Sets. The MIT Press, Cambridge (1998)

6. Wagenknecht, M., Hampel, R., Schneider, V.: Computational aspects of fuzzy arithmetic based on archimedean t-norms. Fuzzy Sets and Systems 123(1), 49–62 (2001)
7. Cross, V., Sudkamp, T.: Similarity and compatibility in fuzzy set theory: assessment and applications. Physica-Verlag GmbH, Heidelberg (2002)
8. Yager, R.R.: Nonmonotonicity and compatibility relations in belief structures. Annals of Mathematics and Artificial Intelligence 34, 161–176 (2002)
9. Kosiński, W., Prokopowicz, P., Ślęzak, P., Ordered, D.: Ordered fuzzy numbers, Bulletin of the Polish Academy of Sciences. Ser. Sci. Math. 51(3), 327–338 (2003)
10. Kosiński, W., Prokopowicz, P., Ślęzak, P., On, D.: algebraic operations on fuzzy numbers. In: Intelligent Information Processing and Web Mining. ASC, vol. 22, pp. 353–362. Springer (2003)
11. Koleśnik, R., Prokopowicz, P., Kosiński, W.: Fuzzy Calculator – usefull tool for programming with fuzzy algebra. In: Rutkowski, L., Siekmann, J.H., Tadeusiewicz, R., Zadeh, L.A. (eds.) ICAISC 2004. LNCS (LNAI), vol. 3070, pp. 320–325. Springer, Heidelberg (2004)
12. Buckley James, J., Eslami, E.: An Introduction to Fuzzy Logic and Fuzzy Sets. Physica-Verlag, A Springer-Verlag Company, Heidelberg (2005)
13. Prokopowicz, P.: Methods based on the ordered fuzzy numbers used in fuzzy control. In: Proc. of the Fifth International Workshop on Robot Motion and Control, RoMoCo 2005, Dymaczewo, Poland, pp. 349–354 (June 2005)
14. Prokopowicz, P.: Using Ordered Fuzzy Numbers Arithmetic in Fuzzy Control. In: Artificial Intelligence and Soft Computing Proc. of the 8th ICAISC, Poland, pp. 156–162. Academic Publishing House EXIT, Warsaw (2006)
15. Kosiński, W.: On fuzzy number calculus. International Journal of Applied Mathematics and Computer Science 16(1), 51–57 (2006)
16. Kosiński, W., Prokopowicz, P.: Fuzziness - Representation of Dynamic Changes, Using Ordered Fuzzy Numbers Arithmetic, New Dimensions in Fuzzy Logic and Related Technologies. In: Proc. of the 5th EUSFLAT, Ostrava, Czech Republic, vol. I, pp. 449–456. University of Ostrava (2007)
17. Prokopowicz, P.: Adaptation of Rules in the Fuzzy Control System Using the Arithmetic of Ordered Fuzzy Numbers. In: Rutkowski, L., Tadeusiewicz, R., Zadeh, L.A., Zurada, J.M. (eds.) ICAISC 2008. LNCS (LNAI), vol. 5097, pp. 306–316. Springer, Heidelberg (2008)
18. Kosiński, W., Prokopowicz, P., Kacprzak, D.: Fuzziness – representation of dynamic changes by ordered fuzzy numbers. In: Seising, R. (ed.) Views on Fuzzy Sets and Systems. STUDFUZZ, vol. 243, pp. 485–508. Springer, Heidelberg (2009)
19. Kacprzak, M., Kosiński, W., Prokopowicz, P.: Implications on Ordered Fuzzy Numbers and Fuzzy Sets of Type Two. In: Rutkowski, L., Korytkowski, M., Scherer, R., Tadeusiewicz, R., Zadeh, L.A., Zurada, J.M. (eds.) ICAISC 2012, Part I. LNCS(LNAI), vol. 7267, pp. 247–255. Springer, Heidelberg (2012)
20. Kosiński, W., Rosa, A., Cendrowska, D., Węgrzyn-Wolska, K.: Defuzzification Functionals Are Homogeneous, Restrictive Additive and Normalized Functions. In: Rutkowski, L., Korytkowski, M., Scherer, R., Tadeusiewicz, R., Zadeh, L.A., Zurada, J.M. (eds.) ICAISC 2012, Part I. LNCS, vol. 7267, pp. 274–282. Springer, Heidelberg (2012)
21. Kosiński, W., Prokopowicz, P., Rosa, A.: Defuzzification Functionals of Ordered Fuzzy Numbers. IEEE Transactions on Fuzzy Systems 21(6), 1163–1169 (2013), doi:10.1109/TFUZZ.2013.2243456

22. Prokopowicz, P.: Flexible and Simple Methods of Calculations on Fuzzy Numbers with the Ordered Fuzzy Numbers Model. In: Rutkowski, L., Korytkowski, M., Scherer, R., Tadeusiewicz, R., Zadeh, L.A., Zurada, J.M. (eds.) ICAISC 2013, Part I. LNCS(LNAI), vol. 7894, pp. 365–375. Springer, Heidelberg (2013)
23. Marszałek, A., Burczyński, T.: Modelling Financial High Frequency Data Using Ordered Fuzzy Numbers. In: Rutkowski, L., Korytkowski, M., Scherer, R., Tadeusiewicz, R., Zadeh, L.A., Zurada, J.M. (eds.) ICAISC 2013, Part I. LNCS(LNAI), vol. 7894, pp. 345–352. Springer, Heidelberg (2013)
24. Kacprzak, D., Kosiński, W., Kosiński, W.K.: Financial Stock Data and Ordered Fuzzy Numbers. In: Rutkowski, L., Korytkowski, M., Scherer, R., Tadeusiewicz, R., Zadeh, L.A., Zurada, J.M. (eds.) ICAISC 2013, Part I. LNCS(LNAI), vol. 7894, pp. 259–270. Springer, Heidelberg (2013)
25. Kacprzak, M., Kosiński, W., Węgrzyn-Wolska, K.: Diversity of opinion evaluated by ordered fuzzy numbers. In: Rutkowski, L., Korytkowski, M., Scherer, R., Tadeusiewicz, R., Zadeh, L.A., Zurada, J.M. (eds.) ICAISC 2013, Part I. LNCS(LNAI), vol. 7894, pp. 271–281. Springer, Heidelberg (2013)
26. Prokopowicz, P., Golsefid, S.M.M.: Aggregation Operator for Ordered Fuzzy Numbers Concerning the Direction. In: Rutkowski, L., Korytkowski, M., Scherer, R., Tadeusiewicz, R., Zadeh, L.A., Zurada, J.M. (eds.) ICAISC 2014, Part I. LNCS, vol. 8467, pp. 267–278. Springer, Heidelberg (2014)
27. Bednarek, T., Kosiński, W., Węgrzyn-Wolska, K.: On Orientation Sensitive Defuzzification Functionals. In: Rutkowski, L., Korytkowski, M., Scherer, R., Tadeusiewicz, R., Zadeh, L.A., Zurada, J.M. (eds.) ICAISC 2014, Part II. LNCS(LNAI), vol. 8468, pp. 653–664. Springer, Heidelberg (2014)
28. Czerniak, J.M., Apiecionek, Ł., Zarzycki, H.: Application of Ordered Fuzzy Numbers in a New OFNAnt Algorithm Based on Ant Colony Optimization. In: Kozielski, S., Mrozek, D., Kasprowski, P., Małysiak-Mrozek, B. z. (eds.) BDAS 2014. CCIS, vol. 424, pp. 259–270. Springer, Heidelberg (2014)

Learning Rules for Hierarchical Fuzzy Logic Systems with Selective Fuzzy Controller Activation

Krzysztof Renkas[1](✉), Adam Niewiadomski[1], and Marcin Kacprowicz[1,2]

[1] Institute of Information Technology
Lodz University of Technology
ul. Wólczańska 215,
90-924 Łódz, Poland
[2] Institute of Social Sciences and Computer Science,
Higher Vocational State School
ul. Mechaników 3,
87-800 Włocławek, Poland
800561@edu.p.lodz.pl, adam.niewiadomski@p.lodz.pl,
marcin.kacprowicz@pwsz.wloclawek.pl

Abstract. This paper focuses on problems related to learning rules using numerical data for the *Hierarchical Fuzzy Logic Systems (HFLS)* described in [9]. Learning rules for *Fuzzy Logic Systems (FLS)* or *Fuzzy Controller (FC)* in short could be accomplished by using many different approaches, building one, complex rulebase using all available input and output variables. Using hierarchical structure we could avoid this problem by problem division into subproblems with smaller dimensions. "Hierarchical" means that fuzzy sets produced as output of one of fuzzy controllers are then processed as an inputs of another one as the sets of auxiliary variables. The main problem is to learn rulebase with numerical data, which does not contain any data for those auxiliary variables. The main scope of this paper is to present an algorithm that is being a solution to this problem and provides support for selective activation of unit FC. The proposal presented in this paper operates on a type-1 HFLS, built with the fuzzy controllers (in the sense of Mamdani). An example of single-player games, i.e. where the "enemy" is controlled by agents is used.

Keywords: Hierarchical fuzzy logic systems · Learning fuzzy rules · Hierarchical fuzzy controller · Nonlinear control systems · Selective unit fuzzy controller activation · Simulation in computer games

1 Introduction

This paper addresses issues of simulations in computer games and data processing. In particular, we are interested in computational intelligence methods based on FLS that make it possible to simulate an enemy in single-player games. The new solution proposed here is to learn HFLS rulebase using numerical data. Our proposal is based on the Wang & Mendel learning algorithm created for the traditional FLSs purposes, newly adapted for HFLSs with selective FC activation (see Subsection 3.2). The main reason is to provide rulebase characterized by real human player behaviours still deriving benefits

© Springer International Publishing Switzerland 2015
L. Rutkowski et al. (Eds.): ICAISC 2015, Part I, LNAI 9119, pp. 260–270, 2015.
DOI: 10.1007/978-3-319-19324-3_24

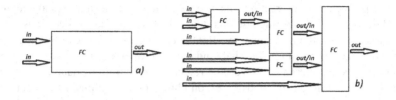

Fig. 1. Examples of two fuzzy controllers, traditional (a) and hierarchical (b)

from the hierarchical structure. The main concept of the system is not changed with respect to [9] and the general structure looks the same (see Figure 2). This concept says that outputs of one FC are then considered as input of another FC. Final output of this system is one crisp value. Furthermore, not every of combined controllers works during each iteration of inference. Figure 1 shows examples of two controllers: a traditional one (a) and hierarchical (b).

In general, fuzzy logic systems or fuzzy controllers are useful in the case when a controlled process is not linear and the use of traditional controllers may appear inefficient. Fuzzy controller is a control unit based on fuzzy logic [19], which makes decisions based on knowledge containing the rules like *IF ... THEN ...;* with unspecified predicates [17]. Those rules are expressed by natural language using *Linguistic Variables (LV)*. Below we can see the example of four rules:

```
RULE 0 : IF TANK_IS_BEING_ATTACKED IS YES THEN ACTION IS ATTACK;
RULE 1 : IF RISK IS ZERO AND SUPPORT IS ZERO
    THEN ACTION IS PATROL;
RULE 2 : IF RISK IS SMALL AND SUPPORT IS ZERO
    THEN ACTION IS WAIT;
...
RULE 15: IF RISK IS SMALL AND SUPPORT IS BIG THEN ACTION IS ATTACK;
```

The above rules belong to the rulebase that is used by inference engine during choosing tank actions in the computer game called *Tank 1990-2012* created by the author. Having simple problem using linguistic variables that are understandable for everyone, anyone could be an expert who could create a rulebase to solve some intuitive problems that do not require specialist knowledge.

However, having for example ten rulebases created by different 'experts', we could have ten **different** rulebases, despite the simplicity of the problem and the limited number of LV. Consequently the inference engine using those rulebases could make different decisions for the same input data. Knowledge based inference is not an objective but subjective inference, because it makes decisions based on expert or expert's knowledge, which represents subjective opinions. Moreover, creating rulebase by more than one expert there might be a problem, that different experts may propose different, contradictory decisions. One of the solutions to this problem is type-2 fuzzy sets application, that provide an uncertainty support. This solution proposed as *Type-2 Hierarchical Fuzzy Logic Systems (T2HFLS)* is described in [10,11].

Another problem is that creating rules we are trying to do it in a logical way using reasoned decisions. Created rulebase could be 'ideal' giving 'ideal' decisions, not always consistent with the real decisions. Real decisions are influenced by many other factors, e.g. if the sun is shining or what kind of music we are listening to.

A very interesting alternative is learning rulebase with a training data. During learning we could use different methods based on clustering algorithms, neural networks, genetic algorithms and more. In this paper we will focus only on learning rules using the numerical data, that represents the real behaviours of different computer games players.

The rest of the paper is organized as follows: Section 2 contains some literature references with basic Wang & Mendel method description. The main concept of HFLS architecture for game purposes is described in Subsection 3.1. Modified learning algorithm providing hierarchical structure support is proposed in subsection 3.2. In Section 4, tests and the results are described. The last Section 5 contains conclusions and some future directions of the research.

2   Literature References

At the start to better understand the HFLS we could recall to [18]. In [7,8,12,16] authors introduce HFLS for many different problems, i.e. controlling agricultural robots in a natural environment, truck backer-upper system or grouping cars into platoons and controlling the velocity and the gap between cars in single lane platoons.

Authors in [14] says that using fuzzy models all parameters should be learnt in appropriate way by using experimental data and respective learning algorithms. Authors of [13] introduce learning a two layer hierarchical fuzzy controller using cooperative co-evolution, comparing results with the results from a classical evolutionary algorithm. Application of genetic and bacterial programming algorithms for learning hierarchical interpolative fuzzy rules is described in [2]. Fuzzy *Feature Subset Selection (FFS)* for learning purposes is described in [4,5] using Wang & Mendel method, in [6] using fuzzy rough set or genetic algorithm in [3].

Learning Fuzzy Rules Algorithm - Basic Method. As the basic rules learning method we would like to introduce the *Wang & Mendel (WM)* method [15], which is designed for traditional FLSs. Learning rules in this method is based on a numerical or a numerical and a linguistic data. In short, this method consists of five steps:

1. divides the input and output domains of the given numerical data into fuzzy regions
2. generates fuzzy rules from the given data
3. assigns a degree of each of the generated rules for the purpose of resolving conflicting rules
4. creates a combined fuzzy rulebase based on both the generated rules and linguistic rules of human experts
5. determines a mapping from input domain to output domain based on the combined fuzzy rulebase using a defuzzifying procedure

This method is simple and is a one-pass build up method, that does not require time consuming training. Complete algorithm is described in [15].

3   Hierarchical Fuzzy Logic System and Learning Rules Algorithms

3.1   The Architecture of Hierarchical Fuzzy Logic System in Computer Games

The proposed HFLS structure combines all of FC's into one system, where the output of one FC becomes the input of another one. Not each of the combined controllers works during each iteration of inference. Figure 2 shows the discussed structure.

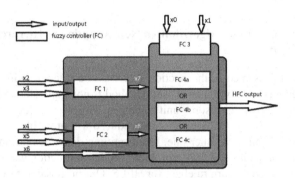

Fig. 2. General diagram of designed HFLS structure

The chosen issue to solve has been defined as controlling military vehicles during clashes in computer games. General rules of the game were drawn from *Tank 1990*[1] developed by *Namco*. Designed HFLS correspond to our issue using FC's 1 and 2 as the controllers computing the level of risk x_7 and support x_8. These variables are transferred as an input to the tank action controller $4a, \ldots, 4c$. Only one of these FCs is activated in the current iteration depending on the strategy chosen by the FC 3. Offensive, defensive and mixed strategies are allowed. The controlling system selects actions for each tank in battalion. The final decision allows to escape, attack, stay at the current position and to patrol the immediate surroundings. The fuzzy controllers are based on Mamdani's model with fuzzy antecedents and fuzzy consequents.

Selective FC Activation.   Selective activation of unit fuzzy controller mechanism enables to activate or deactivate selected fuzzy controller under certain conditions. Unit fuzzy controllers could be organized into blocks. Fuzzy controllers managed by this mechanism should differ from each other using different fuzzy rules, t-norms, t-conorms or defuzzification methods during inference. This mechanism could make system much more flexible.

Input Data and Controller Knowledge.   Input data for inference comes from the simulator and it is expressed by the following LV's: opponent tanks count (x_0), average

---

[1] Basic information about the game *Battle City*, an earlier version of the game *Tank 1990* [1].

force of opponent tanks (x_1), distance to the nearest opponent tank (x_2), force difference between our tank and nearest opponent tank (x_3), number of allies – tanks that
belong to our battalion (x_4), average force of allies (x_5) and tank is being attacked (x_6).
Knowledge base includes six unit rulebases created by the author without any learning methods. Examples of rules from offensive tank action rulebase are presented in
Section 1.

The Simulator Game *Tank 1990-2012* was created as a simulator for testing and demonstrating designed controller and rulebase. This simulator has been implemented in Java.

3.2 Learning Fuzzy Rules Algorithm - a New Adaption to Hierarchical Fuzzy Logic Systems

The WM method presented in the Section 2 learns one rulebase with complex rules
using all antecedents and consequents. This method is not applicable in HFLS because
of using rulebase consisting of some unit rulebases. Moreover, rules from HFLS additionally operate on auxiliary LV, which are produced as output of one controller and
then processed as input of another one. Input training data does not include numerical data for those variables which is a problem. In this subsection we present our new
method, that is adapted to learn rulebase for HFLS. Our proposal is based on the Wang
& Mendel method (see Section 2).

Input. Operating on many input variables and one output we need to have training data
as a set of pairs of the input and output values, i.e.:

$$(x_1(t), x_2(t), \ldots, x_n(t); y(t)). \tag{1}$$

where $t = 1, 2, \ldots T$ is an index of the sample data, T is a number of the training data,
$x_i(t)$ is an input value of the input variable x_i for the given sample data t, n is a number
of input variables, $y(t)$ is an input value of the output variable y.

Our Algorithm. **STEP 1:** divide input and output domains into fuzzy regions. For each
input and output variable (x_i, y) we need to indicate the minimum and the maximum
value getting the intervals for each variable using numerical data. For auxiliary variables
we need to define these values. We need to divide each of the defined intervals into
$2N_i + 1$ regions, where $i = 1..n$. N_i could be different for each variable. For each region
we need to define label and membership function to yield FSs of a given variable.

STEP 2: define groups of variables. For each unit FC of our HFLS we need to define
one group denoting input and output variables.

STEP 3: generate separate rulebase for each group of variables. When the output variable for a given group is not the auxiliary variable, generate fuzzy rules using all combinations of input and output LV. The generated rules contain conflicting rules (different
conclusions for the same conditions). Otherwise, the expert should generate rules or
define generation process. We should not take into account consequent values during
generating rules. It means that generated rulebase should not contain conflicting rules.

STEP 4: compute the rule's degree denoted by $D(R_k)$ for each sample data and for each of the generated rules, for all unit rulebases. Degree is an algebraic product of input values membership values to LV fuzzy sets and could be expressed as follows:

$$D(R_k) = \mu_{A_1}(x_1) \cdot \mu_{A_2}(x_2) \cdot \ldots \cdot \mu_{A_n}(x_n) \cdot \mu_B(y) = \mu_B(y) \prod_{i=1}^{n} \mu_{A_i}(x_i). \tag{2}$$

where R_k is rule expressed as follows:

$$R_k : \text{ IF } x_1 \text{ IS } A_1 \text{ AND } \ldots \text{ AND } x_n \text{ IS } A_n \text{ THEN } y \text{ IS } B. \tag{3}$$

Equation (2) could be used if the output LV for a given rulebase is not auxiliary variable. Otherwise, we need to assume that membership value for this variable is equal to 1 on the faith of the expert knowledge. In that case we could simplify equation (2) to:

$$D(R_k) = \mu_{A_1}(x_1) \cdot \mu_{A_2}(x_2) \cdot \ldots \cdot \mu_{A_n}(x_n) = \prod_{i=1}^{n} \mu_{A_i}(x_i). \tag{4}$$

We assume the value obtained using (4) as a membership value for a given value of auxiliary LV during computing degree for another unit rulebases where this LV occurs as an antecedent.

STEP 5: remove conflicting rules, leaving rules with the highest degree for a given set of conditions. Additionally we could remove rules with the degree less than some α value, where $0 \leq \alpha \leq 1$.

The proposed method is able to learn a HFLS rulebase however, referring to the designed HFLS structure for the game Tank 1990-2012 purposes, we could notice that this algorithm is not fully compatible in our case. The designed structure says that we have three separate rulebases for tank actions. Only one of those rulebase participates during inference for the whole battalion during a single iteration. Decision which one of those three rulebases is used depends on the chosen strategy. To fit our proposal to the designed structure we propose two variants of modification to provide selective activation of unit FC support.

Variant 1 During learning tank action rulebases, method learn each of them using alternative equation (5) during computing degree.

$$D(R_k) = D_{Strategist}(t, s)\mu_B(y) \prod_{i=1}^{n} \mu_{A_i}(x_i). \tag{5}$$

$D_{Strategist}(t, s)$ is the best degree for strategist rules whose conclusions are equal to a given strategy s. In short in this case degrees of learned rules using sample data t additionally take into account the best degree for strategist rules, which choose a strategy that is associated with a given rulebase.

Variant 2 Learning tank action rulebases, method learn only one rulebase strictly associated with the strategy, that is equal to a strategy conclusion of strategist rule with the highest degree. In short, the method learn only one rulebase for a given sample of data.

4   Tests and Results

Training Data The training data comes from a modified game entitled *Tank 1990-2012* and could be expressed as follows:

$$x_0(t), x_1(t), x_2(t), x_3(t), x_4(t), x_5(t), x_6(t), y(t) \qquad (6)$$

where variables x_i are described in Subsection 3.1, y is an final decision as the tank action. In the original version computer tanks are controlled by the HFLS, player tank vehicle is controlled by human player. Modification enables a second player to participate, that is able to choose tank actions for computer tanks. Second player decides which of the tanks is obliged to perform a selected action. All tanks selection is enabled. Training data contains over 10 000 samples collected from five users on different days, example samples of training data are listed below.

```
3, 1.67, 27, 0.0, 1, 3.0, 0, 4
3, 1.5, 18, 0.0, 1, 0.5, 0, 2
3, 1.67, 50, 0.0, 0, 0.0, 0, 3
...
```

4.1   Tests

Processing training data using WM method described in Section 2 and two variants of proposed method one complex FLS rulebase and two HFLS rulebases were learned. At the beginning of the results subsection summary and comparison of all rulebases are described. Summary and comparison refers to the number of learned rules, their degrees and power of the whole rulebase expressed by a proposed measure (see Definition 1). This summary refers also to the rulebase originally created by the expert.

During tests only original rulebase and two new HFLS rulebases are taken into account. The first test applies to general behaviour of the game. In this test case the game *Tank 1990-2012* was launched 72 times for each rulebase counting losses in subsequent stages taking stage 11 as the last one. The second test includes comparison of the times needed to get victory by battalion controlled by HFLS using different rulebases. Game was run 50 times for each rulebase, player tank could not move or perform any actions.

4.2   Results

Table 1 contain comparison of all mentioned rulebases with the different fuzzy set's types used during designing LVs. Some results are shown on Figures 3 and 4.

Definition 1. *Rulebase Power, denoted as RP, is a measure for comparing general degree for the whole rulebase. RP is expressed as a weighted average of obtained number of rules rc_i, whose degrees are in the defined ranges, relative to the total number of rules R. Each range should have associated weight $w_i = 0+(i-1)\cdot\frac{1}{N-1} : w_i \in [0, 1], w_i < w_{i+1}$, where $i = 1..N$, N is the number of all ranges. RP could be expressed as:*

$$RP = \frac{\sum_{i=1}^{N} rc_i \cdot w_i}{R}. \qquad (7)$$

Table 1. Summary of the original rulebase created by an expert and the rulebases learned by the Wang & Mendel and our new methods. Rulebases characterized by the hierarchical structure were tested using both variants of our new method. Results grouped into two sections by different FS type sets used during defining LV during learning process (concerns WM, New v1 and v2).

	Original;v1	Original;v2	Wang & Mendel	New;v1	New;v2
count of non conflicting rules	78	78	1458	81	81
section 1, used FS type: triangular					
rules with D = 0 [%]	30,77%	33,33%	65,02%	3,70%	6,17%
rules with D = 1 [%]	51,28%	51,28%	0,00%	16,05%	16,05%
conflicting rules [%]	0,00%	0,00%	75,00%	66,67%	66,67%
rulebase power RP	0,61%	0,59%	0,08%	0,49%	0,48%
section 2, used FS types: triangular, L, gamma					
rules with D = 0 [%]	30,77%	33,33%	61,52%	2,47%	2,47%
rules with D = 1 [%]	51,28%	51,28%	0,27%	20,99%	20,99%
conflicting rules [%]	0,00%	0,00%	75,00%	66,67%	66,67%
rulebase power RP	0,61%	0,59%	0,11%	0,60%	0,60%

$RP \in [0, 1]$. *If RP equals 0, that means that degree of all rules include into deprecated range with a zero weight. RP equal to 1 means that degree's of all rules include into the range with the highest degree values.*

Table 2 shows the results of the first and the second test. As it is shown playing the game with learned rulebases it is harder to win. Decisions in newer versions are more varied and may surprise in comparison to the original rulebase. Moreover, the difference is imperceptible during testing learned two rulebase variants. Also we could notice that learned rulebases need less time to get victory.

Table 2. Losses in the following stages (72 tests) and average time necessary to win (50 tests) playing the game *Tank 1990-2012* for different rulebases

stage number	1	2	3	4	5	6	7	8	9	10	11	defeat	victory	time
Original	3	10	8	12	11	8	9	6	4	1		72 (100%)	0 (0%)	29.8s
New;v1	3	13	8	15	15	6	10	1	1			72 (100%)	0 (0%)	21.6s
New;v2	5	9	7	18	13	10	9	0	1			72 (100%)	0 (0%)	23.1s

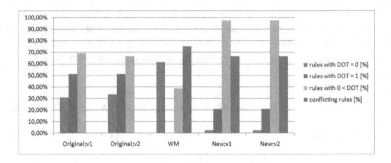

Fig. 3. Graph with percentage summary presented in Table 1 in the second section for tested rule-bases about rules with a given degree in relation to all learned non conflicting rules, percentage of conflicting rules in relation to all learned rules (including conflicting rules)

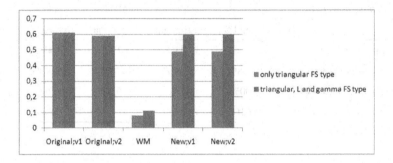

Fig. 4. Graph with rulebase power values for tested rulebases using only triangular FS type and three different types (triangular, L, gamma) defining LVs (see Table 1, Sections 1 and 2).

5   Conclusions and Future Work

The tests run prove correctness of the proposed method for learning rulebases for HFLSs. This algorithm is based on Wang & Mendel method for traditional FLSs, but we newly adapt it to hierarchical FLSs distinguish by a non-trivial hierarchical structure. This is possible because of providing auxiliary LV and selective activation of unit FC support. This gives us much more flexibility during designing structure of HFLS with different relationships between unit FC.

The results obtained during test cases show positive impact on the tank control using learned rulebases. Chosen decisions are interesting and sometimes unpredictable which could surprise in a positive way.

The summary presented in Table 1 in the first section shows a little worse general rulebase power of learned rules using our method (about 0.5) in comparison to the rulebase prepared by an expert (about 0.6). This difference is related to the definition of used variables. Variables in original rulebase were designed using triangular, trape-zoidal, rectangle, L and gamma fuzzy set types. Only triangular fuzzy set type was used defining variables at the beginning of our learning algorithm process. The results presented in Table 1 in the second section confirm our theory. In this test case during defining variables except the triangular FS type were used L and gamma FS types. We could notice that rulebase power has increased and is quite the same as the original rulebase power (about 0.6). We may suppose that using another fuzzy set types we could reach much higher rulebase power.

Another interesting observation is that the original rulebase contains about 30% of rules with the degree equal to 0, which means that 30% of rules during inference are fired unnecessarily. In comparison rulebases learned using our method contain only about 6% of unnecessarily rules, reducing this value to 2.5% using additional FS types.

Moreover, analysing the results we could notice that the first modification variant of our method got slightly better results than the second variant. However, using different fuzzy set types defining linguistic variables, the learning results become the same and we could not talk about superiority of one variant over the other.

During future research we could improve our method to be more independent, i.e. defining LV by algorithm selecting the best number of used FS with optimal types, learn rules with auxiliary LV as output, not involving the expert during generating those rules. Our future research may also direct towards learning rules for type-2 FS. During future research it is important to present application of our solution to another class of problems unrelated to the controlling vehicles in computer games.

References

1. Battle city description, http://pl.wikipedia.org/wiki/Battle_City
2. Balazs, K., Koczy, L.: Hierarchical-interpolative fuzzy system construction by genetic and bacterial programming algorithms. In: 2011 IEEE International Conference on Fuzzy Systems (FUZZ), pp. 2116–2122 (June 2011)
3. Chakraborty, B.: Genetic algorithm with fuzzy fitness function for feature selection. In: Proceedings of the 2002 IEEE International Symposium on Industrial Electronics, ISIE 2002, vol. 1, pp. 315–319 (2002)
4. Cintra, M., de Arruda, C., Monard, M.: Fuzzy feature subset selection using the wang & mendel method. In: Eighth International Conference on Hybrid Intelligent Systems, HIS 2008, pp. 590–595 (Septemeber 2008)
5. Cintra, M., Martin, T., Monard, M., Camargo, H.: Feature subset selection using a fuzzy method. In: International Conference on Intelligent Human-Machine Systems and Cybernetics, IHMSC 2009, vol. 2, pp. 214–217 (August 2009)
6. Guo, C., Zheng, X.: Feature subset selection approach based on fuzzy rough set for high-dimensional data. In: 2014 IEEE International Conference on Granular Computing (GrC), pp. 72–75 (October 2014)
7. Hagras, H., Callaghan, V., Colley, M., Carr-West, M.: A behaviour based hierarchical fuzzy control architecture for agricultural autonomous mobile robots. Journal of Autonomous Robots 13, 37–52 (2002)
8. Kim, H.M., Dickerson, J., Kosko, B.: Fuzzy throttle and brake control for platoons of smart cars. Fuzzy Sets and Systems 84, 209–234 (1996)
9. Renkas, K., Niewiadomski, A.: Hierarchical fuzzy logic systems and controlling vehicles in computer games. Journal of Applied Computer Science (JACS) 22(1), 201–212 (2014), http://it.p.lodz.pl/file.php/12/2014-1/jacs-1-2014-RenkasNiewiadomski.pdf

10. Renkas, K., Niewiadomski, A.: Hierarchical fuzzy logic systems and their extensions based on type-2 fuzzy sets. In: Indrzejczak, A., Kaczmarek, J., Zawidzki, M. (eds.) Trends in Logic XIII. Lodz University Press, Poland (2014)
11. Renkas, K., Niewiadomski, A.: Hierarchical fuzzy logic systems: Current research and perspectives. In: Rutkowski, L., Korytkowski, M., Scherer, R., Tadeusiewicz, R., Zadeh, L.A., Zurada, J.M. (eds.) ICAISC 2014, Part I. LNCS, vol. 8467, pp. 295–306. Springer, Heidelberg (2014), http://dx.doi.org/10.1007/978-3-319-07173-2_26
12. Riid, A., Rstern, E.: Fuzzy hierarchical control of truck and trailer. In: BEC 2002: Proceedings of the 8th Biennial Baltic Electronics Conference, October 6-9, pp. 141–144 (2002)
13. Stonier, R., Young, N.: Co-evolutionary learning and hierarchical fuzzy control for the inverted pendulum. In: The 2003 Congress on Evolutionary Computation, CEC 2003, vol. 1, pp. 467–473 (December 2003)
14. Vachkov, G., Fukuda, T.: Structured learning of fuzzy models for reduction of information dimensionality. In: 1999 IEEE International on Fuzzy Systems Conference Proceedings, FUZZ-IEEE 1999, vol. 2, pp. 963–968 (August 1999)
15. Wang, L.X., Mendel, J.: Generating fuzzy rules by learning from examples. IEEE Transactions on Systems, Man and Cybernetics 22(6), 1414–1427 (1992)
16. Wang, L.X.: Modeling and control of hierarchical systems with fuzzy systems. Automatica 33(6), 1041–1053 (1997)
17. Yager, R.R., Filev, D.P.: Essentials of Fuzzy Modeling and Control. A Wiley-Interscience publication, John Wiley & Sons (1994)
18. Yager, R.: On a hierarchical structure for fuzzy modeling and control. IEEE Transactions on Systems, Man and Cybernetics 23(4), 1189–1197 (1993)
19. Zadeh, L.A.: The concept of a linguistic variable and its applications to approximate reasoning (i). Information Sciences 8, 199–249 (1975)

A New Approach to the Rule-Base Evidential Reasoning with Application

Pavel Sevastjanov[✉], Ludmila Dymova, and Krzysztof Kaczmarek

Institute of Comp.& Information Sci., Czestochowa University of Technology,
Dabrowskiego 73, 42-200 Czestochowa, Poland
sevast@icis.pcz.pl

Abstract. In this paper, a new approach to the rule-base evidential reasoning ($RBER$) based on a new formulation of fuzzy rules is presented. We have shown that the traditional fuzzy logic rules lose an important information when dealing with the intersecting fuzzy classes, e.g., such as *Low* and *Medium*, and this property may lead to the controversial results. In the framework of our approach, an information of the values of all membership functions representing the intersecting (competing) fuzzy classes is preserved and used in the fuzzy logic rules. As $RBER$ methods are based on the synthesis of fuzzy logic and the Dempster-Shafer theory of evidence (DST), the problem of the combination of basic probability assignments (*bpas*) from different sources of evidence arises. The classical Dempster's rule of combination is usually used for this purpose. The classical Dempster's rule may provide controversial results in the case of great conflict and is not idempotent one. We show that the Dempster's rule may provide unreasonable results not only in the case of large conflict, but in the case of complete absence of conflict, too. At the end, we show that in the cases of small and large conflict, the use of simple averaging rule for combination of *bpas* seems to be a best choice. The developed approach is illustrated by the solution of simple, but real-world problem of diagnostics of type 2 diabetes.

Keywords: Fuzzy logic · Dempster-Shafer Theory of evidence · Combination rules

1 Introduction

In our papers [6,7,18,19], we have developed the method based on the synthesis of fuzzy logic and the Dempster-Shafer theory (DST), which was used to the solution of some real-world decision making problems.

This method is based on the classical Dempster's rule of combination of evidence from different sources. Generally, the method provides good results, but in some cases the unreasonable results were obtained. In the part of such cases, undesirable results were coursed by a large conflict between evidence, which often cannot be eliminated when dealing with the real-world problem (it is well known that the Dempster's rule provide controversial results in such situations).

L. Rutkowski et al. (Eds.): ICAISC 2015, Part I, LNAI 9119, pp. 271–282, 2015.
DOI: 10.1007/978-3-319-19324-3_25

On the other hand, in some cases we also have obtained unreasonable results, when the conflict was very small or even equal to zero.

Inspired by these results, we have carried out a study aimed to find a more appropriate combination rules.

Therefore, in this paper, using critical examples, we analyse the known combination rules (including their aggregations) and show their restriction and drawbacks.

At the end, we show that in the cases of small and large conflict, the use of simple averaging rule for combination of basic probability assignments (*bpas*) seems to be a best choice.

The core of *DST* is the rule of combination of evidence from different sources. The classical Dempster's rule [20] assumes that information sources are independent and uses the so-called orthogonal sum to combine multiple belief structures. Zadeh has underlined in [24,25] that this rule may provide counterintuitive results in the case of considerable conflict.

Therefore a wide variety of rules for evidence combination is proposed in the literature. The review and classification of them (obviously, not exhaustive) is presented, for example in the works [17,22].

To avoid the problem concerned with the classical Dempster's rule in the case of high conflict, the different hybrid rules were proposed in the literature. Dubois and Prade [4] proposed to use the combination of non-normalised Dempster's rule and modified disjunction rule defined in [3,5]. Different combinations of the Dempster's and Dubois and Prade's rules were proposed in the literature (see [1,9,10,12,14,23]). Usually such rules are based on weighted sums of conjunction and disjunction rules.

But we did not find in the literature hybrid rules based on Dempster's rule and averaging rules considered in [11,13,15,17]. Therefore, in the current paper, with the use of critical examples we compare the Dempster's and averaging rule and show that in the cases of small and large conflict, the use of simple averaging rule for combination of *bpas* seems to be a best choice.

The developed approach is illustrated by the solution of simple, but real-world problem of diagnostics of type 2 diabetes.

We have found that the traditional fuzzy logic rules lose an important information, when dealing with the intersecting fuzzy classes, e.g., such as *Low* and *Medium*, and this property may lead to the controversial results. In the framework of the proposed in the current paper approach, an information of the values of all membership functions representing the intersecting (competing) fuzzy classes is preserved and used in the fuzzy logic rules.

The rest of paper is set out as follows. In Section 2, we recall the basics of *DST* and some important problems concerned with the combination of evidence, analyse some most popular hybrid rules of combination and show that in the cases of small and large conflict, the use of simple averaging rule for combination of *bpas* seems to be a best choice. Section 3 presents a new approach to the rule-base evidential reasoning which makes it possible to use an information of values of all membership functions representing the intersecting (competing) fuzzy classes in the fuzzy logic rules. Based on real-world examples of type 2 diabetes diagnostics, we have shown that the new approach provides reasonable and intuitively obvious results in the cases when the known approaches (see [6,7,18,19]) lead to the controversial or wrong results. Finally the concluding section summarises the paper.

2   The Problems Concerned with the Known Combination Rules in DST

Firstly we recall briefly the basics of DST needed for the subsequent analysis.

The origins of DST go back to the work by Dempster [2] who developed a system of upper and lower probabilities. Following this work his student Shafer [20] provided a more thorough explanation of belief functions.

Assume A are subsets of X. It is important to note that a subset A may be treated also as a question or proposition and X as a set of propositions or mutually exclusive hypotheses or answers. A DS belief structure has associated with it a mapping m, called basic probability assignment (bpa), from subsets of X into a unit interval, $m : 2^X \to [0,1]$ such that $m(\emptyset) = 0$, $\sum_{A \subseteq X} m(A) = 1$. The subsets of X for which the mapping does not assume a zero value are called focal elements.

The core of the evidence theory is the rule of combination of evidence from different sources. Currently a wide variety of rules for evidence combination is proposed in the literature. A review of them is presented, for example by Sentz and Ferson [17].

The most popular in the different applications of DST are the conjunction Dempster's rule of combination) and the Dubois and Prade's [3,4] disjunctive combination rule.

Let m_1 and m_2 be ($bpas$). The Dempster's rule is defined as follows.

$$m_{12}(A) = \frac{\sum_{B \cap C = A} m_1(B)m_2(C)}{1 - K}, A \neq \emptyset, m_{12}(\emptyset) = 0, \tag{1}$$

where $K = \sum_{B \cap C = \emptyset} m_1(B)m_2(C)$ K is called the degree of conflict which measures the conflict between pieces of evidence and the process of dividing by $1 - K$ is called normalisation.

The main problem with this rule is that it provides counterintuitive results when the conflict K is close to its maximal value equal to 1.

Dubois and Prade disjunctive combination rule is defined as follows [3,5]:

$$m_{12}(X) = \sum_{X_1 \cup X_2 = X} m_1(X_1)m_2(X_2). \tag{2}$$

It is noted by Sentz and Ferson [17] "The union does not generate any conflict and does not reject any of the information asserted by the sources. As such, no normalisation procedure is required ". Nevertheless this rule is not idempotent one.

Let us consider the following critical example:

Example 1.

$m_1(A) = 0.1, m_1(B) = 0.6, m_1(A, B) = 0.3,$
$m_2(A) = 0.1, m_2(B) = 0.6, m_2(A, B) = 0.3.$

There is no conflict between two sources of evidence in this example. Nevertheless, from Dempster's rule (1) we get:

$K = 0.12, m_{12}(A) = 0.0795, m_{12}(B) = 0.8182, m_{12}(A, B) = 0.1022.$

Using Dubois and Prade's disjunctive combination rule (2) we get:

$m_{12}(A) = 0.19, m_{12}(B) = 0.84, m_{12}(A, B) = 0.51.$

We can see that since Dempster's and Dubois and Prade's rules are not idempotent, they cannot provide the true result of combination ($m_{12}(A) = 0.1$, $m_{12}(B) = 0.6$, $m_{12}(A, B) = 0.3$) of the considered not conflicting sources of evidence. It is worth noting that the results obtained in the considered example using Dempster's and Dubois and Prade's rules, differ substantially from the true result.

Hence, the hybrid combinations of Dempster's and Dubois and Prade's rules may provide non-acceptable results when we deal with the absence of conflict or a low conflict between *bpas*.

On the other hand, using the simplest averaging rule in this example, we obtain the true result $m_{12}(A) = 0.1$, $m_{12}(B) = 0.6$, $m_{12}(A, B) = 0.3$.

Although, the averaging rule of combination is idempotent and has some other desirable properties, it is not often used in the framework of *DST* and we have found only a few papers, where averaging rules were used ([11,13,15,16,17]).

Nevertheless, in our recent paper [8] we showed that the averaging rule is justified enough and provides reasonable results in the case of large conflict and a true result in the case when there is no conflict between sources of evidence.

Let us consider the following examples [8] :

Example 2. $m_1(A) = 0, m_1(B) = 0, m_1(A, B) = 1,$
$m_2(A) = 0, m_2(B) = 0.75, m_2(A, B) = 0.25.$

Example 3.
$m_1(A) = 0.01, m_1(B) = 0.01, m_1(A, B) = 0.98,$
$m_2(A) = 0.01, m_2(B) = 0.6, m_2(A, B) = 0.39.$

Example 4.
$m_1(A) = 0.7, m_1(B) = 0.2, m_1(A, B) = 0.1,$
$m_2(A) = 0.2, m_2(B) = 0.7, m_2(A, B) = 0.1.$

Example 5.
$m_1(A) = 0.1, m_1(B) = 0.6, m_1(A, B) = 0.3,$
$m_2(A) = 0.1, m_2(B) = 0.6, m_2(A, B) = 0.3.$

Example 6.
$m_1(A) = 0.3, m_1(B) = 0.4, m_1(A, B) = 0.3,$
$m_2(A) = 0.3, m_2(B) = 0.4, m_2(A, B) = 0.3.$
Example 7.
$m_1(A) = 0.98, m_1(B) = 0.01, m_1(A, B) = 0.01,$
$m_2(A) = 0.01, m_2(B) = 0.98, m_2(A, B) = 0.01.$
Example 8.
$m_1(A) = 1, m_1(B) = 0, m_1(A, B) = 0,$
$m_2(A) = 0, m_2(B) = 1, m_2(A, B) = 0.$
Example 9.
$m_1(A) = 0.3, m_1(B) = 0, m_1(A, B) = 0.7,$
$m_2(A) = 0.3, m_2(B) = 0, m_2(A, B) = 0.7.$

Let us compare the results obtained using Dempster's rule (1), and the averaging rule $m(A) = \frac{1}{N} \sum_{i=1}^{N} m_i(A)$ on the base of examples 2-9.

The results are presented in Tables 1 and 2.

Table 1. The results obtained using Dempster's rule (1)

Example	$m_{12}(A)$	$m_{12}(B)$	$m_{12}(A, B)$
2	0	0.75	0.25
3	0.01388	0.6559	0.3845
4	0.48936	0.48936	0.0213
5	0.07954	0.81818	0.10227
6	0.35526	0.52631	0.11842
7	0.49873	0.49873	0.00253
8	0/0	0/0	0/0
9	0.51	0	0.49

Table 2. The results obtained using the averaging rule

Example	$m_{12}(A)$	$m_{12}(B)$	$m_{12}(A, B)$
2	0	0.375	0.625
3	0.01	0.305	0.685
4	0.45	0.45	0.1
5	0.1	0.6	0.3
6	0.3	0.4	0.3
7	0.495	0.495	0.01
8	0.5	0.5	0
9	0.3	0	0.7

It is seen that in the examples 2 and 3, the sums (from both *bpas*) of values of arguments in favor of (A, B) are greater than in favor of B. Therefore, it is intuitively obvious that in these examples after combination we should expect $m_{12}(A, B) > m_{12}(B)$. We can see that such results are obtained for averaging rule (see Tables 2), but Dempster's rule provides counterintuitive results (see Table 1).

All the analysed rules provide intuitively obvious results for the examples 4 and 7.

In the examples 5 and 6, we deal with the identical *bpas*. Therefore, only idempotent averaging rule provides true results. In the example 8, the result of Dempster's rule is not defined as in this case we deal with the dividing by 0 since $K=1$ and $1-K=0$.

In this example, the averaging combination rule rules provides good results which can be naturally treated as fifty-fifty chances for A and B.

Therefore, we can say that the averaging rule performs better than the Dempster's rule, as it provides true results in both asymptotical cases: in the case of full conflict and in the case of lack of conflict. It is worth noting that in practice we often deal with *bpas* characterised by relatively low conflict. It is clear that in such cases the use of not idempotent Dempster's rule may provide inappropriate numerical results (see examples 5 and 6).

Let us consider the example 9. In this case, we have no conflict at all and $m_1(A) < m_1(A, B)$, $m_2(A) < m_2(A, B)$, $m_1(B) = m_2(B) = 0$. Nevertheless, in Table 1 for this example we can see $m_{12}(A) > m_{12}(A, B)$. Obviously, such a result is in contradiction with the common sense. The true result provides only the averaging rule (see Table 2).

A good property of averaging rule is that it provides normalised combined *bpas* if initial *bpas* are normalised too. It is seen that using averaging rule, it is possible in a natural way to take into account the reliability (or weighs) of combined sources of evidence.

Summarising, we can say that the averaging rule can be used solely to combine *bpas*. Of course, this rule seems to be too simple, but simple methods are not always bad or wrong ones.

On the other hand, we belief that choosing an appropriate combination rule is a context dependent problem.

The advantages of the averaging rule in comparison with the Dempster's rule will be illustrated in the following section.

3   A New Approach to the Rule-Base Evidential Reasoning

To present our approach in a more transparent form, in this section we shall use a relatively simple example of building the expert system for diagnosing type 2 diabetes. It is important also that in spite of simplicity this system is the real-world one. The following tests are recommended by the World Health Organization (WHO) for diagnosing of the type 2 diabetes:

Test 1. A fasting plasma glucose test measures blood glucose in a person who has not eaten anything for at least 8 hours.

Test 2. An oral glucose tolerance test measures blood glucose after a person fasts at least 8 hours and 2 hours after the person drinks a glucose- containing beverage.

These tests are used to detect diabetes and pre-diabetes. Although, WHO proposes crisp intervals for blood glucose which correspond to the health (H), Pre-diabetes (H,D) and diabetes (D), in practice doctors use for diagnostics, e.g., such fuzzy concepts as Low, Medium and Big blood glucose, which can be presented by corresponding membership functions as in Fig.1, where μ_L, μ_M, μ_B correspond to the $\mu_{Low}, \mu_{Medium}, \mu_{Big}$, respectively. Here we shall treat the di-

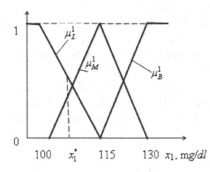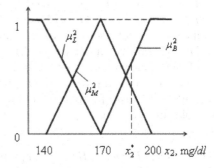

Fig. 1. Test 1 (blood glucose x_1) and Test 2 (blood glucose x_2)

agnosis Pre-diabetes as an intermediate one when a doctor hesitates in choice between the Health and Diabetes diagnoses. Therefore, the diagnosis Pre-diabetes in the spirit of DST can be treated as the compound hypothesis (H,D). Based on the known approaches to the rule-base evidential reasoning ([6,19]) we get the following rules:

$$
\begin{aligned}
&IF\,x_1\ is\,Low\,Then\,m_1^*(H) \ = \ \mu_L^1(x_1),\\
&IF\,x_1\,is\,Medium\,Then\,m_1^*(H,D) = \mu_M^1(x_1);\\
&IF\,x_1\,is\,Big\,Then\,m_1^*(D) = \mu_B^1(x_1),\\
&IF\,x_2\ is\,Low\,Then\,m_2^*(H) \ = \ \mu_L^2(x_2),\\
&IF\,x_2\,is\,Medium\,Then\,m_2^*(H,D) = \mu_M^2(x_2);\\
&IF\,x_2\,is\,Big\,Then\,m_2^*(D) = \mu_B^2(x_2),
\end{aligned}
\tag{3}
$$

where $bpas\ m_1^*(H),\ m_1^*(H,D),\ m_1^*(D)$ and $m_2^*(H),\ m_2^*(H,D),\ m_2^*(D)$ are treated as the pieces of evidence in favor of H, (H,D) and D, respectively, and should be additionally normalised :

$$
\begin{aligned}
&m_1(H) = m_1^*(H)/S_1,\ m_1(H,D) = m_1^*(H,D)/S_1,\ m_1(D) = m_1^*(D)/S_1,\\
&m_2(H) = m_2^*(H)/S_2,\ m_2(H,D) = m_2^*(H,D)/S_2,\ m_2(D) = m_2^*(D)/S_2,\\
&S_1 = m_1^*(H) + m_1^*(H,D) + m_1^*(D),\ S_2 = m_2^*(H) + m_2^*(H,D) + m_2^*(D).
\end{aligned}
$$

For $x_1 = x_1^*$ and $x_2 = x_2^*$ (see Fig.1) using the above rules (3) and the conventional fuzzy logic, from the first test we get the diagnosis H (with $m_1^*(H) = \mu_L^1(x_1^*)$) and from the second one - D (with $m_2^*(D) = \mu_B^1(x_2^*)$).

Since these two tests are different sources of evidence, to obtain the final diagnosis they should be combined using an appropriate combination rule. Nevertheless, the use of classical fuzzy logic may lead to the counterintuitive results. That may be explained as follows. Following to rules of classical fuzzy logic, in the test 1, we take into account only the diagnosis H, whereas the diagnosis (H,D) is possible as well with a non-zero value of membership function $\mu_M^1(x_1^*)$ (see Fig.1). Similarly, in the test 2 we are not taking into account the possible diagnosis (H,D).

Another problem of classical approach is that it is possible in the considered case to use two different rules:

$If\ (x_1\ is\ Low)\ and\ (x_2\ is\ Medium)\ then\ Diabetes$ and
$If\ (x_1\ is\ Low)\ and\ (x_2\ is\ Medium)\ then\ Pre-diabetes.$

Since we cannot use these rules simultaneously, we need an additional information to choose a correct rule and this information usually may be found only out of the framework of classical fuzzy logic.

Summarising, we can say that the known methods of rule-base evidential seasoning lead to the loss of important information which may affect the final results. To avoid this problem, we propose to represent the rules in the example presented in Fig. 1 as follows:

$$IF(x_1 = x_1^*)\,Then\,m_1^*(H) = \mu_L^1(x_1^*),\ m_1^*(H,D) = \mu_M^1(x_1^*), m_1^*(D) = \mu_B^1(x_1^*),$$
$$IF(x_2 = x_2^*)\,Then\,m_2^*(H) = \mu_L^2(x_2^*),\ m_2^*(H,D) = \mu_M^2(x_2^*), m_2^*(D) = \mu_B^2(x_2^*).$$
$$(4)$$

To represent the advantages of proposed approach, consider the critical example presented in Fig.1.

Using conventional fuzzy logic, from (3) we get $bpas\ m_1^*(H) = 0.55$ and $m_2^*(D) = 0.6$. In this case, we can say only that we deal with a high conflict between the pieces of evidence and cannot obtain a reasonable solution (diagnosis) in the considered real-world example. It is important that in this case we cannot say anything about the value of $m_{12}^*(H, D)$.

On the other hand, according to the doctor's opinion, in our case the diagnosis Pre-diabetes seems to be more justified than Diabetes and Diabetes is more preferable than Health. The Pre-diabetes is intuitively obvious for the doctor in the considered example. Moreover, in his informal, but based on common sense analysis, the doctor considered the values $m_1^*(H) = 0.55, m_1^*(H, D) = 0.45, m_1^*(D) = 0$ and $m_2^*(H) = 0, m_2^*(H, D) = 0.4, m_2^*(D) = 0.6$ as the arguments in favour of corresponding diagnoses. It is easy to see that the sum of arguments in favour of Pre-diabetes $m_1^*(H, D) + m_2^*(H, D)$ is grater than the sum of arguments in favour of Diabetes $m_1^*(D) + m_2^*(D)$ which is greater than $m_1^*(H) + m_2^*(H)$.

Using a new approach, from (4) for our example we get

$$(x_1 = x_1^*)\,then\,(m_1^*(H) = 0.55, m_1^*(H, D) = 0.45, m_1^*(D) = 0),$$
$$(x_2 = x_2^*)\,then\,(m_2^*(H) = 0, m_2^*(H, D) = 0.4, m_2^*(D) = 0.6). \qquad (5)$$

We can see that obtained $bpas$ are normalised. Then using the averaging combination rule, we get $m_{12}(H) = 0.275, m_{12}(H, D) = 0.425, m_{12}(D) = 0.3$.

We can see that this result qualitatively coincides with the results of informal, but based on common sense analysis presented above.

On the other hand, using the Dempster's rule (1), we obtain $m_{12}(H) = 0.328$, $m_{12}(H, D) = 0.269$, $m_{12}(D) = 0.402$.

It is seen that this result can be considered as controversial one, as it doesn't qualitatively coincide with the results of above analysis.

Let us consider the critical example presented in Fig.2.

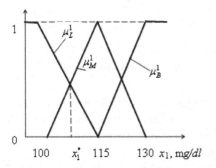 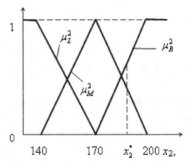

Fig. 2. Test 1 (blood glucose x_1) and Test 2 (blood glucose x_2)

In this case, the use of classical fuzzy logic leads to obtaining from (3) two possible results: $m_1^*(H) = 0.5$, $m_2^*(D) = 0.6$ and $m_1^*(H, D) = 0.5$, $m_2^*(D) = 0.6$. It is seen that in this case we deal with an ambiguity and have no reasons to choose the right result.

On the other hand, using a new approach, from (4) for this example we get

$$(x_1 = x_1^*)\, then\, (m_1^*(H) = 0.5, m_1^*(H, D) = 0.5, m_1^*(D) = 0), \\ (x_2 = x_2^*)\, then\, (m_2^*(H) = 0, m_2^*(H, D) = 0.44, m_2^*(D) = 0.6). \tag{6}$$

Then using the averaging combination rule, we get $m_{12}(H) = 0.25$, $m_{12}(H, D) = 0.45$, $m_{12}(D) = 0.3$.

This result seems to be intuitively obvious, whereas the use of the Dempster's rule (1) provides $m_{12}(H) = 0.286$, $m_{12}(H, D) = 0.286$, $m_{12}(D) = 0.428$.

The last result seems to be not intuitively clear since we have

$m_{12}(H) = m_{12}(H, D)$, whereas the sum $m_1^*(H) + m_2^*(H)$ is lesser than the sum $m_1^*(H, D) + m_2^*(H, D)$.

So far we have considered the examples characterised by the significant conflict between sources of evidence . Therefore, let us consider the example presented in Fig.3, where the conflict is absent.

Since in this case $m_1^*(H) = m_2^*(H) = 0.4$, $m_1^*(H, D) = m_2^*(H, D) = 0.6$ and $m_1^*(D) = m_2^*(D) = 0$, it is clear that in this case the only right result of combination of evidence should be $m_{12}(H) = 0.4$, $m_{12}(H, D) = 0.6$ and $m_{12}(D) = 0$.

The use of classical fuzzy logic and rules (3) provides only $m_{12}^*(H, D) = 0.6$ and this result cannot be treated as a satisfactory one.

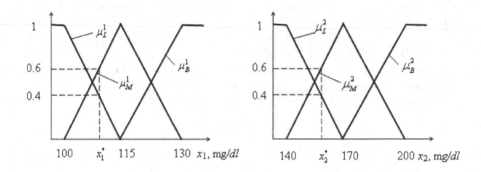

Fig. 3. Test 1 (blood glucose x_1) and Test 2 (blood glucose x_2)

Using the averaging combination rule, in this case from (4) we get the right result $m_{12}(H) = 0.4$, $m_{12}(H, D) = 0.6$ and $m_{12}(D) = 0$, whereas using the Dempster's rule (1) we obtain the result which seems to be undoubtedly wrong: $m_{12}(H) = 0.48$, $m_{12}(H, D) = 0.36$ and $m_{12}(D) = 0$.

Summarising, we can say that based on the considered critical examples we have shown that the proposed new approach to the rule-base evidential reasoning performs better than known ones in the cases of large and small conflict. We have shown that the classical Dempster's combination rule may provide controversial and undoubtedly wrong result not only in the case of large conflict, but when the conflict is absent, too, whereas the use of averaging combination rule makes it possible to avoid these problems.

4   Conclusion

A new approach to the rule-base evidential reasoning ($RBER$) based on a new formulation of fuzzy rules is presented. As $RBER$ methods are based on the synthesis of fuzzy logic and the Dempster-Shafer theory of evidence (DST), the problem of the combination of basic probability assignments (*bpas*) from different sources of evidence arises. The classical Dempster's rule of combination is usually used for this purpose. Since the classical Dempster's rule may provide controversial results in the case of great conflict and is not idempotent one, we provide a brief comparative analysis of the most known rules of combination and their aggregations. We show that the Dempster's rule may provide unreasonable results not only in the case of large conflict, but in the case of complete absence of conflict, too. At the end, we show that in the cases of small and large conflict, the use of simple averaging rule for combination of *bpas* seems to be a best choice.

The introduction of such new formulation of fuzzy rules was inspired by our experience in the solution of decision-making problems with the use of $RBER$. We have shown that the traditional fuzzy logic rules lose an important information, when dealing with the intersecting fuzzy classes, e.g., such as *Low* and *Medium*, and this undesirable property may lead to the controversial results.

In the framework of our approach, an information of the values of all membership functions representing the intersecting (competing) fuzzy classes is preserved and used in the fuzzy logic rules.

A good property of averaging rule is that it provides normalised combined *bpa*s if initial *bpa*s are normalised too. It is obvious that using averaging rule, it is possible in a natural way to take into account the reliabilities (or weighs) of combined sources of evidence.

The developed approach is illustrated by the solution of simple, but real-world problem of diagnostics of type 2 diabetes.

Acknowledgements. The research has been supported by the grant financed by National Science Centre (Poland) on the basis of decision number DEC-2013/11/B/ST6/00960.

References

1. Delmotte, F., Dubois, L., Desodt, A., Borne, P.: Using trust in uncertainty theories. Information and Systems Engineering 1, 303–314 (1995)
2. Dempster, A.P.: Upper and lower probabilities induced by a muilti-valued mapping. Ann. Math. Stat. 38, 325–339 (1967)
3. Dubois, D., Prade, H.: A Set-Theoretic View on Belief Functions: Logical Operations and Approximations by Fuzzy Sets. International Journal of General Systems 12, 193–226 (1986)
4. Dubois, D., Prade, H.: Representation and combination of uncertainty with belief functions and possibility measures. Computational Intelligence 4, 244–264 (1988)
5. Dubois, D., Prade, H.: On the combination of evidence in various mathematical frameworks. In: Aamm, J., Luisi, T. (eds.) Reliability Data Collection and Analysis, pp. 213–241 (1992)
6. Dymova, L., Sevastianov, P., Bartosiewicz, P.: A new approach to the rule-base evidential reasoning: Stock trading expert system application. Expert Systems with Applications 37, 5564–5576 (2010)
7. Dymova, L., Sevastianov, P., Kaczmarek, K.: A stock trading expert system based on the rule-base evidential reasoning using Level 2 Quotes. Expert Systems with Applications 39, 7150–7157 (2012)
8. Dymova, L., Sevastjanov, P., Tkacz, K., Cheherava, T.: A new measure of conflict and hybrid combination rules in the evidence theory. In: Rutkowski, L., Korytkowski, M., Scherer, R., Tadeusiewicz, R., Zadeh, L.A., Zurada, J.M. (eds.) ICAISC 2014, Part II. LNCS, vol. 8468, pp. 411–422. Springer, Heidelberg (2014)
9. Florea, M.C., Dezert, J., Valin, P., Smarandache, F., Jousselme, A.L.: Adaptative combination rule and proportional conflict redistribution rule for information fusion. Presented at the Conference "Cognitive Systems with Interactive Sensors", Paris (2006), arXiv:cs/0604042v1
10. Florea, M.C., Jousselme, A.-L., Bossé, É., Grenier, D.: Robust combination rules for evidence theory. Information Fusion 10, 183–197 (2009)
11. Horiuchi, T.: Decision Rule for Pattern Classification by Integrating Interval Feature Values. IEEE Trans. Pattern Analysis and Machine Intelligence 20, 440–448 (1998)

12. Inagaki, T.: Interdependence between Safety-Control Policy and Multiple-Sensor Schemes Via Dempster-Shafer Theory. IEEE Transactions on Reliability 40, 182–188 (1991)
13. Josang, A., Daniel, M., Vannoorenberghe, P.: Strategies for Combining Conflicting Dogmatic Beliefs. In: Proceedings of the 6th International Conference on International Fusion, vol. 2, pp. 1133–1140 (2003)
14. Martin, A., Osswald, C.H., Dezert, J., Smarandache, F.: General Combination Rules for Qualitative and Quantitative Beliefs. Journal of Advances in Information Fusion 3, 67–89 (2008)
15. Matsuyama, T.: Belief Formation From Observation and Belief Integration Using Virtual Belief Space in Dempster-Shafer Probability Model. In: Proc. Multisensor Fusion and Integration for Intelligent Systems (MFI 1994), pp. 379–386 (1994)
16. Murphy, C.K.: Combining Belief Functions When Evidence Conflicts. Decision Support Systems 29, 1–9 (2000)
17. Sentz, K., Ferson, S.: Combination of Evidence in Dempster-Shafer Theory. Sandia National Laboratories SAND 2002-0835 (2002)
18. Sevastianov, P., Dymova, L.: Synthesis of fuzzy logic and Dempster-Shafer Theory for the simulation of the decision-making process in stock trading systems. Mathematics and Computers in Simulation 80, 506–521 (2009)
19. Sevastianov, P., Dymova, L., Bartosiewicz, P.: A framework for rule-base evidential reasoning in the interval setting applied to diagnosing type 2 diabetes. Expert Systems with Applications 39, 4190–4200 (2012)
20. Shafer, G.: A mathematical theory of evidence. Princeton University Press (1976)
21. Smarandache, F.: An In-Depth Look at Information Fusion Rules and the Unification of Fusion Theories, Computing Research Repository (CoRR), Cornell University arXiv, vol. cs.OH/0410033 (2004)
22. Smarandache, F.: Unification of Fusion Theories (UFT), May 16-27. NATO Advanced Study Institute, Albena (2005)
23. Smets, P.: The alpha-junctions: combination operators applicable to belief functions. LNCS, vol. 1244, pp. 131–153. Springer (1997)
24. Zadeh, L.A.: Review of Books: A Mathematical Theory of Evidence. The AI Magazine 5, 81–83 (1984)
25. Zadeh, L.: A simple view of the Dempster-Shafer theory of evidence and its application for the rule of combination. AI Magazine 7, 85–90 (1986)

Bias-Correction Fuzzy C-Regressions Algorithm

Miin-Shen Yang[(⊠)], Yu-Zen Chen, and Yessica Nataliani

Department of Applied Mathematics, Chung Yuan Christian University,
Chung-Li 32023, Taiwan
msyang@math.cycu.edu.tw

Abstract. In fuzzy clustering, the fuzzy c-means (FCM) algorithm is the most commonly used clustering method. However, the FCM algorithm is usually affected by initializations. Incorporating FCM into switching regressions, called the fuzzy c-regressions (FCR), has also the same drawback as FCM, where bad initializations may cause difficulties in obtaining appropriate clustering and regression results. In this paper, we proposed the bias-correction fuzzy c-regressions (BFCR) algorithm by incorporating bias-correction FCM (BFCM) into switching regressions. Some numerical examples were used to compare the proposed algorithm with some existing fuzzy c-regressions methods. The results indicated the superiority and effectiveness of the proposed BFCR algorithm.

Keywords: Fuzzy clustering · Fuzzy c-means (FCM) · Switching regression · Fuzzy c-regressions (FCR) · Bias-correction fuzzy c-regression (BFCR).

1   Introduction

In fuzzy clustering, the fuzzy c-means (FCM) algorithm [1] is the best-known and most commonly used method. Previous studies in the literature have proposed numerous extensions of FCM clustering (see [3,5,6,8,11]). However, the FCM and its generalizations may be affected by initializations. Recently, Yang and Tian [9] proposed a bias-correction FCM (BFCM) with a learning schema to adjust bias effects of initial values. This method can make bias correction for initial values and it can also produce better clustering results than FCM. Regression analysis is used to model the function relation between independent and dependent variables. In general, a single regression model is used for fitting a data set. However, the data set may contain more than one regression model, say c regressions. This c-regression model is also called switching regression. It is widely applied to data analysis. Since Quandt [7] and Chow [2] initiated the research on switching regression, it had been widely studied and applied. Hathaway and Bezdek [4] first combined switching regression with the FCM algorithm, and referred it fuzzy c-regressions (FCR). Afterwards, Yang et al. [10] proposed alpha-cut FCR to improving noise and outlier effects for FCR [4]. However, these c-regressions algorithms are also affected by initializations. In this paper, we proposed the bias-correction fuzzy c-regressions (BFCR) algorithm by incorporating the BFCM clustering into switching regression such that the BFCR becomes a robust c-regressions algorithm to initializations. The rest of this paper is organized as follows. In Section 2, we briefly review the FCM, FCR and alpha-cut FCR algorithms. In Section 3, we first consider a

© Springer International Publishing Switzerland 2015
L. Rutkowski et al. (Eds.): ICAISC 2015, Part I, LNAI 9119, pp. 283–293, 2015.
DOI: 10.1007/978-3-319-19324-3_26

bias-correction term with a learning schema. We then propose the BFCR algorithm. In Section 4, comparisons of the BFCR with some fuzzy c-regressions methods are made. Finally, conclusions are stated in Section 5.

2   FCM, FCR and Alpha-Cut FCR

The FCM algorithm [1,8] is iterated by using the necessary conditions for a minimizer of the objective function J_{FCM} expressed as follows:

$$J_{FCM}(\mu, a) = \sum_{i=1}^{c} \sum_{j=1}^{n} \mu_{ij}^{m} d(x_j, a_i) \tag{1}$$

where the weighting exponent $m > 1$ is a fuzziness index, $\mu = \{\mu_1, \cdots, \mu_c\}$ with $\mu_{ij} = \mu_i(x_j)$ is a fuzzy c-partition, $a = \{a_1, \cdots, a_c\}$ over the s-dimensional real space R^s is the set of c cluster centers, and $d(x_j, a_i)$ is a dissimilarity measure. The necessary conditions for a minimizer (μ, a) of J_{FCM} are the following updating equations:

$$\mu_{ij} = \frac{d(x_j, a_i)^{-1/(m-1)}}{\sum_{k=1}^{c} d(x_j, a_k)^{-1/(m-1)}} \tag{2}$$

$$a_i = \frac{\sum_{j=1}^{n} \mu_{ij}^{m} x_j}{\sum_{j=1}^{n} \mu_{ij}^{m}} \tag{3}$$

where the Euclidean distance $\sqrt{d(x_j, a_i)} = \|x_j - a_i\|$ is used.

Suppose that, we have a set of data $\{(x_1, y_1), \cdots, (x_n, y_n)\}$ with each independent observation $x_j = (x_{j1}, \cdots, x_{jp}) \in \mathfrak{R}^p$ and corresponding dependent observation $y_j \in \mathfrak{R}$. The objective of switching regression is to find c linear regressions expressed as follows: for $i = 1, \cdots, c$

$$\hat{y}_{j,i} = \beta_{i0} + \beta_{i1} x_{j1} + \cdots + \beta_{ip} x_{jp} \tag{4}$$

that should fit best for the data structure. The combination of switching regression with FCM is referred to as fuzzy c-regressions (FCR) by Hathaway and Bezdek [4], and it minimizes the objective function J_{FCR} expressed as follows:

$$J_{FCR} = \sum_{i=1}^{c} \sum_{j=1}^{n} \mu_{ij}^{m} d(y_j, \hat{y}_{j,i}) \tag{5}$$

with $d(y_j, \hat{y}_{j,i}) = (y_j - \hat{y}_{j,i})^2$. Thus, the updating equations for the minimization are

$$\mu_{ij} = \frac{d(y_j, \hat{y}_{j,i})^{-1/(m-1)}}{\sum_{k=1}^{c} d(y_j, \hat{y}_{j,k})^{-1/(m-1)}} \tag{6}$$

$$\vec{\beta}_i = \begin{bmatrix} \beta_{i0} \\ \vdots \\ \beta_{ip} \end{bmatrix} = [X'D_iX]^{-1}X'D_iY \tag{7}$$

where X denotes the matrix in $\mathfrak{R}^{n\times(p+1)}$ having $(1,x_j)=(1,x_{j1},\cdots,x_{jp})$ as its jth row; Y denotes the vector in $\mathfrak{R}^n$ having y_j as its jth component; and D_i denotes the diagonal matrix in $\mathfrak{R}^{n\times n}$ having μ_{ij}^m as its jth diagonal element.

In FCR, there are some drawbacks, where noise and outliers may cause difficulties in obtaining appropriate regression line results from the FCR algorithm. Alpha-cut fuzzy c-regressions (FCRα) algorithm [10] is a method to improve FCR. The FCRα algorithm is implemented by adding a α term into FCR to adjust the influence of noise and outliers (see also Yang et al. [10]). If the membership value μ_{ij} of the data point (x_j,y_j) is larger than a given α value, then the point (x_j,y_j) will exactly belong to the ith cluster (linear regression) with membership value of 1, but $\mu_{i'j}=0$ for all $i'\neq i$.

3   Bias-Correction Fuzzy C-Regression

In general, the FCR and FCRα algorithms may be affected by initializations. That is, the FCR and FCRα algorithms obtain poor regression line results when poor initializations are given. To overcome this drawback, we propose a bias-correction term to reduce the effects of poor initializations. The similar method can be referred to bias-correction FCM (BFCM) algorithm, proposed by Yang and Tian [9]. We combine BFCM with c-regressions and called it the bias-correction fuzzy c-regression (BFCR).

In the BFCR, we add a bias-correction term to the FCR. The BFCR algorithm is iterated by using the necessary conditions for a minimizer of the objective function J_{BFCR} expressed as follows:

$$J_{BFCR} = \sum_{i=1}^{c}\sum_{j=1}^{n}\mu_{ij}^m d(y_j,\hat{y}_{j,i}) - w\sum_{k=1}^{n}\sum_{i=1}^{c}\mu_{ik}^m \ln(p_i) \tag{8}$$

subject to $\sum_{i=1}^{c}\mu_{ik}=1$ and $\sum_{i=1}^{c}p_i=1$. Thus, the necessary conditions for a minimizer of J_{BFCR} are the following updating equations:

$$\mu_{ik} = \frac{\left(d(y_j,\hat{y}_{j,i})-w\ln(p_i)\right)^{-1/(m-1)}}{\sum_{j=1}^{c}\left(d(y_j,\hat{y}_{j,i})-w\ln(p_j)\right)^{-1/(m-1)}} \tag{9}$$

$$\vec{\beta}_i = \begin{bmatrix} \beta_{i0} \\ \vdots \\ \beta_{ip} \end{bmatrix} = [X'D_iX]^{-1}X'D_iY \tag{10}$$

$$p_i = \frac{\sum_{k=1}^{n} \mu_{ik}^m}{\sum_{j=1}^{c}\sum_{k=1}^{n} \mu_{jk}^m} \tag{11}$$

$$w^{(t)} = e^{\frac{-t}{100}} \tag{12}$$

Thus, the BFCR algorithm can be described as follows:

BFCR Algorithm

Step 1 : Fix $2 \leq c \leq n$ and fix any $\varepsilon > 0$.

   Give an initial $\mu^{(0)}$ and let $t = 0$.

Step 2 : Learn the parameter $w^{(t)}$ using equation (12).

Step 3 : Compute the regression line parameter $\vec{\beta}_i$ using equation (10).

Step 4 : Substitute data point into regression line to get $\hat{y}_{j,i}$ with equation (4).

Step 5 : Compute the probability weight $p_i^{(t+1)}$ by equation (11).

Step 6 : Update $\mu^{(t+1)}$ using equation (9).

Step 7 : Compare $\mu^{(t+1)}$ to $\mu^{(t)}$ in a convenient matrix norm $\|\cdot\|$.

   IF $\|\mu^{(t+1)} - \mu^{(t)}\| < \varepsilon$, STOP

   ELSE $t = t+1$ and return to step 2.

4   Comparisons and Experimental Results

In this section, three examples are used to compare the proposed BFCR algorithm with the FCR and FCRα algorithms. We consider several randomly generated data sets from the model $y_{j,i} = \beta_{i0} + \beta_{i1}x_{j,1} + \varepsilon_i$, $\varepsilon_i \sim N(0, \sigma_i^2)$ where some noisy points are also added. The effectiveness of the algorithms is indicated by the total counts of poor results and total sums of squared residuals from the BFCR, FCR and FCRα algorithms by 50 random initializations.

Example 1 In this example, we make comparisons of the proposed BFCR with FCR. We consider the 2-regressions model $y_{j,i} = \beta_{i0} + \beta_{i1}x_{j,1} + \varepsilon_i$, $i = 1,2$ with $\varepsilon_i \sim N(0, \sigma_i^2)$. The first case is two parallel lines with parameters $\beta_{10} = 0.014$, $\beta_{11} = 0.671$, $\beta_{20} = -2.526$, and $\beta_{21} = 0.513$. According to $\varepsilon_i \sim N(0, \sigma_i^2)$, we generate 100 data points with 50 data points of $\sigma_1^2 = 2$ and 50 data points of $\sigma_2^2 = 2$, as shown in Fig. 1(a). The second case is two crossed lines with parameters $\beta_{10} = 0.006$, $\beta_{11} = 0.004$, $\beta_{20} = -0.031$, $\beta_{21} = 0.986$. Similarly, 100 data points are generated according to $\sigma_1^2 = 2$ and $\sigma_2^2 = 2$, as shown in Fig. 1(b). For each case, we implement the algorithms 50 times with random initializations. In Table 1, when m=2, the total count of poor results from FCR is 32 that is much more than 14 from BFCR. The results of FCR with m=2 and BFCR with m=2 are shown in Figs. 1 and 3. When m=4, FCR may fit the models well, as shown in Fig. 2. However, the total count of poor results from FCR when m=4 is 17 that is still more than 14 from BFCR (m=2). Furthermore, we add some noisy points in the two data sets. The total counts of poor results from FCR and BFCR are also shown in Table 1. When m=2, the total count of poor results from FCR is also more than those from BFCR. The results of FCR with m=2 and BFCR with m=2 for parallel with noises are shown in Figs. 4 and 6. The results of FCR with m=4 are shown in Fig. 5. We also apply these algorithms to the two-curve data set. The results of FCR and BFCR are shown in Fig. 7. From the results of Table 1, we find that the proposed BFCR is actually more stable and robust than FCR for different models under random initializations and noisy cases. The BFCR algorithm can also get better results under smaller fuzziness index m.

Table 1. Total count of poor results obtained by FCR and BFCR

	FCR (m=2)	FCR (m=4)	BFCR (m=2)
Parallel data	32	17	14
Crossed data	17	2	1
Parallel with noises	30	17	15
Crossed with noises	2	1	1
Curve data	24	20	15

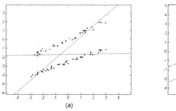 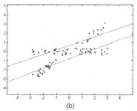

Fig. 1. FCR poor results for the two generated data sets when m=2; (a)Two parallel lines; (b)Two crossed lines

Example 2 In this example, we make comparisons of the proposed BFCR with FCR. We consider the 3-lines model $y_{j,i} = \beta_{i0} + \beta_{i1}x_{j,1} + \varepsilon_i$, $i = 1,2,3$ with parameters $\beta_{10} = 4.362$, $\beta_{11} = 2.049$, $\beta_{20} = -9.998$, $\beta_{21} = 1.988$, $\beta_{30} = 5.030$, and $\beta_{21} = -3.070$.

According to $\varepsilon_i \sim N(0, \sigma_i^2)$, we generate 150 data points with 50 data points of $\sigma_1^2 = 8$, 50 data points of $\sigma_2^2 = 5$, and 50 data points of $\sigma_3^2 = 7$, as shown in Fig. 8. We implement the algorithms 50 times with random initializations. In Table 2, when m=2 and m=4, the total counts of poor results from FCR is 27 and 23, respectively, that are more than 22 from BFCR. The results of FCR with m=2, m=4 and BFCR with m=2 are shown in Fig. 9. Furthermore, we also consider the total sum of squared residuals for the three lines by these 50 times of implementations, as shown in Table 3. Overall, the proposed BFCR algorithm presents better results than the FCR algorithm for the 3-lines data set. The BFCR algorithm can also get better results under smaller fuzziness index m.

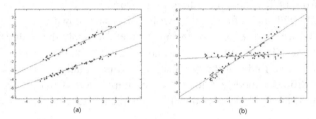

Fig. 2. FCR good results for the two generated data sets when m=4; (a)Two parallel lines; (b)Two crossed lines

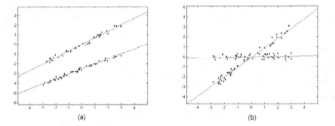

Fig. 3. BFCR good results for the two generated data sets when m=2;(a)Two parallel lines; (b)Two crossed lines

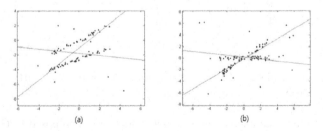

Fig. 4. FCR results for the two generated data sets with some noises when m=2; (a)Two parallel lines; (b)Two crossed lines

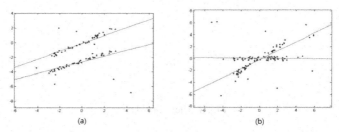

Fig. 5. FCR results for the two generated data sets with some noises when m=4; (a)Two parallel lines; (b)Two crossed lines

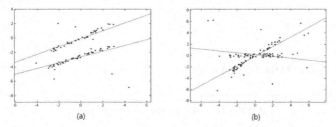

Fig. 6. BFCR results for the two generated data sets with some noises when m=2; (a)Two parallel lines; (b)Two crossed lines

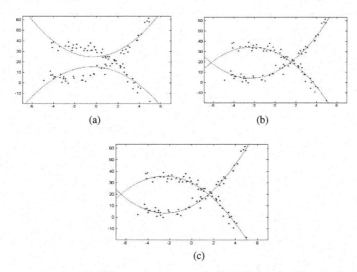

Fig. 7. Two-curve data set; (a) FCR results when m=2; (b) FCR results when m=4; (c) BFCR results when m=2

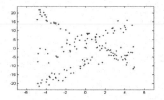

Fig. 8. The 3-line data set

Table 2. Total count of poor results obtained by FCR and BFCR

	FCR (m=2)	FCR (m=4)	BFCR (m=2)
3-line data set	27	23	22

Table 3. Total sum of squared residuals obtained by FCR and BFCR

	FCR (m=2)	FCR (m=4)	BFCR (m=2)
The first line	125.8	190.6	125.8
The second line	388.1	339.0	217.6
The third line	419.4	418.0	331.2

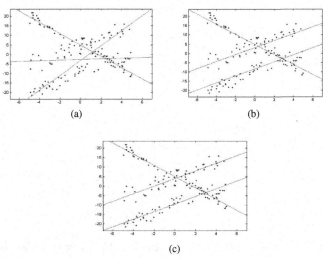

Fig. 9. The 3-line data set; (a) FCR results when m=2; (b) FCR results when m=4; (c) BFCR results when m=2

Example 3 In this example, we use the same data sets of Example 1, as shown in Figs. 1, 4 and 7. We make comparisons of the proposed BFCR with FCRα as α=0.65.

In Table 4, we can find that the total count of poor results from FCRα with m=2 is more than the other methods. When m=4, FCRα can fit the models very well. These results of FCRα and BFCR are shown in Figs. 10, 11 and 12. However, the results of BFCR is quite well with m=2. In this case, we can also see that BFCR can get good results with smaller fuzziness index m and overcome initialization and noisy effects. The results indicate the superiority of the proposed BFCR algorithm. We also consider these algorithms to the two-curve data set. The results of FCRα and BFCR are shown in Table 4 and Fig. 13. Overall, the proposed BFCR algorithm presents better results than the FCRα algorithm as α=0.65.

Table 4. Total count of poor results obtained by FCRα and BFCR

	FCRα (m=2, α=0.65)	FCRα (m=4, α=0.65)	BFCR (m=2)
Parallel data	21	11	11
Crossed data	16	3	0
Parallel with noises	28	22	15
Crossed with noises	12	1	0
Curve data	25	14	15

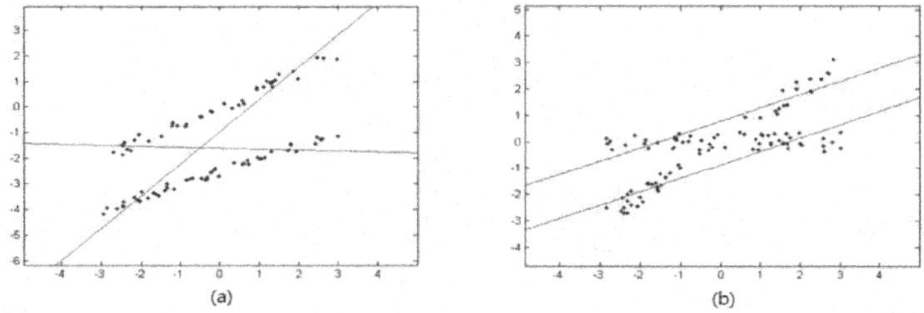

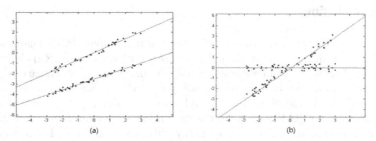

(a)   (b)

Fig. 10. FCRα results for the two generated data sets when m=2 and α=0.65; (a)Two parallel lines; (b)Two crossed lines

(a)   (b)

Fig. 11. FCRα results for the two generated data sets when m=4 and α=0.65; (a)Two parallel lines; (b)Two crossed lines

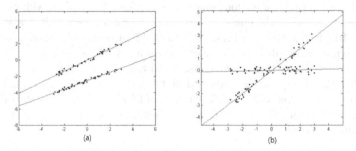

Fig. 12. BFCR results for the two generated data sets when m=2; (a)Two parallel lines; (b)Two crossed lines

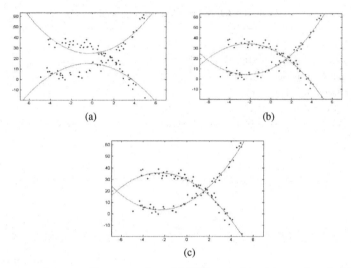

Fig. 13. Two-curve data set with some noises; (a) FCRα results when m=2 and α=0.65; (b) FCRα results when m=4 and α=0.65; (c)BFCR results when m=2

5   Conclusions

Hathaway and Bezdek [4] proposed the fuzzy c-regressions (FCR) algorithm and Yang et al. [10] then proposed the alpha-cut fuzzy c-regressions (FCRα) algorithm to improve FCR. However, initializations usually influence the performance of the FCR and FCRα algorithms. In this paper, we proposed the bias-correction fuzzy c-regression (BFCR) algorithm. The method considers adding a bias-correction term into FCR such that the BFCR algorithm with a bias-correction term can adjust the effects of poor initializations to most fuzzy clustering algorithm. From numerical comparisons, we find that the BFCR algorithm is more robust to initializations and noises than FCR and FCRα. Furthermore, the BFCR algorithm can get better results with lower fuzziness index *m*. The FCR and FCRα algorithms need to have a higher fuzziness index *m* for obtaining better results. In summary, the results indicate the superiority and effectiveness of the proposed BFCR algorithm.

References

1. Bezdek, J.C.: Pattern Recognition with Fuzzy Objective Function Algorithms. Plenum Press, New York (1981)
2. Chow, G.: Tests of the equality between two sets of coefficients in two linear regressions. Econometrica 28, 561–605 (1960)
3. Gustafson, D.E., Kessel, W.C.: Fuzzy clustering with a fuzzy covariance matrix. In: Proc., pp. 761–766. IEEE CDC, San Diego (1979)
4. Hathaway, R.J., Bezdek, J.C.: Switching regression models and fuzzy clustering. IEEE Transactions on Fuzzy Systems 1, 195–204 (1993)
5. Hoppner, F., Klawonn, F., Kruse, R., Runkler, T.: Fuzzy Cluster Analysis: Methods for Classification Data Analysis and Image Recognition. Wiley, New York (1999)
6. Krishnapuram, R., Keller, J.M.: A possibilistic approach to clustering. IEEE Transactions on Fuzzy Systems 1, 98–110 (1993)
7. Quandt, R.E.: Tests of the hypothesis that a linear regression system obeys two separate regimes. Journal of the American Statistical Association 55, 324–330 (1960)
8. Yang, M.S.: A survey of fuzzy clustering. Mathematical and Computer Modeling 18, 1–16 (1993)
9. Yang, M.S., Tian, Y.C.: Bias-correction fuzzy clustering algorithms. Information Sciences (2015) (in press)
10. Yang, M.S., Wu, K.L., Hsieh, J.N., Yu, J.: Alpha-cut implemented fuzzy clustering algorithms and switching regressions. IEEE Transactions on Systems, Man, and Cybernetics-Part B 38, 588–603 (2008)
11. Yu, J., Yang, M.S.: Optimality test for generalized FCM and its application to parameter selection. IEEE Transactions on Fuzzy Systems 13, 164–176 (2005)

Interval Type-2 Locally Linear Neuro Fuzzy Model Based on Locally Linear Model Tree

Zahra Zamanzadeh Darban[1] and Mohammad Hadi Valipour[2(✉)]

[1] Department of Computer Engineering and Information Technology,
Amirkabir University of Technology, Tehran, Iran
[2] Research Center for Developing Advanced Technologies, Tehran, Iran
zamanzadeh@aut.ac.ir, valipour@rcdat.ir

Abstract. In this paper a new interval Type-2 fuzzy neural network will be presented for function approximation. The proposed neural network is based on Locally Linear Model Tree (LOLIMOT) which is a fast learning algorithm for Locally Linear Neuro-Fuzzy Models (LLNFM). In this research, main measures are to be robust in presence of outlier data and be fast in refining steps. The proposed combination between LOLIMOT learning algorithm and interval type 2 fuzzy logic systems presents a good performance both in robustness and speed measures. The results show that the proposed method has good robustness in presence of noise as we can see in experiments conducted using corrupted data. Also this method has eligible speed as it can be seen in the results.

Keywords: LLNFM · LOLIMOT · Type-2 fuzzy systems · Interval Type-2 fuzzy sets

1 Introduction

Recently, studying on Type-2 fuzzy inference systems and Type-2 fuzzy neural networks have been conducted [1]. Type-2 Fuzzy Logic Systems (FLSs) are extensions of Type-1 FLSs [2] that provide more degrees of freedom through uncertainty on Type-1 fuzzy membership. Type-2 fuzzy sets are difficult to understand and utilization because of the three-dimensional fuzzy sets. Also, it is computationally more complicated than using Type-1 fuzzy sets, but it has some advantages such as learning, adaptation, fault-tolerance and generalization [3].

All operations of interval Type-2 fuzzy rules defined by Zadeh's [2] extension's principle that can be derived from a set of Type-2 fuzzy rules. A Type-2 membership has grade which can be any subset in [0, 1], on the primary membership [4]. Indeed, for each primary membership, there is a secondary membership that represents the possibilities for the primary membership. To simplify the computation of construction Type-2 fuzzy rules, the secondary membership functions (MFs) can be set to either zero or one and called interval Type-2 sets.

Researches on the area of fuzzy rule extraction of Type-2 fuzzy sets are limited. Our main objective is to develop an interval Type-2 fuzzy neural networks based on the construction of Type-2 fuzzy sets with LOLIMOT learning method. The Interval

© Springer International Publishing Switzerland 2015
L. Rutkowski et al. (Eds.): ICAISC 2015, Part I, LNAI 9119, pp. 294–304, 2015.
DOI: 10.1007/978-3-319-19324-3_27

Type-2 fuzzy neural network (IT2FNN) is a multi-layer network with interval Type-2 fuzzy signals and interval Type-2 fuzzy weights, Gaussian, generalized bell and sigmoid transfer function with principles of Type-2 fuzzy inference system. Briefly the proposed method is an Interval Type-2 Locally Linear Neuro Fuzzy Model based on Locally Linear Model Tree (IT2LL).

This paper is organized as follows. In Section 2 and 3, we explain LOLIMOT and interval Type-2 fuzzy logic system respectively. In Section 4 the structure of the proposed Type-2 fuzzy neural network and rule extraction will be declared in details. Simulation and experimental results of function approximation are presented in Section 5. Concluding comments are included in Section 6.

2   Locally Linear Model Tree (LOLIMOT)

2.1   Structure

The basic network structure of a locally linear neuro fuzzy model is depicted in Fig. 1. Every neuron consists of a local linear model which called LLM, and a validity function Φ, which defines the validity of the LLM within the input space.

Locally linear neuro-fuzzy models (LLNFM) with locally linear model tree (LOLIMOT) learning algorithm has been introduced in [5]. The network output is calculated as a weighted sum of the outputs of the local linear models, where the validity function is interpreted as the operating point dependent weighting factors. The validity functions are typically chosen as normalized Gaussians. The most important factor for the success of LOLIMOT is divide and conquers strategy that is used in it.

The LOLIMOT is an incremental tree construction algorithm, which divides the input space axes in an orthogonal way. In Fig. 2 the LOLIMOT algorithm for the first five iteration steps with a two dimensional input space is depicted.

2.2   Learning Algorithm

In this section, a mathematical formulation of LLNFM with LOLIMOT learning algorithm is described [5]. The fundamental approach with locally linear neuro-fuzzy models divides the input space into small subspaces with fuzzy validity functions. Any produced linear part with its validity function can be described as a fuzzy neuron. Thus the whole model is a neuro-fuzzy network with one hidden layer and a linear neuron in the output layer. The network structure is shown in [5].

In (1) input-output relation of LLNFM is presented. In this formula i is number of neurons, u is the model input, p is number of input dimension, N equals the number of input samples and w denotes the weights of the neuron [5].

$$\hat{y}_i = w_{i0} + w_{i1}u_1 + \ldots + w_{ip}u_p$$

$$thus \qquad \hat{y} = \sum_{i=1}^{M} y_i \Phi_i(\underline{u}) \tag{1}$$

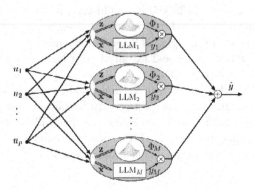

Fig. 1. Network structure of a static local linear neuro-fuzzy with neurons for input u [5]

The validity functions are chosen as normalized Gaussians. Normalization is necessary for a proper interpretation of validity functions. In (2) validity function formulation is represented.

$$\Phi_i(\underline{u}) = \frac{\mu_i(\underline{u})}{\sum_{j=1}^{M} \mu_j(\underline{u})} \quad where$$

$$\mu_i(\underline{u}) = \exp(\frac{(u_1 - c_{i1})^2}{-2\sigma_{i1}^2}) \times ... \times \exp(\frac{(u_p - c_{ip})^2}{-2\sigma_{ip}^2})$$

(2)

Each Gaussian validity function has two parameters: center and standard deviation .Also there are weight parameters of the nonlinear hidden layer. Optimization or learning methods are used to adjust fine tuning of two sets of parameters, weights and the parameters of validity functions.

Local optimization of linear parameters is simply obtained by Least Squares technique. The global parameter vector contains elements. In (3) these parameters are shown.

$$\underline{w} = [w_{10} \quad w_{11} \quad ...w_{1p}... \quad w_{M0} \quad ...w_{Mp}]$$

(3)

Associated regression matrix for measured data samples is formulated in (4). Thus the weights will be obtained by solving (5) as shown in (6).

$$\underline{X} = [\underline{X}_1 \quad \underline{X}_2 \quad ...\underline{X}_M]$$

$$\underline{X}_i = \begin{bmatrix} 1 & u_1(1) & \cdots & u_p(1) \\ 1 & u_1(2) & \cdots & u_p(2) \\ \vdots & \vdots & \cdots & \vdots \\ 1 & u_1(N) & \cdots & u_p(N) \end{bmatrix}$$

(4)

$$\underline{\hat{y}} = \underline{X}\,\underline{Q}\,\underline{\hat{w}}$$

$$Q_i = \begin{bmatrix} \Phi_i(\underline{u}(1)) & 0 & \cdots & 0 \\ 0 & \Phi_i(\underline{u}(2)) & \cdots & 0 \\ \vdots & \vdots & \cdots & \vdots \\ 0 & 0 & \cdots & \Phi_i(\underline{u}(N)) \end{bmatrix} \tag{5}$$

$$\hat{w} = (X^T Q X)^{-1} X^T Q y \tag{6}$$

Tree based methods are appropriate because of their simplicity and intuitive constructive algorithm. LOLIMOT is an incremental based on three iterative steps: first the worst Local Linear Model is defined according to local loss functions. This LLM neuron is selected to be divided. In the second step all divisions of this LLM on input space are constructed and checked. Finally the best division for the new neuron must be added. For further information about LOLIMOT algorithm refer to [5].

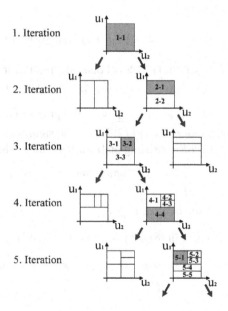

Fig. 2. Operation of the LOLIMOT in the first five iterations for a two dimensional input space [5]

In Fig. 2 the first five iterations of LOLIMOT algorithm for a two dimensional input space is shown. The computation complexity of LOLIMOT grows linearly with number of neurons. This computation complexity is comparable with other algorithms. The remarkable properties of locally linear neuro-fuzzy model, its transparency and intuitive construction, lead to the use of Least Squares for rule antecedent parameters and incremental learning procedures for rule consequent parameters.

3   Interval Type-2 Fuzzy Logic System

An Interval Type-2 fuzzy set can represent and handle uncertain information effectively. That is, interval Type-2 fuzzy sets let us model and minimize the effects of uncertainties in rule-base interval Type-2 fuzzy logic systems (IT2FLS). A general interval Type-2 fuzzy logic system is depicted in Fig. 3. An IT2FLS is very similar to a type-1 fuzzy logic systems (FLS) [6] the major structural difference being that the defuzzifier block of type-1 FLS is replaced by the output processing block in an interval Type-2 FLS, which consists of type-reduction followed by defuzzification.

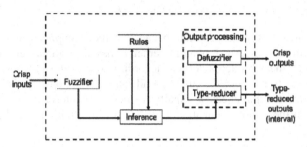

Fig. 3. General Type-2 fuzzy logic system [6]

In Interval Type-2 fuzzy set, an IT2 FS is bounded from the above and below by two T1 FSs, $\overline{A}$ and $\underline{A}$, which are called *upper MF* (UMF) and *lower MF* (LMF), respectively. The area between $\overline{A}$ and $\underline{A}$ is the footprint of uncertainty (FOU) [6].

In practice the computations in an IT2FLS can be significantly simplified. Consider the rule base of an IT2FLS consisting of *M* rules assuming the following form:

$$R^{m} : \ IF \ x_1 \ is \ \tilde{A}_1^{m} \ and \dots and \ x_I \ is \ \tilde{A}_p^{m} \tag{7}$$
$$m = 1, 2, \dots, M$$

Assume the input vector is $x' = (x_1', x_2', \dots, x_p')$. So we can compute the membership of x_i' on each A_i^m. In (8) the firing interval of mth rule, $F^m(x')$ is Computed.

$$F^m(x') = [\mu_{\underline{A}_1^m}(x_1') \times .. \times \mu_{\underline{A}_p^m}(x_p'), \ \mu_{\overline{A}_1^m}(x_1') \times .. \times \mu_{\overline{A}_1^m}(x_p')] \tag{8}$$
$$m = 1, 2, \dots, M$$

4   Proposed Method

In this section, we explained our proposed interval Type-2 fuzzy neural network which is 3 layer network based on local linear neuro-fuzzy. The operation of the each layer is described as follows.

Layer 1: As realized from Fig. 4. this layer is the input layer of the network. Each input has *p* dimensions with crisp value entered to layer 2. According to this, each of *N* input to network represents as follow:

$$u(i) = [1 \quad u_1(i) \quad \dots \quad u_p(i)] \quad i = 1, 2, \dots, N \tag{9}$$

Layer 2: This layer contains M neuron which are the main parts of the network. Each neuron consists of a LLM, and a validity function Φ which are the output of each rule. So each neuron has two output, O^{2-1} is output of its rule and O^{2-2} which is output of LLM.

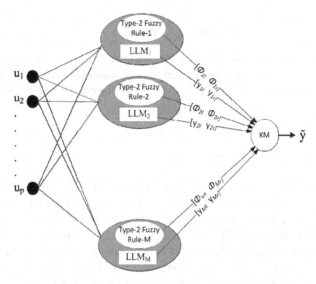

Fig. 4. Interval Type-2 locally linear neuro-fuzzy model

To make each rule interval, each dimension of the rule should become interval. To do this, we change all p MFs of the rule according to (10) which $i=1, \dots, M$.

$$\begin{cases} if & MF_i - \alpha < 0 & [0 \quad MF_i + \alpha] \\ if & MF_i + \alpha > 1 & [MF_i - \alpha \quad 1] \\ else & [MF_i - \alpha \quad MF_i + \alpha] \end{cases} \tag{10}$$

Where α is a value in range (0 1).
After that we can calculate the firing power of each rule:

$$[\mu_{il} \quad \mu_{ir}] = \prod_{j=1}^{p} [MF_{jl} \quad MF_{jr}] \tag{11}$$

As the rules are interval and defined by UMF and LMF, The validity function for any input $u(i)$ is interval which is shown by Φ_{il} and Φ_{ir}. These validity functions are Gaussian and normalized for vector input u as formulated in (12).

$$\Phi_{il}(\underline{u}) = \frac{\mu_{il}(\underline{u})}{\sum_{j=1}^{M} \mu_{jl}(\underline{u})}$$

$$\Phi_{ir}(\underline{u}) = \frac{\mu_{ir}(\underline{u})}{\sum_{j=1}^{M} \mu_{jr}(\underline{u})} \qquad (12)$$

$$O^{2-1} = [\Phi_{il}(\underline{u}) \quad \Phi_{ir}(\underline{u})]$$

Thus the weights which obtained by (6) are interval and we have w_{il} and w_{ir} for each rule. According to the calculated weights, the output of each LLM is interval as shown in Fig. 4. The output y_i of each neuron should be computed by (13).

$$\hat{y}_{il} = w_{il0} + w_{il1}u_1 + \ldots + w_{ilp}u_p$$

$$\hat{y}_{ir} = w_{ir0} + w_{ir1}u_1 + \ldots + w_{irp}u_p \qquad (13)$$

$$O^{2-2} = [\hat{y}_{il} \quad \hat{y}_{ir}]$$

Layer 3: The output sets of the LLM and validity functions are Type-2 fuzzy sets. To obtain embedded type-1 fuzzy sets for each neuron, a type-reduced method, centroid type reduction, is used in type-reducer. The efficient algorithm, called the Karnik-Mendel (KM) algorithm [7], has been developed for centroid type reduction.

KM Algorithm get validity functions (Φ_{il} and Φ_{ir}) and output of LLMs (y_{il} and y_{ir}) as input. In this way, it reduce type of output to type-1 fuzzy and calculate output of the Type-2 LLNFM simultaneously. The output of the network is:

$$O^3 = \tilde{y} = KM(y_l, \ y_r, \ \Phi_l, \ \Phi_r) \qquad (14)$$

4.1   Structure Learning

There are no general guidelines that can be applied to specify the optimal number of fuzzy rules and its corresponding initial values for the FNN. In this study, we propose a Type-2 LOLIMOT method which consists of incremental learning procedures, linear regression, and fuzzy rule extraction to solve this problem. The flowchart of the structure identification for The Type-2 fuzzy static local linear neuro-fuzzy and the process is depicted in Fig. 5.

LOLIMOT convert the worst rule of the existing rules to 2 rules via dividing it in a dimension which is caused that rule worst. Changing LOLIMOT method working to Type-2 fuzzy, we change all membership functions of rules to interval Type-2 fuzzy which intervals have the equal size. Therefore, we have Type-2 fuzzy rules and in each iteration.

The interval Type-2 local linear neuro-fuzzy has a network structure as shown in Fig. 4. The brief description of the functionality and the operation of the whole neural networks is as follows:

The input data enter to fuzzification layer which contains neuron realizes a LLM and M interval rules with an associated validity function that determines the region of validity of the LLM.

To change LOLIMOT to Type-2, Adding new rules with LOLIMOT and learning of the Adding new rules with LOLIMOT and learning of the 2 fuzzy, construct the validity functions for the beginning input space. Set M = 1 and start with one LLM, which covers the whole input space with the interval uncertainty. Then, find the worst Type-2 fuzzy rule with calculating the loss function for each of the local linear models (LLM). A local loss function is used, with a squared output error:

$$LF_i = \sum_{j=1}^{N} e^2(j) * (\Phi_{il} + \Phi_{ir}) * (\underline{u}(j)) \tag{15}$$

The worst LLM is $max_i(LF_i)$ where $i = 1, \dots M$.

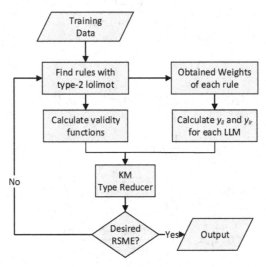

Fig. 5. Structure identification for learning interval Type-2 locally linear neuro-fuzzy model

After finding the worst LLM, check all half division in every p dimension. To select the best division and relocation of two new rules with the worst rule, we should calculate validity functions of each rules obtained by division.

The best among p alternatives is chosen based on generating minimum mean square error (mse) of the network output, because our target is to achieve desired mse with minimum number of rules. Then, the validity functions will be added to the model and the number of LLM is incremented to M + 1. Adding new rules by LOLIMOT and learning of the local linear neuro-fuzzy is continued until the mse is reached to the desired mse or don't change in several iterations.

5   Experiments and Results

We have conducted 6 experiments using 6 non-linear functions, in order to test the proposed method. These functions are described as below in equations (16) to (21).

$$f_1(x) = 3x(x-1)(x-1.9)(x-0.7)(x+1.8) \tag{16}$$

$$f_2(x) = 10[\sin(4x+0.1) + \sin(14x) \\ + \sin(10x+0.2) + \sin(17x+0.3)] \tag{17}$$

$$f_3(x) = 5\tan^{-1} \left(\frac{\begin{array}{c} 2000(x-0.1)(x-0.3)(x-0.5) \\ \times (x-0.9)(x-1.1)(x+0.2) \\ \times (x+0.4)(x+0.6)(x+0.8)(x+1) \end{array}}{x^2 + 1.5x + 1} \right) \tag{18}$$

$$f_4(x_1,x_2) = 3x_1(x_1-1)(x_1-1.9)(x_1-0.7) \\ \times (x_1 + 1.8)\sin(x_2) \tag{19}$$

$$f_5(x_1,x_2) = \frac{1}{10} f_2(x_1) \\ \times \left(10e^{-\left(\frac{x-0.1}{0.25}\right)^2} - 8e^{-\left(\frac{x+0.75}{0.15}\right)^2} - 4e^{-\left(\frac{x-0.8}{0.1}\right)^2} \right) \tag{20}$$

$$f_6(x_1,x_2) = 10\frac{\sin(10x_1^2 + 5x_2^2 - 6x_2)}{10x_1^2 + 5x_2^2 - 6x_2} \tag{21}$$

The uncorrupted training dataset consist of randomly of 300 generated instances, with corresponding inputs and output of f1 to f6. Also a set of 100 uncorrupted instances, generated in the same way, has been used as testing dataset. A corrupted training instance is composed of the same output as the corresponding uncorrupted one but with the input corrupted by adding a random value from a normal distribution with zero mean and standard deviation σ=0.1. In these experiments, three corrupted dataset are used, in which 10%, 20% and 30% of the instances are randomly corrupted. Samples of the test functions are shown in Fig. 6.

In all of the experiments, for fair comparison between methods, the same number of rules are used in simulations. Methods, which are used in respective experiments are LLNFM based on LOLIMOT (T1LL), Type 2 Interval LLNFM based on LOLIMOT (IT2LL) and TSK Fuzzy Neural Network (T1FNN) [8].

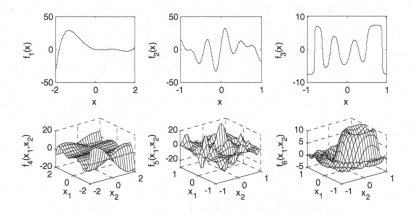

Fig. 6. Samples of the test functions.

Table 1. Experiment Results for f_1, f_2, f_3, f_4, f_5 and f_6

| | uncorrupted data | | | | | | | | | | |
| | f1 | | f2 | | f3 | | f4 | | f5 | | f6 | |
	tr	te	tr	te	tr	te	tr	te	tr	te	tr	te
IT2LL	0.0019	0.0018	0.0032	0.0032	0.0089	0.0088	0.0253	0.0258	0.0685	0.0613	0.0292	0.0275
T1LL	0.0043	0.0046	0.0071	0.0070	0.0114	0.0118	0.0647	0.0662	0.1127	0.1019	0.0795	0.0773
T1FNN	0.0014	0.0014	0.0028	0.0030	0.0070	0.0066	0.0283	0.0299	0.0634	0.0690	0.0332	0.0376
	10% corrupted data										
	f1		f2		f3		f4		f5		f6	
	tr	te	tr	te	tr	te	tr	te	tr	te	tr	te
IT2LL	0.0741	0.0204	0.1225	0.0370	0.3507	0.1023	0.0438	0.0273	0.1128	0.0652	0.0496	0.0287
T1LL	0.0825	0.0311	0.1379	0.0454	0.2206	0.0808	0.0943	0.0768	0.1678	0.1213	0.1210	0.0870
T1FNN	0.0799	0.0234	0.1675	0.0526	0.4042	0.1092	0.0513	0.0414	0.1100	0.0994	0.0574	0.0507
	20% corrupted data										
	f1		f2		f3		f4		f5		f6	
	tr	te	tr	te	tr	te	tr	te	tr	te	tr	te
IT2LL	0.1066	0.0412	0.1843	0.0767	0.5034	0.1925	0.0569	0.0281	0.1581	0.0635	0.0669	0.0297
T1LL	0.1431	0.0891	0.2245	0.1361	0.3773	0.2307	0.1134	0.0813	0.1924	0.1250	0.1430	0.0972
T1FNN	0.1092	0.0584	0.2211	0.1265	0.5477	0.2873	0.0626	0.0571	0.1342	0.1320	0.0746	0.0737
	30% corrupted data										
	f1		f2		f3		f4		f5		f6	
	tr	te	tr	te	tr	te	tr	te	tr	te	tr	te
IT2LL	0.1158	0.0530	0.2007	0.0906	0.5575	0.2640	0.0702	0.0292	0.1840	0.0684	0.0790	0.0313
T1LL	0.1982	0.1519	0.3170	0.2346	0.5065	0.3796	0.1287	0.1001	0.2139	0.1539	0.1605	0.1112
T1FNN	0.1139	0.0983	0.2242	0.2190	0.5907	0.4856	0.0809	0.0685	0.1806	0.1534	0.0902	0.0838

The results are shown in Table 1 and Table 2, where the training and testing error (abbreviated with "tr" and "te", respectively) are root mean square error (RSME).

As it can be seen in Table 1 and Table 2, IT2LL estimates are better than T1LL and also are comparable with T1FNN results. For corrupted data with progressively increased corruption, IT2LL is more robust to input space outliers. The results show that the outliers outperform T1LL and T1FNN estimates. It seems that T1LL cannot handle the noise and T1FNN may overfit the training data.

On the other hand there is a comparison between refining times of these three methods. As it shown in Fig. 7, T1LL's refining time for each function, is less than other methods. The refining time for IT2LL and T1FNN is not very different.

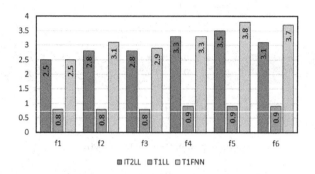

Fig. 7. Refining time for each function in three methods

6   Conclusion

A new interval Type-2 fuzzy neural network for function approximation has been introduced in this paper. The proposed neural network was a combination of Locally Linear Neuro-Fuzzy Model and Interval Type-2 Fuzzy Logic System. The learning algorithm, which has been modified to use in proposed method, was Locally Linear Model Tree which is one of the fast learning algorithm for LLNFM. Regarding the simulation results, it can be concluded that the proposed method is fast and also is robust in presence of outliers.

References

1. Karnik, N.N., Mendel, J.M., Liang, Q.: Type-2 Fuzzy Logic Systems. IEEE Trans. on Fuzzy Systems 7(6), 643–658 (1999)
2. Zadeh, L.A.: Fuzzy Sets. Information and Control 8, 338–353 (1965)
3. Wu, D., Mendel, J.M.: Uncertainty Measures for Interval Type-2 Fuzzy Sets. Information Sciences 77(23), 5378–5393 (2007)
4. Mendel, J.M.: Type-2 Fuzzy Sets and Sytems: An Overview. Computational Intelligence Magazine 2(1), 20–29 (2007)
5. Nelles, O.: Local Linear Model Tree for On-line Identification of Time Variant Nonlinear Dynamic Systems. In: International Conference on Artificial Neural Networks (ICANN), pp. 115–120 (1996)
6. Liang, Q., Mendel, J.M.: Interval Type-2 Fuzzy Logic Systems: Theory and Design. IEEE Transactions on Fuzzy Systems 8, 535–550 (2000)
7. Karnik, N.N., Mendel, J.M.: Centroid of a Type-2 Fuzzy Set. Information Sciences 132(1-4), 195–220 (2001)
8. Takagi, T., Sugeno, M.: Fuzzy identification of systems and its applications to model-ing and control. IEEE Trans. Systems, Man, Cybernetics SMC 15(1), 116–132 (1985)

Evolutionary Algorithms and Their Applications

Hybrids of Two-Subpopulation PSO Algorithm with Local Search Methods for Continuous Optimization

Aneta Bera[✉] and Dariusz Sychel

Faculty of Computer Science and Information Technology, West Pomeranian University of Technology, Żołnierska 49, 71-210 Szczecin, Poland
{abera,dsychel}@wi.zut.edu.pl

Abstract. The paper studies the problem of continuous function optimization. Proposed are twelve hybrids of known methods such as Particle Swarm Optimization (also in a two-subpopulation version), quasi-Newton method and Nelder-Mead method. Described modifications are introduced in order to improve performance and increase the accuracy of known methods. Algorithms are tested against eight benchmark functions and compared with classical versions of: Particle Swarm Optimization algorithm, Newton's, quasi-Newton and Nelder-Mead methods. Presented results allow to indicate two methods that perform satisfactorily in most cases.

Keywords: Optimization · Particle swarm optimization · Quasi-Newton method · Simplex algorithm · Hybrid algorithms

1 Introduction

1.1 A Survey of Continuous Function Optimization Approaches

One of the commonly used optimization algorithms is Particle Swarm Optimization (PSO), originally proposed in 1995 by Kennedy and Eberhart [4]. In this algorithm, we deal with a set of particles that form a swarm. The swarm keeps information about velocities, positions and best positions (found so far) of its particles. Therefore, known is also the best position discovered by the whole swarm. The particles move around the search space looking for the most favorable positions (global minimum / maximum). Their movement is affected by two factors:

- φ_p — cognitive scaling — this factor has an impact on the individual behavior of each particle; if it is greater than the social scaling parameter, the solution found by the swarm will not be as important as its own solution;
- φ_g — social scaling— when it is greater than the cognitive scaling parameter, the particle will rather follow the swarm.

The velocity of a particle can be calculated as:

$$v_{i+1,j} = \omega v_{i,j} + \varphi_p r_p (p_{\text{best},j} - x_{i,j}) + \varphi_g r_g (g_{\text{best}} - x_{i,j}),$$

© Springer International Publishing Switzerland 2015
L. Rutkowski et al. (Eds.): ICAISC 2015, Part I, LNAI 9119, pp. 307–318, 2015.
DOI: 10.1007/978-3-319-19324-3_28

where: i is the iteration number, j is the particle index, $p_{\text{best},j}$ is the best known position of j-th particle, g_{best} is the best known position of the swarm, ω is an inertia weight, r_p, r_g are random numbers drawn from the uniform distribution over $(0, 1)$.

Then, the particle position in updated as:

$$x_{i+1,j} = x_{i,j} + v_{i+1,j}.$$

Methods of determining parameter values — cognitive scaling, social scaling and inertia weight — were the main focus of many papers. In 1998 Shi and Eberhart showed the influence of inertia weight on the algorithm's runtime [10]. They concluded that for $\omega \approx 0.8$ swarms find the solution in the smallest number of iterations. The values of the cognitive and social scaling parameters have significant influence on the algorithm's convergence time. Shi and Eberhart in 1999 proposed the values of these parameters to be around 2 [9]. The main disadvantage of PSO algorithm is that when high accuracy is required the algorithm needs a large number of iterations to find the solution.

Newton's method is an iterative optimization algorithm searching for minima of multivariate functions [7]. To apply this method, the function must be continuous up to the second derivative and convex. This method updates the previous coordinates with following formula: $x_{k+1} = x_k - \nabla^2 f_k^{-1} \nabla f_k$, where $\nabla^2 f_k$ is a Hessian and ∇f_k is a gradient. To avoid calculations of Hessian it is possible to apply the quasi-Newton method. In this approach approximation of Hessian is calculated. Newton's and Quasi-Newton methods will always find the "closest" local minimum.

In 1965 Nelder and Mead presented a method for multivariate function optimization based on the motion of simplex (known in literature as Nelder–Mead method) [6]. The proposed approach consists in comparing function values at $n + 1$ vertices of a simplex, when the search space is n-dimensional. The vertex with the highest (worst) value is replaced by a different point, forming a new simplex. For that, three operations are used: reflection, contraction and expansion. The process is repeated until convergence. This method tends to stuck in local minima.

In 2006 Coelho and Mariani presented a hybrid method that combines PSO algorithm with quasi-Newton method [8]. In their approach, PSO is applied to find an initial candidate for a global optimum. Then, the candidate is used as a starting position for quasi-Newton method.

In 2009 Thomas and Reed proposed new hybrid methods which combined the advantages of PSO and quasi-Newton method [11]. The main goal of the authors was to create a hybrid that will find the global minimum within a reasonable time. The authors have considered three criteria for switching between algorithms: (1) diversity of the swarm (introduced by Ali and Kaelo in [2]); (2) no change in the discovered solution; (3) limit on the number of iterations. The authors also proposed to implement a repulse technique and to collect information provided by successive quasi-Newton iterations. The collected information is used when creating a new swarm. Finally, five modifications were presented:

- Hybrid 1 — The collected information is used to define positions and velocities for all new particles;
- Hybrid 2 — The collected information is used only to define positions for all new particles, velocities are random;
- Hybrid 3 — The collected information is used to define positions and velocities for a subset of new particles;
- Hybrid 4 — The collected information is used only to define positions for a subset of new particles, velocities are random;
- Hybrid 5 — Positions and velocities of new particles are random; this version looks as if it does not use the information from the gradient method.

The results reported in [11] seem to be very promising, especially first hybrid for Rastrigin function of five variables which had the 100% efficiency. However it needed over 2000 PSO generations.

1.2   Motivation

Methods described in this paper are modifications and combinations of the methods cited above. Our motivation was to create hybrids that will be more accurate than in [8] without a significant increase in execution time. One of the methods implemented in this paper (PSO_Quasi_mod_1) is a slight modification of the approach from [8] or Hybrid 5 from [11]. In order to reduce the execution time, the repulse technique used in [11] was omitted. Furthermore, two switching criteria were used: swarm concentration and limit on the number of iterations. These modifications were used in hybrids of two-subpopulation PSO [12] with local search method.

2   Proposed Modifications

We propose hybrid methods based on the following two combinations: either the two-subpopulation PSO [12] and the quasi-Newton method [7] or the two-subpopulation PSO [12] and the simplex [6] method. We have combined these two algorithms in the hope to speed up the calculations and to improve the performance.

The first method is based on the hybrid presented by Thomas and Reed in 2009 in [11]. The method was adapted and implemented according to Algorithm 1 (further referred to as **PSO_Quasi_mod_1**).

The second of proposed modifications is based on a two-subpopulation PSO first proposed in 2012 by Zhe-ping et al. [12]. This modification uses two swarms which share the best global location — g_{best}. The first swarm's behavior is geared more towards for particles individuality. Its task is to explore i.e. to search the function surface to detect potentially interesting areas for further exploitation. Particles in the second swarm tend to congregate. The purpose of this swarm is to examine the area around some discovered location. When one of the subpopulations concentrates, it is restarted. If the second swarm is the one which was restarted, quasi-Newton method is started to correct the accuracy of the solution. The swarm concentration is assessed by the average Euclidean distance from all particles to the best position. The proposed modification (further referred to as **PSO_Quasi_mod_2**) is represented by the Algorithm 2.

Algorithm 1. Hybrid of PSO and a local search method

Create new swarm s
for $t = 1, 2, \ldots, T$ **do**
    Perform a single step of PSO with s
    if s is concentrated **then**
        Start a local search with the starting position as g_{best} from s
        Memorize the best coordinates and value
        Create a new swarm s
Choose the minimal value from the found ones

Algorithm 2. Hybrid of two-subpopulation PSO and a local search method

---

Create two swarms s_1, s_2
for $t = 1, 2, \ldots, T$ **do**
    Search for minimum with both s_1 and s_2
    if s_2 is concentrated **then**
        Start a local search method with the starting position as g_{best} from s_1 and s_2
        Memorize the best coordinates and value
        Create a new swarm s_2
    if s_1 is concentrated **then**
        Create a new swarm s_1
Choose the minimal value from the found ones

The third modification (further referred to as **PSO_Quasi_mod_3**) is similar to the one presented above. The only difference is the moment when the best position g_{best} is updated. This change takes place after each particle movement. In the former version, g_{best} is updated after all particles have moved.

The fourth modification (further referred to as **PSO_Quasi_mod_4**) is an extension of the first. In this version we added a constriction factor $\chi \in (0, 1)$ in the velocity equation presented by Eberhart and Shi in 2000 [3]: $v_{i+1,j} = \chi(\omega v_{i,j} + \varphi_p r_p(p_{\text{best},j} - x_{i,j}) + \varphi_g r_g(g_{\text{best}} - x_{i,j}))$. The purpose of the constriction factor is to reduce oscillations near the optimum and to improve accuracy.

The fifth modification (further referred to as **PSO_Quasi_mod_5**) is also an extension of the first approach. In this version a simpler mechanism of limiting speed was proposed — when the velocity exceeds some predefined maximum threshold it is cut. Thanks to that solution the space is searched through more densely. When this threshold is set to a small value, a large number of iterations is needed to concentrate the swarm.

The sixth modification (further referred to as **PSO_Quasi_mod_6**) assumes the independence of both swarms. Each swarm has its own g_{best}. Findings of first swarm have no influence on the second one and vice versa. When one of the swarms concentrates, quasi-Newton method is launched with value found by this swarm. Then the said swarm is restarted and the founded position of minimum is memorized.

The paper proposes also six hybrids: **PSO_Simplex_mod_1**, ..., **PSO_Simplex_mod_6**. They are counterparts of the aforementioned hybrids with quasi-Newton method replaced by Nelder-Mead method.

3   Benchmark Functions

We focus on eight known test functions from [1]. Problems in finding the global minimum are caused by function's multimodality or by their shape (large flat areas and canyons). Table 1 presents the chosen functions and the *overall success rate* (reported in [1]), which means what fraction of all algorithms registered in the website succeeded in finding the minimum.

Table 1. Benchmark chosen test functions „hardness" [1]

Function	Type	Overall Success rate [%]
Ackley	uni-modal	48.25
Easom	uni-modal	26.08
Griewank	multi-modal	6.08
Langermann	multi-modal	45.67
Michalewicz	multi-modal	81.25
Schwefel	multi-modal	62.67
SineEnvelope	multi-modal	2.17
Xin-She Yang	multi-modal	1.08

Ackley is a multivariate function that has many local minima that are located around the global minimum, which is its biggest difficulty. For Easom the minimum is surrounded by a large flat area that can be a problem especially for gradient based algorithms. Grienwank has many local minima placed evenly over the entire space, and the challange is to find the correct one. Langermann function has many local minima placed unevenly — similarly as Schwefel function. Next two functions (Michalewicz and SinEnvelope) have canyons which may be a reason for not reaching the global minimum. Xin-She Yang is the last function that has characteristic steep ridges.

Figure 1 presents the chosen benchmark functions. In our tests we use variants with two variables.

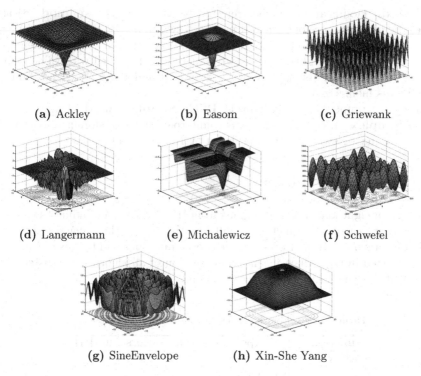

(a) Ackley   (b) Easom   (c) Griewank

(d) Langermann   (e) Michalewicz   (f) Schwefel

(g) SineEnvelope   (h) Xin-She Yang

Fig. 1. Chosen benchmark functions

4 Tests

In every single test the random generator was initialized with the same seed. An algorithm was considered to be successful when the following accuracy goal was met: $|F_{\min} - F(g_{\text{best}})| \leq 10^{-6}$, where $F_{\min}$ is the is the global minimum value of a particular function and $F(g_{\text{best}})$ is the final solution found by a hybrid. This condition was presented in [1]. For all functions 50 repetitions were performed to determine the overall *success rate* of an algorithm, which we report in the subsequent tables. Within a repetition the maximum number of iterations for the PSO algorithm was set to $T = 100$. Swarms in all versions had similar parameters. For Classic_PSO, PSO_Quasi_mod_1 and PSO_Simplex_mod_1 φ_g was set to 2.4, φ_p was 2.0 and ω was 0.85. In other methods which use two populations s_1 and s_2 the parameters were set as: $\varphi_g = 2.0$, $\varphi_p = 2.4$, $\omega = 0.85$ for s_1 and $\varphi_g = 2.4$, $\varphi_p = 2.0$, $\omega = 0.25$ for s_2, as in [9,10]. Velocities limits and the swarm concentration were selected based on search area size and functions shapes. Research was conducted in MATLAB 2012b on notebook with Intel i5-480M processor, 8GB memory and Windows 8.1. Detailed results are provided in Tables 2, 3, 4 and 5.

For the Ackley function modifications 2, 3 and 6 proved to be the most efficient, what can be seen in Table 2. In addition, the use of the Simplex method after switching, proved to be favorable when it comes to the quality of the solution.

Table 2. Test results for Ackley function

	Version	Particles count: 40 or 20 + 20		Particles count: 100 or 50 + 50	
		Success rate [%]	Aver. Time [s]	Success rate [%]	Aver. Time [s]
	Ackley, domain: $[-30, 30]^2$, *velocity limit:* 50, *swarm concentration:* 1				
1	Classical_PSO	0	0.3368	0	0.8603
2	Newton	0	0.0345	0	0.0343
3	Quasi-Newton	0	0.0128	0	0.0120
4	Simplex	0	0.0082	0	0.0084
5	PSO + quasi-Newton [8]	28	0.4100	14	0.9460
6	PSO_Quasi_mod_1	18	0.4273	24	0.9552
7	PSO_Quasi_mod_2	100	0.4515	100	0.9693
8	PSO_Quasi_mod_3	100	0.4519	100	0.9931
9	PSO_Quasi_mod_4	74	1.3405	82	1.6244
10	PSO_Quasi_mod_5	100	0.5028	100	1.0546
11	PSO_Quasi_mod_6	100	0.5760	100	0.9991
12	PSO_Simplex_mod_1	100	0.4286	100	0.9713
13	PSO_Simplex_mod_2	98	0.6449	94	1.1319
14	PSO_Simplex_mod_3	94	0.6379	96	1.1606
15	PSO_Simplex_mod_4	100	1.9014	100	2.6239
16	PSO_Simplex_mod_5	90	0.6921	96	1.2242
17	PSO_Simplex_mod_6	100	0.7177	100	1.2084

Results for the Easom, Griewank and Langerman functions are presented in Table 3. For Easom function Simplex method gave similar results as quasi-Newton but was slower. Furthermore modifications from 2 to 6 achieved similar quality. For the Griewank function the modification that is the most successful is 4 which outperformed other hybrids. Simplex method achieves slightly better results. Tests results for the Langermann function demonstrate that regardless of the local search method modification 2 achieves the best results.

Results for the Michalewicz, Schwefel and Sine Envelope functions are presented in Table 4. For Michalewicz function it may be noted that all modifications have similar quality, but for a given parameters the algorithms which use quasi-Newton method are faster. With the given swarm parameters the best method for the Schwefel function was modification 1 for smaller swarm and 3 for bigger swarm. For the Sine Envelope function the best modification was 4.

From the results for the Xin-She Yang function in Table 5 it can be inferred that modifications 2 and 3 are most efficient.

Due to limited space only two examples of optimization for higher dimensionality could be presented. Table 6 presents the test results for Ackley and Schwefel functions of three variables. It can be inferred that modifications 3 and 5 are most efficient for smaller particles count, for bigger one it is the modification 2.

Table 3. Test results for Easom, Griewank and Langermann functions

	Version	Particles count: 40 or 20 + 20		Particles count: 100 or 50 + 50	
		Success rate [%]	Aver. Time [s]	Success rate [%]	Aver. Time [s]
	Easom, domain: $[-100, 100]^2$, velocity limit: 50, swarm concentration: 1				
1	Classical_PSO	0	0.3218	0	0.8093
2	Newton	0	0.0702	0	0.0692
3	Quasi-Newton	0	0.0034	0	0.0034
4	Simplex	0	0.0077	0	0.0077
5	PSO + quasi-Newton [8]	100	0.3291	100	0.8202
6	PSO_Quasi_mod_1	98	0.3474	100	0.8413
7	PSO_Quasi_mod_2	100	0.3497	100	0.8457
8	PSO_Quasi_mod_3	100	0.3587	100	0.8649
9	PSO_Quasi_mod_4	100	0.4229	100	1.0050
10	PSO_Quasi_mod_5	100	0.3918	100	0.9331
11	PSO_Quasi_mod_6	100	0.3639	100	0.8644
12	PSO_Simplex_mod_1	98	0.4054	100	0.9199
13	PSO_Simplex_mod_2	100	0.4404	100	0.9108
14	PSO_Simplex_mod_3	100	0.4416	100	0.9383
15	PSO_Simplex_mod_4	100	0.6196	100	1.1876
16	PSO_Simplex_mod_5	100	0.4598	100	1.0172
17	PSO_Simplex_mod_6	100	0.5064	100	0.9918
	Griewank, domain: $[-600, 600]^2$, velocity limit: 300, swarm concentration: 5				
1	Classical_PSO	0	0.3167	0	0.8069
2	Newton	0	0.0282	0	0.0328
3	Quasi-Newton	0	0.0091	0	0.0093
4	Simplex	0	0.0074	0	0.0077
5	PSO + quasi-Newton [8]	2	0.3182	6	0.8183
6	PSO_Quasi_mod_1	2	0.3238	8	0.8213
7	PSO_Quasi_mod_2	24	0.3391	40	0.8370
8	PSO_Quasi_mod_3	32	0.3479	50	0.8454
9	PSO_Quasi_mod_4	32	0.4933	62	1.1224
10	PSO_Quasi_mod_5	20	0.3771	36	0.9184
11	PSO_Quasi_mod_6	28	0.3484	48	0.8461
12	PSO_Simplex_mod_1	6	0.3990	8	0.9087
13	PSO_Simplex_mod_2	26	0.3986	38	0.8832
14	PSO_Simplex_mod_3	32	0.4012	50	0.9042
15	PSO_Simplex_mod_4	40	1.0430	64	1.6665
16	PSO_Simplex_mod_5	18	0.4301	36	0.9803
17	PSO_Simplex_mod_6	30	0.4975	46	0.9441
	Langermann, domain: $[0, 10]^2$, velocity limit: 5, swarm concentration: 0.2				
1	Classical_PSO	0	0.3493	0	0.9100
2	Newton	2	0.0631	0	0.0757
3	Quasi-Newton	0	0.0121	0	0.0152
4	Simplex	0	0.0081	0	0.0090
5	PSO + quasi-Newton [8]	44	0.3687	74	0.7733
6	PSO_Quasi_mod_1	44	0.3880	74	0.7865
7	PSO_Quasi_mod_2	60	0.3631	80	0.8712
8	PSO_Quasi_mod_3	44	0.3752	78	0.8869
9	PSO_Quasi_mod_4	56	0.4179	76	1.0218
10	PSO_Quasi_mod_5	50	0.4032	86	0.9935
11	PSO_Quasi_mod_6	46	0.3869	78	0.8932
12	PSO_Simplex_mod_1	36	0.4190	46	0.9304
13	PSO_Simplex_mod_2	60	0.4601	80	0.9359
14	PSO_Simplex_mod_3	42	0.4491	78	0.9472
15	PSO_Simplex_mod_4	40	0.4696	54	1.0726
16	PSO_Simplex_mod_5	46	0.5067	84	1.0272
17	PSO_Simplex_mod_6	46	0.5405	74	1.0115

The near zero level of accuracy of the classical PSO algorithm for all tested functions was caused by the requirements i.e. limit on the number of iterations and required accuracy goal imposed on the running modifications.

Table 4. Test results for Michalewicz, Schwefel and SineEnvelope functions

		Particles count: 40 or 20 + 20		Particles count: 100 or 50 + 50	
	Version	Success rate [%]	Aver. Time [s]	Success rate [%]	Aver. Time [s]
	Michalewicz, domain: $[0, \pi]^2$, velocity limit: $\frac{\pi}{2}$, swarm concentration: 0.2				
1	Classical_PSO	0	0.3452	0	0.8567
2	Newton	10	0.0736	14	0.0738
3	Quasi-Newton	10	0.0117	14	0.0114
4	Simplex	10	0.0083	16	0.0085
5	PSO + quasi-Newton [8]	100	0.4346	100	0.9952
6	PSO_Quasi_mod_1	100	0.4428	100	1.0097
7	PSO_Quasi_mod_2	100	0.4507	100	1.0058
8	PSO_Quasi_mod_3	100	0.4598	100	1.0217
9	PSO_Quasi_mod_4	100	0.4353	100	1.0483
10	PSO_Quasi_mod_5	100	0.4739	100	1.1029
11	PSO_Quasi_mod_6	100	0.4499	100	1.0187
12	PSO_Simplex_mod_1	100	0.4490	100	0.9801
13	PSO_Simplex_mod_2	100	0.8919	100	1.4328
14	PSO_Simplex_mod_3	100	0.9086	100	1.4126
15	PSO_Simplex_mod_4	100	0.4981	100	1.1086
16	PSO_Simplex_mod_5	100	0.7491	100	1.3789
17	PSO_Simplex_mod_6	100	0.8331	100	1.4160
	Schwefel, domain: $[-500, 500]^2$, velocity limit: 250, swarm concentration: 5				
1	Classical_PSO	0	0.3546	0	0.8989
2	Newton	2	0.0568	4	0.0573
3	Quasi-Newton	8	0.0105	4	0.0103
4	Simplex	0	0.0082	0	0.0079
5	PSO + quasi-Newton [8]	72	0.3711	98	0.9062
6	PSO_Quasi_mod_1	90	0.3876	96	0.9124
7	PSO_Quasi_mod_2	82	0.3973	98	0.9235
8	PSO_Quasi_mod_3	90	0.3916	98	0.9267
9	PSO_Quasi_mod_4	78	0.4608	98	1.0726
10	PSO_Quasi_mod_5	70	0.4598	98	1.0043
11	PSO_Quasi_mod_6	88	0.4007	98	0.9164
12	PSO_Simplex_mod_1	90	0.4528	96	0.9660
13	PSO_Simplex_mod_2	76	0.4810	92	1.0081
14	PSO_Simplex_mod_3	80	0.4912	96	1.0244
15	PSO_Simplex_mod_4	70	0.7167	78	1.2841
16	PSO_Simplex_mod_5	70	0.5464	94	1.1373
17	PSO_Simplex_mod_6	38	0.5576	50	1.0918
	SineEnvelope, domain: $[-100, 100]^2$, velocity limit: 50, swarm concentration: 0.2				
1	Classical_PSO	0	0.3727	0	0.9529
2	Newton	2	0.0759	0	0.0738
3	Quasi-Newton	0	0.0080	0	0.0075
4	Simplex	0	0.0082	0	0.0080
5	PSO + quasi-Newton [8]	4	0.4374	4	0.8264
6	PSO_Quasi_mod_1	0	0.4451	6	0.8410
7	PSO_Quasi_mod_2	16	0.3611	50	0.8714
8	PSO_Quasi_mod_3	18	0.3638	44	0.9079
9	PSO_Quasi_mod_4	28	0.4023	66	0.9862
10	PSO_Quasi_mod_5	12	0.3894	36	0.9632
11	PSO_Quasi_mod_6	14	0.3912	48	1.0489
12	PSO_Simplex_mod_1	0	0.4489	6	0.9459
13	PSO_Simplex_mod_2	16	0.4363	50	0.9364
14	PSO_Simplex_mod_3	20	0.4349	44	0.9465
15	PSO_Simplex_mod_4	28	0.5370	66	1.0753
16	PSO_Simplex_mod_5	16	0.4613	38	1.0096
17	PSO_Simplex_mod_6	18	0.4951	50	0.9864

In order to verify the statistical relevance of proposed algorithmic modifications, Fisher's Exact Test was used [5][1], Table 7 presents results. Numbers in the first row and column represent modifications. The characters in a specific cell

---

[1] A single experiment is binary: 1 - success in finding the optimum, 0 - failure.

represent comparison results for eight two variables test functions. As a reference method PSO + quasi-Newton [8] was used, methods 1–4 were skipped.

Table 5. Test results for Xin-She Yang function

	Version	Particles count: 40 or 20 + 20		Particles count: 100 or 50 + 50	
		Success rate [%]	Aver. Time [s]	Success rate [%]	Aver. Time [s]
	Xin-She Yang, domain: $[-20, 20]^2$, *velocity limit:* 10, *swarm concentration:* 5				
1	Classical_PSO	0	0.3463	0	1.4392
2	Newton	2	0.0760	0	0.1411
3	Quasi-Newton	4	0.0162	0	0.0357
4	Simplex	0	0.0084	0	0.0148
5	PSO + quasi-Newton [8]	4	0.6356	8	1.6215
6	PSO_Quasi_mod_1	70	0.9035	98	1.7183
7	PSO_Quasi_mod_2	84	0.9285	100	1.3642
8	PSO_Quasi_mod_3	88	0.8812	100	1.4474
9	PSO_Quasi_mod_4	84	0.8443	96	1.5432
10	PSO_Quasi_mod_5	82	0.9545	100	1.5613
11	PSO_Quasi_mod_6	76	2.4807	98	2.6932
12	PSO_Simplex_mod_1	70	2.9485	94	2.1279
13	PSO_Simplex_mod_2	84	2.2649	98	1.9827
14	PSO_Simplex_mod_3	88	2.0782	100	1.9956
15	PSO_Simplex_mod_4	82	1.9207	94	2.0642
16	PSO_Simplex_mod_5	80	2.7427	98	2.0744
17	PSO_Simplex_mod_6	76	8.4259	96	6.7819

Table 6. Test results Ackley and Schwefel functions of three variables

	Version	Particles count: 40 or 20 + 20		Particles count: 100 or 50 + 50	
		Success rate [%]	Aver. Time [s]	Success rate [%]	Aver. Time [s]
	Ackley, domain: $[-30, 30]^3$, *velocity limit:* 15, *swarm concentration:* 1				
1	Classical_PSO	0	1.2635	0	3.2354
3	Quasi-Newton	0	0.0592	0	0.0572
5	PSO + quasi-Newton [8]	0	1.4795	2	3.5194
6	PSO_Quasi_mod_1	0	1.5772	2	3.3860
7	PSO_Quasi_mod_2	98	1.6241	100	3.8690
8	PSO_Quasi_mod_3	100	1.6441	100	3.7458
9	PSO_Quasi_mod_4	18	3.8084	16	6.2393
10	PSO_Quasi_mod_5	100	2.1060	100	4.0490
11	PSO_Quasi_mod_6	90	2.0603	100	4.4613
	Schwefel, domain: $[-500, 500]^3$, *velocity limit:* 250, *swarm concentration:* 10				
1	Classical_PSO	0	0.2946	0	0.8115
3	Quasi-Newton	2	0.0130	2	0.0142
5	PSO + quasi-Newton [8]	28	0.3826	70	0.8502
6	PSO_Quasi_mod_1	28	0.3434	70	0.8278
7	PSO_Quasi_mod_2	38	0.3495	74	0.8540
8	PSO_Quasi_mod_3	48	0.3777	68	0.8861
9	PSO_Quasi_mod_4	38	0.4288	56	1.0075
10	PSO_Quasi_mod_5	48	0.3943	64	0.9571
11	PSO_Quasi_mod_6	36	0.3675	62	0.8692

According to presented results, modifications 7 (PSO_Quasi_mod_2), 8 (PSO_Quasi_mod_3), 13 (PSO_Simplex_mod_2) and 14 (PSO_Simplex_-mod_3) give the best results — they were never significantly worse than other modifications.

Table 7. Fisher's Exact Test results, where: - means that differences are not statistically significant (p-value greater than 0.05), > means that modification in row is better than the one in column, < contrarily; last three columns contain results summary

	5	6	7	8	9	10	11	12	13	14	15	16	17	-	>	<
5	-,- / -,- / <,< / -,<	<,- / <,- / <,- / -,<	<,- / <,- / <,< / <,<	<,- / <,- / <,< / <,<	<,- / <,- / <,- / <,<	<,- / <,- / <,- / -,<	<,- / -,- / <,- / -,<	<,- / <,- / <,- / -,<	<,- / <,- / <,- / -,-	<,- / <,- / <,- / <,<	<,- / <,- / <,- / <,<	<,- / <,- / <,- / -,<	<,- / <,- / <,> / <,<	42	1	53
6	-,- / -,- / >,> / -,>	<,- / <,- / -,- / <,-	<,- / <,- / -,- / <,<	<,- / <,- / -,- / <,-	<,- / <,- / -,> / <,-	<,- / <,- / -,- / <,-	<,- / -,- / -,- / -,-	<,- / <,- / -,- / <,-	<,- / <,- / -,- / <,-	<,- / <,- / -,> / <,-	<,- / <,- / -,> / <,-	<,- / <,- / -,> / <,-	<,- / <,- / -,- / <,-	56	7	33
7	>,- / >,- / >,- / -,>	>,- / >,- / -,- / >,-		-,- / -,- / -,- / -,-	>,- / -,- / -,- / -,-	-,- / -,- / -,- / -,-	-,- / -,- / -,- / -,-	-,- / >,> / -,- / -,-	-,- / -,- / -,- / -,-	-,- / -,- / -,- / -,-	-,> / -,- / -,- / -,-	-,- / -,- / -,> / -,-	-,- / -,- / -,- / -,-	83	13	0
8	>,- / >,- / >,> / >,>	>,- / >,- / -,- / >,>	-,- / -,- / -,- / -,-		>,- / -,- / -,> / -,-	-,- / -,- / -,- / -,-	-,- / -,- / -,- / -,-	-,- / >,- / -,- / >,>	-,- / -,- / -,- / -,-	-,- / -,- / -,- / -,-	-,- / -,> / -,> / -,-	-,- / -,> / -,> / -,-	-,- / -,> / -,> / -,-	78	18	0
9	>,- / >,- / >,- / >,>	>,- / >,- / -,- / >,-	<,- / -,- / -,- / -,-	<,- / -,- / -,- / -,-		<,- / -,- / -,- / -,-	<,- / -,- / -,- / -,-	<,- / >,> / >,> / -,-	<,- / -,- / -,- / -,-	<,- / -,- / -,- / -,-	<,- / -,- / -,- / -,>	<,- / -,- / -,- / -,>	<,- / -,- / -,> / -,>	74	12	10
10	>,- / >,- / >,- / -,>	>,- / >,- / -,< / >,-	-,- / -,- / -,- / -,-	-,- / -,- / -,< / -,-	>,- / -,- / -,- / -,-		-,- / -,- / -,< / -,-	-,- / -,- / -,< / >,-	-,- / -,- / -,- / -,-	-,- / -,- / -,- / -,-	<,- / -,- / -,- / -,-	-,- / -,- / -,> / -,-	-,- / -,- / -,> / -,-	81	10	5
11	>,- / >,- / >,- / -,>	>,- / >,- / -,- / >,-	-,- / -,- / -,- / -,-	-,- / -,- / -,- / -,-	>,- / -,- / -,- / -,-	-,- / -,- / -,> / -,-		>,- / -,- / -,- / >,-	-,- / -,- / -,- / -,-	-,- / -,- / -,- / -,-	-,- / -,> / -,> / -,-	-,- / -,> / -,> / -,-	-,- / -,- / -,- / -,-	82	14	0
12	>,- / -,- / >,> / -,>	>,- / -,- / -,- / -,-	<,< / <,- / -,- / <,-	<,- / -,- / -,- / <,<	<,< / -,- / -,> / <,-	-,- / -,- / -,< / <,-	<,- / <,- / -,- / <,-		<,< / -,- / -,- / <,-	<,- / -,- / -,- / <,<	<,- / -,> / -,> / <,-	-,- / >,> / >,> / <,-	<,- / -,> / -,> / <,-	63	10	23
13	>,- / >,- / >,- / -,>	>,- / >,- / -,- / >,-	-,- / -,- / -,- / -,-	-,- / -,- / -,- / -,-	>,- / -,- / -,- / -,-	-,- / -,- / -,- / -,-	-,- / -,- / -,- / -,-	>,> / -,- / -,- / >,-		-,- / -,- / -,- / -,-	-,- / -,> / -,> / -,-	-,- / -,- / -,> / -,-	-,- / -,- / -,- / -,-	83	13	0
14	>,- / >,- / >,- / >,>	>,- / >,- / -,- / >,>	-,- / -,- / -,- / -,-	-,- / -,- / -,- / -,-	>,- / -,- / -,- / -,-	-,- / -,- / -,- / -,-	-,- / -,- / -,- / -,-	-,- / >,- / >,> / >,>	-,- / -,- / -,- / -,-		-,- / -,- / -,- / -,-	-,- / -,- / -,> / -,-	-,- / -,- / -,- / -,-	82	14	0
15	>,- / >,- / >,- / >,>	>,- / >,- / -,< / >,-	-,< / -,- / -,- / -,-	-,- / -,< / -,< / -,-	>,- / -,- / -,- / -,-	-,- / -,- / -,- / -,-	>,- / -,- / -,< / >,-	>,- / >,- / -,< / >,-	-,< / -,< / -,- / -,-	-,- / -,- / -,- / -,-		>,- / >,- / -,- / -,-	-,- / -,> / -,> / -,-	76	14	6
16	>,- / >,- / >,- / -,>	>,- / >,- / -,< / >,-	-,- / -,- / -,- / -,-	-,- / -,- / -,< / -,-	>,- / -,- / -,- / -,-	-,- / -,- / -,- / -,-	-,- / -,- / -,< / >,-	-,- / -,- / -,< / >,-	-,- / -,- / -,- / -,-	-,- / -,- / -,- / -,-	<,- / -,- / -,- / -,-		-,- / -,- / -,> / -,-	81	10	5
17	>,- / >,- / >, / >,>	>,- / >,- / -,< / >,-	-,- / -,- / -,< / -,-	-,- / -,- / -,< / -,-	>,- / -,- / -,< / -,-	-,- / -,- / -,< / -,-	-,- / -,- / -,< / -,-	-,- / -,- / -,< / >,-	-,- / -,- / -,< / -,-	-,- / -,- / -,< / -,-	-,- / -,- / -,< / -,<	-,- / -,- / -,< / <,<		73	11	12

5   Conclusions

Owing to the multi-start technique to protect against stopping in a local minimum the proposed hybrid methods were successful in finding potentially beneficial areas, despite small swarm sizes. The use of two smaller, but depending on each other, swarms helped to improve the efficiency of optimization algorithms even more, without significant impact on the execution time.

The use of local search methods such as quasi-Newton or Simplex with better exploitation properties allowed to reduce the number of the iterations of the PSO algorithm which is necessary to find a solution with given accuracy. This results in a decrease the execution time. Application of both quasi-Newton or Simplex methods resulted in obtaining similar quality of solutions.

Experiments have shown that modifications PSO_Quasi_mod_2, PSO_-Quasi_mod_3, PSO_Simplex_mod_2 and PSO_Simplex_mod_3 were the most effective. These variants reached the high performance with a satisfactory small execution time (similar to classic PSO) for most of the tested functions.

To improve the performance for functions such as Sine Envelope, Langerman and Griewank, the following changes can be considered: increasing the number of iterations, increasing the size of the swarm, or choosing a more favorable swarm parameters for this type of functions. However, for purposes of this research we decided to keep identical parameters for all functions.

References

1. Global Optimization Benchmarks and AMPGO, http://infinity77.net/global_optimization/test_functions.html (accessed September 26, 2014)
2. Ali, M.M., Kaelo, P.: Improved particle swarm algorithms for global optimization. Applied Mathematics and Computation 196(2), 578–593 (2008)
3. Eberhart, R., Shi, Y.: Comparing inertia weights and constriction factors in particle swarm optimization. In: Proceedings of the 2000 Congress on Evolutionary Computation, vol. 1, pp. 84–88 (2000)
4. Kennedy, J., Eberhart, R.: Particle swarm optimization. In: Proceedings of IEEE International Conference on Neural Networks, 1995, vol. 4, pp. 1942–1948 (November 1995)
5. MathWorld: Fisher's Exact Test (1999-2015), http://mathworld.wolfram.com/FishersExactTest.html, (accessed December 27, 2014)
6. Nelder, J.A., Mead, R.: A Simplex Method for Function Minimization. The Computer Journal 7(4), 308–313 (1965)
7. Nocedal, J., Wright, S.: Numerical Optimization. Springer series in operations research and financial engineering, Springer (1999)
8. dos Santos Coelho, L., Mariani, V.: Particle Swarm Optimization with Quasi-Newton Local Search for Solving Economic Dispatch Problem. In: IEEE International Conference on Systems, Man and Cybernetics, SMC 2006, vol. 4, pp. 3109–3113 (October 2006)
9. Shi, Y., Eberhart, R.C.: Empirical study of particle swarm optimization. In: Proceedings of the 1999 Congress on Evolutionary Computation, CEC 1999, vol. 3. IEEE (1999)
10. Shi, Y., Eberhart, R.: Parameter selection in particle swarm optimization. In: Porto, V.W., Waagen, D. (eds.) EP 1998. LNCS, vol. 1447, pp. 591–600. Springer, Heidelberg (1998)
11. Thomas, N., Reed, M.: A hybrid algorithm for continuous optimisation. In: IEEE Congress on Evolutionary Computation, CEC 2009, pp. 2584–2589 (May 2009)
12. Zhe-ping, Y., Chao, D., Jia-jia, Z., Dong-nan, C.: A novel two-subpopulation particle swarm optimization. In: 10th World Congress on Intelligent Control and Automation (WCICA), pp. 4113–4117 (July 2012)

Parallel Coevolutionary Algorithm
for Three-Dimensional Bin Packing Problem

Wojciech Bożejko[1(✉)], Łukasz Kacprzak[1] and Mieczysław Wodecki[2]

[1] Department of Automatics, Mechatronics and Control Systems
Faculty of Electronics, Wrocław University of Technology
Wyb. Wyspiańskiego 27, 50-370 Wrocław, Poland
wojciech.bozejko@pwr.edu.pl
lukasz.kacprzak@pwr.edu.pl
[2] Institute of Computer Science, University of Wrocław
Joliot-Curie 15, 50-383 Wrocław, Poland
mieczyslaw.wodecki@ii.uni.wroc.pl

Abstract. The work considers the problem of three-dimensional bin packaging (3D-BPP), where a load of maximum volume is put in a single container. To solve the above mentioned problem there was a coevolutionary parallel algorithm used basing on the separate evolution of cooperating subpopulations of possible solutions. Computational experiments were conducted in a neighbourhood of clusters and aimed to examine the impact of parallelization algorithm on the computation time and the quality of the obtained solutions.[1]

1 Introduction

The three-dimensional bin packing problem (3D-BPP) is a major industrial issue which has a number of practical applications. In a variant of maximizing, the problem boils down to filling the empty space inside a single rectangular cuboid (called *bin*, hereafter referred to as container) with boxes of the greatest volume. With proper management of the available space it is possible to reduce the costs associated with the storage of goods and their transport. The three-dimensional bin packing problem belongs to difficult optimization problems, which is therefore ranked amongst the class of NP-hard problems.

Many heuristic approaches , especially evolutionary algorithms, are used to find approximate solutions to problems, both for one-, two- and three-dimensional packing. However, in connection to the fact that these methods are general and do not use detailed information about the problem, many researchers supplement them with additional heuristic, more suitable for the specific nature of the issue and accepted limitations. Such heuristics are usually responsible for finding acceptable positions for objects in containers (2D packing), or boxes in containers (3D packing) and are (called *decoding procedure*). Method of action

---

[1] The work was partially supported by the OPUS grant DEC-2012/05/B/ST7/00102 of Polish National Centre of Science.

L. Rutkowski et al. (Eds.): ICAISC 2015, Part I, LNAI 9119, pp. 319–328, 2015.
DOI: 10.1007/978-3-319-19324-3_29

in decoding procedure determines the (*packing strategy*). The role of an evolutionary algorithm, used together with a decoding procedure, may boil down to find the best order (method) of packing, in which items or boxes, will be used by heuristic.

Stawowy [12] developed an evolutionary algorithm for one-dimensional packing problem. The aim of this study was to create a possibly simple algorithm, solving the problem at a level similar to more specialized algorithms. The offspring is created with the use of mutation of operators, without a crossover phase. Tan et al. [11] proposed an evolutionary algorithm for two-dimensional packing problem. The authors do not represent a feasible solution as a vector, but as a structure, called a particle, which creates a set of swarm (called *particle swarm*). A single particle contains information not only on the quantity of used containers (called *bin*) but also on arranged in them rectangular objects, and the best results. The work formulates a mathematical model for two-dimensional packing problem with additional restrictions. The center of gravity of the total load was taken into account.

The works of He et al. [6], Wu et al. [13] or Karabulut and Mustafa [9] presented the problem of three-dimensional packing, wherein boxes are placed in a container of fixed length and width but of varying height. In a variant of the problem considered by He et al. [6] and Wu et al. [13] boxes can have different sizes and arbitrary rotation. A single solution is represented as a chromosome, containing information about the order of packing boxes and a kind of rotation of each of them. A decoding procedure uses concept of reference points (called*extreme points*, *reference points*). The authors [6] improved the idea proposed in [13]. The framework has been created (*global search framework*- GSF) using the concept of the *evolutionary gradient*. Karabulut and Mustafa [9] proposed a method for finding positions of boxes in a container, called *Deepest Bottom Left with Fill Method* (DBLF), which is an extension of the procedure given by Hopper [8], for two-dimensional packing problem . The method inserts a box on the first allowed position, located in the deepest possible (*deepest*), the lowest (*bottom*) and the left-side of the container (*left*). Boxes do not have the possibility of rotation.

In their works Goncalves and Resende [7], Bortfeld and Gehring [2], Kang et al. [10] discuss the problem of filling in a single container with fixed dimensions. Kang et al. [10] developed a packing strategy presented by Karabulut and Mustafa [9]. There has been introduced the concept of a rectangular spatial object (ang. *cuboid space object*). The object represents the space inside the container, inside which it is possible to pack the boxes. Using of objects is aimed at, among others, reducing computation time. The boxes of volume and sizes which do not fit into the space occupied by the object are ignored at this stage of algorithm's acting. Goncalves and Resende [7] have developed a parallel algorithm in which the chromosome contains the information about the order of packing boxes into the container and a layer in which the box can be placed. Layer is a rectangular structure (vertical or horizontal), consisting of boxes of the same type used for filling the empty space inside the container (called *maximal spaces*). The authors present a procedure for coupling of free space -(*MaxJoin*). Bortfeld and Gehring [2] presented a genetic algorithm for which the packing strategy is based on a layered technique. The work considers several practical constraints of the problem, i.e. the number of boxes' rotations, restrictions on the load stability, its weight and balance.

Bischoff and Ratcliff [1] held a discussion on the methodology of solving the problem of container filling (called *Container loading problem*). They discussed a wide range of restrictions of the above mentioned issue, designed the procedure that generates multiple instances of the problem, leading to better assessment of the quality of the algorithms developed by researchers who furtherly extended the problem.

2   Problem Definition

The three-dimensional bin packing problem (3D-BPP), in the considered variant, relies in packing of such a number of boxes into a single container that, with the fulfillment of all adopted restrictions, the total volume of load was as large as possible. The container K(see Figure 1), has a form of a rectangular cuboid

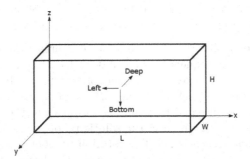

Fig. 1. Container

with fixed dimensions: length L, width W, height H and volume V. There is a set of boxes $P = \{p_0, p_1, \ldots, p_{n-1}\}$, type $T = \{t_0, t_1, \ldots, t_{m-1}\}$ and rotation $R = \{0, 1, 2, 3, 4, 5\}$, representing possible rotations of boxes. Each box $p_i \in P$ has a certain type u_i, defining its dimensions and possible rotation, i.e. $u_i = t_k$, dla $k \in \{0, 1, \ldots, m-1\}$, $i = 0, 1, \ldots, n-1$, $u \in U = \{u_0, u_1, \ldots, u_{n-1}\}$. A given type $t_k \in T$ can be written in the form of: $t_k = (l_k, w_k, h_k, MR_k)$, where $MR_k \subseteq R$ and determines available rotations, whereas l_k, w_k, h_k denote respectively: the length, width and height of the box. The set MR_k may contain from one to six rotations. A solution $e = (PZ_e, q_e)$ of the packing problem under consideration defines a set of packed boxes $PZ_e \subseteq P$, $PZ_e = \{c_0, c_1, \ldots, c_{q_e}\}$, where q_e is the number of boxes in the set PZ_e. The solution e to be found must take the form in which the sum of the volume of packed boxes:

$$\max_{0 \leq c_0 \leq c_1 \leq \ldots \leq c_{q_e-1} \leq n-1} \sum_{z=0}^{q_e-1} v_z$$

was maximum and fulfilling the following constraints:

- box c_z must lie entirely within the container, parallel to the side walls, in one of the available type of rotations,
- box c_z cannot occupy the space previously occupied by the packed boxes,
- box c_z must be placed on the bottom of the container, or on top of another.

To determine the position of boxes there are used coordinates in the Cartesian coordiante system of reference. A set of boxes P may be of unrestricted character, ranging from slightly heterogeneous(*weakly heterogeneous*) to highly heterogeneous (*strongly heterogeneous*). If the set is weakly heterogeneous, it means that the instance of the problem has few types, with plenty of boxes for each of them, whereas a strongly heterogeneous set consists of many types of boxes, with a small quantity of each type.

3   Algorithm Descripion

The proposed algorithm combines the features of a genetic algorithm and heuristic used as a decoding procedure. This section describes the representation adopted for the solution, the method of determining the position of boxes in a container (decoding procedure) and the coevolutionary algorithm.

Representation of Solution. An individual is represented as a chromosome composed of two parts: Sequence and Rotation (see Figure 2). The first one contains the sequence of boxes, the second one corresponding to each box - rotation number, used to pack the boxes into a container. Each part of the chromosome has a length equal to a number of boxes in the set P, regardless of how many of them will be used in the solution. For a number of boxes equal to n the chromosome length is $2n$. The rotation number stored at position d_s corresponds to a box number stored in a place a_s of a chromosome. The division of the chromosome into two parts is also used in the work [6, 13]. On the basis of the chromosome using the decoding procedure, the actual form of a solution e is calculated. In reference to the $n \geq q_e$, which means that not all decoded in the chromosome boxes must be included in the set PZ_e, an individual represents the solution e in an approximate way. A case, in which $q_e = n$ means that the solution e is optimal. In the further part the terms: solution, chromosome and individual will be the same.

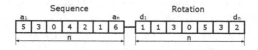

Fig. 2. Chromosome

Decoding Procedure. The task of the decoding procedure is to find possible positions in the container for the greatest number of boxes, whose sequence is decoded by the chromosome. In practice, for solution e, this means finding elements q_e forming the set PZ_e. Heuristic used for this purpose was based on the version of the method presented in the work [9], for bin packing problem with variable height of the container (called *strip packing*). Block diagram of the procedure is shown in Figure 3. In the first step (Initial calculations), the boxes are turned, depending on specific rotation defined in the second part of the chromosome. Then the procedure leads us to place boxes in the container, according to the given sequence. An important element is the position list used to hold the currently available coordinates that are considered when looking for a free place into which b_s box can be packed. If there are no boxes in the container, the position list contains only the coordinates (0,0,0), which is the beginning of the container. In case when the list contains more items, they are

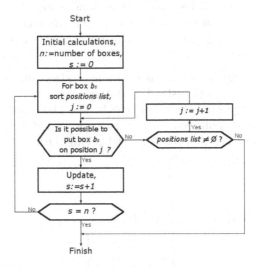

Fig. 3. Scheme of decoding procedure

arranged according to the following order: depth (*deep*, a minimum value on the y-axis), bottom (textit bottom, the smallest possible value of the z-axis), left (textit left, and the lowest value on the x-axis). In order to determine whether it is possible to insert the considered b_s box in the selected position j, heuristic checks if it fits completely within the container and whether it does not disturb the space occupied by the pre-packaged boxes. If the insertion is possible, the position j is removed from the list, and in its place there are three new ones added, created by the location of the box b_s. These positions have coordinates $(x_j + l_s, y_j, z_j)(x_j, y_j + w_s, z_j)(x_j, y_j, z_j + h_s)$ and are referred to as *reference points* or *extreme points*) [6, 13] . Then, in case of the remaining boxes, the procedure takes more of them into consideration, sorting an updated list of available positions and checking the opportunity to insert them in one of the positions, otherwise, the procedure is terminated. If you insert a b_s box in

j position is not possible, the heuristic tries to put them in different positions from the list until its termination. The fulfillment of the condition *position list* $\neq \emptyset$ (see Figure 3) means that in the *position list* there are coordinates not taken into consideration within the context of b_s box. When it is not possible to place the box on any of the available positions, the procedure stops.

At the end of working of decoding procedure, the adaptation (cost) function value is calculated for the given solution e:

$$F(e) = \frac{\sum_{z=0}^{q_e-1} v_z}{V} 100\%,$$

for $e = (PZ_e, q_e)$, where v_z is the volume of subsequently packed boxes $c_z \in PZ_e$, $|PZ_e| = q_e$ a V is the volume of container K. Information concerning the value of adaptation function and packed boxes (their dimensions, the coordinates in the container, the type of rotation) are stored and directly related to the concerned individual, therefore, the procedure is restarted for a given chromosome only in case of its modification.

Coevolutionary Algorithm. A coevolutionary algorithm is a parallel multi-track algorithm, based on the island migration model. It explores the space of solutions using parallel threads in the search. The processes exchange between themselves information obtained during the exploration of their own trajectories, with the result that the algorithm is ranked among the subclass of co-operating algorithms [3–5].

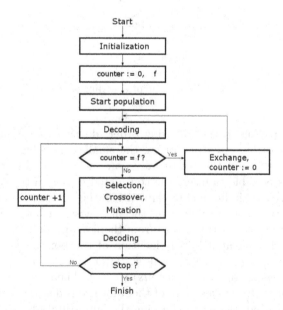

Fig. 4. Scheme of coevolutionary algorithm

A block scheme algorithm, for a single process, was illustrated in Figure 4. All stages of its operation, apart from an exchange step, are accomplished by the given processor independently of the others. The algorithm can also be run in a sequential version and in such a case, it is treated as a parallel algorithm with a single process (the exchange is omitted).

In the first step (Initialization) there are entered data concerning the problem and the initial values are given to necessary variables. Then, each process creates its own starting subpopulation of random individuals. For all chromosomes of each initial subpopulation there is a separate decoding decoding procedure. In the next step, there are two possible situations: (1) *counter* $\neq f$, which means that there was no moment of exchange of individuals between processes and there are genetic operations executed, such as Selection, Crossover and Mutation, after which the new or modified individuals are subject to decoding, (2) *counter* $= f$, and therefore there is a migration of individuals between the individual threads, and if necessary it leads to Decoding.

In the Selection step, each process examines the average quality of solutions of its subpopulation and rejects all having the value of the adaptation function which is below average. In the algorithm there have been implemented two types of Crossover operator: one point and two point with the use of PMX method. In most cases, parents are chosen from a pool of individuals that survived the selection process. However, with certain probability, the choice of parent from the group of rejected solutions may be possible, which is a one of the methods of prevention stagnation.

The mutation may occur in two ways. Since the sequence of boxes decoded in the chromosome is important for the decoding procedure, the first one is the random swapping of two fields with the numbers of boxes and the corresponding rotations. The second method changes the value of the rotation field in a single chromosome, therefore, the associated with it box has a changed rotation when trying to place it in a container by heuristic. The new value of the rotation may not be prohibited by the type to which the box belongs to. The exchange is a key element of the coevolutionary algorithm. In view of the fact that the algorithm was created with the cluster environment, it has been implemented with the use of MPI library. The processes are combined in pairs, in which communication occurs. Each of the two processors emits part of the sub-populations and sends it to another thread. The solutions sent are replaced with the new arrivals. The communication between processors is a non-locking one (functions: *MPI_Isend(),MPI_Irecv()*), and groups of individuals are transferred between them in the form of compressed data packets (functions: *MPI_Pack(),MPI_Unpack()*). The main task of the Exchange, is the diversification of the various sub-populations.

4 Computational Experiments

Calculations were conducted on the Supernova cluster placed in the Wrocław Centre for Networking and Supercomputing, which consists of 573 nodes and

6368 computation cores. Benchmark problem instances were generated basing on procedure proposed in [1]. Fourteen test instances were used in computational experiments, for the number of possible boxes from 3 to 20, with the constant size of the contatiner. The algorithm was executed up to 20 times for each instances:

 − sequentially on 1 processor,
 − parallelly, with using 2,4 and 8 processors.

Each processor was placed in separate node of the cluster, with 2GB of the local RAM memory per node.

Table 1. Results of computations for 1 and 2 processors

problem	types	1 processor			2 processors		
		$F_{aver}[\%]$	$F_{best}[\%]$	$t_{aver}[\min]$	$F_{aver}[\%]$	$F_{best}[\%]$	$t_{aver}[\min]$
bench1_03	3	72.0	72.7	80.4	72.9	74.2	65.8
bench1_31	3	77.3	79.7	209.6	76.9	79.4	176.4
bench2_01	5	79.7	80.7	31.4	80.1	83.4	27.5
bench2_02	5	79.7	82.3	85.8	79.2	81.2	68.5
bench3_01	8	78.8	82.0	75.3	80.0	82.9	43.1
bench3_25	8	74.1	75.8	160.0	74.6	76.9	124.5
bench4_01	10	78.2	80.1	53.7	78.5	81.4	39.7
bench4_02	10	77.6	79.9	185.2	77.9	79.4	157.1
bench5_04	12	76.5	79.6	234.2	76.5	78.8	191.9
bench5_17	12	77.6	78.6	128.8	78.1	80.5	38.1
bench6_01	15	77.4	78.1	146.0	76.7	78.5	107.7
bench6_02	15	76.7	78.3	257.8	76.7	78.2	112.6
bench7_01	20	77.0	78.5	69.8	77.1	78.8	45.1
bench7_02	20	76.6	77.9	119.2	76.3	78.7	83.3
Average		**77.1**	**78.9**	**131.2**	**77,3**	**79.5**	**91.3**

Tables 1 and 2 show results of computations for different number of processors. F_{aver} and F_{best} denote the average and the best found adaptation (cost) function value for each benchmark instance, respectively. The average time of computations for each instance is denoted by t_{aver}. As we can see, quality of solutions measured by the average and the best found solution increase with growing of the number of processors used.

Table 3 presents average speedups comparison. Growing of the speedup can observed for the processor number increasing. For test instances bench6_02 and bench5_17 for 2 processors, as well as for bench5_17 for 4 processors the superlinear speedup was observed. Detailed explaining of this anomaly will be an issue of the further research, it is probably connected with the specify of the cluster environment.

Table 2. Results of computations for 4 and 8 processors

problem	types	4 processors			8 processors		
		$F_{\text{aver}}[\%]$	$F_{\text{best}}[\%]$	$t_{\text{aver}}[\min]$	$F_{\text{aver}}[\%]$	$F_{\text{best}}[\%]$	$t_{\text{aver}}[\min]$
bench1_03	3	72.6	75.0	50.0	71.7	72.7	13.8
bench1_31	3	76.4	78.6	72.9	76.5	78.3	55.3
bench2_01	5	79.9	84.0	12.5	79.2	81.3	8.5
bench2_02	5	79.5	81.1	42.8	79.1	81.5	22.1
bench3_01	8	78.9	82.3	33.	78.2	79.1	17.9
bench3_25	8	73.6	74.5	45.9	72.8	74.6	38.0
bench4_01	10	78.5	82.1	27.3	77.4	79.4	15.0
bench4_02	10	77.5	80.3	69.2	76.4	77.7	29.9
bench5_04	12	76.3	79.0	71.3	75.5	78.1	49.8
bench5_17	12	77.8	79.2	30.2	76.8	79.7	18.4
bench6_01	15	77.1	79.0	51.0	75.9	78.2	41.2
bench6_02	15	76.5	78.7	91.2	75.3	77.4	38.3
bench7_01	20	76.0	78.2	39.7	76.0	77.2	39.8
bench7_02	20	76.1	78.5	61.7	75.2	76.5	46.9
Average		**76.9**	**79.3**	**49.9**	**76.1**	**78.0**	**31.1**

Table 3. Obtained speedups for a given processors number

instance	2 processors	4 processors	8 processors
bench1_03	1.22	1.61	5.83
bench1_31	1.19	2.88	3.79
bench2_01	1.14	2.51	3.69
bench2_02	1.25	2.00	3.88
bench3_01	1.75	2.23	4.21
bench3_25	1.29	3.49	4.21
bench4_01	1.35	1.97	3.58
bench4_02	1.18	2.31	6.19
bench5_04	1.22	3.28	4.70
bench5_17	3.38	4.26	7.00
bench6_01	1.36	2.86	3.54
bench6_02	2.29	2.83	6.74
bench7_01	1.55	1.76	1.76
bench7_02	1.43	1.93	2.54
Average	**1.54**	**2.57**	**4.40**

5   Conclusions

Parallel coevolutionary algorithm for the three-dimensional bin packaging problem is proposed in the paper. Proposed algorithm is based on the island model, which makes possible of communication and solutions exchange between subpopulations. Parallelization of the algorithm gives an effect of processing time shortening (average time for all benchmark instances 131.2 seconds for 1 processor vs. 31.1 seconds for 8 processors) with comparable solutions quality.

References

1. Bischoff, E.E., Ratcliff, M.S.W.: Issues in the Development of Approaches to Container Loading. Omega, Int. J. Mgmt. Sci. 23(4), 377–390 (1995)
2. Bortfeld, A., Gehring, H.: A hybryd genetic algorithm for the container loading problem. European Journal of Operational Research 131, 143–161 (2001)
3. Bożejko, W., Wodecki, M.: Parallel genetic algorithm for minimizing total weighted completion time. In: Rutkowski, L., Siekmann, J.H., Tadeusiewicz, R., Zadeh, L.A. (eds.) ICAISC 2004. LNCS (LNAI), vol. 3070, pp. 400–405. Springer, Heidelberg (2004)
4. Bożejko, W., Wodecki, M.: Parallel Evolutionary Algorithm for the Traveling Salesman Problem. Journal of Numerical Analysis, Industrial and Applied Mathematics 2(3-4), 129–137 (2007)
5. Bożejko, W., Wodecki, M.: Solving Permutational Routing Problems by Population-Based Metaheuristics. Computers & Industrial Engineering 57, 269–276 (2009)
6. He, Y., Wu, Y., de Souza, R.: A global search framework for practical three-dimensional packing with variable carton orientations. Computers & Operations Research 39(2012), 2395–2414 (2012)
7. Goncalves, J.F., Resende, M.G.C.: A parallel multi-population biased random-key genetic algorithm for a container loading problem. Computers & Operations Research 39, 179–190 (2012)
8. Hopper, E.: Two-dimensional Packing Utilising Evolutionary Algorithms and other Meta- Heuristic Methods, PhD Thesis, University of Wales (2000)
9. Karabulut, K., İnceoğlu, M.M.: A hybrid genetic algorithm for packing in 3D with deepest bottom left with fill method. In: Yakhno, T. (ed.) ADVIS 2004. LNCS, vol. 3261, pp. 441–450. Springer, Heidelberg (2004)
10. Kang, K., Moon, I., Wang, H.: A hybrid genetic algorithm with a n packing problem. Applied Mathematics and Computation 219, 1287–1299 (2012)
11. Liu, D.S., Tan, K.C., Huang, S.Y., Goh, C.K., Ho, W.K.: On solving multiobjective bin packing problems using evolutionary particle swarm optimization. European Journal of Operational Research 190, 357–382 (2008)
12. Stawowy, A.: Evolutionary based heuristic for bin packing problem. Computers & Industrial Engineering 55, 465–474 (2008)
13. Wu, Y., Li, W., Goh, M., de Souza, R.: Three-dimensional bin packing problem with variable bin height. European Journal of Operational Research 202, 347–355 (2010)

Adaptive Differential Evolution: SHADE with Competing Crossover Strategies

Petr Bujok[✉] and Josef Tvrdík

Department of Computer Science, University of Ostrava,
Centre of Excellence IT4Innovations,
Institute for Research and Applications of Fuzzy Modeling,
30. dubna 22, 70103 Ostrava, Czech Republic
{petr.bujok,josef.tvrdik}@osu.cz
http://prf.osu.eu/kip/

Abstract. Possible improvement of a successful adaptive SHADE variant of differential evolution is addressed. Exploitation of exponential crossover was applied in two newly proposed SHADE variants. The algorithms were compared experimentally on CEC 2013 test suite used as a benchmark. The results show that the variant using adaptive strategy of the competition of two types of crossover is significantly more efficient than other SHADE variants in 7 out of 28 problems and not worse in the others. Thus, this SHADE with competing crossovers can be considered superior to original SHADE algorithm.

Keywords: Global optimization · Differential evolution · Self-adaptation · Competing crossover · Experimental comparison · CEC 2013 test suite

1 Introduction

Differential evolution (DE) is stochastic evolutionary method which searches for the global optimum of the objective function heuristically. It was introduced by Storn and Price in 1997 [5] in order to solve the real-valued problems. Despite of its simplicity, DE is a robust global optimizer that outperforms frequently other well-known optimization algorithms. This is the reason that DE is very often applied to many real problems [4]. On the other hand, the settings of DE control parameters affects the efficiency of the search substantially. This matter was very intensively studied including the way of their adaptive and self-adaptive setting, for a comprehensive summary of recent results see [1,3].

In this paper, two widely-used crossovers are applied to an efficient adaptive DE variant known under acronym SHADE (Section 3) in literature. The competition of two different crossover strategies using better of them in different stages of searching enables the solution of the problems. Alternation of the various crossovers promises better results in solving the optimization problems. The performance of the newly proposed algorithm is compared with the original SHADE on CEC 2013 test suite.

The remaining text of the paper is organized as follows. Basics of differential evolution algorithm is explained in Section 2 and the newly proposed SHADE

© Springer International Publishing Switzerland 2015
L. Rutkowski et al. (Eds.): ICAISC 2015, Part I, LNAI 9119, pp. 329–339, 2015.
DOI: 10.1007/978-3-319-19324-3_30

variant including competitive adaptation is described in the Sections 3 and 4. CEC 2013 test suite with the experiment settings are introduced in Section 5. Results of experimental comparison of the algorithms are presented in Sections 6 and some remarks are provided in Section 7.

2 Differential Evolution Algorithm

DE algorithm uses a population of N points - candidates of the solutions in the search domain. The population is developed during the whole search process using evolutionary operators, i.e. *selection, mutation* and *crossover*. Mutation is controlled by F parameter, $F > 0$, and crossover is controlled by parameter CR, $0 \leq CR \leq 1$. The combination of mutation and crossover is called DE *strategy* and it is denoted by the abbreviation of $DE/m/n/c$. A symbol m specifies the kind of mutation, n is used for the number of differences in mutation, and c indicates the type of crossover. Various values of F and CR can be used in each strategy. DE has a few control parameters only. Besides setting the population size N and defining the stopping condition necessary for all evolutionary algorithms, the selection of DE strategy and setting the values of F and CR is all what must be done. However, the DE performance is sensitive to the values of these parameters and their appropriate setting is problem-dependent.

3 Adaptive Variant of Differential Evolution - SHADE

Success-History Based Parameter Adaptation for Differential Evolution (SHADE) algorithm was introduced by Tanabe and Fukunaga in 2013 [7]. This very efficient optimization method was derived from the original algorithm Adaptive Differential Evolution With Optional External Archive (JADE) proposed by Zhang and Sanderson [11]. The main extension of SHADE compared to original JADE is in a history-based adaptation of the control parameters F and CR. Both JADE and SHADE variants use an efficient greedy *current-to-pbest* mutation strategy, where the new mutant vector $\boldsymbol{u}_i$ is generated from four mutual individuals – current individual $\boldsymbol{x}_i$, randomly chosen individual from the p best points $\boldsymbol{x}_{pbest}$, randomly selected point $\boldsymbol{x}_{r1}$ from P and randomly selected point $\boldsymbol{x}_{r2}$ from $P \bigcup A$, as it is formed in the equation (1).

$$\boldsymbol{u}_i = \boldsymbol{x}_i + F_i \cdot (\boldsymbol{x}_{pbest} - \boldsymbol{x}_i) + F_i \cdot (\boldsymbol{x}_{r1} - \boldsymbol{x}_{r2}), \tag{1}$$

where the point $\boldsymbol{x}_{pbest}$ is randomly selected from the p best points of P.

Opposite to JADE, the parameter of p for selecting the $\boldsymbol{x}_{pbest}$ is generated randomly for each point of the population according to the equation (2):

$$p_i = rand[2/N,\ 0.2], \tag{2}$$

and the point $\boldsymbol{x}_{pbest}$ is selected from the $p_i \times 100\%$ best points of P. After mutation, the binomial crossover operation is used for generating the trial point $\boldsymbol{y}_i$ (3).

$$\boldsymbol{y}_{i,j} = \begin{cases} \boldsymbol{u}_{i,j}, & if\ rand_j(0,1) \leq CR\ or\ j = rand_j(1,D) \\ \boldsymbol{x}_{i,j}, & otherwise. \end{cases} \tag{3}$$

The changed coordinates are dispersed uniformly over the dimensions $1, 2, \ldots, D$. The crossover operator combines selected elements of mutant vector $\boldsymbol{u}_i$ with the current individual $\boldsymbol{x}_i$ and in order to get a trial vector $\boldsymbol{y}_i$.

If the function value of the newly composed trial point $f(\boldsymbol{y}_i)$ is better than the $f(\boldsymbol{x}_i)$, the new point replaces the old one and the old solution is inserted into archive A. The values of the successful control parameters F and CR are also stored into auxiliary memories S_F and S_{CR}.

When the size of the archive exceeds the size of the population P, superfluous randomly chosen points are deleted from the archive. The purpose of the archive is to store old good solutions from previous generations and use them for the mutation according to (1).

The parameters M_F and M_{CR} for generating new values of the control parameters F and CR are updated using the stored successful values S_F and S_{CR} from auxiliary memories. The new value of M_F is computed as weighted arithmetic mean of the current values S_F and value of M_{CR} is computed as weighted Lehmer mean of the current values from S_{CR}. The values of M_F and M_{CR} remain the same if no successful point was created in the last generation.

4   Adaptive DE with Competition of Crossover Strategies

SHADE algorithm has appeared the best DE algorithm in CEC 2013 competition [6]. However, even SHADE fails in some hard problems defined by composition of several multi-modal functions and high level of dimension, where SHADE algorithm is not able to provide an acceptable solution. That is why we proposed the enhanced SHADE algorithm with the competition of crossover strategies. The binomial crossover (3) is used in the original algorithm for creating the new trial point $\boldsymbol{y}_i$ from current point $\boldsymbol{x}_i$ and mutant vector $\boldsymbol{u}_i$. Some recent results show that exponential crossover (4) can be efficient in problems, where binomial variant performs poorly [8,10]. The exponential crossover is defined by the following rule:

$$
\boldsymbol{y}_{i,j} = \begin{cases} \boldsymbol{u}_{i,j}, \, for \ j = \langle n \rangle_D, \ \langle n+1 \rangle_D, \ldots, \langle n+L-1 \rangle_D \\ \boldsymbol{x}_{i,j}, \, otherwise, \end{cases} \tag{4}
$$

The brackets $\langle \rangle_D$ represent the function modulo with modulus D. The starting position of crossover (n) is chosen randomly from $1, \ldots, D$, and L consecutive elements (counted in circular manner) are taken from the mutant vector $\boldsymbol{u}_i$. Probability of replacing the kth element in the sequence $1, 2, \ldots, L, \ \ L \leq D$, decreases exponentially with increasing k in dependence on CR, next element is replaced if $rand_j(0,1) < CR$. Thus, L adjacent elements are changed in exponential crossover.

The exponential crossover is exploited in newly proposed enhanced variants of SHADE. In one of them, the exponential crossover is simply used instead of the binomial one. In the second variant, both types of crossover alternate. Each variant of crossover has its value of probability to be used and the value of probability is updated according to the success in previous generations of new points. Thereafter, a more successful variant is used more probably than the variant which is not able to generate successful individuals. The scheme for selecting variant of the crossover is borrowed from the competitive DE [9]. The advantage of this scheme is to adapt the search to the currently solved problem. A pseudo-code of SHADE variant with two types of crossover is illustrated in Algorithm 1.

Algorithm 1. SHADE with Competition of Crossover Types

Initialize population $P = (\boldsymbol{x}_1, \boldsymbol{x}_2, \ldots, \boldsymbol{x}_N)$
Evaluate $f(\boldsymbol{x}_i)$, $i = 1, 2, \ldots N$
Set all M_{CR} and M_F to 0.5
Initialize empty archive A
while $FES < MaxFES$ **do**
  Initialize S_{CR}, S_F empty
  for $i = 1, 2, \ldots, N$ **do**
    Select r_i randomly from $[1, H]$
    $CR_i = \text{randn}(M_{CR,r_i}, 0.1)$
    $F_i = \text{randc}(M_{F,r_i}, 0.1)$
    $p_i = \text{rand}[p_{min}, 0.2]$
    Generate trial vector $\boldsymbol{y}_i$ by selected strategy (roulette wheel)
  end for
  for $i = 1, 2, \ldots, N$ **do**
    if $f(\boldsymbol{y}_i) \leq f(\boldsymbol{x}_i)$ **then**
      Insert $\boldsymbol{y}_i$ into Q
    else
      Insert $\boldsymbol{x}_i$ into Q
    end if
    if $f(\boldsymbol{y}_i) < f(\boldsymbol{x}_i)$ **then**
      $\boldsymbol{x}_i \to A$
      $CR_i \to S_{CR}$, $F_i \to S_F$
      Increase counter of success the strategy a) **or** b)
    end if
  end for
  if $\text{size}(A) > \text{size}(P)$ **then**
    Delete randomly chosen individuals from A
  end if
  if $\text{size}(S_{CR}) > 0$ **and** $\text{size}(S_F) > 0$ **then**
    Update M_{CR} and M_F based on S_{CR} and S_F
  end if
  $P \leftarrow Q$
end while

At the beginning the population of N potential solutions $P = (\boldsymbol{x}_1, \boldsymbol{x}_2, \ldots, \boldsymbol{x}_N)$ is uniformly distributed in the search area. Then all H values of both historical memories $M_{CR,i}$ and $M_{F,i}$, $i = 1, 2, \ldots, H$ for generating the control parameters

CR and F are initialized to 0.5. The archive A for storing the old good solutions is set as empty.

In the main cycle, temporary memories S_F and S_{CR} for saving of the successful values of the control parameters F and CR are set empty in each generation. The values of distribution parameters needed for their random updating are chosen randomly from M_F and M_{CR} for each point of the population. The control parameter of mutation F is generated from Cauchy distribution with the parameter M_{F,r_i} and 0.1 and the control parameter of crossover CR is generated from Gauss distribution with the mean value M_{CR,r_i} and standard deviation 0.1, where r_i is randomly selected index from $1, 2, \ldots, H$. The unfeasible values of F and CR are regenerated according to the rules of original JADE algorithm [11].

After setting the control parameters of mutation and crossover, the control parameter p_i for selecting the best point x_{pbest} is set according to (2). Then the mutant vector u_i is constructed applying mutation current-to-$p$best (1). The new trial point y_i is generated by using either binomial or exponential crossover variant.

At the beginning of the evolution, the counters of successes of the crossover variants are set to equal values $q_k = 1/K$, where $K = 2$ is the number of the crossover variants. Both crossover variants have the same probability to be used for generating the new trial point at the start. After each newly generated trial point y_i, the counter of (3) or (4) is increased by one. After each generation, the probabilities are updated based on the counters of the successes:

$$q_k = \frac{n_k + n_0}{\sum_{k=1}^{K} (n_k + n_0)}, \tag{5}$$

where n_k is the current count of the kth crossover variant successes, n_0 is an input parameter to prevent from a dramatic change in q_k and all probabilities are reset to starting values if any q_k decreases below some given δ, $\delta > 0$.

Finally, parameters M_F and M_{CR} are updated using the stored successful values S_F and S_{CR} from auxiliary memories as it is described in Section 3. The values of M_F and M_{CR} remain the same if no successful point was created in the last generation. The main cycle of the algorithm is repeated until the stopping condition is achieved.

5   Experimental Setting

CEC 2013 test suite was employed to compare the efficiency of the algorithms. This suite was defined by Liang et al. for a special section of the Congress on Evolutionary Computation [2]. The suite consists of 28 minimization problems with various hardness, each of these problems has the best known solution. Three categories of the test problems from the suite are shown in Table 1.

The search space $[-100, 100]^D$ is the same for all the test problems. True function value at the global minimum point of each test problem $f(x^*)$ is also known and the correctness of solution found by an algorithm can be compared with $f(x^*)$.

Table 1. Categories of the test problems CEC 2013

Category	Functions	Unrotated	Rotated
Unimodal	1–5	1,5	2–4
Multimodal	6–20	11,14,17,19,20	6–10,12,13,15,16,18
Composition	21–28	22	21,23–28

The error of the solution found by an algorithm is defined as $f(x_{min}) - f(x^*)$, where $f(x_{min})$ is the function value of the solution found by the algorithm.

Three algorithm were compared in experiments, namely original SHADE, SHADE using exponential crossover instead of the binomial one, and SHADE with competition of two types of crossover. The algorithms are denoted by labels *SHADE*, *SHADE-exp*, and *SHADE-cc*, respectively hereafter. In the case of *SHADE-exp* just *EXP* is used if it is necessary to save space in tables. All the

Table 2. Basic characteristics of the original SHADE

Problem	Best	Worst	Median	Mean	Std
1	0	0	0	0	1.13E-13
2	9.00E+03	2.31E+05	5.78E+04	6.92E+04	4.47E+04
3	3.18E+00	2.05E+07	8.48E+04	1.56E+06	4.25E+06
4	5.90E-03	9.68E-01	**6.45E-02**	1.58E-01	2.12E-01
5	0	0	0	0	5.09E-14
6	2.81E-05	29.06	7.77	7.93	7.90
7	37.92	130.48	82.60	81.73	19.20
8	20.33	20.98	**20.65**	20.67	0.17
9	20.36	32.57	**27.53**	27.50	2.21
10	7.40E-03	0.1059	0.051765	0.052106	2.78E-02
11	0	0	0	0	2.78E-14
12	35.89	117.37	68.65	70.46	18.53
13	64.97	178.20	120.17	118.32	24.59
14	7.88E-08	8.33E-02	2.08E-02	2.39E-02	2.15E-02
15	2546.0	4252.2	3465.1	3427.5	343.2
16	7.94E-02	1.24E+00	**8.11E-01**	7.00E-01	3.52E-01
17	30.43	30.43	30.43	30.43	0.00
18	83.58	159.29	123.22	122.77	17.08
19	1.19	2.73	1.76	1.76	0.29
20	9.81	15.00	**11.67**	12.23	1.54
21	200.0	443.5	300.0	329.3	85.5
22	48.65	167.33	121.88	119.54	24.98
23	3127.3	5014.0	4258.6	4241.9	380.6
24	214.8	283.4	272.6	267.7	13.4
25	276.6	300.5	**291.5**	291.2	6.1
26	200.0	370.1	200.0	210.0	39.7
27	894.3	1122.0	1022.9	1016.4	55.9
28	100.0	300.0	300.0	296.1	28.0

algorithms are implemented in Matlab 2010a and all computations were carried out on a standard PC with Windows 7, Intel(R) Core(TM)2 CPU 6320, 1.86GH 1.87GH, 2GB RAM.

The tests were carried out at one problem dimension, $D = 30$. The population size was set to $N = 100$ for all the algorithms and test problems. The values of the remaining parameters controlling the competition of strategies were set to $n_0 = 2$, $\delta = 1/10$. The size of the archive and auxiliary memories is chosen $H = N$.

Other experimental setting follows the requirements given in the report [2], i.e. 51 repeated runs per the test function. The run stops if the prescribed number of the function values MaxFES $= D \times 10000 = 300000$ is reached. The values of the function error less than 1×10^{-8} are treated as zero in further processing because such a value of the error is considered sufficiently small for an acceptable approximation of the solution.

Table 3. Basic characteristics of the SHADE-exp

Problem	Best	Worst	Median	Mean	Std
1	0	0	0	0	9.44E-14
2	6.41E+03	1.83E+05	5.94E+04	6.88E+04	4.15E+04
3	2.68E-01	1.42E+08	9.86E+03	9.45E+06	2.35E+07
4	6.82E-02	1.36E+01	1.40E+00	2.24E+00	2.71E+00
5	0	0	0	0	2.23E-14
6	0	26.41	7.16	6.72	6.37
7	35.59	94.11	68.84	68.96	12.70
8	20.34	21.01	20.68	20.70	0.17
9	24.20	31.10	28.03	27.94	1.67
10	7.40E-03	2.69E-01	5.17E-02	5.85E-02	4.68E-02
11	0	0	0	0	2.28E-14
12	43.17	104.54	68.73	67.89	13.41
13	68.37	175.61	124.36	123.53	20.22
14	0	6.25E-02	2.08E-02	1.67E-02	1.91E-02
15	2776.3	4077.0	3432.6	3423.9	299.5
16	5.34E-01	1.22E+00	8.53E-01	8.76E-01	1.61E-01
17	30.43	30.43	30.43	30.43	0.00
18	81.21	128.88	107.49	106.11	11.54
19	0.86	1.55	1.24	1.25	0.14
20	10.93	15.00	12.63	12.71	0.87
21	200.0	443.5	300.0	332.2	86.9
22	23.91	119.05	**55.85**	64.79	30.41
23	3779.7	5102.4	4404.5	4377.2	320.2
24	239.5	278.6	265.3	264.3	8.9
25	281.4	306.5	295.8	294.9	5.5
26	200.0	200.0	200.0	200.0	0.0
27	777.2	1118.7	1033.3	1025.7	59.8
28	100.0	300.0	300.0	292.2	39.2

Table 4. Basic characteristics of the SHADE-cc

Problem	Best	Worst	Median	Mean	Std
1	0	0	0	0	7.40E-14
2	1.68E+04	1.98E+05	**4.76E+04**	5.97E+04	3.36E+04
3	8.37E-02	8.11E+06	**4.16E+03**	2.32E+05	1.15E+06
4	2.85E-03	1.21E+00	1.87E-01	3.05E-01	2.63E-01
5	0	0	0	0	2.23E-14
6	0	26.41	**5.42**	5.95	6.93
7	30.31	104.84	**59.99**	62.70	16.95
8	20.39	21.00	20.75	20.73	0.16
9	22.49	30.64	28.32	28.01	1.62
10	7.40E-03	1.75E-01	**4.92E-02**	5.31E-02	3.43E-02
11	0	0	0	0	2.19E-14
12	33.96	96.59	**58.22**	60.15	13.25
13	61.28	161.68	**108.43**	111.84	21.36
14	0	1.25E-01	2.08E-02	2.45E-02	2.52E-02
15	2455.6	3908.5	**3372.0**	3317.1	364.7
16	6.23E-01	1.28E+00	8.94E-01	9.05E-01	1.31E-01
17	30.43	30.43	30.43	30.43	0.00
18	80.50	132.54	**101.56**	101.75	9.35
19	0.95	2.14	1.37	1.39	0.26
20	10.53	14.68	12.22	12.20	0.92
21	200.0	443.5	300.0	315.0	85.6
22	29.70	145.54	97.47	86.90	35.18
23	3361.7	5059.9	**4177.9**	4190.4	352.3
24	231.1	282.0	**257.4**	257.2	11.8
25	282.1	302.3	293.0	292.7	5.3
26	200.0	202.4	200.0	200.1	0.4
27	862.6	1055.6	**986.7**	978.6	53.5
28	100.0	1461.8	300.0	341.0	227.0

6 Results

The basic results for three algorithms in comparison are presented in Tables 2, 3 and 4, where the statistical characteristics computed from 51 runs are shown. The least values of median value found among three algorithms are printed in bold. The comparison of the convergence speed for four selected problems is presented in Figure 1. The evolution of the search is divided into eleven stages as prescribed in [2] and the medians of the function values are depicted. We can see different influence of strategy on convergence speed in different stages of the evolutionary process and its problem-dependence but the convergence of SHADE-cc variant appeared the best in these test problems.

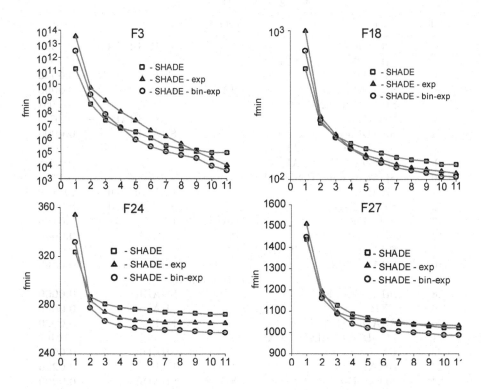

Fig. 1. Comparison of the convergence speed of the presented algorithms, functions 3, 18, 24, 27

Table 6 presents the relative frequency of using the exponential crossover in SHADE-cc variant. The exponential crossover is used more frequently in almost all problems, the values of the frequency vary from 50 % up to 67 %.

Statistical comparison of algorithm efficiency assessed by Kruskal-Wallis test is given in Table 5. When the difference among three algorithms was significant (in all the problems except one), multiple comparison by Kruskal-Wallis method was applied in order to find which algorithm is different. Thus, the rank of algorithms is evaluated. The counts of the unique wins as well as the second best and the worst places are summarized at bottom of the table. The SHADE-cc variant with the crossover competition is the best seven-times while the others are the best only three-times. The best places are shared in remaining fifteen problems.

Table 5. Kruskal-Wallis test

Problem	Best	Second	Third	P-value
1	SHADE		EXP, SHADE-cc	**0.0331**
2	SHADE-cc, SHADE, EXP			0.4400
3	**SHADE-cc**		EXP, SHADE	**0.0040**
4	SHADE	SHADE-cc	EXP	**0.0000**
5	SHADE-cc, EXP, SHADE			0.6051
6	**SHADE-cc**		EXP, SHADE	0.0790
7	SHADE-cc, EXP		SHADE	**0.0000**
8	SHADE, EXP, SHADE-cc			0.2428
9	SHADE, EXP, SHADE-cc			0.2418
10	SHADE-cc, EXP, SHADE			0.9055
11	SHADE		EXP, SHADE-cc	0.1699
12	**SHADE-cc**		EXP, SHADE	**0.0036**
13	**SHADE-cc**	SHADE	EXP	**0.0176**
14	EXP	SHADE-cc	SHADE	**0.0000**
15	SHADE-cc, EXP, SHADE			0.3578
16	SHADE, EXP		SHADE-cc	**0.0363**
17	no significant difference			
18	SHADE-cc, EXP		SHADE	**0.0000**
19	EXP	SHADE-cc	SHADE	**0.0000**
20	SHADE, SHADE-cc		EXP	**0.0029**
21	SHADE-cc, SHADE, EXP			0.6107
22	EXP	SHADE-cc	SHADE	**0.0000**
23	**SHADE-cc**	SHADE	EXP	**0.0226**
24	**SHADE-cc**	EXP	SHADE	**0.0000**
25	SHADE, SHADE-cc		EXP	**0.0106**
26	EXP, SHADE-cc		SHADE	**0.0001**
27	**SHADE-cc**		SHADE, EXP	**0.0000**
28	EXP, SHADE, SHADE-cc			0.8778
SHADE	3	2	7	
SHADE-cc	7	4	1	
EXP	3	1	5	

Table 6. Frequency of using the exponential crossover in SHADE-cc

Prob	Exp	Prob	Exp	Prob	Exp	Prob	Exp
F1	55%	F8	50%	F15	64%	F22	67%
F2	57%	F9	65%	F16	61%	F23	64%
F3	60%	F10	56%	F17	64%	F24	63%
F4	52%	F11	61%	F18	61%	F25	63%
F5	57%	F12	63%	F19	65%	F26	57%
F6	57%	F13	63%	F20	61%	F27	63%
F7	63%	F14	65%	F21	57%	F28	57%

7   Conclusion

Experimental comparison has shown that exploitation of exponential crossover can increase the efficiency of the SHADE algorithm, at least in some optimization problems. The newly proposed variant of SHADE algorithm with the crossover competition has appeared significantly more efficient in 7 out of 28 test problems and in 15 problems achieved results competitive with original algorithm. Further research will be focused on improvement of existing adaptive variants of differential evolution by using a competition of DE strategies.

Acknowledgments. This work was supported by University of Ostrava from the project SGS15/PřF/2015 and partially supported by the European Regional Development Fund in the IT4Innovations Centre of Excellence project (CZ.1.05/1.1.00/02.0070).

References

1. Das, S., Suganthan, P.N.: Differential evolution: A survey of the state-of-the-art. IEEE Transactions on Evolutionary Computation 15, 27–54 (2011)
2. Liang, J.J., Qu, B., Suganthan, P.N., Hernandez-Diaz, A.G.: Problem definitions and evaluation criteria for the CEC 2013 special session on real-parameter optimization (2013), http://www.ntu.edu.sg/home/epnsugan/
3. Neri, F., Tirronen, V.: Recent advances in differential evolution: a review and experimental analysis. Artificial Intelligence Review 33, 61–106 (2010)
4. Price, K.V., Storn, R., Lampinen, J.: Differential Evolution: A Practical Approach to Global Optimization. Springer (2005)
5. Storn, R., Price, K.V.: Differential evolution - a simple and efficient heuristic for global optimization over continuous spaces. J. Global Optimization 11, 341–359 (1997)
6. Tanabe, R., Fukunaga, A.: Evaluating the performance of shade on cec 2013 benchmark problems. In: IEEE Congress on Evolutionary Computation 2013, pp. 1952–1959. IEEE Computational Intelligence Society (2013)
7. Tanabe, R., Fukunaga, A.: Success-history based parameter adaptation for differential evolution. In: 2013 IEEE Congress on Evolutionary Computation (CEC), pp. 71–78 (June 2013)
8. Tvrdík, J.: Exponential crossover in competitive differential evolution. In: Matoušek, R. (ed.) 14th International Conference on Soft Computing, MENDEL 2008, Brno, Czech Republic, June 18-20, pp. 44–49 (2008)
9. Tvrdík, J.: Adaptation in differential evolution: A numerical comparison. Applied Soft Computing 9(3), 1149–1155 (2009)
10. Zaharie, D.: Influence of crossover on the behavior of differential evolution algorithms. Applied Soft Computing 9, 1126–1138 (2009)
11. Zhang, J., Sanderson, A.C.: JADE: Adaptive differential evolution with optional external archive. IEEE Transactions on Evolutionary Computation 13, 945–958 (2009)

A Parallel Approach for Evolutionary Induced Decision Trees. MPI+OpenMP Implementation

Marcin Czajkowski[✉], Krzysztof Jurczuk, and Marek Kretowski

Faculty of Computer Science, Bialystok University of Technology,
Wiejska 45a, 15-351 Bialystok, Poland
{m.czajkowski,k.jurczuk,m.kretowski}@pb.edu.pl

Abstract. One of the important and still not fully addressed issues in evolving decision trees is the induction time, especially for large datasets. In this paper, the authors propose a parallel implementation for Global Decision Tree system that combines shared memory (OpenMP) and message passing (MPI) paradigms to improve the speed of evolutionary induction of decision tree. The proposed solution is based on the classical master-slave model. The population is evenly distributed to available nodes and cores, and the time consuming operations like fitness evaluation and genetic operators are executed in parallel on slaves. Only the selection is performed on the master node. Efficiency and scalability of the proposed implementation is validated experimentally on artificial datasets. It shows noticeable speedup and possibility to efficiently process large datasets.

Keywords: Evolutionary algorithms · Decision trees · Parallel computing · MPI · OpenMP

1 Introduction

Evolutionary algorithms (EA) [14] are metaheuristic nature-inspired algorithms that represent techniques for solving a wide variety of difficult optimization problems. Their mechanisms such as mutation, recombination, natural selection and survival of the fittest are inspired by the biological evolution. One of the main drawbacks of EA is relatively high computational complexity. This issue is especially important for current data mining applications [6], where larger and larger datasets are processed and analyzed.

Fortunately EA are naturally prone to parallelism and the process of artificial evolution can be implemented in various ways [1]. It is possible to parallelize time consuming operations or to parallelize the whole evolutionary process itself. The first approach is often based on the master-slave model [7] and aims at speeding up the calculation without changing the original sequential algorithm. The second approach leads to a variety of distributed (coarse-grained) and cellular (fine-grained) algorithms that differ from the sequential implementation.

In the recent past evolutionary algorithms were successfully applied to evolve decision trees as an alternative to the greedy top-down approaches [2]. However,

© Springer International Publishing Switzerland 2015
L. Rutkowski et al. (Eds.): ICAISC 2015, Part I, LNAI 9119, pp. 340–349, 2015.
DOI: 10.1007/978-3-319-19324-3_31

evolving decision trees is usually more costly and time-consuming and considerably limits their popularity comparing to the greedy strategies. In the recent survey [2] on the evolutionary induction of decision trees, authors put on the first place in the future trends the need of speeding up the evolutionary tree induction.

In this paper, the authors investigate how the evolutionary induction of decision tree can be parallelized using both shared address space (OpenMP [3]) and message passing (MPI [16]) paradigms on a cluster of nodes with multi-core chips. The main objectives of this work are to accelerate the Global Decision Tree (GDT) system and to allow efficient evolutionary induction of decision trees on large datasets.

The first attempt to parallelize the GDT solution was proposed in [13]. The authors investigated parallel and distributed solutions for global induction of decision trees. In this paper, we rewrite and significantly extend that parallel implementation and introduce hybrid MPI+OpenMP approach that may provide a better efficiency than e.g. pure MPI version [15]. In addition, the proposed solution focuses not only on the algorithm speedup but also on algorithm's ability to efficiently process large datasets.

This paper is organized as follows. The next section provides a brief background on the GDT system. Section 3 describes our approach for parallel implementation of evolutionary tree induction in detail. Section 4 presents experimental validation of the proposed solution and comparison results on artificial datasets. In the last section, the paper is concluded and possible future works are sketched.

2 Global Decision Tree System

The GDT general structure follows a typical framework of evolutionary algorithms [14] with an unstructured population and a generational selection. It is able to induce univariate [10], oblique [11] and mixed [12] classification trees.

Decision trees are complicated tree structures, in which number of nodes, type of the tests and even number of test outcomes are not known in advance. Therefore, in the GDT system individuals are not specially encoded and are represented in their actual form as a typical classification trees. Depending on the tree type (univariate, oblique, mixed), each test in internal node concerns one or more attributes. In case of univariate tests, a test representation depends on the considered attribute type. For nominal attributes at least one attribute value is associated with each branch starting in the node, which means that an internal disjunction is implemented. Typical inequality tests with two outcomes are used for continuous-valued features. Only precalculated candidate thresholds [5] are considered as potential splits. In an oblique test with binary outcome a splitting hyperplane is represented by a fixed-size table of real values corresponding to a weight vector and a threshold. The inner product is calculated to decide where an example is routed.

Initial individuals are created by applying the simple top-down algorithm based on a dipolar principle [9] to randomly selected sub-samples of the learning set [12]. Ranking linear selection [14] is used as a selection mechanism. Additionally, in each iteration a single individual with the highest value of fitness function in current population is copied to the next one (elitist strategy). Evolution terminates when the maximum number of generations (default value: 1000) is reached.

To maintain genetic diversity, two specialized genetic operators corresponding to the classical mutation and cross-over were proposed. They are applied with a given probability to a tree (default value is 0.8 for mutation and 0.2 for cross-over). Mutation operator starts with randomly choosing the type of node (equal probability to select leaf or internal node). Next, the ranked list of nodes of the selected type is created and a mechanism analogous to the ranking linear selection is applied to decide which node will be affected. Depending on the type of node, the ranking takes into account the location of the internal node (internal nodes in lower parts of the tree are mutated with higher probability) and the number of misclassified objects (nodes with worse classification accuracy are mutated with higher probability). Modifications performed by the mutation operator depend on the tree type and the node type (i.e. if the considered node is a leaf node or an internal node) and cover different variants:

– changing the sub-trees or tests in the internal nodes;
– pruning the internal nodes or expanding the leaves that contain objects from different classes.

Cross-over operator starts with selecting positions in two affected individuals. Depending on the recombination variant, randomly selected nodes may:

– exchange subtrees (if exists);
– exchange tests associated with the nodes (only when non-terminal nodes are chosen and the numbers of outcomes are equal);
– exchange branches in random order which start from the selected nodes (only when non-terminal nodes are chosen and the numbers of outcomes are equal).

Successful application of any operator results in a necessity for relocation of the learning examples between tree parts rooted in the modified nodes.

Fitness function is one of the most important and sensitive factor in the design of EA. It drives the evolutionary search process by measuring how good a single individual is in terms of meeting the problem objective. In context of decision trees a direct minimization of the reclassification quality measured on a learning set usually leads to the overfitting problem. This problem is partially mitigated by defining a stopping condition and by applying a post-pruning [4] in typical top-down induction of decision trees [17]. In case of the evolutionary induced decision trees, this problem may be mitigated by a term incorporated into the fitness function. In the GDT system the fitness function is maximized and has the following form:

$$Fitness(T) = Q_{Reclass}(T) - \alpha \cdot Comp(T),$$

where $Q_{Reclass}(T)$ is the reclassification quality of the tree T and α is the relative importance of the classifier complexity (default value is 0.005). The tree complexity term $Comp(T)$ can be viewed as a penalty for over-parametrization. It includes the tree size (calculated as the number of leaves) and for oblique and mixed trees also the complexity of attributes in the internal nodes.

3 Parallel Implementation of Global Decision Tree System

In this section, the parallel implementation of the GDT system is proposed. At first, an efficient fitness calculation is shortly discussed and next, distributed (MPI) and shared (OpenMP) memory solutions are described.

In a typical EA the evaluation of fitness of individuals in population is the most time consuming operation. As it is calculated independently for every individual, this process can be easily parallelized by distributing population evenly among available nodes (slaves). The master node executes the remaining operations of the evolution.

In case of the GDT system, the aforementioned approach cannot be directly applied. The information about the learning vectors is stored in each node of decision trees. This way the genetic operators can efficiently and directly obtain the fitness corresponding to the individual [12], [8]. The actual fitness calculation is embedded into the post mutation and cross-over processing, when the learning vectors in the affected parts of the tree (or trees) are relocated. This mechanism increases the memory complexity of the induction but significantly reduces its computational complexity. As a consequence, the most time consuming elements of the algorithm are genetic operators and they should be performed in parallel.

Figure 1 illustrates the proposed hybrid parallel approach for the evolutionary induced decision tree algorithm. It can be observed that at the first step the master node spreads individuals from the population over slave nodes using message-passing strategy. In the next step, in each slave node the calculations are spread over cores which run the algorithm blocks in parallel.

It should be recalled that the shared memory approach is strongly linked and limited by the available hardware (e.g. 8 cores in one node), whereas within the distributed memory approach it is usually easier to create more numerous configurations.

3.1 Distributed Memory Approach

In each evolutionary loop, the master evenly distributes individuals between the nodes (slaves). To avoid wasting resources, the chunk of population is left on the master which also works as a slave. Migration the individuals between nodes is performed with the framework of the message-passing interface and requires:

- packing the tree structures into a flat message;
- transfer the message between nodes (sending/receiving);
- unpacking the message into the corresponding tree.

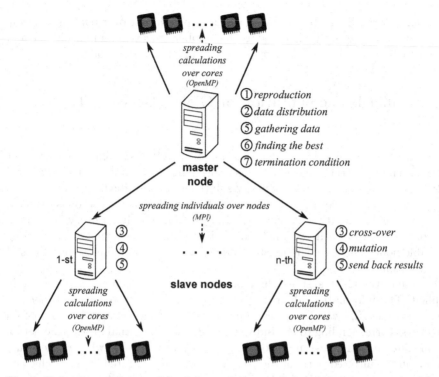

Fig. 1. Hybrid parallel approach of the evolutionary induced decision tree algorithm

The packed tree structure contains information about its size, the tests in the internal nodes' and additional nodes statistics (e.g. number of learning vectors), that speeds up the reconstruction during the message unpacking in the target node. In order to minimize the message size, the information about learning vectors associated with the tree nodes is not included in the message.

The certain parts of EA like reproduction (with elitism) and terminal condition verification are executed on the master node. However, to perform the selection, the fitness value of the distributed individuals has to be known. To avoid unnecessary unpacking-packing operations (for trees will not be selected into the next generation) on the master, the fitness value of the migrated individual is also transferred. Additionally, a certain number of individuals from the given slave node may survive (or be replicated) and in the next iteration they could be scheduled to be sent back to that node. This observation gives another possibility to eliminate unproductive calculation. However, it raises a risk that the individuals in particular a node may not change much (or be very similar). To keep the original sequential algorithm and avoid some kind of island models, we sent the cloned trees to random slave nodes to keep the sub-population diversified at each slave and to avoid crossing with identical or very similar individuals.

In the previously presented research [13] on the parallel GDT implementation, the redistribution of learning vectors was performed after unpacking each individual on the target node. The whole tree was reconstructed before starting the mutation and cross-over operations. Then, after successful application of a genetic operator, the redistribution of learning vectors of an affected node (and eventual sub-nodes) was performed.

This process of associating each instance with appropriate leaf is very time-consuming, especially on large datasets. In order to limit redistribution of the data, we propose to reconstruct only those nodes that will be affected. In addition, there is only a need to fit learning vectors that fall to the affected node since the redistribution of eventual sub-nodes is not necessary. If a genetic operator will be successful, the learning vectors in the sub-tree will be relocated anyway. This way, instead of reallocating all learning vectors in whole tree, we only set a part of the data in the node (without its eventual sub-nodes) that is selected for mutation or cross-over. It can be also noticed that if the root tree node is to be affected by a genetic operator, the preceding processing is reduced only to associating the whole dataset to the root node. The GDT assumption that internal nodes in lower parts of the tree are mutated with higher probability also enhances a possible speedup of the proposed implementation as it is expected that the lower parts of the tree held fewer learning vectors that need to be assigned.

3.2 Shared Memory Approach

The shared memory approach is applied in every slave node (including master which works also as a slave). We assume that all cores within the node operate independently but share the same memory resources. Access and modification of the same memory space by one core is visible to all other cores, therefore, no data communication between the cores is required. However, additional synchronization during write/read operations is needed in order to insure appropriate access to shared memory.

In Figure 1 we see that each slave node spreads calculations further. The calculations in the chosen algorithm blocks concerning different individuals are spread over cores. This way, all variants of genetic operation together with redistribution of learning vectors can be performed in parallel. In case of mutation, each core processes a single individual at a time, whereas during cross-over, pairs of affected individuals are processed in parallel. Parallelization with shared memory approach is also applied on the master node for the distribution and gathering population from other nodes. In addition, all trees that were transformed into leaves after application of genetic operators are extended into sub-trees in parallel by cores at each slave node.

4 Experiments

In this section we show the performance of the proposed parallel version of the GDT system. Two sets of experiments were performed. At first, the efficiency of the parallel MPI and OpenMP implementation is presented for four datasets.

Next, more detailed information is illustrated for one selected dataset with respect to speedup and size of the dataset.

4.1 Setup

Experimental verification was performed with the mixed version of the GDT system. All presented results were obtained with a default settings of parameters from the sequential version of the GDT system. We have tested four artificially generated datasets with different characteristics described in Table 1 and illustrated in Figure 2. All datasets are composed of 100 000 instances and have different characteristics like number of attributes and classes or the type of optimal splits.

In the paper we focus only on the time performance of the GDT system, therefore, results for the classification accuracy are not enclosed. However, for all tested datasets, the GDT system managed to induce trees with optimal structures and almost perfect accuracies (99%-100%). For detailed accuracy results, we refer reader to our previous papers [10,12].

In the performed experiments a cluster of sixteen SMP servers (nodes) running Ubuntu 12 and connected by an Infiniband network (20 Gb/s) was used. Each server was equipped with 16GB RAM, 2xXeon X5355 2.66GHz CPUs with total number of cores equal 8. We used the Intel version 15.1 compiler, MVAPICH version 2.2 and OpenMP version 3.0. Within each node, only the shared memory approach (OpenMP) was applied whereas between the nodes the message-passing interface (MPI) was used.

4.2 Results

In the first experiment, the authors focus on the overall speedup of the proposed hybrid MPI-OpenMP approach. Table 2 presents the obtained mean speedup for different datasets (100 000 instances). Only the best combination of nodes and cores is shown and it looked as follows for all four datasets:

- results for 2 cores: 1 node with 2 OpenMP threads;
- results for 4 cores: 1 node with 4 OpenMP threads;
- results for 8, 16, 32, 64 cores: 8 nodes with 1, 2, 4, 8 OpenMP threads per node, respectively.

Table 1. Datasets' characteristics: name, number of instances, number of attributes, number of classes and the type of splits in the internal nodes

Dataset	Instances	Attributes	Classes	Splits
Chess 3x3	100 000	2	2	univariate
Cross	100 000	2	5	univariate
Diamond	100 000	2	2	oblique
Zebra	100 000	10	2	oblique

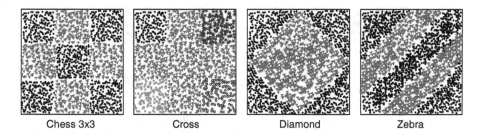

Chess 3x3   Cross   Diamond   Zebra

Fig. 2. Examples of artificial datasets

Table 2. Mean speedup reported for different number of cores

Dataset	Speedup on different number of cores					
	2	4	8	16	32	64
Chess 3x3	1.62	2.75	6.14	8.06	12.97	15.34
Cross	1.67	2.61	4.90	7.80	9.69	10.59
Diamond	1.86	2.62	4.61	7.10	9.35	10.58
Zebra	1.66	2.61	4.43	5.60	8.91	9.93

It is clearly visible that the hybrid parallel algorithm is able to noticeable decrease the computation time. The best speedup for 64 cores (8 cluster nodes - 1 MPI process per node and 8 OpenMP threads inside each node) is obtained for the dataset *Chess 3x3*. We can observe that the speedup differences between 32 and 64 cores are relatively small considering doubling the number of cores. One of the reasons is the size of the population (default: 64 individuals). To achieve effective parallelization, the number of cores should not exceed half of the population because for some operations like cross-over, each core performs calculations on two individuals. The second reason why the efficiency for the higher number of cores is getting smaller results from the Amdahl's law [7] as some parts of the algorithm have to run sequentially.

It should be noticed, that in previous work [13] speedup of the parallel implementation of GDT system on similar datasets were between 2 and 3 for 8 processing units. Here, we manage to achieve speedups between 4 and 6.

Fig. 3(a) shows how the number of used OpenMP threads per node influences the simulation time. Results are obtained for the dataset *Chess 3x3* (100 000 instances). Each time all cores on the used nodes are allocated. Although the population size equals 64, it is still profitable to use 8 nodes (8 MPI processes) with 8 OpenMP threads per each node.

The detailed results for different dataset (*Chess 3x3*) size are presented in Fig. 3(b). It shows the optimal results for the different number of used cores. For example, the 16 used cores means: i) for 10 000 instances - 4 cluster nodes - 1 MPI process per node and 4 OpenMP threads inside each node, or ii) for 1

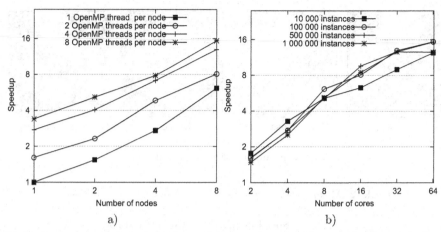

Fig. 3. Performance of the hybrid parallel algorithm of evolutionary induced decision tree: a) speedup across nodes with different number of OpenMP threads per node, b) speedup for different dataset size

000 000 instances - 8 cluster nodes - 1 MPI process per node and 2 OpenMP threads inside each node. Each time all cores on the used nodes are allocated. It is visible that the algorithm deals successfully both with small and large dataset sizes. It is true for a few cores as well as for more processing units.

Time comparison of the average loop time of the GDT solution shows that it is scalable in context of the data size. The sequential GDT system performs evolutionary loop in an average 0.037 second for *Chess 3x3* dataset with 10 000 instances and 31.71 seconds for 1 million instances. The default number of generations in the GDT system equals 1 000, therefore, the tree induction time for the sequential algorithm and the largest dataset takes almost 9 hours (+ the time to read the dataset and create initial population) whereas using parallel implementation is reduced up to 42 minutes when 64 cores are used.

5   Conclusion and Future Works

In the paper, the hybrid parallelization of the evolutionary induction of decision tree is investigated. The authors manage to successfully speed up the evolutionary induction of decision trees and efficiently process large datasets. Proposed implementation takes an advantage of modern parallel machines and may provide an efficient acceleration on high-performance computing clusters as well as on low-cost commodity hardware.

We will continue to work with the presented approach to adapt it to evolutionary induction of regression and model trees. Moreover, future work will deal with a GPGPU paralellization.

Acknowledgments. This project was funded by the Polish National Science Centre and allocated on the basis of decision 2013/09/N/ST6/04083. The second and third author was supported by the grant S/WI/2/2013 from Bialystok University of Technology.

References

1. Alba, E., Tomassini, M.: Parallelism and evolutionary algorithms. IEEE Transactions on Evolutionary Computation 6(5), 443–462 (2002)
2. Barros, R.C., Basgalupp, M.P., Carvalho, A.C., Freitas, A.A.: A survey of evolutionary algorithms for decision-tree induction. IEEE Transactions on Systems Man and Cybernetics Part C Applications and Reviews 42(3), 291–312 (2012)
3. Chapman, B., Jost, B.G., Pas, R., van der Kuck, D.J.: Using OpenMP: Portable Shared Memory Parallel Programming. MIT Press (2007)
4. Esposito, F., Malerba, D., Semeraro, G.: A comparative analysis of methods for pruning decision trees. IEEE Transactions on Pattern Analysis and Machine Intelligence 19(5), 476–491 (1997)
5. Fayyad, U., Irani, K.: Multi-interval discretization of continuous-valued attributes for classification learning. In: Proc. of IJCAI, pp. 1022–1027 (1993)
6. Freitas, A.: Data mining and knowledge discovery with evolutionary algorithms. Natural Computing Series. Springer (2002)
7. Grama, A., Karypis, G., Kumar, V., Gupta, A.: Introduction to Parallel Computing. Addison-Wesley (2003)
8. Kalles, D., Papagelis, A.: Lossless fitness inheritance in genetic algorithms for decision trees. Soft Computing 14(9), 973–993 (2010)
9. Kretowski, M.: An evolutionary algorithm for oblique decision tree induction. In: Rutkowski, L., Siekmann, J.H., Tadeusiewicz, R., Zadeh, L.A. (eds.) ICAISC 2004. LNCS (LNAI), vol. 3070, pp. 432–437. Springer, Heidelberg (2004)
10. Kretowski, M., Grześ, M.: Global learning of decision trees by an evolutionary algorithm. In: Information Processing and Security Systems, pp. 401–410 (2005)
11. Kretowski, M., Grześ, M.: Evolutionary learning of linear trees with embedded feature selection. In: Rutkowski, L., Tadeusiewicz, R., Zadeh, L.A., Żurada, J.M. (eds.) ICAISC 2006. LNCS (LNAI), vol. 4029, pp. 400–409. Springer, Heidelberg (2006)
12. Kretowski, M., Grześ, M.: Evolutionary induction of mixed decision trees. International Journal of Data Warehousing and Mining 3(4), 68–82 (2007)
13. Kretowski, M., Popczyński, P.: Global induction of decision trees: from parallel implementation to distributed evolution. In: Rutkowski, L., Tadeusiewicz, R., Zadeh, L.A., Zurada, J.M. (eds.) ICAISC 2008. LNCS (LNAI), vol. 5097, pp. 426–437. Springer, Heidelberg (2008)
14. Michalewicz, Z.: Genetic algorithms + data structures = evolution programs, 3rd edn. Springer (1996)
15. Rabenseifner, R., Hager, G., Jost, G.: Hybrid MPI/OpenMP parallel programming on clusters of multi-core SMP nodes. In: Proc. of the 17th Euromicro International Conference on Parallel, Distributed and Network-based Processing, pp. 427–436 (2009)
16. Pacheco, P.: Parallel Programming with MPI. Morgan Kaufmann Publishers (1997)
17. Rokach, L., Maimon, O.Z.: Data mining with decision trees: theory and application. Machine Perception Artificial Intelligence 69 (2008)

Automatic Grammar Induction for Grammar Based Genetic Programming

Dariusz Palka and Marek Zachara[✉]

AGH University of Science and Technology,
30 Mickiewicza Av., 30-059, Krakow, Poland
{dpalka,mzachara}@agh.edu.pl

Abstract. This paper discusses selected aspects of evolutionary search algorithms guided by grammars, such as Grammar Guided Genetic Programming or Grammatical Evolution. The aim of the paper is to demonstrate that, when the efficiency of the search process in such environment is considered, it is not only the language defined by a grammar that is important, but also the form of the grammar plays a key role. In the most common current approach, the person who sets up the search environment provides the grammar as well. However, as demonstrated in the paper, this may lead to a sub-optimal efficiency of the search process. Because an infinite number of grammars of different forms can exist for a given language, manual construction of the grammar which makes the search process most effective is generally not possible. It seems that a desirable solution would be to have the optimal grammar generated automatically for the provided constrains. This paper presents possible solutions allowing for automatic grammar induction, which makes the search process more effective.

Keywords: Grammar induction · Meta-grammar GA

1 Introduction

Grammars are one of the most important structures in Computer Science. They can be used to impose restrictions on a represented structure. This ability is important in the evolutionary search algorithms driven by grammars such as Grammar Guided Genetic Programming or Grammatical Evolution (GE). So far, the main focus in the GE field has been placed on the language defined by the supplied grammar and the efficiency of the evolution-related algorithms [4]. However, as it is demonstrated in this paper, the form of the grammar used in GE plays an important role. An example provided in section 4.1 shows that using different forms of grammar for the same language leads to a significant change in the distribution of the generated individuals, thus influencing the efficiency of the search process. Because an infinite number of grammars of different forms can exist for a given language, it is usually not feasible to analyze their efficiency 'manually' while setting up the search environment. In most cases it will not even be possible to estimate the efficiency of the considered form of the grammar against other possible forms.

© Springer International Publishing Switzerland 2015
L. Rutkowski et al. (Eds.): ICAISC 2015, Part I, LNAI 9119, pp. 350–360, 2015.
DOI: 10.1007/978-3-319-19324-3_32

It does, therefore, seem important to provide some mechanisms which will allow for automatic grammar induction (also known as grammatical inference) on the basis of the constrains provided. This paper presents a possible approach to this task, utilizing the GE for the purpose of grammar induction with provided constrains. As demonstrated, such an approach based on Grammatical Evolution is suitable for the presented objective. The form of the grammar generated using this method has proved to be superior to a number of manually provided grammar forms.

The paper is structured as follows. Section 2 shortly describes the role of grammar in Genetic Programming, section 3 provides examples of the impact of grammar on the efficiency of evolutionary search process driven by this grammar, section 4 presents a proposed method of automatic grammar induction and shows the result obtained for the grammar of integer constants, while discussion and conclusions can be found in section 5.

2   The Role of a Grammar in Genetic Programming

In a standard Genetic Programming (GP) form, individuals, i.e. computer programs obtained, are an unrestricted composition of available functions and terminals (typically the only constraint is imposed on the depth of a syntax tree, which prevents the uncontrolled growth of the average size of an individual, which is called a code bloat problem).

As it is observed in [3], using unrestricted syntax trees as program representations in GP can address a wide range of problems. However, we often want to provide some form of additional search space restrictions. For example, if a terminal set contains integer and boolean constants (such as 0, 1, 2, ... and TRUE, FALSE), the generated program can contain expressions like '0 - TRUE', which must be carried on. One way to solve this is to invalidate such programs, but in this case most generated programs must be invalidated, which dramatically decreases the efficiency of the search process. Another solution is to provide semantics for all possible syntactic combinations like '0 - TRUE', which can be possible in simple problems but can rapidly become unwieldy. The alternative is to use a grammar to provide syntactic restrictions on generated programs (represented as syntax trees). The need for constrained syntactic structures have been suggested from GP inceptions, which is discussed in chapter 19 of Koza's first book [3].

Using grammars in GP has many advantages [4]:

- it provides declarative search space restrictions
- it allows for defining homologous operators
- it is the basis for flexible extensions

There are two common types of evolutionary algorithms in which a grammar is used to guide the evolution process, i.e.:

- Grammatically-based Genetic Programming (also called Grammar Guided Genetic Programming) [12] - where the genotype is represented as a tree structure (derivation tree) - the same as in a standard GP form
- Grammatical Evolution [9] [10] - where the genotype is a linear string, which is then decoded to a context-free derivation tree

Grammatical Evolution is now one of the most rapidly developing variations of GP methods [4], and it has been successfully used in a wide range of applications [2] [6] [5] [8].

Because a grammar guides the whole evolutionary process in GP techniques, its role is crucial. Especially, the efficiency of the search process is determined by a grammar and the restrictions marshalled by this grammar.

3   The Impact of the Grammar Form on the Efficiency of the Search Algorithm

As can be seen below, not only are the search space restrictions defined by a grammar important in the efficiency of search space, but also the form of a grammar matters.

The most commonly used types of grammars in GP are context-free grammars, because they are sufficient to define most languages commonly used in GP programming (the languages in which the phenotype expressed as a derivation tree is evaluated). Because an infinite number of context-free grammars can exist for a given context-free language, it is important whether the search process depends on the grammar form and how to select the form which can be most promising in terms of the efficiency of the search process.

The impact of the grammar form on the efficiency of the search process of Grammatical Evolution is shown below for three different problems.

The GEVA software [1] was used to find solutions to each example problem. In each test case the following configuration parameters were used: the maximal number of generations of the evolution process was 5000, the population size was 100, the selection type was tournament selection, the crossover probability was 0.9, and the mutation probability was 0.02. Except for the parameter 'maximum number of generations', the same values of parameters as in the example 'Symbolic Regression' in GEVA software were used.

In each example the efficiency of the search process for three standard forms of grammars was compared

- Backus-Naur Form (BNF) - the most general form of a context-free grammar
- Chomsky normal form (CNF) - where the production rules could be in the form $A ::= BC$ or $A ::= a$ (A, B, C are nonterminal symbols and a is a terminal symbol)
- Greibach normal form (GNF) - where all production rules are in the form $A ::= aA_1 A_2 \ldots A_n$ ($A, A_1, \ldots A_n$ are nonterminals, a is a terminal symbol)

3.1   Point 2D

In this problem the aim is to find unknown coordinates of a point in discrete 2D space. The fitness function is defined as a square of the distance from a searched point to the candidate point found by GE algorithm:

$$fitness = (x_p - x_c)^2 + (y_p - y_c)^2 \tag{1}$$

where:

x_p is x coordinate of the unknown (searched) point
y_p is y coordinate of the unknown (searched) point
x_c is x coordinate of the candidate point
y_c is y coordinate of the candidate point

The search space is limited by the interval of x [0, 99] and the interval of y [0, 99], so in this case the search space contains 10 000 different points. The grammar in BNF is as follows:

```
<point>   ::= <num> , <num>
<num> ::= <digit> | <digit> <digit>
<digit>   ::= 0 | 1 | 2 | 3 | 4 | 5 | 6 | 7 | 8 | 9
```

The grammar for the same language in CNF is:

```
<point> ::= <num> <x>
<x> ::= <comma> <num>
<num> ::=   <digit> <digit> | 0 | 1 | 2 | 3 | 4
    | 5 | 6 | 7 | 8 | 9
<digit>   ::= 0 | 1 | 2 | 3 | 4 | 5 | 6 | 7 | 8 | 9
<comma> ::= ,
```

And the grammar in GNF is:

```
<point> ::= 0 <digit> <x> | 1 <digit> <x>
    | 2 <digit> <x> | 3 <digit> <x> | 4 <digit> <x>
    | 5 <digit> <x> | 6 <digit> <x> | 7 <digit> <x>
    | 8 <digit> <x> | 9 <digit> <x> | 0 <x> | 1 <x>
    | 2 <x> | 3 <x> | 4 <x> | 5 <x> | 6 <x> | 7 <x>
    | 8 <x> | 9 <x>
<x> ::= , <num>
<num> ::= 0 <digit> | 1 <digit> | 2 <digit> | 3 <digit>
    | 4 <digit> | 5 <digit> | 6 <digit> | 7 <digit>
    | 8 <digit> | 9 <digit> | 0 | 1 | 2 | 3 | 4 | 5
    | 6 | 7 | 8 | 9
<digit> ::= 0 | 1 | 2 | 3 | 4 | 5 | 6 | 7 | 8 | 9
```

The standard convention for a context-free grammar was used, where the symbols in angle brackets are the nonterminal symbols, symbol '|' means the alternative right side of productions, and other symbols on the right hand side of productions are the terminal symbols. The symbol on the left hand side of the first production rule is the start symbol.

The 1 000 runs of the GE process for each grammar type were executed, and, as a result, the first generation in which the correct solution was found (i.e. the generation in which the solution with the fitness value = 0) was recorded.

In Figure 1 the cumulative distribution function for the generation in which the solution was found is presented for each grammar form.

Table 1 presents the arithmetic mean and standard deviation of the first generation in which the solution was found.

As can be seen in this example, the best results were obtained using the BNF grammar.

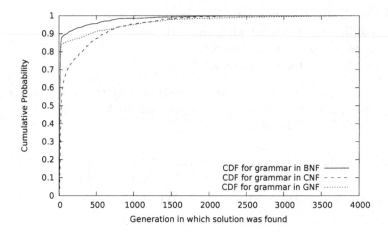

Fig. 1. The plot of the cumulative distribution function for the Point 2D problem

Table 1. The results of Point 2D Problem

	BNF	CNF	GNF
arithmetic mean	63.9	188.8	146.3
standard deviation	224.8	352.8	435.4

3.2   Symbolic Regression

The objective in this example is to find a mathematical expression of the function that best fits a given dataset. A dataset is produced by a function $f(x) = x^3 + x$, for 50 values of x in the interval [-5.0, 5.0].

In this example an expression in the prefix form was looked for. The grammars were as follows:

The grammar in BNF form

```
<expr> ::= <op> <expr> <expr> | <var>
<op>   ::= + | - | * | /
<var>  ::= x0 | 1.0
```

The grammar in CNF form

```
<expr> ::= <op> <v> | x0 | 1.0
<v> ::= <expr> <expr>
<op>   ::= + | - | * | /
```

The grammar in GNF form

```
<expr> ::= + <v> | - <v> | * <v> | / <v> | x0 | 1.0
<v> ::= + <v> <expr> | - <v> <expr> | * <v> <expr>
    | / <v> <expr> | x0 <expr> | 1.0 <expr>
```

The cumulative distribution function for the generation in which a solution was found is presented in Figure 2. The arithmetic mean and standard deviation of the results obtained are presented in Table 2.

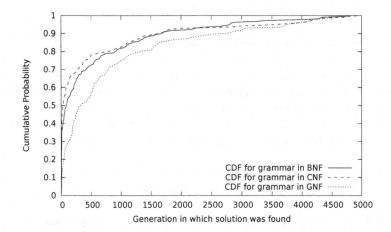

Fig. 2. The plot of the cumulative distribution function for the Symbolic Regression problem

Table 2. The results of Symbolic Regression Problem

	BNF	CNF	GNF
arithmetic mean	535.8	518.6	828.6
standard deviation	956.4	1057.9	1141.2

In this example the grammar in CNF yielded slightly better results than the grammar in BNF.

4   Automatic Induction of Grammars Suitable for the Problem Solved

As can be seen from the above examples, the grammar form has an important impact on the efficiency of the searching process. But in most cases it is impossible to a'priori define the best suitable grammar for a given problem. Even if extra knowledge about the searching space is available, defining the grammar manually may be hard and impractical. However, if extra knowledge about the searching space is available or can be obtained, the GE process can be used to find a proper form of grammar to guide the evolutionary process in GE. This approach is a kind of meta evolution, which has two nested GE stages: during the outer one the grammar (called solution grammar) for inner GE stage is evolved, and during the inner stage this grammar is used to guide the process of the evolutionary search for the solution of a specified problem. This technique of meta evolution for GE is called Grammatical Evolution by Grammatical Evolution or abbreviated as $(GE)^2$ [11].

4.1 Evolution of a Grammar for Integer Values

The efficiency of meta evolution is shown by the example of generating a context-free grammar for integer constant values. The grammar generating constant values is a typical part of many grammars, such as grammars for symbolic regression or grammars for generating programs in arbitrary programming languages, etc.

Also, the extra restrictions for generated integers are provided:

- all values should be placed in the range [0, 99]
- the values should have the uniform distribution

The uniform distribution of generated integer values is important because, in most cases, this makes the search process more effective.

Figure 3 presents the results of the cumulative distribution function for three manually provided grammars in the form of BFN, CNF and GNF.

These grammars are modified parts of the grammars for the Point 2D problem presented above. The modifications guarantee that the created values have the proper form and are in the [0, 99] range.

The grammar in BNF form:

```
<intval>  ::= <digit09> | <digit19> <digit09>
<digit19>  ::= 0 | 1 | 2 | 3 | 4 | 5 | 6 | 7 | 8 | 9
<digit09>  ::= 0 | <digit19>
```

The grammar in CNF form:

```
<intval>  ::=  <digit19> <digit09> | 0 | 1 | 2 | 3 | 4
    | 5 | 6 | 7 | 8 | 9
<digit19>  ::= 1 | 2 | 3 | 4 | 5 | 6 | 7 | 8 | 9
<digit09>  ::= 0 | 1 | 2 | 3 | 4 | 5 | 6 | 7 | 8 | 9
```

The grammar in GNF form:

```
<intval>  ::= 1 <digit09> | 2 <digit09> | 3 <digit09>
    | 4 <digit09> | 5 <digit09> | 6 <digit09>
    | 7 <digit09> | 8 <digit09> | 9 <digit09>
    | 0 | 1 | 2 | 3 | 4 | 5 | 6 | 7 | 8 | 9
<digit09>  ::= 0 | 1 | 2 | 3 | 4 | 5 | 6 | 7 | 8 | 9
```

The figure shows that all these grammars lead to an ineffective search process. In all cases more than half of the values generated from a grammar are placed in the interval [0, 9]. To automatically generate grammar for integer values, the meta-grammar Genetic Algorithm [7] [11] was applied. The meta grammar (grammars' grammar), which dictates the form of solution grammars is as follows:

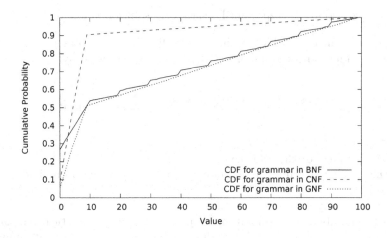

Fig. 3. The plot of the cumulative distribution function for manually provided grammars

```
<syntax> ::= <rule> | <rule> <syntax>
<rule> ::= <rule-name> <assign> <list> <line-end>
<list> ::= <symbol> | <symbol> <whitespace> <list>
<symbol> ::= <terminal> | <rule-name>
<assign> ::= "::="
<line-end> ::= "\n"
<whitespace> ::= " "
<rule-name> ::= NT1 | NT2 | NT3 | NT4 | NT5 | NT6
<terminal> ::= <digit>
<digit> ::= 0 | 1 | 2 | 3 | 4 | 5 | 6 | 7 | 8 | 9
```

This meta grammar allows for constructing any solution grammar in the BNF form, which can use nonterminals $NT1$, $NT2$, ..., $NT6$ and terminals 0, 1, ..., 9. The meta-grammar Genetic Algorithm is as follows:

1. the first generation of solution grammars are created with the use of the meta grammar
2. the requested number N_g of integer values is created for each syntactically correct solution grammar
3. the distribution of values created in step 2 is compared with the uniform distribution, and, on this basis, the fitness value for the grammar is calculated
4. for each syntactically incorrect grammar the value *FitIncorrect* is assigned as the fitness value
5. on the basis of fitness values, candidates (i.e. solution grammars) for the next generation are selected using tournament selection
6. next generation of grammars is created from selected candidates (from step 5) using genetic operations - reproduction, crossover and mutation. The genetic operations are driven by the meta grammar (i.e. created solutions grammars assume the form dictated by the meta grammar)

7. the process loops to step 2 until a satisfying solution is found

The fitness function, which evaluates the distributions obtained for a given solution grammar with the uniform distribution, is expressed by:

$$fitness = P_{va} * N_0 + P_{inv} * N_{inv} + \sum_{i=0}^{99} |N_i - \frac{N_g}{100}| \qquad (2)$$

where:

P_{va} is the penalty for the absence of the value
N_0 is the number of values in the interval $[0, 99]$ for which no individuals are generated
P_{inv} is the penalty for an invalid value
N_{inv} is the number of generated individuals, which are syntactically incorrect (for example, sentences with length equal zero or containing nonterminals)
N_i is the number of generated individuals (integer values) which equal i
N_g is the total number of generated individuals (integer values)

This form of the fitness function prefers solution grammars for which all values in the required interval $[0, 99]$ are reachable and no syntactically incorrect individuals may be created. Figure 4 presents the results of the best solution grammar fitness in each generation.

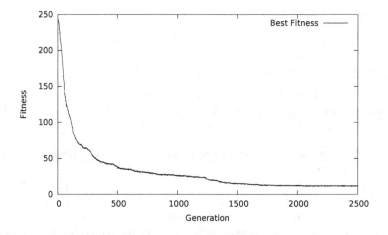

Fig. 4. The plot of fitness for the best individuals (solution grammars)

The cumulative distribution function for the best grammars in the last generation is shown in Figure 5. As seen from this figure, the grammar found by meta-grammar Genetic Algorithm after 2500 generations gives almost an ideal uniform distribution, and slight deviations from the uniform distribution result from the stochastic nature of generating integer values from solution grammars.

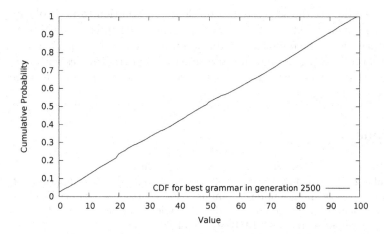

Fig. 5. The plot of the cumulative distribution function for the best individual (solution grammar) in the last generation

The best solution grammar found in the last generation is as follows:

```
<NT3> ::= 0 | 5 <NT5> | <NT1> 8 | <NT5> 5 | <NT5> <NT1>
       | <NT5> <NT1> | 20 | <NT1> 4 | <NT1> 5 | <NT5> <NT1>
       | <NT1> 7 | <NT1> 9 | <NT1> 1 | <NT1> 1 | 3 <NT1>
       | <NT5> <NT1> | <NT1> 7 | 5 <NT1> |   <NT5> | <NT5> 3
       | <NT1> 9 | <NT1> | <NT5> <NT1> | <NT1> 3 | 0 <NT6>
       | <NT1> 4 | <NT1> 0 | <NT1> 6 | 2 <NT5> | 6 <NT1>
       | <NT1> 0 | <NT1> 6 |  <NT1> 2 | <NT1> 3 | <NT1> 0
       | <NT1> 2 | <NT5> <NT1> | <NT1> 5 | <NT1> 2
       | <NT5> <NT5> | <NT1> 8 | <NT1> | 50
<NT5> ::= 5 | 4 | 2 | 2 | 8 | 1 | 9 | 7
<NT4> ::= <NT2> | <NT2>
<NT2> ::= 9 | <NT3> 5 | 79 | 3 <NT3>
<NT1> ::= 8 | 1 | 6 | 9 | 4 | 7 | 3
<NT6> ::= 5 | <NT5> 4 | <NT1> | 52 | 6 | 2 | 5 | <NT5>
```

Such grammar can be then used as a part of universal (meta) grammar for any problem which requires integer constant as a part of the solution.

5   Conclusion

This paper demonstrated that the grammar form used in Grammar Based Genetic Programming has a great influence on the efficiency of the search process. It can be hard or even impossible to provide a grammar manually in a form which makes the evolutionary search process effective. In such cases the process of automatic grammar induction, which is a kind of meta-Grammar Genetic Algorithm presented in this paper, can be applied. In this process Genetic Evolution algorithm is applied to search for an optimal form of the solution grammar, which is next used during the second stage of Genetic Evolution to find solutions of a specified problem (such as the problem of generating integer constant in a defined interval with the uniform distribution presented in the paper). This process is useful in finding a grammar in a suitable form which complies with constrains provided. The induced grammar can be then used as a whole or as a part of a bigger meta grammar.

References

1. GEVA software, http://ncra.ucd.ie/Site/GEVA.html
2. Hemberg, E., Ho, L.T.W., O'Neill, M., Claussen, H.: A comparison of grammatical genetic programming grammars for controlling femtocell network coverage. Genetic Programming and Evolvable Machines 14(1), 65–93 (2013), http://dx.doi.org/10.1007/s10710-012-9171-8
3. Koza, J.: Genetic programming: On the programming of computers by means of natural selection. The MIT Press, Cambridge (1992)
4. McKay, R.I., Hoai, N.X., Whigham, P.A., Shan, Y., O'Neill, M.: Grammar-based genetic programming: a survey. Genetic Programming and Evolvable Machines 11(3-4), 365–396 (2010), http://dx.doi.org/10.1007/s10710-010-9109-y
5. Nicolau, M., O'Neill, M., Brabazon, A.: Applying genetic regulatory networks to index trading. In: Coello, C.A.C., Cutello, V., Deb, K., Forrest, S., Nicosia, G., Pavone, M. (eds.) PPSN 2012, Part II. LNCS, vol. 7492, pp. 428–437. Springer, Heidelberg (2012), http://dx.doi.org/10.1007/978-3-642-32964-7_43
6. Nicolau, M., Saunders, M., O'Neill, M., Osborne, B., Brabazon, A.: Evolving interpolating models of net ecosystem CO_2 exchange using grammatical evolution. In: Moraglio, A., Silva, S., Krawiec, K., Machado, P., Cotta, C. (eds.) EuroGP 2012. LNCS, vol. 7244, pp. 134–145. Springer, Heidelberg (2012), http://dx.doi.org/10.1007/978-3-642-29139-5_12
7. O'Neill, M., Brabazon, A.: mGGA: The meta-grammar genetic algorithm. In: Keijzer, M., Tettamanzi, A., Collet, P., van Hemert, J., Tomassini, M. (eds.) EuroGP 2005. LNCS, vol. 3447, pp. 311–320. Springer, Heidelberg (2005)
8. O'Neill, M., Brabazon, A.: Evolving a logo design using lindenmayer systems, postscript & grammatical evolution. In: IEEE Congress on Evolutionary Computation, pp. 3788–3794. IEEE (2008), http://dx.doi.org/10.1109/CEC.2008.4631311
9. O'Neill, M., Ryan, C.: Grammatical evolution. IEEE Trans. Evolutionary Computation 5(4), 349–358 (2001), http://dx.doi.org/10.1109/4235.942529
10. O'Neill, M., Ryan, C.: Grammatical Evolution: Evolutionary Automatic Programming in a Arbitrary Language, Genetic programming, vol. 4. Kluwer Academic Publishers (2003)
11. O'Neill, M., Ryan, C.: Grammatical evolution by grammatical evolution: The evolution of grammar and genetic code. In: Keijzer, M., O'Reilly, U.-M., Lucas, S., Costa, E., Soule, T. (eds.) EuroGP 2004. LNCS, vol. 3003, pp. 138–149. Springer, Heidelberg (2004)
12. Whigham, P.A.: Grammatically-based genetic programming. In: Rosca, J.P. (ed.) Proceedings of the Workshop on Genetic Programming: From Theory to Real-World Applications, Tahoe City, California, USA, pp. 33–41 (July 9, 1995)

On the Ability of the One-Point Crossover Operator to Search the Space in Genetic Algorithms

Zbigniew Pliszka[1] and Olgierd Unold[2(✉)]

[1] Wroclaw Public Library, Sztabowa 95, 53-310 Wroclaw, Poland
[2] Department of Computer Engineering, Faculty of Electronics
Wroclaw University of Technology, Wyb. Wyspianskiego 27, 50-370 Wroclaw, Poland
olgierd.unold@pwr.edu.pl
http://olgierd.unold.staff.iiar.pwr.edu.pl/

Abstract. In this paper we study the search abilities of binary one-point crossover (1ptc) operator in a genetic algorithm (GA). We show, that under certain conditions, GA is capable of using only a 1ptc operator to explore the entire search space, fighting premature convergence. Further, we prove that to restore the entire space from any two binary chromosomes, each of length n, at least $2^{n-1} - 1$ one-point crossover operations is needed. This number can serve as a measure for comparing the search speed of the different algorithms. Moreover, we propose an algorithm spanning the search space in the minimal number of crossovers.

Keywords: Evolutionary Computation · Genetic Algorithm · One-point Crossover · Premature Convergence

1 Introduction

The genetic algorithm (GA), invented in 1960s by Holland [10], seems to be one of the most studied topics in evolutionary algorithm (EA) literature. GAs are robust search and optimization algorithms based on natural selection in environments and natural genetics in biology. What is interesting, GA examines not just one solution, but a pool of probable solutions simultaneously, which are organized as chromosomes and form a population. GA incrementally generates new chromosomes by applying selection, crossover and mutation operators, until the population finally reaches a state, where diversity is minimal (so called convergence). The set of all possible chromosomes forms the search space. The most common way of encoding chromosome in GA is a fixed binary string. It is well-known that crossover operator plays a key role in the evolutionary process, especially in preserving the genetic diversity [3,31]. Various crossover operators are used in GA, and among them the simplest one is the one-point crossover belonging to so-called *mask-based crossover operators* [30]. This operator selects a crossover point within a chromosome then interchanges two parent chromosomes at this point to produce two new offspring. Note that any multi-point crossover

© Springer International Publishing Switzerland 2015
L. Rutkowski et al. (Eds.): ICAISC 2015, Part I, LNAI 9119, pp. 361–369, 2015.
DOI: 10.1007/978-3-319-19324-3_33

can be seen as 1ptcs assembling [22]. Moreover, in [24] we proved the theorem which says that each crossover exchanging can be represented as a composition of 1ptcs. It means, that the maximum exploration opportunities within a class of exchanging crossovers has one-point crossover, and each other type of crossover operator can retain–at best–this ability!

In this paper we show, that under certain conditions, GA is capable to span (explore) the entire search space adequately, using only one-point crossover operator.

Lets stress here and now that any evolutionary algorithm, including GA, usually tries to avoid exploring the entire space of possible solutions. However, knowing the search abilities of genetic operators is essential for the proper design of the algorithm and to prevent undesirable properties, such as a premature convergence.

Further, we propose a measure for comparing the search speed of a set by different algorithms. For a n-element set this measure is the minimal number of 1ptcs necessary to explore the entire binary space, i.e. $2^{n-1} - 1$. We show how to construct an algorithm spanning the space of binary chromosomes in the minimal number of steps. The use both of the measure and the algorithm was illustrated by the problem of finding palindromes.

2   Related Work

The issue posed by this paper has been a long time study in the field of genetic algorithms [6,29], but the problem of spanning the space of binary chromosomes seems to be still insufficiently explored in the literature and certainly prematurely abandoned.

In [21] the conditions for one-point crossover operator in GA were defined which must be met by the operator for exploring all the search space of binary chromosomes. A somewhat related problem is the problem of too early convergence of GA (convergence refers to some measure of the genetic diversity of the population). A number of attempts were undertaken to avoid this undesirable phenomenon (for a comparative survey see [19]). The authors presented a wide range of solutions. Some of them argue that sufficient operator is a mutation [9] or that such discussion is pointless without reference to particular fitness function or coding method [15]. Another group of authors proposed adaptive probabilities of genetic operators [2,4,5] or drew attention to the impact of selective pressure [1,14]. It is worth noticing a bit controversial proposal of inserting a random individual into a pool [11].

The dynamics of evolutionary algorithms expressed by the NK model, only partly related to the problem of binary search space, has been recently studied [13,32].

What is interesting, while most of the research prove the usefulness of the crossover operator in EAs [7,8,12,17,18], [26] showed the problem, called Ignoble Trails, in which mutation-only EA finds solutions much faster than using crossing-over.

Recently, the influence of crossover in multi-objective EAs is studied [16,27].

3   Some Properties of the Space of Binary Chromosomes

Subject of this study is the following set:

$A^n = \{(a_n, a_{n-1}, \ldots, a_i, \ldots, a_1) : \forall i \in \{1, 2, \ldots, n\}, a_i \in \{0, 1\}\}$.

Its elements represent all possible binary chromosomes of equal length n, where n is a natural number higher than 1. Only one-point crossover is performed on the pairs of elements of this set. This limitation is more apparent than real, however. In [22] we showed that any multi-point crossover is a combination of one-point crossovers. The proof is to be found in [24].

In the previous works [20,21,22,23,24] some definitions and properties of the binary space under study was introduced. In the following, the key definitions and results are summarized.

Definition 1. *An initial or primary population is a set of chromosomes (elements) from the A^n space.*

We assume that all elements of such a set take part in the first selection process for the parent pool.

Definition 2. *We say that the A^n space is ancestral, if all its elements can be obtained from a primary population of repeatedly applying finite number of times only one-point crossover operators.*

Note that the above definition does not reject the chromosomes received from the primary population by the other genetic operations (like mutation or inversion). The only requirement is that there is a potential ability to generate all chromosomes from the space using only 1ptcs.

Definition 3. *Two chromosomes a_t and a_k in A^n are called polar chromosomes if and only if for each coordinate these chromosomes have opposite values.*

For example two chromosomes: (01100) and (10011) are polar in A^5 space. Note that the distance between polar chromosomes is constant and equals n. Some other properties of polar chromosomes were given in [23].

Theorem 1. *The whole space A^n is ancestral if and only if there are the elements in the primary population P, which have the following properties: for each position (locus), we have two elements from P having different (in terms of dual opposing) values.*

This theorem is proven in [20] for binary Hadamard space, which is isomorphic with A^n space (see [23]).

Theorem 2 follows from Theorem 1 immediately.

Theorem 2. *If a primary population $P \subseteq A^n$ contains a pair of polar chromosomes, then the whole space A^n is an ancestral space.*

4   An Optimal Algorithm for Exploring the Space of Binary Chromosomes

Before we prove a theorem allowing us to construct an efficient (in terms of number of operations used) algorithm for searching A^n space, we introduce some definitions and designations.

The space A^n consisting of binary chromosomes generated by 1ptc from two primary chromosomes (i.e. making primary population) can be presented by a binary tree, called CT - crossover tree. In Figure 1, the binary space A^5 in the CT form is shown. In the root node of CT there are two primary chromosomes: (00000), (11111) with their phenotypes 0 and 31, respectively.

We say that the chromosome h in CT is located on the level $k \geqslant 1$ when there is $k - 1$ nodes between the root node of the tree and h. The primary population of chromosomes is located on the 0 level. In the Figure 1, chromosome (00111), with phenotype 7, is situated on the level 3. There are two intermediate nodes to the root: (00011) - phenotype 3 and (00001) - phenotype 1.

The child chromosome is obtained by using one-point crossover from parent chromosomes. In the Figure 1, chromosome (11101) - phenotype 29 from the level 2 - is the child of two chromosomes (00001) - 1 and (11111) - 31 from the level 1. Affiliate chromosome (parent) is the chromosome associated with another parent chromosome to perform a crossover operation. For example, a primary population in CT is a pair of affiliate chromosomes.

Now we will prove a simple but important for our discussion theorem.

Theorem 3. *Any algorithm established to restore (span) the entire space A^n from any two chromosomes with a one-point crossover operator needs at least $2^{n-1} - 1$ operations.*

Proof (of Theorem 2). Note that 1ptc operator gives always two offspring chromosomes. Let us assume (as we show below this is a realistic assumption) that each of the fresh chromosome is new (i.e. not obtained earlier) and chromosomes in the child pair differ from each other.

Since in A^n we have 2^n chromosomes and the whole population starts from two primary chromosomes, then the minimal number of 1ptcs to be performed to explore the entire space is $(2^n - 2)/2 = 2^{n-1} - 1$. $\qquad\qquad\square$

It is therefore not possible to create an algorithm exploring the whole binary space A^n performing less than $2^{n-1} - 1$ one-point crossovers.

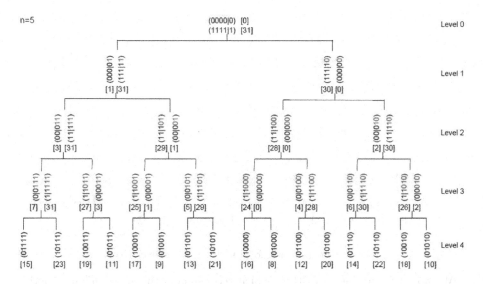

Fig. 1. Exemplary binary space A^5 with the primary population (00000) and (11111). Square brackets are used to denote a phenotype of chromosome.

Listing 1.1. Algorithm CT122

```
1   Input:
2   n                   // size of the space under study
3   hr0                 // input chromosome
4   Begin
5    Tree(1,1,0) = hr0
6    Tree(1,2,0) = 2^n-1-Tree(1,1,0)
7    For c = 1 To n-1
8     Begin //c
9      For j = 1 To 2^(c-1)
10      Begin //j
11       Tree(2*j-1,1,c) = Tree(j,1,c-1) -
12                         (Tree(j,1,c-1)Mod(2^c)) +
13                         (Tree(j,2,c-1)Mod(2^c))
14       Tree(2*j,1,c) = Tree(j,2,c-1) -
15                         (Tree(j,2,c-1)Mod(2^c)) +
16                         (Tree(j,1,c-1)Mod(2^c))
17       If c < n-1 Then
18         Begin //If
19          Tree(2*j-1,2,c) = Tree(j,2,c-1)
20          Tree(2*j,2,c) = Tree(j,1,c-1)
21         End    //If
22      End //j
23     End //c
24   End.
```

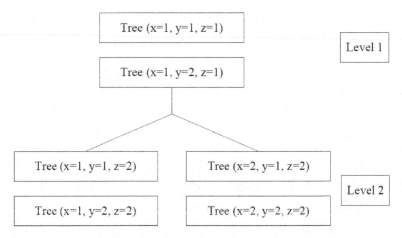

Fig. 2. *Tree* notation for a node in a crossover tree

We now present the algorithm, which reconstructs the space A^n in exactly $2^{n-1} - 1$ one-point crossovers. In the algorithm presented below (Listing 1.1) and called CT122 (Crossover Tree 1-point 2 children 2 parents algorithm), spanning binary space A^n over a binary tree, each chromosome (except the primary ones) is generated by 1ptc operation. The primary population consists of polar chromosomes. Cutting is always performed after $k + 1$ allele for all chromosomes from k level, counting from the right side. The parent chromosomes in each node (except the root node) are created by affiliating the child with one of its parent chromosome, i.e. by using so called backcrossing [28].

Each node in CT122 is denoted by $Tree(x, y, z)$ (see Figure 2), where:

- x counts the nodes for a given level of CT, from the left to the right,
- y distinguishes partners for crossing operation: the value of 1 has the first parent obtained as a result of crossing on the previous level (generation), the second affiliating chromosome, taken from its parental couple, has the value of 2,
- z depicts the level of the node.

According to the above notation $Tree(x, y, 1)$ for the binary tree from Figure 1 gives the following set of chromosomes: (00001) - phenotype 1, (11111) - 31, (11110) - 30, and (00000) - 0. For the same tree, $Tree(3, 1, 4)$ denotes the chromosome (10011) with the phenotype 19.

The proof of the correctness of the Algorithm CT122 is relatively easy, and here omitted. Note that between chromosomes arranged in a tree node, occur the following properties (the reader easily sees them in Figure 1):

- a pair of the chromosomes at the same level c receives the remainders of the division by 2^c according to the rule: the first offspring and the second parent, as well as the second offspring and the first parent, have the same reminders,

- the first offspring from the level c and its first parent, as well as the second offspring from the level c and its second parent, have the same alleles from positions $c + 1$ to n,
- the affiliated chromosomes coupled with a children at the level $c \leqslant n - 1$ in the lines 11-16 of the CT122 Algorithm (see the restriction in the line 17) have the following properties in respect to their partners chosen in the lines 19-20:
  - equal remainders of the division by 2^c,
  - different alleles between affiliated chromosomes at the position $c + 1$.

5   CT122 Algorithm in Palindrome Recognition

Now the question can be raised, what is the use of the minimal number of one-point crossovers performed to explore the entire search space, and introduced in Theorem 2? How and where can the CT122 Algorithm be used? For example, we can apply this number to compare two different algorithms searching a set.

Let us consider the apparently simple task of finding palindromes. This problem is intensively exploited in bioinformatics, e.g. to find palindromic sequences in proteins [25].

Assume, we want to find all palindromes in the space A^n. From the Theorem 2 we know without any computation, that the fastest algorithm can generate all 2^n chromosomes from A^n space in $2^{n-1} - 1$ crossovers. But by knowing some properties of CT122 algorithm we are able to reduce the number of operations twice! In this case we explore two facts:

- the chromosome is a palindrome if and only if the polar-to-it chromosome is a palindrome,
- in the tree CT generated by CT122 algorithm, each polar pair of chromosomes (except by pair of polar chromosomes located in the root node at the level 0) has one each chromosome in two sub-trees, which root nodes contain chromosomes located at the level 1.

Taking into account above properties, we can determine all palindromes in A^n space, scanning two primary chromosomes and only one of the sub-tree, which in its root node has one of the child chromosome from the level 1 (in Figure 2 chromosome (00001) - phenotype 1 or (11110) - 30. It means, that we need to scan only $2 + \frac{2^n - 2}{2} = 2^{n-1} + 1$ chromosomes, what requires $1 + \frac{2^{n-1} - 1 - 1}{2} = 2^{n-2}$ crossovers. Comparing these two algorithms, we can notice, that the second algorithm performs $\frac{2^{n-1} + 1}{2^{n-2}} \cong 2$ times less operations.

6   Conclusions

The paper considered problem of exploring the binary space A^n using only one-point crossover genetic operator. The result obtained entitle us to claim, that 1ptc operator does not have to lead to a too rapid convergence. Its ability to penetrate the space is determined by two factors: starting pool and selection.

This conclusion is somewhat supported by the literature: [4,5] and especially [1] pay attention to the problem of selection, and even apparently extreme proposition of inserting a random chromosome [11], is in fact an attempt to maintain diversity of starting pool. Theorem 1 shows that if the replenishment of the current pool will be ensured by, for example, the presence of at least one pair of polar chromosomes, then the genetic algorithm can escape from the local trap. The results indicate the need to control the selection impact for reducing the possibility of exploration and exploitation properties of crossover operator.

References

1. Bäck, T.: Evolutionary Algorithms in Theory and Practice. Oxford University Press, New York (1996)
2. Choubey, N.S., Kharat, M.U.: Approaches for Handling Premature Convergence in CFG Induction Using GA. Advances in Intelligent and Soft Computing 96, 55–66 (2011)
3. Da Ronco, C.C., Benini, E.: GeDEA-II: A Simplex Crossover Based Evolutionary Algorithm Including the Genetic Diversity as Objective. Engineering Letters 21, 1 (2013)
4. Davis, L.: Adapting operator probabilities in genetic algorithms. In: International Conference on Genetic Algorithms 1989, pp. 61–69 (1989)
5. Davis, L.: Handbook of genetic algorithms. New York Van Nostrand Reinhold (1991)
6. De Jong, K.A., Spears, W.M.: A formal analysis of the role of multi-point crossover in genetic algorithms. Annals of Mathematics and Artificial Intelligence 5(1), 1–26 (1992)
7. Dietzfelbinger, M., Naudts, B., Van Hoyweghen, C., Wegener, I.: The analysis of a recombinative hill-climber on H-IFF. IEEE Transactions on Evolutionary Computation 7(5), 417–423 (2003)
8. Fischer, S., Wegener, I.: The one-dimensional Ising model: mutation versus recombination. Theoretical Computer Science 344(2-3), 208–225 (2005)
9. Fogel, D.B.: Evolving artificial intelligence. Doctoral dissertation University of California (1992)
10. Holland, J.H.: Adaptation in Natural and Artificial System. University of Michigan Press, Ann Arbor (1975)
11. Jones, T.: Crossover, macromutation and population-based search. In: Proceedings of the Sixth International Conference on Genetic Algorithms, pp. 73–80 (1995)
12. Kötzing, T., Sudholt, D., Theile, M.: How crossover helps in pseudo-boolean optimization. In: Proceedings of the 13th Annual Genetic and Evolutionary Computation Conference (GECCO 2011), Dublin, Ireland, pp. 989–996 (2011)
13. Ochoa, G., Verel, S., Daolio, F., Tomassini, M.: Local Optima Networks: A New Model of Combinatorial Fitness Landscapes. In: Recent Advances in the Theory and Application of Fitness Landscapes, pp. 233–262. Springer, Heidelberg (2014)
14. McGinley, B.: Maintaining Healthy Population Diversity Using Adaptive Crossover, Mutation, and Selection. IEEE Transactions on Evolutionary Computation 15, 692–714 (2011)
15. Michalewicz, Z.: Genetic Algorithms + Data Structures = Evolution Programs. Springer (1996)

16. Neumann, F., Theile, M.: How crossover speeds up evolutionary algorithms for the multicriteria all-pairs-shortest-path problem. In: Schaefer, R., Cotta, C., Kołodziej, J., Rudolph, G. (eds.) PPSN XI. LNCS, vol. 6238, pp. 667–676. Springer, Heidelberg (2010)

17. Neumann, F., Oliveto, P.S., Rudolph, G., Sudholt, D.: On the effectiveness of crossover for migration in parallel evolutionary algorithms. In: Proceedings of the 13th ACM Conference on Genetic and Evolutionary Computation (GECCO 2011), Dublin, Ireland, pp. 1587–1594 (2011)

18. Oliveto, P., He, J., Yao, X.: Analysis of population-based evolutionary algorithms for the vertex cover problem. In: Proceedings of the IEEE Congress on Evolutionary Computation (CEC 2008), Hong Kong, China, pp. 1563–1570 (2008)

19. Pandey, H.M., Chaudhary, A., Mehrotra, D.: A comparative review of approaches to prevent premature convergence in GA. Applied Soft Computing 24, 1047–1077 (2014)

20. Pliszka, Z., Unold, O.: Metric Properties of Populations in Artificial Immune Systems. In: Proceedings of the International Multiconference on Computer Science and Information Technology (AAIA 2010), Wisla, Poland, pp. 113–119 (2010)

21. Pliszka, Z., Unold, O.: How to predict future in a world of antibody-antigen chromosomes. In: Ganzha, M., Maciaszek, L., Paprzycki, M. (eds.) Proceedings of the Federated Conference on Computer Science and Information Systems, pp. 91–96. IEEE (2011)

22. Pliszka, Z., Unold, O.: Efficient crossover and mutation operator in genetic algorithm. Elektronika (LII), 166–170 (2011) (in Polish)

23. Pliszka, Z., Unold, O.: On some properties of binary chromosomes and states of artificial immune systems. Int. J. of Data Analysis Techniques and Strategies 4(3), 277–291 (2012)

24. Pliszka, Z., Unold, O.: On multi-individual crossing over in evolutionary algorithms. Elektronika (LV) (9/2014), 140–141 (in Polish)

25. Prasanth, N., Kirti Vaishnavi, M., Sekar, K.: An algorithm to find all palindromic sequences in proteins. Journal of Biosciences 38(1), 173–177 (2013)

26. Richter, J.N., Wright, A., Paxton, J.: Ignoble trails-where crossover is provably harmful. In: Rudolph, G., Jansen, T., Lucas, S., Poloni, C., Beume, N. (eds.) PPSN 2008. LNCS, vol. 5199, pp. 92–101. Springer, Heidelberg (2008)

27. Qian, C., Yu, Y., Zhou, Z.-H.: An analysis on recombination in multi-objective evolutionary optimization. In: Proceedings of the 13th ACM Conference on Genetic and Evolutionary Computation (GECCO 2011), Dublin, Ireland, pp. 2051–2058 (2011)

28. Schweitzer, J.A., Martinsen, G.D., Whitham, T.G.: Cottonwood hybrids gain fitness traits of both parents: a mechanism for their long-term persistence? American Journal of Botany 89(6), 981–990 (2002)

29. Spears, W.M.: Crossover or mutation? In: FOGA, pp. 221–237 (1992)

30. Syswerda, G.: Uniform crossover in genetic algorithms. In: Schaffer, J.D. (ed.) Proceedings of the International Conference on Genetic Algorithms, pp. 2–9. Morgan Kaufmann Publishers, San Mateo (1989)

31. Uy, N.Q., Hoai, N.X., O'Neill, M., McKay, R.I., Phong, D.N.: On the roles of semantic locality of crossover in genetic programming. Information Sciences 235, 195–213 (2013)

32. Verel, S., Ochoa, G., Tomassini, M.: Local optima networks of NK landscapes with neutrality. IEEE Transactions on Evolutionary Computation 15(6), 783–797 (2011)

Multiple Choice Strategy for PSO Algorithm Enhanced with Dimensional Mutation

Michal Pluhacek[1][(✉)], Roman Senkerik[1], Ivan Zelinka[2], and Donald Davendra[2]

[1] Faculty of Applied Informatics, Tomas Bata University in Zlin,
Nam T.G. Masaryka 5555, 760 01 Zlin, Czech Republic
`pluhacek@fai.utb.cz, senkerik@fai.utb.cz`
[2] Faculty of Electrical Engineering and Computer Science, Technical University of
Ostrava, 17. listopadu 15,708 33 Ostrava-Poruba, Czech Republic
`{ivan.zelinka,donald.davendra}@vsb.cz`

Abstract. In this study the promising Multiple-choice strategy for PSO (MC-PSO) is enhanced with the blind search based single dimensional mutation. The MC-PSO utilizes principles of heterogeneous swarms with random behavior selection. The performance previously tested on both large-scale and fast optimization is significantly improved by this approach. The newly proposed algorithm is more robust and resilient to premature convergence than both original PSO and MC-PSO. The performance is tested on four typical benchmark functions with variety of dimension settings.

Keywords: PSO · MC-PSO · Swarm intelligence · Optimization

1 Introduction

Since its introduction the Particle Swarm Optimization algorithm (PSO) [1]-[4] attracts high attention of the evolutionary computing community. In comparison with other promising evolutionary computation techniques (ECTs) such as Ant Colony optimization [5] or Differential Evolution [6] the PSO remains in the center of the theoretical research to this date. There have been numerous redesigns and modifications of the original PSO scheme. One of the very promising trends is the heterogeneous swarm approach [7],[8] in which multiple types of particle behavior are defined and assigned to specific particles according to various rules. One of the latest PSO modifications incorporating the heterogeneous swarm principle and to some extent principles of the SOMA algorithm [9] is the

This work was supported by Grant Agency of the Czech Republic - GACR P103/15/06700S, further by financial support of research project NPU I No. MSMT-7778/2014 by the Ministry of Education of the Czech Republic and also by the European Regional Development Fund under the Project CEBIA-Tech No. CZ.1.05/2.1.00/03.0089, partially supported by Grant of SGS No. SP2015/142 and SP2015/141 of VSB - Technical University of Ostrava, Czech Republic and by Internal Grant Agency of Tomas Bata University under the project No. IGA/FAI/2015/057.

© Springer International Publishing Switzerland 2015
L. Rutkowski et al. (Eds.): ICAISC 2015, Part I, LNAI 9119, pp. 370–378, 2015.
DOI: 10.1007/978-3-319-19324-3_34

Multiple-choice Strategy for PSO (MC-PSO) introduced in 2013 [10],[11]. Originally developed as fast-paced PSO core variant [10], the MC-PSO proved itself to be very robust method even for the large-scale optimization [11]. In this paper the MC-PSO is re-analyzed and enhanced with dimensional mutation method based on the blind search. Using this approach it is possible to further improve the performance of MC-PSO as is presented. The paper is structured as follows: In the following section the PSO basics are summed up. The original MC-PSO and the new re-design description follows. In section 4 the benchmark functions are described. Results section 5 is followed by results discussion and conclusion.

2   Particle Swarm Optimization Algorithm

The original PSO took inspiration from behavior of fish and birds. The knowledge of global best found solution (noted $gBest$) is shared among the particles in the swarm. Furthermore each particle has the knowledge of its own (personal) best found solution (noted $pBest$). The last important part of the algorithm is the velocity of each particle that is taken into account during the calculation of the particle movement. The new position of each particle is then given by (1) , where x_i^{t+1} is the new particle position; x_i^t refers to current particle position and v_i^{t+1} is the new velocity of the particle.

$$x_i^{t+1} = x_i^t + v_i^{t+1} \tag{1}$$

To calculate the new velocity the distance from pBest and gBest is taken into account alongside with current velocity (2).

$$v_{ij}^{t+1} = w \cdot v_{ij}^t + c_1 \cdot Rand \cdot (pBest_{ij} - x_{ij}^t) + c_2 \cdot Rand \cdot (gBest_j - x_{ij}^t) \tag{2}$$

Where:
v_i^{t+1} – New velocity of the ith particle in iteration t+1. (component j of the dimension D).
w – Inertia weight value.
v_i^t – Current velocity of the ith particle in iteration t. (component j of the dimension D).
c_1, c_2 – Acceleration constants.
$pBest_i$ – Local (personal) best solution found by the ith particle. (component j of the dimension D).
$gBest$ – Best solution found in a population.
x_{ij}^t – Current position of the ith particle (component j of the dimension D) in iteration t.
$Rand$ – Pseudo random number, interval (0, 1).

Finally the linear decreasing inertia weight [2], [4] is used. The dynamic inertia weight is meant to slow the particles over time thus to improve the local search capability in the later phase of the optimization. The inertia weight has two control parameters w_{start} and w_{end}. A new w for each iteration is given by (3), where t stands for current iteration number and n stands for the total number of iterations. The typical values used in this study were $w_{start} = 0.9$ and $w_{end}=0.4$.

$$w = w_{start} - \frac{((w_{start} - w_{end}) \cdot t)}{n} \tag{3}$$

3   Multiple-choice Strategy for Particle Swarm Optimization Algorithm (MC-PSO) with mutation (MCm-PSO)

The difference between original MC-PSO [10], [11] and the PSO (section 2) is that a pool of different velocity calculation formulas is defined. Afterwards when new velocity is calculated, one of pre-defined formulas is randomly used. There are four different formulas and the probability of selection of particular one is given by three numbers b_1, b_2 and b_3. These numbers represent border values for different behavior rules and they follow the pattern: $b_1 < b_2 < b_3$. In this study the following values were used: $b_1 = 0.2$, $b_2 = 0.4$, $b_3 = 0.7$. Afterwards during the calculation of new velocity of each particle a random number r is generated from the interval <0, 1>. The selection process of new velocity calculation formula can be described as follows:

If r b_1 the new velocity of particle is given by (4):

$$v_i^{t+1} = 0 \tag{4}$$

If $b_1 < r$ b_2 the new velocity of particle is given by (5):

$$v_i^{t+1} = w \cdot v_i^t + c \cdot Rand \cdot (x_r^t - x_i^t) \tag{5}$$

If $b_2 < r$ b_3 the new velocity of particle is given by (6):

$$v_i^{t+1} = w \cdot v_i^t + c \cdot Rand \cdot (pBest_i - x_i^t) \tag{6}$$

If $b_3 < r$ the new velocity of particle is given by (7):

$$v_i^{t+1} = w \cdot v_i^t + c \cdot Rand \cdot (gBest - x_i^t) \tag{7}$$

Where $x_r(t)$ is the position of randomly chosen particle and $c = 2$.

This initial design proved to be very promising [10], [11]. This study focused on further possibility of performance improvement of the MC-PSO. During the performance testing of original MC-PSO the formula (4) proved to be very beneficial for the optimization process however also the initial implementation of this rule was very ineffective. Despite that the new velocity equaled zero and thus the particle did not change its position the cost function (CF) value of the particle was still re-evaluated wasting the computational time. Despite benefit of stationary particles analyzed in [10], [11] there was no self-improvement quality for stationary particles. To address these issues a dimensional mutation based on blind search is proposed here to further improve the behavior rule originally given by (4) as follows:

The new velocity $v_i{}^{t+1}$ is set to 0. Furthermore a single dimensional mutation occurs as follows:

Firstly a copy of active particle is stored in "trial particle". Afterwards dimension index is selected randomly. Finally random number from interval defined by the lower and upper bounds specified for that dimension is generated and stored into a trial particle corresponding to the dimension index. If the trial particle CF value is better than the *pBest* of the active particle, the active particle is replaced by the trial particle. Otherwise the active particle remains intact. For clarity the algorithm can be described as series of following steps:

Step 1: Copy $x_i{}^t$ to x_{trial}.
Step 2: Choose random integer number $r_1 = \text{Rand}(1,\text{D})$.
Step 3: Mutate the given dimension component of trial vector to random real number from the bounds. Using: j= r_1; $x_{trial,j}=$ Rand(low$_j$, high$_j$).
Step 4: If CF(x_{trial}) < pBest value then $x_i{}^t = x_{trial}$.

In this new design the stationary particle performs a simple try to improve its quality however keeps the benefits of stationary particles that help keep population diversity.

This new design was noted MCm-PSO (for Multiple Choice mutating PSO) and its performance has been investigated in the experimental section of this paper.

4 Test Functions

The following set of four common test functions was used in this study with different dimensional setting.
The Sphere function is given by (8).

$$f(x) = \sum_{i=1}^{\dim} x_i^2 \tag{8}$$

Function minimum:
Position for E_n: $(x_1,x_2 \ldots x_n) = E_n$: $(x_1,x_2 \ldots x_n) = (0,0,\ldots, 0)$
Value for E_n: $y = 0$

The Rosenbrock's function is given by (9).

$$f(x) = \sum_{i=1}^{\dim -1} 100(x_i^2 - x_{i+1})^2 + (1 - x_i)^2 \tag{9}$$

Function minimum:

Position for E_n: $(x_1, x_2 \ldots x_n) = (1,1,\ldots,1)$
Value for E_n: $y = 0$

The Rastrigin's function is given by (10).

$$f(x) = 10 \dim + \sum_{i=1}^{\dim} x_i^2 - 10 \cos(2\pi x_i) \qquad (10)$$

Function minimum:
Position for E_n: $(x_1, x_2 \ldots x_n) = (0,0,\ldots,0)$
Value for E_n: $y = 0$

Schwefel's function is given by (11).

$$f(x) = \sum_{i=1}^{\dim} -x_i \sin(\sqrt{|x|}) \qquad (11)$$

Optimum position for E_n: $(x_1, x_2 \ldots x_n) = (420.969, 420.969, \ldots, 420.969)$
Optimum value for E_n: $y = $ -418.983·$dimension$

5   Experiment Setup

Within all performance testing three PSO versions were used. The first one was the original PSO with linear decreasing inertia weight (as described in section 2) noted PSO. The second version was the original multiple choice strategy described in section 3 (noted MC-PSO). The last one was the new MC-PSO with dimensional mutation noted MCm-PSO.

In the performance testing, test functions, which are described in section 4, were used for all described versions of PSO algorithm. 200 separate runs were performed and statistically analyzed.

Control parameters were set up based on the previous numerous experiments and literature [1] - [4], [10], [11] as follows:

Population size: 40
Generations: 500
w_{start}: 0.9
w_{end}: 0.4
Dimension: 10, 40, 100, 400

The aim of the experiment was to evaluate the performance of MCm-PSO on different types of fitness landscapes and also in low, mid and high dimensions.

6   Results

Following tables and figures show the results of the performance testing. Best mean CF value and best overall result in tables are highlighted. As mentioned

Table 1. Results for the Sphere function (dim = 40)

	PSO	MC-PSO	MCm-PSO
Mean CF Value:	2.78818	1.0697	**0.325628**
Std. Dev.:	0.906801	0.403835	0.109858
CF Value Median:	2.75675	1.00552	0.311603
Max. CF Value:	5.63421	2.67571	0.695595
Min. CF Value:	0.928909	0.382715	**0.125516**

Table 2. Results for the Rosenbrock's function (dim = 40)

	PSO	MC-PSO	MCm-PSO
Mean CF Value:	112.823	72.4695	**44.326**
Std. Dev.:	28.0613	20.9571	3.77064
CF Value Median:	107.292	66.8194	43.7688
Max. CF Value:	237.04	202.052	86.9006
Min. CF Value:	61.712	47.1052	**39.7329**

Table 3. Results for the Rastrigins' function (dim = 40)

	PSO	MC-PSO	MCm-PSO
Mean CF Value:	125.604	126.963	**68.4728**
Std. Dev.:	21.4819	22.9898	14.9334
CF Value Median:	125.215	127.973	66.9011
Max. CF Value:	190.721	182.807	124.582
Min. CF Value:	58.0376	70.51	**31.1679**

Table 4. Results for the Schwefel function (dim = 40)

	PSO	MC-PSO	MCm-PSO
Mean CF Value:	-5826,09	-7594,65	**-9449**
Std. Dev.:	636,65	728,5	723,511
CF Value Median:	-5787,1	-7597,19	-9470,39
Max. CF Value:	-4261,96	-5713,8	-7271,65
Min. CF Value:	-7669,49	-9990,89	**-11229,9**

previously different statistical indicators were derived from the results. An example of statistical overview is given in Table 1 – 4. For dim = 40. For easier comparison of overall performance basic mean results comparison is given in Table 5 – 8. And finally to illustrate the effect of proposed modification on the performance and convergence behavior of the MC-PSO the example of *gBest* history for all three algorithms is given in Fig. 1 and 2.

Table 5. Mean results comparison for the Sphere function

Dim	PSO	MC-PSO	MCm-PSO
10	**3.00E-07**	0.000127422	8.68E-05
40	2.78818	1.0697	**0.325628**
100	27.3926	11.0538	**4.8809**
400	251.701	84.5689	**64.228**

Table 6. Mean results comparison for the Rosenbrock's function

Dim	PSO	MC-PSO	MCm-PSO
10	**4.96751**	6.26294	6.11422
40	112.823	72.4695	**44.326**
100	723.136	314.311	**186.018**
400	6764.76	1901.3	**1521.33**

Table 7. Mean results comparison for the Rastirgin's function

Dim	PSO	MC-PSO	MCm-PSO
10	6.09292	12.6528	**3.87228**
40	125.604	126.963	**68.4728**
100	581.487	560.083	**327.834**
400	3396.87	3269.47	**2702.17**

Table 8. Mean results comparison for the Schwefel's function

Dim	PSO	MC-PSO	MCm-PSO
10	-2810.65	-3037.36	**-3779.11**
40	-5826.09	-7594.65	**-9449**
100	-9282.35	-13068.3	**-15110**
400	-18600.1	-27650.2	**-29774.7**

7   Results Analysis

Tables 1 – 4 give the complete results overview for the case of dim = 40. It is clear that the performance on newly proposed MCm-PSO is superior to both the PSO and the MC-PSO in terms of mean, median and best result value. It should also be pointed out that the MCm-PSO achieved the lowest Std. Dev. value therefore the newly proposed algorithm seems to be the most reliable of the three.

Based on Fig. 1 and 2 it seems that the MCm-PSO is able to evade the premature converge that both the PSO and the MC-PSO suffer from. Also it seems that the MCm-PSO is achieving best results during the whole course of optimization. This seems very promising for future applications of this method for task of very fast and real-time optimization where time constrains are important factor.

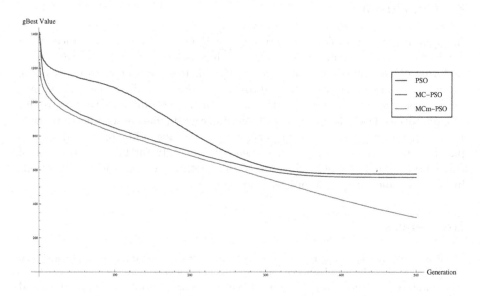

Fig. 1. Mean *gBest* history comparison – Rastrigin's function; dim: 100; runs: 200

Finally based on mean results comparison given in tables 5 – 8 the performance of MCm-PSO was superior to both other algorithms in 14 from 16 experiments. The performance of MCm-PSO was superior in all high-dimensional cases

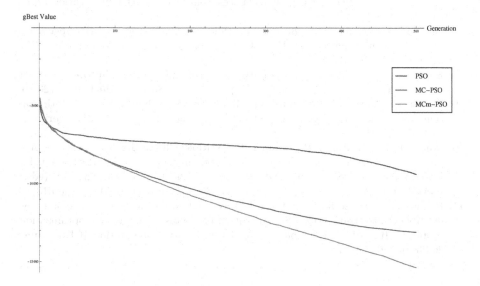

Fig. 2. Mean *gBest* history comparison – Schwefel's function; dim: 100; runs: 200

8   Conclusions

In this study the Multiple-choice strategy for PSO algorithm was enhanced with single-dimensional mutation. The aim is to improve the affectivity of the design in terms of computational time use and to increase the chances of avoiding premature convergence and thus improving the overall performance. This novel design was tested on a set of well-known benchmark functions that represent different fitness landscape shapes and four different dimension settings were used. Based on presented data the performance of the algorithm presented in this paper seems very promising and encourages not only further development of this method but also the application of this method on real-world applications in both fast and large scale optimization.

References

1. Kennedy, J., Eberhart, R.: Particle swarm optimization. In: IEEE International Conference on Neural Networks, pp. 1942–1948 (1995)
2. Yuhui, S., Eberhart, R.: A modified particle swarm optimizer. In: IEEE World Congress on Computational Intelligence, May 4-9, pp. 69–73 (1998)
3. Kennedy, J.: The particle swarm: social adaptation of knowledge. In: IEEE International Conference on Evolutionary Computation, pp. 303–308 (1997)
4. Nickabadi, A., Ebadzadeh, M.M., Safabakhsh, R.: A novel particle swarm optimization algorithm with adaptive inertia weight. Applied Soft Computing 11(4), 3658–3670 (2011)
5. Dorigo, M.: Ant Colony Optimization and Swarm Intelligence. Springer (2006)
6. Storn, R., Price, K.: Differential Evolution A Simple and Efficient Heuristic for global Optimization over Continuous Spaces. Journal of Global Optimization 11(4), 341–359 (1997)
7. de Oca, M.A.M., Pena, J., Stutzle, T., Pinciroli, C., Dorigo, M.: Heterogeneous particle swarm optimizers. In: IEEE Congress on Evolutionary Computation CEC 2009, pp. 698–705 (2009)
8. Engelbrecht, A.P.: Heterogeneous Particle Swarm Optimization. In: Dorigo, M., et al. (eds.) ANTS 2010. LNCS, vol. 6234, pp. 191–202. Springer, Heidelberg (2010)
9. Zelinka, I.: SOMA Self-Organizing Migrating Algorithm. In: New Optimization Techniques in Engineering. STUDFUZZ, vol. 141, pp. 167–217. Springer, Heidelberg (2004)
10. Pluhacek, M., Senkerik, R., Zelinka, I.: Multiple Choice Strategy A Novel Approach for Particle Swarm Optimization Preliminary Study. In: Rutkowski, L., Korytkowski, M., Scherer, R., Tadeusiewicz, R., Zadeh, L.A., Zurada, J.M. (eds.) ICAISC 2013, Part II. LNCS, vol. 7895, pp. 36–45. Springer, Heidelberg (2013)
11. Pluhacek, M., Senkerik, R., Zelinka, I.: Investigation on the performance of a new multiple choice strategy for PSO Algorithm in the task of large scale optimization problems. In: 2013 IEEE Congress on Evolutionary Computation (CEC), June 20-23, pp. 2007–(2011)

A Hybrid Differential Evolution-Gradient Optimization Method

Wojciech Rafajłowicz[✉]

Wojciech Rafajłowicz is with the Department of Computer Engineering, Faculty of Electronics, Wrocław University of Technology, Wybrzeże Wyspiańskiego 27, 50 370 Wrocław, Poland
wojciech.rafajlowicz@pwr.wroc.pl

Abstract. In this paper a new three level, hybrid optimization method is proposed. Differential evolution is hybridized with traditonal gradient optimization. Some ideas from simulated annealing are also employed. Usefulness of the proposed method is supported by numerical simulations.

1 Introduction

Unconstrained optimization problems arise as a simplification of common problems in nearly all branches of science and engineering. Traditionally, global artificial intelligence optimization methods were contrasted with more classic optimization algorithms which are inherently local. Recently these hybrid methods that join both of these methods are under investigation. In most cases two artificial intelligence methods are merged together. In contrast, in this paper we propose to combine the differential evolution method with gradient based local search.

Differential evolution is a method proposed by Kenneth Price and Reiner Stron in a technical report [14] in 1995. From that time this method has become increasingly popular as one of the most efficient methods. This method provides better results than a simple evolutionary search, retaining its abilities to search for non-local solutions. It was successfully used in many applications like [8].

The gradient method is traditionally attributed to Newton. In its geometric interpretation, a parabolic approximation of a real-valued goal function $f(\mathbf{x})$, $\mathbf{x} \in \mathbf{R}^n$ is used in order to calculate a step $\mathbf{p} \in \mathbf{R}^n$ of further search. A step $\mathbf{p}$ is calculated by solving the following system of linear equations:

$$H_f(\mathbf{x})\,\mathbf{p} = -\nabla_f(\mathbf{x}) \tag{1}$$

where $\nabla f(\mathbf{x})$ is the gradient of the goal function f at a current point $\mathbf{x}$, while H_f is its Hessian. Then, in subsequent steps the method moves toward the optimum (or saddle point), if it starts in a vicinity of it (see, e.g., [13] for modifications of the Newton method in order to ensure convergence from any staring point).

In this paper we propose an alternative approach. An artificial intelligence method from the class of differential evolution methods is joined with the classic

© Springer International Publishing Switzerland 2015
L. Rutkowski et al. (Eds.): ICAISC 2015, Part I, LNAI 9119, pp. 379–388, 2015.
DOI: 10.1007/978-3-319-19324-3_35

Newton algorithm, leading to a hybridized approach. We will show that such combination has many advantages, mainly balancing capabilities of faster convergence to local optimum and searching for the global one. Additionally, some ideas from other methods will be included.

It should be mentioned that a number of approaches to hybridization have been proposed, including ant colony optimization [22] or particle swarm optimization [12]. Also two methods, namely Neadler-Mead and bidirectional random optimization were combined together in [1]. The approach proposed here combines two methods that are both based on the idea of differentiation, but one of them is local, while the other one is global.

The paper is organized as follows. We firstly recall the idea of differential evolution, then its connections to gradient optimization are shown. Subsequently, the new method is proposed and numerical results are provided.

2   Differential Evolution

Differential evolution (DE) is a meta-heuristic method of optimization. The basics of the method can be found in [15] or in the book [16]. In this method gradients are not directly computed, but two random agents from the population are selected on at random. Then, their difference is used with some coefficient F, usually selected from $(0, 2]$ interval.

Remarks.

- The DE method can be easily parallelized.
- It can be also modified to solve many classes of problems.
- The DE method is called evolutionary, however it is different than a typical biologically inspired evolution methods presented, for example, in [4], [5].

Below, we provide an outline of the DE method. In a typical case differential evolution requires a population consisting of vectors from $\mathbf{R}^n$ which is the domain of the goal function $f(x)$.

- Choose parameters for differential evolution $CR \in (0, 1)$ that governs a random strategy described below and the step size $F \in (0, 2)$. Initialize a starting population by selecting $m > 3$ vectors from $\mathbf{R}^n$. Usually, the selection is done at random and m is taken to be not less than n.
- Until reaching a stopping criterion, for each element $\mathbf{x} = [x_1, x_2, \dots, x_n]^T$ of the current population perform the following steps. Here and below T is the transposition of a vector.

  Step 1 Choose at random three elements from the current population $\mathbf{a} = [a_1, a_2, \dots, a_n]^T$, $\mathbf{b} = [b_1, b_2, \dots, b_n]^T$ and $\mathbf{c} = [c_1, c_2, \dots, c_n]^T$ such that $\mathbf{a} \neq \mathbf{b}$, $\mathbf{b} \neq \mathbf{c}$ and $\mathbf{a} \neq \mathbf{c}$. Choose a random number R from $1 \dots n$ (the current working dimension for all vectors).

  Step 2 For each dimension $k = 1, \dots, n$ perform the following steps.

      1. Choose random r from $[0, 1]$.

2. If $r < CR$ or $k = R$, then set $y_k = a_k + F \cdot (b_k - c_k)$,

3. else set $y_k = x_k$.

Step 3 For the resulting $\mathbf{y} = [y_1, y_2, \ldots, y_n]^T$ calculate $f(\mathbf{y})$. If $f(\mathbf{y}) < f(\mathbf{x})$ then put $\mathbf{x} = \mathbf{y}$. Check for global best. Select the next $\mathbf{x}$ from the current population (other than $\mathbf{x}$'s already considered) and go to Step 1.

3 Connections of the Differential Evolution Method with Gradient Optimization

To motivate the proposed way the hybridization, it is expedient to discuss connections of the DE method with a gradient based optimization algorithm. To this end, let us consider a unimodal goal function. For the sake of simplicity we consider only three points around minimum (see Fig. 1). It can frequently happen when population is centered around the optimum.

We can think about $\mathbf{a}, \mathbf{b}$ and $\mathbf{c}$ as vectors anchored at zero. According to the DE method, $\mathbf{b} - \mathbf{c}$ give us the direction[1] of search. This free vector is added to $\mathbf{a}$. This results in the new point $\mathbf{y}$. In our simple example new $\mathbf{y}$ matches the optimum exactly[2], if $F = 1$ (see Fig. 2). Thus, a differential evolution algorithm indicates in this case a proper direction toward the minimum. One can expect that this conveys to a multidimensional case. The above interpretation can be summarized as follows. If a current population contains points in the vicinity of the minimizer, then the DE method is able to produce search directions that are close to the gradient of f. As it is known, the search along gradient directions quickly brings us to the neighborhood of the minimizer, but then its rates of convergence drastically slow down. Then, it is expedient to switch a search direction to one dictated by the Newton method. These considerations motivate the hybrid method described in the next section. Note however, that the DE method – due to the randomization at Step 2.2 – has an advantage over the classic method of the steepest descent along the gradient direction, namely it has an ability of searching for a global optimum. For this reason, we combine the Newton step with it, instead of with the latter one.

4 Proposed Hybrid Method

In this section we describe the proposed hybrid method in its basic form (Subsection 4.1) and then we discuss its possible modifications and improvements (Subsection 4.2).

4.1 Basic Method

The DE method, such as described in the previous section has several drawbacks. It can find a point near a optimum (possibly near the global one, but we never

---

[1] In fact, this direction is additionally modified by a random selection at Steps 2.2 and 2.3, but we postpone this fact in our interpretation.

[2] Clearly, in general case we can expect to be only closer to the minimizing point.

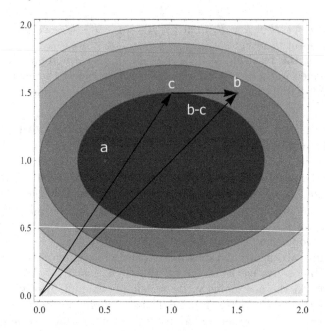

Fig. 1. Points **a**, **b** and **c** as vectors anchored at zero

can be sure). On the other hand, a precise location of the exact optimum can be prohibitively time consuming.

The well-know way of speeding up the search near optimum is to apply the Newton method. Hence, we propose to modify DE algorithm in a way that after making a the DE step an additional step is done in the Newton direction. We shall further call this approach the DE-Newton method. Thus, the modified method consists of the following steps.

- Choose parameters for differential evolution $CR \in (0, 1)$ that governs a random strategy described below and the step size $F \in (0, 2)$. Initialize a starting population by selecting $m > 3$ vectors from $\mathbf{R}^n$. Usually, the selection is done at random and m is taken to be not less than n.
- Until reaching a stopping criterion, for each element $\mathbf{x} = [x_1, x_2, \ldots, x_n]^T$ of the current population perform the following steps. Here and below T is the transposition of a vector.

  Step 1 Choose at random three elements from the current population $\mathbf{a} = [a_1, a_2, \ldots, a_n]^T$, $\mathbf{b} = [b_1, b_2, \ldots, b_n]^T$ and $\mathbf{c} = [c_1, c_2, \ldots, c_n]^T$ such that $\mathbf{a} \neq \mathbf{b}$, $\mathbf{b} \neq \mathbf{c}$ and $\mathbf{a} \neq \mathbf{c}$. Choose a random number R from $1 \ldots n$ (the current working dimension for all vectors).

  Step 2 For each dimension $k = 1, \ldots, n$ perform the following steps.
  1. Choose random r from $[0, 1]$.
  2. If $r < CR$ or $k = R$, then set $y_k = a_k + F \cdot (b_k - c_k)$,
  3. else set $y_k = x_k$.

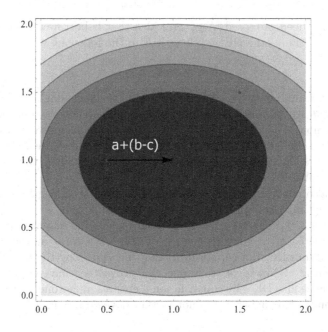

Fig. 2. New point **y**, resulting from DE method, is close to the minimum

Newton's improvement For the resulting $\mathbf{y} = [y_1, y_2, \ldots, y_n]^T$ the gradient and the Hessian are calculated. Linear equation $H_f(\mathbf{y})\,p = -\nabla_f(\mathbf{y})$ is solved and $\mathbf{y} = \mathbf{y} + \mathbf{p}$

Step 3 Calculate $f(\mathbf{y})$. If $f(\mathbf{y}) < f(\mathbf{x})$ then put $\mathbf{x} = \mathbf{y}$. Check for global best. Select the next **x** from the current population (other than **x**'s already considered) and go to Step 1.

As one can notice, the above algorithm differs from the one described in Section 2 by adding only one step called Newton's improvement. Notice, that at each iteration of the DE method we propose to make only a step in the Newton direction. The rationale behind this is the following. If f is a quadratic function, then the Newton method finds the optimum in one step. Thus, if DE finds a point that is close to optimum and f can be sufficiently accurately approximated there by a quadratic function, then one step of the Newton method brings us very close to the optimum. On the other hand, if we are far from the optimum, then the Newton method may not be so successful and we do not waste time on additional calculations of the Hessian. These considerations do not exclude that in some cases it can be useful to repeat the Newton step several times.

4.2 Additional Modifications

The main advantage of differential evolution is its ability to explore a large part of a goal function domain. In some papers a hybrid mixing with the simulated annealing have been proposed. A general idea that is borrowed from simulated annealing is to change the DE step length F in the following way

$$F = \eta + \theta\, e^{-i/N}, \tag{2}$$

where i is current iteration number and N is the total number of iterations, while η and θ are parameters that in our simulation experiments have been selected as follows: $\eta = 0.2$, $\theta = 0.25$. The parameter F bears some resemblance to temperature change in the simulated annealing method. More about it can be found in [2]. We shall refer to the DE-Newton method with F tuned according to (2) as the SA-DE-Newton method.

One can also consider the selection of the Newton step length, as it is done in the local optimization algorithms, i.e., instead of setting $\mathbf{y} = \mathbf{y} + \mathbf{p}$ one can consider $\mathbf{y} = \mathbf{y} + \gamma\mathbf{p}$, where $\gamma > 0$ is selected by the line search in $\mathbf{p}$ direction. This would increase the convergence rate in the local sense at the expense of computational burden. Notice, however, that incorporating the line search and admitting repeated Newton's steps one can prove the convergence of such a method, because also DE – by construction – ensures monotone decrease of f at each iteration. In this paper we do not further develop this idea.

5   Numerical Results

Our aim in this section is to test the proposed the SA-DE-Newton method and to compare it with the DE-Newton and the classic DE method. We do not compare the SA-DE-Newton with the classic Newton method, because it does not have an ability to search for global maxima. As a test goal function the following, bivariate one, is selected:

$$f(\mathbf{x}) = -\frac{sin^3(2\pi x_1)sin(2\pi x_2)}{x_1^3(x_1 + x_2)}, \quad \mathbf{x} = [x_1,\, x_2]^T. \tag{3}$$

This function, known as a very difficult g08 benchmark problem, has many local minima, as illustrated in Fig. 3. Notice that we consider the g08 problem of searching for a global minimum, but without constrains. This, in fact, makes it more difficult because without them the global minimum is near nonlinearity around 0.   Comparing decrease of f in subsequent iterations that is drawn in Fig. 4, Fig. 5 and Fig. 6 for the same starting point, one can observe the following.

DE Differential evolution method is relatively successful in finding a good solution. We can see that it happened near the final iterations of the method. It is difficult to say how many of them should be made in order to reach the global minimum. In the case of stopping after 180 iterations we may be left with an intermediate solution only (see Fig. 4).

DE-Newton The hybridization, by adding an additional Newton step, leads not only to finding a slightly deeper optimum, but also the solution is achieved much faster – in just 50 iterations (fig. 5).

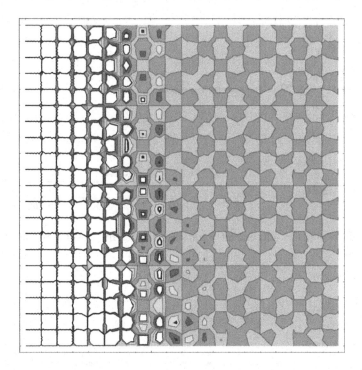

Fig. 3. The contour plot of multimodal g08 test problem

SA-DE-Newton If F in the DE-Newton method is tuned as in (2) with $\eta = 0.2$, $\theta = 0.25$, then we are closer to the global minimum than using the DE-Newton method. Namely, $f \approx -1325$ is obtained, whilethe DE-Newton method obtained $f \approx -1300$. The price for this is not too large, because the DE-Newton method for the first time achieved $f \approx -1300$ after 15 iterations, while the SA-DE-Newton attained $f \approx -1325$ after 60 iterations with almost the same computational burden in each iteration.

Summarizing, the analysis of the above results seems to support the following conclusions:

- The two versions of the proposed hybrid method outperform the DE approach both with respect to the achieved value of f and – even more convincingly – with respect to the number of iterations.
- DE-Newton method is faster than the SA-DE-Newton, but it may stop before reaching the global minimum.
- SA-DE-Newton method is only slightly slower than DE-Newton method, but we have a chance to find a point closer to the global minimum.

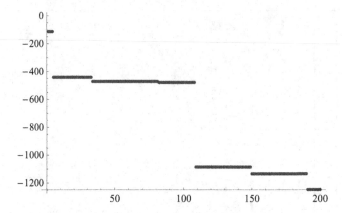

Fig. 4. Values of (3) in subsequent iterations of differential evolution algorithm (for comparisons)

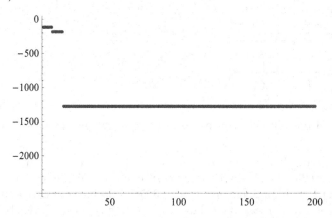

Fig. 5. Values of (3) in subsequent iterations of DE-Newton method

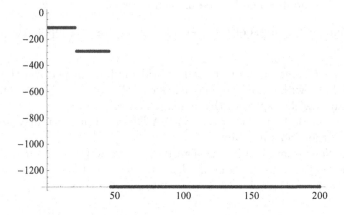

Fig. 6. Values of (3) in subsequent iterations of SA-DE-Newton method

6   Conclusions and Directions of Further Research

We have shown that the proposed hybrid methods the DE-Newton and the SA-DE-Newton of unconstrained optimization can be useful in solving multi-modal problems. Hybridization also provides some possibilities for parallelization of the proposed algorithm, which in general is difficult in classical methods.

It can also form a base for solving constrained problems. Many methods of handling constraints have been proposed, e.g., the idea of applying Fletcher's filter in random search meta-heuristic methods, in an evolutionary method [18] and then in [19].

Many methods of handling constraints in differential evolution were proposed. Some of them are simple penalty function or merit function as evaluated in [9]. In [11] a complicated set of comparison criterions has been proposed that were close in spirit to the filter idea. Most further work like [6] concentrate on initial population and special cross-over methods. Others, like [7] propose using more vectors from the population for reproduction.

One may hope that also the approach proposed here can be sufficiently efficient in solving optimization problems with constraints, using the guidelines of applying stochastic search methods that have been proposed in [20], [21].

Modified differential evolution can also be used in difficult learning problems, such as described in [3].

Acknowledgements.. Calculations have been carried out in Wroclaw Centre for Networking and Supercomputing (http://www.wcss.wroc.pl).

The author would like to express his deep appreciation to Professor Roman Galar for discussions on evolutionary methods.

Sincere thanks are also addressed to the anonymous referee for her/his patience in pointing out ways of improving the style of the presentation.

References

1. Ahandani, M.A., Vakil-Baghmisheh, M.T., Talebi, M.: Hybridizing Local Search Algorithms for Global Optimization Computational Optimization and Applications (2014) (article in Press)
2. Brownlee J.: Clever Algorithms. Nature-Inspired Programming Recipes. LuLu. (January 2011) ISBN: 978-1-4467-8506-5
3. Cpałka, K., Rutkowski, L.: Evolutionary Learning of Flexible Neuro-Fuzzy Structures. In: Recent Advances in Control and Automation, pp. 398–407. Akademicka Oficyna Wydawnicza EXIT (2008)
4. Galar, R.: Handicapped Individua in Evolutionary Processes. Biol. Cybern. 53, 1–9 (1985)
5. Galar, R.: Evolutionary Search with Soft Selection. Biol. Cybern. 60, 357–364 (1989)
6. Gong, W., Cai, Z.: A Multiobjective Differential Evolution Algorithm for Constrained Optimization. In: 2008 IEEE Congress on Evolutionary Computation (2008)

7. Gordián-Rivera, L.-A., Mezura-Montes, E.: A Combination of Specialized Differential Evolution Variants for Constrained Optimization. In: Pavón, J., Duque-Méndez, N.D., Fuentes-Fernández, R. (eds.) IBERAMIA 2012. LNCS, vol. 7637, pp. 261–270. Springer, Heidelberg (2012)

8. Lobato, F.S., Valder, S., Neto, A.: Solution of Singular Optimal Control Problems Using the Improved Differential Evolution Algorithm. Journal of Artificial Intelligence and Soft Computing Research 1(3), 195–206 (2011)

9. de Melo, V., Grazieli, L., Costa, C.: Evaluating differential evolution with penalty function to solve constrained engineering problems. Expert Systems with Applications 39, 7860–7863 (2012)

10. Mezura-Montes, E., Coello, C.A.: A Simple Multimembered Evolution Strategy to Solve Constrained Optimization Problems. IEEE Transactions on Evolutionary Computation 9(1), 1–17 (2005)

11. Mezura-Montes, E., Coello Coello, C.A., Tun-Morales, E.I.: Simple Feasibility Rules and Differential Evolution for Constrained Optimization. In: Monroy, R., Arroyo-Figueroa, G., Sucar, L.E., Sossa, H. (eds.) MICAI 2004. LNCS (LNAI), vol. 2972, pp. 707–716. Springer, Heidelberg (2004)

12. Muranaka, K., Aiyoshi, E.: Computational Properties of Hybrid Methods with PSO and DE. Electronics and Communications 97(4), 58–66 (2014) (in Japan)

13. Nocedal, J., Wright, S.J.: Numerical Optimization. Springer Science, New York (2006)

14. Storn, R., Price, K.: Differential evolution a simple and efficient adaptive scheme for global optimization over continuous spaces. Technical report (1995)

15. Storn, R., Price, K.: Differential evolution a simple and efficient heuristic for global optimization over continuous spaces. Journal of Global Optimization 11, 341–359 (1997)

16. Price, K., Storn, R., Lampinen, J.: Differential Evolution A Practical Approach to Global Optimization. Springer, Heidelberg (2005)

17. Rafajłowicz, E., Styczeń, K., Rafajłowicz, W.: A modified filter SQP method as a tool for optimal control of nonlinear systems with spatio-temporal dynamics. International Journal of Applied Mathematics and Computer Science 22(2) (2012)

18. Rafajłowicz, E., Rafajłowicz, W.: Fletcher's Filter Methodology as a Soft Selector in Evolutionary Algorithms for Constrained Optimization. In: Rutkowski, L., Korytkowski, M., Scherer, R., Tadeusiewicz, R., Zadeh, L.A., Zurada, J.M. (eds.) EC 2012 and SIDE 2012. LNCS, vol. 7269, pp. 333–341. Springer, Heidelberg (2012)

19. Rocha, A.M.A.C., Costa, M.F.P., Fernandes, E.M.G.P.: An Artificial Fish Swarm Filter-Based Method for Constrained Global Optimization. In: Murgante, B., Gervasi, O., Misra, S., Nedjah, N., Rocha, A.M.A.C., Taniar, D., Apduhan, B.O. (eds.) ICCSA 2012, Part III. LNCS, vol. 7335, pp. 57–71. Springer, Heidelberg (2012)

20. Skowron, M., Styczeń, K.: Evolutionary search for globally optimal constrained stable cycles. Chemical Engineering Science 61(24), 7924–7932 (2006)

21. Skowron, M., Styczeń, K.: Evolutionary search for globally optimal stable multicycles in complex systems with inventory couplings. International Journal of Chemical Engineering (2009)

22. Xue, Y., Zhong, S., Ma, T., Cao, J.: A Hybrid Evolutionary Algorithm for Numerical Optimization Problem Intelligent Automation and Soft Computing (2014) (article in Press)

On the Tuning of Complex Dynamics Embedded into Differential Evolution

Roman Senkerik[1](✉), Michal Pluhacek[1], Ivan Zelinka[2], Donald Davendra[2],
Zuzana Kominkova Oplatkova[1], and Roman Jasek[1]

[1] Faculty of Applied Informatics, Tomas Bata University in Zlin,
Nam T.G. Masaryka 5555, 760 01 Zlin, Czech Republic
{senkerik,pluhacek,oplatkova,jasek}@fai.utb.cz
[2] Faculty of Electrical Engineering and Computer Science, Technical University of
Ostrava, 17. listopadu 15,708 33 Ostrava-Poruba, Czech Republic
{donald.davendra,ivan.zelinka}@vsb.cz

Abstract. This research deals with the hybridization of the two softcomputing fields, which are chaos theory and evolutionary computation.
This paper aims on the experimental investigations on the chaos-driven
evolutionary algorithm Differential Evolution (DE) concept. This research represents the continuation of the satisfactory results obtained
by means of chaos embedded (driven) DE, which utilizes the chaotic dynamics in the place of pseudorandom number generators This work is
aimed at the tuning of the complex chaotic dynamics directly injected
into the DE. To be more precise, this research investigates the influence
of different parameter settings for discrete chaotic systems to the performance of DE. Repeated simulations were performed on the IEEE CEC
13 benchmark functions set in dimension of 30. Finally, the obtained
results are compared with canonical DE and jDE.

Keywords: Differential Evolution · Complex dynamics · Deterministic
chaos · Dissipative system

1 Introduction

This research deals with the hybridization of the two softcomputing fields, which
are chaos theory and evolutionary computation techniques (ECT's). These days
the evolutionary algorithms (EA's) are known as powerful tool for almost any
difficult and complex optimization problem. Differential Evolution (DE) [1] is
one of the most potent heuristics available.

This work was supported by Grant Agency of the Czech Republic - GACR
P103/15/06700S, further by financial support of research project NPU I No.
MSMT-7778/2014 by the Ministry of Education of the Czech Republic and also
by the European Regional Development Fund under the Project CEBIA-Tech No.
CZ.1.05/2.1.00/03.0089, partially supported by Grant of SGS No. SP2015/142
and SP2015/141 of VSB - Technical University of Ostrava, Czech Republic and
by Internal Grant Agency of Tomas Bata University under the project No.
IGA/FAI/2015/057.

© Springer International Publishing Switzerland 2015
L. Rutkowski et al. (Eds.): ICAISC 2015, Part I, LNAI 9119, pp. 389–399, 2015.
DOI: 10.1007/978-3-319-19324-3_36

A number of DE variants have been recently developed with the emphasis on adaptivity/selfadaptivity [2], ensemble approach [3] or utilization for discrete domain problems. The importance of randomization as a compensation of limited amount of search moves is stated in the survey paper [4]. This idea has been carried out in subsequent studies describing various techniques to modify the randomization process [5], [6] and especially in [7], where the sampling of the points is tested from modified distribution. Together with this persistent development in such mainstream research topics, the basic concept of chaos driven DE have been introduced.

Recent research in chaos driven heuristics has been fueled with the predisposition that unlike stochastic approaches, a chaotic approach is able to bypass local optima stagnation. This one clause is of deep importance to evolutionary algorithms. A chaotic approach generally uses the chaotic map in the place of a pseudo random number generator [8]. This causes the heuristic to map unique regions, since the chaotic map iterates to new regions. The task is then to select a very good chaotic map as the pseudo random number generator.

Several papers have been recently focused on the connection of DE and chaotic dynamics either in the form of hybridizing of DE with chaotic searching algorithm [9] or in the form of chaotic mutation factor and dynamically changing weighting and crossover factor in self-adaptive chaos differential evolution (SACDE) [10]. Focus of our research is the direct embedding of chaotic systems in the form of chaos pseudo random number generator (CPRNG) into the DE (ChaosDE) [11].

Also the PSO (Particle Swarm Optimization) algorithm with elements of chaos was introduced as CPSO [12]. The concept of ChaosDE proved itself to be a powerful heuristic also in combinatorial problems domain [13]. At the same time the chaos embedded PSO with inertia weigh strategy was closely investigated [14], followed by the introduction of a PSO strategy driven alternately by two chaotic systems [15]. Recently the chaos driven firefly algorithm has been introduced [16].

The organization of this paper is following: Firstly, the motivation for this research is proposed. The next sections are focused on the description of the concept of chaos driven DE and the experiment background. Results and conclusion follow afterwards.

2   Motivation

This research is an extension and continuation of the previous successful initial experiment with chaos driven DE (ChaosDE) [17], [18] with basic test functions. In this paper the concept of DE/rand/1/bin strategy is experimentally investigated. To be more precise this research is focused on the influence of parameter tuning for the discrete chaotic systems to the performance of DE.

From the previous research it follows, that very promising results were obtained through the utilization of Delayed Logistic, Lozi, Burgers and Tinkerbelt chaotic maps. These discrete dissipative chaotic maps have unique properties with connection to DE: either strong progress towards global extreme with weak overall statistical results (e.g. average cost function value, higher std. dev. value, tendency to premature stagnation); or continuously stable and very satisfactory performance of searching process.

The Lozi map remains a very intense subject of research in the area of chaos driven ECT's thanks to its unique sequencing and other unique attributes [19]. The Lozi map (as well as the most of the discrete chaotic systems) has accessible parameters, which have to be set up by numerous experiments, by apriori knowledge or according to the literature sources. This opens up the possibility for the investigation on the influence of the parameter settings for the Lozi map to the performance of chaos driven heuristic with the Lozi map embedded.

3   Differential Evolution

DE is a population-based optimization method that works on real-number-coded individuals [1]. DE is quite robust, fast, and effective, with global optimization ability. It does not require the objective function to be differentiable, and it works well even with noisy and time-dependent objective functions. Due to a limited space and the aims of this paper, the detailed description of well known differential evolution algorithm basic principles is insignificant and hence omitted. Please refer to [1], [20] for the detailed description of the used DERand1Bin strategy (both for ChaosDE and Canonical DE) as well as for the complete description of all other strategies.

4   The Concept of ChaosDE

The general idea of ChaosDE and CPRNG is to replace the default pseudorandom number generator (PRNG) with the discrete chaotic map. As the discrete chaotic map is a set of equations with a static start position, we created a random start position of the map, in order to have different start position for different experiments (runs of EA's). This random position is initialized with the default PRNG, as a one-off randomizer. Once the start position of the chaotic map has been obtained, the map generates the next sequence using its current position.

The first possible way is to generate and store a long data sequence (approx. 50-500 thousands numbers) during the evolutionary process initialization and keep the pointer to the actual used value in the memory. In case of the using up of the whole sequence, the new one will be generated with the last known value as the new initial one.

The second approach is that the chaotic map is not re-initialized during the experiment and any long data series is not stored, thus it is imperative to keep the current state of the map in memory to obtain the new output values.

As two different types of numbers are required in ChaosDE; real and integers, the modulo operators is used to obtain values between the specified ranges, as given in the following equations (1) and (2):

$$rndreal = mod(abs(rndChaos), 1.0) \tag{1}$$

$$rndint = mod(abs(rndChaos), 1.0) \times Range + 1 \qquad (2)$$

Where *abs* refers to the absolute portion of the chaotic map generated number *rndChaos*, and *mod* is the modulo operator. *Range* specifies the value (inclusive) till where the number is to be scaled.

5   Chaotic Lozi Map

In this work, Lozi chaotic map (3) was used as the CPRNG for DE. Direct output iterations of the chaotic maps were used for the generation of real numbers in the process of crossover based on the user defined *CR* value and for the generation of the integer values used for selection of individuals.

The Lozi map is a discrete two-dimensional chaotic map. The map equations are given in (3). The typical parameter setting is: $a = 1.7$ and $b = 0.5$ as suggested in [21]. For these values, the system exhibits typical chaotic behavior and with this parameter setting it is used in the most research papers and other literature sources.

$$X_{n+1} = 1 - a\,|X_n| + bY_n$$
$$Y_{n+1} = X_n \qquad (3)$$

The Lozi map generates chaotic sequences with the unique structure and sequencing of following output values for the parameter setting: $a \in \langle 1.3,\ 1.7 \rangle$ and $b \in \langle 0.1,\ 0.5 \rangle$. However not every combinations are leading to the expected chaotic behavior. The illustrative example of such a complex behavior is depicted in Fig. 1, which shows the dependence of output values x and y on the parameter b (a is fixed to 1.7).

6   Experiment Design

The experiment encompasses three main parts:

– Tuning of mutation and crossover parameters (F and CR) for ChaosDE.
– Investigation on the settings of adjustable parameters of discrete chaotic map used as a CPRNG.
– Performance comparison of DE, jDE [22] and ChaosDE with selected combination of mutation, crossover and chaotic map adjustable parameters on IEEE CEC 2013 benchmark set [23].

The first and second parts utilize the set of four simple test functions, since the idea was to keep the investigation process distinct and to easily track the influence of chaotic dynamics.

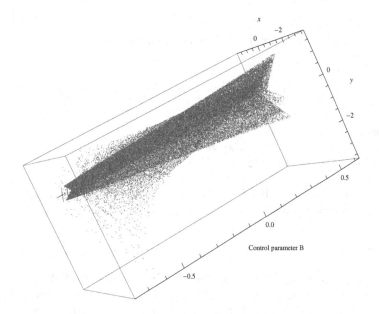

Fig. 1. 3D bifurcation diagram of the chaotic Lozi map – a is fixed to 1.7

7   Simple Benchmark Functions

For the purpose of ChaosDE, Canonical DE and jDE investigation on DE control and chaotic map parameters, Schwefel's test function (4), shifted 1st De Jong's function (5), shifted Ackley's original function in the form (6), shifted Rastrigin's function (7) were selected.

$$f(x) = \sum_{i=1}^{\dim} -x_i \sin\left(\sqrt{|x_i|}\right) \tag{4}$$

Function minimum:
Position for E_n: $(x_1, x_2 \ldots x_n) = (420.969, 420.969, \ldots, 420.969)$
Value for E_n: $y = -418.983 \cdot dim$
Function interval: <-500, 500>.

$$f(x) = \sum_{i=1}^{\dim} (x_i - s_i)^2 \tag{5}$$

Function minimum:
Position for E_n: $(x_1, x_2 \ldots x_n) = s$; Value for E_n: $y = 0$
Function interval: <-5.12, 5.12>.

$$f(x) = -20 \exp\left(-0.02\sqrt{\tfrac{1}{D}\sum_{i=1}^{\dim}(x_i - s_i)^2}\right) - \exp\left(\tfrac{1}{D}\sum_{i=1}^{\dim}\cos 2\pi(x_i - s_i)\right) +$$
$$+20 + \exp(1)$$

$$\tag{6}$$

Function minimum:

Position for E_n: $(x_1, x_2 \ldots x_n) = s$; Value for E_n: $y = 0$

Function interval: $<-30, 30>$.

$$f(x) = 10 \dim + \sum_{i=1}^{\dim} (x_i - s_i)^2 - 10 \cos(2\pi x_i - s_i) \tag{7}$$

Function minimum:

Position for E_n: $(x_1, x_2 \ldots x_n) = s$; Value for E_n: $y = 0$

Function interval: $<-5.12, 5.12>$.

Where s_i is a random number from the 90% range of function interval; s vector is randomly generated before each run of the optimization process.

8   Results

Experiments were performed in the combined environments of Wolfram Mathematica and C language, canonical DE and jDE therefore used the built-in C language pseudo random number generator Mersenne Twister C representing traditional pseudorandom number generators in comparisons. All experiments used different initialization, i.e. different initial population was generated in each run.

Within this research, one type of experiment was performed. It utilizes the maximum number of generations fixed at 1500 generations, Population size of 75 and dimension $dim = 30$. Maximum cost function evaluation was therefore 112500 for all experiments. This allowed the possibility to analyze the progress of all studied DE variants within a limited number of generations and cost function evaluations.

8.1   Mutation and Crossover Parameter Settings for Chaos Driven DE

Firstly, two ChaosDE control parameters for mutation and crossover (F and CR) were finely tuned in the range $<0.1, 0.9>$ with the step of 0.1. Experiments were performed with the typical settings for the Lozi map ($a = 1.7$, $b = 0.5$). We have used such an experiment design, since different a and b combinations (i.e. different chaotic dynamics) have significantly lower influence for DE performance within F and CR tuning than CR and F themselves. Corresponding examples of contours plots are depicted in Fig. 2 for two selected simple benchmark functions.

From the experiment, it follows that the best results are obtained with the combination $F = 0.4$, $CR = 0.4$.

8.2   Parameter Settings for Chaotic Lozi Map

In the second part of experiment, two accessible control parameters (a and b) of chaotic discrete Lozi map were finely tuned within the ranges: $a \in \langle 1.3, 1.7 \rangle$ and

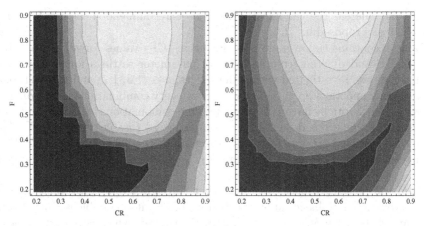

Fig. 2. Contours plots of average results for 50 repeated runs, from left to right: Schwefel's test function (left) and shifted Rastrigin's function (right), dim = 30

Table 1. Parameters tuning for Lozi map

DE Version	Original Schwefel's test function	shifted 1st De Jong's function	shifted Ackley's original function	shifted Rastrigin's function
Canonical DE	-5384.8	2.4E-21	1.78E-10	168.5168
jDE	**-12569.5**	3.18E-15	2.48E-07	32.42622
a=1.3 b=0.1	-6323.84	66.93173	17.35857	208.913
a=1.3 b=0.2	-9760.51	5.001269	9.939031	67.4757
a=1.4 b=0.1	-11774.1	0.042298	1.731801	24.85462
a=1.4 b=0.2	-12228.6	4.05E-19	2.05E-10	16.45284
a=1.4 b=0.3	-12412.9	3.56E-28	0.011731	**15.83748**
a=1.5 b=0.1	-11462.4	0	**4E-15**	95.21326
a=1.5 b=0.2	-11479.9	0	**4E-15**	97.04095
a=1.5 b=0.3	-11290.4	0	**4E-15**	97.93962
a=1.5 b=0.4	-12070.2	0	**4E-15**	89.73319
a=1.6 b=0.1	-11768.9	0	4.12E-15	98.31299
a=1.6 b=0.2	-11677.5	0	**4E-15**	101.3721
a=1.6 b=0.3	-11759	0	**4E-15**	100.9559
a=1.6 b=0.4	-11000.6	0	3.88E-15	108.1069
a=1.6 b=0.5	-10602.5	0	**4E-15**	105.949
a=1.7 b=0.1	-11966.2	0	4.12E-15	98.42761
a=1.7 b=0.2	-10990.7	0	**4E-15**	102.5946
a=1.7 b=0.3	-10618	0	**4E-15**	107.0337
a=1.7 b=0.4	-9866.49	0	**4E-15**	111.6011
a=1.7 b=0.5	-9058.77	0	**4E-15**	114.8259

$b \in \langle 0.1, 0.5 \rangle$ with the incremental step $= 0.1$. ChaosDE has utilized the mutation and crossover parameter settings from the previous experiment: $F = 0.4$,

$CR = 0.4$, whereas the canonical DE has used recommended setting $F = 0.5$, $CR = 0.9$ as proposed in [16].

Table 1 contains the average Cost Function (CF) values for all 50 repeated runs of DE and different combinations of parameter settings for chaotic Lozi map, which was investigated within the ranges: $a \in \langle 1.3, 1.7 \rangle$ and $b \in \langle 0.1, 0.5 \rangle$ with the incremental step $= 0.1$. However not every combinations are leading to the expected chaotic behavior, thus the missing combinations in Table 1 indicate that such combinations do not lead to the expected (usable) chaotic behavior. With the increasing of the parameter a, the suitable chaotic behavior for CPRNG occurs within the wider range of parameter b. Bold number represents the best result.

From the presented data, it is clear that through simple implementation of chaotic dynamic into basic canonical strategy of DE, it is possible to outperform the state of the art representative of adaptive strategy, which is jDE, in three of four case studies with limited maximum number of generations.

Finally following settings for ChaosDE with Lozi map gives very promising results: $F = 0.4$, $CR = 0.4$, $a = 1.4$, $b = 0.3$ for Schwefel's and Rastrigin's test function. For the remaining two cases, the different combination of $a = 1.5$, $b = 0.4$ proved to be also a good choice.

8.3   Performance Comparison on CEC13 Benchmark Set

In this experiment, the performance of ChaosDE with selected combinations of parameters settings for CPRNG, jDE, Canonical DE with two different settings $F = 0.4$, $CR = 0.4$ (to be comparable with ChaosDE), and $F = 0.5$, $CR = 0.9$ were tested on the IEEE CEC 2013 benchmark set. Results are given in Table 2 showing the average final CF values of all 50 runs ($D = 30$, max. generations $= 1500$, pop. size $= 75$).

9   Conclusions

This work was aimed at the experimental analysis of the complex chaotic dynamics directly injected into the DE. To be more precise, this research investigates the influence of parameter tuning to the performance of chaos driven DE. Both settings for mutation and crossover DE control parameters and adjustable chaotic system parameters were experimentally investigated here. Furthermore this paper compared the ChaosDE with state-of-the art representative, which is simple adaptive jDE.

Results lend weigh to the argument that through tuning of parameters of chaotic Lozi map unique properties with connection to DE have been revealed. The findings can be summarized as follows:

– The high sensitivity of the DE to the selection, parameters settings and internal dynamics of the chaotic PRNG is fully manifested within all case studies.

Table 2. Performance comparison for ChaosDE, jDE, Canonical DE (CanDE) on CEC 13 Benchmark Set, dim = 30, max. Generations = 1500; *Bold values represent the best performance, italic equal: based on Friedman Rank Tests

	f min	ChaosDE 1.4 0.3	ChaosDE 1.5 0.4	CanDE 0.4 0.4	CanDE 0.5 0.9	jDE
f1	-1400	*-1400*	*-1400*	*-1400*	*-1400*	*-1400*
f2	-1300	6.36 E07	8.17 E07	8.71 E07	**1.84 E06**	1.20 E07
f3	-1200	2.74 E07	**1.29 E06**	1.30 E06	2.41 E06	2.27 E06
f4	-1100	56740.35	57426.93	54083.25	**12998.92**	24176.48
f5	-1000	-993.908	*-1000*	*-1000*	*-1000*	*-1000*
f6	-900	-860.45	-872.433	-877.276	-876.359	**-883.662**
f7	-800	-761.446	-788.442	-781.269	**-798.411**	-787.59
f8	-700	*-679.019*	*-679.013*	*-679.004*	*-679.02*	*-679.031*
f9	-600	-560.074	-559.75	-560.666	-560.058	**-565.196**
f10	-500	-498.594	**-499.795**	-498.732	-498.976	-498.97
f11	-400	**-381.755**	-304.57	-313.009	-240.304	-365.637
f12	-300	-109.226	-108.865	-110.953	-110.015	**-134.237**
f13	-200	-9.92991	-8.79018	-14.9001	-12.6618	**-22.0975**
f14	-100	**2020.009**	4219.34	3890.948	6675.347	2120.024
f15	100	7620.809	7532.795	7712.248	7602.119	**7340.324**
f16	200	202.6942	**202.652**	*202.6532*	202.8108	202.6974
f17	300	390.5675	438.1732	422.1826	501.9207	**385.4481**
f18	400	616.8802	**616.1296**	622.3375	616.9574	620.9147
f19	500	513.4088	513.8151	511.0433	515.866	**507.8474**
f20	600	612.593	**612.5352**	612.5527	612.5541	*612.5353*
f21	700	992.7185	**980.1435**	985.118	1001.532	1015.886
f22	800	4142.029	5494.466	5211.529	8016.171	**3610.891**
f23	900	8894.33	8814.177	8632.869	8699.092	8575.498
f24	1000	1222.877	*1201.455*	1204.168	**1200.622**	1208.364
f25	1100	1414.14	1410.514	1411.526	**1356.466**	1398.31
f26	1200	1412.658	1405.587	1407.445	1400.047	1400.423
f27	1300	2328.621	1820.004	2265.583	**1619.784**	1886.461
f28	1400	1701.41	*1700*	*1700*	*1700*	*1700*
Overall*		2+, 2=	6+,5=	0+, 4=	6+, 3=	8+,5=

- With simple test functions, the performance of ChaosDE is better in the most cases than jDE and Canonical DE. This makes the ChaosDe concept easy to use (plug-in) for (simple) real optimization tasks.
- With complex CEC13 benchmark set, the performance of ChaosDE (with particular combination of parameters) is worse than jDE, but better than canonical DE.
- ChaosDE requires lower values of CR and F for almost any CPRNG and benchmark test function.
- Presented experiment workflow was checked also reversibly, i.e. firstly the parameters of chaotic map were tuned, and thereafter the mutation and crossover parameters of DE were finely tuned for several selected combina-

tions. This was more time demanding, since more combinations occurred. Due to the limited space, results are not presented here. Nevertheless, still the same findings of lower values of CR and F were confirmed.

− Fine complex tuning with little steps of two basic DE parameters and another two up to six (depends on the chaotic map) accessible parameters of used chaotic systems may lead to the difficult combinatorial task. This issue opens up the possibility of examining the impact of an adaptation to generation of pseudorandom numbers, and thus influence on the results obtained by DE.

References

1. Price, K.V.: An Introduction to Differential Evolution. In: Corne, D., Dorigo, M., Glover, F. (eds.) New Ideas in Optimization, pp. 79–108. McGraw-Hill Ltd. (1999)
2. Qin, A.K., Huang, V.L., Suganthan, P.N.: Differential Evolution Algorithm With Strategy Adaptation for Global Numerical Optimization. IEEE Transactions on Evolutionary Computation 13(2), 398–417 (2009)
3. Mallipeddi, R., Suganthan, P.N., Pan, Q.K., Tasgetiren, M.F.: Differential evolution algorithm with ensemble of parameters and mutation strategies. Applied Soft Computing 11(2), 1679–1696 (2011)
4. Neri, F., Tirronen, V.: Recent advances in differential evolution: a survey and experimental analysis. Artif. Intell. Rev. 33(1-2), 61–106 (2010)
5. Weber, M., Neri, F., Tirronen, V.: A study on scale factor in distributed differential evolution. Information Sciences 181(12), 2488–2511 (2011)
6. Neri, F., Iacca, G., Mininno, E.: Disturbed Exploitation compact Differential Evolution for limited memory optimization problems. Information Sciences 181(12), 2469–2487 (2011)
7. Iacca, G., Caraffini, F., Neri, F.: Compact Differential Evolution Light: High Performance Despite Limited Memory Requirement and Modest Computational Overhead. J. Comput. Sci. Technol. 27(5), 1056–1076 (2012)
8. Aydin, I., Karakose, M., Akin, E.: Chaotic-based hybrid negative selection algorithm and its applications in fault and anomaly detection. Expert Systems with Applications 37(7), 5285–5294 (2010)
9. Liang, W., Zhang, L., Wang, M.: The chaos differential evolution optimization algorithm and its application to support vector regression machine. Journal of Software 6(7), 1297–1304 (2011)
10. Zhenyu, G., Bo, C., Min, Y., Binggang, C.: Self-Adaptive Chaos Differential Evolution. In: Jiao, L., Wang, L., Gao, X.-B., Liu, J., Wu, F. (eds.) ICNC 2006. LNCS, vol. 4221, pp. 972–975. Springer, Heidelberg (2006)
11. Davendra, D., Zelinka, I., Senkerik, R.: Chaos driven evolutionary algorithms for the task of PID control. Computers & Mathematics with Applications 60(4), 1088–1104 (2010)
12. dos Santos Coelho, L., Mariani, V.C.: A novel chaotic particle swarm optimization approach using Henon map and implicit filtering local search for economic load dispatch. Chaos, Solitons & Fractals 39(2), 510–518 (2009)
13. Davendra, D., Bialic-Davendra, M., Senkerik, R.: Scheduling the Lot-Streaming Flowshop scheduling problem with setup time with the chaos-induced Enhanced Differential Evolution. In: 2013 IEEE Symposium on Differential Evolution (SDE), April 16-19, pp. 119–126 (2013)

14. Pluhacek, M., Senkerik, R., Davendra, D., Kominkova Oplatkova, Z., Zelinka, I.: On the behavior and performance of chaos driven PSO algorithm with inertia weight. Computers & Mathematics with Applications 66(2), 122–134 (2013)
15. Pluhacek, M., Senkerik, R., Zelinka, I., Davendra, D.: Chaos PSO algorithm driven alternately by two different chaotic maps - An initial study. In: 2013 IEEE Congress on Evolutionary Computation (CEC), June 20-23, pp. 2444–2449 (2013)
16. Gandomi, A.H., Yang, X.S., Talatahari, S., Alavi, A.H.: Firefly algorithm with chaos. Communications in Nonlinear Science and Numerical Simulation 18(1), 89–98 (2013)
17. Senkerik, R., Pluhacek, M., Zelinka, I., Oplatkova, Z.K., Vala, R., Jasek, R.: Performance of Chaos Driven Differential Evolution on Shifted Benchmark Functions Set. In: Herrero, A., et al. (eds.) International Joint Conference SOCO 2013-CISIS 2013-ICEUTE 2013. AISC, vol. 239, pp. 41–50. Springer, Heidelberg (2014)
18. Senkerik, R., Davendra, D., Zelinka, I., Pluhacek, M., Kominkova Oplatkova, Z.: On the Differential Evolution Driven by Selected Discrete Chaotic Systems: Extended Study. In: 19th International Conference on Soft Computing, MENDEL 2013, pp. 137–144 (2013)
19. Lozi, R.: Engineering of Mathematical Chaotic Circuits. In: Zelinka, I., Chen, G., Rössler, O.E., Snasel, V., Abraham, A. (eds.) Nostradamus 2013: Prediction, Model. & Analysis. AISC, vol. 210, pp. 17–29. Springer, Heidelberg (2013)
20. Price, K.V., Storn, R.M., Lampinen, J.A.: Differential Evolution - A Practical Approach to Global Optimization. Natural Computing Series. Springer, Heidelberg (2005)
21. Sprott, J.C.: Chaos and Time-Series Analysis. Oxford University Press (2003)
22. Brest, J., Greiner, S., Boskovic, B., Mernik, M., Zumer, V.: Self-adapting control parameters in differential evolution: A comparative study on numerical benchmark problems. IEEE Transactions on Evolutionary Computation 10, 646–657 (2006)
23. Liang, J.J., Qu, B.-Y., Suganthan, P.N., Hernandez-Diaz, A.G.: Problem Definitions and Evaluation Criteria for the CEC 2013 Special Session and Competition on Real-Parameter Optimization, Technical Report 201212, Computational Intelligence Laboratory, Zhengzhou University, Zhengzhou China and Technical Report, Nanyang Technological University, Singapore (2013)

Classification and Estimation

Mathematical Characterization of Sophisticated Variants for Relevance Learning in Learning Matrix Quantization Based on Schatten-p-norms

Andrea Bohnsack[1,2], Kristin Domaschke[2], Marika Kaden[2,3], Mandy Lange[2,3], and Thomas Villmann[2,3(✉)]

[1] Staatliche Berufliche Oberschule Kaufbeuren,
Kaufbeuren, 87600, Germany
[2] Computational Intelligence Group,
University of Applied Sciences Mittweida, 09648 Mittweida, Germany
[3] Institut für Computational Intelligence
und intelligente Datenanalyse e.V. (CIID), 09648 Mittweida, Germany
thomas.villmann@hs-mittweida.de

Abstract. In this paper we investigate possibilities of relevance learning in learning matrix quantization and discuss their mathematical properties. Learning matrix quantization can be seen as an extension of the learning vector quantization method, which is one of the most popular and intuitive prototype based vector quantization algorithms for classification learning. Whereas in the vector quantization approach vector data are processed, learning matrix quantization deals with matrix data as they occur in image processing of gray-scale images or in time-resolved spectral analysis. Here, we concentrate on the consideration of relevance learning when learning matrix quantization is based on the Schatten-p-norm as the data dissimilarity measure. For those matrix systems exist more relevance learning variants than for vector classification systems. We contemplate several approaches based on different matrix products as well as tensor operators. In particular, we discuss their mathematical properties related to the relevance learning task keeping in mind the stochastic gradient learning scheme for both, prototype as well as relevance learning.

1 Introduction

Classification of big data is still a challenging task in machine learning. Frequently, vector data are processed, which may have large data dimensions depending on the task. Nowadays, more complex data are in the focus. For example, the health status of a patient is described by means of structured data records as a composite of heterogeneous components which require dedicated data processing [35]. Other complex data are gray-scale images or time-resolved spectra. Classification learning of those complex data is often executed by vectorization of the data in advance and application of vector based methods afterwards.

Many machine learning classifiers were developed to process vectorial data ranging from prototype based methods like Support Vector Machines (SVMs,

© Springer International Publishing Switzerland 2015
L. Rutkowski et al. (Eds.): ICAISC 2015, Part I, LNAI 9119, pp. 403–414, 2015.
DOI: 10.1007/978-3-319-19324-3_37

[27]) or the family of Learning Vector Quantizers (LVQs, [19]) to classification trees and deep learning architectures [8,2]. Thereby, the family of LVQs provide an intuitive and robust algorithmic approach approximating a Bayes classification decision scheme [17,18], which frequently achieves promising results. Usually, these methods are based on the Euclidean metric to judge the dissimilarity between the data. Non-Euclidean dissimilarities were also considered including correlations, divergences or kernels depending on the given data structure [30,31,32]. One of the key extensions of the Euclidean LVQ is relevance learning, which weights the vector dimensions to improve the performance [4,13]. It can be further improved taking the data dimension correlations into account [28].

Obviously, these methods can also be applied to matrix data after vectorization. However, this preprocessing may destroy spatial relations contained in a matrix, so that this important information is lost. One possibility to overcome this dilemma is feature extraction based on spatial features. Gabor filters are frequently applied in image processing [5,29,34,33], whereas time-resolved spectra maybe decomposed by two-dimensional Fourier expansions ore wavelet decompositions [23,21].

Recently, a matrix variant for LVQ was proposed such that matrix data can be processed directly keeping the basic principles of LVQ [7]. The resulting learning matrix quantization (LMQ) remains a prototype based classifier with prototypes now being matrices. The dissimilarity measure for discrimination between the matrix data and prototypes is determined by the Schatten-p-norm [26], which is a natural extension of the l_p-norm for vectors [10,14]. The most prominent case is $p = 2$, which is the Frobenius norm.

As already mentioned, the automatic weighting of the vector dimensions for the classification performance improvement is a vitally extension of the (Euclidean) LVQ known as *relevance learning* [13]. Relevance learning as well as matrix learning can easily be plugged in LVQ based on l_p- norms as it is shown in [20]. Yet, these ideas cannot immediately be adopted for LMQ based on Schatten-p-norms because of the more rich algebraic structure, as we will explain in this paper. Thus, this contribution considers, how adequate concepts of relevance learning could be realized in LMQ. Thereby, the aim of this paper is rather to investigate relevance learning concepts from a formal mathematical point than give numerical simulation results.

For this purpose, first we briefly recapitulate LVQ based on l_p-norms together with concepts of relevance learning. Thereafter we turn over to LMQ based on Schatten-p-norms as the matrix data counterpart and consider the algebraic possibilities of relevance learning. We emphasize at this point that we are not dealing with numerical properties and behavior but restricting ourselves to the investigation of the mathematical characteristics. Numerical evaluations should be studied for promising candidate models for relevance learning in the future.

2   Learning Vector Quantization Based on l_p-norms and Relevance Learning

2.1   Basic Learning Vector Quantization Based on l_p-norms

LVQ was introduced by KOHONEN as an intuitive prototype based learning classifier [17]. LVQ assumes a prototype set $W = \{\mathbf{w}_k \in \mathbb{R}^n, k = 1 \dots M\}$ with class labels $y_{\mathbf{w}_k} \in \mathcal{C} = \{1, \dots, C\}$ such that there is at least one prototype per class and $\mathcal{C}$ is the class index set. The training data $\mathbf{v} \in V \subseteq \mathbb{R}^n$ are also equipped with class labels $x_{\mathbf{v}} \in \mathcal{C}$ representing the classes to be learned by the LVQ model.

LVQ models distribute the prototypes $\mathbf{v} \in \mathbb{R}^n$ in the data space during the learning phase. After training, a new data vector $\mathbf{v} \in \mathbb{R}^n$ is assigned to a class via a winner takes all rule

$$\mathbf{v} \overset{LVQ}{\longmapsto} y_{\mathbf{w}_s} \tag{2.1}$$

with

$$s = argmin_{k=1\dots M} d(\mathbf{v}, \mathbf{w}_k) \tag{2.2}$$

and $d(\mathbf{v}, \mathbf{w})$ is a mathematical dissimilarity measure [24], e.g. the squared Euclidean distance. A more general choice would be a l_p-dissimilarity

$$d_p(\mathbf{v}, \mathbf{w}) = \left(\|\mathbf{v} - \mathbf{w}\|_p \right)^p = |\mathbf{v} - \mathbf{w}|^p \tag{2.3}$$

based on the l_p-norm $\|\mathbf{v} - \mathbf{w}\|_p = \sqrt[p]{\sum_{i=1}^n |v_i - w_i|^p}$. The prototype $\mathbf{w}_s$ is denoted as the overall winner. The basic LVQ learning principle is that prototypes are attracted by those training data samples, which have the same class labels and are repulsed otherwise. The original LVQ variants LVQ1...LVQ3 differ in their particular training schemes, however, all realize after learning an approximated Bayes-classifier [18]. The disadvantage of these models is that the learning schemes are only heuristically motivated.

The generalized learning vector quantization (GLVQ) model overcomes this disadvantage [25]. It is a cost function based modification of the intuitive LVQ, approximating the classification error as the objective to be minimized. GLVQ based on l_p-norms assumes a classifier function

$$\mu(\mathbf{v}) = \frac{d_p^+(\mathbf{v}) - d_p^-(\mathbf{v})}{d_p^+(\mathbf{v}) + d_p^-(\mathbf{v})} \in [-1, 1] \tag{2.4}$$

where $d_p^+(\mathbf{v}) = d_p(\mathbf{v}, \mathbf{w}^+)$ denotes the dissimilarity between the data vector $\mathbf{v}$ and the closest prototype $\mathbf{w}^+$ with the same class label $y_{\mathbf{w}^+} = x_{\mathbf{v}}$, and $d_p^-(\mathbf{v}) = d_p(\mathbf{v}, \mathbf{w}^-)$ is the dissimilarity value for the best matching prototype $\mathbf{w}^-$ with a class label $y_{\mathbf{w}^-}$ different from $x_{\mathbf{v}}$. Hence, $\mu(\mathbf{v})$ becomes non-positive if a data sample $\mathbf{v}$ is correctly classified. The cost function to be minimized is

$$E_{GLVQ}(W) = \frac{1}{2} \sum_{\mathbf{v} \in V} f(\mu(\mathbf{v})) \tag{2.5}$$

where f is a monotonically increasing squashing function usually chosen as a differentiable sigmoid or the identity function. The sigmoid choice allows a smooth approximation of the classification error [16]. Further, it can be shown that GLVQ maximizes the hypothesis margin $d_p^+ (\mathbf{v}) - d_p^- (\mathbf{v})$ [6,3,12]. Learning in GLVQ is performed by the *stochastic* gradient descent learning for the cost function E_{GLVQ} with respect to the winning prototypes $\mathbf{w}^+$ and $\mathbf{w}^-$ for a randomly chosen training sample $\mathbf{v} \in V$. The updates can be written as

$$\Delta \mathbf{w}^\pm \propto - \frac{\partial f}{\partial \mu (\mathbf{v})} \cdot \frac{\partial \mu (\mathbf{v})}{\partial d_p^\pm (\mathbf{v})} \cdot \frac{\partial d_p^\pm (\mathbf{v})}{\partial \mathbf{w}^\pm} \qquad (2.6)$$

with

$$\frac{\partial d_p^\pm}{\partial \mathbf{w}^\pm} = -p \left| \mathbf{z}^\pm \right|^{\circ (p-1)} \circ \frac{\partial g (\mathbf{z}^\pm)}{\partial \mathbf{z}^\pm}$$

are the formal derivatives of $d_p (\mathbf{v}, \mathbf{w})$, $\mathbf{z}^\pm = \mathbf{v} - \mathbf{w}^\pm$, and the element-by-element function $g (\mathbf{x}) = |\mathbf{x}|$ [20]. Further, $|\mathbf{z}|^{\circ (p-1)}$ denotes the element-by-element power of the vector $\mathbf{z}$.

Several extensions were proposed to adapt this basic GLVQ scheme according to specific classification tasks. A recent overview can be found in [15].

2.2   Relevance Learning in GLVQ

One of the most successful modifications is relevance learning in GLVQ (GRLVQ, [4,13]). The idea is to weight the data vector dimensions according to their relevance for better classification performance. Thus, in the GRLVQ, the dissimilarity measure $d_p (\mathbf{v}, \mathbf{w})$ is replaced by

$$d_{p,\mathbf{r}} (\mathbf{v}, \mathbf{w}) = |\mathbf{r} \circ (\mathbf{v} - \mathbf{w})|^p \qquad (2.7)$$

with the relevance vector $\mathbf{r}$ consisting of the relevance weights r_i with normalization $\sum_{i=1}^n |r_i|^p = 1$. Here, $\mathbf{r} \circ \mathbf{x}$ denotes the element-by-element Hadamard product. The *relevances r_i weight each data dimension independently* and can also be adapted by stochastic gradient learning according to

$$\Delta \mathbf{r} \propto - \frac{\partial f}{\partial \mu (\mathbf{v})} \cdot \left(\frac{\partial \mu (\mathbf{v})}{\partial d_{p,\mathbf{r}}^+ (\mathbf{v})} \cdot \frac{\partial d_{p,\mathbf{r}}^+ (\mathbf{v})}{\partial \mathbf{r}} + \frac{\partial \mu (\mathbf{v})}{\partial d_{p,\mathbf{r}}^- (\mathbf{v})} \cdot \frac{\partial d_{p,\mathbf{r}}^- (\mathbf{v})}{\partial \mathbf{r}} \right) \qquad (2.8)$$

with

$$\frac{\partial d_{p,\mathbf{r}}^\pm (\mathbf{v})}{\partial \mathbf{r}} = \left| \mathbf{r} \circ \mathbf{z}^\pm \right|^{\circ (p-1)} \circ \frac{\partial g (\mathbf{z}^\pm)}{\partial \mathbf{z}^\pm} \circ \mathbf{z}^\pm .$$

A further generalization can be obtained if also correlations between vector dimensions are considered. The respective variant is known as *generalized matrix* LVQ (GMLVQ, [28]) with the dissimilarity measure

$$d_{p,\Omega} (\mathbf{v}, \mathbf{w}) = |\Omega (\mathbf{v} - \mathbf{w})|^p \qquad (2.9)$$

and $\Omega \in \mathbb{R}^{m \times n}$ is a mapping matrix. Then, the symmetric matrix $\Lambda = \Omega^T \Omega$ can be interpreted after learning as a *classification correlation matrix* combining those data dimensions, which supports the class separabilities. The diagonal elements Λ_{ii} can be seen as relevance weights comparable to the weights r_i in GRLVQ . Analogously to (2.8) we obtain

$$\Delta\Omega_{ij} \propto -\frac{\partial f}{\partial \mu\left(\mathbf{v}\right)} \cdot \left(\frac{\partial \mu\left(\mathbf{v}\right)}{\partial d_{p,\Omega}^{+}\left(\mathbf{v}\right)} \cdot \frac{\partial d_{p,\Omega}^{+}\left(\mathbf{v}\right)}{\partial \Omega_{ij}} + \frac{\partial \mu\left(\mathbf{v}\right)}{\partial d_{p,\Omega}^{-}\left(\mathbf{v}\right)} \cdot \frac{\partial d_{p,\Omega}^{-}\left(\mathbf{v}\right)}{\partial \Omega_{ij}} \right) \tag{2.10}$$

with

$$\frac{\partial d_{p,\Omega}^{\pm}}{\partial \Omega} = p\left(\left|\mathbf{s}^{\pm}\right|^{\circ(p-1)} \circ \frac{\partial g\left(\mathbf{s}^{\pm}\right)}{\partial \mathbf{s}^{\pm}} \right) \mathbf{z}^{T}$$

and $\mathbf{s}^{\pm} = \Omega\mathbf{z}^{\pm}$ for stochastic gradient descent optimization with respect to the mapping matrix Ω [20].

3 Learning Matrix Quantization Based on Schatten-p-norms and Variants of Relevance Learning

3.1 Learning Matrix Quantization Based on Schatten-p-norms

In the following we contemplate matrix data and the *generalized learning matrix quantization* (GLMQ) based on Schatten-p-norms as adequate counterpart of GLVQ based on l_p-norms. Thus the data are considered to be matrices $\mathbf{V} \in V_{m,n} \subseteq \mathbb{R}^{m\times n}$, and, adequately, the prototype set W of GLMQ also consists of matrices $\mathbf{W}_k \in \mathbb{R}^{m\times n}$ and the l_p-norm has to be replaced by an appropriate matrix norm. Mathematically, the vector space $\mathbb{R}^{m\times n}$ of matrices equipped with a norm is a Banach space $\mathfrak{B}_{m,n}$. Respective matrix norms have to fulfill the usual norm axioms. A matrix norm $\|\bullet\|_M$ based on a vector norm $\|\bullet\|_V$ by

$$\|\mathbf{A}\|_M = \max_{\|\mathbf{v}\|_V=1} \|\mathbf{A}\mathbf{v}\|_V$$

is denoted as *natural norm induced by* $\|\bullet\|_V$. Natural matrix norms also fulfill the additional property of sub-multiplicity, i.e. they satisfy the Cauchy-Schwarz-inequality $\|\mathbf{X} \cdot \mathbf{Y}\|_M \leq \|\mathbf{X}\|_M \cdot \|\mathbf{Y}\|_M$ [10]. Examples of non-sub-multiplicative norms are the maximum norm $\|\mathbf{A}\|_{\max} = \max_{i,j} |a_{ij}|$ or the Ky-Fan-norm being the sum of the first K singular values of the matrix [14]. Another important matrix norm based on all singular values is the Schatten-p-norm

$$s_p\left(\mathbf{A}\right) = \|\sigma\left(\mathbf{A}\right)\|_p \tag{3.1}$$

defined by the l_p-norm of the vector $\sigma\left(\mathbf{A}\right)$ of the singular values of the matrix $\mathbf{A} \in \mathbb{R}^{m\times n}$ [26]. Schatten-p-norms have been proven to be successful in classification learning of images and time-resolved spectra [11,7]. These sub-multiplicative norms can be calculated alternatively as

$$s_p\left(\mathbf{A}\right) = \sqrt[p]{tr(|\mathbf{A}|^p)} \tag{3.2}$$

where $tr(\bullet)$ is the trace operator and $|\mathbf{A}| = \sqrt[p]{\mathbf{A}^*\mathbf{A}}$ is the *positive matrix root*[1]. For $p = 2$, the Schatten-p-norm reduces to the prominent Frobenius norm $s_2(\mathbf{A}) = \sqrt{tr(\mathbf{A}\mathbf{A}^T)} = \sqrt{tr(\mathbf{A}^T\mathbf{A})}$, which is the natural matrix norm induced by the Euclidean vector norm and has found wide applications.

Based on these mathematical properties we take

$$\delta_p(\mathbf{V}, \mathbf{W}) = (s_p(\mathbf{V} - \mathbf{W}))^p \tag{3.3}$$

as a dissimilarity measure for GLMQ comparable to $d_p(\mathbf{v}, \mathbf{w})$ in GLVQ emphasizing the case $p = 2$. The respectively GLMQ cost function adapted from (2.5) for an arbitrary p-value $p > 0$ reads as

$$E_{GLMQ}(W) = \frac{1}{2} \sum_{\mathbf{V} \in V_{m,n}} f(\mu(\mathbf{V})) . \tag{3.4}$$

with the modified classifier function

$$\mu(\mathbf{V}) = \frac{\delta_p^+(\mathbf{V}) - \delta_p^-(\mathbf{V})}{\delta_p^+(\mathbf{V}) + \delta_p^-(\mathbf{V})} \in [-1, 1] \tag{3.5}$$

where $\delta_p^\pm(\mathbf{V})$ plays the same role as $d_p^\pm(\mathbf{v})$ for GLVQ. Applying now the analog formalism as for GLVQ, we obtain the formal prototype update rules

$$\Delta\mathbf{W}^\pm \propto -\frac{\partial f}{\partial \mu(\mathbf{V})} \cdot \frac{\partial \mu(\mathbf{V})}{\partial \delta_p^\pm(\mathbf{V})} \cdot \frac{\partial \delta_p^\pm(\mathbf{V})}{\partial \mathbf{W}^\pm} \tag{3.6}$$

for $\mathbf{W}^\pm$. For $p = 2$, we simply get $\frac{\partial \delta_p^\pm(\mathbf{V})}{\partial \mathbf{W}^\pm} = -2(\mathbf{V} - \mathbf{W}^\pm)$.

3.2   Relevance Learning in GLMQ

In the following we will discuss variants of relevance learning for GLMQ. Obviously, the algebraic structure of the Banach space $\mathfrak{B}_{m,n}^p$ of matrices equipped with the Schatten-p-norm is more complex as the simpler $\mathbb{R}^n$. In particular, there are several possibilities to define kinds of relevance learning depending on the algebraic composition. We investigate them distinguishing matrix compositions with a relevance matrix $\mathbf{R}$ and tensor composites with a relevance tensor $\mathbf{T}$. Thereby, of particular interest is always the case $p = 2$, corresponding to the Frobenius-norm to be applied.

---

[1] The positive root of a positive semi-definite symmetric matrix $\mathbf{S}$ is given by the following definition: Let $\mathbf{O}^T\mathbf{S}\mathbf{O} = \mathbf{D}$ with $\mathbf{D}$ is diagonal and $\mathbf{O}$ being an orthogonal matrix. Let $\mathbf{D}^{\frac{1}{2}}$ be the diagonal matrix obtained from $\mathbf{D}$ taking the *positive* roots of the diagonal elements. Then $\mathbf{S}^{\frac{1}{2}} = \mathbf{O}\mathbf{D}^{\frac{1}{2}}\mathbf{O}^T$ is the positive matrix root and $\mathbf{S} = \mathbf{S}^{\frac{1}{2}}\mathbf{S}^{\frac{1}{2}}$. Frequently, the attribute 'positive' is omitted.

Relevance Matrix Compositions

Hadamard-Relevance-Learning (HRL) The obvious counterpart to the vector variant $d_{p,r}$ from (2.7) for Schatten-p-norms would be

$$\delta_{p,\mathbf{R}\circ}(\mathbf{V},\mathbf{W}) = (s_p(\mathbf{R}\circ(\mathbf{V}-\mathbf{W})))^p \tag{3.7}$$

with the *relevance matrix* $\mathbf{R}$ *weighting independently each entry of a data matrix* $\mathbf{V}$ by the Hadamard product. For $p = 2$, this approach yields $\delta_{2,\mathbf{R}\circ}(\mathbf{V},\mathbf{W}) = tr\left((\mathbf{R}\circ(\mathbf{V}-\mathbf{W}))(\mathbf{R}\circ(\mathbf{V}-\mathbf{W}))^T\right)$. The formal relevance update as the stochastic gradient of (3.4) becomes

$$\Delta\mathbf{R} \propto -\frac{\partial f}{\partial\mu(\mathbf{V})}\cdot\left(\frac{\partial\mu(\mathbf{V})}{\partial\delta_{p,\mathbf{R}\circ}^{+}(\mathbf{V})}\cdot\frac{\partial\delta_{p,\mathbf{R}\circ}^{+}(\mathbf{V})}{\partial\mathbf{R}} + \frac{\partial\mu(\mathbf{V})}{\partial\delta_{p,\mathbf{R}\circ}^{-}(\mathbf{V})}\cdot\frac{\partial\delta_{p,\mathbf{R}\circ}^{-}(\mathbf{V})}{\partial\mathbf{R}}\right) \tag{3.8}$$

where $\frac{\partial\delta_{2,\mathbf{R}\circ}^{\pm}(\mathbf{V})}{\partial\mathbf{R}} = 2\mathbf{R}\circ(\mathbf{V}-\mathbf{W}^{\pm})\circ(\mathbf{V}-\mathbf{W}^{\pm})$ is obtained for $p = 2$. It is accompanied by the respective prototype derivatives (3.6) involving the term $\frac{\partial\delta_{2,\mathbf{R}\circ}^{\pm}(\mathbf{V})}{\partial\mathbf{W}^{\pm}} = -2\mathbf{R}\circ\mathbf{R}\circ(\mathbf{V}-\mathbf{W}^{\pm})$ for $p = 2$. We denote this variant as Hadamard-Relevance-Learning (HRL).

Multiplicative Relevance Learning (MRL) Alternatively to the HRL we can think about the weighting

$$\delta_{p,\mathbf{R}}(\mathbf{V},\mathbf{W}) = (s_p(\mathbf{R}\cdot(\mathbf{V}-\mathbf{W})))^p \tag{3.9}$$

using the ordinary matrix multiplication. Here, a *weighted linear relevance mixing* is applied, taking partially linear combinations of matrix entries into account. The relevance update is analog to (3.8) paying attention to the new derivative $\frac{\partial\delta_{p,\mathbf{R}}(\mathbf{V})}{\partial\mathbf{R}}$ to be involved. For $p = 2$ we get $\frac{\partial\delta_{2,\mathbf{R}}^{\pm}(\mathbf{V})}{\partial\mathbf{R}} = 2\mathbf{R}\cdot(\mathbf{V}-\mathbf{W}^{\pm})\cdot(\mathbf{V}-\mathbf{W}^{\pm})^T$. The respective prototype update involves the term $\frac{\partial\delta_{2,\mathbf{R}}^{\pm}(\mathbf{V})}{\partial\mathbf{W}^{\pm}} = -2\mathbf{R}^T\cdot\mathbf{R}\cdot(\mathbf{V}-\mathbf{W}^{\pm})$ and the method is referred here as (left) *Multiplicative Relevance Learning* (MRL). Note that also a right-hand multiplication could be considered, which can be processed analogously.

QR-*Relevance Learning (QR-RL)* In [1] the following matrix norm was introduced

$$n_{p,\mathbf{Q},\mathbf{R}}(\mathbf{A}) = \sqrt[p]{tr\left((\mathbf{Q}\cdot\mathbf{A}\cdot\mathbf{R}^T\cdot\mathbf{A}^T)^{\frac{p}{2}}\right)} \tag{3.10}$$

with positive definite matrices $\mathbf{Q}$ and $\mathbf{R}$ for $p = 2$, which can be used to identify fMRI-voxel-time-series for adequately chosen matrices $\mathbf{Q}$ and $\mathbf{R}$ to scale spatial and time resolution. Yet, it can easily be verified that (3.10) is also a norm for $p = 2q$ and $q \in \mathbb{N}$. Thus, a relevance based dissimilarity would be obtained as

$$\delta_{p,\mathbf{QR}}(\mathbf{V},\mathbf{W}) = tr\left(\left(\mathbf{Q}\cdot(\mathbf{V}-\mathbf{W})\cdot((\mathbf{V}-\mathbf{W})\cdot\mathbf{R})^T\right)^{\frac{p}{2}}\right) \tag{3.11}$$

which is, for $\mathbf{R} = \mathbb{E}$ being the unit matrix, strongly related to the (left) MRL. Similar, $\mathbf{Q} = \mathbb{E}$ corresponds to the right-hand multiplication MRL. For $p = 2$ and $\mathbf{Z}^{\pm} = (\mathbf{V} - \mathbf{W}^{\pm})$, we obtain the derivatives

$$\frac{\partial \delta_{2,\mathbf{QR}}^{\pm}(\mathbf{V})}{\partial \mathbf{W}^{\pm}} = -\mathbf{Q}^T \mathbf{Z}^{\pm} \mathbf{R}^T - \mathbf{Q} \mathbf{Z}^{\pm} \mathbf{R}$$

for the prototype update. Because $\mathbf{Q}$ and $\mathbf{R}$ are assumed to be positive definite, we suppose decompositions $\mathbf{Q} = \tilde{\mathbf{Q}}^T \tilde{\mathbf{Q}}$ and $\mathbf{R} = \tilde{\mathbf{R}}^T \tilde{\mathbf{R}}$. Then we get the derivatives

$$\frac{\partial \delta_{2,\mathbf{QR}}^{\pm}(\mathbf{V})}{\partial \tilde{\mathbf{R}}} = \left(\mathbf{Z}^{\pm}\right)^T \mathbf{Q}^T \left(\mathbf{Z}^{\pm}\right) \tilde{\mathbf{R}} + \tilde{\mathbf{R}}^T \left(\mathbf{Z}^{\pm}\right)^T \mathbf{Q}^T \left(\mathbf{Z}^{\pm}\right)$$

as well as

$$\frac{\partial \delta_{2,\mathbf{QR}}^{\pm}(\mathbf{V})}{\partial \tilde{\mathbf{Q}}} = \left(\mathbf{Z}^{\pm}\right) \mathbf{R} \left(\mathbf{Z}^{\pm}\right)^T \tilde{\mathbf{Q}} + \left(\mathbf{Z}^{\pm}\right) \mathbf{R}^T \left(\mathbf{Z}^{\pm}\right)^T \tilde{\mathbf{Q}}$$

for the relevance updates.

Kronecker-Relevance-Learning (KRL). The Kronecker-product $\mathbf{K} = \mathbf{A} \otimes \mathbf{B}$ between matrices $\mathbf{A} \in \mathbb{R}^{m_1 \times n_1}$ and $\mathbf{B} \in \mathbb{R}^{m_2 \times n_2}$ is known from tensor analysis [9,22]. It composites the matrices in vector space such that $\mathbf{K} \in \mathbb{R}^{m_1 m_2 \times n_1 n_2}$, i.e. a huge dimensionality is created. Thus, a respective relevance compositions might offers a high variability to relate the matrix elements. Therefore, Kronecker-product based relevance learning in GLMQ seems to provide a reliable method, having in mind the idea of high-dimensional embedding as known from support vector machines (SVM, [27]). Thus we consider the dissimilarity measure

$$\delta_{p,\mathbf{R}\otimes}(\mathbf{V}, \mathbf{W}) = (s_p(\mathbf{R} \otimes (\mathbf{V} - \mathbf{W})))^p \qquad (3.12)$$
$$= tr(|\mathbf{R} \otimes (\mathbf{V} - \mathbf{W})|^p)$$

which can be simplified to

$$\delta_{p,\mathbf{R}\otimes}(\mathbf{V}, \mathbf{W}) = tr\left(\left(\sqrt[†]{\mathbf{R}^T \mathbf{R} \otimes (\mathbf{V} - \mathbf{W})^T (\mathbf{V} - \mathbf{W})}\right)^p\right). \qquad (3.13)$$

For $p = 2q$ this reduces to

$$\delta_{2q,\mathbf{R}\otimes}(\mathbf{V}, \mathbf{W}) = tr\left(\left(\mathbf{R}^T \mathbf{R} \otimes (\mathbf{V} - \mathbf{W})^T (\mathbf{V} - \mathbf{W})\right)^q\right) \qquad (3.14)$$

and, in particular for the most intriguingly case $p = 2$, we get

$$\delta_{2,\mathbf{R}\otimes}(\mathbf{V}, \mathbf{W}) = tr\left(\mathbf{R}^T \mathbf{R} \otimes (\mathbf{V} - \mathbf{W})^T (\mathbf{V} - \mathbf{W})\right)$$
$$= tr\left(\mathbf{R}^T \mathbf{R}\right) tr\left((\mathbf{V} - \mathbf{W})^T (\mathbf{V} - \mathbf{W})\right)$$

whereby the commutative properties of the Kronecker product were used to achieve the last equation [22]. From this last transformation we learn that the structure of the relevance matrix $\mathbf{R}$ would be ignored despite the trace value for $p = 2$. Hence, the suspected variability is degenerated to one parameter and, therefore, meaningless for relevance learning in GLMQ.

Relevance Tensor Compositions

Tensor as multi-linear maps applied to matrices offer another kind of composition. Mathematically, matrices are tensors of 2nd order whereas vectors are tensors of first order. In this sense, the mapping $\boldsymbol{\Omega}\,(\mathbf{v} - \mathbf{w})$ used in (2.9) for GMLVQ can be taken as a tensor composite $\overset{\langle 2 \rangle}{\boldsymbol{\Omega}}\,[\mathbf{z}]$ resulting a tensor of first order (vector). Now the idea is to translate this to GLMQ dissimilarities.

Relevance Tensors of fourth order We consider the tensor induced mapping

$$\overset{\langle 4 \rangle}{\mathbf{T}}\,[\mathbf{Z}] = \mathbf{X}$$

where the matrix difference $\mathbf{Z} = \mathbf{V} - \mathbf{W}$ is projected onto a matrix $\mathbf{X}$ by $X_{ij} = \sum_{k,l} T_{ijkl} D_{kl}$. This would correspond to a dissimilarity measure

$$\delta_{p,\,\overset{\langle 4 \rangle}{\mathbf{T}}\,[\bullet]}(\mathbf{V}, \mathbf{W}) = \left(s_p \left(\overset{\langle 4 \rangle}{\mathbf{T}}\,[\mathbf{V} - \mathbf{W}] \right) \right)^p$$

based on Schatten-p-norms. However, $\mathbf{Z}$ as well as $\mathbf{X}$ belong to matrix vector spaces forming linear mappings as known from linear algebra. For those tensor composites, we can always find a base representation in these vector spaces such that the tensor composite is equivalent to a Kronecker-product-composite [9,22]. Hence, the respective relevance learning variability is the same as for the previously investigated KRL. In particular, it is also algebraically degenerating for the most interesting case $p = 2$.

Relevance Tensors of third order In this last possibility we consider tensors of third order such that

$$\mathbf{t} = \overset{\langle 3 \rangle}{\mathbf{T}}\,[\mathbf{V} - \mathbf{W}] \tag{3.15}$$

delivers a result vector $\mathbf{t}$ with $t_i = \sum_{jk} T_{ijk}\,(V_{jk} - W_{jk})$. Using this ansatz, the Schatten-p-norm reduces to the l_p-norm and we get

$$\delta_{p,\,\overset{\langle 3 \rangle}{\mathbf{T}}\,[\bullet]}(\mathbf{V}, \mathbf{W}) = \left\| \overset{\langle 3 \rangle}{\mathbf{T}}\,[\mathbf{V} - \mathbf{W}] \right\|_p^p \tag{3.16}$$

the derivative of which can be easily calculated. On a first glance, it looks like a counterpart to the matrix mapping $\boldsymbol{\Omega}\,(\mathbf{v} - \mathbf{w})$ applied in GMLVQ. However, it is not, because the dimensionality of the result of the tensor operation is a vector (tensor of zero order), whereas the difference $\mathbf{V} - \mathbf{W}$ is a tensor of second order. Otherwise, the mapping in GMLVQ preserves the orders of the tensors.

4 Conclusion and Future Work

In this paper we contemplate variants of relevance learning for learning matrix quantization. Thereby we assume that the dissimilarity measure for comparison of prototypes and data samples (matrices) is the Schatten-p-norm. The investigations in this paper are done on a conceptional algebraic level rather than accompanied by numerical simulations to verify the mathematical properties and characteristics of respective relevance-composite based dissimilarities. We figure out potential relevance learning models, which should be studied according to their numerical behavior in the future. In particular, composites based on usual matrix multiplication and Hadamard multiplication seems to be promising candidates, the latter one being equivalent to relevance learning known from learning vector quantization. Kronecker multiplication is meaningless in the most considered case $p = 2$. Auspicious tensor composites are tensors of third order whereas tensors of fourth order deliver degenerating results for $p = 2$.

References

[1] Allen, G., Grosenick, L., Taylor, J.: A generalized least squares matrix decomposition. Journal of the American Statistical Association, Theory & Methods 109(505), 145–159 (2012)

[2] Bengio, Y.: Learning deep architectures for AI. Foundations and Trends in Machine Learning 2(1), 1–127 (2009)

[3] Biehl, M., Hammer, B., Schneider, P., Villmann, T.: Metric learning for prototype-based classification. In: Bianchini, M., Maggini, M., Scarselli, F., Jain, L. (eds.) Innovations in Neural Information Paradigms and Applications. SCI, vol. 247, pp. 183–199. Springer, Berlin (2009)

[4] Bojer, T., Hammer, B., Schunk, D., von Toschanowitz, K.T.: Relevance determination in learning vector quantization. In: Proceedings of the 9th European Symposium on Artificial Neural Networks, ESANN 2001, D-Facto, Evere, Belgium, pp. 271–276 (2001)

[5] Cichocki, A., Amari, S.: Adaptive Blind Signal and Image Processing. John Wiley (2002)

[6] Crammer, K., Gilad-Bachrach, R., Navot, A., Tishby, A.: Margin analysis of the LVQ algorithm. In: Becker, S., Thrun, S., Obermayer, K. (eds.) Advances in Neural Information Processing (Proc. NIPS 2002), vol. 15, pp. 462–469. MIT Press, Cambridge (2003)

[7] Domaschke, K., Kaden, M., Lange, M., Villmann, T.: Learning matrix quantization and variants of relevance learning. In: Verleysen, M. (ed.) Proceedings of the European Symposium on Artificial Neural Networks, Computational Intelligence and Machine Learning (ESANN 2015), Louvain-La-Neuve, Belgium, page submitted (2015), i6doc.com

[8] Duda, R., Hart, P.: Pattern Classification and Scene Analysis. Wiley, New York (1973)

[9] Goldhorn, K.-H., Heinz, H.-P., Kraus, M.: Moderne mathematische Methoden der Physik, vol. 1. Springer, Heidelberg (2009)

[10] Golub, G., Loan, C.V.: Matrix Computations, 4th edn. Johns Hopkins Studies in the Mathematical Sciences. John Hopkins University Press, Baltimore (2013)

[11] Gu, Z., Shao, M., Li, L., Fu, Y.: Discriminative metric: Schatten norms vs. vector norm. In: Proc. of the 21st International Conference on Pattern Recognition (ICPR 2012), pp. 1213–1216 (2012)

[12] Hammer, B., Strickert, M., Villmann, T.: Relevance LVQ versus SVM. In: Rutkowski, L., Siekmann, J.H., Tadeusiewicz, R., Zadeh, L.A. (eds.) ICAISC 2004. LNCS (LNAI), vol. 3070, pp. 592–597. Springer, Heidelberg (2004)

[13] Hammer, B., Villmann, T.: Generalized relevance learning vector quantization. Neural Networks 15(8-9), 1059–1068 (2002)

[14] Horn, R., Johnson, C.: Matrix Analysis, 2nd edn. Cambridge University Press (2013)

[15] Kaden, M., Lange, M., Nebel, D., Riedel, M., Geweniger, T., Villmann, T.: Aspects in classification learning - Review of recent developments in Learning Vector Quantization. Foundations of Computing and Decision Sciences 39(2), 79–105 (2014)

[16] Kaden, M., Riedel, M., Hermann, W., Villmann, T.: Border-sensitive learning in generalized learning vector quantization: an alternative to support vector machines. Soft Computing, page in press (2015)

[17] Kohonen, T.: Learning vector quantization for pattern recognition. Report TKK-F-A601, Helsinki University of Technology, Espoo, Finland (1986)

[18] Kohonen, T.: Learning Vector Quantization. Neural Networks 1(suppl. 1), 303 (1988)

[19] Kohonen, T.: Self-Organizing Maps. Springer Series in Information Sciences, vol. 30. Springer, Heidelberg (1995) (2nd Extended Edition 1997)

[20] Lange, M., Zühlke, D., Holz, O., Villmann, T.: Applications of l_p-norms and their smooth approximations for gradient based learning vector quantization. In: Verleysen, M. (ed.) Proc. of European Symposium on Artificial Neural Networks, Computational Intelligence and Machine Learning (ESANN 2014), Louvain-La-Neuve, Belgium, pp. 271–276 (2014), i6doc.com

[21] Leung, A., Chau, F., Gao, J.: A review on applications of wavelet transform techniques in chemical analysis: 1989–1997. Chemometrics and Intelligent Laboratory Systems 43(1), 165–184 (1998)

[22] Liu, S., Trenkler, G.: Hadamard, Khatri-Rao, Kronecker and other matrix products. International Journal of Information and System Sciences 4(1), 160–177 (2008)

[23] Osowski, S., Nghia, D.D.: Neural networks for classification of 2-d patterns. In: 2000 5th International Conference on Signal Processing Proceedings. 16th World Computer Congress 2000, WCC 2000—ICSP 2000, vol. 3, pp. 1568–1571. IEEE, Piscataway (2000)

[24] Pekalska, E., Duin, R.: The Dissimilarity Representation for Pattern Recognition: Foundations and Applications. World Scientific (2006)

[25] Sato, A., Yamada, K.: Generalized learning vector quantization. In: Touretzky, D.S., Mozer, M.C., Hasselmo, M.E. (eds.) Proceedings of the 1995 Conference on Advances in Neural Information Processing Systems 8, pp. 423–429. MIT Press, Cambridge (1996)

[26] Schatten, R.: A Theory of Cross-Spaces. Annals of Mathematics Studies, vol. 26. Princeton University Press (1950)

[27] Schölkopf, B., Smola, A.: Learning with Kernels. MIT Press, Cambridge (2002)

[28] Schneider, P., Hammer, B., Biehl, M.: Adaptive relevance matrices in learning vector quantization. Neural Computation 21, 3532–3561 (2009)

[29] Sonka, M., Hlavac, V., Boyle, R.: Image Processing, Analysis and Machine Vision, 2nd edn. Brooks Publishing (1998)

[30] Strickert, M., Seiffert, U., Sreenivasulu, N., Weschke, W., Villmann, T., Hammer, B.: Generalized relevance LVQ (GRLVQ) with correlation measures for gene expression analysis. Neurocomputing 69(6-7), 651–659 (2006) ISSN: 0925-2312

[31] Villmann, T., Haase, S.: Divergence based vector quantization. Neural Computation 23(5), 1343–1392 (2011)

[32] Villmann, T., Haase, S., Kaden, M.: Kernelized vector quantization in gradient-descent learning. Neurocomputing 147, 83–95 (2015)

[33] Walter, J., Arnrich, B., Scheering, C.: Learning fine positioning of a robot manipulator based on gabor wavelets. In: Proceedings of the International Joint Conference on Neural Networks, vol. 5, pp. 137–142. Univ. of Bielefeld, IEEE, Piscataway, NJ (2000)

[34] Yoshimura, H., Etoh, M., Kondo, K., Yokoya, N.: Gray-scale character recognition by gabor jets projection. In: Proceedings of the 15th International Conference on Pattern Recognition, ICPR 2000, vol. 2, pp. 335–338. IEEE Comput. Soc., Los Alamitos (2000)

[35] Zühlke, D., Schleif, F.-M., Geweniger, T., Haase, S., Villmann, T.: Learning vector quantization for heterogeneous structured data. In: Verleysen, M. (ed.) Proc. of European Symposium on Artificial Neural Networks (ESANN 2010), Evere, Belgium, pp. 271–276. d-side publications (2010)

Adaptive Active Learning with Ensemble of Learners and Multiclass Problems

Wojciech Marian Czarnecki[✉]

Faculty of Mathematics and Computer Science,
Jagiellonian University, Cracow, Poland
wojciech.czarnecki@uj.edu.pl
http://czarnecki.gmum.net

Abstract. Active Learning (AL) is an emerging field of machine learning focusing on creating a closed loop of learner (statistical model) and oracle (expert able to label examples) in order to exploit the vast amounts of accessible unlabeled datasets in the most effective way from the classification point of view.

This paper analyzes the problem of multiclass active learning methods and proposes to approach it in a new way through substitution of the original concept of predefined utility function with an ensemble of learners. As opposed to known ensemble methods in AL, where learners vote for a particular example, we use them as a black box mechanisms for which we try to model the current competence value using adaptive training scheme.

We show that modeling this problem as a multi-armed bandit problem and applying even very basic strategies bring significant improvement to the AL process.

Keywords: Active learning · Ensemble · Classification · Multiclass

1 Introduction

Classical supervised machine learning methods require big labeled datasets to construct good models. Unfortunately, in real life applications it is often the case that, while large amounts of data may be available, a significant portion of them misses the true labeling. Obtaining such information commonly requires substantial amounts of time/costs (like labeling video recordings, tagging text corpora or synthesis and testing of new kinds of drugs). *Active learning* [24] addresses this issue by introducing the label querying step into the model's training process to minimize the total cost of building the most accurate classifier.

To the authors' best knowledge, not much work has addressed the problem of dealing with active learning ensembles. There has been many approaches to build active learning strategies on the ensembles of models [25] or extreme hypotheses [13] but they all operate on the different level of abstraction.

In this paper we present a method of creating a complex active learning strategy from an ensemble of existing strategies. We model the problem of adaptively

© Springer International Publishing Switzerland 2015
L. Rutkowski et al. (Eds.): ICAISC 2015, Part I, LNAI 9119, pp. 415–426, 2015.
DOI: 10.1007/978-3-319-19324-3_38

selecting the best ones as a well known multi-armed bandit problem, which is used as a model in many fields of computer science [12] and machine learning [7]. We analyze the generic scheme of such approach and define few families of possible reward functions. Then we focus on applicability of particular selection strategies in this context.

2   Related Work

This work is a continuation of the short communicate entitled "Adaptive Active Learning as the multi-armed bandit problem" [10]. Results from this paper significantly extend previous ones through more theoretical analysis of the process, deeper analysis of empirical behaviour, extension to multiclass problems and more valuable reward function.

There are many active learning strategies working with ensembles of learners in the sense of classifiers. Approaches such as Query by Disagreement (QBD [13]) or Query by Committee (QBC [25]) assume that there is one, fixed utility function which analyzes multiple classifiers (elements of an ensemble) and a meta-strategy which makes a consensus decision (such as majority voting or entropy). In this work we analyze a problem one layer of abstraction higher where by learner we shall denote its utility function. So we are working in the scenario where we have multiple utility functions, working on a single machine learning model (which can be an ensemble itself, in fact we perform evaluation using entropy QBD querying as an element of a learners ensemble).

3   Adaptive Active Learner

In the classic Active Learning pool based approach [26,27] we have a set of unlabeled data $\mathcal{U}$ and a learner defined by its utility function u such that

$$u : \mathcal{H} \times \mathcal{U} \to \mathbb{R}.$$

In a given iteration we have hypothesis (model) h and simply select sample to label it with

$$q = \arg\max_{x \in \mathcal{U}} u(h, x).$$

This means that if we denote by h_i the hypothesis in i'th iteration, by A the training algorithm which given training set returns a hypothesis and an oracle over K-class problem $o : \mathcal{U} \to \{1, ..., K\}$, we obtain:

$$h_{i+1} = \mathrm{A}(\{(q_k, o(q_k))\}_{k=1}^{i}),$$

where

$$q_i = \arg\max_{x \in \mathcal{U}_i} u(h_i, x)$$

$$\mathcal{U}_{i+1} = \mathcal{U}_i \setminus \{q_i\}.$$

If we look at the time dimension of our dynamical learning process it appears that only h depends on time (as classifier learns over time), while u is considered a constant function.

The Adaptive Active Learner (A^{2}L) proposed by Czarnecki et al. [10] assumes that also u itself depends on time and can benefit from past experiences, meaning that

$$q_i = \arg\max_{x \in \mathcal{U}_i} u_i(h_i, x)$$

and there is some adaptive process f such that

$$u_{i+1} = f((h_k)_{k=1}^i, (u_k)_{k=1}^i, (q_k)_{k=1}^i, (o(q_k))_{k=1}^i),$$

where $(a_k)_{k=1}^i$ denotes *sequence* of a_i from $k = 1$ to i.

In general f could be any function returning an utility function so the problem of finding a good one is extremely complex. In the following sections we will focus on a narrowing of space of possible f to the family of functions on some finite set.

3.1 A^{2}L for Ensemble of Learners

Let us assume that we are given a finite set of learners, denoted by their corresponding utility functions

$$L = \{u^{(1)}, ..., u^{(K)}\}$$

and that in each iteration we simply choose one of these learners to query (see Fig. 1), using some previous knowledge on their competences in current task and timeframe.

One of possible statistical models which can help us perform adaptation over time is the multi-armed bandit problem [23]. Given some finite set of processes (bandits) we iteratively sample (play) them and receive a value (reward). The aim of this model is to maximize the cumulative reward over time having no prior knowledge regarding particular bandits. We only observe results of playing at given machine. The problem of finding the best strategy can be stated as a minimization of, so called, regret $\mathcal{R}$, defined as a difference between the sum of gained rewards and the sum of rewards obtained by some hypothetical optimal selection.

$$\underset{s}{\text{minimize}} \ \mathcal{R}(s) = \sum_{k=1}^{T} r_k^{opt} - \sum_{k=1}^{T} r_k^s \iff \underset{s}{\text{maximize}} \sum_{k=1}^{T} r_k^s,$$

where r_k^s is the reward obtained in kth iteration using strategy s and opt is the optimal strategy.

In order to model A^{2}L using MAB as in [10] we consider learners as machines and querying them as playing. The only thing missing is some reward function r which we want to optimize and we can plug in any existing MAB algorithm (such as ε-greedy [16], UCB [3], EXP3 [4], ...) as f.

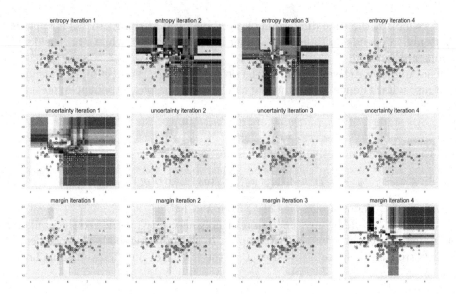

Fig. 1. Visualization of A^2L with three learners (rows) over 4 iterations (columns) on two first dimensions of Iris dataset with Random Forest classifier. In each iteration only one learner is selected and its decision (yellow square sample) is chosen (the only not transparent plot) to query. Circles denote labeled samples while triangles unlabeled ones.

$$f((h_k)_{k=1}^i, (u_k)_{k=1}^i, (q_k)_{k=1}^i, (o(q_k))_{k=1}^i) := \text{MAB}((u_k)_{k=1}^i, (r_k)_{k=1}^i),$$

where
$$r_i = r((h_k)_{k=1}^i, (u_k)_{k=1}^i, (q_k)_{k=1}^i, (o(q_k))_{k=1}^i).$$

One of the simplest reward functions one can define is a characteristic function of predicting an incorrect label

$$r((h_k)_{k=1}^i, (u_k)_{k=1}^i, (q_k)_{k=1}^i, (o(q_k))_{k=1}^i) = r_{0/1}(h_i, q_i, o(q_i)) = 1_{h_i(q_i) \neq o(q_i)}.$$

Using such reward function we prefer strategies querying points which are currently incorrectly labeled by our classifier. As a result we maximize accuracy of the underling machine learning model.

Theorem 1. *Given A^2L with UCB1 strategy, set of active learners L and $r_{0/1}$ reward function, assuming that given learner's reward in each iteration is stochastic and independent on process history the maximum number of missed (not queried) mislabeled points which could be found using different selection of learners after T iterations is $\mathcal{O}(\log T)$. In general this bound cannot be improved.*

Proof. This is a direct consequence of the UCB1 MAB bounds on regret function and the fact that $r_{0/1}$ equals 1 if and only if current hypothesis mislabels given point. This bound realizes the theoretical lower bound of MAB error [3] of $\Omega(\log T)$ so in general it cannot be asymptotically improved.   □

Slightly more complex reward function is to measure the increase in the generalization capabilities of a particular model under given evaluation metric m on some representative[1] validation set V.

$$r_m(h_i, h_{i-1}; V) = m(h_i(V), \mathbf{o}(V)) - m(h_{i-1}(V), \mathbf{o}(V)).$$

Using such reward function we can get even better theoretical bound on the learning process.

Theorem 2. *Given* A^2L *with UCB1 strategy, set of active learners* L *and* r_m *reward function, assuming that given learner's reward in each iteration is stochastic and independent on process history, the achieved generalization capabilities in terms of metric* m *is at most* $\mathcal{O}(\log T)$ *worse than the one achieved by optimal selection of learners after* T *iterations. In general this bound cannot be improved.*

Proof. This is a direct consequence of the UCB1 MAB bounds on reward function and the fact that

$$\sum_{k=1}^{T} r_{m_k} = \sum_{k=1}^{T} [m(h_k(V), \mathbf{o}(V)) - m(h_{k-1}(V), \mathbf{o}(V))]$$
$$= m(h_T(V), \mathbf{o}(V)) - m(h_0(V), \mathbf{o}(V))$$

is the generalization capability of a given model, dependent only on the final hypothesis h_T and the initial hypothesis h_0. Optimality is analogous to the one from Theorem 1.   □

3.2   Multi-armed Bandit Algorithms

In this section we briefly summarize multi-armed bandits (MAB) algorithms used in this work. According to extensive evaluation on both artificial and real datasets [16] it has been shown that ε-greedy and UCB, very simple methods of MAB perform well in reality. We use following notation to denote mean reward of jth learner

$$\bar{r}_j = \sum_{k \in P_j} \frac{r_k}{|P_j|},$$

where $P_j = \{k : u_k = u^{(j)}\}$ is a set of iterations' indices where jth learner was used.

---

[1] in Practical Considerations section we shortly discuss how to get such set V.

ε-greedy With probability $1 - \varepsilon$ we select learner which maximized the mean rewards obtained till this iteration, so we choose u_b such that

$$b = \underset{j \in \{1,...,K\}}{\arg\max} \, \bar{r}_j.$$

And with probability ε we just select random b from uniform distribution over learners. In other words for most of the time (assuming that $\varepsilon < 0.5$) we use the most promising learner so far, and for the rest of time we randomly explore other strategies. This is a very greedy approach which might lead to highly suboptimal results if learners competences change over time.

Upper Confidence Bound (UCB1) proposed by Auer, Cesa-Bianchi and Fisher [3] as an elegant approach to the idea of Lai and Robbins [17]. It has been shown that such approach achieves the minimal regret bound of $\Omega(\log T)$ if we assume constant variance of each machine.

$$b = \underset{j \in \{1,...,K\}}{\arg\max} \left(\bar{r}_j + \sqrt{\tfrac{2 \log T}{|P_j|}} \right).$$

This method achieves surprisingly good results in numerous applications, including its extension to the game trees structure (Upper Confidence Bounds applied to Trees, UCT) which is currently one of the best AI methods for GO [12], beating even deep convolutional networks [8].

Upper Confidence Bound Tuned (UCB1 Tuned) according to authors [3] including the machine's variance helps in determining the most promising exploration candidates.

$$b = \underset{j \in \{1,...,K\}}{\arg\max} \left(\bar{r}_j + \sqrt{\tfrac{\log T}{|P_j|} \min\left(\tfrac{1}{4}, \underset{k \in P_j}{\mathrm{var}}\left(r_k\right) + \sqrt{\tfrac{2 \log T}{|P_j|}} \right)} \right),$$

however to our best knowledge this method lacks many success stories [16].

4   Practical Considerations

Proposed approach, as well as most of the existing utility functions, is independent on the choice of underlying classifier. However, from the practical point of view one should use a model which:

- supports multiclass classification, preferably directly[2],
- is able to return a confidence $P(y|x)$ of classification instead of just a label,

---

[2] models such as SVM do not support such operation but using Platt's scaling one can add this type of functionality at the cost of loss of mathematical cohesion of the method.

– is capable of assessing its own generalization capabilities without creating hold out set never-used during training process.

While two first elements are satisfied by nearly any modern classifier including neural networks [20], true multiclass Support Vector Machines [9] or Extreme Learning Machines [14]. However, last element is much more complex, and requires classifier to be based on bagging [5] or other ensemble technique which allows model to use, at the same time, all data for training and have a set of observations which can be used for unbiased error estimation.

Recent extensive evaluation studies showed that Random Forest [6] is one of the best behaving classifiers available in modern machine learning libraries [11]. This model satisfies all three requirements we listed above and furthermore it works quite well even with very rough estimation of the hyperparameters. This makes it one of the best candidates to use with A^2L (and most other existing active learning strategies).

5   Evaluation

Now we proceed to empirical evaluation of proposed method. Following experiments were performed using code written in Python with use of scikit-learn library [21]. We use three datasets, DIGITS [1], being a collection of 1797 low-resolution (8x8 pixels) hand written digits scans; MNIST [18], the well known dataset of 70,000 hand scans of postal codes and finally CIFAR-10 [15], a dataset of thousands of 32x32 pixels images of various objects from 10 classes. We use Random Forest classifier as a base method. For explanation of this particular choice refer to the Practical Considerations section. Each experiment starts with a small set of randomly selected labeled examples (2 samples from each class for MNIST and DIGITS, and 100 samples from each class for CIFAR-10[3].). For digits recognition we use raw pixels values as the input to the classifier while for images recognition we first perform randomized PCA dimensionality reduction to map $\mathbb{R}^{32 \times 32}$ to $\mathbb{R}^{20}$.

During these experiments we show three strengths of A^2L, namely:

1. ability to exploit diverse characteristics of given set of learners,
2. small vulnerability to the redundant learners,
3. possibility to model completely novel strategies.

Let us focus on the evaluation process. We propose to look at two different tasks which might be the aim of active learning scenario. First, the most natural one is to create a good predictive model using only subset of the training data. We will call this a concept learning, as we are interested in building a classifier which solves the problem for some underlying data densities and so we assume that there are (possibly infinitely many) samples besides our unlabeled pool. The second possibility is to assume that the pool is actually the whole input space

---

[3] CIFAR-10 is much harder dataset and RF needs more knowledge to start modeling actual concepts

and we are interested in correct classification of these samples using as small labeling queries as possible. We will refer to this scenario as finite set learning, as we assume that there are no samples besides the pool. Even though these problems might look similar there is at least one fundamental difference between them. The second problem can be solved efficiently through querying the hardest points, as they will be automatically correctly classified, while leaving the easy samples to our model. In the first scenario this is a much more complex problem as the hardest examples are not necessarily are the ones giving most knowledge about the concept being modeled. Both these approaches have their justification and practical applications so we will analyze both scenarios. In order to measure the concept learning capabilities we will use the hold out set to estimate the generalization capabilities which is different than the pool of samples, while for the finite set learning we will estimate generalization on all samples from the pool minus queried points. Table 1 summarizes popular learners' utility functions used for multiclass active learning.

Table 1. Popular utility functions, $P(h(x) = l)$ is models confidence in classifying x as l. By hash we denote perfect hashing function which guarantees random ordering of values.

method	$u(h, x)$
uncertainty	$- \max_l P(h(x) = l)$
margin	$\max_l P(h(x) = l) - \max_{l' \neq l} P(h(x) = l')$
entropy	$- \sum_l P(h(x) = l) \log P(h(x) = l)$
passive	$\text{hash}(x)$

During experiments on DIGITS dataset all strategies significantly speeded up the learning process (as compared to passive learning, see Table 2) and led to about 86% accuracy in the concept learning scenario and over 95% in finite set learning. One can easily deduce that learners were able to eliminate hard examples from the dataset. Margin based method appeared to perform the best, while entropy learner was much weaker. We applied basic ε-greedy A^2L with the learners' ensemble consisting of margin, uncertainty and entropy learners. Not only was this strategy able to deal with existence of weak learner, but achieved results even better than any of the basic methods (despite these approaches yield highly correlated utility functions [24]). This shows some basic resistance to the existence of redundant learners in the ensemble.

After removal of the entropy learner and change to the more complex strategy (UCB1 with r_{Acc} reward function) we were able to tweak the learning curve and achieve above 89% concept learning ability. This is about 3% increase of the final accuracy after sampling just 200 images as compared to the best learner's result and over 10% better than the passive approach.

During an active learning process some classes might be easy to separate even in the very early stage of the experiment despite the fact that their particular

Table 2. Comparison of different strategies on Pen-based DIGITS dataset

| DIGITS | Finite | | Concept | |
200 iterations	Mean Acc	Final Acc	Mean Acc	Final Acc
Passive	81.56 ± 0.07	91.90	78.65 ± 0.04	80.91
Uncertainty	86.16 ± 0.09	95.09	81.05 ± 0.04	86.34
Entropy	80.96 ± 0.09	91.74	81.82 ± 0.03	82.74
Margin	86.41 ± 0.10	95.36	82.17 ± 0.04	86.80
$A^2L\ r_{0/1}$ 0.5-greedy {entropy, margin, uncertainty}	86.38 ± 0.10	95.37	$\mathbf{84.08 \pm 0.05}$	**87.77**
$A^2L\ r_{Acc}$ UCB1 { margin, uncertainty}	86.91 ± 0.09	95.75	$\mathbf{83.51 \pm 0.04}$	**89.06**
$A^2L\ r_{Acc}$ UCB1 $\{u_0, u_1, u_2, u_3, \cdots, u_9\}$	85.85 ± 0.09	94.58	$\mathbf{84.95 \pm 0.04}$	**89.11**
$A^2L\ r_{Acc}$ UCB1Tuned $\{u_0, u_1, u_2, u_3, \cdots, u_9\}$	85.54 ± 0.09	95.73	82.12 ± 0.04	**86.97**

samples still lie in the "uncertain" zone of the input space. As the result uncertainty, margin or entropy sampling will query their labels even though this part of the classification is already completed. In order to deal with this problem we propose to create a family of learners u_i such that they do not query points for which current model returns different label than i. On the rest of the samples they work as simple uncertainty sampling[4].

$$u_i(h, x) = \begin{cases} -\infty & , \text{ if } h(x) \neq i \\ -P(h(x) = i) & , \text{ if } h(x) = i \end{cases}$$

It is easy to notice that such utility function cannot be expressed as single learner (as it would be equivalent of 1 vs all learning with just ith classifier) nor with voting schemes (as each u_i has disjoint competence subspaces meaning that $\forall x \exists! i : u_i(x) \neq -\infty$) so it would degenerate to the uncertainty sampling. However in the A^2L scenario this family gives us ability to select in each iteration which class is now the most important one and sample from it.

Such learner slightly increases the score on DIGITS dataset (Table 2), however in more complex task of MNIST problem (Table 3) the difference is not that big. One should notice, that this approach is based on uncertainty sampling, and as compared to the non-class based approach it outperforms it by nearly 10% in concept learning and over 12% in finite set learning.

Once we switch to the variance analysis enriched UCB strategy – UCB1Tuned, we get adaptation, which outperforms all basic methods with about 2% in final accuracy on MNIST dataset (in both tasks) and over 5% of mean accuracy, meaning that learning process is much more stable (we achieve good results not only after full 500 iterations but also "in between"). The same method is able to

---

[4] one can analogously define such family for other basic utility functions such as margin or entropy.

Table 3. Comparison of different strategies on MNIST dataset

MNIST 500 iterations	Finite Mean Acc	Final Acc	Concept Mean Acc	Final Acc
Passive	71.86 ± 0.09	78.50	73.48 ± 0.08	78.89
Uncertainty	66.16 ± 0.07	72.01	70.86 ± 0.07	77.24
Entropy	64.68 ± 0.08	72.09	67.54 ± 0.07	76.66
Margin	68.84 ± 0.16	82.05	71.98 ± 0.17	85.90
$A^2L\ r_{0/1}$ UCB1 $\{u_0, u_1, u_2, u_3, \cdots, u_9\}$	$\mathbf{75.36 \pm 0.10}$	**84.20**	$\mathbf{78.33 \pm 0.09}$	85.82
$A^2L\ r_{Acc}$ UCB1 $\{u_0, u_1, u_2, u_3, \cdots, u_9\}$	73.32 ± 0.10	81.63	$\mathbf{77.47 \pm 0.10}$	84.10
$A^2L\ r_{Acc}$ UCB1Tuned $\{u_0, u_1, u_2, u_3, \cdots, u_9\}$	74.33 ± 0.10	**84.27**	$\mathbf{77.75 \pm 0.10}$	**86.02**
$A^2L\ r_{Acc}$ 0.5-greedy $\{u_0, u_1, u_2, u_3, \cdots, u_9\}$	74.36 ± 0.11	**84.03**	$\mathbf{77.46 \pm 0.10}$	**86.20**

Table 4. Comparison of different strategies on CIFAR-10 dataset

CIFAR-10 350 iterations	Finite Mean Acc	Final Acc	Concept Mean Acc	Final Acc
Passive	26.72 ± 0.02	29.27	24.31 ± 0.02	28.61
Uncertainty	24.81 ± 0.01	27.89	26.20 ± 0.02	27.70
Entropy	25.05 ± 0.02	27.94	23.94 ± 0.02	27.78
Margin	27.28 ± 0.02	29.86	27.97 ± 0.02	30.86
$A^2L\ r_{Acc}$ UCB1 margin $\{u_0, u_1, u_2, u_3, \cdots, u_9\}$	27.13 ± 0.02	29.94	27.12 ± 0.02	30.20
$A^2L\ r_{Acc}$ UCB1 $\{\text{margin, uncertainty}\}$	26.99 ± 0.02	**31.07**	28.14 ± 0.02	**31.26**
$A^2L\ r_{Acc}$ UCB1Tuned margin $\{u_0, u_1, u_2, u_3, \cdots, u_9\}$	$\mathbf{27.88 \pm 0.02}$	**30.31**	$\mathbf{29.09 \pm 0.02}$	**33.13**

increase final scores also on much harder, CIFAR-10 (Table 4) dataset for about 3% on concept learning and brings a bit weaker effect on the finite set learning.

6 Discussion and Conclusions

Multiclass learning is still a challenge for active learning. In binary classification uncertainty sampling is quite successful despite its naive approach. In multiclass approach its natural generalization appears to perform quite weak. Adaptive Active Learning, proposed in this paper, tackles this problem and proposes generic framework in which we can generalize uncertainty sampling to the multiclass scenario. Resulting strategy outperforms (as shown in the evaluation section) state of the art multiclass methods in most cases. Furthermore, proposed approach appears to be able to deal (to some extent) with redundant learners and select the most promising strategies. There seems to be a strong correlation between problems complexity and required multi-armed bandit strategy needed to achieve best results.

It remains an open question whether very simple generalization to the multi-class ensembles is the best approach especially when dealing with large classes space (such as hundreds in CIFAR-100 or thousands in Wikipedia). This would cause linear growth of the ensemble size and could be hard to comprehend by MAB methods [16]. One could investigate some grouping/class clustering methods such as those used in HCOC [22] model.

There are also more complex strategies for MAB problems, including Exp family [4], ShiftBand methods [2], as well as a more advanced methods adding feature vectors to each machine such as LinUCB [19]. These methods could be very beneficial in our task where we can associate various strategies statistics such as variance (which helped UCB1 to achieve better scores through UCB1Tuned heuristic) to actually learn the exact relation between these effects.

Aknowledgments. The paper was partially funded by National Science Centre Poland Found grant no. 2013/09/N/ST6/03015.

References

1. Alimoglu, F., Alpaydin, E.: Methods of combining multiple classifiers based on different representations for pen-based handwritten digit recognition. In: Proceedings of the Fifth Turkish Artificial Intelligence and Artificial Neural Networks Symposium (TAINN 1996). Citeseer (1996)
2. Auer, P.: Using confidence bounds for exploitation-exploration trade-offs. Journal of Machine Learning Research 3, 397–422 (2003)
3. Auer, P., Cesa-Bianchi, N., Fischer, P.: Finite-time analysis of the multiarmed bandit problem. Machine Learning 47(2-3), 235–256 (2002)
4. Auer, P., Cesa-Bianchi, N., Freund, Y., Schapire, R.E.: The nonstochastic multi-armed bandit problem. SIAM Journal on Computing 32(1), 48–77 (2003)
5. Breiman, L.: Bagging predictors. Machine Learning 24(2), 123–140 (1996)
6. Breiman, L.: Random forests. Machine Learning 45(1), 5–32 (2001)
7. Carpentier, A., Lazaric, A., Ghavamzadeh, M., Munos, R., Auer, P.: Upper-confidence-bound algorithms for active learning in multi-armed bandits. In: Kivinen, J., Szepesvári, C., Ukkonen, E., Zeugmann, T. (eds.) ALT 2011. LNCS, vol. 6925, pp. 189–203. Springer, Heidelberg (2011)
8. Clark, C., Storkey, A.: Teaching deep convolutional neural networks to play go. arXiv preprint arXiv:1412.3409 (2014)
9. Crammer, K., Singer, Y.: On the algorithmic implementation of multiclass kernel-based vector machines. The Journal of Machine Learning Research 2, 265–292 (2002)
10. Czarnecki, W.M., Podolak, I.: Adaptive active learning as a multi-armed bandit problem. Frontiers in Artificial Intelligence and Applications, pp. 989–990 (2014)
11. Fernández-Delgado, M., Cernadas, E., Barro, S., Amorim, D.: Do we need hundreds of classifiers to solve real world classification problems? The Journal of Machine Learning Research 15(1), 3133–3181 (2014)

12. Gelly, S., Silver, D.: Monte-Carlo tree search and rapid action value estimation in computer Go. Artificial Intelligence 175(11), 1856–1875 (2011)
13. Haussler, D.: Learning conjunctive concepts in structural domains. Machine Learning 4(1), 7–40 (1994)
14. Huang, G.B., Zhu, Q.Y., Siew, C.K.: Extreme learning machine: theory and applications. Neurocomputing 70(1), 489–501 (2006)
15. Krizhevsky, A., Hinton, G.: Learning multiple layers of features from tiny images. Computer Science Department, University of Toronto, Tech. Rep. (2009)
16. Kuleshov, V., Precup, D.: Algorithms for the multi-armed bandit problem. Journal of Machine Learning Research 1, 397–422 (2000)
17. Lai, T.L., Robbins, H.: Asymptotically efficient adaptive allocation rules. Advances in Applied Mathematics 6(1), 4–22 (1985)
18. LeCun, Y., Cortes, C.: Mnist handwritten digit database. AT&T Labs [Online] (2010), http://yann.lecun.com/exdb/mnist
19. Li, L., Chu, W., Langford, J., Schapire, R.E.: A contextual-bandit approach to personalized news article recommendation. In: Proceedings of the 19th International Conference on World Wide Web, pp. 661–670. ACM (2010)
20. Ou, G., Murphey, Y.L.: Multi-class pattern classification using neural networks. Pattern Recognition 40(1), 4–18 (2007)
21. Pedregosa, F., Varoquaux, G., Gramfort, A., Michel, V., Thirion, B., Grisel, O., Blondel, M., Prettenhofer, P., Weiss, R., Dubourg, V., et al.: Scikit-learn: Machine learning in python. The Journal of Machine Learning Research 12, 2825–2830 (2011)
22. Podolak, I.T., Roman, A.: Theoretical foundations and experimental results for a hierarchical classifier with overlapping clusters. Computational Intelligence 29(2), 357–388 (2013)
23. Robbins, H.: Some aspects of the sequential design of experiments. In: Lai, T., Siegmund, D. (eds.) Herbert Robbins Selected Papers, pp. 169–177. Springer, New York (1985)
24. Settles, B.: Active Learning, vol. 6. Morgan & Claypool Publishers (2012)
25. Seung, H.S., Opper, M., Sompolinsky, H.: Query by committee. In: Proceedings of the Fifth Annual Workshop on Computational Learning Theory, COLT 1992, pp. 287–294. ACM (1992)
26. Sindhwani, V., Melville, P., Lawrence, R.D.: Uncertainty sampling and transductive experimental design for active dual supervision. In: Proceedings of the 26th Annual International Conference on Machine Learning, ICML 2009, pp. 953–960. ACM (2009)
27. Xu, Z., Akella, R., Zhang, Y.: Incorporating diversity and density in active learning for relevance feedback. In: Amati, G., Carpineto, C., Romano, G. (eds.) ECIR 2007. LNCS, vol. 4425, pp. 246–257. Springer, Heidelberg (2007)

Orthogonal Series Estimation of Regression Functions in Nonstationary Conditions

Tomasz Galkowski[1][(⊠)] and Miroslaw Pawlak[2]

[1] Institute of Computational Intelligence
Czestochowa University of Technology, Czestochowa, Poland
`tomasz.galkowski@iisi.pcz.pl`
[2] Information Technology Institute, University of Social Sciences, Lodz, Poland
Department of Electrical and Computer Engineering
University of Manitoba, Winnipeg, Canada
`pawlak@ee.umanitoba.ca`

Abstract. The article concerns of the problem of regression functions estimation when the output is contaminated by additive nonstationary noise. We investigate the model $y_i = R(\mathbf{x_i}) + Z_i$, $i = 1, 2, \ldots n$, where $\mathbf{x_i}$ is assumed to be the set of deterministic inputs (d-dimensional vector), y_i is the scalar, probabilistic outputs, and Z_i is a measurement noise with zero mean and variance depending on n. $R(.)$ is a completely unknown function. The problem of finding function $R(.)$ may be solved by applying non-parametric methodology, for instance: algorithms based on the Parzen kernel or algorithms derived from orthogonal series. In this work we present the orthogonal series approach. The analysis has been made for some class of nonstationarity. We present the conditions of convergence of the estimation algorithm for the variance of noise growing up when number of observations is tending to infinity. The results of numerical simulations are presented.

1 Preliminary and Algorithm

The article is concerning the systems described by the following equation

$$y_i = R(\mathbf{x_i}) + Z_i, \, i = 1, ..., n \tag{1}$$

where y_i is the probabilistic scalar output, $\mathbf{x}_i$ is the deterministic d-vector input, Z_i is the random variable measurement noise. There are a few known non-parametric approaches for fitting unknown function $R(.)$ for one- and multi-dimensional cases: the Parzen-Rosenblatt methods (see e.g. [6], [7], [8], [9], [11], [12], [23]), methods derived from orthogonal series expansions (see e.g. [25], [35], [36], [37], [39], [41]) or type-1 and type-2 neuro-fuzzy structures [17], [18], [22], [45], [46], [47], [48], [50], [51], [53]. In non-parametric methodology no a-priori assumption on mathematical form of unknown function $R(.)$ is undertaken, in opposition to such methods like splines or linear regression. In bibliography one may find the theorems on convergence of mentioned algorithms. The non-stationary situations, frequently appearing in stream data ([16], [24]), have been

© Springer International Publishing Switzerland 2015
L. Rutkowski et al. (Eds.): ICAISC 2015, Part I, LNAI 9119, pp. 427–435, 2015.
DOI: 10.1007/978-3-319-19324-3_39

investigated rarely (e.g. [13], [28], [29], [38], [42], [43]). Recently, non-parametric methodology based on the Parzen kernel has been studied in [10]). Similar algorithms have been also applied for identification, recognition and/or control of some classes of non-linear dynamical systems (e.g. [1], [2], [3], [4], [5], [15], [19], [20], [21], [32], [33], [34], [39], [40], [44], [49], [52], [54]).

Consider the d-dimensional space $Q_d = \left\{\mathbf{x} \in [0,1]^d\right\}$. Let $n^{1/d} = m$ be an integer and $p = 1, ..., d$; $i_p = 1, ..., m$. Let us partition the unit interval $[0,1]$ on the p-th axis into m subsets Δx_{i_p}. Define the Cartesian product

$$\Delta x_{i_1} \otimes \Delta x_{i_2} \otimes \cdots \otimes \Delta x_{i_d} = Q_{d,i}.$$

Let $Q_{d,i} \wedge Q_{d,j} = \emptyset$ for $i \neq j$ and $\bigcup_{i=1}^{m} Q_{d,i} = Q_d$.

The inputs $\mathbf{x}_i$ are selected to satisfy $\mathbf{x}_i \in Q_{d,i}$.

Let $g_k(.)$, $k = 0, 1, 2, ...$, be the orthogonal system of functions in the interval $[0,1]$. Then, the system of all possible products $g_{k_1}(x_1) \cdot g_{k_2}(x_2) \cdot ... \cdot g_{k_d}(x_d)$, $k_j = 0, 1, 2, ..., j = 1, 2, ..., d$, is an orthogonal system of functions in the d-dimensional cube $Q_d = [0,1]^d$.

Define the "kernel" function $K_n(.)$ as follows:

$$K_n(\mathbf{x}, \mathbf{u}) = \sum_{k_1=0}^{N} \sum_{k_2=0}^{N} \cdots \sum_{k_d=0}^{N} g_{k_1}(x_1) g_{k_2}(x_2) ... g_{k_d}(x_d) \cdot g_{k_1}(u_1) g_{k_2}(u_2) ... g_{k_d}(u_d) =$$
$$= \sum_{|\mathbf{k}| \leq N} g_{\mathbf{k}}(\mathbf{x}) g_{\mathbf{k}}(\mathbf{u})$$

(2)

where number N depends on n and

$$N(n) \to \infty \text{ as } n \to \infty \tag{3}$$

Now the estimator of multivariate function $R(\mathbf{x})$ in Q_d is given by:

$$\hat{R}(\mathbf{x}) = \sum_{i=1}^{n} y_i \int_{Q_{d,i}} K_n(\mathbf{x}, \mathbf{u}) d\mathbf{u} \tag{4}$$

The above procedure has been proposed in unidimensional case by Rutkowski [30], and further investigated by Rutkowski [31], Galkowski and Rutkowski [7]. Procedure (4) can be rewritten in the more suitable form:

$$\hat{R}(\mathbf{x}) = \sum_{|\mathbf{k}| \leq N(n)} g_{\mathbf{k}}(\mathbf{x}) \hat{a}_{\mathbf{k},n} \tag{5}$$

where

$$\hat{a}_{\mathbf{k},n} = \sum_{i=1}^{n} y_i \int_{Q_{d,i}} g_{\mathbf{k}}(\mathbf{u}) d\mathbf{u} \tag{6}$$

Algorithm (4) is "integral" type of non-parametric methods. There are also known and investigated other types of similar algorithms based on orthogonal series, for instance Greblicki and Pawlak [14]. Note that procedure (4) is not a trivial extension of the one-dimensional algorithm because of the construction of partition of set Q_d. In the following we shall denote the length of the interval Δx_{i_p}, $i_p = 1, ..., m$, $p = 1, ..., d$ as $\left| \Delta x_{i_p} \right|$. The main result of this work is concerned with the extension of algorithm (4) to handle non-stationary noise.

2   Convergence of the Algorithm

Assume that $R(.)$ is continuous and restricted function in $Q_d = [0, 1]^d$. Suppose that:

$$EZ_i = 0, \ i = 1, ..., n \tag{7}$$

We shall prove that under some conditions estimator (4) is convergent even if the variance of measurement noise is divergent to infinity.

Theorem 1. *(Mean Square Error Convergence): If (7) holds, and*

$$EZ_n^2 = \sigma_n^2 = s_n \tag{8}$$

$$\Delta_n = \max_{1 \leq i_p \leq N} \left| \Delta x_{i_p} \right| = O\left(n^{-1/d} \right), \ p = 1, ..., d \tag{9}$$

and

$$s_n n^{-1} N^d \to 0 \tag{10}$$

then

$$E\left[\hat{R}_n(\mathbf{x}) - R(\mathbf{x}) \right]^2 \to 0 \ if \ n \to \infty \tag{11}$$

for every point $x \in (0, 1)^d$ in which

$$\sum_{|\mathbf{k}| \leq N(n)} a_{\mathbf{k}} g_{\mathbf{k}}(\mathbf{x}) \to R(\mathbf{x}) \tag{12}$$

where

$$a_{\mathbf{k}} = \int_Q R(\mathbf{u}) g_{\mathbf{k}}(\mathbf{u}) d\mathbf{u} \tag{13}$$

Proof. Obviously

$$E\left[\hat{R}_n(\mathbf{x}) - R(\mathbf{x}) \right]^2 \leq \mathrm{var} \hat{R}_n(\mathbf{x}) + 2E\left[\hat{R}_n(\mathbf{x}) - R_n^*(\mathbf{x}) \right]^2 + 2[R_n^*(\mathbf{x}) - R(\mathbf{x})]^2 \tag{14}$$

where

$$R_n^*(\mathbf{x}) = \sum_{|\mathbf{k}| \leq N(n)} g_{\mathbf{k}}(\mathbf{x}) \sum_{i=1}^n \int_{Q_{d,i}} R(\mathbf{u}) g_{\mathbf{k}}(\mathbf{u}) \, d\mathbf{u}. \tag{15}$$

Using notation (2), by the Cauchy-Schwartz inequality we have the following bound for variance:

$$
\mathrm{var}\hat{R}_n\left(\mathbf{x}\right) = \left(\sum_{i=1}^{n} \sum_{|\mathbf{k}| \leq N(n)} g_{\mathbf{k}}\left(\mathbf{x}\right) \int_{Q_{d,i}} g_{\mathbf{k}}\left(\mathbf{u}\right) d\mathbf{u} \right)^2 \mathrm{var}Z_i =
$$

$$
\left(\sum_{i=1}^{n} \int_{Q_{d,i}} K_n\left(\mathbf{x},\mathbf{u}\right) d\mathbf{u} \right)^2 \mathrm{var}Z_i \leq \qquad (16)
$$

$$
\leq s_n \sum_{i=1}^{n} \int_{Q_{d,i}} K_n^2\left(\mathbf{x},\mathbf{u}\right) d\mathbf{u} \int_{Q_{d,i}} d\mathbf{u} \leq c_1 s_n n^{-1} N^d
$$

For the second term in (14) we have the bound

$$
\left| E\hat{R}(\mathbf{x}) - R_n^*(\mathbf{x}) \right| \leq \sum_{j=1}^{n} \int_Q |R(\mathbf{x}_i) - R(\mathbf{u})| K_n(\mathbf{x},\mathbf{u}) d\mathbf{u} \qquad (17)
$$

The convergence of (17) follows from fact that the distance $|R(\mathbf{x}_i) - R(\mathbf{u})|$ is arbitrarily small if $n \to \infty$.

The convergence of last term in (14) follows directly from the assumption (12).

This completes the proof.

3   Simulation Example

Figure 1 presents an example of simulation of non-parametric function fitting using the trigonometric series. Testing function is as follows:

$$
R(x) = \begin{cases} 0.3 + 2\exp(-2x)\sin(9x) & \text{for } x \leq 0.65 \\ 0.8 + 2\exp(-2x)\cos(12x - 2\pi) & \text{for } x > 0.65 \end{cases} \qquad (18)
$$

We made several simulations in the case when the output has a non-stationary additive noise. The parameter N is of course the natural number. We increase N gradually from $N = 1$ to $N = 5$ as is indicated in Figure 2. We assume that the sequence s_n is of type

$$
s_n = O\left(n^\beta\right), \ \beta > 0 \qquad (19)
$$

Assuming $x \in (0,1)^d$, for sufficiently large n we have the bound

$$
\mathrm{var}\hat{R}_n(\mathbf{x}) \leq c_1 n^{-1+\beta} N^d(n), \ c_1 = const \qquad (20)
$$

So, the exponent β must be selected very carefully to assure the mean square convergence of the estimator (5). The simulations were performed for unidimensional case $d = 1$. We performed series of tests in 50 evenly spaced in $(0,1)$ points, for the number of generated measurements growing up from $n = 150$

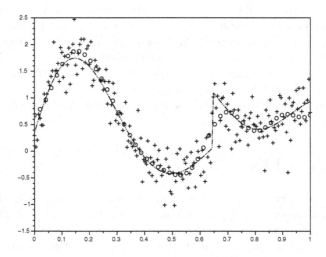

Fig. 1. Example of non-parametric orthogonal series function fitting

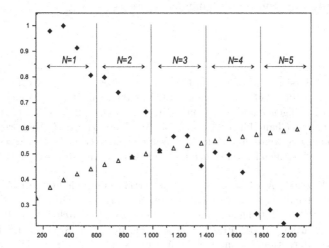

Fig. 2. Mean square error graph for series of simulation experiments

to $n = 2150$. We assume the sequence $s_n = 0.2n^\beta$, $\beta = 0.2$. Number of summands N in Fourier series was increased gradually, with increasing number of observations n.

As the measure of performance we use the mean square error

$$Err_n = \frac{1}{M}\sqrt{\sum_{m=1}^{M}\left(\hat{R}_n(x_m) - R(x_m)\right)^2} \tag{21}$$

where $M = 50$ is the number of testing points. Figure 2 shows graphs of the mean square error Err_n (marked with black diamonds), and the increasing - according to number n - variance of the noise s_n (marked with triangles). Note that the graphs were rescaled to obtain better view of their course. The visible irregularities in the graphs course could arise because of the independent processes of noise generation for each sample set.

The simulations results confirmed the convergence of the mean square error if the conditions of Theorem 1 hold.

4   Remarks and Extensions

The function recovery algorithm based on the orthogonal series in the presence of non-stationary noise has been constructed. The theorem on the mean square error convergence was formulated and proved. Under suitable conditions the algorithm is convergent even if the noise variance is divergent to infinity. We presented graphical results of performed simulations basing on the Fourier series. It could be mentioned that the error tends to zero when the number of observations n is growing up. Our aim in the future research is to apply such estimators to optimal control of dynamical systems (see e.g. [20], [53], [54]).

References

1. Apolloni, B., Bassis, S., Mesiano, C., Rinaudo, S., Ciccazzo, A., Marotta, A.: Statistical Parameter Identification of Analog Integrated Circuit Reverse Models. Journal of Artificial Intelligence and Soft Computing Research 1(2), 115–134 (2011)
2. Chaibakhsh, A., Chaibakhsh, N., Abbasi, M., Norouzi, A.: Orthonormal Basis Function Fuzzy Systems for Biological Wastewater Treatment Processes Modeling. Journal of Artificial Intelligence and Soft Computing Research 2(4), 343–356 (2012)
3. Chu, J.L., Krzyzak, A.: The recognition of partially Occluded Objects With Support Vector Machines, Convolutional Neural Networks and Deep Belief Networks. Journal of Artificial Intelligence and Soft Computing Research 4(1), 5–19 (2014)
4. Cpałka, K., Rutkowski, L.: Flexible Takagi-Sugeno Fuzzy Systems. In: Proceedings of the International Joint Conference on Neural Networks 2005, Montreal, pp. 1764–1769 (2005)
5. Cpałka, K., Rutkowski, L.: A New Method for Designing and Reduction of Neuro-fuzzy Systems. In: Proceedings of the 2006 IEEE International Conference on Fuzzy Systems (IEEE World Congress on Computational Intelligence, WCCI 2006), Vancouver, BC, Canada, pp. 8510–8516 (2006)
6. Galkowski, T., Rutkowski, L.: Nonparametric recovery of multivariate functions with applications to system identification. Proceedings of the IEEE 73, 942–943 (1985)
7. Galkowski, T., Rutkowski, L.: Nonparametric fitting of multivariable functions. IEEE Transactions on Automatic Control AC-31, 785–787 (1986)
8. Galkowski, T.: Nonparametric estimation of boundary values of functions. Archives of Control Science 3(1-2), 85–93 (1994)

9. Gałkowski, T.: Kernel estimation of regression functions in the boundary regions. In: Rutkowski, L., Korytkowski, M., Scherer, R., Tadeusiewicz, R., Zadeh, L.A., Zurada, J.M. (eds.) ICAISC 2013, Part II. LNCS (LNAI), vol. 7895, pp. 158–166. Springer, Heidelberg (2013)

10. Galkowski, T., Pawlak, M.: Nonparametric Function Fitting in the Presence of Nonstationary Noise. In: Rutkowski, L., Korytkowski, M., Scherer, R., Tadeusiewicz, R., Zadeh, L.A., Zurada, J.M. (eds.) ICAISC 2014, Part I. LNCS (LNAI), vol. 8467, pp. 531–538. Springer, Heidelberg (2014)

11. Gasser, T., Muller, H.G.: Kernel estimation of regression functions. Lecture Notes in Mathematics, vol. 757, pp. 23–68. Springer, Heidelberg (1979)

12. Greblicki, W., Rutkowski, L.: Density-free Bayes risk consistency of nonparametric pattern recognition procedures. Proceedings of the IEEE 69(4), 482–483 (1981)

13. Greblicki, W., Rutkowska, D., Rutkowski, L.: An orthogonal series estimate of time-varying regression. Annals of the Institute of Statistical Mathematics 35(2), 215–228 (1983)

14. Greblicki, W., Pawlak, M.: Fourier and Hermite series estimates of regression functions. Ann. of the Inst. of Stat. Math. 37(3A), 443–453 (1985)

15. Hashimoto, K., Doki, K., Doki, S.: Estimation of Next Human Action and Its Timing Based on The Human Action Model Considering Time Series Information of The Situation. Journal of Artificial Intelligence and Soft Computing Research 2(3), 223–233 (2012)

16. Jaworski, M., Duda, P., Pietruczuk, L.: On fuzzy clustering of data streams with concept drift. In: Rutkowski, L., Korytkowski, M., Scherer, R., Tadeusiewicz, R., Zadeh, L.A., Zurada, J.M. (eds.) ICAISC 2012, Part II. LNCS (LNAI), vol. 7268, pp. 82–91. Springer, Heidelberg (2012)

17. Korytkowski, M., Rutkowski, L., Scherer, R.: On combining backpropagation with boosting. In: IEEE International Joint Conference on Neural Network (IJCNN) Proceedings, vols. 1-10, Vancouver, July 16-21, pp. 1274–1277 (2006)

18. Korytkowski, M., Rutkowski, L., Scherer, R.: From Ensemble of Fuzzy Classifiers to Single Fuzzy Rule Base Classifier. In: Rutkowski, L., Tadeusiewicz, R., Zadeh, L.A., Zurada, J.M. (eds.) ICAISC 2008. LNCS (LNAI), vol. 5097, pp. 265–272. Springer, Heidelberg (2008)

19. Korytkowski, M., Nowicki, R., Rutkowski, L., Scherer, R.: AdaBoost Ensemble of DCOG Rough–Neuro–Fuzzy Systems. In: Jędrzejowicz, P., Nguyen, N.T., Hoang, K. (eds.) ICCCI 2011, Part I. LNCS, vol. 6922, pp. 62–71. Springer, Heidelberg (2011)

20. Kroll, A.: On choosing the fuzziness parameter for identifying TS models with multidimensional membership functions. Journal of Artificial Intelligence and Soft Computing Research 1(4), 283–300 (2011)

21. Lobato, F.S., Steffen Jr., V., Neto, A.J.S.: Solution of singular optimal control problems using the improved differential evolution algorithm. Journal of Artificial Intelligence and Soft Computing Research 1(3), 195–206 (2011)

22. Nowicki, R.: Rough Neuro-Fuzzy Structures for Classification With Missing Data. IEEE Transactions on Systems Man and Cybernetics Part B-Cybernetics 39(6), 1334–1347 (2009)

23. Parzen, E.: On estimation of a probability density function and mode. Analysis of Mathematical Statistics 33(3), 1065–1076 (1962)

24. Pietruczuk, L., Duda, P., Jaworski, M.: A new fuzzy classifier for data streams. In: Rutkowski, L., Korytkowski, M., Scherer, R., Tadeusiewicz, R., Zadeh, L.A., Zurada, J.M. (eds.) ICAISC 2012, Part I. LNCS (LNAI), vol. 7267, pp. 318–324. Springer, Heidelberg (2012)

25. Rafajlowicz, E.: Nonparametric orthogonal series estimators of regression - A class attaining the optimal convergence in L2. Statistics and Probability Letters 5(3), 219–224 (1987)

26. Rafajlowicz, E., Schwabe, R.: Halton and Hammersley sequences in multivariate nonparametric regression. Statistics and Probability Letters 76(8), 803–812 (2006)

27. Rutkowski, L.: Sequential estimates of probability densities by orthogonal series and their application in pattern classification. IEEE Transactions on Systems, Man, and Cybernetics SMC-10(12), 918–920 (1980)

28. Rutkowski, L.: On Bayes risk consistent pattern recognition procedures in a quasi-stationary environment. IEEE Transactions on Pattern Analysis and Machine Intelligence PAMI-4(1), 84–87 (1982)

29. Rutkowski, L.: On-line identification of time-varying systems by nonparametric techniques. IEEE Transactions on Automatic Control AC-27, 228–230 (1982)

30. Rutkowski, L.: On system identification by nonparametric function fitting. IEEE Trans. on Autom. Control AC-27, 225–227 (1982)

31. Rutkowski, L.: Orthogonal series estimates of a regression function with application in system identification. In: Probab. and Statist. Inference, pp. 343–347. D. Reidel Publ. Comp. (1982)

32. Rutkowski, L.: On nonparametric identification with prediction of time-varying systems. IEEE Transactions on Automatic Control AC-29, 58–60 (1984)

33. Rutkowski, L.: Nonparametric identification of quasi-stationary systems. Systems and Control Letters 6, 33–35 (1985)

34. Rutkowski, L.: The real-time identification of time-varying systems by nonparametric algorithms based on Parzen kernels. International Journal of Systems Science 16, 1123–1130 (1985)

35. Rutkowski, L.: A general approach for nonparametric fitting of functions and their derivatives with applications to linear circuits identification. IEEE Transactions on Circuits Systems CAS-33, 812–818 (1986)

36. Rutkowski, L.: Sequential pattern recognition procedures derived from multiple Fourier series. Pattern Recognition Letters 8, 213–216 (1988)

37. Rutkowski, L.: An application of multiple Fourier series to identification of multivariable nonstationary systems. International Journal of Systems Science 20(10), 1993–2002 (1989)

38. Rutkowski, L.: Non-parametric learning algorithms in the time-varying environments. Signal Processing 18(2), 129–137 (1989)

39. Rutkowski, L., Rafajlowicz, E.: On optimal global rate of convergence of some nonparametric identification procedures. IEEE Transaction on Automatic Control AC-34(10), 1089–1091 (1989)

40. Rutkowski, L.: Identification of MISO nonlinear regressions in the presence of a wide class of disturbances. IEEE Transactions on Information Theory IT-37, 214–216 (1991)

41. Rutkowski, L.: Multiple Fourier series procedures for extraction of nonlinear regressions from noisy data. IEEE Transactions on Signal Processing 41(10), 3062–3065 (1993)

42. Rutkowski, L.: Adaptive probabilistic neural-networks for pattern classification in time-varying environment. IEEE Trans. Neural Networks 15, 811–827 (2004)

43. Rutkowski, L.: Generalized regression neural networks in time-varying environment. IEEE Trans. Neural Networks 15, 576–596 (2004)

44. Rutkowski, L., Przybył, A., Cpałka, K., Er, M.J.: Online Speed Profile Generation for Industrial Machine Tool Based on Neuro-fuzzy Approach. In: Rutkowski, L., Scherer, R., Tadeusiewicz, R., Zadeh, L.A., Zurada, J.M. (eds.) ICAISC 2010, Part II. LNCS (LNAI), vol. 6114, pp. 645–650. Springer, Heidelberg (2010)
45. Rutkowski, L., Przybyl, A., Cpałka, K.: Novel on-line speed profile generation for industrial machine tool based on flexible neuro-fuzzy approximation. IEEE Transactions on Industrial Electronics 59, 1238–1247 (2012)
46. Rutkowski, L., Pietruczuk, L., Duda, P., Jaworski, M.: Decision trees for mining data streams based on the McDiarmid's bound. IEEE Transactions on Knowledge and Data Engineering 25(6), 1272–1279 (2013)
47. Rutkowski, L., Jaworski, M., Pietruczuk, L., Duda, P.: Decision trees for mining data streams based on the gaussian approximation. IEEE Transactions on Knowledge and Data Engineering 26(1), 108–119 (2014)
48. Rutkowski, L., Jaworski, M., Pietruczuk, L., Duda, P.: The CART decision tree for mining data streams. Information Sciences 266, 1–15 (2014)
49. Starczewski, A.: A cluster validity index for hard clustering. In: Rutkowski, L., Korytkowski, M., Scherer, R., Tadeusiewicz, R., Zadeh, L.A., Zurada, J.M. (eds.) ICAISC 2012, Part II. LNCS (LNAI), vol. 7268, pp. 168–174. Springer, Heidelberg (2012)
50. Starczewski, J., Rutkowski, L.: Interval type 2 neuro-fuzzy systems based on interval consequents. In: Rutkowski, L., Kacprzyk, J. (eds.) Neural Networks and Soft Computing, pp. 570–577. Physica-Verlag, Springer-Verlag Company, Heidelberg, New York (2003)
51. Starczewski, J., Rutkowski, L.: Connectionist Structures of Type 2 Fuzzy Inference Systems. In: Wyrzykowski, R., Dongarra, J., Paprzycki, M., Waśniewski, J. (eds.) PPAM 2001. LNCS, vol. 2328, pp. 634–642. Springer, Heidelberg (2002)
52. Starczewski, J., Scherer, R., Korytkowski, M., Nowicki, R.: Modular Type-2 Neuro-fuzzy Systems. In: Wyrzykowski, R., Dongarra, J., Karczewski, K., Wasniewski, J. (eds.) PPAM 2007. LNCS, vol. 4967, pp. 570–578. Springer, Heidelberg (2008)
53. Theodoridis Dimitris, C., Boutalis Yiannis, S., Christodoulou Manolis, A.: Robustifying analysis of the direct adaptive control of unknown multivariable nonlinear systems based on a new neuro-fuzzy method. Journal of Artificial Intelligence and Soft Computing Research 1(1), 59–79 (2011)
54. Tran, V.N., Brdys, M.A.: Optimizing Control by Robustly Feasible Model Predictive Control and Application to Drinkwater Distribution Systems. Journal of Artificial Intelligence and Soft Computing Research 1(1), 43–57 (2011)

A Comparison of Shallow Decision Trees Under Real-Boost Procedure with Application to Landmine Detection Using Ground Penetrating Radar

Przemysław Klęsk$^{(\boxtimes)}$, Mariusz Kapruziak, and Bogdan Olech

Faculty of Computer Science and Information Technology
West Pomeranian University of Technology
ul. Żołnierska 49, 71-210, Szczecin, Poland
{pklesk,mkapruziak,bolech}@wi.zut.edu.pl

Abstract. An application of Ground Penetrating Radar to landmine detection is presented. Using our prototype GPR system, we collect high-resolution 3D images, so called C-scans. By sampling 3D windows from C-scans, we generate large data sets for learning. We focus on experimentations with different recipes for growing shallow decision trees under the real-boost procedure. A particular attention is paid to the exponential criterion working as impurity function, in comparison to well known impurities. In the light of a theoretical bound on true error, driven from the properties of boosting, we check how greedy learning approaches translate in practice (for our GPR data) onto test error measures.

1 Introduction

1.1 Ground Penetrating Radar (GPR) and Landmine Detection

The GPR technology is a fairly new one, developed and studied extensively in the last two decades. GPRs allow to 'see' objects with different dielectric properties from the medium (soil), in particular non-metal objects. High trust GPR systems for mine detection require very large data sets to collect and to learn from. In other fields of application, e.g. construction industry or archeology, high accuracy or even the automatic detection itself are commonly not needed.

There are three types of GPR images one can work with. An A-scan is the simplest one-dimensional radagram defined over the depth (or time) axis only. A linear collection of A-scans forms a B-scan. Finally, a collection of B-scans forms a C-scan i.e. a 3D image over: accross-track × along-track × depth coordinates. For more elementary information on GPR we address the reader to [5].

Landmine detecting systems typically report their accuracy in terms of: sensitivity and FAR (false alarm rate), or the AUC[1] measure. Despite a relevant

---

This work was partially financed by the Ministry of Science and Higher Education in Poland (R&D project no. 0 R00 0091 12, agreement signed on 30.11.2010).

[1] Area Under Curve — area under the ROC curve (Receiver Operating Characteristic).

© Springer International Publishing Switzerland 2015
L. Rutkowski et al. (Eds.): ICAISC 2015, Part I, LNAI 9119, pp. 436–447, 2015.
DOI: 10.1007/978-3-319-19324-3_40

progress in the last decade, see e.g. [7,10,11,9,3,4], even the latest GPR-based detectors struggle with false alarms due to: soil inhomogeneities, clutter, rocks, water pockets, mine resembling objects, etc., and thus are still deficient. For example, in [3] Frigui et. al. present an advanced approach involving: a two-sensor system (GPR+EMI) and discrimation based on edge histogram descriptor using HMM algorithms. The data collected from two test lanes in U.S. included 875 scans (311 out of which represented mines). The following results are reported: sensitivity $\approx$ 95% and FAR $\approx$ 10%. In [4], authors focus on reconstruction[2] approaches and apply a detection algorithm based on averaged energy — integrations over A-scans. Reported AUCs are categorized into: small mines (AUC = 88.69%), medium mines (AUC = 99.02%) and big mines (AUC = 99.97%). In particular, the authors manage to obtain 100% sensitivity at the cost of the following FARs: $\approx$ 8% (small mines), $\approx$ 1% (medium mines), $\approx$ 0.1% (big mines).

Fig. 1 shows our prototype GPR system. It is a frequency-domain radar, generating microvawes from 500 MHz to 18 GHz, with a 1 cm resolution of successive A-scans. The prototype is based on a VNA and an antenna system of our construction. The transmitting antenna is a form of Vivaldi [1] and the receiving antenna is a shielded loop. All drives are based on stepping motors. The motion of the vehicle is controlled remotely. Raw data from scans is transferred through WiFi to a host computer (Xeon 2.4 GHz 2 × 8 core). All the software (for control, imaging, learning, and detection) was programmed in C#. Fig. 2 shows an

Fig. 1. Our prototype GPR system shown out-doors and on a laboratory test stand

example of a successful detection by our system for a metal antitank (AT) mine. Please note the characteristic hyperbolic patterns in GPR images.

1.2 Some Properties of Boosting with Real-Valued Weak Classifiers

This paper focuses on a specific aspect of our GPR research project [6], namely: learning with decision trees under boosting. To set up the reader's attention we first remind the real-boost learning procedure [8,2]. Then, we enumerate some of its properties that form the ground for further considerations and discussion.

---

[2] Attempts to reconstruct natural geometric shapes of buried objects based on hyperbolic patterns visible originally in GPR images.

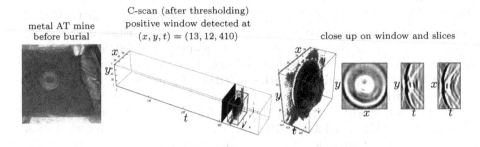

C-scan (after thresholding)

metal AT mine   positive window detected at
before burial $(x, y, t) = (13, 12, 410)$ close up on window and slices

Fig. 2. Example of detection on a metal AT mine. C-scan taken over $\approx 1\,\text{m}^2$ area.

Let $D = \{(\mathbf{x}_i, y_i)\}_{i=1,\ldots,m}$ be the set of training examples, where $\mathbf{x}_i = (x_{i1}, \ldots, x_{id})$ are vectors of features and $y \in \{-1, 1\}$ are class labels. In the Algorithm 1, $w_k(i)$ denotes the weight of i-th training example on the k-th round of boosting.

Algorithm 1. RealBoost(D)

1: start with uniform weights on data examples $w_1(i) := 1/m, \quad i = 1, \ldots, m$;
2: **for** $k = 1, 2, \ldots, K$ **do**
3:     train a new weak classifier f_k using current weights $w_k(i)$ to form
4:     an estimation of the conditional probability function $\widehat{P}_{w_k}(y = 1|\mathbf{x})$; and set:
5:     $f_k(\mathbf{x}) := 1/2 \log\left(\widehat{P}_{w_k}(y = 1|\mathbf{x}) \Big/ \left(1 - \widehat{P}_{w_k}(y = 1|\mathbf{x})\right)\right)$;
6:     update weights:
7:     $Z_k := \sum_{i=1}^{m} w_k(i)\, e^{-y_i f_k(\mathbf{x}_i)}$,
8:     $w_{k+1}(i) := w_k(i)\, e^{-y_i f_k(\mathbf{x}_i)}/Z_k, \quad i = 1, \ldots, m$;
9: **return** ensemble classifier $F(\mathbf{x}) := \sum_{k=1}^{K} f_k(\mathbf{x})$, with its decision: $\operatorname{sgn} F(\mathbf{x})$;

Friedman, Hastie and Tibshirani [2] demonstrated, in statistical terms, that boosting can be understood as an *additive model* for *logistic regression*. The reweighing mechanism plays a role akin to the errors residua technique. In logistic regression one tries to approximate the logarithmic odds ratio $F^*(\mathbf{x}) = \log\big(P(y = 1|\mathbf{x})/(1 - P(y = 1|\mathbf{x}))\big)$ — logit transform — using a linear model $F^*(\mathbf{x}) \approx a_0 + a_1 x_1 + \ldots + a_d x_d$. Solving the transform for probability yields the sigmoid function $P(y = 1|\mathbf{x}) = 1/\big(1 + e^{-F^*(\mathbf{x})}\big)$. In real-boost, one approximates *half* the logit transform $F^*(\mathbf{x}) = 1/2 \log\big(P(y = 1|\mathbf{x})/(1 - P(y = 1|\mathbf{x}))\big)$ by a sum of weak classifiers $F^*(\mathbf{x}) \approx f_1(\mathbf{x}) + \cdots + f_k(\mathbf{x})$, so in general simple but possibly multivariate functions. Solving for probability yields $P(y = 1|\mathbf{x}) = 1/\big(1 + e^{-2F^*(\mathbf{x})}\big)$. Therefore, both models are equivalent up to the factor of 2).

It is easy to check that half the logit transform is the minimizer of the *exponential criterion*: $\mathbb{E}\big(e^{-yF(\mathbf{x})}\big)$, where the expectation is taken with respect to the unknown joint probability distribution from which data pairs $(\mathbf{x}, y)$ are drawn. If the perfect function F^* (the minimizer) could be somehow found immediately then the boosting procedure could be stopped after just one round. Weak learners provide only rough approximations, therefore multiple rounds are needed.

The exponential criterion can also be viewed as a smooth upper bound on misclassification error, as noted by Schapire and Singer [8]. This leads to a more sensitive learning. Even if the training error is zero, a further learning will still try to decrease the criterion and yield a purer, more confident solution (greater $|F(\mathbf{x})|$ values) with a larger separation margin.

Boosting almost never overfits. As new summands are added the test error typically decreases and then stabilizes, instead of ultimately increasing. One can construct counter-examples (e.g. 'a ball in a ball' in [2]) but, as noted by Breiman in his comments to [2], hundreds of real-world data sets confirm the proper boosting behaviour. Some of the conjectures why boosting avoids overfitting are that: (1) late f_k summands have a mild effect on regions close to the decision boundary and none effect on pure regions, (2) parameters are tuned stage-wise rather then all at once, which makes the model complexity smaller than the sum of individual complexities of weak classifiers.

2   Motivation Lemmas

Below we formulate two lemmas that were a motivatation for our experiments. The lemmas are direct consequences of results from [2] due to Friedman et. al.

Let $\mathcal{P}$ denote the joint probability distribution (population), unknown in practice, from which data examples $(\mathbf{x}_i, y_i)$ are drawn i.i.d. Let $\mathcal{P}$ be described by a density function $p(\mathbf{x}, y) = p(\mathbf{x})P(y|\mathbf{x})$. For a real-valued classifier F, consider the following two error criterions defined as expectations with respect to p:

$$Q_p^{\mathrm{err}}(F) = \mathbb{E}_p\Big([\mathrm{sgn}\, F(\mathbf{x}) \neq y]\Big) = \int_{\mathbf{x}} \sum_{y \in \{-1,1\}} [\mathrm{sgn}\, F(\mathbf{x}) \neq y] p(\mathbf{x}, y)\, d\mathbf{x}, \quad (1)$$

$$Q_p^{\mathrm{exp}}(F) = \mathbb{E}_p\Big(e^{-yF(\mathbf{x})}\Big) = \int_{\mathbf{x}} \sum_{y \in \{-1,1\}} e^{-yF(\mathbf{x})} p(\mathbf{x}, y)\, d\mathbf{x} \quad (2)$$

($[\cdot]$ is an indicator function, returning 1 if its argument is true and 0 otherwise). The Q_p^{err} criterion is equal to the probability of misclassification by F and is commonly known as the *true error*[3]. In a learning experiment, by calculating the misclassification frequency on some finite test sample one obtains an estimate of true error. The Q_p^{exp} is the *exponential criterion*. Its sample-based version is well known from boosting and can be applied in it for two purposes: (1) to reweight examples, (2) to train weak classifiers. However, we should remark that different strategies, even randomized, can be met for the second purpose.

Lemma 1 *Consider a population-based version of the real-boost procedure that is aware of $\mathcal{P}$. Think of the sequence of weighing density functions involved in the procedure on successive rounds: $w_1(\mathbf{x}, y), w_2(\mathbf{x}, y), \ldots$ calculated as :*

$$w_1(\mathbf{x}, y) := p(\mathbf{x}, y), \quad (3)$$

$$w_{k+1}(\mathbf{x}, y) := w_k(\mathbf{x}, y)e^{-yf_k(\mathbf{x})}/Z_k, \qquad k = 1, \ldots, K; \quad (4)$$

---

[3] Also referred to as *true risk* in Vapnik's Statistical Learning Theory.

where $Z_k := \int_{\mathbf{x}} \sum_{y \in \{-1,1\}} e^{-y f_k(\mathbf{x})} w_k(\mathbf{x}, y) \, d\mathbf{x}$ are normalizing constants. Then, the product of Z_k constants is equal to the exponential criterion for the ensemble classifier: $\prod_{k=1}^{K} Z_k = Q_p^{exp}(F)$.

Lemma 2 *Suppose the population-based version of real-boost perfomed k rounds, arriving at a partial solution $F_k = f_1 + \cdots + f_k$ and a weighing density $w_{k+1}(\mathbf{x}, y)$. The procedure is about to make an update of solution to $F_{k+1} := F_k + f_{k+1}$ on the next round. Then, the following bound holds true for the updated solution:*

$$Q_p^{err}(F_k + f_{k+1}) \leqslant Q_p^{exp}(F_k + f_{k+1}) = Q_p^{exp}(F_k) \cdot Q_{w_{k+1}}^{exp}(f_{k+1}). \qquad (5)$$

It implies that the true error can be minimized by greedily minimizing the exponential criterion for summands f_k using weighing densities on successive rounds.

Proofs are straightforward derivations and we move them to appendix A.

The lemmas pertain to the population related case. In practice, we always carry out the learning using some finite training sample (a data set). On one hand it is well known that minimization of some error criterion on a training sample does not have to translate to a small test value of the criterion, especially when the model is complex. On the other hand, as stated earlier, practical evidence shows that boosting almost never overfits. Having *both* last statements in mind, one may be tempted to check if a replacement of the right-hand-side in the bound (5) by counterparts based on a training sample could still translate to minimization of true error. In other words, we ask if some recipe for growing shallow trees that tries to minimize directly the exponential criterion on a training sample (e.g. by using the criterion as the impurity for splits selection), and does it greedily on each boosting round, could work accordingly to the lemma 2. Contrarily, perhaps one could do better by applying the training error as impurity but still using the exponential criterion to reweight examples?

Please note that there are actually *two* levels of greediness in the context of growing decision trees under boosting. The outer level is the boosting procedure itself. The inner level is the tree growing recursion — on each call of the recursion chosen is a split that minimizes the expected impurity of its direct descendants (children nodes); one neglects how this choice affects the expected impurity of grandchildren, or great-grandchildren, and so forth.

In the light of the lemmas, in experiments we focus on two elements while growing shallow trees: (1) choice of impurity function, (2) choice of tree depth; and we observe the resulting quantities of interest like: train/test error criterions, sensitivities, FARs, AUC measures. We give little attention to such topics as e.g.: preprocessing of GPR images, extraction of features, subsampling of negative windows; though, the absolutely necessary elements are shortly described.

3 Impurities and Tree Splits Under Boosting

For a fixed tree node, suppose that $\{i\}$ denotes the set of indices limited only to examples falling into that node. Let $W_+ = \sum_{\{i:\, y_i = 1\}} w_k(i)$ and $W_- =$

$\sum_{\{i:\ y_i=-1\}} w_k(i)$, where k is the number of the current boosting round. Further, let $(\nu, 1-\nu)$ represent the probability distribution of two classes conditional on that node, where $\nu = W_+/(W_+ + W_-)$ and $1-\nu = W_-/(W_+ + W_-)$.

Below, we enumerate three common variants of impurity functions: misclassification error ($\mathrm{imp^{err}}$), Gini index ($\mathrm{imp^{gini}}$), entropy ($\mathrm{imp^{entr}}$), and as the fourth we add the *exponential criterion* ($\mathrm{imp^{exp}}$) to the list. Recall that tree nodes shall respond with half the logit transform. Note that the exponential criterion satisfies the conditions imposed on impurity functions, namely: (1) non-negativeness, (2) maximum attained for the uniform distribution, (3) minimum, equal 0, for deterministic distributions, (4) symmetry for distribution permutations.

$$\mathrm{imp^{err}}(\nu) = \begin{cases} \nu, & 0 \leqslant \nu < \frac{1}{2}; \\ 1-\nu, & \frac{1}{2} \leqslant \nu \leqslant 1. \end{cases} \tag{6}$$

$$= \tfrac{1}{2} - \left|\nu - \tfrac{1}{2}\right|. \tag{7}$$

$$\mathrm{imp^{gini}}(\nu) = 1 - \nu^2 - (1-\nu)^2 \tag{8}$$

$$= 2\nu(1-\nu) = \tfrac{1}{2} - 2\left(\nu - \tfrac{1}{2}\right)^2. \tag{9}$$

$$\mathrm{imp^{entr}}(\nu) = -\left(\nu\log\nu + (1-\nu)\log(1-\nu)\right) \tag{10}$$

$$= \log 2 - 2\left(\nu - \tfrac{1}{2}\right)^2 - \tfrac{4}{3}\left(\nu - \tfrac{1}{2}\right)^4 - \tfrac{32}{15}\left(\nu - \tfrac{1}{2}\right)^6 + O\left(\nu - \tfrac{1}{2}\right)^8. \tag{11}$$

$$\mathrm{imp^{exp}}(\nu) = \nu e^{-1/2\log(\nu/(1-\nu))} + (1-\nu)e^{1/2\log(\nu/(1-\nu))} \tag{12}$$

$$= 2\sqrt{\nu(1-\nu)} = \sqrt{1 - 4\left(\nu - \tfrac{1}{2}\right)^2}. \tag{13}$$

For each listed impurity, we first write down the formula according to a common definition, then we show an equivalent representations in terms of the $|\nu - 1/2|$ expression (for entropy we use Taylor series expansion about the $1/2$ point). These additional representations indicate the symmetry, but are also meant to show that the listed impurities can be regarded as successive upper bounds on one another: $\mathrm{imp^{err}}(\nu) \leqslant \mathrm{imp^{gini}}(\nu) \leqslant \mathrm{imp^{entr}}(\nu) \leqslant \mathrm{imp^{exp}}(\nu)$.

Consider a split on a j-th variable at a value v. Let suitable sums of weights in the left (L) and right (R) parts be: $W_{L(j,v)} = \sum_{\{i:\ x_{ij}<v\}} w_k(i)$, $W_{R(j,v)} = \sum_{\{i:\ x_{ij}\geqslant v\}} w_k(i)$. Also, let $\nu_{L(j,v)}$ and $\nu_{R(j,v)}$ represent suitable left and right conditionals. Then, the best split is selected according to the rule:

$$\underset{(j,v)}{\arg\min} \frac{W_{L(j,v)}}{W_{L(j,v)}+W_{R(j,v)}}\mathrm{imp}\left(\nu_{L(j,v)}\right) + \frac{W_{R(j,v)}}{W_{L(j,v)}+W_{R(j,v)}}\mathrm{imp}\left(\nu_{R(j,v)}\right). \tag{14}$$

4   Experiments

4.1   Learning Material

The collected learning material consisted of 210 C-scans, each taken from an area of $\approx 1\,\mathrm{m}^2$ on our laboratory test stand filled with garden soil[4]. There were

---

[4] Garden soil is regarded as more difficult for GPR than sand or gravel.

three groups in the material: 70 scans with a metal AT mine (TM-62M, height 128 mm, diameter 320 mm), 70 scans with a plastic AT mine (PT-Mi-Ba III, height 110 mm, diameter 330 mm) and 70 scans non-mine objects (boxes, cans, cables, bricks, shafts, discs). The material was divided into train (80%) and test (20%) parts, with even proportions of the three groups. Finally, a procedure traversing all the scans with a sliding 3D window ($67 \times 67 \times 39$) was executed. Examples of 3D windows formed suitable train and test sets. We decided to train separate detectors for the metal and the plastic mine, therefore there were actually two pairs of train/test sets; the metal mine was a negative example for the "plastic detector" and vice-versa. All positive windows (containing a mine) were memorized with a 2-pixel tolerance along each dimension. For negative windows (background or clutter) we applied undersampling with probability $5 \cdot 10^{-4}$. These proceedings led to train sets containing about 85 000 negative examples and 7 000 positives examples. Test sets were proportionally four times smaller. Due to a large number of features extracted (described in the next section) — 15 625 features for each example, the train sets were 5.6 GB large.

4.2 Features Extraction

To extract features we applied *piecewise 3D Fourier approximations* of low orders with respect to image windows. Each window was divided into a regular $5 \times 5 \times 5$ grid of cuboids and for each cuboid, spanning from (x_1, y_1, t_1) to (x_2, y_2, t_2), Fourier coefficients were calculated as:

$$c_{k_x, k_y, k_t} = \frac{\sum\limits_{x=x_1}^{x_2} \sum\limits_{y=y_1}^{y_2} \sum\limits_{t=t_1}^{t_2} i(x, y, t) e^{-2\pi i \left(k_x \frac{x - x_1}{x_2 - x_1 + 1} + k_y \frac{y - y_1}{y_2 - y_1 + 1} + k_t \frac{t - t_1}{t_2 - t_1 + 1} \right)}}{(x_2 - x_1 + 1)(y_2 - y_1 + 1)(t_2 - t_1 + 1)}, \quad (15)$$

where: $-n \leqslant k_x, k_y, k_t \leqslant n$ indicate harmonic orders of a coefficient with n being the maximum, $i(x, y, t)$ is the pixel intensity, and $i = \sqrt{-1}$ is the imaginary unit. Real and imaginary parts of the coefficients were taken as the features. Due to the complex conjugacy, the number of distinct real and imaginary parts is $(2n + 1)^3$ in total, rather than $2 \cdot (2n + 1)^3$. For computational reasons we imposed $n = 2$ as the maximum harmonic order. Therefore, the effective number of features, taking into account all cuboids, was $d = 125 \cdot (2n + 1)^3 = 15\,625$.

4.3 Results of Experiments

In all experiments we imposed a constant number of weak classifiers ($K = 500$). We varied impurities and depths of shallow trees; obtaining trees with 2, 4 or 8 terminal nodes at maximum. The trees with 2 terminals are also known as decision stumps. In reported results we use the labels: err2, gini2, entr2, exp2, err4, ..., exp8, to indicate the type of impurity and the number of terminals.

We first report the results at the 'windows level of detail' i.e. with each 3D window treated as a separate object under classification. Later, we report the results at the 'images level of detail' i.e. for whole C-scans and after the post-processing. The postprocessing step groups each cluster of multiple detected windows (lying close to each other) into a single indication. By that, the second level is less meticulous and gives more optimistic numbers. For example, the windows 'turned on' lying just outside the 2-pixel tolerance of an accurate mine location (mild false alarms) can be absorbed by a postprocessed group.

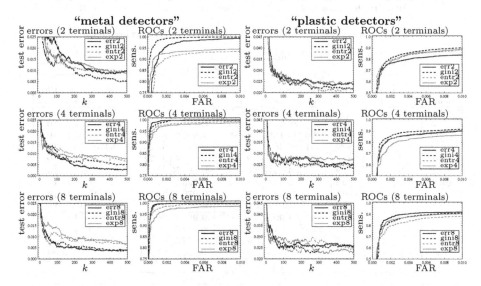

Fig. 3. Test errors and ROC curves for all detectors.

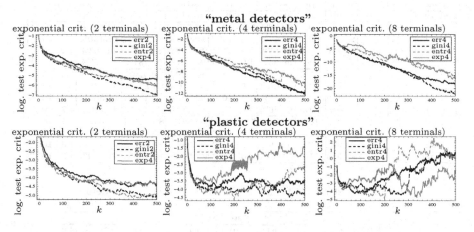

Fig. 4. Test values of exponential criterion on logarithmic scale for all detectors

Fig. 3 shows test errors and ROC curves for both types of detectors: "metal detectors" (dedicated for the metal AT mine) and "plastic detectors" (dedicated for the plastic AT mine). Results for "metal detectors" were in general better, therefore we adjusted plot ranges for readability to: $[0.0, 0.025]$ for test error, and $[0.75, 1.0]$ for sensitivity, while for "plastic detectors" the corresponding ranges are $[0.020, 0.045]$ and $[0.5, 1.0]$. Fig. 4 illustrates test values of the exponential criterion on the logarithmic scale. Table 1 summarizes results at the 'window level of detail' (AUC_α notation in the table stands for the normalized AUC measure obtained up to point α of FAR axis). Table 2 reports detections for whole C-scans. In the tables we distinguished the best detectors by frames.

Table 1. Test results for all detectors at 'windows level of detail'

	train results		test results							
name	error	log. exp. crit.	error	log. exp. crit.	sens.	FAR	AUC	$AUC_{0.01}$	$AUC_{0.001}$	FAR at sens. 1/2
zero-rule	n.a.	n.a.	7.27%	n.a.	0.00%	0.0	0.000%	0.000%	0.000%	0.0
err2	0.00%	−8.4	0.94%	−5.5	88.24%	$9.4 \cdot 10^{-4}$	99.947%	95.438%	74.400%	$4.7 \cdot 10^{-5}$
gini2	0.00%	−9.2	**0.53%**	**−7.0**	**93.13%**	$3.8 \cdot 10^{-4}$	**99.987%**	**98.977%**	**93.188%**	$4.7 \cdot 10^{-5}$
entr2	0.00%	−9.3	0.89%	−6.1	88.30%	$4.7 \cdot 10^{-4}$	97.711%	90.264%	72.476%	$9.4 \cdot 10^{-5}$
exp2	0.00%	−9.4	0.89%	−6.1	88.36%	$5.2 \cdot 10^{-4}$	99.029%	92.727%	84.272%	$4.7 \cdot 10^{-5}$
err4	0.00%	−27.1	**0.31%**	**−12.0**	**96.12%**	$2.8 \cdot 10^{-4}$	**99.993%**	**99.480%**	**96.365%**	$4.7 \cdot 10^{-5}$
gini4	0.00%	−28.6	0.50%	**−12.3**	93.43%	$2.3 \cdot 10^{-4}$	99.988%	99.138%	94.679%	$4.7 \cdot 10^{-5}$
entr4	0.00%	−29.7	0.66%	−10.9	91.22%	$2.8 \cdot 10^{-4}$	99.970%	97.946%	91.852%	$4.7 \cdot 10^{-5}$
exp4	0.00%	−30.8	0.77%	−9.9	89.67%	$1.9 \cdot 10^{-4}$	99.955%	97.373%	91.463%	$4.7 \cdot 10^{-5}$
err8	0.00%	−60.3	**0.40%**	−18.3	**94.99%**	$3.3 \cdot 10^{-4}$	**99.994%**	**99.601%**	**97.192%**	$4.7 \cdot 10^{-5}$
gini8	0.00%	−67.2	0.41%	**−22.0**	94.69%	$2.3 \cdot 10^{-4}$	99.992%	99.445%	96.160%	$4.7 \cdot 10^{-5}$
entr8	0.00%	−69.8	0.63%	−16.2	91.52%	$1.9 \cdot 10^{-4}$	99.982%	98.715%	94.089%	$4.7 \cdot 10^{-5}$
exp8	0.00%	−64.4	0.69%	−16.0	90.93%	$3.3 \cdot 10^{-4}$	99.925%	97.141%	90.337%	**0.00**

"plastic detectors"										
	train results		test results							
name	error	log. exp. crit.	error	log. exp. crit.	sens.	FAR	AUC	$AUC_{0.01}$	$AUC_{0.001}$	FAR at sens. 1/2
zero-rule	n.a.	n.a.	7.60%	n.a.	0.00%	0.0	0.000%	0.000%	0.000%	0.0
err2	0.00%	−7.2	2.36%	−4.4	70.06%	$9.4 \cdot 10^{-4}$	95.710%	76.851%	44.663%	$5.6 \cdot 10^{-4}$
gini2	0.00%	−8.7	2.21%	−5.0	72.17%	$1.0 \cdot 10^{-3}$	96.030%	**82.049%**	**46.430%**	$4.7 \cdot 10^{-4}$
entr2	0.00%	−8.7	**2.18%**	−5.0	**72.57%**	$9.0 \cdot 10^{-4}$	**96.194%**	80.396%	46.363%	$4.2 \cdot 10^{-4}$
exp2	0.00%	−8.8	2.39%	−4.3	69.83%	$1.0 \cdot 10^{-3}$	95.234%	79.781%	40.377%	$5.6 \cdot 10^{-4}$
err4	0.00%	−21.7	2.50%	−3.5	68.11%	$8.0 \cdot 10^{-4}$	**96.436%**	82.529%	46.927%	$5.2 \cdot 10^{-4}$
gini4	0.00%	−24.6	**2.30%**	−4.4	**70.63%**	$7.5 \cdot 10^{-4}$	94.910%	**84.879%**	47.768%	$5.2 \cdot 10^{-4}$
entr4	0.00%	−26.0	2.51%	−2.6	67.83%	$6.6 \cdot 10^{-4}$	95.297%	83.143%	**48.501%**	$4.7 \cdot 10^{-4}$
exp4	0.00%	−18.8	2.76%	−1.5	64.86%	$9.4 \cdot 10^{-4}$	95.170%	78.440%	42.246%	$4.7 \cdot 10^{-4}$
err8	0.00%	−49.5	2.58%	0.7	66.91%	$7.0 \cdot 10^{-4}$	96.291%	**86.253%**	50.437%	$4.7 \cdot 10^{-4}$
gini8	0.00%	−55.7	2.50%	0.7	68.06%	$7.5 \cdot 10^{-4}$	95.571%	83.659%	45.147%	$5.2 \cdot 10^{-4}$
entr8	0.00%	−59.9	2.43%	−0.2	69.09%	$8.5 \cdot 10^{-4}$	95.302%	80.823%	48.544%	$4.3 \cdot 10^{-4}$
exp8	0.00%	−57.0	**2.35%**	−1.6	**70.06%**	$8.0 \cdot 10^{-4}$	**96.526%**	84.409%	**53.880%**	$4.3 \cdot 10^{-4}$

Table 2. Test results for all detectors at 'images level of detail'

"metal detectors"												
	err2	gini2	entr2	exp2	err4	gini4	entr4	exp4	err8	gini8	entr8	exp8
sensitivity	14/14	14/14	14/14	14/14	**14/14**	**14/14**	**14/14**	14/14	**14/14**	**14/14**	13/14	14/14
FAR	3/42	1/42	1/42	4/42	**0/42**	**0/42**	**0/42**	1/42	**0/42**	**0/42**	1/42	3/42

"plastic detectors"												
	err2	gini2	entr2	exp2	err4	gini4	entr4	exp4	err8	gini8	entr8	exp8
sensitivity	13/14	13/14	13/14	13/14	13/14	13/14	**13/14**	13/14	**13/14**	**13/14**	13/14	13/14
FAR	14/42	4/42	4/42	11/42	2/42	1/42	**0/42**	5/42	**0/42**	**0/42**	6/42	12/42

The following tendencies can be seen overall in the results. **"Metal detectors"** achieved very good results with best test errors smaller than 0.5% and most of AUCs greater than 99.9%. The test errors decreased for trees with more terminals, and although the best-of-all error was achieved for the err4 variant the results on average (especially AUCs) appear to be better for 8-terminal trees. The misclassification error working as impurity turned out to be best choice for larger trees. Surprisingly, the exponential criterion was in most cases leading to the worst test measures (of any kind). **"Plastic detectors"** obtained test errors slightly greater than 2% and best AUCs $\approx$ 96.5%. The overall tendencies are less apparrent, in particular the choice of impurity function is not clear. As regards the size of trees, test errors appear the smallest for decision stumps, but AUC measures, especially for initial parts of ROC curves ($AUC_{0.01}$, $AUC_{0.001}$), favour larger trees. Moreover, the 4 and 8-terminal trees were clearly better at 'images level of detail', producing fewer false alarms. It is also interesting to note that test values of the exponential criterion were not stable for larger trees as new weak classifiers were added (Fig. 4), even though simultaneously the corresponding test errors were leveled off. Our supposition is that this behaviour is due to a certain small number of misclassified test examples (close to the decision boundary but on the wrong side) which exhibit very high $e^{|F_k(\mathbf{x})|}$ values.

We should also note that for train sets the greedy usage of exponential criterion as impurity obviously led to the smallest values of that criterion for stumps, but for more terminals it was not necessarily the case (third column in Table 1).

Results at the 'images level of detail' show that 5 variants of "metal detectors" succeeded in achieving a perfect score (14/14 sensitivity and 0/42 FAR). None of the "plastic detectors" managed to detect correctly all mines.

5   Conclusions

We generated large data sets (over $9 \cdot 10^5$ examples and $1.5 \cdot 10^4$ features) by sampling densely 3D windows from a collection of GPR C-scans. The collection itself was of moderate size — 210 scans describing two types of antitank mines and various non-mine objects. Boosted decision trees proved to be well suited for our application and resistant to overfitting. Many of tested ensembles obtained close to perfect results in terms of sensitivity and FAR.

Experimentations with different recipes for growing trees showed that the exponential criterion working as impurity function almost never transposed to best test results. This contradicts an intuition one might draw from a theoretical bound (motivation lemma 2) true for the population case when the joint distribution is explicitly known.

The future direction for us is to include in the research more types of soil and mines (in particular antipersonnel mines). A larger learning material will give a more accurate view on how well our prototype system can actually work in more difficult and variable conditions.

A   Proofs of Lemmas

Proof (Lemma 1). We expand the weighing density $w_{K+1}(\mathbf{x}, y)$, obtained after the last boosting round, using (4):

$$w_{K+1}(\mathbf{x}, y) = w_K(\mathbf{x}, y)e^{-yf_K(\mathbf{x})}/Z_K = w_{K-1}(\mathbf{x}, y)e^{-y(f_{K-1}(\mathbf{x})+f_K(\mathbf{x}))}/(Z_{K-1}Z_K)$$

$$= \cdots = p(\mathbf{x}, y)e^{-y\sum_{k=1}^{K} f_k(\mathbf{x})}/(Z_1 \cdots Z_K) = p(\mathbf{x}, y)e^{-yF(\mathbf{x})} \Big/ \prod_{k=1}^{K} Z_k.$$

The result follows by summation (over y) and integration (over $\mathbf{x}$) side-wise. □

Proof (Lemma 2). First, note that $[\operatorname{sgn} F(\mathbf{x}) \neq y] = [yF(\mathbf{x}) < 0] \leqslant e^{-yF(\mathbf{x})}$, therefore $Q_p^{\mathrm{err}}(F) \leqslant Q_p^{\mathrm{exp}}(F)$. Further:

$$Q_p^{\mathrm{exp}}(F_k + f_{k+1}) = \int_{\mathbf{x}} \sum_{y \in \{-1,1\}} e^{-y(F_k(\mathbf{x})+f_{k+1}(\mathbf{x}))} p(\mathbf{x}, y)\,\mathbf{dx}$$

$$= \prod_{q=1}^{k} Z_q \cdot \int_{\mathbf{x}} \sum_{y \in \{-1,1\}} e^{-yf_{k+1}(\mathbf{x})} \underbrace{e^{-yF_k(\mathbf{x})}p(\mathbf{x}, y)\Big/\prod_{q=1}^{k} Z_q}_{w_{k+1}(\mathbf{x},y)}\,\mathbf{dx}$$

$$= Q_p^{\mathrm{exp}}(F_k) \cdot Q_{w_{k+1}}^{\mathrm{exp}}(f_{k+1}). \quad \square$$

References

1. Azodi, H., Zhuge, X., Yarovoy, A.: Balanced Antipodal Vivaldi Antenna with Novel Transition from Feeding Line to the Flares. In: Proceedings of the 5th European Conference on Antennas and Propagation (EUCAP), pp. 1279–1283 (2011)
2. Friedman, J., Hastie, T., Tibshirani, R.: Additive logistic regression: a statistical view of boosting. The Annals of Statistics 28(2), 337–407 (2000)
3. Frigui, H., et al.: Context-dependent multisensor fusion and its application to land mine detection. IEEE Trans. on Geoscience and Remote Sensing 48(6) (2010)
4. Gonzalez-Huici, M., Catapano, I., Soldovieri, F.: A Comparative Study of GPR Reconstruction Approaches for Landmine Detection. IEEE Journal of Selected Topics in Applied Earth Observations and Remote Sensing PP(99), article#: 2321276 (2014)
5. Jol, H.M.: Ground Penetrating Radar: Theory and Applications. Elsevier, Oxford (2009)
6. Klęsk, P., Godziuk, A., Kapruziak, M., Olech, B.: Landmine Detection in 3D Images from Ground Penetrating Radar Using Haar-Like Features. In: Rutkowski, L., Korytkowski, M., Scherer, R., Tadeusiewicz, R., Zadeh, L.A., Zurada, J.M. (eds.) ICAISC 2013, Part I. LNCS (LNAI), vol. 7894, pp. 559–567. Springer, Heidelberg (2013)
7. Marble, J.A.: Advances in Surface Penetrating Technologies for Imaging, Detection and Classification. PhD thesis, University of Michigan, Michigan, USA (2007)
8. Schapire, R.E., Singer, Y.: Improved boosting using confidence-rated predictions. Machine Learning 37(3), 297–336 (1999)

9. Seyfried, D., et al.: Information extraction from ultrawideband ground penetrating radar data: A machine learning approach. In: 7th German Microwave Conference (GeMiC 2012), pp. 1–4 (2012)
10. Yarovoy, A.: Landmine and unexploaded ordnance detection and classification with ground penetrating radar. In: Jol, H.M. (ed.) Ground Penetrating Radar: Theory and Applications, pp. 445–478. Elsevier, Oxford (2009)
11. Zhu, Q., Collins, L.M.: Application of feature extraction methods for landmine detection using the Wichmann/Niitek Ground-Penetrating Radar. IEEE Transactions on Geoscience and Remote Sensing 43(1) (2005)

A New Interpretability Criteria for Neuro-Fuzzy Systems for Nonlinear Classification

Krystian Łapa[1(✉)], Krzysztof Cpałka[1], and Alexander I. Galushkin[2]

[1] Institute of Computational Intelligence, Częstochowa University of Technology, Częstochowa Poland
{krystian.lapa,krzysztof.cpalka}@iisi.pcz.pl
[2] Moscow Institute of Physics and Technology, Moscow Oblast, Russia
neurocomputer@yandex.ru

Abstract. In this paper a new approach for construction of neuro-fuzzy systems for nonlinear classification is introduced. In particular, we concentrate on the flexible neuro-fuzzy systems which allow us to extend notation of rules with weights of fuzzy sets. The proposed approach uses possibilities of hybrid evolutionary algorithm and interpretability criteria of expert knowledge. These criteria include not only complexity of the system, but also semantics of the rules. The approach presented in our paper was tested on typical nonlinear classification simulation problems.

1 Introduction

The process of construction methods for the nonlinear classification is focused mostly on reaching high accuracy. The other important aim is to achieve a good clarity and interpretability of classification rules. It allows to better understand considered problem. These both aims are contradictory, so the balance between accuracy and interpretability of classifier is often investigated in the literature (see e.g. [28,36,37,71]).

A number of methods are used for nonlinear classification, i.e. neuro-fuzzy systems (see e.g. [35,47,48,55,67,90,95,102]). In those systems the knowledge is gathered in a form of rules *ifthen*. These rules contain linguistic variables and variables corresponding to fuzzy sets and their parameters. Methods for increasing interpretability of neuro-fuzzy system rules take an important place in the literature. This interpretability arises not only from complexity of the system, but also from semantics of the rules (see e.g. [2,30]). In the area of those research is worth to list methods focused on: **(a)** Definition and implementation of new criteria of interpretability of fuzzy rules (see e.g. [1,30,86,87]). **(b)** Appropriate aggregation of those criteria (see e.g. [3,18,31,99]) and using multi-objective methods (see e.g. [57,85,86,100]). **(c)** Use of population-based algorithms to obtain interpretable systems (see e.g. [49,60,65,74]). **(d)** Use of possibilities of non-supervising learning in the field of initialization of fuzzy rules for increasing interpretability (see e.g. [4,41,72,88]). **(e)** Use of possibilities of gradient and evolutionary methods for reduction and scaling of fuzzy rules and fuzzy sets (see e.g. [39,45,46,63]). **(f)** Use of extended structures of neuro-fuzzy systems

© Springer International Publishing Switzerland 2015
L. Rutkowski et al. (Eds.): ICAISC 2015, Part I, LNAI 9119, pp. 448–468, 2015.
DOI: 10.1007/978-3-319-19324-3_41

in purpose to increase both the accuracy and interpretability of neuro-fuzzy rules (see e.g. [20,21,79], [80]). **(g)** Extending notation of neuro-fuzzy rules for additional possibilities in the field of more precise description of considering problems (see e.g. [42,59,72,73,89]). It is worth to mention that there are many papers that focus on reviewing methods that concentrate on interpretability and interpretability-accuracy trade-off (see e.g. [1,30,86,87]). For example, in [30] authors are focused on splitting types of methods in the context of interpretability into following quadrants of interpretability: **(a)** complexity at the rule base level (it refers to i.e. number of rules, number of inputs used), **(b)** complexity at the fuzzy partition level (it refers to i.e. number of antecedences and consequents), **(c)** semantics at the rule base level (it refers to i.e. level of active rules for individual input sets), **(d)** semantics at the fuzzy partition level (it refer to i.e. equal covering the search space by fuzzy sets, shape and place of the fuzzy sets).

In this paper we propose a new method for increasing the interpretability of neuro-fuzzy systems for nonlinear classification. Neuro-fuzzy systems (see e.g. [29,52]) combine the natural language description of fuzzy systems (see e.g. [6,61]) and the learning properties of neural networks (see e.g. [7,8,9,10,11,12,13,14,15,51,94,98]). In particular we propose: **(a)** a new approach for construction and tuning of neuro-fuzzy systems (including flexible neuro-fuzzy systems, see e.g. [19,22,23,103,108,109]) **(b)** a new interpretability criteria for increasing interpretability of expert knowledge taking into account not only the complexity of the system but also semantics of the rules.

It is worth to note that many computational intelligence methods (see e.g. [5,24,25,26,62,81,82,91,92,93]) are succesfully used in pattern recognition (see e.g. [38,75,76,77,84]), modelling (see e.g. [16,69,83,97,104,105,106,107]) and many other (see e.g. [32,33,34,50]) issues.

This paper is presented as follows: in Section 2 a description of proposed system and its tuning process for nonlinear classification is presented. In Section 3 a new interpretability criteria to increase interpretability for neuro-fuzzy systems are shown. The results of simulations are presented in Section 4, finally the conclusions are described in Section 5.

2   Description of Neuro-Fuzzy System for Nonlinear Classification and Algorithm for Its Tuning

2.1   System Description

We consider multi-input, multi-output neuro-fuzzy system mapping $\mathbf{X} \to \mathbf{Y}$, where $\mathbf{X} \subset \mathbf{R}^n$ and $\mathbf{Y} \subset \mathbf{R}^m$. The flexible fuzzy rule base consists of a collection of N fuzzy if-then rules in the form

$$R^k : \left[\left(\begin{array}{l} \text{IF } \left(\bar{x}_1 \text{ is } A_1^k\right) \left| w_{k,1}^A \text{ AND} \dots \text{AND} \left(\bar{x}_n \text{ is } A_n^k\right) \right| w_{k,n}^A \\ \text{THEN } \left(y_1 \text{ is } B_1^k\right) \left| w_{1,k}^B, \dots, \left(y_m \text{ is } B_m^k\right) \right| w_{m,k}^B \end{array} \right) \left| w_k^{\text{rule}} \right. \right], \quad (1)$$

where n is a number of inputs, m is a number of outputs, $\bar{\mathbf{x}} = [\bar{x}_1, \ldots, \bar{x}_n] \in \mathbf{X}$, $\mathbf{y} = [y_1, \ldots, y_m] \in \mathbf{Y}$, $A_1^k, \ldots, A_n^k$ are fuzzy sets characterized by membership functions $\mu_{A_i^k}(x_i)$, $i = 1, \ldots, n$, $k = 1, \ldots, N$, $B_1^k, \ldots, B_m^k$ are fuzzy sets characterized by membership functions $\mu_{B_j^k}(y_j)$, $j = 1, \ldots, m$, $k = 1, \ldots, N$, $w_{k,i}^A \in [0,1]$, $i = 1, \ldots, n$, $k = 1, \ldots, N$, are weights of antecedents, $w_{j,k}^B \in [0,1]$, $k = 1, \ldots, N$, $j = 1, \ldots, m$, are weights of consequences, $w_k^{\text{rule}} \in [0,1]$, $k = 1, \ldots, N$, are weights of rules. In logical approach output signal $\bar{y}_j$, $j = 1, \ldots, m$, of the neuro-fuzzy system can be described by the formula

$$\bar{y}_j = \frac{\sum\limits_{r=1}^{R} \bar{y}_{j,r}^{\text{def}} \cdot \mathop{T^*}\limits_{k=1}^{N} \left\{ S^* \left\{ 1 - \mathop{T^*}\limits_{i=1}^{n} \left\{ \mu_{A_i^k}(\bar{x}_i); w_{k,i}^A \right\}, \mu_{B_j^k}(\bar{y}_{j,r}^{\text{def}}); 1, w_{j,k}^B \right\}; w_k^{\text{rule}} \right\}}{\sum\limits_{r=1}^{R} \mathop{T^*}\limits_{k=1}^{N} \left\{ S^* \left\{ 1 - \mathop{T^*}\limits_{i=1}^{n} \left\{ \mu_{A_i^k}(\bar{x}_i); w_{k,i}^A \right\}, \mu_{B_j^k}(\bar{y}_{j,r}^{\text{def}}); 1, w_{j,k}^B \right\}; w_k^{\text{rule}} \right\}},$$

(2)

where $T^* \{\cdot\}$ and $S^* \{\cdot\}$ are weighted triangular norms (see e.g. [20,21,78], [79,80]), $\bar{y}_{j,r}^{\text{def}}$, $j = 1, \ldots, m$, $r = 1, \ldots, R$, are discretization points, R is a number of discretization points. For more details see our previous papers, e.g. [20,21,78].

2.2 Description of tuning algorithm

For selection of structure and parameters of system (2) we propose an evolutionary algorithm (see e.g. [27,54,53,66,68,96,101]). In the process of evolution (evolution of parameters) all parameters of the neuro-fuzzy system (2) will be found. Moreover, in the process of evolution (evolution of the structure) we will find the number of inputs n, the number of rules N, the number of antecedents and consequents (number of fuzzy sets) and the number of discretization points R. The algorithm is based on the Pittsburgh approach ([58,78]), on the evolutionary strategy (μ, λ) for selecting parameters of system (2), on the classical genetic algorithm for choosing structure of system (2) and on the bees algorithm for fixing parameters of reduced systems (2).

The evolutionary strategy (μ, λ) starts with a random generation of the initial parents population $\mathbf{P}$ containing μ individuals. Next, a temporary population $\mathbf{T}$ is created by means of reproduction, whose population contains λ individuals, while $\lambda \geq \mu$. Reproduction consists in a multiple random selection of λ individuals out of the population $\mathbf{P}$ (multiple sampling) and placing the selected ones in temporary population $\mathbf{T}$. Individuals of the population $\mathbf{T}$ undergo crossover and mutation operations as a result of which an offspring population $\mathbf{O}$ is created, which also has size λ. The purpose of the repair procedure of the population $\mathbf{O}$ is to correct the parameters if they reach inadmissible values. The new population $\mathbf{P}$ containing μ individuals is selected only out of the best λ individuals of the population $\mathbf{O}$. The bees algorithm mimics the food foraging behaviour of honey bee colonies and it is used to tuning parameters of system (2). The aim of using this algorithm is to tune the parameters of the system with recently reduced structure and to repair damaged accuracy. The behaviour of the bees can be described as follows: **(a)** For every μ population chromosomes of $\mathbf{P}$ and μ chromosomes are generated (scout bees), **b)** For every chromosome of $\mathbf{B}$ a search territory area is calculated (as an area of solution explorations coded in the population $\mathbf{P}$). For every iteration of the algorithm the area of exploration is decreased, **(c)** After this modification, chromosomes from $\mathbf{B}$ are repaired and evaluated (analogically to evolutionary strategy (μ, λ)), **(d)** In the last step one solution (with best fitness function value) is picked from each group of scout bees and moved into the population $\mathbf{P}$. More details about bees algorithm can be found in [64].

Coding of Parameters and Structure. The parameters of system (2) are coded in the following chromosome (Pittsburgh approach)

$$
\mathbf{X}_{ch}^{\mathrm{par}} = \left\{ \begin{array}{c}
\bar{x}_{1,1}^{A}, \sigma_{1,1}^{A}, \ldots, \bar{x}_{n,1}^{A}, \sigma_{n,1}^{A}, \ldots \\
\bar{x}_{1,Nmax}^{A}, \sigma_{1,Nmax}^{A}, \ldots, \bar{x}_{n,Nmax}^{A}, \sigma_{n,Nmax}^{A}, \\
\bar{y}_{1,1}^{B}, \sigma_{1,1}^{B}, \ldots, \bar{y}_{m,1}^{B}, \sigma_{m,1}^{B}, \ldots \\
\bar{y}_{1,Nmax}^{B}, \sigma_{1,Nmax}^{B}, \ldots, \bar{y}_{m,Nmax}^{B}, \sigma_{m,Nmax}^{B}, \\
w_{1,1}^{A}, \ldots, w_{1,n}^{A}, \ldots, w_{Nmax,1}^{A}, \ldots, w_{Nmax,n}^{A}, \\
w_{1,1}^{B}, \ldots, w_{m,1}^{B}, \ldots, w_{1,Nmax}^{B}, \ldots, w_{m,Nmax}^{B}, \\
w_{1}^{\mathrm{rule}}, \ldots, w_{Nmax}^{\mathrm{rule}}, \\
\bar{y}_{1,1}^{\mathrm{def}}, \ldots, \bar{y}_{1,Rmax}^{\mathrm{def}}, \ldots, \bar{y}_{m,1}^{\mathrm{def}}, \ldots, \bar{y}_{m,Rmax}^{\mathrm{def}}
\end{array} \right\} = \left\{ X_{ch,1}^{\mathrm{par}}, \ldots, X_{ch,L}^{\mathrm{par}} \right\},
$$

(3)

where $L = Nmax \cdot (3 \cdot n + 3 \cdot m + 1) + Rmax \cdot m$ is the length of the chromosome $\mathbf{X}_{ch}^{\mathrm{par}}$, $ch = 1, \ldots, \mu$ for the parent population or $ch = 1, \ldots, \lambda$ for the temporary population, $\{\bar{x}_{i,k}^{A}, \sigma_{i,k}^{A}\}$, $i = 1, \ldots, n$, $k = 1, \ldots, N$, are parameters of Gaussian membership functions $\mu_{A_i^k}(x_i)$ of the input fuzzy sets $A_1^k, \ldots, A_n^k$ (were used in our simulations), $\{\bar{y}_{j,k}^{B}, \sigma_{j,k}^{B}\}$, $k = 1, \ldots, N$, $j = 1, \ldots, m$, are parameters of Gaussian membership functions $\mu_{B_j^k}(y_j)$ of the output fuzzy sets $B_1^k, \ldots, B_m^k$, $Nmax$ is the maximum number of rules, $Rmax$ is the maximum number of discretization points. The maximum number of rules $Nmax$ should be selected individually to the problem from the range $[1, Nmax]$. Analogously, the maximum number of discretization points $Rmax$ should also be selected individually to the problem from the range $[1, Rmax]$ ([20,21,78]). The purpose of the algorithm is also to select the number of antecedents (from the range $[1, n]$) and consequents (from the range $[1, m]$) within each rule from rule base. The reduction of the system is done using additional chromosome $\mathbf{X}_{ch}^{\mathrm{red}}$. Its genes take binary values and indicate which rules, antecedents, consequents, inputs, and discretization points are selected. The chromosome $\mathbf{X}_{ch}^{\mathrm{red}}$ is given by

$$
\mathbf{X}_{ch}^{\mathrm{red}} = \left\{ \begin{array}{c}
x_1, \ldots, x_n, \\
A_1^1, \ldots, A_n^1, \ldots, A_1^{Nmax}, \ldots, A_n^{Nmax}, \\
B_1^1, \ldots, B_m^1, \ldots, B_1^{Nmax}, \ldots, B_m^{Nmax}, \\
\mathrm{rule}_1, \ldots, \mathrm{rule}_{Nmax}, \\
\bar{y}_{1,1}^{\mathrm{def}}, \ldots, \bar{y}_{1,Rmax}^{\mathrm{def}}, \ldots, \bar{y}_{m,1}^{\mathrm{def}}, \ldots, \bar{y}_{m,Rmax}^{\mathrm{def}}
\end{array} \right\} = \left\{ X_{ch,1}^{\mathrm{red}}, \ldots, X_{ch,L^{\mathrm{red}}}^{\mathrm{red}} \right\}, \quad (4)
$$

where $L^{\text{red}} = Nmax \cdot (n+m+1) + n + Rmax \cdot m$ is the length of the chromosome $\mathbf{X}_{ch}^{\text{red}}$. Its genes indicate which rules ($rule_k$, $k = 1, \ldots, Nmax$), antecedents (A_i^k, $i = 1, \ldots, n$, $k = 1, \ldots, Nmax$), consequents (B_j^k, $j = 1, \ldots, m$, $k = 1, \ldots, Nmax$), inputs ($\bar{x}_i$, $i = 1, \ldots, n$), and discretization points ($\bar{y}^r$, $r = 1, \ldots, Rmax$) are taken to the system. We can easily notice that the number of inputs used in the system and encoded in the chromosome ch can be determined as follows

$$n_{ch} = \sum_{i=1}^{n} \mathbf{X}_{ch}^{\text{red}} \{x_i\}, \tag{5}$$

where $\mathbf{X}_{ch}^{\text{red}} \{x_i\}$ means gene of the chromosome $\mathbf{X}_{ch}^{\text{red}}$ associated with the input x_i (as previously mentioned, if the value of the gene is 1, the associated input is taken into account during work of the system). The number of rules (N_{ch}) used in the system and encoded in the chromosome ch may be determined analogously. Implementation of the strategy (μ, λ) uses an additional chromosome

$$\sigma_{ch}^{\text{par}} = \left(\sigma_{ch,1}^{\text{par}}, \ldots, \sigma_{ch,L}^{\text{par}} \right). \tag{6}$$

This allows the implementation of the mechanism of self-adaptive range of mutation (see e.g. [78]). At the beginning of the operation of evolutionary strategy the range is large, while during the convergence its gradual reduction is observed. This results in a smooth transition from exploration (occurring at the beginning of the algorithm) to exploitation of the promising areas.

Evolution of Parameters and Structure. This hybrid population-based method allows for tuning both structure and parameters of system (2) with various interpretability criteria. It is worth to mention that: **(a)** An evolutionary strategy (μ, λ) is used for tuning the parameters of system (2). It processes chromosomes $\mathbf{X}_{ch}^{\text{par}}$ and σ_{ch}^{par} from the population $\mathbf{P}$, $\mathbf{T}$ and $\mathbf{O}$. The details about crossover and mutation operators from this strategy can be found in [78]. **(b)** For the structure evolution of system (2), a classic genetic algorithm is chosen. It processes chromosomes $\mathbf{X}_{ch}^{\text{red}}$ from the population $\mathbf{P}$, $\mathbf{T}$ and $\mathbf{O}$. The details about crossover and mutation operators from this strategy can be found in [58]. It is important to mention that genetic algorithm works together with evolutionary strategy (μ, λ) and it allows to reduce any element of the system structure, such as antecedences, consequents, inputs, rules and discretization points. **(c)** A bees algorithm is additionally used for tuning parameters of the system (2). It processes chromosomes $\mathbf{X}_{ch}^{\text{par}}$ from the population $\mathbf{B}$. The purpose of the use of the bees algorithm is to search neighbourhood around chromosomes from population $\mathbf{B}$ (chromosomes with reduced structure of the system) and replace them with fitter solutions. The details about bees algorithm can be found in [64]. **(d)** The important mechanism of our method is an evaluation process of the chromosomes from populations $\mathbf{P}$, $\mathbf{T}$, $\mathbf{O}$ and $\mathbf{B}$ described in next subsection. It takes into account an accuracy-interpretability trade-off and allows to obtain a balanced dependent from weights of the fitness function components solutions (see e.g. [30]).

Chromosome Population Evaluation. Each individual $\mathbf{X}_{ch}$ of the parental and temporary populations is represented by a sequence of chromosomes $\langle \mathbf{X}_{ch}^{par}, \sigma_{ch}^{par}, \mathbf{X}_{ch}^{red} \rangle$, given by formulas (3), (4) and (6). Genes of two first chromosomes take real values, whereas the genes of the last chromosome take integer values from the set $\{0, 1\}$. The system aims to minimize the following fitness function

$$\text{ff}\left(\mathbf{X}_{ch}\right) = T^* \left\{ \begin{array}{c} \text{ffaccuracy}\left(\mathbf{X}_{ch}\right), \text{ffinterpretability}\left(\mathbf{X}_{ch}\right); \\ w_{\text{ffaccuracy}}, w_{\text{ffinterpretability}} \end{array} \right\}, \qquad (7)$$

where $T^*\{\cdot\}$ is the algebraic weighted t-norm (see e.g. [20,21,78]), $w_{\text{ffaccuracy}} \in (0, 1]$ is a weight of the component $\text{ffaccuracy}\left(\mathbf{X}_{ch}\right)$ and $w_{\text{ffinterpretability}}$ is a weight of the component $\text{ffinterpretability}\left(\mathbf{X}_{ch}\right)$. The component $\text{ffaccuracy}\left(\mathbf{X}_{ch}\right)$ determines the accuracy of the system (2) i.e. average normalized percentage classification error for all data from learning sequence. A purpose of normalization of the component $\text{ffaccuracy}\left(\mathbf{X}_{ch}\right)$ is to ensure an influence on every component of the function (7). The component $\text{ffinterpretability}\left(\mathbf{X}_{ch}\right)$ determines complexity-based (component $\text{ffint}_A\left(\mathbf{X}_{ch}\right)$) and semantic-based (components $\text{ffint}_B\left(\mathbf{X}_{ch}\right)$-$\text{ffint}_G\left(\mathbf{X}_{ch}\right)$) interpretability of the system (2) encoded in the tested chromosome

$$\text{ffinterpretability}\left(\mathbf{X}_{ch}\right) =$$
$$T^* \left\{ \begin{array}{c} \text{ffint}_A\left(\mathbf{X}_{ch}\right), \text{ffint}_B\left(\mathbf{X}_{ch}\right), \text{ffint}_C\left(\mathbf{X}_{ch}\right), \text{ffint}_D\left(\mathbf{X}_{ch}\right), \\ \text{ffint}_E\left(\mathbf{X}_{ch}\right), \text{ffint}_F\left(\mathbf{X}_{ch}\right), \text{ffint}_G\left(\mathbf{X}_{ch}\right); \\ w_{\text{ffintA}}, w_{\text{ffintB}}, w_{\text{ffintC}}, w_{\text{ffintD}}, w_{\text{ffintE}}, w_{\text{ffintF}}, w_{\text{ffintG}} \end{array} \right\}, \qquad (8)$$

where $w_{\text{ffintA}} \in (0, 1]$ denotes weight of the component $\text{ffint}_A\left(\mathbf{X}_{ch}\right)$, etc. The individual components of the formula (8) are defined in the next section.

3 A New Interpretability Criteria for Neuro-Fuzzy System for Nonlinear Classification

In this section a new interpretability criteria for neuro-fuzzy system for nonlinear classification are described, each criterion is a component of fitness function responsible for interpretability (8) of the system. The criteria are defined as follows:

(a) The component $\text{ffint}_A\left(\mathbf{X}_{ch}\right)$ determines complexity of the system (2) i.e. a number of reduced elements of the system (rules, input fuzzy sets, output fuzzy sets, inputs, and discretization points) in relation to length of the chromosome $\mathbf{X}_{ch}^{red}$ (it allows to increase complexity-based interpretability)

$$ffint_A\left(\mathbf{X}_{ch}\right) = \frac{\left(\begin{array}{c} \sum\limits_{i=1}^{n} \mathbf{X}_{ch}^{\text{red}}\left\{x_i\right\} \cdot \sum\limits_{k=1}^{Nmax} \mathbf{X}_{ch}^{\text{red}}\left\{\text{rule}_k\right\} \cdot \mathbf{X}_{ch}^{\text{red}}\left\{A_i^k\right\}+ \\ + \sum\limits_{j=1}^{m} \sum\limits_{k=1}^{Nmax} \mathbf{X}_{ch}^{\text{red}}\left\{\text{rule}_k\right\} \cdot \mathbf{X}_{ch}^{\text{red}}\left\{B_j^k\right\}+ \\ + \sum\limits_{j=1}^{m} \sum\limits_{r=1}^{Rmax} \mathbf{X}_{ch}^{\text{red}}\left\{\bar{y}_{m,r}^{\text{def}}\right\} \end{array}\right)}{N_{ch} \cdot (n_{ch} + m) + m \cdot Rmax}, \tag{9}$$

where $\mathbf{X}_{ch}^{\text{red}}\left\{x_i\right\}$ means a gene of the chromosome $\mathbf{X}_{ch}^{\text{red}}$ associated with the input x_i, etc.

(b) The component $ffint_B\left(\mathbf{X}_{ch}\right)$ minimizes number of rules fired at the same time in the system (2) for fuzzy sets

$$ffint_B\left(\mathbf{X}_{ch}\right) = 1 - \frac{1}{Z} \sum_{z=1}^{Z} \frac{\left(\max\limits_{k=1,\ldots,Nmax}\left\{\mathbf{X}_{ch}^{\text{red}}\left\{\text{rule}_k\right\} \cdot \tau_k\left(\bar{\mathbf{x}}_z\right)\right\}\right)^2}{\sum\limits_{k=1}^{Nmax} \mathbf{X}_{ch}^{\text{red}}\left\{\text{rule}_k\right\} \cdot \tau_k\left(\bar{\mathbf{x}}_z\right)}, \tag{10}$$

where $\bar{\mathbf{x}}_z$ is a vector of input signals learning sequence ($z = 1, \ldots, Z$), Z is the number of samples of learning sequence and $\tau_k\left(\bar{\mathbf{x}}_z\right)$ is the flexible firing strength of the k-th rule described by the formula

$$\tau_k\left(\bar{\mathbf{x}}\right) = \mu_{\mathbf{A}^k}\left(\bar{\mathbf{x}}\right) = \overset{n}{\underset{i=1}{T^*}}\left\{\mu_{A_i^k}\left(\bar{x}_i\right); w_{k,i}^A\right\}. \tag{11}$$

(c) The component $ffint_C\left(\mathbf{X}_{ch}\right)$ maximizes a fitness of training data to input fuzzy sets of the system (2) encoded in the tested chromosome

$$ffint_C\left(\mathbf{X}_{ch}\right) = \frac{\sum\limits_{z=1}^{Z} \sum\limits_{i=1}^{n} \mathbf{X}_{ch}^{\text{red}}\left\{x_i\right\} \cdot \left(1 - \max\limits_{k=1,\ldots,Nmax}\left\{\mathbf{X}_{ch}^{\text{red}}\left\{\text{rule}_k\right\} \cdot \mu_{A_i^k}\left(\bar{x}_{z,i}\right)\right\}\right)}{Z \cdot n_{ch}}. \tag{12}$$

(d) The component $ffint_D\left(\mathbf{X}_{ch}\right)$ reduces overlapping of input and output fuzzy sets of the system (2) encoded in the tested chromosome

$$\text{ffint}_D\left(\mathbf{X}_{ch}\right) =$$

$$\frac{1}{4} \cdot \left(\frac{\displaystyle\sum_{i=1}^{n_{ch}} \sum_{k=1}^{\text{noifs}(i)-1} \left(\left| c_{\text{ffintc}} - \exp\left(-\left(\frac{\mathbf{X}_{ch}^{\text{supp}}\left\{\bar{x}_{i,k}^{A}\right\} - \mathbf{X}_{ch}^{\text{supp}}\left\{\bar{x}_{i,k+1}^{A}\right\}}{\mathbf{X}_{ch}^{\text{supp}}\left\{\sigma_{i,k}^{A}\right\} + \mathbf{X}_{ch}^{\text{supp}}\left\{\sigma_{i,k+1}^{A}\right\}} \right)^{2} \right) \right| + \\ \left| -\exp\left(-\left(\frac{\mathbf{X}_{ch}^{\text{supp}}\left\{\bar{x}_{i,k}^{A}\right\} - \mathbf{X}_{ch}^{\text{supp}}\left\{\bar{x}_{i,k+1}^{A}\right\}}{\mathbf{X}_{ch}^{\text{supp}}\left\{\sigma_{i,k}^{A}\right\} - \mathbf{X}_{ch}^{\text{supp}}\left\{\sigma_{i,k+1}^{A}\right\}} \right)^{2} \right) \right| \right)}{\displaystyle\sum_{i=1}^{n_{ch}} (\text{noifs}(i)-1)} + \right.$$

$$\left. + \frac{\displaystyle\sum_{j=1}^{m} \sum_{k=1}^{\text{noofs}(j)-1} \left(\left| c_{\text{ffintc}} - \exp\left(-\left(\frac{\mathbf{X}_{ch}^{\text{supp}}\left\{\bar{y}_{j,k}^{B}\right\} - \mathbf{X}_{ch}^{\text{supp}}\left\{\bar{y}_{j,k+1}^{B}\right\}}{\mathbf{X}_{ch}^{\text{supp}}\left\{\sigma_{j,k}^{B}\right\} + \mathbf{X}_{ch}^{\text{supp}}\left\{\sigma_{j,k+1}^{B}\right\}} \right)^{2} \right) \right| + \\ \left| -\exp\left(-\left(\frac{\mathbf{X}_{ch}^{\text{supp}}\left\{\bar{y}_{j,k}^{B}\right\} - \mathbf{X}_{ch}^{\text{supp}}\left\{\bar{y}_{j,k+1}^{B}\right\}}{\mathbf{X}_{ch}^{\text{supp}}\left\{\sigma_{j,k}^{B}\right\} - \mathbf{X}_{ch}^{\text{supp}}\left\{\sigma_{j,k+1}^{B}\right\}} \right)^{2} \right) \right| \right)}{\displaystyle\sum_{j=1}^{m} (\text{noofs}(j)-1)} \right),$$

$$\tag{13}$$

where $\mathbf{X}_{ch}^{\text{supp}}$ stands for additional chromosome with list of non-reduced fuzzy sets

$$\mathbf{X}_{ch}^{\text{supp}} = \left\{ \begin{array}{c} \bar{x}_{1,1}^{A}, \sigma_{1,1}^{A}, \bar{x}_{1,2}^{A}, \sigma_{1,2}^{A}, \ldots, \\ \bar{x}_{n_{ch},1}^{A}, \sigma_{n_{ch},1}^{A}, \bar{x}_{n_{ch},2}^{A}, \sigma_{n_{ch},2}^{A}, \ldots, \\ \bar{y}_{1,1}^{B}, \sigma_{1,1}^{B}, \bar{y}_{2,N_{ch}}^{B}, \sigma_{2,N_{ch}}^{B}, \ldots, \\ \bar{y}_{m,N_{ch}}^{B}, \sigma_{m,N_{ch}}^{B}, \bar{y}_{2,N_{ch}}^{B}, \sigma_{2,N_{ch}}^{B}, \ldots \end{array} \right\} = \left\{ X_{ch,1}^{\text{supp}}, \ldots, X_{ch,L^{\text{supp}}}^{\text{supp}} \right\}, \tag{14}$$

where $L^{\text{supp}} = 2 \cdot \left(\displaystyle\sum_{i=1}^{n_{ch}} \text{noifs}\,(i) + \displaystyle\sum_{j=1}^{m} \text{noofs}\,(j) \right)$ stands for length of the chromosome $\mathbf{X}_{ch}^{\text{supp}}$. Moreover, a number of fuzzy sets for input i from equation (13) can be reached using function $\text{noifs}\,(i)$ defined as follows

$$\text{noifs}\,(i) = \sum_{k=1}^{N_{ch}} \mathbf{X}_{ch}^{\text{red}}\left\{\text{rule}_{k}\right\} \cdot \mathbf{X}_{ch}^{\text{red}}\left\{A_{i}^{k}\right\}. \tag{15}$$

A number of fuzzy sets for output j can be calculated analogously. The lists of parameters encoded in the chromosome $\mathbf{X}_{ch}^{\text{supp}}$ does not have specified final elements - their amount depends on a structure of the chromosome $\mathbf{X}_{ch}^{\text{red}}$. It is worth to mention that lists of parameters are sorted by centres of fuzzy sets. Single rows from the $\mathbf{X}_{ch}^{\text{supp}}$ contain parameters connected with specified input and output fuzzy sets. Due to that this approach is different from the one that uses chromosome $\mathbf{X}_{ch}^{\text{red}}$.

(e) The component $\text{ffint}_E\left(\mathbf{X}_{ch}\right)$ increases the integrity of the shape of the input and output fuzzy sets associated with the inputs and outputs of the system (2) encoded in the tested chromosome

$$
\mathrm{ffint}_D\left(\mathbf{X}_{ch}\right) =
$$

$$
\left(\begin{array}{c}
\displaystyle\sum_{i=1}^{n} \mathbf{X}_{ch}^{\mathrm{red}}\left\{x_i\right\} \cdot \sum_{k1=1}^{Nmax} \mathbf{X}_{ch}^{\mathrm{red}}\left\{\mathrm{rule}_{k1}\right\} \cdot \\[2mm]
\cdot \left(1 - \dfrac{\min\left(\mathbf{X}_{ch}^{\mathrm{par}}\left\{\sigma_{i,k1}^{A}\right\}, \frac{1}{N_{ch}} \sum\limits_{k2=1}^{Nmax}\left(\mathbf{X}_{ch}^{\mathrm{red}}\left\{\mathrm{rule}_{k2}\right\}\cdot\mathbf{X}_{ch}^{\mathrm{par}}\left\{\sigma_{i,k2}^{A}\right\}\right)\right)}{\max\left(\mathbf{X}_{ch}^{\mathrm{par}}\left\{\sigma_{i,k1}^{A}\right\}, \frac{1}{N_{ch}} \sum\limits_{k2=1}^{Nmax}\left(\mathbf{X}_{ch}^{\mathrm{red}}\left\{\mathrm{rule}_{k2}\right\}\cdot\mathbf{X}_{ch}^{\mathrm{par}}\left\{\sigma_{i,k2}^{A}\right\}\right)\right)}\right) + \\[2mm]
\dfrac{\sum\limits_{k1=1}^{Nmax} \mathbf{X}_{ch}^{\mathrm{red}}\left\{\mathrm{rule}_{k1}\right\} \cdot }{} \\[2mm]
+ \displaystyle\sum_{j=1}^{m} \cdot \left(1 - \dfrac{\min \mathbf{X}_{ch}^{\mathrm{par}}\left\{\sigma_{j,k1}^{B}\right\}, \frac{1}{N_{ch}} \sum\limits_{k2=1}^{Nmax}\left(\mathbf{X}_{ch}^{\mathrm{red}}\left\{\mathrm{rule}_{k2}\right\}\cdot\mathbf{X}_{ch}^{\mathrm{par}}\left\{\sigma_{j,k2}^{B}\right\}\right)}{\max\left(\mathbf{X}_{ch}^{\mathrm{par}}\left\{\sigma_{j,k1}^{B}\right\}, \frac{1}{N_{ch}} \sum\limits_{k2=1}^{Nmax}\left(\mathbf{X}_{ch}^{\mathrm{red}}\left\{\mathrm{rule}_{k2}\right\}\cdot\mathbf{X}_{ch}^{\mathrm{par}}\left\{\sigma_{j,k2}^{B}\right\}\right)\right)}\right) \\[2mm]
\hline
n_{ch}+m
\end{array}\right), \quad (16)
$$

where $\mathbf{X}_{ch}^{\mathrm{par}}\left\{\sigma_{i,k}^{A}\right\}$ stands for a gene of the chromosome $\mathbf{X}_{ch}^{\mathrm{par}}$ associated with the parameter $\sigma_{i,k}^{A}$ (the width of the Gaussian function used in the simulations), $\mathbf{X}_{ch}^{\mathrm{par}}\left\{\sigma_{j,k}^{B}\right\}$ means gene of the chromosome $\mathbf{X}_{ch}^{\mathrm{par}}$ associated with the parameter $\sigma_{j,k}^{B}$.

(f) The component $\mathrm{ffint}_F\left(\mathbf{X}_{ch}\right)$ increases complementarity of the input fuzzy sets of system (2) encoded in the tested chromosome

$$
\mathrm{ffint}_F\left(\mathbf{X}_{ch}\right) = \frac{\displaystyle\sum_{z=1}^{Z}\sum_{i=1}^{n}\left(\cdot\max\left(1, \left|1 - \dfrac{\mathbf{X}_{ch}^{\mathrm{red}}\left\{x_i\right\}\cdot}{\displaystyle\sum_{k=1}^{Nmax}\mathbf{X}_{ch}^{\mathrm{red}}\left\{\mathrm{rule}_k\right\}\cdot\mu_{A_i^k}\left(\bar{x}_{z,i}\right)}\right|\right)\right)}{Z\cdot n_{ch}}.
$$
$$(17)$$

(g) The component $\mathrm{ffint}_G\left(\mathbf{X}_{ch}\right)$ increases readability of the antecedents and weights of rules of system (2) encoded in the tested chromosome

$$
\mathrm{ffint}_G\left(\mathbf{X}_{ch}\right) = 1 - \dfrac{\left(\begin{array}{c}\displaystyle\sum_{k=1}^{Nmax}\mathbf{X}_{ch}^{\mathrm{red}}\left\{\mathrm{rule}_k\right\}\cdot\left(\dfrac{\sum\limits_{i=1}^{n}\mathbf{X}_{ch}^{\mathrm{red}}\left\{x_i\right\}\cdot\mu_w\left(w_{i,k}^{A}\right)}{n_{ch}}\right) + \\[2mm] + \displaystyle\sum_{k=1}^{Nmax}\mathbf{X}_{ch}^{\mathrm{red}}\left\{\mathrm{rule}_k\right\}\cdot\mu_w\left(w_k^{\mathrm{rule}}\right)\end{array}\right)}{2\cdot N_{ch}}, \quad (18)
$$

where $\mu_w\left(w_{i,k}^{A}\right)$ is a function defining congeries around values 0, 0.5 and 1 (in simulations we assumed that $a = 0.25$, $b = 0.50$ i $c = 0.75$). This function is described as follows

$$
\mu_w\left(x\right) = \begin{cases} \frac{a-x}{a} & \text{for } x \geq 0 \text{ and } x \leq a \\ \frac{x-a}{b-a} & \text{for } x \geq a \text{ and } x \leq b \\ \frac{c-x}{c-b} & \text{for } x \geq b \text{ and } x \leq c \\ \frac{x-c}{1-c} & \text{for } x \geq c \text{ and } x \leq 1 \end{cases} . \quad (19)
$$

Table 1. Values of the weights of the components ffaccuracy $(\mathbf{X}_{ch})$ and ffinterpretability $(\mathbf{X}_{ch})$ for variants considered in simulation: Case I-Case V. Weights of remaining criteria was set as follows: $w_{\text{ffintA}} = 0.50$, $w_{\text{ffintB}} = 0.10$, $w_{\text{ffintC}} = 0.10$, $w_{\text{ffintD}} = 1.00$, $w_{\text{ffintE}} = 1.00$, $w_{\text{ffintF}} = 0.10$, $w_{\text{ffintG}} = 0.20$.

Name of the weight	Case I	Case II	Case III	Case IV	Case V
ffaccuracy $(\mathbf{X}_{ch})$	1.00	1.00	1.00	0.75	0.25
ffinterpretability $(\mathbf{X}_{ch})$	0.25	0.75	1.00	1.00	1.00

Table 2. The accuracy (%) of the neuro-fuzzy classifier (2) for learning phase, testing phase and average value of them both for simulation variants Case I-Case V

Problem	Sequence	Case					Other authors testing results
		I	II	III	IV	V	
wine	testing	92.21	91.53	90.59	88.48	87.88	85.00-98.61
recognition	learning	98.95	98.70	98.73	98.31	97.50	[43,70]
problem	average	95.58	95.11	94.66	93.39	92.69	
glass	testing	73.81	71.98	64.29	59.43	50.08	49.99-74.00
identification	learning	76.77	75.19	73.10	71.09	68.86	[17,43,70]
problem	average	75.29	73.58	68.69	65.26	59.47	
Pima Indians	testing	75.39	74.92	73.34	70.86	69.08	45.90-80.00
diabetes	learning	79.40	78.61	77.10	74.56	71.63	[17,44]
problem	average	77.40	76.77	75.22	72.71	70.35	
iris	testing	93.33	93.00	91.33	90.83	88.50	81.80-97.84
classification	learning	98.42	98.59	98.15	98.24	98.24	[17,40]
problem	average	95.88	95.80	94.74	94.54	93.37	
Wisconsin	testing	96.27	96.12	95.90	95.72	95.56	90.00-97.24
breast cancer	learning	97.97	97.83	97.94	97.42	96.88	[40,70]
problem	average	97.12	96.97	96.92	96.57	96.22	

4   Simulation Results

In our simulations we considered five typical problems from field of nonlinear classification ([56]): **(a)** wine recognition problem, **(b)** glass identification problem, **(c)** Pima Indians diabetes problem, **(d)** iris classification problem, **(e)** Wisconsin breast cancer problem. For each problem a 10-fold cross validation was used, and the process was repeated 5 times. Moreover, for each simulation problem a five variants of learning were applied. Each variant had different set of weights of fitness function (7) - see Table 1. These variants can be described as follows: **(a)** Case "high accuracy", where an accuracy component (2) is the most important in the chromosome evaluation (marked further as "Case I"). **(b)** Case "high interpretability", where the interpretability component (2) is the most important in the chromosome evaluation ("Case V"). **(c)** Case "balanced accuracy and interpretability", where both components of the fitness function have the same meaning (equal values of the weights) ("Case III"). **(d)** Two cases between

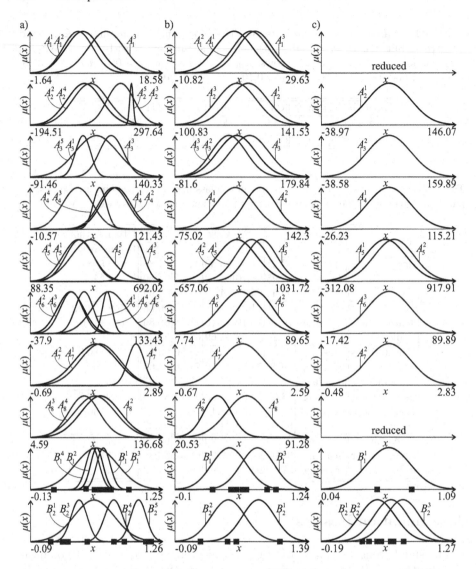

Fig. 1. Example input and output fuzzy sets of the neuro-fuzzy system (2) for the Pima Indians diabetes problem for three various settings of the function (7): a) Case I, b) Case III, c) Case V. The position of the discretization points was marked as black rectangles.

described above cases: Case II (case between Case I and Case III), Case IV (case between Case III and Case V). Obtained results are presented on Fig. 3 and in Table 2. Other relevant simulation properties can be summarized as follows: (a) For the system (2) algebraic triangular norms were used. (b) The following properties of evolutionary algorithm were assumed: the number of chromosomes in the population was set to 100, the algorithm performs 10 000 steps (gener-

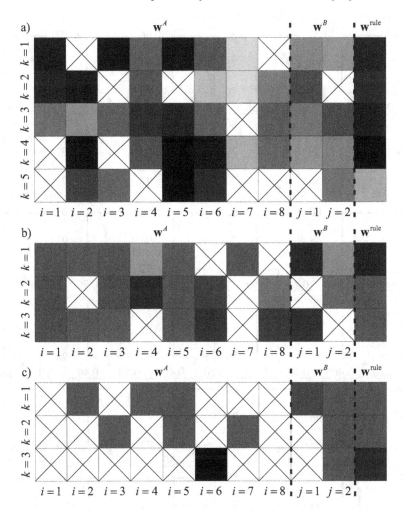

Fig. 2. Example weights representation in the neuro-fuzzy system (2) (dark areas correspond to low values of weights and vice versa) for Pima Indians diabetes problem for different weights configuration of the function (7): a) Case I, b) Case III, c) Case V

ations), the crossover probability was set as $p_c = 0.8$, the mutation probability was set as $p_m = 0.2$, the mutation intensity was set as $\sigma = 0.3$.

The conclusions from simulations can be summarized as follows: **(a)** The effect of the weights of (7) is significant, which can be seen on Fig. 3. **(b)** Case III from the simulations allowed to reach good interpretability of fuzzy sets (see Fig. 1 and Fig. 2) and high accuracy (see Table 2). **(c)** Case I allowed (as expected) to achieve significantly higher accuracy of the system (see Table 2) in comparison with other cases and satisfactory results in comparison with other authors' results.

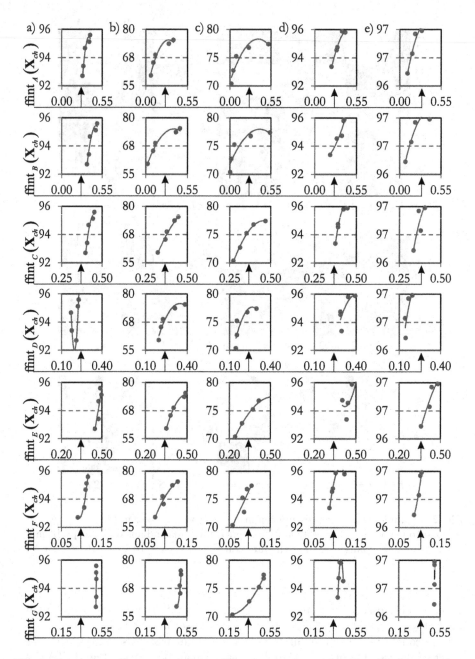

Fig. 3. Dependence between accuracy (%) of neuro-fuzzy classifier (2) (average for learning and testing phase) and values of interpretability components ffint$_A$ ($\mathbf{X}_{ch}$)-ffint$_G$ ($\mathbf{X}_{ch}$) for considered simulation variants Case I-Case V for following simulation problems: a) wine recognition problem, b) glass identification problem, c) Pima Indians diabetes problem, d) iris classification problem, e) Wisconsin breast cancer problem

5   Conclusions

In this paper, we proposed a new approach to the construction of interpretable neuro-fuzzy systems for nonlinear classification. It allows to select a structure and parameters of the neuro-fuzzy classifier. Moreover, it allows to take into account different interpretability criteria. The method for selection and configuration of those criteria is very flexible. Due to that fact it allows to obtain the balance between accuracy and interpretability of neuro-fuzzy system classifier in a convenient way. Simulations confirmed the effectiveness of the proposed approach.

Acknowledgment. The project was financed by the National Science Centre (Poland) on the basis of the decision number DEC-2012/05/B/ST7/02138.

References

1. Alonso, J.M.: Embedding HILK in a three-objective evolutionary algorithm with the aim of modeling highly interpretable fuzzy rule-based classifiers, pp. 15–20. European Centre for Soft Computing (2010)
2. Alonso, J.M., Cordon, O., Quirin, A., Magdalena, L.: Analyzing interpretability of fuzzy rule-based systems by means of fuzzy inference-grams. In: 1st World Conference on Soft Computing, pp. 181.1–181.8 (2011)
3. Alonso, J.M., Magdalena, L., Guillaume, S.: HILK: A new methodology for designing highly interpretable linguistic knowledge bases using the fuzzy logic formalism. International Journal of Intelligent Systems 23(7), 761–794 (2008)
4. Aziz, D., Ali, M.A.M., Gan, K.B., Saiboon, I.: Initialization of Adaptive Neuro-Fuzzy Inference System Using Fuzzy Clustering in Predicting Primary Triage Category. In: 2012 4th International Conference on Intelligent and Advanced Systems (ICIAS), pp. 170–174. Dept. of Electr., Electron. & Syst. Eng., Univ. Kebangsaan (2012)
5. Bartczuk, Ł., Dziwiński, P., Starczewski, J.T.: New method for generation type-2 fuzzy partition for FDT. In: Rutkowski, L., Scherer, R., Tadeusiewicz, R., Zadeh, L.A., Zurada, J.M. (eds.) ICAISC 2010, Part I. LNCS (LNAI), vol. 6113, pp. 275–280. Springer, Heidelberg (2010)
6. Bartczuk, Ł., Dziwiński, P., Starczewski, J.T.: A new method for dealing with unbalanced linguistic term set. In: Rutkowski, L., Korytkowski, M., Scherer, R., Tadeusiewicz, R., Zadeh, L.A., Zurada, J.M. (eds.) ICAISC 2012, Part I. LNCS, vol. 7267, pp. 207–212. Springer, Heidelberg (2012)
7. Bilski, J.: Momentum modification of the RLS algorithms. In: Rutkowski, L., Siekmann, J.H., Tadeusiewicz, R., Zadeh, L.A. (eds.) ICAISC 2004. LNCS (LNAI), vol. 3070, pp. 151–157. Springer, Heidelberg (2004)
8. Bilski, J., Rutkowski, L.: Numerically robust learning algorithms for feed forward neural networks. Advances in Soft Computing, pp. 149–154 (2003)
9. Bilski, J., Smoląg, J.: Parallel realisation of the recurrent RTRN neural network learning. In: Rutkowski, L., Tadeusiewicz, R., Zadeh, L.A., Zurada, J.M. (eds.) ICAISC 2008. LNCS (LNAI), vol. 5097, pp. 11–16. Springer, Heidelberg (2008)

10. Bilski, J., Smoląg, J.: Parallel Realisation of the Recurrent Elman Neural Network Learning. In: Rutkowski, L., Scherer, R., Tadeusiewicz, R., Zadeh, L.A., Zurada, J.M. (eds.) ICAISC 2010, Part II. LNCS (LNAI), vol. 6114, pp. 19–25. Springer, Heidelberg (2010)

11. Bilski, J., Smoląg, J.: Parallel Realisation of the Recurrent Multi Layer Perceptron Learning. In: Rutkowski, L., Korytkowski, M., Scherer, R., Tadeusiewicz, R., Zadeh, L.A., Zurada, J.M. (eds.) ICAISC 2012, Part I. LNCS (LNAI), vol. 7267, pp. 12–20. Springer, Heidelberg (2012)

12. Bilski, J., Smoląg, J.: Parallel approach to learning of the recurrent jordan neural network. In: Rutkowski, L., Korytkowski, M., Scherer, R., Tadeusiewicz, R., Zadeh, L.A., Zurada, J.M. (eds.) ICAISC 2013, Part I. LNCS (LNAI), vol. 7894, pp. 32–40. Springer, Heidelberg (2013)

13. Bilski, J., Smoląg, J.: Parallel architectures for learning the RTRN and Elman dynamic neural networks. IEEE Trans. Parallel and Distributed Systems PP(99) (2014)

14. Bilski, J., Smoląg, J., Galushkin, A.I.: The Parallel Approach to the Conjugate Gradient Learning Algorithm for the Feedforward Neural Networks. In: Rutkowski, L., Korytkowski, M., Scherer, R., Tadeusiewicz, R., Zadeh, L.A., Zurada, J.M. (eds.) ICAISC 2014, Part I. LNCS (LNAI), vol. 8467, pp. 12–21. Springer, Heidelberg (2014)

15. Bilski, J., Litwiński, S., Smoląg, J.: Parallel realisation of QR algorithm for neural networks learning. In: Rutkowski, L., Siekmann, J.H., Tadeusiewicz, R., Zadeh, L.A. (eds.) ICAISC 2004. LNCS (LNAI), vol. 3070, pp. 158–165. Springer, Heidelberg (2004)

16. Bartczuk, Ł., Przybył, A., Koprinkova-Hristova, P.: New method for nonlinear fuzzy correction modelling of dynamic objects. In: Rutkowski, L., Korytkowski, M., Scherer, R., Tadeusiewicz, R., Zadeh, L.A., Zurada, J.M. (eds.) ICAISC 2014, Part I. LNCS (LNAI), vol. 8467, pp. 169–180. Springer, Heidelberg (2014)

17. Bostanci, B., Bostanci, E.: An Evaluation of Classification Algorithms Using Mc Nemar's Test. In: Bansal, J.C., Singh, P.K., Deep, K., Pant, M., Nagar, A.K. (eds.) Proceedings of Seventh International Conference on Bio-Inspired Computing: Theories and Applications (BIC-TA 2012). AISC, vol. 201, pp. 15–26. Springer, India (2013)

18. Chen, J.L., Hou, Y.L., Xing, Z.Y., Jia, L.M., Tong, Z.Z.: A Multi-objective Genetic-based Method for Design Fuzzy Classification Systems. IJCSNS International Journal of Computer Science and Network Security 6(8), 110–117 (2006)

19. Cpałka, K., Łapa, K., Przybył, A., Zalasiński, M., Rutkowski, L.: A new method for designing neuro-fuzzy systems for nonlinear modelling with interpretability aspects. Neurocomputing 135, 203–217 (2014)

20. Cpałka, K.: A New Method for Design and Reduction of Neuro-Fuzzy Classification Systems. IEEE Transactions on Neural Networks 20, 701–714 (2009)

21. Cpałka, K.: On evolutionary designing and learning of flexible neuro-fuzzy structures for nonlinear classification. Nonlinear Analysis Series A: Theory, Methods and Applications 71, 1659–1672 (2009)

22. Cpałka, K., Zalasiński, M.: On-line signature verification using vertical signature partitioning. Expert Systems with Applications 41, 4170–4180 (2014)

23. Cpałka, K., Zalasiński, M., Rutkowski, L.: New method for the on-line signature verification based on horizontal partitioning. Pattern Recognition 47, 2652–2661 (2014)

24. Dziwiński, P., Bartczuk, Ł., Starczewski, J.T.: Fully controllable ant colony system for text data clustering. In: Rutkowski, L., Korytkowski, M., Scherer, R., Tadeusiewicz, R., Zadeh, L.A., Zurada, J.M. (eds.) SIDE 2012 and EC 2012. LNCS, vol. 7269, pp. 199–205. Springer, Heidelberg (2012)

25. Dziwiński, P., Starczewski, J.T., Bartczuk, Ł.: New linguistic hedges in construction of interval type-2 FLS. In: Rutkowski, L., Scherer, R., Tadeusiewicz, R., Zadeh, L.A., Zurada, J.M. (eds.) ICAISC 2010, Part II. LNCS (LNAI), vol. 6114, pp. 445–450. Springer, Heidelberg (2010)

26. Dziwiński, P., Bartczuk, Ł., Przybył, A., Avedyan, E.D.: A New Algorithm for Identification of Significant Operating Points Using Swarm Intelligence. In: Rutkowski, L., Korytkowski, M., Scherer, R., Tadeusiewicz, R., Zadeh, L.A., Zurada, J.M. (eds.) ICAISC 2014, Part II. LNCS (LNAI), vol. 8468, pp. 349–362. Springer, Heidelberg (2014)

27. El-Abd, M.: On the hybridization on the artificial bee colony and particle swarm optimization algorithms. Journal of Artificial Intelligence and Soft Computing Research 2(2), 147–155 (2012)

28. Fazzolari, M., Alcalá, R., Herrera, F.: A multi-objective evolutionary method for learning granularities based on fuzzy discretization to improve the accuracy-complexity trade-off of fuzzy rule-based classification systems: D-MOFARC algorithm. Applied Soft Computing 24, 470–481 (2014)

29. Gabryel, M., Cpałka, K., Rutkowski, L.: Evolutionary strategies for learning of neuro-fuzzy systems. In: Proceedings of the I Workshop on Genetic Fuzzy Systems, Granada, pp. 119–123 (2005)

30. Gacto, M.J., Alcalá, R., Herrera, F.: Interpretability of linguistic fuzzy rule-based systems: An overview of interpretability measures. Information Sciences 181, 4340–4360 (2011)

31. Gacto, M.J., Alcalá, R., Herrera, F.: A Multiobjective Evolutionary Algorithm for Tuning Fuzzy Rule Based Systems with Measures for Preserving Interpretability. In: Proc. of the Joint International Fuzzy Systems Association World Congress and the European Society for Fuzzy Logic and Technology Conference (IFSA/EUSFLAT 2009) (2009)

32. Gałkowski, T.: Kernel estimation of regression functions in the boundary regions. In: Rutkowski, L., Korytkowski, M., Scherer, R., Tadeusiewicz, R., Zadeh, L.A., Zurada, J.M. (eds.) ICAISC 2013, Part II. LNCS (LNAI), vol. 7895, pp. 158–166. Springer, Heidelberg (2013)

33. Galkowski, T., Pawlak, M.: Nonparametric function fitting in the presence of nonstationary noise. In: Rutkowski, L., Korytkowski, M., Scherer, R., Tadeusiewicz, R., Zadeh, L.A., Zurada, J.M. (eds.) ICAISC 2014, Part I. LNCS (LNAI), vol. 8467, pp. 531–538. Springer, Heidelberg (2014)

34. Galkowski, T., Rutkowski, L.: Nonparametric fitting of multivariate functions. IEEE Trans. Automatic Control AC-31(8), 785–787 (1986)

35. Gao, M., Hong, X., Harris, C.J.: Construction of Neurofuzzy Models For Imbalanced Data Classification. IEEE Transactions on Fuzzy Systems 22(6), 1472–1488 (2014)

36. Ghandar, A., Michalewicz, Z.: An experimental study of Multi-Objective Evolutionary Algorithms for balancing interpretability and accuracy in fuzzy rule base classifiers for financial prediction. In: 2011 IEEE Symposium on Computational Intelligence for Financial Engineering and Economics, pp. 1–6 (2011)

37. Gorzałczany, M.B., Rudziński, F.: Accuracy vs. interpretability of fuzzy rule-based classifiers: An evolutionary approach. In: Rutkowski, L., Korytkowski, M.,

Scherer, R., Tadeusiewicz, R., Zadeh, L.A., Zurada, J.M. (eds.) EC 2012 and SIDE 2012. LNCS, vol. 7269, pp. 222–230. Springer, Heidelberg (2012)

38. Grycuk, R., Gabryel, M., Korytkowski, M., Scherer, R., Voloshynovskiy, S.: From single image to list of objects based on edge and blob detection. In: Rutkowski, L., Korytkowski, M., Scherer, R., Tadeusiewicz, R., Zadeh, L.A., Zurada, J.M. (eds.) ICAISC 2014, Part II. LNCS (LNAI), vol. 8468, pp. 605–615. Springer, Heidelberg (2014)

39. Guillaume, S., Charnomordic, B.: Generating an Interpretable Family of Fuzzy Partitions From Data. IEEE Transactions on Fuzzy Systems 12(3), 324–335 (2004)

40. Hossen, J., Sayeed, S., Yusof, I., Kalaiarasi, S.M.A.: A Framework of Modified Adaptive Fuzzy Inference Engine (MAFIE) and Its Application. International Journal of Computer Information Systems and Industrial Management Applications 5, 662–670 (2013)

41. Icke, I., Rosenberg, A.: Multi-objective Genetic Programming for Visual Analytics. In: Silva, S., Foster, J.A., Nicolau, M., Machado, P., Giacobini, M. (eds.) EuroGP 2011. LNCS, vol. 6621, pp. 322–334. Springer, Heidelberg (2011)

42. Ishibuchi, H., Nakashima, T.: Effect of the rule weights in fuzzy rule-based classification systems. IEEE Trans. Fuzzy Syst. 9, 506–515 (2001)

43. Jensen, R., Cornelis, C.: Fuzzy-Rough Nearest Neighbour Classification. In: Peters, J.F., Skowron, A., Chan, C.-C., Grzymala-Busse, J.W., Ziarko, W.P. (eds.) Transactions on Rough Sets XIII. LNCS, vol. 6499, pp. 56–72. Springer, Heidelberg (2011)

44. Kalaiselvi, C., Nasira, G.M.: A Novel Approach for the Diagnosis of Diabetes and Liver Cancer using ANFIS and Improved KNN. Research Journal of Applied Sciences, Engineering and Technology 8(2), 243–250 (2014)

45. Kaur, G.: Similarity measure of different types of fuzzy sets. School of Mathematics and Computer Applications, Tharpar University (2010)

46. Kenesei, T., Abonyi, J.: Interpetable Support Vector Machines in Regression and Classification - Application In Process Engineering. Hungarian Journal of Industrial Chemistry, Veszprém 35, 101–108 (2007)

47. Korytkowski, M., Nowicki, R., Rutkowski, L., Scherer, R.: AdaBoost Ensemble of DCOG Rough–Neuro–Fuzzy Systems. In: Jędrzejowicz, P., Nguyen, N.T., Hoang, K. (eds.) ICCCI 2011, Part I. LNCS, vol. 6922, pp. 62–71. Springer, Heidelberg (2011)

48. Korytkowski, M., Nowicki, R., Scherer, R.: Neuro-fuzzy rough classifier ensemble. In: Alippi, C., Polycarpou, M., Panayiotou, C., Ellinas, G. (eds.) ICANN 2009, Part I. LNCS, vol. 5768, pp. 817–823. Springer, Heidelberg (2009)

49. Kumar, G., Rani, P., Devaraj, C., Victoire, D.: Hybrid Ant Bee Algorithm for Fuzzy Expert System Based Sample Classification. IEEE/ACM Transactions on Computational Biology and Bioinformatics 11(2), 347–360 (2014)

50. Laskowski, Ł., Laskowska, M.: Functionalization of SBA-15 mesoporous silica by Cu-phosphonate units: Probing of synthesis route. Journal of Solid State Chemistry 220, 221–226 (2014)

51. Laskowski, Ł., Laskowska, M., Jelonkiewicz, J., Boullanger, A.: Spin-glass implementation of a Hopfield neural structure. In: Rutkowski, L., Korytkowski, M., Scherer, R., Tadeusiewicz, R., Zadeh, L.A., Zurada, J.M. (eds.) ICAISC 2014, Part I. LNCS (LNAI), vol. 8467, pp. 89–96. Springer, Heidelberg (2014)

52. Łapa, K., Zalasiński, M., Cpałka, K.: A new method for designing and complexity reduction of neuro-fuzzy systems for nonlinear modelling. In: Rutkowski, L., Korytkowski, M., Scherer, R., Tadeusiewicz, R., Zadeh, L.A., Zurada, J.M. (eds.)

ICAISC 2013, Part I. LNCS (LNAI), vol. 7894, pp. 329–344. Springer, Heidelberg (2013)

53. Lobato, F.S., Steffen Jr., V.: A new multi-objective optimization algorithm based on differential evolution and neighborhood exploring evolution strategy. Journal of Artificial Intelligence and Soft Computing Research 1(4), 259–267 (2011)

54. Lobato, F.S., Steffen Jr., V., Silva Neto, A.J.: Solution of singular optimal control problems using the improved differential evolution algorithm. Journal of Artificial Intelligence and Soft Computing Research 1(3), 195–206 (2011)

55. Luukka, P.: A New Nonlinear Fuzzy Robust PCA Algorithm and Similarity Classifier in Classification of Medical Data Sets. International Journal of Fuzzy Systems 13(3), 153–163 (2011)

56. Machine Learning Repository [Online], https://archive.ics.uci.edu/ml/datasets.html (accessed: December 16, 2014)

57. Marquez, A.A., Marquez, F.A., Peregrin, A.: A multi-objective evolutionary algorithm with an interpretability improvement mechanism for linguistic fuzzy systems with adaptive defuzzification. In: 2010 IEEE International Conference on Fuzzy Systems (FUZZ), pp. 1–7 (2010)

58. Michalewicz, Z.: Genetic Algorithms + Data Structures = Evolution Programs. Springer (1999)

59. Nauck, D., Kruse, R.: How the Learning of the RuleWeight Affects the Interpretability of the Fuzzy Systems. In: Proceedings of 1998 IEEE International Conference on Fuzzy Systems, vol. 2, pp. 1235–1240 (1998)

60. Nouri, J.D., Abadeh, S.M., Mohammadi, G.F.: HYEI: A New Hybrid Evolutionary Imperialist Competitive Algorithm for Fuzzy Knowledge Discovery. Advances in Fuzzy Systems 2014, 1–9 (2014)

61. Nowicki, R., Rutkowski, L., Scherer, R.: A method for learning of hierarchical fuzzy systems. In: Intelligent Technologies - Theory and Applications, pp. 124–129 (2002)

62. Pławiak, P., Tadeusiewicz, R.: Approximation of phenol concentration using novel hybrid computational intelligence methods. Applied Mathematics and Computer Science 24(1) (2014)

63. Paiva, R.P., Dourado, A.: Interpretability and learning in neuro-fuzzy systems. Fuzzy Sets and Systems 147, 17–38 (2004)

64. Pham, D.T., Ghanbarzadeh, A., Koc, E., Otri, S., Rahim, S., Zaidi, M.: The Bees Algorithm, A Novel Tool for Complex Optimisation Problems. In: Proceedings of the 2nd International Virtual Conference on Intelligent Production Machines and Systems, pp. 454–459 (2006)

65. Pouyan, B.M., Yousefi, R., Ostadabbas, S., Nourani, M.: A Hybrid Fuzzy-Firefly Approach for Rule-Based Classification. In: The Twenty-Seventh International Flairs Conference (2014)

66. Prampero, P.S., Attux, R.: Magnetic particle swarm optimization. Journal of Artificial Intelligence and Soft Computing Research 2(1), 59–72 (2012)

67. Przybył, A., Er, M.J.: The idea for the integration of neuro-fuzzy hardware emulators with real-time network. In: Rutkowski, L., Korytkowski, M., Scherer, R., Tadeusiewicz, R., Zadeh, L.A., Zurada, J.M. (eds.) ICAISC 2014, Part I. LNCS (LNAI), vol. 8467, pp. 279–294. Springer, Heidelberg (2014)

68. Przybył, A., Jelonkiewicz, J.: Genetic algorithm for observer parameters tuning in sensorless induction motor drive. In: Neural Networks and Soft Computing, pp. 376–381 (2003)

69. Przybył, A., Smoląg, J., Kimla, P.: Distributed control system based on real time ethernet for computer numerical controlled machine tool (in Polish). Przegląd Elektrotechniczny 86(2), 342–346 (2010)

70. Qu, Y., Shang, C., Shen, Q., Parthalain, M., Wei, W.N.: Kernel-based fuzzy-rough nearest neighbour classification. In: 2011 IEEE International Conference on Fuzzy Systems (FUZZ), pp. 1523–1529 (2011)

71. Rey, M.I., Galende, M., Sainz, G.I., Fuente, M.J.: Checking orthogonal transformations and genetic algorithms for selection of fuzzy rules based on interpretability-accuracy concepts. In: 2011 IEEE International Conference on Fuzzy Systems, pp. 1271–1278 (2011)

72. Riid, A., Rustern, E.: Interpretability improvement of fuzzy systems: Reducing the number of unique singletons in zeroth order Takagi-Sugeno systems. In: 2010 IEEE International Conference on Fuzzy Systems (FUZZ), pp. 1–6 (2010)

73. Riid, A., Rüstern, E.: Interpretability, Interpolation and Rule Weights in Linguistic Fuzzy Modeling. In: Fanelli, A.M., Pedrycz, W., Petrosino, A. (eds.) WILF 2011. LNCS (LNAI), vol. 6857, pp. 91–98. Springer, Heidelberg (2011)

74. Rini, D.P., Shamsuddin, S.M., Yuhaniz, S.S.: Balanced the Trade-offs Problem of ANFIS using Particle Swarm Optimization. Telkomnika 11(3), 611–616 (2013)

75. Rutkowski, L.: On Bayes risk consistent pattern-recognition procedures in a quasi-stationary environment. IEEE Trans. Pattern Analysis and Machine Intelligence 4(1), 84–87 (1982)

76. Rutkowski, L.: Online Identification of Time-Varying Systems by Nonparametric Techniques. IEEE Trans. Automatic Control 27(1), 228–230 (1982)

77. Rutkowski, L.: On nonparametric identification with prediction of time-varying systems. IEEE Trans. Automatic Control 29(1), 58–60 (1984)

78. Rutkowski, L.: Computational Intelligence. Springer (2008)

79. Rutkowski, L., Cpałka, K.: Flexible structures of neuro-fuzzy systems. In: Sincak, P., Vascak, J. (eds.) Quo Vadis Computational Intelligence. STUDFUZZ, vol. 54, pp. 479–484. Springer, Heidelberg (2000)

80. Rutkowski, L., Cpałka, K.: Compromise approach to neuro-fuzzy systems. In: Sincak, P., Vascak, J., Kvasnicka, V., Pospichal, J. (eds.) Intelligent Technologies - Theory and Applications, vol. 76, pp. 85–90. IOS Press (2002)

81. Rutkowski, L., Jaworski, M., Pietruczuk, L., Duda, P.: Decision Trees for Mining Data Streams Based on the Gaussian Approximation. IEEE Transactions on Knowledge and Data Engineering 26, 108–119 (2014)

82. Rutkowski, L., Jaworski, M., Pietruczuk, L., Duda, P.: The CART decision tree for mining data streams. Information Sciences 266, 1–15 (2014)

83. Rutkowski, L., Przybył, A., Cpałka, K., Er, M.J.: Online speed profile generation for industrial machine tool based on neuro-fuzzy approach. In: Rutkowski, L., Scherer, R., Tadeusiewicz, R., Zadeh, L.A., Zurada, J.M. (eds.) ICAISC 2010, Part II. LNCS (LNAI), vol. 6114, pp. 645–650. Springer, Heidelberg (2010)

84. Rutkowski, L., Rafajłowicz, E.: On optimal global rate of convergence of some nonparametric identification procedures. IEEE Trans. Automatic Control 34(10), 1089–1091 (1989)

85. Sánchez, G., Jiménez, F., Sánchez, J.F., Alcaraz, J.M.: A Multi-objective Neuroevolutionary Algorithm to Obtain Interpretable Fuzzy Models. In: Meseguer, P., Mandow, L., Gasca, R.M. (eds.) CAEPIA 2009. LNCS, vol. 5988, pp. 51–60. Springer, Heidelberg (2010)

86. Shukla, P.K., Tripathi, S.P.: A Review on the Interpretability-Accuracy Trade-Off in Evolutionary Multi-Objective Fuzzy Systems (EMOFS). Information 3, 256–277 (2012)

87. Shukla, P.K., Tripathi, S.P.: A new approach for tuning interval type-2 fuzzy knowledge bases using genetic algorithms. Journal of Uncertainty Analysis and Applications 2, 4 (2014)
88. Shukla, P.K., Tripathi, S.P.: Handling High Dimensionality and Interpretability-Accuracy Trade-Off Issues in Evolutionary Multiobjective Fuzzy Classifiers. International Journal of Scientific & Engineering Research 5(6) (2014)
89. Siminski, K.: Rule Weights in a Neuro-Fuzzy System with a Hierarchical Domain Partition. Int. J. Appl. Math. Comput. Sci. 20(2), 337–347 (2010)
90. Sood, A., Aggarwal, S.: Crossroads in Classification: Comparison and Analysis of Fuzzy and Neuro-Fuzzy Techniques. International Journal of Computer Applications (0975-8887) 24(2), 13–17 (2011)
91. Starczewski, J., Rutkowski, L.: Connectionist structures of type 2 Fuzzy Inference Systems. In: Wyrzykowski, R., Dongarra, J., Paprzycki, M., Waśniewski, J. (eds.) PPAM 2001. LNCS, vol. 2328, pp. 634–642. Springer, Heidelberg (2002)
92. Starczewski, J., Rutkowski, L.: Interval type 2 neuro-fuzzy systems based on interval consequents. Advances in Soft Computing, pp. 570–577 (2003)
93. Starczewski, J.T., Bartczuk, Ł., Dziwiński, P., Marvuglia, A.: Learning methods for type-2 FLS based on FCM. In: Rutkowski, L., Scherer, R., Tadeusiewicz, R., Zadeh, L.A., Zurada, J.M. (eds.) ICAISC 2010, Part I. LNCS (LNAI), vol. 6113, pp. 224–231. Springer, Heidelberg (2010)
94. Szarek, A., Korytkowski, M., Rutkowski, L., Scherer, R., Szyprowski, J.: Application of neural networks in assessing changes around implant after total hip arthroplasty. In: Rutkowski, L., Korytkowski, M., Scherer, R., Tadeusiewicz, R., Zadeh, L.A., Zurada, J.M. (eds.) ICAISC 2012, Part II. LNCS (LNAI), vol. 7268, pp. 335–340. Springer, Heidelberg (2012)
95. Szarek, A., Korytkowski, M., Rutkowski, L., Scherer, R., Szyprowski, J.: Forecasting wear of head and acetabulum in hip joint implant. In: Rutkowski, L., Korytkowski, M., Scherer, R., Tadeusiewicz, R., Zadeh, L.A., Zurada, J.M. (eds.) ICAISC 2012, Part II. LNCS (LNAI), vol. 7268, pp. 341–346. Springer, Heidelberg (2012)
96. Szczypta, J., Przybył, A., Cpałka, K.: Some aspects of evolutionary designing optimal controllers. In: Rutkowski, L., Korytkowski, M., Scherer, R., Tadeusiewicz, R., Zadeh, L.A., Zurada, J.M. (eds.) ICAISC 2013, Part II. LNCS (LNAI), vol. 7895, pp. 91–100. Springer, Heidelberg (2013)
97. Szczypta, J., Przybył, A., Wang, L.: Evolutionary approach with multiple quality criteria for controller design. In: Rutkowski, L., Korytkowski, M., Scherer, R., Tadeusiewicz, R., Zadeh, L.A., Zurada, J.M. (eds.) ICAISC 2014, Part I. LNCS (LNAI), vol. 8467, pp. 455–467. Springer, Heidelberg (2014)
98. Tadeusiewicz, R., Chaki, R., Chaki, N.: Exploring Neural Networks with C#. CRC Press, Taylor & Francis Group, Boca Raton (2014)
99. Troiano, L., Ranilla, J., Díaz, I.: Interpretability of Fuzzy Association Rules as means of Discovering Threaths to Privacy (CMMSE 2010). International Journal of Computer Mathematics, 325–333 (2011)
100. Wang, H., Kwong, S., Jin, Y., Wei, W., Man, K.F.: Multi-objective hierarchical genetic algorithm for interpretable fuzzy rule-based knowledge extraction. Fuzzy Sets and Systems 149(1), 149–186 (2005)
101. Woźniak, M., Kempa, W.M., Gabryel, M., Nowicki, R.: A finite-buffer queue with single vacation policy-analytical study with evolutionary positioning. Int. Journal of Applied Mathematics and Computer Science 24, 887–900 (2014)

102. Yang, Z., Wang, Y., Ouyang, G.: Adaptive Neuro-Fuzzy Inference System for Classification of Background EEG Signals from ESES Patients and Controls. The Scientific World Journal 2014, 1–8 (2014)
103. Zalasiński, M., Cpałka, K.: A new method of on-line signature verification using a flexible fuzzy one-class classifier, pp. 38–53. Academic Publishing House EXIT (2011)
104. Zalasiński, M., Łapa, K., Cpałka, K.: New Algorithm for Evolutionary Selection of the Dynamic Signature Global Features. In: Rutkowski, L., Korytkowski, M., Scherer, R., Tadeusiewicz, R., Zadeh, L.A., Zurada, J.M. (eds.) ICAISC 2013, Part II. LNCS (LNAI), vol. 7895, pp. 113–121. Springer, Heidelberg (2013)
105. Zalasiński, M., Cpałka, K.: Novel algorithm for the on-line signature verification. In: Rutkowski, L., Korytkowski, M., Scherer, R., Tadeusiewicz, R., Zadeh, L.A., Zurada, J.M. (eds.) ICAISC 2012, Part II. LNCS (LNAI), vol. 7268, pp. 362–367. Springer, Heidelberg (2012)
106. Zalasiński, M., Cpałka, K.: New approach for the on-line signature verification based on method of horizontal partitioning. In: Rutkowski, L., Korytkowski, M., Scherer, R., Tadeusiewicz, R., Zadeh, L.A., Zurada, J.M. (eds.) ICAISC 2013, Part II. LNCS (LNAI), vol. 7895, pp. 342–350. Springer, Heidelberg (2013)
107. Zalasiński, M., Cpałka, K.: Novel Algorithm for the On-Line Signature Verification Using Selected Discretization Points Groups. In: Rutkowski, L., Korytkowski, M., Scherer, R., Tadeusiewicz, R., Zadeh, L.A., Zurada, J.M. (eds.) ICAISC 2013, Part I. LNCS (LNAI), vol. 7894, pp. 493–502. Springer, Heidelberg (2013)
108. Zalasiński, M., Cpałka, K., Er, M.J.: New Method for Dynamic Signature Verification Using Hybrid Partitioning. In: Rutkowski, L., Korytkowski, M., Scherer, R., Tadeusiewicz, R., Zadeh, L.A., Zurada, J.M. (eds.) ICAISC 2014, Part II. LNCS (LNAI), vol. 8468, pp. 216–230. Springer, Heidelberg (2014)
109. Zalasiński, M., Cpałka, K., Hayashi, Y.: New Method for Dynamic Signature Verification Based on Global Features. In: Rutkowski, L., Korytkowski, M., Scherer, R., Tadeusiewicz, R., Zadeh, L.A., Zurada, J.M. (eds.) ICAISC 2014, Part II. LNCS (LNAI), vol. 8468, pp. 231–245. Springer, Heidelberg (2014)

Multi-class Nearest Neighbour Classifier for Incomplete Data Handling

Bartosz A. Nowak[1,2], Robert K. Nowicki[2(✉)], Marcin Woźniak[3], and Christian Napoli[4]

[1] Department of Mathematical Methods in Computer Science, University of Warmia and Mazury, ul. Słoneczna 54, 10-710 Olsztyn, Poland
bnowak@matman.uwm.edu.pl
[2] Institute of Computational Intelligence, Czestochowa University of Technology, Al. Armii Krajowej 36, 42-200 Czestochowa, Poland
{bartosz.nowak,robert.nowicki}@iisi.pcz.pl
[3] Institute of Mathematics, Silesian University of Technology, Kaszubska 23, 44-101 Gliwice, Poland
Marcin.Wozniak@polsl.pl
[4] Department of Mathematics and Informatics, University of Catania, Viale A. Doria 6, 95125 Catania, Italy
napoli@dmi.unict.it

Abstract. The basic nearest neighbour algorithm has been designed to work with complete data vectors. Moreover, it is assumed that each reference sample as well as classified sample belong to one and the only one class. In the paper this restriction has been dismissed. Through incorporation of certain elements of rough set and fuzzy set theories into k-nn classifier we obtain a sample based classifier with new features. In processing incomplete data, the proposed classifier gives answer in the form of rough set, i.e. indicated lower or upper approximation of one or more classes. The basic nearest neighbour algorithm has been designed to work with complete data vectors and assumed that each reference sample as well as classified sample belongs to one and the only one class. Indication of more than one class is a result of incomplete data processing as well as final reduction operation.

Keywords: Nearest neighbour · Missing values · Rough sets

1 Introduction

The nearest neighbours algorithm (k-nn) is one of the most widely known classification methods [1, 9]. Despite its simplicity, or thanks to it, k-nn is still one of the most resultant ones. The main idea is quite simple. The classifier which works in input space $\Omega = \Re^n$ has the set of reference samples with known membership to one of m classes. The s–th reference sample x_r can be described by the vector $\overline{\mathbf{v}}_r = [\overline{v}_{r,1}, \ldots, \overline{v}_{r,i}, \ldots, \overline{v}_{r,n}, \omega(x_r)]$. The set is knowledge of the classifier. The goal of the method is to indicate one of m classes for the sample x described

© Springer International Publishing Switzerland 2015
L. Rutkowski et al. (Eds.): ICAISC 2015, Part I, LNAI 9119, pp. 469–480, 2015.
DOI: 10.1007/978-3-319-19324-3_42

by the vector $\overline{\mathbf{v}} = [\overline{v}_1, \ldots, \overline{v}_i, \ldots, \overline{v}_n]$. In the first step we calculate distances d_r between classified sample x and each reference sample x_r, i.e.

$$d_r = \|\overline{\mathbf{v}}_r - \overline{\mathbf{v}}\|, \tag{1}$$

where a wide variety of definitions of the norm $\|\cdot\|$ can be implemented. In the second step classifier should select k reference samples which are nearest to classified one. The order of reference samples is insignificant, however to make the selection at least partial sorting is necessary. We can apply in this process some fast input data aggregation methods [48–50]. Finally, classifier counts the representatives of particular classes in selected samples. The most strongly represented class is assigned to the classified sample x. So, the definition of the norm $\|\cdot\|$ and cardinality of selected samples (parameter k) are the only parameters of the algorithm. Let us also note, that in the case of classic k-nn algorithm we hav two assumptions. Firstly, each reference sample belongs to exactly one class and the classifier indicates only one class for classified sample (excepting the draw in the final step). Secondly, the usually applied norms require that all elements of vector $\overline{\mathbf{v}}_r$ and vector $\overline{\mathbf{v}}$ have known values. We would like to face with these two limitations. Why? Because these are not fulfilled in real classification tasks.

The restriction of one class for one sample is in general unnatural. Let us take a red fresh tomato from a greengrocer. It undoubtedly can by classified as good one to make a sandwich and as good one to make a tomato soup and as good one to make a Greek salad. Many models of cars are good to drive to shopping or lift a child to school and go to the theatre. So one class is not enough. We have proposed and presented in the paper fuzzy-like solution to extend k-nn classifier and make it capable to realize multiple classification.

The problem of incomplete input data is inherent in many real applications of decision–making systems. In the industry, some information could be unavailable due to e.g. the measuring instrument failure, temporary exceeding the measure range in some port of monitoring process. In medical diagnosis procedures some tests are omitted because of the patient state, unacceptable cost, lack of reagents or rejected by the community because of beliefs. Moreover, it could be deemed unnecessary by a doctor. The decision support system cannot remain idle in such cases. Of course, this problem can be relatively easily solved by marginalization or imputation. In the marginalization the input space Ω is temporary reduced [7, 37] to the lower dimensionality of consideration space to the features of known values. Therefore, some elements of the system are just turned off. Thus sometimes the elimination of all incomplete samples includes also the marginalization. However, it is eventually accepted only in course of designing decision systems. When we use the imputation, the unknown values are replaced by estimated ones. The palette of available methods is generally unlimited. The most primitive ones are confined to insertion of random, average or most common values. More sophisticated ones apply EM (Expectation Maximization) or k nearest neighbour algorithms, neural networks and fuzzy systems.

In the paper has been proposed alternative solution - rough sets [33]. In this theory an object can be classified to a positive region of the class (i.e. the object certainly belongs to the class), to a negative region of the class (i.e. the object certainly not belongs to the class) or to a boundary region of the class (i.e. it is not possible to determine if the object belongs to the class or not). Membership to these regions depends on the quality of object description. If this description is good enough, the object belongs either to the positive or negative regions. If the description is too weak, then the object belongs to the boundary region. In the rough set theory [33] as well as in the theory of evidence [45], we do not use the individual elements but some granules [34]. The granules contain elements which are indistinguishable basing on knowledge that we dispose. Thus, the size and the shape of granules depend on the used (known) knowledge about the elements. Obviously, the solutions combined nearest neighbour algorithm with rough set theory and fuzzy logic are already present in the literature. Researchers have included to his/her systems also other methods inspired by nature. Some examples are [3, 17–19, 21, 42, 46, 47, 51]. However our proposition is different. In it, when all input features have known and available values, the classifier works as elemental k–nn system. In the case, when some value is missing all possible outputs of the classifier are estimated. When only one decision is possible, the feature with missing value could be considered negligible and the classified sample is assigned to lower approximation (positive region) of classes indicated by the classifier. When more than one decision is possible, the classified sample is assigned to upper approximation of each class indicated by the classifier. Obviously, it is not possible to test all features with missing values. In presented solution we use the intervals and specific procedure shown below. Moreover, the final answer of the classifier is based on type reduction similar to used in neuro-fuzzy inference system.

2   Interval-Type Rough k-nn Algorithm

The paper contains proposition of the algorithm which extends k-nn method by support of interval-type value of attributes and fuzzy-rough type answer. Although the algorithm considers whole spectrum of values inside all intervals, it analyses data only in limited set of important points, but with nearly the same results. This type of input values can be caused by imprecision or missing data. In the paper we use notation that value of i-th attribute of s-th sample is defined as $[\bar{v}_{s,i*}, \bar{v}_{s,i}^{*}]$. All intervals are normalized by the algorithm to $[0, 1]$ range:

$$
\bar{v}_{i*}^{norm} = \frac{\bar{v}_{i*}^{org} - v_i^{min}}{v_i^{max} - v_i^{min}}, \bar{v}_i^{*norm} = \frac{\bar{v}_i^{*org} - v_i^{min}}{v_i^{max} - v_i^{min}}, \tag{2}
$$

where $[v_{i*}^{org}, \bar{v}_{s,i}^{*org}]$ is original value of i-th attribute, $[v_{i*}^{norm}, \bar{v}_{s,i}^{*norm}]$ is normalized value of this attribute, v_i^{min}, v_i^{max} are minimal and maximal possible values of this interval. Missing values of attribute are replaced by the most possible wide interval ($[0, 1]$). Because of interval-type of input values, the distance is also interval. In the paper the distance between samples x_a and x_b is similar to typical taxicab metric:

$$d_*(x_a, x_b) = \sum_{i=1...n} \begin{cases} 0 \text{ if } [v_{a,i*}, v^*_{a,i}] \cap [v_{b,i*}, v^*_{b,i}] \neq \emptyset \\ \min \begin{cases} |v_{a,i*} - v^*_{b,i}|, \\ |v^*_{a,i} - v_{b,i*}| \end{cases} \text{else,} \end{cases} \tag{3}$$

$$d^*(x_a, x_b) = \sum_{i=1...n} \max \begin{cases} |v_{a,i*} - v^*_{b,i}|, |v_{a,i*} - v_{b,i*}|, \\ |v^*_{a,i} - v_{b,i*}|, |v^*_{a,i} - v^*_{b,i}| \end{cases}. \tag{4}$$

For simplification of notation, the distance between current test sample and reference one (x_s) is defined as $[d_{s*}, d^*_s]$. The algorithm uses vector $\mathbf{d}^{srt}$ which stores sorted values of all beginnings end endings (d_{s*}, d^*_s) of distance intervals. Repeated values of this vector $(\mathbf{d}^{srt})$ are removed. Another information required by the method is stored in vectors ψ_*, ψ^*. They define how many samples have respectively ends or starts of the distance interval $([d_*, d^*])$ smaller or equal to defined distance represented by $\mathbf{d}^{srt}$:

$$\psi_{c*} = \left|\{x_s : d^*_s \leq d^{srt}_c\}\right|, \psi^*_c = \left|\{x_s : d_{s*} \leq d^{srt}_c\}\right|. \tag{5}$$

The algorithm also uses matrices $\mathbf{\Psi}_*, \mathbf{\Psi}^*$. The matrix $\mathbf{\Psi}_*$ stores numbers of reference samples that have ends of distance intervals not greater than specified distance and are members of defined class. Content of $\mathbf{\Psi}^*$ is the same, but beginnings of distance intervals are considered:

$$\Psi_{c,j*} = \left|\{x_s : d^*_s \leq d^{srt}_c \wedge x_s \in \omega_j\}\right|, \Psi^*_{c,j} = \left|\{x_s : d_{s*} \leq d^{srt}_c \wedge x_s \in \omega_j\}\right|, \tag{6}$$

where ω_j is j-th class, m is number of classes. An example values for $\Psi_{c,j*}$ and $\Psi^*_{c,j}$ are visible in Figure 1. In the paper we assume that single sample may belong to any number of classes or even to none, therefore $\sum_{j=1}^m (\Psi_{c,j*})$ is not always equal to ψ_{c*}, and $\sum_{j=1}^m (\Psi^*_{c,j})$ is not necessarily the same as ψ^*_c. The algorithm defines $\neg\Psi_{c,j*}, \neg\Psi^*_{c,j}$:

$$\neg\Psi_{c,j*} = \left|\{x_s : d^*_s \leq d^{srt}_c \wedge x_s \notin \omega_j\}\right| = \psi_{c*} - \Psi_{c,j*}, \tag{7}$$

$$\neg\Psi^*_{c,j} = \left|\{x_s : d_{s*} \leq d^{srt}_c \wedge x_s \notin \omega_j\}\right| = \psi^*_c - \Psi^*_{c,j}, \tag{8}$$

which are opposite to $\Psi_{c,j*}, \Psi^*_{c,j}$ (Eq. 6). In the standard k-nn algorithm, $\psi_* = \psi^*$, $\mathbf{\Psi}_* = \mathbf{\Psi}^*$ and only reference samples which have distance not grater than $d^{str}_{c_{max}}$ would be chosen for voting. The index c_{max} is the same as index of the first element in ψ that has value not smaller than the main parameter of k-nn algorithm. Therefore, typical k-nn would choose the following samples for voting:

$$\{x_s : d_s \leq d^{str}_{c_{max}}\}, c_{max} = \arg\min_c(\psi_c \geq k). \tag{9}$$

The rate of samples that belong to specified class may be defined (for k-nn) as follows:

$$\tau_j = \frac{\Psi_{c_{max},j}}{\psi_{c_{max}}}. \tag{10}$$

In the paper $\mathbf{d}_*$ is not necessarily the same as $\mathbf{d}^*$ and authors observed, that there are possible solutions for k-nn algorithm for all distances $d^{str}_{c_{min}}$, $d^{str}_{c_{min}+1}, \ldots, d^{str}_{c_{max}}$, where:

$$c_{min} = \arg\min_c \left(\overline{\psi}_c \geq k\right), \; c_{max} = \arg\min_c \left(\underline{\psi}_c \geq k\right). \tag{11}$$

The distance $d_{c_{min}}$ is the first distance, where at least k distances have already started or ended, whereas $d_{c_{max}}$ is the first distance, where at least k distances have ended. Proposed algorithm calculates minimum (τ_{j*}) and maximum (τ_j^*) rate of reference samples that may belong to specified class (ω_j) and which are the k (or more in case of a tie) nearest neighbours of test sample. In order to calculate these values algorithm must iterate through distances $d^{str}_{c_{min}}, d^{str}_{c_{min}+1}, \ldots, d^{str}_{c_{max}}$. The number of samples which are members of single class (and are not members) depends on d_c and are in ranges $[\Psi_{c,j*}, \Psi_{c,j}^*]$, $[\neg\Psi_{c,j*}, \neg\Psi_{c,j}^*]$, respectively. Also the number of these samples, which are members or not of that class, must be not less than k. The case in which the previous conditions are satisfied and the number of samples equals k', $k' > k$ means situation, when $(k+1)$-th, $(k+2)$-th ... (k')-th nearest neighbours are in the same distance as k-th nearest distance (a tie), therefore they must be considered during voting. During computation of τ_j^* the highest possible $(\Psi_{j,c}^*)$ number of samples that belong to ω_j is selected, as well as lowest possible (up to $\Psi_{j,c*}$) number of samples which are not members of the class is chosen. There are three cases:

1. In the first one $\Psi_{j,c}^* + \neg\Psi_{c,j*} < k$, therefore the number of chosen samples which are not member of current class equals $k - \Psi_{j,c}^*$.
2. When $\Psi_{j,c}^* + \neg\Psi_{c,j*} = k$, the number of chosen samples which are not members of current class are set to $k = \neg\Psi_{c,j*}$.
3. In the last case $\Psi_{j,c}^* + \neg\Psi_{c,j*} > k$ the number of chosen samples which are not members of current class equals $\neg\Psi_{c,j*}$.

$$\tau_j^* = \max_{c=c_{min}\ldots c_{max}} (\tau_{c,j}^*), \tag{12}$$

$$\tau_{c,j}^* = \begin{cases} \dfrac{\Psi_{c,j}^*}{k} & \text{if } (\Psi_{c,j}^* + \neg\Psi_{c,j}^*) < k \\[2mm] \dfrac{\Psi_{c,j}^*}{k} & \text{if } (\Psi_{c,j}^* + \neg\Psi_{c,j*}) = k \\[2mm] \dfrac{\Psi_{c,j}^*}{\Psi_{c,j}^* + \neg\Psi_{j,c*}} & \text{if } (\Psi_{c,j}^* + \neg\Psi_{c,j*}) > k. \end{cases} \tag{13}$$

After transformation:

$$\tau_j^* = \max_{c=c_{min}\ldots c_{max}} \left(\frac{\Psi_{c,j}^*}{\max\left\{k, \Psi_{c,j}^* + \neg\Psi_{\sim c,j*}\right\}} \right). \tag{14}$$

Similarly to τ_j^*, during calculation of τ_{j*} the smallest possible number of samples that belong to the current class are selected, and number of samples which are not members of current classes equal $\neg\Psi_{c,j*}$. There are also three cases:

1. When $\Psi_{c,j*} + \neg\Psi_{c,j}^* < k$, the number of samples that belong to current class equal $k - \neg\Psi_{c,j*}$.
2. If $\Psi_{c,j*} + \neg\Psi_{c,j}^* < k$, then number of samples that belong to current class defined by $\Psi_{c,j*}$.
3. Otherwise number of samples that belong to current class is set to $\Psi_{c,j*}$.

$$\tau_{j*} = \min_{c=c_{min}\ldots c_{max}} (\tau_{c,j*}), \tag{15}$$

$$\tau_{c,j*} = \begin{cases} \dfrac{k - \neg\Psi_{c,j}^*}{k} & \text{if } (\Psi_{c,j*} + \neg\Psi_{c,j}^*) < k \\[2mm] \dfrac{\Psi_{c,j*}}{k} & \text{if } (\Psi_{c,j*} + \neg\Psi_{c,j}^*) = k \\[2mm] \dfrac{\Psi_{c,j*}}{\Psi_{c,j*} + \neg\Psi_{c,j}^*} & \text{if } (\Psi_{c,j*} + \neg\Psi_{c,j}^*) > k. \end{cases} \tag{16}$$

After transformation,

$$\tau_{j*} = \min_{c=c_{min}\ldots c_{max}} \left(\frac{\max\left\{ k - \neg\Psi_{c,j}^*, \Psi_{c,j*} \right\}}{\max\left\{ k, \Psi_{c,j*} + \neg\Psi_{c,j}^* \right\}} \right). \tag{17}$$

For the same example as in Figure 1 the values of $\tau_{c,j*}$ and $\tau_{c,j}^*$ are shown in Figure 2.

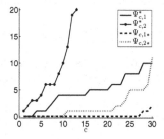

Fig. 1. Values of $\Psi_{c,j*}$ and $\Psi_{c,j}^*$ for 90% samples of BCW database and artificial test sample with values of all attributes equal 0.5 (after normalisation), and the first attribute with missing values. For this example $c_{min} = 8$, $c_{max} = 30$.

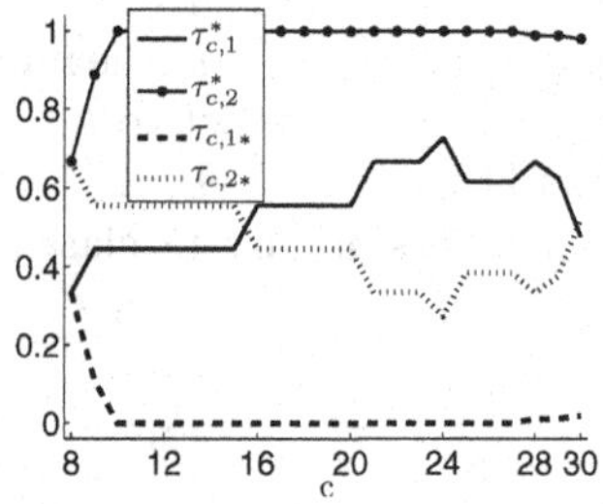

Fig. 2. Values of $\tau_{c,j*}$ and $\tau_{c,j}^*$ for the same situation as in Figure 1

3   Simulations

The authors have examined influence of existence of missing values in test sample on results of the system. Proposed algorithm was tested using 10-fold cross validation [22] and databases from UCI Repository [8]. Therefore all results are averages for 10 simulations. For test purposes five databases were chosen, and

Table 1. Properties of used databases from UCI repository and used value of k parameter

Data set name	k	number of samples	number of attributes	number of classes
Glass Identification	11	214	9	2
Ionosphere	9	351	34	2
Iris	5	150	4	3
Wine	11	178	13	3
Breast Cancer Wisconsin (BCW)	13	699	9	2

Table 2. Results for Ionosphere Data Set

list of removed attributes	results [%] φ	ψ
$\emptyset$	13.1	0
v_{29}	7.7	13.7
v_{18}, v_{29}	4.5	25.1
v_{10}, v_{18}, v_{29}	0.8	52.1
$v_{10}, v_{18}, v_{29}, v_{33}$	0	77.2
$v_8, v_{10}, v_{18}, v_{29}, v_{33}$	0	86.3
$v_8, v_{10}, v_{15}, v_{18}, v_{29}, v_{33}$	0	91.2
$v_7, v_8, v_{10}, v_{15}, v_{18}, v_{29}, v_{33}$	0	98
$v_7, v_8, v_{10}, v_{15}, v_{18}, v_{27}, v_{29}, v_{33}$	0	100

parameter k was set empirically for all of them in range $[5, 13]$. The number of samples was equal from 214 to 699, the number of attributes from 4 to 34 and number of classes from 2 to 3. Properties of used databases, and chosen values of k are visible in Table 1.

Proposed algorithm returns interval-type answer $([\tau_{j*}, \tau_j^*])$ for each class for classification of test sample. This type of result is also lower (τ_{j*}) and upper (τ_j^*) approximation of membership of test sample to the class ω_j. All used datasets were published for benchmarking of classifiers. Although in used data sets single sample is member of only one of available classes, the algorithm operates separately for each class, so it can be used for cases, where single sample is member of any number of classes. Proposed algorithm was tested [2] using two criteria:

1. The first criterion compute rate of incorrect classification of sample to each class using threshold 0.5,

$$\varphi(X^{(t)}) = 1 - \frac{1}{m \cdot M^{(t)}} \sum_{s=1}^{M^{(t)}} \sum_{j=1}^{m} \begin{cases} 1 & \text{if} \begin{pmatrix} \tau_{j,s}^* > 0.5 \\ \wedge \tau_{j,s*} > 0.5 \\ \wedge x_s^{(t)} \in \omega_j \end{pmatrix} \vee \begin{pmatrix} \tau_{j,s}^* < 0.5 \\ \wedge \tau_{j,s*} < 0.5 \\ \wedge x_s^{(t)} \notin \omega_j \end{pmatrix}, \\ 0 & \text{otherwise,} \end{cases}$$

(18)

where $X^{(t)}$ is set of test samples, $M^{(t)}$ is number of test samples, m is number of classes, $x_s^{(t)} \in \omega_j$ defines that test sample ought to be member of j-th class.

Table 3. Results for Glass Identification Data Set

list of removed attributes	results [%] φ	ψ
v_9	0.5	33.7
v_8	0	79.4
v_7	0	41.2
v_6	0	69.2
v_5	0.5	23.4
v_4	0	37.3
v_3	0	95.3
v_2	0	28.6
v_1	0.5	34.7
$\emptyset$	8	0
v_8	0	79.4
v_2, v_8	0	100

Table 4. Results for Iris Data Set

list of removed attributes	results [%] φ	ψ
v_4	0	74.9
v_3	0	71.3
v_2	0	51.6
v_1	0	49.1
$\emptyset$	3.6	0
v_1	0	49.1
v_1, v_2	0	93.3
v_1, v_2, v_4	0	100

Table 5. Results Wine Data Set

list of removed attributes	results [%] φ	ψ
v_{13}	0	39.9
v_{12}	0	32.7
v_{11}	0	28
v_{10}	0	34.8
v_9	0	27.4
v_8	0	23.8
v_7	0	31
v_6	0	25.6
v_5	0	30.3
v_4	0	22.8
v_3	0	21.9
v_2	0	32.2
v_1	0	34.2
$\emptyset$	1.5	0
v_4	0	22.8
v_2, v_4	0	73.2
v_2, v_4, v_8	0	98.1
v_2, v_4, v_5, v_8	0	100

Table 6. Results for Breast Cancer Wisconsin Data Set

list of removed attributes	results [%] φ	ψ
v_9	0.1	24.3
v_8	0	27.6
v_7	0.4	18.8
v_6	0.3	30.9
v_5	0.1	19.3
v_4	0.3	24
v_3	0.1	21.3
v_2	0.1	23.5
v_1	0.6	20.9
$\emptyset$	2.9	1.6
v_8	0	27.6
v_8, v_9	0	94.7
v_2, v_8, v_9	0	100

2. The second criterion compute rate of situation, where classifier refuses to answer if test sample is member of a class,

$$\psi(X^{(t)}) = \frac{1}{m \cdot M^{(t)}} \sum_{s=1}^{M^{(t)}} \sum_{j=1}^{m} \begin{cases} 1 & \text{if } \left(\begin{matrix} \tau_{j,s}^* \geq 0.5 \\ \wedge \tau_{j,s*} \leq 0.5 \end{matrix} \right), \\ 0 & \text{otherwise.} \end{cases} \tag{19}$$

The results of evaluation of proposed algorithm are presented in Tables 2, 3, 4, 5, 6. With increase of number of removed values of attributes level of φ fall towards 0, in cost of increase of ψ.

4   Conclusions

Proposed algorithm is generalization of k-nn method. It returns interval type membership of test sample to each class, caused by interval-type value of attributes. In the research intervals were used only to represent missing values, but could be also used to present uncertainty of processed data. Proposed algorithm caused, that after increase of the set of removed values of attributes rate of wrong classification has not increased. It occurs because classifier does not give incorrect answers as the result of missing values, in other words if the classification is proper for complete input vector, it is also proper in case of incomplete data. In this properties result is similar like in rough-neuro-fuzzy classifiers presented in [30–32]. Moreover, processing with the rates τ allows to build system more suitable to work with samples belong to more than on class. The experimental studies confirm the expectations. It can be expected that such type of classifiers can be useful as component of ensemble of various decision systems [4–6, 10–16, 23, 41, 43, 44]. Special expectations arise from reports of new hardware implementations of such systems e.g. neural networks [29] using of magnetic molecules for realization of neurons [27, 28]. A big challenge will be to apply an ensembles consist of proposed k-nn subsystems together with decision trees and fuzzy systems to data in form of stream [20, 35, 36, 38–40] and stereo vision [24–26].

Acknowledgments. The project was funded by the National Science Centre under decision number DEC-2012/05/B/ST6/03620.

References

1. Aldahdooh, R.T., Ashour, W.: DSMK-means "Density-based split-and-merge k-means clustering algorithm". Journal of Artificial Intelligence and Soft Computing Research 3(1), 51–71 (2013)
2. Anguita, D., Ghelardoni, L., Ghio, A., Ridella, S.: A survey of old and new results for the test error estimation of a classifier. Journal of Artificial Intelligence and Soft Computing Research 3(4), 229–242 (2013)
3. Bao, Y., Du, X., Ishii, N.: Improving performance of the k-nearest neighbor classifier by tolerant rough sets. In: Proceedings of the Third International Symposium on Cooperative Database Systems for Advanced Applications, CODAS 2001, pp. 167–171 (2001)
4. Bilski, J., Smolag, J.: Parallel architectures for learning the RTRN and Elman dynamic neural networks. IEEE Transactions on Parallel and Distributed Systems PP(99) (2014)

5. Bilski, J., Smoląg, J., Galushkin, A.I.: The parallel approach to the conjugate gradient learning algorithm for the feedforward neural networks. In: Rutkowski, L., Korytkowski, M., Scherer, R., Tadeusiewicz, R., Zadeh, L.A., Zurada, J.M. (eds.) ICAISC 2014, Part I. LNCS (LNAI), vol. 8467, pp. 12–21. Springer, Heidelberg (2014)

6. Bilski, J.: Momentum modification of the RLS algorithms. In: Rutkowski, L., Siekmann, J.H., Tadeusiewicz, R., Zadeh, L.A. (eds.) ICAISC 2004. LNCS (LNAI), vol. 3070, pp. 151–157. Springer, Heidelberg (2004)

7. Chang, Y., Wang, Y., Chen, C., Ricanek, K.: Improved image-based automatic gender classification by feature selection. Journal of Artificial Intelligence and Soft Computing Research 1(3), 241–253 (2011)

8. collective work: UCI machine learning repository, http://archive.ics.uci.edu/ml/datasets.html

9. Cover, T., Hart, P.: Nearest neighbor pattern classification. IEEE Transactions on Information Theory 13(1), 21–27 (1967)

10. Cpałka, K., Rutkowski, L.: Flexible Takagi-Sugeno fuzzy systems. In: Proceedings of IEEE International Joint Conference on Neural Networks, IJCNN 2005, vol. 3, pp. 1764–1769. IEEE (2005)

11. Cpałka, K., Łapa, K., Przybył, A., Zalasiński, M.: A new method for designing neuro-fuzzy systems for nonlinear modelling with interpretability aspects. Neurocomputing 135, 203–217 (2014)

12. Cpałka, K., Rebrova, O., Nowicki, R., Rutkowski, L.: On design of flexible neuro-fuzzy systems for nonlinear modelling. International Journal of General Systems 42(6), 706–720 (2013)

13. Gabryel, M., Korytkowski, M., Scherer, R., Rutkowski, L.: Object detection by simple fuzzy classifiers generated by boosting. In: Rutkowski, L., Korytkowski, M., Scherer, R., Tadeusiewicz, R., Zadeh, L.A., Zurada, J.M. (eds.) ICAISC 2013, Part I. LNCS (LNAI), vol. 7894, pp. 540–547. Springer, Heidelberg (2013)

14. Gabryel, M., Rutkowski, L.: Evolutionary learning of mamdani-type neuro-fuzzy systems. In: Rutkowski, L., Tadeusiewicz, R., Zadeh, L.A., Żurada, J.M. (eds.) ICAISC 2006. LNCS (LNAI), vol. 4029, pp. 354–359. Springer, Heidelberg (2006)

15. Gabryel, M., Rutkowski, L.: Evolutionary designing of logic-type fuzzy systems. In: Rutkowski, L., Scherer, R., Tadeusiewicz, R., Zadeh, L.A., Zurada, J.M. (eds.) ICAISC 2010, Part II. LNCS (LNAI), vol. 6114, pp. 143–148. Springer, Heidelberg (2010)

16. Gaweda, A.E., Scherer, R.: Fuzzy number-based hierarchical fuzzy system. In: Rutkowski, L., Siekmann, J.H., Tadeusiewicz, R., Zadeh, L.A. (eds.) ICAISC 2004. LNCS (LNAI), vol. 3070, pp. 302–307. Springer, Heidelberg (2004)

17. He, M., Ping Du, Y.: Research on attribute reduction using rough neighborhood model. In: International Seminar on Business and Information Management, ISBIM 2008, vol. 1, pp. 268–270 (December 2008)

18. Ishii, N., Torii, I., Bao, Y., Tanaka, H.: Modified reduct: Nearest neighbor classification. In: 2012 IEEE/ACIS 11th International Conference on Computer and Information Science (ICIS), pp. 310–315 (May 2012)

19. Ishii, N., Torii, I., Bao, Y., Tanaka, H.: Mapping of nearest neighbor for classification. In: 2013 IEEE/ACIS 12th International Conference on Computer and Information Science (ICIS), pp. 121–126 (June 2013)

20. Jaworski, M., Duda, P., Pietruczuk, L.: On fuzzy clustering of data streams with concept drift. In: Rutkowski, L., Korytkowski, M., Scherer, R., Tadeusiewicz, R., Zadeh, L.A., Zurada, J.M. (eds.) ICAISC 2012, Part II. LNCS, vol. 7268, pp. 82–91. Springer, Heidelberg (2012)

21. Keller, J., Gray, M., Givens, J.: A fuzzy k-nearest neighbor algorithm. IEEE Transactions on Systems, Man and Cybernetics SMC-15(4), 580–585 (1985)
22. Kohavi, R.: A study of cross-validation and bootstrap for accuracy estimation and model selection. In: Prceedings on the International Join Conference on Artficial Intelligence (IJCAI), Montreal, Canada, pp. 1137–1143 (1995)
23. Korytkowski, M., Rutkowski, L., Scherer, R.: From ensemble of fuzzy classifiers to single fuzzy rule base classifier. In: Rutkowski, L., Tadeusiewicz, R., Zadeh, L.A., Zurada, J.M. (eds.) ICAISC 2008. LNCS (LNAI), vol. 5097, pp. 265–272. Springer, Heidelberg (2008)
24. Laskowski, Ł.: Objects auto-selection from stereo-images realised by self-correcting neural network. In: Rutkowski, L., Korytkowski, M., Scherer, R., Tadeusiewicz, R., Zadeh, L.A., Zurada, J.M. (eds.) ICAISC 2012, Part I. LNCS, vol. 7267, pp. 119–125. Springer, Heidelberg (2012)
25. Laskowski, Ł.: A novel hybrid-maximum neural network in stereo-matching process. Neural Computing and Applications 23(7-8), 2435–2450 (2013)
26. Laskowski, Ł., Jelonkiewicz, J.: Self-correcting neural network for stereo-matching problem solving. Fundamenta Informaticae 138, 1–26 (2015)
27. Laskowski, Ł., Laskowska, M.: Functionalization of SBA-15 mesoporous silica by cu-phosphonate units: Probing of synthesis route. Journal of Solid State Chemistry 220, 221–226 (2014)
28. Laskowski, Ł., Laskowska, M., Balanda, M., Fitta, M., Kwiatkowska, J., Dzilinski, K., Karczmarska, A.: Mesoporous silica SBA-15 functionalized by nickel-phosphonic units: Raman and magnetic analysis. Microporous and Mesoporous Materials 200, 253–259 (2014)
29. Laskowski, Ł., Laskowska, M., Jelonkiewicz, J., Boullanger, A.: Spin-glass implementation of a Hopfield neural structure. In: Rutkowski, L., Korytkowski, M., Scherer, R., Tadeusiewicz, R., Zadeh, L.A., Zurada, J.M. (eds.) ICAISC 2014, Part I. LNCS (LNAI), vol. 8467, pp. 89–96. Springer, Heidelberg (2014)
30. Nowicki, R.: On combining neuro-fuzzy architectures with the rough set theory to solve classification problems with incomplete data. IEEE Transactions on Knowledge and Data Engineering 20(9), 1239–1253 (2008)
31. Nowicki, R.: Rough neuro-fuzzy structures for classification with missing data. IEEE Transactions on Systems, Man, and Cybernetics, Part B: Cybernetics 39(6), 1334–1347 (2009)
32. Nowicki, R.: On classification with missing data using rough-neuro-fuzzy systems. International Journal of Applied Mathematics and Computer Science 20(1), 55–67 (2010)
33. Pawlak, Z.: Rough Sets: Theoretical Aspects of Reasoning About Data. Kluwer, Dordrecht (1991)
34. Pedrycz, W., Bargiela, A.: Granular clustering: a granular signature of data. IEEE Transactions on Systems, Man, and Cybernetics, Part B: Cybernetics 32(2), 212–224 (2002)
35. Pietruczuk, L., Duda, P., Jaworski, M.: A new fuzzy classifier for data streams. In: Rutkowski, L., Korytkowski, M., Scherer, R., Tadeusiewicz, R., Zadeh, L.A., Zurada, J.M. (eds.) ICAISC 2012, Part I. LNCS, vol. 7267, pp. 318–324. Springer, Heidelberg (2012)
36. Pietruczuk, L., Duda, P., Jaworski, M.: Adaptation of decision trees for handling concept drift. In: Rutkowski, L., Korytkowski, M., Scherer, R., Tadeusiewicz, R., Zadeh, L.A., Zurada, J.M. (eds.) ICAISC 2013, Part I. LNCS (LNAI), vol. 7894, pp. 459–473. Springer, Heidelberg (2013)

37. Romaszewski, M., Gawron, P., Opozda, S.: Dimensionality reduction of dynamic mesh animations using ho-svd. Journal of Artificial Intelligence and Soft Computing Research 3(4), 277–289 (2013)
38. Rutkowski, L., Jaworski, M., Pietruczuk, L., Duda, P.: Decision trees for mining data streams based on the gaussian approximation. IEEE Transactions on Knowledge and Data Engineering 26(1), 108–119 (2014)
39. Rutkowski, L., Pietruczuk, L., Duda, P., Jaworski, M.: Decision trees for mining data streams based on the mcdiarmid's bound. IEEE Transactions on Knowledge and Data Engineering 25(6), 1272–1279 (2013)
40. Rutkowski, L., Jaworski, M., Pietruczuk, L., Duda, P.: The CART decision tree for mining data streams. Information Sciences 266, 1–15 (2014)
41. Rutkowski, L., Przybył, A., Cpałka, K., Er, M.J.: Online speed profile generation for industrial machine tool based on neuro-fuzzy approach. In: Rutkowski, L., Scherer, R., Tadeusiewicz, R., Zadeh, L.A., Zurada, J.M. (eds.) ICAISC 2010, Part II. LNCS (LNAI), vol. 6114, pp. 645–650. Springer, Heidelberg (2010)
42. Sarkar, M.: Fuzzy-rough nearest neighbors algorithm. In: 2000 IEEE International Conference on Systems, Man, and Cybernetics, vol. 5, pp. 3556–3561 (2000)
43. Scherer, R., Rutkowski, L.: A fuzzy relational system with linguistic antecedent certainty factors. In: Rutkowski, L., Kacprzyk, J. (eds.) Proceedings of the Sixth International Conference on Neural Network and Soft Computing. Advances in Soft Computing, pp. 563–569. Springer, Heidelberg (2003)
44. Scherer, R.: Neuro-fuzzy relational systems for nonlinear approximation and prediction. Nonlinear Analysis 71, e1420–e1425 (2009)
45. Shafer, G.: A Mathematical Theory of Evidence. Princeton University Press, Princeton (1976)
46. Verbiest, N., Cornelis, C., Jensen, R.: Fuzzy rough positive region based nearest neighbour classification. In: 2012 IEEE International Conference on Fuzzy Systems (FUZZ-IEEE), pp. 1–7 (June 2012)
47. Villmann, T., Schleif, F., Hammer, B.: Fuzzy labeled soft nearest neighbor classification with relevance learning. In: Proceedings of the Fourth International Conference on Machine Learning and Applications, pp. 11–15 (December 2005)
48. Woźniak, M., Marszałek, Z., Gabryel, M., Nowicki, R.K.: Modified merge sort algorithm for large scale data sets. In: Rutkowski, L., Korytkowski, M., Scherer, R., Tadeusiewicz, R., Zadeh, L.A., Zurada, J.M. (eds.) ICAISC 2013, Part II. LNCS (LNAI), vol. 7895, pp. 612–622. Springer, Heidelberg (2013)
49. Woźniak, M., Marszałek, Z., Gabryel, M., Nowicki, R.K.: On quick sort algorithm performance for large data sets. In: Skulimowski, A.M.J. (ed.) Looking into the Future of Creativity and Decision Support Systems, pp. 647–656. Progress & Business Publishers, Cracow (2013)
50. Woźniak, M., Marszałek, Z., Gabryel, M., Nowicki, R.K.: Triple heap sort algorithm for large data sets. In: Skulimowski, A.M.J. (ed.) Looking into the Future of Creativity and Decision Support Systems, pp. 657–665. Progress & Business Publishers, Cracow (2013)
51. Yager, R.: Using fuzzy methods to model nearest neighbor rules. IEEE Transactions on Systems, Man, and Cybernetics, Part B: Cybernetics 32(4), 512–525 (2002)

Cross-Entropy Clustering Approach to One-Class Classification

Przemysaw Spurek[1(✉)], Mateusz Wójcik[2], and Jacek Tabor[1]

[1] Faculty of Mathematics and Computer Science, Jagiellonian University,
Łojasiewicza 6, 30-348 Kraków, Poland
{przemyslaw.spurek,jacek.tabor}@ii.uj.edu.pl
[2] Faculty of Electrotechnics, Automation, AGH University of Science and
Technology, Computer Science and Biomedical Engineering
Al. Mickiewicza 30, 30-059 Kraków, Poland
mateuszjanwojcik@gmail.com

Abstract. Cross-entropy clustering (CEC) is a density model based
clustering algorithm. In this paper we apply CEC to the one-class classification, which has several advantages over classical approaches based on
Expectation Maximization (EM) and Support Vector Machines (SVM).
More precisely, our model allows the use of various types of gaussian models with low computational complexity. We test the designed method on
real data coming from the monitoring systems of wind turbines.

Keywords: Covariance matrixa · Gaussian filter · Mathematical mor-
phology · Electron microscopy

1 Introduction

One-class classification, also called novelty detection, outliers detection, or data
description [10,14,16] can be used to detect uncharacteristic observations. It is
also useful when the background class contains enormous variations making its
estimation unfeasible, for example in the case of background class in object detection (the background class should contain everything except the object to
be detected). Another typical example is given by the classification of active
chemical compounds, where the inactive class is usually totally non representative, as the scientists rarely publish information about chemically nonactive
compounds [13,19,21]. One-class classification is also necessary when samples
can be obtained only from a single known class.

This situation is encountered in the case of data from the monitoring systems
of wind turbines [4,6,8,9]. The growing number of that kind of systems causes the
necessity for analysis of gigabytes of data obtained every day. Apart from the development of several advanced diagnostic methods for this type of machinery, there is
a need for a group of methods which can act as an "early warning tools". The idea

The paper was supported by the National Centre for Research and Development
under Grant no. WND-DEM-1-153/01.

L. Rutkowski et al. (Eds.): ICAISC 2015, Part I, LNAI 9119, pp. 481–490, 2015.
DOI: 10.1007/978-3-319-19324-3_43

of this approach could be based on data driven algorithm which would decide on a similarity of current data to the data which are already known. Using the one class classification method, data from a turbine which is in good condition could be classified as a one class. If there are data points outside the determined class, it means that an unknown operational state of the turbine appeared and an expert should be informed about the situation. Thus, this simple approach can be used in the case when there are no failure states known. In this paper some of the one class classification methods are tested against the data from vertical axis wind turbine prototypes which are innovative machines developed in Poland (no failure has occurred yet for this kind of turbines). The tests were performed on 4-D data covering the period from 18.04.2014 till 29.04.2014, recorded every 1 second by an on-line monitoring system. The data set contained only the basic values that define the operational state of a turbine: wind speed, rotational speed of the rotor and the AC/DC power generated by the turbine. Negative values of AC power mean that the power was absorbed. The recorded data were not averaged. The data set included 985837 measurements. It should be also mentioned that the operational states classification is one of subtasks of a complex task of the intelligent wind turbines monitoring what is highly multifaceted in terms of scientific research [5,7].

The most straightforward method for obtaining one class classifier is to estimate the probability density of the data and to set a density value threshold. This approach was successfully applied within the use of Gaussian Mixture Models (GMM) and have been widely used in classification [3,10,25,24] and general density estimation tasks. They are also suitable for one-class classification.

Other class of algorithms widely used in outliers detection is given by kernel methods like one-class Support Vector Machines (1-SVM) [17] or Support Vector Data Description (SVDD) [26]. These methods inherit provable generalization properties from learning theory [17] and can handle high dimensional feature spaces. Contrary to EM the complexity of the methods is high.

In this paper we propose a new approach to one class classification problem which is strongly related to GMM, and is based on the cross-entropy clustering [20,22,23] (CEC). The CEC model uses similar approach like GMM, but using different combination of models [23]. Moreover, in the case of CEC implementation the data is covered by finite set of ellipsoids or balls. Consequently it is easier to compute and visualize classification border. It occurs that at the small cost of minimally worse density approximation [23] we gain speed in implementation[1] and the ease of using more complicated density models. In particular spherical CEC has lower computational complexity then spherical EM. Moreover, we can modify clusters on-line by adding new data which could be of high importance in the case of monitoring wind turbines.

This paper is arranged as follows. In the next section the theoretical background of CEC and comparison with GMM will be presented. We also describe how to adapt CEC to one-class classification problem. Last section presents numerical experiments.

---

[1] We can often use the Hartigan approach to clustering which is faster and typically finds better minima.

2   One Class Classification

Classical approaches to one class problems are usually based on two different ideas. In the first one we directly look for the decision borders. The main disadvantages of SVM based model is a problem with numerical complexity of the method and high number of parameters. In consequence, decision border depend on large number of constraints.

The second one is constructed in two steps. First we estimate a density model and after that we construct the decision algorithm. EM based approaches uses reasonably small number of parameters with good flexibility of changing decision border. More precisely, the model is constructed before the classification process is started. This kind of methods give good results if we have reasonably large set with quite small dimension [18] (lower then 10). In such situation density estimation works effectively.

In the case of data form the monitoring systems of wind turbines we have large amount of data in $\mathbb{R}^4$. Consequently, density based model give essentially better results. Nevertheless, for data in higher dimensional spaces SVM (thanks to kernel trick) works nice.

Since our work is based on the CEC method and one class classification (based on density estimation) we start by introducing CEC in relation to GMM which uses EM (Expectation Maximization) approach.

Let us recall that the standard Gaussian densities in $\mathbb{R}^d$ are defined by

$$N(\mathrm{m}, \Sigma)(\mathrm{x}) := \frac{1}{(2\pi)^{d/2}\det(\Sigma)^{1/2}} \exp\left(-\frac{1}{2}\|\mathrm{x} - \mathrm{m}\|_{\Sigma}^2\right),$$

where m denotes the mean, Σ is the covariance matrix and $\|v\|_{\Sigma}^2 := v^T \Sigma^{-1} v$ is the square of Mahalanobis norm. In general EM aims at finding $p_1, \ldots, p_k \geq 0$, $\sum_{i=1}^k p_i = 1$ and $f_1, \ldots, f_k$ Gaussian densities (where k is given beforehand and denotes the number of densities which convex combination builds the desired density model) such that the convex combination

$$f := p_1 f_1 + \ldots p_k f_k$$

optimally approximates the scatter of our data $X = \{x_1, \ldots, x_n\}$ with respect to MLE cost function

$$\mathrm{MLE}(f, X) := -\sum_{l=1}^n \ln(p_1 f_1(x_l) + \ldots + p_n f_n(x_l)). \tag{1}$$

The EM procedure consists of the Expectation and Maximization steps. While the Expectation step is relatively simple, the Maximization usually needs complicated numerical optimization even for relatively simple Gaussian models [12,11,2].

A goal of CEC is to minimize the cost function, which is a minor modification of that given in (1) by substituting sum with maximum:

$$\mathrm{CEC}(f, X) := -\sum_{l=1}^n \ln(\max(p_1 f_1(x_l), \ldots, p_n f_n(x_l))). \tag{2}$$

Time between Old Faithful eruptions

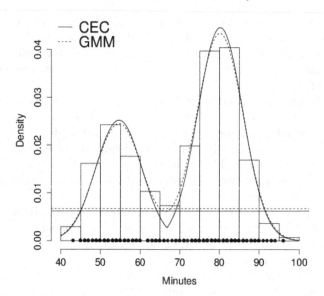

Fig. 1. The Old Faithful waiting data fitted by GMM and CEC with 95% level of point classified to X_+

Instead of focusing on the density estimation as its main tasks, CEC aims itself directly at the clustering problem.

Let it be remarked that the seemingly small difference in the cost function between (1) and (2) has profound consequences, which follow from the fact that the densities in (2) do not "cooperate" to build the final approximation of f. Roughly speaking, the advantage is obtained because models do not mix with each other, since we take the maximum instead of the convex mixture.

As it was mentioned the CEC model is given by following formula:

$$f = \max(p_1 f_1(x_l), \dots, p_n f_n(x_l)),$$

where f_i are Gaussian densities. The density based one–class classification need an estimation of probability distribution f, data set X and probability of belonging to arbitrary given distribution $\varepsilon \in [0, 1]$. As an output we obtain assignment of points to two group X_+ which we interpret as an element from distribution and X_- which contain outliers.

Decision border α is given by level set construct such empirical probability of belonging to the class X_+ is equal ε:

$$\frac{|\{x \in X : f(x) \le \alpha\}|}{|X|} = \varepsilon.$$

where $|\cdot|$ denote the cardinality of a set.

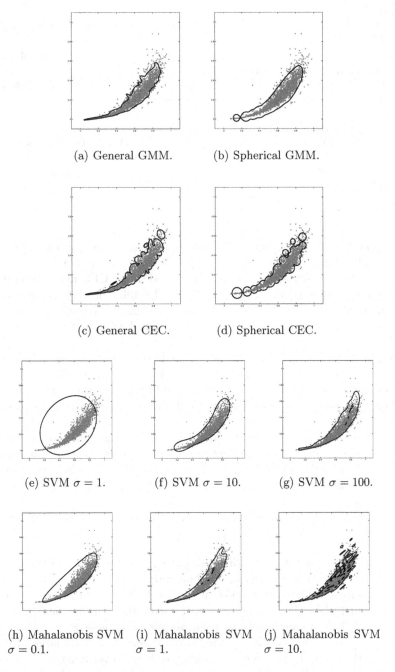

(a) General GMM.   (b) Spherical GMM.

(c) General CEC.   (d) Spherical CEC.

(e) SVM $\sigma = 1$.   (f) SVM $\sigma = 10$.   (g) SVM $\sigma = 100$.

(h) Mahalanobis SVM   (i) Mahalanobis SVM   (j) Mahalanobis SVM
$\sigma = 0.1$. $\sigma = 1$. $\sigma = 10$.

Fig. 2. Comparison of decision border in the case of different one-class classification algorithms on Abalon dataset from the UCI repository

---

Algorithm 1. Density based classifier:

---

input
   $X \subset \mathbb{R}^d$ ▷ training data
   $Y \subset \mathbb{R}^d$ ▷ testing data
   $\varepsilon \geq 0$ ▷ level of decision
construction of the model
   $f : \mathbb{R}^d \to \mathbb{R}_+$ ▷ density estimation
   Compute decision border α *such, that* $\frac{|\{x \in X : f(x) \leq \alpha\}|}{|X|} \approx \varepsilon$
   for $y \in Y$ **do**
      if $f(y) < \alpha$ **then**
         y *add to* Y_+ ▷ classified as the positive class
      else
         y *add to* Y_- ▷ classify to outliers
      end if
   end for

The pseudo code of density based one-class classification (we can us CEC or EM algorithm for density estimation) is presented in Algorithm 1.

The result of density estimation obtain by GMM and CEC models on the Old Faithful waiting data [1] we present on Fig. 2. The difference between models are quite small. We also see that the 95% border is similar. Consequently, applying CEC method we obtain similar results like in EM with lower computational time.

Since we have only one class, it is nontrivial to construct a reasonable criterion for verifying the correctness of classification process [17,15]. To do so we use standard measure of sensitivity and and introduce a new approach to measure specificity. In the first case we want to verify how many true positive examples are in testing set.

Let X be a data coming from the density $f : \mathbb{R}^d \to \mathbb{R}_+$. Since we do not have two classes we assume that some percentage ε of data are sampled from random variable X_+ and other ones are treated as outliers X_-. We construct a decision border on training set such, that $\frac{|X_+|}{|X|} \leq \varepsilon$. Consequently, sensitivity can be measured by

$$\left| \frac{|Y_+|}{|Y|} - \frac{|X_+|}{|X|} \right|$$

where Y is testing and X is training set. The smaller the above value, the more "stable" is the considered classification boundary.

We measure specificity by a different approach. The problem lies in the fact that we want to be able to generate negative examples without being explicitly given second class. To do so, without using additional knowledge, we assume that elements from the second class have uniform distribution on some large cube containing all the positive class. Such reasoning leads us to verifying which decision border contains smaller number of elements of negative class. This equivalently can be stated as finding those decision border which has inside the minimal volume.

Remark 1. Let us observe that for a known density this reduces to the level sets. For density $f\colon \mathbb{R}^d \to \mathbb{R}_+$ and $\varepsilon \in [0,1]$ consider all $U \subset \mathbb{R}^d$ such that

$$\int_U f(x)dx = \varepsilon$$

Then the above is minimal if U is given by $U = f^{-1}([a,\infty])$, where a is such that $\int_{f^{-1}([a,\infty])} f(x)dx = \varepsilon$.

Table 1. Comparison of the CEC, GMM and SVM in the case of one class classification

		abalone 1	abalone 2	turbion 1	turbion 2
CEC	Time	0,272	0,218	24,793	133,735
	Testing rate	95,57%	95,89%	95,03%	98,66%
	Volum	5.361	5.470	0.005	0.001
	Parameters	$30 \cdot 7 = 210$	$29 \cdot 7 = 203$	$29 \cdot 13 = 377$	$30 \cdot 13 = 390$
EM	Time	0,863	0,211	23,025	53,955
	Testing rate	93,82%	92,3%	95,23%	98,63%
	Volume	4.807	4.595	0.006	0.001
	Parameters	$30 \cdot 7 = 210$	$29 \cdot 7 = 203$	$15 \cdot 13 = 195$	$30 \cdot 13 = 390$
SVM $\sigma = 1$	Time	0,014	0,019	48,792	1034,062
	Testing rate	95,13%	95,73%	95,55%	98,03%
	Volume	20.575	21.068	0.524	0.161
	Parameters	$85 \cdot 3 = 255$	$84 \cdot 3 = 252$	$4288 \cdot 4 = 17152$	$19717 \cdot 4 = 78872$
SVM $\sigma = 10$	Time	0,021	0,017	48,563	1067,091
	Testing rate	94,8%	94,65%	96,44%	97,98%
	Volume	6.65	6.567	0.316	0.099
	Parameters	$86 \cdot 3 = 258$	$85 \cdot 3 = 255$	$4288 \cdot 4 = 17152$	$19718 \cdot 4 = 78872$
SVM $\sigma = 100$	Time	0,033	0,022	49.4126	1137.22
	Testing rate	93,42%	93,34%	96.28%	97.75%
	Volume	5.55	5.672	0.081	0.018
	Parameters	$100 \cdot 3 = 300$	$112 \cdot 3 = 336$	$4289 \cdot 4 = 17156$	$19718 \cdot 4 = 78872$
CEC spherical	Time	0.109	0.011	21.76	151.54
	Testing rate	93.26%	94.34%	94.87%	98,45%
	Volume	5.395	6.029	0.03	0.003
	Parameters	$28 \cdot 4 = 112$	$28 \cdot 4 = 112$	$29 \cdot 5 = 145$	$30 \cdot 5 = 150$
EM spherical	Time	0.863	0.211	23.025	53.955
	Testing rate	93,82%	92,3%	95,23%	98,63%
	Volume	4.807	4.595	0.006	0.001
	Parameters	$30 \cdot 4 = 120$	$30 \cdot 4 = 120$	$30 \cdot 5 = 150$	$30 \cdot 5 = 150$
SVM Mahalanobis $\sigma = 0.1$	Time	0.016	0.022	49.33	1459.01
	Testing rate	95.25%	94.93%	96.55%	94.87%
	Volume	8.636	8.562	0.116	0.012
	Parameters	$87 \cdot 3 = 261$	$87 \cdot 3 = 261$	$4289 \cdot 4 = 17156$	$19718 \cdot 4 = 78872$
SVM Mahalanobis $\sigma = 1$	Time	0.026	0.025	53.023	1061.36
	Testing rate	94.18%	93.30%	95.43%	97.85%
	Volume	5.851	5.546	0.011	0.002
	Parameters	$96 \cdot 3 = 288$	$96 \cdot 3 = 288$	$4316 \cdot 4 = 17264$	$19732 \cdot 4 = 78928$
SVM Mahalanobis $\sigma = 10$	Time	0.121	0.118	64.950	1209.17
	Testing rate	86.64%	87.20%	94.60%	98.20%
	Volume	4.836	4.652	0.006	0.001
	Parameters	$441 \cdot 3 = 1323$	$414 \cdot 3 = 1242$	$4486 \cdot 4 = 17944$	$19852 \cdot 4 = 79408$

3   Experiments

In this section we present the results of CEC one-class classification method in relation to GMM and SVM. Let us start from Abalone data from UCI repository [27]. For our experiments we restrict the data to two dimensions, which enabled to plot the decision border and visually compare quality of classifiers (see Fig. 2), and divided the data into two groups: teaching (40%) and testing (60%). We trained CEC, GMM and SVM algorithms in such a way that 95% of training data are classified to X_+. In our experiments we apply classical and spherical versions of EM and CEC. Analogically, we use SVM with different kernels (spherical and Mahanalobis) with varied kernel width.

As it was discussed in the previous section we prefer the classifier which minimizes volume of area dedicated for the positive class and which has similar percentage of points positively classified simultaneously in training and testing sets. In the case of abalone data set, CEC, EM and SVM gives similar results. Nevertheless, SVN uses more parameters then density based approaches with similar measure of volume and testing rate, see two first column in Tab. 1. By using circles instead ellipses we reduce the number of parameters and consequently also the possibility of overfitting. The result of general and spherical version of CEC we present in Fig. 3.

In the second example we use real data from monitoring system of wind turbine. The tests were performed on 4-D data covering the period from 18.04.2014 till 29.04.2014, recorded every 1 second by an on-line monitoring system. The data set included up to 985837 measurements. It occurs that the data are situated in fact in lower dimensional subspace and are strongly correlated in one direction, as the last eigenvalue of covariance matrix is essentially smaller then three first: 350102.91, 2006.03, 126.14, 0.76. Therefore, we used PCA (Principal

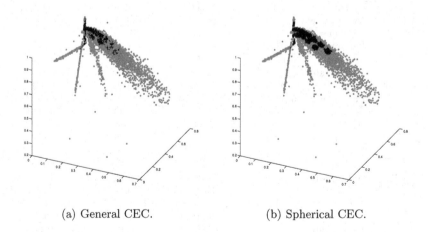

(a) General CEC.   (b) Spherical CEC.

Fig. 3. The result of classical and spherical CEC in 3D data form monitoring of wind turbines

Component Analysis) for extracting three most important dimensions, which also enables easier visualization of the results, see Fig. 3.

In the case of this large amount of data we observe the difference between computational complexity of CEC approach and EM and SVM algorithms, see two last columns in Tab. 1. The difference between computation time in the case of spherical version of EM and CEC shows further advantage of our method. In the case of turbine dataset we obtain similar testing rate like in EM and SVM. The basic difference lies in the number of parameters and computation time.

4   Conclusions

In this paper a new approach to one-class classification problem was presented. The method is based on Cross-Entropy Clustering algorithm. More precisely, we use density estimation which is a mix of Gaussian distribution and thresholding border constructed so that 5% of data is classified as outliers. We obtained similar results to EM based approach with smaller computational complexity, larger flexibility for applying more complicated models and possibility of applying on-line version. The method was verified on data from turbine monitoring system.

References

1. Azzalini, A., Bowman, A.: A look at some data on the old faithful geyser. Applied Statistics, 357–365 (1990)
2. Banfield, J.D., Raftery, A.E.: Model-based gaussian and non-gaussian clustering. Biometrics, 803–821 (1993)
3. Barnett, V., Lewis, T.: Outliers in statistical data, vol. 3. Wiley, New York (1994)
4. Barszcz, T., Bielecka, M., Bielecki, A., Wójcik, M.: Wind turbines states classification by a fuzzy-ART neural network with a stereographic projection as a signal normalization. In: Dobnikar, A., Lotrič, U., Šter, B. (eds.) ICANNGA 2011, Part II. LNCS, vol. 6594, pp. 225–234. Springer, Heidelberg (2011)
5. Barszcz, T., Bielecka, M., Bielecki, A., Wójcik, M.: Wind speed modelling using weierstrass function fitted by a genetic algorithm. Journal of Wind Engineering and Industrial Aerodynamics 109, 68–78 (2012)
6. Barszcz, T., Bielecki, A., Wójcik, M.: ART-type artificial neural networks applications for classification of operational states in wind turbines. In: Rutkowski, L., Scherer, R., Tadeusiewicz, R., Zadeh, L.A., Zurada, J.M. (eds.) ICAISC 2010, Part II. LNCS (LNAI), vol. 6114, pp. 11–18. Springer, Heidelberg (2010)
7. Bielecki, A., Barszcz, T., Wójcik, M.: Modelling of a chaotic load of wind turbines drivetrain. Mechanical Systems and Signal Processing 54-55, 491–505 (2015)
8. Bielecki, A., Barszcz, T., Wójcik, M., Bielecka, M.: Art-2 artificial neural networks applications for classification of vibration signals and operational states of wind turbines for intelligent monitoring. Diagnostyka 14(4), 21–26 (2013)
9. Bielecki, A., Barszcz, T., Wójcik, M., Bielecka, M.: Hybrid system of ART and RBF neural networks for classification of vibration signals and operational states of wind turbines. In: Rutkowski, L., Korytkowski, M., Scherer, R., Tadeusiewicz, R., Zadeh, L.A., Zurada, J.M. (eds.) ICAISC 2014, Part I. LNCS (LNAI), vol. 8467, pp. 3–11. Springer, Heidelberg (2014)

10. Bishop, C.M.: Novelty detection and neural network validation. In: IEE Proceedings - Vision, Image and Signal Processing, vol. 141, pp. 217–222. IET (1994)
11. Celeux, G., Govaert, G.: Gaussian parsimonious clustering models. Pattern Recognition 28(5), 781–793 (1995)
12. Davis-Stober, C., Broomell, S., Lorenz, F.: Exploratory data analysis with MATLAB. Psychometrika 72(1), 107–108 (2007)
13. Guner, O.: History and evolution of the pharmacophore concept in computer-aided drug design. Current Topics in Medicinal Chemistry 2(12), 1321–1332 (2002)
14. Hodge, V.J., Austin, J.: A survey of outlier detection methodologies. Artificial Intelligence Review 22(2), 85–126 (2004)
15. Lukashevich, H., Nowak, S., Dunker, P.: Using one-class svm outliers detection for verification of collaboratively tagged image training sets. In: IEEE International Conference on Multimedia and Expo, ICME 2009, pp. 682–685. IEEE (2009)
16. Markou, M., Singh, S.: Novelty detection: a review–part 1: statistical approaches. Signal Processing 83(12), 2481–2497 (2003)
17. Schölkopf, B., Platt, J.C., Shawe-Taylor, J., Smola, A.J., Williamson, R.C.: Estimating the support of a high-dimensional distribution. Neural Computation 13(7), 1443–1471 (2001)
18. Silverman, B.W.: Density estimation for statistics and data analysis, vol. 26. CRC Press (1986)
19. Śmieja, M., Warszycki, D., Tabor, J., Bojarski, A.J.: Asymmetric clustering index in a case study of 5-ht1a receptor ligands. PloS One 9(7), e102069 (2014)
20. Spurek, P., Tabor, J., Zając, E.: Detection of disk-like particles in electron microscopy images. In: Burduk, R., Jackowski, K., Kurzynski, M., Wozniak, M., Zolnierek, A. (eds.) CORES 2013. AISC, vol. 226, pp. 411–417. Springer, Heidelberg (2013)
21. Stahura, F.L., Bajorath, J.: Virtual screening methods that complement hts. Combinatorial Chemistry & High Throughput Screening 7(4), 259–269 (2004)
22. Tabor, J., Misztal, K.: Detection of elliptical shapes via cross-entropy clustering. In: Sanches, J.M., Micó, L., Cardoso, J.S. (eds.) IbPRIA 2013. LNCS, vol. 7887, pp. 656–663. Springer, Heidelberg (2013)
23. Tabor, J., Spurek, P.: Cross-entropy clustering. Pattern Recognition 47(9), 3046–3059 (2014)
24. Tarassenko, L., Nairac, A., Townsend, N., Buxton, I., Cowley, P.: Novelty detection for the identification of abnormalities. International Journal of Systems Science 31(11), 1427–1439 (2000)
25. Tax, D.M.J., Duin, R.P.W.: Outlier detection using classifier instability. In: Amin, A., Dori, D., Pudil, P., Freeman, H. (eds.) SPR 1998 and SSPR 1998. LNCS, vol. 1451, pp. 593–601. Springer, Heidelberg (1998)
26. Tax, D.M., Duin, R.P.: Support vector data description. Machine Learning 54(1), 45–66 (2004)
27. Waugh, S.: Extending and benchmarking cascade-correlation. Dept of Computer Science, University of Tasmania, Ph. D. Dissertation (1995)

Comparison of the Efficiency of Time and Frequency Descriptors Based on Different Classification Conceptions

Krzysztof Tyburek[1(✉)], Piotr Prokopowicz[1], Piotr Kotlarz[1], and Repka Michał[2]

[1] Institute of Mechanics and Applied Computer Science
Kazimierz Wielki University, Bydgoszcz, Poland
[2] Faculty of Mining and Geology, Technical University of Ostrava, Ostrava,
Czech Republic
{krzysiekkt,piotrekp,piotrk}@ukw.edu.pl, michal.repka@vsb.cz
http://www.imis.ukw.edu.pl

Abstract. Extraction and detailed analysis of sound files using the MPEG 7 standard descriptors is extensively explored. However, an automatic description of the specific field of sounds of nature still needs an intensive research. This publication presents a comparison of effectiveness of time and frequency descriptors applied in recognition of species of birds by their voices. The results presented here are a continuation of the research/studies on this subject. Three different conceptions of classification - the WEKA system as classical tool, linguistically modelled fuzzy system and artificial neural network were used for testing the descriptors effectiveness. The analysed sounds of birds come from 10 different species of birds: Corn Crake, Hawk, Blackbird, Cuckoo, Lesser Whitethroat, Chiffchaff, Eurasian Pygmy Owl, Meadow Pipit, House Sparrow and Firecrest. For the analysis of the physical features of a song, MPEG 7 standard audio descriptors were used.

Keywords: MPEG 7 · Audio descriptors · Fuzzy system · Linguistic modeling · Fuzzy classification · Neural networks

1 Introduction

Automatic recognition of elements of surrounding sounds is of significant, practical importance, from safety aspects, through aesthetic, to ecological. However, since recognizing the sources of all surrounding voices is hardly possible, the selected aspects will be the subject of present research. Moving Picture Experts Group proposed the MPEG-7 standard, named "Multimedia Content Description Interface" (see [4,5]), which defines universal mechanisms for the extracting descriptors. Generally descriptors are defined on the basis of the analysis of digital signals and index of their most important factors. It is a basic tool for the algorithmization of classification of different kinds of sounds.

The MPEG 7 Audio standard contains descriptors and description schemes that can be divided (see [5,6]) into two classes: generic lowlevel tools and applicationspecific tools. The generic tools, referred to in the standard as the audio

© Springer International Publishing Switzerland 2015
L. Rutkowski et al. (Eds.): ICAISC 2015, Part I, LNAI 9119, pp. 491–502, 2015.
DOI: 10.1007/978-3-319-19324-3_44

description framework apply to any audio signal and include the scalable series, lowlevel descriptors (LLDs) and the unform silence segment.

The application of specific tools limit their application domain in order to achieve more descriptive power and include general sound recognition, indexing tools and description tools. The lowlevel audio descriptors have very general applicability in describing audio. There are seventeen temporal and spectral descriptors (see [5,6]) that can be divided into six groups. A typical LLD may be instantiated either as a single value for a segment or a sampled series. Two names for those descriptors are used, following the application requirements: AudioLLDScalarType and AudioLLDVectorType. The first type is inherited for scalar values and describes a segment with a single summary, such as power or fundamental frequency, while the second one is inherited for vector types and describes a series of sampled values of such spectra, respectively.

The study presented in this paper focuses on the recognition of voices of species of birds. The main aim is to specify the type of descriptors, which enable an easy distinction between the sources of the bird's sounds. In this part, special attention was paid to the division of the descriptors into two categories: time and frequency domains. As the choice of descriptors is crucial for the successful recognition of the particular sounds, the information about which kind of them gives better results, vital for further research on this subject. The comparison of the usefulness of the kinds of descriptors is tested with the three different conceptions of classification. The first one is done by the Weka system, as a standard, being an appropriate reference tool. The next one is a fuzzy system based on a special linguistic model. Whereas the third one is an artificial neural network.

2   Sound Description with the MPEG 7

Descriptors of sound should allow to recognize classes of objects being the source of these sounds. Sound features included in MPEG-7 Audio are based on the research performed so far in this area and comprise technologies for sound description (sound, in the widest sense). The audio description framework in MPEG-7 includes 17 temporal and spectral descriptors divided into the following groups:

1. basic: instantaneous waveform and power values
2. basic spectral: log-frequency power spectrum envelopes, spectral centroid, spectrum spread and spectrum flatness.
3. signal parameters: fundamental frequency and harmony of signal.
4. timbral temporal: log attack time and temporal centroid
5. timbral spectral: spectral centroid, harmonic spectral centroid and harmonic spectral deviation, harmonic spectral spread, harmonic spectral variation.
6. spectral basis representations: spectrum basis and spectrum projection [8].

2.1   Time Domain Parameterization

For the purpose of correct description of sounds waveform it is necessary to define the descriptor. The descriptor is represented as a fraction of time of separating phases to time of all phases.

1. Log - time of the ending transient (TET) l_{tk}, which is given by:

$$l_{tk} = log(t_{pk} - t_{max}) \tag{1}$$

   where: t_{max} is the time at which the maximal amplitude has been reached, t_{pk} is the time at which the level of 10 % of maximal value has been reached in the decay stage.

2. The Log–Attack–Time Descriptor characterizes the "attack" of a sound, the time it takes for the signal to rise from silence to the maximum amplitude. This feature signifies the difference between a sudden and a smooth sound. The Log-Attack-Time is given by:

$$l_{tp} = log(t_{max} - t_{pp}) \tag{2}$$

   where: t_{max} is the time at which the maximal amplitude has been reached, t_{pp} is the begin of rise of signal.

3. ZC - (zero crossing) which describes the number of X axis crossing in the analyzed window in the time domain. In these experiments the length of window was $n = 1000$ samples. The onset of the window was at the begining of the signals rise . The length of the window was sufficiently long for all the samples in the experiments

2.2   Frequency Domain Parameterization

Since the frequency domain may contain important information concerning features of the sound it is worthwhile to introduce its parameterization. The base of parameterization of sound spectrum is Fourier transform, wavelet analysis, cepstrum or Wigner–Ville'a transform. The following parameters describing frequency domain of signal were applied:

1. Brightness

$$Br = \frac{\sum\limits_{i=0}^{n} A(i) \cdot i}{\sum\limits_{i=0}^{n} A(i)} \tag{3}$$

   where: $A(i)$ is amplitude of the i-th partial (harmonic), i - the frequency of the i-th partial.

2. Irregularity of spectrum

$$Ir = log(20 \sum_{i=2}^{N-1} | log\frac{A(i)}{\sqrt[3]{A(i-1) \cdot A(i) \cdot A(i+1)}} |) \tag{4}$$

where: $A(i)$ is amplitude of the i-th partial (harmonic)

N - number of available harmonics

3. Contents of the selected groups of harmonics in spectrum – including even/odd partials ratio descriptors (Ev,Odd).

$$Ev = \frac{\sqrt{\sum_{k=1}^{M} A(i)_{2k}^2}}{\sqrt{\sum_{n=1}^{N} A(i)_{n}^2}} \tag{5}$$

$$Odd = \frac{\sqrt{\sum_{k=2}^{L} A(i)_{2k-1}^2}}{\sqrt{\sum_{n=1}^{N} A(i)_{n}^2}} \tag{6}$$

where: $A(i)$ is amplitude of the i–th partial (harmonic)

N - number of available harmonic in spectrum

$M = [N/2]$ and $L = [N/2 + 1]$

a	b	c	d	e	f	g	h	i	j	Classified
82	0	0	0	0	1,8	0	0	16	0	a = Corn Crake
0	98	1,8	0	0	0	0	0	0	0	b = Hawk
0	1,8	95	0	0	0	3,6	0	0	0	c = Blackbird
0	0	1,8	96	0	0	1,8	0	0	0	d = Cuckoo
0	0	0	0	100	0	0	0	0	0	e = Lesser Whitethroat
0	0	0	0	0	100	0	0	0	0	f = Chiffchaff
0	0	0	0	0	0	100	0	0	0	g = Eurasian Pygmy Owl
0	0	0	0	0	0	0	98	0	1,8	h = Meadow Pipit
22	0	0	0	0	0	0	0	78	0	i = House Sparrow
0	0	0	0	0	0	0	5,5	0	95	j = Firecrest

Fig. 1. Error matrix for classification of sound of 10 kind of bird. Used k-NN, cross-validation method ($k = 10$). General recognition 94,18%. Vector of features from time domain has been used.

3   The Research Methodology

The purpose of the research was to find two vectors of features which enable automatic classification of the sound of a bird. These vectors should contain features of sound from time and frequency domains. For the parameterization of frequency domain state window length was proposed (see [16]). It was applied for all the samples. State window length is the fragment of the signal (in time domain) taken at the same point of time. State window length contains constant amount of samples. The beginning of this window was taken when the level of

10% of maximal value was reached. The length of the window is determined by the resolution of spectrum, according to the following formula:

$$f_r = \frac{f_s}{n} \tag{7}$$

where: f_r is the spectrum resolution
f_s – sampling frequency (44100 Hz)
n - number of samples.

a	b	c	d	e	f	g	h	i	j	Classified
65	0	0	0	0	7,3	0	20	7,3	0	a = Corn Crake
0	27	0	7,3	29	15	18	0	0	3,6	b = Hawk
0	0	53	3,6	3,6	9,1	5,5	7,3	18	0	c = Blackbird
0	11	3,6	45	9,1	13	3,6	0	7,3	7,3	d = Cuckoo
0	24	0	7,3	36	15	11	0	1,8	5,5	e = Lesser Whitethroat
5,5	16	9,1	9,1	5,5	25	3,6	11	13	1,8	f = Chiffchaff
0	22	9,1	3,6	11	1,8	44	0	0	9,1	g = Eurasian Pygmy Owl
16	1,8	9,1	0	0	11	0	51	9,1	1,8	h = Meadow Pipit
5,5	0	15	5,5	3,6	16	3,6	18	31	1,8	i = House Sparrow
0	13	5,5	18	3,6	1,8	7,3	1,8	3,6	45	j =Firecrest

Fig. 2. Error matrix for classification of sound of 10 kind of bird. Used k-NN, cross-validation method ($k = 10$). General recognition 42,36%. Vector of features from frequency domain has been used (Ev, Odd, Ir descriptors).

In this study, f_r equal to 10Hz was assumed. It means that the number of samples which were used in the analysis equaled 4410. If testing sound is shorter than the length of the window (n=4410), then the absent values should be supplemented with zeros until n=4410. Selected fragments of signals in the time domain were treated as DFT and this spectrum was analyzed. Moreover, Blackman window was used in the analysis.

4 The Results of the Analysis of WEKA System

During the research, WEKA was used With the cross–validation method and algorithms: k–Nearest Neighbors, Random forest and JRip. Some of the results of classification of 10 kind of bird are presented on Fig.1.

The results of the experiments clearly show that indexing of time domain brings better solution for automatic recognition of bird species by their song. The best results were reached by k-NN algorithm and three time descriptors: TET, LAT and ZC. General recognition of 94,18% was reached. Moreover, individual recognitions of each class of birds were above 80 % (except house sparrow - 78%). It is worth pointing out that three classes of birds (Lesser Whitethroat, Chiffchaff, Eurasian Pygmy Owl) had 100% efficiency of recognition. The other species of birds showed high recognition too. A very important aspect was the fact that descriptors for the time domain are sensitive to articulation, which is their weak point.

a	b	c	d	e	f	g	h	i	j	Classified
91	0	0	0	0	1,8	0	0	7,3	0	a = Corn Crake
0	93	7,3	0	0	0	0	0	0	0	b = Hawk
0	7,3	85	1,8	0	0	1,8	0	3,6	0	c = Blackbird
0	0	1,8	96	0	0	1,8	0	0	0	d = Cuckoo
0	0	0	0	100	0	0	0	0	0	e = Lesser Whitethroat
1,8	1,8	0	0	0	96	0	0	0	0	f = Chiffchaff
0	0	0	0	0	0	100	0	0	0	g = Eurasian Pygmy Owl
0	0	0	0	0	0	0	96	0	3,6	h = Meadow Pipit
15	0	0	0	0	3,6	0	0	82	0	i = House Sparrow
0	0	0	0	0	0	0	5,5	0	95	j = Firecrest

Fig. 3. Error matrix for classification of sound of 10 kind of bird. Used Random Forest, cross-validation method (k=10). General recognition 93,45%. Vector of features from time domain has been used.

Unfortunately, the frequency descriptors did not provide satisfactory results in the recognition of species of birds (general and individual). Fig.3 shows the results of classification of 10 classes of birds - random forest was used. General recognition was only 62,55

a	b	c	d	e	f	g	h	i	j	Classified
84	0	0	0	0	3,6	0	11	1,8	0	a = Corn Crake
0	62	1,8	1,8	16	11	3,6	0	0	3,6	b = Hawk
0	3,6	65	1,8	1,8	9,1	1,8	1,8	15	0	c = Blackbird
0	1,8	5,5	78	3,6	3,6	3,6	0	0	3,6	d = Cuckoo
0	25	1,8	1,8	44	7,3	11	0	0	9,1	e = Lesser Whitethroat
7,3	11	5,5	0	13	47	0	11	5,5	0	f = Chiffchaff
0	5,5	3,6	1,8	5,5	1,8	76	0	0	5,5	g = Eurasian Pygmy Owl
16	0	0	0	0	11	0	65	7,3	0	h = Meadow Pipit
15	0	16	1,8	1,8	11	1,8	9,1	44	0	i = House Sparrow
0	5,5	5,5	3,6	15	0	7,3	0	3,6	60	j = Firecrest

Fig. 4. Error matrix for classification of sound of 10 kind of bird. Used Random Forest, cross-validation method ($k = 10$). General recognition 62,55%. Vector of features from frequency domain has been used (Ev, Odd, Ir, Br descriptors).

5   Model of Classification with a Fuzzy System

In this study Mamdani type of fuzzy system was used for classification. It is based on the concept presented earlier [16,17]. The main advantage of linguistic description is its clarity. In addition, the proposed method is flexible. It allows adding new classes to the classifier without the re-adaptation of the existing elements of the model. Adding a new class involves only new data for that class.

General parameters of the fuzzy system:

- method of fuzzyfication - singleton,
- method of aggregation for premise parts of rules - min,
- operator of implication - min,
- defuzzyfication - middle of maximum.

All the data used in the defining model of system were normalized to the interval $[0, 1]$. Proposed system was realized using the Matlab environment, and its fuzzy logic toolbox.

5.1 Input Variables

The system aims at detecting a species of birds basing on its sound, described by the chosen descriptors. So, the set of the descriptors is an input of the fuzzy system. Each descriptor is represented by a separate linguistic variable. The method proposes spliting the input variables into the fuzzy sets characteristic for each species. This way for each input of linguistic variables we introduce ten sets characteristic of the following species of birds: *CornCrake*, *Hawk*, *Blackbird*, *Cuckoo*, *LesserWhitethroat*, *Chiffchaff*, *EurasianPygmyOwl*, *MeadowPipit*, *HouseSparrow*, *Firecrest*. Each of them is a triangular fuzzy set (see LR fuzzy sets notation in [1]) and is calculated basing on the available data. Similar approach to another problem - the classification of flowers (irises) - was presented in [9].

The method for the construction of an input variable's fuzzy set indicating given species is presented by the formula:

$$Bird_i = \Lambda(x; x_{mean} - 2 \cdot \Delta_L, x_{mean}, x_{mean} + 2\Delta_R), \qquad (8)$$

where: i - number of bird specie $\Delta_L = x_{mean} - x_{min}$, $\Delta_R = x_{max} - x_{mean}$, $x_{min}/x_{max}/x_{mean}$ – the minimum/maximum/mean value of the descriptor for the given species.

This way we constructed all the fuzzy sets for every input of the linguistic variables, which represented the audio descriptors. It may be surprising, but we ignored the properties usually expected from the fuzzy model such as completeness or continuity (see [3]). We also did not expect the values of the fuzzy membership functions to sum to unity within a linguistic variable.

5.2 Output Variables and Basis of Rules

The outputs were simplified to two valued linguistic variables defined on the interval $[0, 1]$. The 0 value means lack of recognition of the given species, whereas 1 means full identification. As we applied one rule for each class, we achieved ten rules. For the specific input of linguistic variables the rule base was very intuitive. The model for the defining rules can be expressed linguistically as follows:

$$IF\ in_1\ is\ Bird_1\ AND\ in_2\ is\ Bird_1\ AND\ ...\ in_i\ is\ Bird_1\ THEN$$
$$Bird_1\ is\ recognized\ and\ Bird_2\ is\ rejected\ AND\ ...\ Bird_i\ is\ rejected \qquad (9)$$

The purpose of each rule was to select the one of the several kinds of birds. This way we obtained ten answers from the fuzzy system, which belong to the numerical interval $[0, 1]$. Thanks to that, the final result of classification could be easily and clearly–cut determined using *winner takes all*principle. This means that the largest output value indicates an identified species of birds assigned to the given audio signal. Such method of modelling fuzzy systems for classification has one main advantage - the simplicity of expansion. Adding next species of the birds does not violate the existing structure. It just needs adding the next fuzzy set of characteristics for the new species and a rule that recognizes the new class of data. Similarly, if we want to import another descriptor to the classifier, the changes also are simple, intuitive and independent of the existing solution.

5.3   Classification Procedure

Testing the efficiency of the proposed fuzzy classifier was done as follows:

- all data was divided into two sets: Training and Testing,
- fuzzy classifier was created basing on the Training data set,
- the created fuzzy classifier was applied for the Testing set, and wrong recognitions were calculated.

In the further part of the paper the term **dividing point** will be used for description of the percent of all data used as Training set. The dividing data is realized randomly. After setting the dividing point, the training part of the data is randomly selected. What is left, is used as the Testing set. Selecting of data keeps proportions for the subset data for every class. Which means that if the dividing point is 60, then the training set is chosen as 60% of the data from each class separately. Efficiency is presented as a percentage of wrong recognitions for the Testing set. For the correctness of the research the procedure was applied for different dividing points from 40 to 88 with step 2. Moreover, for each dividing point the testing procedure was run ten times more than the amount of available data representing a singular class. The result for every dividing point is the average of all start-ups.

Figure 5 shows the effectiveness of a time domain descriptors. We can observe the range of errors from about eleven to about thirteen. This shows a relatively good usefulness of that kind of descriptors. For descriptors of frequency domain, the results were significantly below 50% of errors, thus there is no need for presenting them as they are definitely less useful in this case.

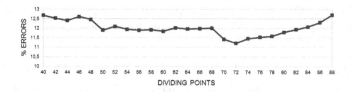

Fig. 5. Effectiveness of time domain descriptors tested by fuzzy system

5.4   Future Application of Fuzzy Numbers in Signal Description

The algorithm of calculating the descriptors plays a fundamental role in the presented study. The MPEG-7 descriptors are mathematical formulas, which operate on numerical data acquired from the audio signal. However, there is a potential to describe some audio parameters linguistically. So there is place for imprecise methods i.e. application of fuzzy numbers. One of the author's directions of future work is the use fuzzy numbers represented by the Ordered Fuzzy Numbers (OFN) model to define signal descriptors.

OFNs ([7,12,13,15,18]) are a quite recent proposition for modeling the calculations on imprecise values in a similar way as the fuzzy numbers. Most important property of OFNs, in this case, is flexibility of calculations [15], so they can be easily applied in different mathematical formulas, as for example MPEG-7 descriptors.

6   The Results of the Research for Neural Classifier

To compare the effectiveness of descriptors (spectrum and time), a neural classifier was used. For the purpose of testing, 50 samples were used for each of the 10 species of birds. The experimental/training set consisted of 30 samples for each species, and the control/testing set contained 20 samples. The applied learning method is based on the delta rule for neural network being a single-layer network. As comparison criteria for evaluating the effectiveness of the two types of descriptors (spectrum and time) the parameter of the speed of neural network learning was used. The test data was divided into 3 sets obtained by using, respectively: the time function descriptor and the spectral function descriptor (Ir - Irregularity of Spectrum, Br - Brightness of sound). For each test data set, tests of neural network learning were performed using two different activation functions: threshold and sigmoid. The learning process was carried out at different learning coefficients, and in case of neurons with sigmoid function at different beta coefficients. In the conducted tests, the applied neural network consisted of 10 identical neurons with two different activation functions ([2]).

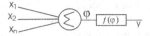

Fig. 6. Model of neuron

The model of this neural network is presented by the formula:

$$\varphi = \sum_{i=1}^{n} x_i * w_i = x * w^T, w = [w_1, w_2, ..., w_i], x = [x_1, x_2, ..., x_i]. \qquad (10)$$

where:n - index of input neuron ($n = 10$),ϕ - membrane potential, w - matrix of weights, x - matrix inputs.

$$f = \begin{cases} 0,5\varphi > p \\ -0,5\varphi < p \end{cases} \qquad (11)$$

where: f - active function,p - threshold,φ - membrane potential.

$$f = \frac{2}{1 + e^{\beta x}} - 1 \tag{12}$$

where: f - active function, $\beta \epsilon (0, 1]$.

The choice of the p-value and as well as the neural response via the function f was selected by numerical experiments, which are associated with the selection of proper parameters of the training process. The process of neural network training employed a continuous activation function; a threshold function is applied in the process of testing. The delta rule in the version for the threshold activation function was used in the training process. The general form delta rule for permanent active function was applied $(f(\varphi))$(see [14]).

$$r = \sigma = [d_i - f(w_i^t x)] f'(w_i^t x) \tag{13}$$

Adjustment of neuron weights:

$$\sigma w_i = c(d_i - y_i) f'(net_i) x_i \tag{14}$$

where: r - signal learner, σ w - correction weights, c - constant learning process, d - error learning, y - matrix outputs, active function, x - matrix inputs.

During the learning process, the focus was on comparing how learning takes place for each of the three data sets obtained thanks to applying the above-mentioned descriptors. The first conclusion that can be drawn is that an indication of those bird species which the network learns to recognize the fastest. It was assumed that the learning process will be carried out for 30 periods (each consisting of 30 data sets for one species). Only on the basis of this phase of the experiment, an overwhelming superiority of time function descriptors over spectral function descriptors can be noticed.

Table 1. The number of cycles of the learning process after which recognition rate reached 25% $*Ir$ - Irregularity of Spectrum, $**Br$ - Brightness of sound

	Time sigmoid activation function	Time threshold activation function	$IR*$ sigmoid activation function	$IR*$ threshold activation function	BR $*$ $*$ sigmoid activation function	BR $*$ $*$ threshold activation function
Corn Crake	18	26	≥ 30	≥ 30	≥ 30	≥ 30
Hawk	12	16	≥ 30	≥ 30	≥ 30	≥ 30
Blackbird	20	21	25	25	≥ 30	≥ 30
Cuckoo Lesser	9	12	≥ 30	≥ 30	≥ 30	≥ 30
Whitethroat	20	22	≥ 30	≥ 30	≥ 30	≥ 30
Primrose	10	10	26	13	≥ 30	≥ 30

The results (see Tab.1) clearly show that: the BR spectrum descriptor is definitely the worst one in terms of learning process efficiency; the IR descriptor is slightly better, but it seems that achieving classification efficiency of 70 to 90%

after further research cannot be expected; however, the time function descriptor is definitely very good and promising.

The next stage of the research was to assess the subject in which the network learning process is carried out for the data from the training set. Experiments were conducted with different activation functions and different parameters of the learning process. The results of the tests are shown in the chart below.

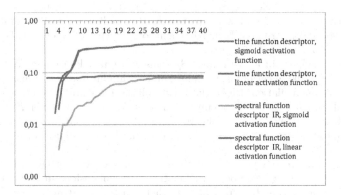

Fig. 7. The process of testing descriptors

It can be concluded that time function descriptors are by far more efficient than spectral descriptors. This conclusion applies, of course, to testing of samples of bird voices. Given the speed of the learning process, such conclusion can be drawn. It would certainly be confirmed when studying the effectiveness (recognition rate) of the learning process, which will be the subject of further research, using more complex neural structures.

7   Conclusions

All the methods used in the paper showed that, for presented application the time domain descriptors are better than frequency. The difference is very significant so, this is a useful sign for the future study on this subject. As the next step in the search for tools to automatic recognition of species of birds by their voices, the main concentration will be directed on the time domain features.

References

1. Dubois, D., Prade, H.M.: Fuzzy sets and systems: Theory and applications. Academic Press, New York (1980)
2. Mc Culloch, Pitts, W.: A Logical Calculus of the Ideas Immanent in Nervous Activity. Neurocomputing: Foundations of Research, str. 15–27 (1988)
3. Driankov, D., Hellendoorn, H., Reinfrank, M.: An Introduction to fuzzy control. Springer, Heidelberg (1996)

4. Manjunath, B.S., Salembier, P., Sikora, T. (eds.): Introduction to MPEG-7. Multimedia Content Description Interface. John Wiley & Sons, Chichester (2002)
5. Martinez, J.M.: MPEG-7 Overview, Klangenfurt (2002)
6. Lindsay, A.T., Burnett, I., Quackenbush, S., Jackson, M.: Fundamentals of audio descriptions. In: Manjunath, B.S., Salembier, P., Sikora, T. (eds.) Introduction to MPEG-7: Multimedia Content Description Interface, pp. 283–298. John Wiley and Sons, Ltd. (2002)
7. Kosiński, W., Prokopowicz, P., Ślęzak, D.: Ordered fuzzy numbers. Bulletin of the Polish Academy of Sciences, Ser. Sci. Math. 51(3), 327–338 (2003)
8. Wieczorkowska, A., Wróblewski, J., Synak, P.: Application of Temporal Descriptors to Musical Instrument Sound Recognition. Journal of Intelligent Information Systems, KL1796-06, 71–93 (2003)
9. Siler, W., Buckley, J.: Fuzzy Expert Systems and Fuzzy Reasoning. Wiley (2005)
10. Tyburek, K.: Classification of string instruments in multimedia database especially for pizzicato articulation, Ph.D. thesis (in Polish), Institute of Fundamental Technological Research Polish Academy of Sciences Warsaw (November 2006)
11. Tyburek, K., Cudny, W., Kosiński, W.: Pizzicato sound analysis of selected instruments In the frequency domain. Image Processing & Communications 11(1), 53–57 (2006)
12. Kosiński, W., Prokopowicz, P.: Fuzziness - Representation of Dynamic Changes, Using Ordered Fuzzy Numbers Arithmetic, New Dimensions in Fuzzy Logic and Related Technologies. In: Proc. of the 5th EUSFLAT, Ostrava, Czech Republic, vol. I, pp. 449–456. University of Ostrava (2007)
13. Kosiński, W., Prokopowicz, P., Rosa, A.: Defuzzification Functionals of Ordered Fuzzy Numbers. IEEE Transactions on Fuzzy Systems 21(6), 1163–1169 (2013), doi:10.1109/TFUZZ.2013.2243456
14. Hannagan, T., Grainger, J.: Learning diagnostic features: The delta rule does Bubbles. Journal of Vision 13(8), 17, 1–11 (2013)
15. Prokopowicz, P.: Flexible and Simple Methods of Calculations on Fuzzy Numbers with the Ordered Fuzzy Numbers Model. In: Rutkowski, L., Korytkowski, M., Scherer, R., Tadeusiewicz, R., Zadeh, L.A., Zurada, J.M. (eds.) ICAISC 2013, Part I. LNCS (LNAI), vol. 7894, pp. 365–375. Springer, Heidelberg (2013)
16. Tyburek, K., Prokopowicz, P., Kotlarz, P.: Fuzzy System for the Classification of Sounds of Birds Based on the Audio Descriptors. In: Rutkowski, L., Korytkowski, M., Scherer, R., Tadeusiewicz, R., Zadeh, L.A., Zurada, J.M. (eds.) ICAISC 2014, Part II. LNCS (LNAI), vol. 8468, pp. 700–709. Springer, Heidelberg (2014)
17. Tyburek, K., Prokopowicz, P., Kotlarz, P.: Computational intelligence in a classification of audio recordings of nature. In: Proc. of the 6th International Conference on Fuzzy Computation Theory and Applications, pp. 187–192. Scitepress - Science and Technology Publications, Rome (2014) ISBN: 978-989-758-053-6
18. Prokopowicz, P., Golsefid, S.M.M.: Aggregation Operator for Ordered Fuzzy Numbers Concerning the Direction. In: Rutkowski, L., Korytkowski, M., Scherer, R., Tadeusiewicz, R., Zadeh, L.A., Zurada, J.M. (eds.) ICAISC 2014, Part I. LNCS (LNAI), vol. 8467, pp. 267–278. Springer, Heidelberg (2014)

CNC Milling Tool Head Imbalance Prediction Using Computational Intelligence Methods

Tomasz Żabiński[1], Tomasz Mączka[1], Jacek Kluska[1(✉)], Maciej Kusy[1],
Piotr Gierlak[2], Robert Hanus[1], Sławomir Prucnal[2], and Jarosław Sęp[2]

[1] Faculty of Electrical and Computer Engineering, Rzeszów University of Technology,
Powstańców Warszawy 12, 35-959 Rzeszów, Poland
{tomz,tmaczka,jacklu,mkusy,rohan}@prz.edu.pl
[2] Faculty of Mechanical Engineering and Aeronautics,
Rzeszów University of Technology,
Powstańców Warszawy 12, 35-959 Rzeszów, Poland
{pgierlak,spktmiop,jsztmiop}@prz.edu.pl

Abstract. In this paper, a mechanical imbalance prediction problem
for a milling tool heads used in Computer Numerical Control (CNC)
machines was studied. Four classes of the head imbalance were examined. The data set included 27334 records with 14 features in the time
and frequency domains. The feature selection procedure was applied in
order to extract the most significant attributes. Only 3 out of 14 attributes were selected and utilized for the representation of each signal.
Seven computational intelligence methods were applied in the prediction
task: K–Means clustering algorithm, probabilistic neural network, single
decision tree, boosted decision trees, multilayer perceptron, radial basis
function neural network and support vector machine. The accuracy, sensitivity and specificity were computed in order to asses the performance
of the algorithms.

Keywords: CNC machines · Milling tool head imbalance · Condition
monitoring · Computational intelligence methods

1 Introduction

This paper describes how machine learning methods can be effectively used to
predict CNC milling tool heads mechanical imbalance on the basis of data registered by the industrial monitoring platform. Balancing of rotating cutting tools
(milling cutters, drills) in CNC machines is a common industrial practice and is
typically done by the use of special balancing machines as a part of the process
setting phase. Detection of tool head imbalance is an important task from a
practical point of view. Tool head imbalance has significant influence on dura-
bility of CNC machines and quality of produced parts. Due to the necessity for
limiting defective parts production and time savings, an online prediction of the
imbalance state of the tool mounted in the machine spindle is desirable. The need
of online CNC tools imbalance monitoring is particularly important in aviation

L. Rutkowski et al. (Eds.): ICAISC 2015, Part I, LNAI 9119, pp. 503–514, 2015.
DOI: 10.1007/978-3-319-19324-3_45

industry, as the unit cost of manufactured parts is high, and elements which do not meet quality standards generate high financial losses. The prototype system for CNC milling tool head imbalance prediction has been created on the basis of production processes monitoring platform described in [1] and [2].

In this paper, the first results of the project phase devoted to the platform adaptation to aviation industry requirements in the field of CNC machines and machining processes condition monitoring, are described. This phase determines hardware and software tools which satisfy industrial requirements and allow intelligent monitoring methods development. The system testbed has been deployed in Haas Factory Outlet (HFO) and Haas Technical Education Center (HTEC) located in Rzeszow University of Technology. Further descriptions in this paper will be referred to the testbed. The system consists of modern industrial automation equipment and software tools used for rapid prototyping of data acquisition and intelligent monitoring solutions. For data acquisition and processing as well as for communication purposes, industrial personal computer (IPC) [3] equipped with real-time subsystem TwinCAT 3 [5] and general operating Windows 7 system is used. Dedicated software, that works on IPC, performs diverse tasks simultaneously, both in real-time subsystem and in Windows 7. The IPC's real-time software automatically acquires data concerning machine and process state on the basis of communication with machine control system and by the use of electrical signals provided by additional sensors. The application for Windows 7 provides Human System Interface (HSI) [4] for machine operators. It also communicates with real-time software modules, peripheral devices (e.g. barcode reader, etc.) and with the server layer. Ethernet is used for communication between IPC and the server. Data is stored in PostgreSQL database and web services are used for communication between devices. The hardware structure of the platform is shown in Fig. 1.

In the real-time layer of IPC software, a separate Programmable Logic Controller (PLC) task created using Structured Text language (norm IEC 61131) in TwinCAT 3 environment is used to read data from CNC machine control system and from digital and analog input terminals. Another real-time task created using Matlab/Simulink software and automatic code generation tools (Matlab Coder [6] and Simulink Coder [7]) are used to perform data processing. Data collection is done using Matlab/Simulink External Mode (Fig. 2).

This paper is composed of the following sections. Section 2 describes the CNC tool imbalance problem and data acquisition and analysis system. In Section 3, computational intelligence methods used in this research are discussed. Section 4 shows the results and in Section 5 the conclusions are formulated.

2   CNC Tool Mechanical Imbalance Problem and Data Acquisition System Description

Mechanical vibrations of the cutting tool are one of the factors that negatively affects quality of parts produced by CNC machines, i.e. machining accuracy and roughness of the machined surface. They can arise for two reasons: (1) the

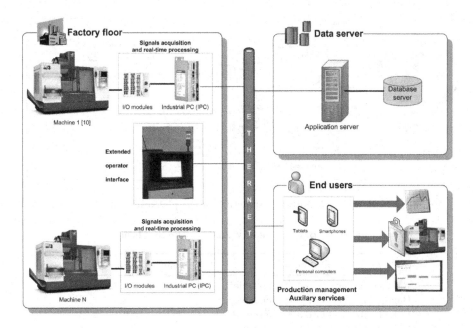

Fig. 1. Hardware structure of the platform

imbalance of the rotating parts of the CNC machine and (2) the forces generated at the contact point of the cutting tool with the workpiece. In this article the first problem is referred to. All rotating parts of the CNC machine such as a spindle, a tool-holder and a tool have to be balanced. In fact, imbalance always appears due to inaccuracies arising from the design, manufacturing, assembling and working state of these elements [8]. The imbalance is defined as the state which exists in a spindle-tool system when vibration force or motion is imparted to its bearings as a result of centrifugal forces [9]. In general, it occurs when forces generated by, or acting on, the rotating element are not in a state of equilibrium.

This article presents an analysis of the tool imbalance for the Haas VM-3 CNC machine [10] shown in Fig. 3. This machine is used for the production of high-precision elements. The machine is equipped with a 12000 rpm (revolutions per minute) inline direct-drive spindle. Tools are held in the spindle drawbar by the use of taper holder. In this study, a milling tool head with seven replaceable cutting plates was used (see Fig. 4). To determine the tool imbalance, we utilized the Haimer Tool Dynamic 2009 balancing machine [11].

Permissible imbalances for machine elements are defined in the norm ISO 1940–1:2003 [12]. On the basis of this standard, the balance quality grade that should be achieved for the individual elements, i.e. spindle unit, drawbar components, milling tool head of the spindle-tool system is specified. The balance quality grade is denoted by a capital letter G with a number, which specifies the maximum permissible velocity in [mm/s] of vibration caused by imbalance.

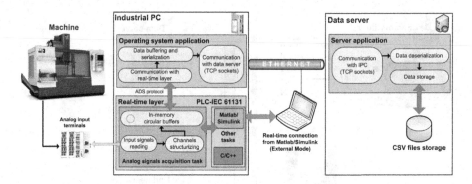

Fig. 2. Software structure of the platform

Table 1. Balance quality grades of milling head

State of the milling head	imbalance [g·mm]	class
Balance in class G 0,4 (acceptable)	0.8	1
Balance in class G 2,5 (acceptable)	4.8	2
Balance in class G 6,3 (unacceptable)	9.1	3
Balance in class G 40 (unacceptable)	18.6	4

The SI unit for imbalance is kilogram meter [kg·m], but for balancing purposes a more practical unit is gram millimeter [g·mm]. The milling tool head consists of a head with replaceable cutting plates, cone for mounting in the spindle and place for drilling balancing holes (see Fig. 4). Permissible balance quality grade for milling tool head according to the norm is G 2,5.

In Table 1, four cases of milling head imbalance levels which were examined during experiments are shown. Balance quality grades G 0,4 and G 2,5 are acceptable, balance quality grade G 6,3 is not permitted due to deterioration of produced parts quality, while the balance quality grade G 40 may result in damage of the spindle unit. The four mentioned classes will be predicted by a classification system.

Experiments described in this paper were conducted in the industrial testbed. The imbalance classes were obtained by mounting cutting plates of different weight in the milling head tool, which ran with the 12000 rpm service speed. This speed corresponds to the frequency of 200 Hz. Precise imbalance value for each class and experiment was examined using the balancing machine. The CNC machine was equipped with one acceleration sensor Hansford HS-100ST mounted on the spindle. During the experiments, the data from the sensor was collected using the platform described in Section 1. The dedicated C6920 IPC and EL3632 analog input module with oversampling from Beckhoff were used for acceleration sensor signal acquisition. IPC was used for signal acquisition and communication with the server and PC station equipped with Matlab/Simulink system, which performed data collection in External Mode. The PC station

Fig. 3. Haas VM-3 CNC machine

received the data from IPC and stored it as binary Matlab files on a hard drive. The signal duration and the sampling interval were equal to 640 ms and 40 μs, respectively. The real-time module for data acquisition ran with main sampling interval 2 ms. Analog input module oversampling factor, defined as the number of probes per one main sampling interval, was set to 50.

Various features of acceleration signal were used in time and frequency domain analysis. Frequency domain signal was obtained with the use of the 16384-point Fast Fourier Transform (FFT) calculated separately for each 640 ms data buffer. Features of the signals used in this study were calculated for each 640 ms data buffer. They are described as follows:

1. Features of the acceleration signal in the time domain:
    (a) T1: maximum,
    (b) T2: minimum,
    (c) T3: mean,
    (d) T4: kurtosis,
    (e) T5: skewness,
    (f) T6: 3rd moment,
    (g) T7: root mean square (RMS),
    (h) T8: standard deviation.

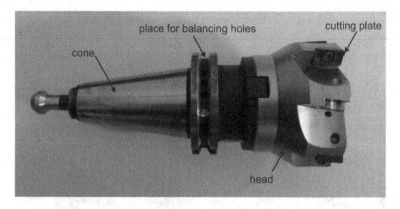

Fig. 4. Milling tool head

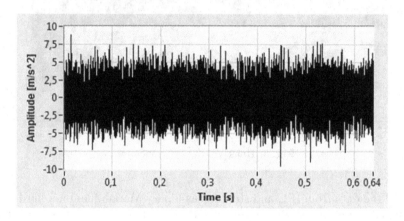

Fig. 5. Exemplary plot of the time signal (class 1)

2. Features of the acceleration signal in the frequency domain:

   (a) F1: RMS amplitude spectrum in the frequency range 190 Hz – 210 Hz,
   (b) F2: RMS amplitude spectrum in the frequency range 390 Hz – 410 Hz,
   (c) F3: RMS amplitude spectrum in the frequency range 10 Hz – 500 Hz,
   (d) F4: RMS amplitude spectrum in the frequency range 500 Hz – 1000 Hz,
   (e) F5: area under the amplitude spectrum in the frequency range 10 Hz – 500 Hz,
   (f) F6: area under the amplitude spectrum in the frequency range 500 Hz – 1000 Hz.

Exemplary plot of the acceleration signal in the time domain is presented in Fig. 5. In Fig. 6, the plot of acceleration signal amplitude spectrum in the frequency range 0 Hz – 1100 Hz and graphical representation of the features F1–F4 are shown.

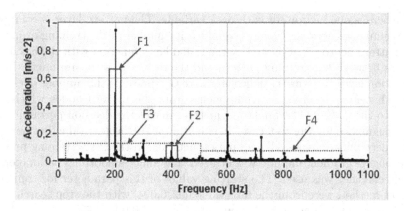

Fig. 6. Graphical representation of the features F1–F4

3   Computational Intelligence Methods Used in the Study

In this research, we used the following classification algorithms:

1. K–Means clustering (K–Means),
2. probabilistic neural network (PNN),
3. single decision tree (SDT),
4. boosted decision trees (BDT),
5. multilayer perceptron (MLP),
6. radial basis function neural network (RBF),
7. support vector machine (SVM).

Since the models are well described in the literature, e.g. in [13], only the short description is here presented. All the classifiers were simulated in DTREG software [14].

3.1   K–Means Method

K–Means method is a clustering algorithm used to group records based on similarity of values for a set of input fields [15]. The basic idea is to try to discover K clusters, such that the records within each cluster are similar to each other and distinct from records in other clusters. The grouping process relies on the iterative minimization of the sum of squared distances computed between input data and the cluster center. In the experiments, the model was trained with $K \in \{2, 3, \ldots, 200\}$ clusters per target category. The model was created with 195 clusters for each class. Predictions were made by using the closest cluster.

3.2   Probabilistic Neural Network

PNN is a feedforward model proposed by Specht [16]. This network consists of an input layer, a pattern layer, a summation layer and an output layer. In the input layer, there is one neuron for each data variable. The pattern layer is composed of the number of neurons which is equal to the number of the training examples. Each pattern neuron is activated by the radial basis function with the Euclidean distance between the training pattern and the test case as the argument. In the summation layer there are G neurons, where G represents the number of classes. Each gth neuron receives the components from the pattern nodes which only belong to the class g. The final, output layer makes the decision pertaining the class assignment for the test case. It is based on the largest value between the signals determined among all summation neurons. In the PNN training process, the conjugate gradient method was utilized. The single smoothing parameter (σ) for this classifier was used. The starting values of this parameter for conjugate gradient method were from the interval $[0.002, 0.004]$ with the step search equal to 5. The optimal value of σ was found to be equal 0.0036067.

3.3   Single Decision Tree

SDT is a decision model originally described in [17]. The algorithm of SDT searches for all possible variables and values in order to find the best split – the question that splits the data into two parts until some stopping criterion is satisfied. In this study, Gini and entropy fitting algorithms were applied to split variables, the minimum rows allowed in a node was 5, the minimum size for node to split was equal to 10 and the maximum tree levels were set to 6. We did not apply any pruning algorithm to simplify the structure of the tree.

3.4   Boosted Decision Trees

Boosting is a technique for improving the accuracy of a predictive function by applying the function repeatedly in a series and combining the output of each function with weighting so that the total error of the prediction is minimized. The tree boost algorithm used in [14] was developed by Friedman [18] and is optimized for improving the accuracy of models built on decision trees. For K classification problems, BDT builds K parallel series to model the probability of each possible category. At the end of the process, the probability values for the categories are compared and the one that minimizes misclassification cost is chosen as the best predicted category. In our work, the maximum number of trees was chosen to be 100 while the depth of individual trees was set to 5. Minimum size for node to split was equal to 10.

3.5   Multilayer Perceptron

MLP is the feedforward neural network [19]. It is composed of an input layer, a number of hidden layers and an output layer. The neurons in the hidden and output layer are activated by some transfer functions. The number of hidden layers along with the number of hidden neurons is an open problem which is usually solved experimentally. In this research, MLP with single hidden layer was simulated. The number of hidden neurons was taken from the set $\{2, 3, \ldots, 20\}$. Both hidden and output layer were activated using logistic transfer function. Scaled conjugate gradient method was applied for MLP training. The optimal MLP structure was 3 input neurons, 5 hidden neurons and 4 output neurons.

3.6   Radial Basis Function Network

RBF neural network is a feedforward network composed of an input layer, a radial basis hidden layer and a linear output layer. The hidden layer is composed of radial basis function neurons centered on an input vector. The number of neurons is determined during the training process. In this work, an evolutionary approach was applied for this purpose [20]. The linear output layer calculates the weighted sum of the hidden layer outputs. For the classification problems, there are four nodes in the output layer, which represent a target category. RBF was trained up to 100 radial basis neurons with the spread constant from the interval: $[0.01, 400]$. The optimal RBF structure was obtained for 25 neurons.

3.7   Support Vector Machine

SVM [21] is a classification algorithm which constructs an optimal separating hypersurface for the input vectors with associated class labels ± 1. The equation of this hypersurface is found by solving the quadratic programming problem. The radial basis and polynomial kernel functions were utilized to perform training and classification of SVM. The grid search was used in order to determine optimal parameters of SVM: $C \in \{10^{-1}, 10^0, 10^1, 10^2, 10^3, 10^4, 10^5\}$ - the upper bound for Lagrange multipliers and $\gamma \in \{1.2, 1.5, 2, 5, 10, 50, 80, 100, 200, 500\}$ - the spread constans for radial basis kernel function. The optimal SVM classifier was obtained for the kernel functions with: $C = 1$, $\gamma = 0.5$. The number of support vectors was equal to 2143.

4   Results

The input data consists of 27334 records. Each record is composed of 14 attributes: eight features of acceleration signal in the time domain (T1–T8) and six features of acceleration signal in the frequency domain (F1–F6). Four class data classification problem is considered: balance in class G 0,4 (class 1), balance in class G 2,5 (class 2), balance in class G 6,3 (class 3) and balance in class G 40 (class 4). In this work, we apply the feature selection procedure in order to extract the most significant features out of all 14 attributes. This procedure steps through the predictor variables one at a time. It randomly shuffles the values of the selected variable across the rows of the dataset (same set of values, just randomly moved to different rows), and it evaluates the accuracy of the predictions using the randomly moved variable values. If the variable is important, randomizing the order of its values greatly degrades the accuracy of the predictions. If the variable is unimportant, the order of its values has little or no impact on the

Table 2. The accuracy, sensitivity and specificity for all classes obtained by applying considered computational intelligence methods

Classifier	class 1			class 2			class 3			class 4		
	Acc	Sen	Spe	Acc	Sen	Spe	Acc	Sen	Spe	Acc	Sen	Spe
K–Means	1	1	1	1	1	1	1	1	1	1	1	1
PNN	1	1	1	1	1	1	1	1	1	1	0.999	1
SDT	1	1	1	1	1	1	0.999	0.999	0.999	0.999	0.999	1
BDT	1	1	1	1	1	1	0.999	0.999	0.999	0.999	0.999	0.999
MLP	1	1	1	1	1	1	0.999	0.998	0.999	0.999	0.998	0.999
RBF	1	1	1	0.999	0.998	1	0.998	0.995	0.999	0.998	0.998	0.998
SVM	1	1	1	1	0.999	1	0.998	0.996	0.999	0.998	0.998	0.998

accuracy of the model. It then ranks the importance of the variables based on the amount of degradation that occurred by randomizing the values and scales the scores so the most important has a relative importance of 100. After application of this procedure, 3 out of all 14 attributes were selected.: RMS amplitude spectrum in the frequency range 190 Hz – 210 Hz, RMS amplitude spectrum in the frequency range 390 Hz – 410 Hz and RMS amplitude spectrum in the frequency range 10 Hz – 500 Hz named F1, F2 and F3, respectively. For the data set composed of 27334 records with three features we performed four class classification problem. Table 2 presents the accuracy (Acc), the sensitivity (Sen) and the specificity (Spe) obtained for K–Means, PNN, SDT, BDT, MLP, RBF, and SVM models obtained using 10-fold cross validation testing method. Since there are four classes among the data the results are presented for each class.

It should be emphasized that class 1 was ideally predicted by all the algorithms. For K–Means model the highest prediction ability results were obtained. Therefore, for this classifier we present the confusion matrix (Table 3). As shown, all the diagonal elements of this matrix are different than 0 while the remaining ones are equal to 0. It means that this classifier has ideal overall prediction ability.

Table 3. The confusion matrix obtained for K–Means classifier

		Predicted class			
		class 1	class 2	class 3	class 4
	class 1	9625	0	0	0
Actual class	class 2	0	5888	0	0
	class 3	0	0	6176	0
	class 4	0	0	0	5645

5   Conclusions

In this article, we considered the CNC milling tool head imbalance prediction problem in Haas VM-3 Machine. Four classes of the head imbalance were examined. The data set consisted of 27334 records with 14 features in the time and frequency domains. The feature selection procedure was applied in order to extract the most significant attributes. As the result, 3 out of 14 attributes were selected and utilized for the representation of each signal: RMS amplitude spectrum in the frequency range 190 Hz – 210 Hz, RMS amplitude spectrum in the frequency range 390 Hz – 410 Hz and RMS amplitude spectrum in the frequency range 10 Hz – 500 Hz. The results of the analysis indicate that the best features for the diagnosis of imbalance are: F1, F2 and F3. This is consistent with the interpretation of the imbalance phenomenon on the basis of mechanics. Information about the state of imbalance is contained mainly in the band of spectrum derived from the angular frequency (represented by the feature F1) and its first harmonic (represented by the feature F2). From the standpoint of the imbalance state classification, a low frequency band analysis is also important (represented by the feature F3).

Seven well known computational intelligence methods were applied: K–Means clustering algorithm, probabilistic neural network, single decision tree, boosted decision trees, multilayer perceptron, radial basis function neural network and support vector machine. The accuracy, sensitivity and specificity were used to asses the performance of the algorithms. The values of these indicators were very high for all the models. However, for the K–Means algorithm, they were all equal to one.

It was experimentally proven that it is possible to detect, with high accuracy, different grades of CNC tool head imbalance by utilization of computational intelligence methods. Tool head imbalance detection should be used in machine monitoring procedure performed when new tool is installed or after particular period of its working time. It is worth to emphasize that implementation of proposed imbalance monitoring approach in real-time mode seems to be possible. The result of the feature selection procedure shows that only 3 attributes of acceleration signal are sufficient for accurate imbalance prediction. The imbalance prediction ability of all seven tested computational methods is very high and almost the same. Because of that, for real-time purposes the method with the lowest computational power requirements can be selected. However, further research is required in this field.

Acknowledgements. This research was partially supported by the Grant INNO-TECH–K2/IN2/41/182370/NCBR/13 from the National Centre for Research and Development in Poland and by U-533/DS/M

References

1. Mączka, T., Żabiński, T.: Platform for Intelligent Manufacturing Systems with elements of knowledge discovery. In: Manufacturing System, pp. 183–204. InTech, Croatia (2012)
2. Żabiński, T., Mączka, T., Kluska, J., Kusy, M., Hajduk, Z., Prucnal, S.: Failures Prediction in the Cold Forging Process Using Machine Learning Methods. In: Rutkowski, L., Korytkowski, M., Scherer, R., Tadeusiewicz, R., Zadeh, L.A., Zurada, J.M. (eds.) ICAISC 2014, Part I. LNCS(LNAI), vol. 8467, pp. 622–633. Springer, Heidelberg (2014)
3. IPC–BECKHOFF New Automation Technology, http://www.beckhoff.com/ipc
4. Żabiński, T., Mączka, T.: Implementation of Human-System Interface for Manufacturing Organizations. In: Hippe, Z.S., Kulikowski, J.L., Mroczek, T. (eds.) Human – Computer Systems Interaction. AISC, Part I, vol. 98, pp. 13–31. Springer, Heidelberg (2012)
5. TwinCAT 3, http://www.beckhoff.com/english/twincat/twincat-3.htm
6. Matlab Coder, http://www.mathworks.com/products/matlab-coder/
7. Simulink Coder, http://www.mathworks.com/products/simulink-coder/
8. Shen, C., Wang, G., Wang, S., Liu, G.: The Imbalance Source of Spindle-Tool System and Influence to Machine Vibration Characteristics. In: Second International Conference on Digital Manufacturing & Automation (2011)
9. Smith, G.T.: Cutting tool technology: industrial handbook. Springer-Verlag London Limited (2008)
10. Haas VM-3 CNC machine, http://int.haascnc.com
11. HAIMER Tool Dynamic (2009), www.haimer.com
12. ISO 1940–1:2003 Mechanical vibration - Balance quality requirements for rotors in a constant (rigid) state - Part 1: Specification and verification of balance tolerances
13. Wu, X., Kumar, V., Quinlan, J.R., et al.: Top 10 algorithms in data mining. Knowledge Information Systems 14, 1–37 (2008)
14. Sherrod, P.H.: DTREG predictive modelling software, http://www.dtreg.com
15. Hartigan, J.A., Wong, M.A.: A k-means clustering algorithm. Journal of the Royal Statistical Society - Series C (Applied Statistics) 1, 100–108 (1979)
16. Specht, D.F.: Probabilistic neural networks. Neural Networks 3, 109–118 (1990)
17. Breiman, L., Friedman, J.H., Olshen, R.A., Stone, C.J.: Classification and regression trees. Wadsworth, Belmont (1984)
18. Friedman, J.H.: Greedy Function Approximation: A Gradient Boosting Machine. IMS Reitz Lecture (1999)
19. Rumelhart, D., McClelland, J.: Parallel Distributed Processing. MIT Press, Cambridge (1986)
20. Chen, S., Wang, X., Harris, C.J.: Experiments with repeating weighted boosting search for optimization in signal processing applications. IEEE Trans. Systems Man Cybernetics Part B Cybernetics 35, 682–693 (2005)
21. Vapnik, V.: The Nature of Statistical Learning Theory. Springer, New York (1995)

Computer Vision, Image and Speech Analysis

A Feature-Based Machine Learning Agent for Automatic Rice and Weed Discrimination

Beibei Cheng[1] and Eric T. Matson[2(✉)]

[1] Microsoft
Redmond, WA, USA
bcx93@mst.edu
[2] Purdue University
M2M Lab/Department of Computer and Information Technology
West Lafayette IN, USA
ematson@purdue.edu

Abstract. Rice is an important crop utilized as a staple food in many parts of the world and particularly of importance in Asia. The process to grow rice is very human labor intensive. Much of the difficult labor of rice production can be automated with intelligent and robotic platforms. We propose an intelligent agent which can use sensors to automate the process of distinguishing between rice and weeds, so that a robot can cultivate fields. This paper describes a feature-based learning approach to automatically identify and distinguish weeds from rice plants. A Harris Corner Detection algorithm is firstly applied to find the points of interests such as the tips of leaf and the rice ear, secondly, multiple features for each points surrounding area are extracted to feed into a machine learning algorithm to discriminate weed from rice, last but not least, a clustering algorithm is used for noise removal based on the points position and density. Evaluation performed on images downloaded from internet yielded very promising classification result.

1 Introduction

Rice is an important crop utilized and depended on as a staple food in the diet of many people. This dependence spans many parts of the world and is of particular importance in many parts of Asia. The process to grow rice is not currently as automated as are many other dependent staple crops across the world such as wheat, corn or sorghum. These crops are produced in large fields with efficient techniques, large machinery and mass production. Unlike these crops, the production of rice remains a very human labor intensive practice. Given the statement of belief by the IEEE Robotics and Automation Society [1], the automation of agriculture can be enhanced with robotic, and therefore agent-oriented systems.

Agriculture is humankinds oldest and still its most important economic activity, providing the food, feed, fiber, and fuel necessary for

© Springer International Publishing Switzerland 2015
L. Rutkowski et al. (Eds.): ICAISC 2015, Part I, LNAI 9119, pp. 517–527, 2015.
DOI: 10.1007/978-3-319-19324-3_46

our survival. With the global population expected to reach 9 billion by 2050, agricultural production must double if it is to meet the increasing demands for food and bioenergy. Given limited land, water and labor resources, it is estimated that the efficiency of agricultural productivity must increase by 25% to meet that goal, while limiting the growing pressure that agriculture puts on the environment. Robotics and automation can play a significant role in society meeting 2050 agricultural production needs. For six decades robots have played a fundamental role in increasing the efficiency and reducing the cost of industrial production and products.

Much of the difficult labor of rice production can be automated with intelligent and robotic platforms. We propose an intelligent agent architecture which can use sensors to automate the process of distinguishing between rice and weeds, so that a robot can cultivate fields. This agent system will be used to control a platform, such as Bonirob as shown in Fig. 1. The Bonirob [2] is an example of a row crop robotic platform that can be utilized in tillage and general crop production.

Fig. 1. Bonirob (IEEE RAS)

1.1 Motivation

As a good source of protein and a staple food in many parts of the world, rice is mostly planted in Asia and subtropical/tropical zone of Africa. Weedy plants which are growing with rice not only cost time and energy for farmers to get rid of them, but also cost rice damage and lost earnings. Nowadays, with the development of agriculture technology, we are looking for an automatic rice/weed discrimination method in order to produce rice in a more efficient way.

The cycle of rice growing can be divided into five stages as showing in Fig. 2 [3]. Rice ear starts growing up after the heading stage, where rice can be obtained from, as shown in Fig. 3 marked by pink circle. There is a plenty of weeds in the rice farm, Fig. 4 - 7 shows four typical types of common weeds in rice fields [4].

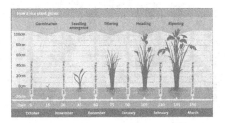

Fig. 2. The cycle of rice

Fig. 3. Rice ear and leaf tips

1.2   Background and Related Work

Several approaches to rice/weed classification have been proposed with varying degree of success. Ryohei et al proposed a method of rice plant detection based on rice ear [5]. Xavier et al developed an approach using crop rows extraction to get rid of the weed [6]. Hong et al used feature extraction and artificial neural network for crop/weed segmentation [7]. However, there are drawbacks in each existing approach: although rice ear can be used as an important feature to distinguish rice from weed in [5], the weed inside young rice plant (without rice ear) has to be identified as well, which is even more critical since weed often causes more damages to young rice; different from crop in [6], the rice is planted in the water and is growing in both vertical and horizontal direction, which is impossible to use the straight row to eliminate weed; [7] requires to segment each individual plant before extracting its features, while it is hard to separate them since the leaves of rice are overlapping each other as shown in Fig. 9.

After addressing the above drawbacks, this paper proposed a general solution to discriminate weed in different rice growing stages. The solution is briefly

Fig. 4. Sagittaria Trifolia

Fig. 5. Semen Euphorbiae

Fig. 6. Alligator Alternanthera

Fig. 7. Barnyardgrass

described as below. First, instead of segmenting the edge of rice/weed, the corner points (i.e. the tips of leaf, the rice ear as shown in Fig. 3) are detected by using *Harris Corner Algorithm.* Second, multiple features for each points surrounding area are extracted to represent the color of that area, the coarseness of that area and so on. Thirdly, some machine learning algorithms are utilized to train those features in order to get a classifier to deliver high discrimination accuracy. The detail of the methodology is given in the next session.

This paper is organized with the methods in section 2, experiments and results in section 3, conclusions in section 4 and finally the future work in section 5.

2   Methods

An overview of methods used is shown in Fig. 8. A pre-processing algorithm - Harris corner detection is used for the points of interests localization and characterization. Feature sets for all the detected Harris points are generated. Its subset is used to train the decision tree. Then the trained decision tree is applied to the entire feature sets in order to remove the rice points. A post-processing algorithm DBSCAN is used to filter the false positive weed points. The following shows each processing step in detail.

2.1   Sample Image

Fig. 9 is an image with size 1125x1500 downloaded from the internet with some weeds named Semen Euphorbia inside the rice. As you can see, some rice plants have ear while some do not. The following shows the steps how to find out the weed from the rice.

2.2   Harris Corner Detection

The tips of roots/branches/leaves/gains from both weed and rice are corner points. Based on the fact that Corner is detected based on the significant change

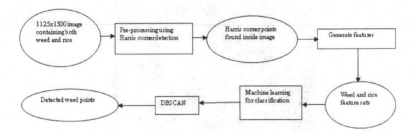

Fig. 8. Overview weed discrimination from rice

in all directions while edge has no change along the edge direction, Harris corner detection algorithm [8] is firstly applied to mark the region of interest as shown in Fig. 9. Fig. 9 is firstly divided into 480x360 sub-region from top left to bottom right. Harris points are then calculated based on each sub-region. Fig. 10 demonstrates the overall detected Harris points.

Fig. 9. Original Image (Rice with Semen Euphorbia in the center)

2.3   Feature Extraction

Relevant features extracted from a 40x40 window with the Harris corner pixel at the center include color features and texture features. Color features measure the absolute color and the change of color while the textual features measure the smoothness, coarseness and regularity of that area. The color features are item 1 to 6, in Table 1. The textual features are item 7 to 14. However, these textual features use only histograms, which carry no information regarding the relative positions of pixels with respect to each other. To solve this problem, a co-occurrence matrix [9] is used which considers pixel position. Additional textual features from these co-occurrence matrices are labeled from item 15 to item 24 in Table 1.

Fig. 10. Output Image with Harris Points

2.4   Feature Evaluation

After the 24 features listed in Table 1 are extracted from each point in Fig. 10, the ground truth for each point is also manually labeled(0 represent rice while 1 represent weed). Each features information gain [10] is calculated and three features (item 11, 13 and 14) are removed because their information gain is zero. Fig. 11 and Fig. 12 demonstrates the data visualization with red dots representing rice points and blue dots representing weed points for the worst two features combination (feature 11 and feature 13) and the best features combination (feature 6 and feature 22), respectively.

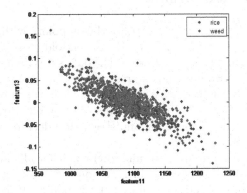

Fig. 11. Data distribution in feature 11 and feature 13 plane

2.5   Machine Learning Algorithm

Supervised Learning: Therefore, the training data set including the points twenty-one features and the ground truth is used to train multiple machine learning algorithms such as Decision Tree [11], Support Vector Machine [13], Neural Network [10].

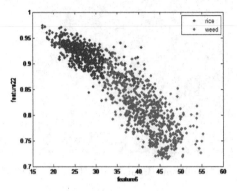

Fig. 12. Data distribution in feature 6 and feature 22 plane

Clustering Algorithm: Grouping the more similar objects in the same group, clustering algorithm is an unsupervised learning method. Density-based spatial clustering of applications with noise (DBSCAN) [12] is the clustering algorithm chosen in this research. The DBSCAN identifies clusters in large spatial data sets by looking at the local density of database elements. It is applied here to remove the false positive Harris Points of weed based on the different density between weed area and rice area.

3   Experiments and Results

The experimental data set consists of 1261 Harris points with 561 rice points while 700 weed points as shown in Figure 10. A ten-fold cross validation is used to set up the training and testing data sets. The data set is divided into ten parts where 9/10 is used for training and the rest is used for testing. This procedure is repeated ten times. The accuracy of the classifier is based on averaging the accuracy of the ten test sets. Table 2 presents the accuracy result by applying different machine learning algorithms, and shows that decision tree delivers the best classification result.

Fig. 13 provides the ten-fold cross validation result for all Harris points after applying the trained decision tree classifier. As you can see, most of Harris points of the weed are correctly discriminated except few points of rice are incorrectly detected as the weed. DBSCAN is then applied for grouping those Harris points based on their position. For DBSCAN algorithm, the number of objects in a neighborhood of an object is set to be 8 and the neighborhood radius is set to be 50. As shown in Fig.14, those false positive weeds with black color are removed because of their low density.

Table 1. Extracted Features

Feature Set	Label	Measure	Description
Color Features	1	Mean Red	the average red value inside a window
	2	Mean Green	the average green value inside a window
	3	Mean Blue	The average blue value inside window
	4	Std Red	The standard deviation of red inside window
	5	Std Green	The standard deviation of green inside window
	6	Std Blue	The standard deviation of blue inside window
Textual Features	7	Mean of histogram	the first moment of gray image
	8	Variance of histogram	The second moment of gray image
	9	Skewness of histogram	The third moment of gray image
	10	Flatness of histogram	The fourth moment of gray image
	11	Contrast of histogram	The intensity contrast of gray image
	12	Maximum of histogram	The uniformity of gray image
	13	Correlation of histogram	The correlation of gray image
	14	Closeness of histogram	The homogeneity of gray image
	15 16	Contrast	The intensity contrast of correlation matrices
	17 18	Correlation	The correlation of correlation matrices
	19 20	Uniformity	The uniformity of correlation matrices
	21 22	Closeness	The homogeneity of correlation matrices
	23 24	Strongest	response The maximum probability of correlation matrices

Table 2. Performance comparison for different machine learning algorithms

	TPRate	FPRate	Precision	Recall
Decision Tree	0.982	0.019	0.982	0.977
SVM	0.952	0.047	0.953	0.952
Naive Bayes	0.929	0.066	0.931	0.929

Fig. 13. Output Image with weed discrimination after decision tree classification

Fig. 14. Output Image with weed discrimination after DBSCAN clustering

4   Conclusions

As the importance of rice grains are paramount to the health and security of people in many parts of the world, the increased efficiency introduced by intelligent agent systems and robotics, will be critical in the coming years. As the emphasis has been placed on agricultural robotics by many government and academic agencies to fulfill these needs, the technology to enable humans to reduce the human effort and time required to produce rice will be important. The human time can be used for higher level practice, while the lower lever and lower capability tasks of rice production can be relegated to machines.

One of the time consuming tasks is that of cultivation and reduction of noxious and resource draining weed species. Reducing the weeds will allow all ground nutrients to be focused on the efficient production of rice or other needed grains. We have proposed and developed an intelligent agent which can use sensors to automate the process of distinguishing between rice and weeds, so that a robot can take on the former human task of field cultivation. If the robot cannot distinguish between the weed and the crop, it is impossible to deploy robots for this time consuming and arduous environment task. So, in this paper, we describe a feature-based learning approach to automatically identify and distinguish weeds from rice plants.

This paper proposes a framework for weed and rice identification based on image feature analysis and machine learning techniques. Harris point finder is applied to the preprocessing of the images. Multiple features associated with the weed/rice types are then extracted. Machine learning algorithms are employed to classify weed from rice and then DBSCAN is used to remove the false positive weed. The experimental results demonstrate that integration of various image processing techniques, feature extraction techniques, and machine learning methods as proposed in this paper can achieve high classification accuracy.

5   Future Work

This current work results in an agent that can do rudimentary work to distinguish between rice plants and common weed types. The future work includes the inclusion of more weed types to differentiate from rice. Secondly, the implementation of this system on a rice field robot for navigation and elementary cultivation testing. Finally, the generalized methodology will be used to create a method employable in any production crop scenario.

References

1. IEEE RAS Agricultural Robotics, http://www.ieee-ras.org/agricultural-robotics
2. Ruckelshausen, A., Biber, P., Dorna, M., Gremmes, H., Klose, R., Linz, A., Rahe, F., Resch, R., Thiel, M., Trautz, D., Weiss, U.: BoniRob an autonomous field robot platform for individual plant phenotyping. In: Proceedings of the Joint International Agricultural Conference, Wageningen (2009)

3. The Rice Growing and Production Process,
   http://www.rga.org.au/f.ashx/rice_growing.pdf
4. General Weed Types,
   http://wenku.baidu.com/view/e0bb770a844769eae009ed6a.html
5. Masuda, R., Nakayama, K., Nomura, K.: Rice plant detection in heading team for autonomous robot navigation. In: XVII World Congress of the International Commission of Agricultural and Biosystems Engineering (CIGR), Qubec City, Canada, June 13-17 (2010)
6. Burgos-Artizzu, X.P., Ribeiro, A., Guijarro, M., Pajares, G.: Real-time image processing for crop/weed discrimination in maize fields. Comput. Electron. 75, 337–346 (2011)
7. Jeon, H.Y., Tian, L.F., Zhu, H.: Robust crop and weed segmentation under uncontrolled outdoor illumination. Sensors 11, 6270–6283 (2011)
8. Harris, C., Stephens, M.: A combined corner and edge detector. In: Alvey Vision Conference, pp. 147–152 (1988)
9. Haralick, R.M., Shanmugam, K.: Itshak Dinstein, Textural Features for Image Classification. IEEE Transactions on Systems, Man, and Cybernetics SMC 3, 610–621 (1973)
10. Mitchell, T.M.: Machine Learning. The Mc-Graw-Hill Companies, Inc. (1997)
11. Breiman, L.: Classification and Regression Trees. CRC Press, Boca Raton (1984)
12. Ester, M., Kriegel, H.-P., Sander, J., Xu, X.: A density-based algorithm for discovering clusters in large spatial databases with noise. In: Simoudis, E., Han, J., Fayyad, U.M. (eds.) Proceedings of the Second International Conference on Knowledge Discovery and Data Mining (KDD 1996), pp. 226–231. AAAI Press (1996)
13. Cortes, C., Vapnik, V.: Support-vector networks. Machine Learning 20(3), 273 (1995)

Relation of Average Error in Prolate Spheroidal Wave Functions Algorithm for Bandlimited Functions Approximation to Radius of Information

Michał Cholewa[✉]

Institute of Theoretical and Applied Informatics, Polish Academy of Sciences;
Bałtycka 5, 44-100 Gliwice, Poland
mcholewa@iitis.pl

Abstract. This article focuses on calculation of how close the estimated average error of Prolate Spheroidal Wave Functions (PSWFs) approaches the actual radius of information in the presence of both jitter and approximation and quantization error. The existing upper bound of the estimation is here paired with lower bound and compared to bounds on information radius. Performed calculation are to obtain the precision of error estimation.

1 Introduction

Prolate Spheroidal Wave Functions (PSWF), eigenfunctions of certain integral operator form an orthonormal base for linear space of bandlimited signals. The ortogonality of PSWFs in $L^2(-\infty, \infty)$ as well as their other properties led to construction of an approximation algorithm for bandlimited signals based on obtaining the coordinates of a signal in PSWF base. The PSWF approximation algorithm is, on grounds of Smolyak's Lemma, optimal with respect to error. This optimality is, however, guaranteed only in case where both approximation and quantization error δ and jitter γ are equal to zero.

Optimality of PSWF algorithm led to further research concerning its behavior when working with distorted data, namely, how the algorithm reacts to approximation and quantization error δ and jitter γ. The work of Dąbrowska in [3] established an estimation of pessimistic error of PSWF algorithm on subset of bandlimited functions. Kowalski in [9] worked on estimation of the algorithm's average error. His calculations were performed under the assumption that $\gamma = 0$. In [2] his work was extended by estimating the bound on average error including non-zero jitter γ. The calculations shown, that the average error is bounded by expression linearly dependent on jitter.

This work further extends the result of [2] by inserting them into context of radius of information, the ultimate lower bound for error.

The main goal of the article is to estimate the radius and diagonal of information operator for PSWFs algorithm (in respect to Gaussian measure ξ as defined

© Springer International Publishing Switzerland 2015
L. Rutkowski et al. (Eds.): ICAISC 2015, Part I, LNAI 9119, pp. 528–540, 2015.
DOI: 10.1007/978-3-319-19324-3_47

in [9], and reminded in Appendix B) in presence of jitter and approximation and quantization error, then to relate them to calculated estimates of average error. The result will show how predictable and how close to actual radius of information the PSWF algorithm can get.

This paper is organized as follows: In Section 3 we state the problem we aim to solve and introduce the PSWF algorithm. Then, in Section 4 we present the main result of this article, which is the estimation of the information radius for PSWF algorithm (with $\gamma > 0, \delta > 0$) and present the relation the average error has to radius of information (as Theorem 1). Finally, in Section 5 we conclude the presented work. This article also has two Appendices - Appendix A offers more detailed description of PSWFs and some of their properties we will refer to. Appendix B defines the measure we will be using for averaging the radius of information of the PSWF algorithm.

2 Related Work

The theory of optimal algorithms (in approach presented by Traub and Woźniakowski [19]), as important field of computer science. It has been vastly researched, with works such as Milanese's [12] and it is the ground for many further research, with the one of the main result being Smolyak's Lemma [17] determining existence of linear optimal algorithm once certain assumptions are met. The Smolyak's lemma allowed the certainty in finding fast optimal algorithm to many convex problems - one of which is the problem of approximation in unitary spaces.

The signal recovery itself, due to its wide practical applications was approached from several angles, such as bi-orthogonal systems in [5] by Genossar, and work by Kowalski and Kacewicz in [6]. More recent results include Tropp's [20] where author successfully applied greedy algorithm of Orthogonal Matching Pursuit (OMP), as well as bilinear transforms presented in [21].

The algorithms for digital approximation meet with several difficulties that can diminish their precision, such as the infinite-dimensionality of natural signal space, the problem which is described by works such as Khare and George in [8]. Other issue is the fact that the systems usually deal with distorted input data. That problem for approximations in unitary spaces was addressed by Kowalski and Kacewicz in [6,7] and Kowalski, Stegner and Sikorski in [11].

The Prolate Spheroidal Wave Functions (PSWF) were introduced in 1961 by Slepian et al in [16] as orthogonal functions spanning bandlimited signal space. Then Fuchs in [4] approaches them from the area of eigenfunctions of integral equations. As orthonormal system spanning bandlimited signal space PSWFs were researched and used as base for approximation algorithms notably by Lindquist and Wager in [14], where they were used for analysis of fMRI images. They have also been used as a base for finite fractional Fourier transform in [13] or as base for solving partial differential equations in [1].

That set of properties make prolate spheroidal wave functions a good option for approximation algorithms. In [9], Kowalski proves that Prolate Spheroidal

Wave Functions algorithm is an optimal algorithm in case of precise data (with $\gamma = 0, \delta = 0$). The adding the jitter factor is presented by Kowalski and Dąbrowska in [10], which is followed by [3] in which Dąbrowska researches the effect of jitter and approximation and quantization error on PSWF algorithm in pessimistic case for energy-limited subset of bandlimited functions. Further research in [2] extends the obtained analysis by providing the upper bound of the PSWF algorithm's average error with $\gamma > 0, \delta > 0$.

3   Problem Statement

The goal of this paper is estimate the distance of average error of the Prolate Spheroidal Wave Function algorithm for approximation of signals (functions) to its radius of information. Such calculation is meant to analyze the predictability of the average error, by which we understand the precision of its estimation.

The PSWF algorithm domain is the subset of space

$$B(\Omega_0) = \left\{ \int_{-\Omega_0}^{\Omega_0} X(\omega)e^{i\omega \cdot} d\omega : X \in L_2(-\Omega_0, \Omega_0) \right\}. \tag{1}$$

Here, $0 < \Omega_0 < \infty$, and $L_2(-\Omega_0, \Omega_0)$ denotes the space of all square integrable complex-valued functions on the interval $(-\Omega_0, \Omega_0)$. The functions in $B(\Omega_0)$ are said to be band-limited to the level of Ω_0.

The PSWF algorithm approximates functions from $B(\Omega_0)$ on finite interval $[-\tau, \tau]$, defined as

$$B(\Omega_0, \tau) = \left\{ f \in L_2(-\tau, \tau) : \sum_{i=0}^{\infty} \frac{|\langle f, \phi_i \rangle|}{\lambda_i} < \infty \right\}. \tag{2}$$

Here ϕ_i is the i-th Prolate Spheroidal Wave Function and λ_i is its energy concentration on interval $[-\tau, \tau]$.

This approach is finite information oriented (we assume we can have only finite amount of information about the function) and that this information is additionally distorted by quantization error $\delta = (\delta_0, \ldots, \delta_{n-1}), \delta_i < \Delta$ and jitter $\gamma = (\gamma_0, \ldots, \gamma_{n-1}), \gamma_i < \Gamma$.

That is, we shall assume that signals in the space $B(\Omega_0, \tau)$ are given through an information operator of the form $\Re : B(\Omega_0, \tau) \longrightarrow \mathbb{C}^n$

$$\Re(f, \gamma, \delta) = (L_0(f, \gamma_0, \delta_0), L_1(f, \gamma_1, \delta_1), \ldots, L_{n-1}(f, \gamma_{n-1}, \delta_{n-1})) \tag{3}$$

where $L_i : B(\Omega_0, \tau) \longrightarrow \mathbb{C}$ is defined as

$$L_i(f, \gamma_i, \delta_i) = \int_{-\tau-\gamma_i}^{\tau+\gamma_i} f(t)\phi_i(t)dt + \delta_i \tag{4}$$

with ϕ_i being the i-th normalized Prolate Spheroidal Wave Function (PSWF, for detailed description see Appendix A).

Approximation using the PSWF algorithm Φ is given as

$$\Phi\left(\Re(f,\gamma,\delta)\right) = \sum_{i=0}^{n-1} L_i(f,\gamma_i,\delta_i)\phi_i. \tag{5}$$

As the PSWF algorithm works with finite information, its error is bounded from below by radius of information

$$r(\Re,\Gamma,\Delta) = \sup_{x\in\mathbb{R}^n} \inf_{f\in B(\Omega_0,\tau)} \sup_{g\in\Re^{-1}(x)} \|f-g\|. \tag{6}$$

For our estimation we will be however using the term of diameter of information as defined in [19,18]

$$d(\Re,\Gamma,\Delta) = \sup_{f,g:\Re(f)=\Re(g)} \|f-g\|, \tag{7}$$

which is connected to radius the following way

$$r(\Re,\Gamma,\Delta) \leq d(\Re,\Gamma,\Delta) \leq 2r(\Re,\Gamma,\Delta). \tag{8}$$

The average error of the PSWF algorithm with presence of jitter and approximation and quantization error was estimated in [2]. In this article, we will estimate the relation between average radius of information and average error of the PSWF algorithm, when $\Gamma > 0, \Delta > 0$, as calculated in [2] using norm $\|f\| = \langle f,f\rangle^{\frac{1}{2}}$, where $\langle f,g\rangle = \int_{-\tau}^{\tau} f(t)g(t)dt$.

We will calculate the radius of information *average over* $B(\Omega_0,\tau)$, while *pessimistic in respect to both* γ *and* δ. The averaging will be done with respect to the zero mean Gaussian measure ξ such that the ϕ_i are eigenfunctions of the correlation operator. A detailed definition of measure ξ can be found in Appendix B.

4   Main Result

Upper bound of the algorithm is provided by [2] as

Theorem 1. *Let Φ be the PSWF algorithm for bandlimited signal approximation, as defined in Section 3 and let ξ be a Gaussian measure defined in Appendix B. Let then jitter $\gamma = [\gamma_0,\ldots,\gamma_{n-1}], |\gamma_i| < \Gamma$, and approximation and quantization error $\delta = [\delta_0,\ldots,\delta_{n-1}], |\delta_i| < \Delta$. Then, the average error of algorithm Φ satisfies*

$$e^{\mathrm{avg}}(\Gamma,\Delta,\Phi) \leq M(\beta) + (n\Delta)^{\frac{1}{2}} + J(n,\Gamma), \tag{9}$$

where

$$J(n, \Gamma) \leq \sum_{k=0}^{n-1} \sum_{i=0}^{\infty} \sqrt{\beta_i \lambda_i} 2 \Big(|\phi_i(\tau)| |\phi_k(\tau)| \Gamma$$

$$\cdot \Big(1 + \sum_{w=1}^{\infty} \frac{(\Omega \alpha_k \Gamma)^w}{w(w+1)2^w} + \sum_{j=1}^{\infty} \frac{(\Omega \alpha_i \Gamma)^j}{j(j+1)2^j} +$$

$$+ \sum_{w=1}^{\infty} \sum_{j=1}^{\infty} \frac{1}{(w+j+1)wj} \left(\frac{\Omega \alpha_i \Gamma}{2} \right)^j \left(\frac{\Omega \alpha_k \Gamma}{2} \right)^w \Big) \Big)$$

(10)

and

$$M(\beta) = 2 \left(\sum_{k=n}^{\infty} \beta_k \lambda_k \right)^{\frac{1}{2}}.$$

(11)

For lower bound we will utilize the fact, that $e^{avg}(0, \Delta, \Phi) \leq e^{avg}(\Gamma, \Delta, \Phi)$. That brings us to

$$e^{avg}(\Gamma, \Delta, \Phi) \geq \sup_{\delta_k \leq \Delta} \int_{B(\Omega_0, \tau)} \left[\| \sum_{k=n}^{\infty} \langle f, \phi_k \rangle \phi_k \|^2 + \| \sum_{k=0}^{n-1} \delta_k \phi_k \|^2 \right]^{\frac{1}{2}} \xi(df)$$

$$\geq \sup_{\delta_k \leq \Delta} \left[\int_E \| \sum_{k=n}^{\infty} \langle f, \phi_k \rangle \phi_k \|^2 + \| \sum_{k=0}^{n-1} \delta_k \phi_k \|^2 \xi(df) \right]^{\frac{1}{2}}$$

$$\geq ((M(\beta))^2 + n\Delta)^{\frac{1}{2}}.$$

(12)

Which ultimately allows us to formulate the following bounds for average error estimate

$$((M(\beta))^2 + n\Delta)^{\frac{1}{2}} \leq e^{avg}(\Gamma, \Delta, \Phi) \leq M(\beta) + (n\Delta)^{\frac{1}{2}} + J(n, \Gamma).$$

(13)

That means that the actual average error lies within the interval of length

$$J(n, \Gamma) + A(\Delta, \beta, n),$$

(14)

where $A(\Delta, \beta, n) = M(\beta) + (n\Delta)^{\frac{1}{2}} - ((M(\beta))^2 + n\Delta)^{\frac{1}{2}}$

We can easily estimate that $A(\Delta, \beta, n) \leq \sqrt{2M(\beta)(n\Delta)^{1/2}}$ and, since $\Gamma \ll \Delta$,

$$J(n, \Gamma) \ll A(\Delta, \beta, n).$$

(15)

4.1   The Radius of Information

In this section we will focus on estimating the radius of information $r(\Re, \Gamma, \Delta)$. It is an important step in assessment of the algorithm's quality, as it is necessary to relate the average error to the radius of information, which is the lowest possible error of any algorithm.

Even the algorithm that has very well estimated error can still need improvement if this error is far from the radius of its information.

We know that

$$\frac{1}{2}d(\Re, \Gamma, \Delta) \leq r(\Re, \Gamma, \Delta) \leq d(\Re, \Gamma, \Delta), \tag{16}$$

where

$$d(\Re, \Gamma, \Delta) = \sup_{\{f,g \in B(\Omega_0, \tau) : \Re(f) = \Re(g)\}} \|f - g\|, \tag{17}$$

which $\forall_{f \in B(\Omega_0, \tau)}$ is given as follows:

$$\Re(f) = \left[\int_{-\tau - \gamma_k}^{\tau + \gamma_k} f(t)\phi_k(t)dt + \delta_k \right]_{k=0}^{n-1} \tag{18}$$

$$\Re(g) = \left[\int_{-\tau - \eta_k}^{\tau + \eta_k} f(t)\phi_k(t)dt + \sigma_k \right]_{k=0}^{n-1}, \tag{19}$$

where $|\gamma_k|, |\eta_k| \leq \Gamma$ and $|\delta_k|, |\sigma_k| \leq \Delta$.

Lemma 1. *For $f, g \in B(\Omega_0, \tau)$ if $\forall k \leq n - 1$, we have*

$$\langle f, \phi_k \rangle \phi_k = \langle g, \phi_k \rangle \phi_k - 2\Delta\phi_k, \tag{20}$$

Then

$$\exists_{\delta_k, \sigma_k \leq \Delta} \exists_{\gamma_k, \eta_k \leq \Gamma} \Re(f) = \Re(g). \tag{21}$$

Proof. Let $\delta_k = -\Delta$ i $\sigma_k = \Delta$ and $\gamma_k = \eta_k = 0$. Then

$$\begin{aligned}
\Re(f) &= [\langle f, \phi_k \rangle \phi_k - \Delta\phi_k]_{k=0...n-1} = \\
&= [\langle g, \phi_k \rangle \phi_k + 2\Delta\phi_k - \Delta\phi_k]_{k=0...n-1} = \\
&= [\langle g, \phi_k \rangle \phi_k + \Delta\phi_k]_{k=0...n-1} = \quad \Re(g) \quad (22)
\end{aligned}$$

$\square$

Lemma 2. *For $f, g \in B(\Omega_0, \tau)$ if $\forall_{k \leq n-1}$ we have*

$$\langle f, \phi_k \rangle \phi_k = \langle g, \phi_k \rangle \phi_k \tag{23}$$

and

$$\langle f, \phi_k \rangle \phi_k = -\langle g, \phi_k \rangle \phi_k \forall k \geq n. \tag{24}$$

Then

$$\exists_{\delta_k, \sigma_k \leq \Delta} \exists_{\gamma_k, \eta_k \leq \Gamma} \Re(f) = \Re(g). \tag{25}$$

Proof. Let $\delta_k = \sigma_k \leq \Delta$ oraz $\eta_k = \gamma_k = 0$. Then

$$
\begin{aligned}
\Re(f) &= & [\langle f, \phi_k \rangle \phi_k + \delta_k \phi_k]_{k=0\ldots n-1} = \\
&= & [\langle f, \phi_k \rangle \phi_k + \sigma_k \phi_k]_{k=0\ldots n-1} = \\
&= & [\langle g, \phi_k \rangle \phi_k + \sigma_k \phi_k]_{k=0\ldots n-1} = & \Re(g) \quad (26)
\end{aligned}
$$

$\square$

Lemma 3. *For $f, g \in B(\Omega_0, \tau)$, if $\forall_{k \leq n-1}$ we have*

$$
\langle f, \phi_k \rangle \phi_k = \langle g, \phi_k \rangle \phi_k + \left(\int_{-\tau}^{-\tau+\Gamma} + \int_{\tau-\Gamma}^{\tau} f(t) \phi_k(t) \right) \phi_k, \quad (27)
$$

then

$$
\exists_{\delta_k, \sigma_k \leq \Delta} \exists_{\gamma_k, \eta_k \leq \Gamma} \Re(f) = \Re(g). \quad (28)
$$

Proof. Let $\sigma_k = \delta_k = 0$ and $\gamma_k = -\Gamma$ i $\eta_k = 0$. Then

$$
\begin{aligned}
\Re(f) &= \left[<f, \phi_k> \phi_k - \int_{-\tau}^{-\tau+\Gamma} + \int_{\tau-\Gamma}^{\tau} f(t)\phi_k(t)dt\phi_k \right]_{k=0}^{n-1} = \\
&= \left[\langle g, \phi_k \rangle \phi_k + \left(\int_{-\tau}^{-\tau+\Gamma} + \int_{\tau-\Gamma}^{\tau} f(t)\phi_k(t) \right) \phi_k - \right. \\
&\quad \left. - \int_{-\tau}^{-\tau+\Gamma} + \int_{\tau-\Gamma}^{\tau} f(t)\phi_k(t)dt\phi_k \right]_{k=0}^{n-1} = \\
&= [\langle g, \phi_k \rangle \phi_k]_{k=0\ldots n-1} = \Re(g). \quad (29)
\end{aligned}
$$

$\square$

Lemma 4. *Let $\Re(f) = \left\{ [y_0, y_1, \ldots, y_{n-1}]^t : y_i = \int_{-\tau-\Gamma}^{\tau+\Gamma} f(t)\phi_i(t)dt + \Delta \right\}$ for every $f \in B(\Omega_0, \tau)$. Then the diameter of information*

$$
\begin{aligned}
d(\Re, \Gamma, \Delta) &\geq \int_{B(\Omega_0,\tau)} \left\| 2 \sum_{k=n}^{\infty} \langle f, \phi_k \rangle + \sum_{k=0}^{n-1} 2\Delta\phi_k + \right. \\
&\quad \left. + \sum_{k=0}^{n-1} \left(\int_{-\tau}^{-\tau+\Gamma} + \int_{\tau-\Gamma}^{\tau} f(t)\phi_k(t)dt \right) \phi_k \right\| \xi(df). \quad (30)
\end{aligned}
$$

Proof. Let $\gamma_k = -\Gamma$ i $\eta_k = 0$ and $\delta_k = -\Delta$, $\sigma_k = \Delta$ and let $g \in B(\Omega_0, \tau)$ and

$$f = \sum_{k=0}^{n-1} \langle g, \phi_k \rangle \phi_k - 2\Delta\phi_k - \sum_{k=n}^{\infty} \langle g, \phi_k \rangle \phi_k -$$

$$- \sum_{k=0}^{n-1} \left(\int_{-\tau}^{\tau+\Gamma} + \int_{\tau-\Gamma}^{\tau} g(t)\phi_k(t) dt \right) \phi_k. \tag{31}$$

Then from lemmas 1, 2 i 3
$\Re(f) = \Re(g)$.
So

$$d(\Re, \Gamma, \Delta) \geq \sup_{g \in B(\Omega_0, \tau)} \|g - f\| \geq \int_{B(\Omega_0, \tau)} \left\| 2 \sum_{k=n}^{\infty} \langle g, \phi_k \rangle + \sum_{k=0}^{n-1} 2\Delta\phi_k \right.$$

$$\left. + \sum_{k=0}^{n-1} \left(\int_{-\tau}^{-\tau+\Gamma} + \int_{\tau-\Gamma}^{\tau} g(t)\phi_k(t) dt \right) \phi_k \right\| \xi(dg). \tag{32}$$

$\square$

We can continue by estimating

$$d(\Re, \Gamma, \Delta) \geq \int_{B(\Omega_0, \tau)} \left\| 2 \sum_{k=n}^{\infty} \langle f, \phi_k \rangle + \sum_{k=0}^{n-1} 2\Delta\phi_k \right\| \xi(df) =$$

$$= 2 \int_{B(\Omega_0, \tau)} \left\| \sum_{k=n}^{\infty} \langle f, \phi_k \rangle + \sum_{k=0}^{n-1} \Delta\phi_k \right\| \xi(df). \tag{33}$$

Knowing, that

$$\frac{1}{2} d(\Re, \Gamma, \Delta) \leq r(\Re, \Gamma, \Delta) \tag{34}$$

and

$$r(\Re, \Gamma, \Delta) \leq e^{avg}(\Gamma, \Delta, \Phi). \tag{35}$$

Obviously at this point we want the lower bound of the error to be close to lower bound of the radius of information $r(\Re, \Gamma, \Delta)$. And indeed, it is, since

$$r(\Re, \Gamma, \Delta) \geq \int_{B(\Omega_0, \tau)} \left\| \sum_{k=n}^{\infty} \langle f, \phi_k \rangle + \sum_{k=0}^{n-1} \Delta\phi_k \right\| \xi(df), \tag{36}$$

which is the lower bound of error of PSWF algorithm. We thus obtain

$$(M(\beta) + n^2\Delta^2)^{\frac{1}{2}} \leq r(\Re, \Gamma, \Delta) \leq$$

$$\leq e^{avg}(\Gamma, \Delta, \Phi) \leq M(\beta) + (n\Delta)^{\frac{1}{2}} + J(n, \Gamma). \tag{37}$$

Which means, that we can place both the radius of information and the value of average error of the PSWF algorithm in the interval of length

$$M(\beta) + (n\Delta)^{\frac{1}{2}} + J(n, \Gamma) - (M(\beta) + n^2\Delta^2)^{\frac{1}{2}}. \tag{38}$$

The above calculations show, that estimation in Theorem 1 has a practical sense and the PSWF approximation algorithm can be still considered close to optimal error.

5 Conclusion

The extended analysis of the PSWF bandlimited function approximation algorithm allows us to extend the results by Kowalski in [9] and author in [2] in the average case distorted by both approximation and quantization error and jitter.

It was proven in this article that average error estimation of PSWF algorithm in the presence of jitter is not only well bounded from above but also predictable, by which we mean that we can bound it well from both above and below and place it close to the radius of information.

Acknowledgements. This work has been supported by the means provided by National Science Centre, based on decision no DEC-2012/07/N/ST6/03656.

Appendix A: Prolate Spheroidal Wave Functions

We will begin by defining Prolate Spheroidal Wave Functions and stating some of their properties.

It is known that for every real number c, values of parameter κ, so that the differential equation

$$\forall_{t\in(-1,1)}(1 - t^2)u''(t) - 2tu'(t) + (\kappa - c^2t^2)u(t) = 0, \tag{39}$$

has non-zero solution, can be ordered to create increasing sequence of positive numbers

$$0 < \kappa_0(c) < \kappa_1(c) < \kappa_2(c) < \dots.$$

Moreover, for $\kappa = \kappa_k(c)$ there exists a single function $\psi_k : [-1, 1] \longrightarrow \mathbb{R}$ such as

1. $\int_{-1}^{1} |\psi_k(t)|^2 dt = 1$
2. $\psi_k(1) > 0$

Let us then put $c = \Omega_0\tau$ and define a normalized Prolate Spheroidal Wave Function $\phi_k^* : [-\tau, \tau] \to \mathbb{R}$ as follows:

$$\phi_k^*(t) = \frac{1}{\sqrt{\tau}}\psi_k(\frac{t}{\tau}), k = 0, 1, \dots. \tag{40}$$

As stated in [10], each ϕ_k^* is continuously dependent on Ω_0 and τ, and for fixed values of Ω_0 and τ can be expanded to an entire function of $t \in \mathbb{C}$. Lets then assume that ϕ_k is the extension of ϕ_k^* to an entire function.

Such extensions of a normalized PSWFs have a number of properties that are widely discussed in [9,15,16,22], of which we will use

(A) Each ϕ_k is continuous and for $t \in \mathbb{R}, \phi_k(t) \in \mathbb{R}$
(B) Each $\phi_k, k = 0, 1, \ldots$ is bandlimited to Ω_0 and has limited energy. Moreover, the set of $\{\phi_k\}_{k=0}^\infty$ is orthonormal in $L_2(-\tau, \tau)$ and complete in $B(\Omega_0, \tau)$.
(C) Functions ϕ_k are even for even k and odd for odd k.

The above properties make PSWFs fitting tool for representation of bandlimited signals. We can present $B(\Omega_0, \tau)$, a set of bandlimited signals in $L_2(-\tau, \tau)$ as:

(D) $B(\Omega_0, \tau) = \left\{ f \in L_2(-\tau, \tau) : \Sigma_{k=0}^\infty \frac{|\langle f, \phi_k \rangle|^2}{\lambda_k} < \infty \right\}.$

From [9] and the definition of ϕ_k we get that of all the functions in $B(\Omega_0, \tau)$ orthogonal to $\phi_0, \phi_1, \ldots, \phi_{k-1}$, ϕ_k has the highest energy concentration on interval $(-\tau, \tau)$, namely $\lambda_k(c)$.

$$\lambda_k(c) = \sup \left\{ \frac{\|f\|_{2,\tau}^2}{\|f\|_{2,\infty}^2} : f \in B(\Omega_0, \tau), (f, \phi_j) = 0, j = 0, 1, \ldots, k-1 \right\}. \quad (41)$$

Values $\lambda_k(c)$ satisfy the following:

(E) $\lambda_{[2c/\pi]-1} \geq 1/2, \lambda_{[2c/\pi]+1} \leq 1/2$
   and
(F) $e^{-1/12} \frac{\pi c}{2I_k(k+1/2)} \left(\frac{c}{2\pi k} \right)^{2k} < \lambda_k(c) < \frac{2c}{\pi^2 k^2} \left(\frac{ec}{2k} \right)^2 k,$
   where $I_k = \int_{-\pi/2}^\infty \left(\frac{\sin x}{x} \right)^{2k} dx$ and $k \geq 2c/\pi$.

We can also remind the two facts about how the ϕ_k functions behave at the end of the interval $[-\tau, \tau]$. We will begin with the equation proved by Slepian in [15] and Fuchs [4], that allows to get the value of ϕ_k at the ends of the integration interval.

(G) (from Slepian, Fuchs [4,15]) With previously defined ψ_k, λ_k, c we have

$$|\phi_k(\tau)| = \sqrt{\frac{\Omega}{2} \frac{d \ln \lambda_k}{dc}}. \quad (42)$$

(H) (from DĂĚbrowska [3]) Let $\alpha_k = \max \left\{ |\frac{\kappa_k}{c} - c|, c \right\}$ and $c \geq 2$. Then

$$|\phi_k^{(j)}(\tau)| \leq (j-1)! \left(\frac{\Omega \alpha_k}{2} \right) |\phi_k(\tau)|. \quad (43)$$

Appendix B: Measure

Defining a measure in space $B(\Omega_0, \tau)$ is a crucial decision when dealing with the average case. In our case the space in question is infinite-dimensional, therefore the measure cannot be uniform. Following [9], we will use Gaussian measures.

Let then ξ be a measure on $B(\Omega_0, \tau)$. Since $\phi_k(t)$ have real values for real arguments t, $B(\Omega_0, \tau)$ can be treated as Cartesian product $H \times H$, where

$$H = H(\Omega_0, \tau) = \left\{ g \in \mathcal{L}_2(-\tau, \tau) : \sum_{k=0}^{\infty} \frac{\langle g, \phi_k \rangle}{\lambda_k} < \infty \right\} \tag{44}$$

and $\mathcal{L}_2(\tau, \tau)$ is the space of all real-valued functions in $L_2(-\tau, \tau)$.

To be precise, $B(\Omega_0, \tau)$ is isomorphic to Hilbert space $H \times H$ with the inner product $\langle \cdot, \cdot \rangle$ and norm $||| \cdot |||$, defined as $\langle (u, v), (x, y) \rangle = \langle u, x \rangle + \langle v, y \rangle$ and $|||(u, v)||| = \langle (u, v), (u, v) \rangle^{1/2}$, where (u, v) and (x, y) are elements of $H \times H$, and $\langle \cdot, \cdot \rangle$ is the inner product in $\mathcal{L}_2(-\tau, \tau)$. The bijection between those two spaces is

$$B(\Omega_0, \tau) \ni f \to \mathbf{I}(f) = (u, v) \in H \times H, \tag{45}$$

where $u = \mathrm{Re}(f)$, and $v = \mathrm{Im}(f)$.

Every Gaussian measure m on real Hilbert space is uniquely defined by its mean element $\overline{m}$ and correlation operator C_m. Moreover, the set of all the possible correlation operators can be seen as symmetric semi-positive defined finite trace operators.

We then define Gaussian measure μ on H, by defining its mean element $\overline{\mu}$ as 0 and correlation operator C_μ satisfying $C_\mu \phi_k = \beta_k \phi_k$, $k = 0, 1, \ldots$, where $\beta_k \geq 0$ and $\mathrm{Tr} C_\mu = \sum_{k=0}^{\infty} \beta_k < \infty$. So the characteristic functional for μ is

$$\chi_\sigma(u) = e^{\left(-\frac{1}{2} \langle C_\mu u, u \rangle \right)}. \tag{46}$$

Now we can define measure on $H \times H$ as product $\sigma = \mu \times \mu$. As the characteristic function σ satisfies the equation

$$\chi_\sigma((u, v)) = \chi_\mu(u) \chi_\mu(v), \forall_{u, v \in H}, \tag{47}$$

we see, that $\forall_{u, v \in H}$,

$$\chi_\sigma((u, v)) = e^{-\frac{1}{2} \langle C_\mu u, u \rangle} e^{-\frac{1}{2} \langle C_\mu v, v \rangle} = e^{-\frac{1}{2} \langle (C_\mu u C_\mu v), (u, v) \rangle}. \tag{48}$$

Defined σ is the Gaussian measure on $H \times H$ with mean element $\overline{\sigma}(u, v) = (0, 0)$ and correlation operator

$$C_\sigma(u, v) = (C_\mu u, C_\mu v), \forall_{u, v \in H}. \tag{49}$$

Particularly

$$C_\sigma(0, \phi_k) = \beta_k(0, \phi_k)$$
$$C_\sigma(\phi_k, 0) = \beta_k(\phi_k, 0), k = 0, 1, \ldots \tag{50}$$

We finally can define measure ξ on (Ω_0, τ) as

$$\xi(\mathbf{I}^{-1}(A)) = \sigma(A \times B) = \mu(A)\mu(B). \tag{51}$$

References

1. Chen, Q.-Y., Gottlieb, D., Hesthaven, J.S.: Spectral methods based on prolate spheroidal wave functions for hyperbolic pdes. SIAM Journal on Numerical Analysis 43(5), 1912–1933 (2006)
2. Cholewa, M.: Estimation of the average error of prolate spheroidal wave functions approximation algorithm for bandlimited signals. Submitted to Journal of Complexity (2015)
3. Dąbrowska, D.: The effects of distortions in arguments and values of samples in optimal signal recontruction. In: To do Justice in Love: Memorial Book from Cardinal Stefan Wyszyński University for His Eminence Cardinal Józef Glemp in 20th Anniversary of His Service as Primate Bishop, pp. 424–490 (2001) (in Polish)
4. Fuchs, W.H.J.: On the eigenvalues of of an integral equation arising in the theory of band-limited signals. Journal of Mathematics Analysis and Applications 9, 317–330 (1964)
5. Genossar, T.: Optimal bi-orthonormal approximation of signals. IEEE Transactions on Systems, Man and Cybernetics 22(3), 449–460 (1992)
6. Kacewicz, B.Z., Kowalski, M.A.: Recovering signals from inaccurate data. In: Curves and Surfaces in Computer Vision and Graphics II, Int. Soc. Opt. Eng., pp. 68–74 (1992)
7. Kacewicz, B.Z., Kowalski, M.A.: Approximating linear functionals on unitary spaces in the presence of bounded data errors with applications to signal recovery. J. Adaptive Control Signal Process. 9, 19–31 (1995)
8. Khare, K., George, N.: Hilbert spaces induced by hilbert space valued functions. J. Phys. Ser. A 36, 10011–10021 (2003)
9. Kowalski, M.A.: On approximation of band-limited signals. Journal of Complexity 5, 283–302 (1989)
10. Kowalski, M.A., Dábrowska, D.: Approximating band- and energy-limited signals in the presence of jitter. Journal of Complexity 14, 557–570 (1998)
11. Kowalski, M.A., Stegner, F., Sikorski, K.A.: Selected Topics in Approximation and Computation. Oxford University Press (1995)
12. Milanese, M.: Optimal algorithms theory for robust estimation and prediction. IEEE Transactions on Automatic Control 30(8), 730–738 (1985)
13. Pei, S.C., Ding, J.J.: Discrete-to-discrete prolate spheroidal wave functions and finite duration discrete fractional Fourier transform. In: IEEE Transactions on European Signal Processing Conferecne (2007)
14. Shkolinsky, Y., Tygert, M., Rokhlin, V.: Approximation of bandlimited functions. Appl. Comput. Harmon. Anal. 21, 413–420 (2006)
15. Slepian, D.: Some asymptotic expansions for prolate spheroidal wave functions. Journal of Mathematics and Physics 44, 99–143 (1965)
16. Slepian, D., Pollak, H.O.: Prolate spheroidal wave functions - fourier analysis and uncertainty. Bell Syst. Tech. J. 40, 43–64 (1961)
17. Smolyak, S.A.: On optimal restoration in functions and functionals in them: unpublished candidate dissertation. Moscow State University (1965)
18. Traub, J.F., Wasilkowski, G.W., Woźniakowski, H.: Information-Based Complexity. Academic Press (1988)
19. Traub, J.F., Woźniakowski, H.: A general theory of optimal algorithms. ACM Monograph Series (1980)

20. Tropp, J.A.: Signal recovery from random measurements via orthogonal matching pursuit. IEEE Transactions on Information Theory 53(11), 4655–4666 (2007)
21. Venkataraman, A.: Signal approximation using the bilinear transform. Massachusetts Institute of Technology (2007)
22. Wang, L.-L., Zhang, L.: An improved estimate of PSWF approximation and approximation by mathieu functions. J. Math. Anal. Appl. 379, 35–47 (2011)

Algebraic Logical Meta-Model of Decision Processes - New Metaheuristics

Ewa Dudek-Dyduch[✉]

Department of Automatics and Biomedical Engineering
AGH University of Science and Technology, Karków, Poland
edd@agh.edu.pl

Abstract. The paper presents a formal approach to developing new heuristic methods for finding solutions of discrete optimization problems. The presented approach is based on algebraic-logical meta-model of multistage decision process (ALMM of DMP) that has been developed by the author. Definitions are provided for two deterministic classes of multistage decision processes: common multistage decision processes (cMDP) and multistage dynamic decision processes (MDDP). The paper presents some part of research results pertaining to heuristic methods utilising ALMM of MDP. It lays out a three stage concept of heuristic method synthesis involving local optimization together with two heuristic methods based on the said concept: Machine Learning Based on ALMM of DMP and the Substitute Task Method.

Keywords: Machine learning · Discrete optimization problems · Multistage decision process · Heuristic methods · Algebraic-logical meta-model · ALMM of DMP · Local optimization · Substitution task method

1 Introduction

The paper covers the development of new heuristic methods of solving discrete optimization problems and NP hard problems in particular. Solutions for a vast majority of such problems can be presented as sequences of decisions, thus multistage decision process can be applied to obtain the solution.

A huge number of heuristic algorithms have been published for NP hard problems, but there have been just a few heuristic methods. The most popular methods, apart from the ones utilizing local optimization, are ones mirroring biological processes such as evolutionary programming (genetic algorithms), methods based on swarm intelligence and artificial immune system [25,34] neural network learning [33,32,26].

The author's research suggests that new heuristic methods can be established based on a very general formal multistage decision process model.

The notion of a multistage decision process is understandable and has been used for long. Multistage processes have been used to model and control (decision making) not only deterministic processes, but also stochastic and fuzzy ones [27]. This paper takes a specific deterministic multistage decision process modeling

© Springer International Publishing Switzerland 2015
L. Rutkowski et al. (Eds.): ICAISC 2015, Part I, LNAI 9119, pp. 541–554, 2015.
DOI: 10.1007/978-3-319-19324-3_48

paradigm called Algebraic-Logical Meta-Model of Multistage Decision Process (ALMM of MDP), characterized by high level of generalization.

ALMM of MDP facilitates convenient representation of all kinds of information regarding the problem to be solved, in particular the information defining the states, decisions, algorithm used to generate consecutive states and various temporal relationships and restrictions of the process. Furthermore, ALMM of MDP enables us to define various problem properties, in particular ones for which a particular heuristic method may be applied.

The main aim of this paper is to present how ALMM of MDP is applied to create new heuristic methods and justify their concepts. The paper presents some earlier research related to heuristic methods utilizing ALMM of MDP. It provides three stage concept of heuristic method synthesis involving local optimization as well as two heuristic methods based on the said concept: Machine Learning Based on ALMM of DMP and the Substitute Task Method.

The paper consists of 6 sections. The algebraic-logical meta-model is presented in the 2nd section. The three-stage method for designing heuristic algorithms with local optimization is described in the 3rd section. Machine learning method based on ALMM of DMP and Substitute task method are given in the 4th and in 5th sections respectively. Final conclusions are stated in section 6.

2   Algebraic-Logical Meta-Model of Multistage Decision Process

The algebraic-logical meta-model of multistage decision process (ALMM of DMP) is a general model development paradigm for deterministic problems, for which solutions can be presented as a sequence of decisions. In other words, ALMM of DMP is a general formal model development paradigm for deterministic decision processes, with the latter being understood as processes that require the development of a sequence or a set of decisions for a certain goal to be achieved. What is important, the number of decisions that have to be determined (or taken) does not have to be known beforehand. In other words, the specific form of the solution may not be known in advance.

The idea of an ALMM of DMP paradigm was proposed and developed by the author [7,1,2,3,6,14]. In early works, various terms were used to describe the very same idea (compact knowledge based model [4], discrete deterministic or determinable processes [3], discrete event processes [6] in order to emphasize different aspects of this general modelling concept or to adjust to its current area of application [5].

Based on ALMM of DMP formal models (so-called AL models) may be established for a very broad class of discrete optimization problems from a variety of application areas, thus yielding to the meta-model designation. In [1,3,4,7,6] that lays the groundwork for the basic ALMM of DMP theory, the author herein has presented i. a. AL models for discrete manufacturing process control, for logistics problems (the salesman problem), for knapsack problem, while in [2,8,10,13,24] she presented a model for a complex real-life problem encompassing both manufacturing and logistics. The last of these, referred to as "scheduling preparatory work in mines", will be presented in section 4.

ALMM of DMP (abbreviated as ALMM) provides a structured way of recording knowledge of the goal and all relevant restrictions that exist within the problems modelled. In line with this idea, all information is split into pre-defined basic components with appropriate links, defined both through algebraic and logical formulae.

Using this paradigm, the author has provided, i.a. in [7,1], the definition of two base classes for multistage decision processes: a common process, denoted here as cMDP (or AL-cMDP to emphasize the algebraic-logical description) and a dynamic process, denoted as MDDP (or AL-MDDP). Let us review them briefly.

Definition 1. Common multistage decision process is a process that is specified by the sextuple cMDP= (U, X, x_0, f, X_N, X_G) where U is a set of decisions, X is a set of states, $f : U \times X \rightarrow X$ is a partial function called a transition function, (it does not have to be determined for all elements of the set $U \times X$), x_0, $X_N \subset X$, $X_G \subset X$ are respectively: an initial state, a set of not admissible states, and a set of goal states, i.e. the states in which we want the process to take place at the end. Subsets X_G and X_N are disjoint i.e. $X_G \cap X_N = \varnothing$.

Because not all decisions defined formally make sense in certain situations, the transition function f is defined as a partial one. As a result, all limitations concerning the decisions in a given state x can be defined in a convenient way by means of so-called sets of possible decisions $U_p(x)$, and defined as: $U_p(x) = \{u \in U : (u, x) \in Dom\ f\}$.

The formal definition of multistage dynamic decision process(MDDP) quoted below refers to dynamic decision processes, i.e. processes wherein both the constraints and the transition function (and in particular the possible decision sets) depend on time. Therefore, the concept of the so-called "generalized state" has been introduced, defined as a pair containing both the state and the time instant.

Definition 2. Multistage dynamic decision process is a process that is specified by the sextuple MDDP= (U, S, s_0, f, S_N, S_G) where U is a set of decisions, $S = X \times T$ is a set named a set of generalized states, X is a set of proper states, $T \subset \Re + \cup\{0\}$ is a subset of non negative real numbers representing the time instants, $f : U \times S \rightarrow S$ is a partial function called a transition function, (it does not have to be determined for all elements of the set $U \times S$), $s_0 = (x_0, t_0)$, $S_N \subset S$, $S_G \subset S$ are respectively: an initial generalized state, a set of not admissible generalized states, and a set of goal generalized states, i.e. the states in which we want the process to take place at the end. Subsets S_G and S_N are disjoint i.e. $S_G \cap S_N = \varnothing$.

The transition function is defined by means of two functions, $f = (f_x, f_t)$ where $f_x : U \times X \times T \rightarrow X$ determines the next state, $f_t : U \times X \times T \rightarrow T$ determines the next time instant. It is assumed that the difference $\Delta t = f_t(u, x, t) - t$ has a value that is both finite and positive.

Thus, as a result of the decision u that is taken or realized at the proper state x and the moment t, the state of the process changes for $x' = f_x(u, x, t)$ that is observed at the moment $t' = f_t(u, x, t) = t + \Delta t$.

Just like in definition 1, the transition function f is defined as a partial one. As a result, all limitations concerning the decisions in a given state s can be defined in a convenient way by means of so-called sets of possible decisions $U_p(s)$, and defined as: $U_p(s) = \{u \in U : (u, s) \in Dom\ f\}$.

For both defined multistage decision processes, in the most general case, sets U and X may be presented as a Cartesian product $U = U^1 \times U^2 \times ... \times U^m$, $X = X^1 \times X^2 \times ... \times X^n$ i.e. $u = (u^1, u^2, ..., u^m)$, $x = (x^1, x^2, ..., x^n)$. In particular, u^i, $i = 1, 2..m$ represent separate decisions that must or may be taken at the same time (for definition 2) or at the same stage (for definition 1) and relate to particular objects. There are no limitations imposed on the sets; in particular they do not have to be numerical. Thus values of particular coordinates of a state or a decision may be names of elements (symbols) as well as some objects (e.g. finite set, sequence etc.). The most significant characteristics unique for the proposed ALMM of DMP paradigm is the fact that state coordinates can be higher order variables.

The sets X_N, S_N, X_G, S_G and Up are formally defined with the use of both algebraic and logical formulae, hence the algebraic-logic model descriptor. The AL-MDDP paradigm can be used for very convenient establishment of discrete manufacturing process (DMP) models. Thus, in the author's papers related to discrete manufacturing process control, the AL-MDDP may be (and is) treated as an equivalent to a general formal model of discrete manufacturing processes [5,7,8,13].

If for the sake of further discourse the status of a multistage decision process as a common or a dynamic one is not relevant, we will refer to a multistage process in general and denote it as MDP (or AL-MDP). The definition of a multistage decision process covering both process classes, that is both cDMP and MDDP, was provided in [7] and quoted, i.a. [15].

Based on the meta-model given herein, algebraic-logical models (AL models) may be created for individual problems consisting of seeking admissible or optimal solutions. In case of an admissible solution, an AL model is equivalent to a suitable multistage decision process, hence it is denoted as process $\boldsymbol{P}$. An **optimization** problem then is denoted as a $(\boldsymbol{P}, \boldsymbol{Q})$ pair where $\boldsymbol{Q}$, is a criterion. An optimization task (instance of the problem) is denoted as a (P, Q). A sequence of consecutive states from the initial state to a final state (goal or non-admissible), computed by the transition function forms a process trajectory.

3   Three-Stage Method for Designing Local Optimization Heuristic Algorithms

The most popular heuristic algorithms are those based on local optimization. The criterions for local optimization (heuristics) are created by means of intuition and very often more than one heuristic is proposed for the same problem. They are verified by means of computer experiments or sometimes by means of error estimation. The questions arise:

- can we create preference function or local optimization task not intuitively but consciously and, if so, in which way?
- can we compare formally different algorithms of this type and indicate the introduced simplification?
- in which way should we modify the local optimization task in order to obtain a better trajectory?

The three-stage method for designing local optimization heuristic algorithms provided below helps us in answering the above questions. The method was first described in [14,7], then referred to in [12,15]. It is suitable for both MDP classes. As the AL-MDDP paradigm is the broader one, we are going to use its designations in the further part of this discourse but we will skip the "generalized" descriptor for the state s. Let us recall the method briefly.

At the first stage, one formulates some conditions for the optimal (suboptimal) or only admissible solution. They refer directly to subsets of decisions, or/and determine the state sets that are advantageous S_{A_i}, $i = 1, 2 \ldots$ or disadvantageous S_{DA_i}, $i = 1, 2..$ from the criterion point of view or for a possibility of generating an admissible trajectory. The conditions can also define some indirect aims, particularly the ones defining the state sets to be achieved in shortest time or under the minimal value of a special auxiliary criterion.

At the second stage, one determines a local optimization problem. In order to do it, the information about the distinguished, at the first stage, "advantageous" or "disadvantageous" states is used. Obviously, one also uses the information about the set of goal states S_G, set of not admissible states S_N and information about the sets of possible decisions. As we need the generated trajectory to run only through the advantageous states and to avoid the disadvantageous ones, it seems most natural to introduce any "measure of distance" in the state space, and to assume some local criterions. Maximizations (minimizations) of the criterions correspond to maximizations (minimization) of "distances" to the particular distinguished sets of states. In [7], the author has proposed to use different semimetrics (or metrics in a subspace of the state space) for the measurement of these distances. Therein, she also provided the basic and most useful semimetrics (metrics). As it is known, semimetric, denotes here by ψ, differs from metric in that it does not have to fulfill the condition $\psi(a, b) = 0 \Leftrightarrow a = b$.

Taking into account the change of the global criterion Q (local change or/and estimated value of $Q(s)$ as it is defined by A^* strategy [31] and maximization (minimization) of the mentioned distances, we obtain the substitute local problem. (It is assumed that the criterion Q is separable [7]). This new problem is usually a multicriterion one.

At the third stage, one should determine the manner of solving the local multicriteria optimisation task. The basic ideas of multicriterion decision approach [35,7] can be applied here. However, Pareto analysis cannot be applied here due to computational complexity. Furthermore, decision coordinate values may not belong to the number space as contrasted with [30]. In [7,1,15], the author laid out ways of solving multicriterion decision problems that are most useful here.

Let us recap significant components of the 3-stage method:

- the local optimization problem was defined as a multicriterion problem,
- a way of developing a local optimization problem was provided, basing on distances between the current state s and the state subsets S_G, S_N and S_{A_i}, S_{DA_i}, $i = 1, 2..$ reachable from s as well as a criterion estimated value,
- a use of semimetric (or metric in subspace of the state space) to determine the distance was proposed and a series of semimetrics that may be used was provided,
- various ways of solving the local multicriterion problem were provided,
- the idea of using some indirect objects was raised, particularly ones defining the state sets to be achieved in shortest time or under the minimal value of a special auxiliary criterion; this idea constitutes a basis of the multi-objective approach as well as of decomposed generation of an optimized trajectory.

Combinations of the above mentioned components enable the development of various metaheuristics and algorithms based on them. Below two heuristic methods built from the selected components are provided.

4   Machine Learning Based on the Paradigm ALMM of DMP

The original concept of the learning method presented below and referred to as prime Learning Method based on ALMM on DMP (or, more shortly, Learning Method Based on ALMM) was first published in [24,2], then in [10,11,12], with Dyduch T. and Dudek-Dyduch E. as the authors. The method was then further developed in [28,17,21,16].

The objective of the method is to find solutions for some classes of discrete optimization problems. The said problems are modelled using AL-cDMP or AL-MDDP paradigms but we will use AL-MDDP in the further part of this discourse. (P, Q) problems for which we may use learning algorithms have to be characterized by finiteness of all their trajectories and a separable Q criterion. The Q criterion separability property was defined in [7,1] (then also referred to in [29]. Separability is a property of an algorithm which calculates quality criterion for a sequence of decisions $\tilde{u}$, and thus for designated by him trajectory $\tilde{s}$. Roughly speaking criterion is separable if we can calculate its value for the next state of a trajectory knowing criterion value in the previous state and the decision taken at that time. Particularly useful are the property of additive separability of criterion [7].

4.1   Prime (Basic) Concept of Learning Method Based on ALMM of DMP

Prime Learning Method Based on ALMM consists of an iterative generation of consecutive possibly improving trajectories (solutions). The trajectory generation is based on a specially constructed local multicriterion optimization task used to select the best decision $u \in U_p(s)$ at each state of the trajectory. The multicriterion problem is solved by means of scalarization. A single criterion $q(u, s)$ is developed, as a weighted sum of components for individual criteria. The weight coefficients are improved during the learning process.

(a) Developing a Local Optimization Criterion

A local multicriterion task consists of criteria taking into account various types of requirements and restrictions. The first criterion concerns the value of the global criterion Q for the generated trajectory. It consists of the increase of the criterion resulting from the realization of the considered decision and the estimated value of the criterion for the final trajectory sections, which follows the possible realization of the considered decision. This part of the criterion is suitable for problems, which criterion Q is additively separable [1,7].

The next criterions relate to additional limitations or requirements. The criteria utilize estimated distances in the state space between the state s in which the considered decision has been taken and the reachable subsets of non admissible state set S_N, goal set S_G as well as reachable subsets of the distinguished advantageous sets S_{A_i} or disadvantageous sets S_{DA_i}. In order to determine distances between state s and the state subsets, an appropriate semimetrics is used.

The multicriterion problem is solved by means of scalarization. A single criterion $q(u, s)$ is developed as a weighted sum of components for individual criteria. The basic form of the local criterion $q(u, s)$ is represented as follows:

$$q\left(u, s\right) = \Delta Q\left(u, s\right) + \,\hat{}Q\left(u, s\right) + a_1\varphi_1\left(u, s\right) + \ldots + a_i\varphi_i\left(u, s\right) + \ldots + a_n\varphi_n\left(u, s\right)$$

where $\Delta Q(u, s)$ - increase of the criterion value as a result of decision u, undertaken in the state s, $\hat{}Q(u, s)$ - estimation of the quality index value for the final trajectory section after the decision u has been realized, $\varphi_i(u, s)$ - components reflecting additional limitations or additional requirements in the space of states, $i = 1, 2, \ldots, n$, a_i - coefficient which defines the weight of i-th component $\varphi_i(u, x, t)$ in the criterion $q(u, x, t)$.

(b) Learning Process

The significance of particular local criterion components may vary. The more significant a given component is, the higher value of its coefficient should be. It is difficult to define optimal weights a'priori. They depend both on the considered optimization problem as well as the input data for the particular optimization task (instance). The knowledge gathered in the course of trajectory generation (experiments performed by the algorithm) are used to modify these coefficients. On the other hand, coefficient values established for the best trajectory represent aggregated knowledge obtained in the course of experiments.

Each generated trajectory is analyzed by the learning algorithm. If it is not admissible, the reasons of the failure are examined. For example, it is examined through which subsets of not advantageous states the trajectory has passed. A role of the criterion components connected with these subsets should be strengthened for the next trajectory i.e. the weights (priorities) of these components increase. When the generated trajectory is admissible, the role of the components responsible for the trajectory quality can be strengthened, i.e. their weights can be increased. Based on the gained information, the local optimization task is being improved during simulation experiments. This process is treated as learning or intelligent searching algorithm.

Let us summarize the original components of prime learning method. These include:

- A concept of developing a local optimization task as a multicriterion one converted to a single-criterion one by means of scalarization, in particular
  - taking into account information on advantageous and disadvantageous state subsets (including information on S_G and S_N sets) as well as utilizing information on distances from a given trajectory's state s to individual distinguished subsets of the state set,
  - using semimetrics (or metrics in subspace of the state space) to estimate the said distances.
- A learning process concept consisting of algorithmic analysis of consecutive trajectories and appropriate modification of weight coefficients relevant components of the local criterion.

Compared to other learning methods, the Prime Learning Method Based on ALMM is unique in terms of the following characteristics:

1. The objective for which the method was developed: finding solutions for discrete optimization problems.
2. Knowledge supply: the knowledge is fed into the algorithm through an algebraic-logical model of the problem (P, Q) and a multicriterion local optimization task converted into a single-criterion one by means of scalarization.
3. Recording/storing the acquired knowledge: the knowledge is stored in the local criterion weight coefficient values.
4. The concept of knowledge acquisition and utilisation: generating consecutive trajectories occurs during the solution searching and consists of analysing the trajectories and in particular the sets they pass through; on that base, the algorithm updates weight coefficient values for individual components of the local optimization criterion.
5. It is learning with no supervisor. The algorithm generates trajectories (conducts experiments), analyses the obtained admissible and non-admissible solutions and proceeds to change its acting depending on the generated trajectories and their analysis results obtained.

It must be pointed out that the knowledge of the problem is provided in an aggregated form. The transition function is given in an algorithmic form. Thus, consequences of decisions are not known beyond a single step. Moreover, a priori definitions of the $U_p(s)$ sets for individual states are not known either. This is a reason why the algorithm has to "learn" how to generate an admissible trajectory that is as good as possible.

4.2   Extension of Prime Learning Method Based on ALMM of DMP

Essential extensions of prime learning method were proposed by Dyduch T. and Dudek-Dyduch E. in [10,11]. The papers included utilization of additional expert knowledge decreasing the power of $U_p(s)$ sets. If one posses additional expert knowledge then a better algorithm can be proposed. If some state subsets S_{d_i}, $i = 1, 2..$ are distinguished and for these subsets some rules for decision choice R_i, $i = 1, 2, ..$ are given by an expert then algorithm can verify to which subset the new generated state belongs and realises the suitable rule R_i. If rules given by expert exclude some decisions then matching sets of possible decisions $U_p(s)$ are decreased. Similarly, knowledge acquired throughout the learning experiments is used to further limit the $U_p(s)$ sets.

The next addition to the prime learning method was introduced by Kucharska E. [28,21]. The new elements proposed include:

(a) modifications related to the local criterion [28,29] consisting of:
   (i) including additional components depending on decisions only within the local criterion,
   (ii) changing the local criterion form (omitting some components) in case when certain state subsets are not reachable anymore,
(b) hybrid combination of the prime learning method with some elements utilised by searching methods such as pruning [29] and others [28,21].

4.3   Exemplary Problem

Both methods i.e Learning Method Based on ALMM and Substitute Tasks Method were tested using an extremely complex NP-hard problem combining scheduling and related both to logistics and to equipment transportation. It is real-world problem that takes place when scheduling preparatory works in mines.

The set of headings in the mine must be driven in order to render the exploitation field accessible. The headings form a net formally, represented by a nonoriented multigraph $G = (I, J, P)$ where the set of branches J and the set of nodes I represent the set of headings and the set of heading crossings respectively, and relation $P \subset (I \times J \times I)$ determines connections between the headings (a partial order between the headings). There are two kinds of driving machines, that differ in efficiency, cost of driving and necessity of transport. The first kind machines (set $M1$) are more effective but a cost of driving by means of them is much higher than for the second kind (set $M2$). Additionally, the first kind machines must be transported when driving starts from another heading crossing than the one in which the machine is, while the second type machines need no transport. Driving a heading cannot be interrupted before its completion and can be done only by one machine a time. There are given due dates for some of the headings, lengths of the headings, and for both kind of machines: efficiency and cost of a length unit driven, cost of the time unit waiting, speed of machine transport and transport cost per a length unit. One must determine the order of heading driving and the machine by means of which each heading should be driven so that the total cost of driving be minimal and each of headings be complete before its due date. This problem may be presented as a scheduling problem with state dependent resources or a scheduling problem with state dependent retooling. The first AL models for the said problem were developed by the author [8,2,10,11,12], then AL models for some variants of the problem were presented in [28,19,22].

The performed experiments confirmed efficiency of both methods.

5   The Idea of the Substitution Tasks Method

Substitution tasks method has been proposed by Dutkiewicz L. in [19,23]. Then some theoretical background for the method has been developed in [9,20].

5.1   Development of Substitution Tasks

The method is a constructive one in which whole trajectories are generated. While generating the solution, in each state s a decision is made on the basis of a specially constructed optimization task named substitution task $ST(s)$. The substitution task may be different in each state of the process. Substitution tasks are created to facilitate the decision making at a given state by substituting global optimization task with a simpler local task. After determining the best decision $u^*(s)$, the next process state S' is generated. Then, an automatic analysis of the new process state is performed and, on the basis of information gained, a new or modified substitution task is defined. Thus, in each iteration of the method, computations are performed at two levels:

1. The level of automatic analysis of the process and constructing a substitution task.
2. The level of determining possibly optimal decision for the substitution task and computing the next state.

Substitution task $ST(s) = (P_{ST}, Q_{ST})$, where: P_{ST} - a certain substitution multi-stage process and Q_{ST} - substitution criterion. Substitution task construction presented in [20] is based upon the concept of so-called intermediate goals. Intermediate goal d is defined as reaching by the process, as soon as possible, a certain set of states S_d. In scheduling problems, it is most often the case that the subset of states associated with the intermediate goals consists of such states in which the distinguished tasks (or one task) is completed. The distinguished intermediate goals are used to define the set of goal states of the substitution process P_{ST}. Thus for the substitution process a new set of final states $S_{G_{ST}}$ is defined, the initial state $s_{0_{ST}}$ is the current state s of the basic process P, whilst the transition function and the sets U, S, S_N, are the same as for the basic process P. As a result, the substitution process is defined as follows.

$$P_{ST}(s) = (U, S, \ s_{0_{ST}}, f, S_N, S_{G_{ST}})$$

It needs to be emphasized that the substitution task $ST(s)$ is for choosing only one single decision in the state s and not for determining a sequence of decisions leading the process P_{ST} from this state to the set of final states $S_{G_{ST}}$.

5.2   Automatic Analysis and Creation of Substitution Tasks

The following question arises: is it possible to define how substitution tasks should be constructed for any type of problem? The answer is: yes but the problem must be presented by AL model. The rules for goal determining and procedures based on them strongly depend on the given optimization problem. For some problem instances, the goals may also be defined by an expert. This article presents a method for goal determining based on the definition of the set of non-admissible states S_N. It contains the theory elements introduced in [6,9,20]. The set S_N is defined through a logical formula ϕ_N. $S_N = \{s : \phi_N(s)\}$, in particular: $\phi_N(s) = \phi_1(s) \cup \phi_2(s) \cup ...\phi_k(s)$. Each constraint ϕ_i is connected with a subset of non-admissible states $S(\phi_i)$ for which $\phi_i(s)$ is true. Therefore: $S_N(s) = S(\phi_1) \cup S(\phi_2) \cup ...S(\phi_k)$ where $S(\phi_i) = \{s : \phi_i(s)\}$. Let us notice that while generating subsequent states of the trajectory, the set of states that may be reachable by means of an admissible decision sequences undergoes changes.

Definition 3. The subset $S_{Rch}(s_i)$ is reachable from the state s_i if and only if there is a sequence of decisions $(u_i, u_{i+1}, ...u_{i+k-1})$ such that for the generated part of the trajectory $(s_{i+1}, s_{i+2}, ...s_{i+k})$ the state s_{i+k} belongs to S_{Rch}. If such a sequence does not exist the subset is not reachable from s_i.

Definition 4. The constraint ϕ_j is active in the state s_i if the set $S(\phi_j)$ defined, through that constraint is reachable from the state si. Otherwise, the constraint ϕ_j is inactive in a given state.

Properties given in definition 4 can easily be verified in a process of automatic analysis as a part of an algorithm based on the method.

There is a large class of problems which are characterized by the following property: if a constraint is no longer active at a certain trajectory state s, then it remains inactive in all further states of any trajectories that starts from the state s. We called this property *a permanent constraint inactivity*. A major part of the known scheduling problems has this property. For the needs of the further discussion, let us assume that the considered optimization problem possesses this property as well. The set of constraints active in a given state defines the subset $S_{NA}(s) \subseteq S_N$ and referred to as active non-admissible set. The more constraints inactive in a given state, the smaller the active set of non-admissible states, and the higher the chances for generating an admissible trajectory. At the same time there is much more freedom in the decision-making process (higher possibility of making decisions which are advantageous in the context of the criterion).

The general idea is to generate a trajectory in such a way as to deactivate certain constraints and at the same time make the subsets of S_N unreachable in an advantageous order. Thus, intermediate goal d_i will be to reach the subset of states S_{d_i}, for which a certain constraint ϕ_i becomes inactive. The set D will be implied by the subset of active constraints that we want to deactivate in a possibly shortest time. The priorities will define the scheduling of eliminating active constraints, that is most favorable order in which the trajectory should reach the subsets of states connected with these goals. In order to define the substitution process P_{ST}, it is necessary to define a new set of goal sates $S_{G_{ST}}$. This set is defined on the basis of the distinguished subset of intermediate goals

$D_W(s) \subseteq D$. When choosing the subset $D_W(s)$ it is most often the case that priorities of goals are taken into consideration. Afterwards, a set of final states $S_{G_{ST}}$ of the substitution process $P_{ST}(s)$ is defined as intersection of all subsets defined by particular intermediate goals $d_i \in D_W(s)$ $(i = 1, 2, ... k)$.

Summing up, construction of a substitution task in a given state s is realized through the following steps: definition of the set of goals D, definition of priorities in the set of goals D, choice of the set $D_W(s)$ of goals for realization, and definition of the set of final states $S_{G_{ST}}$ for the substitution process P_{ST}.

The method of selecting decision u^* is strongly dependent upon the substitution task (see example). Due to the fact that the entire problem is formally presented as an AL model, both analysis and substitution task creation methods can be algoritmized.

6   Conclusion

The paper presents the development of new heuristic methods of solving discrete optimization problems. The methods are based on algebraic-logical meta model of multistage decision process (ALMM of DMP). It provides three stage concept of heuristic method synthesis involving local optimization as well as two heuristic methods based on the said concept: Machine Learning Based on ALMM of DMP and the Substitution Task Method. Both methods will be implemented in a special software tool for solving discrete optimization problems, named ALMM Solver [18].

References

1. Dudek-Dyduch, E.: Information systems for production management. Wyd. Poldex, Kraków (2002) (in Polish) ISBN 83-88979-12-4
2. Dudek-Dyduch, E.: Learning based algorithm in sheduling. Journal of Intelligent Manufacturing (JIM) 11(2), 135–143 (accepted to be published 1998)
3. Dudek-Dyduch, E.: Discrete determinable processes - compact knowledge-based model. Notas de Matematica No 137. Universidad de Los Andes, Merida (1993)
4. Dudek-Dyduch, E.: Heuristic algorithms - formal approach based on compact knowledge-based model. Notas de Matematica No 138. Universidad de Los Andes, Merida (1993)
5. Dudek-Dyduch, E.: Problemy reprezentacji wiedzy w systemach ekspertowych wspomagających sterowanie DPP. In: Inżynieria Wiedzy i Systemy Ekspertowe, Prace II Krajowej Konferencji, tom I, pp. 147-154. Politechnika Wrocławska, Wroław (1993)
6. Dudek-Dyduch, E.: Control of discrete event processes - branch and bound method. In: Proc. of IFAC/Ifors/Imacs Symposium Large Scale Systems: Theory and Applications, Chinese Association of Automation, vol. 2, pp. 573–578 (1992)
7. Dudek-Dyduch, E.: Formalization and analysis of problems of discrete manufacturing processes. Scientific bulletin of AGH University, Automatics, vol. 54 (1990) (in Polish)
8. Dudek-Dyduch, E.: Simulation of some class of discrete manufacturing processes. In: Proc. of European Congress on Simulation, Praha (1987)

9. Dudek-Dyduch, E., Dutkiewicz, L.: Substitution tasks method for discrete optimization. In: Rutkowski, L., Korytkowski, M., Scherer, R., Tadeusiewicz, R., Zadeh, L.A., Zurada, J.M. (eds.) ICAISC 2013, Part II. LNCS, vol. 7895, pp. 419–430. Springer, Heidelberg (2013)

10. Dudek-Dyduch, E., Dyduch, T.: Learning algorithms for scheduling using knowledge based model. In: Rutkowski, L., Tadeusiewicz, R., Zadeh, L.A., Żurada, J.M. (eds.) ICAISC 2006. LNCS (LNAI), vol. 4029, pp. 1091–1100. Springer, Heidelberg (2006)

11. Dudek-Dyduch, E., Dyduch, T.: Hybrid learning method for discrete manufacturing control using knowledge based model. In: Proc. of the Third Int Conf. on Informatics, Control, Automation and Robotics, Setubal, Portugal, pp. 160–166 (2006)

12. Dudek-Dyduch, E., Dyduch, T.: Intelligent search algorithms in scheduling. In: Trapl, R. (ed.) Cybernetics and Systems 1996, Vienna, pp. 1228–1232 (1996)

13. Dudek-Dyduch, E., Dyduch, T.: Formal approach to optimization of discrete manufacturing processes. In: Hamza, M.H. (ed.) Proc. of the Twelfth IASTED Int. Conference Modelling, Identification and Control. Acta Press Zurich (1993)

14. Dudek-Dyduch, E., Dyduch, T.: Scheduling some class of discrete processes. In: Proc. of 12th IMACS World Congress, Paris (1988)

15. Dudek-Dyduch, E., Fuchs-Seliger, S.: Approximate algorithms for some tasks in management and economy. System, Modelling, Control 1(7) (1993)

16. Dudek-Dyduch, E., Kucharska, E.: Learning method for co-operation. In: Jędrzejowicz, P., Nguyen, N.T., Hoang, K. (eds.) ICCCI 2011, Part II. LNCS, vol. 6923, pp. 290–300. Springer, Heidelberg (2011)

17. Dudek-Dyduch, E., Kucharska, E.: Optimization Learning Method for Discrete Process Control. In: ICINCO 2011, vol. 1, pp. 24–33 (2011)

18. Dudek-Dyduch, E., Kucharska, E., Dutkiewicz, L., Rączka, K.: ALMM Solver - A Tool for Optimization Problems. In: Rutkowski, L., Korytkowski, M., Scherer, R., Tadeusiewicz, R., Zadeh, L.A., Zurada, J.M. (eds.) ICAISC 2014, Part II. LNCS(LNAI), vol. 8468, pp. 328–338. Springer, Heidelberg (2014)

19. Dutkiewicz, L.: Two-Level Algorithms for Optimization of Production Processes with Resources Depending on System State. PhD thesis (2005) (in Polish)

20. Dutkiewicz, L., Dudek-Dyduch, E.: Substitution Tasks Method for Co-operation. In: Badica, A., Trawinski, B., Nguyen, N.T. (eds.) Recent Developments in Computational Collective Intelligence. SCI, vol. 513, pp. 103–113. Springer, Heidelberg (2014)

21. Dutkiewicz, L., Kucharska, E.: Metody optymalizacyjne oparte na ogólnym schemacie modelu algebraiczno-logicznego. Pomiary, Automatyka, Robotyka 15, 178–182 (2011)

22. Dutkiewicz, L., Kucharska, E., Kraszewska, M.: Scheduling of preparatory work in mine - Simulation algorithms. Mineral Resources Management 24(3), 79–93 (2008) (in Polish)

23. Dutkiewicz, L., Kucharska, E., Rączka, K., Grobler-Dębska, K.: ST Method Based Algorithm for the Supply Routes for Multi-location Companies Problem. In: Kacprzyk, J. (ed.) AISC, pp. 2194–5357 (to appear) ISSN 2194-5357

24. Dyduch, T., Dudek-Dyduch, E.: Learning based algorithm in sheduling. In: Proc. of Int. Conf. on Industrial Engineering and Production Management, Lyon, vol. 1, pp. 119–128 (1997)

25. El-Abd, M.: On the hybridization of the artificial Bee Colony and Particle Swarm Optimization Algorithms. Journal of Artificial Intelligence and Soft Computing Research 2(2) (2012)

26. Horzyk, A.: How Does Generalization and Creativity Come into Being in Neural Associative Systems and How Does It Form Human-Like Knowledge?. Neurocomputing, 238–257 (2014), doi: 10.1016/j.neucom.2014.04.046
27. Kacprzyk, J.: Multistage Fuzzy Control: A Model-Based Approach to Control and Decision-Making. Wiley, Chichester (1997)
28. Kucharska, E.: Application of an algebraic-logical model for optimization of scheduling problems with retooling time depending on system state. PhD thesis (2006) (in Polish)
29. Kucharska, E., Dudek-Dyduch, E.: Extended Learning Method for Designation of Cooperation. In: Nguyen, N.T. (ed.) TCCI XIV 2014. LNCS, vol. 8615, pp. 136–157. Springer, Heidelberg (2014)
30. Lobato, F.S., Steffen Jr., J.V.: A New Multi-objective Optimization Algorithm Based on Differential Evolution and Neighborhood Exploring Evolution Strategy. Journal of Artificial Intelligence and Soft Computing Research 1(4) (2011)
31. Pearl, J.: Heuristics: Intelligent Search Strategies for Computer Problem Solving. Addison-Wesley Comp., Menlo Park (1984)
32. Tadeusiewicz, R., Izworski, A.: Learning in Neural Network - Unusual Effects of "Artificial Dreams". In: King, I., Wang, J., Chan, L.-W., Wang, D. (eds.) ICONIP 2006, Part II. LNCS, vol. 4232, pp. 211–218. Springer, Heidelberg (2006)
33. Tadeusiewicz, R., Izworski, A., Bulka, J., Wochlik, I.: Unusual Effects of Artificial Dreams Encountered During Learning in "Neural Networks". In: Yeung, D.S., Wang, X., Zhan, L., Huang, J. (eds.) Proceedings of 2005 International Conference on Machine Learning and Cybernetics, vol. 7, pp. 4205–4209. IEEE Press (IEEE catalog number 05EX1059), Guangzhou (2005)
34. Vijayalakshmi, G.A., Pai, M.T.: Metaheuristic Optimization of Marginal Risk Constrained Long-Short Portfolios. Journal of Artificial Intelligence and Soft Computing Research 2(2) (2012)
35. Vincke, P.: Multicriteria decision-aid. John Wiley & Sons (1992)

Specific Object Detection Scheme Based on Descriptors Fusion Using Belief Functions

Mariem Farhat[1(✉)], Slim Mhiri[2], and Moncef Tagina[1]

[1] National School of Computer Science, University of Manouba, Tunisia
`mariem.farhat@ensi.rnu.tn`,
[2] CRISTAL Laboratory, GRIFT research group, Tunisia

Abstract. Here, a comparative study of information fusion methods for instance object detection is proposed. Instance object detection is one of mean service that robots needs. Classical approaches are based on extracting discriminant and invariant features. However those features still have a limitation to represent all kinds of objects and satisfy all requirements (discrimination and invariance). Since no single feature can work well in various situations, we need to combine several features so that the robot can handle all kind of daily life objects. Our task consists in defining a strategy that can work on various objects and backgrounds without any prior knowledge. In this paper we propose a scheme to combine two descriptors using belief function theory. First, objects are extracted from image and described by two complementary descriptors: Dominant Color Descriptor for color description and Zernike Moments for shape description. Second, similarity indicators is computed between object of interest descriptors and each extracted object descriptors. Finally, those measures are combined into a belief functions in order to build a final decision about the object presence in the image taking the information uncertainty and imprecise into consideration. We have evaluated our approach with different methods of information fusion such as the weighted vote approach, the possibility theory and so forth.

Keywords: Object detection · Global descriptor · Local descriptor · dominant color descriptor · Zernike moments · Belief functions

1 Introduction

Object instance detection is a very popular and known problem in computer vision which attracts the attention of many researchers. Although it is similar to many other issues like object detection, object recognition and image based retrieval but in reality there are quite a few differences between them. This problem can be considered as one of the most important step in grasping object by a robot manipulator. The main goal of object instance detection, the issue with which we grapple in this paper, is to attempt to find and locate a specific object in an image. Accordingly, we propose, via the current research, a strategy for object instance detection. It allows the robot to find the desired object designed by the user in an interface that reflects the scene image. So, we consider our

© Springer International Publishing Switzerland 2015
L. Rutkowski et al. (Eds.): ICAISC 2015, Part I, LNAI 9119, pp. 555–565, 2015.
DOI: 10.1007/978-3-319-19324-3_49

strategy is implemented using the vision system proposed in [12]. It is based on two cameras observing the same scene in two arbitrary views as following:

- The fixed camera observes the whole scene and returns an image in the user interface. Through this image, the user can select the desired object to grasp.
- The mobile camera is fixed on the top of the grasper and returns the view observed by the robot. This camera must guide the manipulator to attend the desired object for grasping.

Given this configuration, our goal is to decide whether the desired object exists in the current view of the mobile camera or not. That is what we call Object instance detection. This target leads to many challenges:

- Computational time: We handle a real time application, so the computational time is a crucial criterion for the success of the grasping task.
- Generic: In order to cover the objects of everyday life, the proposed strategy must be efficient with all object types.
- No prior knowledge: we must consider that the objects of everyday life we do not have any prior knowledge about the desired object.
- Automatic: In order to achieve the task in a full automatic manner; our robot must operate without any human intervention.
- Stable under changes: The object can appear under different image projections giving rise to many other challenges. In fact, an object instance may have a dramatically varied appearance due to viewpoint transformations and self-occlusions (parts of the object are only visible from some viewpoints).
- Complexity of the background: the background surrounding the object may also vary.

Many researchers have proposed strategy for achieving this goal. In [12], authors use the traditional template matching based methods and SIFT matching based methods. Unfortunately this method generates very few or no keypoints if the objects are very plain and do not have much detail. Therefore, SIFT is not well suited to recognize objects such as single color coffee mugs or pieces of fruit. Although, SIFT based method has low computation and is stable under changes, there is still non generic solution. Since no single method can work well in various situations, the most promising recent studies combine several methods. In [10], authors propose a scheme to classify situations depending on the characteristics of object of interest, the background and the user demand so that the robots can use an appropriate one automatically. This strategy requires a pre-processing to identify which situation to handle. In [16], authors present a cascade template matching framework for object instance detection. Triplet of feature descriptors [13] is proposed for detection and recognition. These triplets are labeled via modified K-means clustering algorithm, which is followed by inverse lookup matching and triplet votes. Although this subject has attracted much researcher interest and seems to be easy, it remains unresolved. Most of presented works do not meet the challenges of the problem. The most crucial question is how to combine different descriptors to have riche and accurate decision for any type of objects and scenes taking account of constraints defined by the grasping object task. In this paper, we present our work that aims to provide a new way for the resolution of this problem. We have focused our attention in the manner of the combination of different descriptors associated to the desired object. In order to take benefit of the complementarity of many descriptors, we choose a fusion and not a cascade matching template. Our main contribution is the application of the belief function theory for the descriptor fusion in order to manage the imprecise and uncertain information. In the reminder of this paper, we first discuss some related works on instance object detection. Second, our approach and contribution is presented in details. Following that, comparisons between our approach and those identified in literature ones are shown with discussions and analysis. Finally, the whole work is concluded.

2 Review of Class-Specific Object Detection Methods Based On Combination

In this paragraph, we present all combination based methods regardless of specific or class object detection. The combination can be made in different manners: cascade [5,1], hierarchically [7], and a real fusion. The fusion based methods can be divided in two categories depending on whether the merger is done before or after the step of measuring the similarity (or classification) [14]:

– Early fusion: in this case, features are merged by simple vector concatenation that constitutes a single global vector [14,15]. In [9] authors combine between many local features : scale Invariant Transform Features (SIFT), subsampled gray values, basic intensity moments and moment invariants as input to the boosting classifier in recognizing object classes. Others have proposed to combine local and global features in order to take of benefits of each [10,11,9].
– Late fusion: in this case, decisions of different descriptors are merged. For such case a merger is effective, it is usually necessary to normalize different distances so that they all have a similar dynamicity. If only labels are available, a majority vote [3,4] is used. If continuous outputs like posteriori probabilities are supplied, an average or some other linear combinations have been suggested [8,6,7,6]. If the classifier outputs are interpreted as fuzzy membership values, belief values or evidence, fuzzy rules, and belief functions are used.

The specific object detection is based on modeling visual information. The accuracy and reliability of the method depend on the choice of visual features and the confidence degree granted to data and measurements. This information is given by descriptors, which describe the object, can be imprecise and uncertain information. Furthermore, many instances of the same object may appear in the same image (e.g. two soons, each with a different color). Moreover, for a robotic service task, the method must consider all possible types of objects that can occur in different poses. Another important constraint is the reliability of the method which must avoid fault and minimize errors. The combination between different sources of information generates a conflict which must be managed in an intelligent way. Therefore, the combination method to use must take into consideration this type of incompleteness. At present, researchers are facing difficulties in determining the combination of methods that could produce optimal results. For that goal, we propose a late fusion scheme based on belief functions to combine between two descriptors to color and shape. Then we compare between our method and two other fusion methods: the majority vote and the possibility methods method.

3   Proposed Approach for Specific Unknown Object Detection

To overcome the above problems, we propose a novel object detection method using one object image. The problem, as it was described, is dealing with the detection of the presence of an unknown object R in an image I by searching an object O_i in the image I which is highly similar to the desired object R. The proposed method does not require a complicated pre-processing – such as the camera calibration – and is a time-efficient approach. Fig. 1 shows the overall procedure of the proposed object instance detection method. Given an input image, our method proceeds in three steps. In the first step, we do an image segmentation to extract the different objects O_i contained on the image. In the second step, we compute two descriptors : Color descriptor - Dominant Color and Shape descriptor - Zernike Moments. As images can be acquired in two completely different camera angles, the color description may be insufficient to describe the object in question essentially in the case where it is not homogeneous. A description of the object shape can enrich the signature of the object. So, we choose to combine a shape descriptor with a color descriptor. So, we compute the distance between the descriptor of each extracted object O_i and the descriptor of R. In the third step, a combination of decisions from each descriptor is done by belief functions theory to manage the uncertainty, imprecision and incomplete data.

4   Application of the Evidence Theory On Specific Object Detection

4.1   Modeling Information

In order to associate the object of interest R to one of extracted objects, we define a frame of discernment as:

$$\Theta = \{O_1, O_2, ..., O_N\} \tag{1}$$

Where O_i is hypothesis. Each O_i means that O_i is our object of interest $R(O_i = R)$. N is the number of extracted object. We define S_1 and S_2 respectively for Zernike and Dominant Color descriptors. To estimate mass functions, there are two main methods: Probabilistic and Distance based methods [17]. Probabilistic methods [2] require the knowledge of $p(S_i/O_j)$. Distance based methods [17] assign a mass function to O_j dependent on its similarity to R. So, we choose the distance based method to compute the mass function as bellow:

$$m_j^i(O_i) = \alpha_j * exp(-d_{i,j}) \tag{2}$$

Where α_j is a parameter that prevents the allocation of the whole mass function for one source. It reflects the uncertainty in the characterization of information provided by i.th source. In addition, the constraint $\alpha_j < 1$ guarantees the possibility of combining m_i with any other mass function. $d_{(i,j)}$ represents distance between the descriptors of R and O_i. As O_i is the unique focal element; we have:

$$m_j^i(\Theta) = 1 - m_j^i(O_i) \tag{3}$$

and for each H_k:

$$m_j^i(H_i) = 0 \forall k \neq i \tag{4}$$

This can be explained by the fact that: when computing the mass function of H_i based on similarity distance, the descriptor has no idea about the mass function of H_k(e.g. the similarity distance between O_k and R). So, having $m_j^i(H_k) = 0$ doesn't mean that H_k is impossible but it means that we ignore the precise degree to assign to H_k (Fig.2). We estimate α_i as a measure of source conflict:

Table 1. mass functions of the source S_1

m1 O1	O2	O3	ignore
0,601884622	0	0	0,398115
0	0,50304714	0	0,496953
0	0	0,558313354	0,441687

$$\alpha_j = (1 - (Conf(s,j))^\lambda)^{\frac{1}{\lambda}} \tag{5}$$

In our case, sources are two descriptors: Zernike moment and Dominant Color descriptor. So the conflict parameter $Conf(s,j)$ which defines distance between sources is given as following:

$$Conf(1,2) = d(m_1, m_2) \tag{6}$$

$$d(m_1, m_2) = \sqrt{1/2^t(m_1 - m_2)D(m_1 - m_2)} \tag{7}$$

4.2   Combination Rules

As described below, when computing the mass function of H_i based on similarity distance, the descriptor has no idea about the mass function of H_k. So, the fusion is given in two steps: first we combine mass functions of different decisions for the same source. Second, we combine different decisions of different sources. In order to combine mass functions provided by each source for each class, there are many approaches. Conjunctive combination or Smets operator supposes that all sources are reliable. We first combine mass functions for each source using the conjunctive combination and supposing that each of them is reliable. So we compute $m_j(H_i)$ for $i = 1...n$ using the equation:

$$m_j(H_i) = \bigoplus m_j^i(H_i) = \frac{m_j^i(H_i) \prod_{i \neq q} m_j^q(\Theta)}{K} \tag{8}$$

$$m_j(\Theta) = \frac{\prod_{q=1n} m_j^q(\Theta)}{K} \tag{9}$$

$$K = \sum_{i=1}^{n} m_j^i(O_i) \prod_{i?q} m_j^q(\Theta) + \prod_{q=1n} m_j^q(\Theta) \tag{10}$$

Where K is a normalize factor that guarantees the condition of closed word: $\sum_i m(H_i) = 1$. Usually, this factor denotes a conflict factor between sources. In our case, K represents the auto conflict factor that reflects the uncertainty of the data provided by the source S_i. Then, we combine all mass functions $m_j(H_i)$ for each hypothesis based on the conjunctive combination, a global $m(H_i) = \bigoplus m_j(H_i)$ is obtained as:

$$m(H_i) = \sum_{O_k \cap O_l \cap \cap O_q = O_i} m_1(H_k) m_2(H_l) \tag{11}$$

$$m(\Theta) = m_1(\Theta) m_2(\Theta) \tag{12}$$

Where $m_1(\Theta)$ is the mass of ignorance of the source S_1 and $m_2(\Theta)$ is the mass of ignorance of the source S_2.

4.3   Decision Rules

We define a credibility function as:

$$bel(H) = \sum_{Y \subset H, Y \neq \phi} m(Y) \tag{13}$$

We will choose an element $H \in 2^\Theta$, if it has the maximum of credibility:

$$bel(H_d) = max_{1 < i < n} bel(H_i) \tag{14}$$

and

$$bel(H_d) \succeq bel(H_d^c) \tag{15}$$

The addition of the second condition implies that we cannot take H_i as a final decision if it is ambiguous, that is to say, we take H_i only if we believe more in class H_i^c than in its opposite. We have to note that this criterion is based on the measure of doubt introduced by Shafer.

5   Results and Experiments

We have done several experiments on a number of images of virtual scene. We have designed different virtual scenes and captured two views for each one. One view represents the complete scene as shown in Fig.2 and the the other view represents the object of interest as shown in Fig.4. We have considered different scenarios: object of interest doesn't belong to the scene Fig.3 ((b), (c), (d), (e), (f), (g)), a scene that contain a similar object with a different color Fig.3 ((b), (c), (e)), a scene that contain a different object with the same color as the desired object Fig.3 ((e), (f)) and the case of a scene that contain the desired object and a different object with the same color Fig.3 ((f)). We have also captured the

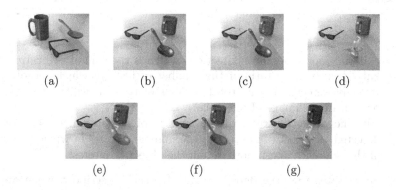

(a)   (b)   (c)   (d)

(e)   (f)   (g)

Fig. 1. Different scene images

Fig. 2. Object of interest under different geometric transformations

object of interest under different geometric transformations: rotation, translation and scale (Fig.5). Three performance measures were obtained by comparing the object detected using each method and the reference data:

- Detection rate: is calculated using the ratio of the number of tests in which the object is correctly detected to the number of tests in which the object is present in the image of reference;

Table 2. table name

Transformation				
Rotation				
Translation				
Scale				
Occlusion				

- False alarm: represents false detections which is the sum of two ratios:
  - False positive: the ratio of the number of tests in which the object is wrongly detected to the total number of tests in which the object is present in the image of reference;
  - False negative: the ratio of the number of test in which the object is detected as object of interest to the number of tests in which the image of the reference doesn not contain the object of interest.

Fig.6 demonstrates that the detection rate for each descriptor, when applied lonely, is modest compared to the fusion methods. In the case of majority vote,

Table 3. Descriptors results

	Detection rate	False positive	False negative
Zernike	0,363636	0,16	0,538462
Dominant Color	0,340909	0,48	0,239316

we choose a weighted vote principle. As the Fig.6 shows, the majority vote method gives the worst result in term of detection rate. We can notice that the detection performance of the fusion (even with the worst method) 0,431818 is much better than results obtained by each single feature 0,363636-0,340909. It justifies the importance and the fusion of its contribution in the improvement of

Table 4. Combination methods results

Detection Methods	Detection rate	False positive	False negative
Fusion based on vote method	0,431818	0,44	0,435897
Fusion based on possibility theory with Min operator	0,818182	0,28	0,854701
Fusion based on possibility theory with Conj operator	0,522727	0,76	0,888889
Fusion based on possibility theory with Prod Operator	0,5	0,68	0,803419
Fusion based on evidence theory	0,454545	0,12	0,153846

results thanks to the complementarity of these features. We observe also, that fusion based on vote method increase results for false alarm (false positive and false negative). In fact, vote method is a linear fusion of sources without any conflict resolution. We can improve results for vote method if we use another source that will support the decision of one or other source. Unlike vote method, evidence method minimizes false alarm as it redistributes the conflict term on decisions. Furthermore, the process don not consider a decision only in case we believe on it more than we believe on its opposite. In the context of the possibility theory, for the combination step we have tested different operators. The detection rates given in Fig.8 show that the best result is reached for the t-norm min (with 0,818182). For the evidence theory based method, we can notice that it has a modest result compared to those of possibility theory. But, it is more robust to bad features and gives the best result for false alarm. The detection rate is relatively low (0,454545) and this can be justified by two arguments. First, the decision rule is more restrict then decision rule of possibility theory; we must believe in the hypothesis more than in its opposite. Second, the combination rule used in belief functions method distributes the conflict term in a uniform manner which does not promote a decision. To make results more significant, we define *ratio 1* between the detection rate and false alarm. When the ratio is , it means that the method has false detection more than a positive one. This makes the evidence based method (0.602462) more efficient than other methods. Min operator for possibility based method has a close result (1.386856) as illustrated in Fig.9. We have also defined ratio 2 between detection rate and false negative. False negative means the method predicts that the object exists while it do not which is worse. Comparing methods using *ratio 2*, we can notice that evidence based method has more interesting results and is further than others.

Table 5. results of fusion methods for *ratio1* and *ratio2*

	Ratio 1	Ratio 2
Vote	2,028393907	1,009446109
Evidence	0,602462	0,338462
possibility_min	1,386856	1,044634
possibility_conj	3,154398	1,700484
possibility_prod	2,966838	1,606838

6   Conclusion

In this paper, we proposed a method for object detection using a later fusion between two descriptors: color dominant descriptor and Zernike moment descriptor. We have focused our attention in the manner of the combination of different descriptors to describe the desired object. In order to take benefit of the complementary of many descriptors, we choose a fusion and not a cascade matching template. Our main contribution is the application of the belief function theory for the descriptor fusion in order to manage the imprecise and uncertain information. The main contribution is the fusion based on the belief functions theory which overcomes the source conflict and relies on credibility function to make a decision. As the results show, the fusion of descriptor is more reliable than the template based method using each descriptor alone. We have tested several fusion methods and we have concluded that evidence method gives the most interest results. For the same images, SIFT gives few matches which cannot be used to detect the presence of the object. We can add one other descriptor to describe the texture of the objects. So we can handle a simple and complex shape object in one hand, and a textured and texturless object in another hand. We can also use the auto conflict that exists in the mass function of each source to predict the fiability parameter.

References

1. El-Shishiny, H., Abdel-Mottaleb, M.S., El-Raey, M., Shoukry, A.: A multistage algorithm for fast classification of patterns. Pattern Recognition Letters 10(4), 211–215 (1989)
2. Appriou, A.: Probabilit et incertitude en fusion de donnes multi-senseurs. Titre part- Office national d'tudes et de recherches aerospatiales (1991)
3. Kimura, F., Shridhar, M.: Handwritten numerical recognition based on multiple algorithms. Pattern Recognition 24(10), 969–983 (1991)
4. Franke, J., Mandler, E.: A comparison of two approaches for combining the votes of cooperating classifiers. In: Proceedings of 11th IAPR International Conference on Pattern Recognition: Conference B: Pattern Recognition Methodology and Systems, vol. II, pp. 611–614. IEEE (1992)

5. Pudil, P., Novovicova, J., Blaha, S., Kittler, J.: Multistage pattern recognition with reject option. In: Proceedings of 11th IAPR International Conference on Pattern Recognition Conference B: Pattern Recognition Methodology and Systems, vol. II, pp. 92–95. IEEE (1992)

6. Xu, L., Krzyzak, A., Suen, C.Y.: Methods of combining multiple classifiers and their applications to handwriting recognition. IEEE Transactions on Systems, Man and Cybernetics 22(3), 418–435 (1992)

7. Zhou, J., Pavlidis, T.: Discrimination of characters by a multi-stage recognition process. Pattern Recognition 27(11), 1539–1549 (1994)

8. Hashem, S., Schmeiser, B.: Improving model accuracy using optimal linear combinations of trained neural networks. IEEE Transactions on Neural Networks 6(3), 792–794 (1995)

9. Opelt, A., Pinz, A., Fussenegger, M., Auer, P.: Generic object recognition with boosting. IEEE Transactions on Pattern Analysis and Machine Intelligence 28(3), 416–431 (2006)

10. Mansur, A., Hossain, M. A., Kuno, Y.: Integration of multiple methods for class and specific object recognition. In: Bebis, G., et al. (eds.) ISVC 2006. LNCS, vol. 4291, pp. 841–849. Springer, Heidelberg (2006)

11. Opelt, A., Pinz, A., Zisserman, A.: Fusing shape and appearance information for object category detection (2006)

12. Dune, C., Marchand, E., Leroux, C.: One click focus with eye-in-hand/eye-to-hand cooperation. In: IEEE International Conference on Robotics and Automation, pp. 2471–2476. IEEE (2007)

13. Zitnick, C.L., Sun, J., Szeliski, R., Winder, S.: Object instance recognition using triplets of feature symbols. Microsoft Research Technical Report (2007)

14. Oliveira, L., Nunes, U.: On integration of features and classifiers for robust vehicle detection. In: 11th International IEEE Conference on Intelligent Transportation Systems, ITSC 2008, pp. 414–419. IEEE (2008)

15. Sun, X., Chen, M., Hauptmann, A.: Action recognition via local descriptors and holistic features. In: IEEE Computer Society Conference on Computer Vision and Pattern Recognition Workshops, CVPR Workshops 2009, pp. 58–65 (2009)

16. Xie, C., Li, J., Wang, T., Wang, J., Lu, H.: Real-Time Cascade Template Matching for Object Instance Detection. In: The Era of Interactive Media, pp. 433–443. Springer, New York (2013)

17. Denoeux, A.: A k-nearest neighbour classification rule based on Dempster-Shafer theory. IEEE Trans. Syst. Man. and Cyber. 25(5), 804–813 (1995)

Video Key Frame Detection Based on SURF Algorithm

Rafał Grycuk[1], Michał Knop[1(✉)], and Sayantan Mandal[2]

[1] Institute of Computational Intelligence, Częstochowa University of Technology
Al. Armii Krajowej 36, 42-200 Częstochowa, Poland
{rafal.grycuk,michal.knop}@iisi.pcz.pl
http://iisi.pcz.pl
[2] Nanyang Technological University, Singapore, Singapore

Abstract. In this paper we present a new method for key frame detection. Our approach is based on a well known algorithm: Speeded-Up Robust Features (SURF), which is a crucial step of our method. The frames are compared by a SURF matcher, which allows to count the corresponding keypoints. The proposed method provides better results for professional and high resolution videos. The simulations we conducted proved the effectiveness of our approach. The algorithm requires only one input parameter.

Keywords: SURF · Key frame detection · Video compression · Image Key Point

1 Introduction

In recent years popularity of digital movies has been increased. Efficient techniques based on video content analysis have become the main method for indexing systems. Therefore, video content analysis is a very interesting area of research. The video can be treated as a stream of incoming images which is a problem widely investigated in the literature [9][16][32][33][34][39][40]. However it does not take into account the relationship between neighboring images. Therefore, it is more efficient to divide the video stream into different scenes. Key frame detection is a process that divides a movie into physical scenes. There are many key frame detection methods [3][21][23][37][41]. The process of matching two consecutive frames is a challenging issue. This problem can be solved in many ways, such as histogram based methods [8][27], the correlation of images [18][29] or entropy [17]. However, most algorithms are sensitive to noise and movements of the camera or objects. Their implementation is challenging due to lack of information on the image content. Some researchers try to find a method that may improve the key frame detection efficiency, such as using the keypoints of the image (e.g. SURF, SIFT). After extracting key frames from the video we can use them in other applications such as video compression, video on demand or video analysis. In our work, we used methods based on the SURF algorithm. In the proposed approach, we used image keypoints (interest points) to compare frames and retrieve key frames.

© Springer International Publishing Switzerland 2015
L. Rutkowski et al. (Eds.): ICAISC 2015, Part I, LNAI 9119, pp. 566–576, 2015.
DOI: 10.1007/978-3-319-19324-3_50

2   Related Works

2.1   Correlation Coefficient Method

The correlation coefficient is a number indicating the linear dependency between two random variables or two sets of data [15]. This parameter makes it possible to distinguish between the following transition types: cuts, gradual transitions and motion. For the cuts, the difference between the two frames is large, and the correlation of these frames is low. For a gradual transition, the pixel values of two adjacent frames are different, but are similar in the edges and textures, so the correlation in the spatial domain is high [22]. A histogram of brightness changes slightly for motion scenes that take place on the same background. However, for scenes of gradual transition or cuts, it changes gradually or abruptly [18].

Differences between objects motion in the scene and the scene change can be obtained by comparison of the key frames with subsequent frames. The key frame histogram H_{kf} can be defined as:

$$H_{kf}(r_k) = n_k, \tag{1}$$

where r_k is the k-th level of brightness, n_k is the number of pixels in frame with the brightness level r_k.

For N frames in the video, we calculate the histogram H_i, i $= 2,3, ..., $ N. The correlation between H_{kf} and H_i can be defined as:

$$corr(H_{kf}, H_i) = \frac{\sum_{j=0}^{m}(H_{kf}(j) - h_{kf})(H_i(j) - h_i)}{\sqrt{\sum_{j=0}^{m}(H_{kf}(j) - h_{kf})^2 \sum_{j=0}^{m}(H_i(j) - h_i)^2}}, \tag{2}$$

where m is the number of brightness scale levels r_k; h_{kf}, h_i are mean values of H_{kf} and H_i [31], respectively, and can be defined as:

$$h_i = \frac{1}{m} \sum_{j=0}^{m} H_i(j). \tag{3}$$

Then, the correlation value computed from eq. (2) is compared with a threshold. If the correlation value is lower than the assumed threshold, the algorithm determines a new key frame [18].

2.2   Entropy Method

Knop et al. [17] proposed a method based on entropy to determine the complexity of information stored in each frame. The general formula for the entropy on the grayscale video materials is as follows:

$$E_j = -\sum_{i=0}^{N} p_i log(p_i), \tag{4}$$

where E_j is a characteristic value calculated from the current frame, p_i is the next pixel from this frame, and N is a number of whole pixels in the current image. Since we used HSV color gamut, we must calculate the value of the entropy value for each coefficient in the palette. The individual components of the HSV model are not equal. The hue H is the most important in the process of determining the coefficient. Even the slightest change of its value should lead to detecting scene changes. The color saturation S has a bit less importance because, even larger changes are for us fully acceptable. The value of the color V has the lowest importance for us. Hence, the final value of entropy for each frame in the HSV color space will be calculated from the following formula:

$$F_n(E) = a \cdot E_j(H) + b \cdot E_j(S) + c \cdot E_j(V) \qquad (5)$$

Parameters of a, b and c correspond to weighting factors for the entropy, component of HSV and the their values are successively set to 0.9, 0.3 and 0.1 respectively [30]. To detect new a key frame this method compares the current key frame with subsequent frames. The following formula was used for the comparison operation:

$$E_{j,k} = \frac{|E_j - E_k|}{E_k}, \qquad (6)$$

where j is the number of our current frame and k is the current key frame. The first key frame is always the first image taken at start of the video. The next key frames are calculated based on the comparison result (see formula (6)). If the entropy value is lower than the assumed threshold, the algorithm determines a new key frame.

2.3   SURF

SURF (Speeded-Up Robust Features) is an algorithm used to detect and describe local features of an image. It was presented for the first time in [2], but currently is used in various systems e.g. image recognition [19][26], 3D reconstruction, image description [36], segmentation [12][14], image analysis [35], content based image retrieval [13][28], object tracking [11], image databases [4][5][6][7][20], and many others.

SURF is based on SIFT, and it uses Integral Images instead of DOG (Difference of Gaussian), which allows to work much faster than SIFT [24][25]. It can also be accelerated by a GPU [38] and it has a parallel implementation [42]. SURF is based on image keypoints (interesting points), which allows to extract local features from an image. For each keypoint, which indicates local image feature, we generate a feature vector, which can be used for further processing. SURF contains four main steps [1][2][10]:

1. Computing Integral Images,
2. Fast-Hessian Detector,
   - The Hessian,
   - Constructing the Scale-Space,
   - Accurate Interest Point Localization,

3. Interest Point Descriptor,
   - Orientation Assignment
   - Descriptor Components
4. Generating vectors describing the keypoint.

A SURF keypoint consists of two vectors. First one contains: point position (x, y), scale (Detected scale), response (Response of the detected feature, strength), orientation (Orientation measured anti-clockwise from +ve x-axis), laplacian (Sign of laplacian for fast matching purposes). The second one describes the intensity distribution of the pixels within the neighborhood of the point interest (64 or 128 values). In order to generate keypoints SURF require one input parameter $minHessian$. The method is resistant to change of scale and rotation, which allows it to match corresponding keypoints in similar images (frames).

3   Proposed Method

The proposed method for key frame detection is based on the SURF algorithm. Our approach consists of several stages. The first step divides input video into individual frames. Next, we need to create two variables $current$, $next$ and load the first frame to the $current$ variable and the second one to the $next$ variable. Then the frames are compared by the SURF algorithm. This stage is crucial. In result of this comparison we obtain a $factor$, which is in range $(0 \le factor \le 1)$, where 0 means - no similarity and 1 - complete similarity. The following step compares this $factor$ with the threshold t value. If the $factor$ is lower then t, the $next$ frame is labeled as a key frame. The t value is passed as the input parameter of our algorithm. The final step is to set $next$ frame as $current$ and get the following frame. If $next$ frame is empty, the algorithm stops functioning. The pseudo code describes all steps of our method (see Algorithm 1).

The key stage of the algorithm is the comparison step, performed by the SURF detector. We use SURF to find corresponding keypoints on both images. ($current$, $next$). Then we count them and calculate $factor$. $Factor$ is percentage value of correctly found keypoints from first frame on the second one. Thus, the correctness of SURF detection is crucial. The following pseudo code can also be represented by a block diagram (see Fig.1).

4   Experimental Results

Algorithm stages were implemented in .NET C# using and Emgu CV libraries which are wrapper for OPEN CV (C++). The compare step is based on EMGU CV. Other steps were implemented by the authors. In our experiments we set $minHessian$ parameter to 500. This value was determined empirically.

After the first step, we obtained the numbered frames. Every experiment shows which frame is labeled as a key frame.Tab.1 presents a list of factors. The first column represents the frame number and second one contains a $factor$ computed between them. Fig. 2 and Fig.3 represents corresponding keypoints

INPUT: Video, t, *video*
OUTPUT: Detected key frames, *keyFrameList*
framesList:= ExtractFramesFromVideo(*video*);
current := LoadFrame();
next := LoadFrame();
while *next != NULL* **do**
  matchedKeyPointsCount := CompareFrameBySURFDetector(*current*, *next*);
  factor := *matchedKeyPointsCount*/*allKeyPoints*;
  if *factor < t* **then**
    next.IsKeyFrame := true;
    keyFrameList.Add(next);
  end
  current := *next*;
  next := LoadFrame();
end

Algorithm 1. Key frame detection steps

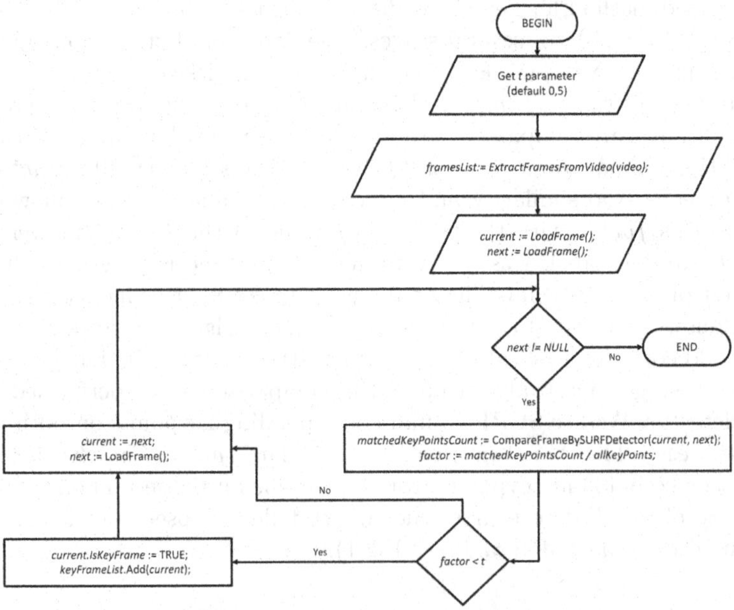

Fig. 1. Block diagram of the proposed method

connected with a line. As can be seen in similar frames (fig.2), many of keypoints are found on both frames. It should be noted, that on every frame we have the same label in left bottom corner (see Fig. 3). It presents some difficulty, but our algorithm overcomes this issue.

In Table 1 we can distinguish two types of frames. In the first type the comparison factor is high (close to 1) and in the second one the factor is low (close

Fig. 2. Detection of corresponding keypoints in similar frames

Fig. 3. Detection of corresponding keypoints in dissimilar frames

to 0). As can be seen, frames: 40-41, 236-237, 282-283, 331-332 and 458-459 have low similarity. Thus, the second frame of each pair have been labeled as key frames (KF, see Fig. 4). The experiment we performed proved that key frames were correctly found. The method was improved relatively to existing approaches [17]. In our approach the algorithm did not detect key frames between 41-236, when the foreground object (person) was moved beyond the scene.

Experiment 2 is presented in Figure 5. The input video was obtained from and AR.Drone 2.0, which has an embedded HD camera (1280x720). The rapid fluctuations of camera causes fast objects movement, thus the corresponding keypoints located on the current frame cannot be found on the next. A very interesting issue is the value of threshold, which is set to 0.1. This value was obtained empirically. Procedure of threshold selection allowed to reduce a number of false-positive detected frames.

Fig. 4. Experiment 1. The detected key frames are labeled with (KF) label. Threshold (t) value was set to 0.4.

Table 1. Calculated factors. Due to lack of space non important frames have been removed.

Frames IDs	Factor
1-2	0.8
2-3	0.8
38-39	0.8
39-40	0.8
40-41	0.1
41-42	0.9
42-43	0.8
234-235	0.8
235-236	0.9
236-237	0.2
237-238	0.9
238-239	0.9
280-281	0.8
281-282	0.8

Frames IDs	Factor
282-283	0.3
283-284	1
284-285	0.8
329-330	0.8
330-331	0.8
331-332	0.2
332-333	1
333-334	0.9
456-457	0.8
457-458	0.9
458-459	0.2
459-460	1
460-461	0.9

Fig. 5. Experiment 2. The detected key frames are labeled with (KF) label. Threshold (t) value were set to 0.1.

Fig. 6. Experiment 3. The detected key frames are labeled with (KF) label. Threshold (t) value was set to 0.2.

Fig. 6 represents the last simulation. This experiment is similar to Exp.1, but in this one we have tested our method on a video with different types of lighting (light, dark). As can be seen, the presented approach has proved to be effective.

5   Final Remarks

The presented method is a novel approach for key frame detection. Simulations verified the correctness of the algorithm. The presented approach requires only one input parameter - threshold (t). During the experiments we discovered, that the proposed method has better results in professional videos, because this type of video has better lighting and objects transitions are slower. Thus, the keypoints detected on them do not have an immediate effect on a frame's factor. Amateur videos are often recorded without a tripod, thus the movements of the camera are more rapid. The algorithm is more effective in high resolution videos, but it requires more execution time (more keypoints are detected on high resolution frames). The method has been tested on various videos, but due to lack of space we had to narrow the presented simulations. In addition our algorithm is resistant to any markers located on the video.

Acknowledgments. The work presented in this paper was supported by a grant BS/MN-1-109-301/14/P "Clustering algorithms for data stream - in reference to the Content-Based Image Retrieval methods (CBIR)".

The work presented in this paper was supported by a grant BS/MN 1-109-302/14/P "New video compression method using neural image compression algorithm".

References

1. Bay, H., Ess, A., Tuytelaars, T., Van Gool, L.: Speeded-up robust features (surf). Computer Vision and Image Understanding 110(3), 346–359 (2008)
2. Bay, H., Tuytelaars, T., Van Gool, L.: SURF: Speeded up robust features. In: Leonardis, A., Bischof, H., Pinz, A. (eds.) ECCV 2006, Part I. LNCS, vol. 3951, pp. 404–417. Springer, Heidelberg (2006)
3. Bazarganigilani, M.: Optimized image feature selection using pairwise classifiers. Journal of Artificial Intelligence and Soft Computing Research 1(1), 147–153 (2011)
4. Chromiak, M., Dobrowolski, D.: Content repository in object oriented data model. Annales UMCS, Informatica 13(2), 17–27 (2013)
5. Chromiak, M., Stencel, K.: The linkup data structure for heterogeneous data integration platform. In: Kim, T.-H., Lee, Y.-H., Fang, W.-C. (eds.) FGIT 2012. LNCS, vol. 7709, pp. 263–274. Springer, Heidelberg (2012)
6. Chromiak, M., Stencel, K.: A data model for heterogeneous data integration architecture. In: Proceedings of Beyond Databases, Architectures, and Structures 10th International Conference, BDAS 2014, Ustron, Poland, May 27-30, pp. 547–556 (2014)
7. Chromiak, M., Wisniewski, P., Stencel, K.: Exploiting order dependencies on primary keys for optimization. In: Proceedings of the 23th International Workshop on Concurrency, Specification and Programming, Chemnitz, Germany, September 29-October 1, pp. 58–68 (2014)

8. Cierniak, R., Knop, M.: Video compression algorithm based on neural networks. In: Rutkowski, L., Korytkowski, M., Scherer, R., Tadeusiewicz, R., Zadeh, L.A., Zurada, J.M. (eds.) ICAISC 2013, Part I. LNCS(LNAI), vol. 7894, pp. 524–531. Springer, Heidelberg (2013)

9. Cruz Chvez, M.A., Martnez Oropeza, A.: B-tree algorithm complexity analysis to evaluate the feasibility of its application in the university course timetabling problem. Journal of Artificial Intelligence and Soft Computing Research 3(4), 251–263 (2013)

10. Evans, C.: Notes on the opensurf library. University of Bristol, Tech. Rep. CSTR-09-001 (January 2009)

11. Gabryel, M., Korytkowski, M., Scherer, R., Rutkowski, L.: Object detection by simple fuzzy classifiers generated by boosting. In: Rutkowski, L., Korytkowski, M., Scherer, R., Tadeusiewicz, R., Zadeh, L.A., Zurada, J.M. (eds.) ICAISC 2013, Part I. LNCS(LNAI), vol. 7894, pp. 540–547. Springer, Heidelberg (2013)

12. Grycuk, R., Gabryel, M., Korytkowski, M., Romanowski, J., Scherer, R.: Improved digital image segmentation based on stereo vision and mean shift algorithm. In: Wyrzykowski, R., Dongarra, J., Karczewski, K., Waśniewski, J. (eds.) PPAM 2013, Part I. LNCS, vol. 8384, pp. 433–443. Springer, Heidelberg (2014)

13. Grycuk, R., Gabryel, M., Korytkowski, M., Scherer, R.: Content-based image indexing by data clustering and inverse document frequency. In: Kozielski, S., Mrozek, D., Kasprowski, P., Małysiak-Mrozek, B., Kostrzewa, D. (eds.) BDAS 2014. CCIS, vol. 424, pp. 374–383. Springer, Heidelberg (2014)

14. Grycuk, R., Gabryel, M., Korytkowski, M., Scherer, R., Voloshynovskiy, S.: From single image to list of objects based on edge and blob detection. In: Rutkowski, L., Korytkowski, M., Scherer, R., Tadeusiewicz, R., Zadeh, L.A., Zurada, J.M. (eds.) ICAISC 2014, Part II. LNCS(LNAI), vol. 8468, pp. 605–615. Springer, Heidelberg (2014)

15. Hobson, S., Austin, J.: Improved storage capacity in correlation matrix memories storing fixed weight codes. Journal of Artificial Intelligence and Soft Computing Research 1(2), 97–102 (2011)

16. Hu, Y., Frank, C., Walden, J., Crawford, E., Kasturiratna, D.: Mining file repository accesses for detecting data exfiltration activites. Journal of Artificial Intelligence and Soft Computing Research 2(1), 31–41 (2012)

17. Knop, M., Dobosz, P.: Neural video compression algorithm. In: Choraś, R.S. (ed.) Image Processing & Communications Challenges 6. AISC, vol. 313, pp. 61–68. Springer, Heidelberg (2015)

18. Knop, M., Cierniak, R., Shah, N.: Video compression algorithm based on neural network structures. In: Rutkowski, L., Korytkowski, M., Scherer, R., Tadeusiewicz, R., Zadeh, L.A., Zurada, J.M. (eds.) ICAISC 2014, Part I. LNCS(LNAI), vol. 8467, pp. 715–724. Springer, Heidelberg (2014)

19. Kostadinov, D., Voloshynovskiy, S., Ferdowsi, S., Diephuis, M., Scherer, R.: Robust face recognition by group sparse representation that uses samples from list of subjects. In: Rutkowski, L., Korytkowski, M., Scherer, R., Tadeusiewicz, R., Zadeh, L.A., Zurada, J.M. (eds.) ICAISC 2014, Part II. LNCS(LNAI), vol. 8468, pp. 616–626. Springer, Heidelberg (2014)

20. Kowalski, T.M., Chromiak, M., Kuliberda, K., Wislicki, J., Adamus, R., Subieta, K.: Query optimization by indexing in the ODRA OODBM. Annales UMCS, Informatica 9(1), 77–97 (2009)

21. Lee, P.M., Hsiao, T.C.: Applying lcs to affective image classification in spacial-frequency domain. Journal of Artificial Intelligence and Soft Computing Research 4(2), 99–123 (2014)

22. Li, Z., Liu, G.: A novel scene change detection algorithm based on the 3d wavelet transform. In: 15th IEEE International Conference on Image Processing, ICIP 2008, pp. 1536–1539 (2008)

23. Liu, G., Wen, X., Zheng, W., He, P.: Shot boundary detection and keyframe extraction based on scale invariant feature transform. In: Eighth IEEE/ACIS International Conference on Computer and Information Science, ICIS 2009, pp. 1126–1130 (2009)

24. Lowe, D.G.: Object recognition from local scale-invariant features. In: The Proceedings of the Seventh IEEE International Conference on Computer Vision, vol. 2, pp. 1150–1157. IEEE (1999)

25. Lowe, D.G.: Distinctive image features from scale-invariant keypoints. International Journal of Computer Vision 60(2), 91–110 (2004)

26. Najgebauer, P., Nowak, T., Romanowski, J., Rygał, J., Korytkowski, M., Scherer, R.: Novel method for parasite detection in microscopic samples. In: Rutkowski, L., Korytkowski, M., Scherer, R., Tadeusiewicz, R., Zadeh, L.A., Zurada, J.M. (eds.) ICAISC 2012, Part I. LNCS, vol. 7267, pp. 551–558. Springer, Heidelberg (2012)

27. Nowak, T., Gabryel, M., Korytkowski, M., Scherer, R.: Comparing images based on histograms of local interest points. In: Wyrzykowski, R., Dongarra, J., Karczewski, K., Waśniewski, J. (eds.) PPAM 2013, Part I. LNCS, vol. 8384, pp. 423–432. Springer, Heidelberg (2014)

28. Nowak, T., Najgebauer, P., Romanowski, J., Gabryel, M., Korytkowski, M., Scherer, R., Kostadinov, D.: Spatial keypoint representation for visual object retrieval. In: Rutkowski, L., Korytkowski, M., Scherer, R., Tadeusiewicz, R., Zadeh, L.A., Zurada, J.M. (eds.) ICAISC 2014, Part II. LNCS(LNAI), vol. 8468, pp. 639–650. Springer, Heidelberg (2014)

29. Nowak, T., Najgebauer, P., Rygał, J., Scherer, R.: A novel graph-based descriptor for object matching. In: Rutkowski, L., Korytkowski, M., Scherer, R., Tadeusiewicz, R., Zadeh, L.A., Zurada, J.M. (eds.) ICAISC 2013, Part I. LNCS(LNAI), vol. 7894, pp. 602–612. Springer, Heidelberg (2013)

30. Qu, Z., Lin, L., Gao, T., Wang, Y.: An improved keyframe extraction method based on hsv colour space. Journal of Software 8(7) (2013)

31. Radwan, N.I., Salem, N.M., El Adawy, M.I.: Histogram correlation for video scene change detection. In: Wyld, D.C., Zizka, J., Nagamalai, D. (eds.) Advances in Computer Science, Eng. & Appl. ASC, vol. 166, pp. 765–773. Springer, Heidelberg (2012)

32. Rutkowski, L., Jaworski, M., Pietruczuk, L., Duda, P.: Decision trees for mining data streams based on the gaussian approximation. IEEE Transactions on Knowledge and Data Engineering 26(1), 108–119 (2014)

33. Rutkowski, L., Pietruczuk, L., Duda, P., Jaworski, M.: Decision trees for mining data streams based on the mcdiarmid's bound. IEEE Transactions on Knowledge and Data Engineering 25(6), 1272–1279 (2013)

34. Rutkowski, L., Jaworski, M., Pietruczuk, L., Duda, P.: The {CART} decision tree for mining data streams. Information Sciences 266, 1–15 (2014)

35. Rygał, J., Najgebauer, P., Nowak, T., Romanowski, J., Gabryel, M., Scherer, R.: Properties and structure of fast text search engine in context of semantic image analysis. In: Rutkowski, L., Korytkowski, M., Scherer, R., Tadeusiewicz, R., Zadeh, L.A., Zurada, J.M. (eds.) ICAISC 2012, Part I. LNCS, vol. 7267, pp. 592–599. Springer, Heidelberg (2012)

36. Rygał, J., Romanowski, J., Scherer, R., Ferdowsi, S.: Novel algorithm for translation from image content to semantic form. In: Rutkowski, L., Korytkowski, M., Scherer, R., Tadeusiewicz, R., Zadeh, L.A., Zurada, J.M. (eds.) ICAISC 2014, Part I. LNCS(LNAI), vol. 8467, pp. 783–792. Springer, Heidelberg (2014)
37. Seeling, P.: Scene change detection for uncompressed video. In: Technological Developments in Education and Automation, pp. 11–14. Springer, Netherlands (2010)
38. Terriberry, T.B., French, L.M., Helmsen, J.: Gpu accelerating speeded-up robust features. In: Proc. Int. Symp. on 3D Data Processing, Visualization and Transmission (3DPVT), pp. 355–362. Citeseer (2008)
39. Thiagarajan, R., Rahman, M., Gossink, D., Calbert, G.: A data mining approach to improve military demand forecasting. Journal of Artificial Intelligence and Soft Computing Research 3(4), 205–214 (2014)
40. Vivekanandan, P., Nedunchezhian, R.: Mining rules of concept drift using genetic algorithm. Journal of Artificial Intelligence and Soft Computing Research 1(2), 135–145 (2011)
41. Wang, X., Weng, Z.: Scene abrupt change detection. In: 2000 Canadian Conference on Electrical and Computer Engineering, vol. 2, pp. 880–883 (2000)
42. Zhang, N.: Computing optimised parallel speeded-up robust features (p-surf) on multi-core processors. International Journal of Parallel Programming 38(2), 138–158 (2010)

Automatic Diagnosis of Melanoid Skin Lesions Using Machine Learning Methods

Katarzyna Grzesiak-Kopeć[(✉)], Leszek Nowak, and Maciej Ogorzałek[1]

Department of Information Technologies, Jagiellonian University in Krakow, Kraków,
Poland
{katarzyna.grzesiak-kopec,leszek.nowak,maciej.ogorzalek}@uj.edu.pl

Abstract. Dermatology is one of the fields where computer aided diagnostic is developing rapidly. The presented research concentrates on
creation of automatic methods for melanoid skin lesions diagnosis using
machine learning methods. In the experiments 1010 samples described in
[5] are used. There are 275 melanoma cases and 735 benign ones. Three
different machine learning methods are applied, namely the Naive Bayes
classifier, the Random Forest, the K* instance-based classifier, and Attributional Calculus. The obtained results confirm that clinical history
context and dermoscopic structures together with the selected machine
learning methods may be an important and accurate diagnostic tool.

Keywords: Computer aided diagnostic · Machine learning · Melanoma

1 Introduction

The incidence of melanoma skin cancer has been significantly increasing over
the past decades. Even though it accounts to less than 2% of skin cancer cases,
it is the most malignant one with very high mortality rate. In the world every
57 minutes one person dies of melanoma. In 2014, according to the American
Cancer Society, about 76.100 new melanomas will be diagnosed and about 9.710
people are expected to die of melanoma in the US. When detected early, the
overall 5-year survival rate for patients is about 98%. It falls to 62% when the
disease reaches the lymph nodes, and to 16% when the disease reaches metastasis
to distant organs [2]. This is why the effective early clinical recognition of this
neoplasm becomes a critical problem. Even experienced and well-trained derma-
tologists with the use of dermoscopy and different clinical diagnostic approaches
such as the ABCD rule, the Menzies scoring method or 7-point checklist [11]
achieve about $75 - 85\%$ diagnostic efficiency for the early melanoma cases [3].

The clinical diagnosis is very complex and highly dependent on experience
of the doctor. Analysis and diagnosis of cutaneous lesions can be enhanced by
applying computers to perform the task. Recently many different software packages have been developed to support physicians. Some of them take into account
geometry, color and texture [12], some use image processing methods [18]. Some
packages combine both the dermoscopic images with the clinical history context

© Springer International Publishing Switzerland 2015
L. Rutkowski et al. (Eds.): ICAISC 2015, Part I, LNAI 9119, pp. 577–585, 2015.
DOI: 10.1007/978-3-319-19324-3_51

and information like age, gender, location etc. [1]. Many specific applications calculating A, B and C values from the ABCD rule are available [16],[17].

We strongly believe that the computer aided diagnosis support system combining image processing, feature extraction and classification has the potential to bring new knowledge about melanoma skin cancer [15]. There are however some features for which automatic calculation is very difficult or even impossible. For example, the parameter D of the ABCD rule is very hard to define and calculate. D stands for the dermoscopic structures and specific patterns visible in the images. Taking all this aspects into account, besides the image processing research, we have decided to consider the features provided in The Interactive Atlas of Dermoscopy [5] and to analyze their influence on the pigmented skin lesions diagnosis. The 7-point checklist diagnostic method [11] requires the identification of 7 from the considered dermoscopic criteria. Furthermore, one of the important factors affecting the final diagnosis is the age of the patient, which cannot be calculated and must be fed to the computer system.

2   Computer Aided Diagnosis

The computer-assisted medical diagnosis is especially valuable if it both classifies observations and provides an explanation for the decision as well. This is why we have decided to take into account not only the static data analysis but also a complementary approach called knowledge mining [14]. Three different approaches from the statistical learning techniques have been chosen: the Naive Bayes classifier [20], the Random Forest [7] and the K* instance-based classifier [8]. The WEKA [10] tool implementation was applied. For rules explaining the elaborated pattern classification the Attributional Calculus (AC) implemented in the AQ21 multitask learning and knowledge mining program was used [19].

2.1   Data Set Description

In all computer experiments we used 1010 sample images as described in [5]. There are 275 melanoma cases and 735 benign ones. Such a number of examples may be considered sufficient to make a reliable generalization and to evaluate the impact of each feature on the final diagnosis. All the preliminary information regarding the selected attributes (features) are derived from [5].

14 properties of skin lesions were taken into account: age, sex, location, diameter, elevation, global feature, pigment network, streaks, pigmentation, regression structures, globules, blue whitish veil, hypo-pigmentation and vascular structures. All the introduced features are considered to be diagnostic significant. The patients were aged from 2 to 90. The age was divided into 6 groups: *baby* from 0 to 10, *teenager* from 11 to 19, *young* from 20 to 30, *adult* from 31 to 50, *old* from 51 to 70 and *very_old* from 71 to 90.

Among global properties, patterns like parallel, multicomponent or lacunar ones were taken into account. One of the important local dermoscopic features is the pigment network, regular grid of brownish lines over a diffuse light-brown background, which depicts the dermoscopic hallmark of melanocytic lesion

(Fig. 1). Streaks are brownish-black linear structures of variable thickness that can be found in both benign and malignant skin lesions and their geometric arrangement is essential for diagnosis (Fig. 1). The pigmentation extends from dark-brown to gray-black and because of this diversity its diagnostic significance is limited. The same insufficient diagnostic relevance occurs with hypopigmentation. Nevertheless, localized irregular and diffuse irregular pigmentation suggest malignancy. The regression structures are white and blue areas that generally can be recognized as melanoma. Globules (dots) can be found not only in malignant melanocytic proliferations but in benign ones as well (Fig. 2). However, in any case they vary in shape and distribution. The blue-whitish veil is almost exclusively the characteristic of malignant melanomas and Spitz/Reed nevi (Fig. 2). The vascular structures have been classified and assigned to certain types of skin lesions [6].

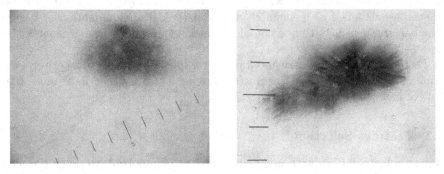

Fig. 1. Typical pigment network and streaks

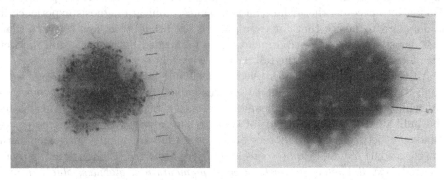

Fig. 2. Typical dots/globules and blue-whitish veil

For calculating the ABCD score the Asymmetry, Border, Color and Differential structures criteria have to be evaluated. For evaluation of the D parameter, the following, inter alia, dermoscopic features are used: pigment network, streaks, dots and globules. The diagnostic procedure requires the doctor to examine magnified images of skin lesion. The nature of this features is very hard to to define,

Table 1. The clinical diagnosis accuracy

Physician	Sensitivity	Specificity
Experts	90%	59%
Dermatologists	81%	60%
Trainees	85%	36%
General practitioners	62%	63%

detect and assess. The statistical study [13] confirms that this method relies upon medical practitioner skills (Table 1).

The incidence of these attributes and blue-whitish veil in the examined data set is presented in Fig. 3. The numerical characteristics are shown in tables where the columns denote: (Feature name) the structural feature categories, (Count) the total number of samples with the feature category, (Melanoma) the number of samples classified as melanoma by histopathological examination of tissues. The bar graph depicts the percentage of melanoma lesions (red) versus benign ones (blue).

The demonstrated numerical data confirm differential structures criteria discriminant power. For each feature there is one category that have more than 50% of melanoma samples.

2.2   Features Selection

Having a large dataset with many attributes, it is important to select the most relevant ones before starting the machine learning process. In some cases, neglecting the data preprocessing may lead to slow and inefficient learning procedure. Taking into account the melanoma skin cancer clinical diagnosis experience it is not hard to notice that for example the sex attribute is less relevant than vascular structures. The experiments were performed both on the full dataset with all attributes and on the full dataset with selected subset of features.

All the methods for features selection available in the WEKA package were applied. The most discriminant power was gained by the method *CfsSubsetEval* which evaluated the significance of a subset of attributes by considering the individual predictive ability of each feature along with the degree of redundancy between them. Subsets of features that are highly correlated with the class while having low intercorrelation were preferred. Eight attributes were selected: *age, diameter, network, streaks, pigmentation, globules, blue_w_v* and *vascular_structures*.

Also the simplified promise criterion [4] implemented in AQ21 software was used to determine which attributes are likely to be the most relevant. The ones that did not exceed the acceptance threshold parameter set to 0.31 were rejected. In this way six attributes were indicated for further consideration: *diameter, elevation, network, reg_structures, blue_w_v* and *vascular_structures*.

Pigment Network	Count	Melanoma
absent	399	100 (25, 06%)
atypical	230	139 (60, 43%)
typical	381	36 (9, 45%)

Streaks	|Count|	Melanoma
absent_s	652	101 (15, 49%)
irregular_s	251	158 (62, 95%)
regular_s	107	16 (14, 95%)

Globules	|Count|	Melanoma
absent_g	228	31 (13, 60%)
irregular_g	448	228 (50, 89%)
regular_g	334	16 (4, 79%)

Blue Whitish Veil	|Count|	Melanoma
absent_b	815	154 (18, 89%)
present_b	195	121 (62, 05%)

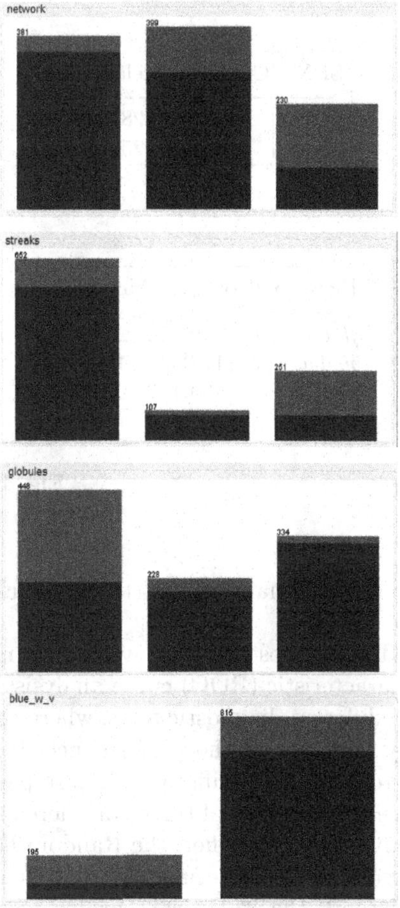

Fig. 3. The incidence of pigment network, streaks, dots/globules and blue whitish veil dermoscopic features

Since two features, namely *sex* and *elevation*, did not exceed in any category the 50% of samples classified as melanoma (Fig. 4), another two experiments were carried out. In the first case only the *sex* attribute was removed from the feature vector. In the second one both the *sex* and the *elevation* attributes were eliminated from the learning process.

2.3   Results

For each selected learning method 5 experiments with a different feature vector were set up. The $10 - fold$ cross validation test was applied for each classifier to gain a justifiable estimation of its accuracy. The $n - fold$ cross validation procedure randomly divides the whole data set into n subsets of samples. After that, n different models are trained using data from $n - 1$ sets and validated

SEX	Count	Melanoma
female	521	151 (28, 98%)
male	489	124 (25, 36%)

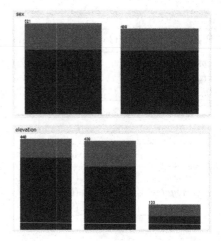

Elevation	Count	Melanoma
flat	448	92 (20, 53%)
nodular	123	56 (45, 53%)
palpable	439	127 (28, 93%)

Fig. 4. Elevation

using the remaining one (the holdout fold). The process is repeated for each of the n folds.

The diagnostic efficiency of a test may be evaluated using Receiver Operating Characteristic (ROC) curve analysis [9]. ROC curves are also useful in comparing different diagnostic tests, where the area under the ROC curve (AUC) is the key indicator of the performance. It shows sensitivity (the true positive rate) in relation to specificity (the false positive rate). The AUC was chosen to measure the accuracy of three considered statistical learning approaches, namely the Naive Bayes classifier, the Random Forest and the K* instance-based classifier. Results of the experiments are presented in Table 2 where the columns denote: (Method) the statistical learning method, (Attr No) the number of considered attributes, (Correct Class) the percentage of correctly classified instances, (TP Rate) sensitivity, (FP Rate) specificity, (AUC) the area under the ROC curve.

The conducted experiments show that all the selected statistical learning techniques have comparable levels of performance. For each classifier the best results were achieved after removing the *sex* attribute from the samples. The highest score of $AUC = 0.922$ was obtained by the Random Forest, the second best was the K* instance-based classifier with $AUC = 0.92$ and the Naive Bayes classifier reached $AUC = 0.917$. Also the Random Forest with 13 attributes gained the highest percentage of correctly classified instances 87.3267%. The interesting fact is that the rate of correctly classified instances does not decrease rapidly with the smaller count of selected features. Such an observation could perhaps be a sign that with statistically sufficient data set the feature vector could be reduced without losing the performance accuracy.

The AQ21 learning technique has the binary output, and thus the percentage of correctly (incorrectly) classified patterns is used as the accuracy measure. The outcome of this learning approach application is given in Table 3. Three columns have not changed, namely (Method) the learning method, (Attr No) the number

Table 2. Results for the Naive Bayes classifier, the Random Forest and the K* instance-based classifier

Method	Attr No	Correct Class	TP Rate	FP Rate	AUC
	14	85.9406%	0.859	0.203	**0.917**
	13	86.3366%	0.863	0.199	**0.917**
NB	12	86.2376%	0.862	0.202	0.916
	8	**86.8317%**	0.868	0.202	0.916
	6	81.8812%	0.819	0.343	0.861
	14	**86.5347%**	0.865	0.253	0.914
	13	86.4356%	0.864	0.262	**0.922**
RF	12	86.3366%	0.863	0.256	0.907
	8	84.9505%	0.85	0.254	0.895
	6	81.8812%	0.819	0.32	0.84
	14	86.3366%	0.863	0.249	0.913
	13	**87.3267%**	0.873	0.239	**0.92**
K*	12	87.2277%	0.872	0.23	0.915
	8	85.9406%	0.859	0.251	0.909
	6	83.1683%	0.832	0.384	0.873

Table 3. Results for the AQ21 learning program

Method	Attr No	Correct Class	Avg Rules No	Avg Conditions No
	14	83.27%	16.80	116.60
	13	**84.16%**	15.30	104.10
AQ21	12	82.38%	14.80	89.20
	8	68.81%	7.20	16.20
	6	61.49%	4.00	4.50

of considered attributes, and (Correct Class) the percentage of correctly classified instances. The last two columns denote respectively: (Avg Rules No) the average number of rules and (Avg Conditions No) the average number of conditions. As in the case of statistical learning techniques, the AQ21 gain the highest score while working with 13 attributes describing samples **84.16%**. However, on the contrary to them, further reducing the number of attributes resulted in a rapid decline in the classification performance. This may mean that the clinical diagnosis based features are specific for certain cases and can not be generalized.

3   Conclusions and Future Prospects

The main aim of the research was to verify whether automatic diagnosis of melanoma based on the clinical history context and dermoscopic structures can be accurate and bring new knowledge about melanoma skin cancer. The paper presents the results obtained using three different statistical learning techniques, namely the Naive Bayes classifier, the Random Forest and the K* instance-based classifier, and the AQ21 multitask learning and knowledge mining program. On the one hand, the experiments confirmed the discriminant power of selected criteria and $AUC = 0.922$ was achieved with the Random Forest. But on the other hand, the knowledge mining procedure using the AQ21 implementation of the Attributional Calculus was unable to perform satisfactory classification of samples having a reduced feature vector. It seems that the clinical diagnosis based features lack generalizability and are closely related to specific melanoid skin lesions. It would be of great assistance if some global characteristics for such a lesions are recognized. This will be the next step of our research. We are going to follow-up study by combining image processing and feature extraction with the clinical data set based classification. Such a holistic non-invasive approach is likely to overcome the weaknesses of both procedures. The most *difficult* samples will be recognized and if necessary a boosting technique will be applied.

References

1. Alcn, J.F., Ciuhu, C., Kate, W., et al.: Automatic imaging system with decision support for inspection of pigmented skin lesions and melanoma diagnosis. IEEE J. Select. Top. Sign. Process. 3(1), 14–25 (2009)
2. American Cancer Society, Cancer Facts & Figures (2014), http://www.cancer.org/acs/groups/content/research/documents/webcontent/acspc-042151.pdf (accessed November 16, 2014)
3. Argenziano, G., Soyer, H.P., Chimenti, S., et al.: Dermoscopy of pigmented skin lesions: results of a consensus meeting via the Internet. J. Am. Acad. Dermatol. 48, 679–693 (2003)
4. Baim, P.: The PROMISE Method For Selecting Most Relevant Attributes For Inductive Learning Systems, Reports of the Intelligent Systems Group, ISG 82-1, UIUCDCS-F-82-898, Department of Computer Science, University of Illinois, Urbana (September 1982)
5. Argenziano, G., Soyer, H.P., De Giorgio, V., et al.: Interactive atlas of dermoscopy. Edra Medical Publishing & New Media, Milan (2000)
6. Argenziano, G., Scalvenzi, M., Staibano, S., et al.: Dermatoscopic pitfalls in differentiating pigmented Spitz naevi from cutaneous melanomas. Br. J. Dermatol. 141, 788–793 (1999)
7. Breiman, L.: Random Forests. Machine Learning 45(1), 5–32 (2001)
8. Cleary, J.G., Trigg, L.E.: K*: An Instance-based Learner Using an Entropic Distance Measure. In: 12th International Conference on Machine Learning, pp. 108–114 (1995)
9. van Erkel, A.R., Pattynama, P.M.: Receiver operating characteristic (ROC) analysis: Basic principles and applications in radiology. European Journal of Radiology 27(2), 88–94 (1997)
10. Hall, M., Frank, E., Holmes, G., et al.: The WEKA Data Mining Software: An Update. SIGKDD Explorations 11(1), 10–18 (2009)
11. Johr, R.H.: Dermoscopy: Alternative Melanocytic Algorithms - The ABCD Rule of Dermatoscopy, Menzies Scoring Method, and 7-Point Checklist. Clinics in Dermatology 20, 240–247 (2002)
12. Manousaki, A.G., Manios, A.G., Tsompanaki, E.I., et al.: A simple digital image processing system to aid in melanoma diagnosis in an everyday melanocytic skin lesion unit: a preliminary report. Int. J. Dermatol. 45(4), 402–410 (2006)

13. Menzies, S.W., Bischof, L., Talbot, H., et al.: The Performance of SolarScan. An Automated Dermoscopy Image Analysis Instrument for the Diagnosis of Primary Melanoma. Archive of Dermatology, 1388–1396 (2005)
14. Michalski, R.S., Kaufman, K., Pietrzykowski, J., et al.: Natural Induction and Conceptual Clustering: A Review of Applications, Reports of the Machine Learning and Inference Laboratory, MLI 06-3, George Mason University, Fairfax, VA (June 2006) (updated: August 23, 2006)
15. Nowak, L.A., Pawłowski, M.P., Grzesiak-Kopeć, K., Ogorzałek, M.J.: Color calibration model of skin lesion images for computer-aided diagnostic. In: Proc. Operations Research and its Applications in Engineering, Technology and Management 2013 (ISORA 2013), pp. 1–5 (2013)
16. Ogorzałek, M., Surówka, G., Nowak, L., Merkwirth, C.: Computational intelligence and image processing methods for applications in skin cancer diagnosis. In: Fred, A., Filipe, J., Gamboa, H. (eds.) BIOSTEC 2009. CCIS, vol. 52, pp. 3–20. Springer, Heidelberg (2010)
17. Ogorzałek, M.J., Nowak, L., Surówka, G., Alekseenko, A.: Modern Techniques for Computer-Aided Melanoma Diagnosis. In: Murph, M. (ed.) Melanoma in the Clinic - Diagnosis, Management and Complications of Malignancy. InTech (2011) ISBN: 978-953-307-571-6
18. Surówka, G., Grzesiak-Kopeć, K.: Different Learning Paradigms for the Classification of Melanoid Skin Lesions Using Wavelets. In: Conf. Proc. IEEE Eng. Med. Biol. Soc., pp. 3136–3139 (2007)
19. Wojtusiak, J.: AQ21 Users Guide, Reports of the Machine Learning and Inference Laboratory, MLI 04-3, George Mason University, Fairfax, VA (September 2004) (updated in September 2005)
20. Zhang, H.: The Optimality of Naive Bayes. In: FLAIRS Conference (2004)

An Edge Detection Using 2D Gaussian Function in Computed Tomography

Michal Knas[1](✉), Robert Cierniak[1], and Olga Rebrova[2]

[1] Institute of Computational Intelligence, Czestochowa University of Technology,
Armii Krajowej 36, 42-200 Czestochowa, Poland
michal.knas@iisi.pcz.pl
[2] Department of Medical Cybernetics and Informatics, The Russian National
Reasearch Medical University, Moscow, Russia

Abstract. In this paper, we propose an iterative algorithm for edge detection. The presented method uses a 2D Gaussian function and Prewitt operator. Firstly, the selection of edge points has been achieved by a statistical method. Secondly, the boundary tracking has been performed by the rotation of the Gaussian function and by changing function's variables. The algorithm has been tested using a medical phantom. Additionally, an implementation on multicore GPUs has been designed for a better performance.

1 Introduction

Currently in medical practice, many techniques of medical imaging are being used, which significantly facilitate the identification of diseases. In many cases, those techniques allow for a diagnosis of many pathological and physiological changes in the human body. This gives greater effectiveness in saving lives and more appropriate method selection for the treatment of patients.

One of the most commonly used medical imaging techniques is Computed Tomography (CT). It can carry out very detailed research, in order to detect hematomas, aneurysms, cancer, brain tumors, hydrocephalus, stroke and other diseases. However, it uses X radiation which may bring changes in the human body and increase risk of cancer. To reduce this problem, it is strongly recommended to decrease a radiation dose [1–4]. This causes a deterioration of the image quality, resulting in a significant reduction of the Signal to Noise Ratio (SNR). If we want diagnostic three-dimensional visualization methods, such as volume rendering (VR) and shaded surface display (SSD), to be useful, then we have to conduct series of operations. It is required to solve the problem of highly heterogeneous structures, which human tissues are [5, 6].

The main part of defining borders between organs, is edge detection. There are many approaches to this problem. Most of them are based on first-order or second-order derivative, with pre- or post-processing of noise and thickness (of detected edges) reduction, or a combination of them [7–11]. In our case, the priority is to choose methods that will allow for a very precise definition of the boundaries, even better than resolution of collected data from medical

© Springer International Publishing Switzerland 2015
L. Rutkowski et al. (Eds.): ICAISC 2015, Part I, LNAI 9119, pp. 586–593, 2015.
DOI: 10.1007/978-3-319-19324-3_52

equipment. This will provide possibility of diagnostically useful image rendering. To solve this problem, we decided for the most part to use statistical methods. They are computationally complex, although can give very accurate results. Taking into account the enormous volume of data in computed tomography, the data stream mining may be potentially considered for better performance in future research work [12–18].

2   Proposed Algorithm

Our algorithm for edge detection has four main steps. The first operation is a convolution with the Prewitt operator. For better results, instead of the standard two directions approach, we use rotating mask, [19, 20] as a base for further steps, which are described below.

2.1   Gaussian Matching

Main part of our edge detection algorithm, is matching two dimensional Gaussian function with an image after convolution with the Prewitt operator. For the better performance, we take 25 elements from the image and we try to set the parameters of the function to achieve a minimal square error.

In our method, we use the following equations:

$$x = x - x_o \ , \ y = y - y_o \tag{1}$$

$$x' = x cos(\alpha) - y sin(\alpha) \ , \ y' = x sin(\alpha) + y cos(\alpha) \tag{2}$$

$$f(x', y') = A \exp\left(-\left(\frac{(x')^2}{2\sigma_x^2} + \frac{(y')^2}{2\sigma_y^2}\right)\right) \tag{3}$$

where (x, y) are coordinates of central subpixel, A is the image value with the Prewitt operator in (x, y) position, and x_o and y_o are limited to the range $[-0.5, 0.5)$.

First of all, in order to minimize the error, we set $sigma_x$ to vary between 0.1 and 0.9 and tenfold larger $sigma_y$ to give a shape of tunnel for our function. Then we rotate it by changing α from 0 to 180 degrees, what is shown in Fig. 1.

The best angle is selected by calculating the MSE. Then, for better precision, we move the tunnel around the pixel. For clearer visualization, this operation is presented in one dimension in Fig. 2.

After those operations, the algorithm takes a preliminary decision whether a given point is a part of the edge. The MSE is minimized, which means the best match. The equation below(4) shows the criterion that has to be satisfied to mark a subpixel as boundary.

$$MSE_{min} < k \cdot E_{x,y} M_{x,y} \Big(\sum_{\substack{-2 \le i \le 2 \\ -2 \le j \le 2}} M_{x+i,y+j} \Big) \tag{4}$$

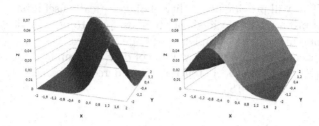

Fig. 1. Gaussian tunnel (left $\alpha = 30°$, right $\alpha = 160°$)

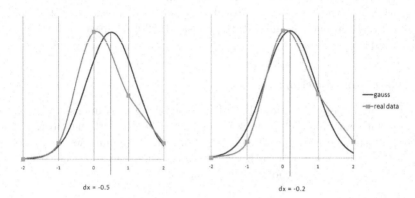

Fig. 2. Gaussian matching

The only parameter that has to be set independently is an experimentally chosen coefficient k, and it allows us to make a threshold. The matrix $E = [E_{x,y}]$ consists of values that increase permissible error if edge tracing is successfully completed. This parameter is fully described in subsection 2.3. The $M = [M_{x,y}]$ consists of convolved image by the Prewitt operator.

2.2   Preliminary Non-Edge-Point Removing

Before proceeding to the final step of our algorithm, we decided to remove some points that have been selected as a part of boundary, simply in order to avoid unexpected edge tracking and to reduce the number of calculations. Taking into account the continuous nature of the edge, there is very low probability, that within the twenty-five subpixel, only the middle one is part of the edge. Therefore, we decided to deselect those points. Even if we did not detect any boundary in this area, the last stage of our algorithm will allow for re-selection with greater probability.

2.3 Edge Tracing

Last stage of our method is similar to the Edge Tracking by Hysteresis in Canny Edge Detector [21] or Ant Colony Algorithm [22]. It is a validation, whether the edge can be found in the neighborhood. However, the neighboring subpixels are not screened only for being a point of the edge, but also whether the angle that was adapted by Gaussian function matching is directed to and in line with angle of the mid-point. If there are multiple matches, those which are nearest to the values selected on the basis of the matrix with the Prewitt mask. To reduce the number of calculations, depending on the vertical, horizontal or diagonal line direction, different groups of subpixels are examined. Fig. 3 shows examples of this operation.

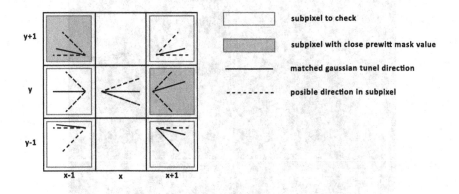

Fig. 3. Edge Tracing by Gaussian

If terms are correct, then value of the parameter $E_{x,y}$ is increased, or in the opposite case decreased. When all points of the image are checked, the method continues to perform the Gaussian matching step (Sub. 2.1) of the algorithm.

3 Experimental Results

We carried out some computer simulations to verify whether our modifications will give better results than standard approaches.

To create experimental environment, we used Microsoft Visual Studio 2010 with CUDAfy.NET 1.27 library and NVIDIA CUDA Toolkit 5.5 to achieve better performance. Tests were performed on NVIDIA GTX 680 and on Intel Core2Quad Q8400. The testing platform was Windows 8.1.

It was necessary to use the GPU. Proposed algorithm is highly complex computationally. Every stage of our process depends on how precise we want to be, although even with a small matching accuracy there is a plenty of calculations. If we rotate our tunnel, which consists of only 25 subpixels, by 15 degrees, and we move it by half of the distance between the pixels, there is 2700 calculations (1, 2, 3) and comparisons between the mask and the calculated values in only one point of the image. Since we work only on matrices, we could make a strong parallelization, reducing the time of one iteration below 3s, when the image has resolution of 512×512 pixels.

Our algorithm was tested on two sets of data that contains mathematical model of the human head cross section with resolution 512×512.

In the first phase of testing, we checked whether Gaussian matching and edge tracking works. Fig. 4 shows the initial, middle and final effects of the proposed method. In this experiment, we have not added any noise, σ_x was set to 0.1, d_x and d_y were set to 0.5, and k was set to 0.08.

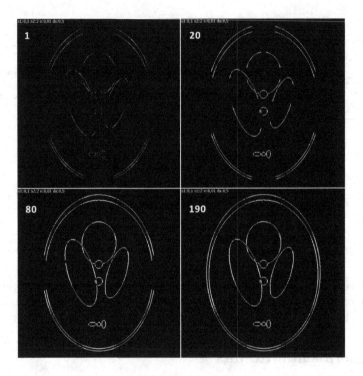

Fig. 4. Performance of the proposed algorithm1 at: 20, 80 and 190 iterations

The second experiment was conducted to test our algorithm in the case of presence of noise, and to compare it with a standard threshold. However, both methods and the Prewitt operator do not include edge thinning, therefore we decided to show results when MSE is minimal for our algorithm, with the same error for reference method, what is depicted in Fig. 5.

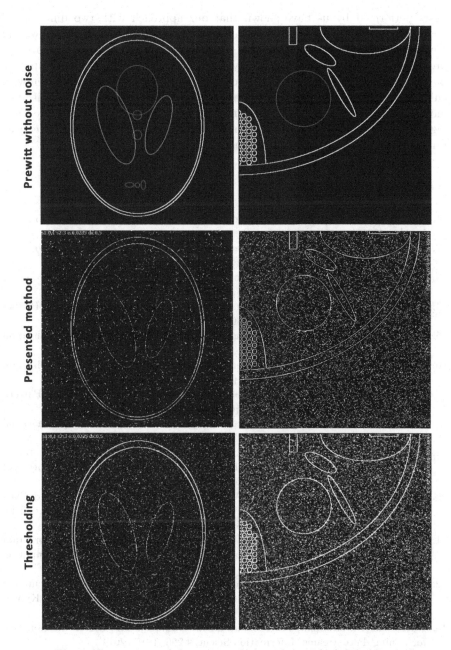

Fig. 5. Comparison of the presented algorithm with thresholding

4   Conclusion

Tests performed by us have shown that our approach with two dimensional Gaussian function matching and tunnel edge tracking works properly. As we can see in Fig. 5, visual results are better than those obtained using a standard approach. However, our algorithm is very complex and requires massive computing power. Presently, it is too much time consuming to work in real time, even with enhanced hardware. Nevertheless, the additional advantage of our algorithm is more precise determination of boundary. Depending on the accuracy of the shifting Gaussian function, we are able to obtain a very precise image that can be further used as a detailed medical presentation.

References

1. Cierniak, R.: X-Ray Computed Tomography in Biomedical Engineering. Springer, London (2011)
2. Li, A.: Acute adverse reactions to magnetic resonance contrast media - gadolinium chelates. British Journal of Radiology 79 (2006)
3. Bush, W.H., Swanson, D.P.: Acute reactions to intravascular contrast media. Types, risk factors, recognition, and specific treatment. AJR (1991)
4. Bush, W.H., McClennan, B.L., Swanson, D.P.: Contrast media reactions. Prediction, prevention, and treatment. Postgrad. Radiol. (1993)
5. Prince, J.L., Links, J.: Medical imaging signals and system. Pearson Education (2006)
6. Calhoun, P., Kuszyk, B.: Three-dimensional Volume Rendering of Spiral CT Data: Theory and Method. Radiographics (1999)
7. Canny, J.: A Computational Approach To Edge Detection. IEEE Trans. Pattern Analysis and Machine Intelligence 8(6), 679–698 (1986)
8. Ziou, D., Tabbone, S.: Edge detection techniques: An overview. International Journal of Pattern Recognition and Image Analysis 8(4), 537–559 (1998)
9. Salazar-Gonzalez, A., Li, Y., Liu, X.: Automatic Graph Cut Based Segmentation of Retinal Optic Disc by Incorporating Blood Vessel Compensation. Journal of Artificial Intelligence and Soft Computing Research 2(3), 235–246 (2012)
10. Karimi, B., Krzyzak, A.: A Novel Approach for Automatic Detection and Classification of Suspicious Lesions in Breast Ultrasound Images. Journal of Artificial Intelligence and Soft Computing Research 3(4), 265–276 (2013)
11. Biniaz, A., Abbasi, A.: Fast FCM with Spatial Neighborhood Information for Brain MR Image Segmentation. Journal of Artificial Intelligence and Soft Computing Research 3(1), 15–26 (2013)
12. Rutkowski, L., Jaworski, M., Pietruczuk, L., Duda, P.: Decision trees for mining data streams based on the gaussian approximation. IEEE Transactions on Knowledge and Data Engineering 26(1), 108–119 (2014)
13. Rutkowski, L., Jaworski, M., Pietruczuk, L., Duda, P.: The CART decision tree for mining data streams. Information Sciences 266, 1–15 (2014)
14. Jaworski, M., Duda, P., Pietruczuk, L.: On fuzzy clustering of data streams with concept drift. In: Rutkowski, L., Korytkowski, M., Scherer, R., Tadeusiewicz, R., Zadeh, L.A., Zurada, J.M. (eds.) ICAISC 2012, Part II. LNCS, vol. 7268, pp. 82–91. Springer, Heidelberg (2012)

15. Rutkowski, L., Pietruczuk, L., Duda, P., Jaworski, M.: Decision trees for mining data streams based on the McDiarmids bound. IEEE Transactions on Knowledge and Data Engineering 25(6), 1272–1279 (2013)
16. Vivekanandan, P., Nedunchezhian, R.: Mining Fules of Concept Drift Using Genetic Algorithm. Journal of Artificial Intelligence and Soft Computing Research 1(2), 135–145 (2011)
17. Hu, Y., Frank, C., Walden, J., Crawford, E., Kasturiratna, D.: Mining File Repository Accesses for Detecting Data Exfiltration Activites. Journal of Artificial Intelligence and Soft Computing Research 2(1), 31–41 (2012)
18. Cruz Chvez, M.A., Martnez Oropeza, A.: B-Tree Algorithm Complexity Analysis to Evaluate the Feasibility of its Application in the University Course Timetabling Problem. Journal of Artificial Intelligence and Soft Computing Research 3(4), 251–263 (2013)
19. Knas, M., Cierniak, R.: Computed tomography images denoising with Markov Random Field model parametrized by Prewitt mask. Image Processing & Communications Challenges 6, 53–58 (2015)
20. Kaushal, M., Singh, A., Singh, B., Kaushal, M.: Adaptive Thresholding for Edge Detection in Gray Scale Images. International Journal of Engineering Science and Technology 2 (2010)
21. Moeslund, T.B.: Image and Video Processing Notes. Canny Edge Detection (March 23, 2009)
22. Biniaz, A., Ataollah, A.: Segmentation and edge detection based on modified ant colony optimization for iris image processing. Journal of Artificial Intelligence and Soft Computing Research 3(2), 133–141 (2013)

Facial Displays Description Schemas for Smiling vs. Neutral Emotion Recognition

Karolina Nurzyńska[1]([✉]) and Bogdan Smołka[2]

[1] Institute of Informatics, Silesian University of Technology,
ul. Akademicka 16, 44-100 Gliwice, Poland
Karolina.Nurzynska@polsl.pl
[2] Institute of Automatic Control, Silesian University of Technology,
ul. Akademicka 16, 44-100 Gliwice, Poland
Bogdan.Smolka@polsl.pl

Abstract. The possibility of correct automatic recognition of emotion is of high importance in many research domains. In this paper the choice of relevant face regions for smile detection is investigated. Firstly, three facial display division schemas are compared. Afterwards, for the most promising, some region masks are suggested. The presented approach differs in feature vector length. The performance of classification between smiling and neutral facial display proved that applying masks, hence shortening the feature vector, does not decrease the accuracy but even improves the result.

Keywords: Local binary patterns · Classification · Smile detection

1 Introduction

Knowing human emotional state enables better understanding of the other person. In daily life the experience and intuition are used to judge other persons' attitude, frankness, and in consequence their approach to us. However, no matter how much one tries to discover the real feelings of others, very often we allow ourselves to be deceived. Therefore, there is a need to develop techniques which enable automatic recognition between spontaneous and artificial emotion display. This issue is very important during recruitment of workers in security sector (e.g. police officers) to check their truthfulness. Other applications could be used for customer quality service development or in the law cases to decide whether the accused person is telling the truth or not. Moreover, in case of patients suffering from schizophrenia such systems could help in medical treatment.

The problem of emotion recognition has been addressed for many years. It started with application of the optical flow [13] to muscle movement tracking, which were applied to decipher presented emotion. Afterwards, the holistic methods and explicit measures were exploited [7], [3]. More recently the Facial Action Coding System (FACS) [6], describing which muscles are activated in each emotion expression, was used to recognize subtle emotions [5].

© Springer International Publishing Switzerland 2015
L. Rutkowski et al. (Eds.): ICAISC 2015, Part I, LNAI 9119, pp. 594–605, 2015.
DOI: 10.1007/978-3-319-19324-3_53

Since local binary patterns, (LBP), texture operator was so successfully used for face recognition, it should not be surprising that soon it was exploited for facial expression classification, too. The work [20] presents results of emotion classification on the *Cohn-Kanade* database with very good performance. In this approach the uniform version of this texture operator was employed and classified with application of support vector machine, (SVM), with different kernels. Moreover, authors suggest a *boosted-LBP* to improve the classification accuracy. Finally, the work [11] compares their solution for facial expression classification based on LBP with other approaches, such as: gradient maps, Tsallis entropy of Gabor filtered images using *Jaffe* database. Combination of suggested methods gives 94% accuracy for all basic emotions. Yet more comparison concerning facial expression recognition can be found in [18].

Applying LBP operator for facial display emotion recognition is very successful. Yet, it suffers from some shortcomings. One of them is the length of a feature vector, which influences the computational time, but also the classification technique feasibility. Therefore in this paper, the relation between the image description schema, feature vector length, and recognition accuracy is investigated. The authors suggest application of specially designed masks to keep the classification accuracy with simultaneous feature vector length diminishing.

2   Local Binary Patterns

Local binary patterns [19] operator describes image content in a form of a histogram, where each bin corresponds to a code describing a small texture area, as depicted in Fig. 1. There are several approaches to code image regions' content. Those exploited in presented research are detailed below.

2.1   Basic LBP Operator

In case of texture operator approach, for each image pixel its local neighbourhood is considered in order to calculate some code describing the content of a region. The local binary patterns, (LBP), code is given as [14,15,16]:

$$LBP_{P,R}(x_c, y_c) = \sum_{p=0}^{P-1} s(g_p - g_c) \cdot 2^p, \qquad (1)$$

where g_c is grey value of the central pixel, g_p is the value of the neighbours, and s is a threshold function based on the difference sign defined as follows:

$$s(z) = \begin{cases} 1, & z \geq 0, \\ 0, & z < 0. \end{cases} \qquad (2)$$

The method assumes a circular neighbourhood of radius R and P points sampled with equal spacing. Assuming (x, y) coordinates for g_c the positions, (x_p, y_p) of neighbouring points are: $x_p = x + R\cos(2\pi p/P)$, $y_p = y - R\sin(2\pi p/P)$, where $p = 0, \ldots, P-1$. The steps of this algorithm are visualized in Fig. 1.

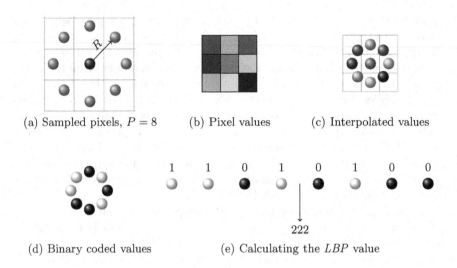

(a) Sampled pixels, $P = 8$ (b) Pixel values   (c) Interpolated values

1   1   0   1   0   1   0   0

222

(d) Binary coded values   (e) Calculating the *LBP* value

Fig. 1. *LBP* operator calculation

2.2 Uniform Patterns

It was noticed [19] that the most descriptive labels are when there are up to two transitions between 0 and 1 in the operator written as a series of bits, eg. 00100000 (see Fig. 2), and those patterns are defined as a 'uniform' patterns, (*uLBP*). Other, with higher number of transitions are considered non-uniform and are given a single label (i.e. are placed in one histogram bin). This approach diminishes the number of different labels to $P(P-1)+3$ for P sampling points.

2.3 Rotation Invariant *LBP*

When the texture rotates, it corresponds to the rotation of the data in the histogram [2], [19]. This phenomenon results in various features vector calculated for the same but rotated texture. Notwithstanding, since the neighbouring points are sampled in the circular neighbourhood, they might be rotated before

Fig. 2. Some examples for uniform patterns

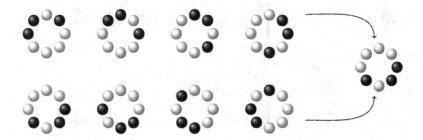

Fig. 3. Example of rotation invariant local binary patterns determination

the value calculation. When assuming that the patterns are stored in an array, where the column, n, corresponds to number of 1-bits, and row to rotation, r, it is possible to easily recalculate the pattern $U(n,r)$ depending on the rotation according to the formula:

$$U_P(n,r) \text{ rotated by } \alpha = a\frac{360}{P} \doteq U_P(n, r+a \mod P), a = 0,\ldots,P-1. \quad (3)$$

Following presented consideration, it is possible to normalize histogram of the rotated texture by invariant mapping:

$$riLBP_{P,R} = \min_i ROR(LBP_{P,R}, i), \quad (4)$$

where $ROR(x,i)$ is a circular bitwise right rotation of a bit sequence x by i steps. Figure 3 depicts application of this operator.

2.4 Rotation Invariant and Uniform *LBP*

It is obvious that the rotation of the texture also influences the uniform patterns. Therefore, the rotation invariant version of this operator was also suggested *riuLBP*. In this case, the rotation operator is applied for the local binary patterns which have up to two transitions between 0 and 1 bits. This solution diminishes the number of histogram bins to $P+2$.

3 Databases

In the literature several image databases are used to evaluate proposed algorithms for emotion recognition. The databases have various quality, number of subjects, and image resolution. This features influence enormously the algorithms performance. Moreover, considering recognition only of neutral and smiling facial display, these datasets have up to dozen separate subjects. Therefore a combined database was created. The exploited image sets are described below.

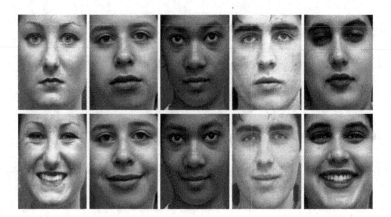

Fig. 4. *Cohn-Kanade* image database. Examples of neutral expression are presented in the top row, whereas the smiling ones in the bottom row.

3.1 *Cohn-Kanade* Image Database

In late 70s Ekman and Friesen [6] created a Facial Action Coding System, (FACS), which enables description of individual or group muscle action in human face. Each action is numbered and called an Action Unit, which enables building description of muscles activation in case of emotion visible in face. Cohn-Kanade AU-Coded Facial Expression Database [4], [12] exploits the Ekman technique for emotion description. It includes image sequences from neutral to target display of basic emotions (e.g. joy, surprise, anger, fear, disgust).

For the described research, images from 82 sequences were chosen which depicted the neutral and smiling expression. The image resolution is 640×480 pixels with 8-bit precision for grayscale values. The images differ in lighting conditions and the subjects do not wear glasses or other covering elements, as well as do not have beards. The same set of subjects represent neutral and smiling expressions. Some examples are presented in Fig. 4.

3.2 *Feret* Image Database

Feret database [21] was prepared for facial recognition system evaluation by the Defence Advanced Research Project Agency (DARPA) and the National Institute of Standards and Technology (NIST). For the described in this paper experiments, 62 images were chosen to represent the neutral and smiling expression. The subjects differ in each group. Moreover, it is possible to have different images for the same person in one group. Figure 5 presents examples of this database.

3.3 *All* Database

The small size of existing datasets is problematic when proper evaluation of algorithms is considered. In order to eliminate the influence of particular database

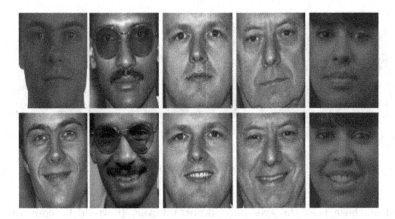

Fig. 5. *Feret* image database. Examples of neutral expression are presented in the top row, whereas the smiling ones in the bottom row.

a collective dataset was prepared. It contains images from the two presented above datasets but also from other popular image sets, like: Nottingham originals, Iranian, Utrecht, and Pain [22]. The combined dataset has in total 712 images equally divided between the two groups.

4   Image Divisions and Masks

While determining the FACS [6] it was noticed that only selected muscles take part in facial display change for emotion expression. Therefore, creating a single *LBP* histogram for whole face image might be too general. In consequence, the feature vector built to describe emotions is a concatenation of several histograms calculated for image parts as presented in Fig. 6. In some research, authors include the general *LBP* histogram for a whole image as a part of the concatenated feature vector [1], but according to our research this operation does not influence the facial expression recognition accuracy, hence is omitted.

Another problem constitutes the choice of division schema. It is known that during the smile not only the lips shape changes but also muscles around them

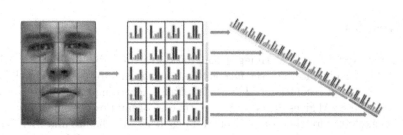

Fig. 6. Creation of the concatenated feature vector with the *LBP* texture operator.

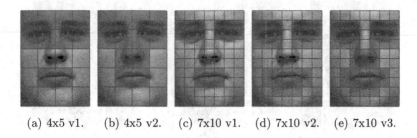

(a) 4x5 v1.   (b) 4x5 v2.   (c) 7x10 v1.   (d) 7x10 v2.   (e) 7x10 v3.

Fig. 7. Examined masks setups.

as well as those near the eyes play important role. It would be convenient to describe these regions in detail. Yet, while choosing the best image division one need to have in mind, that the sub-image must be large enough to densely fill the histogram. Moreover, the number of sub-images corresponds to the feature vector length, which should not be too long. As a result of this considerations, for face images of resolution 112×150, three division schemas were addressed in presented research:

4x5 that results in 20 sub-images, each with resolution 28×30 pixels and 840 elements in the histogram,

4x10 that results in 40 sub-images, each with resolution 28×15 pixels and 420 elements in the histogram,

7x10 that results in 70 sub-images, each with resolution 16×15 pixels and 240 elements in the histogram.

Several parts of such generated image divisions seem to be excessive, as they describe these regions of the face which do not take part in expression generation. Researchers in [1] suggested to use weights to discriminate between the significant and unessential image parts. This is interesting solution, but it demands to work with specially designed classifier, which is not a goal of this research. Therefore, in presented work a mask approach is suggested, in order to verify, which facial region contains the most discriminative information. For the division schemas which proved to work well, a few masks were suggested. Figure 7 presents the developed masks.

5   Results

In the presented research, the images in all databases are normalized to monochromatic 8-bit per pixel format, the face is found using detector described in [9] and scaled to constant resolution of 112×150 pixels. According to previous research [17], the linear SVM gives the best accuracy in case of emotion classification, therefore it is exploited for this comparison of image division schemas and then region masks. Due to the small number of images, the 10-fold cross-validation technique is applied.

The goal of the first experiment was to compare the classification accuracy when one of the three suggested image division schemas was applied. In each case, all texture operators were compared: *LBP*, *uLBP*, *riLBP*, and *riuLBP* with radius, R, varying from 1 to 3.

Table 1 gathers results for *Cohn-Kanade* database. The correct classification ratio for this image set is very high, in many cases above 90%. Generally, analysing data one can notice that the performance, nevertheless of chosen division schema, is much better when *uLBP* or *LBP* texture operator is applied, and reaches more than 92%, with the best result 97%. When comparing the outcome for different radiuses applied in the texture operator, it is easily seen that the performance diminishes when the radius equals 3. Regarding the outcomes for the best texture operators (*LBP*, and *uLBP*) it is difficult to conclude which division schema is the best, however it seems that the division 4×5 and 4×10 perform a little better.

The recognition accuracy between smiling and neutral facial displays in case of *Feret* database is given in Tab. 2. Despite the generally lower precision of presented methods (between 70-88%) when comparing to *Cohn-Kanade* database, similar behaviour might be noticed. Once again the *LBP* and *uLBP* texture operators outperform rotation invariant versions achieving correct classification ratio in the range 85-88%. Similarly, it is difficult to claim which from the division schemas is the best, however one can see that here the best results were recorded for 4×10 and 7×10 approaches. Finally, the radiuses do not influence the recognition performance.

Similar research were conducted on the *All* database, since it is the most general one. From the gathered outcomes summarised in Tab. 3 following conclusions

Table 1. *Cohn-Kanade* database. Smiling vs. neutral display correct classification ratio.

	Division schemas								
	4×5			4×10			7×10		
	$R = 1$	$R = 2$	$R = 3$	$R = 1$	$R = 2$	$R = 3$	$R = 1$	$R = 2$	$R = 3$
uLBP	**96.34**	95.73	**96.34**	**96.95**	**96.34**	94.52	95.73	95.12	92.68
LBP	**97.56**	95.73	94.51	**96.34**	95.71	95.09	95.12	95.09	92.68
riLBP	79.88	89.02	88.41	87.80	93.29	89.02	89.63	89.02	88.41
riuLBP	85.98	89.02	91.46	88.41	90.24	90.85	87.20	84.76	90.24

Table 2. *Feret* database. Smiling vs. neutral display correct classification ratio.

	Division schemas								
	4×5			4×10			7×10		
	$R = 1$	$R = 2$	$R = 3$	$R = 1$	$R = 2$	$R = 3$	$R = 1$	$R = 2$	$R = 3$
uLBP	85.48	86.29	85.48	86.29	**87.90**	85.48	**88.71**	87.90	87.90
LBP	83.87	86.29	87.90	87.10	87.10	87.90	87.90	83.55	83.87
riLBP	62.10	72.58	74.19	75.00	77.42	77.42	80.65	78.23	79.03
riuLBP	70.16	67.74	75.00	71.77	76.61	74.19	81.45	78.23	75.00

Table 3. *All* database. Smiling vs. neutral display correct classification ratio.

| | Division schemas | | | | | | | | |
| | 4×5 | | | 4×10 | | | 7×10 | | |
	$R=1$	$R=2$	$R=3$	$R=1$	$R=2$	$R=3$	$R=1$	$R=2$	$R=3$
uLBP	85.69	84.99	83.31	87.24	85.83	86.54	86.68	85.83	83.31
LBP	85.83	86.82	86.40	87.80	**88.92**	**89.34**	**88.63**	87.24	86.82
riLBP	70.41	74.33	73.91	75.32	80.36	80.79	81.49	84.71	79.94
riuLBP	73.49	75.32	74.89	72.23	77.14	73.35	77.98	78.96	76.02

might be drawn. First of all, the *LBP* and *uLBP* texture operators work better than *riLBP* and *riuLBP*. It is difficult to observe the influence of radius change on the classification accuracy. Although, the best results were recorded for 4×10 and 7×10 image division schema, the improvement in those cases is so small, that it is difficult to relay on it. In consequence it was decided that the mask should be created for 4×5 division schema, which is characterised by smaller number of sub-images, and 7×10 division schema, which is the most detailed approach.

The second experiment compared the influence of applied mask on the smiling vs. neutral facial display recognition. Here five different masks presented in Fig. 7 were considered. The experiments were performed for each database and the results are presented in Tabs. 4-9.

In the search for the beneficial mask it is good to analyse together tables with results for 4 × 5 and 7 × 10 masks. In case of *Cohn-Kanade* image data set (see Tabs. 4 and 5) the highest correct classification ratio was recorded for 4 × 5 v2. with *uLBP* texture operator used for radius equal to 3. However other combinations of parameters for this mask as well as those for 7×10 v3. are not far behind. Application of 7 × 10 v3. for *Feret* image database seems most useful as can be noticed from Tabs. 6 and 7. Similar behaviour can be seen for the *All* database

Table 4. *Cohn-Kanade* database. Smiling vs. neutral facial display correct classification ratio with 4×5 masks.

| | Division schemas | | | | | |
| | 4×5 v1. | | | 4×5 v2. | | |
	$R=1$	$R=2$	$R=3$	$R=1$	$R=2$	$R=3$
uLBP	**96.32**	93.25	95.09	95.09	95.71	**97.55**
LBP	95.71	95.09	93.25	**96.32**	**96.32**	93.87

Table 5. *Cohn-Kanade* database. Smiling vs. neutral facial display correct classification ratio with 7×10 masks.

| | Division schemas | | | | | | | | |
| | 7×10 v1. | | | 7×10 v2. | | | 7×10 v3. | | |
	$R=1$	$R=2$	$R=3$	$R=1$	$R=2$	$R=3$	$R=1$	$R=2$	$R=3$
uLBP	**96.32**	95.09	92.02	**96.32**	95.71	95.71	**96.93**	**96.93**	**96.32**
LBP	93.87	92.64	93.87	93.87	95.09	94.48	**96.32**	**96.32**	**96.32**

Table 6. *Feret* database. Smiling vs. neutral facial display correct classification ratio with 4×5 masks.

	Division schemas					
	4×5 v1.			4×5 v2.		
	$R=1$	$R=2$	$R=3$	$R=1$	$R=2$	$R=3$
uLBP	75.81	83.87	82.26	78.23	84.68	80.65
LBP	76.61	87.90	85.48	83.06	85.48	84.68

Table 7. *Feret* database. Smiling vs. neutral facial display correct classification ratio with 7×10 masks.

	Division schemas								
	7×10 v1.			7×10 v2.			7×10 v3.		
	$R=1$	$R=2$	$R=3$	$R=1$	$R=2$	$R=3$	$R=1$	$R=2$	$R=3$
uLBP	81.45	83.06	75.81	76.90	85.48	85.48	86.29	87.10	85.48
LBP	86.29	83.87	81.45	**88.71**	86.29	84.68	**89.52**	87.10	**88.71**

Table 8. *All* database. Smiling vs. neutral facial display correct classification ratio with 4×5 masks.

	Division schemas					
	4×5 v1.			4×5 v2.		
	$R=1$	$R=2$	$R=3$	$R=1$	$R=2$	$R=3$
uLBP	78.96	80.08	77.28	82.30	81.07	78.40
LBP	80.50	80.93	82.89	81.07	82.75	84.01

Table 9. *All* database. Smiling vs. neutral facial display correct classification ratio with 7×10 masks.

	Division schemas								
	7×10 v1.			7×10 v2.			7×10 v3.		
	$R=1$	$R=2$	$R=3$	$R=1$	$R=2$	$R=3$	$R=1$	$R=2$	$R=3$
uLBP	83.03	80.93	78.12	86.40	84.01	82.75	86.40	84.29	84.15
LBP	85.97	84.71	85.55	86.82	86.12	86.82	86.96	87.10	**89.34**

(see Tabs. 8 and 9). Looking at these results and comparing them with the mask shape, it can be stated that in order to describe the smile, not only the region of the eyes and lips are necessary, but also the nose conveys crucial information.

Finally, the best outcome for image division presented in Tabs. 1-3 with those achieved with mask application is given in Tabs. 4-9. Regardless of the reduction of number of valid sub-images, the overall image recognition accuracy did not suffer. For the *Cohn-Kanade* database it stays at the same level of 97.56%, for the *Feret* it grows a little bit from 88.71% to 89.52%, and did not change in case of *All* database – 89.34%. It is also worth mentioning, that applying the masks is connected with feature vector length decreasing of almost 50% (refer to Tab. 10 for details) maintaining the same recognition accuracy with lowering

Table 10. Feature vector length for each division schema and applied mask.

	Feature vector length							
	4×5			4×10		7×10		
Texture operator	v1.	v2.				v1.	v2.	v3.
LBP	5120	2560	3072	10240	17920	4608	7936	9472
uLBP	1180	590	708	2360	4130	1062	1829	2183
	Percent of the original feature vector length							
	100	50	60	100	100	26	44	53

the computational costs both on the side of image description calculation as well as in time of the classification.

6 Conclusions

The work presents the influence of image division schema application on the recognition accuracy between smiling and neutral facial displays. In the research classification performance for three different image division schemas, when whole image was considered, and a mask approach, when only distinguished parts of image are incorporated into feature vector, were compared. The gathered results shown that shortening the feature vector length, due to mask application, does not worsen the classification accuracy. Moreover, in some cases the result improved a little bit. Choice of a proper mask, however, has some impact on the recognition accuracy, as the best masks prove to be those which contain information from the regions of eyes, lips, and nose.

Acknowledgement. This work has been supported by the Polish National Science Centre (NCN) under the Grant: DEC-2012/07/B/ST6/01227 and was performed using the infrastructure supported by POIG.02.03.01-24-099/13 grant: GCONiI - Upper-Silesian Center for Scientific Computation.

References

1. Ahonen, T., Hadid, A., Pietikäinen, M.: Face recognition with local binary patterns. In: Pajdla, T., Matas, J. (eds.) ECCV 2004, Part I. LNCS, vol. 3021, pp. 469–481. Springer, Heidelberg (2004)
2. Ahonen, T., Matas, J., He, C., Pietikäinen, M.: Rotation invariant image description with local binary pattern histogram fourier features. In: Salberg, A.-B., Hardeberg, J.Y., Jenssen, R. (eds.) SCIA 2009. LNCS, vol. 5575, pp. 61–70. Springer, Heidelberg (2009)
3. Bartlett, M.S., Hager, J.C., Ekman, P., Sejnowski, T.J.: Measuring facial expressions by computer image analysis. Psychophysiology 36(2), 253–263 (1999)
4. Cohn, J.F., Zlochower, A.J., Lien, J., Kanade, T.: Automated face analysis by feature point tracking has high concurrent validity with manual FACS coding. Psychophysiology 36, 35–43 (1999)

5. Cohn, J., Zlochower, A., Lien, J.-J.J., Kanade, T.: Feature-point tracking by optical flow discriminates subtle differences in facial expression. In: Proc. 3rd IEEE Intern. Conf. on Autom. Face and Gesture Recog., pp. 396–401 (1998)

6. Ekman, P., Friesen, W.: Facial action coding system: a technique for the measurement of facial movement. Consulting Psychologists Press (1978)

7. Essa, I.A., Pentland, A.P.: Coding, analysis, interpretation, and recognition of facial expressions. IEEE Trans. Pattern Anal. Mach. Intell. 19(7), 757–763 (1997)

8. Heusch, G., Rodriguez, Y., Marcel, S.: Local binary patterns as an image preprocessing for face authentication. In: 7th International Conference on Automatic Face and Gesture Recognition, pp. 6–14 (2006)

9. Kawulok, M., Szymanek, J.: Precise multi-level face detector for advanced analysis of facial images. IET Image Processing 6(2), 95–103 (2012)

10. Lanitis, A., Taylor, C.J., Cootes, T.F.: Automatic interpretation and coding of face images using flexible models. IEEE Trans. Pattern Anal. Mach. Intell. 19(7), 743–756 (1997)

11. Liao, S., Fan, W., Chung, A.C.S., Yeung, D.-Y.: Facial expression recognition using advanced local binary patterns, Tsallis entropies and global appearance features. In: IEEE International Conference on Image Processing, pp. 665–668 (2006)

12. Lien, J.-J.J., Kanade, T., Cohn, J., Li, C.: Detection, tracking, and classification of action units in facial expression. Journal of Robotics and Autonomous System 31, 131–146 (2000)

13. Mase, K.: An application of optical flow – extraction of facial expression. In: IAPR Workshop on Machine Vision Applications, pp. 195–198 (1990)

14. Ojala, T., Pietikäinen, M., Harwood, D.: A comparative study of texture measures with classification based on featured distributions. Pattern Recognition, 51–59 (1996)

15. Ojala, T., Pietikäinen, M., Mäenpää, T.: A generalized Local Binary Pattern operator for multiresolution gray scale and rotation invariant texture classification. In: Singh, S., Murshed, N., Kropatsch, W.G. (eds.) ICAPR 2001. LNCS, vol. 2013, pp. 397–406. Springer, Heidelberg (2001)

16. Ojala, T., Pietikäinen, M., Mäenpää, T.: Multiresolution Gray-Scale and Rotation Invariant Texture Classification with Local Binary Patterns. IEEE Trans. Pattern Anal. Mach. Intell. 24(7), 971–987 (2002)

17. Nurzynska, K., Smolka, B.: Optimal Classification Method for Smiling vs. Neutral Facial Display Recognition. Journal of Medical Informatics and Technology 23, 87–94 (2014)

18. Pantic, M., Rothkrantz, L.J.M.: Automatic analysis of facial expressions: the state of the art. IEEE Transactions on Pattern Analysis and Machine Intelligence 22, 1424–1445 (2000)

19. Pietikäinen, M., Zhao, G., Hadid, A., Ahonen, T.: Computer vision using local binary patterns. Computational imaging and vision, vol. 40, pp. 13–49. Springer (2011)

20. Shan, C., Gong, S., McOwan, P.W.: Facial expression recognition based on local binary patterns: A comprehensive study. Image and Vision Computing 27(6), 803–816 (2009)

21. FERET database, http://www.itl.nist.gov/iad/humanid/feret/feret_master.html (July 04, 2014)

22. Iranian, Nottingham, Pain, Utrecht database, http://pics.psych.stir.ac.uk (July 04, 2014)

Image Segmentation in Liquid Argon Time Projection Chamber Detector

Piotr Płoński[1(✉)], Dorota Stefan[2], Robert Sulej[3], and Krzysztof Zaremba[1]

[1] Institute of Radioelectronics, Warsaw University of Technology,
Nowowiejska 15/19,00-665 Warsaw, Poland
{pplonski,zaremba}@ire.pw.edu.pl
[2] Istituto Nazionale di Fisica Nucleare, Sezione di Milano e Politecnico,
Via Celoria 16, I-20133 Milano, Italy
dorota.stefan@ifj.edu.pl
[3] National Center for Nuclear Research,
A. Soltana 7, 05-400 Otwock/Swierk, Poland
Robert.Sulej@cern.ch

Abstract. The Liquid Argon Time Projection Chamber (LAr-TPC) detectors provide excellent imaging and particle identification ability for studying neutrinos. An efficient and automatic reconstruction procedures are required to exploit potential of this imaging technology. Herein, a novel method for segmentation of images from LAr-TPC detectors is presented. The proposed approach computes a feature descriptor for each pixel in the image, which characterizes amplitude distribution in pixel and its neighbourhood. The supervised classifier is employed to distinguish between pixels representing particle's track and noise. The classifier is trained and evaluated on the hand-labeled dataset. The proposed approach can be a preprocessing step for reconstructing algorithms working directly on detector images.

Keywords: Liquid argon · Time projection chambers · Image Segmentation · Pixel classification · Feature descriptor

1 Introduction

The Liquid Argon Time Projection Chamber (LAr-TPC) detector idea was proposed by C.Rubbia in 1977 [23]. It provides excellent imaging ability of charged particles, making it ideal for studying neutrino oscillation parameters, sterile neutrinos existence [22], Charge Parity violation, violation of baryonic number conservation and dark matter searches. The LAr-TPC technique is used in several projects around the world [16], [2], [1], [14], [11]. The ICARUS T600 [11] was the largest working detector located at Gran Sasso in the underground Italian National Laboratory operating on CNGS beam (CERN[1] Neutrinos to Gran Sasso). In this study, the T600 will be used as a reference detector as other existing or planned LAr-TPC detectors have the similar construction and settings.

---

[1] CERN - European Organization for Nuclear Research

© Springer International Publishing Switzerland 2015
L. Rutkowski et al. (Eds.): ICAISC 2015, Part I, LNAI 9119, pp. 606–615, 2015.
DOI: 10.1007/978-3-319-19324-3_54

In the LAr-TPC detector a charged particle produces both scintillation light and ionization electrons along its path. The scintillation light, which is poor compared to ionisation charge, is detected by photomultipliers which trigger the read-out process. Free electrons from ionizing particles drift in an uniform electric field toward the anode. They can drift to macroscopic distances because its diffussion approximate value 4.8 cm^2/s in highly purified liquid argon is much slower than electron drift velocity 1.59 mm/μs. The anode consists of three wire planes, so-called Induction1, Induction2, Collection. A signal is induced in a non-destructive way on the first two wire planes, which are practically transparent to the drifting electrons. The signal on the third wire plane (Collection) is formed by collecting the ionization charge. It is also the source of the calorimetric measurement. The wires in consecutive planes are oriented in three different degrees with respect to the horizontal with 3 mm spacing between wires in the plane. This allows to localize the signal source in the XZ plane, whereas Y coordinate is calculated from wire signal timing and electron drift velocity[2]. Signal on wires is amplified and digitized with 2.5 MHz sampling frequency which results in 0.64 mm spatial resolution along the drift coordinate. The digitized waveforms from consecutive wires placed next to each other form a 2D projection images of an event. The image size resolution is 0.64 mm x 3 mm.

The registered images are input for reconstruction and particle identification algorithms, which estimate physical quantities from events observed in the detector. To our knowledge, all recently presented analysis assume that images are preprocessed into so-called set of hits [1], [3], [21]. Each hit represents a position of signal on wire coming from particle's track. Hit has information about the beginning, the end and the peak of the particle's track signal on wire. Hits are obtained by fitting a multiple reference signal pulses on wire's signal. This approach has some limitations. The hit fitting algorithm distinguishes signal from particle's track and noise based on defined threshold value, which can fail in case of noise with high amplitude. This can be a common case during analysis of images deconvoluted with impulse response of the wire signal readout chain, because the signal-to-noise ratio descends. What is more, the hit unit can be imprecise in case of multiple tracks overlapping in the same position in the image. These drawbacks can be overcame by constructing algorithms working directly on raw images. In this paper, the novel method for images segmentation from LAr-TPC detectors is presented, which can be used as a preprocessing step for reconstruction and identification algorithms working directly on images from detector. Furthermore, this segmentation method can be used to improve hit fitting procedure by replacing identification of particle's track based on threshold value. The presented approach use a supervised classifier working on a feature descriptor which characterizes the amplitude distribution in pixel and its neighbourhood. The classifier is trained and evaluated on a hand-labeled dataset. The performance of the proposed method is compared with segmentation based on threshold value. The importance of proposed features is studied.

---

[2] Coordinate system labeling is given for reference.

2 Methods

2.1 Proposed Feature Descriptor

Describing image by set of features is a common approach in computer vision [15], [18], [19], [13], [9]. The feature vector is constructed to obtain the relevant information from the image data. Herein, in order to characterize distribution of signal in the pixel and its neighbourhood a feature descriptor is constructed, consisting of 42 features, which are described below:

- Pixel value, proportional to the charge value;
- Signal statistics, which describe the amplitude distribution in the pixel and its neighbourhood, represented by: maximum, minimum, median, mean and standard deviation computed for 3x3, 5x5 and 7x7 kernel sizes;
- Difference of Gaussians, which is substraction of two blurred images with Gaussian kernel with different standard deviations, which can be viewed as band-pass filter. Used pairs of standard deviations are : $\{0.5, 2\}$, $\{0.5, 3\}$, $\{0.5, 4\}$, $\{0.75, 2\}$, $\{0.75, 3\}$, $\{0.75, 4\}$, $\{1, 2\}$, $\{1, 3\}$, $\{1, 4\}$;
- Image gradient magnitude, which detects sudden changes in the amplitude, the Prewitt operator was used for gradient computation;
- Ordered eigenvalues of image's Hessian as well as sum and multiplication of them, which describes the second order of local image intesity;
- Ordered eigenvalues of image's tensor, together with sum and multiplication of them for kernel sizes 3x3, 5x5, 7x7, which indicates the strength of the directional intensity change.

The similar configuration of proposed features is often used in image analysis in medicine [4], [24]. Recently, the usage of image tensor eigenvalues was proposed for detecting points of interest and delta electrons in images from LAr-TPC detector [17].

2.2 Datasets Creation

To generate datasets the FLUKA software [7] and T600 detector parameters were used. The events were generated for 2 GeV energy. From obtained events 50 images for Induction2 and Collection views were independently selected. The two views were chosen to present the performance of the proposed method on two sources of images which have different characteristics of the signal. All images were deconvoluted with impulse response of wire signal readout chain of each plane and resized to have similar resolution on both axis. The dedicated application with Graphical User Interface was used to manually label the dataset. The pixels representing particle's track are noted as a positive class whereas noise pixels as a negative class. For each pixel in the dataset the feature vector was computed according to the description in Section 2.1. The feature vector together with class label of the pixel form a sample in the dataset. The dataset was divided into train and test subsets. There are 40 events in the train subset and 10 events in the test subset in each considered plane. The number of samples in each subset for Induction2 and Collection views are presented in Table 1. They are different because the readout procedure is triggered by photomultipliers only on subset of wires, from which particle's track is registered. The classes are highly imbalanced in considered datasets. The ratios of positives to negatives in train dataset are 1:305 and 1:109 for Induction2 and Collection views, respectively.

Table 1. The number of samples in train and test subsets for Induction2 and Collection views. Positive samples represent particle's track pixels whereas negative samples represent noise

	Induction2		Collection	
	Negative	Positive	Negative	Positive
Train	15,648,122	51,300	7,290,844	66,749
Test	4,427,377	10,437	2,061,778	16,988

2.3   Classifiers

In the proposed approach, the created feature descriptor is an input for the classifier, which response is a probability whether pixel represents particle's track in the image. The Logistic Regression (LR) [10] and Random Forest [5], [20] algorithms were used as classifiers. They were trained on all features described in Section 2.1 contrary to the Decision Stump (DS) [25] trained only on considered pixel's amplitude value. The performance of the DS is baseline because it is commonly used in analysis by physicists. To asses the classifier's performance the precision recall graph was used, where

$$Precision = \frac{TP}{TP + FP}, \tag{1}$$

$$Recall = \frac{TP}{TP + FN}. \tag{2}$$

The TP stands for true positives - correctly classified positive samples, FP are false positives - negative samples incorrectly classified, and FN are false negatives, which are positive samples improperly classified as negatives.

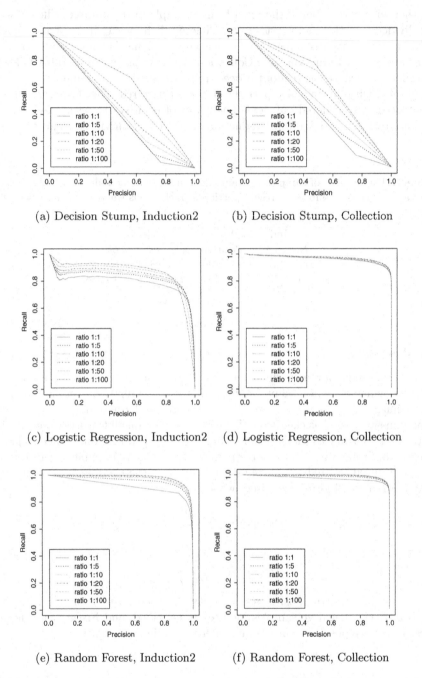

(a) Decision Stump, Induction2   (b) Decision Stump, Collection

(c) Logistic Regression, Induction2   (d) Logistic Regression, Collection

(e) Random Forest, Induction2   (f) Random Forest, Collection

Fig. 1. The precision recall graphs for Decision Stump, Logistic Regression and Random Forest classifiers for Induction2 and Collection views. Classifiers were trained with different ratios of positive to negative classes in train set and evaluated on all samples from test set.

3   Results

Due to the facts that classes are highly imbalanced and there is a large number
of samples, the train datasets were downsampled. The classifiers were trained
on different class ratios: 1:1, 1:10, 1:20, 1:50, 1:100 - with constant number of
positive samples and changing the number of negative samples. All the samples
from the test set were used in evaluation of the classifiers performance. There
were used 100 trees in RF algorithm for both views, later the selection of optimal
number of trees in the forest is reported. The precision recall graphs for DS, LR
and RF are presented in the Fig.1. The accuracy of DS classifier increases with
increasing number of negative samples in the train set because the threshold
value in decision rule can be more precisely estimated for larger dataset. For
LR and RF the similar behavior can be observed, especially for Induction2.
The more data is available the more accurate classifiers can be trained. From
this point, the 1:100 classes ratio is used in tha analysis for both views. The
comparison of used classifiers' performance is presented in the Fig.2. The RF
classifier outperforms DS and LR on both views. The RF algorithm, which is
an ensemble of unpruned decision trees, is able to learn more about data than
DS and LR. The difference in performance between RF and other algorithms
is larger on Induction2 than on the Collection. Therefore, the Induction2 signal
seems to be more complex to classify than Collection signal.

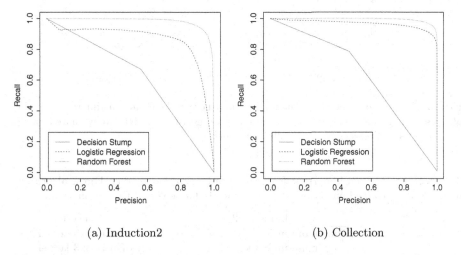

(a) Induction2   (b) Collection

Fig. 2. The comparison of classifiers preformance learned with train set with class ratio
1:100 of positive to negative samples and evaluated on all test samples, for Induction2
and Collection views

The RF performance for different number of trees was examined. The precision recall graphs for trees number $\{10, 20, 50, 100, 200, 500, 1000\}$ for class ratio
1:100 for Induction2 and Collection are presented in Fig.3. The RF achieves

the highest performance starting from 100 trees in the ensemble for Induction2 and the classifier accuracy does not significantly change with adding more trees. Whereas, the classification performance is the highest starting from 50 trees in the forest for Collection view. The higher number of trees in the forest is needed to learn a dataset in the Induction2 than in the Collection view. This once more indicates that Induction2 signal is more complex in classification than the Collection signal.

The response of the classifier is a probability that pixel represents particle's track. The examples of all examined classifiers responses on the test event from Induction2 are presented in the Fig.4. It can be observed that for DS and LR there are more breaks on tracks than on response from RF. Therefore, the RF output is preferable for further reconstructing algorithms.

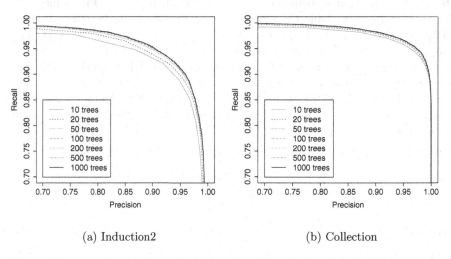

(a) Induction2   (b) Collection

Fig. 3. The precision recall graphs for Random Forest algorithm for different number of trees used, trained on class ratio of positives to negatives 1:100 and evaluated on all test samples for Induction2 and Collection views

Table 2. The top ten important features according to the Random Forest algorithm with 100 trees trained on classes ratio 1:100 for Induction2 and Collection views

Rank	Induction2	Collection
1	maximum in 5x5 kernel	mean in 3x3 kernel
2	maximum in 3x3 kernel	median in 3x3 kernel
3	maximum in 7x7 kernel	mean in 5x5 kernel
4	standard deviation in 5x5 kernel	tensor 1st eigenvalue in 3x3 kernel
5	standard deviation in 3x3 kernel	median in 5x5 kernel
6	tensor 1st eigenvalue in 3x3 kernel	maximum in 5x5 kernel
7	standard deviation in 7x7 kernel	standard deviation in 5x5 kernel
8	mean in 3x3 kernel	mean in 7x7 kernel
9	pixel amplitude	maximum in 3x3 kernel
10	median in 3x3 kernel	maximum in 7x7 kernel

One of the key features of the RF algorithm is that the variable importance can be easily obtained from learned model [5]. The top ten features for Induction2 and Collection views are listed in Table 2. It is worth to notice, that there are different features selected as the most important for Induction2 and Collection. It is interesting that pixel amplitude was selected as the ninth of the most important features for Induction2 and is not present in the top ten important

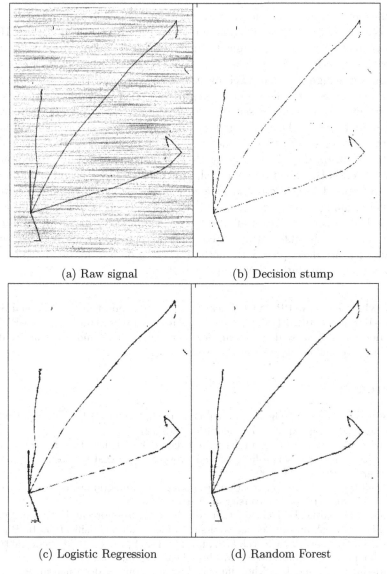

(a) Raw signal   (b) Decision stump

(c) Logistic Regression   (d) Random Forest

Fig. 4. (a) The raw signal of test event from Induction2. (b,c,d) The response of the classifiers for considered test event. The classifiers were trained on classes ratio 1:100.

features for Collection dataset. Although based on only this variable the decision of pixel representation was done in the threshold method. All the proposed features described in Section 2.1 used in the RF training are important in classification, since elimination of the least important features decreases the classifier performance on each view.

4 Conclusions

The efficient computerized methods for automatic analysis of observed events are required to fully exploit the imaging potential of the LAr-TPC detectors. Herein, the novel method for image segmentation is presented. In the proposed approach the feature descriptor for each pixel in the image is computed. It describes the distribution of signal in the pixel and its neighbourhood. Based on constructed features the classifier makes a decision whether pixel represents particle's track or noise. The two popular classifiers were examined, namely: Logistic Regression and Random Forest. The classifier was trained and evaluated on the hand-labeled dataset on images from two distinct views. The proposed method outperforms with large margin the widely used method of image thresholding based on pixel amplitude on both Induction2 and Collection views. The method is an universal and can be used for various characteristic of the signal in the image after the classifier training. The performance of the method can be further improved by using other classifiers, like Multi-Layer Perceptron [8] or extending the feature vector. It would be interesting to compare the proposed method working on prepared feature descriptor with method working on automatically constructed features from Convolutional Neural Network [6].

Acknowledgements. PP and KZ acknowledge the support of the National Science Center (Harmonia 2012/04/M/ST2/00775). Authors are grateful to the ICARUS Collaboration and Polish Neutrino Group for useful suggestions and constructive discussions during a preliminary part of this work.

References

1. Anderson, C., et al.: The ArgoNeuT Detector in the NuMI Low-Energy beam line at Fermilab. Journal of Instrumentation 7 (2012)
2. Autiero, D., et al.: Large underground, liquid based detectors for astro-particle physics in Europe: scientific case and prospects. Journal of Cosmology and Astroparticle Physics 11 (2007)
3. Bennieston, A.J.: Reconstruction techniques for fine-grained neutrino detectors, Doctoral dissertation, University of Warwick (2013)
4. Andres, B., Köthe, U., Helmstaedter, M., Denk, W., Hamprecht, F.A.: Segmentation of SBFSEM volume data of neural tissue by hierarchical classification. In: Rigoll, G. (ed.) DAGM 2008. LNCS, vol. 5096, pp. 142–152. Springer, Heidelberg (2008)
5. Breiman, L.: Random Forests. Machine Learning 45, 5–32 (2001)
6. Ciresan, D., Meier, U., Schmidhuber, J.: Multi-column deep neural networks for image classification. In: The IEEE Conference on Computer Vision and Pattern Recognition, pp. 3642–3649 (2012)

7. Ferrari, A., Sala, P.R., Fasso, A., Ranft, J.: FLUKA: a multi-particle transport code, CERN-2005-10, INFN TC 05 11, SLAC-R-773 (2005)
8. Graczyk, K.M., Płonski, P., Sulej, R.: Neural network parameterizations of electromagnetic nucleon form-factors. Journal of High Energy Physics 2010, 1–30 (2010)
9. Grycuk, R., Gabryel, M., Korytkowski, M., Romanowski, J., Scherer, R.: Improved Digital Image Segmentation Based on Stereo Vision and Mean Shift Algorithm. In: Wyrzykowski, R., Dongarra, J., Karczewski, K., Waśniewski, J. (eds.) PPAM 2013, Part I. LNCS, vol. 8384, pp. 433–443. Springer, Heidelberg (2014)
10. Hastie, T., Friedman, J., Tibshirani, R.: The elements of statistical learning. Springer (2009)
11. The ICARUS Collaboration, Design, construction and tests of the ICARUS T600 detector, Nuclear Instruments and Methods in Physics Research, vol. A527 (2004)
12. The ICARUS Collaboration, The trigger system of the ICARUS experiment for the CNGS beam, Journal of Instrumentation, vol. 9 (2014)
13. Kostadinov, D., Voloshynovskiy, S., Ferdowsi, S., Diephuis, M., Scherer, R.: Robust Face Recognition by Group Sparse Representation That Uses Samples from List of Subjects. In: Rutkowski, L., Korytkowski, M., Scherer, R., Tadeusiewicz, R., Zadeh, L.A., Zurada, J.M. (eds.) ICAISC 2014, Part II. LNCS (LNAI), vol. 8468, pp. 616–626. Springer, Heidelberg (2014)
14. The LBNE Collaboration, The Long-Baseline Neutrino Experiment - Exploring Fundamental Symmetries of the Universe, FERMILAB-PUB-14-022, arXiv:1307.7335 (2014)
15. Lowe, D.: Distinctive Image Features from Scale-Invariant Keypoints. International Journal of Computer Vision 60, 91–110 (2004)
16. The MicroBooNE Collaboration, Proposal for a New Experiment Using the Booster and NuMI Neutrino Beamlines: MicroBooNE, FERMILAB-PROPOSAL-0974 (2007)
17. Morgan, B.: Interest Point Detection for Reconstruction in High Granularity Tracking Detectors. Journal of Instrumentation 5 (2010)
18. Najgebauer, P., Nowak, T., Romanowski, J., Gabryel, M., Korytkowski, M., Scherer, R.: Content-Based Image Retrieval by Dictionary of Local Feature Descriptors. In: Proceedings of the International Joint Conference on Neural Networks (2014)
19. Nowak, T., Gabryel, M., Korytkowski, M., Scherer, R.: Comparing Images Based on Histograms of Local Interest Points. In: Wyrzykowski, R., Dongarra, J., Karczewski, K., Waśniewski, J. (eds.) PPAM 2013, Part I. LNCS, vol. 8384, pp. 423–432. Springer, Heidelberg (2014)
20. Płoński, P., Zaremba, K.: Visualizing Random Forest with Self-Organising Map. In: Rutkowski, L., Korytkowski, M., Scherer, R., Tadeusiewicz, R., Zadeh, L.A., Zurada, J.M. (eds.) ICAISC 2014, Part II. LNCS (LNAI), vol. 8468, pp. 63–71. Springer, Heidelberg (2014)
21. Stefan, D., Sulej, R., et al.: Precise 3D Track Reconstruction Algorithm for the ICARUS T600 Liquid Argon Time Projection Chamber Detector. Advances in High Energy Physics, 2013
22. Sulej, R.: Sterile neutrino search with the ICARUS T600 in the CNGS beam. In: XV Workshop on Neutrino Telescopes, PoS Neutel (2013)
23. Rubbia, C.: The Liquid-Argon Time Projection Chamber: a new concept for neutrino detectors, CERN Report (1977)
24. Rudzki, M.: Vessel detection method based on eigenvalues of the hessian matrix and its applicability to airway tree segmentation. In: Proceedings of the 11th International PhD Workshop OWD, pp. 100–105 (2009)
25. Wayne, I., Pat, L.: Induction of One-Level Decision Trees. In: Proceedings of the Ninth International Conference on Machine Learning (1992)

Massively Parallel Change Detection with Application to Visual Quality Control

Ewaryst Rafajłowicz[✉] and Karol Niżyński

Department of Automatic Control and Mechatronics, Faculty of Electronics,
Wrocław University of Technology, Wrocław, Poland
`ewaryst.rafajlowicz@pwr.wroc.pl`

Abstract. Our aim in this paper is to extend the results on parallel change detection recently discussed in [15], where such a detector has been proposed. Here, we emphasize its adaptive abilities to follow changing background and relax some theoretical assumptions on random errors, extending possible applications of the detector. We also discuss its implementation in NVidia CUDA technology and provide results of its extensive testing when applied to copper visual quality control, which is a challenge due to the need for massively parallel calculations in real-time.

1 Introduction

Classical change detectors, such as the Shewhart chart, CUSUM and EWMA charts have been designed for detecting changes in one or at most tens time series (see [8] for a comprehensive review of control charts and [14], [10] for recently proposed nonparametric control charts). Detecting changes in image sequences (video streams) requires following grey levels of millions of pixels. The simplest and widely used method is to subtract subsequent images and apply thresholding to the resulting image (see, e.g., [1]). This approach is fast, but has a serious and well-known drawback, namely, if even a slight change of background has appeared, then it is detected, independently whether objects of interest have changed or not. This drawback leads to false alarms at least in the following cases:

a) a camera observes a terrain in order to detect moving objects, e.g., running peoples or moving cars, while even small changes in sunshine intensity or moving leaves on trees invoke a false alarm,
b) a camera is used to detect defects on a moving surface, e.g., of a hot metal – then slight changes in background temperature will be detected as moving defects.
This paper is motivated by the latter example. High resolution industrial cameras are well suited for quality monitoring of such processes (see [6]).

In this paper we further develop a change detector that was recently proposed by the first author in [15]. We put emphasis on its theoretical properties under less restrictive assumptions and then, we shall concentrate on its massively parallel implementation on graphical Processing Units (GPU) using NVidia CUDA technology. Finally, we provide the results of testing the algorithm. The tests have been run on video sequences of a copper slab.

© Springer International Publishing Switzerland 2015
L. Rutkowski et al. (Eds.): ICAISC 2015, Part I, LNAI 9119, pp. 616–625, 2015.
DOI: 10.1007/978-3-319-19324-3_55

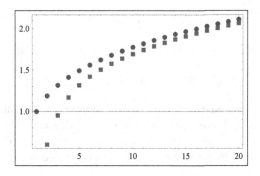

Fig. 1. Adaptation of the parallel change detector to a slowly changing background. Dots simulate a background of one pixel that is changing as $n^{1/4}$, while squares show the background estimate, obtained for $\alpha = 0.6$.

The idea is based on exponentially weighted moving average smoothing (EWMAS), but the detector itself is different than the one that is used in the classic EWMA chart, because EWMAS also uses the idea of vertical weighting [13], [14].

The proposed change detector can also be used in the stream of research called spatial statistics (see [2] and the bibliography cited therein) and in geoscience (see [4], [16]). It suffices to replace a rectangular image domain by the one that is appropriate for the application at hand or even by a set of sites or a graph nodes. We refer the reader to [12] and [17] for other approaches that are useful in change detection in image sequences.

2   A Bundle of Background-Adaptive Jump Detectors

Let $x \in \Omega$ denote a spatial position of a pixel at rectangular image Ω. When necessary, we shall also use the notation $\kappa(i, j) \in \Omega$, $i, j = 1, 2, \ldots$ for pixels' positions. By $t = 1, 2, \ldots$ we denote time instants when images from a camera are sampled.

Observed integer or real-valued grey-levels of an image $Y(x, t)$ are the results of observing an unknown function $m(x, t)$ with random additive errors $\varepsilon(x, t)$ that have zero mean and finite variance σ^2 i.e.,

$$Y(x, t) = m(x, t) + \varepsilon(x, t), \quad x \in \Omega, t = 1, 2, \ldots. \tag{1}$$

We assume that:

– there exists the probability density function (p.d.f.) of ε, denoted by f_ε, which does not depend on x and t,
– f_ε is symmetric,
– f_ε is known (e.g., f_ε has Gaussian distribution $N(0, \sigma^2)$),
– $Y(x, t)$ and $Y(x', t')$ are uncorrelated for $t \neq t', t, t' = 1, 2, \ldots, x, x' \in \Omega$, even if $x = x'$

These assumptions will be used only when theoretical properties of our jump detector are investigated. The assumption that f_ε is known is used only for selecting a parameter

$H > 0$ that dictates heights of jumps to be detected. In practice, H can be selected experimentally.

We assume that at a certain (unknown) time instant $t_0 > 1$ for the first time

$$Y(x, t_0) = M(x) + r(x, t_0) + \varepsilon(x, t_0), \quad x \in \Omega \tag{2}$$

where $M(x)$ is a background, which is unknown, while $r(x, t_0)$ is a jump to be detected. Also unknown is $r(x, t_0)$, but we assume that it is bounded away from 0, i.e., there exists $R > 0$ such that $|r(x, t_0)| > R$, $x \in \Omega$. We allow $r(x, t_0 + \tau) = 0$, (defects vanish), but $\tau > 0$ should be sufficiently large in comparison to the frame rate in order to be able to detect defects.

The second parameter that we have to choose is the smoothing parameter $0 < \alpha < 1$. It influences adaptivity properties of the algorithm presented below to possible background changes. Larger values of α correspond to faster adaptation. The third ingredient is the size $J \geq 0$ of a $(2J + 1) \times (2J + 1)$ window that is used for possible averaging of $Y(x, t)$'s in a neighborhood of pixel $x \in \Omega$, but in such a way that the averaged regions are non-overlapping. More precisely, we cover Ω by $(2J + 1) \times (2J + 1)$ just touching squares with centers at equidistant pixels, say $\kappa(i, j) \in \Omega$, $i, j = 1, 2, \ldots$. Then, we define

$$\hat{Y}(\kappa(i, j), t) = (2J + 1)^{-2} \sum_{|h| \leq J} \sum_{|v| \leq J} Y(\kappa(i + h, j + v), t). \tag{3}$$

Notice, that we admit $J = 0$ and then, $\kappa(i, j)$'s are placed at all pixels in Ω and $\hat{Y}(\kappa(i, j), t) = Y(\kappa(i, j), t)$. This case is considered as the basic one in this paper. We mention the averaged version (3) with $J > 0$ for the following reasons:
– it may happen that random errors are so intensive that averaging is necessary,
– the number of available parallel processors is much smaller than the number of pixels in Ω, a frame rate is large and it is not possible to run computations in real-time.

Define by $\hat{m}(\kappa(i, j), t)$ the estimate of the background at pixel $\kappa(i, j)$ in t-th time instant, assuming that there was no essential change at this pixel at time t. The following recurrent formula is used for an adaptive background update:

$$\hat{m}(\kappa(i, j), t + 1) = (1 - \alpha)\hat{m}(\kappa(i, j), t) + \tag{4}$$

$$+ \begin{cases} \alpha \hat{m}(\kappa(i, j), t), & \text{if } |\hat{Y}(\kappa(i, j), t) - \hat{m}(\kappa(i, j), t)| > H \\ \alpha \hat{Y}(\kappa(i, j), t) & \text{if } |\hat{Y}(\kappa(i, j), t) - \hat{m}(\kappa(i, j), t)| \leq H \end{cases}$$

From (4) it is clear that $\hat{m}(\kappa(i, j), t + 1)$ is updated only if there is no an essential jump, i.e., a possible jump is less than $H > 0$. In other words, (4) resembles the EWMA chart with three essential differences:

1) $\hat{m}(\kappa(i, j), t + 1)$ is changed only when a new observation is close to it, i.e., $\hat{m}(\kappa(i, j), t)$ estimates the process mean, adapting to it, but only in-control states.
2) Notice that in the EWMA chart also undetected jumps are added to the current state of the chart.
3) In the classic EWMA chart the present chart's state is compared to a threshold. Here, the decision is based on the difference between $\hat{Y}$ and $\hat{m}$.

Parallel Change Detector – The Main – On-line – Loop

Step 0 – Initialization. Set $t = 0$. For each pixel $kappa(i, j)$, $i, j = 1, 2, \ldots$ set the initial background $\hat{m}(\kappa(i, j), 0)$ to a value that is typical for the controlled process when there are no changes in its quality.

Step 1 – Image Acquisition and Preparation. Acquire new image $Y(\kappa(i, j), t)$, $i, j = 1, 2, \ldots$. Calculate $\hat{Y}(\kappa(i, j), t)$, $i, j = 1, 2, \ldots$ according to (3) (if $J > 0$).

Step 2 – Run in Paralle.l for current image at time t For every pixel $\kappa(i, j)$, $i, j = 1, 2, \ldots$ calculate elements of a binary matrix $B(\kappa(i, j)t)$ in the following way:

$$B(\kappa(i, j), t) = \begin{cases} 1, & if \quad |\hat{Y}(\kappa(i, j), t) - \hat{m}(\kappa(i, j), t)| > H \\ 0, & \text{otherwise} \end{cases} \tag{5}$$

Step 3 – Adaptive Background Update. Set $t = t + 1$. Calculate new background estimate $\hat{m}(\kappa(i, j), t)$ for each pixel $i, j = 1, 2, \ldots$. Go to Step 1.

For the most efficient parallel implementation, the above main loop requires as many parallel processor units as the number of pixels $\kappa(i, j)$, $i, j = 1, 2, \ldots$. Its simplicity allows for running it on graphical processor units (GPU), e.g., in NVidia CUDA technology, leading to massively parallel implementation that can be run on-line, even for relatively fast processes, as documented later in this paper.

Decision Unit

A decision unit that is described below should be placed on a processor that runs in parallel with the GPUs'. This processor is activated for each acquired frame, after finishing calculations of each full pass of the parallel change detector.

Select $\theta_0 \geq 0$ as a threshold below which we decide there were no changes at a current image and $\theta_1 > \theta_0$ as a threshold for setting an alarm that the production quality visible at a current image is not satisfactory.

First Decision. If $\sum_{i,j} B(\kappa(i, j), t) \leq \theta_0$, go to Step 1 of the main loop, otherwise, execute the routine *Removing small clusters* that is described below.

Removing Small Clusters. Interpret $B(., t)$ as a binary image and apply image processing tools like morphological erosion or blob analysis (see [1]) in order to remove single pixels or small clusters of them by setting the corresponding $B(\kappa(i, j), t) = 0$. Go to *Second decision*.

Fig. 2. Defects detected on the copper slab – two subsequent frames

Second Decision. If $\sum_{i,j} B(\kappa(i,j),t) > \theta_1$, then declare ALARM and go to Step 1 of the main loop (or stop the production process when it is necessary – the decision here is problem-dependent).

3   Tuning the Change Detector and its Correctness

In order to tune a bundle of change detectors it suffices to consider only one of them, since they are exactly the same and work in parallel. Later on, we return to use $x \in \Omega$ as a shorthand notation for a typical pixel coordinates $\kappa(i,j)$.

Tuning
1) Select a confidence level $0 < \beta < 1$ (typically, $\beta = 0.95$ or 0.99).
2) Calculate $\mathscr{E}$ such that with probability β, $|\varepsilon(x,t)| \leq \mathscr{E}$, i.e., $\mathscr{E}$ is such that $\int_{-\mathscr{E}}^{\mathscr{E}} f_\varepsilon(x)\, dx = \beta$.

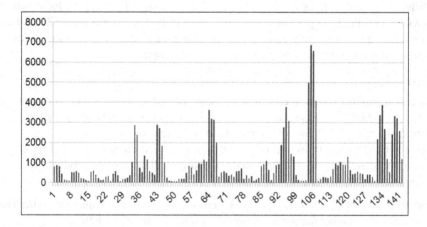

Fig. 3. The number of pixels with defects detected on the copper slab – 142 subsequent frames, corresponding to about 20 sec. of the production process

Remark 1. *If $f_\varepsilon(x)$ is unknown, then $\mathscr{E}$ can be estimated from empirical data as follows. From past images select those without defects and having a similar background. Split them into parts. Average the first part of them to estimate the background. Subtract the estimated background from the second part of of selected images in order to obtain estimates of errors. Use estimated errors to obtain empirical quantiles of f_ε (see [11] and the bibliography therein for methods of estimating quantiles).*

3) Select $H > 0$ such that $H \geq 2\mathscr{E}$. This choice ensures that the probability of false alarm is not larger than $1 - \beta$. On the other hand, if we want to detect large jumps immediately with high probability, it is reasonable to select $H = 2\mathscr{E}$ (see below).

4) Select smoothing parameter $0 < \alpha < 1$. Typically, $\alpha \in [0.3, 0.6]$, when we expect faster changes of a background and $\alpha \in (0.6, 0.95]$, when the background changes rather slowly.

5) Set $\hat{m}(x, 0) = Y(x, 0)$.

Correctness of the Background Estimation. In this subsection we assume that $m(x, t) = M(x)$, $x \in \Omega$ i.e., the background is constant in time. In such a case, one should expect that no alarm is declared or if it is, then the probability of such an event is low.

Property 1. *When the background is constant in time, then*
1) for each pixel $x \in \Omega$ the probability of false alarm is not larger than $1 - \beta$,
2) $|M(x) - \hat{m}(x, t)| \leq \mathcal{E}$ with probability not less than β for all $x \in \Omega$ and all $t > 1$.

Indeed, $|\varepsilon(x, t)| > \mathcal{E}$ with probability $1 - \beta$, but we have selected $H \geq 2\mathcal{E}$. To prove 2), let us define

$$\hat{\varepsilon}(x, t) = (1 - \alpha)\hat{\varepsilon}(x, t - 1) + \alpha\varepsilon(x, t), \quad t = 1, 2, \ldots \tag{6}$$

with the initial condition $\hat{\varepsilon}(x, 0) = \varepsilon(x, 0)$. Then, 2) follows by induction, since $|\varepsilon(x, t)| \leq \mathcal{E}$ with probability β.

Adaptation to Slow Background Changes. Property 1 means that the proposed procedure is able to estimate correctly any background that is constant in time. In Fig. 1 it is documented that it can also adapt to a slowly changing background. As one can notice, after about 12 frames proper tracking is obtained. More generally, the proposed background estimation scheme is able to track changes of the form n^γ for $0 < \gamma < 1$.

Immediate Change Detection of Large Jumps. By large changes we mean those for which $R > 4\mathcal{E}$. As we shall demonstrate, they can be detected immediately[1], i.e., at the first frame at which they occur.

Property 2. *If $R > 4\mathcal{E}$ and $H > 0$ is selected so that $2\mathcal{E} \leq H < R - 2\mathcal{E}$. Then the jump is detected immediately with probability at least β, at each site $x \in \Omega$ where it appears.*

The proof repeat steps in [15] with the exception that now errors are contained in $[-\mathcal{E}, \mathcal{E}]$ with probability β.

4   Parallel Implementation, Tuning the Decision Unit and Example

In this section we provide details of implementing and testing. Also details concerning a practical approach to tuning the decision unit are provided.

---

[1] For immediate detection it suffices to require $R > 3\mathcal{E}$ and to select H such that $\mathcal{E} \leq H < R - 2\mathcal{E}$, but selecting H only slightly above $\mathcal{E}$ and below $2\mathcal{E}$ increases the probability of false alarm above $1 - \beta$.

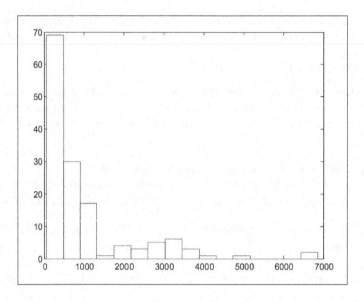

Fig. 4. Histogram of the number of pixels with defects detected on the copper slab – 142 subsequent frames, corresponding to about 20 sec. of the production process

4.1   Parallel Implementation and its Efficiency

The proposed change detector has been implemented in C/C++ using the following tools and packages: MS Visual Studio 2012, NVIDIA Nsight Visual Studio, CUDA Toolkit v5.5 and OpenCV v. 2.4.8 together with GPU module. The results of testing are shown in Fig. 3 for $\alpha = 0.3$, $H = 6.5$.

The mean execution times (obtained by averaging them from 30 frames, 1280 x 960) are shown in Tab. 1. GPU calculations have been run on NVidia GeForce GTX 760 2048 MB, while – for comparison – CPU time is provided for Intel Core i5-4690K 3.5 GHz. From the point of view of on-line quality control it is important that the parallel algorithm allows for the monitoring of about 45 fps, which is sufficient for moderately fast processes (assuming that a camera covers 0.5 meters along a production line movement, it allows to control a process that runs 22.5 m/sec.). On the other hand, mathematically the same algorithm when executed on a typical serial CPU allows the control of only rather slow processes with the rate 4.5 fps.

Table 1. Mean execution time of one frame on CPU (third column) and on GPU (second) which the sum of pure execution time using CUDA (first column) and the time for loading data to GPU memory and back to the CPU.

	CUDA	GPU	CPU
Time [sec.]	0.000047	0.022217	0.220965

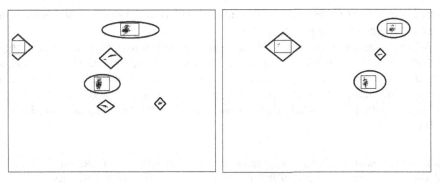

Fig. 5. Small groups of pixels to be removed – encircled by diamonds The same "pattern" of defects detected on two subsequent frames – marked by ellipses

4.2   Example

In continuous production processes (see [3]) any defects, having different grey levels than the proper surface, are easier to detect as moving objects.

In order to illustrate the theory, the parallel change detector has been applied to detect defects (darker places) on a bright (proper) surface of a hot copper slab continuously moving before a camera. Slow changes of the proper surface temperature make the task more difficult. Applying the proposed approach with $\alpha = 0.5$ and $H = 6$ grey levels (scale $[0, 255]$) provides the results shown in Fig. 2.

Almost the same number of changed pixels (3888 and 3847) have been detected at subsequent images, demonstrating the reliability of detection. In Fig. 3 one can also observe groups of bars with similar heights that correspond to the number of defects detected at subsequent frames. On the other hand, this figure indicates a good production quality, since the total number of pixels considered is 1280 x 960.

4.3   Tuning the Decision Unit

The above example is a convenient vehicle to discuss how to tune the decision unit (described in Section 2) in practice.

The first decision is based on the threshold θ_0 which indicates that the number of detected pixels is rather low and negligible. The mean number of detected pixels at subsequent frames (see Fig. 3) equals 980, but it is not a proper threshold because it includes also frames with a large number of defects. This is confirmed by a large dispersion that is equal to 1232 pixels and by the histogram in Fig. 4. A much better candidate for θ_0 is the median (510 marked pixels).

The next step is to remove small clusters of pixels. This step is illustrated in Fig. 5, where the blob analysis has been used. More advanced techniques, e.g., as those used in [5] for other purposes, can also be used at this stage. Notice that an additional factor in making decision as to whether a given cluster should be removed or not is its position at subsequent frames. Notice that the removed clusters (encircled) does not appear at the same positions at frames that follow a given frame. By contrast, clusters that have not been removed (inside elliptic contours), are also not very large, but they move with the constant speed of the production line.

When the number of remaining marked pixels is still large (larger than θ_1) and they are present in three or four subsequent frames (see Fig. 2), then an ALARM state is declared. The analysis of Fig. 4 indicates that $\theta_1 = 3400$ is a good choice, because it is a local maximum of the histogram, taking into account that 1000 of marked pixels amounts to about 0.1% of all pixels. In practice, $\theta_1 = 3400$ as the alarm threshold is still too low.

Acknowledgements.. This paper was supported by the National Council for Research of the Polish Government under grant 2012/07/B/ST7/01216, internal code 350914 of Wrocław University of Technology.

References

1. Davies, E.R.: Machine Vision: Theory, Algorithms, Practicalities. Morgan Kaufmann (2005)
2. Gaetan, C., Guyon, X.: Spatial Statistics and Modeling. Springer, Berlin (2010)
3. Garcia Rube, D.F., et al.: Shape Inspection System for Variable-Luminance Steel Plates with Real-Time Adaptation Capabilities to Luminance Variations. Real-Time Imaging 8, 303–315 (2002)
4. Hima, E.P.: Video Objects Detection Using Spatial and Temporal Segmentation. International Journal of Science and Research 2(7) (July 2013)
5. Karimi, B., Krzyżak, A.: A novel approach for automatic detection and classification of suspicious lesions in breast ultrasound images. Journal of Artificial Intelligence and Soft Computing 3(3), 265–276 (2013)
6. Malamasa, E.N., et al.: A survey on industrial vision systems, applications and tools. Image and Vision Computing 21, 171–188 (2003)
7. Megahed, F.M., Woodall, W.H., Camelio, J.A.: A review and perspective on control charting with image data. Journal of Quality Technology 43(2), 83–98 (2011)
8. Montgomery, D.C.: Introduction to Statistical Quality Control. Wiley, New York (1996)
9. Panigrahi, N., Mohan, B.K., Athithan, G.: Differential Geometric Approach to Change Detection Using Remotely Sensed Images. Journal of Advances In Information Technology 2(3), 134–138 (2011)
10. Pawlak, M., Rafajłowicz, E., Steland, A.: On detecting jumps in time series: nonparametric setting. Journal of Nonparametric Statistics 16(3/4), 329–347 (2004)
11. Pepelyshev, A., Rafajłowicz, E., Steland, A.: Estimation of the quantile function using Bernstein-Durrmeyer polynomials. Journal of Nonparametric Statistics, 1–20 (2013)
12. Prause, A., Steland, A.: Detecting changes in spatial-temporal image data based on quadratic forms. In: Steland, A., Rafajłowicz, E., Szajowski, K. (eds.) Stochastic Models, Statistics and Their Applications. Springer Proceedings in Mathematics & Statistics, vol. 122, pp. 122–130. Springer, Berlin (2015)
13. Rafajłowicz, E.: SUSAN edge detector reinterpreted, simplified and modified. In: International Workshop on Multidimensional (nD) Systems, Aveiro, Portugal, pp. 69–74 (2007)
14. Rafajłowicz, E., Pawlak, M., Steland, A.: Nonparametric sequential change-point detection by a vertically-trimmed box method. IEEE Transactions on Information Theory 56(7), 3621–3634 (2010)

15. Rafajłowicz, E.: Detection of essential changes in spatio-temporal processes with applications to camera based quality control. In: Steland, A., Rafajłowicz, E., Szajowski, K. (eds.) Stochastic Models, Statistics and Their Applications. Springer Proceedings in Mathematics & Statistics, vol. 122, pp. 382–389. Springer, Berlin (2015)
16. Ristivojevic, M., Konrad, J.: Space-Time Image Sequence Analysis: Object Tunnels and Occlusion Volumes. IEEE Transactions on Image Processing 15(2), 364–376 (2006)
17. Skubalska-Rafajłowicz, E.: Change-point detection of mean vector with fewer observations than the dimension using instantaneous normal random projections. In: Steland, A., Rafajłowicz, E., Szajowski, K. (eds.) Stochastic Models, Statistics and Their Applications. Springer Proceedings in Mathematics & Statistics, vol. 122, pp. 154–161. Springer, Berlin (2015)

A Fuzzy Logic Approach for Gender Recognition from Face Images with Embedded Bandlets

Zain Shabbir[1], Absar Ullah Khan[1], Aun Irtaza[2],
and Muhammad Tariq Mahmood[3]([✉])

[1] Department of Electrical Engineering,
University of Engineering and Technology, Taxila, Pakistan
zain07.uet@gmail.com, absar.ullah@hotmail.com
[2] Department of Computer Science,
University of Engineering and Technology, Taxila, Pakistan
aun.irtaza@uettaxila.edu.pk
[3] School of Computer Science and Engineering,
Korea University of Technology and Education, Cheonan, Korea
tariq@koreatech.ac.kr

Abstract. In this paper we have proposed a gender recognition system through facial images. We have used three different techniques that involve Bandlet Trans-form (a multi-resolution technique), LBP (Local Binary Pattern) and mean to create the feature vectors of the images. To classify the images for gender, we have used fuzzy c mean clustering. SUMS and FERET databases were used for testing. Experimental results have shown that the maximum average accuracy was achieved using SUMS, 97.1% has been achieved using Band-lets and mean technique, Bandlets and whole image LBP has shown 85.13% and Bandlets with blocked based LBP has shown 87.02% average accuracy.

Keywords: Bandlet · Gender recognition · LBP · Fuzzy c-mean · Multi-resolution

1 Introduction

One of the most important information gathered from faces is gender, moreover an efficient gender classification technique can significantly increase the performance of different applications that include efficient human to machine inter-face system, person recognition. It can also be used for several commercial and law enforcement applications. Gender recognition is also vital as a prior step to facial recognition [1]. Gender recognition is actually a common job for human beings. Despite of this, the accuracy to recognize gender for human being can decrease surprisingly in particular situations, an online gender recognition test [1] results that the accuracy to recognize gender is just 74%.

Algorithms for gender recognition systems generally involve whole body information but there are certain scenarios in which whole information is not available or in case camera is so close that just face is captured, in such cases algorithm

© Springer International Publishing Switzerland 2015
L. Rutkowski et al. (Eds.): ICAISC 2015, Part I, LNAI 9119, pp. 626–637, 2015.
DOI: 10.1007/978-3-319-19324-3_56

is designed that does gender recognition by just using information from faces. In the recent times, a lot of research has been started in biometrics, specifically in facial recognition systems [3] because of the increased computational power of recent computers. This advancement is also leading research in gender recognition system that is a specific domain of facial recognition systems. In facial recognition systems there are generally three basic parts: source, feature extraction, and classification as shown in Fig. 1. In case of gender recognition source is images from the data set, second step is feature extraction, this process is applied on each and every image from the data set and the last step is the classifier that classifies the gender on the basis of features.

In literature, many methods have been proposed for gender recognition using facial information. Different techniques involve LBP[4], Support Vector Machines (SVM)[5], Weber Local Descriptor (WLD)[6], Discrete Wavelet Transform (DWT)[7], Principal Component Analysis (PCA)[8] and Interlaced Derivative Pattern (IDP)[9]. Some techniques also involve the combination of two techniques to improve the results. Different databases are available and used for classification.

Fig. 1. A general scheme for facial recognition systems

In this paper we are using three combined approaches that use (Bandlets + LBP), (Bandlets + block based LBP) and the third approach is (Bandlets + mean) for the feature extraction purpose and after that fuzzy c mean clustering is used for the classification of gender. Bandlets is the technique that uses multiresolution features of images because image contains many geometric structures that carry different information, these geometric structures can be used to improve the representation of image. Wavelet transform is one of the techniques that can be used for geometric representation but it lacks where it comes sharp transitions in images and these transitions are well handled by Bandlets. We represent image with geometric flow of vectors using Bandlets approach, if the image has regular variations these vectors provide the local directions. These orthogonal Bandlets bases are created by sub dividing image into the blocks where the geometric flow is parallel. Experimental results demonstrate the effectiveness of the proposed approach.

The rest of the paper has been arranged as follows. Section 2 discusses the Proposed Approach, Section 3 includes the Experimental Results, Section 4 covers Discussion and Future Work while Section 5 concludes the discussion.

2   Proposed Approach

There are three main steps in our system for gender recognition. First one is data acquisition, the second one is making features with three techniques and third one is categorization of the facial images with respect to the gender. Block diagram of all the three schemes proposed is shown in Fig. 2. The first technique involves the Bandletization of the facial images from the data set and then LBP is applied on that Bandletized image for feature vector creation. In 2nd technique, first the input image is decomposed into several sub-bands of different scales, each sub-band is then divided into blocks and then LBP is applied on that, afterwards LBP histogram is extracted from each block of sub-band and these histograms are used to create a feature vector of the image.

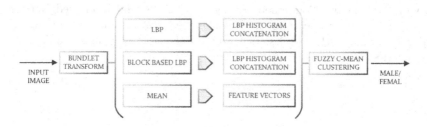

Fig. 2. Block diagram of proposed schemes

The Bandlet basis are created using Wavelet basis which are enveloped along the flow of the geometry as shown in Fig. 3, which helps in taking advantage of the image regularity. There are certain conditions that are applied on the geometry to obtain orthonormal Bandlet basis. When applying Bandlet transform, the image is divided into different square blocks with varying resolution. In each block (Ω_i) there must be at least one contour specifying the edge in that block within the flow of the geometry. If there is no contour in that block it means that image intensity is regular and uniformly distributed in that block, when we compute Wavelet basis and approximate those basis in $L^2(\Omega)$ domain, Bandlet basis are computed.

$$
\begin{cases}
\phi_{j,m}(x) = \phi_{j,m1}(x1)\,\phi_{j,m2}(x2) \\
\psi_{j,m}^{H}(x) = \phi_{j,m1}(x1)\,\psi_{j,m2}(x2) \\
\psi_{j,m}^{V}(x) = \psi_{j,m1}(x1)\,\phi_{j,m2}(x2) \\
\psi_{j,m}^{D}(x) = \psi_{j,m1}(x1)\,\psi_{j,m2}(x2)
\end{cases}
\tag{1}
$$

where $(j, m1, m2) \in I_\Omega$. In the above Equation, I_Ω shows the index geometry set of the block Ω, $\phi_{j,m}(x)$ is the rough scale calculation, $\psi_{j,m}^{H}(x)$ denotes high horizontal frequency, $(j, m)^{V}(x)$ denotes high vertical frequency, $(j, m)^{D}(x)$ denotes high diagonal frequency coefficients that are decomposed by Discrete Wavelet transform. Wavelets transform $\psi(t)$ with expansion j and translation

k is calculated by taking product of elementary orthogonal operators and the result is produced as follows.

$$\psi_{j,k}(t) = 2^{\frac{-j}{2}} \psi\left(2^{-j}t - k\right).$$ (2)

$$\phi_{j,k}(t) = 2^{\frac{-j}{2}} \psi\left(2^{-j}t - k\right).$$ (3)

In order to compute Bandlet orthonormal basis in geometric flow of region Ω using the expression (1), wavelet basis will be replaced as follows.

$$\left\{ \begin{array}{l} \phi_{j,m}(x) = \phi_{j,m1}(x1)\,\phi_{j,m2}(x2 - c(x1)) \\ \psi^{H}_{j,m}(x) = \phi_{j,m1}(x1)\,\psi_{j,m2}(x2 - c(x1)) \\ \psi^{V}_{j,m}(x) = \psi_{j,m1}(x1)\,\phi_{j,m2}(x2 - c(x1)) \\ \psi^{D}_{j,m}(x) = \psi_{j,m1}(x1)\,\psi_{j,m2}(x2 - c(x1)) \end{array} \right\}$$ (4)

where $j, m > j, m1, m2$. In the above equation $c(x)$ is defined as the flow line of the geometry changes of the translation parameter that changes with the geometry change and it is expressed as

$$c(x) = \int_{\min x}^{x} c(u)du$$ (5)

It has also been observed that the size of the division that we use while dividing the image affects the direction of geometric vector flow, if we use smaller block size then Bandlet function can accurately define the edges available in that block. The change in edges with the variation in number of blocks can be observed in the Fig. 4. It can be seen that when we use smaller block size the number of blocks increases which results in large number of edges and the geometry flow is smooth while when we increase the block size it decreases the number of blocks in the image and that results in reduced number of edges which results in slightly coarse image representation.

Fig. 3. Bandlet segmentation in which each arrow is showing the flow of the vector in each region. (Source: IEEE Transaction on Image Processing, Vol:14, p:426

After the Bandlets have been implemented on our data set images, the next step that comes is the implementation of LBP for the extraction of feature vectors from the Bandletized images. LBP is a very well-known technique that is

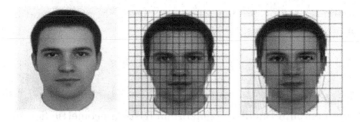

Fig. 4. Representation of geometric flow with different block sizes (a) original image, (b) 4x4 small block size, (c) 8x8 large block size. (Source: Face Image from faceresearch.org)

used as local texture descriptor to describe faces. LBP is very efficient technique due to its stability to monotonic changes in grey level, its efficiency of computation and its distinction power. While implementing LBP, a 3x3 window is created and a threshold is created with reference to the center pixel, now each value in the 3x3 window is compared with the center value. If the value is greater than the center value, the value is converted to '1' and if it is less than the center threshold value, the value is converted to '0'. Then the value is converted into the decimal in order starting from the top right most value as shown in Fig. 5. A histogram at each block is created and every histogram is concatenated afterwards, then this concatenated histogram is used as a texture descriptor. If there are different scales in images, a neighborhood approach is used in LBP. In this case an R radius circle is drawn from the center pixel and P sample points are taken from the edge of the circles then bilinear interpolation is performed to obtain the value of the sampled points P in the circle. (P, R) term is used to represent the neighborhood notation. Fig. 6 shows the neighborhood approach for different values of P and R.

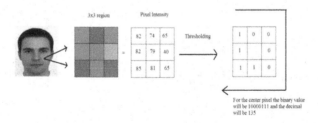

Fig. 5. Basic LBP operation (Source: IEEE 20th IWSSIP 2013, p:60)

Let us take the coordinates of the center pixel as (xc, yc) then the coordinates of the neighbors (xp, yp) can be measured by using Equations (7) and (8).

$$x_p = x_c + Rcos\left(\frac{2\pi p}{P}\right) \tag{6}$$

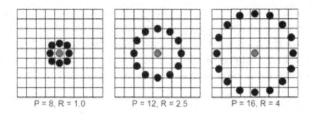

Fig. 6. Circular neighbour for three values of P and R

$$y_p = y_c + Rsin\left(\frac{2\pi p}{P}\right) \tag{7}$$

Now lets assume if the gray value of the center pixel is gc and gray value of the pixel in the neighbour is gp with the value of P ranging in between 0, P-1 then pattern A in the local neighbourhood of the pixel (xc, yc) can be defined as:

$$A = t\left(g_c, g_0, \ldots, g_{p-1}\right) \tag{8}$$

Once we are able to create the LBP for every pixel in the image then feature vectors are constructed. The above mentioned method implies the implementation of the LBP on the entire image. Our second approach is to efficiently extract the features while applying LBP on the image divided in k blocks, after that histogram is calculated on each block and then these histograms are concatenated, the complete process is shown in Fig. 7.

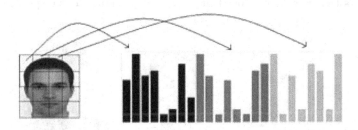

Fig. 7. Block based LBP approach (Source: Face Recognition with Local Binary Patterns, Bachelor Assignment, p:14)

Our third approach for feature extraction includes the calculation of mean on the Bandletized images as Bandlet transformed images provide the contours where there are edges, so in order to efficiently create features we used this statistical approach to distinguish between male and female images using facial specifications. After obtaining the feature vectors, next step is to classify the images by using those feature vectors, we have used fuzzy c mean clustering for the classification of the images. In fuzzy clustering each point of the feature vectors has a chance of association to any cluster instead of belonging to just single cluster, so the points at edges can belong to the cluster of less degree instead of belonging to the centre one. Fuzzy c-mean algorithm is based on the optimization of the basic c-mean cost function formulated by Bezdek and Dunn which is given below:

$$J(Z;U,V) = \sum_{i=1}^{c} \sum_{k=1}^{N} (\mu_{ik})^m \|z_k - v_i\|_A^2 \tag{9}$$

where $U = [\mu_{ik}] \in M_{fc}$ is known as the fuzzy partition matrix of Z, $V = [v_1, v_2, ..., v_c]$ is defined as the cluster centers vector, which we have to determine, $D^2_{ikA} = \|z_k - v_i\|_A^2 = (z_k - v_i)^T A (z_k - v_i)$ is defined as the square inner product distance normal and $m \in [1, \infty)$ is a parameter used to determine the resulting cluster fuzziness. The cost function actually shows the variance of zk from vi. In fuzzy c mean clustering, any point has coefficients that describe the degree of that point belonging to certain cluster. By using fuzzy c mean clustering the centre of the cluster is obtained by calculating the mean of all the points. And then distance is measured with each centre vector to the image feature vector, after that each image is assigned a cluster, in our case as we are classifying gender, there will be 2 clusters, one for male and other for female. Equation 10 rep-resents the centre of each cluster.

$$c_k = \frac{\sum x w_k(x)^m x}{\sum x w_k(x)^m} \tag{10}$$

A point x has different set of coefficients that give the degree of being in the kth cluster wk(x). By using fuzzy c-means, the centroid of a cluster is the mean of all points that is weighted by their degree of belonging to the specific cluster.

Fig. 8. Original and Transformed images (Source: Face Images from SUMS Database)

3 Experiments and results

For experiment, we selected three different tests to perform. We have used SUMS and FERET databases in our experiment. SUMS database contains 400 images, out of which 200 are male and 200 are female, each of 200 x 200 resolution. All images are of good quality and are grayscale. Images have different poses and varying facial expressions. Images also contain people of different ages, with and without hair, with and without glasses and having differ-ent ethnic backgrounds. While FERET has 1564 set of images.

As we have performed 3 different tests which are Bandlet + mean, Bandlet + LBP on whole image, Bandlet + block based LBP, so, results of these ex-periments have been compared with previous techniques. Features have been extracted based on these techniques. In first experiment, we have applied Ban-dlet Trans-form on all images of database then these Bandlet transformed images were subtracted from original images. These difference images have been divided into different size blocks. In this experiment 8x8, 4x4 and 2x2 blocks have been made. When image is divided into 64 blocks, mean is calculated on each block. Hence, each block corresponds to a mean value. Blocks on black portion cor-respond to zero mean value while blocks corresponding to edges result in some non-zero value. Similarly mean values are calculated when image is divided into 8 and 4 blocks. These 64 mean values from 64 blocks, 16 mean values from 16 blocks and 4 mean values from 4 blocks are concatenated to make 84 entities feature vector of the image. Feature vectors of all the images from the database are generated and stored in a matrix. Fuzzy c-mean clustering is applied on these feature vectors using 2 clusters and results are achieved. 97.1% average accuracy was achieved in this experiment when SUMS database was used and 93.3% aver-age accuracy was achieved when FERET was used. A set of original images and Bandlet transformed images have been shown in Fig. 8.

In 2nd experiment, Bandlets and LBP on whole image (taking as a single block) are used to form feature vectors. In this case total no. of entities in the feature vector were 256. After forming feature vector matrix, fuzzy c-mean clus-tering was applied using 2 clusters. Average accuracy achieved in this ex-periment was 85.13% and 81.01% when SUMS and FERET databases were used respectively.

In our 3rd experiment, same Bandlet transformed images were obtained but these transformed images were divided into blocks and LBP was applied on each block, after combining LBP histogram of each block, feature vector was formed. The length of feature vector was 16384 when 64 blocks were formed and aver-age accuracy of the experiment was 87.02% when SUMS database was used and 84.3% average accuracy was achieved when FERET was used. In these experi-ments whole database was our test set. In the work of [21] ,they has compared different techniques for gender recognition, our results compared with previ-ous techniques have also been tabulated in Table 1. It has been observed that experiment 1, in which we used Bandlet and mean, gives more accurate results than Bandlet + LBP and Bandlet + Block based LBP. When our first technique was compared with previously proposed techniques such as SVM, Threshold Adaboost, LUT Adaboost, Mean Adaboost, LBP+SVM, PCA (com-pared in [20]), gives more accurate results. The comparison has been shown in Figures 9 and 10.

4   Discussion and Future Work

In our experiments, we have used face database as it is without any pre-processing. While in [20], authors first perform face detection algorithm on the whole database and discard those images which are not detected by the algorithm. After perform-ing face detection, gender recognition techniques are applied which results in more accurate results. So, in future our achieved results can be more improved by pre-processing steps that is by 1st applying face detection algorithm on the database and discarding those images which are not detected by the algorithm and then applying the proposed (Bandlet + mean) technique.

Table 1. comparison

Methods	Feature Extraction	Classifier Used	Test Database	Average Accuracy (%)
Lee [10]	Regression function	SVM	WEB Images	81.1
Demirkus [11]	SIFT	Bayesian	Video Sequence	90
Li [12]	DCT Spatial	GMM	YGA	92.5
Aghajanian [13]	Patchbased	Bayesian	Web images	89
Xu [14]	Haar-like fiducial distances	SVM-RBF 5-CV	92.38	
Makinen [15]	Various - pixels, LBPH,Haar-like	Mix	FERET web images	92.86/83.14
Lian [16]	LBP histogram	SVM polynomial	CAS-PEAL	94.08
Baluja [17]	Pixel comp.	SVM	5-CV	93.5
Buchala [18]	PCA SVM RBF	5-CV	92.25	
Shakhnarovich [19]	Haar-like	Adaboost	5-CV Video seqs.	79,90
ErnoMkinen [20]	LBP	Neural Network	FERET	91.11
ErnoMkinen [20]	LBP	SVM	FERET	73.88
ErnoMkinen [20]	LBP	SVM	WWW	76.01
ours 1	Bandlet+ mean	Fuzzy c-mean	SUMS/FERET	97.1/93.3
ours 2	Bandlet+ LBP whole	Fuzzy c-mean	SUMS/FERET	85.13/81.01
ours 3	Bandlet+ Blocked LBP	Fuzzy c-mean	SUMS/FERET	87.02/84.3

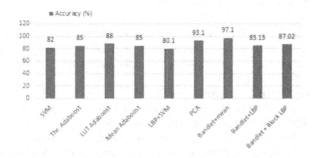

Fig. 9. Comparison graph when SUMS database was used

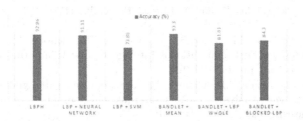

Fig. 10. Comparison graph when SUMS database was used

5 Conclusion

In this paper. we have proposed Bandlet transform based three method for gender classification. We carried out 3 different experiments for gender recognition which are: (Band-let + mean), (Bandlet + LBP whole image), (Bandlet + Blocked LBP) and then we observed that 1st technique (Bandlet + mean) gives the best result among these. When this technique was compared with previously renowned techniques, the proposed technique was also more efficient. The maximum average accuracy achieved was 97.1%.

Acknowledgements. This research was supported by Basic Science Research Program through the National Research Foundation (NRF) Korea funded by the Ministry of Science, ICT & Future Planning (MSIP)(2013-R1A1A2-008180).

References

1. Ullah, I., Hussain, M., Muhammad, G., Aboalsamh, H., Bebis, G., Mirza, A.: Gender Recognition from Faces Using Bandlet and Local Binary Patterns. In: 20th International Conference on Systems, Signals and Image Processing (IWSSIP), Bucharest, pp. 59–62 (2013)
2. Test my Brain, http://www.testmybrain.org
3. Faundez-Zanuy, M.: On the vulnerability of biometric security systems. IEEE Aerospace Electron. System Mag. 1996, 3–8 (2004)
4. Ahonen, T., Hadid, A., Pietikäinen, M.: Face Description with Local Binary Patterns: Application to Face Recognition. IEEE Trans. Pattern Analysis and Machine Intelligence 28(12), 2037–2041 (2006)
5. Zang, J., Lu, B.L.: A support vector machine classifier with automatic confidence and its application to gender classification. Neurocomputing 74, 1926–1935 (2011)
6. Ullah, I., Hussain, M., Muhammad, G., Aboalsamh, H., Bebis, G., Mirza, A.: Gender recognition from face images with local WLD descriptor. In: 19th International Conference on Systems, Signals and Image Processing (IWSSIP), Vienna, pp. 417–420 (2012)
7. Ozbudak, O., Tukel, M., Seker, S.: Fast Gender Classification. In: IEEE International Conference on Computational Intelligence and Computing Research (IC-CIC), Coimbatore, pp. 1–5 (2010)
8. Kekre, H.B., Thepade, S.D., Chopra, T.: Face and Gender Recognition Using Principal Component Analysis. (IJCSE) International Journal on Computer Science and Engineering 02(04), 959–964 (2010)
9. Shobeirinejad, A., Gao, Y.: Gender Classification Using Interlaced Derivative Patterns. In: 20th International Conference on Pattern Recognition (ICPR 2010), Brisbane, pp. 1509–1512 (2010)
10. Lee, P.H., Hung, J.Y., Hung, Y.P.: Automatic Gender Recognition Using Fusion of Facial Strips. In: 2010 20th International Conference on Pattern Recognition (ICPR), pp. 1140–1143 (2010)
11. Demirkus, M., Toews, M., Clark, J.J., Arbel, T.: Gender classification from unconstrained video sequences. In: 2010 IEEE Computer Society Conference on Computer Vision and Pattern Recognition Workshops (CVPRW), pp. 55–62 (2010)
12. Li, Z., Zhou, X.: Spatial gaussian mixture model for gender recognition. In: 2009 16th IEEE International Conference on Image Processing (ICIP), pp. 45–48 (2009); Rai, P., Khanna, P.: Gender classification using Radon and Wavelet Transforms. In: 2010 International Conference on Industrial and Information Systems (ICIIS), pp. 448–451 (2010)
13. Aghajanian, J., Warrell, J., Prince, S.J.D., Rohn, J.L., Baum, B.: Patch-based within object classification. In: 2009 IEEE 12th International Conference on Computer Vision, pp. 1125–1132 (2009)
14. Xu, Z., Lu, L., Shi, P.: A hybrid approach to gender classification from face images. In: 19th International Conference on Pattern Recognition, ICPR 2008, pp. 1–4 (2008)
15. Mäkinen, E., Raisamo, R.: An experimental comparison of gender classification methods. Pattern Recognition Letters 29(10), 1544–1556 (2008)
16. Lian, H.-C., Lu, B.-L.: Multi-view gender classification using local binary patterns and support vector machines. In: Wang, J., Yi, Z., Żurada, J.M., Lu, B.-L., Yin, H. (eds.) ISNN 2006. LNCS, vol. 3972, pp. 202–209. Springer, Heidelberg (2006)

17. Baluja, S., Rowley, H.A.: Boosting sex identification performance. International Journal of Computer Vision 71(1), 111–119 (2007)
18. Buchala, S., Loomes, M.J., Davey, N., Frank, R.J.: The role of global and feature based information in gender classification of faces: a comparison of human performance and computational models. International Journal of Neural Systems 15, 121–128 (2005)
19. Shakhnarovich, G., Viola, P., Moghaddam, B.: A unified learning framework for real time face detection and classification. In: Proceedings of Fifth IEEE International Conference on Automatic Face Gesture Recognition, pp. 16–23 (2002)
20. Mäkinen, E., Raisamo, R.: An Experimental Comparison of Gender Classification Methods. Pattern Recognition Letters 29(10), 1544–1556 (2008)
21. Boon Ng, C., HaurTay, Y., Goi, B.M.: Vision-based Human Gender Recognition: A Survey, ArXiv e-prints (April 2012)

Interpretation of Image Segmentation in Terms of Justifiable Granularity

Piotr S. Szczepaniak[(✉)]

Institute of Information Technology, Lodz University of Technology,
ul. Wólczańska 215, 90-924 Lodz, Poland
piotr.szczepaniak@p.lodz.pl

Abstract. The principle of justifiable granularity, as formulated in [1], defines intuitively motivated requirements for an information granule to be meaningful. In the paper, granulation of images obtained by their segmentation is considered. In this context, such concepts as representation of granules and their relations, representation of concepts, consideration of context, detection and treatment of outliers, and recognition method, are of importance. The granular approach is related to intelligent analysis of all kinds of data, not only the computer images.

Keywords: Image segmentation · Justifiable granularity · Patch approach · Active hypercontour

1 Introduction

The term 'granule' is understood as a group, cluster, or class of clusters in a universe of discourse. Within the 'granular computing', theory, methodologies and techniques which deal with processing of information granules are conceptually located [2], [3]. Usually, granulation of information is considered when intelligent analysis of numerical data is performed, and the discussion is related to the task of proximity-based fuzzy clustering, e.g. [1], [4]. However, in a natural way one links the semantics of the term 'granulation' with the detection of segments on computer images. The literature on image segmentation is very rich, with a diversity of approaches [5].

In this paper, we do not aim at a survey of segmentation methods, as well as not at survey of data clustering methods. We concentrate at the issue of definition of information granularity levels (section 2) which can be formulated for parametrized image segmentation (section 3) and we relate those problems to pattern recognition mechanism (section 4) which benefits from the results of basic data (image) analysis. The contents of the paper is completed by consideration of outliers in terms of the concept of information granularity (section 5).

2 Information Granularity in Images

Real images are composed of patches, which are regions of diverse shapes. To form each shape, we assign to it certain information, or meaning. Computer

© Springer International Publishing Switzerland 2015
L. Rutkowski et al. (Eds.): ICAISC 2015, Part I, LNAI 9119, pp. 638–648, 2015.
DOI: 10.1007/978-3-319-19324-3_57

images are collections of pixels. The standard task in image analysis is segmentation - the search for regions that are similar in terms of color, texture, or other feature. Segmentation results may strongly differ from each other, even if the same method is applied, but with different parameters.

Depending on the segmentation method

    a) one interprets the obtained form of shape;

    b) one performs the search for predefined shapes of segments.

Segmentation is in fact a kind of information granulation, which can be performed on diverse levels.

    Assuming that pixels create the *zero level* and that one aims at forming groups of pixels, according to their gray level, we can say that the vector composed of pixel coordinates and the value of its gray level is the *zero level* information $[x_i, y_i, g_i]$ (Fig. 1 a).

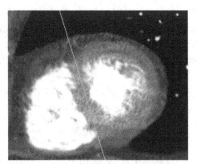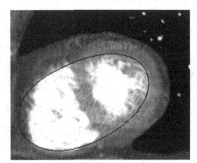

a) *zero level*; *j*=0   b) (*j* + *1*)-th level
original image – heart   jointly segmented both ventricles

Fig. 1. Example of medical image analysis

It is easy to presume that the search jointly for two ventricles in one stage of the method applied was performed using both, the *zero level* information and external (expert) information about the expected form of the shape to be found on the original image (Fig. 1). Neglecting the external shape information, one would accept the pixels, which lie along the white line in Fig. 1, a) between the ventricles and are similar to those which constitute the background; in consequence, the desired result would not be achieved.

    Technically, the original pixel space is transformed by the segmentation method into a smaller collection of segments, which can be interpreted as granules of the 1st level, leaving aside whether the granulated image thus obtained is more informative than the original one or not. It is also possible to group the smaller segments into a 2nd level of elements, according to the degree of their proximity. For example, the semantic graphs can be created, or simple clustering like k-NN can be performed, depending on the goal of image analysis and interpretation.

3   Parametrized Segmentation and Justifiable Granularity

A lot of methods of low-level image segmentation have been developed. Some of them can operate on higher than *zero level* of granulation For example, the two- or multi-layer Kohonen neural network [6], [7]. Frequently, low-level methods can not perform image content interpretation because the direct incorporation of expert knowledge is impossible.

Originally, *active contour* methods, e.g. [8], [9], [10], [11], were also developed as tools for a low-level image segmentation. The main idea of this approach is to find an optimal contour in the space of considered contours representing (surrounding) certain region in the image (Fig. 1 b). The search is performed in an evolution process (optimization) in which the given objective function, called energy, evaluates the quality of a contour. Usually, the energy function is composed of two components, namely *internal* and *external*, which express the demands to the shape of contour and features of the ground, respectively. Because of the internal part of the energy, contours provide the ability to use the high-level information.

Moreover, contours are contextual classifiers of pixels (a part of pixels belongs to the interior and another one - to the exterior of a given contour), but *active* contours are also methods of *optimal construction of classifiers* [12], [13]. For advanced forms of active contours, namely Cognitive Hierarchical Active Partitions - CHAP, see [14], [15], [16] and [17].

Segmentation methods are usually controlled by a set of parameters:

pixel space → parametrized granulation → space of contours (segments)

The mentioned active contours are good examples of that kind of contour (classifier) representation. Here, just two methods are briefly presented: snakes [9] and *potential active hypercontours* [11], [13].

Snakes [9]
The parametric form of continuous snake contour $c\,(s)$ is defined as follows

$$c \in F\left(\,[\,a,b\,]\,,\, R^2\right) \tag{1}$$

where
s - parameter, $a \leq s \leq b$;
$x \in F\left(\,[\,a,b\,]\,,\, R\,\right)$ and $y \in F\left(\,[\,a,b\,]\,,\, R\,\right)$.

Usually, the contour is differentiable and closed, i.e. $c\,(a) = c\,(b)$. Moreover, it does not intersects own curve – Fig. 2. Uneven distribution of parameter s is allowed. In this way, the space C of contours $c\,(s)$ determines the space of admissible image segments which can be found on the image. The contour is a classifier, which distinguishes between object (segment) and background.

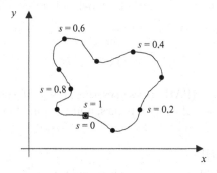

Fig. 2. Example of snake; here $a = 0$, $b = 1$

Potential active hypercontours (PAH) are an implementation of *active hypercontours* introduced in [12]; see also [11], [13].

Let X – called feature space – be a metric space with metric $\rho : X \times X$.

The potential hypercontour h is determined by set D^c of labelled control points x_i^c and potential functions assigned to them: P_i^c, $i = 1, 2, \ldots, N^c$ (Fig. 3).

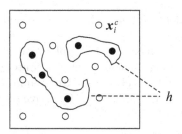

Fig. 3. Hypercontour h composed by two contours and determined by control points $\{\bullet, \circ\}$

Each control point x_i^c is a source of potential P_i^c. The frequently used forms are:

– exponential $\qquad\qquad P_i^c = \Psi_i \, exp \left(-\mu_i \, \rho^2 (x_i^c, x) \right)$

– inverse $\qquad\qquad P_i^c = \dfrac{\Psi_i}{1 + \mu_i \, \rho^2 (x_i^c, x)}$

where real numbers Ψ_i and μ_i are parameters characterizing the potential field of each control point. The value of P_i^c decreases with the distance. Note that the number of control points, their distribution and field parameters fully determine the shape of the contour.

Since each control point is labelled, i.e. one disposes of pairs (x_i^c, l_i^c) then h is in fact a classifier and it can be formally defined as follows:

$$C(x) = arg \max_{l \in L} \sum_v^a P_i^c(x_i^c, x) \, \delta(l_i^c, l)$$

where L is set of labels, l_i^c, l denote labels of x_i^c and the examined one, respectively, while

$$\delta = \begin{cases} 0 & for \ l \neq l_i^c \\ 1 & for \ l = l_i^c \end{cases}.$$

Potential active contour (PAH) possesses the ability of *evolution*, in line with the change of the location of control points, and with modification of parameters of potential functions.

Justifiable Granularity

The principle of justifiable granularity, as formulated in [1], defines the intuitively motivated requirements for an information granule to be considered meaningful:

a) *Experimental evidence.* The numeric evidence accumulated within the bounds of the granule considered has to be as *high* as possible. It should reflect as big amount of data as possible to make the data set legitimate.

b) *Well-articulated semantics.* At the same time, the granule should be as specific as possible. It should carry a well-defined semantics (meaning). The agreement with our perception of knowledge about the problem is desired.

Since these two requirements are in conflict, the method of finding a compromise is of practical importance.

In the granulation performed by the application of the active contour approach, the vehicle for finding the compromise is contour optimization. However, in contrary to the above intuitively formulated requirements a) and b), the demands for justifiable granularity generated by active contours are more objective and they can be termed as:

(a) *attribution,*   (b) *evidence,*   (c) *specification.*

They are respectively related to: (a) the features of the contour like elasticity and rigidity, (b) the environment in which the contour operates (image background), and (c) our expectations to the final shape of the contour being the result of automatic image analysis (the knowledge about the object searched).

Optimization of the Contour

The quality of contours generated by a given method (snake, potential, and others) is evaluated during the execution of the method. In general, three elements (features) are considered and evaluated:

- current contour shape features - represented and evaluated by the value of E_{int} called *internal energy*; *attribution*;
- features of the background (image) and position of the contour on the image - image energy E_{img}; *evidence*;
- external knowledge or (user) demands related to contour - constraint energy E_{con}; *specification*.

The general objective function E (called energy) used for evaluation of the contour is usually of the form:

$$E = E_{int} + E_{img} + E_{con} = E_{int} + E_{ext}'$$

where external energy $E_{ext} = E_{img} + E_{con}$. The classic internal energy is of the form [9]:

$$E_{ext} = \int_0^1 \frac{\alpha(s) \mid v'(s) \mid^2 + \beta(s) \mid v''(s) \mid^2}{2} \, ds$$

where:

$s \in [\, 0, 1 \,]$ – position of the point on the contour,

$v(s) = x(s), y(s)$ – coordinates of the considered point,

$\alpha \in [\, 0, 1 \,]$ – elasticity parameter,

$\beta \in [\, 0, 1 \,]$ – rigidity parameter.

To sum up, the search for optimal hypercontour is performed by optimization of performance index E called *energy*

$$E : H \to R^+ \cup \{\, 0 \,\} \text{ with } H \text{ being the space of all available hypercontours.}$$

It has been proven in [12] that each hypercontour generates the corresponding classification function. This statement is true if the space X is metric. In E almost any type of information can be used assuming that we are able to implement this information in a computer oriented form, such as mathematical formula, output of neural network, output of fuzzy system, etc. We can also decide if the classification is *supervised* or *unsupervised*, with the former being more intuitive. The idea of using expert opinion was proposed in the unsupervised classification problem [19] where expert estimated the proximity between pairs of objects from the training set.

The search for the optimal hypercontour may be conducted in many ways, e.g. by the use of simulated annealing or genetic algorithm, both of which perform a global search without using gradient.

Another interesting and powerful mechanism is *adaptation*. Discrimination ability of the given hypercontour is limited and it depends on the number of control points (assuming that other parameters are fixed). The flexibility of the potential active hypercontours (PAH) can be improved if we incorporate the change of the number of control points into the optimization procedure. The rate of misclassification in some areas of space X can be the reason for introducing a number of new control points (*local tuning* is possible).

4 Pattern Recognition

In Section 2, we defined the *zero level* information as vectors whose elements are pixel coordinates and the value of gray level. On the pixel image, applying a low-level method, a set of elements of higher granularity can be detected. Consequently, the search for *second level* information can be performed. For

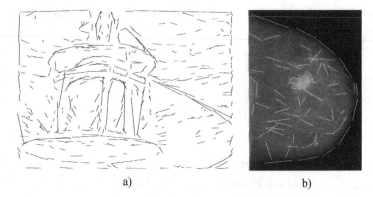

Fig. 4. Second-level information -line segments detected by method acting on zero-level a) a metallic object; b) radiological image of breast.

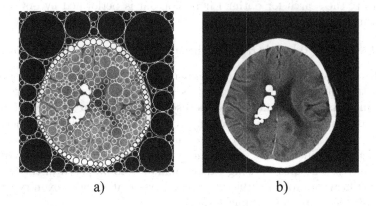

Fig. 5. Brain: granulation - patches in the form of circles a) group of patches similar to the prototype; b) final result shown on the original image.

example, line segments (Fig. 4) or small patches (Fig. 5 - in the form of circles) can be detected. Generalization of the granulation for 3D is also possible (Fig. 6).

The recognition can be performed using active contours because they can also operate on elements of higher granularity which are called patches, or, more generally, spatches [14], [15]. A spatch (spatial patch) can be literally anything from single pixels, through model-based objects like lines or circles, to any set of pixels. Moreover, spatches may or may not have a direct translation to images' pixel space. Nevertheless, recognized objects are considered to be describable by sets of spatches. The search is performed on the set of spatches, e.g. line segments previously detected by some low-level method - spatch approach.

Using line segments, one arises at the task of recognition of shapes composed of those segments. The recognition task can be difficult, like in the case of real physical objects (birds, ships, vehicles, and the like) or easier - when alphanumeric

Fig. 6. Brain 3D - balls as spatial patches

characters, or geometrical figures need to be recognized, e.g. square, rectangle, circle, ellipse, etc.

The form of energy should be such that in the form of its minima the *concept* of the shape to be recognized is reflected. In other words, the external *domain expert knowledge* or *user expectation* be implemented. Operation on elements of high granularity (spatch approach) in a natural way leads to the use of linguistic descriptions of desired shapes, which allows one to express the domain knowledge in a way resembling a natural language. At least three approaches are available:

- concepts are transformed into mathematical formulae;
- knowledge is encapsulated in rules formulated in a natural language; the reasoning process is implemented in fuzzy controller based on those rules;
- graphs represent knowledge about image and concept; vertices represent (semantically defined) objects; edges - linguistic relations between the objects detected.

Looking for some formal interpretation, one can formulate the following statements:

- Each element (e.g. pixel, line segment, spatch, etc.) can be described by its features (for pixel - coordinates and colour components).
- Contour acting on the elements of j-th level of granularity ($j = 0, 1, 2, \ldots$) determines potential sets $\vartheta(i)$ representing possible results of recognition.
- Each given set $\vartheta(i)$ is evaluated by the energy. Consequently, the energy function can be interpreted as concept recogniser.
- The decision is taken because of the optimisation of the energy function. This is the reason why we can speak about decision function d which is able to find a proper set $\vartheta(i)$.
- The energy function can model any arbitrary concepts and relations. The high-level knowledge is usually obtained from domain experts or by the use of machine learning approach.

In the case of graph representation, the optimal prototype matching is performed [14].

The existence and successful applicability of recognition methods on diverse levels of information granularity is of key importance for performing the complex data analysis. However, all the elements should be smartly composed, i.e., the way of justifiable granulation, representation of granules and their relations, representation of concepts, consideration of context, detection and treatment of outliers, and recognition method. These remarks apply to the analysis of all kinds of data, not only the computer images.

5   Outliers and Granulation

In the theory of numeric data analysis, a number of concepts for definition of outliers are formulated. The most common ones can be reflected in the following statement: an observation which is significantly different from predominant number of other observations is called an *outlier* [18], [19].

Let us illustrate it again on the heart image - Fig. 7. Single light points in the upper right part of the image are outliers (both in the original image Fig. 7a) and in Fig. 7b), the binary version being the result of tresholding). These outliers are not of importance for the task of search for main objects - heart ventricles. The goal of image processing is here the reason why those isolated points will not be considered during objects' clustering performed on higher levels $j > 1$. In other words, during further granulation such isolated information granules, as well as noise, are ignored.

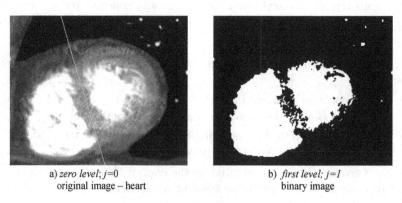

a) *zero level; j=0*
original image – heart

b) *first level; j=1*
binary image

Fig. 7. Segmentation using thresholding

The definition of an outlier derived from the above observation and generalized to the granulation of information can be formulated as follows.

Def. 1 Outlier – information granule of the j-th level which is not a subject of granulation on the j+1-th level ($j = 0, 1, 2, 3, \ldots$).

□

Note that for the reasoning process (to call medical diagnosis as an example), background, outliers, and existence of noise, as well as other image information can be significant, but this statement is not in conflict with the rules of granulation process.

Generally, there exist several methods (supervised or unsupervised ones) designed for either for noise removal or detection, as well as for application-specific outliers detection. Here again, the form of implementation of justifiable granularity gains in importance.

6   Conclusions

In the paper, the approach defined within the term 'granular computation' is interpreted and illustrated using the task of image segmentation. The principle of justifiable granularity [1] (which defines intuitively motivated requirements for information granule being meaningful) has been interpreted in terms of the image segmentation task. Advanced segmentation methods, like active contours, are particularly helpful to illustrate the granular computing concepts and their interpretation. For example, we can expect that the more acceptable pixels are included into the determined segment (bounded by contour c) , the better, and consequently, the more legitimate the segment becomes. At the same time, the granule should be as *specific* as possible It should come with a well-defined semantics (meaning). This point of view on the segmentation task is in agreement with our perception of knowledge about the expected features of the shape of a segment or of the related contour. Since the two above-mentioned requirements are in conflict, the method of finding a compromise is of practical importance.

In the granulation performed by the application of the active contour approach, the compromise is found via contour optimization. However, the demands for justifiable granularity generated by active contours can be defined more precisely and the executable mechanisms of practical usability can be described.

Acknowledgment.. The author thanks to A. Tomczyk, B. Lis, K. Jojczyk, S. Walczak, and J. Lazarek (Lodz University of Technology) for their effort in computational experiments, and to P. Grzelak, and C. Wolski from the Barlicki University Hospital in Lodz for making medical images available, as well as to K. Stokfiszewski (Lodz University of Technology) for technical support.

References

1. Pedrycz, W., Al-Hamouz, R., Morfeq, A., Balamash, A.: The Design of Free Structure Granular Mappings: The Use of the Prniciple of Justifiable Granularity. IEEE Trans. on Cybernetics 43, 2105–2113 (2013)
2. Pedrycz, W.: Granular computing in data mining. In: Last, M., Kandel, A. (eds.) Data Mining and Computational Intelligence. Springer, Singapore (2001)
3. Lin, T.Y., et al. (eds.): Data mining, rough sets and granular computing. Physica-Verlag, Berlin (2002)

4. Pedrycz, W., Loia, V.: P-FCM: A proximity-based fuzzy clustering. Fuzzy Sets and Systems 128, 21–41 (2004)
5. Sonka, M., Hlavac, V., Boyle, R.: Image processing, analysis and machine vision. Chapman and Hall, Cambridge (1993)
6. Tomczyk, A., Szczepaniak, P.S., Lis, B.: Generalized Multi-layer Kohonen Network and Its Application to Texture Recognition. In: Rutkowski, L., Siekmann, J.H., Tadeusiewicz, R., Zadeh, L.A. (eds.) ICAISC 2004. LNCS (LNAI), vol. 3070, pp. 760–767. Springer, Heidelberg (2004)
7. Lis, B., Szczepaniak, P.S., Tomczyk, A.: Multi-layer Kohonen Network and Texture Recognition. In: Grzegorzewski, P., Krawczak, M., Zadrożny, S. (eds.) Soft Computing Tools, Techniques and Applications. Akademicka Oficyna Wydawnicza EXIT, Warszawa (2004)
8. Grzeszczuk, R., Levin, D.: Brownian Strings: Segmenting Images with Stochastically Deformable Models. IEEE Trans. on Pattern Analysis and Machine Intelligence 19(10), 100–1013 (1997)
9. Kass, M., Witkin, W., Terzopoulos, S.: Snakes: Active Contour Models. Int. Journal of Computer Vision 1(4), 321–333 (1988)
10. Caselles, V., Kimmel, R., Sapiro, G.: Geodesic Active Contours. Int. Journal of Computer Vision 22(1), 61–79 (2000)
11. Tomczyk, A., Szczepaniak, P.S.: Adaptive Potential Active Hypercontours. In: Rutkowski, L., Tadeusiewicz, R., Zadeh, L.A., Żurada, J.M. (eds.) ICAISC 2006. LNCS (LNAI), vol. 4029, pp. 692–701. Springer, Heidelberg (2006)
12. Tomczyk, A.: Active Hypercontours and Contextual Classification. In: Proceedings of the 5th International Conference on Intelligent Systems Design and Applications – ISDA 2005, Wroclaw, Poland, pp. 256–261. IEEE Computer Society Press (2005)
13. Tomczyk, A., Szczepaniak, P.S.: On the Relationship between Active Contours and Contextual Classification. In: Kurzyński, M., et al. (eds.) Proceedings of the 4th Int. Conference on Computer Recognition Systems – CORES 2005, pp. 303–310. Springer, Heidelberg (2005)
14. Tomczyk, A., Pryczek, M., Walczak, S., Jojczyk, K., Szczepaniak, P.S.: Spatch Based Active Partitions with Linguistically Formulated Energy. Journal of Applied Computer Science 18(1), 87–115 (2010)
15. Pryczek, M., Tomczyk, A., Szczepaniak, P.S.: Active Partition Based Medical Image Understanding with Self Organized, Competitive Spatch Eduction. Journal of Applied Computer Science 18(2), 67–78 (2010)
16. Jojczyk, K., Pryczek, M., Tomczyk, A., Szczepaniak, P.S., Grzelak, P.: Cognitive Hierarchical Active Partitions Using Patch Approach. In: Bolc, L., Tadeusiewicz, R., Chmielewski, L.J., Wojciechowski, K. (eds.) ICCVG 2010, Part I. LNCS, vol. 6374, pp. 35–42. Springer, Heidelberg (2010)
17. Tomczyk, A., Szczepaniak, P.S., Pryczek, M.: Cognitive hierarchical active partitions in distributed analysis of medical images. Journal of Ambient Intelligence and Humanized Computing, 1–11 (2012)
18. Aggarwal, C.C.: Outlier Analysis. Kluwer Academic Publishers, Boston (2013)
19. Hawkins, D.: Identification of Outliers. Chapman and Hall (1980)

Information Granules in Application to Image Recognition

Krzysztof Wiaderek[1]([✉]), Danuta Rutkowska[1,2],
and Elisabeth Rakus-Andersson[3]

[1] Institute of Computer and Information Sciences, Czestochowa University
of Technology, 42-201 Czestochowa, Poland
{krzysztof.wiaderek,danuta.rutkowska}@icis.pcz.pl
[2] Information Technology Institute, University of Social Sciences,
90-113 Lodz, Poland
[3] Department of Mathematics and Natural Sciences, Blekinge Institute
of Technology, S-37179 Karlskrona, Sweden
elisabeth.andersson@bth.se

Abstract. The paper concerns specific problems of color digital image recognition by use of the concept of fuzzy and rough granulation. This idea employs information granules that contain pieces of knowledge about digital pictures such as color, location, size, and shape of an object to be recognized. The object information granule (OIG) is introduced, and the Granular Pattern Recognition System (GPRS) proposed, in order to solve different tasks formulated with regard to the information granules.

1 Introduction

The main idea of this paper is to propose an intelligent system that can solve specific image recognition problems by use of information granules that can be created by means of fuzzy sets [25] or rough sets [11]. For details concerning the theory of fuzzy sets, rough sets, as well as information granules, see also e.g. [18], [16], [17], [20], [15].

The subject of this paper is a continuation of the topics presented in [23] and [24], where the concept of fuzzy granulation [27] is considered. Now, we focus our attention on the rough set approach to information granulation [20], [15]. Moreover, the previous papers concern mostly the color and location attributes but now we mainly study the shape attribute. In addition, we introduce the OIG (object information granule), propose the GPRS (Pattern Recognition System), and formulate different image recognition problems depending on the information included in the OIG.

The paper is organized as follows. In Section 2, information granules are depicted in application to image recognition, and also the OIG is introduced. Those particular information granules are described in Sections 4, 5, 6, and 7. In Section 3, the GPRS is portrayed. In Section 8, examples of problems that can be solved by the GPRS are formulated. One of the image recognition tasks is considered

© Springer International Publishing Switzerland 2015
L. Rutkowski et al. (Eds.): ICAISC 2015, Part I, LNAI 9119, pp. 649–659, 2015.
DOI: 10.1007/978-3-319-19324-3_58

in Section 7 with regard to the shape information granule created by use of the rough set theory. Conclusions and final remarks are presented in Section 9.

2   Information Granules

The concept of information granules in application to pattern recognition is introduced in [13], and then employed in many publications, e.g. [14], [10].

In our approach, presented in this paper as well as in [23] and [24], we consider various kinds of granules. With regard to color digital pictures, obviously the smallest granule is a pixel, commonly known as the picture element. Every pixel is characterized by two attributes: color and location. Thus, we can say that the pixels include information about values of these attributes.

The macropixels, introduced in [23], constitute groups of neighbouring pixels that can be viewed as fuzzy granules. Of course, crisp macropixels may also be considered as crisp granules. The crisp macropixels are applied in the rough granulation, mentioned in [24] as the subject of further research, and developed in this paper. In both cases, the macropixels are treated as granules that contain information about color and location.

Two other attributes. i.e. size and shape may be associated with the macropixels. However, in this paper, we propose to use the so-called multipixels that are groups of neighbouring macropixels (see Section 6). The multipixels are characterized by four attributtes: color, location, size, and shape.

It is obvious that granulation is a hierarchical concept (see also [27]). In our approach, we have an example of such hierarchy: pixel, macropixel, multipixel, and the whole digital picture as an information granule.

The OIG (object information granule) is also introduced in this paper, with regard to the specific problem of digital picture recognition considered with reference to the GPRS. In a particular case, the OIG is represented by a macropixel or multipixel with specified values of the attributes such as color, location, size, shape. The OIG may include only partial information about these attributes, accepting their unknown values. This refers to the image recognition tasks formulated in Section 8.

3   Color Digital Picture Recognition

In this paper, the problem of color digital picture recognition based on the granulation approach considered in [23] and [24] is developed. In Section 8 examples of different kinds of the recognition tasks, depending on the knowledge about the object to be recognized, are presented. In general, we can describe the problem according to the illustration in Fig.1. Our main goal is to create a granular pattern recognition system that recognizes a picture (or pictures) from a collection of color digital pictures (images) based on the object information granule (OIG).

As a matter of fact, the problem does not concerns the typical image recognition but rather detection of the picture characterized by the OIG. Therefore, we do not need to employ special feature selection techniques such those used

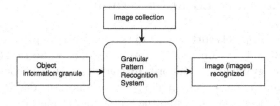

Fig. 1. Granular image recognition system

e.g. in face recognition [1] or gender classification [7]. Moreover, our approach does not require any methods for image segmentation like e.g. those applied in medical image processing [19], [4], [9], [6], and any algorithms for edge detection (see e.g.[5]). We do not focus our attention on details like e.g. in face recognition or even ageing effects visible on faces [1] and facial expressions [3].

The newest system for recognizing faces, FaceNet produced by Google, performs recognition (who is this person), verification (is this the same person), and clustering (find common people among these faces). This system uses an artificial intelligence technique called deep learning [22]. Our system, proposed in Fig.1, does not require neural networks and learning methods. Instead of recognizing details, the aim of our system is to detect a color digital picture (or pictures) including a roughly (or in a fuzzy way) described object.

The OIG is presented at the input of the system (GPRS) sketched in Fig.1. The OIG is the granule that includes information about attributes of the object that characterizes the picture to be recognized (detected) and retrieved from the collection of pictures (images). The following attributes are considered within the OIG: color, location, size, and shape. Values of these attributes may be viewed as fuzzy granules or roughly defined granules (within the framework of the rough set theory). Thus, in our approach, the OIG is composed of color, location, size, and shape granules; each of them is described in the next sections, respectively.

The Granular Pattern Recognition System (GPRS), portrayed in Fig.1, is a knowledge-based system that realizes an inference algorthm by means of appropriate fuzzy rules and/or the rules formulated using the rough set theory. In both cases, the rule base includes information granules represented by fuzzy and/or rough sets, respectively. As a result of the inference process the system recognizes the picture, from the image collection, that matches the OIG presented at the input, according to the IF-THEN rules (fuzzy and rough).

Depending on the problem to be solved (see Section 8), the OIG may include information about selected attributes. Thus, the GPRS performs the inference taking into account every pixel or bigger granules like macropixels and multi-pixels (described in the next sections) located in particular regions of a digital picture. It is important that hierarchical granulation is employed.

4   Macropixels and Location Granules

The concept of macropixels with regard to the color digital picture recognition is introduced in [23] and developed in [24]. As mentioned in Section 2, macropixels are considered as granules. An algorithm that creates the macropixels is described in [24], and refers to the pixel space granulation. Particular pixels are viewed as the smallest granules while the whole digital picture is treated as the biggest granule within the pixel space.

With regard to the macropixels and the pixel space granulation, the location attribute is very significant, when the size and shape of the macropixels are determined. Thus, the macropixels generated by the above mentioned algorithm include information about their location in the digital picture. Therefore, we call them location granules, and consider as crisp or fuzzy granules. For details, see [23] and [24].

5   Color Granules

The color space granulation with regard to the digital picture recognition is studied in [23] and [24]. The color attribute of the pixels, and macropixels, is very important - in addition to the location attribute - when color digital images are considered.

Apart from the location attribute, we may focus our attention on the macropixels of a specific color. In this case, such macropixels are viewed as color granules that include information about the color.

Details concerning the color space granulation are presented in [23] and [24], where the color areas (regions) of the CIE chromaticity triangle [8] are treated as fuzzy areas, with fuzzy boundaries between them. Thus, in addition to the commonly used RGB tree-dimensional space, the fuzzy color areas of the CIE color space is employed in order to create the color granules.

6   Size Granules

The size attribute is also considered in [23] and [24], mostly with regard to the size of macropixels generated by the algorithm presented in [24]. Depending on the image recognition task (see Section 8), an appropriate size of the macropixels should be used, e.g. small or medium size fuzzy granules.

With regard to the size granules, an important issue is a scaling problem of the digital pictures that can be of different resolution and size. However, it is easy to employ a simply algorithm that transforms different images to one particular size.

Referring to the size granules, we also propose to use the multipixels, introduced in Section 2, that are groups of the neighbouring macropixels. Examples of the multipixels as crisp (non-fuzzy) granules are presented in Section 7, in application to the rough set approach, with regard to the shape granules.

7   Shape Granules

The shape attribute is mentioned in [24] and the rough set approach introduced by Pawlak [11], [12] is proposed to create the shape granules. Within the framework of the rough set theory, the shape of an object can easily be determined by the lower and upper approximations of the group of macropixels corresponding to the object in the picture.

Figure 2 illustrates a part of a picture, e.g. the right top corner, with an object in the form of hat shape; see also [24]. The picture is granulated by use of macropixels, decribed in Section 4. The macropixels labeled by X, in Fig.2, represent lower approximation while both the macropixels indicated by X and X portray upper approximation.

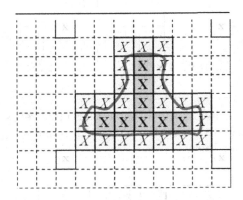

Fig. 2. Part of a picture presented a hat shape object

Table 1 may be used as a decision table that refers to the shape presented in Fig.2. With regard to that particular hat shape, the macropixels labeled by X and X are subsets of the set of macropixels $U_0 = \{\Omega_1, \Omega_2, ..., \Omega_M\}$. The set U_0 constitutes the rectangle region of the color digital picture, confined by the corner macropixels marked by slightly visible "x". This region may correspond to the above mentioned right top corner of the picture. Of course, in this case we do not need to analyse the whole picture but only this part. However, in general, the set of macropixels $U = \{\Omega^1, \Omega^2, ..., \Omega^N\}$ that constitutes the whole area of the digital picture should be taken into account in the decision table. It is obvious that U_0 is included in U.

In Table 1, for each macropixel belonging to U, values of attributes $A = \{a_1, a_2, ..., a_k\}$ and d are presented. The former are called conditional and the latter decision attributes. The sets of values are denoted as $V_{a_i} = \{v_{a_{i_1}}, v_{a_{i_2}}, ..., v_{a_{i_N}}\}$ for $i = 1, ..., k$, for the conditional attributes, and $V_d = \{v_{d_1}, v_{d_2}, ..., v_{d_N}\}$, for the decision attribute, respectively. The typical set of values for the decision attribute is $V_d = \{Yes, No\}$.

In the simplest case, the conditional attributes may refer to color and location, with regard to the macropixels illustrated in Fig.2. For the macropixels labeled by X the decision value is Yes, for those indicated by X the decision may be Yes or No, and for others remaining the decision value is No. This means that the particular macropixels certainly belong, roughly belong, and not belong to the hat shape, respectively. For each macropixel, the decision value depends on values of every conditional attribute. Of course, in this case we can use the set of macropixels U_0 instead of U, so Table 1 includes 42 rows.

Table 1. Decision table

	a_1	a_2	...	...	a_i	...	a_k	d
Ω^1	$v_{a_{1_1}}$	$v_{a_{2_1}}$	...	...	$v_{a_{i_1}}$	...	$v_{a_{k_1}}$	v_{d_1}
Ω^2	$v_{a_{1_2}}$	$v_{a_{2_2}}$	...	...	$v_{a_{i_2}}$	...	$v_{a_{k_2}}$	v_{d_2}
...								
Ω^n	$v_{a_{1_n}}$	$v_{a_{2_n}}$	...	...	$v_{a_{i_n}}$	...	$v_{a_{k_n}}$	v_{d_n}
...								
Ω^N	$v_{a_{1_N}}$	$v_{a_{2_N}}$	...	...	$v_{a_{i_N}}$	...	$v_{a_{k_N}}$	v_{d_N}

Based on Table 1, in its particular simplest form that refers to Fig.2, applying the rough set theory, we obtain the multipixel granules G_l, for $l = 1, ..., 14$ presented in Fig.3 and Table 2.

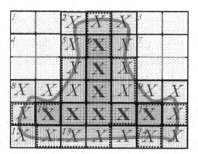

Fig. 3. An example of multipixel granules

Figure 3 shows the part of Fig.2 that portrays the hat shape object, and is confined to the area of the picture that includes the set of 42 macropixels, $U_0 = \{\Omega_1, \Omega_2, ..., \Omega_M\}$, where $M = 42$. In addition, the multipixels are marked, and numbered in the same way as in Table 2 (first column). The multipixels are granules generated by use of an equivalence relation [10] defined in the rough set theory as an indiscernibility relation [12]. Simply speaking, the multipixel granules are groups of macropixels characterized by the same attribut values, so they are viewed as indiscernibility classes.

The following values of the color and location attributes are considered, and included in Table 2:

$$V_{color} = V_c = \{g, yr, r\}, \text{ where } g - \text{green}, \ yr - \text{yellow} - \text{red}, r - \text{red},$$
$$V_{location} = V_l = \{LU, MU, RU, LC, MC, RC, LD, MD, RD\},$$

where $LU, MU, RU, LC, MC, RC, LD, MD, RD$ denote Left Upper, Middle Upper, Right Upper, Left Central, Middle Central, Right Central, Left Down, Middle Down, Right Down, respectivly.
For details concerning the attribute values, see [23].

The first two columns of Table 2 present multipixels G_l, for $l = 1, ..., 14$, created as groups of macropixels Ω_j, for $j = 1, ..., 42$, by means of the rough set approach. The next two columns refer to the color and location attributes of the multipixels, and the last column includes decision d corresponding to Table 1. However, the decision columns contain decision values for macropixels Ω_j and multipixels G_l in Tables 1 and 2, respectively. Therefore, Table 2 is called the modified decision table. In both tables, the set of values of the decision attribute is $V_d = \{Yes, No\}$, and describes belonginess of the macropixels (multipixels) to the hat shape portrayed in Figs.2 and 3.

Table 2. Modified decision table

G_l	groups of macropixels Ω_j	color	location	d
1	$\{1,2\}$	g	LU	No
2	$\{3,5\} \cup \{4\}$	yr	MU	$No \cup Yes$
3	$\{6,7\}$	g	RU	No
4	$\{8,9,15,16\}$	g	RC	No
5	$\{10,12\} \cup \{17,19,24,26\}$	yr	MC	$No \cup Yes$
6	$\{11,18,25,31,32.33\}$	r	MC	Yes
7	$\{13,14,20,21\}$	g	RC	No
8	$\{22,23\} \cup \{29\}$	yr	LC	$No \cup Yes$
9	$\{27,28\} \cup \{35\}$	yr	RC	$No \cup Yes$
10	$\{30\}$	r	LC	Yes
11	$\{34\}$	r	RC	Yes
12	$\{36\} \cup \{37\}$	yr	LD	$No \cup Yes$
13	$\{40\} \cup \{38,39\}$	yr	MD	$No \cup Yes$
14	$\{42\} \cup \{41\}$	yr	RD	$No \cup Yes$

Let us notice that the decision values No, Yes, $No \cup Yes$, in Table 2, inform that the corresponding multipixel granules do not belong, certainly belong, roughly belong to the hat shape, respectively.

From Table 2 we can generate rules for the Granular Pattern Recognition System, portrayed in Fig.1, in addition to fuzzy rules that may be formulated using different information granules.

8 Examples of Image Recognition Problems

Different image recognition problems can be formulated and solved based on the granulation approach by use of the information granules. With regard to the color digital picture recognition, depending on the knowledge about the object to be recognized, different types of the granules can be applied. The granules that include information about all the attributes, i.e. color, location, size, and shape, may be used when we possess knowledge concerning each of them. In the case when we have only partial knowledge we apply the specific granules corresponding to the knowledge about the object.

Figure 4 portrays the attributes, i.e. color, location, size, and shape, and relations between them within an information granule that contains knowledge about the object to be recognized in a color picture. The color attribute is most important, because other attributes, i.e. location, size, and shape, must be considered along with the color. Therefore, Fig.4 presents "color" in the center, and arrows that connect the "color" with "location", "size", and "shape", respectively. This means that the information granule may include partial knowledge that refers only to the color or to the color with location or color with size or color with shape, respectively. In addition, in Fig.4 we see connections between "location" and "size", "location" and "shape", "size" and "shape", that refer to the "color". Thus, as Fig.4 illustrates, we can consider partial knowledge, according to the following one, two, or three, attributes, and the case of color with location and size and shape, as follows:

- color
- color + location
- color + size
- color + shape
- color + location + size
- color + location + shape
- color + size + shape
- color + location + size + shape

Based on the knowledge contained in the information granule, the following examples of image recognition problems may be formulated. From a large collection of color digital pictures, find e.g. a picture (or pictures) that include:

- an object of a color close to red.
- an object of a color close to red, located in the center.
- a big object of a color close to red.
- an object of a color close to red, and round shape
- a big object of a color close to red, located in the center.
- an object of a color close to red, round shape, and located in the center.
- a big object of a color close to red, and round shape.
- a big object of a color close to red, round shape, and located in the center.

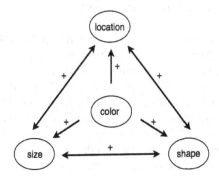

Fig. 4. Attributes and relations within an information granule

In Fig.4, the "color", "location", "size", and "shape" can be viewed as fuzzy granules with linguistic values, such as "color close to red", "big size", "round shape" (which means approximately round), location in the center (or right top corner). The linguistic values are represented by membership functions of fuzzy sets. Those granules compose the information granule that include knowledge about the object.

Other kinds of very interesting problems refer to the image understanding (see e.g.[21]). In the case of the color digital picture recognition and understanding we propose to consider the information granules that also include linguistic information about the picture. The linguistic description of the picture, in the natural language, should be automatically transformed to the form that expresses both the syntactic and semantic aspect of its meaning. This may be possible to realize within the framework of computing with words that is the theory introduced and developed by Zadeh [26].

The first step to extend the problems considered in this paper in the direction to image understanding is to increase the number of objects to be recognized in a picture and describe relations between the objects. For example, with regard to a big object of a color close to red, located in the center of a picture, and a small object of color close to yellow, located in the right corner at the top of the picture, the following linguistic description can be produced. The picture presents two objects, with medium distance between them, one object is bigger, darker, and located in higher position than another. In this way, similar relations may discribe a picture that presents more different objects. An information granule can include additional attribute value that is the number of objects, and relations between them, as well as their color, location, size, and shape.

As we see, the image recognition problems differ depending on the knowledge about the picture, from the information only about the color of one object in the picture to the linguistic description concerning many objects and relations between them.

9   Conclusions and Final Remarks

This paper concerns the concept of fuzzy granulation introduced by Zadeh [27], and developed by Pedrycz (e.g. [13]), and the rough set approach to the granulation proposed by Pawlak [12] and studied by other researchers, e.g. [20], [10]. The fuzzy and rough granulation is employed in the GPRS - the system presented in Section 3, for solving the image recognition tasks formulated in Section 8.

Color and shape attributes are very important in problems of image retrieval and classification; see e.g. [2] where shape representation techniques are considered. In this paper, we employ the rough set approach to create the shape granules. However, as mentioned in [24], the fuzzy set theory may be applied in order to describe the granules. In such a case, specific mathematical functions should be used as membership functions of fuzzy sets that approximate the shape granules. As a matter of fact, in this approach, fuzzy multipixels must be employed as the granules of particular shapes.

The information granules considered in this paper, and the GPRS will be developed, and the image recognition problems with regard to the OIG and the inference of the GPRS are subjects of our further research.

References

1. Akhtar, Z., Rattani, A., Foresti, G.L.: Temporal analyzis of adaptive face recognition. Journal of Artificial Intelligence and Soft Computing Research 4(4), 243–255 (2014)
2. Bazarganigilani, M.: Optimized image feature selection using pairwise classifiers. Journal of Artificial Intelligence and Soft Computing Research 1(2), 147–153 (2011)
3. Becker-Asano, C., Ishiguro, H.: Intercultural differences in decoding facial expressions of the android robot geminoid F. Journal of Artificial Intelligence and Soft Computing Research 1(3), 215–231 (2011)
4. Biniaz, A., Abbasi, A.: Fast FCM with spatial neighborhood information for brain MR image segmentation. Journal of Artificial Intelligence and Soft Computing Research 3(1), 15–25 (2013)
5. Biniaz, A., Abbasi, A.: Segmentation and edge detection based on modified ant colony optimization for iris image processing. Journal of Artificial Intelligence and Soft Computing Research 3(2), 133–141 (2013)
6. Bruzdzinski, T., Krzyzak, A., Fevens, T., Jelen, L.: Web-based framework for breast cancer classification. Journal of Artificial Intelligence and Soft Computing Research 4(2), 149–162 (2014)
7. Chang, Y., Wang, Y., Chen, C., Ricanek, K.: Improved image-based automatic gender classification by feature selection. Journal of Artificial Intelligence and Soft Computing Research 1(3), 241–253 (2011)
8. Fortner, B., Meyer, T.E.: Number by Color. A Guide to Using Color to Understand Technical Data. Springer (1997)
9. Karimi, B., Krzyzak, A.: A nowel approach for automatic detection and classification of suspicious lesions in breast ultrasound images. Journal of Artificial Intelligence and Soft Computing Research 3(3), 265–276 (2013)
10. Pal, S.K., Meher, S.K., Dutta, S.: Class-dependent rough-fuzzy granular space, dispersion index and classification. Pattern Recognition 45, 2690–2707 (2012)

11. Pawlak, Z.: Rough Sets. Theoretical Aspects of Reasoning about Data. Kluwer Academic Publishers, Dordrecht (1991)
12. Pawlak, Z.: Granularity of knowledge, indiscernibility and rough sets. In: Fuzzy Systems Proceedings. IEEE World Congress on Computational Intelligence, vol. 1, pp. 106–110 (1998)
13. Pedrycz, W., Vukovich, G.: Granular computing in pattern recognition. In: Bunke, H., Kandel, A. (eds.) Neuro-Fuzzy Pattern Recognition, pp. 125–143. World Scientific (2000)
14. Pedrycz, W., Park, B.J., Oh, S.K.: The design of granular classifiers: a study in the synergy of interval calculus and fuzzy sets in pattern recognition. Pattern Recognition 41, 3720–3735 (2008)
15. Peters, J.F., Skowron, A., Synak, P., Ramanna, S.: Rough sets and information granulation. In: De Baets, B., Kaynak, O., Bilgiç, T. (eds.) IFSA 2003. LNCS (LNAI), vol. 2715, pp. 370–377. Springer, Heidelberg (2003)
16. Rakus-Andersson, E.: Fuzzy and Rough Techniques in Medical Diagnosis and Medication. Springer (2007)
17. Rakus-Andersson, E.: Approximation and rough classification of letter-like polygon shapes. In: Skowron, A., Suraj, Z. (eds.) Rough Sets and Intelligent Systems - Professor Zdzisław Pawlak in Memoriam. ISRL, vol. 43, pp. 455–474. Springer, Heidelberg (2013)
18. Rutkowska, D.: Neuro-Fuzzy Architectures and Hybrid Learning. Springer (2002)
19. Salazar-Gonzales, A., Li, Y., Liu, X.: Automatic graph cut based segmentation of retinal optic disc by incorporating blood vessel compensation. Journal of Artificial Intelligence and Soft Computing Research 2(3), 235–245 (2012)
20. Skowron, A., Stepaniuk, J.: Information granules: Towards foundations of granular computing. International Journal of Intelligent Systems 16(1), 57–85 (2001)
21. Tadeusiewicz, R., Ogiela, M.R.: Why Automatic Understanding? In: Beliczynski, B., Dzielinski, A., Iwanowski, M., Ribeiro, B. (eds.) ICANNGA 2007. LNCS, vol. 4432, pp. 477–491. Springer, Heidelberg (2007)
22. Taigman, Y., Yang, M., Ranzato, M.A., Wolf, L.: Deepface: Closing the gap to human-level performance in face verification. In: Proc. IEEE Conference on Computer Vision and Pattern Recognition (CVPR), pp. 1701–1708 (2014)
23. Wiaderek, K., Rutkowska, D.: Fuzzy granulation approach to color digital picture recognition. In: Rutkowski, L., Korytkowski, M., Scherer, R., Tadeusiewicz, R., Zadeh, L.A., Zurada, J.M. (eds.) ICAISC 2013, Part I. LNCS (LNAI), vol. 7894, pp. 412–425. Springer, Heidelberg (2013)
24. Wiaderek, K., Rutkowska, D., Rakus-Andersson, E.: Color digital picture recognition based on fuzzy granulation approach. In: Rutkowski, L., Korytkowski, M., Scherer, R., Tadeusiewicz, R., Zadeh, L.A., Zurada, J.M. (eds.) ICAISC 2014, Part I. LNCS (LNAI), vol. 8467, pp. 319–332. Springer, Heidelberg (2014)
25. Zadeh, L.A.: Fuzzy sets. Information and Control 8, 338–353 (1965)
26. Zadeh, L.A.: Fuzzy logic = computing with words. IEEE Transactions on Fuzzy Systems 4, 103–111 (1996)
27. Zadeh, L.A.: Toward a theory of fuzzy information granulation and its centrality in human reasoning and fuzzy logic. Fuzzy Sets and Systems 90, 111–127 (1997)

Can We Process 2D Images Using Artificial Bee Colony?

Marcin Woźniak[1]($\boxtimes$), Dawid Połap[1], Marcin Gabryel[2], Robert K. Nowicki[2], Christian Napoli[3], and Emiliano Tramontana[3]

[1] Institute of Mathematics, Silesian University of Technology,
Kaszubska 23, 44-101 Gliwice, Poland
Marcin.Wozniak@polsl.pl
[2] Institute of Computational Intelligence, Czestochowa University of Technology,
Al. Armii Krajowej 36, 42-200 Czestochowa, Poland
Marcin.Gabryel@iisi.pcz.pl, Robert.Nowicki@iisi.pcz.pl
[3] Department of Mathematics and Informatics, University of Catania,
Viale A. Doria 6, 95125 Catania, Italy
napoli@dmi.unict.it, tramontana@dmi.unict.it

Abstract. This paper is to discuss a matter of preprocessing 2D input images by selected methods of Evolutionary Computation. In the following sections we try to analyze possibility of using Artificial Bee Colony algorithm to preprocess input images for classification purposes. Experiments have been performed with the examined method applied on a set of test images, to present and discuss efficacy and precision of recognition.

Keywords: Image processing · Evolutionary computation · Artificial bee colony algorithm

1 Introduction

Image recognition is one of the processes, where dedicated computer systems may help to classify input objects. However, this is non-trivial operation and the efficacy is of a paramount importance. Therefore in this paper we try to analyze an application of selected Computational Intelligence (CI) method, in particular Artificial Bee Colony Algorithm (ABCA), combined with a sobel filter version what creates a simplified 2D input image recognition system.

CI gives interesting solutions that are imitating the behavior of real organisms to efficiently assist in various problems solving. They find application in positioning, simulation, optimization, control and management. Evolutionary Strategies (ES) efficiently help to create learning sets for Artificial Intelligence (AI) control systems as presented in [8] and [3] or dynamic systems [23]. Moreover, CI powers the resolution of complicated differential and integral equations like in positioning queueing systems: [7], [26], [18], [25] and [24]. CI can be applied in the optimization of optimal osmotic parameters (see [31]), optimal clustering methods (see [6]), evaluation in games (see [21], [20]), simulation of iron cast and

© Springer International Publishing Switzerland 2015
L. Rutkowski et al. (Eds.): ICAISC 2015, Part I, LNAI 9119, pp. 660–671, 2015.
DOI: 10.1007/978-3-319-19324-3_59

heat transfer (see [9] and [10]), benchmark tests [30] and cloud-computing work-flow management [4]. As You see CI can provide many methods that are efficient in various operations. In this paper we describe the application of Artificial Bee Colony Algorithm (ABCA) in image processing.

1.1   Related Works

CI is efficient in image preprocessing. Firefly Algorithm was used in image com-pression [11], gray-scale image watermarking [14] and Key-Point classification [27], [17]. Cuckoo Search Algorithm has efficient application in intelligent video target racking [22], satellite image segmentation [2] and recognition [29].

Such examples convince to examine ABCA as a part of simplified 2D image classifier. Therefore, we discuss an approach to object classification based on the application of ABCA with a sobel filter that operates on 2D input images, so as to simplify object recognition. First experiments for sample images from open test images databases[1][2] are presented and discussed in the following sections.

2   Sobel Filter

Sobel operator evaluates directional gradient of the luminosity. Then, it reveals the edges of the depicted objects as the pixels with high gradient value. These points are characterized by sharp-cut variations of luminosity (e.g. the sudden variation of luminosity for a well-lit object on a dark background provides the bright edge).

In the examined solution, a sobel based recognition in gray scale images is obtained by an edge detection approach using derivative preprocessing. In order to recognize shapes, the edges are detected by applying a sobel filter based on a differential operator, see [5] and [1]. Applied sobel operator approximates the two dimensional gradient of a luminance function by a convolution with an integer filter applied along the axial directions. In order to detect the edges contained in a gray scale image $\mathcal{I}$, the sobel operator makes use of the second order differential operator. Therefore it is a kind of an orthogonal gradient operator in local form. For a continuous function $f : \mathbb{R}^2 \to \mathbb{R}$ and a given image point $\mathbf{x_i} = (x_{i,1}, x_{i,2})$, the gradient can be expressed as:

$$df = \nabla f \cdot d\mathbf{x_i} = [\partial_1 f, \partial_2 f] \cdot [dx_{i,1}, dx_{i,2}], \tag{1}$$

where partial derivatives $\partial_1 f$, $\partial_2 f$ are computed for each pixel location. In the applied method, an approximation is achieved as a convolution of kernels for a small area of neighbor pixels. $\partial_1 f$ and $\partial_2 f$ use a separate kernel each, so there are two applied kernels combined into a simplified gradient operator:

$$S1 = \begin{pmatrix} -1 & -2 & -1 \\ 0 & 0 & 0 \\ 1 & 2 & 1 \end{pmatrix}, \quad S2 = \begin{pmatrix} -1 & 0 & -1 \\ -2 & 0 & 2 \\ -1 & 0 & 1 \end{pmatrix}. \tag{2}$$

---

[1] www.imageprocessingplace.com
[2] http://sipi.usc.edu/database/

One of the kernels from (2) has a maximum response for the vertical edge and the other has a maximum response for the horizontal edge of the input object. Therefore, in the applied method, the maximum value of the two convolutions is used as the output bit of each input image point. As a result, we get an image of the edge amplitude. In order to obtain the edges of the image, starting by its associated luminance intensity matrix I, for every pixel $\mathbf{x_i} = (x_{i,1}, x_{i,2})$ of the image we compute the following functions:

$$g_1(\mathbf{x_i}) = g_1(x_{i,1}, x_{i,2}) = \sum_{m=1}^{3} \sum_{n=1}^{3} S1_{mn} \cdot I(x_{i,1} + m - 2, x_{i,2} + n - 2),$$

$$g_2(\mathbf{x_i}) = g_2(x_{i,1}, x_{i,2}) = \sum_{m=1}^{3} \sum_{n=1}^{3} S2_{mn} \cdot I(x_{i,1} + m - 2, x_{i,2} + n - 2), \qquad (3)$$

$$g(\mathbf{x_i}) = g(x_{i,1}, x_{i,2}) = g_1^2(\mathbf{x_i}) + g_2^2(\mathbf{x_i}),$$

where $S1_{ij}, S2_{ij}, g_1$ and g_2 are taken form the classical Sobel approach. In classic version, once the values of the functions in (3) are obtained for each pixel, the edges are defined as the pixels in the subset of points $\mathcal{E} \subset \mathcal{I}$ so that:

$$\forall \mathbf{x_i} \in \mathcal{E} \Rightarrow \begin{cases} g(\mathbf{x_i}) > 4\langle g^2 \rangle \\ g_1(\mathbf{x_i}) > g_2(\mathbf{x_i}) \\ g(\mathbf{x_i}) \geq g(x_{i,1}, x_{i,2} - 1) \\ g(\mathbf{x_i}) \geq g(x_{i,1}, x_{i,2} + 1) \end{cases} \vee \begin{cases} g(\mathbf{x_i}) > 4\langle g^2 \rangle \\ g_1(\mathbf{x_i}) < g_2(\mathbf{x_i}) \\ g(\mathbf{x_i}) \leq g(x_{i,1} - 1, x_{i,2}) \\ g(\mathbf{x_i}) \leq g(x_{i,1} + 1, x_{i,2}) \end{cases}, \qquad (4)$$

basing on the g_1, g_2 and g computed in (3). When a sobel filter is applied to 2D input image $\mathcal{I}$, a new indexed image is depicted as a plain representation of the points of $\mathcal{E} \subset \mathcal{I}$, as defined in (4). The indexed image coordinate system is a representation of $\mathcal{I}$, whereby all the values are zeros, except for the coordinates of the points in $\mathcal{E}$ which are ones. Such representation is lossy since it does not carry the values given by the functions in (3) but only a logical representation of the set $\mathcal{E}$.

To obtain an advanced identification of the edges retaining partial information, such as the values of the functions in (3), Sobel filter must be modified. For each point of $\mathcal{I}$, instead of obtaining $\mathcal{E}$ from (4), we used the value of $g(\mathbf{x_i})$ and its square root:

$$\forall \mathbf{x_i} \in \mathcal{I} \Rightarrow \tilde{g}(\mathbf{x_i}) = \sqrt{g(\mathbf{x_i})} = \sqrt{g_1^2(\mathbf{x_i}) + g_2^2(\mathbf{x_i})}. \qquad (5)$$

Using g and $\tilde{g}$ functions defined in (3) and (5), edges become blurred. However now they are more suitable for proposed recognition, since higher values are obtained with respect to the other points of image $\mathcal{I}$. The bright patterns, become the shapes for applied CI method which can now solve simplified detection. Let us present the applied version of the sobel filter method, see Algorithm 1.

3   Artificial Bee Colony Algorithm

ABCA is one of CI methods. One of the first versions was presented in [12] and [32]. In the idea, ABCA is inspired by the behavior of honey bees.

Algorithm 1. Simplified sobel filter algorithm

Start,
Import image $\mathcal{I}$ to Im,
Calculate the number of pixels columns and rows in 2D input image Im,
Create the 3×3 filters $S1$ and $S2$ using (2),
while $n \leq rows$ **do**
 while $m \leq columns$ **do**
  $Grays[m][n]$ = ccvmean($Im[m][n]$),
  // ccvmean is the mean of color channels values
  Compute g, g_1 and g_2 on $Grays[m][n]$ using (3),
  if $f\_selection$ specifies it **then**
   $g\_tilde[m][n]$=sqrt($g[m][n]$),
  end
  // Apply the filter to the 2D input image
 end
end
Save g as a bitmap grayscale image GIm,
switch $f\_selection$ **do**
 case *1* Save g as a grayscale image GIm,
 case *2* Save g_tilde as a grayscale image $G\_tildeIm$,
 case *3*
  Save g as a grayscale image GIm,
  Save g_tilde as a grayscale image $G\_tildeIm$,
 endsw
endsw
Stop.

During searching for food, bees have developed a variety of techniques to communicate with each other. This communication is related to the sources of nectar and helps to determine the location of best source. One of such techniques is a waggle dance. Performing it, bees are providing information about distance from the hive to the source of the nectar, it's direction and quality.

In implemented ABCA, bees are divided into groups. There are scouts, who are searching for food in a random way over the given space. Then there are on-lookers and finally employed bees. After coming hive, scouts perform the waggle dance in which the information about the nectar is provided. Onlookers watch waggle dance, and then choose the best places to go for searching. In the method we treat a bee as a point in the image. The bee stays at each point until it finds (by contacting with other bees) a better location. If there is a new, better place of nectar source in the image (the bee gets the information from others) then the present source is abandoned and the employed bee goes for searching of it. Therefore it becomes a scout. The bee is flying and searching for nectar. At the end of each epoch we compare all the bees (the information is given to others in a waggle dance). This comparison gives an information, where the best nectar sources (according to the fitness function) are placed. Thus the bees from this part of the image keep their positions and the others are flying toward this direction to find better nectar sources.

In the hive, at the end of each epoch the bees are performing waggle dance. They watch others to get information about best nectar source positions. An onlooker bee chooses the best food place according to the formula:

$$p(\mathbf{x_i}) = \frac{\Phi(\mathbf{x_i})}{\sum_{i=1}^{i=n} \Phi(\mathbf{x_i})}, \tag{6}$$

where $\Phi(\mathbf{x_i})$ is a value of the fitness function calculated for each dancing bee. Having this information the population is sorted according to fitness, and in this way the set of best nectar sources (location of these employed bees) is evaluated. Therefore other onlookers can go to search for food in this direction. They fly in random ways and their position over the input image is modified by the equation:

$$\mathbf{x_i}^{t+1} = \mathbf{x_i}^t + \alpha_k \cdot \Delta\mathbf{x_{ik}}, \tag{7}$$

where k is randomly chosen index of the bee among those placed in best nectar sources, α_k is a random number between $[-1, 1]$ and $\Delta\mathbf{x_{ik}}$ is calculated as:

$$\Delta\mathbf{x_{ik}} = (x_{ij} - x_{kj}), \tag{8}$$

where j is randomly chosen spatial coordinate of the chosen bee. In this way we model a waggle dance in the hive, selection of the best nectar sources (best fitness function points) and movement of all the bees toward selected direction in each epoch.

An ABCA implementation is quite simple. At the very beginning we create a random population of n bees. Each bee is a point in the image. We will evaluate it by getting the brightness of the pixel (potential Key-Points). In the next step, we check fitness function for each of them and sort the entire population according to this value. After that we select m best bees among them. The best bees are transferred to next round and the process starts from the beginning. An implementation of the method is presented in Algorithm 2.

3.1   Image Processing Method

A digital 2D image $\mathcal{I}$ consists of points, each having a position and special properties. The position of a pixel with given coordinates $\mathbf{x_i} = (x_{i,1}, x_{i,2})$ and its properties (i.e. brightness or saturation) are crucial for classification. This combination brings unique information about the objects in the picture. However, correct classification depends on the right decision (i.e. recognition), which is based on some features. Thus, a *Key-Point* is a pixel in a 2D input image $\mathcal{I}$ with peculiar properties making it important for object recognition. A *Key-Area* is containing many Key-Points that all together compose an object (shape, crucial parts, etc.) to recognize. In other words, to find the object of the interest computer can search for areas in the picture that contain many points of the same kind. Sobel filter is applied for preprocessing 2D input images to be passed to an ABCA simplified recognition.

Algorithm 2. ABCA to classify 2D images Key-Points

Start,
Define all coefficients: n-size of population, m-number of chosen best bees,
number of *generations* and number of *bees*,
Define fitness function for the algorithm using (9),
Create a random initial population of *bees* in 2D image,
$t = 0$,
while $t \leq generation$ **do**

    Evaluate *bees* population using (6),

    Sort *bees* according to the value of fitness function,

    Select m best locations among all *bees*,

    Using (7) move the *bees* toward nectar source (best locations) defined in (8),

    Next generation $t + +$,

end
Values from last population with best fitness are the solution,
Stop.

Each bee is representing a single pixel. A population of bees is then simulated in order to move from point to point and search for specific areas. Searching is based on a simplified fitness function that reflects brightness of each filtered image point

$$\Phi(\mathbf{x}_i) = \Phi((x_{i,1}, x_{i,2})) = \begin{cases} 0.1 \ldots 1 & \text{saturation} \\ 0 & \text{other} \end{cases}, \qquad (9)$$

where $\Phi(\mathbf{x}_i)$ denotes the quality of the evaluated pixel reflected in the scale from 0.0 to 1.0, where color saturation changes from black to white. Therefore using ABCA with fitness function (9) for sobel filtered input images we are to build a simplified 2D image processing. Using filtering we extract the borders of input objects, which will be marked in white on a dark background. Therefore, these filtered images are proper input for ABCA classifier. When bees fly in search for nectar, they pick points with the best fitness within the range of their flight. Then, from all points we take m best locations, where fitness function is highest. These points are taken to the next round and the rest of the population is moved toward them, as defined in the algorithm. Finally, the last generation cover areas of interest. Experiments were performed for 400 bees in 20 generations with $\alpha = 0.3$ and $m = 30$. Let us see some sample results.

4   Experimental Results

We tried to examine the behavior of the proposed classifier on various 2D images (see Section 1). Results are presented to discuss potential efficiency. Fig. 1 to Fig. 5 present the classifier steps. Firstly, the leftmost top image in each Figure presents the original input image. Then, going towards the right on the first row, we can see the image after the first sobel filtering, then the filtered image with ABCA recognized Key-Points (in red). The second row shows (from left to right) the image after the second filtering operation, the filtered image with ABCA recognized Key-Points (in red), and, finally the main result: classified 2D input image, where Key-Points are presented on top of the original input image (each one in red).

Fig. 1. 2D input image recognition process over construction images

We can see that proposed solution can find shapes of recognized objects. ABCA is able to recognize objects, however applied sobel filtering is helping a lot to improve classification. If we look at images closely, we see that in recognition without filtering ABCA finds only location. However after filtering the recognition is much improved. Depending on the input object, recognition over first filtering gives good quality. However sometimes second filtering is even more crucial to help to exact shape (see Fig. 4 and Fig. 5).

4.1   Conclusions

It is possible to process images by an ad-hoc combination of sobel filter with ABCA as a simplified CI classifier. Performed calculations are very simple. We just use formulas (1) – (4) to filter input image and then (6) – (8) to calculate the position of Key-Areas in examined images. The classifier covers recognized objects with Key-Points. If the input images have many points with the same value, the classification process may be more complicated. On the other hand, the system efficacy is self-increased if we are looking for Key-Points with high contrast in relation to surroundings. Moreover, it is possible to increase the

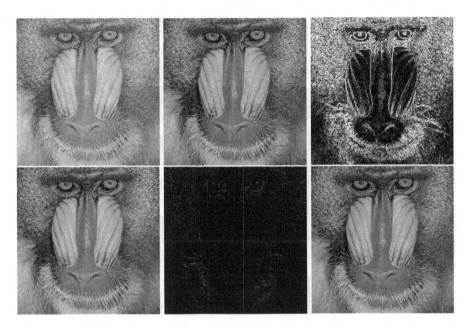

Fig. 2. 2D input image recognition process over facial images

Fig. 3. 2D input image recognition process over landscape images

Fig. 4. 2D input image recognition process over single objects

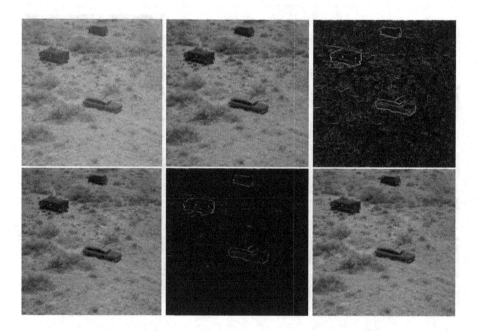

Fig. 5. 2D input image recognition process over many objects

classifier efficiency in some ways. The first step would be introducing more precise sobel kernels or filtering functions. The second step is to have more efficient ABCA motion or information processing. Finally, we can introduce better fitness function. Furthermore, we will try to build a classifier for large collections [4] of input images using fast methods [16], [28] and [13].

Better filtering or ABCA models will be considered in the future research. However, introducing a special recognition function is non-trivial task. The fitness function is the most sensitive part of the classifier. To increase its efficiency in classification we must define a special function for the various classes of objects, i.e. different for blocks or buildings, for faces and other appearance features, etc. From our first research findings, we can state that it is very unlikely to have one function for all classified objects types. Therefore another attempt to improve it would be to use some dedicated AI methods, like neural networks [15] or fuzzy systems [19].

5 Final Remarks

We can state that the presented classifier can find objects of interest, and therefore answer to the question given in the title is positive.

This feature makes it a promising tool for Artificial Intelligence recognition systems. The solution discussed in this article can also work as a part of sophisticated image classifiers. We decided to apply sobel operator for image filtering for its low complexity and coarse precision, which both have importance for the problem of edge detection. Applied ABCA is easy to implement and allows easily exploration of the entire input image without complicated mathematical operations. However the precision in recognition can be improved. In further research, we plan to work on sobel filter precision, by applying other kernels and ABCA method by improving motion or decision.

References

1. Anusha, G., Prasad, T., Narayana, D.: Implementation of sobel edge detection on fpga. International Journal of Computer Trends and Technology 3(3), 472–475 (2012)
2. Bhandari, A., Singh, V., Kumar, A., Singh, G.: Cuckoo search algorithm and wind driven optimization based study of satellite image segmentation for multilevel thresholding using kapurs entropy. Expert Systems with Applications 41(7), 3538–3560 (2014)
3. Bonanno, F., Capizzi, G., Sciuto, G.L., Napoli, C., Pappalardo, G., Tramontana, E.: A cascade neural network architecture investigating surface plasmon polaritons propagation for thin metals in openMP. In: Rutkowski, L., Korytkowski, M., Scherer, R., Tadeusiewicz, R., Zadeh, L.A., Zurada, J.M. (eds.) ICAISC 2014, Part I. LNCS (LNAI), vol. 8467, pp. 22–33. Springer, Heidelberg (2014)
4. Borowik, G., Woźniak, M., Fornaia, A., Giunta, R., Napoli, C., Pappalardo, G., Tramontana, E.: A software architecture assisting workflow executions on cloud resources. International Journal of Electronics and Telecommunications 61(1), 17–23 (2015)

5. Canny, J.: A computational approach to edge detection. IEEE Transactions on Pattern Analysis and Machine Intelligence (6), 679–698 (1986)

6. Chen, M., Ludwig, S.: Particle swarm optimization based fuzzy clustering approach to identify optimal number of clusters. Journal of Artificial Intelligence and Soft Computing Research 4(1), 43–56 (2014)

7. Gabryel, M., Nowicki, R.K., Woźniak, M., Kempa, W.M.: Genetic cost optimization of the $GI/M/1/N$ finite-buffer queue with a single vacation policy. In: Rutkowski, L., Korytkowski, M., Scherer, R., Tadeusiewicz, R., Zadeh, L.A., Zurada, J.M. (eds.) ICAISC 2013, Part II. LNCS (LNAI), vol. 7895, pp. 12–23. Springer, Heidelberg (2013)

8. Gabryel, M., Woźniak, M., Nowicki, R.K.: Creating learning sets for control systems using an evolutionary method. In: Rutkowski, L., Korytkowski, M., Scherer, R., Tadeusiewicz, R., Zadeh, L.A., Zurada, J.M. (eds.) SIDE 2012 and EC 2012. LNCS, vol. 7269, pp. 206–213. Springer, Heidelberg (2012)

9. Hetmaniok, E., Nowak, I., Słota, D., Zielonka, A.: Determination of optimal parameters for the immune algorithm used for solving inverse heat conduction problems with and without a phase change. Numer. Heat Transfer B 62, 462–478 (2012)

10. Hetmaniok, E., Słota, D., Zielonka, A.: Experimental verification of immune recruitment mechanism and clonal selection algorithm applied for solving the inverse problems of pure metal solidification. Int. Comm. Heat & Mass Transf. 47, 7–14 (2013)

11. Horng, M.H.: Vector quantization using the firefly algorithm for image compression. Expert Systems with Applications 39(1), 1078–1091 (2012)

12. Karaboga, D., Basturk, B.: Artificial bee colony (ABC) optimization algorithm for solving constrained optimization problems. In: Melin, P., Castillo, O., Aguilar, L.T., Kacprzyk, J., Pedrycz, W. (eds.) IFSA 2007. LNCS (LNAI), vol. 4529, pp. 789–798. Springer, Heidelberg (2007)

13. Marszałek, Z., Połap, D., Woźniak, M.: On preprocessing large data sets by the use of triple merge sort algorithm. In: Proceedings of International Conference on Advances in Information Processing and Communication Technologies - IPCT 2014, Rome, Italy, June 7-8, pp. 65–72. The IRED, Seek Digital Library (2014)

14. Mishra, A., Agarwal, C., Sharma, A., Bedi, P.: Optimized gray-scale image watermarking using dwt svd and firefly algorithm. Expert Systems with Applications 41(17), 7858–7867 (2014)

15. Napoli, C., Pappalardo, G., Tramontana, E.: A hybrid neuro–wavelet predictor for QoS control and stability. In: Baldoni, M., Baroglio, C., Boella, G., Micalizio, R. (eds.) AI*IA 2013. LNCS, vol. 8249, pp. 527–538. Springer, Heidelberg (2013)

16. Napoli, C., Pappalardo, G., Tramontana, E.: Using modularity metrics to assist move method refactoring of large systems. In: Seventh International Conference on Complex, Intelligent, and Software Intensive Systems - CISIS 2013, pp. 529–534 (July 2013)

17. Napoli, C., Pappalardo, G., Tramontana, E., Marszałek, Z., Połap, D., Woźniak, M.: Simplified firefly algorithm for 2D image key-points search. In: Proceedings of the IEEE Symposium Series on Computational Intelligence - SSCI 2014: 2014 IEEE Symposium on Computational Intelligence for Human-like Intelligence - CIHLI 2014, Orlando, Florida, USA, December 9-12, pp. 118–125. IEEE (2014)

18. Napoli, C., Papplardo, G., Tramontana, E.: Improving files availability for bittorrent using a diffusion model. In: IEEE 23rd International Workshop on Enabling Technologies: Infrastructure for Collaborative Enterprises - WETICE 2014, pp. 191–196 (June 2014)

19. Niewiadomski, A.: Imprecision Measures for Type-2 Fuzzy Sets: Applications to Linguistic Summarization of Databases. In: Rutkowski, L., Tadeusiewicz, R., Zadeh, L.A., Zurada, J.M. (eds.) ICAISC 2008. LNCS (LNAI), vol. 5097, pp. 285–294. Springer, Heidelberg (2008)
20. Swiechowski, M., Mandziuk, J.: Self-adaptation of playing strategies in general game playing. IEEE Trans. Comput. Intellig. and AI in Games 6(4), 367–381 (2014)
21. Waledzik, K., Mandziuk, J.: An automatically generated evaluation function in general game playing. IEEE Trans. Comput. Intellig. and AI in Games 6(3), 258–270 (2014)
22. Walia, G.S., Kapoor, R.: Intelligent video target tracking using an evolutionary particle filter based upon improved cuckoo search. Expert Systems with Applications 41(14), 6315–6326 (2014)
23. Woźniak, M.: Fitness function for evolutionary computation applied in dynamic object simulation and positioning. In: Proceedings of the IEEE Symposium Series on Computational Intelligence - SSCI 2014: 2014 IEEE Symposium on Computational Intelligence in Vehicles and Transportation Systems - CIVTS 2014, Orlando, Florida, USA, December 9-12, pp. 108–114. IEEE (2014)
24. Woźniak, M.: On positioning traffic in nosql database systems by the use of particle swarm algorithm. In: Proceedings of XV Workshop DAGLI OGGETTI AGLI AGENTI - WOA 2014, Catania, Italy, September 25-26. CEUR Workshop Proceedings (CEUR-WS.org), RWTH Aachen University, paper 5 (2014)
25. Woźniak, M., Kempa, W.M., Gabryel, M., Nowicki, R.K.: A finite-buffer queue with single vacation policy - analytical study with evolutionary positioning. International Journal of Applied Mathematics and Computer Science 24(4), 887–900 (2014)
26. Woźniak, M., Kempa, W.M., Gabryel, M., Nowicki, R.K., Shao, Z.: On applying evolutionary computation methods to optimization of vacation cycle costs in finite-buffer queue. In: Rutkowski, L., Korytkowski, M., Scherer, R., Tadeusiewicz, R., Zadeh, L.A., Zurada, J.M. (eds.) ICAISC 2014, Part I. LNCS (LNAI), vol. 8467, pp. 480–491. Springer, Heidelberg (2014)
27. Woźniak, M., Marszałek, Z.: An idea to apply firefly algorithm in 2D image key-points search. In: Dregvaite, G., Damasevicius, R. (eds.) ICIST 2014. CCIS, vol. 465, pp. 312–323. Springer, Heidelberg (2014)
28. Woźniak, M., Marszałek, Z., Gabryel, M., Nowicki, R.K.: Modified merge sort algorithm for large scale data sets. In: Rutkowski, L., Korytkowski, M., Scherer, R., Tadeusiewicz, R., Zadeh, L.A., Zurada, J.M. (eds.) ICAISC 2013, Part II. LNCS (LNAI), vol. 7895, pp. 612–622. Springer, Heidelberg (2013)
29. Woźniak, M., Połap, D.: Basic concept of cuckoo search algorithm for 2D images processing with some research results. In: Proceedings of the 11th International Conference on Signal Processing and Multimedia Applications - SIGMAP 2014, Vienna, Austria, August 28-30, pp. 164–173. SciTePress - INSTICC (2014)
30. Woźniak, M., Połap, D.: On some aspects of genetic and evolutionary methods for optimization purposes. International Journal of Electronics and Telecommunications 61(1), 7–16 (2015)
31. Yeomans, J.: A parametric testing of the firefly algorithm in the determination of the optimal osmotic drying parameters of mushrooms. Journal of Artificial Intelligence and Soft Computing Research 4(4), 257–266 (2015)
32. Zou, W., Zhu, Y., Chen, H., Zhu, Z.: Cooperative approaches to artificial bee colony algorithm. In: Proceedings of International Conference on Computer Application and System Modeling-ICCASM 2010, pp. V9–44–V9–48. IEEE (2010)

Workshop: Large-Scale Visual Recognition and Machine Learning

Improving Effectiveness of SVM Classifier
for Large Scale Data

Jerzy Balicki, Julian Szymański[(✉)], Marcin Kępa,
Karol Draszawka, and Waldemar Korłub

Department of Computer Systems Architecture,
Faculty of Electronics, Telecommunications and Informatics
Gdańsk University of Technology, Gdańsk, Poland
{jerzy.balicki,julian.szymanski,kadr,
waldemar.korlub}@eti.pg.gda.pl, marc.kepa@gmail.com

Abstract. The paper presents our approach to SVM implementation in parallel environment. We describe how classification learning and prediction phases were pararellised. We also propose a method for limiting the number of necessary computations during classifier construction. Our method, named *one-vs-near*, is an extension of typical *one-vs-all* approach that is used for binary classifiers to work with multiclass problems. We perform experiments of scalability and quality of the implementation. The results show that the proposed solution allows to scale up SVM that gives reasonable quality results. The proposed *one-vs-near* method significantly improves effectiveness of the classifier construction.

Keywords: SVM · Wikipedia · Documents categorization · Parallel classification

1 Introduction

The size of the internet and globally stored data is growing with every year. Today the estimated number of indexed web pages is somewhere between 20 and 50 billion pages [1]. Automatic categorization of this evergrowing data becomes a real challenge. Even smaller text documents repositories, such as the Wikipedia reaching 4.5 million articles organized with hundreds of thousands of categories [2], require the aid of automatic categorization. The building of accurate text classifiers is a hard task by itself and the huge size of the data makes this problem even more challenging. There are many existing approaches to this problem, with different results both in terms of accuracy and performance [3] [4] [5] [6] [7] [8], but there is still need for improvements in this area.

The aim of the work presented here was to create a classifier capable of automatic categorization of text documents from repositories containing over 100k categories with acceptable performance and quality. The experiments, aimed at evaluating our classification solution, have been performed using Wikipedia data, created with our application that allows to construct its machine-processable representation [9].

The structure of this article is as follows. The next section briefly describes SVM classifiers and the way they are incorporated to solve multiclass classification problems. Section 3 describes our proposition to speed up and boost performance of SVM

© Springer International Publishing Switzerland 2015
L. Rutkowski et al. (Eds.): ICAISC 2015, Part I, LNAI 9119, pp. 675–686, 2015.
DOI: 10.1007/978-3-319-19324-3_60

in highly multiclass classification tasks. Then, in section 4 we present details of our parallel implementation of the proposed method. The experiments using this implementation, along with empirical results on Wikipedia datasets, are given in section 5. Last section concludes the paper and gives the ideas for further research in this area.

2   SVM Classifier in a Typical Multiclass Setting

One of the most effective methods of text classification is Support Vector Machines [10]. SVM in its base form is a binary classifier. Mathematically, SVM classifier is a hyperplane $h()$ in high dimensional feature space (examples are typically projected into that space by a kernel function), which is convex-optimized during training so that it separates the classes leaving maximal possible space (margins) between them. Prediction step can be summarized in a simple equation $a = h(x)$, where a is the activation of the hyperplane, and x is the feature vector (possibly transformed by a kernel) of a testing object. The sign of a decides which class is predicted, whereas the absolute value of a indicates the confidence of this decision. With advanced optimization algorithms used by SVM, time complexity of training such a hyperplane is $O(m_{train})$, where m_{train} is number of training examples.

Although there are attempts to directly deal with multiclass problems using reformulated SVMs [11,12], most often such problems are decomposed into binary classifications and incorporate typical SVM classifiers summarized above.

In a popular *one–vs–all* scheme (also more correctly referred to as *one–vs–rest*), for each class a separate hyperplane is trained by treating examples from that class as positives and all the rest examples in the dataset as negatives. During prediction a test object is assigned to a class which hyperplane's activation a is the highest (*winner takes all* strategy). Complexity of calculating the whole model in this setting is $O(m_{train} \cdot N)$, where N denotes the number of classes. In case of prediction, assigning labels to m_{test} test objects can be performed in a $O(m_{test} \cdot N)$ time. For large datasets comprising lots of classes and objects, both training and prediction is computationally expensive to the extent where it becomes impractical to perform training and prediction sequentially and thus parallel techniques are necessary. Moreover, for very big datasets, the requirement that the whole dataset is needed for training a single hyperplane, can lead to memory problems. Another important issue with this approach is that it divides data into positive and negative classes which are very imbalanced, especially for highly multiclass problems. For example, assuming that there are 100k classes of equal size, the proportion of positive to negative examples would be 1:99999. This high imbalance can lead to poor quality of predictions.

The second popular scheme is called *one–vs–one*. Here, a separate SVM classifier is trained for each pair of classes, yielding $N(N - 1)/2$ hyperplanes. The prediction in such a system is most often done with *Max Wins* approach, in which the class with the biggest number of *votes* from all classifiers is chosen, although more advanced techniques are possible [13]. Although the number of hyperplanes grows quadratically with N, each classifier requires examples only from two classes and not from the whole dataset, therefore the learning phase theoretically could still be $O(m_{train} \cdot N)$, while there are no problems with fitting data into memory and imbalanced data. Unfortunately, this complexity estimation does not hold for datasets, where objects can belong to more than one class (multi-label classification tasks). Also, the testing phase, assuming standard *Max Wins* approach, is $O\left(N^2\right)$. Therefore, for large-scale multi-label problems (and categorizing Wikipedia articles belongs to this family), *one–vs–one* scheme becomes impractical. The comparative study of these multiclass SVM settings, as well as less popular ones, can be found in [14].

It is important to note, that the Wikipedia classification belongs to a multi-label family of problems, where a given document can be (and almost always is) associated with more that one category label. In such cases, the *winner takes all* algorithm of *one–vs–all* strategy is replaced with the following procedure. Each article is tested against every category in the dataset and the final result consists of categories with activation scores that exceed a specified threshold value. The number of categories returned as well as the minimum acceptable level of activation are parametrized. It should be noticed that changing these parameters has great impact on accuracy of the classifier. Having large computational resources (as training has to be repeated many times) this task can be optimized to select the parameters giving the best results.

3   *One–vs–near* Method

Since the number of categories has a crucial influence on classifier performance, we propose a solution to limit the number of necessary comparisons by modifying standard *one–vs–all* scheme. During SVM training instead of comparing every class with set of all others we compare it *only to the most similar ones*.

This scheme we call *one–vs–near*. It allows to limit the number of articles m_{train}, required to train during a single binary classifier construction, by reducing the dataset only to the most similar categories. This solution makes certain assumptions that need to be met for it to work properly.

 – The dataset should contain many distinguishable categories.
 – It should be possible to find nearest neighbors of each category in a short time.
 – The neighboring categories should allow to create an accurate classifier.

All these conditions should be easily met in a sparse dataset such as the Wikipedia machine processable representation based on bag of words [15] and its extensions [16]. Because of the huge number of categories and articles, it should be possible to limit the training dataset size for each binary classifier. This solution should give us the following advantages:

 – The memory consumption should be limited.
 – The training performance should be better due to smaller size of the training set.
 – The accuracy of the resulting classifier should be comparable to the one trained on the entire dataset, if above assumptions are satisfied, or even better due to noise reduction.
 – The problem of highly unbalanced datasets should be mitigated.

Since the SVM uses the support vectors to create the hyperplane only the datapoints at the border between categories are significant to the result. This means that most of the dataset should be redundant and only the points in the neighboring categories are needed to create an accurate classifier. This situation is symbolically represented in Fig. 1.

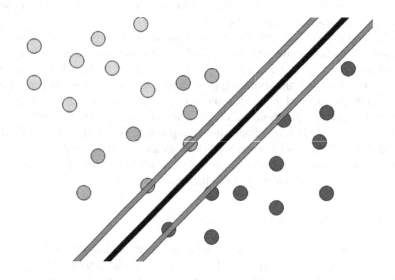

Fig. 1. Schematic example motivating *one–vs–near* approach

In this example we can see that only the border points of categories represented as red and green dots are needed in order to create the support vectors and plot the optimal hyperplane. The points of the category represented with blue dots are therefore redundant, and have no impact at the resulting classifier.

The neighboring classes are computed by a kNN classifier using cosine distance, typical in text processing [17]. To obtain nearest categories, instead of comparing distances of a test document feature vector to training feature vectors, the kNN classifier computes the distances between every category centroid – we model distances between categories by distances between their centroids.

4   Parallel Implementation Details

Besides the speedups obtained due to our *one–vs–near* multiclass scheme, the construction of scalable text classifier requires the use of a parallel computations environment. As presented before, both the training and the prediction task related to each SVM hyperplane are intrinsically independent, therefore the job of decomposing the problem between parallel computational nodes is straightforward. In fact, each task is either a category to train (in the training phase) or an article, for which classes are to be predicted (in the prediction phase). Each computational node picks up tasks from the task queue.

In our implementation each of computed hyperplanes is saved into a separate file and for each category prediction this file should be read. SVM training for large data can be parallelized by running a single class training procedure in one thread. Managing to distribute training procedures related to all classes over different computational nodes allows to construct a scalable classifier. Our implementation uses a file queue in order to distribute training tasks between processes. This allows us to run the classifier in parallel on many computing nodes using common network file system.

The prediction phase of the classifier requires to test each article from the test set against every hyperplane. Just as in the training phase, this problem can also be parallelized – the procedure is run in parallel threads and the use of file queue allows to run the program on many computing nodes.

In our implementation computations were parallelized in two ways. First, the jobs are spread across multiple machines. Then, on each machine multiple processor cores are used to speed up the whole process. Synchronization between computing nodes was obtained using Network File System (NFS) and file locking. With NFS, every machine works in the same directory, having access to the same files and saving results in the same folder. All the jobs to be done are stored in a single TODO file. The TODO file contains names of hyperplanes to train in case of training and list of objects to predict labels for in case of prediction. Every computing node can obtain certain number of jobs from the TODO file and run these jobs using available cores. Having done that it can receive new jobs and so on.

In addition to machine level parallelization the architecture allows for each node to run its computations in parallel threads. This means that eg. having 5 nodes each with 4 logical processors gives us 20 parallel threads in total. Both the number of nodes and threads running on each node is parametrized and can be changed depending on available hardware.

As manually starting the software on each node is time consuming and prone to errors we did MPI Message Passing Interface implementation [18] to run and initialize the program on specified nodes with a single command as well as to assign ranks to each process in order to identify them. The ranks are used for logging the computations of each node in a separate file and in some cases to assign certain parts of the problem to separate threads on separate nodes. Since the filesystem queue performed with acceptable results there was no need for any additional tasks division scheme like master-slave.

5   Experiments

To evaluate effectiveness of our approach we perform series of tests. They were planned to check performance, scalability and accuracy of the classifier. Initial tests have been performed with smaller size data and without cross validation in order to make them feasible to run with limited time and computing power. The final tests have been performed using large scale datasets.

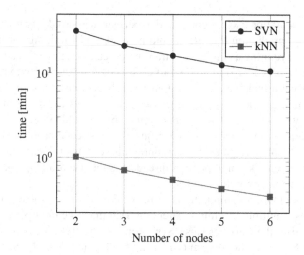

Fig. 2. SVM and kNN performance

5.1 SVM and kNN Training Scalability

For evaluation of SVM and kNN scalability we use data prepared from Wikipedia that contained 530 categories and 853283 articles. The average density of feature vectors equals 0.004%, which gives 876 MB file. The results were computed on our computer cluster with usage of different number of nodes. Each node consists of four logical processors, the time results are shown in Fig. 2.

The aim of this test was to approximate the performance of SVM classifier construction in relation to the number of computational nodes. As we can see the classifier scales quite well as it was expected. Whats more, we can see that the kNN classifier is faster by a magnitude, which confirms the most important assumption of the one–vs–near scheme, that we can find neighbours of each category in a short time.

5.2 Tests of Accuracy on Small Data

In order to assess the quality of the SVM classifier we perform a test of its accuracy. To limit the time of the experiment we run this test on the dataset with limited number of elements, same as in the previous experiment. The tests were performed using 10-fold cross-validation. The measured values contains precision, recall and the F-score. These values are presented in Tab. 1.

- $Precision = true\_positive/(true\_positive + false\_positive)$
- $Recall = true\_positive/(true\_positive + false\_negative)$
- $F - score = 2 * Precision * Recall/(Precision + Recall)$

Big number of examples per category allowed to train an accurate classifier. The results of the experiments presented in sections 5.1 and 5.2 indicate the classifier will scale up well and can reach acceptable results of classification quality.

Table 1. SVM classification results

True positives	False positives	False negatives	Precision	Recall	F-score
888306	203669	339974	81.34%	72.32%	76.56%

5.3   Scalability in the Function of Datasets Size

To check how the classifiers architecture works on large data we perform experiments with different sizes of big data packages. Beside computational effectiveness, the main concern here was the memory required on each computing node to load a dataset. To overcome that problem it was required to implement additional parameter that specifies the size of processed data block. For this experiment different sets of data were created with different numbers of articles.

Five various datasets were created from the full Wikipedia using Matrix'u application [9] based on 8th March 2013 [19] dump. They differ in the number of articles filtered out from them, the number of small categories merged with their parents and finally the number of the remaining small categories removed (categories with not enough examples to train a general classifier). Their description is shown in Tab. 2.

Table 2. Large scale datasets

Name	File size	Num. of cat.	Num. of art.	Vector density
Dataset1	2.1 GB	127402	2331707	0,0017%
Dataset2	2.4 GB	125573	2675198	0,0017%
Dataset3	2.7 GB	146444	3067138	0,0017%
Dataset4	3.0 GB	156829	3517048	0,0017%
Dataset5	4.4 GB	163986	3520309	0,0024%

The tests were run on two different clusters of computers with different hardware configurations:

Department Cluster: processor: Intel(R) Xeon(TM) CPU 2.80GHz, 4 physical, 8 logical cores, L2 Cache size: 2048KB, Memory: 4054340 kB, Swap 3076436 kB.

Lab 527: processor: Intel(R) Core(TM) i7-2600K CPU 3.40GHz, 4 physical, 8 logical cores, L2 cache size: 256K, L3 cache size, Memory: 8172568 kB, Swap 2111484 kB.

Each dataset was run on each cluster in order to test the memory consumption as well as to compare the performance between different hardware configurations. Both clusters consisted of 8 computing nodes with four threads per node, giving a total of 32 threads. The results of these tests are presented in Fig. 3

As expected, the execution times in this test are bigger for datasets containing more articles and categories and having bigger density. The lab527 cluster shows better performance than the department cluster for all datasets, most likely due to the hardware specification. The most interesting result of this test is the scaling of the classifier on the department cluster. The execution times grew nonlineary with the size of the dataset. This can be explained by the memory limitations of each node on this cluster. The times

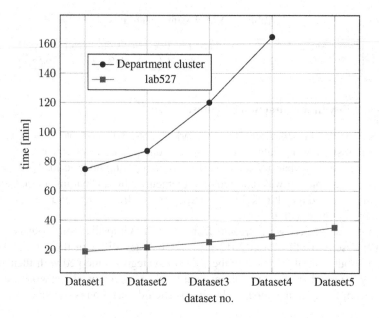

Fig. 3. kNN training scalability for large data

used for memory initialization by the system grew rapidly with dataset sizes closing to the maximum size of system memory.

5.4 *One–vs–near* Accuracy in Relation to the Number of Neighbors

This test was designed in order to measure the accuracy of the *one–vs–near* strategy in relation to the number of category neighbours and to compare it with the accuracy of the *one–vs–all* scheme. The test was conducted for a predefined set of parameters and the only variable parameter was the number of neighbours. As an evaluation dataset, here we use the same dataset as in section 5.2. The assessment of the *one–vs–near* accuracy was performed with use of 10-fold cross-validation. The results of this test are shown in Fig. 4.

As we can see in Fig. 4 the *one–vs–near* strategy starts to perform quite well above particular treshold of k neighbors. The results for the *one–vs–near* strategy were worse than the *one–vs–all* scheme if smaller number of class neighbors has been selected. Increase of that parameter leads to improvement of the results. Increasing the number of k neighbors over 400 makes the strategy practically equivalent to *one–vs–all*. This is intuitive as the number of category's nearest categories limits in the total number of all the other categories. It should be noticed proposed approach consumes additional computation time required to calculate neighbors. In next section we show how this addition processing is compensated by more effective classifier learning.

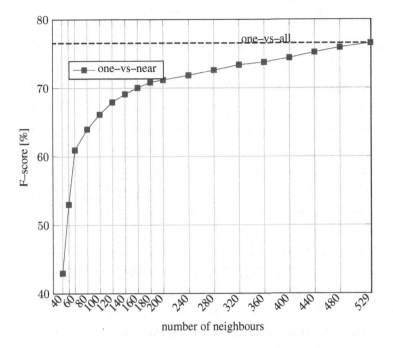

Fig. 4. *One-vs-near* accuracy compared to *one-vs-all*

5.5 *One–vs–near* Performance

Another factor we measure is the performance of the *one–vs–near* approach in relation to the number of neighbors. The results performed on lab527 cluster and dataset #5 are shown in Fig. 5.

What can be observed from the graphs given in Fig. 5 is that the decreasing number of classes used for classifier construction significantly reduces the computation time. The gain is significant up to using 500 neighboring classes. This fact together with previously observed improvement of the classifier quality constructed with smaller number of classes (see Fig. 4) constitute a strong argument that *one–vs–near* scheme can be used as a general method for SVM improvement.

However, it should be noticed that the *one–vs–near* method adds a fixed factor to the computations that comes from computing the neighbouring classes. This additional time can be observed in the graph when the total number of neighbouring classes exceeds 1000. Above that point *one-vs-all* strategy starts to perform better than one-vs-near. In our application we use a simple comparison of one class with others, but this time can be significantly reduced incorporating dedicated indexes [20].

Despite increasing computation cost, the memory requirements of the strategy proposed by us, interestingly, are still below requirements of *one–vs–all* approach. Our solution allows us to limit the memory consumption using the cost of additional computations. If the number of neighbouring classes would contain all examples from the

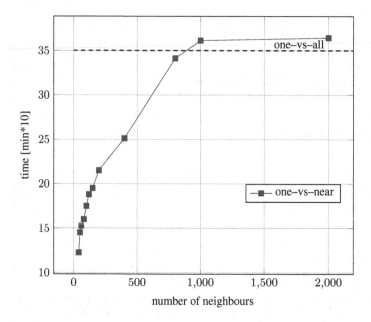

Fig. 5. *One–vs–near* performance in relation to the number of neighbors

dataset, it would cause maximum memory requirements that would be as big as for the *one–vs–all* scheme.

6   Conclusions and Future Work

In our research we developed and evaluated a parallel approach to classification of text documents with SVM. The algorithm was designed to be used with large scale text document repositories in mind, such as the Wikipedia. The proposed solution scales up well and gave acceptable accuracy results. Additionally, a new approach to improve effectiveness of classification – *one–vs–near* scheme – was implemented and tested. Proposed scheme provides accuracy comparable, to typical *one–vs–all* scheme while significantly improving time needed to classifier construction.

Although the problem of text documents classification was extensively tested in many works (eg. [5] [3] [21]), there is still some room for further research and improvements in this area. There are many yet untested approaches to this problem that might be worth testing.

One of such possible approaches is an application of different methods for neighbors search, such as the one proposed by Holloway et al [22]. It would be valuable to compare its quality and performance with the centroid based approach. Another idea would be to seek for neighboring articles instead of whole categories although this could be very demanding performance–wise. It would be also interesting to test the *one–vs–near* classifier with different kinds of SVM solvers and their parameters. Proposed approach can also be useful for identifying inner categories relations [23].

One thing that did not present satisfying results in our research was the memory usage reduction. Storage of large matrixes in the form of neighbor list can be possibly improved using some sort of array data DBMS, such as SciDB [24], to store the feature vectors, instead of plain text files. This would further improve the performance of the classifier and allow to limit the batch size and thus the memory requirements.

Another potentially interesting approach would be to make the initial classification on some reduced set of higher level categories (only if categories are organized in a hierarchical structure, as in case of Wikipedia categories) and then continue the more detailed classification only on the set of neighboring categories. However, the accuracy of such solution could be greatly decreased since errors from each classification stage would multiply.

As mentioned before, the developed classifier presents promising results in the Wikipedia classification task. There are many different approaches to automatic classification that have not been tested yet or at least not in the context of text documents classification. Some of which were mentioned in this section. It is an interesting topic and there is still a lot of potentially valuable research to be done in this area of computer science. A big challenge will be to develop some classifiers using a quantum-inspired algorithms [25] as well as some immune algorithms.

Acknowledgements. The work was supported by founds of Department of Computer Systems Architecture of Faculty of Electronics, Telecommunications and Informatics Gdańsk University of Technology.

References

1. de Kunder, M.: The size of the world wide web (2014), http://www.worldwidewebsize.com/ (Online; accessed May 22, 2014)
2. Wikipedia: Size of wikipedia (2014), http://en.wikipedia.org/wiki/Wikipedia:Size_of_Wikipedia (Online; accessed January 25, 2014)
3. Gantner, Z., Schmidt-Thieme, L.: Automatic content-based categorization of wikipedia articles. In: Proceedings of the 2009 Workshop on The People's Web Meets NLP: Collaboratively Constructed Semantic Resources, People's Web 2009, pp. 32–37. Association for Computational Linguistics, Stroudsburg (2009)
4. Han, E.-H., Karypis, G.: Centroid-based document classification: Analysis and experimental results. In: Zighed, D.A., Komorowski, J., Żytkow, J.M. (eds.) PKDD 2000. LNCS (LNAI), vol. 1910, pp. 424–431. Springer, Heidelberg (2000)
5. Fan, R.E., Chang, K.W., Hsieh, C.J., Wang, X.R., Lin, C.J.: Liblinear: A library for large linear classification. Journal of Machine Learning Research 9, 1871–1874 (2008)
6. Miao, Y., Qiu, X.: Hierarchical centroid-based classifier for large scale text classification. In: Large Scale Hierarchical Text Classification (2009)
7. Chu, C.T., Kim, S.K., Lin, Y.A., Yu, Y., Bradski, G.R., Ng, A.Y., Olukotun, K.: Map-reduce for machine learning on multicore. In: Schölkopf, B., Platt, J.C., Hoffman, T. (eds.) NIPS, pp. 281–288. MIT Press (2006)
8. Balicki, J., Korłub, W., Szymanski, J., Zakidalski, M.: Big data paradigm developed in volunteer grid system with genetic programming scheduler. In: Rutkowski, L., Korytkowski, M., Scherer, R., Tadeusiewicz, R., Zadeh, L.A., Zurada, J.M. (eds.) ICAISC 2014, Part I. LNCS (LNAI), vol. 8467, pp. 771–782. Springer, Heidelberg (2014)

9. Szymański, J.: Wikipedia Articles Representation with Matrix'u. In: Hota, C., Srimani, P.K. (eds.) ICDCIT 2013. LNCS, vol. 7753, pp. 500–510. Springer, Heidelberg (2013)

10. Joachims, T.: Text categorization with support vector machines: Learning with many relevant features. Springer (1998)

11. Crammer, K., Singer, Y.: On the algorithmic implementation of multiclass kernel-based vector machines. The Journal of Machine Learning Research 2, 265–292 (2002)

12. Lee, Y., Lin, Y., Wahba, G.: Multicategory support vector machines: Theory and application to the classification of microarray data and satellite radiance data. Journal of the American Statistical Association 99, 67–81 (2004)

13. Platt, J.C., Cristianini, N., Shawe-Taylor, J.: Large margin dags for multiclass classification. In: Advances in Neural Information Processing Systems, vol. 12, pp. 547–553. MIT Press (2000)

14. Duan, K.-B., Keerthi, S.S.: Which is the best multiclass SVM method? An empirical study. In: Oza, N.C., Polikar, R., Kittler, J., Roli, F. (eds.) MCS 2005. LNCS, vol. 3541, pp. 278–285. Springer, Heidelberg (2005)

15. Szymański, J.: Comparative analysis of text representation methods using classification. Cybernetics and Systems 45, 180–199 (2014)

16. Szymański, J.: Words context analysis for improvement of information retrieval. In: Nguyen, N.-T., Hoang, K., Jędrzejowicz, P. (eds.) ICCCI 2012, Part I. LNCS, vol. 7653, pp. 318–325. Springer, Heidelberg (2012)

17. Baeza-Yates, R., Ribeiro-Neto, B., et al.: Modern information retrieval, vol. 463. ACM Press, New York (1999)

18. Gabriel, E., Fagg, G.E., Bosilca, G., Angskun, T., Dongarra, J.J., Squyres, J.M., Sahay, V., Kambadur, P., Barrett, B., Lumsdaine, A., Castain, R.H., Daniel, D.J., Graham, R.L., Woodall, T.S.: Open MPI: Goals, concept, and design of a next generation MPI implementation. In: Proceedings of the 11th European PVM/MPI Users' Group Meeting, Budapest, Hungary, pp. 97–104 (2004)

19. Wikipedia: Wikipedia database dump (2014), http://dumps.wikimedia.org/enwiki/20140102/ (Online; accessed January 25, 2014)

20. Kryszkiewicz, M., Skonieczny, L.: Faster clustering with DBSCAN. In: Intelligent Information Processing and Web Mining, Proceedings of the International IIS: IIPWM 2005 Conference held in Gdansk, Poland, June 13-16, pp. 605–614 (2005)

21. Hsu, C.W., Chang, C.C., Lin, C.J.: A practical guide to support vector classification. Technical report, Department of Computer Science, National Taiwan University (2003)

22. Holloway, T., Bozicevic, M., Börner, K.: Analyzing and visualizing the semantic coverage of wikipedia and its authors: Research articles. Complex 12, 30–40 (2007)

23. Szymański, J.: Mining relations between wikipedia categories. In: Zavoral, F., Yaghob, J., Pichappan, P., El-Qawasmeh, E. (eds.) NDT 2010. CCIS, vol. 88, pp. 248–255. Springer, Heidelberg (2010)

24. Cudré-Mauroux, P., Kimura, H., Lim, K.T., Rogers, J., Simakov, R., Soroush, E., Velikhov, P., Wang, D.L., Balazinska, M., Becla, J., et al.: A demonstration of scidb: a science-oriented dbms. Proceedings of the VLDB Endowment 2, 1534–1537 (2009)

25. Balicki, J.: An adaptive quantum-based multiobjective evolutionary algorithm for efficient task assignment in distributed systems. In: Proceedings of the WSEAES 13th International Conference on Computers, ICCOMP 2009, Stevens Point, Wisconsin, USA, pp. 417–422. World Scientific and Engineering Academy and Society (WSEAS) (2009)

Reducing Time Complexity of SVM Model by LVQ Data Compression

Marcin Blachnik[✉]

Department of Management and Informatics, Silesian University of Technology,
Katowice, Krasińskiego 8, Poland
marcin.blachnik@polsl.pl

Abstract. The standard SVM classifier is not adjusted to processing large training set as the computational complexity can reach $O(n^3)$. To overcome this limitation we discuss the idea of reducing the size of the training data by initial preprocessing of the training set using Learning Vector Quantization (LVQ) neural network and then building the SVM model using prototypes returned by the LVQ network. As the LVQ network scales linearly with n, and in contrast to clustering algorithms utilizes label information it seems to be a good choice for initial data compression.

1 Introduction

One of the state of the art classification algorithms is support vector machine (SVM) [10], which in the last two decades proved its quality being the winner in many of the classification challenges. Since every coin has two sides, providing good classification accuracy usually leads to high computational complexity. This issue is becoming more important as the sizes of the datasets increase. The scale of this problem demonstrates Fig. (1)), which presents an average number of samples in the classification dataset submitted to the UCI repository [1] in each year (note logarithmic Y axis).

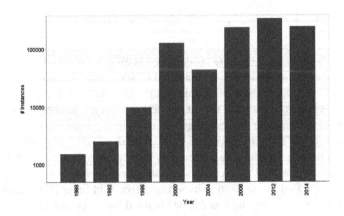

Fig. 1. Evolution of the number of samples of the datasets in UCI repository per year

© Springer International Publishing Switzerland 2015
L. Rutkowski et al. (Eds.): ICAISC 2015, Part I, LNAI 9119, pp. 687–695, 2015.
DOI: 10.1007/978-3-319-19324-3_61

The standard SVM is not adjusted to that issue because its high computational complexity, which may be of order $O(n^3)$. In this paper we discuss the idea of reducing the size of the training data by initial preprocessing of the training set using Learning Vector Quantization (LVQ) neural network and then building the SVM model using prototypes (vectors) returned by the LVQ network. As the LVQ network scales linearly with n, and in contrast to clustering algorithms the LVQ network utilizes label information, the whole process of building the prediction model can be significantly accelerated without any important impact on classification accuracy.

To avoid ambiguity and to provide coherence we use to following notation: a classification task is defined as a mapping $y = M(\mathbf{x})$ where $\mathbf{x} \in \Re^m$, which returns a value $y^t \in [v_1, v_2, \ldots, v_L]$. The challenge is to find such a model $M(\cdot)$ having a training set $[\mathbf{X}, \mathbf{y}]$, which consists of n samples $\mathbf{X} = [\mathbf{x}^1, \mathbf{x}^2, \ldots, \mathbf{x}^n]^T$ and $\mathbf{y} = [y_1, y_2, \ldots, y_n]^T$.

The paper is organized as follows: the next section (2) briefly describes the SVM classifier and shows how in some case process large training sets, then the next section (3) presents the LVQ algorithm and its application to training size reduction. The following section (4) provides description of the experiments and obtained results. Finally in the last section general conclusions are provided with the plans for the future work.

2   SVM Algorithm

In the case of SVM algorithm a classification model $M(\mathbf{x})$ is represented as a separating hyperplane defined in the feature space obtained using some mapping function $\Phi(\mathbf{x})$ which maps input data into this space. The hyperplane is determined by a set of support vectors $\mathbf{sv}_i$, which are the samples from the training set situated in between the classification margin. Considering the properties of the dot product in the feature space $\Phi(\mathbf{x}_a) \cdot \Phi(\mathbf{x}_b)$, to classify an input vector $\mathbf{x}$ it is not necessary to find its direct representation of $\mathbf{x}$ in the feature space, instead this dot product can be simply calculated using a kernel function $K(||\mathbf{x_a} - \mathbf{x_b}||)$, what leads to the equation (1)

$$M(\mathbf{x}) = sign\left(\sum_{i=1}^{n} \alpha_i K\left(||\mathbf{x} - \mathbf{sv}_i||\right)\right) \tag{1}$$

The dimensionality of the feature space depends on the mapping function Φ and in some cases may lead to an infinite-dimensional or very high dimensional space. As it was introduced, the main limitation of this algorithm is its computational complexity, which becomes a serious problem for infinite feature spaces, as obtained by a typical Gaussian kernel. In that case the computational complexity scales between $O(n) = n^2$ and $O(n) = n^3$ [2]. If the feature space is finite and rather low (comparable to the input space), then the acceleration can be achieved by a direct mapping of the input data into the feature space, as a kind of preprocessing step, and solving a linear optimization problem ($O(n)$) to find the separating hyperplane (see LibLinear [3]). An example of the finite feature space representation can be obtained for polynomial kernels.

A linear SVM has even more advantages, it allows not only to reduce the computational complexity of the training phase, but also allows to reduce the complexity of the prediction phase to $O(1)$. It is possible by converting the decision function from the support vector representation as in (1) into a feature space representation of a classical linear model

$$y = sign\left(\mathbf{a}^T \cdot \mathbf{x}\right) \tag{2}$$

where $\mathbf{a} = [a_1, a_2, \ldots a_m]$ are attribute factors, which in the case of linear SVM can be obtained by

$$a_j = \sum_{i=1}^{n} \alpha_i x_{ij} \tag{3}$$

where x_{ij} is the value of j'th feature of vector $\mathbf{x}_{ij}$. It is assumed that the vector $\mathbf{x}$ is explicitly represented in the feature space.

The approach presented above can be only applied to a finite-dimensional feature space where the space can be directly calculated. However, this does not apply to a non-linear SVM, which utilizes the kernel trick, as in the case of Gaussian kernel (which is usually the default choice for most SVMs). In this scenario, to handle massive datasets another solution needs to be applied. The most natural approach is input data compression, where instead of n only n' most representative samples are used to build the model, where $n' < n$. This can be implemented by instance selection methods, which were designed to improve accuracy by noise reduction and speed-up the k-NN classifier. For example this was studied in [5,7,9,4]. Another solution is data clustering, which allows to replace the original input samples by means of a small groups of data. This can be done by k-means, vector quantization (VQ) or any other clustering algorithm, which represents clusters as some reference points. As the clustering can be applied to large n, the algorithm should have low computational complexity. As well k-means as VQ clustering satisfy this requirements with their linear complexity.

The compression based methods have one more advantage. As the complexity of the decision making process depends on the size of the training dataset (sum over n) by reducing n we also speed up the prediction phase proportionally to the compression ratio n/n'.

An extension to the standard clustering algorithms can be obtained by learning vector quantization (LVQ) algorithm (described below), which also uses label information during the self organization process.

3   The LVQ Algorithm

The Learning Vector Quantization or LVQ [8] algorithm belongs to the family of self organizing neural networks. In this type of networks a neuron also called codebook or prototype (these names will be used interchangeably) is defined as a vector in the input space $\mathbf{p} \in \Re^m$ and in case of the LVQ network also incorporates label information y_p. To annotate access to the label information of a prototype or training vector an $c(\cdot)$ operator will be used ($y_p = c(\mathbf{p})$).

One of the standard training methods of self organizing networks is based on the winner takes all principle. According to this principle only the most activated neuron is updated during the training phase. From another point of view, one may say that LVQ derives from clustering methods because codebooks represent cluster centers, but the update rule incorporates label information. The update rule of the standard LVQ is defined as (4) and (5)

$$\mathbf{p}_j^{t+1} = \mathbf{p}_j^t + \alpha \cdot (\mathbf{x}_i - \mathbf{p}_j^t) \tag{4}$$

$$\mathbf{p}_j^{t+1} = \mathbf{p}_j^t - \alpha \cdot (\mathbf{x}_i - \mathbf{p}_j^t) \tag{5}$$

where $\mathbf{p}_i^t$ denotes i's codebook of total c codebooks in iteration t. These two equations are used alternatively, one or the other depending on the label equality between the closest codebook $\mathbf{p}_j$ and current input vector $\mathbf{x}_i$.

The scheme of this algorithm is presented in sketch (1). From that sketch we can easily see that the computational complexity of the LVQ algorithm is linear in terms of the number of samples n and in terms of the number of attributes m $O(n, m) = n \cdot m \cdot l$ and it also linearly depends on the number of training iterations l. This is an important advantage over other classification methods. As stated above the LVQ algorithm can

---

Algorithm 1. LVQ algorithm

Data: Training set $T = \{(\mathbf{x}_1, y_1), \ldots (\mathbf{x}_n, y_n)\}$
Input: c - the number of codebooks,
        α - initial learning rate,
        l - the number of iterations
Result: Set of codebooks P

1   $P \leftarrow$ RandomInstances(T, c)
2   **for** $i = 1 \ldots l$ **do**
3      $k = \underset{j=1\ldots c}{argmin} \left(D\left(\mathbf{x}_i, \mathbf{p}_j\right) \right)$
4   **if** $c(\mathbf{x}_i) = c(\mathbf{p}_k)$ **then**
5         $\mathbf{p}_k \leftarrow \mathbf{p}_k + \alpha \cdot (\mathbf{x}_i - \mathbf{p}_k)$
     else
6         $\mathbf{p}_k \leftarrow \mathbf{p}_k - \alpha \cdot (\mathbf{x}_i - \mathbf{p}_k)$
     end
7      $alpha = \dfrac{alpha}{1 + alpha}$
  end
  return P

---

be considered a kind of clustering method, similarly to the standard Vector Quantization clustering algorithm, which differs only in the update rule ignoring equation 5. This small difference has a huge impact on the self organizing process, so that the prototypes (a king of cluster centers) represent dense clusters of input vectors and preserve label information. This leads to the next conclusion that the codebooks should represent the compressed structure of the data very accurately, maintaining all the important properties of the training set and thus can be used as the preprocessing step, compressing the training set before building a classification model.

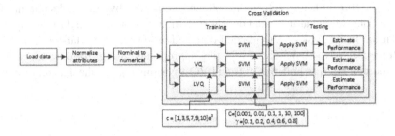

Fig. 2. Data flow diagram

The above-described facts of liner computational complexity and proper data representation allows to define a thesis that the LVQ algorithm is very well suited for large dataset compression for reducing computational complexity of the SVM classifier in both the training and prediction process.

4   Experiments

4.1   Experiment Settings

To validate the thesis presented in previous section we provided a set of experiments comparing classification accuracy of the pure SVM model trained on the whole training set with the model built on the data obtained as prototypes from the LVQ network and the VQ clustering algorithm. The general scheme of the experiments is provided in Fig. (2)

Table 1. Datasets used in the experiment

Name	# Attributes	# Classes	# Samples
Segment	19	7	2310
Texture	40	11	5500
Phoneme	5	2	5404
Ring	20	2	7400
Spambase	57	2	4597
Twonorm	20	2	7400

It started from loading the data, then the attributes of the dataset were normalized to fit into the range $[0, 1]$ and in the case of nominal attributes they were converted into numerical ones using a standard binary representation. Finally the performance of the 10-fold cross validation was evaluated. During the training phase of the cross validation step simultaneously three SVM models were build, which differs in data compression method. The first model was obtained directly on the input data, the next two models used codebooks as an input data provided by the VQ and LVQ algorithm. The number of codebooks of the VQ and LVQ algorithm were changed in range $c = [100, 300, 500, 700, 900, 1000]$ and initialized by stratified sampling from the input data, such that the codebooks distribution was proportional to the input data distribution. In the case of VQ method obtained prototypes were labeled considering class frequency of the input data. Adjusting appropriate settings for the SVM model is very important because both the VQ and LVQ algorithm change the data representation

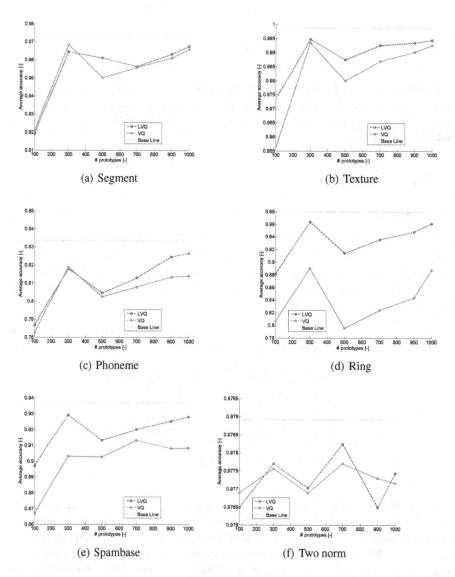

(a) Segment   (b) Texture

(c) Phoneme   (d) Ring

(e) Spambase   (f) Two norm

Fig. 3. Relation between the number of prototypes used by the LVQ and VQ algorithms and the corresponding accuracy of SVM. The baseline represents the accuracy of SVM trained on the whole training set.

so these classifiers has to be optimized for each input data independently. The set of parameters evaluated for the SVM classifier are $C = [0.001, 0.01, 0.1, 1, 10, 100]$ and $\gamma = [0.1, 0.2, 0.4, 0.6, 0.8]$.

The experiments were evaluated on 6 datasets obtained from the Keel project repository [6]. The detailed list of datasets used in the experiments with the basic description such as number of attributes, samples, and classes is provided in table 1.

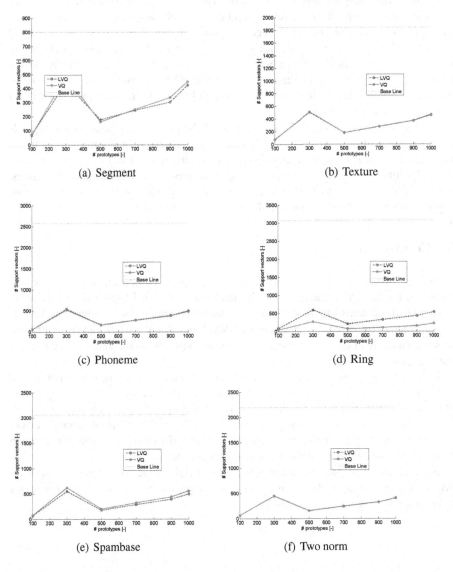

(a) Segment

(b) Texture

(c) Phoneme

(d) Ring

(e) Spambase

(f) Two norm

Fig. 4. Relation between the number of prototypes used by the LVQ and VQ algorithms and the number of support vectors of the SVM. The baseline represents the number of support vectors of SVM trained on the whole training set.

4.2 Results

The most important issue discussed in this paper is the relation between the level of compression and the accuracy of the SVM classifier. The obtained results, which show this relation are presented in Figure (3), but instead of direct value of compression the number of prototypes returned by the LVQ and VQ algorithms is given.

In almost all presented figures the LVQ network overcomes the VQ clustering algorithm. In some examples as in *Phone me*, *Two Norm* or *Segment* datasets the difference is not significant especially for lower number of codebooks, but in some other cases as in *Spambase* or *Ring* the difference is significant. For these two dataset the LVQ algorithm allows for over 3% accuracy increase compared to the standard clustering method. Moreover, the difference between the accuracy of SVM for correctly chosen number of prototypes (maximum accuracy) and the SVM trained on the whole dataset differed only by 0.5%, while in the case of the VQ network the difference could reach 10% as for the *Ring* dataset.

Another important issue is the complexity of the prediction phase, which depends on the number of support vectors. The results are presented in Figure (4). As it can be observed there is no significant difference between the LVQ and VQ methods. Both these algorithms reduce total number of support vectors of the SVM around 3 to 5 times, what is equivalent to 3 to 5 times acceleration of the prediction process. The level of support vector reduction depends on the initial size of the datasets.

5   Conclusions

As it was shown, the LVQ method seems to be a good choice for training-data size reduction for the SVM classifier. In all presented cases the LVQ-based compression overcome the clustering method preserving identical computational complexity, and allowed to achieve comparable results to the SVM trained on the whole dataset. Although in some cases as in *Phone me* the accuracy was about 1% lower than the accuracy of the SVM trained of the whole dataset.

In both cases when the dataset compression was performed, a significant acceleration was observed also in the prediction phase. The acceleration of the training part is obvious, as the size of the input data decreases, but proposed approach also has significant impact on the number of support vectors. As the total number of support vectors is upper bounded by the number of training instances, the final prediction time is much sorter in all cases when the dataset compression was performed.

A drawback of proposed solution is the need of right choice of the number of codebooks. A general rule is "higher is better" but it reduces the compression. This seems to be an interesting topic for research.

References

1. Asuncion, A., Newman, D.: UCI machine learning repository (2007),
   http://www.ics.uci.edu/~mlearn/MLRepository.html
2. Bottou, L., Lin, C.J.: Support vector machine solvers. In: Large Scale Kernel Machines,
   pp. 301–320 (2007)
3. Fan, R.E., Chang, K.W., Hsieh, C.J., Wang, X.R., Lin, C.J.: Liblinear: A library for large
   linear classification. Journal of Machine Learning Research 9, 1871–1874 (2008)
4. Garcia, S., Derrac, J., Cano, J.R., Herrera, F.: Prototype selection for nearest neighbor classification: Taxonomy and empirical study. IEEE Transactions on Pattern Analysis and Machine
   Intelligence 34(3), 417–435 (2012)
5. Grochowski, M., Jankowski, N.: Comparison of instance selection algorithms II. Results and
   comments. In: Rutkowski, L., Siekmann, J.H., Tadeusiewicz, R., Zadeh, L.A. (eds.) ICAISC
   2004. LNCS (LNAI), vol. 3070, pp. 580–585. Springer, Heidelberg (2004)
6. Herrera, F.: Keel, knowledge extraction based on evolutionary learning, Spanish National Projects TIC2002-04036-C05, TIN2005-08386-C05 and TIN2008-06681-C06 (2005),
   http://www.keel.es
7. Jankowski, N., Grochowski, M.: Comparison of instances seletion algorithms I. Algorithms
   survey. In: Rutkowski, L., Siekmann, J.H., Tadeusiewicz, R., Zadeh, L.A. (eds.) ICAISC
   2004. LNCS (LNAI), vol. 3070, pp. 598–603. Springer, Heidelberg (2004)
8. Kohonen, T.: Learning vector quantization. In: Self-Organizing Maps, pp. 203–217. Springer
   (1997)
9. Kordos, M., Rusiecki, A.: Improving MLP neural network performance by noise reduction.
   In: Dediu, A.-H., Martín-Vide, C., Truthe, B., Vega-Rodríguez, M.A. (eds.) TPNC 2013.
   LNCS, vol. 8273, pp. 133–144. Springer, Heidelberg (2013)
10. Schölkopf, B., Smola, A.: Learning with Kernels. MIT Press, Cambridge (2002)

Secure Representation of Images Using Multi-layer Compression

Sohrab Ferdowsi[1], Sviatoslav Voloshynovskiy[1(✉)], Dimche Kostadinov[1],
Marcin Korytkowski[2], and Rafał Scherer[2]

[1] Department of Computer Science, University of Geneva,
Battle Bât. A, 7 route de Drize, 1227 Carouge, Switzerland
`svolos@unige.ch`
[2] Institute of Computational Intelligence, Częstochowa University of Technology
Al. Armii Krajowej 36, 42-200 Częstochowa, Poland

Abstract. We analyze the privacy preservation capabilities of a previously introduced multi-stage image representation framework where
blocks of images with similar statistics are decomposed into different
codebooks (dictionaries). There it was shown that at very low rate
regimes, the method is capable of compressing images that come from the
same family with results superior to those of the JPEG2000 codec. We
consider two different elements to be added to the discussed approach
to achieve a joint compression-encryption framework. The first visual
scrambling is the random projections were the random matrix is kept secret between the encryption and decryption sides. We show that for the
second approach, scrambling in the DCT domain, we can even slightly
increase the compression performance of the multi-layer approach while
making it safe against de-scrambling attacks. The experiments were carried out on the *ExtendedYaleB* database of facial images.

Keywords: Image compression · Image scrambling · Dictionary learning · Rate-distortion theory · Privacy preservation

1 Introduction

Representation of visual data is a fundamental problem in many areas of artificial
intelligence. In general, one seeks a representation which is as concise as possible
in terms of memory storage, as fast as possible in terms of computation and as
precise as possible in terms of fidelity to the original data.

Moreover, in many applications like medical imaging, biometric data and multimedia management, the security and privacy preservation issues are also among
the major factors that should be seriously taken into account. In these applications, the image data could be of sensitive nature that should not be revealed. As
an assumption, one can consider that a set of images and their encoded versions,
also possibly some information about their encoding algorithm are available in a
public domain. Therefore, a safe and privacy preserving representation scheme
should impede an attacker who knows the general structure of the representation method being used and aims at reconstructing the original images from

© Springer International Publishing Switzerland 2015
L. Rutkowski et al. (Eds.): ICAISC 2015, Part I, LNAI 9119, pp. 696–705, 2015.
DOI: 10.1007/978-3-319-19324-3_62

their representation by increasing the computational cost and the necessary data resources needed for the attack.

In this work, we consider the framework introduced in [1] for image representation and in particular image compression when the images have a similar source. We investigate the privacy preserving capabilities of this approach and add visual scrambling elements to make the representation more secure.

The paper is organized as follows. In section 2 we review the multi-layer image representation framework and in section 2.1 we analyze the security issues with this framework. In section 3 we introduce two different methods to increase the privacy preserving capabilities of the discussed framework and analyze their behavior. The first method is based on random projections and the second method scrambles the images in their DCT domain. Section 4 discusses the experimental setup and the results. We conclude the paper in section 5.

2 Multi-layer Image Representation

A framework to represent images into multi layers of decomposition was recently introduced in [1]. The method is based on qunatizing the image patches in the direct gray-scale domain into several codeworks (atoms) for the first stage. In the next stages, the quantization residual is quantized to a new set of codewords.

Fig. 1 shows this idea. $\mathbf{X} \in \mathcal{R}^n$ is the random vector representing the vectorized patches of images and $\mathbf{x}(j)$ is its jth realization. $\hat{\mathbf{x}}_1(j), \cdots \hat{\mathbf{x}}_L(j)$ are the results of quantization of the jth patch at each stage and $\hat{\mathbf{x}}(j) = \hat{\mathbf{x}}_1(w_1(j)) + \cdots + \hat{\mathbf{x}}_L(w_L(j))$ is the final estimation of $\mathbf{x}(j)$. An index vector $\mathbf{w}(j) = [w_1(j), \cdots, w_L(j)]^T$ will be used to represent the estimation of the jth patch.

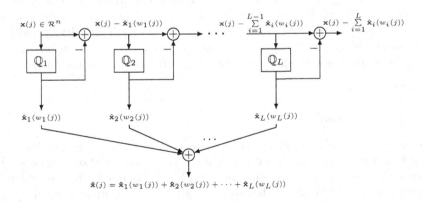

Fig. 1. Multi-layer quantization of a vectorized image patch $\mathbf{x}(j)$ to the vector $\hat{\mathbf{x}}(j)$. $\mathbb{Q}_i(\cdot), 1 \leq i \leq L$ is the quantizer of the ith layer and $w_i(j)$ is the the corresponding index at that layer. Quantizer $\mathbb{Q}_i(\cdot)$ has 2^{nR_i} codewords, where R_i is the rate of compression at i^{th} stage.

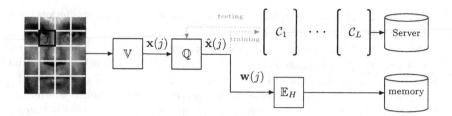

Fig. 2. Compression of an image from its blocks. $\mathbb{V}$ is the vectorizing operator, $\mathbb{Q}$ is the multi-layer quantizer and $\mathbb{E}_H$ is the entropy encoding. The codewords in each of the codebooks $\mathcal{C}_1, \cdots \mathcal{C}_L$ will be kept on a server while the encoded indices will be stored in memory as the representation of images.

Fig. 2 illustrates the compression stages to be carried out in this representation scheme. The decompression procedure is simply the inverse of compression.

In this decomposition, each codeword of $\mathcal{C}_i$, $\hat{\mathbf{X}}_i$ has the same dimension as $\mathbf{X}$. Each codebook $\mathcal{C}_i$ contains 2^{nR_i} codewords, or equivalently the corresponding indices have an alphabet of $|\mathbf{W}_i| = 2^{nR_i}$ in each layer. Therefore, the equivalent alphabet size of the corresponding indices of the final estimation, $\hat{\mathbf{X}}$ is upper bounded as

$$|\hat{\mathbf{W}}| \leq 2^{nR_1} \times \cdots \times 2^{nR_L} = 2^{n(R_1 + \cdots R_L)}.$$

This means that, by this multi-layer decomposition, the image patch could be represented by an equivalent dictionary with a maximum number of atoms equals to $2^{nR_c} = 2^{2(R_1 + \cdots R_L)}$.

This is very appealing since the equivalent alphabet size is growing exponentially with the number of layers. If a one-layer structure was to be used, like in k-means based VQ, we would need to store all these atoms in memory which would practically be infeasible, while in fact, in the multi-layer structure, we only store $2^{nR_1} + \cdots + 2^{nR_L}$ atoms. Moreover, the search complexity and also the sample complexity, the amount of training data required to achieve a certain performance in a machine learning setup will also be reduced the same as memory.

2.1   Security Analysis

We assume that an attacker has access to a number of training data from the same family of images, along with their respective representations (indices). To analyze the security of this scheme, one should ask the question, given the representation of a probe image, how can the attacker reconstruct the content of the compressed image? In particular, we are interested in estimating the amount of training data needed for the attacker to do the reconstruction and also the computational complexity of this attack procedure.

We imagine that the attacker has a database $\mathcal{X} = [\mathbf{x}(1)^T, \cdots \mathbf{x}(M)^T]$ of training data which could be similar to the database used to train the codebooks, where $\mathbf{x}(j)^T \in \mathcal{R}^n$ is a column vector of an image patch. For any $\mathbf{x}(j), 1 \le j \le M$, the attacker has also a set of indices $\mathbf{w}_1(j), \cdots \mathbf{w}_L(j)$, where $\mathbf{w}_i(j)$ is a column vector consisting of k_i elements with only one element equal to one(active) and the rest equal to zero and where k_i is the number of codewords in an unknown codebook $\mathcal{C}_i$ with $1 \le i \le L$.

Therefore, the attacker can write the system of equations as below.

$$\mathbf{x}(1)^T = \mathcal{C}_1 \mathbf{w}_1(1) + \cdots + \mathcal{C}_L \mathbf{w}_L(1)$$
$$\mathbf{x}(2)^T = \mathcal{C}_1 \mathbf{w}_1(2) + \cdots + \mathcal{C}_L \mathbf{w}_L(2)$$
$$\vdots$$
$$\mathbf{x}(M)^T = \mathcal{C}_1 \mathbf{w}_1(M) + \cdots + \mathcal{C}_L \mathbf{w}_L(M)$$

(1)

This can be written in a matrix form as:

$$\mathcal{X}^T = \mathcal{C}W \tag{2}$$

Where $\mathcal{X}$ is defined as above and $\mathcal{C}_{n \times K}$ is the concatenation of all codebooks with $K = \sum_{i=1}^{L} k_i$ and $W_{K \times M}$ is the concatenation of all $\mathbf{w}_j(i)$'s corresponding to one $\mathbf{x}(i)$ in its $i^{\mathbf{th}}$ column.

The pseudo-inverse of W does not exist since its sparsity pattern imposes the rank of WW^T to be not complete for the multi-layer case. Therefore, this equation cannot be solved to derive the value of unknown $\mathcal{C}$.

However, instead of directly solving equation (2), the attacker can estimate the values of $\mathcal{C}_j$ sequentially, starting from the first layer and then continuing to the next layers. For example, one can gather all $\mathbf{x}(j)$'s that have the same $\mathbf{w}_1$ and sum them up. As long as the number of $\mathbf{x}$'s is enough, assuming that $\mathcal{C}_i$'s are zero mean, an estimation of the corresponding codeword of $\mathcal{C}_1$ will be derived. Having estimated the codewords of C_1, then other codebooks could also be estimated accordingly.

Therefore, one can conclude that this data representation scheme is not safe against attacks. In the next section, we investigate two different modifications to this approach to boost its privacy preservation capabilities.

3   Privacy Preserving Multi-layer Image Representation

In this section we consider the problem of joint compression-scrambling. In particular, we search for an image representation which is as compact as possible, while it should be able to cope with the distortions introduced by the compression and also not prone to security attacks. In section 3.1 we investigate the idea of Random Projections as an element to be added to the previous setup. Then in 3.2 we consider randomizing the images in the DCT domain.

Fig. 3 sketches the general idea of joint compression-scrambling.

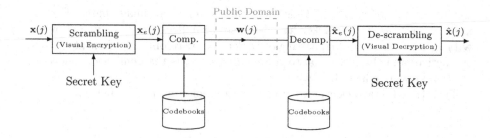

Fig. 3. The joint compression-scrambling scenario where the image data are scrambled(visually encrypted) using a secret key and then compressed. The image representations(indices), along with the details of the compression algorithm may be available to public.

3.1 Random Projections Based Scrambling

Random projections are extensively used in dimensionality reduction due to their capabilities to preserve pairwise distances of data points [2]. Although we are not interested here in dimensionality reduction, random projections are appealing for us. Because, while keeping the essentials of the original data, we can have a randomization in their structure and thus more security.

Fig. 4 shows the structure of the system with random projections. $A_{b \times b}$ is a random matrix with elements independently drawn from an identical zero-mean Gaussian distribution and then orthogonalized, where b is the size of square patches from images. $x(i)$ is an image patch in the form of a square matrix before vectorization.

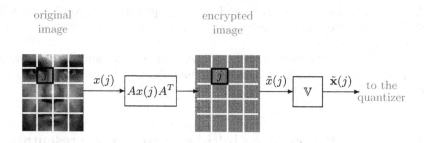

Fig. 4. Encryption of the images with random projections. $\mathbb{V}$ is the vectorizing operator

After the compression and decompression stages, the de-scrambling of the data is simply the reverse operations of those in Fig. 4. However, having the random matrix A as a secret key between the encryption and decryption sides and not disclosed to the public domain, the attacker cannot practically reconstruct the data given their representation and a set of training images. The reason is that in the construction of $\tilde{x}(j) = Ax(j)A^T$, the random matrix A is multiplied by the image patch from both sides. Therefore, even in the case where only one stage of quantization is used where equation (2) can be solved in the non-encrypted case, the attacker cannot infer anything from the structure of the codebooks and indices, even by having access to an increasing number of training data.

A drawback of this encryption method, however, is a reduction in compression performance. Random projections are shown to decrease correlation in data [3]. In fact, the entropy of the transformed coefficients is increased. As a result, more rate is required to achieve the same distortion. Therefore, the performance of quantizers will be decreased, especially in the initial stages where the images are considerably correlated in nature. In section 4, we show experimentally how this method is decreasing the compression performance.

3.2   DCT Domain Scrambling

The randomization can also be performed in the DCT domain. Fig. 5 shows the proposed DCT-based encryption, the main contribution of this paper.

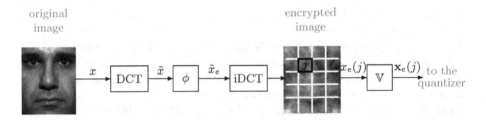

Fig. 5. Scrambling of the images in the DCT domain. ϕ is the randomizer in the DCT domain and $\mathbb{V}$ is the vectorizing operator.

After computing the DCT coefficients of an image, a random matrix $B_{b \times b}$ with values drawn equi-probably from a binary alphabet $\{\pm 1\}$ will be multiplied element-wise (Hadamard product) with the DCT coefficients of that image and then converted back to the pixel value domain. The matrix $B_{b \times b}$ could be generated for each block specifically, or it can be generated universally for all blocks. We can write:

$$\tilde{x} = MxM^T$$
$$\tilde{x}_e = \phi(\tilde{x}) = \tilde{x} \circ B \qquad (3)$$
$$x_e = M^T\tilde{x}_eM,$$

where M is the orthogonal DCT matrix.

As in the random projection based encryption, the attacker cannot reconstruct the images as long as the random matrix B is kept secret, or, even if only one universal matrix is used for all blocks, he has to guess its values among the 2^n possible values with $n = b^2$, which makes it computationally intractable.

It should be pointed out that in this way of scrambling, the magnitude information of images is revealed. However, as can be seen in Fig. 5, the scrambled images do not have any meaningful visual resemblance to the original images since in the images, the phase information is very important rather than the magnitude information. The reader is refered to [4] for more explanations on this method of scrambling. The DCT-based scrambling is also closely related to the DFT scrambling based on phase randomization [5].

An important advantage of this encryption method is that the correlation among the data is not reduced here as much as in the random projection based encryption. In fact, entropy of the scrambled data in this case is the same as the original data, since changing the sign of the DCT coefficients does not increase their entropy. Therefore, the performance of quantization is expected to be superior. Moreover, as will be shown in section 4, the blocking artifacts present in the previous methods are completely removed since every image block $x(j)$ contains information about the whole image that it comes from and hence causes a smoothness, although the blocks will be processed independently afterwards.

4   Experimental Results

In this section we experimentally study the proposed methods and validate them on the *CroppedYaleB* [6], a database of facial images with varying lighting conditions. We randomly chose 1600 images for training the codebooks and tested on another 400 images from the same database.

Fig. 6 shows the average Peak Signal-to-Noise Ratio (PSNR) for different methods versus their corresponding Bits Per Pixel (BPP) values. $L = 20$ layers were used in the methods with $k_i = 256, 128, 32, 16$ codewords for the first, second, third and forth quarters of the 20 layers, respectively.

As can be seen from the curves, the joint compression-scrambling in the DCT domain does not decrease the quality of compression of the method discussed in [1]. It should be noted, however, that the quality of compression increases less rapidly with the increase of rate compared to the JPEG2000 codec. The reason is, in the current simple experimental setup, many optimizations are neglected. For example, the number of codewords in each codebook, the design of different codebooks for different rate regimes, variable length code allocation for different patches based on their variance are among the immediate points to be considered in future versions of this family of methods.

Fig. 7 shows the results of compression of these methods for two different rates.

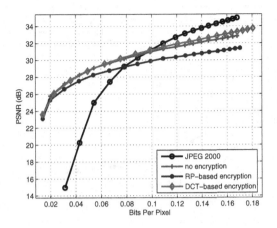

Fig. 6. PSNR vs. BPP, averaged over 400 test images

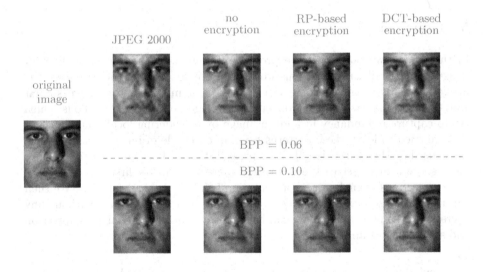

Fig. 7. Visual comparison of different methods for two different BPP values

It is interesting to point out that the blocking artifacts are removed in the DCT-based scrambling. Fig. 8 compares the rate-distortion behavior of the methods on the test data. It is verified here that the DCT-based scrambling, unlike its random projection counterpart, does not decrease the rate-distortion performance.

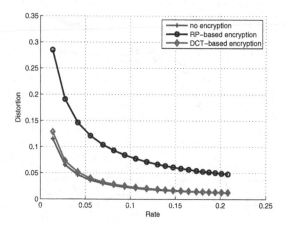

Fig. 8. Rate-Distortion curve, averaged over the normalized data from 400 images. The rate here can also be interpreted as bits per pixel since their values are the same.

5   Conclusions

In this paper, we addressed the problem of joint compression-scrambling for images. Specifically, in a previous work, we were considering the case were the images to be compressed come from the same family and thus have similar statistics. In this case, unlike conventional image compression methods which try to capture redundancy in a given image by considering local image properties, we tried to learn these patterns from an ensemble of images. In this work, we focused on the encryption of this representation and considered two remedies for the problem of security and privacy preservation. We first discussed random projections to make the representation less vulnerable to attacks. We then considered the scrambling in the DCT domain and showed that, without any decrease in the performance, we can have a framework for the joint compression and scrambling of images.

Acknowledgments. The research has been partially supported by a grant from Switzerland through the Swiss Contribution to the enlarged European Union PSPB-125/2010.

References

1. Ferdowsi, S., Voloshynovskiy, S., Kostadinov, D.: Sparse Multi-Layer image approximation: Image compression. In: European Signal Processing Conference 2015 (EUSIPCO 2015) (submitted to), Nice, France (August 2015)
2. Johnson, W.B., Lindenstrauss, J.: Extensions of lipschitz mappings into a hilbert space. In: Conference in Modern Analysis and Probability (New Haven, Conn., 1982). Contemp. Math., vol. 26, pp. 189–206 (1984)

3. Farhadzadeh, F., Voloshynovskiy, S., Koval, O.J.: Performance analysis of content-based identification using constrained list-based decoding. IEEE Transactions on Information Forensics and Security 7(5), 1652–1667 (2012)
4. Diephuis, M., Voloshynovskiy, S., Koval, O., Beekhof, F.: Robust message-privacy preserving image copy detection for cloud-based systems. In: 10th Workshop on Content-Based Multimedia Indexing, CBMI 2012 (2012)
5. Grytskiv, Z., Voloshynovskiy, S., Rytsar, Y.: Cryptography and steganography of video information in modern communications. Facta Universitatis 11(1), 115–125 (1998)
6. Lee, K., Ho, J., Kriegman, D.: Acquiring linear subspaces for face recognition under variable lighting. IEEE Trans. Pattern Anal. Mach. Intelligence 27(5), 684–698 (2005)

Image Indexing and Retrieval Using GSOM Algorithm

Marcin Gabryel[1]([✉]), Rafał Grycuk[1], Marcin Korytkowski[1],
and Taras Holotyak[2]

[1] Institute of Computational Intelligence, Częstochowa University of Technology
Al. Armii Krajowej 36, 42-200 Częstochowa, Poland
{marcin.gabryel,rafal.grycuk,marcin.korytkowski}@iisi.pcz.pl
http://iisi.pcz.pl
[2] Computer Science Department, University of Geneva,
7 Route de Drize, Geneva, Switzerland
http://sip.unige.ch

Abstract. Growing Self Organized Map (GSOM) algorithm is a well-known unsupervised clustering algorithm which a definite advantage is that both the map structure as well as the number of classes are automatically adjusted depending on the training data. We propose a new approach to apply it in the process of the image indexation and retrieval in a database. Unlike the classic bag-of-words (BoW) algorithm with k-means clustering, it is completely unnecessary to predetermine the number of classes (words). Thanks to that, the process of indexation can be fully automated. What is more, numerous modifications of the classic algorithm were added, and as a result, the retrieval process was considerably improved. Results of the experiments as well as comparison with BoW are presented at the end of the paper.

1 Introduction

Effective browsing and searching large image databases based on their content is one of the most important challenges of computer science. It is required in many various fields of life e.g. medicine, architecture, forensic, publishing, fashion, archives and many others. The aim can be a retrieval of a similar image. Retrieving mechanisms use image recognition methods. This is a sophisticated process which requires the use of algorithms from many different areas such as computational intelligence [21] in particularly fuzzy systems [5, 6, 13], rough neuro-fuzzy systems [18, 19], evolutionary algorithms [7, 12, 16] and mathematics [22] and image processing [3, 17].

One of the most popular and widely spread algorithm used for indexation and images retrieval is the bag-of-words model (BoW) [8, 14], known also as a bag of features. This algorithm is based on a concept of text search methods within collections of documents. Single words are stored in dictionaries with emphasis on appearing in various documents. BoW in a similar way creates dictionaries of characteristic features appearing in images. Additionally, classification process

L. Rutkowski et al. (Eds.): ICAISC 2015, Part I, LNAI 9119, pp. 706–714, 2015.
DOI: 10.1007/978-3-319-19324-3_63

enables during the search to determine what type of image class we are dealing with. In [14] we can find a detailed description of BoW and associated algorithms.

While working with the classic BoW algorithm we can easily notice its drawback as it is required to determine an initial number of classes for the k-means clustering algorithm. Afterwards, a classifier is used (in most cases the Support Vector Machine algorithm) which task is to provide an arbitrary class to which a searched image belongs to [8]. In such model there is no possibility of returning a list of similar images stored in a database. The method which we present in contradiction to BoW does not require the knowledge of the number of classes creating words in a dictionary. It allows to find the most similar images to the examined one and the additional classifier is no longer required. One of modifications proposed in the paper is called neuronal activity thresholding and it is used during creating images histograms. Once the threshold is applied, neuron which is activated the least in the whole class is eliminated. The research proved that this fact significantly improves the classification efficiency. Ultimate decision concerning a class to which a given image belongs, is taken through the majority voting.

The article is divided into several parts. In Section 2 we can find familiar algorithms such as Speeded Up Robust Features (SURF) and GSOM. Those are the ones which we use in our method. In the following section there is also a description of our idea of an indexing images and creating new databases algorithms with the use of GSOM algorithm. In the last section we present the results of experiments as well as the summary of our work.

2   Algorithms Used in the Proposed Approach

The proposed method of image indexing and retrieval implements several algorithms. In this section we present the GOSM algorithm which is used for clustering and for the reduction of initial interest point number and the SURF algorithm which task is to find and describe those points.

2.1   SURF

SURF (Speeded Up Robust Features) is a robust local feature detector, first presented in [2] by Herbert Bay in 2006. It is partly inspired by the SIFT descriptor [15]. SURF gives description of the image by selecting characteristic keypoints. This method combines selection of keypoints with calculating 64-element vector (a descriptor). In SURF, integral image and filter approximation of block Hessian determinant is applied. To detect interesting points, a special Hessian-matrix approximation is used. For features, orientation is based on information from circular region around the pixel. Then, a square region aligned to selected orientation is constructed and the SURF descriptor is extracted from it. It uses the sum of the Haar wavelet responses around an interest point. The local feature around the point is described by a 64-number vector.

2.2 GSOM

GSOM algorithm (Growing Self-Organizing Map) was invented in 1995 [11]. In fact it is a modification of SelfOrganizing Map (SOM) which additionally was equipped in the ability of expansion. The number of neurons is adjusted to data during learning. There are many papers where we can find a description of the GSOM algorithm [23] or the Growing Hierarchical Self-Organizing Map (GHSOM) [9, 20]. In this section we present our modified version of the original GHSOM algorithm [11].

The network we consider consists of $n \times m$ neurons N_j, where $j = 1, ..., N_c$, N_c - number of neurons, $N_c = n \cdot m$, n - number of rows and m - number of columns. Initially, we create a network made of four neurons. They are placed on every vertex of a square. Learning data are vectors $\mathbf{x}_i = (x_{i1}, x_{i2}, ...x_{iK})$, where $i = 1, ..., M$, M – number of vectors, K - vector dimension). Every neuron N_j has a weight vector $\mathbf{w}_j = (w_{j1}, ...w_{jK})$. In our case, in order to allow parallel algorithm operation we used a modified version of the SOM algorithm. Single iteration of learning consists of six steps:

1. Set the vector of changes $\mathbf{dx}_i$ so that $dx_{jk} = 0$, $j = 1, ..., K$, $k = 1, ..., N_c$.
2. Repeat for every $i = 1, ..., M$ steps 3-6.
3. Find such a neuron N_s that fulfils the inequality

$$\|\mathbf{w}_s - \mathbf{x}_i\| \leq \|\mathbf{w}_j - \mathbf{x}_i\|. \tag{1}$$

4. Modify changes vector $\mathbf{dx}_s$

$$\mathbf{dx}_s = \mathbf{dx}_s + (\mathbf{x}_s - \mathbf{x}_i). \tag{2}$$

5. Increase the counter of winnings

$$\tau_s = \tau_s + 1. \tag{3}$$

6. Modify weight of all neurons

$$\mathbf{w}_j = \mathbf{w}_j - \alpha \cdot \mathbf{dx}_j/t_j, \text{ for } t_j \neq 0. \tag{4}$$

Afterwards, the expansion algorithm is used. Initially, a neuron N_q is found for which inequality is as follows:

$$\tau_q \geq \tau_j. \tag{5}$$

If the number τ_q exceeds a fixed number τ_{max}, what happens is the expansion of a network in one of four directions. We assume that the neuron N_f is a neuron which value τ_f is the highest of all neighbouring neurons N_q. Between neurons N_q and N_f a new column (or row) is inserted. Weights of a new neuron $N_{q'}$ are determined as follows:

$$\mathbf{w}'_q = 0.5 \cdot (\mathbf{w}_q + \mathbf{w}_f). \tag{6}$$

The number of columns m (or rows n) as well as the general number of neurons N_c are increased. All counters of winnings are reset

$$\tau_j = 0, \, i = 1, ..., N_c. \tag{7}$$

After the predetermined number of generated iteration there are N_c groups with the centres of clusters which coordinates are $\mathbf{w}_j$.

3 Indexing and Retrieval Using GSOM Algorithm

The presented algorithm consists of several modules. Just as in the case of BoW, we initially create a dictionary of words. Based on them we obtain histogram, containing the presence of those words in each single image.

1. Consider images database I_i, where $i = 1, ..., L$, L number of images.
2. Find the characteristic points (for example with SURF algorithm) x_{ij}, $i = 1, ..., L$, $j = 1, .., K$, K - the dimension of the vector describing characteristic point (for SURF $K = 64$).
3. Group the points x_{ij} with the use of GSOM algorithm. Obtain group centres $\mathbf{w}_j$, $j = 1, ..., N_c$.
4. Create histograms $h_i = [h_{i1}, h_{i2}, ..., h_{iN}]$, where

$$h_{ij} = \sum_{j=1}^{N_c} \delta_{ji}, \tag{8}$$

$$\delta_{ji} = \begin{cases} 1 \text{ if } \|\mathbf{w}_j - \mathbf{x}_k\| \leq \|\mathbf{w}_k - \mathbf{x}_k\| \text{ for } \mathbf{x}_k \in \mathbf{I}_i \\ 0 \text{ otherwise} \end{cases}. \tag{9}$$

Variable δ_{ji} is an indicator if a neuron N_j is the closest vector (a winner) for any sample from an image $\mathbf{I}_i$.

A novel, active neurons thresholding method is used in the presented algorithm. This approach is responsible for calculating the activity of neurons for every class of image. After that, the element of histogram h_{ij}, which on account of too weak activity of neuron N_j in a given class did not reach the threshold θ, is reset. The algorithm consists of two steps:

1. For every class c calculate the activity of neurons α_{jc}

$$\alpha_{jc} = \sum_{j=1}^{N_c} \delta_{ji}, \ \mathbf{I}_i \subset c. \tag{10}$$

2. If inequality

$$\alpha_{jc} < \theta \tag{11}$$

is satisfied, then

$$h_{ji} = 0, \text{ for } \mathbf{I}_i \subset c. \tag{12}$$

Our experiments clearly confirm that removing inactive neurons boosts the classification efficiency. In the next chapter we depicted detailed results.

Image search $\mathbf{I}_t$ in the database consists in preparation of a histogram $\mathbf{h}_t$ in accordance with the algorithm described above. Next, we look for the closest histograms calculating the L1 norm between them:

$$d_{fi} = \sum_{j=1}^{K} |h_{fi} - h_{ji}|, \ i = 1, ..., K. \tag{13}$$

Ultimate decision concerning a class of an image $\mathbf{I}_t$, is taken through the majority voting. An image $\mathbf{I}_t$ belongs to the class c if in this particular class is the highest number of sorted L/C images with regard to distance d_{fi}.

4   Experiments

We present two experiments to show the effectiveness of the algorithm. In the first one we present to what extent applying the neuron activation threshold in the histogram creation improves search and classification of images. The second experiment shows the efficiency of the new algorithm in comparison to the BoW algorithm implemented with the use of functions available in the OpenCV library [4]. The research is performed on the Caltech 101 image database (collected by L. Fei-Fei et al. [10]). Four categories of images were chosen: planes, cars, cats and motorcycles. For every category images were divided into the learning part (80% of the available number of images) and the testing part (20%).

Our algorithm was implemented in Java language with the use of parallel computing (Concurrent library) as well as JavaCV [1] library function. JavaCV is a library which adopts functions available in OpenCV for Java language needs. We used this function in order to generate characteristic points with the use of the SURF algorithm.

Tables 1 and 2 present effectiveness of images classification for various values of neuron activity threshold. We can easily observe that adding this modification considerably improved classification efficiency. Graphs of these dependencies are presented in Fig. 2 and 3.

The algorithm was compared with the BoW algorithm which was implemented with standard functions of OpenCV according to [8]. In this particular algorithm points are grouped by the k-means clustering. Next, a classifier is learned by the Support Vector Machine algorithm (SVM). The results of single groups as well as comparison of all classes are presented in Table 3. The classification performed with the use of our algorithm is more efficient than the BoW with k-means and the classifier.

Table 1. Influence of neuronal activity thresholding on the effectiveness of classification for $\tau_{max} = 1000$

τ_{max}	treshold of neuron activity	efficiency %
1000	0	85.59
1000	5	85.59
1000	7	86.44
1000	10	86.44
1000	12	87.29
1000	15	85.59
1000	20	83.90

Fig. 1. Sample images from the Caltech 101 database for the four categories used in the experiments

Table 2. Influence of neuronal activity thresholding on the effectiveness of classification for $\tau_{max} = 2000$

τ_{max}	treshold of activity neurons	efficiency %
2000	0	86.44
2000	5	86.44
2000	10	86.44
2000	15	86.44
2000	20	86.44
2000	25	87.29
2000	30	87.29
2000	35	88.16
2000	40	86.44

Table 3. Comparison algorithm efficiencies for the test images

image type	classic BoW efficiency	our algorithm efficiency
plane	88.37%	93.18%
cars	82.61%	91.66%
wild cats	70.83%	84.00%
motorbike	91.66%	80.00%
all	84.21%	88.16%

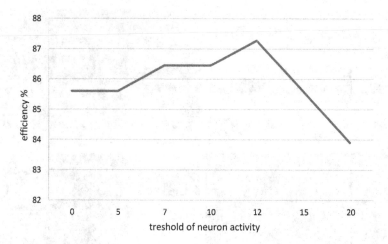

Fig. 2. Influence of neuronal activity thresholding on the effectiveness of classification for $\tau_{max} = 1000$

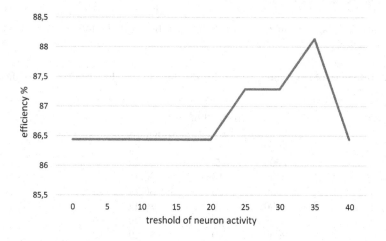

Fig. 3. Influence of neuronal activity thresholding on the effectiveness of classification for $\tau_{max} = 2000$

5   Final Remarks

As we have presented in the paper, content-based image classification with the GSOM algorithm, despite its clear and simple construction, has many advantages. What is worth mentioning, the lack of a classifier at the output does not cause any effectiveness loss. Moreover, the described thresholding method of inactive neurons contributed to increase in efficacy of the algorithm. In future, we would like to improve the effectiveness of the algorithm for greater number of classes. What is more, to modify inactive neuron handling in such a way that their number will be adjusted to every class separately. Our ultimate goal however is to implement this algorithm in a relational database (for example Microsoft SQL Server or MySQL) to expand its functionality with the possibility of content-based images search and retrieval.

Acknowledgements. This work was supported by the Polish National Science Centre (NCN) within project number DEC-2011/01/D/ST6/06957.

References

[1] Audet, S.: JavaCV (2014), http://bytedeco.org/ (Online; accessed December 1, 2014)

[2] Bay, H., Tuytelaars, T., Van Gool, L.: SURF: Speeded up robust features. In: Leonardis, A., Bischof, H., Pinz, A. (eds.) ECCV 2006, Part I. LNCS, vol. 3951, pp. 404–417. Springer, Heidelberg (2006), http://dx.doi.org/10.1007/11744023_32

[3] Biniaz, A., Abbasi, A.: Fast FCM with spatial neighborhood information for brain mr image segmentation. Journal of Artificial Intelligence and Soft Computing Research 3(1), 15–25 (2014)

[4] Bradski, G.: The OpenCV Library. Dr. Dobb's Journal of Software Tools (2000)

[5] Chen, M., Ludwig, S.: Particle swarm optimization based fuzzy clustering approach to identify optimal number of clusters. Journal of Artificial Intelligence and Soft Computing Research 4(1), 43–56 (2014)

[6] Cpalka, K., Rutkowski, L.: Flexible takagi-sugeno fuzzy systems. In: Proceedings of the 2005 IEEE International Joint Conference on Neural Networks, IJCNN 2005, vol. 3, pp. 1764–1769 (July 2005)

[7] Cpalka, K.: On evolutionary designing and learning of flexible neuro-fuzzy structures for nonlinear classification. Nonlinear Analysis: Theory, Methods & Applications 71(12), e1659 – e1672 (2009),
http://www.sciencedirect.com/science/article/pii/S0362546X09002831

[8] Csurka, G., Dance, C.R., Fan, L., Willamowski, J., Bray, C.: Visual categorization with bags of keypoints. In: Workshop on Statistical Learning in Computer Vision, ECCV, pp. 1–22 (2004)

[9] Dittenbach, M., Merkl, D., Rauber, A.: The growing hierarchical self-organizing map. In: IEEE-INNS-ENNS International Joint Conference on Neural Networks, vol. 6, p. 6015. IEEE Computer Society (2000)

[10] Fei-Fei, L., Fergus, R., Perona, P.: Learning generative visual models from few training examples: An incremental bayesian approach tested on 101 object categories. In: Conference on Computer Vision and Pattern Recognition Workshop, CVPRW 2004, p. 178 (June 2004)

[11] Fritzke, B.: Growing grid – a self-organizing network with constant neighborhood range and adaptation strength. Neural Processing Letters 2(5), 9–13 (1995), http://dx.doi.org/10.1007/BF02332159

[12] Koshiyama, A.S., Vellasco, M.M.B.R., Tanscheit, R.: Gpfis-control: A genetic fuzzy system for control tasks. Journal of Artificial Intelligence and Soft Computing Research 4(3) (March 2015)

[13] Lapa, K., Przybył, A., Cpałka, K.: A new approach to designing interpretable models of dynamic systems. In: Rutkowski, L., Korytkowski, M., Scherer, R., Tadeusiewicz, R., Zadeh, L.A., Zurada, J.M. (eds.) ICAISC 2013, Part II. LNCS (LNAI), vol. 7895, pp. 523–534. Springer, Heidelberg (2013), http://dx.doi.org/10.1007/978-3-642-38610-7_48

[14] Liu, J.: Image retrieval based on bag-of-words model. CoRR abs/1304.5168 (2013), http://arxiv.org/abs/1304.5168

[15] Lowe, D.G.: Distinctive image features from scale-invariant keypoints. International Journal of Computer Vision 60(2), 91–110 (2004)

[16] Ludwig, S.: Repulsive self-adaptive acceleration particle swarm optimization approach. Journal of Artificial Intelligence and Soft Computing Research 4(3), 189–204 (2015)

[17] Najgebauer, P., Nowak, T., Romanowski, J., Rygał, J., Korytkowski, M., Scherer, R.: Novel method for parasite detection in microscopic samples. In: Rutkowski, L., Korytkowski, M., Scherer, R., Tadeusiewicz, R., Zadeh, L.A., Zurada, J.M. (eds.) ICAISC 2012, Part I. LNCS, vol. 7267, pp. 551–558. Springer, Heidelberg (2012)

[18] Nowicki, R.: Rough–neuro–fuzzy system with MICOG defuzzification. In: Proceedings of IEEE International Conference on Fuzzy Systems, IEEE World Congress on Computational Intelligence, Vancouver, BC, Canada, pp. 1958–1965 (July 2006)

[19] Nowicki, R.: Nonlinear modelling and classification based on the MICOG defuzzification. Journal of Nonlinear Analysis, Series A: Theory, Methods & Applications 7(12), e1033–e1047 (2009)

[20] Rauber, A., Merkl, D., Dittenbach, M.: The growing hierarchical self-organizing map: exploratory analysis of high-dimensional data. IEEE Transactions on Neural Networks 13(6), 1331–1341 (2002)

[21] Starczewski, J., Scherer, R., Korytkowski, M., Nowicki, R.: Modular type-2 neuro-fuzzy systems. In: Wyrzykowski, R., Dongarra, J., Karczewski, K., Wasniewski, J. (eds.) PPAM 2007. LNCS, vol. 4967, pp. 570–578. Springer, Heidelberg (2008)

[22] Woźniak, M., Kempa, W.M., Gabryel, M., Nowicki, R.K.: A finite-buffer queue with single vacation policy - analytical study with evolutionary positioning. International Journal of Applied Mathematics and Computer Science 24(4), 887–900 (2014)

[23] Zhu, G., Zhu, X.: The growing self-organizing map for clustering algorithms in programming codes. In: 2010 International Conference on Artificial Intelligence and Computational Intelligence (AICI), vol. 3, pp. 178–182 (October 2010)

Multi-layer Architecture For Storing Visual Data Based on WCF and Microsoft SQL Server Database

Rafał Grycuk[1(✉)], Marcin Gabryel[1], Rafał Scherer[1],
and Sviatoslav Voloshynovskiy[2]

[1] Institute of Computational Intelligence, Częstochowa University of Technology
Al. Armii Krajowej 36, 42-200 Częstochowa, Poland
{rafal.grycuk,marcin.gabryel,rafal.scherer}@iisi.pcz.pl
http://iisi.pcz.pl
[2] Computer Science Department, University of Geneva,
7 Route de Drize, Geneva, Switzerland
http://sip.unige.ch

Abstract. In this paper we present a novel architecture for storing visual data. Effective storing, browsing and searching collections of images is one of the most important challenges of computer science. The design of architecture for storing such data requires a set of tools and frameworks such as SQL database management systems and service-oriented frameworks. The proposed solution is based on a multi-layer architecture, which allows to replace any component without recompilation of other components. The approach contains five components, i.e. Model, Base Engine, Concrete Engine, CBIR service and Presentation. They were based on two well-known design patterns: Dependency Injection and Inverse of Control. For experimental purposes we implemented the SURF local interest point detector as a feature extractor and K-means clustering as indexer. The presented architecture is intended for content-based retrieval systems simulation purposes as well as for real-world CBIR tasks.

Keywords: WCF · Microsoft SQL server · Dependency injection · Inversion of control · Entity framework · Multi-layer architecture · k-means · SURF · Content-based image retrieval

1 Introduction

Images are created everyday in tremendous amount and there is ongoing research to make it possible to efficiently search these vast collections by their content. Generally, this work can be divided into image classification [4][18] and image retrieval [17]. Recognizing images and objects on images relies on suitable feature extraction which can be basically divided into several groups, i.e. based on color representation [28], textures [48], shape [50][52], edge detectors [42][43][53] or local invariant features, e.g. SURF [2], SIFT [34] or ORB [46]. Matching features

© Springer International Publishing Switzerland 2015
L. Rutkowski et al. (Eds.): ICAISC 2015, Part I, LNAI 9119, pp. 715–726, 2015.
DOI: 10.1007/978-3-319-19324-3_64

can be also performed by several methods, e.g. clustering, nearest neighbour, bag of features [21] or soft computing [15][30].

There are many content-based image processing systems developed so far. A good review of such systems is provided in [51]. To the best of our knowledge no other system uses similar set of tools to the system proposed in the paper. Now we describe briefly the most important tools used to design the proposed framework.

1.1 Windows Communication Foundation

Windows Communication Foundation (WCF) is a framework based on Service-Oriented Architecture [14][27]. WCF allows to send data asynchronously between two service and client endpoints. Service endpoints can be deployed on IIS server or be hosted locally. The messages can be send as XML (value types) or binary file (complex types) [9][29][35][39]. WCF consist of following features:[45][49] Service Orientation, Interoperability, Multiple Message Patterns, Service Metadata, Data Contracts, Security, Multiple Transports and Encodings, Reliable and Queued Messages, Durable Messages, Transactions, AJAX and REST Support, Extensibility.

1.2 SQL Sever

MS SQL Server is a database management system for storing various types of data, fully supporting cloud computing technologies [5][11][12][16]. It provides a set of tools to extract data from various devices or sources, even at datacenters. MS SQL query language, T-SQL (Transact-SQL), allows for both structural or procedural queries [6][10][13][31][37][38]. The DBMS (Database Management System) is based on a client-server architecture. The platform is composed of the following services:[33][41]

- Database engine - allows to execute queries and is necessary to run the server,
- Integration Services (SSIS, SQL Server Integration Services) - ETL (Extraction, Transformation and Loading) platform responsible for data migration from the heterogeneous data sources,
- SQL Agent - answerable for performing tasks according to the specified schedule,
- Full-text Filter Daemon Launcher - allow to perform full-text searches on text columns,
- Reporting Services (SSIS, SQL Server Reporting Services) - responsible for designing and deploying reports,
- Analysis Services (SSAS, SQL Server Analysis Services) - allows to create multidimensional cubes and executing MDX (Multidimensional Expressions) queries [25],

DBMS store data in a relational form (tables and their relations) and allows to select information by executing queries. Many frameworks perform object relational mapping. In this paper we use Entity Framework (EF) with Code First approach [1][8][32].

1.3   Dependency Injection and Inverse of Control

Re-usability of existing components is crucial in modern software engineering. The aim of this approach is to combine separate layers into one application. This is a challenging task, because as the application complexity increases, so do dependencies [7]. The best practice for tone down proliferation of dependencies is by using Dependency Injection (DI) design pattern allowing to inject objects into a class constructor. Thus, the creation of the object does not rely on a class. The initialization logic is rarely reusable outside of created component. That pattern provides a layer of abstraction for the injected object, thus we can implement the concrete logic in the other component and inject it in the class constructor by the interface. DI [39] is an implementation of Inverse of Control (IoC)[20][44][47]. Figure 1 shows the typical class dependencies. Such a scheme entails the following problems [36]:

1. Any code changes of *ServiceA* forces changes in *ClassA*, thus the recompilation of all components is required,
2. All classes must be implemented and available at the compile time,
3. Classes are difficult to test and to achieve components isolation,
4. Contradicts the (DRY) Don't Repeat Yourself principle.

To resolve this issue we used the Dependency Injection [7][20]. A Conceptual view of DI is presented in Figure 2.

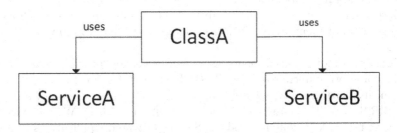

Fig. 1. Problem illustration of tightly coupled dependencies. *ClassA* uses *ServiceA* and *ServiceB*. This is a simple representation of *ClassA* dependencies on *ServiceA* and *ServiceB*.

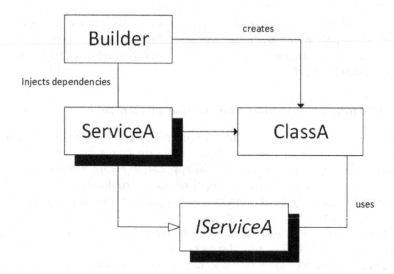

Fig. 2. Solution of the problem formulated in Fig. 1. The Inverse of Control pattern can be implemented by Dependency Injection. *Builder* creates *ClassA* which uses abstract interface *IServiceA*. Dependencies of *ServiceA* are injected to *ClassA* by inheritance.

2   Proposed Architecture For Storing Visual Data

Proposed architecture is based on two main components. The first one is SQL database which is Microsoft SQL Server, and the second one is Windows Communication Foundation (WCF). Our approach consists of five main layers (tiers):

1. Model - which contains data model generated by the Entity Framework (6.1) with Code First approach,
2. Base Engine - consist of several abstract classes or interfaces which can be used to implement user solutions, but they provide appropriate business logic,
3. Concrete Engine - implements user logic based on previous the layer (in this paper we implemented the SURF descriptors for feature extraction and k-means clustering [26] for indexing),
4. CBIR Service (for more about CBIR see [23][22]) - which is WCF service that allows to invoke engine methods as Service Oriented Applications (SOA).
5. Endpoint (Client) - presentation layer for invoking service methods, it can be desktop, web or mobile application. All the user needs to do, is to add service reference and invoke methods.

The agility applied in the presented approach is important, because it is not restricted to any particular implementation and it can be applied in various solutions. The architecture is presented in Fig. 3a.

   The Base Engine and Concrete Engine layers are based on two design patterns, i.e. Dependency Injection (DI) and Inverse of Control (IoC) described

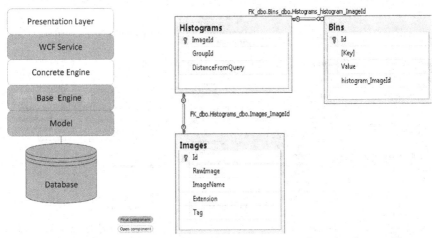

(a) Multi-tier architecture for storing visual data. Final components are compiled release of dll's and open components are user implementation.

(b) Entity diagram based on database tables.

Fig. 3. Multi-layer architecture and entity diagram of the proposed approach

in Section 1.3. These patterns allowed to separate the containers and maintain the S.O.L.I.D. principles [39]. Components are composed of a set of classes or interfaces. Each component has a representation in UML (Unified Modeling Language) diagram. Figure 5a shows the model layer, which contains five classes and two interfaces. Classes: *Bin*, *Histogram* and *Image* were generated by the Entity Framework and they correspond with the database tables presented in Fig. 3b. Interface *IRepositoryBase* is a generic interface which provides the basic C.R.U.D. (create, read, update and delete) operations. The methods allow to operate on any types of objects. The *GenericRepository* implements *IRepositoryBase* interface. In addition, the *dataContext* field is generic, thus the concrete implementation does not contains any dependencies. The *GenericRepository* class is based on the Singleton pattern, to create instance which user needs to use static method *GetInstance*. A very interesting interface is *IFeature*, which allows to implement any type of image features (an image descriptor).

Fig. 4b represents a class diagram for the Base Engine layer, which contains items for feature extraction (*IFeatureExtractor*), feature indexation (*Feature Indexer*), operations executions (*IExecutor*, *ExecutorBase*) and simulation (*SimulationEvaluator*, *RetrievalFactors*). *IExecutor* provides abstract methods for following operations: index creation and deletion, query execution and image insertion. It contains one property: repository. *IFeatureExtractor* is

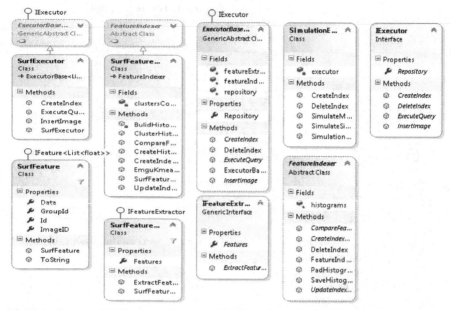

(a) Class diagram for Concrete Engine layer

(b) Class diagram for Base Engine layer

Fig. 4. Class diagrams for Concrete Engine and Base Engine layers

responsible for feature extraction and contains: *Features* property and Extract-Features method. The first one stores previously extracted features, the second one extracts features from image passed as a parameter. The method is only a definition, thus the class that will implement that interface must contain its own version. *FeatureIndexer* consists of one field (histograms) which is a composition relation with the *Histogram* class. Methods are abstract, thus they require concrete implementation in the inherited class. *ExecutorBase* is a base class that uses the dependency injection to initiate object, that allows to inject logic. The *RetrievalFactors* contains fields that describes the query results. The Concrete Engine layer (see Fig. 4a) is designed and presented for simulation purposes. We implemented SURF [3][19][24] as a feature extractor and k-means method as a indexer. Figure 5b shows diagram for the CBIR Service layer. Each WCF service consists of the following items:

- Interface - defines the method e.g. *IImage Retrival Service*,
- Implementation class - implements the method's body e.g. *Image Retrieval Service*,
- Contract (optional) - required to retrieve data from the service *Image Contract*.

CBIR Service component contains two services: simulation service is used to perform simulations on the created index. The most interesting methods are

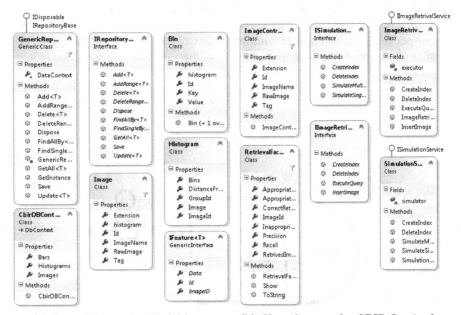

(a) Class diagram for Model layer   (b) Class diagram for CBIR Service layer

Fig. 5. Class diagrams for Model and CBIR Service layers

SimulateMultiQuery and SimulateSingleQuery. The first one returns a list of *RetrievalFactors* and performs multi query. The second one executes a single query. The image retrieval service allows to execute queries. The difference between SimulateSingleQuery and ExecuteQuery methods are the following: ExecuteQuery returns a list of retrieved images, SimulateSingleQuery returns a list of factors (*precision, recall*) which allows to evaluate index efficiency. The proposed architecture was designed in .NET framework and written in C#.

3   Experimental Results

Experiments were carried out using the designed architecture. The created endpoint was a desktop application with service reference to CBIR Service. Research includes experiments on various objects with background described by the SURF local interest point descriptor [34]. Test images were taken from the Corel database. We chose images with various types of objects. In experiments we used 90% of each class for index creating and 10% as query images. In Tab.1 we presented the retrieved factors for each query image. Tab. 2 shows retrieved images for a query image (the image with border).

For the purposes of the performance evaluation we use two measures; precision and recall [40]. Fig. 6 shows the performance measures of the image retrieval. The *AI* is a set of appropriate images, that should be returned as being similar to the query image. The *RI* represents a set of returned images by the system. *Rai* is a group of properly returned images. *Iri* represents improperly returned images, *anr* proper not returned and *inr* improper not returned images. The presented measure allows to define *precision* and *recall* by the following formulas [40]:

$$precision = \frac{|rai|}{|rai + iri|},$$ (1)

$$recall = \frac{|rai|}{|rai + anr|}.$$ (2)

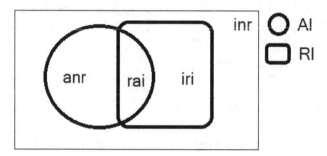

Fig. 6. Performance measures diagram

Image Id	RI	AI	rai	iri	anr	Precision	Recall
1 (1).jpg	19	33	21	12	7	13	7
1 (2).jpg	21	33	31	3	18	3	19
1 (20).jpg	19	33	21	12	7	13	7
1 (21).jpg	19	33	21	12	7	13	7
2 (1).jpg	14	33	27	7	7	7	8
2 (10).jpg	12	33	28	6	6	6	7
2 (11).jpg	19	33	24	9	9	10	10
2 (17).jpg	12	33	28	6	6	6	7
3 (1).jpg	22	33	23	11	12	11	12
3 (10).jpg	21	33	23	10	11	11	12
3 (11).jpg	18	33	27	7	11	7	12
3 (15).jpg	21	33	29	4	17	4	17

Table 1. Simulation results for multi query. Measures were normalized and presented as percentage value [%]

Table 2. Query results. Eighteen example images from the experiment. The image with border is the query image

4   Final Remarks

The presented approach is a novel architecture for storing visual data. We used SQL Server and WCF services as a core of our method. The proposed solution for storing visual data has no dependencies with concrete implementation, thus we can simulate any CBIR method. Our approach allows creating any type of endpoint: desktop, web or mobile application. It can be used as core back-end solution. The performed experiments proved effectiveness of our method. Our paper present a part of a larger system that allows to search and identify specific classes of objects.

Acknowledgments. The work presented in this paper was supported by a grant BS/MN-1-109-301/14/P "Clustering algorithms for data stream - in reference to the Content-Based Image Retrieval methods (CBIR)". The work presented in this paper was supported partially by a grant from Switzerland through the Swiss Contribution to the enlarged European Union.

References

[1] Adya, A., Blakeley, J.A., Melnik, S., Muralidhar, S.: Anatomy of the ado.net entity framework. In: Proceedings of the 2007 ACM SIGMOD International Conference on Management of Data, pp. 877–888. ACM (2007)

[2] Bay, H., Ess, A., Tuytelaars, T., Van Gool, L.: Speeded-up robust features (surf). Comput. Vis. Image Underst. 110(3), 346–359 (2008)

[3] Bay, H., Tuytelaars, T., Van Gool, L.: SURF: Speeded up robust features. In: Leonardis, A., Bischof, H., Pinz, A. (eds.) ECCV 2006, Part I. LNCS, vol. 3951, pp. 404–417. Springer, Heidelberg (2006)

[4] Bazarganigilani, M.: Optimized image feature selection using pairwise classifiers. Journal of Artificial Intelligence and Soft Computing Research 1(2), 147–153 (2011)

[5] Ben-Gan, I.: Microsoft SQL Server 2012 T-SQL Fundamentals. Pearson Education (2012)

[6] Biniaz, A., Abbasi, A.: Segmentation and edge detection based on modified ant colony optimization for iris image processing. Journal of Artificial Intelligence and Soft Computing Research 3(2), 133–141 (2013)

[7] Caprio, G.: Design patterns-dependency injection. MSDN Magazine, 103–110 (2005)

[8] Castro, P., Melnik, S., Adya, A.: Ado.net entity framework: raising the level of abstraction in data programming. In: Proceedings of the 2007 ACM SIGMOD International Conference on Management of Data, pp. 1070–1072. ACM (2007)

[9] Chappell, D.: Introducing windows communication foundation in .net framework 4. Retrieved May 11, 2011 (2010)

[10] Chen, M., Ludwig, S.A.: Particle swarm optimization based fuzzy clustering approach to identify optimal number of clusters. Journal of Artificial Intelligence and Soft Computing Research 4(1), 43–56 (2014)

[11] Chromiak, M., Stencel, K.: The linkup data structure for heterogeneous data integration platform. In: Kim, T.-H., Lee, Y.-H., Fang, W.-C. (eds.) FGIT 2012. LNCS, vol. 7709, pp. 263–274. Springer, Heidelberg (2012)

[12] Chromiak, M., Stencel, K.: A data model for heterogeneous data integration architecture. In: Proceedings of the 10th International Conference on Beyond Databases, Architectures, and Structures, BDAS 2014, Ustron, Poland, May 27-30, pp. 547–556 (2014)

[13] Chu, J.L., Krzyźak, A.: The recognition of partially occluded objects with support vector machines, convolutional neural networks and deep belief networks. Journal of Artificial Intelligence and Soft Computing Research 4(1), 5–19 (2014)

[14] Cibraro, P., Claeys, K., Cozzolino, F., Grabner, J.: Professional WCF 4: Windows Communication Foundation with .NET 4. John Wiley & Sons (2010)

[15] Cpalka, K.: On evolutionary designing and learning of flexible neuro-fuzzy structures for nonlinear classification. Nonlinear Analysis: Theory, Methods & Applications 71(12), e1659–e1672 (2009)

[16] Delaney, K., Freeman, C.: Microsoft SQL Server 2012 Internals. Microsoft Press (2013)

[17] Drozda, P., Sopyła, K., Górecki, P.: Online crowdsource system supporting ground truth datasets creation. In: Rutkowski, L., Korytkowski, M., Scherer, R., Tadeusiewicz, R., Zadeh, L.A., Zurada, J.M. (eds.) ICAISC 2013, Part I. LNCS (LNAI), vol. 7894, pp. 532–539. Springer, Heidelberg (2013)

[18] Drozda, P., Sopyła, K., Górecki, P.: Different orderings and visual sequence alignment algorithms for image classification. In: Rutkowski, L., Korytkowski, M., Scherer, R., Tadeusiewicz, R., Zadeh, L.A., Zurada, J.M. (eds.) ICAISC 2014, Part I. LNCS (LNAI), vol. 8467, pp. 693–702. Springer, Heidelberg (2014)

[19] Evans, C.: Notes on the opensurf library. University of Bristol, Tech. Rep. CSTR-09-001 (January 2009)

[20] Fowler, M.: Inversion of control containers and the dependency injection pattern (2004)

[21] Grauman, K., Darrell, T.: Efficient image matching with distributions of local invariant features. In: IEEE Computer Society Conference on Computer Vision and Pattern Recognition, CVPR 2005, vol. 2, pp. 627–634 (June 2005)

[22] Grycuk, R., Gabryel, M., Korytkowski, M., Romanowski, J., Scherer, R.: Improved digital image segmentation based on stereo vision and mean shift algorithm. In: Wyrzykowski, R., Dongarra, J., Karczewski, K., Waśniewski, J. (eds.) PPAM 2013, Part I. LNCS, vol. 8384, pp. 433–443. Springer, Heidelberg (2014), http://dx.doi.org/10.1007/978-3-642-55224-3_41

[23] Grycuk, R., Gabryel, M., Korytkowski, M., Scherer, R.: Content-based image indexing by data clustering and inverse document frequency. In: Kozielski, S., Mrozek, D., Kasprowski, P., Małysiak-Mrozek, B. (eds.) BDAS 2014. CCIS, vol. 424, pp. 374–383. Springer, Heidelberg (2014)

[24] Grycuk, R., Gabryel, M., Korytkowski, M., Scherer, R., Voloshynovskiy, S.: From single image to list of objects based on edge and blob detection. In: Rutkowski, L., Korytkowski, M., Scherer, R., Tadeusiewicz, R., Zadeh, L.A., Zurada, J.M. (eds.) ICAISC 2014, Part II. LNCS (LNAI), vol. 8468, pp. 605–615. Springer, Heidelberg (2014)

[25] Harinath, S., Pihlgren, R., Lee, D.G.Y., Sirmon, J., Bruckner, R.M.: Professional Microsoft SQL Server 2012 Analysis Services with MDX and DAX. John Wiley & Sons (2012)

[26] Hartigan, J.A., Wong, M.A.: Algorithm as 136: A k-means clustering algorithm. Applied Statistics, 100–108 (1979)

[27] Hirschheim, R., Welke, R., Schwarz, A.: Service-oriented architecture: Myths, realities, and a maturity model. MIS Quarterly Executive 9(1), 37–48 (2010)

[28] Huang, J., Kumar, S., Mitra, M., Zhu, W.J., Zabih, R.: Image indexing using color correlograms. In: Proceedings of the 1997 IEEE Computer Society Conference on Computer Vision and Pattern Recognition, pp. 762–768 (June 1997)

[29] Klein, S.: Professional WCF programming: .NET development with the Windows communication foundation. John Wiley & Sons (2007)

[30] Łapa, K., Zalasiński, M., Cpałka, K.: A new method for designing and complexity reduction of neuro-fuzzy systems for nonlinear modelling. In: Rutkowski, L., Korytkowski, M., Scherer, R., Tadeusiewicz, R., Zadeh, L.A., Zurada, J.M. (eds.) ICAISC 2013, Part I. LNCS (LNAI), vol. 7894, pp. 329–344. Springer, Heidelberg (2013)

[31] Leblanc, P.: Microsoft SQL Server 2012 Step by Step. Pearson Education (2013)

[32] Lerman, J., Miller, R.: Programming Entity Framework: Code First. O'Reilly Media, Inc. (2011)

[33] Lobel, L., Brust, A.: Programming Microsoft® SQL Server® 2012. O'Reilly Media, Inc. (2012)

[34] Lowe, D.G.: Distinctive image features from scale-invariant keypoints. Int. J. Comput. Vision 60(2), 91–110 (2004)

[35] Mackey, A.: Windows communication foundation. In: Introducing .NET 4.0, pp. 159–173. Springer (2010)

[36] Magazine, M.: Design patterns: Dependency injection (2005)

[37] Makinana, S., Malumedzha, T., Nelwamondo, F.V.: Quality parameter assessment on iris images. Journal of Artificial Intelligence and Soft Computing Research 4(1), 21–30 (2014)

[38] Mallik, S., Mukhopadhyay, A., Maulik, U.: Integrated statistical and rule-mining techniques for dna methylation and gene expression data analysis. Journal of Artificial Intelligence and Soft Computing Research 3(2), 101–115 (2013)

[39] Martin, M., Martin, R.C.: Agile principles, patterns, and practices in C#. Pearson Education (2006)

[40] Meskaldji, K., Boucherkha, S., Chikhi, S.: Color quantization and its impact on color histogram based image retrieval (2009)

[41] Mistry, R., Misner, S.: Introducing Microsoft® SQL Server® 2012. O'Reilly Media, Inc. (2012)

[42] Ogiela, M.R., Tadeusiewicz, R.: Syntactic reasoning and pattern recognition for analysis of coronary artery images. Artificial Intelligence in Medicine 26(1), 145–159 (2002)

[43] Ogiela, M.R., Tadeusiewicz, R.: Nonlinear processing and semantic content analysis in medical imaging-a cognitive approach. IEEE Transactions on Instrumentation and Measurement 54(6), 2149–2155 (2005)

[44] Prasanna, D.R.: Dependency injection. Manning Publications Co. (2009)

[45] Rosen, M., Lublinsky, B., Smith, K.T., Balcer, M.J.: Applied SOA: service-oriented architecture and design strategies. John Wiley & Sons (2012)

[46] Rublee, E., Rabaud, V., Konolige, K., Bradski, G.: Orb: An efficient alternative to sift or surf. In: 2011 IEEE International Conference on Computer Vision (ICCV), pp. 2564–2571 (November 2011)

[47] Seemann, M.: Dependency injection in .NET. Manning (2012)

[48] Śmietański, J., Tadeusiewicz, R., Łuczyńska, E.: Texture analysis in perfusion images of prostate cancer-a case study. International Journal of Applied Mathematics and Computer Science 20(1), 149–156 (2010)

[49] Tsai, W.T., Sun, X., Balasooriya, J.: Service-oriented cloud computing architecture. In: 2010 Seventh International Conference on Information Technology: New Generations (ITNG), pp. 684–689. IEEE (2010)

[50] Veltkamp, R.C., Hagedoorn, M.: State of the art in shape matching. In: Lew, M.S. (ed.) Principles of Visual Information Retrieval, pp. 87–119. Springer, London (2001)

[51] Veltkamp, R.C., Tanase, M.: Content-based image retrieval systems: A survey. Department of Computing Science, Utrecht University, pp. 1–62 (2002)

[52] Zalasiński, M., Cpałka, K.: New approach for the on-line signature verification based on method of horizontal partitioning. In: Rutkowski, L., Korytkowski, M., Scherer, R., Tadeusiewicz, R., Zadeh, L.A., Zurada, J.M. (eds.) ICAISC 2013, Part II. LNCS (LNAI), vol. 7895, pp. 342–350. Springer, Heidelberg (2013)

[53] Zitnick, C.L., Dollár, P.: Edge boxes: Locating object proposals from edges. In: Fleet, D., Pajdla, T., Schiele, B., Tuytelaars, T. (eds.) ECCV 2014, Part V. LNCS, vol. 8693, pp. 391–405. Springer, Heidelberg (2014)

Object Localization Using Active Partitions and Structural Description

Mateusz Jadczyk and Arkadiusz Tomczyk[✉]

Institute of Information Technology,
Lodz University of Technology,
ul. Wolczanska 215, 90-924 Lodz, Poland
arkadiusz.tomczyk@p.lodz.pl

Abstract. In this work a method of object localization on the basis of its expected structure is presented. An active partition approach is used for that purpose where, instead of pixels, line segments are used to represent image content. The expectation about object being sought is expressed in the form of model where the expected line segments are specified explicitly. Both image representation and model take into account relations between segments and thus both can be considered as graphs constituting their structural description. The best subsets of line segments are sought in a systematic search process with properly defined model fit function. It allows to identify a subset of segments that resembles the given model even if the segments are detected imprecisely.

Keywords: Active contour · Active partition · Graph matching · Structural description

1 Introduction

In the paper a practical realization of active partition concept is presented. Active partitions are a generalization of active contour methods where, instead of contours dividing set of image pixels into subsets representing object and background, partitions of a set containing more complex elements are sought. In this work images are described using line segments detected automatically by means of the method presented in [1] being a variation of LSD technique proposed in [2]. The additional assumption is that only the shape of the objects is considered and not the colors of image pixels.

To localize objects, active contours define an energy function, expressing expectations about objects that are sought, which becomes an objective function of some optimization process. The type of this process depends mainly on the form of the energy and on the assumed contour model ([3,4,5]). In this work expectations are expressed in the form of a sample shape model which should be found in the image. Because of the specificity of image description this model as well as the whole image can be interpreted as graphs. Consequently, in the discussed case the optimization task can be reduced to the problem of searching of the best subgraph or subgraphs of the image graph that are similar to that model.

© Springer International Publishing Switzerland 2015
L. Rutkowski et al. (Eds.): ICAISC 2015, Part I, LNAI 9119, pp. 727–736, 2015.
DOI: 10.1007/978-3-319-19324-3_65

The results of the proposed method are illustrated with two cases: detection of warning signs in real world scenes and detection of circular regions in mammograms. The paper is organized as follows: first the active partition concept is introduced and structural representation is described, next a fit function allowing to identify and evaluate the searched subsets of segments is presented, finally, last two sections describe and discuss the obtained results.

2   Active Partitions

As it was mentioned above, the idea of active partitions comes from active contours where the optimal object contour is sought in the image. The objective of this search has a form of energy function and the search itself is an optimization process. Since most of the optimization procedures are iterative algorithms, there exists a solution candidate in every iteration. The observation of the solution sequence makes an impression that the contour explores the image and that is why contours are called active. It does not mean, however, that only such iterative optimization procedures are allowed in that group of segmentation techniques.

In earlier works it was noticed that a contour represents a decision boundary of a certain classifier that divides the whole set of pixels into those that represent an object and those that represent a background ([6]). This observation has its consequences. Usually classifier models can be applied to any type of the classified object so, perhaps, instead of dividing a set of pixels some other image representations could be of use here. If the search of the optimal partition of that set is an iterative optimization process it may be, by analogy, called an active partition method.

Some alternative representations have already been proposed in [7] where image was represented as a set of line segments or circular regions. Such an alternative representation has beyond doubt its advantages as it reduces the number of the elements describing the image which allows to compress the higher-level knowledge in the attributes of these elements.

In this work the image is represented using automatically detected set S of line segments representing these areas of the image where the intensity changes in the similar way (Fig. 1b). To find an acceptable partition the systematic search is performed. The algorithm iterates through all of the segments in the image graph and uses described further fit function F for computing the model fit score for a single base segment. The best fit identifies the optimal partition. Additionally, such an approach allows to make a ranking of all of the fit scores. Therefore, also suboptimal solutions (partitions) can be found apart from the best ones.

3   Structural Description

As the systematic consideration of all the subsets would be unacceptable because of the computational costs, the information about neighboring line segments of a given segment is considered to reduce the complexity of the algorithm. This is why both model and image are represented by a graph structure. The graph

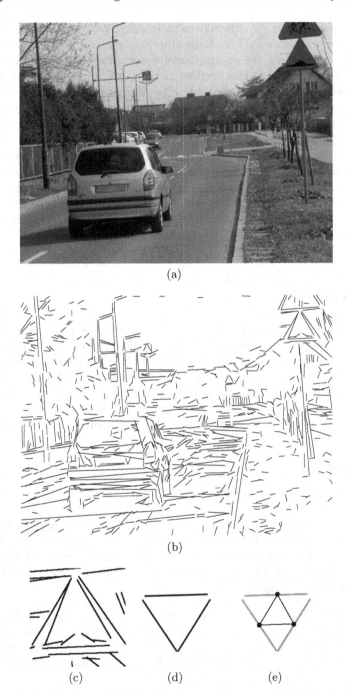

Fig. 1. The input of the method: (a) - original image, (b) - detected line segments, (c) - fragment with detected line segments of warning sign, (d) - model, (e) - graph representation of the model

used in the paper, however, differs from an intuitive view of the graph composed of line segments which would normally store segment end points as vertices and segments as edges. Here, the graph structure stores the segments extracted from the image as vertices. For two vertices in the graph to be connected (to have an edge between them), they need to be in close proximity to each other (Fig. 1e). In practice, only the vertices are explicitly defined in the image while the relations between them are found during the course of action of the algorithm. For the model the edges are defined explicitly.

It must be emphasized that such a representation allows to keep both standard and additional information about the set of line segments in the attributes of vertices and edges. In case of vertices these can be: coordinates of segment end points, characteristic of the image on both sides of such segment, etc., whereas for edges it can be: the distance between segments, their relative orientation, etc. Further in this paper, however, only the information about segment end points is used.

4   Fit Function

The goal of the fit function $F : S \to 2^S \times \mathbb{R}$ is to assign to a given base segment the subset of segments in the image which together approximately resemble the given model. Additionally, it should also measure this similarity with a decimal number from the range 0 to 1, where 1 translates to an exact match. There are two main difficulties while constructing such a function. Firstly, the object in the image can have size and orientation other than a model. Secondly, one segment in the model may be explained by a sequence of segments in the image.

4.1   Extensions

The fit function uses a concept of extensions (prolongations) as some of the object contour segments might have been split into many separate segments in the process of their detection. To find those extensions, the applied procedure takes a segment and tries to find all extensions of the segment, starting with the starting and ending points. The segments neighboring the considered point are found, then iterated on the nearest-first basic, and the following conditions are checked for each of them:

- The first condition is that an angle between the lines determined by the base segment and neighbor's segment has to be smaller than $a = 15$ degrees. If two separate segments formed a single segment in reality, they are supposedly placed at similar angle in the image. If this first condition fails, the next neighbor is taken under inspection.
- Next it is checked if the neighboring segment starts in close enough proximity with respect to the analyzed segment. The algorithm makes sure that the segment starts within the circle of a diameter equal to a given number of pixels. The exact diameter is dependent on the analyzed segment's length

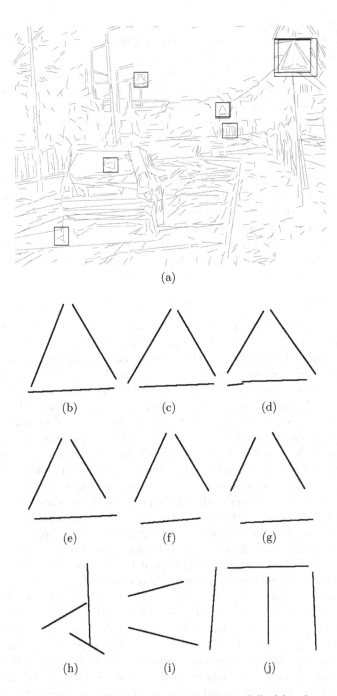

Fig. 2. Sample result for road images (with triangle model): (a) - detected segments and potential warning signs, (b) - (j) - detected 9 subsets of line segments in order of their decreasing fit score value.

and based on the coefficient $d = 0.1$, cannot however be less than $d_{min} = 15$ and more than $d_{max} = 25$ pixels. If the neighboring segment is close enough, one more condition is checked.

- If many segments are added as extensions and all of them are at big (but still within the limit) angles, it may turn out that the resultant segment is positioned at a wrong angle with respect to the base segment. To prevent it, before an segment is treated as an extension, it is checked if the summed segment obtained as a result lies at the angle not greater than $a_{max} = 15$ degrees compared to the base segment.

If all of the conditions have been satisfied, the base segment is extended by this neighbor. The resultant summed segment is used as a new reference point for checking the extension conditions. Each time a new segment is added as an extension, all of the segments found so far are added together as one extended segment to the list. This way all the possible combinations for one side of the segment are stored, and not only the longest possible extension.

4.2   Matching

The computation of the fit function result works as follows: it treats one of the segments of the image as a base segment and finds all of its possible extensions in both directions (starting from the starting and ending points of the given segment). It then iterates through all of the found extensions and then all of the model's segments one by one. For each model segment, the model graph is transformed and adjusted (scaled and rotated) so that the given model segment is aligned with the current extension. This way the locations where other segments in the subgraph are expected to be, to fit the model precisely, are known. Having adjusted the model graph according to one of the model segments, other model segments are iterated in order to find matches for them (one model segment is already perfectly aligned) among the segments in the image subgraph. The next step is to designate neighbors in the image graph of the extended base segment to be inspected. It is assumed that segments in the model graph are given in the known order - one by one, depending on their location. The approach allows to make the algorithm more efficient as it is known where the next model segment should be located. This way only neighbors at the predicted side of the segment can be searched through. Once a list of neighbors has been obtained, it is iterated. Again, for each neighbor it is required to find all of its extensions and iterate through them. Each extension is treated as a normal segment by the following simplification - it starts where the first segment in the extension starts and ends where the last segment in the extension ends. Next stage is to check how well each extension matches the currently processed model segment. The extension which matches the model segment most is then stored as a partial match.

There are three factors influencing the overall score for an extension-segment match. These are the angle between the vectors, the offset of the starting point and the offset of the ending point. Thanks to the transformed model, it is exactly known where the extension should be located to fit the model segment most.

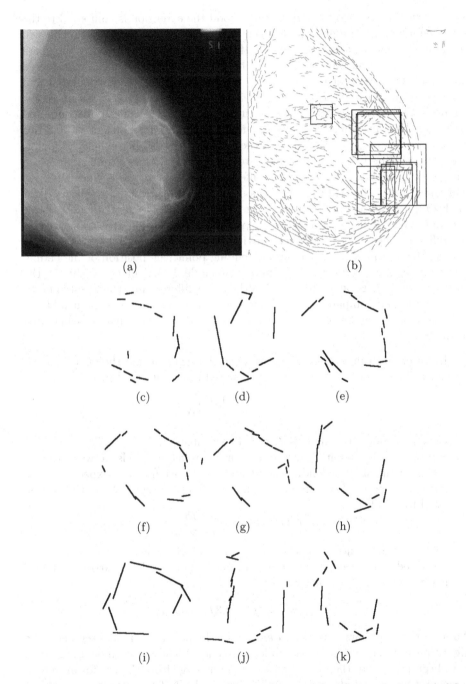

Fig. 3. Sample result for mamograms (with circle model): (a) - original image, (b) - detected segments and circular region, (c) - (k) - detected 9 subsets of line segments in order of their decreasing fit score value

The information is used to compute how good the extension is compared to the expected segment. The first thing taken into consideration is the angle between the model segment and the extension. If at this point it is above the threshold $r_{max} = 50$, the extension is assumed not to be a match at all and is not considered any more. Otherwise, a rotation fit f_r based on this angle is calculated and the algorithm proceeds. The next step is checking the starting position of the segment. The starting point has to be within a circle of a given radius (computed based on the transformed model segment's length and a coefficient $t = 0.8$ but not greater than $t_{max} = 100$) having the center in the predicted starting point. If so, the starting point fit f_s is calculated depending on the difference between the perfect and actual position. The difference is also stored as it will be needed while predicting the ending point's position. A similar procedure is used for analyzing the ending point, but with one difference. The predicted ending point is updated based on the actual starting point of the extension. It is translated by the difference between the perfect starting point and the actual starting point. Having the new position of the perfect ending point, the position of the ending point of the extension is checked against the circle. If it is placed within it, the ending point fit f_e is calculated. Having the three different fits, the wighted fit f_w is computed and compared with the best fit found so far among the neighbors. If it turns out to be better, the best fit is updated. All those fits are calculated in the following way:

- Rotation fit evaluates the angle between the segment and the expected segment. The angle of 15 degrees is translated to the fit equal to 0.7:

$$f_r = \exp(-\frac{\ln 0.7}{15}\alpha)$$

  where α denotes the angle between the segments
- Starting/ending point fit evaluates the difference in pixels between the location of the starting/ending point and the location of the expected starting/ending point. The difference equal to 15% of the segment length is translated to 0.75 fit:

$$f_s/f_e = \exp(-\frac{\ln 0.75}{0.15}\frac{d}{l})$$

  where d is difference in pixels and l represents the length of the segment
- Weighted fit is a weighted average obtained from rotation, starting and ending fits with the following weights:

$$f_w = 0.35f_r + 0.3f_s + 0.3f_e$$

After all the neighbors have been iterated for the particular model segment, the algorithm proceeds to the next model segment. When all the model segments have been processed, the overall fit score (an average from the fits for all model segments) is calculated and stored. Having used all of the model segments as perfectly aligned to the extension, other extensions of the base segment are processed. When all the loops are finished, the result of the F function is selected as the best found average value and the segments leading to that score.

Table 1. Statistics of warning sign detection for a small (selected) and large (all) set of images

(a)

Selected images	
# of images	49
# of images with all signs	43 (87,76%)
# of signs	67
# of localized signs	59 (88,06%)
# of signs at position = 1	30 (44,78%)
# of signs at position ≤ 5	46 (68,66%)
# of signs at position ≤ 10	47 (70,15%)

(b)

All images	
# of images	184
# of images with all signs	139 (75,54%)
# of signs	243
# of localized signs	189 (77,78%)
# of signs at position = 1	98 (40,33%)
# of signs at position ≤ 5	136 (55,97%)
# of signs at position ≤ 10	143 (58,85%)

5   Results

To evaluate the presented approach, road images were considered where triangular warning sings were to be detected (Fig. 1). Before the experiment the images were carefully inspected and the signs were marked with the smallest rectangle containing every of them (too small signs were ignored). This allowed to automatically summarize the results of detection since those rectangles were compared with rectangles enclosing detected segments. To identify the reasons of incorrect detections the smaller set of selected images was considered as it allowed to visually assess the result. The statistics of the results are presented in Tab. 1. The sample detection output is presented in Fig. 2.

The closer analysis of those results reveals that the proposed method successfully localizes most of the warning signs in the images. It means that not only signs are detected but also the fit function F gives them one of the highest scores. Results in Tab. 1 and the examination of detected subsets of segments in Fig. 2 give an evidence that the ordering of those subsets is reasonable as well. The visual inspection of outcomes for the images in the smaller set suggests that the main cause of that problem is detection of line segments (in all 8 cases at least one border line of a sign was not represented by any line segment).

To proof that method can be applied to different kinds of problems, a task of circular region detection in mammograms was considered. The images were obtained from MIAS database available at http://www.mammoimage.org. Some of those regions may be significant from diagnostic point of view since they may represent a malignant circumscribed or spicular lesion. The preliminary results, for a model with 6 segments approximating circle, are presented in Fig. 3. They are promising but show that because of the specificity of the images quite a large number of such circular regions may be detected.

6 Summary

In this paper a method of automatic detection of given structures was presented. It was evaluated in a problem of warning road signs detection. The results shows that even if no information about colors of the pixels is considered the modified representation of the image content allows to localize the desired objects. This new representation of the image significantly reduces the amount of information that must be processed but at the same time is the most crucial element influencing the results. There can be two problems. Firstly, if not all of the segments are detected properly, some of the objects might not be found. Secondly, too many segments may cause that there may exist many reasonable solutions. All of that problems might be overcome if the color information was also considered. It can be used in line segment detection to eliminate some regions or to identify segments that separate regions of different colors (and not only of different intensities), it can be applied after object detection to reject some of them and it finally can be used between these two phases to eliminate some segments before further processing. The consideration of the afore-mentioned aspects was not a goal of this work but it will be under further investigation.

Acknowledgement. This project has been funded with support from National Science Centre, Republic of Poland, decision number DEC-2012/05/D/ST6/03091.

References

1. Tomczyk, A.: Detection of Line Segments. Journal of Applied Computer Science 22(2), 81–90 (2014)
2. von Gioi, R.G., Jakubowicz, J., Morel, J.-M., Randall, G.: LSD: a Line Segment Detector. Image Processing On Line 2, 35–55 (2012)
3. Kass, M., Witkin, A., Terzopoulos, D.: Snakes: Active contour models. International Journal of Computer Vision, 321–331 (1988)
4. Caselles, V.: Geometric models for active contours. In: Proceedings of the International Conference on Image Processing, pp. 9–12 (1995)
5. Cootes, T., Taylor, C., Cooper, D., Graham, J.: Active shape model - their training and application. CVGIP Image Understanding 61(1), 38–59 (1994)
6. Tomczyk, A., Szczepaniak, P.S.: Adaptive potential active contours. Pattern Analysis and Application 14, 425–440 (2011)
7. Tomczyk, A., Szczepaniak, P.S., Pryczek, M.: Cognitive hierarchical active partitions in distributed analysis of medical images. Journal of Ambient Intelligence and Humanized Computing 4(3), 357–367 (2012)

Supervised Transform Learning for Face Recognition

Dimche Kostadinov[1(✉)], Sviatoslav Voloshynovskiy[1], Sohrab Ferdowsi[1], Maurits Diephuis[1], and Rafał Scherer[2]

[1] Computer Science Department, University of Geneva,
7 Route de Drize, Geneva, Switzerland
http://sip.unige.ch,
dimche.kostadinov@unige.ch
[2] Institute of Computational Intelligence, Częstochowa University of Technology
Al. Armii Krajowej 36, 42-200 Częstochowa, Poland

Abstract. In this paper we investigate transform learning and apply it to face recognition problem. The focus is to find a transformation matrix that transforms the signal into a robust to noise, discriminative and compact representation. We propose a method that finds an optimal transform under the above constrains. The non-sparse variant of the presented method has a closed form solution whereas the sparse one may be formulated as a solution to a sparsity regularized problem. In addition we give a generalized version of the proposed problem and we propose a prior on the data distribution across the dimensions in the transform domain.

Supervised transform learning is applied to the MVQ [10] method and is tested on a face recognition application using the YALE B database. The recognition rate and the robustness to noise is superior compared to the original MVQ based on k-means.

Keywords: Supervised sparsifying transform · Sparse representation · Dictionary learning · Face recognition

1 Introduction

Sparse signal representation approximates a signal using a linear combination of a few basis vectors from a given basis set, in contrast the sparsifying transform makes the signal approximately sparse using a transformation matrix. It recent years signal sparsity has been widely exploited in many applications like: pattern recognition, signal image processing, language modelling, text analysis, gene separation, mapping and many others.

Transform domain processing is a classical tool in signal processing, starting from *basic analytic transforms* (cosine, sine [1], Fourier [16], wavelet [17]), to many *analysis transforms* (factor analysis [4], principal component analysis (PCA) [9], independent component analysis like: zero-phase component analysis (ZCA) [3], linear discriminant analysis (LDA) [13], Fisher discriminant analysis (FDA) [6]), to *decomposition methods* as eigenvalue value decompositions

© Springer International Publishing Switzerland 2015
L. Rutkowski et al. (Eds.): ICAISC 2015, Part I, LNAI 9119, pp. 737–746, 2015.
DOI: 10.1007/978-3-319-19324-3_66

and many matrix decomposition methods [11]. In addition alternative models that have been studied for sparse signal representations are: the *synthesis model* [12], the *analysis model*, the *noisy signal analysis model* [14] and *the sparsifying transform model* [15].

The proposed supervised transform (ST) is similar in nature to the analysis transforms like: PCA, ZCA, LDA and FLD. PCA is a statistical procedure that uses an orthogonal transformation to convert a set of observations of possibly correlated variables into a set of linearly uncorrelated variables called principal components. A whitening transformation is a decorrelation transformation that transforms a set of random variables having a known covariance matrix into a set of new random variables whose covariance is the identity matrix (meaning that they are uncorrelated and all have variance 1). The PCA transformation is not unique. Indeed, the PCA whitening transformation data will stay whitened after any arbitrary rotation (multiplication with an arbitrary orthogonal matrix). The defining property of the ZCA transformation (sometimes also called "Mahalanobis transformation") is that it results in whitened data that is as close as possible to the original data (in the least squares sense). LDA is also closely related to PCA and factor analysis in that they both look for linear combinations of variables which best explain the data, and LDA explicitly attempts to model the difference between the classes of data. LDA is a generalization of Fisher's linear discriminant, a method used in statistics, pattern recognition and machine learning to find a linear combination of features that characterizes or separates two or more classes of objects or events. The resulting combination may be used as a linear classifier, or, more commonly, for dimensionality reduction before later classification.

In the most favourable case, when the training and observation signal models are known, stationary and noise free, signal transformation may not be necessary (except when one considers the computational complexity and the memory requirements). However, in many applications the training and observation models are unknown or highly non-stationary and one only has a few training samples. If one considers recognition tasks then the recognition system basically learns a classifier in a "blind" way using only the available distorted training samples and expects that the observation model will exhibit similar behavior to the training model. In this scenario, one may analyse the signal in the original domain and alternately transform it in a more suitable domain considering complexity, memory requirements and robustness to distortions.

Here we focus on learning a transformation matrix that may transform the signal into robust to noise, discriminative and compact representation. The transform learning is a part of a multiple level, multi-resolution image representation, considered in the scope of the multi-resolution vector quantization (MVQ) model presented in [10].

A computer simulation is performed using the supervised transform learning (STL). The transform is used as a part of the MVQ model and is compared with the MVQ model that uses k-means for the codebook design. Both approaches are evaluated in terms of their recognition rate for a certain range of distortions and their memory requirements.

This paper is organized as follows. Section 2 formalizes the problem. In Section 3 we present and describe the proposed transform. The results of the computer simulations are presented in Section 4 and Section 5 concludes the paper.

Notation: Capital bold letters are used to denote real valued matrices, $\mathbf{W} \in \Re^{N \times KM}$, small bold letters to denote real valued vectors: $\mathbf{x} \in \Re^N$. The estimate of $\mathbf{x}$ is denoted as $\hat{\mathbf{x}}$. All vectors have finite length, explicitly defined where appropriate.

2 Problem Formulation

Assume that there are K subjects where each subject $k \in \{1, \cdots, K\}$ has M available training samples. Equivalently in matrix notation, one assumes that a data matrix $\mathbf{W} \in \Re^{N \times KM}$ is given, where the columns of $\mathbf{W}$ represent the available training samples $\mathbf{x}_j$ (e.g. images represented as vectors by column concatenation), $j \in \{1, \cdots, KM\}$. The number of training samples in total is KM. The matrix representation is as follows:

$$\mathbf{W} = [\mathbf{x}_1, \mathbf{x}_2, \mathbf{x}_3, ..., \mathbf{x}_{KM}] \in \Re^{N \times KM}. \tag{1}$$

The goal is to find a transformation matrix $\mathbf{T}$ such that all the transformed samples $\mathbf{Tx}_i$ from one subject k are similar with respect to a particular similarity measure and any two transformed samples $\mathbf{Tx}_i$ and $\mathbf{Tx}_j$ that come from two different subjects $i \in k, j \in l, l \neq k$ are different. Figure 1 shows an illustration of this goal. One may note that the supervised part consists only in the fact that given a number of samples KM and a number of subjects K it is assumed (known) that every sample comes from a single, particular subject.

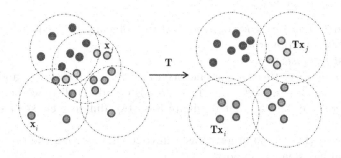

Fig. 1. Idealized transform that produces a robust, discriminative and compact data representation.

3   Supervised Transform Learning

The first part formalizes the supervised transform learning as an optimization problem. The second part presents a prior on the data distribution across the dimensions in the transform domain.

3.1   Proposed Method

Supervised transform learning (STL) may be formulated as the following problem:

$$\min_{\mathbf{T}} \underbrace{\frac{1}{2}\|\mathbf{TW} - \mathbf{C}\|_F^2}_{A} + \underbrace{\frac{\alpha}{2}\sum_{i=1}^{KM}\sum_{j\neq k}^{KM}\pi_{i,j}\|\mathbf{Tx}_i - \mathbf{Tx}_j\|_2^2}_{B} +$$

$$\underbrace{\frac{\beta}{2}\sum_{k=1}^{K}\sum_{i=1}^{KM}\xi_{k,i}\|\mathbf{Tx}_i - \mathbb{E}[\mathbf{Tx}_k]\|_2^2}_{C}. \tag{2}$$

where $\| * \|_F$ is a Frobenius norm, the matrix $\mathbf{C} = [\mathbf{c}_1, \cdots, \mathbf{c}_{KM}]$ contains a specified vectors $\mathbf{c}_i$ called ideal codes that will be introduced bellow, $\mathbf{T} \in \Re^{Z \times N}$, α, β and γ are Lagrangian parameters and $\mathbb{E}[\mathbf{Tx}_k]$ is the empirical expected value of all the transform codes that come from subject k:

$$\mathbb{E}[\mathbf{Tx}_k] = \frac{1}{M}\sum_{i=M(k-1)+1}^{M(k-1)+M}\mathbf{Tx}_i, k \in \{1, \cdots, K\}. \tag{3}$$

The term A in (2) introduces a penalty for the difference between the ideal code $\mathbf{c}_i$ that will be defined later and the transform code $\mathbf{Tx}_i$ using the transformation $\mathbf{T}$ and the data sample $\mathbf{x}_i$. Assume that this ideal code $\mathbf{c}_i$ is known, than this term enforces the transform code $\mathbf{Tx}_i$ to equal the ideal code $\mathbf{c}_i$. The ideal code $\mathbf{c}_i$ is introduced as follows:

Definition 1. The ideal code $\mathbf{c}_i$ in context to problem (2) is a code that satisfies the following constraints:

1. robust to noise;

2. discriminative: the distance between any two ideal codes $\mathbf{c}_i$ and $\mathbf{c}_j$ that come from one class $i, j \in k, k \in \{1, \cdots, K\}$ is 0 and the distance between any two ideal codes $\mathbf{c}_i$ and $\mathbf{c}_j$ that originate from two different classes $i \in k, j \in l$, $l \neq k$ is infinity;

3. compact: there is no other transform code that satisfies the previous constraints and has smaller support.

The term B enforces penalties on the differences between a pair of transform codes. The $\pi_{i,j}$ for a pair of transform codes that come from same subject $k, k \in \{1, \cdots K\}$ is equal to 1 and for a pair of transform codes that come from two different subject is equal to -1. This term enforces the transform codes that come from the same subject to be similar and the transform codes that come from different subject to be dissimilar.

The term C enforces penalties between a transform code and the expected value per subject of the transform codes. The idea and the role of $\xi_{i,j}$ is similar to the second term and $\pi_{i,j}$ except that instead of pairwise constrains it imposes the transform codes that comes from a particular subject k to be similar to the expected transform code of the same subject k. Similarly it imposes the same transform code to be dissimilar with the expected transform code of the rest subjects $l \neq k$.

All the terms in problem (1) may be expressed alternatively as follows:

$$\|\mathbf{TW} - \mathbf{C}\|_F^2 = \mathrm{Tr}\left([\mathbf{TW} - \mathbf{C}]^T[\mathbf{TW} - \mathbf{C}]\right),$$

$$\sum_{i=1}^{KM}\sum_{j \neq i}^{KM} \pi_{i,j}\|\mathbf{Tx}_i - \mathbf{Tx}_j\|_2^2 = \mathrm{Tr}\left([\mathbf{TWS}_p]^T[\mathbf{TWS}_p]\right) - \mathrm{Tr}\left([\mathbf{TWD}_p]^T[\mathbf{TWD}_p]\right),$$

$$\sum_{k=1}^{K}\sum_{i=1}^{KM} \xi_{k,i}\|\mathbf{Tx}_i - \mathbb{E}[\mathbf{Tx}_k]\|_2^2 = \mathrm{Tr}\left([\mathbf{TWS}_\mathbb{E}]^T[\mathbf{TWS}_\mathbb{E}]\right) - \mathrm{Tr}\left([\mathbf{TWD}_\mathbb{E}]^T[\mathbf{TWD}_\mathbb{E}]\right), (4)$$

where $\mathrm{Tr}(.)$ denotes the trace of matrix, $\mathbf{S}_p \in \{-1, +1\}^{KM \times \frac{M(M-1)}{2}}$ and $\mathbf{D}_p \in \{-1, +1\}^{KM \times \frac{M(K-1)(M(K-1)-1)}{2}}$ are sparse matrices that are used to enforce the pairwise constraints and have only two non-zero elements per column (one positive and one negative), $\mathbf{S}_\mathbb{E} \in \Re^{KM \times KM}$ and $\mathbf{D}_\mathbb{E} \in \Re^{KM \times KM}$ are also sparse matrices that are used to enforce the constraints between transform code and the subject expected transform code.

Therefore problem (1) may be expressed using an equivalent matrix trace formulation:

$$\min_{\mathbf{T}} \mathrm{Tr}([\mathbf{TW} - \mathbf{C}]^T[\mathbf{TW} - \mathbf{C}] + \alpha\left([\mathbf{TWS}_p]^T[\mathbf{WWS}_p] - [\mathbf{WXD}_p]^T[\mathbf{TWD}_p]\right) +$$

$$\beta\left([\mathbf{TWS}_\mathbb{E}]^T[\mathbf{TWS}_\mathbb{E}] - [\mathbf{TWD}_\mathbb{E}]^T[\mathbf{TWD}_\mathbb{E}]\right)). \tag{5}$$

Denoting the objective function in problem (2) as $F(\mathbf{T})$, the first order derivative of $F(\mathbf{T})$ may be expressed as:

$$F'(\mathbf{T}) = \underbrace{\mathbf{TWW}^T}_{A_1'} - \underbrace{\mathbf{CW}^T}_{A_2'} + \alpha\mathbf{T}\left(\underbrace{[\mathbf{WS}_p][\mathbf{WS}_p]^T - [\mathbf{WD}_p][\mathbf{WD}_p]^T}_{G_p}\right) +$$

$$\beta\mathbf{T}\left(\underbrace{[\mathbf{WS}_\mathbb{E}][\mathbf{WS}_\mathbb{E}]^T - [\mathbf{WD}_\mathbb{E}][\mathbf{WD}_\mathbb{E}]^T}_{G_\mathbb{E}}\right). \tag{6}$$

Denoting $[\mathbf{WS}_p][\mathbf{WS}_p]^T - [\mathbf{WD}_p][\mathbf{WD}_p]^T$ as $\mathbf{G}_p$, $[\mathbf{WS}_\mathbb{E}][\mathbf{WS}_\mathbb{E}]^T - [\mathbf{WD}_\mathbb{E}][\mathbf{WD}_\mathbb{E}]^T]$ as $\mathbf{G}_\mathbb{E}$ and setting the derivative to zero, one obtains the closed form solution:

$$\mathbf{T} = \mathbf{CW}^T\left[\mathbf{WW}^T + \alpha\mathbf{G}_p + \beta\mathbf{G}_\mathbb{E}\right]^{-1}. \tag{7}$$

Considering a sparsity constraint on the transform codes $\mathbf{Tx}_i$ an extended and generalized version of problem (7), that we name here as supervised sparsifying transform learning (SSTL) may be formulated as follows:

$$\min_T \frac{1}{2}\phi\left(\mathbf{T}\left(\mathbf{WW}^T + \alpha\mathbf{G}_p + \beta\mathbf{G}_\mathrm{E}\right) - \mathbf{CW}^T\right) + \gamma\sum_{i=1}^{KM}\varphi\left(\mathbf{Tx}_i\right), \qquad (8)$$

where $\phi(.)$ represents an error function (e.g. Forbenius-norm, Huber [8] or Tukey [2]) and $\varphi(.)$ is a penalty that enforcers sparsity. One such function is the following [18]:

$$\sum_{i=1}^{KM}\varphi\left(\mathbf{Tx}_i\right) = \sum_{i=1}^{KM}\left(\|\mathbf{Tx}_i\|_1\right)^2. \qquad (9)$$

In addition if one constrains the solution of (8) to be positive $\mathbf{T} \geq 0$, then (9) equals $\mathrm{Tr}([\mathbf{TW}]^T\mathbf{E}[\mathbf{TW}])$, where the matrix $\mathbf{E} \in \{1\}^{Z \times Z}$ is a square matrix of all ones. Alternatively one may use the nuclear norm defined as:

$$\|\mathbf{TW}\|_* = \mathrm{Tr}(\sqrt{[\mathbf{TW}]^T[\mathbf{TW}]}). \qquad (10)$$

3.2 Prior on the Data Distribution Across the Dimensions in the Transform Domain

Knowing the ideal codes $\mathbf{c}_i, i \in \{1, \cdots, KM\}$ one may solve efficiently (10) and thereby find the optimal transformation matrix $\mathbf{T}$. However given an unknown probability distribution of data $\mathbf{W}$, unknown probability distribution of codes $\mathbf{C}$, small number of distorted data samples $\mathbf{W}$, one alternative is to make a priory assumption about the codes $\mathbf{c}_i$. Adopting this approach one assumes in probability that:

$$C(i,j) \sim P\left(C(i,j)\right), 1 \leq i \leq Z, 1 \leq j \leq KM, \qquad (11)$$

$C(i,j)$ is distributed under some probability distribution $P\left(C(i,j)\right)$ and $C(i,j)$ denotes the (i,j) element of matrix $\mathbf{C}$.

The prior on the data distribution across the dimensions in the transform domain is considered by using the first order derivative of the similarity penalty term A in (2) with respect to $\mathbf{T}$.

Proposition 1. Assume that the term A_2' in (6) (the second term of the first order derivative of term A in (2) with respect to $\mathbf{T}$) is bounded and is distributed according to a particular probability distribution. Then the proposed prior may be expressed as:

$$\left(\mathbf{CW}^T\right)(i,j) \sim P\left(\left(\mathbf{CW}^T\right)(i,j)\right), 1 \leq i \leq Z, 1 \leq j \leq N, \qquad (12)$$

where $P\left((\mathbf{CW}^T)(i,j)\right)$ is a probability distribution.

A well known information theory result is that for a a given, fixed support, the probability distribution from all the probability distribution that has the highest entropy is the uniform one [5].

Corollary 1. The uniform probability distribution of the second term in the first order derivative of the term A in equation 2 achieves the highest entropy of all the posible probability distributions and by this the solution to problem (2) is such that the resulting transformation $\mathbf{T}$, transforms all the data form the base domain in the transform domain where the data is equlikely distributed among all the dimensions in the transformed domain under the constraints B, C in (2).

In this way the informative content of every dimension in the transform domain under the constraints B, C in (2) is maximized.

4 Computer Simulation

In this section we present the results of the computer simulation, preformed on the MVQ method to compare the recognition rate and the robustness under several assumptions. The MVQ model consists of three main parts: decomposition, codebook generation, encoding, decoding (recognition) and result fusion. By a decomposition we refer to image partitioning into local block where MVQ basically uses local codebooks. Two types of MVQ codebooks are analysed:

a)*one using a set of available training data samples*;
b)*one without using a training data set.*

4.1 Used Data Set

The computer simulation is carried out on the publicly available face dataset Extended Yale B [7]. This database consists of 2414 frontal face images of 38 subjects captured under various laboratory-controlled *extreme lighting variability*. All the images from this database are converted to gray scale, cropped and normalized to 192x168 pixels.

4.2 Experimental Set-up

There are three experiments, where it is analysed the codebook impact on the recognition rate and the robustness to noise. In every experiment the dimensionality of the transform domain is set to be $Z = 512$.

A codebook constructed using the k-means algorithm with training samples is compared with one that is generated using:

1. *a prior distribution, with no use of a training samples, (*$\mathbf{T}$ *is generated from 4 different distributions: Laplace, Gaussian, Uniform in the range* $[0, 1]$ *and Uniform on the set* $\{-1, +1\}$;

2. *a prior distribution about the ideal code* $\mathbf{C}$ *in the transform domain and using the training samples (basically using the term* $\mathbf{CW}^T$ *in (7) we make a prior assumption about the ideal codes* $\mathbf{C}$ *in the transform domain),* $\mathbf{C}$ *is generated* *from 4 different distributions: Laplace, Gaussian, Uniform in the range* $[0, 1]$ *and Uniform on the set* $\{-1, +1\}$;

3. *the STL method, using the training samples* ($\mathbf{CW}^T$ *is generated from 4 different distributions: Laplace, Gaussian, Uniform in the range* $[0, 1]$ *and Uniform on the set* $\{-1, +1\}$).

As image feature we refer to a basic, elementary image pixel values. All of the three experiments are preformed on 4 different downsampled images feature dimensions. Considering the decomposition, the local block size is set to 3×3. To be unbiased in our validation of the results we use 5-fold cross validation, where for single validation for each subject, half of the images are selected at random for training and the remainder for testing.

4.3 Results

From Table 1 one may note that when one does not use training samples, the recognition rate is low compared to MVQ that uses k-means algorithm for the low dimensional features. At the highest dimensional feature the recognition rate is still smaller, however is comparable with the one of MVQ that uses k-means.

Table 1. MVQ recognition rate results on Yale B database at different image feature dimensions

1. MVQ recognition rates (%) on Yale B using prior on the transformation T				
Dimension	30	56	120	504
$\mathbf{T} \sim$ Laplace	32	50	72	96
$\mathbf{T} \sim$ Gauss	32	49	72	95
$\mathbf{T} \sim$ Uniform	30	49	73	96
$\mathbf{T} \sim$ Uniform $\{-1, +1\}$	34	53	77	95
k-means	**53**	**75**	**97**	**99**

Table 2. MVQ recognition rate results on Yale B database at different image feature dimensions

2. MVQ recognition rates (%) on Yale B using prior on the ideal code C				
Dimension	30	56	120	504
$\mathbf{C} \sim$ Laplace	59	75	93	99
$\mathbf{C} \sim$ Gauss	59	76	93	99
$\mathbf{C} \sim$ Uniform	59	76	93	99
$\mathbf{C} \sim$ Uniform $\{-1, +1\}$	**59**	**76**	93	**99**
k-means	53	75	**97**	99

One may confirm from the results shown in Table 2 that when one uses MVQ with training data samples even with a prior distribution about the ideal code **C**, the recognition rate is improved and even higher compared to MVQ that uses k-means algorithm. The results shown on Table 3 confirm that with the uniform

Table 3. MVQ recognition rate results on Yale B database at different image feature dimensions, using the proposed transform learning method and prior on the data distribution across the dimensions in the transform domain

3. MVQ recognition rates (%) on Yale B using prior on the data distribution across the dimensions in the transform domain				
Dimension	30	56	120	504
$\mathbf{CW}^T \sim$ Laplace	64	83	96	100
$\mathbf{CW}^T \sim$ Gauss	69	86	97	100
$\mathbf{CW}^T \sim$ Uniform	71	88	98	100
$\mathbf{CW}^T \sim$ Uniform $\{-1, +1\}$	**71**	**89**	**98**	**100**
k-means	53	75	97	99

prior on the data distribution across the dimensions in the transform domain the MVQ method with the proposed STL method achieves highest recognition rates across all the feature dimensions. Moreover the results in Table 3 show that MVQ with the STL method outperforms the MVQ with k-means at every feature dimension and that the MVQ with the STL method has a recognition rate of 100% at the highest feature dimension.

5   Conclusion

In this paper we proposed a generalized (including: generalized error term, non-sparse and sparse) transform learning for a robust, discriminative and compact representation and a prior on the data distribution across the dimensions in the transform domain. The non sparse variant and the sparse one have closed form solution and a solution to a sparsity regularized problem, respectively. Supervised transform learning was used in the MVQ [10] method and was tested on a face recognition application using the YALE B database. The computer simulation confirm that the recognition rate and the robustness to noise is superior compared to the original MVQ based on k-means.

Acknowledgements. The research has been partially supported by a grant from Switzerland through the Swiss Contribution to the enlarged European Union PSPB-125/2010.

References

1. Ahmed, N., Natarajan, T., Rao, K.R.: Discrete cosine transfom. IEEE Trans. Comput. 23(1), 90–93 (1974)
2. Beaton, A.E., Tukey, J.W.: The Fitting of Power Series, Meaning Polynomials, Illustrated on Band-Spectroscopic Data. Technometrics 16(2), 147–185 (1974)
3. Bell, A.J., Sejnowski, T.J.: The "independent components" of natural scenes are edge filters. Vision Research 37, 3327–3338 (1997)
4. Child, D.: The Essentials of Factor Analysis. Bloomsbury Academic (2006)
5. Cover, T.M., Thomas, J.A.: Elements of Information Theory (Wiley Series in Telecommunications and Signal Processing). Wiley-Interscience (2006)
6. Fisher, R.A.: The use of multiple measurements in taxonomic problems. Annals of Eugenics 7(2), 179–188 (1936)
7. Georghiades, A.S., Belhumeur, P.N., Kriegman, D.J.: From few to many: Illumination cone models for face recognition under variable lighting and pose. IEEE Transactions on Pattern Analysis and Machine Intelligence 23, 643–660 (2001)
8. Huber, P.J.: Robust estimation of a location parameter. Annals of Mathematical Statistics 35(1), 73–101 (1964)
9. Jolliffe, I.: Principal Component Analysis. Springer Series in Statistics. Springer (2002)
10. Kostadinov, D., Voloshynovskiy, S., Diephuis, M.: Visual information encoding for face recognition: sparse coding vs vector quantization. In: 4th Joint WIC IEEE Symposium on Information Theory and Signal Processing in the Benelux, Eindhoven, Netherlands, vol. 35 (May 2014)
11. Lay, D.C.: Linear Algebra and Its Applications, 4th edn. Addison-Wesley (2006)
12. Elad, M., Milanfar, P., Rubinstein, R.: Analysis versus synthesis in signal priors. Inverse Problems 23(3), 947–968 (2007)
13. Martinez, A.M., Kak, A.C.: Pca versus lda. IEEE Transactions on Pattern Analysis and Machine Intelligence 23, 228–233 (2001)
14. Rubinstein, R., Peleg, T., Elad, M.: Analysis k-svd: A dictionary-learning algorithm for the analysis sparse model. IEEE Transactions on Signal Processing 61(3), 661–677 (2013)
15. Ravishankar, S., Bresler, Y.: ℓ_0 sparsifying transform learning with efficient optimal updates and convergence guarantees. CoRR abs/1501.02859 (2015)
16. Bracewell, R.N.: The Fourier Transform and Its Applications. Electrical engineering series. McGraw Hill (2000)
17. Stphane, M.: A Wavelet Tour of Signal Processing: The Sparse Way, 3rd edn. Academic Press (2008)
18. Zdunek, R., Cichocki, A.: Non-negative matrix factorization with quasi-newton optimization. In: Rutkowski, L., Tadeusiewicz, R., Zadeh, L.A., Żurada, J.M. (eds.) ICAISC 2006. LNCS (LNAI), vol. 4029, pp. 870–879. Springer, Heidelberg (2006)

Fast Dictionary Matching for Content-Based Image Retrieval

Patryk Najgebauer[1], Janusz Rygał[1], Tomasz Nowak[1], Jakub Romanowski[1],
Leszek Rutkowski[2], Sviatoslav Voloshynovskiy[3], and Rafał Scherer[1](✉)

[1] Institute of Computational Intelligence, Częstochowa University of Technology
al. Armii Krajowej 36, 42-200 Częstochowa, Poland
{patryk.najgebauer,janusz.rygal,tomasz.nowak,jakub.romanowski,
leszek.rutkowski,rafal.scherer}@iisi.pcz.pl
http://iisi.pcz.pl
[2] University of Social Sciences in Łódź
Sienkiewicza 9, 90-113 Łódź, Poland
[3] Computer Science Department, University of Geneva,
7 Route de Drize, Geneva, Switzerland

Abstract. This paper describes a method for searching for common sets of descriptors between collections of images. The presented method operates on local interest keypoints, which are generated using the SURF algorithm. The use of a dictionary of descriptors allowed achieving good performance of the content-based image retrieval. The method can be used to initially determine a set of similar pairs of keypoints between images. For this purpose, we use a certain level of tolerance between values of descriptors, as values of feature descriptors are almost never equal but similar between different images. After that, the method compares the structure of rotation and location of interest points in one image with the point structure in other images. Thus, we were able to find similar areas in images and determine the level of similarity between them, even when images contain different scenes.

Keywords: Content-based image retrieval · Local interest points · Image matching

1 Introduction

Content-based image analysis is important part of many areas of science and engineering. It can be used for face recognition [1], medical imaging [3][7][8], military science [12] and general purpose image analysis [4]. Image comparison based on their content is a complex process and still far from the excellence of the human vision. The main problem is a difference between human perception and that what can be analysed by computers. Humans focus on the remembering semantic description of an image without details as well as events, actions and objects represented by images. At the same time, they are not able to reconstruct exactly what they saw, as we remember overall image context. Humans recognize image objects by linking the situation presented on the image and

© Springer International Publishing Switzerland 2015
L. Rutkowski et al. (Eds.): ICAISC 2015, Part I, LNAI 9119, pp. 747–756, 2015.
DOI: 10.1007/978-3-319-19324-3_67

the information about it learned previously. Computers cannot find simply a relationship between images and the semantic description of objects being the content of the image. On the other hand, they are very detailed in the analysis and thanks to their precision they are able to do things such as fingerprint[5] or signature [13] recognition much faster and better than humans.

Algorithms generating local keypoints are often used for general purposes. Unfortunately they generate huge amount of information, which has to be compared afterwards. This feature implicates large complexity of computation both while generating and comparing keypoints. Using keypoints, we can focus on certain areas of the image and skip the rest.

Keypoints have also spatial relationships, which are useful in comparison of similar areas in images regarding to their rotation and shift in different images. We cannot simply search for each keypoint in an image for its equivalent in the other image as some keypoints could exist only in one image.

1.1   SURF Algorithm

One of the fastest algorithms nowadays for local interest point detection and description is the SURF algorithm [2][10]. One of the advantages of SURF over other algorithms is good performance, which is achieved by comparing areas in images and not single pixels. This approach has also a disadvantage: it is impossible to divide an image into circular areas. The algorithm can function only with square areas, which can cause some inaccuracies in estimated values, when an image is for example rotated 45 degrees. The algorithm searches for areas, in which local values of second derivatives are the highest, i.e. for local extremes. It is a typical function of algorithms of the blob detection family (Fig. 1)[11]. It also estimates the size and the rotation of the keypoint, which is important for the exploration of dependencies between keypoints. The most im-

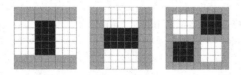

Fig. 1. SURF smallest 9x9 pixels blob detector

portant information, which is generated for each keypoint, is its descriptor. The descriptor allows to recognize a keypoint and represents local gradient around the keypoint. In the basic version of the SURF algorithm, the descriptor is built from 64 floating-point values. These values are grouped in 4 element chunks, which describe each of sixteen subregion of the descriptor: X-axis derivatives, Y-axis derivatives, modulus of the X-axis derivatives and modulus of the Y-axis derivatives

$$V = \left(\sum dx, \sum dy, \sum |dx|, \sum |dy| \right) . \tag{1}$$

Subregions create a 4x4 matrix that cover the keypoint localization in image (Fig. 2).

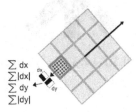

Fig. 2. Descriptor structure, 4x4 matrix of 4 values from subregion (V_{sub})

2 Description of the Problem

As already mentioned, comparison of descriptors has to be done by tresholding their difference, otherwise it will be almost impossible to match them to keypoints from a different image. For example, Table 1 presents distribution of differences in values of similar descriptors (Fig. 3) with the sum of absolute differences (SAD, L^1 norm) equal to 0.4753. In this case, we consider the keypoints with SAD lower than 0.5 as similar.

Table 1. Differences between V_{sub} of two similar keypoints descriptor

$V_{sub}x/y$	1	2	3	4
1	0.0000	0.0059	0.0031	-0.0047
2	-0.0098	0.0144	0.0349	0.0159
3	-0.0495	-0.0214	-0.0159	0.0079
4	-0.0770	-0.0062	-0.0120	-0.0173

Presented keypoints and their orientations are identical for humans, but according to the values of descriptors, they are different. After generation of keypoints in the process of comparison of two images, we have two sets of keypoints. The number of keypoints depends on the size of images and the amount of details. Often, for images larger than 1280x800 pixels, the number of keypoints exceeds 1000. The easiest and the most common approach of comparison of keypoints between images is to compare each keypoint with the rest, but when we deal with a large number of keypoints, the number of needed computations is very high. For example, 1000 of key points implicates 1 million of comparisons. To reduce the number of comparisons, keypoints should be ordered somehow and some of them should be passed over during the comparison process.

Fig. 3. An example of similar SURF keypoints with 0.47 value of difference between descriptor components

Another challenge by the estimation of similar parts is the problem of keypoints being lost during image transformations. The cause for this problem is different configuration of the same keypoints after the transformation. Usually images representing the same content contain only part of similar keypoints, another image can contain of course a different set of keypoints.

3   Method Description

For better performance the proposed method uses a special, dictionary-based form of keypoint representation [6][9]. Dictionary-based structure accelerates the comparison process by allowing to skip most of keypoint combinations.

3.1   Dictionary Creation

Before performing matching images, the method prepares images by keypoint detection and generating the dictionary structure for each single image (see Fig. 4).

Fig. 4. Flowchart presenting the process of dictionary creation

Descriptor dictionary is created from 64 element vectors which are local interest point descriptors of an image. The method puts separate elements of the descriptor in the dictionary beginning from the first element. The dictionary is built in a similar way to the B-tree, where the first element of dictionary contains the list of first elements of descriptors.

The elements of descriptors which are similar and their values do not exceed estimated limits, are grouped and will be represented as a single element of the dictionary. An example of grouping is presented in Fig. 5 for the first element of descriptors with the number between 2 and 6. The rest of descriptor elements,

Descriptor Number	Number of descriptor element				
	1	2	3	4	5
1	-0.1021	0.2031	0.1229	-0.0551	0.2168
2				-0.0551	-0.0720
3		0.1846	0.2229	0.1779	-0.0068
4	0.0451				0.2168
5		0.4722	-0.1021	-0.0067	0.0205
6			-0.0551	0.2168	0.1780
7	0.2687	0.1846	-0.0067	0.0205	-0.0068
8		0.5151	0.2168	0.1779	0.2168
9	0.4552	0.1847	-0.0068	-0.0551	-0.0721
10			0.0205	-0.0068	0.2168

Fig. 5. Exemplary part of the descriptor dictionary

from which another elements are built, are derivatives of the first group. Thanks to grouping, we can decrease the number of similar, duplicated elements of descriptors. Thanks to the presented approach, building index of descriptors is also faster, especially when we deal with a very large number of descriptors. The rest of data of keypoints such as position, size or orientation are contained in the last part of the word associated with the descriptor. The last step of the process of creation of the dictionary is conversion of data to a binary file as it is sufficient to generate the dictionary only once.

3.2 Comparison Between Descriptors and Dictionary

Every image from the analyzed set has its own descriptor dictionary stored in a form of a binary file (see Section 3.1). Now, let us assume that we have a new query image and we want to find similar images in the large collection of images. The first step is to create a dictionary of its feature descriptors and store it in a binary file. Fig. 6 presents a flowchart of such image retrieval.

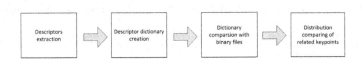

Fig. 6. Flowchart of image retrieval searching in the set of images

The next step is a comparison of the query image dictionary with the dictionaries from the binary files. Descriptors values are similar if their sum of absolute differences (SAD) is less than the threshold. Comparison of two dictionaries is presented in the Fig. 7, where the dark background represents a common part.

Number of descriptor element

Descriptor Number	1	2	3	4	5
1	-0.1021	0.2031	0.1229	-0.0551	0.2168
2				-0.0551	-0.072
3		0.1846	0.2229	0.1779	-0.0068
4	0.0451				0.2168
5		0.4722	-0.1021	-0.0067	0.0205
6			-0.0551	0.2168	0.1780
7	0.2687	0.5151	0.2168	0.1779	0.2168
8		0.1846	-0.0067	0.0205	-0.0068
9	0.4552	0.1846	-0.0068	-0.0551	-0.0720
10			0.0205	-0.0068	0.2168

Dictionary form binary file
Number of descriptor element

	1	2	3	4	5
1	0.042	0.5111	-0.1021	-0.0067	0.0205
2			-0.0551	0.2168	0.1780
3	0.1187	0.1846	-0.0067	0.0205	-0.0068
4		0.5151	0.2168	0.1779	0.2168
5	0.2687	0.1846	-0.0205	-0.0068	0.2168
6			-0.0068	0.03	-0.0068

Fig. 7. Exemplary part of two compared dictionaries

3.3   Matching Determined Sets of Keypoints

The dictionary comparing process returns a set of pairs of similar keypoints. The next step is to examine keypoint distribution between images. Each pair will be excluded, if their distribution in the relation to the rest of pairs indicates wrong connection. Fig. 8 describes an example of keypoint distribution between two images. Each point has its own counterpart in the second set. The method compares the direction and the distance between keypoints from the same set. For example, angles β_{12} and α_{12} have the same value as β_{12}' and α_{12}' from the second set. Distances d12 and d12' are also similar. Thus, in this case we can

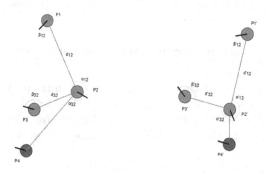

Fig. 8. Example of keypoints pair checking by mapping them between images

assume, that points P1 and P2 are related. In other case we mark points as not related, e.g. P4 and P4'.

4   Experimental Results

In this section we show some examples of the proposed method for content-based image retrieval on the test images presented in Fig. 9. For better presentation, we chose images, which are only slightly different.

Table 2 contains test results of comparison between each image with all other from Fig. 6. "No. of points" column is the number of descriptors extracted from

Fig. 9. Images used in the experiments

the image. "Matched" column is the number of related descriptors between current and all other images. "Comparisons" is the number of descriptors compared by using the dictionary. "Combination" is the number of all possible combinations of descriptors between images. As we can see, the number of comparisons in the proposed method is significantly smaller in relation to the number of all combinations. In our tests, the number of compared descriptors is only 0.18% of all possible combination.

Table 2. Results of comparisons between dictionaries.

Images	No. of points	Matched	Comparisons	Combinations	Performance
01	367	225	19522	3733124	0.52%
02	257	26	3691	2614204	0.14%
03	727	103	15373	7395044	0.21%
04	80	101	1747	813760	0.21%
05	408	112	10773	4150176	0.26%
06	24	22	413	244128	0.17%
07	729	0	0	7415388	0.00%
08	414	20	7676	4211208	0.18%
09	845	20	7674	8595340	0.09%
10	359	128	5137	3651748	0.14%
11	318	128	5107	3234696	0.16%
12	213	44	3815	2166636	0.18%
13	891	52	13049	9063252	0.14%
14	785	61	19567	7985020	0.25%
15	435	162	10068	4424820	0.23%
16	295	95	10575	3000740	0.35%
17	489	154	10408	4974108	0.21%
18	650	116	14754	6611800	0.22%
19	417	186	13569	4241724	0.32%
20	464	104	13479	4719808	0.29%
21	1005	5	134	10222860	0.00%

Fig. 10 presents the results of search for common set of keypoints from image number 17. The largest image is our query image. The others are found similar images. Related points are marked on each image. Larger points are the centers of keypoints that describe common area.

Table 3 presents detailed values from comparison procedure between images from Fig. 10. Only part of keypoints were connected, but this number allows selecting a common part of both images. In this case, a single image has been incorrectly marked as related to the query image. It was caused by a similarity between descriptors and their orientation.

Fig. 10. Sample of detected groups of descriptors between images

Table 3. Results of comparison between images from Fig.10

No. image (query)	No. of keypoints	No. image (compared)	No. of keypoints	Math	Comparisons
17	489	4	80	31	290
17	489	15	435	17	1491
17	489	18	650	20	2197
17	489	19	417	57	1708
17	489	20	464	23	1723

5   Conclusion

Analysing results of our test, we can say that creation of the dictionary allows to significantly decrease the number of operations, which have to be done in the process of image comparison. In our case, the number of operation has been reduced to the 0.18 of all operations. The approach obtains better results in the case of larger sets of images. Images related to the query image can be found much faster in comparison to the standard all-to-all approach. Moreover, saving the dictionary in a binary file allows for more efficient image multiple comparison and reuse of data.

Acknowledgements. This work was supported by the Polish National Science Centre (NCN) within project number DEC-2011/01/D/ST6/06957.

References

1. Akhtar, Z., Rattani, A., Foresti, G.L.: Temporal analysis of adaptive face recognition. Journal of Artificial Intelligence and Soft Computing Research 4(4), 243–255 (2014)
2. Bay, H., Ess, A., Tuytelaars, T., Van Gool, L.: Speeded-up robust features (surf). Comput. Vis. Image Underst. 110(3), 346–359 (2008)

3. Bruzdzinski, T., Krzyzak, A., Fevens, T., Jelen, L.: Web-based framework for breast cancer classification. Journal of Artificial Intelligence and Soft Computing Research 4(2), 149–162 (2014)

4. Chu, J.L., Krzyżak, A.: The recognition of partially occluded objects with support vector machines and convolutional neural networks and deep belief networks. Journal of Artificial Intelligence and Soft Computing Research 4(1), 5–19 (2014)

5. Drozda, P., Sopyła, K., Górecki, P.: Online crowdsource system supporting ground truth datasets creation. In: Rutkowski, L., Korytkowski, M., Scherer, R., Tadeusiewicz, R., Zadeh, L.A., Zurada, J.M. (eds.) ICAISC 2013, Part I. LNCS (LNAI), vol. 7894, pp. 532–539. Springer, Heidelberg (2013)

6. Edelkamp, S., Schroedl, S.: Heuristic Search: Theory and Applications. Elsevier Science (2011)

7. Karimi, B., Krzyzak, A.: A novel approach for automatic detection and classification of suspicious lesions in breast ultrasound images. Journal of Artificial Intelligence and Soft Computing Research 3(4), 265–276 (2013)

8. Makinana, S., Malumedzha, T., Nelwamondo, F.V.: Quality parameter assessment on iris images. Journal of Artificial Intelligence and Soft Computing Research 4(1), 21–30 (2014)

9. Najgebauer, P., Nowak, T., Romanowski, J., Gabryel, M., Korytkowski, M., Scherer, R.: Content-based image retrieval by dictionary of local feature descriptors. In: 2014 International Joint Conference on Neural Networks, IJCNN 2014, Beijing, China, July 6-11, pp. 512–517 (2014)

10. Pena, M.: A Comparative Study of Three Image Matching Algorithms: Sift, Surf, and Fast. BiblioBazaar (2012)

11. Wang, L., Ju, H.: A robust blob detection and delineation method. In: International Workshop on Education Technology and Training and 2008 International Workshop on Geoscience and Remote Sensing, ETT and GRS 2008, vol. 1, pp. 827–830 (December 2008)

12. Wang, X., Japkowicz, N., Matwin, S.: Automated approach to classification of mine-like objects using multiple-aspect sonar images. Journal of Artificial Intelligence and Soft Computing Research 4(2), 133–148 (2014)

13. Zalasiński, M., Cpałka, K.: New approach for the on-line signature verification based on method of horizontal partitioning. In: Rutkowski, L., Korytkowski, M., Scherer, R., Tadeusiewicz, R., Zadeh, L.A., Zurada, J.M. (eds.) ICAISC 2013, Part II. LNCS (LNAI), vol. 7895, pp. 342–350. Springer, Heidelberg (2013)

Recognition and Modeling
of Atypical Children Behavior

Aleksandra Postawka[(⊠)] and Przemysław Śliwiński

Faculty of Electronics, Wroclaw University of Technology, Wroclaw, Poland
{aleksandra.postawka,przemyslaw.sliwinski}@pwr.edu.pl

Abstract. According to reports from medical community the number of autistic children's birth is more and more alarming. Early diagnosis and regular rehabilitation are crucial. The problem with verbal and emotional communication is very common. In a form of short survey, a few similar issues and their solutions have been examined in terms of input data type, feature selection, pattern recognition and formal mathematical modeling. Then we propose a system for autistic children rehabilitation, surveillance and emotions translation. These new solutions have been compared with those reported in the literature. The preliminary experiments provide rather satisfactory results.

Keywords: Markov model · Hidden Markov Model (HMM) · Action recognition · Skeleton · Kinect-type sensors

1 Introduction

Children are not aware of danger which can be brought by some situations and sometimes a moment is enough to cause a disaster. Each child requires a lot of attention, so it can be imagined how protective autistic children's parents should be - it is much harder to predict child's intentions and further motions. In many cases autistic children cannot communicate their feelings and basic needs. Their behavior seems to be logical but in their own criteria, not typical for people around them [1].

There are a few issues which may be undertaken to improve autistic children's and their parents' lives. Firstly, with action recognition function it would be possible to create a *system for children rehabilitation*, which besides being attractive for children may improve their abilities necessary for everyday life. Such a system would allow for tracking the progress of an exercise and for precise evaluation of a therapy progress. Secondly, the *system of hints* for basic activities may be created (e.g. clothing) - by checking progress of the whole task the next subtask can be illustrated. Since the way of task execution depends on current emotions, the system might be used for *emotions recognition*. Another important issues are *potential danger prevention* or *child's surveillance* - modeling child's standard behavior within defined room, we can notice whether the observed activities deviate from norm. Some actions may be labeled as dangerous and in the event of their occurrence an alarm should be raised. It is said that as many autistic people as many autisms - each is different and requires individual approach [2]. This distinguishes the investigated problem from the existing research. Nevertheless, formal models have the capability of learning [11] and can adapt to specific behavior.

© Springer International Publishing Switzerland 2015
L. Rutkowski et al. (Eds.): ICAISC 2015, Part I, LNAI 9119, pp. 757–767, 2015.
DOI: 10.1007/978-3-319-19324-3_68

During the last 15 years on the market have appeared new technologies that generate powerful possibilities for such problem solution [13]. One of the prominent example is the Microsoft's *Kinect* sensor which provides the capability of human motions tracking while being *non-invasive and respecting person's privacy*. This feature is very important when it comes to supervision systems, especially for incapacitated people.

There are also many well known formal tools based on machine learning, like e.g. statistical modeling or pattern recognition, which make it possible to fully take advantage of the technical innovations. In this work *a few similar issues and their solutions* have been examined in various categories in order to find the most promising approach. The categories have been distinguished due to the successive stages of system design.

The rest of paper is organized as follows. The first part is devoted to the survey, in particular, in Section 2 the set of similar problems has been presented. Section 3 concerns problems mentioned in previous section, focusing on acquired data type and methods used for feature extraction. In Section 4 the focus is placed on clustering and classifying methods. The problem of mathematical model selection in different problems solutions is depicted in Section 5. A short summary of the reviewed literature in the issue of autistic children's behavior recognition is presented in Section 6. In the remaining part the personal experiences in work done so far have been described in Section 7. The overall conclusions for new system design appear in Section 8.

2   Applications

The research on action recognition has various motivations, often resulting from human needs. Probably the most popular issue is *taking care of elderly*. Many articles deal with the problem of older person supervision or abnormal situation detection, e.g.: [3–8]. For instance, [3] concerns the problem of movements recognition on the stairs, as stairs are a frequent reason of accidents and older people are particularly vulnerable for such danger. In [4] the issue of unusual human activity detection using wearable sensors is described. This solution is dedicated mainly for elderly suffering from Alzheimer or Parkinson diseases. [5] and [6] undertake the problem of fall detection through position recognition. The application has been designed especially for elders who live alone. Also [7] deals with fall detection, but they focus on horizontal position detection of elderly or hospital patients. In [8] the life-logging system has been described.

Action recognition has also many applications in everyday life, like *dance gestures recognition* [9], *tennis action recognition* [10] or *American sign language (ASL) recognition* [11]. There are also many studies motivated by *game development* and *human computer interaction*, e.g. [12, 13]. Apart from research aimed at specified applications a lot of articles focus on action recognition just as the issue of *methods*: [14–16].

3   Data Type and Feature Extraction

According to the literature the input data for action recognition is being collected from various kinds of sensors: video cameras, depth sensors. Because of variation in features and capabilities provided by different data sensors, we split the collected bibliography into categories, depending on used devices.

Kinect. In [5] for data collection the RGB and depth images obtained from Kinect camera are used. The feature vector contains center of the mass, vertical speed and standard deviation of all the points belonging to the observed person. In [7] the data is obtained from the *Kinect SDK* as 20 skeleton joints. The points are normalized and such feature vector is forwarded to the classifier. Authors in [8] as the input data use the 15-joint structure provided by *Open NI* library. Because of different body orientations, locations and proportions the data are normalized. The feature vector's elements are calculated as the sum of motion magnitudes during a time period. Authors in [9] deal with dance gestures recognition and proposed an angular model based on 16-joint skeleton. The skeleton has been divided into 3 parts: torso, first-degree joints and second-degree joints. The feature vector consists of 8 pairs of angles calculated for first- and second-degree joints in the way dependent on the parent group. In [12] for 7 right hand actions recognition two normalized vectors are used - each designated by two joints belonging either to a forearm or an upper forearm. Also [13], for the gesture recognition problem uses the skeleton structure included in *Microsoft SDK*. Significant contribution have only left and right hands and elbows. The features have been defined as vectors designated by these points and the spine joint. In [14] the skeleton movements have been modeled as curves in the *Lie group* structure. The set of training curves for each category is warped by the *Dynamic Time Warping algorithm* to the nominal curve representing one action.

Video or Image Sequences. Authors in [3] use the raw video stream so that in contrast to Kinect some additional operations are needed. Moving down the stairs is represented as a time sequence of feature vectors obtained by optical flow computation. Fall detection in [6] is based on body acceleration dependences over the time. The intensity of motions is described by *Cmotion* coefficient, calculated for specified number of history video frames and used as a feature for HMM (Hidden Markov Model). There are also some other features extracted (axial ratio, context information histogram, estimated height) for posture recognition. In [10] the features are extracted from the time-sequential images using the mesh features, i.e. the binarized image is divided into squares and the ratio of black pixels in each square is a separate feature. In the problem of ASL recognition [11], the feature vector comprises hand's positions, angle of axis of least inertia and eccentricity of bounding ellipse, all for both hands. In [15] for subsequent video frames the body joint angles are calculated and mapped by feature vector quantization to HMM symbols. The feature vector describes the human body in the category of degrees of freedom. Authors in [16] use the image sequences obtained from the video. After the optical flow for subsequent frames is computed, the obtained measurements are split into channels and finally transformed into a histogram.

Sensors. In [4] data is obtained from wearable sensors. The feature extraction is based on HMMs - for each trace the probability of each considered activity is calculated.

4   Clustering and Classifying Methods

After obtaining the feature vector usually some clustering and classification is needed. Sometimes it is the last stage of recognition process but often it is just the preparation for further modeling. The reviewed papers have been assigned to categories depending on proposed algorithms.

Various Algorithms. The classification process in [7] involves assigning a new sample to one of 3 classes: sitting, standing or lying down. In the open source tool *KNIME* the 4 methods have been compared: *Backpropagation Neural Network* (*BPNN*), *Support Vector Machine* (*SVM*), *decision tree* and *naïve Bayes*. The *BPNN* comprises 3 layers: input, hidden and output with 60, 10 and 3 nodes, respectively. For *SVM* the polynomial kernel is chosen. For chosen parameters values the best results have been obtained by *BPNN* (100%) and *SVM* (99.8%). *Decision tree* and *naïve Bayes* classify with 93.2% and 93.7% accuracy, respectively. Gestures classification in [13] uses i.a. *NN* classifier.

k-means. The feature vector with the size of 1×60 obtained in [8] is clustered by the *k-means* algorithm so that the codebook of observations is created. The new sample is classified to cluster with the lowest distance and the appropriate code is assigned. In [12] the parameter k is set to 5 as the optimal value, therefore each action to be recognized comprises five stages. In [16] the *k-means* algorithm has been applied to histograms clustering problem in order to obtain HMM symbols (clustering centers).

Support Vector Machine (SVM). In [4] authors deal with the problem of abnormal activity detection basing on normal data, so one of the aims is to correctly recognize normal activities. Authors decided to use *One-Class SVM* with a *GRBF* kernel. False negative rate is minimized, because abnormal activities should not be classified as normal. The curves in [14] have been classified using the *one-vs-rest linear SVM*.

Quantization. Sometimes the features are one-dimensional and therefore it is possible to define the thresholds values in empirical way. For example in [6] the *Cmotion* value is quantized into four levels and then treated as the observation symbols in HMM. Also in [10] matching the samples with codewords has been done by the vector quantization operation. As codewords, 12 images and corresponding feature vectors for each of 6 categories (gestures) have been selected. The feature vector quantization into the codewords has been also applied to [15]. The codebook is composed of 32 codewords.

Relevance Vector Machine (RVM). In [6] the axial ratio, context information histogram and the estimated height compose the feature vector used for *RVM* learning technique. *RVM* is based on Bayesian inference and is used for obtaining sparse solutions for regression or classification [6]. It is used here for horizontal position detection.

5   Statistical Models and Learning Algorithms

The reviewed articles have been divided into categories, depending on discussed models. For human action modeling problem various statistical models have been proposed, but probably *Hidden Markov Model* (*HMM*) is the one most frequently used.

Conditional Random Field (CRF). In a moving down the stairs problem [3], division into singular steps is performed either manually or using *CRF* method. For training the *CRFs* authors use a *limited memory quasi-Newton* algorithm. Training data is obtained from manual stair event segmentation. The labeling is acquired by the *Viterbi algorithm*.

Hidden Markov Model (HMM). In [4] a set of *HMMs* is created for different types of normal activities. These models are used to obtain feature vectors for SVM classification. Apart from normal activities models the general *HMM* for all normal traces is trained - to calculate the probability that the given trace is normal (specified threshold value). For traces recognized as abnormal new *HMM*s are created. In *HMM*s created in [5] each of 8 recognized postures is represented by a separate state. The probability of being in the given state is calculated by *forward-backward algorithm*. In fall detection problem [6] the *HMM* is trained by the modified *Baum-Welch algorithm* which enables learning process for multiple observations. The 3-state model is trained with 8 fall sequences. The evaluation problem has been solved by the *forward-backward algorithm*. In [8] the 4-state *left-to-right HMM*s are created in order to model activities. The models are trained using the *Baum-Welch algorithm*. Tennis gestures [10] are modeled by 36-state *HMM*s. Authors use *Baum-Welch algorithm* and *forward algorithm* (evaluation). ASL recognition [11] is also based on *left-to-right HMM*s. The number of states reflects the number of stages for a given sign. Because of different complexity of various signs the *skip transitions* are used - the traces can be abbreviated. In [12] 3-state *HMM*s are used to model right arm movements. Authors use *Baum-Welch algorithm* and *backward algorithm* (evaluation). In [15] 4-state *left-to-right HMM*s' topology describes subsequent stages of modeled activities. [16] for action recognition uses *HMM*s trained with *Baum-Welch algorithm* and evaluated by *forward-backward algorithm*.

6   The Proposed Approach

Kinect sensor and the skeleton structure included in Microsoft SDK make it possible to track the person's characteristic body points without image preprocessing operations which are necessary for human silhouette extraction while using the video camera. Because of this convenience and broad perspectives presented in [7], [9], [12–14] it has been decided to use Kinect as data source. The system for autistic children proposed in this paper may be divided into subparts by their requirements.

a) rehabilitation system and system of hints need action recognition algorithm - the former for recognizing the stage of assigned exercise, the latter for recognizing the stage of chosen activity. Each action consists of a sequence of human positions. In the system these positions sequences may be modeled as a Moore machine.

b) child's surveillance and potential danger prevention is a more complicated task. In contrast to previously described system's subpart, the information about activity that is being performed is not given. The problem is similar to the issues depicted in [6], [8], [10–12], [14–16] where the solution is based on *HMM*s. *HMM*s' hidden states may be understood as the stages of modeled activities ([8], [11], [15]) where each state's output is a discrete probability distribution [11]. This feature enables modeling real life motions, which are not deterministic [11] (possible indecisions, delays). Due to broad perspectives *HMM*s have been chosen for activity modeling.

c) emotions recognition using the behavior model is different from issues depicted in articles listed in previous sections, yet it is a bit similar to posture recognition in [5], where postures are reflected by hidden states. In the problem of emotions recognition there has been taken an assumption that the way of behavior (position sequence) is dependent on current child's emotions and emotions can be represented by hidden states. In the problem set defined in b) and c) appears the issue of Hidden Markov Models. To describe discrete *HMM* the following notation will be used.

> Let $\lambda = \{A, B, \pi\}$ be a complete parameter set of the *HMM* model. Then:
> T - length of observation sequence
> N - number of hidden states
> M - number of observation symbols
> $Q = \{q_i\}$, $i \in \{1, 2, \cdots, N\}$ - set of states
> $V = \{v_i\}$, $i \in \{1, 2, \cdots, M\}$ - set of possible observation symbols
> $A = \{a_{ij}\}$, $a_{ij} = Pr(q_j$ at $t+1 \mid q_i$ at $t)$ - state transition probability distribution matrix
> $\{a_{ij}\}$ - probability of transiting from state q_i to state q_j
> $B = \{b_j(k)\}$, $b_j(k) = Pr(v_k$ at $t \mid q_j$ at $t)$ - observation symbol probability distribution matrix
> $\{b_j(k)\}$ - probability of generating observation symbol v_k in state q_j
> $\pi = \{\pi_i\}$, $\pi_i = Pr(q_i$ at $t = 1)$ - initial state distribution
> $O = O_1, O_2, \cdots, O_T$ - observation sequence

Within the issue of *HMM* there are three basic computational problems [6]:

Evaluation. First we refer to the standard approach in which each model is scored separately. Given a *HMM* model λ evaluate the posterior probability $Pr(O \mid \lambda)$ of an observed symbol sequence O.

In the literature this problem is being solved by *forward algorithm* [10], *backward algorithm* [12] or *forward-backward algorithm* [5,6], [16]. In the issue described in this paper the problem of evaluation appears in tasks included in groups b) and c).

Next, since it is interesting to evaluate ("score") and compare the presented algorithms in a formal manner, we introduce the model assessment algorithm based on the *aggregative modelling technique*, proposed for memoryless models in [19] and extended to finite-memory nonlinear one in [20].

Remark 1. For HMM models, which have infinite memory (that is, their output processes have non-compactly supported correlation functions), the formal proof of the presented algorithm is under study.

Given $D > 2$ HMM-based models m_d, $d = 1, \ldots, D$, we build the *empirical aggregative model* as their convex combination

$$m(t, \lambda) = \sum_{d=1}^{D} \lambda_d m_d(t), \text{ such that } \|\lambda\|_1 = 1 \text{ and } 0 \leq \lambda_d \leq 1 \text{ for all } d.$$

The weights $\{\lambda_d\}$ are obtained from the observation sequence of the length $T = 1, 2, \ldots$ using the standard optimization routine (*e.g.* the Matlab's 'quadprog'). The resulting model can be useful twofold:

1. as a selector (choosing the model with the largest λ_d as the most probable one) of the best single model.
2. as the aggregative model $m(t, \lambda)$ (under the assumption that the linear combination of m_d is meaningful.)

Denote by $m(t, \lambda^*)$ the *optimal aggregative model*, that is, the best convex combination of the models $m_d(t)$. It was shown in the papers referenced above that the 'expected non-optimality' of the $m(t, \lambda)$ w.r.t. $m(t, \lambda^*)$ is, for finite memory models m_d, of order $\mathcal{O}(\sqrt{T^{-1} \ln D})$, that is, it is virtually independent of the number of models

D, and holds even for the case when $D \gg T$, allowing evaluation of a bulk number of models using only small or moderate observation sequences. Moreover, for $D > \sqrt{T}$ such a rate cannot be (significantly) reduced.

Remark 2. In the *model selection problem* this means that the empirical model is – with growing number of measurements – not only converging to the best model in the dictionary but also, even for small T (smaller than D) is the best attainable model; see *e.g. [21, Th. 2].*

Remark 3. In the *aggregation problem* it allows, *e.g.* by combining the row vectors of the models' transition matrices to create aggregated models which matrices remain the (right) stochastic ones, that is, the resulting models remain the Markov ones.

Decoding. Given a *HMM* model λ and an observation sequence O decode a hidden state sequence that is the most likely to generate O.

For decoding the sequence of hidden states the *Viterbi algorithm* can be used [17]. This problem will be depicted in the group c).

Learning. Given an observation sequence O train the *HMM* model λ to maximize the probability $Pr(O \mid \lambda)$.

Learning the *HMM* model is usually realized with *Baum-Welch algorithm* [6], [8], [10], [12], [16]. The problem of learning *HMM*s concerns groups b) and c).

The way of feature vector extraction is dependent on its further application. If only the motion recognition is needed the position recognition is not necessary, e.g. [12]. In the system described in this paper the information about child's position is desirable and the accuracy of this diagnosis is very important.

In this paper the novel method of feature extraction for a few basic positions (standing, sitting, lying down, kneeling, bending) is suggested. Such position recognition can be based on significant differences between distances calculated for projections of pairs of joints onto given plane and between distances along given axis. For instance, standing and sitting positions can be differentiated by the distance between hip and knees centers, projected onto the plane OXZ while sitting position and kneeling position can be distinguished by the distance between knees and feet centers, projected onto the OY axis. To such understood features the decision tree or cascaded classifier can be adopted.

7 Preliminary Results

Kinect provides the capability of tracking two people simultaneously, returning the skeleton structure of 20 joints. However, despite many advantages of skeleton tracking, experiments reveal some limitations of the Kinect v1 depth sensor technology.

At the beginning of current study, similarly like in [7], 3 basic positions have been chosen: standing, sitting and lying down. Then some skeleton data have been collected and each sample has been manually assigned into proper class. However, it has been observed that it was *impossible to register the natural lying down position* - all joints got lost and in effect skeleton was not tracked any more. The similar result can be observed when the person kneels or their forearms are crossed. It seems that this inconvenience has been resolved in the recently released second version of Kinect (2014), which is based on much more accurate time-of-flight technology. Moreover the system has been trained by a number of data, including some ambiguous images where joints have been applied manually. Because of novelty of this technology only few articles with practical application can be found, e.g. [18]. However due to Microsoft's advertising videos and overall information the research with *Kinect v2 may provide satisfactory results.*

Because of mentioned inconvenience in Kinect v1, temporarily only two main positions have been left. After collecting classified data the features have been extracted as described in Section 6. The hip and knees centers have been projected onto the plane OXZ and their distance has been calculated. Then the data have been visualized in Matlab as histograms (Fig. 1(a)). The diagrams are nearly completely separable what confirms that the method is well chosen. For each histogram the density function has been generated (Fig. 1(b)) so that the intersection of the curves could be calculated.

The position recognition with the use of obtained classifier is very accurate. Wrong answers occur only in the transitional positions (neither standing, nor sitting). Bayes error is unavoidable, but we can use this property as some preliminary knowledge - if the previous position was 'sitting' and the classifier indicates the uncertain range we can make an assumption that the person is going to stand up. Such knowledge can be crucial in danger prediction system - it is much more important to minimize false-negative than false-positive error rate. The examples of program execution have been presented in Fig. 2. Human is visualized as a skeleton and the marking 'SI' and 'ST' is used for sitting and standing positions, respectively. Gray lines denote not accurate sensor readings.

As mentioned, potentially dangerous behavior may be detected basing on the model of standard child's behavior within a specified room. In order to create such a model the probabilities of being in each position given part of the room have been collected. During the test one person has been observed by Kinect sensor for about 15 minutes. The generated probability a priori map has been shown in Fig. 3. The value in the grayscale illustrates the probability value - white denotes 1.0 and black denotes 0.0.

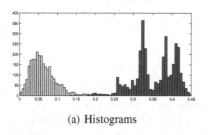

(a) Histograms

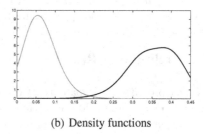

(b) Density functions

Fig. 1. Histograms for Euclidean distance between chosen points projected on OXY plane for standing (left) and sitting (right) classes (a) and density functions estimated from these data (b)

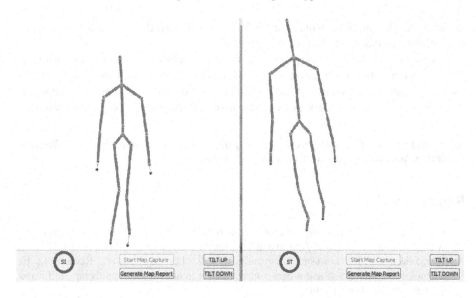

Fig. 2. Examples of program execution - position recognition ('ST' - standing, 'SI' - sitting)

Fig. 3. Probability map (a priori probability of being in specified position given part of the room)

8   Conclusions

In this paper the system for autistic children rehabilitation, surveillance and emotions translation has been proposed. A set of articles concerning the similar problems has been reviewed, paying special attention to the input data type, feature selection, pattern recognition and formal modeling. Moreover, the formal assessment method for comparison and evaluation of the existing heuristic models was proposed.

The functions of the planned system have been assigned into groups depending on their requirements. For each group, basing on the reviewed literature, possible solutions have been described.

The models applied in the reviewed papers are selected according to a heuristic reasoning rather than derived from a formal reasoning. Hidden Markov Models enable modeling real life motions, which are not deterministic [11]. Because of broad perspectives HMMs have been chosen for activity modeling.

In a majority of the reviewed papers, the feature selection step is somehow arbitrary. The methods are chosen intuitively, basing on authors observations. In this paper a novel method for features extraction in the position recognition problem has been proposed. The preliminary experiments based on these assumptions provide satisfactory results.

Acknowledgement. This work was supported by the statutory funds of the Faculty of Electronics S40265, Wroclaw University of Technology, Wroclaw, Poland.

References

1. Ricks, D., Wing, L.: Language, Communication, and the Use of Symbols in Normal and Autistic Children. Journal of Autism and Childhood Schizophrenia 5, 191-221 (1975)
2. Landowska, A., Kołakowska, A., Anzulewicz, A., Jarmołkowicz, P., Rewera, J.: E-technologies in diagnosis and progress measurement in autistic children therapy in Poland (in Polish). E-mentor 4 (2014)
3. Snoek, J., Hoey, J., Stewart, L., Zemel, R.: Automated Detection of Unusual Events on Stairs. Image and Vision Computing 27, 153-166 (2009)
4. Yin, J., Yang, Q., Junfen Pan, J.: Sensor-Based Abnormal Human-Activity Detection. IEEE Transactions on Knowledge and Data Engineering 20, 1082-1090 (2008)
5. Dubois, A., Charpillet, F.: Human Activities Recognition with RGB-Depth Camera using HMM. 35th Annual International Conference on the IEEE EMBS 4666-4669 (2013)
6. Jiang, M., Chen, Y., Zhao, Y., Cai, A.: A Real-Time Fall Detection System Based on HMM and RVM. Visual Communications and Image Processing, 1-6 (2013)
7. Patsadu, O., Nukoolkit, Ch., Watanapa, B.: Human Gesture Recognition Using Kinect Camera. Ninth International Joint Conference on Computer Science and Software Engineering, 28-32 (2012)
8. Jalal, A., Kamal, S., Kim, D.: A Depth Video Sensor-Based Life-Logging Human Activity Recognition System for Elderly Care in Smart Indoor Environments. Sensors 14, 11735-11759 (2014)
9. Raptis, M., Kirovski, D., Hoppe, H.: Real-Time Classification of Dance Gestures from Skeleton Animation. Symposium on Computer Animation, 147-156 (2011)
10. Yamato, J., Ohya, J., Ishii, K.: Recognizing Human Action in Time-Sequential Images using Hidden Markov Model. IEEE Computer Society Conference on Computer Vision and Pattern Recognition, 379-385 (1992)
11. Starner, T.: Visual Recognition of American Sign Language Using Hidden Markov Models. Massachusetts Institute of Technology (1995)
12. Liu, T., Song, Y., Gu, Y., Li, A.: Human Action Recognition Based on Depth Images from Microsoft Kinect. Fourth Global Congress on Intelligent Systems, 200-204 (2013)
13. Lai, K., Konrad, J., Ishwar, P.: A gesture-driven computer interface using Kinect. IEEE Southwest Symposium on Image Analysis and Interpretation, 185-188 (2012)
14. Vemulapalli, R., Arrate, F., Chellappa, R.: Human Action Recognition by Representing 3D Skeletons as Points in a Lie Group. IEEE Conference on Computer Vision and Pattern Recognition, 588-595 (2014)
15. Uddin, Z., Thang, D., N., Kim, T.-S.: Human Activity Recognition via 3-D Joint Angle Features and Hidden Markov Models. Proceedings of 2010 IEEE 17th International Conference on Image Processing, 713-716 (2010)

16. Ji, X., Wang, C., Li, Y., Wu, Q.: Hidden Markov Model-based Human Action Recognition Using Mixed Features. Journal of Computational Information Systems, 3659-3666 (2013)
17. Forney, D.: The Viterbi Algorithm. Proceedings of the IEEE 61 (1973)
18. Kajastila, R., Hamalainen, P.: Augmented Climbing: Interacting With Projected Graphics on a Climbing Wall. CHI Extended Abstracts' 14, 1279-1284 (2014)
19. Juditsky, A., Nemirovski, A.: Functional aggregation for nonparametric regression. Annals of Statistics 28 (3), 681-712 (2000)
20. Wachel, P., Śliwiński, P.: Aggregative modelling of nonlinear systems. IEEE Signal Processing Letters 33 (9), 1482-1486 (2015)
21. Tsybakov, A.B.: Optimal rates of aggregation. Learning Theory and Kernel Machines. Springer, 303-313 (2003)

Intelligent Fusion of Infrared and Visible Spectrum for Video Surveillance Application

Rania Rebai Boukhriss[1(✉)], Emna Fendri[2], and Mohamed Hammami[2]

[1] Miracl-ISIMS, Sfax University, Sakiet Ezzit, Sfax, Tunisia
[2] Miracl-FS, Sfax University, Road Sokra, Sfax, Tunisia
rania.rebai@hotmail.fr, fendri.msf@gnet.tn, Mohamed.Hammami@fss.rnu.tn

Abstract. In video surveillance, we can rely on either a visible spectrum or an infrared one. In order to profit from both of them, several fusion methods were proposed in literature: low-level fusion, middle-level fusion and high-level fusion. The first one is the most used for moving objects' detection. It consists in merging information from visible image and infrared one into a new synthetic image to detect objects. However, the fusion process may not preserve all relevant information. In addition, perfect correlation between the two spectrums is needed. In This paper, we propose an intelligent fusion method for moving object detection. The proposed method relies on one of the two given spectrum at once according to weather conditions (darkness, sunny days, fog, snow, etc.). Thus, we first extract a set of low-level features (visibility, local contrast, sharpness, hue, saturation and value), then a prediction model is generated by supervised learning techniques. The classification results on 15 sequences with different weather conditions indicate the effectiveness of the extracted features, by using C4.5 as classifier.

Keywords: Image fusion · Classification · Weather conditions · Moving object detection

1 Introduction

Moving object detection in complex scenes is an active research topic in computer vision. The related research area includes intelligent video analysis, which can be applied to monitor outdoors areas such as airports, streets, highways, subways and parking lots etc. The research diversity is justified by the complexity of the problem and the variability of its challenges, still incompletely resolved, like detection in night-time, in total occlusion and in presence of non-stationary background objects. Therefore, we relied on two categories of cameras: visible ones and infrared ones which provide as respectively visible (VIS) spectrum and infrared (IR) spectrum.

In the literature, several methods[1],[2],[3],[4],[5],[6] have been proposed for moving object detection in VIS spectrum. These methods are based either on background modeling [1],[2],[3], on optical flow [4],[5],[6], or on inter-frame difference [7],[8],[9]. However, these methods suffer from many limitations such as

© Springer International Publishing Switzerland 2015
L. Rutkowski et al. (Eds.): ICAISC 2015, Part I, LNAI 9119, pp. 768–777, 2015.
DOI: 10.1007/978-3-319-19324-3_69

failure to face camouflage, night or poor visibility conditions (fog, snow, rain, etc.).

In order to overcome these limitations, many works [10],[11],[12] propose to use IR sensor. We can distinguish two approaches to detect moving object from IR sensor: pixel/region-based approaches [12],[13],[14] and model-based approaches [13],[14],[15],[16]. These methods achieve a good performance especially in night and/or poor visibility conditions, but fail in presence of some climatic conditions like a hot sunny day or when the object has low contrast (not warmer than the background) [17],[18].

Face to limitations of the use, at once, of visible or infrared spectrums, recent researches [14],[17],[19],[20] propose to use both Visible and Infrared sensors. A fusion between the information provided by VIS and IR cameras for moving object detection would offer complementary solutions: relying on visible images in sunny days, we achieve a good detection and can extract a rich content; while the use of infrared sensor seems to give better results for moving object detection in presence of darkness, limited levels of luminosity, shadows, light reflections, or some weather variations. Visible and infrared fusion aims to perform correct moving object detection all over the day (morning, afternoon and night) for particular hot objects such as persons and vehicles [21].

In the literature, moving object detection using both visible and infrared spectrums suppose merging information in different levels: low-level, medium-level or high-level. Experimentations prove that, in some cases, merging information may reduce the quality of moving object detection. Thus, in this paper our main contribution is to propose an intelligent fusion of VIS-IR spectrums based on weather conditions' classification. The rest of this paper is organized as follows: Section 2 provides an overview of literature related to fusion techniques. Section 3 describes the proposed method for VIS-IR spectrums fusion. Section 4 outlines the results of a quantitative and a qualitative evaluation. Finally, Section 5 recapitulates the presented method and outlines future work.

2   State of Art on Fusion Techniques

Moving objects detection' methods relying on Visible/Infrared fusion can be classified into three categories according to the level of processing [17],[18],[22]: Low-level fusion, Medium-level fusion and High-level fusion. In low-level fusion, also called signal, data or pixel-level fusion, fused images are generated by merging pixel information from both spectrums. Therefore, infrared and visible images must be synchronized so that all pixel positions of all the input images correspond to the same location. The most common pixel level fusion techniques [17],[23],[24] are: techniques based on Weighted Averaging, techniques based on Pyramid Transforms and techniques based on a Wavelet Transforms.

In medium-level fusion, also called feature-level fusion, they first extract features from both the infrared spectrum and the visible one. Then, they fuse the extracted features. This fusion could be achieved in two ways: among the two modules of features extraction and features selection or after both of them [19].

Since, one of the essential goals of fusion is to preserve the image features, feature level methods have the ability to yield subjectively better fused images than pixel based techniques [17],[25].

Finally, the last category of fusion methods concerns high-level fusion. In this latter, the fusion is applied either at decision level or at score level. In the fusion at decision level, the classifiers are applied independently to each sensor output. The given decisions are combined to make a final decision [17]. In the score level fusion, multiple classifiers produce a set of scores which represent the probabilities that one object belongs to different possible classes. These score can be combined by a weighted parameter in order to obtain a new score which is then used to make the final decision [19].

The choice of the fusion level depends on the nature of the handled application. In our context, we aim to improve the quality of moving object detection. Thus, we will be interested with low-level fusion. However, in this fusion, we must satisfy a set of constraints [26]: the fusion process should preserve all relevant information on the input imagery in the composite image; the fusion process should not introduce any artifacts or inconsistencies and the fusion process should be shift and rotational invariant. Moreover, low-level fusion techniques suppose that a perfect correlation between the images is performed before performing the fusion itself. When images are not well correlated, it could lead to errors in the image fusion process [19].

For this reasons, we propose an intelligent fusion of VIS-IR videos to profit from the quality of both of them, without having neither to correlate the spectrums nor to generate a fused spectrum that may be different from both of them. To make this manuscript clear to read and easy to grasp, these works will be detailed in next section.

3 Proposed Method

We propose an intelligent fusion method for moving object detection. The proposed method rely either on visible spectrum either on infrared spectrum according to weather conditions and timing of the video acquisition. Thus, the visible spectrum is used in sunny days under normal weather conditions, while the infrared spectrum will be used at night or in presence of fog, rain, snow, etc. Our method is composed of two steps: (i) offline step adopting a data-mining process in order to build the adequate prediction model for abnormal weather classification and (ii) an online step to classify VIS images into image in Normal conditions or in Abnormal conditions and to detect Moving objects in IR spectrum or in VIS spectrum. Fig. 1 shows the framework of the proposed method.

3.1 Offline Step

Our offline step is composed of two major steps: (1) Data preparation step, and (2) Data mining step which aims to build a generic prediction model by the use of several data-mining algorithms.

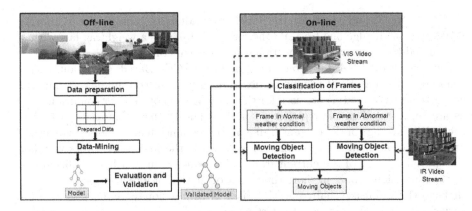

Fig. 1. Proposed method of intelligent fusion VIS-IR for moving object detection

Data Preparation. In this step, we identify efficient weather conditions features in order to build a two-dimensional table from our training corpus. This table is devoted thereafter to the learning step. In our case, the robustness of an image classification technique depends on reliable and strong environmental features. A thorough look on the features that are most commonly employed for describing visibility in the literature provided the grounds for the ultimate selection of eight features for consideration in our work : Visibility, Local Contrast, Sharpness, Hue, Saturation and Value [27] and two temporal features based on the autocorrelation of each pixel's intensities over time [28], detailed below.

Visibility metric. The visibility metric (equation 1) calculates the ratio between contrast and noise of Image estimated by a Gaussian kernel.

$$Visibility = \frac{\sum_L \sum_C \sqrt{IM_{noise^2}}}{L * C} .$$ (1)

Where L and C represent the number of row and column of the image, respectively, IM_{noise} is the image noise filtered by a Gaussian filter.

Local Contrast. This feature calculates the contrast between a pixel and its neighbors (equation 2).

$$I_{Cont}(i) = \frac{I(i) - M_w}{S_w} .$$ (2)

Where M_w and S_w is respectively the mean of the pixels' gray values and the standard deviation of the neighbors window.

Sharpness. Seeing that visible images in normal conditions have sharp edges with large contrast differences, the sharpness was considered as a meaningful feature to classify images. Roser and al. [27] proposed a measure of sharpness (equation 3), based on the average of the Sobel gradient magnitude.

$$T_{adv} = \frac{\sum_i \delta_i \, \rho(i) \, \sqrt{S_X^2(i) + S_Y^2(i)}}{\sum_i \delta_i} .$$ (3)

Where, $S_X(i)$ and $S_Y(i)$ are the Sobel filter values for each pixel i, δ_i informs if the pixel is an edge one (= 1, 0 otherwise), and $\rho(i)$ is a weighting factor that is assumed to be inversely proportional to the local contrast.

Features based on AutoCorrelation Function (ACF). Based on the autocorrelation function (ACF) of the intensities of each pixel in the time, two temporal characteristics (C and S) are used for the classification of weather conditions [28] as are represented in the equations 4 and 5. The feature C indicates whether the spatial average of the current frame of the sequence has weaker time-average autocorrelation of intensity change or not, while the feature S shows whether the spatial average of the current frame of a sequence in weather condition under classification is only in short-time autocorrelation of intensity change or not. In fact, the intensity change at the pixel is proportional to the illumination variation speed. For instance, for fast illumination variation, we notify a strong short-time autocorrelation; however, in presence of rain streaks or snowflakes (two brightness states at a fixed pixel), it leads to weaker time-average ACF value than that of gradual illumination variation.

$$C = \underset{y \in \Omega}{mean} \left(\sum_{k=1}^{T-1} \frac{\hat{\rho}_y(k)}{T} \right). \tag{4}$$

$$S = \underset{y \in \Omega}{mean} \left(\hat{f}_y(k) \right). \tag{5}$$

Where $\hat{\rho}_y(k)$ is equivalent to ACF value at location y in the kth frame interval. Ω is the current frame and T is the limited time length. $\hat{f}(k)$ represents the quadratic fit of $\hat{\rho}(k)$.

Color Features. Weather conditions variation can be detected in case of color variation. We choose to consider the Hue, Saturation and Value of images in HSV color space. This space is known as being the closest one to human perception.

Data Mining. Our goal is to build a predictive model to classify the VIS image in Normal weather conditions or abnormal ones. This prediction model is obtained by supervised learning technique. In supervised learning, the efficiency and genericity of the generated classifier increases when the size of the training set and the number of relevant features increase. Another pertinent setting to consider is the choice of the appropriate learning technique.

Evaluation and Validation. The objective of this step is to evaluate the previous one. It consists in comparison of different prediction models learned in order to determine the best prediction model for images' classification according to weather conditions. Therefore, as for the majority of recent works, we construct the confusion matrix to evaluate the quality of a prediction model. From this confusion matrix we can calculate the Total Correct Classification TCC detailed in the equation 6.

$$TCC = \frac{n_{AA} + n_{BB}}{n_{AA} + n_{AB} + n_{BB} + n_{BA}}. \tag{6}$$

- n_{AA}: represents the number of frames in Abnormal weather conditions correctly classified
- n_{BB}: represents the number of frames in Normal weather conditions correctly classified.
- n_{AB}: represents the number of frames in Abnormal weather conditions classified as in Normal weather conditions.
- n_{BA}: represents the number of frames in Normal weather conditions classified as in Abnormal weather conditions.

3.2   Online Step

In the proposed approach, after the offline step, an online step is carried out. This latter starts with a step of VIS images classification by the extracted prediction model. Then, according to the decision, we perform either moving object detection on VIS spectrum or on IR spectrum.

Classification of Frames. The objective of this step is to classify the images of VIS spectrum into image in Normal weather conditions or in Abnormal weather conditions. This classification is based on the prediction model extracted from the offline step.

Moving Object Detection. As soon as images are classified as in Normal or Abnormal weather conditions, the visible (respectively infrared) spectrum is considered to perform a moving object detection technique. In this work, we have adopted a method based on background modeling with dynamic matrix and spatio-temporal analyses of scenes [29]. This method has shown high performances and robustness in foreground segmentation under various complex scenes conditions such as sudden and gradual illumination changes, ghost and foreground speed.

4   Experimental Results

In order to evaluate our proposed method, we carried out a series of experiments. We performed experiments on a large and representative corpus shown in table 1 and table 2 (15 famous outdoor sequences recorded in typical conditions). This corpus consists of 7 sequences in Normal weather conditions (5440 images) and 8 sequences in Abnormal weather conditions (3525 images). The Abnormal sequences present several challenges such as fog, rain, snow etc. We randomly selected sequences from the database to build up our fixed training (70%) and testing data sets (30%). We ensure that no sequence is used for both training and testing at the same time for each class.

We then have build learning data: an $N*9$ matrix of extracted features from our training corpus (N is the number of pixels from our training corpus). Once learning data were defined, we proceeded to selecting the appropriate learning technique. In fact, in literature, we find several techniques of supervised learning, each with its own advantages and drawbacks. Therefore, the learning is

Table 1. Sequences of image in Abnormal State

Sequences	Number of Frames	Resolution (Pixels)	Used for
Brouillard1[30]	700	720*576	Learning
Set10_RainyDay[1]	1049	640*360	Learning
Set10_SunStrokes[1]	347	640*360	Learning
Set10_Tunnel[1]	216	640*360	Learning
Dtneu_nebel[2]	349	768*576	Learning
Dtneu_winter[2]	299	768*576	Test
Dtneu_schnee[2]	298	768*576	Test
Brouillard2[30]	267	720*500	Test

Table 2. Sequences of image in Normal State

Sequences	Number of Frames	Resolution (Pixels)	Used for
Set3_SuburbanFollow[1]	1171	1280*1024	Learning
Set10_Daylight[1]	902	640*360	Learning
Balcony5_Vis[3]	564	640*480	Learning
qmul_junction[4]	867	360*288	Learning
Set3_SuburbanBridge[1]	851	1280*1024	Learning
Set3_TrailerFollow[1]	800	1280*1024	Test
Set10_Snowy[1]	285	640*360	Test

performed by 3 different learning algorithms: the decision tree C4.5, SVM with Radial Basis Function Kernel and Multilayer Perceptron Neural Network (MLP). Each method is considered as reference in its category. This data mining algorithms were compared according to Total Correct Classification (equation 6). The experimental results are shown in figure 2. We obtained a best classification rate on learning and Test set by C4.5 (81.16%).

Fig. 3 shows some promising results of our method. In fact, the images (a) and (b) are extracted from two sequences which have two bad weather conditions respectively snowy day and fog. These two images are classified in Abnormal conditions. In the other hand, the images (b) and (c) present two scenes in favorable weather conditions that are classified as in the Normal conditions. Note that in the scene of (b) there's snow in the boards of the road but it does not snow when it is recorded. This is due to the characteristics based on the autocorrelation of pixel-wise intensities over time that allow to distinguish the motion blur caused by rain streaks or snowflakes.

---

[1] http://ccv.wordpress.fos.auckland.ac.nz/eisats/
[2] http://i21www.ira.uka.de/image_sequences/
[3] http://www.eeng.dcu.ie/~oconaire/dataset/
[4] http://www.eecs.qmul.ac.uk/~ccloy/index.html

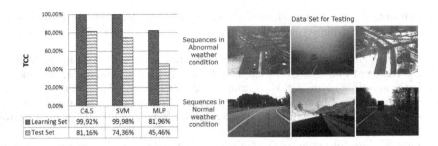

Fig. 2. Results of images' classification as normal/abnormal weather conditions

Fig. 3. Results of classification (a) and (b) are classified in Abnormal weather condition but (c) and (d) are classified in Normal weather condition

5 Conclusion

In this paper, we proposed a novel method of intelligent fusion for moving object detection. This method relies on a classification step of images according to the weather conditions. We consider visible or infrared spectrums according to weather conditions (darkness, sunny days, fog, snow, etc.). For thus, we first extract a set of low-level features (visibility, local contrast, sharpness, two features based on ACF which are C and S, hue, saturation and value), then we generate a prediction model by supervised learning techniques. Experimentations carried out on several sequences with different weather conditions prove the effectiveness of the generated prediction model. Compared to two other learning techniques (SVM and MLP), prediction model generated by C4.5 records the best classification rate with 81.16%. Our future orientations will examine the impact of our contribution on the accuracy of moving object detection in VIS and IR videos.

References

1. Brutzer, S., Höferlin, B., Heidemann, G.: Evaluation of background subtraction techniques for video surveillance. In: IEEE Conference on Computer Vision and Pattern Recognition, Colorado Springs, pp. 1937–1944 (2011)
2. Biswas, S., Sil, J., Sengupta, N.: Background modeling and implementation using discrete wavelet transform, a review. International Journal on Graphics, Vision and Image Processing 11(1), 29–42 (2011)

3. Cristani, M., Farenzena, M., Bloisi, D., Murino, V.: Background subtraction for automated multisensor surveillance: A comprehensive review. EURASIP J. Adv. Sig. Proc. (2010)

4. Roth, S., Black, M.J.: On the spatial statistics of optical flow. In: 10th IEEE International Conference on Computer Vision, Beijing, China, pp. 42–49 (2005)

5. Pathirana, P.N., Lim, A.E.K., Carminati, J., Premaratne, M.: Simultaneous estimation of optical flow and object state: A modified approach to optical flow calculation. In: IEEE International Conference on Networking, Sensing and Control, London, pp. 634–638 (2007)

6. Lim, S., Apostolopoulos, J.G., Gamal, A.E.: Optical flow estimation using temporally over-sampled video. IEEE Transactions on Image Processing, 1074–1087 (2005)

7. Guo, J., Chng, E.S., Deepu, R.: Foreground motion detection by difference-based spatial temporal entropy image. In: IEEE Region 10 Conference, pp. 379–382 (2004)

8. Chang, M., Cheng, Y.: Motion Detection by Using Entropy Image and Adaptive State-Labeling Technique. In: IEEE International Symposium on Circuits and Systems, New Orleans, pp. 3667–3670 (2007)

9. Durus, M., Ercil, A.: Robust Vehicle Detection Algorithm. In: 15th IEEE International Conference on Signal Processing and Communications Applications, Siu, pp. 1–4 (2007)

10. Gilmore, E.T., Ugbome, C., Kim, C.: An IR-based Pedestrian Detection System Imple-mented with Matlab-Equipped Laptop and Low-Cost Microcontroller. International Journal of Computer Science & Information Technology 3(5), 79–87 (2011)

11. Xu, F., Liu, X., Fujimura, K.: Pedestrian Detection and Tracking with Night Vision. IEEE Transactions on Intelligent Transportation Systems 6(5), 63–71 (2005)

12. Fang, Y., Yamada, K., Ninomiya, Y., Horn, B.K.P., Masaki, I.: A shape-independent method for pedestrian detection with far-infrared images. IEEE Transactions on Vehicular Technology 53(6), 1679–1697 (2004)

13. Olmeda, D., Hilario, C., de la Escalera, A., Armingol, J.M.: Pedestrian Detection and Tracking Based on Far Infrared Visual Information. In: Blanc-Talon, J., Bourennane, S., Philips, W., Popescu, D., Scheunders, P. (eds.) ACIVS 2008. LNCS, vol. 5259, pp. 958–969. Springer, Heidelberg (2008)

14. Bertozzi, M., Broggi, A., Rose, M.D., Felisa, M., Rakotomamonjy, A., Suard, F.: A Pedestrian Detector Using Histograms of Oriented Gradients and a Support Vector Machine Classifier. In: IEEE Intelligent Transportation Systems Conference, USA, pp. 143–148 (2007)

15. Nanda, H., Davis, L.: Probabilistic Template Based Pedestrian Detection in Infrared Videos. In: IEEE Intelligent Vehicles Symposium, Paris, France, pp. 15–20 (2002)

16. Dai, C., Zheng, Y., Li, X.: Pedestrian detection and tracking in infrared imagery using shape and appearance. Journal of Computer Vision and Image Understanding 106, 288–299 (2007)

17. Zin, T.T., Takahashi, H., Toriu, T., Hama, H.: Fusion of Infrared and Visible Images for Robust Person Detection. Image Fusion (2011) ISBN: 978-953-307-679-9

18. Goubet, E., Katz, J., Porikli, F.: Pedestrian tracking using thermal infrared imaging. In: Infrared Technology and Applications XXXII Proc. SPIE, vol. 6206 (2006), doi:10.1117/12.673132

19. Apătean, A.D.: Contributions to the Information Fusion, Application to Obstacle Recognition in Visible and Infrared Images. Doctoral thesis (2011)

20. Wang, J., Liang, J., Hu, H., Li, Y., Feng, B.: Performance evaluation of infrared and visible image fusion algorithms for face recognition. In: International Conference on Intelligent Systems and Knowledge Engineering, Chengdu, China, pp. 1–8 (2007)

21. Ó Conaire, C., Cooke, E., O'Connor, N., Murphy, N., Smeaton, A.: Fusion of infrared and visible spectrum video for indoor surveillance. In: 6th International Workshop on Image Analysis for Multimedia Interactive Services, Montreux, Switzerland (2005)

22. Apatean, A., Rogozan, A., Bensrhair, A.: Information Fusion for Obstacle Recognition in Visible and Infrared Images. In: International Symposium on Signals, Circuits and Systems, pp. 1–4 (2009)

23. Blum, R.S., Xue, Z., Zhang, Z.: An Overview of Image Fusion. In: Multi-Sensor Image Fusion and Its Applications, pp. 1–36. Taylor & Francis, Boca Raton (2006)

24. Sadjadi, F.: Comparative Image Fusion Analysais. In: IEEE Computer Society Conference on Computer Vision and Pattern Recognition - Workshops, vol. 8(8), p. 25 (2005)

25. Samadzadegan, F.: Data Integration Related to Sensors, Data and Models. In: International Society for Photogrammetry and Remote Sensing (2004)

26. Yang, B., Zhong-liang, J., Hai-tao, Z.: Review of pixel-level image fusion. Journal of Shanghai Jiaotong University 15(1), 6–12 (2010)

27. Roser, M., Moosmann, F.: Classification of Weather Situations on Single Color Images. In: IEEE Intelligent Vehicles Symposium Eindhoven University of Technology, Eindhoven, The Netherlands, pp. 798–803 (2008)

28. Zhao, X., Liu, P., Liu, J., Tang, X.: Feature extraction for classification of different weather conditions. Frontiers of Electrical and Electronic Engineering 6(2), 339–346 (2011)

29. Hammami, M., Jarraya, S.K., Ben-Abdallah, H.: On line background modeling for moving object segmentation in dynamic scene. Multimedia Tools and Applications 63(3), 899–926 (2013)

30. Hammami, M., Ben Romdhane, N., Ben-Abdallah, H.: An Improved Lane Detection and Tracking Method for Lane Departure Warning Systems. International Journal of Computer Vision and Image Processing 3(3), 1–15 (2013)

Visual Saccades for Object Recognition

Janusz A. Starzyk[1, 2(✉)]

[1] Ohio University, Athens, OH, USA
[2] University of Information Technology and Management, Rzeszow, Poland
starzykj@ohio.edu

Abstract. This paper describes a method for rapid location and characterization of objects in 2D images. It derives optimizing parameters of a normalized Gaussian that best approximates the observed object, simultaneously finding the object location in the observed scene. A similarity measure to this optimized Gaussian is used to characterize the object. Optimization process has global and exponentially fast convergence, thus it can be used to implement saccadic motion for object recognition and scene analysis. This method was inspired by Perlovsky's work on neural dynamic logic used for fast location, characterization, and identification of objects. Developed method was tested and illustrated with an example of an object location and characterization.

Keywords: Object recognition · Visual saccades · Dynamic logic

1   Introduction

This paper addresses an important problem of visual object recognition. Koch argues that while it is possible to imagine the algorithms that could perform object identification and recognition at a specific location, it is difficult to think of such parallel algorithm in which object recognition takes place in the entire field of vision [1]. Such algorithm would face tremendous computational complexity. Koch's work shows that the visual information is processed in a sequence of operations; each one identifies an object at a specific location, while early preprocessing stage may be performed in parallel on the entire image.

Poggio developed computational vision approach to image recognition and understanding [2]. A computational vision system assembles scene description from the input image in which early vision modules extract various features of the observed image like edges, color, texture, size, direction of motion etc. Poggio's computational vision system strived to match performance of human visual system in fast feedforward object categorization. He assumed that such system will perform mostly feedforward parallel operations for high speed processing.

Subsequently, Poggio and his coworkers introduced a set of higher level features for object recognition [3]. These features were obtained from simple features (like edge detectors) combined into complex cells capable of detecting edges in the cell neighborhood, independently on their location and orientation. In [4] authors show that using a hierarchy of feature extraction circuits involving simple and complex

© Springer International Publishing Switzerland 2015
L. Rutkowski et al. (Eds.): ICAISC 2015, Part I, LNAI 9119, pp. 778–788, 2015.
DOI: 10.1007/978-3-319-19324-3_70

cells (similar to those observed by Hubel and Wiesel in research on ganglion cells in early vision) they can match human performance in a simple animal vs. non-animal categorization task. In a similar work, authors developed a tool for visual recognition of complex scenes [5].

Hierarchical organization of an object features and their assemblies is a foundation of the visual saccades based object representation, memory organization and recognition presented in this work. The work reduces tremendous computational complexity indicated by Koch while preserving flexibility in resolution level, scale and rotation of the original object image. The system is compatible with visual memory organization that can use higher order visual features extracted from simple or complex cells obtained from self-organizing feedforward neural networks in the visual input.

Section 2 presents the concept of visual saccades and visual attention. Section 3 describes finding characteristic features that represent an object or its parts using the most similar Gaussian distribution. Section 4 shows an example of object location and characterization. Section 5 contains conclusions and future work.

2   Visual Perception

2.1   Visual Saccades

A visual **saccade** is a fast movement of an eye, head or of an optical device. It is initiated either consciously or subconsciously, and serves as a mechanism for focusing the visual attention on an object or its part [6]. Saccades are used to locate interesting parts of the observed scene in order to recognize the observed objects and build a representation of the observed scene. Saccades are very rapid and end with the gaze fixated on a selected spot. Additional advantage of the saccadic movement is to apply full resolution of the central part of the retina to the observed scene fragment in order to help recognize the observed object. This leads to a better use of the computational resources, improves the processing speed, and increases the recognition accuracy.

Saccadic movements are used to repeatedly revisit the same locations with a high saliency while reconstructing the whole scene. This is particularly useful at the object recognition stage. Once a mental image of the familiar object was made, it may serve as a reference for object recognition. Gradually the observed object and its features are inspected and compared to the internal image model with the best matching model selected for object recognition. Focus of attention associated with visual saccade improves recognition, and provides accurate information about the object location [7].

Features that were used to build such mental image are recalled and are used as guidelines for conscious saccades, to either confirm individual expected details of the model, or are basis for rejection of the inspected image if the observed image does not match with the expectations [8]. In this later case the observed object is considered unknown and a new model may be introduced and stored in the semantic memory.

2.2   Visual Attention

Visually salient features (like brightness, movement, color, etc) are used to attract the visual attention. The visual attention supports efficient management of computing resources, reducing time cost and performing different visual tasks in a normal, cluttered and dynamic environment. It is used in the object recognition in coordination with the object model stored in the semantic memory.

Attention was considered as a mechanism for binding of distributed activations in response to presented stimuli [9]. It is a sequential mechanism used to select one of possibly many elements of the scene. Attention is used to temporarily suppress stimuli that do not belong to the object in attention focus, activating those that are correlated with the object of attention. The mechanism of temporal binding provided by attention may be used to quickly provide connections necessary to bind the activated groups of neurons forming long lasting memories.

Selective visual attention, linked to visual saccades, is needed to recognize objects and to understand a complex scene. The question is which part of the observed scene should be focused on, or how can we know where to look for objects we want to recognize? This task can be accomplished by evaluating saliency of various parts of the observed scene, concentrating attention on the most salient regions. After the winning region is inhibited, the next most prominent salient location is automatically selected through the same mechanism. However, it was determined that saliency is not the only factor for visual attention focus and that a significant portion of visual saccades is affected by associations between the observed artifacts [10].

For fast location and better identification of observed objects, attentional selection of objects was used in [11]. An interesting part of the image was selected using bottom-up attention based on salient features, to provide object location, and subsequently, an object was recognized using grouping based on segmentation. Thus both salient and homogeneous areas were used to locate and identify the object. Attentional modulation of neural activity helps to recognize object in a clattered scene [12].

Since computers process images performing sequential operations, then bottom-up attention algorithms limit the processing effort to analyze selected locations in the image. Koch and Itti have built a complex model of saliency-based spatial attention [13]. In their model a Winner-Take-All (WTA) neural network selects a location based on the saliency map to shift the visual attention to the selected spot, and to examine the image in the selected location.

Tsotsos et al. [14] used inhibition of the examined areas in order to perform attentional based selection and to obtain a selective tuning model of the observed object or scene. He used a top-down WTA attentional selection, with inhibition used for switching attention to the next salient feature.

Clark et al. [15] proposed a model where each task-specific feature detector is associated with a weight representing the relative importance of the particular feature to the current task. Also in his model, WTA operations are used on the saliency map to direct and switch spatial attention (triggering visual saccades). He used color and stereo vision to for attention focus and figure/ground separation.

Grossberg developed adaptive resonance theory (ART) to perform attention based perceptual grouping [16]. He proposed how a machine can learn new objects and events without forgetting those that were previously learned. He also suggested how bottom-up and top-down pathways can be used to focus attention on expected combinations of input features. ART also determines the level of mismatch between bottom-up feature patterns and top-down expectations to trigger memory search, or hypothesis testing, for recognition of objects and categories.

In [17] a hierarchical object-based computational model of visual attention was presented. This model combines object-based with visual saliency based model of visual attention [18] and uses bottom-up and top-down interaction [19,20]. The model integrates object and location based attention with visual representations of features. Top down attention provides priming to search for the expected features.

3   Feature Selection

Fitting models to data typically requires selecting parameters corresponding to various models. However, the number of useful subsets of model parameters is combinatorially large. Thus model-based approaches encountered computational complexity and required treatments of NP complete algorithms. This problem was addressed by Perlovsky [21,22] where he described computational mechanism of going "from vague-fuzzy to crisp," that he called the dynamic logic.

In fast location, characterization and identification of objects using neural dynamic logic an important aspect is fast alignment of the object and its model. However, direct application of the dynamic logic needs a quick estimation of log-similarity between the image and the model. While this can be easily done for special cases (like matching two Gaussian functions), in general no constructive algorithm was proposed, and computational complexity similarity estimation is unknown.

An object may have a complex hierarchical structure of its visual features. Such features can be extracted and recognized using various methods. Representation of objects in the memory, which allow for recognition of objects irrespectively of the different viewing distance, direction, and other conditions, can be obtained using visual features descriptors generated with the SURF (Speeded Up Robust Feature) method [23].

In this paper I introduce a new approach which combines Perlovsky's concept of finding proper parameters to represent the object with the idea of saccading movement and attention switching for fast alignment of the object and its model. This will yield object representation and will help recognition of objects and visual scenes.

Saccadic movement is obtained through rapid finding of object location, orientation and scale on 2D image plane. In this work a two-step approach is used. First, each object in the semantic memory is characterized by its best matching Gaussian model, and then Gaussian functions are used to quickly locate and characterize the image objects. Memory objects are compared with the observed images after proper rotation and scale. In such approach, derivative information needed to find an optimum alignment is easily obtained by combining the observed image with properties of Gaussian function.

3.1   Finding the Most Similar Gaussian Distribution

We will characterize and locate objects in 2D image plane using square root of the normalized Gaussian (based on multivariate normal distribution)

$$f(x, \mu, \Sigma) = \frac{1}{\sqrt{2\pi\sqrt{\det(\Sigma)}}} e^{-\frac{(x-\mu)\,\Sigma^{-1}(x-\mu)^T}{4}}. \tag{1}$$

where $x = [x_1, x_2], \mu = [\mu_1, \mu_2]$, and Σ is 2x2 covariance matrix. Parameters x, μ, and Σ are chosen to maximize similarity S to the target function computed as the normalized inner product between Gaussian and the target function

$$S(\mu, \Sigma, \phi) = \int_{-\infty}^{\infty} f(x, \mu, \sigma) \, \phi(x) \, dx = \frac{f(x,\mu,\sigma)*\phi(x)}{\|f(x,\mu,\sigma)\|\|\phi(x)\|}. \quad (2)$$

To find the optimum values of μ and Σ we need to calculate derivatives $\frac{\partial S(\mu,\Sigma,\bar{y})}{\partial \mu}$ and $\frac{\partial S(\mu,\Sigma,\bar{y})}{\partial \Sigma}$ and set them to zero. First let us find

$$\frac{\partial f(x, \mu, \Sigma)}{\partial \mu} = f(x, \mu, \Sigma) * \left(-\frac{1}{4} \frac{\partial}{\partial \mu} \left(\text{tr}\left(\Sigma^{-1} * (x - \mu)^T * (x - \mu) \right) \right) \right)$$

$$= f(x, \mu, \Sigma) * \left(-\frac{1}{4}(x - \mu) * \Sigma^{-1} \right) \quad (3)$$

where tr(A) is trace of a square matrix $A = [a_{ij}]$, $\text{tr}(A) = \sum_i a_{ii}$. After normalizing both Gaussian and target functions we have:

$$S(\mu, \Sigma, \phi) = \bar{f}(x, \mu, \Sigma) * \bar{y}(x) = \sum_i \bar{f}(x_i, \mu, \Sigma) * \bar{y}(x_i) \quad (4)$$

and derivative of the similarity function is set to 0 to find the optimum value μ.

$$\frac{\partial S(\mu,\Sigma,\bar{y})}{\partial \mu} = \frac{\partial \bar{f}(x,\mu,\Sigma)*\bar{y}}{\partial \mu} = \sum_i \bar{f}(x_i) * \bar{y}_i * \left(-\frac{1}{4}(x_i - \mu) * \Sigma^{-1} \right) = 0. \quad (5)$$

Solving for the optimum values of μ we get:

$$\mu = \frac{\sum_i \bar{f}(x_i,\mu_0,\Sigma_0)*\bar{y}_i*x_i}{\sum_i \bar{f}(x_i,\mu_0,\Sigma_0)*\bar{y}_i}, \quad (6)$$

where x_i is a 2D coordinate vector $x_i = [x_{i1}, x_{i2}]$, and $\bar{f}(x_i)$, and $\bar{y}_i$ are scalar Gaussian and target function values at x_i. In addition from

$$\frac{\partial f(x, \mu, \Sigma)}{\partial \Sigma^{-1}} = f(x, \mu, \Sigma) * \left(\frac{1}{4 * \det(\Sigma^{-1})} * \frac{\partial \det(\Sigma^{-1})}{\partial \Sigma^{-1}} \right)$$

$$+ f(x, \mu, \Sigma) * \frac{\partial \left(-\frac{1}{4} \text{tr}\left(\Sigma^{-1} * (x - \mu)^T * (x - \mu) \right) \right)}{\partial \Sigma^{-1}}$$

$$= f(x, \mu, \Sigma) * \left(\frac{\Sigma^T}{4} - \frac{1}{4}(x - \mu)^T * (x - \mu) \right) \quad (7)$$

where we used

$$\frac{\partial \det(\Sigma^{-1})}{\partial \Sigma^{-1}} = \det(\Sigma^{-1}) * \Sigma^T,$$

we have

$$\frac{\partial S(\mu, \Sigma, \bar{y})}{\partial \Sigma^{-1}} = \frac{\partial \bar{f}(x, \mu, \Sigma) * \bar{y}}{\partial \Sigma^{-1}}$$

$$= \frac{1}{4} \Sigma_i \bar{f}(x_i) * \bar{y}_i * \left(\Sigma^{\mathrm{T}} - (x - \mu)^{\mathrm{T}} * (x - \mu) \right) = 0 \tag{8}$$

Using (6) and (8) μ and Σ can be iteratively updated and the convergence is very fast. We will obtain

$$\mu = \begin{bmatrix} \mu_1 \\ \mu_2 \end{bmatrix} = \begin{bmatrix} \dfrac{\Sigma_i \bar{f}(x_i, \mu_0, \Sigma_0) * \bar{y}_i * x_{i1}}{\Sigma_i \bar{f}(x_i, \mu_0, \Sigma_0) * \bar{y}_i} \\ \dfrac{\Sigma_i \bar{f}(x_i, \mu_0, \Sigma_0) * \bar{y}_i * x_{i2}}{\Sigma_i \bar{f}(x_i, \mu_0, \Sigma_0) * \bar{y}_i} \end{bmatrix}, \tag{9}$$

and

$$\Sigma = \begin{bmatrix} e_{11} & e_{12} \\ e_{21} & e_{22} \end{bmatrix}$$

$$= \frac{1}{\Sigma_i \bar{f}_i * \bar{y}_i} \begin{bmatrix} \displaystyle\sum_i \bar{f}_i * (x_{i1} - \mu_1)^2 * \bar{y}_i & \displaystyle\sum_i \bar{f}_i * (x_{i1} - \mu_1) * (x_{i2} - \mu_2) * \bar{y}_i \\ \displaystyle\sum_i \bar{f}_i * (x_{i1} - \mu_1) * (x_{i2} - \mu_2) * \bar{y}_i & \displaystyle\sum_i \bar{f}_i * (x_{i2} - \mu_2)^2 * \bar{y}_i \end{bmatrix} \tag{10}$$

where for simplicity

$$f_i = \bar{f}(x_i, \mu_0, \Sigma_0) \tag{11}$$

Assume that the set of points that represent a 2D object were rotated by ϑ. In addition, if we scale the object in x and y directions by scaling factors λ_1 and λ_2 and translate it by shifting all the object points on the plane by vector a, we can represent a linear transformation of all points as:

$$Ax + a = R * \Lambda * x + a = \begin{bmatrix} \cos(\vartheta) & -\sin(\vartheta) \\ \sin(\vartheta) & \cos(\vartheta) \end{bmatrix} * \begin{bmatrix} \lambda_1 & 0 \\ 0 & \lambda_2 \end{bmatrix} * x + a \tag{12}$$

Using properties of the covariance matrix we have for a matrix A and a vector a:

$$\Sigma(Ax + a) = cov(Ax + a) = A * \Sigma(x) * A^{\mathrm{T}} \tag{13}$$

Using (13) it is easy to obtain covariance of the translated, rotated and scaled set of points.

To characterize and object we will first need to find Σ and μ of the transformed Gaussian, that maximizes similarity S described by (2). This corresponds to finding the rotation matrix R, scale matrix Λ and mean values μ.

From (12) we have the covariance matrix:

$$\Sigma_G = A * \Sigma_0 * A^{\mathrm{T}} = R * \Lambda * \Lambda^{\mathrm{T}} * R^{\mathrm{T}} = R * \begin{bmatrix} \lambda_{G1}^2 & 0 \\ 0 & \lambda_{G2}^2 \end{bmatrix} * R^{\mathrm{T}} \tag{14}$$

Using diagonalization of a matrix Σ_G we can get

$$\Lambda_G = \begin{bmatrix} \lambda_{G1}^2 & 0 \\ 0 & \lambda_{G2}^2 \end{bmatrix} = X^{-1} * \Sigma_G * X \tag{15}$$

where X is the matrix with eigenvectors of Σ_G as column of X and λ_{G1}^2 and λ_{G2}^2 are equal to eigenvalues of Σ_G. Thus the scale factors in y and x directions λ_{G1} and λ_{G2} can be obtained from (15). In addition, the rotation matrix $R_G = X^{-1}$.

3.2 Fitting Gaussian Function

Fitting Gaussian function is used to characterize the object and to find its location. This is a quickly convergent iterative process and it is a part of object characterization and location procedures. Fitting Gaussian function it is performed by the following algorithm.

Fitting Gaussian Function Algorithm:

1. Start with the initial value for $\mu = \left[\left| \frac{x_{1max} - x_{1min}}{2} \right| \quad \left| \frac{x_{2max} - x_{2min}}{2} \right| \right]$, where x_{1max}, x_{1min}, x_{2max}, and x_{2min} are respectively the maximum and minimum values of x and y coordinates in the observed scene. Notice, that for location and characterization the size of the observed scene is typically larger than the size of the object. Start with initial value for Σ equal to

$$\Sigma = \begin{bmatrix} (x_{1mxo} - x_{1mno})^2 & 0 \\ 0 & (x_{2mxo} - x_{2mno})^2 \end{bmatrix}$$

   where x_{1mxo}, x_{1mno}, x_{2mxo}, and x_{2mno} are respectively the maximum and minimum values of x and y coordinates in the observed image.

2. Compute the square root of the Gaussian function

$$f(x,\mu,\Sigma) = \frac{1}{\sqrt{2\pi\sqrt{\det(\Sigma)}}} e^{-\frac{(x-\mu)\Sigma^{-1}(x-\mu)^T}{4}},$$

   where $x = [x_1 \quad x_2]^T$, $\mu = [\mu_1 \quad \mu_2]^T$ and Σ is 2x2 covariance matrix.

3. Use (9) and (10) to compute new values for μ and Σ.

4. Since both μ and Σ influence computation of the function $f(x,\mu,\Sigma)$ values, we need to iterate repeating steps 2. and 3.

   The algorithm convergence is very fast. Fig. 1 shows the convergence rates for both the covariance matrix and the mean values. As we can see, even after the first iteration the object is located within the distance of 2^3 pixels as the error of the mean value indicates. Considering that the object was located within a 960x740 pixels image this indicates less than 1% error for the first iteration and the error is reduced exponentially to less than 2^{-8} pixel distance after 20 iterations. Such accuracy is seldom required and a single iteration is sufficient to locate the object or its feature, implementing rapid saccading motion to the target area.

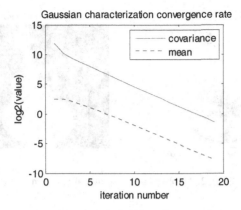

Fig. 1. Convergence of the covariance matrix and the mean values for the Gaussian characterization

3.3   2D Object Characterization

To characterize the object we perform the following operations:

2D Object Characterization Algorithm:

1. Normalize the object image and remove its background.
   a. Object image is reduced to black and white image.
   b. The black and white version of the image is normalized to have norm equal to 1.
2. Position the normalized object image in a bigger picture by shifting its lower left corner by a preset vector μ_C.
3. Fit Gaussian function $\bar{f}(x, \mu, \Sigma)$ to obtain relative location of the Gaussian $\mu_o = \begin{bmatrix} \mu_{o1} \\ \mu_{o2} \end{bmatrix}$ with respect to the lower left corner of the image. This is obtained by subtracting position of the left lower corner of the object image from the coordinates of the Gaussian $\mu_o = \mu_G - \mu_C$.
4. Obtain covariance matrix Σ_o of its best fitting Gaussian function and similarity $S(\mu_o, \Sigma_o, \phi_o) = \bar{f}(x, \mu, \Sigma) * \bar{t}(x)$ measure between the normalized image $\bar{t}(x)$ and this Gaussian.
5. The object image is characterized by $\mu_o, \Sigma_o, and \ S(\mu_o, \Sigma_o, \phi_o)$.

4   Example

To illustrate the discussed approach let us consider an image of an object and its gray scale version shown in Fig. 2. Vertical and horizontal axes correspond to y and x values.

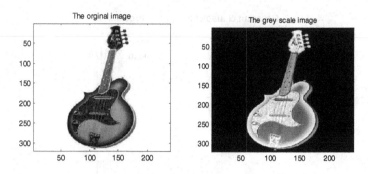

Fig. 2. An object and its grayscale version

This image was shifted in such a way that its upper left corner was moved from the location (1,1) to the position $\mu_C = [320\ 240]^T$ as shown in Fig. 3.

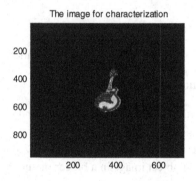

Fig. 3. The object placed in a larger area

The image was characterized using 2D object characterization algorithm by the Gaussian function located at $\mu_G = [\mu_{Gy}\ \mu_{Gx}] = [545.58\ 357.78]^T$ and the optimum Gaussian has its covariance matrix equal to:

$$\Sigma_o = \begin{bmatrix} 1719.7 & -245.2 \\ -245.2 & 677.5 \end{bmatrix}$$

After characterization this image similarity to square root of the optimum Gaussian was determined to be $S(\mu_o, \Sigma_o, \phi_o) = 0.9444$.

5   Conclusions and Future Work

Presented in this paper, quick characterization and location of the object image is a machine implementation of the visual saccades idea for object recognition. Using this approach the observed image is described based on the mean value and the covariance matrix of a 2D Gaussian function that is most similar to the observed image. Similarity measure between the best Gaussian fit and the observed object is used for object characterization. Subsequently, characterized and memorized objects that have specific Gaussian similarity are extracted from the memory, and after proper rotation and scale, are placed in the identified location for recognition.

Mathematical equations that solve the optimization problem to find the most similar Gaussian function are solved explicitly, yielding fast convergence of the iterative algorithm. One iteration of the algorithm typically suffices to find approximate location of the perceived object. More precise determination of the object location, its scale, and rotation require very few iterations and can be quickly computed.

This procedure can be applied either to the entire image, its parts, or to a complex scene. Inhibition of previously visited areas of the image will force saccadic searches to describe and recognize various objects in the observed scene.

Future work is to test this concept in realistic scenes with several objects, to build hierarchical object representations in the semantic memory, and to apply various resolution levels in order to minimize the processing time.

Acknowledgements: This research was supported by The National Science Centre, grant No. 2011/03/B/ST7/02518.

References

1. Koch, C., Ullman, S.: Shifts in selective visual attention: towards the underlying neural circuitry. Matters of Intelligence, 115–141 (1987)
2. Poggio, T., Torre, V., Koch, C.: Computational vision and regularization theory. Image Understanding 3(1-18), 111 (1989)
3. Serre, T., Wolf, L., Poggio, T.: Object recognition with features inspired by visual cortex. In: Computer Vision and Pattern Recognition, CVPR 2005. IEEE Computer (2005)
4. Serre, T., Oliva, A., Poggio, T.: A feedforward architecture accounts for rapid categorization. Proceedings of the National Academy of Sciences 104(15), 6424–6429 (2007)
5. Serre, T., Wolf, L., Bileschi, S., Riesenhuber, M., Poggio, T.: Robust object recognition with cortex-like mechanisms. IEEE Trans. on PAMI 29(3), 411–426 (2007)
6. Kirchner, H., Thorpe, S.J.: Ultra rapid object detection with saccadic eye movements: Visual processing speed revisited. Vision Research 46(11), 1762–1776 (2006)
7. Irwin, D.E., Gordon, R.D.: Eye movements, attention, and trans-saccadic memory. Visual Cognition 5, 127–155 (1998)
8. Herwig, Schneider, W.X.: Predicting object features across saccades: evidence from object recognition and visual search. J. Exp. Psychol. Gen. 143(5), 1903–1922 (2014)
9. Reynolds, J.H., Desimone, R.: The role of neural mechanisms of attention in solving the binding problem. Neuron 24(1), 19–29 (1999)
10. Peters, R.J., Iyer, A., Itti, L., Koch, C.: Components of bottom-up gaze allocation in natural images. Vision Research 45(18), 2397–2416 (2005)
11. Walther, D., Rutishauser, U., Koch, C., Perona, P.: Selective visual attention enables learning and recognition of multiple objects in cluttered scenes. Computer Vision and Image Understanding 100, 41–63 (2005)
12. Walther, D., Itti, L., Riesenhuber, M., Poggio, T., Koch, C.: Attentional selection for object recognition - A gentle way. In: Bülthoff, H.H., Lee, S.-W., Poggio, T.A., Wallraven, C. (eds.) BMCV 2002. LNCS, vol. 2525, pp. 472–479. Springer, Heidelberg (2002)
13. Itti, L., Koch, C.: A saliency-based search mechanism for overt and covert shifts of visual attention. Vision Res. 40(10-12), 1489–1506 (2000)

14. Tsotsos, J.K., et al.: Modelling visual attention via selective tuning. Artificial Intelligence 78, 507–545 (1995)
15. Clark, J.J.: Spatial attention and latencies of saccadic eye movements. Vision Res. 39(3), 583–600 (1998)
16. Grossberg, S.: How does the cerebral cortex work? Learning, attention, and grouping by the laminar circuits of visual cortex. Spatial Vision 12(2), 13–185 (1999)
17. Sun, Y., Fisher, R.: Object-based visual attention for computer vision. Artificial Intelligence 146(1), 77–123 (2003)
18. Itti, L., Koch, C., Niebur, E.: A model of saliency-based visual attention for rapid scene analysis. IEEE Trans. Pattern Anal. Machine Intel. 20(11), 1254–1259 (1998)
19. Wolfe, J.W.: Visual search. In: Pashler, H. (ed.) Attention, pp. 13–73. Psychology Press (1998)
20. Yantis, S.: Control of visual attention. In: Pashler, H. (ed.) Attention, pp. 223–256. Psychology Press (1998)
21. Perlovsky, L.I.: "Vague-to-Crisp" Neural Mechanism of Perception. IEEE Transactions on Neural Networks 20, 1363–1367 (2009)
22. Perlovsky, L.I.: Neural Mechanisms of the Mind: Aristotle, Zadeh and fMRI. IEEE Transactions on Neural Networks 21, 718–733 (2010)
23. Bay, H., Ess, A., Tuytelaars, T., Van Gool, L.: SURF: Speeded Up Robust Features. Comput. Vis. Image Und. 110(3), 346–359 (2008)

Improving Image Processing Performance Using Database User-Defined Functions

Michal Vagač[✉] and Miroslav Melicherčík

Department of Computer Science, Faculty of Science,
Matej Bel University, Tajovského 40, SK-97401 Banská Bystrica, Slovakia
{michal.vagac,miroslav.melichercik}@umb.sk,
http://www.fpv.umb.sk/

Abstract. Writing user-defined functions or stored procedures presents common way in application development using a relational database management system. It allows to embed application code inside of RDBMS. In this paper, we examine an effect of embedding selected computer vision algorithms as user-defined functions in a relational database management system. We show that such a combination can in certain scenarios lead to a performance improvement.

Keywords: Database management systems · Database user defined function · Database trigger · Database stored procedure · Image analysis · Image processing · Color-based image retrieval

1 Introduction

Relational database presents standard way of data storage and organization today. It provides a clear way of defining relations between data. Also, this is benefit when semi-results and results in image processing and image analysis tasks need to be stored. A proper database structure allows easy manipulation with complex and detailed results, gathered for different parameters settings.

Providing support for multimedia objects in relational database management systems (RDBMS) poses many challenges [1]. In contrast to the limited storage requirements of traditional data types, a single record of multimedia data such as image may span several pages. One common alternative is to store multimedia data in database as binary large objects (BLOBs). While modern databases provide effective mechanisms to store very large multimedia objects in a BLOB, where BLOBs are uninterpreted sequences of bytes, which cannot represent the rich internal structure of multimedia data.

Since SQL is a nonprocedural programming language by definition, it lacks procedural constructs (such as iterations or conditions) [2]. While relational databases become increasingly sophisticated, the idea arose to store procedural programming modules inside relational database management systems in compiled (binary) form. There are two main forms of RDBMS procedural routines. These are stored procedures and triggers that embody two different procedural

© Springer International Publishing Switzerland 2015
L. Rutkowski et al. (Eds.): ICAISC 2015, Part I, LNAI 9119, pp. 789–799, 2015.
DOI: 10.1007/978-3-319-19324-3_71

programming approaches – linear and event-driven, correspondingly. A user-defined function (UDF) can be envisioned as a special case of a stored procedure [2]. It provides a mechanism for extending functionality of database server by adding a function that can be evaluated in SQL statements.

In this paper, we evaluate possibilities of embedding selected image processing algorithms into the core of relational database in the form of user-defined functions. Our aim is not to focus on capabilities of the selected algorithms, but on a performance improvement of this way of implementation. Since user-defined functions are basically closer to a processed data, performance improvement is expected.

Using RDBMS user-defined functions, stored procedures or triggers to solve a computer vision problem was already mentioned in the literature. Each time it was just a part of the solution to more complex problem. Aim of our paper is to explore this method as such. At the best of our knowledge this kind of research has never been reported in the literature.

The rest of the paper is structured as follows. Section 2 discusses current research in the field. Since we have not found any evaluation of embedding the computer vision algorithms in the relational database, we focus on papers mentioning this approach as well as a brief description of algorithms used in this paper. The proposed technique is discussed in Section 3 and evaluated by experiments in Section 4. The final section summarizes the paper with a conclusion.

2   Related Work

We found an example of using a stored procedure for image analysis process in work by Ogle and Stonebraker [3]. They wrote a function in their picture retrieval system named Chabot that analyzes color histograms at retrieval time, which have been previously computed and stored in database. The function has two arguments: a color criterion and a color histogram. The function returns *true* if the histogram meets the criterion, *false* if it does not.

Chabot system uses this kind of function to have possibility to call it at run-time as part of the regular querying mechanism. However, the question of time efficiency is not targeted and further examined.

Paper [4] proposes an image-handling extension to the relational database management system PostgreSQL. The extension called PostgreSQL-IE is independent of the application and provides an advantage of being open source and portable. The proposed system extends the functionalities of the structured query language SQL with new functions, which are able to create new feature extraction procedures, new feature vectors as combinations of previously defined features, and new access methods, as well as to compose similarity queries. PostgreSQL-IE makes available a new image data type, which permits the association of various images with a given unique image attribute.

In this paper, we examine contribution of implementing image processing algorithms as user-defined functions in RDBMS in two scenarios. In the first one, we have developed an algorithm to ensure image uniqueness in the database.

To ensure there are no duplicates, each new image being inserted must be compared with all other images already stored in the database. Comparison of two images pixel-by-pixel has several drawbacks – among others it is very resource demanding and two representations of the same image may differ. The process of images comparison (calculation of a similarity between two images) is studied in image retrieval topic. Content-based image retrieval systems (CBIR) aim to provide an automatic way to extract such information from images that depends only on the content of the image. They use low-level visual features such as color, texture, shape and spatial information to retrieve images. We use this knowledge to find a duplicity (and similarity) with other already existing images in the database. Similar problem is described in [5], where authors search for images that are not similar but exact copies of the same image that have undergone some transformation. Their motivation is to find slightly modified versions of copyrighted images. In our implementation, the color based comparison of images is used. Colors of the image are the most commonly described by a color histogram. This kind of descriptor has advantage of being simple, fast to calculate and it is robust to common image transformations. One of the first approaches to compare two images using color histogram was described in paper [6], and was followed by other papers [7,8,9,10,11].

In the second scenario we have implemented basic image analysis algorithms – edge detection and line identification. Aim of the edge detection algorithms is to identify points in an image where the image brightness changes rapidly. One of state-of-the-art edge detectors is Canny edge detector [12]. The first step in Canny edge detection process is noise reduction – the input image is convolved with a Gaussian filter. Then gradients' intensity and direction is determined – filters to detect horizontal, vertical and diagonal edges are used in the blurred image. In the next step, unwanted spurious points are removed. At each point, it is checked if its magnitude is greater than the magnitude of the two neighbors in the gradient direction. If not, point is not considered as edge point. Since in the most cases it is not possible to specify a threshold, which determines that a given intensity gradient corresponds to an edge, thresholding with hysteresis is used (first and second thresholds for the hysteresis procedure are specified). The detected edges are input for a next step – lines identification. This task is solved using Hough Transform. In this method, the straight lines of different angles are passed through each edge point. Parameters of these lines are cast in the Hough parameter space. Maxima of this space show parameters of lines in the image.

3   Image Processing in Database User-Defined Functions

The most of relational database management systems is implemented following a client-server architecture. One of server's tasks is to manage the data. A client – such as a user application – communicates with a server to access the data. It is obvious that even when both – client and server – are located on the same computer, some extra overhead is present. The situation will be even worse, when client and server communicate over network, which is common scenario in enterprise configurations.

In comparison to traditional data types, multimedia data such as images occupy considerably more space. Therefore, it will make bigger difference when data are transfered over network compared to when they are not.

Figure 1 depicts the client-server architecture of relational database management system. Since all three mentioned forms of RDBMS procedural routines (stored procedures, triggers and user-defined functions) are stored in the database data dictionary, they offer already mentioned benefits such as more efficient access to data in the system. In tasks, where it is needed to analyze image data to obtain some short results, it should be beneficial to analyze image data inside of database and avoid transferring it out of the server.

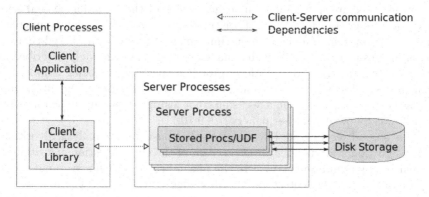

Fig. 1. Client-server architecture of relational database management system. Stored procedures and user-defined functions are defined in a database server

Figure 2 depicts expected difference between client and user-defined function (UDF) version of tested algorithm. Considering mentioned enterprise configuration with separated database and application servers, the application server is in fact a client of the database server. Usually, those two are installed on the same kind of hardware, therefore we can assume that execution time of subjected algorithm will be roughly the same when running in the database server or in the database client (i.e. application server). The only difference of overall execution time depends on the time of communication (data transfer). Another assumption is that time to access data in UDF will be always shorter than time to access data from client application. Gain should be significant especially when the algorithm is repeated several times (e.g. to each record in the database).

4   Experiments and Results

The described approach is considered in general, but motivated by a particular problem – recognition of foot prints and tire prints. The most obvious way is to fill a database with foot print samples, which are used for recognition of specific foot print from crime scene. A problem of this approach is, that it is difficult to

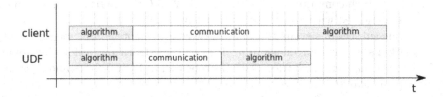

Fig. 2. Embeding an algorithm into RDBMS should be advantageous, when time of communication represents considerable time of overall process

put it into practice (to make a foot print or a tire print, a source of print must be physically available). In our approach, we fill a database with images of shoes and tires. Such images are easily available in the Internet e-shops with shoes and tires. The database will be filled in by an automatic process (web crawler), which will repeatedly download images from the Internet and store them in the database. This way will naturally lead to duplicities, what is one of problems targeted in this paper. Another aspect of the system is a process of tuning image analyzing algorithms – some parameters need to be set up empirically, so repeating execution of algorithms is expected. Therefore, optimal access to images' data is evaluated. When designing our system, a question of optimal implementation of database is arisen. Since we have not found any evaluation of using UDF for such tasks, we developed following experiments.

We have decided to implement our experimental algorithms in POSTGRES [13], an object-relational DBMS (database management system) developed at the University of California, Berkeley. In addition to the standard relational database features, it allows developers to define and create their own custom data types along with supporting functions and operators that define their behavior. User-defined functions can be written in several languages such as PL/pgSQL, C, Perl, Python and Tcl. We stored all image data in single database table. The table consists of BYTEA column for binary image data, CHAR column for MD5 hash and array of FLOATs column for histogram data.

Each algorithm was implemented in several different ways – from only client version to as-much-as-possible server side version (UDF). Performance of different implementations of the algorithm were tested with respect to the number of records in the database, therefore, we executed it on different sizes of the database. All images were stored in jpeg file format – with average resolution at 1155x818 pixels and file size of 308 kB.

Image analysis algorithms were implemented using OpenCV library, which is considered to be the standard library for high-end computer vision.

As it was mentioned above, it is very common in enterprise configurations to split application and database servers. It was expected that embedding algorithm in server should be beneficial especially in this configuration. Therefore, alongside local tests (denoted as local version) we run all tests also in networked configuration (denoted as remote version) – consisting of two networked computers (one running a database server with UDFs, the other running a client application). Each computer has a CPU Intel i3 2.13 GHz, 4 GB of memory and were interconnected with 100 Mbps Ethernet network.

Following subsections evaluate results of two experiments – implementation of an algorithm searching for image duplicities and an algorithm performing some simple image analysis. Each execution was repeated at least 5 times and average value was calculated.

4.1 Image Uniqueness Experiment

Important property of our database is uniqueness of stored data. Since the database can be filled from different sources, this constraint could be violated. This is true especially when the database is filled in by an automated web crawler from certain web sites – same images will be downloaded repeatedly. Comparing just filenames of the images is not enough, since the same picture can be used on different web sites with different names.

As it was mentioned above, comparing all image data is time intensive task. Extracting certain features from the image can significantly improve this process. This way allows image to be described by less data (than all pixel color information), what leads to speedup of the comparison. Also features can describe the image in scale/rotation/crop invariant way. This generalization is beneficial, since it allows us to recognize just slightly modified versions of the image.

In our experiment it is not expected to update images, so uniqueness check will be performed only at image insertion time. Since images will be repeatedly downloaded from the Internet, there is a big chance to repeatedly insert the very same image. For this case, at first MD5 hash will be used to avoid exact duplicities. If MD5 duplicity is discovered, the image is refused immediately. If MD5 hash computed for a new image is not present in the database, comparison based on distance of color histograms is used. If a similarity is detected, the new image is inserted and a relation between this new image and similar image is created. This relation will be marked according to the "level" of similarity.

In the following part, the *client* is a program, which takes an image as its input, connects to the database server and stores the image in a particular table column. *UDF* is a function executing inside of the database server, where image data are stored. According to written above, 4 versions of algorithms were implemented:

1. *Version 1 (no UDFs)*: The client calculates MD5 of an inserted image. Then it searches for calculated MD5 in the database. If found, insertion error is raised. If not, the client calculates histogram of the image. Then it iterates over all histograms in the database, calculates distance between histograms in the database and histogram of the new image. Finally, the new image and its histogram is inserted in the database together with a relationship to the closest histogram from the database.

2. *Version 2 (MD5 check as UDF)*: Database trigger calculating MD5 was defined in the database as UDF. The trigger ensures that for each inserted image MD5 is calculated and stored in particular column (a unique index is defined for the column). Same as in previous case, the client calculates

histogram of the image and iterates over all histograms in the database to find the nearest one. Finally, the image and the image's histogram are stored in the database.

3. *Version 3 (MD5 check and histogram comparison as UDF)*: As in previous case, MD5 database trigger is used. In addition, user-defined function to compare two histograms is defined. The client calculates histogram as in the previous case, but searching for the nearest histogram is done using user-defined function. After the search, the client inserts image and histogram into the database.

4. *Version 4 (only image insertion in client)*: The only client's task is to insert an image. The rest of the algorithm – MD5 check, a histogram calculation and searching for the nearest histogram is implemented in user-defined functions in the server.

A brief overview of the algorithms is summarized in Table 1.

Table 1. Four different versions of algorithm implementation ensuring uniqueness of image in the database

	MD5 check	histogram calculation	histogram comparison
Version 1	client	client	client
Version 2	UDF	client	client
Version 3	UDF	client	UDF
Version 4	UDF	UDF	UDF

As for the MD5 uniqueness implementation, it can by handled by database itself. A solution is to set unique index on MD5 hash column and to create "before insert" trigger to always fill in MD5 hash value. If duplicate image is inserted (MD5 value is already present in the column), for the insert command a rollback is executed. This logic is easily implementable using PL/pgSQL language.

As for color histogram comparison, a situation is more complicated. Even though PL/pgSQL language allows standard arithmetical operations, which would be sufficient for histogram computation, problem is with decoding the image data. For this reason, a trigger handling color histogram comparison was written in language C. This trigger was set to be invoked "after insert" of a new row.

Each version of the algorithm was executed both locally and remotely (database server and application sever on different computers) for empty table, table with 50, 100, 500, 1000, 5000 and 10000 rows gradually. Time was measured for overall client execution when inserting 10 different image files. Figure 3 displays measured results.

From graph results, it is obvious that the biggest speed-up was observed after implementing histogram comparison and search as UDFs inside of database server. It corresponds with assumption of data transfers – in versions 1 and 2 histogram data for each image in the database have to be transfered to client.

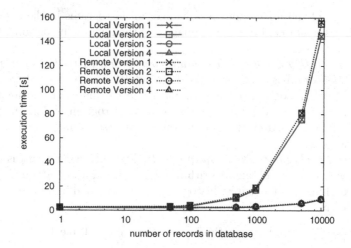

Fig. 3. Dependence of image insertion algorithm execution time on number of records in the database

On the other side, version 4 does not get any significant improvement over version 3 – in this case, the only difference is that histogram of inserted image is calculated in UDF of server in contrary to version 3. That means the only difference is one transfer of histogram from client to server, which does not count too much.

When inserting images remotely, the improvement is even better – even though the difference is small. This is because of the fact, that size of transfered data was not critically high.

4.2 Image Analysis Experiment

Image analysis and feature extraction are important tasks in problem of foot prints and tire prints recognition. It is expected that developed algorithms will be changed frequently during the research. After the modification of an algorithm (or tuning its parameters), it is needed to rerun the algorithm to see, how it performs with data. In this experiment, we are not dealing with specific algorithms' parameters and results. Aim of the experiment is to answer a question, if it is possible to speed-up image analysis by embedding analysis code into RDBMS server.

Since we expected that execution time of algorithm plays important role, we developed 3 different algorithms of different complexity (from the simplest to the most complex):

1. *Random data access*: The simplest algorithm just access binary data of image in random position. In this case, the image is not even decoded – just binary data of jpeg format are accessed.

2. *Edge detection*: The binary data are converted to an image. The image is converted to grayscale and finally edge detection algorithm is applied.
3. *Line identification*: It starts with same steps as in edge detection version, but after that some morphological operations are applied (erosion and dilation) and Hough Transform is used to line identification.

Each algorithm in the end updates database with some results.

All three algorithms were implemented in two different versions:

1. *Version 1 (everything in client)*
2. *Version 2 (everything as UDF)*

UDF version of the algorithms was implemented in language C. Each version of the algorithm was again executed both locally and remotely for table with 50, 100, 500, 1000, 5000 and 10000 rows gradually. Time was measured for overall client execution. Figures 4, 5, 6 display measured results.

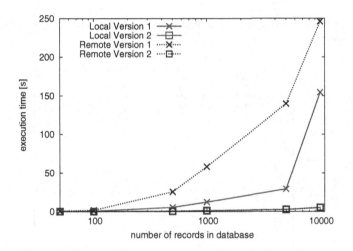

Fig. 4. Dependence of random data access algorithm execution time on number of records in the database

Analyzing the results in figures, it is clearly visible that the biggest performance gain is in the case with the random data access algorithm (Fig. 4). The reason is obvious – when accessing the data from UDF, the data does not have to be transfered to client and can be accessed directly. The algorithm itself is so fast that the time of communication is significant part in overall time.

Not so good performance gain is in the edge detection algorithm (Fig. 5). In this case, the algorithm takes significant time in overall process, so advantage of missing communication (in UDF version) is almost negligible. Even though, the better gain in remote version than in local version is still clearly visible.

The worst results were measured in the third algorithm. Hough Transform was too slow for this situation (Fig. 6). There is practically no difference in client/UDF versions of the algorithm.

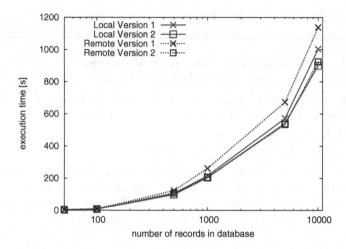

Fig. 5. Dependence of edge detection algorithm execution time on number of records in the database

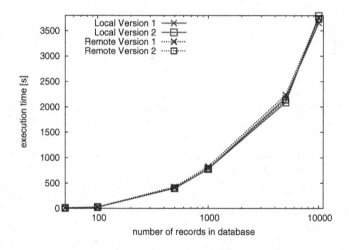

Fig. 6. Dependence of line identification algorithm (Hough Transform) execution time on number of records in the database

5 Conclusions

In the paper, we examined an effect of embedding two selected image processing algorithms as user-defined functions in a relational database management system. In certain scenarios, described approach can lead to a performance improvements. The results show, that usefulness of this approach is highly dependable on a particular situation, where the main variables are size of data and complexity of the algorithm. In general, short algorithms (in sense of time) working with big data stored in database are among others the best candidates. In our experiments, such situation happened when comparing histograms and randomly accessing image data.

On the other side, developing user-defined functions is not in general a trivial task. It is impossible to use standard SQL languages to develop algorithms dealing with complicated structure such as image data. Using of a more general programming language is required (if it is possible, a language with access to a proper computer vision library must be used). When developing UDF, it can be required to use a server API, which is non-trivial task that requires specialized skills that many developers do not possess. Furthermore, the created UDF may not be portable to other database management systems.

The essential question remains, if improvement gained by using user-defined functions is worth all the additional effort.

Acknowledgments. This work was supported by the Slovak Research and Development Agency under the contract No. APVV-0219-12.

References

1. Ortega-Binderberger, M., Chakrabarti, K., Mehrotra, S.: Database Support for Multimedia Applications. In: Castelli, V., Bergman, L.D. (eds.) Image Database, Search and Retrieval of Digital Imagery, pp. 861–210. Wiley, New York (2002)
2. Kriegel, A., Trukhnov, B.M.: SQL Bible. Wiley, Indianapolis (2008)
3. Ogle, V.E., Stonebraker, M.: Chabot: Retrieval from a Relational Database of Images. Computer 28, 40–48 (1995)
4. Guliato, D., de Melo, E.V., Rangayyan, R.M., Soares, R.C.: POSTGRESQL-IE: An Image-handling Extension for PostgreSQL. J. Digit. Imaging 22, 149–165 (2009)
5. Gavrielides, M.A., Šikudová, E., Pitas, I.: Color-Based Descriptors for Image Fingerprinting. Multimedia 8, 740–748 (2006)
6. Swain, M.J., Ballard, D.H.: Color indexing. Computer Vision 7, 11–32 (1991)
7. Schettini, R.: Multicolored object recognition and location. Pattern Recogn. Lett. 15, 1089–1097 (1994)
8. Mehtre, B.M., Kankanhalli, M.S., Narsimhalu, A.D., Man, G.C.: Color matching for image retrieval. Pattern Recogn. Lett. 16, 325–331 (1995)
9. Jain, A.K., Vailaya, A.: Image Retrieval Using Color and Shape. Pattern Recogn. 29, 1233–1244 (1996)
10. Chakravarti, R., Meng, X.: A Study of Color Histogram Based Image Retrieval. In: 2009 Sixth International Conference on Information Technology: New Generations, pp. 1323–1328. IEEE, Las Vegas (2009)
11. Hussain, C.A., Rao, D.V., Praveen, T.: Color Histogram Based Image Retrieval. Int. J. Adv. Engg. Tech. 4, 63–66 (2013)
12. Canny, J.F.: A Computational Approach to Edge Detection. IEEE Transactions on Pattern Analysis and Machine Intelligence 8, 679–698 (1986)
13. PostgreSQL 9.3.5 Documentation, http://www.postgresql.org/docs/9.3/static/

Author Index

Adrian, Weronika T.   II-541
Alfaro-Garcia, Victor Gerardo   I-137
Arioua, Abdallah   II-554
Arjona, Rosario   I-149
Avedyan, Eduard D.   II-364
Ávila, Anderson   II-305

Bagchi, Susmit   II-71
Bai, Aleksander   II-799
Balicki, Jerzy   I-675
Bartczak, Tomasz   I-112
Bartczuk, Łukasz   II-318
Basterrech, Sebastián   II-79
Baturone, Iluminada   I-149
Bera, Aneta   I-307
Bielecki, Wlodzimierz   I-102
Bilski, Jarosław   I-3
Blachnik, Marcin   I-687
Bobek, Szymon   II-565, II-578
Bobrov, Pavel   II-79
Bohnsack, Andrea   I-403
Boukhriss, Rania Rebai   I-768
Boullanger, Arnaud   I-72
Bourahla, Mustapha   II-591
Bouzid, Maroua   I-172
Bożejko, Wojciech   I-319, II-603, II-778
Buche, Patrice   II-554
Bujok, Petr   I-329
Burak, Dariusz   II-191
Burczyński, Tadeusz   II-471, II-483
Buza, Krisztian   II-91

Chen, Yu-Zen   I-283
Cheng, Beibei   I-517
Chmiel, Wojciech   II-223
Chmielewski, Leszek   II-330
Cho, Sung-Bae   II-36
Cholewa, Michał   I-528, II-391
Cierniak, Robert   I-586
Cimino, Mario G.C.A.   II-341
Cpałka, Krzysztof   I-448, II-161, II-175
Croitoru, Madalina   II-554
Czajkowski, Marcin   I-340
Czarnecki, Wojciech Marian   I-415

Damaševičius, Robertas   II-379
Davendra, Donald   I-370, I-389
Diephuis, Maurits   I-737
Domaschke, Kristin   I-403
Draszawka, Karol   I-675
Dudek-Dyduch, Ewa   I-541, II-353, II-504
Dueñas, Juan C.   II-714
Dutkiewicz, Lidia   II-504
Dymova, Ludmila   I-271
Dziwiński, Piotr   II-364
Dzwinel, Witold   II-25

Engelstad, Paal   II-799
Er, Meng Joo   II-161
Ernst, Sebastian   II-214, II-282

Farhat, Mariem   I-555
Fendri, Emna   I-768
Ferdowsi, Sohrab   I-696, I-737, II-142, II-760
Fortin, Jérôme   II-554
Frey, Janusz   II-130
Frolov, Alexander   II-79
Fu, Xiuju   II-3

G., Hugo A. Parada   II-714
Gabryel, Marcin   I-660, I-706, I-715, II-379
Gajowniczek, Krzysztof   II-527
Galkowski, Tomasz   I-427, II-3
Galushkin, Alexander I.   I-448
Gierlak, Piotr   I-503
Gil-Lafuente, Anna Maria   I-137
Głomb, Przemysław   II-391
Górski, Radosław   II-483
Gorzałczany, Marian B.   I-15
Grabowski, Adam   I-160
Grabska, Ewa   II-436
Grodzki, Olgierd   II-565
Grycuk, Rafał   I-566, I-706, I-715
Grzanek, Konrad   II-613
Grzesiak-Kopeć, Katarzyna   I-577

Hammami, Mohamed   I-768
Hammer, Hugo Lewi   II-799
Hanus, Robert   I-503
Hayashi, Yoichi   I-59, II-175
Holotyak, Taras   I-706, II-101
Horecki, Krystian   II-13
Horzyk, Adrian   I-26
Húsek, Dušan   II-79
Hwang, Chao-Ming   I-218

Irtaza, Aun   I-626

Jadczyk, Mateusz   I-727
Jagiełło, Szymon   II-202, II-778
Janowicz, Maciej   II-330
Jasek, Roman   I-389
Jelonkiewicz, Jerzy   I-59, I-72
Jobczyk, Krystian   I-172
Jurczuk, Krzysztof   I-340
Juszczyk, Radosław   II-214

Kacprowicz, Marcin   I-184, I-260
Kacprzak, Łukasz   I-319
Kacprzak, Magdalena   II-625
Kaczmarek, Krzysztof   I-271
Kaczor, Krzysztof   II-637, II-703
Kaden, Marika   I-403
Kadłuczka, Piotr   II-223
Kapruziak, Mariusz   I-436
Karczmarczuk, Jerzy   I-172
Karwowski, Jan   II-402
Kebair, Fahem   II-424
Kępa, Marcin   I-675
Khan, Absar Ullah   I-626
Klęsk, Przemysław   I-436
Klimek, Radosław   II-237, II-412
Klimova, Anna   I-137
Kluska, Jacek   I-195, I-503
Kluza, Krzysztof   II-649, II-703
Knas, Michal   I-586
Knop, Michał   I-566
Kolbusz, Janusz   I-112
Koller, Júlia   II-91
Konkol, Michal   I-207
Koprinkova-Hristova, Petia   II-318
Korłub, Waldemar   I-675
Korytkowski, Marcin   I-696, I-706,
    II-151, II-760
Kostadinov, Dimche   II-151, I-696, I-737
Kotlarz, Piotr   I-491

Kotulski, Leszek   II-237, II-515
Krawczak, Maciej   II-660
Kreinovich, Vladik   II-305
Kretowski, Marek   I-340
Krichen, Saoussen   II-789
Krzyzak, Adam   I-90, II-49
Kubanek, Mariusz   II-101
Kucharska, Edyta   II-504
Kułakowski, Konrad   II-214
Kuo, Hsun-Chih   II-112
Kůrková, Věra   I-39
Kusy, Maciej   I-49, I-503

Lach, Ewa   II-669
Lange, Mandy   I-403
Łapa, Krystian   I-448, II-247
Laskowska, Magdalena   I-72
Laskowski, Łukasz   I-59, I-72
Lazzeri, Alessandro   II-341
Lejmi-Riahi, Hanen   II-424
Leone, Nicola   II-541
Ligęza, Antoni   I-172, II-541

Ma, Jingwen   II-691
Mączka, Tomasz   I-503
Mahmood, Muhammad Tariq   I-626
Mandal, Sayantan   I-566
Mańdziuk, Jacek   II-402, II-679
Manna, Marco   II-541
Marussy, Kristóf   II-91
Marvuglia, Antonino   II-120
Matson, Eric T.   I-517
Mazurkiewicz, Jacek   II-13
Melicherčík, Miroslav   I-789
Mhiri, Slim   I-555
Michal, Repka   I-491
Mitsuishi, Takashi   I-160
Mleczko, Wojciech K.   I-90
Mo, Hongwei   II-691

Najgebauer, Patryk   I-747
Nalepa, Grzegorz J.   II-565, II-578,
    II-703
Napoli, Christian   I-79, I-469, I-660
Nataliani, Yessica   I-218, I-283
Navarro, José M.   II-714
Nejman, Cezary   II-679
Neruda, Roman   I-123
Niewiadomski, Adam   I-184, I-260
Niżyński, Karol   I-616

Nowak, Bartosz A.   I-469
Nowak, Leszek   I-577
Nowak, Tomasz   I-747
Nowicki, Robert K.   I-79, I-90, I-469,
    I-660
Nurzyńska, Karolina   I-594

Ogorzałek, Maciej   I-577
Olas, Tomasz   I-90
Olech, Bogdan   I-436
Oplatkova, Zuzana Kominkova   I-389
Orchel, Marcin   II-727
Orłowski, Arkadiusz   II-330

Pabiasz, Sebastian   II-120
Palacz, Wojciech   II-436
Palka, Dariusz   I-350
Palkowski, Marek   I-102
Pappalardo, Giuseppe   I-79
Pawlak, Miroslaw   I-427
Pawliczek, Piotr   II-25
Pedrycz, Witold   I-249
Pempera, Jarosław   II-603, II-778
Piech, Henryk   II-495
Piegat, Andrzej   I-228, II-448, II-460
Piekoszewski, Jakub   I-15
Pietrzykowski, Marcin   II-460
Pliszka, Zbigniew   I-361
Płoński, Piotr   I-606
Pluciński, Marcin   I-239
Pluhacek, Michal   I-370, I-389
Polański, Andrzej   II-739
Połap, Dawid   I-660
Postawka, Aleksandra   I-757
Poteralski, Arkadiusz   II-471, II-483
Prokopowicz, Piotr   I-249, I-491
Prucnal, Sławomir   I-503
Pruszowski, Przemysław   II-739
Przybył, Andrzej   II-261, II-318
Ptak, Aleksandra   II-495

Rączka, Krzysztof   II-504
Rafajłowicz, Ewaryst   I-616
Rafajłowicz, Wojciech   I-379
Rakus-Andersson, Elisabeth   I-649,
    II-130
Rebrova, Olga   I-586
Reiser, Renata   II-305
Renkas, Krzysztof   I-184, I-260
Rogus, Grzegorz   II-412

Romanowski, Jakub   I-747
Ronao, Charissa Ann   II-36
Rozycki, Pawel   I-112
Rudy, Jarosław   II-202, II-272
Rudziński, Filip   I-15
Rutkowska, Danuta   I-649, II-130
Rutkowski, Leszek   I-747, II-151
Rygał, Janusz   I-747
Ryszka, Iwona   II-436, II-749

Said, Lamjed Ben   II-424
Sałabun, Wojciech   I-228
Scherer, Magdalena   II-151, II-760
Scherer, Rafał   I-696, I-715, I-737, I-747
Schmalfuss, Murilo   II-305
Sędziwy, Adam   II-515
Senkerik, Roman   I-370, I-389
Sęp, Jarosław   I-503
Sevastjanov, Pavel   I-271
Shabbir, Zain   I-626
Ślażyński, Mateusz   II-541, II-578
Śliwiński, Przemysław   I-757
Słupik, Janusz   II-739
Smoląg, Jacek   I-3
Smołka, Bogdan   I-594
Smorawa, Dorota   II-101
Spurek, Przemysaw   I-481
Starczewski, Artur   II-3, II-49
Starczewski, Janusz T.   I-79, II-120
Starosta, Bartłomiej   II-625
Starzyk, Janusz A.   I-778
Staszewski, Paweł   II-142
Stefan, Dorota   I-606
Strug, Barbara   II-749, II-768
Sulej, Robert   I-606
Sychel, Dariusz   I-307
Szarek, Arkadiusz   II-151
Szczesna, Agnieszka   II-739
Szczepaniak, Piotr S.   I-638
Szczepanik, Mirosław   II-471, II-483
Szczypta, Jacek   II-247, II-261
Szkatuła, Grażyna   II-660
Szupiluk, Ryszard   II-527
Szwed, Piotr   II-223
Szymański, Julian   I-675
Szyprowski, Janusz   II-151

Tabor, Jacek   I-481
Tagina, Moncef   I-555
Takeuchi, Yugo   II-292

Tamani, Nouredine II-554
Tomaszewska, Karina II-448
Tomczyk, Arkadiusz I-727
Tramontana, Emiliano I-79, I-660
Turek, Wojciech II-282
Tvrdík, Josef I-329
Tyburek, Krzysztof I-491

Unold, Olgierd I-361

Vagač, Michal I-789
Vaglini, Gigliola II-341
Valipour, Mohammad Hadi I-294
Venkatesan, Rajasekar II-247
Vidnerová, Petra I-123
Villmann, Thomas I-403
Voloshynovskiy, Sviatoslav I-696, I-715,
    I-737, I-747

Wang, Lipo II-261
Węgrzyn-Wolska, Katarzyna II-625
Wiaderek, Krzysztof I-649
Wilamowski, Bogdan M. I-112
Wodecki, Mieczysław I-319, II-603,
    II-778
Wojciechowski, Konrad II-739
Wójcik, Mateusz I-481

Wojnicki, Igor II-282
Woldan, Piotr II-142
Woźniak, Marcin I-79, I-469, I-660,
    II-379
Wyrzykowski, Roman I-90

Yahyaoui, Hiba II-789
Yamamoto, Saori II-292
Yang, Miin-Shen I-218, I-283
Yazidi, Anis II-799
Yeh, Sheng-Tzung II-112
Yuen, David A. II-25

Żabiński, Tomasz I-503
Ząbkowski, Tomasz II-527
Zachara, Marek I-350
Zajdel, Roman I-49
Zalasiński, Marcin II-161, II-175
Zaremba, Krzysztof I-606
Zdunek, Rafał II-59
Żelazny, Dominik II-202, II-272
Zelinka, Ivan I-370, I-389
Zamanzadeh Darban, Zahra I-294
Zhao, Yanyan II-691
Zhou, Nina II-495
Żurada, Jacek M. I-3